SECOND

CANADIAN

EDITION

# Organizational Behaviour

## CONCEPTS, CONTROVERSIES, APPLICATIONS

STEPHEN P. ROBBINS
SAN DIEGO STATE UNIVERSITY

NANCY LANGTON
UNIVERSITY OF BRITISH COLUMBIA

Prentice
Hall

TORONTO

## Canadian Cataloguing in Publication Data

Robbins, Stephen P., 1943-
 Organizational behaviour : concepts, controversies, applications

2nd Canadian ed.
ISBN 0-13-014420-7

1. Organizational behaviour. I. Langton, Nancy. II. Title. III. Title: Organizational behaviour: concepts, controversies, applications.

HD58.7.R62  2000          658.3          C00-931603-5

0-13-014420-7

Vice President, Editorial Director: Michael Young
Executive Acquisitions Editor: Mike Ryan
Marketing Manager: James Buchanan
Developmental Editor: Paul Donnelly
Production Editor: Mary Ann McCutcheon
Copy Editor: Sharon Kirsch
Production Coordinator: Deborah Starks
Page Layout: Zofia Moczulak
Permissions Research: Susan Wallace-Cox
Photo Research: Alene McNeill
Art Director: Mary Opper
Interior and Cover Design: Lisa LaPointe
Cover Image: David Madison/Tony Stone

3 4 5      05 04 03 02 01

Printed and bound in USA

# BRIEF CONTENTS

# CONTENTS

## CHAPTER 8 — Power and Politics

# PREFACE

Welcome to the second Canadian edition of *Organizational Behaviour*. Stephen P. Robbins' book, now in its ninth edition, has long been the number-one-selling textbook on organizational behaviour (OB) in the United States and worldwide. The first Canadian edition enjoyed widespread acclaim across the country and quickly established itself as a leading textbook in the field.

This edition draws upon the strongest aspects of its American cousin, while also expressing its own vision and voice. It provides the context for understanding OB in the Canadian workplace and foregrounds the many Canadian contributions to the field. Indeed, it goes a step further than most OB textbooks prepared for the Canadian marketplace. Specifically, it asks, in many instances:

- Does this theory apply in the Canadian workplace of today?

- How is it likely to apply as the workplace undergoes transformations that have already started?

- What are the implications of the theory for managers and employees working in the 21st century?

It also raises the following issues:

- Can organizations actually change values to create a workplace where diversity is truly respected?

- In what ways do women lead, negotiate, and communicate differently? (Comments by prominent Canadian businesswomen throughout the text provide insights into these issues.)

- How do you manage change in a unionized environment?

- What is it like to work in the new dot-com organization?

While we have kept the features of the previous edition that adopters continue to say they like, there is also a lot that is new.

## General Content and Approach

- *Writing style.* Clarity and readability are hallmarks of this text. Users of the first edition have described it as "conversational," "interesting," "student-friendly," and "very clear and understandable." This revision upholds that tradition.

- *Examples, examples, examples.* From our teaching experience, we know that students may not remember a concept, but they'll remember an example. Moreover, a good example goes a long way in helping students to better understand a concept. You'll find this revision packed full of recent real-world examples drawn from a variety of organizations: business and not-for-profit, large and small, and local and international. We have also used the photos as additional opportunities to provide examples by expanding the captions to give additional information.

- *Three-level model of analysis.* This book continues to organize OB around three levels of analysis. We begin with individual behaviour and then move on to group behaviour. Finally, we add the organization system to capture the full complexity of organizational behaviour.

- *Comprehensive literature coverage.* This book is regularly singled out for its comprehensive and up-to-date coverage of OB from both academic journals as well as business periodicals. It was one of the first OB books to include the topics of diversity, globalization, power and politics, the virtual organization, and the importance of building trust. This Canadian edition is also the first OB textbook worldwide to present up-to-date coverage of two key emerging issues: working in a dot-com world and the toxic workplace.

- *Technology.* An Internet site dedicated to the book is provided at **www.pearsoned.ca/robbins**. The site includes an interactive study guide, links to web sites of many of the organizations mentioned in the text, search tools, and a special section for instructors that includes a syllabus builder and other tools for effective teaching.

- *Skill-building emphasis.* **From Concepts to Skills** boxes show the connections between theories and real-world applications. Exercises at the end of each chapter reinforce critical thinking, behavioral analysis, team building, and Internet-search skills.

- *Relevance.* The text reminds both teacher and student alike that we have entered the 21$^{st}$ century and must contend with a new paradigm of work that may be considerably different from the past. The new paradigm is more globally focused and competitive, relies more heavily on part-time and contract jobs, and places a higher premium on entrepreneurial acumen, either within the traditional workplace structure, as an individual seeking out an alternative job, or as the creator of your own new business.

The text also emphasizes that OB pertains to everyone, from the bottom-rung employee to the CEO, as well as to anyone who has to interact with others to accomplish a task. Gone is the assumption that OB is strictly for managers. We remind you that it is relevant far beyond your "9-to-5" job by concluding each chapter with a summary that outlines the implications for you not only in the workplace, but as an individual.

## New to the Second Canadian Edition

*Contemporary content.* New material on organizational citizenship behaviour, emotions, emotional intelligence (EI), trust, virtual teams, team effectiveness, and leadership have been added. We also examine the values and attitudes of Canada's NAFTA partners and those of various Asian trading partners. Of course, the entire book's research base has been revised and updated for this edition. Coverage of many topics has been expanded and revised, as is detailed in the Chapter-by-Chapter Highlights, on the next page.

*New organization.* This edition features fewer chapters arranged in a more cohesive order. The first three chapters, which comprise Part 1, focus on situating the workplace in the Canadian context. In Part 2, the two chapters on motivation and rewards have been combined to present a more integrated discussion of motivation. The application of motivation theories is made clearer with this revision. In Part 3, the chapter on communication has been combined with the chapter on conflict and negotiation. The result is a more focused discussion of the benefits of communication done well, and the hazards of communication done poorly. In Part 4, the chapter on culture now precedes the chapter on leadership, thus allowing for an understanding of the internal environment of the organization prior to looking at how leadership is implemented.

## Chapter-by-Chapter Highlights

*Chapter 1: What Is Organizational Behaviour?* Presenting an overview of the Canadian workplace as we move into the 21st century, this chapter considers how the effects of globalization, downsizing, and the need to be competitive have affected workplace relations. We consider why managing well makes a difference, and offer a fresh appraisal of what an organization is, and of the various roles that constitute it. Finally, the chapter introduces OB as a field that everyone, and not just managers, needs to know about.

*Chapter 2: Perception, Personality, and Emotion.* This chapter contains a new section on emotions: what they are why they are important. There is also a new discussion of emotional intelligence (EI) and how it is exhibited. Students can assess their EI in a new **Learning About Yourself Exercise**, "What's Your EI at Work?"

*Chapter 3: Values, Attitudes, and Their Effects in the Workplace.* The revisions to this chapter emphasize why we need a better understanding of values. First, we present additional information about the multicultural mix in Canada to indicate how our workplace environments are changing. Then we include new discussions of additional countries with which Canada does trade. Thus you will find a new discussion of values in the Mexican workplace (to reflect our NAFTA connection) and a discussion of *guanxi* (personal connections) in China and its implications for doing business in East and Southeast Asia. The chapter also includes a new discussion of how organizational citizenship behaviour (OCB) relates to job satisfaction. Finally, there is additional discussion on how personal values and organizational values "fit".

*Chapter 4: Motivating Self and Others.* Former chapters 5 and 6 have been streamlined and combined to give a simpler and more coherent view of motivation theories. Applied rewards are discussed in the context of motivation theories. There is a new discussion on other types of performance, beyond productivity and skill, that are being rewarded these days. In addition, more summary exhibits help to visually present differences among various motivation theories.

*Chapter 5: Foundations of Group Behaviour.* A discussion of the effects of friendship on group performance is now included in this chapter. A new **Working With Others Exercise**, "Observing Group Processes" provides students with the opportunity to observe the different roles that occur within a newly developing group, and analyze how these roles affect interpersonal interaction and group productivity.

*Chapter 6: Developing Teamwork.* With the increasing emphasis on the use of teams in the workplace, this chapter addresses some of the growing concerns about teams. There is a clearer, more focused discussion of how to create effective teams. We explore the dynamics of the virtual team: what it looks like and how it works. We also present a discussion on determining the appropriate use of teams, and this is further supplemented by the chapter's CBC Video Case. There is also an expanded discussion of trust, which we see as a key issue in building better work environments. A new **Working With Others Exercise**, "The Paper Tower Exercise," provides students with the opportunity to engage in team building in a fun and creative exercise.

*Chapter 7: Interacting With Others.* This chapter combines former chapter 9 (Communication) and chapter 13 (Conflict and Negotiation), thus joining a relatively theoretical discussion of communication with the applied topics of conflict and negotiation. The intent of this revision was to present a more integrated view of how communication works.

*Chapter 8: Power and Politics.* This chapter offers fuller and more current discussions of empowerment and impression management, two current hot topics in the literature. There is also a new exhibit on the characteristics of empowered employees. The chapter also contains a new discussion on emotional labour, which is another "hot topic" in the field of organizational behaviour. A new **Working With Others Exercise**, "Understanding Power Bases," provides students with the opportunity to apply their knowledge of power bases to a persuasion activity.

*Chapter 9: Organizational Culture.* This chapter contains additional discussion on changing organizational culture, and a new **From Concepts to Skills** box on "How to Read an Organization's Culture." There is also a new section on types of organizational culture.

*Chapter 10: Leadership.* The revisions to this chapter are extensive. The overall organization of the leadership material is new to an OB text. Specifically, we make a distinction between supervising and leading, using Professor Rabindra Kanungo's (McGill University) framework to illustrate these ideas. Additionally, different types of leadership opportunities in organizations are discussed, from supervising to leading, to team leadership to self-leadership and leading without authority. Discussions of self-leadership and grassroots leadership are also new. Finally, in keeping with a commitment to highlight the best Canadian research wherever possible, this chapter highlights Canadian contributions to leadership (Peter Frost, Jane Howell, and Rabindra Kanungo).

*Chapter 11: Decision Making, Creativity, and Ethics.* This chapter contains an updated discussion on groupthink, noting that some research suggests that groupthink can have positive impacts, and that there has been very little empirical research demonstrating the negative effects of groupthink. There is an enhanced discussion of creativity, based on very recent research. The chapter also includes a discussion of electronic brainstorming and notes Queen's University's facilities for this process. Finally there are additional examples and illustrations of how ethics and social responsibility are being applied in Canadian organizations.

*Chapter 12: Organizational Variety.* This chapter takes an extended look at new organizational forms for the 21st century. There is also a new section on team structure, including a performance model for team-based organizations. There is also an updated discussion of downsizing in **HR Implications**, including research recommendations made by Professor Ron Burke at York University's Schulich School of Business. A new **Working With Others Exercise**, "Words-in-Sentences Company," provides students with the opportunity to examine the effects of organizational structure on productivity.

*Chapter 13: Work Design.* This chapter includes updated and expanded coverage of telecommuting and hotelling.

*Chapter 14: Organizational Change.* This chapter includes a new discussion of organizational learning and how it affects the process of organizational change. A new discussion about "Communicating Change" gives much more focused discussion on how to communicate change to employees.

## Pedagogical Features

The pedagogical features of *Organizational Behaviour* are designed to complement and reinforce the textual material. With the introduction of two new features, **OB on the Edge** and **Internet Search Exercises**, this edition offers the most complete assortment of pedagogy available in any OB book on the market.

- The text is developed in a "story-line" format that emphasizes how the topics fit together. Each chapter opens with a **Roadmap** to guide the reader through the discussion, and closes with a **Roadmap Reminder** that recapitulates the key ideas of the chapter and points the way ahead in subsequent chapters.

- Provided in the margins, **Weblinks** give students access to Internet resources for companies and organizations discussed in the text, broadening their grasp of real-world issues. To find a weblink for a particular organization, look it up in the Name and Organization index, where the page on which the weblink appears in boldface. The Destinations button of the book's Companion Website provides hyperlinks and regular updating of the URLs for all weblinks (see **www.pearsoned.ca/robbins**).

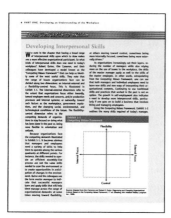

- **From Concepts to Skills** boxes in every chapter demonstrate real-world applications of OB theories.

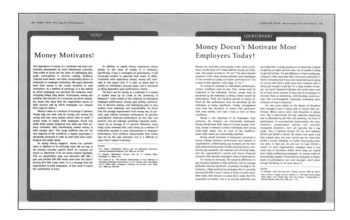

- Positioned in the middle of each chapter, the **Point** and **Counterpoint** pages promote debate on contentious OB issues. Most are new and all have been shortened to present more focused arguments.

- **HR Implications** boxes (Chapters 2 to 14) spotlight those facets of each chapter topic that are relevant to human resources management.

- Exclusive to the Canadian edition, **OB on the Edge** (following Parts 1, 3, and 5) takes a close look at some of the hottest topics in the field: work-related stress, behavioral pathologies that can make an organization "toxic," and the organizational culture of dot-coms. Since it is a stand-alone feature, these topics can be introduced at the instructor's discretion.

- Each chapter concludes with **Learning About Yourself, Working with Others,** and **Ethical Dilemma Exercises.** We have found great value in using application exercises in the classroom. The many new exercises included here are ones that we have found particularly stimulating in our own classrooms. Our students say they like these exercises *and* they learn from them.

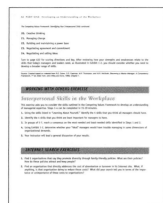

- **Internet Search Exercises** at the end of each chapter help students learn about resources available on the Internet and to use those resources to answer OB-related questions. For each exercise, students should (a) describe in detail the path they took to develop their answer, which includes citing their Internet sources, and (b) provide their answers to the questions asked. Part (a) reinforces that it's as important to know the paths on the Internet that students take to find an answer as it is to find the answer itself.

    Students with little or no Internet experience should check out **http://searchenginewatch.internet.com**. This site is a comprehensive source for learning how to navigate the Internet and specifically how to do Internet searches. For more experienced individuals, we suggest using popular search engines such as AltaVista (www.altavista.com), Excite (www.excite.com), Google! (www.google.com), Lycos (www.lycos.com), MetaCrawler (www.metacrawler.com), and Yahoo! (www.yahoo.com).

- Each chapter concludes with a **Case Incident** that deals with real-world scenarios and requires students to exercise their decision-making skills. Each case will enable an instructor to quickly generate class discussion on a key theme within each chapter.

- **CBC Video Cases** related to segments from the *Venture* series can be found at the end of each chapter. Several new cases have been chosen in keeping with our commitment to providing fresh material with each edition.

- This edition contains a new **Progressive Case**, presented at the end of each Part. Unlike the case incidents, which are chapter-specific, the progressive case requires students to use ideas and concepts presented throughout the text to understand the organizational challenges faced by one entrepreneur building a new business.

## Supplements

One tradition that continues for the Canadian edition of *Organizational Behaviour* is the creation of an outstanding supplements package. The following materials are available:

*Instructor's Resource Manual with CBC Video Guide* (ISBN 0-13-014476-2). Prepared by Nancy Langton, the Instructor's Resource Manual includes learning objectives, chapter outlines and synopses, annotated lecture outlines, teaching guides for in-text exercises, a summary and analysis of the Point/Counterpoint features, and answers to questions found under For Review, For Discussion, Case Incidents, CBC Video Cases, and the Progressive Case. There are additional cases, exercises and teaching materials as well. This supplement will be available on the Companion Website.

*Test Item File* (ISBN 0-13-014477-0). Prepared by Nancy Langton, the Test Item File contains over 3000 items, including multiple choice, true/false, and discussion questions that relate not only to the body of the text but to From Concepts to Skills, Point/Counterpoint, and case materials. For each question we've provided the correct answer, a page reference to the text, a difficulty rating (easy, moderate, or challenging), and a classification (factual/application). For a small set of questions we've indicated that these items have been subjected to discrimination analysis and shown to discriminate well between those who know the material and those who do not.

*Pearson Education Canada Test Manager* (ISBN 0-13-014478-9). This test-generating and grading software allows instructors to assemble their own customized tests from the questions included in the Test Item File.

*Electronic Transparencies in PowerPoint* (ISBN 0-13-014479-7). Prepared by Nancy Langton, this package includes over 400 slides of content and exhibits from the text, prepared for electronic presentation in PowerPoint 7.0.

*Colour Acetates* (ISBN 0-13-030850-1). This package contains more than 120 full-colour transparencies, highlighting key concepts for classroom presentation. (Please contact your Pearson sales representative for details.)

*CBC/Pearson Education Canada Video Library* (ISBN 0-13-014479-7). In an exclusive partnership, the CBC and Pearson Education Canada have worked together to develop an exciting video package consisting of 16 segments from the prestigious series *Venture*. At an average of seven minutes in length, these segments show students issues of organizational behaviour as they affect real Canadian individuals and companies. Teaching notes are provided in the Instructor's Resource Manual with CBC Video Guide.

CBC

*Companion Website with Online Study Guide* (ISBN 0-13-014482-7). Our exciting new Website includes a comprehensive online study guide that presents students with numerous review exercises and research tools. Practice tests with true/false and multiple choice questions offer instant feedback to students. Destinations (hyperlinks to the text's weblinks) and search tools facilitate further research into key organizations and topics discussed in the text. A special section for instructors contains a syllabus builder and other materials. See **www.pearsoned.ca/robbins** and explore.

## Acknowledgments

I have worked with an amazing team at Pearson Education Canada to produce this second edition. Under the direction of Mike Ryan, Executive Acquisitions Editor, the team has worked hard to help me realize the dreams and visions I carried for this project. Working with them reminds me, on a daily basis, that organizational behaviour is a constant, living, breathing experience. It is not just something that occurs in the classroom, or in a "real" job. It happens at all of the different intersections of our lives, as we deal with people on various projects.

When I reviewed my acknowledgements from the first edition, I was struck by how much change there had been in my "project team" since we produced that book. Three key people, including John Fleming, who had initially recruited me to the project, had moved on to jobs with other publishers. I have certainly missed their inputs and involvement this time, while acknowledging the new energetic team that's been part of this journey.

In making my acknowledgments, I would be remiss if I did not thank Steve Robbins for providing a truly excellent vehicle for adaptation. That said, my vision of a Canadian adaptation extended beyond the addition or substitution of a few Canadian examples, to producing a text that seriously addressed the issues of the Canadian workplace. This second edition has given me the opportunity to take more risks and bring new ideas to the project, including the innovative feature *OB on the Edge*.

When I first suggested to Mike Ryan and Lesley Mann (who was the developmental editor on this project until I completed the manuscript), that I wanted to create a new feature for the textbook that "would be like a chapter, but not a chapter" they did what any good editor might do. They said, in unison, "I don't think so." Chapters that were not chapters are just not something one does in publishing a textbook. Despite this initial resistance, *OB on the Edge* did come to fruition, allowing us to present some of the most exciting topics in organizational behaviour in a design that is innovative and fully reflective of the spirit of being "on the edge." I credit Mike and Lesley with sticking with me through the development of this feature, and then doing everything they could to make sure that it visually looked like the product I intended. I also credit Lisa LaPointe with developing the artistic layout of this feature, as well as the rest of the book.

I could tell further positive stories about this team, but I won't. Instead, I'll just thank them for all of their hard work. Mike Ryan is the guiding light of the team. He is also its calming influence during times of troubled seas. I'm not sure I would want to do a project of this magnitude without him there supporting and cheering me on. Lesley Mann was my developmental editor for much of the project, and I am sorry that she has now gone on to other adventures. As with the first edition, Lesley provided great insights, a wealth of material, and unflagging good humour at the bumpy parts in the road throughout the writing process. Paul Donnelly has taken over for Lesley, and in his few short months on the project has exhibited lots of enthusiasm, good will and humour in keeping the project on track. My copyeditor, Sharon Kirsch, was an author's dream. I've often read the praises of other authors for their copyeditors; now I know why. A great one really makes a huge difference. Sharon's attention to detail may be unsurpassed. Mary Ann McCutcheon was the production editor for this project. She was efficient, calm and good spirited, even as tight deadlines loomed large. It was a pleasure to have her direct the production effort. There are a variety of others at Pearson who also had their hand in turning my manuscript into the book that you see, and others who then take this book and market and sell it. To all of them I extend my thanks for jobs well done.

A special thank you is extended to Rob Gareau, co-owner of Human Performance, for agreeing to be the subject of the Progressive Case. His openness in sharing with us the details of his company provided a wealth of material for this book's integrative case. I am one of Rob's appreciative clients, and he certainly helps me keep balance in my own life with our 7 a.m. gym sessions three mornings a week. His training keeps me centred when other things seem like they might spin out of control.

Finally, I want to acknowledge a number of people who provided personal support throughout the process of writing this book. I begin with the 1999-2000 teaching staff of Commerce 292 and 329, our Introduction to Organizational Behaviour courses (Larry Anderson, Ron Camp, Diana Cawood, Sally Maitlis, Martin Martens, Dan Skarlicki, Skip Walter and Charlene Zietsma). We teach an intro course that we all really enjoy, and it is through the creative efforts of all of us that this is possible. Every summer we sit down and revisit the course, make considerable changes, and then try out our new ideas. The OB course is alive, dynamic, and open to change. This energy and enthusiasm gets fed into this textbook in a variety of ways. I am thrilled to work with such a dynamic group of instructors, who contribute considerably to the liveliness of our course, and provide countless insights into how we can make that course better every year. I have tried to capture that excitement in developing the material for this edition of the textbook. My undergraduate students have also contributed greatly to this edition, both with their feedback and with the countless examples and ideas they supplied during the term. One of those students, Harriet To, has worked with me this spring to get the supplements in order and I greatly appreciate her work.

More generally, my Organizational Behaviour and Human Resources Division colleagues at UBC brought various things to my attention, from newspaper articles to research reports, and engaged in various discussions with me about appropriate presentation of material. They also encouraged my writing efforts. I would like to thank them publicly for their support: Merle Ace, Brian Bemmels, Peter Frost, Dev Jennings, Tom Knight, Sally Maitlis, Dave McPhillips, Sandra Robinson, Dan Skarlicki, Mark Thompson, and Skip Walter. Our divisional secretary, Irene Khoo, deserves special mention for helping to keep the project on track, doing some of the word processing, managing the courier packages and faxes, and always being attentive to detail. I could not ask for a better, more dedicated, or more cheerful assistant.

A number of my friends worked hard to make sure that I would maintain my sanity under the pressure of deadlines, dragged me away from my writing from time to time just so I would have a break, and showed a lot of patience with me. Writing a book pulls one away from others sometimes. These include Devon Knight, Rhona Steinberg, Chris O'Rourke and Vera Horiuchi. The members of the Carnavaron Quilt Guild provided Monday night breaks from grueling writing sessions, and always asked how things were going and encouraged me along the way. My coauthors on my research projects, Howard Aldrich and Jennifer Cliff, provide a great deal of support, encouragement and forgiveness as I try to juggle research writing and textbook writing. It is a pleasure to collaborate with both of them and I gain lots from our interactions. Jennifer is also another great source of teaching ideas. Last in this category of friends, but by no means least, Pat and Alan Carlson and their daughter Nicole provide a welcome refuge in California when I need breaks from intensive textbook writing. When it comes to friends, Pat is truly the best in the business.

Finally, I want to acknowledge the many reviewers of this textbook for their detailed and helpful comments. I appreciate the time and care that they put into their reviewing: Bob Boudreau, University of Lethbridge; Martin Martens, University of British Columbia; Ronald J. Burke, York University; Laurie Milton, University of Calgary; Robert A. Cameron, Lakehead University; Linda Piper, Canadore College and Nipissing University; Theresa Feener, Northern Alberta Institute of Technology; Rick Roskin, Memorial University of Newfoundland; Beverly Linnell, Saskatchewan Institute of Technology; and Jennifer Singh, Seneca College of Applied Arts and Technology.

I dedicate this book to my father, Peter X. Langton. He was a man of many talents, and his understanding of organizational behaviour may have been greater than my own. To my family I give silent acknowledgment for everything else.

Nancy Langton
2001

## About the Authors

**STEPHEN P. ROBBINS** received his Ph.D. from the University of Arizona. He previously worked for the Shell Oil Company and Reynolds Metals Company. Since completing his graduate studies, Dr. Robbins has taught at the University of Nebraska at Omaha, Concordia University in Montreal, the University of Baltimore, Southern Illinois University at Edwardsville, and San Diego State University. Dr. Robbins' research interests have focused on conflict, power, and politics in organizations, as well as the development of effective interpersonal skills. His articles on these and other topics have appeared in such journals as *Business Horizons*, the *California Management Review*, *Business and Economic Perspectives*, *International Management*, *Management Review*, *Canadian Personnel and Industrial Relations*, and *The Journal of Management Education*.

In recent years, Dr. Robbins has been spending most of his professional time writing textbooks. His other Prentice Hall books include *Managing Today!*, 2nd edition, *Management*, 6th edition (with Mary Coulter); *Fundamentals of Management*, 3rd edition (with David DeCenzo); *Essentials of Organizational Behavior*, 6th edition; *Training in InterPersonal Skills*, 2nd edition (with Phillip Hunsaker); *Organization Theory*, 3rd edition; and *Supervision Today!*, 3rd edition (with David DeCenzo). These books are used at more than 1000 U.S. colleges and universities, as well as hundreds of schools in Canada, Australia, New Zealand, Singapore, Hong Kong, Malaysia, China, the Philippine Islands, Mexico, the Netherlands, and Scandinavia.

In Dr. Robbins' "other life," he participates in masters' track competition. Since turning 50 in 1993, he has set numerous indoor and outdoor age-group world sprint records. He has won more than a dozen indoor and outdoor U.S. championships at 60m, 100m, 200m, and 400m, and won five gold medals at the World Veteran Championships.

**NANCY LANGTON** received her Ph.D. from Stanford University. Since completing her graduate studies, Dr. Langton has taught at the University of Oklahoma and the University of British Columbia. She teaches at the undergraduate, MBA and Ph.D. level and conducts executive programs on working in a dot-com world, as well as women and management issues. Dr. Langton has received several major three-year research grants from the Social Sciences and Humanities Research Council of Canada, and her research interests have focused on human resource issues in the workplace, including pay equity, gender equity, and leadership and communication styles. She is currently conducting longitudinal research with entrepreneurs in the Greater Vancouver Region, trying to understand the relationship between their human resource practices and the success of their businesses. Her articles on these and other topics have appeared in such journals as *Administrative Science Quarterly*, *American Sociological Review*, *Sociological Quarterly*, *Journal of Management Education*, and *Gender, Work and Organizations*. She has won Best Paper commendations from both the Academy of Management and the Administrative Sciences Association of Canada.

Dr. Langton routinely wins high marks from her students for teaching. She has been nominated many times for the Commerce Undergraduate Society Awards, and has won several honourable mention plaques. In 1998 she won the University of British Columbia Faculty of Commerce's most prestigious award for teaching innovation, The Talking Stick. The award was given for Dr. Langton's redesign of the undergraduate organizational behaviour course as well as the many activities that were a spin-off of these efforts.

In Dr. Langton's "other life," she teaches the artistry of quiltmaking, and one day hopes to win first prize at *Visions*, the juried show for quilts as works of art. In the meantime she teaches art quilt courses on colour and design in her spare time. When she is not designing quilts, she is either reading novels (often suggested by a favourite correspondent), or studying cookbooks for new ideas. All of her friends would say that she makes from scratch the best pizza in all of Vancouver.

## CHAPTER 1

# What Is Organizational Behaviour?

**W**hen Canadian engineer-astronaut Julie Payette blasted off aboard the space shuttle Discovery in May 1999, she was part of NASA's new breed of astronauts, those "with good psychological makeup who can function as part of a group."[1]

### Questions for Consideration

**What is organizational behaviour?**

**What challenges do managers and employees face in the workplace of the 21st century?**

**How will knowledge of organizational behaviour make a difference for you?**

Astronauts didn't always have to have people skills; in fact, in the late 1950s and early 1960s, those at the head of the US space program were expected to have "right stuff" that was equal parts "intelligence, 'rude, animal health' and an ice-cold fearless attitude." In those days astronauts took short flights, while nowadays they are expected to live in space, sometimes for months at a time, as they conduct complex research. Today's "right stuff" is "mood stability, empathy, and good communication skills" in addition to university training. But the important factor is good interpersonal skills.

Evidence from the Russian cosmonaut program and life on the Russian space station Mir showed that good group dynamics significantly helped the success of missions, and that teamwork was an important element of success. This was seen when US navy doctor Jerry Linegar, an ambitious loner, thoroughly demoralized his

Soviet crewmates with his poor attitude and unwillingness to help out during his mission on Mir.

The space program illustrates what most people in organizations need to know: Much of the success in any job involves developing good interpersonal, or people, skills. As you work on class projects in teams, you will begin to appreciate this fact even more. Lawrence Weinbach, former chief executive at the accounting firm of Arthur Andersen & Co., puts it this way: "Pure technical knowledge is only going to get you to a point. Beyond that, interpersonal skills become critical."[2] In fact, the Conference Board of Canada identified the skills that will form the foundation for a high-quality workforce in today's workplace as communication, thinking, learning, working with others, as well as positive attitudes and behaviours and an ability to take responsibility for one's actions.[3]

Knowing how to deal with people is closely tied to an organization's ability to attract and keep high-performing employees. For instance, Robert Eaton, co-chair of DaimlerChrysler AG, views his workforce as an asset that provides his company with a sustainable competitive advantage. "The only way we can beat the competition is with people," says Eaton. "That's the only thing anybody has. Your culture and how you motivate and empower and educate your people is what makes the difference."[4] Howard Schultz, CEO of Starbucks, the rapidly growing Seattle-based coffee retailer that has established specialty coffee shops in cities across Canada, concurs: "Our only sustainable competitive advantage is the quality of our workforce."[5]

Interpersonal skills do not come easily to all people, however. A study of 191 top executives at six Fortune 500 companies sought to answer the question "Why do managers fail?" The single biggest reason for failure, according to these executives, is poor interpersonal skills.[6] The Center for Creative Leadership in Greensboro, North Carolina, estimates that half of all managers and 30 percent of all senior managers have some type of difficulty with people.[7] They also found that about 40 percent of new management hires failed within their first 18 months.[8] When the Center looked into *why* these new hires failed, they found that "failure to build good relationships with peers and subordinates" was the culprit an overwhelming 82 percent of the time.[9]

**Julie Payette**
www.myna.com/~elliott/
Astronauts/PAYETTE.HTM

**NASA**
www.nasa.gov/

**Center for Creative
Leadership**
www.ccl.org/

**Relic Entertainment**
www.relic.com

**organizational behaviour**
A field of study that
investigates the impact that
individuals, groups, and
structure have on behaviour
within organizations, for the
purpose of applying such
knowledge toward improving an
organization's effectiveness.

**Conference Board
of Canada**
www.conferenceboard.ca

When university recruiters are surveyed about what they consider most important for the job effectiveness of MBA graduates, they consistently identify interpersonal skills as most important.[10] Ron Moravek, chief operating officer of Vancouver-based Relic Entertainment, a games development firm, notes that the company's founder and CEO, Alex Garden, was a genius in his own right, but still needed to understand how to communicate in order to run his successful business.[11] John Hunkin, the new chair of Canadian Imperial Bank of Commerce, has been hailed as a team builder, with his success attributed to his interpersonal skills. Wayne Fox, CIBC vice-chair of treasury and balance sheet management, says of Hunkin: "He is a good listener, he is a good team builder and provides a consensus environment."[12]

As these examples indicate, in Canada's increasingly competitive and demanding workplace, neither managers nor employees can succeed on their technical skills alone. They must also have good people skills. This book has been written to help managers, potential managers, and employees develop those people skills. It has also been written to help you think about both group behaviour and business issues from an organizational behaviour perspective. To learn more about the skills needed in today's workplace, you should read From Concepts to Skills on pages 6-7.

## Enter Organizational Behaviour

**Organizational behaviour** (often abbreviated as OB) is a field of study that investigates the impact that individuals, groups, and structure have on behaviour within organizations. Behaviour refers to what people do in the organization, what their attitudes are, how they perform. Because the organizations studied are often business organizations, OB is frequently applied to topics such as absenteeism, employment turnover, productivity, human performance, working in groups, and job satisfaction.

Much of the material of organizational behaviour can be generalized beyond the employment situation, however. The interactions among family members, the voluntary group that comes together to do something about reviving the downtown area, the parents who sit on the board of their child's daycare centre, or even the members of a lunchtime pick-up basketball team can be informed by the study of organizational behaviour. Researchers in OB often apply the knowledge gained from studying individuals, groups, and the effect of structure on behaviour to make organizations work more effectively.

There appears to be general agreement that OB includes core topics from different levels of behaviour: individual (learning, attitude development and perception, motivation); group (group structure and processes, interpersonal communication and conflict); and the larger organizational environment (leadership, power, organizational structure, work design, and change processes). However, there is still considerable debate as to the relative importance of each.[13]

What is organizational behaviour? It's a field of study that focuses on three levels of behaviour in organizations. One level is the individual, such as the Wal-Mart greeter handling out smiley balloons. Another level is the group, such as the three employees of Praxair, a distributor of bottled industrial gases, who meet to discuss their work. The third level is structure, which is depicted here by employees working in cubicles at Bloomberg, a financial media company.

## What Do We Mean by Organization?

**organization**
A consciously coordinated social unit, composed of two or more people, that functions on a relatively continuous basis to achieve a common goal or set of goals.

An **organization** is a consciously coordinated social unit, composed of two or more people, that functions on a relatively continuous basis to achieve a common goal or set of goals. Thus, manufacturing and service firms are organizations, and so are schools, hospitals, churches, military units, retail stores, police departments, and local, provincial, and federal government agencies. As students, you may tend to think that when we say "organization" we are referring to large manufacturing firms, to the exclusion of the variety of other forms of organization that exist. But this would be very short-sighted. Only 16.7 percent of Canadians work in manufacturing organizations. Three-quarters of Canadians work in the service-producing sector of the economy, indicating that a large number of workers are engaged in people-related tasks for at least part of their jobs. Another 16 percent are engaged in wholesale and retail trade. To help you gain a clearer picture of

# From CONCEPTS to SKILLS

## Developing Interpersonal Skills

We note in the chapter that having a broad range of interpersonal skills upon which to draw makes one a more effective organizational participant. So what kinds of interpersonal skills does one need in today's workplace? Robert Quinn, Kim Cameron, and their colleagues have developed a model known as the "Competing Values Framework"[1] that can help us identify some of the most useful skills. They note that the range of issues organizations face can be divided along two dimensions: an internal-external and a flexibility-control focus. This is illustrated in Exhibit 1-1. The internal-external dimensions refer to the extent that organizations focus either inwardly, toward employee needs and concerns, and/or production processes and internal systems; or outwardly, toward such factors as the marketplace, government regulations, and the changing social, environmental, and technological conditions of the future. The flexibility-control dimension refers to the competing demands of organizations to stay focused on doing what has been done in the past vs. being more flexible in orientation and outlook.

Because organizations face the competing demands illustrated in Exhibit 1-1, it becomes obvious that managers and employees need a variety of skills to help them to operate among the various quadrants at different points. For instance, the skills needed to operate an efficient assembly-line process are not the same skills needed to scan the environment or to create opportunities in anticipation of changes in the environment. Quinn and his colleagues use the term *master manager* to indicate that successful managers learn and apply skills that will help them manage across the range of organizational demands; at some times moving toward flexibility, at others moving toward control, sometimes being more internally focused, sometimes being more externally driven.[2]

As organizations increasingly cut their layers, reducing the number of managers while also relying more on the use of teams in the workplace, the skills of the master manager apply as well to the skills of the master employee. In other words, extrapolating from the *Competing Values Framework,* one can see that both managers and individual employees need to learn new skills and new ways of interpreting their organizational contexts. Continuing to use traditional skills and practices that worked in the past is not an option. The growth in self-employment also indicates a need to develop more interpersonal skills, particularly if one goes on to build a business that involves hiring and managing employees.

Using the *Competing Values Framework,* Exhibit 1-2 outlines the many skills required of today's manager.

### Exhibit 1-1
### Competing Values Framework

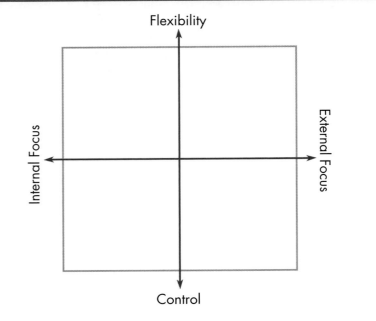

Source: Adapted from Kim Cameron and Robert E. Quinn, *Diagnosing and Changing Organizational Culture: Based on the Competing Values Framework,* 1st ed. (Reading, MA: Addison Wesley Longman Inc., 1999).

It gives you an indication of the complexities of the roles filled by managers and employees facing the changing workplace. The skills are organized in terms of four major roles: maintaining flexibility, maintaining control, maintaining an external focus, and maintaining an internal focus. The Learning About Yourself Exercise will help you identify your own strengths and weaknesses in these skill areas, so that you can have a better sense of how close you are to becoming a successful manager. For instance, on the flexibility side, organizations want to inspire their employees toward high-performance behaviour. Such behaviour includes looking ahead to the future and envisioning possible new directions for the organization. To do these things, employees need to think and act like mentors and facilitators. It is also important to have the skills of innovators and brokers. On the control side, organizations need to set clear goals about productivity expectations, and they have to develop and implement

systems to carry out the production process. To be effective on the production side, employees need to have the skills of monitors, coordinators, directors, and producers. The Working With Others Exercise will help you better understand how closely your views on the ideal skills of managers and leaders match the skills needed to be successful in the broad range of activities that managers and leaders encounter.

At this point, you may wonder whether it is possible for people to learn all of the skills necessary to become a master manager. More important, you may wonder whether one can change one's style, say from more controlling to more flexible. Here's what Peggy Witte, former chair, president, and CEO of Royal Oak Mines, said about how her managerial style changed from controlling to more flexible over time: "I started out being very dictatorial. Everybody in head office reported to me. I had to learn to trust other executives so we could work out problems together."[3] So, while it is probably true that each of us has preferred styles of operating, it is also the case that we can develop new skills if that is something we choose to do.

### Exhibit 1-2
### Skills for Mastery in the New Workplace

Source: R.E. Quinn, *Beyond Rational Management* (San Francisco: Jossey-Bass Inc., 1988), p. 86.

Sources:

[1] R.E. Quinn, *Beyond Rational Management : Mastering the Paradoxes and Competing Demands of High Performance* (San Francisco: Jossey-Bass, 1991); R.E. Quinn, S.R. Faerman, M.P. Thompson, and M.R. McGrath, *Becoming a Master Manager: A Competency Framework*, 1st ed. (New York: John Wiley and Sons, 1990); K. Cameron and R.E. Quinn, *Diagnosing and Changing Organizational Culture: Based on the Competing Values Framework*, 1st ed. (Reading, MA: Addison Wesley Longman Inc., 1999).

[2] R.E. Quinn, S.R. Faerman, M.P. Thompson, and M.R. McGrath, *Becoming a Master Manager: A Competency Framework*, 1st ed. (New York: John Wiley and Sons, 1990).

[3] D. Maley, "Canada's Top Women CEOs," *Maclean's*, October 20, 1997, pp. 52ff.

### Exhibit 1-3
### Percentage of Canadians Employed in Various Industries, 1998

| Industry Category | Percentage employed [1] |
|---|---|
| Agricultural and related service industries | 3.1 |
| Fishing and trapping industries | .2 |
| Logging and forestry industries | .5 |
| Mining (including milling), quarrying and oil well industries | 1.2 |
| Utilities | 1.0 |
| Manufacturing industries | 16.7 |
| Construction industries | 5.4 |
| Transportation and storage industries | 4.0 |
| Communication and other utility industries | 2.4 |
| Wholesale trade industries | 4.1 |
| Retail trade industries | 12.2 |
| Finance and insurance industries | 3.7 |
| Real estate operator and insurance agent industries | 1.8 |
| Business service industries | 7.9 |
| Government service industries | 5.5 |
| Educational service industries | 6.7 |
| Health and social service industries | 10.3 |
| Accommodation, food and beverage service industries | 6.4 |
| Other service industries | 7.2 |
| Goods-producing industries[2] | 27.1 |
| Service-producing industries[3] | 72.9 |

(1) Numbers do not add to 100 percent, due to rounding.

(2) Goods-producing industries include the following industry divisions: Agricultural and Related, Fishing and Trapping, Logging and Forestry Mining, Manufacturing and Construction; as well as the Other Utility Major Group from the Communications and Other Utility Industry Division.

(3) Service-producing industries include the following industry divisions: Transportation and Storage, Wholesale Trade, Retail Trade, Finance and Insurance, Real Estate Operator and Insurance Agent, Business Service, Government Service, Educational Service, Health and Social Service, Accommodation, Food and Beverage Service, Other Services; as well as the Communication Major Group from the Communication and Other Utility Industry Division.

Source: Statistics Canada, Catalogue no. 71F0004-XCB.

**General Motors**
gmcanada.com/english/home/
home.html

**Canada Post**
www.canadapost.ca/

where Canadians are employed, Exhibit 1-3 indicates the percentage of Canadians employed by each industry in 1998.

Besides being more service-oriented than manufacturing-oriented, the organizations in which Canadians work comprise a variety of types. When we think of organizations, we tend to think in terms of size and often envision large organizations, such as General Motors Canada or Canada Post.

**Hudson's Bay Company**
www.hbc.com/english.asp

**Air Canada**
www.aircanada.ca

**The Globe and Mail**
www.globeandmail.com

These large firms represent only three percent of the firms in Canada. Businesses with fewer than 50 employees accounted for 97 percent of the 928 000 firms in Canada in 1996. While big business employs more workers than small business, you might be surprised to learn that the share of jobs in big business is just over 40 percent, while small businesses account for about one-third of the jobs in Canada.[14] You should also be aware that in 1998, about 2.6 million individuals reported that they were self-employed, which represents 18 percent of the labour force. Between 1989 and 1998, there was an increase of 42.5 percent among individuals who were self-employed.[15] Self-employed individuals often do not act as managers, but they certainly interact with other individuals and organizations as part of their work. Thus, the study of organizational behaviour is equally important for the sole proprietor or entrepreneur as for those who work in large organizations.

Beyond the industry location and the size of the organization, other factors affect how organizations operate. Specifically, organizations can be located in the public or private sector; they can be unionized or not; they can be publicly traded or privately held. If they are publicly traded, senior managers typically are responsible to a board of directors, which may or may not take an active role in how the firm is run. The managers themselves may or may not own shares of the firm. If the firm is privately held, it may be run by the owners or the managers may report to the owners. Firms can also operate in the for-profit or nonprofit sectors.

All of these facts, taken as a whole, should suggest to you that when you think of an organization, the likelihood that you are thinking of a "typical" organization is small. It is difficult, given the variety of circumstances under which organizations operate, to indicate what a typical organization might be. The examples in this text try to present various organizations to help you reflect across the many types that exist. Though you might not have considered this before, the college or university you attend is every bit as much a "real" organization as is Hudson's Bay or Air Canada or *The Globe and Mail*. Therefore, the theories we cover should be considered in light of the variety of organizations you may encounter. We try to point out instances where the theory may be less applicable (or especially applicable) to a particular type of organization. In the absence of a caveat, however, you should expect that the discussions in this book apply across the broad spectrum of organizations.

## What Are the Roles Within Organizations?

Many of us carry around a somewhat simplistic view of work organizations that divides the participants into the following categories: owners, leaders and/or managers, and employees. These distinct roles probably most apply to large publicly held organizations. Distinct organizational roles become somewhat blurred when we discuss smaller privately owned firms, however. For instance, the owners of a privately held company generally differ quite significantly from the owners of a large publicly held corporation. Specifically, in a privately held company, ownership may be held by just one person or a small group of people. Sometimes it is held by a group of family members. Usually, though not always, these owners have a more hands-on approach to the running of the organization.

In a publicly held corporation, however, the owners are the shareholders. The shares of a publicly held organization may be concentrated in the hands of relatively few owners, such as when a pension fund or a few share-holders hold a larger number of the shares, or the shares can be widely dispersed. Given the differences in what it means to be an owner, from one person owning the firm outright to many people having an interest mainly in the share prices of the corporation, the influence of the owners on the day-to-day operations of the firm will vary significantly.

When we talk about leadership in organizations, we typically mean the person or persons responsible for setting the overall vision of the organization, although leadership can come from informal sources as well. We discuss leadership extensively in Chapter 10. Not all firms have leaders in the true sense of leadership. While there is an extensive literature comparing and contrasting leaders and managers, we do not feel it necessary to get into that debate here. As Professor John McCallum of the University of Manitoba notes, managers "organize, direct and motivate people, financial capital and hard assets with a specific goal in mind."[16]

Managers and leaders are not the only ones with expanded roles. Employees are being asked to "move beyond their traditional role as inputs to the process of achieving organizational goals."[17] To some extent, then, the roles of managers and employees are becoming blurred in many organizations. Employees are being asked to share in some of the decision processes of managers, rather than simply following orders. In particular, in the high-performance organizations described in the Conference Board of Canada's 1996 report, "Employees are willing to be accountable for their own and the organization's success."[18] To be accountable will mean that employees "take charge of their own careers, decide what skills they need to acquire and determine where they wish to employ these skills."[19]

Organizational behaviour, then, gives all of us more insight into how to work with others, and how to prepare to become employees in the 21st century workplace.

## Today's Challenges in the Canadian Workplace

> Is today's workplace different from the one our parents entered?

Understanding organizational behaviour has never been more important for managers and employees as the Canadian workplace enters the 21st century. Both the shape of the organization and employees' attitudes about the organizations in which they work are changing in ways that require careful consideration. Organizations were once viewed as long-term employers, offering relatively stable employment over one's lifetime. Today's workforce, however, has been increasingly affected by downsizing, creating an environment where employees might well think of themselves as entrepreneurs, in terms of creating their own organizations, or as sellers of their most personal product to their employer: their labour. This new workplace, where fewer workers are hired for life, requires better career management by employees, and demands more commitment and involvement on the part of employees while they're actually employed.

Physical labour is increasingly a smaller requirement in the workplace, at the same time that decision-making abilities, the ability to work in teams, and the ability to respond flexibly to a changing environment have become assets for the organization. Organizations are realizing that their most important asset is their people, and the most important attribute that these employees bring to the workplace is their knowledge. Thus organizations have to identify ways to manage that reflect that people are more valuable than capital assets in many instances.

The workplace that both employees and managers face today differs in some fairly fundamental ways from the workplace that we faced 20 years ago. With that comes a change in behavioural expectations for both employees and managers. The field of organizational behaviour is useful for addressing many of the challenges facing today's workplace. We'll review some of those challenges, including productivity, loss of respect, the demand for job satisfaction, the increase in sharing power, managing in a changing and competitive environment, globalization, and workplace diversity.

## Productivity

**productivity**
A performance measure including effectiveness and efficiency.

**effectiveness**
Achievement of goals.

**efficiency**
The ratio of effective work output to the input required to produce the work.

An organization or group is productive if it achieves its goals and does so by transferring inputs to outputs at the lowest cost. As such, **productivity** implies a concern for both **effectiveness** and **efficiency**.

A hospital, for example, is *effective* when it successfully meets the needs of its clientele. It is *efficient* when it can do so at a low cost. If a hospital manages to achieve higher output from its present staff by reducing the average number of days a patient is confined to a bed or by increasing the number of staff-patient contacts per day, we say that the hospital has gained productive efficiency. A business firm is effective when it attains its sales or market-share goals, but its productivity also depends on achieving those goals efficiently. Measures of such efficiency may include return on investment, profit per dollar of sales, and output per hour of labour. A student team is effective when it puts together a group project that gets a high mark. It is efficient when all the members manage their time appropriately and aren't at each other's throats.

We can also look at productivity from the perspective of the individual employee. Take the cases of Mike and Sally, who are both long-distance truckers. If Mike is supposed to haul his fully loaded rig from Toronto to its destination in Vancouver in 75 hours or less, he is effective if he makes the 4600-kilometre trip within that period. But measures of productivity must take into account the costs incurred in reaching the goal. That's where efficiency comes in. Let's assume that Mike made the Toronto-to-Vancouver run in 68 hours and averaged three kilometres per litre. Sally, on the other hand, also made the trip in 68 hours but averaged four kilometres per litre (rigs and loads are identical). Both Mike and Sally were effective—they accomplished their goal—but Sally was more efficient than Mike because her rig consumed less gas and, therefore, she achieved her goal at a lower cost.

As you study OB, you will begin to understand those factors that influence the effectiveness and efficiency of individuals, of groups, and of the overall organization. You may wonder whether organizations can both maximize profits and treat their employees well. To get an answer to this question, take a look at this chapter's Point/CounterPoint feature on pages 12-13.

## Lack of Respect

**Bombardier**
www.challenger.bombardier.com/

In a 1997 Angus Reid survey, Canadians were asked to name the company they most respected.[20] Forty percent either didn't know or would not state the name of a company they respected. Only one company, Montreal-based Bombardier Inc., received acknowledgment from more than 10 percent of

## POINT

# Successful Organizations Put People First

Intel does it. So does Microsoft, Motorola, W.L. Gore & Associates, Southwest Airlines, Ben & Jerry's Homemade, Hewlett-Packard, Lincoln Electric, and Starbucks. What is it? These companies pursue "people-first" strategies.

There is an increasing amount of evidence that successful organizations put people first. Why? Astute managers have come to learn that their organization's employees are its only true competitive advantage. Competitors can match most organizations' products, processes, locations, distribution channels, and the like. What's far more difficult to copy is a workforce made up of highly knowledgeable and motivated people. The characteristic that differentiates successful companies from their less-successful counterparts in almost every industry is the quality of the people they're able to get and keep.

What kind of practices differentiate people-first organizations? We can list at least four: (1) They value cultural diversity. They actively seek a diverse workforce based on age, gender, and race. (2) They are family-friendly. They help employees balance work and personal responsibilities through programs like flexible work schedules and on-site child-care facilities. (3) They invest in employee training. These organizations spend heavily to make sure employee skills levels are kept current. This not only ensures that employees can handle the latest technologies and processes for the organization but that employees will be marketable to other employers. (4) People-first organizations empower their employees. They push authority and responsibility down to the lowest levels.

Organizations that put people first have a more dedicated and committed workforce. This, in turn, converts into higher employee productivity and satisfaction. These employees are willing to put forth the extra effort—to do whatever is necessary to see that their jobs are done properly and completely. People-first strategies also lead to organizations' being able to recruit smarter, more conscientious, and more loyal employees.

**COUNTERPOINT**

# Successful Companies Put Profits First

Putting "people first" is easy to say. And it's currently politically correct. What manager, in his or her right mind, is going to admit publicly that employees take a back seat to cost-cutting or profitability? It's important, however, not to confuse talk with action.

Putting people first is not necessarily consistent with long-term competitiveness. Managers recognize this fact and are increasingly acting on it. Today's organizations are more typically pursuing a "labour-cost minimization" strategy rather than a people-first strategy.

When you look beyond what managers say, you find most business firms place profits over people. To stay competitive in a global economy, they look for cost-cutting measures. They re-engineer processes and cut the size of their permanent workforce. And they substitute temporary workers for full-time permanent staff.

Organizations with problems typically look to staffing cuts as a first response. And organizations without problems are regularly reviewing their staffing needs to identify redundancies and overstaffing. Their goal is to keep themselves "lean and mean." In today's competitive environment, few organizations have the luxury to be able to provide workers with implied "permanent employment" or to offer anything more than minimal job security.

For almost all organizations today, employees are a variable cost. Staffing levels are kept to a minimum and employees are continually added or deleted as needed.

Interestingly, the labour-cost-minimization strategy appears to be spreading worldwide. It began in Canada and the United States in the early 1990s. Now it has become the model for companies in countries such as Japan, South Korea, and Thailand—places that historically protected their employees in good times and bad. Many firms in these countries have abandoned their permanent-employment, people-first policies. Why? Because such policies are inconsistent with aggressive, low-cost global competition.

Canadian businesses are suffering from a lack of respect, according to a 1997 Angus Reid poll. Montreal-based Bombardier Inc., manufacturer of the Global Express shown here, was the company most frequently cited by respondents as commanding their respect.

**Ontario Power Generation**
www.ontariopowergeneration.com/

Does job satisfaction *really* make a difference?

**Starbucks**
www.starbucks.com

those surveyed.[21] Moreover, while CEOs in the same survey reported that shareholders, managers, and employees had benefited from the recent economic upturn, 70 percent of non-CEO respondents cited managers and shareholders as the beneficiaries, not employees. One consultant claimed that these findings were "an explicit criticism of current Canadian management."[22] A 1999 study by AON Consulting of 1500 workers found that only 47 percent of them would recommend their organizations as "a best place to work."[23]

What has caused this crisis in respect for corporate Canada? Canadian companies have undergone a long wave of downsizing in recent years, cutting employees and reducing costs to increase competitiveness. In many cases, fewer employees also resulted in less service for customers and clients. Canadians have expressed concern about the large number of layoffs that occurred during the 1990s. In the *Maclean's*/CBC News 1996 year-end poll, 58 percent of respondents said it was unacceptable for profitable corporations to lay off workers.[24]

Has downsizing at least paid off to the corporate bottom line? A 1998 report by the American Management Association suggests not.[25] Only one-third of the companies surveyed realized long-term gains to shareholder value after downsizing. Many of the companies that reduced the number of employees were unable to maintain initial increases in productivity and operating costs.[26] Ontario Power Generation's experience serves as a reminder of other negative effects companies face when productive employees are downsized.[27] A 1997 report found that problems with some of Ontario Power Generation's nuclear reactors could be linked to poor management and a lack of staff stemming from the company's downsizing in 1993.

## The Demand for Job Satisfaction

Employees are increasingly demanding job satisfaction out of their jobs. In a recent *Financial Post* survey, 75 percent of the public deemed it extremely important for managers to make employees happy and satisfied. CEOs were not quite in sync, with only 55 percent of them responding similarly.[28] As Robert Gemmel, president and CEO of Toronto-based Salomon Brothers Canada Inc., notes: "Managing people has changed even over the past 10 years. Expectations for job satisfaction have grown. The main challenge is to ensure an environment to help meet expectations."[29] As we will discuss in Chapter 3, overall job satisfaction in the Canadian workplace is relatively high. However, individuals cite several factors that could be improved in the workplace. For instance, in a 1997 Angus Reid survey, 29 percent of employees did not consider their jobs to be mentally challenging.[30]

Dissatisfaction with the workplace is echoed by two twenty-somethings who successfully brought unions to their respective workplaces. Steven Emery worked at a Vancouver Starbucks outlet and did not appreciate Starbucks' Star Labor software, which created shift schedules that looked

**Astral Communications, Inc.**
www.astral.com/splash.asp

**Black Photo Corporation**
www.blacksphoto.com

efficient on paper but caused erratic work schedules. For example, Emery objected to a shift that began at 5 a.m. and ended at 9:30 a.m. "You're supposed to come in at that hour for such a tiny shift? It was crazy."[31]

Wynne Hartviksen started working at a Black Photo Corporation in Ontario while in high school, and then accepted a full-time position after graduating from university. When Black's purchased 103 photo shops owned by Astral Communications, Inc., the workload at Black's skyrocketed, and the shifts became unpredictable, according to Hartviksen. When asked to explain her reasons for organizing a union for Black's employees, Hartviksen explained, "This really, ultimately, isn't about money. Sure we need money, but what we need more is to be able to tolerate our workplaces. It's about justice, which sounds kind of corny, but it's true. We don't want to get fired just because someone feels like it."[32]

The belief that satisfied employees are more productive than dissatisfied employees has been a basic tenet among managers for years. Although some evidence questions that assumed causal relationship, it can be argued that advanced societies should be concerned not only with the quantity of life—that is, with concerns such as higher productivity and material acquisitions—but also with its quality. Those researchers with strong humanistic values argue that satisfaction is a legitimate objective of an organization, which should be responsible for providing employees with jobs that are challenging and intrinsically rewarding.

Job satisfaction may be related to the brain drain problem, that is, the loss of key workers to the United States. A 2000 report indicated that some Canadians are lured to the United States by higher wages and better opportunities, while other Canadians are driven out of Canada because of "poor working conditions and a lack of job opportunities."[33]

Job satisfaction is also of concern because it is negatively related to absenteeism and turnover, which cost organizations considerable amounts of money annually. We will discuss this important topic more thoroughly in Chapter 3.

**absenteeism**
Failure to report to work.

**ABSENTEEISM** The cost of **absenteeism** for 1995 has been estimated at over $15 billion for Canadian firms and $56 billion for US organizations.[34] In Germany, absences cost industrial firms more than 60 billion Deutschmark ($49.4 billion) each year.[35] At the job level, a one-day absence by a clerical worker can cost an employer up to $139 in reduced efficiency and increased managerial workload.[36] These figures indicate the importance to an organization of reducing absenteeism.

It is obviously difficult for an organization to operate smoothly and to attain its objectives if employees fail to report to their jobs. The workflow is disrupted, and often important decisions must be delayed. In organizations that rely heavily upon assembly-line production, absenteeism can be considerably more than a disruption; it can result in a drastic reduction in quality of output, and in some cases, it can bring about a complete shutdown of the production facility. Levels of absenteeism beyond the normal range in any organization have a direct impact on that organization's effectiveness and efficiency.

Are *all* absences bad? Probably not! Although most absences have a negative impact on the organization (especially absences of strategically important individuals), we can conceive of situations in which the organization may benefit by an employee's voluntarily choosing not to come to work. For instance, illness, fatigue, or excess stress can significantly decrease an

Keeping turnover down is a key concern of Canada's high tech firms, many of which can't pay salaries comparable to their U.S. competitors. Vancouver-based Seagate Software sees retention as a priority. So it offers incentives beyond compensation such as opportunity, an excellent working environment, and the chance to continually upgrade skills. Not everything is serious at Seagate, however. Employees can buy Oreo cookies, Haagen Dazs ice cream bars, and pop at cost, and then work off the extra pounds in the weight room.

employee's productivity, and a bad cold or case of the flu might spread, affecting co-workers' productivity as well. In jobs in which an employee needs to be alert—surgeons and airline pilots are obvious examples—it may well be better for the organization and for its clientele if the employee does not report to work rather than show up and perform poorly. The cost of an accident in such jobs could be prohibitive. Even in managerial jobs, where mistakes are less spectacular, performance may be improved when managers excuse themselves from work rather than make a poor decision under stress. However, these examples are clearly atypical. For the most part, we can assume that organizations benefit when employee absenteeism is low.

**turnover**
Voluntary and involuntary permanent withdrawal from the organization.

**TURNOVER** A high rate of **turnover** in an organization results in high recruiting, selection, and training costs. How high are those costs? A conservative estimate would be about $21 000 per employee.[37] A high rate of turnover can also disrupt the efficient running of an organization when knowledgeable and experienced employees leave, and replacements must be found and prepared to assume positions of responsibility.

All organizations, of course, have some turnover. In fact, if the "right" people—the marginal and sub-marginal employees—are leaving the organization, turnover can be positive. It may create the opportunity to replace an underperforming individual with someone who has higher skills or motivation, open up increased opportunities for promotions, and bring individuals with new and fresh ideas to the organization.[38] In today's changing world of work, reasonable levels of employee-initiated turnover facilitate organizational flexibility and employee independence, and they can lessen the need for management-initiated layoffs.

But turnover often involves the loss of people the organization doesn't want to lose. For instance, one study covering 900 employees who had resigned their jobs found that 92 percent earned performance ratings of "satisfactory" or better from their managers.[39] So when turnover is excessive, or when it involves valuable performers, it can be a disruptive factor, hindering the organization's effectiveness. We revisit the issue of job satisfaction in Chapter 3.

## Sharing Power

At the same time that managers are being held responsible for employee satisfaction and happiness, they are also being asked to share more of their power. If you read any popular business periodical nowadays, you'll find that managers are referred to as coaches, advisers, sponsors, or facilitators.[40]

Workers' responsibilities are similarly increasing. In many organizations, employees have become associates or teammates,[41] and the roles of managers and workers have blurred. Decision making is being pushed down to the operating level, where workers are being given the freedom to make choices about schedules, procedures, and solving work-related problems. In the 1980s, managers were encouraged to involve their employees in work-related decisions.[42] Now, managers are going considerably farther by providing employees with full control of their work. Self-managed teams, in which workers operate largely without bosses, have become the rage of the 1990s.[43] Organizations will likely continue this trend of teamwork and worker responsibility into the 21st century. To help you understand how to perform better as a team player, we discuss the dynamics of teams in Chapter 6.

What's going on is that managers are empowering employees. **Empowerment** means managers are putting employees in charge of what they do. In the process, managers are learning how to give up control, and employees are learning how to take responsibility for their work and make appropriate decisions. The roles for both managers and employees are changing, often without much guidance on how to perform these new roles. How widespread are these changes in the workplace? While we have no specific Canadian data, a recent survey by the American Management Association of 1040 executives found that 46 percent of their companies were still operating within a hierarchical structure, but 31 percent defined their companies as empowered.[44] We will discuss the empowerment process further in Chapter 8. This chapter's CBC Video Case looks at the impact of changing managerial functions on some organizations.

## Managing and Working in a Changing and Competitive Environment

In the past, the workplace could be characterized by long periods of stability, interrupted occasionally by short periods of change. Today's workplace would be more accurately described as long periods of ongoing change, interrupted occasionally by short periods of stability! The world that most managers and employees face today is one of "permanent temporariness."

In recent years, Canadian businesses have faced tough competition from the United States, Europe, Japan, and even China, as well as from within the country's borders. To survive, they have had to cut fat, increase productivity, and improve quality. A number of Canadian companies have found it necessary to merge in order to survive. Commenting on the recent merger between Ottawa-based law firm Scott and Aylen and Toronto-based law

---

**Are you ready to assume more responsibility at work?**

**empowerment**
Giving employees responsibility for what they do.

**American Management Association**
www.amanet.org/index.htm

firm Borden and Elliot, David Scott, chair of Scott and Aylen, said that without the merger, Scott and Aylen was "too small to compete with major national and international firms, and too big to grow to a healthy size in a community like Ottawa."[45] Other companies have faced acquisitions or alliances.

Employees, too, have new challenges, including the increased use of new technologies in their workplace. This affects the number of jobs available and the number of skills required. For instance, when Canada Post moved from hand-sorting mail to using automatic mail sorters, some workers lost their jobs and others had to learn how to operate the equipment. In November 1999, Canada Post workers faced another change: The Crown corporation launched an electronic-post office service, advertised as "the first one on the planet."[46] Production employees at companies such as the *Vancouver Sun*, Binney & Smith, and GM Canada now need to know how to operate computerized production equipment. This skill was not part of their job description 15 years ago.

These changes in the workplace mean that the actual jobs that workers perform, and even the managers to whom they report, are in a permanent state of flux. To stay employable under these conditions, workers need to continually update their knowledge and skills to perform new job requirements.[47] Today's managers and employees have to learn to live with flexibility, spontaneity, uncertainty, and unpredictability.

The changing and competitive environment means that not only do individuals have to become increasingly flexible, but organizations do too. They need to learn how to adjust to shifts in demand, technology, and the economy. For example, Burnaby, British Columbia-based George Third and Son fabricates and installs steel structures. The company was founded in 1909. Since then, George Third has undergone a number of changes, including moving into different manufacturing lines. The company owes its survival to the ability to shift with the times. "Corporate survival has depended on change, a feisty willingness to leap off a cliff," says Rob Third, grandson of the founder, and the individual responsible for production and purchasing. Adds brother Brett, who is in charge of marketing, sales, and administration, "We need to make changes to keep going in the business."[48]

In order to make the changes that need to be made, organizations and people must be committed to learning new skills, new ways of thinking, and new ways to do business. In Chapter 2 we will discuss learning, as a reminder of the importance of engaging in continuous learning over the lifetime of both the individual and the firm. We follow this up with a discussion of organizational learning in Chapter 14.

## Managing and Working in a Global Village

Twenty or 30 years ago, national borders acted to insulate most firms from foreign competitive pressures. Now, organizations are no longer constrained by national borders. Trading blocks such as the North American Free Trade Agreement (NAFTA) and the European Union (EU) have significantly reduced tariffs and barriers to trade; capitalism is rapidly replacing government control in Eastern European companies; and North America and Europe no longer have a monopoly on highly skilled labour. The Internet has also enabled companies to become more globally connected, both through international sales and through increasing the opportunities to carry on business. For example, the Internet enables even small firms to bid

**Vancouver Sun**
www.vancouversun.com

**NAFTA Secretariat**
www.nafta-sec-alena.org

**European Union**
www.europa.eu.int

One of the challenges facing Canadian businesses is the increasing globalization of the workplace. McDonald's Canada opened the first McDonald's restaurant in Moscow.

on projects in different countries and compete with larger firms.

The world has truly become a global village. Burger King is owned by a British firm, and McDonald's Canada opened the first McDonald's restaurant in Moscow. Toyota and Honda produce cars here in Canada for export around the world. Hitachi Canadian Industries Ltd. in Saskatoon produces power-generating equipment components for its local market and supplies parts to the parent company in Japan. Oakville, Ontario-based Brew Store partners Gary Deathe and Dean Thrasher have launched brew-on-premise operations in the United States, Japan, and New Zealand. The message? As multinational corporations develop operations worldwide, as companies develop joint ventures with foreign partners, and as workers increasingly pursue job opportunities across national borders, managers and employees must become capable of working with people from different cultures. Managing people well and understanding the interpersonal dynamics of the workplace are not just issues for companies doing business in Canadian society.

Professor John Eggers, of the Richard Ivey School of Business at the University of Western Ontario, has commented on doing business in Asia. He notes, "It is important to remember that business is conducted through relationships much more so than it is in Western countries. It takes years to form and develop the relationships a company needs, and to build the trust necessary to do business. Business in Asia is conducted courteously and respectfully, and at a slower pace—foreign managers who do not act in a polite manner will not be well received."[49]

## Managing and Working in a Culturally Diverse Workplace

One of the most important and broad-based challenges currently facing organizations is adapting to people who are different. The term we use for describing this challenge is *workforce diversity*. Whereas globalization focuses on differences among people from different countries, workforce diversity addresses differences among people within the same country, particularly as this is expressed in corporations.

**workforce diversity**
The heterogeneity of workers in organizations in terms of gender, race, ethnicity, disability, sexual preference, and age, as well as background characteristics such as education, income, and training.

**Workforce diversity** arises because organizations are becoming more heterogeneous in terms of gender, race, and ethnicity, as well as demographic characteristics, such as age, education, and socio-economic status. In addition to the more obvious groups—women, First Nations peoples, Asian Canadians, African Canadians, Indo-Canadians—the workplace also includes people with disabilities, gays and lesbians, and the elderly. Moreover, workforce diversity is an issue in the United States, Australia, South Africa, Japan, and Europe, as well as Canada. For example, the "new" South Africa will increasingly be characterized by Blacks' holding important technical and managerial jobs. Japan has experienced considerable change in its workplace as women, long confined to low-paying temporary jobs, are now employed in permanent careers and even moving into managerial positions. Immigration patterns and relatively open national borders in some countries have also led to changes in workforce diversity. For instance, managers and employees in Canada and Australia are having to learn to work side by side with immigrants from Asia and other countries. Moreover, the creation of the European Union cooperative trade arrangement, which opened up borders throughout much of Western Europe, has increased workforce diversity in organizations that operate in countries such as Germany, Portugal, Italy, and France.

Why should you care about understanding other people?

Haven't organizations always included members of diverse groups? Yes, but they were a small percentage of the workforce and were, for the most part, ignored by large organizations. For instance, before the 1980s, the Canadian workforce was composed predominantly of male Caucasians working full-time to support a nonemployed wife and school-aged children. Now such employees are the true minority! Between 1997 and 2010, white males will account for fewer of the new labour-force entrants as visible minorities increase their participation in the workplace.

We used to assume that people in organizations who differed from the stereotypical employee would somehow assimilate. We now recognize that employees don't set aside their cultural values and lifestyle preferences when they come to work. The challenge for organizations, therefore, is to accommodate diverse groups of people by addressing their different lifestyles, family needs, and work styles.[50] However, what motivates you may not motivate them. Your style of communication may be straightforward and open; they may find that style uncomfortable and threatening. To work effectively with different people, you'll need to understand their culture and how it has shaped them, and learn to adapt your interaction style.

Workforce diversity also has important implications for management practice. Managers need to shift their philosophy from treating everyone alike to recognizing differences. They need to respond to those differences in ways that will ensure employee retention and greater productivity while, at the same time, not discriminating. This shift includes, for instance, providing diversity training and revamping benefit programs to make them more "family-friendly." Diversity, if positively managed, can increase creativity and innovation in organizations, as well as improve decision making by providing different perspectives on problems.[51] When diversity is not managed properly, there is potential for higher turnover, more difficult communication, and more interpersonal conflicts. We will discuss further issues of workplace diversity in Chapter 3.

## Does Managing Well Make a Difference?

Black Photo Corporation's president, Rod Smith, learned that not listening to employee demands can have undesirable consequences when he was confronted with a union drive at Black's. He's not pleased about working with a union. In fact, he argues that "one of the things that you lose when you get unionized is that ability to be compassionate, because the rules are the rules, and they catch people in ways we prefer not to catch them."[52]

Arlis Kaplanis, president and CEO of Toronto-based Teranet Land Information Services Inc., however, understands the importance of managing well. In an industry where turnover is typically 10 to 20 percent, Teranet's annual turnover rate is less than one percent. Kaplanis believes that his low turnover is the result of developing a corporate culture that is both humane

Psychologists at the Center for Creative Leadership systematically study the behaviour of managers in a controlled environment. Through one-way glass, they observe, videotape, and evaluate managers' leadership skills. They also gather data by surveying the managers and their co-workers, bosses, and subordinates. The goal of this scientific study: to teach managers how to lead others in their organizations effectively.

and family-friendly. "My perspective is that the company has two assets—one is the customers, the other is our employees. Both of these assets have to be serviced."[53]

The evidence indicates that managing people well makes for better corporations overall. Exhibit 1-4 shows that many of the firms that made *Report on Business's* 1999 Honour Roll of Most Respected Businesses for people management also scored high on innovation, financial performance, corporate responsibility, and investment value. The *Financial Post's* 50 Best Managed Private Companies for 1997 also showed the importance of managing well. Two of the main characteristics of the top 50 were firms that exhibited "a growing awareness of the need for a team approach, not just at the top, but throughout the organization" and "a growing investment in people using everything from advanced training to increased employee share ownership."[54]

*Fortune* magazine recently published a list of the 100 best companies to work for in the United States. They wanted to know what makes employees love the organization where they work. *Fortune* identified three main traits

### Exhibit 1-4
### Firms That Made *Report on Business's* 1999 Honour Roll of Most Respected Businesses for People Management

| Rank on People Management | Rank on Innovation | Rank on Financial Performance | Rank on Corporate Responsibility | Rank on Investment Value |
|---|---|---|---|---|
| 1. Royal Bank | n/a | 1 | 1 | 2 |
| 2. Bombardier | 2 | 2 | n/a | 1 |
| 3. BCE Inc. | n/a | 3 | 2 | 4 |
| 4. Dofasco | n/a | n/a | n/a | n/a |
| 5. Northern Telecom Ltd. | 1 | 5 | n/a | 3 |
| 6. IBM Canada Ltd. | n/a | n/a | n/a | n/a |
| 7. Bank of Montreal | n/a | 10 | 10 | n/a |
| 8. Alcan Aluminum Ltd. | n/a | n/a | n/a | n/a |
| 9. Magna International Inc. | 4 | 4 | n/a | 5 |
| 10. Imperial Oil | n/a | n/a | 3 | n/a |

Source: S. McKay, "You Snooze, You Lose," *Report on Business Magazine*, April 1999, pp. 71-78.

of best-loved companies: (1) they are run by a powerful, visionary leader; (2) they offer a physical environment that employees like; and (3) they organize their workforces so that employees feel their jobs are important and have meaning.[55]

While the *Financial Post* results showed that managing well added to the bottom line, the *Fortune* study showed more directly the day-to-day return that managers receive from managing well. At *Fortune*'s best companies to work for, turnover is low and employees want to stay with their firms, *even* when they are offered higher-paying jobs by other companies. When asked why they stayed with these companies, employees responded: "cutting-edge technology, exciting work, the chance to change careers within the same company, a shot at a challenging overseas assignment, the promise of promotion from within, flexible or reduced work hours that still keep you on the fast track, truly terrific benefits."[56] None of the employees mentioned money.

The message from each of these surveys: Managing people well pays off. It may also lead to greater organizational commitment. We use the term **organizational commitment** to refer to an employee's emotional attachment to the organization, resulting in identification and involvement with one's organization.[57] This type of commitment is often called *affective commitment* and represents the attitude of managers and employees who go beyond expected behaviours to provide extra service, extra insight, or whatever else is needed to get the job done. There is some concern that organizational commitment carried to an extreme can have negative consequences, in that employees with strong organizational commitment may engage in unethical behaviour to protect the organization. But this should not be a reason to avoid fostering commitment. For example, organizations can foster commitment through communication. When Siemens-Nixdorf Informationssysteme (SNI), the largest European supplier of information technology, needed to reduce the workforce from 52 000 to 35 000 in 1994, the CEO met with 11 000 employees to explain and ask for help in reducing costs. Employees showed a great deal of commitment to the organization, even in the event of downsizing, often working after hours to redesign the operations. Within a year, SNI was operating profitably, and employee satisfaction had almost doubled.

Finally, managing well may improve organizational citizenship. We use the term **organizational citizenship behaviour (OCB)** to describe discretionary behaviour that is not part of an employee's formal job requirements, but that nevertheless promotes the effective functioning of the organization.[58]

Successful organizations need employees who will do more than their usual job duties; who will provide performance that is *beyond* expectations. In today's dynamic workplace, where tasks are increasingly done in teams and where flexibility is critical, organizations need employees who will engage in "good citizenship" behaviours, such as making constructive statements about their work group and the organization, helping others on their team, volunteering for extra job activities, avoiding unnecessary conflicts, showing care for organizational property, respecting the spirit as well as the letter of rules and regulations, and gracefully tolerating the occasional work-related impositions and nuisances.

Organizations want and need employees who will do those things that aren't in any job description. And the evidence indicates that organizations that have such employees outperform those that don't.[59]

**organizational commitment**
An employee's emotional attachment to the organization, resulting in identification and involvement with the organization.

**Siemens-Nixdorf Informationssysteme**
www.siemensnixdorf.com/eng/
homepage/index.html

**organizational citizenship behaviour (OCB)**
Discretionary behaviour that is not part of an employee's formal job requirements but that nevertheless promotes the effective functioning of the organization.

## OB: Making Sense of Behaviour in Organizations

Organizational behaviour is an applied behavioural science that is built upon contributions from a number of behavioural disciplines. The predominant areas are psychology, sociology, social psychology, anthropology, and political science.[60] As we will learn, psychology's contributions have been mainly at the individual, or micro-level, of analysis; the other four disciplines have contributed to our understanding of macro concepts, such as group processes and organization. Exhibit 1-5 presents an overview of the major contributions to the study of organizational behaviour.

**Exhibit 1-5**
**Toward an OB Discipline**

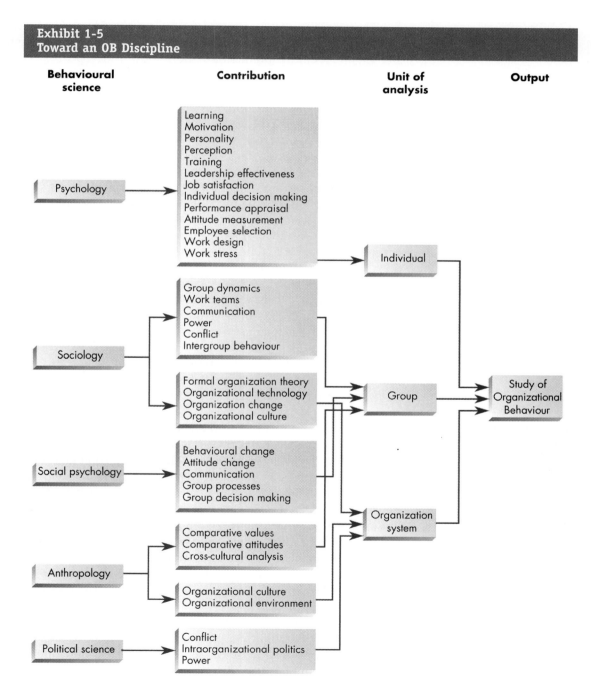

How can OB help us? Whether one wants to respond to the challenges of the Canadian workplace, manage well, or guarantee satisfying and rewarding employment for one's self, an understanding of organizational behaviour pays off. It provides a systematic approach to the study of behaviour in organizations. Underlying this systematic approach is the belief that behaviour is not random—it stems from and is directed toward some end that the individual believes, rightly or wrongly, is in his or her best interest.

Certainly there are differences among individuals. Placed in similar situations, all people don't act exactly alike. However, there are certain fundamental consistencies underlying the behaviour of all individuals that can be identified and then modified to reflect individual differences.

These fundamental consistencies are very important because they allow predictability. When you get into your car, you make some definite and usually highly accurate predictions about how other people will behave. In North America, for instance, you predict that other drivers will stop at stop signs and red lights, drive on the right side of the road, pass on your left, and not cross the solid double line on mountain roads. Notice that your predictions about the behaviour of people behind the wheels of their cars are almost always correct. Obviously, the rules of driving make predictions about driving behaviour fairly easy.

> **Isn't OB just common sense?**

What may be less obvious is that there are rules (written and unwritten) in almost every setting. Therefore, it can be argued that it's possible to predict behaviour (undoubtedly, not always with 100 percent accuracy) in supermarkets, classrooms, doctors' offices, elevators, and in most structured situations. For instance, do you turn around and face the doors when you get into an elevator? Almost everyone does. Is there a sign inside the elevator that tells you to do this? Probably not! Just as we make predictions about drivers, where there are definite rules of the road, we can make predictions about the behaviour of people in elevators, where there are few written rules. In a class of 60 students, if you wanted to ask a question of the instructor, you would raise your hand. You don't clap, stand up, raise your leg, cough, or yell, "Hey, over here!" You have learned that raising your hand is appropriate behaviour in school. These examples support a major contention in this text: Behaviour is generally predictable, and the *systematic study* of behaviour is a means to making reasonably accurate predictions.

**systematic study**
The examination of behaviour in order to draw conclusions, based on scientific evidence, about causes and effects in relationships.

When we use the phrase **systematic study**, we mean looking at relationships, attempting to attribute causes and effects, and basing our conclusions on scientific evidence—that is, on data gathered under controlled conditions, and measured and interpreted in a reasonably rigorous manner. A systematic approach does not mean that those things you have come to believe in an unsystematic way are necessarily incorrect. Some of the conclusions we make in this text, based on reasonably substantive research findings, will support what you always knew was true. You'll also be exposed to research evidence that runs counter to what you might have thought was common sense. In fact, one of the challenges to teaching a subject like organizational behaviour is to overcome the notion, held by many, "that's all common sense."[61]

You'll find that many of the so-called common-sense views you hold about human behaviour are, on closer examination, wrong. Moreover, what one person considers common sense frequently runs counter to another's version of common sense. Are leaders born or made? What is it that motivates people at work nowadays? You probably have answers to such questions, and individuals who have not reviewed the research are likely to differ on their answers. The point is that one of the objectives of this text is to expose you to a systematic analysis of behaviour, in the belief that such analysis will improve your accuracy in explaining and predicting behaviour. If understanding behaviour were simply common sense, we wouldn't observe many of the problems that occur in the workplace, because managers and employees would know how to behave. Unfortunately, as you'll see from examples throughout the textbook, many individuals and managers exhibit less than desirable behaviour in the workplace. With a stronger grounding in organizational behaviour, you might be able to avoid some of these mistakes.

## There Are Few Absolutes in OB

There are few, if any, simple and universal principles that explain organizational behaviour. In contrast, the physical sciences—chemistry, astronomy, physics—have laws that are consistent and apply in a wide range of situations. They allow scientists to generalize about the pull of gravity or to confidently send astronauts into space to repair satellites. But as one noted behavioural researcher aptly concluded, "God gave all the easy problems to the physicists." Human beings are complex. Because they are not alike, our ability to make simple, accurate, and sweeping generalizations is limited. Two people often act very differently in the same situation, and the same person's behaviour changes in different situations. For instance, not everyone is motivated by money, and you behave differently at a religious service than you do at a party.

**contingency approach**
Considers behaviour within the context in which it occurs.

That doesn't mean, of course, that we can't offer reasonably accurate explanations of human behaviour or make valid predictions. It does mean, however, that OB concepts must reflect situational, or **contingency**, conditions. So, for example, OB scholars would avoid stating that effective leaders should always seek the ideas of their employees before making a decision. Rather, we may find that in some situations a participative style is clearly superior, but, in other situations, an autocratic decision style is more effective. In other words, the effectiveness of a particular leadership style depends upon the situation in which it is used, and therefore the OB scholar would try to describe the situations to which each style was suited.

As you proceed through this text, you'll encounter a wealth of research-based theories about how people behave in organizations. But don't expect to find a lot of straightforward cause-and-effect relationships. There aren't many! Organizational behaviour theories mirror the subject matter with which they deal. People are complex and complicated, and so too must be the theories developed to explain their actions.

Consistent with the contingency philosophy, Point/CounterPoint debates are provided in each chapter. These debates are included to reinforce the fact that within the OB field there are many issues over which there is significant disagreement. Directly addressing some of the more controversial issues using the Point/CounterPoint format gives you the opportunity to explore different points of view, discover how diverse perspectives complement and oppose each other, and gain insight into some of the debates currently taking place within the OB field.[62]

So in one chapter, you'll find the argument that leadership plays an important role in an organization's attaining its goals, followed by the argument that there is little evidence to support that claim. Similarly, in other chapters, you'll read both sides of the debate on whether money is a motivator, clear communication is always desirable, and other controversial issues. These arguments are meant to demonstrate that OB, like many disciplines, has disagreements over specific findings, methods, and theories. Some of the Point/CounterPoint arguments are more provocative than others, but each makes some valid points that you should find thought-provoking. The key is to be able to decipher under what conditions each argument may be right or wrong.

## Explaining Organizational Behaviour

Earlier in the chapter we reviewed some of the challenges of the Canadian workplace. So how do we account for variations in things like productivity, absenteeism, turnover, job satisfaction, organizational commitment, and organizational citizenship? Our answer to that question considers that individuals themselves differ, and group and organizational factors also affect behaviour. Exhibit 1-6 presents the three levels of analysis we consider in this textbook, and shows that as we move from the individual level to the organization systems level, we add systematically to our understanding of behaviour in organizations. The three basic levels are analogous to building blocks: Each level is constructed upon the previous level. Group concepts grow out of the foundation laid in the individual section; we overlay structural constraints on the individual and group in order to arrive at organizational behaviour.

**INDIVIDUAL-LEVEL BEHAVIOUR** People enter groups and organizations with certain characteristics that will influence their behaviour. The more obvious of these are personality characteristics, values, and attitudes. These characteristics are essentially intact when an individual joins an organization, and for the most part, there is little that those in the organization can do to alter them. Yet they have a very real impact on behaviour. Therefore, each of these factors will be discussed in Chapters 2 and 3.

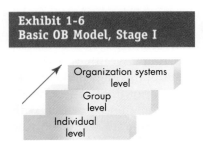

**Exhibit 1-6
Basic OB Model, Stage I**

Organization systems level

Group level

Individual level

Two other individual-level factors that have been shown to affect group and organizational behaviour are perception and motivation. Chapter 2 examines the role of perception in our interactions and understandings. Chapter 4 discusses the importance of rewards for motivating employees, and describes specific rewards that can be used in the workplace. You may find the discussion of motivation and rewards particularly interesting after realizing that a 1997 Angus Reid survey showed that 29 percent of employees do not feel they receive fair or reasonable rewards.[63]

**GROUP-LEVEL BEHAVIOUR** The behaviour of people in groups is more than the sum total of all the individuals acting in their own way. People's behaviour when they are in groups is different from their behaviour when they are alone. Therefore, the next step in the development of an understanding of OB is the study of group behaviour.

Chapter 5 lays the foundation for an understanding of the dynamics of group behaviour. That chapter discusses how individuals in groups are influenced by the patterns of behaviour they are expected to exhibit, what the group considers to be acceptable standards of behaviour, and the degree to which group members are attracted to each other. Chapter 6 translates our understanding of groups to the design of effective work teams. You may be interested in these chapters because in a 1997 Angus Reid survey, only 50 percent of employees report having supportive colleagues.[64] Thus Chapters 5 and 6 discuss ways that individuals could learn to work together more effectively and be more supportive of one another.

Chapters 7 through 11 demonstrate how communication patterns, decision making, and leadership styles affect group behaviour, and show how organizational culture transmits the vision of the organization to its members. Again, these chapters may be of interest to you once you know that a 1997 Angus Reid survey indicated that companies are not communicating enough information to their employees.[65] We discuss the specific topic of communication and how to do a better job at the individual, group, and organizational levels in Chapter 7.

Chapters 7 and 8 examine some of the more complex issues of interaction, including power and politics, and conflict and negotiation. These chapters give you an opportunity to think about how communication processes sometimes become complicated because of office politicking and interpersonal and group conflict.

**ORGANIZATION SYSTEMS-LEVEL BEHAVIOUR** Organizational behaviour reaches its highest level of sophistication when we add formal structure to our previous knowledge of individual and group behaviour. Just as groups are more than the sum of their individual members, so are organizations more than the sum of their member groups. The design of the formal organization, work processes, and jobs all have an impact on the organizational outcomes. These are discussed in detail in Chapters 12 and 13. Finally, in Chapter 14 we will discuss the cycle of organizational change and renewal, and ways to manage that change. As we have noted already, and as will become clear throughout the text, change is a key issue for organizations in the 21st century.

## Putting It All Together

Exhibit 1-7 shows how individual, group, and organizational behaviours link to each other and lead to differences in a person's output, including his or her productivity, absenteeism, turnover, satisfaction, organizational commitment and citizenship, and workplace interactions. The figure should help to explain the reasons for arranging the chapters in this book as they are and help you to explain and predict the behaviour of people at work.

Note that we have included the concepts of change and stress in Exhibit 1-7, acknowledging the dynamics of behaviour and the fact that work stress is an individual, group, and organizational issue. Also note that Exhibit 1-7 includes linkages among the three levels of analysis. For instance, organization structure is linked to leadership. This link is meant to convey that authority and leadership are related: Management exerts its influence on group behaviour through leadership. Similarly, communication is the means by which individuals transmit information; thus, it is the link between individual and group behaviour.

**Exhibit 1-7**
**Basic OB Model, Stage II**

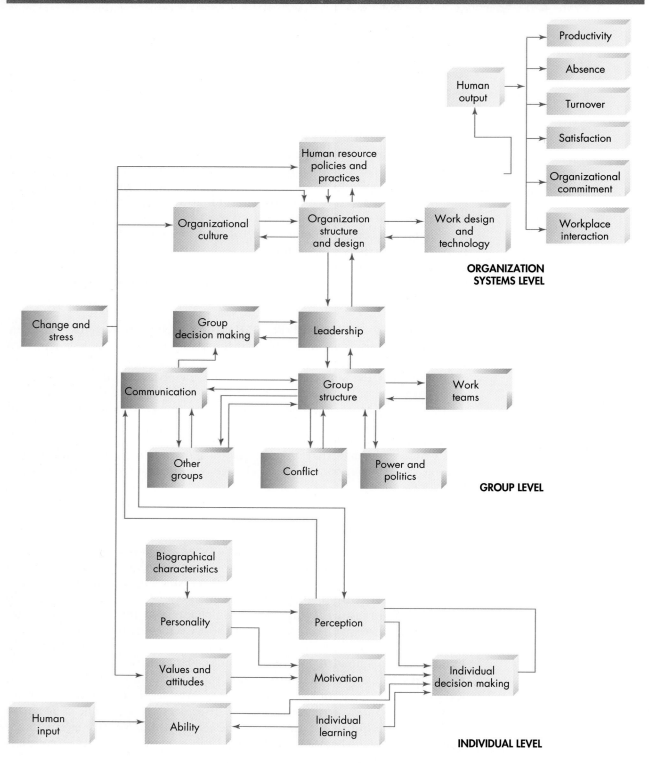

## SUMMARY AND IMPLICATIONS

### For the Workplace

Managers and employees need to develop their interpersonal, or people, skills if they are going to be effective in their jobs. The Conference Board of Canada recently noted that "portable skills such as problem-solving, project management and interpersonal relations are becoming as important as job-specific technical expertise."[66]

Organizational behaviour (OB) is a field of study that investigates the impact that individuals, groups, and structure have on behaviour within an organization, and it then applies that knowledge to make organizations work more effectively. Specifically, OB focuses on how to improve productivity, reduce absenteeism and turnover, and increase employee job satisfaction. OB also instructs us about how people can work together more effectively in the workplace.

We all hold generalizations about the behaviour of people. Some of our generalizations may provide valid insights into human behaviour, but many are erroneous. Organizational behaviour uses systematic study to improve predictions of behaviour that would be made from common sense alone. But, because people are different, we need to look at OB in a contingency framework, using situational variables to moderate cause-effect relationships.

Organizational behaviour offers both challenges and opportunities to everyone in the workplace. It recognizes differences, and helps us to see the value of workforce diversity and practices that may need to be changed when managing and working in different countries. It can help improve quality and employee productivity by showing managers how to empower their people, as well as how to design and implement change programs. It offers specific insights to improve people skills. In times of rapid and ongoing change—what most people in the workplace face today—OB can help us learn to cope in a world of impermanence and to manage a workforce that has undergone the trauma of downsizing.

### For You as an Individual

As you journey through this course in organizational behaviour, bear in mind that the processes we describe are as relevant to you as an individual as they are to organizations, managers, and employees. When you work together with student teams, when you join a student organization, when you volunteer time to some community group, your interactions with the other people in those groups will be affected by your ability to get along with others and to help the group achieve its goals. This chapter's Case Incident about the daycare centre on page 33 is a good example of how organizational behavioural skills are relevant in areas outside of the workplace.

Each of the chapters in this book provides insights that you can use today, even if you are not yet in the workforce. For instance, being aware of how your perceptions and personality affect your interactions with others gives you an opportunity to be somewhat more careful in your initial impression of others. Knowing how to motivate others who are working with you, knowing how to communicate effectively, to negotiate and compromise where necessary, are all elements of getting along in a variety of situations that are not necessarily work-related. Finally, because we live in uncertain times, and guaranteed jobs are no longer part of the Canadian workplace, you will find it helpful to keep yourself in a learning framework throughout your life, rather than confining learning to school. It may be the case that you decide to become an entrepreneur, as many people today are doing. In that case, having organizational behaviour skills becomes even more important to ensure that you can work effectively with your employees.

## ROADMAP REMINDER

This chapter sets the context for why you might want to consider studying organizational behaviour. We also looked at some of the specific challenges that managers face as organizations meet the demands of the 21$^{st}$ century. Finally, we considered some of the demands that you, as an employee, will face. In the next chapter, we introduce the concepts of perception and personality as a reminder that we work together with others, and what we bring as individuals to the workplace affects those around us. We also look at the role of emotions to show how they can both hinder and enhance performance in the workplace.

## For Review

1. Define *organizational behaviour*.
2. What is an organization? Is the family unit an organization? Explain.
3. What is the Competing Values Framework?
4. "Behaviour is generally predictable, so there is no need to formally study OB." Do you agree or disagree with this statement? Why?
5. What are some of the challenges and opportunities that managers face as we move into the 21$^{st}$ century?
6. What are the 3 levels of analysis in our OB model? Are they related? If so, how?
7. Why is job satisfaction an important consideration for OB?
8. What are effectiveness and efficiency, and how are they related to organizational behaviour?

## For Critical Thinking

1. "The best way to view OB is through a contingency approach." Build an argument to support this statement.
2. Why do you think the subject of OB might be criticized as being "only common sense," when one would rarely hear such a criticism of a course in physics or statistics? Do you think this criticism of OB is fair?

3. On a scale of 1 to 10 measuring the sophistication of a scientific discipline in predicting phenomena, mathematical physics would probably be a 10. Where do you think OB would fall on the scale? Why?

4. Millions of workers have lost their jobs due to downsizing. At the same time, many organizations are complaining that they can't find people to fill vacancies. How do you explain this apparent contradiction?

## *LEARNING ABOUT YOURSELF EXERCISE*

# The Competing Values Framework: Identifying Your Interpersonal Skills

**Directions:** From the list below, identify what you believe to be your strongest skills, and then identify those in which you think your performance is weak. You should identify about 4 strong skills and 4 weak skills.

1. Taking initiative

2. Goal setting

3. Delegating effectively

4. Personal productivity and motivation

5. Motivating others

6. Time and stress management

7. Planning

8. Organizing

9. Controlling

10. Receiving and organizing information

11. Evaluating routine information

12. Responding to routine information

13. Understanding yourself and others

14. Interpersonal communication

15. Developing subordinates

16. Team building

17. Participative decision making

18. Conflict management

19. Living with change

*Continued on next page*

*The Competing Values Framework: Identifying Your Interpersonal Skills continued.*

**20.** Creative thinking

**21.** Managing change

**22.** Building and maintaining a power base

**23.** Negotiating agreement and commitment

**24.** Negotiating and selling ideas

Turn to page 632 for scoring directions and key. After reviewing how your strengths and weaknesses relate to the skills that today's managers and leaders need, as illustrated in Exhibit 1-2, you should consider whether you need to develop a broader range of skills.

---

Source: Created based on material from R.E. Quinn, S.R. Faerman, M.P. Thompson, and M.R. McGrath, *Becoming a Master Manager: A Competency Framework,* 1st ed. (New York: John Wiley and Sons, 1990), Chapter 1.

## WORKING WITH OTHERS EXERCISE

# Interpersonal Skills in the Workplace

This exercise asks you to consider the skills outlined in the Competing Values Framework to develop an understanding of managerial expertise. Steps 1-4 can be completed in 15-20 minutes.

**1.** Using the skills listed in "Learning About Yourself," identify the 4 skills that you think all managers should have.

**2.** Identify the 4 skills that you think are least important for managers to have.

**3.** In groups of 5-7, reach a consensus on the most-needed and least-needed skills identified in Steps 1 and 2.

**4.** Using Exhibit 1-2, determine whether your "ideal" managers would have trouble managing in some dimensions of organizational demands.

**5.** Your instructor will lead a general discussion of your results.

## INTERNET SEARCH EXERCISES

**1.** Find 5 organizations that say they promote diversity through family-friendly policies. What are their policies? How do these policies attract and keep people?

**2.** Find an organization that directly addresses the cost of absenteeism or turnover in its Internet site. What, if anything, is that organization doing to reduce those costs? What did your search tell you in terms of the importance or unimportance of these costs to organizations?

## CASE INCIDENT

# I Thought These Problems Happened Only at Work

As the father of two young children, Marshall Rogers thought that serving on the board of Marysville Daycare would be a good way to stay in touch with those who cared for his children during the day. But he never dreamt that he would become involved in union-management negotiations with daycare-centre workers.

Late one Sunday evening, in his ninth month as president of the daycare centre, Rogers received a phone call from Grace Ng, a union representative of the Provincial Government Employees' Union (PGEU). Ng informed Rogers that the daycare workers would be unionized the following week. Rogers was stunned to hear this news. Early the next morning, he had to present his new marketing plan to senior management at Techtronix Industries, where he was vice-president of marketing. Somehow he made it through the meeting, wondering why he hadn't been aware of the employees' unhappiness, and how this action would affect his children.

Following his presentation, Rogers received documentation from the Labour Relations Board indicating that the daycare employees had been working to unionize themselves for over a year. Rogers immediately contacted Xavier Breslin, the board's vice-president, and together they determined that no one on the board had been aware that the daycare workers were unhappy, let alone prepared to join a union.

Hoping that there was some sort of misunderstanding, Rogers called Emma Reynaud, Marysville's supervisor. Reynaud attended most of the board meetings, but she had never mentioned the union-organizing drive. Yet Reynaud now told Rogers that she had actively encouraged the other daycare workers to consider joining the PGEU because the board had not been interested in the workers' concerns, had not increased their wages sufficiently over the last two years, and had not maintained communication channels between the board and the employees.

All of the board members had full-time jobs elsewhere, and many were upper- and middle-level managers in their own companies. They were used to dealing with unhappy employees in their own workplaces, although none had experienced a union-organizing drive. Like Rogers, they had chosen to serve on the board of Marysville to stay informed about the day-to-day events of the centre. They hadn't really thought of themselves as the centre's employer, although, as board members, they represented all the parents of children enrolled at Marysville. Their main tasks on the daycare-centre board had been setting fees for the children and wages for the daycare workers. The board members usually saw the staff members several times a week, when they picked up their children, yet the unhappiness represented by the union-organizing drive was surprising to all of them. When they met at an emergency board meeting that evening, they tried to evaluate what had gone wrong at Marysville.

## Questions

1. If you were either a board member or a parent, how would you know that the employees taking care of your children were unhappy with their jobs?

2. What might you do if you learned about their unhappiness?

3. What might Rogers have done differently as president of the board?

4. In what ways does this case illustrate that knowledge of organizational behaviour can be applied beyond your own workplace?

Source: Nancy Langton and Joy Begley © 1999. (The events described are based on an actual situation, although the participants, as well as the centre, have been disguised.)

# Revenge of the Middle Manager

Today's organizations are becoming flatter, through both downsizing in general and looking for different ways of organizing the work employees do. It's not unusual for employees to have more managerial responsibilities today, in contrast with the time when employees "worked" and managers "supervised." Many employees are expected to manage themselves better and work in teams.

The consequence of these changes is that middle managers are becoming a rare commodity in organizations. And some accounting firms, private investigators, and insurance companies are suggesting that employee fraud is the direct result of the disappearance of middle managers. Organizations have fewer of the people who provided essential checks and balances.

"When we start to remove middle managers we remove a level of supervision," says Norman Inkster, former head of the RCMP and now an executive with consulting firm KPMG. "If you just take it out holus bolus and there's nothing there, then there is a void. And that's how people can take advantage of those opportunities."

Bill Joynt, private investigator and president of Toronto-based The Investigators Group, thinks organizations are making a mistake when they look at the bottom line just in terms of the number of employees on the books. "People aren't stupid. They know no one is watching them and it doesn't take long before it (fraud) starts to happen," he says.

So what do middle managers do in organizations? They communicate, coordinate, and act as "watchdogs," as one management consultant put it. But computers and e-mail help with both communication and coordination, seemingly making managers less essential.

However, as one landlord discovered, improved efficiency through technology can lead to serious losses in other ways. The landlord had two managers handling rent cheques, and part of their job was checking on each other. However, in an effort to cut costs, one manager was laid off. The remaining manager started taking some of the rent cheques, concealing his actions by claiming that apartments were vacant when they weren't. The company's plan to save money through a layoff backfired. They lost at least $70 000 that they know about.

St. Catharine's, Ontario shipbuilder Port Weller Dry Docks is another company that tried to reduce costs by cutting the number of supervisors. Unfortunately, shipbuilding is a complex process, and there were not enough managers left to tell the workers what they were supposed to do. The shipbuilder is now retraining the entire workforce, so that they will know how to work without as many supervisors.

# Questions

1. What might companies do to avoid the problems that come with cutting middle managers?

2. Under what kinds of conditions might we expect that companies will face greater fraud when middle managers are cut?

3. What are ways that companies might balance giving employees more power, while making sure that power is not abused through activities like fraud?

4. What other problems might you expect as you think about the kinds of changes organizations are facing as they enter the 21st century?

Source: Based on "Revenge of the Middle-Managers," *Venture 724*; aired October 12, 1999.

# CHAPTER 2

# Perception, Personality, and Emotion

## Questions for Consideration

**What is perception, and why is it important for understanding the workplace?**

**To what extent does personality affect behaviour?**

**Does understanding emotions lead to better understanding how people interact?**

The former and the current CEOs of Montreal-based Bank of Montreal couldn't be more different.[1] Matthew Barrett, who turned over the reins in February 1999 and is currently CEO of Barclays PLC, Britain's second-largest bank, is only seven months older than his successor, Anthony Comper. Barrett is described as "flashy," Comper as "sober." Barrett is "slick and silver-tongued," while Comper is "a techno-whiz who speaks in jargon." Even their family lives are different. Barrett's second marriage to a jet-setting beautiful younger woman was an "event" in Toronto's social circle. Comper, a devout Roman Catholic, is still married to his first wife of 28 years, Elizabeth.

Barrett is described as a risk-taker, both in his personal life, and with his bank. He proposed the failed bank merger with Royal Bank of Canada. Comper is viewed as "the steady hand at the tiller, the efficient organizer who trusts others to do their work." One observer called Comper's promotion to CEO after Barrett "the revenge of the nerds."

It should be clear from these descriptions that Barrett and Comper have quite different personalities, and no doubt the leadership styles they bring to the Bank of Montreal will be telling. Barrett became CEO in 1989, when the

bank was profitable, but was known for treating employees poorly. Under his leadership, Bank of Montreal became more profitable than ever, and was recognized as a model employer.

Barrett's vision for the 21st century was a merged Bank of Montreal and Royal Bank with Royal chair and CEO John Cleghorn at its head. Unfortunately for Barrett, Finance Minister Paul Martin did not agree with this vision. Many in the financial community attributed the failed merger to Barrett's arrogance. Before announcing the proposed merger, Barrett did not even consult with the federal government about his plan. When Martin forbade the merger, it was not surprising that Barrett decided to step down. After all, Barrett had warned of dire consequences should the merger fail.

Bay Street analysts gave thumbs-up to Comper's appointment, saying "the Bank of Montreal does not need charisma now — it needs a hands-on innovator who can implement restructuring plans with the patience and wisdom of a would-be priest."

Matthew Barrett's arrogance and risk-seeking personality characteristics, and Anthony Comper's more quiet ways, were in place long before each came to head the Bank of Montreal. But these qualities played an important role in shaping the men's actions. *All* our behaviour is somewhat shaped by our perceptions, personalities, emotions, and experiences. In this chapter, we consider the role that perception plays in affecting the way we see the world and the people around us. We also consider how personality characteristics affect our attitudes toward people and situations. We then consider how emotions shape many of our work-related behaviours.

## What Is Perception, and Why Is It Important?

**Perception** can be defined as a process by which individuals organize and interpret their sensory impressions in order to give meaning to their environment. However, what one perceives can be substantially different from objective reality. It need not be, but there is often disagreement about what is objectively real. For example, it is possible that all employees in

**perception**
A process by which individuals organize and interpret their sensory impressions in order to give meaning to their environment.

**Barclays PLC**
www.barclays.co.uk

**Royal Bank of Canada**
www.royalbank.com

**Planet Sun**
www.canoe.ca/PlanetSun

a firm may view it as a great place to work—favourable working conditions, interesting job assignments, good pay, understanding and responsible management—but, as most of us know, it is very unusual to find such agreement.

Why is perception important in the study of OB? Simply because people's behaviour is based on their perception of what reality is, not on reality itself. *The world as it is perceived is the world that is behaviourally important.* Paul Godfrey, the CEO of Toronto-based Sun Media Corp., notes that "a lot of things in life are perception." He claims that as chair of Metropolitan Toronto for 11 years, he had little real power, but people believed he could get things done, and so he did.[2]

## Factors Influencing Perception

How do we explain that individuals may look at the same thing, yet perceive it differently? A number of factors operate to shape and sometimes distort perception. These factors can reside in the *perceiver*, in the object or *target* being perceived, or in the context of the *situation* in which the perception is made. This chapter's Working With Others Exercise on page 83 helps to give you an understanding of the role of perception in evaluating others.

### The Perceiver

When an individual looks at a target and attempts to interpret what he or she sees, that interpretation is heavily influenced by personal characteristics of the individual perceiver. Have you ever bought a new car and then suddenly noticed a large number of cars like yours on the road? It's unlikely that the number of such cars suddenly increased. Rather, your own purchase has influenced your perception so that you are now more likely to notice the other cars. This is an example of how factors related to the perceiver influence what he or she perceives.

A variety of factors affect our perception of an event. Our attitudes and motives, interests, and past experiences all shape the way we perceive an event. For instance, suppose you had a bad experience last term in a large class where students were not able to participate, and you prefer class participation. This term, you are assigned to the largest section of a new course. You dread the class before it begins, because your perception is that you won't be able to participate enough in class. In this case, your attitude, combined with your previous experience, makes it difficult to be open-minded about the new experience.

There are other ways that perceptions affect interpretations of the world around us. For example, we often interpret others' behaviours based on our knowledge of our own behaviour. Thus people who are devious are prone to view others as also being devious.

Finally, expectations can distort your perceptions in that you will see what you expect to see. For example, if you expect police officers to be authoritarian, young people to be unambitious, human resources directors to "like people," or individuals holding public office to be unscrupulous, you may perceive individuals in these categories as such, regardless of their actual traits.

Diversity advocate Ernest Drew, CEO of Hoechst Celanese, set a goal to have at least 34 percent representation of women and minorities at all levels of his company by 2001. To influence managers' perceptions of women and minorities, Drew requires that his top 26 officers join two organizations in which they are a minority. Drew put the policy in place to help managers break out of their comfort zones and experience what it's like to be a minority so they learn "that all people are similar." Drew is a board member of Black Hampton University and of SER-Jobs for Progress, a Hispanic association. He's shown here visiting with Hampton students.

## The Target

A target's characteristics can affect what is perceived. Loud people are more likely to be noticed in a group than are quiet ones. So, too, are extremely attractive or unattractive individuals. Motion, sound, size, and other attributes of a target shape the way we see it.

Because targets are not looked at in isolation, the relationship of a target to its background influences perception, as does our tendency to group close things and similar things together.

What we see depends on how we separate a figure from its general background. For instance, what you see as you read this sentence is black letters on a white page. You do not see funny-shaped patches of black and white because you recognize these shapes and organize the black shapes against the white background. Exhibit 2-1 dramatizes this effect. The object on the left may at first look like a white vase. However, if white is taken as the background, we see two purple profiles. On first observation, the group of objects on the right appears to be some purple modular figures against a white background. Closer inspection will reveal the word *FLY* once the background is defined as purple.

Objects that are close to each other will tend to be perceived together rather than separately. As a result of physical or time proximity, we often put together objects or events that are unrelated. Employees in a particular department are seen as a group. If two people in a four-member department suddenly resign, we tend to assume that their departures were related when, in fact, they may be totally unrelated. Timing may also imply dependence when, for example, a new sales manager is assigned to a territory and, soon after, sales in that territory skyrocket. The assignment

**Exhibit 2-1**
**Figure-Ground Illustrations**

## Exhibit 2-2
### Factors That Influence Perception

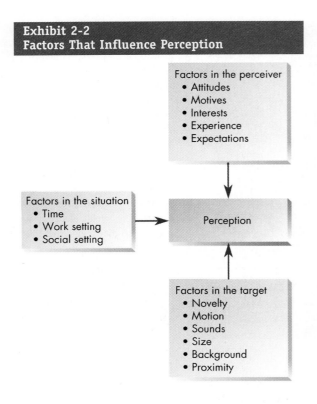

Factors in the perceiver
- Attitudes
- Motives
- Interests
- Experience
- Expectations

Factors in the situation
- Time
- Work setting
- Social setting

Perception

Factors in the target
- Novelty
- Motion
- Sounds
- Size
- Background
- Proximity

of the new sales manager and the increase in sales may not be related—the increase may be due to the introduction of a new product line or to one of many other reasons—but there is a tendency to perceive the two occurrences as being related.

Persons, objects, or events that are similar to each other also tend to be grouped together. The greater the similarity, the greater the probability that we will tend to perceive them as a common group. People who are female, or Black, or members of any other clearly distinguishable group will tend to be perceived as similar not only in physical terms but in other unrelated characteristics as well.

## The Situation

The context in which we see objects or events is important. Elements in the surrounding environment influence our perceptions. You are more likely to notice your employees goofing off if your manager from the head office happens to be in town. Your employees may be acting quite "normally"; however, it is the situation that affects your perception. The time at which an object or event is seen can influence attention, as can location, light, heat, or any number of situational factors. Exhibit 2-2 summarizes the factors influencing perception.

## Perception and Judgment: Attribution Theory

When we observe people, we attempt to develop explanations of why they behave in certain ways. Our perception and judgment of a person's actions, therefore, will be significantly influenced by the assumptions we make about that person's internal state.

**attribution theory**
When individuals observe behaviour, they attempt to determine whether it is internally or externally caused.

**Attribution theory** has been proposed to develop explanations of the ways in which we judge people differently, depending on what meaning we attribute to a given behaviour.[3] Basically, the theory suggests that when we observe an individual's behaviour, we attempt to determine whether it was internally or externally caused. That determination, however, depends largely on three factors: (1) distinctiveness, (2) consensus, and (3) consistency. First, let's clarify the differences between internal and external causation, and then we will elaborate on each of the three determining factors.

*Internally* caused behaviour is that believed to be under the personal control of the individual. *Externally* caused behaviour is seen as resulting from outside causes; that is, the person is seen as having been forced into the behaviour by the situation. For example, if one of your employees is late for work, you might attribute his lateness to his partying into the wee hours of the morning and then oversleeping. This would be an internal attribution. But if you attributed his arriving late to a major automobile accident that tied up traffic on the road that this employee regularly uses, then you would be making an external attribution.

*Distinctiveness* refers to whether an individual displays different behaviours in different situations. Is the employee who arrives late today also the

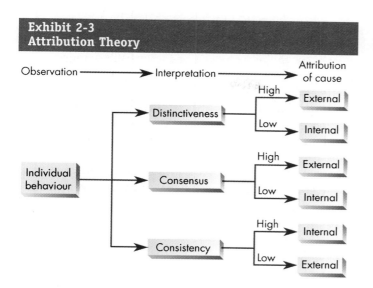

**Exhibit 2-3
Attribution Theory**

source of complaints by co-workers for "goofing off"? What we want to know is whether this behaviour is unusual. If it is, the observer is likely to give the behaviour an external attribution. If this action is not unusual, it will probably be judged as internal.

If everyone who is faced with a similar situation responds in the same way, we can say the behaviour shows *consensus*. Our late employee's behaviour would meet this criterion if all employees who took the same route to work were also late. From an attribution perspective, if consensus is high, you would be expected to give an external attribution to the employee's tardiness; whereas if other employees who took the same route made it to work on time, your conclusion as to causation would be internal.

Finally, an observer looks for *consistency* in a person's actions. Does the person respond the same way over time? Arriving 10 minutes late for work is not perceived in the same way for the employee for whom it is unusual (she hasn't been late for several months) as it is for the employee for whom it is routine (he is regularly late two or three times a week). The more consistent the behaviour, the more likely the observer is to attribute it to internal causes.

Exhibit 2-3 summarizes the key elements in attribution theory. It would tell us, for instance, how to evaluate your employee Kim Randolph's behaviour on a new task. To do this, you would consider whether she generally performs at about the same level on other related tasks as she does on her current task (low distinctiveness). You would also see if other employees frequently perform differently—better or worse—than Kim does on that current task (low consensus). Finally, if Kim's performance on this current task is consistent over time (high consistency), you or anyone else who is judging Kim's work is likely to hold her primarily responsible for her task performance (internal attribution).

> Who do you tend to blame when you make a mistake —yourself or others? Ever wonder why?

One of the more interesting findings from attribution theory is that there are errors or biases that distort attributions. For instance, there is substantial evidence that when we judge the behaviour of other people, we tend to underestimate the influence of external factors and overestimate the influence of internal or personal factors.[4] This is called the **fundamental attribution error** and can explain why a sales manager is prone to attribute the poor performance of his or her sales agents to laziness rather than to the innovative product line introduced by a competitor. There is also a tendency for individuals to attribute their own successes to internal factors, such as ability or effort, while putting the blame for failure on external factors, such as luck. This is called the **self-serving bias** and suggests that feedback provided to employees in performance reviews will be predictably distorted by recipients depending on whether it is positive or negative.

Are these errors or biases that distort attributions universal across different cultures? We can't answer that question definitively, but there is some preliminary evidence that indicates cultural differences. For instance, a study of Korean managers found that, contrary to the self-serving bias, they

**fundamental attribution error**
The tendency to underestimate the influence of external factors and overestimate the influence of internal factors when making judgments about the behaviour of others.

**self-serving bias**
The tendency for individuals to attribute their own successes to internal factors while putting the blame for failures on external factors.

tended to accept responsibility for group failure "because I was not a capable leader" instead of attributing it to group members.[5] There have been enough suicides committed by Japanese executives who feel responsible for the problems of their companies to indicate that many Japanese executives also do not use the "self-serving" bias. In just the first half of 1998, high-profile suicides in Japan included a central banker, three top finance ministry bureaucrats, a politician, and scores of executives. Toru Sekiya, who runs a psychiatric clinic in suburban Tokyo, explains these suicides as follows: "A lot of people used to die for the emperor. Now they die for the company." Professor Toyoma Fuse, from York University, notes that it is rarely the president of the company who commits suicide, however. Usually it is a subordinate; "caught in between the top brass and the workers, he really has to account for both."[6]

Attribution theory was developed largely in the United States on the basis of experiments with Americans, but there is no particular reason to believe it would not apply in Canada. However, the Korean study, as well as evidence from Japan, suggests caution in making attribution theory predictions in non-Western countries or in those with strong collectivist traditions, such as Spain, Portugal, and some of the Eastern European countries.

## Frequently Used Shortcuts in Judging Others

We use a number of shortcuts when we judge others. Perceiving and interpreting what others do is burdensome. As a result, individuals develop techniques for making the task more manageable. These techniques are frequently valuable—they allow us to make accurate perceptions rapidly and provide valid data for making predictions. However, they are not foolproof. They can and do get us into trouble. An understanding of these shortcuts can be helpful toward recognizing when they can result in significant distortions.

> **Did you ever find you'd misjudged a person? Learn why.**

**selective perception**
People selectively interpret what they see based on their interests, background, experience, and attitudes.

**SELECTIVE PERCEPTION**   Any characteristic that makes a person, object, or event stand out will increase the probability that it will be perceived. Why? Because it is impossible for us to assimilate everything we see—only certain stimuli can be taken in. This tendency explains why, as we noted earlier, you are more likely to notice cars like your own. It also explains why some people may be reprimanded by their manager for doing something that, when done by another employee, goes unnoticed. Since we can't observe everything going on about us, we engage in **selective perception**. A classic example shows how vested interests can significantly influence which problems we see.

Dearborn and Simon performed a perceptual study in which 23 business executives read a comprehensive case describing the organization and activities of a steel company.[7] Six of the 23 executives were in the sales function, five in production, four in accounting, and eight in miscellaneous functions. Each manager was asked to write down the most important problem he or she found in the case. Eighty-three percent of the sales executives rated sales important; only 29 percent of the others did so. This, along with other results of the study, led the researchers to conclude that the participants perceived aspects of a situation that were specifically related to the activities and goals of the unit to which they were attached. A group's perception of organizational activities is selectively altered to align with the vested interests they represent. In other words, when the stimuli are ambiguous, as in the steel company case, perception tends to be influenced more by an individual's base of interpretation (that is, attitudes, interests, and background) than by the stimulus itself.

But how does selectivity work as a shortcut in judging other people? Since we cannot assimilate all that we observe, we take in bits and pieces. But those bits and pieces are not chosen randomly; rather, they are selectively chosen according to our interests, background, experience, and attitudes. Selective perception allows us to "speed-read" others, but not without the risk of drawing an inaccurate picture. Because we see what we want to see, we can draw unwarranted conclusions from an ambiguous situation. Suppose there is a rumour going around the office that your company's sales are down and that large layoffs may be imminent. A routine visit by a senior executive from headquarters might then be interpreted as the first step in management's identification of people to be fired, when in reality such an action might be the furthest thing from the mind of the senior executive.

**halo effect**
Drawing a general impression about an individual based on a single characteristic.

**HALO EFFECT**   When we draw a general impression about an individual on the basis of a single characteristic, such as intelligence, sociability, or appearance, a **halo effect** is operating. This phenomenon frequently occurs when students appraise their instructor. Students may give prominence to a single trait, such as enthusiasm, and allow their entire evaluation to be tainted by how they judge the instructor on that one trait. Thus, an instructor may be quiet, assured, knowledgeable, and highly qualified, but if his or her presentation style lacks enthusiasm, those students would probably give the instructor a low rating.

The reality of the halo effect was confirmed in a classic study. Subjects were given a list of traits—such as intelligent, skillful, practical, industrious, determined, and warm—and were asked to evaluate the person to whom those traits applied.[8] When those traits were used, the person was judged to be wise, humorous, popular, and imaginative. When the same list was modified—cold was substituted for warm—a completely different set of perceptions was obtained. Clearly, the subjects were allowing a single trait to influence their overall impression of the person being judged.

The propensity for the halo effect to operate is not random. Research suggests that it is likely to be most extreme when the traits to be perceived are ambiguous in behavioural terms, when the traits have moral overtones, and when the perceiver is judging traits with which he or she has had limited experience.[9]

**contrast effects**
A person's evaluation is affected by comparisons with other individuals recently encountered.

**CONTRAST EFFECTS**   There's an old adage among entertainers who perform in variety shows: Never follow an act that has children or animals in it.

This example demonstrates how **contrast effects** can distort perceptions. We don't evaluate a person in isolation. Our reaction to one person is often influenced by other people we have recently encountered.

An illustration of how contrast effects operate is an interview situation in which one sees a pool of job applicants. Distortions in any given candidate's evaluation can occur as a result of his or her place in the interview schedule. The candidate is likely to receive a more favourable evaluation if preceded by mediocre applicants and a less favourable evaluation if preceded by strong applicants.

**projection**
Attributing one's own characteristics to other people.

**PROJECTION**   It is easy to judge others if we assume that they are similar to us. For instance, if you want challenge and responsibility in your job, you assume that others want the same. Or, you are honest and trustworthy, so you take it for granted that other people are equally honest and trustworthy. This tendency to attribute one's own characteristics to other people—which is called **projection**—can distort perceptions made about others.

People who engage in projection tend to perceive others according to what they themselves are like rather than according to what the person being observed is really like. When observing others who actually are like them, these observers are quite accurate—not because they are perceptive but because they always judge people as being similar to themselves. So when they finally do find someone who is like them, they are naturally correct. When managers engage in projection, they compromise their ability to respond to individual differences. They tend to see people as more homogeneous than they really are.

**stereotyping**
Judging someone on the basis of one's perception of the group to which that person belongs.

**STEREOTYPING**   When we judge someone on the basis of our perception of the group to which he or she belongs, we are using the shortcut called **stereotyping**. According to a popular literary anecdote, F. Scott Fitzgerald engaged in stereotyping when he told Ernest Hemingway, "the rich are very different from you and me," implying that the wealthy have values and behaviour unlike regular people. Hemingway's reply, "yes, they have more money," indicated that he refused to generalize characteristics of people on the basis of their wealth.

Generalization, of course, is not without advantages. It is a means of simplifying a complex world, and it permits us to maintain consistency. It is less difficult to deal with an unmanageable number of stimuli if we use stereotypes. As an example, assume you are a sales manager looking to fill a sales position in your territory. You want to hire someone who is ambitious and hard-working and who can deal well with adversity. You've had good success in the past by hiring individuals who participated in athletics while at university. So you focus your search by looking for candidates who participated in university athletics. In so doing, you have cut down considerably on your search time. Furthermore, to the extent that athletes *are* ambitious, hard-working, and able to deal with adversity, the use of this stereotype can improve your decision making. The problem, of course, is when we inaccurately stereotype.[10] All university athletes are *not necessarily* ambitious, hard-working, or good at dealing with adversity, just as all accountants are *not necessarily* quiet and introspective. Moreover, when we stereotype like this, we run the risk of overlooking highly qualified people who do not meet our stereotypes.

In organizations, we frequently hear comments that represent stereotypes based on gender, age, race, ethnicity, and even weight:[11] "Women won't relocate for a promotion"; "men aren't interested in child care"; "older workers can't learn new skills"; "Asian immigrants are hard-working and conscientious"; "overweight people lack self-discipline." From a perceptual standpoint, if people expect to see these stereotypes, that is what they will perceive, whether or not they are accurate.

Obviously, one of the problems of stereotypes is that they are widespread, despite the fact that they may not contain a shred of truth or that they may be irrelevant. Their being widespread may mean only that many people are making the same inaccurate perception on the basis of a false premise about a group.

Stereotyping cost a contractor in Ontario the opportunity to build the facility for Fern Hill School, a private school located in Oakville, Ontario. The contractor kept speaking to their male architect, instead of co-owners Joanne McLean (right) and Wendy Derrick when pitching his bid. He didn't even give the owners an opportunity to speak during the meeting. The job went to another builder.

## Why Do Perception and Judgment Matter?

People in organizations are always judging each other. For instance, in order to become an organizational member, a person typically goes through an employment interview. Interviewers make perceptual judgments during the interview, which then affect whether the individual is hired. Studies show that if negative information is exposed early in the interview, it tends to be more heavily weighted than if that same information comes out later.[12] When multiple interviewers are present, agreement among interviewers is often poor; that is, different interviewers see different things in the same candidate and thus arrive at different conclusions about the applicant. If the employment interview is an important input into the hiring decision—and it usually is—you should recognize that perceptual factors influence who is hired and, eventually, the quality of an organization's labour force.

The impact of performance evaluations on behaviour will be discussed fully in the HR Implications in Chapter 5. It should be pointed out here, though, that an employee's performance appraisal is another example of something in the workplace that depends very much on the perceptual process.[13] An employee's future is closely tied to his or her appraisal—promotions, pay raises, and continuation of employment are among the most obvious outcomes. The performance appraisal represents an assessment of an employee's work. Although the appraisal can be objective (for example, a salesperson is appraised on how many dollars of sales he or she generates in a given territory), many jobs are evaluated in subjective terms. Subjective measures are easier to implement, they provide managers with greater discretion, and many jobs do not readily lend themselves to objective measures. Subjective measures are, by definition, judgmental. The evaluator forms a general impression of an employee's work. To the degree that managers use subjective measures in appraising employees, what the evaluator perceives to be good or bad employee characteristics or behaviours will significantly influence the outcome of the appraisal.

Hiring and performance appraisals are not the only processes in organizations that are subject to perceptual bias. For instance, we evaluate how much effort our co-workers are putting into their jobs. When a new person joins a work team, he or she is immediately "sized up" by the other team members. As you can see, perception plays a large role in the way that day-to-day activities are carried out in an organization. Personality, which we review below, is another major factor affecting how people relate in the workplace.

## Personality

**Tests, Tests, Tests**
www.queendom.com/tests.html

Why are some people quiet and passive, while others are loud and aggressive? Are certain personality types better adapted for certain job types? What do we know from theories of personality that can help us explain and predict the behaviour of people like Matthew Barrett and Anthony Comper (former and current CEOs of Bank of Montreal), whom we described at the opening of this chapter? How do we explain the risk-taking nature of Peggy Witte, fomer CEO of Royal Oak Mines? In this section, we will attempt to answer such questions.

### What Is Personality?

When we talk of personality, we don't mean that a person has charm, a positive attitude toward life, a smiling face, or is a finalist for "Happiest and Friendliest" in this year's Best Student Contest. When psychologists talk of personality, they mean a dynamic concept describing the growth and development of a person's whole psychological system. Rather than looking at parts of the person, personality looks at some aggregate whole that is greater than the sum of the parts.

**personality**
The sum total of ways in which an individual reacts and interacts with others.

Gordon Allport produced the most frequently used definition of personality more than 60 years ago. He said personality is "the dynamic organization within the individual of those psychophysical systems that determine his unique adjustments to his environment."[14] For our purposes, you should think of **personality** as the sum total of ways in which an individual reacts to and interacts with others. It is most often described in terms of measurable traits that a person exhibits. For an interesting look at how personality can affect business dealings, you might want to read this chapter's Point/Counterpoint discussion on pages 48-49. The discussion centres on how flexible and inflexible personality is. In addition, this chapter's CBC Video Case examines Mogens Smed. It gives you an opportunity to see if you can apply some of these personality concepts to the founder and CEO of SMED International Inc., a Calgary-based builder of office interiors.

**SMED International**
www.smednet.com

### Personality Determinants

An early argument in personality research centred on whether an individual's personality was the result of heredity or of environment. Was the personality predetermined at birth, or was it the result of the individual's interaction with his or her environment? Clearly, there is no simple answer. Personality appears to be a result of both influences. In addition, today we recognize a third factor—the situation. Thus, an adult's personality is now generally considered to be made up of both hereditary and environmental factors, moderated by situational conditions.

**HEREDITY**   Heredity refers to those factors that were determined at conception. Physical stature, facial attractiveness, gender, temperament, muscle composition and reflexes, energy level, and biological rhythms are characteristics that are generally considered to be either completely or substantially influenced by who your parents were: that is, by their biological, physiological, and inherent psychological makeup. The heredity approach argues that the ultimate explanation of an individual's personality is the molecular structure of the genes, located in the chromosomes.

Three different streams of research lend some credibility to the argument that heredity plays an important part in determining an individual's personality. The first looks at the genetic underpinnings of human behaviour and temperament among young children. The second addresses the study of twins who were separated at birth. The third examines the consistency in job satisfaction over time and across situations.

Recent studies of young children lend strong support to the power of heredity.[15] Evidence demonstrates that traits such as shyness, fear, and distress are most likely caused by inherited genetic characteristics. This finding suggests that some personality traits may be built into the same genetic code that affects factors such as height and hair colour.

Researchers have studied more than 100 sets of identical twins who were separated at birth and raised separately.[16] If heredity played little or no part in determining personality, you would expect to find few similarities between the separated twins. But the researchers found a lot in common. For almost every behavioural trait, a significant part of the variation between the twins turned out to be associated with genetic factors. For instance, one set of twins, who had been separated for 39 years and raised 70 kilometres apart, were found to drive the same model and colour car, chain-smoke the same brand of cigarette, own dogs with the same name, and regularly vacation within three blocks of each other in a beach community located 2000 kilometres away. Researchers have found that genetics accounts for about 50 percent of the personality differences and more than 30 percent of the variation in occupational and leisure interests.

Further support for the importance of heredity can be found in studies of individual job satisfaction. Research has uncovered an interesting phenomenon: individual job satisfaction is remarkably stable over time. Even when employers or occupations change, job satisfaction remains relatively stable during one's lifetime.[17] This result is consistent with what you would expect if satisfaction were determined by something inherent in the person rather than by external environmental factors.

If personality characteristics were *completely* dictated by heredity, they would be fixed at birth and no amount of experience could alter them. If you were tense and irritable as a child, for example, that would be the result of your genes, and it would not be possible for you to change those characteristics. But personality characteristics are not completely dictated by heredity.

**ENVIRONMENT**   Among the factors that exert pressures on our personality formation are the culture in which we are raised; our early conditioning; the norms among our family, friends, and social groups; and other influences

> Are people born with their personalities?

## POINT

# Traits Are Powerful Predictors of Behaviour

The essence of trait approaches in OB is that employees possess stable personality characteristics that significantly influence their attitudes toward, and behavioural reactions to, organizational settings. People with particular traits tend to be relatively consistent in their attitudes and behaviour over time and across situations.[1]

Of course, trait theorists recognize that all traits are not equally powerful. They tend to put traits into one of three categories. *Cardinal traits* are those so strong and generalized that they influence every act a person performs. *Primary traits* are generally consistent influences on behaviour, but they may not show up in all situations. Finally, *secondary traits* are attributes that do not form a vital part of the personality, but come into play only in particular situations. For the most part, trait theories have focused on the power of primary traits to predict employee behaviour.

Trait theorists do a fairly good job of meeting the average person's common-sense beliefs. Think of friends, relatives, and acquaintances you have known for a number of years. Do they have traits that have remained essentially stable over time? Most of us would answer that question in the affirmative. If cousin Anne was shy and nervous when we last saw her 10 years ago, we would be surprised to find her outgoing and relaxed now.

Managers seem to have a strong belief in the power of traits to predict behaviour. If managers believed that situations determined behaviour, they would hire people almost at random and put great effort into structuring situations properly. But the employee selection process in most organizations places a great deal of emphasis on how applicants perform in interviews and on tests. Assume you're an interviewer and ask yourself: What am I looking for in job candidates? If you answered with terms such as *conscientious, hard-working, persistent, confident,* and *dependable,* you're a trait theorist!

---

Source:
[1] Some of the points in this argument are from R.J. House, S.A. Shane, and D.M. Herold, "Rumors of the Death of Dispositional Research Are Vastly Exaggerated," *Academy of Management Review*, January 1996, pp. 203-224.

## COUNTERPOINT

# Traits Reflect the Surrounding Situation

Few people would dispute that there are some stable individual attributes that affect reactions to the workplace. But trait theorists go beyond that generality and argue that individual behaviour consistencies are widespread and account for much of the difference in behaviour among people.[1]

There are two important problems with using traits to explain a large proportion of behaviour in organizations. First, organizational settings are strong situations that have a large impact on employee behaviour. Second, individuals are highly adaptive and personality traits change in response to organizational situations.

It has been well-known for some time that the effects of traits are likely to be strongest in relatively weak situations, and weakest in relatively strong situations. Organizational settings tend to be strong situations because they have rules and other formal regulations that define acceptable behaviour and punish deviant behaviour; and they have informal norms that dictate appropriate behaviours. These formal and informal constraints minimize the effects of personality traits.

By arguing that employees possess stable traits that lead to cross-situational consistencies in behaviours, trait theorists are implying that individuals don't really adapt to different situations. But there is a growing body of evidence that an individual's traits are changed by the organizations that individual participates in. If the individual's personality changes as a result of exposure to organizational settings, in what sense can that individual be said to have traits that persistently and consistently affect his or her reactions to those very settings? Moreover, people typically belong to multiple organizations, which often include very different kinds of members. And they adapt to those different situations. Instead of being the prisoners of a rigid and stable personality framework, as trait theorists propose, people regularly adjust their behaviour to reflect the requirements of various situations.

Source:
[1] Based on A. Davis-Blake and J. Pfeffer, "Just a Mirage: The Search for Dispositional Effects in Organizational Research," *Academy of Management Review*, July 1989, pp. 385-400.

The cultural environment in which people are raised plays a major role in shaping personality. In India, children learn from an early age the values of hard work, frugality, and family closeness. This photo of the Harilela family illustrates the importance placed on close family ties. Six Harilela brothers own real estate and hotels throughout Asia. Not only do the brothers work together, but their six families and that of a married sister also live together in a Hong Kong mansion.

that we experience. The environment we are exposed to plays a substantial role in shaping our personalities.

For example, culture establishes the norms, attitudes, and values that are passed along from one generation to the next and create consistencies over time. An ideology that is intensely fostered in one culture may have only a moderate influence in another. For instance, North Americans have had the themes of industriousness, success, competition, independence, and the Protestant work ethic constantly instilled in them through books, the school system, family, and friends. North Americans, as a result, tend to be ambitious and aggressive relative to individuals raised in cultures that have emphasized getting along with others, cooperation, and the priority of family over work and career.

Careful consideration of the arguments favouring either heredity or environment as the primary determinant of personality forces the conclusion that both are important. Heredity sets the parameters, or outer limits, but an individual's full potential will be determined by how well he or she adjusts to the demands and requirements of the environment.

**SITUATION** A third factor, the situation, influences the effects of heredity and environment on personality. An individual's personality, although generally stable and consistent, may be more effective in some situations than others. More specifically, the different demands of different situations call forth different aspects of one's personality. We should not, therefore, look at personality patterns in isolation.[18]

It seems only logical to suppose that situations will influence an individual's personality, but a neat classification scheme that would tell us the impact of various types of situations has so far eluded us. "Apparently we are not yet close to developing a system for clarifying situations so that they might be systematically studied."[19] However, we do know that certain situations are more relevant than others in influencing personality. We also know that situations seem to differ substantially in the constraints they impose on behaviour. Some situations, such as a religious service or an employment interview, constrain many behaviours; other situations, such as a picnic in a public park, constrain relatively few.[20]

Furthermore, although certain generalizations can be made about personality, there are significant individual differences. As we will see, the study of individual differences has come to receive greater emphasis in personality research, which originally sought out more general, universal patterns.

## Personality Traits

**personality traits**
Enduring characteristics that describe an individual's behaviour.

The early work in the structure of personality revolved around attempts to identify and label enduring characteristics that describe an individual's behaviour. Popular characteristics include shy, aggressive, submissive, lazy, ambitious, loyal, and timid. Those characteristics, when they are exhibited in a large number of situations, are called **personality traits**.[21] The more consistent the characteristic and the more frequently it occurs in diverse situations, the more important that trait is in describing the individual.

Researchers have tried to identify the different personality traits, and one researcher identified 16 personality factors that he called the source, or primary, traits.[22] They are shown in Exhibit 2-4.

| Exhibit 2-4 Sixteen Primary Traits | | |
|---|---|---|
| 1. Reserved | vs. | Outgoing |
| 2. Less intelligent | vs. | More intelligent |
| 3. Affected by feelings | vs. | Emotionally stable |
| 4. Submissive | vs. | Dominant |
| 5. Serious | vs. | Happy-go-lucky |
| 6. Expedient | vs. | Conscientious |
| 7. Timid | vs. | Venturesome |
| 8. Tough-minded | vs. | Sensitive |
| 9. Trusting | vs. | Suspicious |
| 10. Practical | vs. | Imaginative |
| 11. Forthright | vs. | Shrewd |
| 12. Self-assured | vs. | Apprehensive |
| 13. Conservative | vs. | Experimenting |
| 14. Group-dependent | vs. | Self-sufficient |
| 15. Uncontrolled | vs. | Controlled |
| 16. Relaxed | vs. | Tense |

These 16 traits have been found to be generally steady and constant sources of behaviour, allowing prediction of an individual's behaviour in specific situations by weighing the characteristics for their situational relevance.

Our personality traits, by the way, are evaluated differently by different people. This is partially a function of perception, which we discussed earlier in the chapter. In Exhibit 2-5, you will note that Lucy tells Linus a few things about his personality.

**THE MYERS-BRIGGS TYPE INDICATOR**  One of the most widely used personality frameworks is called the Myers-Briggs Type Indicator (MBTI).[23] It is essentially a 100-question personality test that asks people how they usually feel or act in particular situations.

On the basis of the answers individuals give to the test, they are classified as extroverted or introverted (E or I), sensing or intuitive (S or N), thinking or feeling (T or F), and perceiving or judging (P or J). These classifications are then combined into 16 personality types. (These types are different from the 16 primary traits in Exhibit 2-4.) To illustrate, let's take several examples. INTJs are visionaries. They usually have original minds and great drive for their own ideas and purposes. They are characterized as sceptical, critical, independent, determined, and often stubborn. ESTJs are organizers. They are realistic, logical, analytical, decisive, and have a natural head for business or mechanics. They like to organize and run activities. The ENTP type is a conceptualizer. He or she is innovative, individualistic, versatile, and attracted to entrepreneurial ideas. This person tends to be resourceful in solving challenging problems but may neglect routine assignments. G.N. Landrum's *Profiles of Genius* profiled 13 contemporary business people who created super-successful firms including Apple Computer, Federal Express, Honda Motors, Microsoft, Price Club, and Sony. He found that all 13 are intuitive thinkers (NTs).[24] This result is particularly interesting because intuitive thinkers represent only about five percent of the population.

Ironically, there is no hard evidence that the MBTI is a valid measure of personality. But lack of evidence doesn't seem to deter its use in a wide range of organizations. A number of popular books are available to help individuals identify both their own and their colleagues' "types." One of the benefits of thinking about individuals by type is that it will give you some insight into how a particular person might react in a situation. However, as we noted above in our discussion of stereotyping, relying solely on personality measures to judge people can have its problems.

**Myers-Briggs Type Indicator (MBTI)**
A personality test that taps four characteristics and classifies people into one of 16 personality types.

**Apple Computer**
www.apple.com/ca

**Federal Express**
www.fedex.com/ca

**Honda Canada**
www.honda.ca/splash.asp

**Microsoft Canada**
www.microsoft.com/canada/default.asp

**Sony Canada**
www.sony.ca

Exhibit 2-5

**Association for
Psychological Type**
www.aptcentral.org/apt.htm

**extroversion**
A personality dimension that
describes someone who is
sociable, talkative, and
assertive.

**agreeableness**
A personality dimension that
describes someone who is
good-natured, cooperative, and
trusting.

**conscientiousness**
A personality dimension that
describes someone who is
responsible, dependable,
persistent, and achievement-
oriented.

**emotional stability**
A personality dimension that
characterizes someone as calm,
enthusiastic, and secure
(positive) vs. tense, nervous,
depressed, and insecure
(negative).

**openness to experience**
A personality dimension that
characterizes someone in terms
of imaginativeness, artistic
sensitivity, and intellectualism.

**THE BIG FIVE MODEL** The MBTI may lack for valid supporting evidence, but that can't be said for the widely accepted five-factor model of personality—more typically called the "Big Five."[25] An impressive body of research supports the notion that five basic personality dimensions underlie all others and encompass most of the significant variation in human personality. The big five factors are:

*Extroversion.* This dimension captures one's comfort level with relationships. Extroverts (high in **extroversion**) tend to be gregarious, assertive, and sociable. Introverts tend to be reserved, timid, and quiet.

*Agreeableness.* This dimension refers to an individual's propensity to defer to others. Highly agreeable people are cooperative, warm, and trusting. People who score low on **agreeableness** are cold, disagreeable, and antagonistic.

*Conscientiousness.* This dimension is a measure of reliability. A highly **conscientious** person is responsible, organized, dependable, and persistent. Those who score low on this dimension are easily distracted, disorganized, and unreliable.

*Emotional stability.* This dimension taps a person's ability to withstand stress. People with positive **emotional stability** tend to be characterized as calm, self-confident, and secure. Those with high negative scores tend to be nervous, anxious, depressed, and insecure.

*Openness to experience.* The final dimension addresses one's range of interests and fascination with novelty. Extremely open people are creative, curious, and artistic. Those at the other end of the **openness to experience** category are more conventional and find comfort in the familiar.

In addition to providing a unifying personality framework, research on the Big Five also has found important relationships between these personality dimensions and job performance.[26] A broad spectrum of occupations was examined: professionals (including engineers, architects, accountants, lawyers), police officers, managers, salespeople, and semi-skilled and skilled employees. Job performance was defined in terms of performance ratings, training proficiency (performance during training programs), and data such as salary level.

All of the factors have been found to have at least some relationship to performance in some situations.[27] Exhibit 2-6 summarizes the key research findings on the relationship of the Big Five personality factors to both individual job performance and team performance.[28] Evidence also finds a relatively strong and consistent relationship between conscientiousness and organizational citizenship behaviour (OCB).[29] This, however, seems to be the only personality dimension that predicts organizational citizenship behaviour.

## Major Personality Attributes Influencing OB

In this section, we want to more carefully evaluate specific personality attributes that have been found to be powerful predictors of behaviour in organizations. The first is related to where one perceives the locus of control in one's life. The others are machiavellianism, self-esteem, self-monitoring, propensity for risk-taking, and Type A personality. In this section, we shall briefly introduce these attributes and summarize what we know about their ability to explain and predict employee behaviour. If you want to know more about your own personal characteristics, this chapter's Learning

**Exhibit 2-6**
**Big Five Personality Factors and Individual Job and Team Performance**

| Big Five Personality Factor | Relationship to Job Performance | Relationship to Team Performance |
|---|---|---|
| *Extroversion* | • Positively related to job performance in occupations requiring social interaction | • Positively related to group performance |
| | • Positively related to training proficiency for all occupations | • Positively related to degree of participation within group |
| *Agreeableness* | • Positively related to job performance in service jobs | • Most studies found no link between agreeableness and performance or productivity in groups |
| | | • Some found a negative link between person's likeability and group performance |
| *Conscientiousness* | • Positively related to job performance for all occupational groups | • Should be positively related to team performance |
| | • May be better than ability in predicting job performance | |
| *Emotional Stability* | • A minimal threshold amount may be necessary for adequate performance; greater degrees not related to job performance | • Should be positively related to group performance |
| | • Positively related to performance in service jobs | |
| | • May be better than ability in predicting job performance across all occupational groups | |
| *Openness to Experience* | • Positively related to training proficiency | • Data unavailable |

Source: Adapted from S.L. Kichuk and W.H. Wiesner, "Work Teams: Selecting Members for Optimal Performance," *Canadian Psychology*, 39(1-2), 1999, pp. 24-26.

About Yourself Exercises on pages 75-82 present you with a variety of personality measures to explore.

**internals**
Individuals who believe that they control what happens to them.

**externals**
Individuals who believe that what happens to them is controlled by outside forces such as luck or chance.

**locus of control**
The degree to which people believe they are in control of their own fate.

**LOCUS OF CONTROL**   Some people believe that they are in control of their own destiny. Other people see themselves as pawns of fate, believing that what happens to them in their lives is due to luck or chance. The first type, those who believe that they control their destinies, have been labelled **internals**, whereas the latter, who see their lives as being controlled by outside forces, have been called **externals**.[30] A person's perception of the source of his or her fate is termed **locus of control**.

A large amount of research comparing internals with externals has consistently shown that individuals who rate high in externality are less satisfied with their jobs, have higher absenteeism rates, are more alienated from the work setting, and are less involved in their jobs than are internals.[31]

Why are externals more dissatisfied? The answer is probably because they perceive themselves as having little control over those organizational outcomes that are important to them. Internals, facing the same situation, attribute organizational outcomes to their own actions. If the situation is unattractive, they believe that they have no one else to blame but themselves. Also, the dissatisfied internal is more likely to quit a dissatisfying job.

The impact of locus of control on absence is an interesting one. Internals believe that health is substantially under their own control through proper habits, so they take more responsibility for their health and have better health habits. Consequently, their incidences of sickness and, hence, of absenteeism, are lower.[32]

We shouldn't expect any clear relationship between locus of control and turnover, because there are opposing forces at work. "On the one hand, internals tend to take action and thus might be expected to quit jobs more readily. On the other hand, they tend to be more successful on the job and more satisfied, factors associated with less individual turnover."[33]

The overall evidence indicates that internals generally perform better on their jobs, but that conclusion should be moderated to reflect differences in jobs. Internals search more actively for information before making a decision, are more motivated to achieve, and make a greater attempt to control their environment. Externals, however, are more compliant and willing to follow directions. Therefore, internals do well on sophisticated tasks—including most managerial and professional jobs—that require complex information processing and learning. In addition, internals are more suited to jobs that require initiative and independence

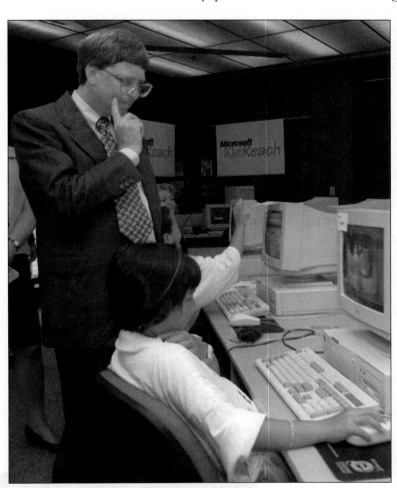

Bill Gates, co-founder of Microsoft, is shown here looking on as a group of children at Toronto's Lillian H. Smith Library surf the Internet. Gates would score high on the conscientiousness dimension of the Big Five model. His success stems from his personality— an intense drive to succeed, persistence, personal intensity, brilliant intellect, and competitiveness. Gates' personality has influenced the culture—and success—of Microsoft and made him the most famous business celebrity in the world.

of action. In contrast, externals should do well on jobs that are well-structured and routine, and in which success depends heavily on complying with the direction of others. If you are interested in determining your locus of control, you might want to complete Learning About Yourself Exercise #1 on page 75.

**machiavellianism**

Degree to which an individual is pragmatic, maintains emotional distance, and believes that ends can justify means.

**MACHIAVELLIANISM**    The personality characteristic of **machiavellianism** (mach) is named after Niccol Machiavelli, who wrote in the 16th century on how to gain and use power. An individual high in machiavellianism is pragmatic, maintains emotional distance, and believes that ends can justify means. "If it works, use it" is consistent with a high-mach perspective.

A considerable amount of research has been directed toward relating high- and low-mach personalities to certain behavioural outcomes.[34] High Machs manipulate more, win more, are persuaded less, and persuade others more than do low Machs.[35] Yet these high-mach outcomes are moderated by situational factors. It has been found that high Machs flourish (1) when they interact face to face with others rather than indirectly; (2) when the situation has a minimum number of rules and regulations, thus allowing latitude for improvisation; and (3) when emotional involvement with details irrelevant to winning distracts low Machs.[36]

Should we conclude that high Machs make good employees? That answer depends on the type of job and whether you consider ethical implications in evaluating performance. In jobs that require bargaining skills (such as labour negotiation) or that offer substantial rewards for winning (as in commissioned sales), high Machs will be productive. But if the ends can't justify the means, if there are absolute standards of behaviour, or if the three situational factors noted in the preceding paragraph are not in evidence, our ability to predict a high Mach's performance will be severely curtailed. If you are interested in determining your level of machiavellianism, you might want to complete Learning About Yourself Exercise #2 on page 76.

**self-esteem**

Individuals' degree of liking or disliking of themselves.

**SELF-ESTEEM**    People differ in the degree to which they like or dislike themselves. This trait is called **self-esteem**.[37] The research on self-esteem (SE) offers some interesting insights into organizational behaviour. For example, self-esteem is directly related to expectations for success. High SEs believe that they possess the ability they need in order to succeed at work. Individuals with high self-esteem will take more risks in job selection and are more likely to choose unconventional jobs than are people with low self-esteem.

The most generalizable finding on self-esteem is that low SEs are more susceptible to external influence than are high SEs. Low SEs are dependent on the receipt of positive evaluations from others. As a result, they are more likely to seek approval from others and more prone to conform to the beliefs and behaviours of those they respect than are high SEs. In managerial positions, low SEs tend to be concerned with pleasing others and, therefore, are less likely to take unpopular stands than are high SEs.

Not surprisingly, self-esteem has also been found to be related to job satisfaction. A number of studies confirm that high SEs are more satisfied with their jobs than are low SEs. If you are interested in determining your self-esteem score, you might want to complete Learning About Yourself Exercise #3 on page 77.

**self-monitoring**
A personality trait that measures an individual's ability to adjust his or her behaviour to external situational factors.

**SELF-MONITORING**  A personality trait that has recently received increased attention in the organizational literature is called **self-monitoring**.[38] It refers to an individual's ability to adjust his or her behaviour to external, situational factors.

Individuals high in self-monitoring show considerable adaptability in adjusting their behaviour to external situational factors. They are highly sensitive to external cues and can behave differently in different situations. High self-monitors are capable of presenting striking contradictions between their public persona and their private self. Low self-monitors can't disguise themselves in that way. They tend to display their true dispositions and attitudes in every situation; hence, there is high behavioural consistency between who they are and what they do.

The research on self-monitoring is in its infancy, so predictions must be guarded. However, preliminary evidence suggests that high self-monitors tend to pay closer attention to the behaviour of others and are more capable of conforming than are low self-monitors.[39] In addition, high self-monitoring managers tend to be more mobile in their careers and receive more promotions (both internal and cross-organizational).[40] We might also hypothesize that high self-monitors will be more successful in managerial positions in which individuals are required to play multiple, and even contradicting, roles. The high self-monitor is capable of putting on different "faces" for different audiences. If you are interested in determining whether you are a high or low self-monitor, you might want to complete Learning About Yourself Exercise #4 on page 78.

Richard Branson's propensity to take risks aligns with his job demands of being an entrepreneur. Branson, founder and chairman of London-based Virgin Group, started risky ventures that compete against industry giants. His Virgin Atlantic airline, for example, has taken market share from British Airways and has earned the reputation as one of the financially healthiest airlines in the world. Branson's risk-taking personality extends to his leisure activities of speedboat racing, sky diving, and ballooning.

**RISK-TAKING**  People differ in their willingness to take chances. Matthew Barrett, the subject of this chapter's opening vignette, and Frank Stronach, the subject of this chapter's Case Incident, are good example of high risk-takers. This propensity to assume or avoid risk has been shown to have an impact on how long it takes managers to make a decision and how much information they require before making their choice. For instance, 79 managers worked on simulated exercises that required them to make hiring decisions.[41] High **risk-taking** managers made more rapid decisions and used less information in making their choices than did the low risk-taking managers. Interestingly, the decision accuracy was the same for both groups.

While it is generally correct to conclude that managers in organizations are risk-aversive,[42] there are still individual differences on this dimension.[43] As a result, it makes sense to recognize these differences and even to consider aligning risk-taking propensity with specific job demands. For instance, a high risk-taking propensity may lead to more effective performance for a stock trader in a brokerage firm because that type of job demands rapid decision making. On the other hand, a willingness to take risks might prove a major obstacle to an accountant who performs auditing activities. The latter job might be better filled by someone with a low risk-taking propensity. If you are interested in determining where you stand on risk-taking, you might want to complete Learning About Yourself Exercise #5 on page 79.

**TYPE A PERSONALITY**  Do you know any people who are excessively competitive and always seem to be experiencing a chronic sense of time urgency? If you do, it's a good bet that those people have a Type A personality. A person with a **Type A personality** is "*aggressively* involved in a *chronic, incessant* struggle to achieve more and more in less and less time, and, if required to do so, against the opposing efforts of other things or other persons."[44] In the North American culture, such characteristics tend to be highly prized and positively associated with ambition and the successful acquisition of material goods.

Type As

- are always moving, walking, and eating rapidly;
- feel impatient with the rate at which most events take place;
- strive to think or do two or more things at once;
- cannot cope with leisure time;
- are obsessed with numbers, measuring their success in terms of how many or how much of everything they acquire.

In contrast to the Type A personality is the Type B, who is exactly opposite. Type Bs are "rarely harried by the desire to obtain a wildly increasing number of things or participate in an endless growing series of events in an ever-decreasing amount of time."[45]

Type Bs

- never suffer from a sense of time urgency with its accompanying impatience;
- feel no need to display or discuss either their achievements or accomplishments unless such exposure is demanded by the situation;

---

**risk-taking**
Refers to a person's willingness to take chances or risks.

**Type A personality**
A personality with aggressive involvement in a chronic, incessant struggle to achieve more and more in less and less time and, if necessary, against the opposing efforts of other things or other people.

- play for fun and relaxation, rather than to exhibit their superiority at any cost;
- can relax without guilt.

Type As are often characterized by impatience, hurriedness, competitiveness, and hostility, but these characteristics tend to emerge when a Type A individual experiences stress or challenge.[46] Type As are fast workers because they emphasize quantity over quality. In managerial positions, Type As demonstrate their competitiveness by working long hours and, not infrequently, making poor decisions because they make them too fast. Stressed Type As are also rarely creative. Because of their concern with quantity and speed, they rely on past experiences when faced with problems. They will not allocate the time that is necessary to develop unique solutions to new problems. They rarely vary in their responses to specific challenges in their milieu; hence, their behaviour is easier to predict than that of Type Bs.

Are Type As or Type Bs more successful in organizations? Despite the Type As' hard work, the Type Bs are the ones who appear to make it to the top. Great salespeople are usually Type As; senior executives are usually Type Bs. Why? The answer lies in the tendency of Type As to trade off quality of effort for quantity. Promotions in corporate and professional organizations "usually go to those who are wise rather than to those who are merely hasty, to those who are tactful rather than to those who are hostile, and to those who are creative rather than to those who are merely agile in competitive strife."[47]

More important than the simple question of promotion is that Type As suffer more serious health consequences when under stress. Stressed Type A individuals tend to exhibit such negative health consequences as higher blood pressure, and their recovery from the stressful situation is slower than that of Type B personalities. These findings suggest why Type A individuals tend to have higher rates of death associated with hypertension, coronary heart disease, and coronary artery disease.[48]

Recent research has looked at the effect of job complexity on the cardiovascular health of both Type A and Type B individuals to see whether Type As always suffered negative health consequences.[49] Type B individuals did not suffer negative health consequences from jobs with psychological complexity. Type A workers who faced high job complexity had higher death rates from heart-related disorders than Type As who faced lower job complexity. These findings suggest that healthwise, Type B workers suffer less when handling more complex jobs than do Type As. It also suggests that Type As who face lower job complexity do not face the same health risks as Type As who face higher job complexity.

If you are interested in determining whether you have a Type A or Type B personality type, you might want to complete Learning About Yourself Exercise #6 on page 81.

> **Do you think it's better to be a Type A or a Type B?**

## Personality and National Culture

There are certainly no common personality types for a given country. You can, for instance, find high and low risk-takers in almost any culture. Yet a country's culture should influence the dominant personality characteristics of its population. Let's build this case by looking at one personality attribute—locus of control.

There is evidence that cultures differ in terms of people's relationship to their environment.[50] In some cultures, such as those in North America, people believe that they can dominate their environment. People in other societies, such as Middle Eastern countries, believe that life is essentially pre-ordained. Notice the close parallel to internal and external locus of control. We should expect a larger proportion of internals in the Canadian and American workforces than in the Saudi Arabian or Iranian workforces.

## Achieving Personality Fit

Twenty years ago, organizations were concerned with personality primarily because they wanted to match individuals to specific jobs. That concern still exists. But, in recent years, interest has expanded to include the individual-organization fit. Why? Because managers today are less interested in an applicant's ability to perform a *specific* job than with his or her *flexibility* to meet changing situations.

**personality-job fit theory**
Identifies six personality types and proposes that the fit between personality type and occupational environment determines satisfaction and turnover.

**THE PERSON-JOB FIT** In the discussion of personality attributes, our conclusions were often qualified to recognize that the requirements of the job moderated the relationship between possession of the personality characteristic and job performance. This concern with matching the job requirements with personality characteristics is best articulated in John Holland's **personality-job fit theory**.[51] The theory is based on the notion of fit between an individual's personality characteristics and his or her occupational environment. Holland presents six personality types. He then proposes that satisfaction and the propensity to leave a job depend on the degree to which individuals successfully match their personalities to an occupational environment.

Each one of the six personality types has a congruent occupational environment. Exhibit 2-7 describes the six types and their personality characteristics, and gives examples of congruent occupations.

Holland has developed a Vocational Preference Inventory questionnaire that contains 160 occupational titles. Respondents indicate which of these occupations they like or dislike, and their answers are used to form personality profiles. Using this procedure, research strongly supports the hexagonal diagram in Exhibit 2-8.[52] This figure shows that the closer two fields, or orientations, are in the hexagon, the more compatible they are. Adjacent categories are quite similar, whereas those diagonally opposite are highly dissimilar.

What does all this mean? The theory argues that satisfaction is highest and turnover lowest when personality and occupation are in agreement. Social individuals should be in social jobs, conventional people in conventional jobs, and so forth. A realistic person in a realistic job is in a more congruent situation than is a realistic person in an investigative job. A realistic person in a social job is in the most incongruent situation possible. The key points of this model are that (1) there appear to be intrinsic differences in personality among individuals, (2) there are different types of jobs, and (3) people in job environments congruent with their personality types should be more satisfied and less likely to voluntarily resign than should people in incongruent jobs. In this chapter's HR Implications on pages 69-71, we review aspects of career development to help you begin to think about how you will manage your career. This chapter has indicated that there is a link between personality and career choices that you might make.

## Exhibit 2-7
## Holland's Typology of Personality and Congruent Occupations

| Type | Personality Characteristics | Congruent Occupations |
|---|---|---|
| *Realistic:* Prefers physical activities that require skill, strength, and coordination | Shy, genuine, persistent, stable, conforming, practical | Mechanic, drill press operator, assembly-line worker, farmer |
| *Investigative:* Prefers activities that involve thinking, organizing, and understanding | Analytical, original, curious, independent | Biologist, economist, mathematician, news reporter |
| *Social:* Prefers activities that involve helping and developing others | Sociable, friendly, cooperative, understanding | Social worker, teacher, counsellor, clinical psychologist |
| *Conventional:* Prefers rule-regulated, orderly, and unambiguous activities | Conforming, efficient, practical, unimaginative, inflexible | Accountant, corporate manager, bank teller, file clerk |
| *Enterprising*: Prefers verbal activities where there are opportunities to influence others and attain power | Self-confident, ambitious, energetic, domineering | Lawyer, real estate agent, public relations specialist, small business manager |
| *Artistic*: Prefers ambiguous and unsystematic activities that allow creative expression | Imaginative, disorderly, idealistic, emotional, impractical | Painter, musician, writer, interior decorator |

Source: Reprinted by special permission of the publisher, Psychological Assessment Resources, Inc., from *Making Vocational Choices*, Copyright 1973, 1985, 1992 by Psychological Assessment Resources, Inc. All rights reserved.

## Exhibit 2-8
## Relationships Among Occupational Personality Types

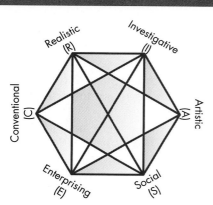

**THE PERSON-ORGANIZATION FIT** As previously noted, attention in recent years has expanded to include matching people to *organizations* as well as *jobs*. Many organizations now face a dynamic and changing environment, and require employees who are able to readily change tasks and move fluidly between teams. To the extent that this applies, it's probably more important that employees' personalities fit with an organization's overall culture than with the characteristics of any specific job.

The person-organization fit essentially argues that people leave jobs that are not compatible with their personalities.[53] Using the Big Five terminology, for instance, we could expect that people high on extroversion fit better with aggressive and team-oriented cultures; people high on agreeableness will match up better with

At Dallas, Texas-based Southwest Airlines people work hard, but they have a good time. They're allowed to let their personalities show. Southwest uses the personality-job fit theory during its selective hiring process. During interviews, applicants must prove that they have a sense of humour. It's a job requirement because it fits with the airline's fun-loving culture. Here a flight attendant pops out of a luggage bin, demonstrating her quirky personality.

a supportive organizational climate than one that focuses on aggressiveness; and people high on openness to experience fit better into organizations that emphasize innovation rather than standardization.[54] Following these guidelines at the time of hiring should lead to selecting new employees who fit better with an organization's culture which, in turn, should result in higher employee satisfaction and reduced turnover.

## Emotions

In April 1999, a former Ottawa transit worker walked into a bus garage and killed four former co-workers before killing himself. He had a history of work-related problems, and had been ordered to take an anger management class after one of his eruptions. He had quit his job in January 1999, but for some reason had still felt the need to kill some of his former co-workers.[55] For this worker, anger led to violence.

Going on a shooting rampage at work is an extreme example, but it does dramatically illustrate the theme of this section: Emotions are a critical factor in employee behaviour.

Given the obvious role that emotions play in our everyday life, it might surprise you to learn that, until very recently, the topic of emotions was given little or no attention within the field of OB. When emotions were considered, the discussion focused on strong negative emotions—especially anger—that interfered with an employee's ability to do his or her job effectively. Emotions were rarely viewed as being constructive or able to stimulate performance-enhancing behaviours.

Certainly some emotions, particularly when exhibited at the wrong time, can reduce employee performance. But this doesn't change the reality that employees bring an emotional component with them to work every day, and that no study of OB could be comprehensive without considering the role of emotions in workplace behaviour.

## What Are Emotions?

Before we can proceed with our analysis, we need to clarify three terms that are closely intertwined. These are *affect*, *emotions*, and *moods*.

**affect**
A broad range of feelings that people experience.

**emotions**
Intense feelings that are directed at someone or something.

**moods**
Feelings that tend to be less intense than emotions and that lack a contextual stimulus.

**Affect** is a generic term that covers a broad range of feelings that people experience. It's an umbrella concept that encompasses both emotions and moods.[56] **Emotions** are intense feelings that are directed at someone or something.[57] Finally, **moods** are feelings that tend to be less intense than emotions and which lack a contextual stimulus.[58]

Emotions are reactions to an object, not a trait. They're object-specific. You show your emotions when you're "happy about something, angry at someone, afraid of something."[59] Research has identified six universal emotions: anger, fear, sadness, happiness, disgust, and surprise.[60] Moods, on the other hand, aren't directed at an object. Emotions can turn into moods when you lose focus on the contextual object. So when a colleague criticizes you for the way you spoke to a client, you might become angry at him. That is, you show emotion (anger) toward a specific object (your colleague). But later in the day, you might find yourself just generally dispirited. You can't attribute this feeling to any single event; you're just not your normal, upbeat self. This affect state describes a mood.

**emotional labour**
When an employee expresses organizationally desired emotions during interpersonal interactions.

A related affect-term that is gaining increasing importance in organizational behaviour is *emotional labour*. All employees expend physical and mental labour when they put their bodies and cognitive capabilities, respectively, into their jobs. But most jobs also require **emotional labour**. This term was first coined by Berkeley professor Arlie Hochschild and refers to the demand organizations make on their employees to display "appropriate" emotions during interpersonal transactions.[61] The concept of emotional labour originally developed in relation to service jobs. Airline flight attendants, for instance, are expected to be cheerful, funeral counsellors sad, and doctors emotionally neutral. But today, the concept of emotional labour seems relevant to almost every job. You're expected, for example, to be

Ellie Rubin (left), co-founder of the international software company The Bulldog Group, interviews young employment applicants. Rubin's ideal employee is a "professional eclectic," a person who is creative, flexible, analytical, communicative, willing to learn, and thinks independently but can work with team members.

Emotional labour is an important component of effective job performance at the Happy Beauty Salon in Long Island, New York. Owner Happy Nomikos, shown here serving customers strawberries and grapes, requires that her nail technicians and hair stylists build customer loyalty by being courteous and cheerful. In interacting with her employees and customers, Nomikos says "I have to keep everyone happy." She hugs loyal customers, jokes with her staff, and offers customers pizza and cake in celebration of employees' birthdays.

courteous and not hostile in interactions with co-workers. And leaders are expected to draw on emotional labour to "charge the troops." Almost every great speech, for instance, contains a strong emotional component that stirs feelings in others.

As we proceed in this section, you'll see that it's because of emotional labour's increasing importance in effective job performance that an understanding of emotion has gained heightened relevance within the field of OB. We discuss emotional labour further in Chapter 8, when we consider impression management's role in politics in the organization.

## Felt vs. Displayed Emotions

| Ever wonder why the grocery clerk is always smiling? |
| :--- |

**felt emotions**
An individual's actual emotions.

**displayed emotions**
Emotions that are organizationally required and considered appropriate in a given job.

Emotional labour creates dilemmas for employees when their job requires them to exhibit emotions that are incongruous with their actual feelings. Not surprisingly, this is a frequent occurrence. There are people you have to work with to whom you find it very difficult to be friendly. Maybe you consider their personality abrasive. Maybe you know they've said negative things about you behind your back. Regardless, your job requires you to interact with these people on a regular basis. So you're forced to feign friendliness.

It can help you to better understand emotions if you separate them into *felt* vs. *displayed*.[62] **Felt emotions** are an individual's actual emotions. In contrast, **displayed emotions** are those that are organizationally required and considered appropriate in a given job. They're not innate; they're learned. "The ritual look of delight on the face of the first runner-up as the new Miss America is announced is a product of the display rule that losers should mask their sadness with an expression of joy for the winner."[63] Similarly, most of us know that we're expected to act sad at funerals, regardless of whether we consider the person's death to be a loss; and to pretend to be happy at weddings, even if we don't feel like celebrating.[64] Effective managers have learned to be serious when giving an employee a negative performance evaluation and to cover up their anger when they've been passed over for promotion. And the salesperson who hasn't learned to smile and appear friendly, but instead reveals his or her true feelings at the moment, isn't typically going to last long on most sales jobs.

The key point here is that felt and displayed emotions are often different. In fact, many people have problems working with others simply because they naively assume that the emotions they see others display is what those others actually feel. This is particularly true in organizations, where role demands and situations often require people to exhibit emotional behaviours that mask their true feelings.

## Can People Be Emotionless?

Are people who seem outwardly calm or apathetic in situations where others are clearly emotionally charged without feeling? Can people be emotion*less*?

Some people have severe difficulty in expressing their emotions and understanding the emotions of others. Psychologists call this *alexithymia* (which is Greek for "lack of emotion").[65] People who suffer from alexithymia rarely cry and are often seen by others as bland and cold. Their own feelings make them uncomfortable, and they're not able to discriminate among their different emotions. Additionally, they're often at a complete loss to understand what others around them feel.

Does this inability to express emotions and read others mean that people who suffer from alexithymia are poor work performers? Not necessarily. Consistent with our discussion on matching personality types with appropriate jobs, people who lack emotion need to be in jobs that require little or no emotional labour. These people are not well-suited to sales and managerial positions. But they might very well be effective performers, for instance, in a job writing program code or in any work that is confined exclusively to computer interaction.

## Gender and Emotions

It's widely assumed that women are more "in touch" with their feelings than men—that they react more emotionally and are better able to read emotions in others. Is there any truth to these assumptions?

The evidence does confirm differences between men and women when it comes to emotional reactions and ability to read others. When the genders are contrasted, women show greater emotional expression than men;[66] they experience emotions more intensely; and they display more frequent expressions of both positive and negative emotions, except anger.[67] In contrast with men, women also report more comfort in expressing emotions. Finally, women are better at reading nonverbal and paralinguistic cues than are men.[68]

What explains these differences? Three possible answers have been suggested. One explanation is the different ways men and women have been socialized.[69] Men are taught to be tough and brave; and showing emotion is inconsistent with this image. Women, on the other hand, are socialized to be nurturing. This may account for the perception that women are generally warmer and friendlier than men. For instance, women are expected to express more positive emotions on the job (shown by smiling) than men, and they do.[70] A second explanation is that women may have more innate ability to read others and present their emotions than do men.[71] Thirdly, women may have a greater need for social approval and, thus, a higher propensity to show positive emotions like happiness.

## Why Should We Care About Emotions in the Workplace?

**Bank of Montreal**
www.bmo.com

**emotional intelligence**
An assortment of noncognitive skills, capabilities, and competencies that influence a person's ability to succeed in coping with environmental demands and pressures.

There are a number of reasons to be concerned about understanding emotions in the workplace. People who know their own emotions and are good at reading others' emotions may be more effective in their jobs. That, in essence, is the theme underlying recent research on *emotional intelligence* (EI).[72] Maria Gonzalez, vice-president of strategic initiatives and corporate planning at Bank of Montreal, believes EI is so important that she suggests, "MBA schools will become obsolete if they don't imbed elements of EI in their programs, as that's what makes people successful in the workplace."[73]

**Emotional intelligence** refers to an assortment of noncognitive skills, capabilities, and competencies that influence a person's ability to succeed in coping with environmental demands and pressures. It's composed of five dimensions:

- *Self-awareness.* Being aware of what you're feeling. It is exhibited by self-confident, realistic self-assessment, and a self-deprecating sense of humour.

- *Self-management.* The ability to manage one's own emotions and impulses. It is exhibited by trustworthiness and integrity, comfort with ambiguity, and openness to change.

- *Self-motivation.* The ability to persist in the face of setbacks and failures. It is exhibited by a strong drive to achieve, optimism, and high organizational commitment.

- *Empathy.* The ability to sense how others are feeling. It is exhibited by expertise in building and retaining talent, cross-cultural sensitivity, and service to clients and customers.

- *Social skills.* The ability to handle the emotions of others. It is exhibited by persuasiveness, and expertise in building and leading groups and teams.

Several studies suggest EI may play an important role in job performance. For instance, one study looked at the characteristics of Bell Lab engineers who were rated as stars by their peers. The scientists concluded that stars were better at relating to others. That is, it was EI, not academic IQ, that characterized high performers. A second study of US Air Force recruiters generated similar findings. Top-performing recruiters exhibited high levels of EI. Using these findings, the US Air Force revamped its selection criteria. A follow-up investigation found that future hires who had high EI scores were 2.6 times more successful than those who didn't. A recent poll of human resource managers asked: How important is it for your workers to demonstrate EI to move up the corporate ladder? Forty percent replied "Very Important." Another 16 percent said "Moderately Important."

The implications from the initial evidence on EI is that employers should consider it as a factor in selection, especially in jobs that demand a high degree of social interaction. Anthony Comper, the recently appointed CEO of Bank of Montreal, certainly agrees with the importance of understanding emotional intelligence. He cites Daniel Goleman's *Working With Emotional Intelligence*[74] as one of his three favourite recent books on leadership.[75] This chapter's From Concepts to Skills gives you some insight into reading the emotions of others.

# From CONCEPTS to SKILLS

## Reading Emotions

Understanding another person's felt emotions is a very difficult task. But we can learn to read others' display emotions. We do this by focusing on verbal, nonverbal, and paralanguage cues.

The easiest way to find out what someone is feeling is to ask them. Saying something as simple as "Are you OK? What's the problem?" can frequently provide you with the information to assess an individual's emotional state. But relying on a *verbal* response has two drawbacks. First, almost all of us conceal our emotions to some extent for privacy and to reflect social expectations. So we might be unwilling to share our true feelings. Second, even if we want to verbally convey our feelings, we may be unable to do so. As we've noted previously, some people have difficulty understanding their own emotions and, hence, are unable to express them verbally. So, at best, verbal responses provide only partial information.

You're talking with a co-worker. Does the fact that his back is rigid, his teeth clenched, and his facial muscles tight tell you something about his emotional state? It probably should. Facial expressions, gestures, body movements, and physical distance are *nonverbal* cues that can provide additional insights into what a person is feeling. The facial expressions shown in Exhibit 2-9, for instance, are a window into a person's feelings. Notice the difference in facial features: the height of cheeks, the raising or lowering of the brow, the turn of the mouth, the positioning of the lips, and the configuration of muscles around the eyes. Even something as subtle as the distance someone chooses to position him- or herself from you can convey that person's feelings, or lack, of intimacy, aggressiveness, repugnance, or withdrawal.

As Janet and I talked, I noticed a sharp change in the tone of her voice and the speed at which she spoke. I was tapping into the third source of information on a person's emotions—*paralanguage*. This is communication that goes beyond the specific spoken words. It includes pitch, amplitude, rate, and voice quality of speech. Paralanguage reminds us that people convey their feelings not only in *what* they say, but also in *how* they say it.

Source: V.P. Richmond, J.C. McCroskey, and S.K. Payne, *Nonverbal Behavior in Interpersonal Relations*, 2nd ed. (Englewood Cliffs, NJ: Prentice Hall, 1991), pp. 117-138; and L.A. King, "Ambivalence Over Emotional Expression and Reading Emotions in Situations and Faces," *Journal of Personality and Social Psychology*, March 1998, pp. 753-762.

**Exhibit 2-9**
**Facial Expressions Convey Emotions**

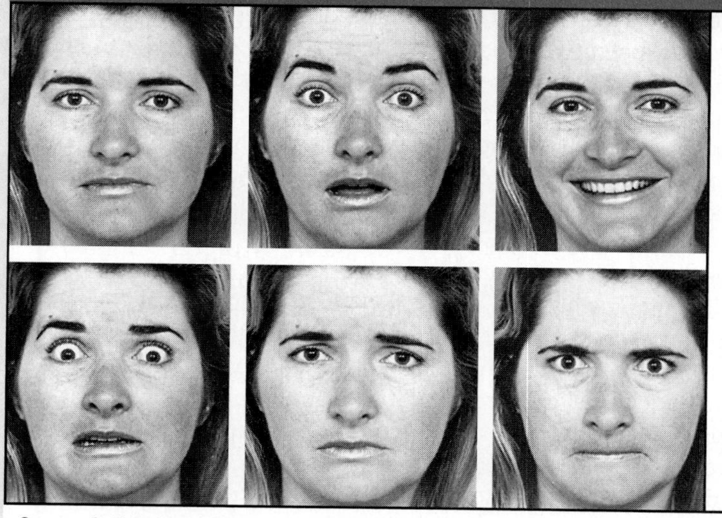

Each picture portrays a different emotion. Try to identify them before looking at the answers. (Top, left to right: neutral, surprise, happiness. Bottom: fear, sadness, anger.)

Source: S. E. Taylor, L.A. Peplan, and D. O. Sears, *Social Psychology*, 9th ed. (Upper Saddle River, N): Prentice Hall, 1997). p. 98; photographs by Paul Ekman, Ph.D. Used with permission.

Emotions also affect decision making, which we cover in Chapter 11. Anxiety, fear, frustration, doubt, happiness, excitement, and similar emotions can all influence one's decision at a particular moment. Given the same objective data, we should expect that people may make different choices when they're angry and stressed out than when they're calm and collected. Negative emotions can result in a limited search for new alternatives and a less vigilant use of information. On the other hand, positive emotions can increase problem-solving and facilitate the integration of information.[76]

You can improve your understanding of decision making by considering "the heart" as well as "the head." People use emotions as well as rational and intuitive processes in making decisions. Failure to incorporate emotions into the study of decision processes will result in an incomplete (and often inaccurate) view of the process.

As we think about what motivates individuals, a topic we'll consider thoroughly in Chapter 4, we might consider the role of emotions. Since people aren't cold, unfeeling machines, their perceptions of situations will significantly influence how much effort they exert. Moreover, when you see people who are highly motivated in their jobs, they're emotionally committed. Are all people emotionally engaged in their work? No! But many are. And if we focus only on rational calculations of inducements and contributions, we fail to be able to explain some behaviours, for instance, those of the individual who forgets to have dinner and works late into the night, lost in the thrill of her work.[77]

Emotions also play a role in leadership, which we cover in Chapter 10. Effective leaders almost all rely on the expression of feelings to help convey their messages. In fact, the expression of emotions in speeches is often the critical element that results in individuals accepting or rejecting a leader's message. "When leaders feel excited, enthusiastic, and active, they may be more likely to energize their subordinates and convey a sense of efficacy, competence, optimism, and enjoyment."[78] Politicians, as a case in point, have learned to show enthusiasm when talking about their chances for winning an election, even when polls suggest otherwise.

Corporate executives know that emotional content is critical if employees are to buy into the executives' vision of the company's future and accept change. When new visions are offered, especially when they contain distant or vague goals, change is often difficult to accept. So when effective leaders want to implement significant changes, they rely on "the evocation, framing, and mobilization of *emotions*."[79] By arousing emotions and linking them to an appealing vision, leaders increase the likelihood that managers and employees alike will accept change.

Whenever conflicts arise, you can be fairly certain that emotions are also surfacing. A manager's success in trying to resolve conflicts, in fact, is often largely due to his or her ability to identify the emotional elements in the conflict and to get the conflicting parties to work through their emotions. And the manager who ignores the emotional elements in conflicts, focusing singularly on rational and task-focused concerns, is unlikely to be very effective in resolving those conflicts.

Finally, negative emotions can lead to a number of deviant workplace behaviours. Anyone who has spent much time in an organization realizes

**employee deviance**
Voluntary actions that violate established norms and that threaten the organization, its members or both.

that people often engage in voluntary actions that violate established norms and threaten the organization, its members, or both. These actions are called **employee deviance**.[80] They fall into categories such as production (that is, leaving early, intentionally working slowly); property (that is, stealing, sabotage); political (that is, gossiping, blaming co-workers); and personal aggression (that is, sexual harassment, verbal abuse).[81] Many of these deviant behaviours can be traced to negative emotions.

For instance, envy is an emotion that occurs when you resent someone for having something that you don't, and that you strongly desire.[82] It can lead to malicious deviant behaviours. Envy, for example, has been found to be associated with hostility, "backstabbing," and other forms of political behaviour, with negatively distorting others' successes and positively distorting one's own accomplishments.[83]

## HR Implications

# Career Development

Our chapter has considered the roles that perception and personality play in judging and getting along with others. We have also examined the extent to which one should consider the match between personality and specific jobs. One thing that we have not discussed in our text to date is how you manage your career, however. We thought this would be an early opportunity, as you are starting to learn about the fundamentals of organizational behaviour, to think about various career issues. Below we discuss both the role of the organization and your role in developing your career.

Few human resource issues have changed as much in the past couple of decades as the role of the organization in its employees' careers.[1] Twenty years ago, when a person was more likely to spend his or her entire work years with the same employer, most medium-sized and large organizations engaged in extensive employee career planning. Such planning focused exclusively on developing employees for opportunities within the specific organization. For instance, organizations would develop sophisticated replacement charts to identify potential promotion candidates for key internal positions. They'd also offer a wide range of in-house career development programs to prepare employees for promotions.

Today, many more organizations are engaged in nearly continuous restructuring through downsizing their operations, re-engineering processes, increasing flexibility. Bank and other mergers lead to layoffs when duplicate jobs are eliminated. New technologies make it possible to do more work with fewer people. And because of globalization, companies are increasingly taking their labour-intensive work to countries with lower labour costs, resulting in fewer jobs within the corporation at home. The Internet and other electronic media have brought about increased availability of information. This allows people to work together in a variety of ways, but it also demands more teamwork and more decentralized decision making. The new technologies are also increasing the speed with which work is expected to be accomplished. Thus individuals are expected to master new ways of keeping up. As a result of all of these changes, employees must take personal responsibility for planning their personal career track. They should not simply leave it to their manager or the company to define their future.

Despite the need for employees to assume personal responsibility for their careers, there are benefits that accrue to organizations that offer career development programs.[2] These include ensuring the right people will be available to meet changing staffing requirements, increasing workforce diversity, and providing employees with more realistic job expectations. Below, we describe both the organization's and employees' responsibilities for career development today.

First, however, let's define what we mean by the term *career*. A **career** is "the evolving sequence of a person's work experiences over time."[3] This definition does not imply advancement or success or failure. Any work, paid or unpaid, pursued over an extended period of time, can constitute a career. In addition to formal job work, it may include school work, home-making, or volunteer work.[4]

## The Organization's Responsibilities

What, if any, responsibility does the organization have for career development under these new rules? Amoco Corp.'s career development program is a model for today's companies.[5] It's designed around employee self-reliance and to help employees reflect on their marketability both inside and outside the oil company. All workers are encouraged to participate in a half-day introduction to the program and in full-day self-assessment and self-development sessions. The company supports its employees by providing information—a worldwide electronic job-posting system, a network of career advisers, and a worldwide directory of Amoco employees and their skills from which company managers can search for candidates for job openings. But the whole program is voluntary and assumes that it's the employees' responsibility to maintain their employability.

The essence of a progressive career development program is built on providing support for employees to continually add to their skills, abilities, and knowledge. This support includes:

1. *Clearly communicating the organization's goals and future strategies*. When people know where the organization is headed, they're better able to develop a personal plan to share in that future.

2. *Creating growth opportunities*. Employees should have the opportunity to get new, interesting, and professionally challenging work experiences.

3. *Offering financial assistance*. The organization should offer tuition reimbursement to help employees keep current.

4. *Providing the time for employees to learn*. The organization should be generous in providing paid time off from work for off-the-job training. Additionally, workloads should not be so demanding that they preclude employees' having the time to develop new skills, abilities, and knowledge.

## The Employee's Responsibilities

Today's employees should manage their own careers like entrepreneurs managing a small business. They should think of themselves as self-employed, even if employed in a large organization.[6] In a world of "free agency," the successful career will be built on maintaining flexibility and keeping skills and knowledge up-to-date. The following suggestions are consistent with being a career activist—taking charge of your own career.[7]

1. *Ensure your employability*. Make sure you have alternatives, should you lose your job. Acquire new skills, pursue opportunities that will stretch you.

2. *Have a fallback position*. Be sure to have multiple options for your career, and try to see yourself in multiple roles. Thus you could be an employee, a contract worker, or a freelance consultant using a wider skill set.

3. *Know your key skills*. You need to know how to package your existent skills and experience in new ways (for example, an architect who has a hobby as a gardener may start a business designing and building greenhouses). Look carefully to identify your key talents and skills, and don't limit yourself to your job title.

4. *Market! market! market!* Even while performing at your highest level, always keep your eyes open for new work assignments, and position yourself for these. Let key people know your skills and

how you can bring value to the organization. Also be sure to network. And be sure to treat everyone you meet as a potential client.

5. *Act Type A, be Type B.* While it is important, often, to have the drive and achievement orientation of Type As, it is also important to have the more relaxed Type B attitude of feeling good about yourself, even if you are not producing at a mile a minute. It is important that your sense of self not be completely tied to your job and the workplace.

6. *Stay culturally current.* Make sure that you're aware of world and cultural events through reading and even participating in online discussion groups. Being in the know helps you establish relationships with other people and can help you manage your career effectively.

7. *Be a compelling communicator.* Everyone is busy these days, so it's important to communicate effectively and efficiently. You may be communi-

cating with people halfway around the globe or individuals who know little about the technical details of what you do, so being clear is important.

8. *Manage your finances.* To reduce your dependence on employment, make sure that you have your finances in order, as this will give you greater opportunities to explore change.

9. *Act like an insider, think like an outsider.* You need to be able to work as a team player, but also to be self-aware and able to evaluate your performance with some objectivity. It is important to be able to think independently. There will be times when you will have to make decisions without the benefit of a group.

10. *Be capable of rewarding yourself.* With increased demands on everyone, you may not receive all of the external feedback you might like. Thus, you have to be able to give yourself a pat on the back when you do things well. Celebrate your successes, and take time to nourish yourself.

Sources:

[1] See H. Lancaster, "You and Only You, Must Stay in Charge of Your Employability," *Wall Street Journal*, November 15, 1994, p. B1; B. Filipczak, "You're On Your Own: Training, Employability, and the New Employment Contract," *Training*, January 1995, pp. 29-36; and M.B. Arthur, P.H. Claman, and R.J. DeFillippi, "Intelligent Enterprise, Intelligent Careers," *The Executive*, November 1995, pp. 7-20.

[2] See, for example, P.O. Benham, Jr., "Developing Organizational Talent: The Key to Performance and Productivity," *SAM Advanced Management Journal*, January 1993, pp. 34-39.

[3] M.B. Arthur, D.T. Hall, and B.S. Lawrence (eds.), *Handbook of Career Theory* (Cambridge: Cambridge University Press, 1989), p. 8.

[4] D.T. Hall, *Careers in Organizations* (Santa Monica, CA: Goodyear, 1976), pp. 3-4.

[5] M. Hequet, "Flat and Happy?" *Training*, April 1995, pp. 29-34.

[6] G. Johns, *Organizational Behavior: Understanding and Managing Life at Work*, 4th ed. (New York: HarperCollins, 1996), p. 622.

[7] For further elaboration of these points, see B. Moses, *Career Intelligence: Mastering the New Work and Personal Realities* (Toronto: Stoddart Publishing Co., Ltd., 1997).

## *SUMMARY AND IMPLICATIONS*

## For the Workplace

**Perception** Individuals behave in a given manner based not on the way their external environment actually is but, rather, on what they see or believe it to be. An organization may spend millions of dollars to create a pleasant work environment for its employees. However, despite these expenditures, an employee who believes that his or her job is lousy will behave accordingly. It is the employee's perception of a situation that becomes the basis for his or her behaviour. The employee who perceives his or her manager as a hurdle reducer who helps the employee do a better job will have one behavioural response to the manager. The employee who sees the same manager as "big brother, closely monitoring every motion, to ensure that I keep working," will differ in his or her behavioural response to that manager. The difference has nothing to do with the reality of the manager's actions; the difference in employee behaviour is due to different perceptions. Managers make similar perception judgments that may not be based in reality; therefore, the way they manage and the way they interact with top executives will be influenced by these perceptions.

The evidence suggests that what individuals perceive from their work situation will influence their productivity more than will the situation itself. Whether a job is actually interesting or challenging is irrelevant. Whether a manager successfully plans and organizes the work of his or her employees, actually helping them to structure their work more efficiently and effectively, is far less important than how employees perceive the manager's efforts. Similarly, issues such as fair pay for work performed, the validity of performance appraisals, and the adequacy of working conditions are not judged by employees in a way that ensures common perceptions; nor can we be assured that individuals will interpret conditions surrounding their jobs in a favourable light. Therefore, to be able to influence productivity, it is necessary to assess how workers *perceive* their jobs.

Absenteeism, turnover, job satisfaction, and organizational commitment are also reactions that arise from the individual's perceptions. Dissatisfaction with working conditions or the belief that there is a lack of promotion opportunity in the organization is a judgment based on an attempt to make some meaning out of one's job. The employee's conclusion that a job is good or bad is an interpretation. Managers must spend time understanding how each individual interprets reality and, where there is a significant difference between what is seen and what exists, try to eliminate the distortions. Failure to deal with the differences when individuals perceive the job in negative terms will result in increased absenteeism and turnover, and lower job satisfaction and commitment.

**Personality**  A review of the personality literature offers general guidelines that can lead to effective job performance. As such, it can improve hiring, transfer, and promotion decisions. Because personality characteristics create the parameters for people's behaviour, they give us a framework for predicting behaviour. For example, individuals who are shy, introverted, and uncomfortable in social situations would probably make poor salespeople. Individuals who are submissive and conforming might not be effective as advertising "idea" people.

Can we predict which people will be high performers in sales, research, or assembly-line work on the basis of their personality characteristics alone? The answer is "no." But a knowledge of an individual's personality can aid in reducing mismatches, which, in turn, can lead to reduced turnover and higher job satisfaction.

We can look at certain personality characteristics that tend to be related to job success, test for those traits, and use the data to make selection more effective. Some individuals accept rules, conformity, and dependence and rate high on authoritarianism. They are likely to feel more comfortable in, say, a structured assembly-line job, as an admittance clerk in a hospital, or as an administrator in a large public agency than as a researcher or an employee whose job requires a high degree of creativity. Be aware, though, that measuring personality is not an exact science, and as you no doubt learned from the discussion of attribution theory, it is easy to attribute personality characteristics in error.

**Emotions** Can managers control the emotions of their colleagues and employees? No. Emotions are a natural part of an individual's makeup. Where managers err is if they ignore the emotional elements in organizational behaviour and assess individual behaviour as if it were completely rational. As one consultant aptly put it, "You can't divorce emotions from the workplace because you can't divorce emotions from people."[84] Managers who understand the role of emotions will significantly improve their ability to explain and predict individual behaviour.

Do emotions affect job performance? Yes. They can *hinder* performance, especially negative emotions. That's probably why organizations, for the most part, try to extract emotions out of the workplace. But emotions can also *enhance* performance. How? Two ways.[85] First, emotions can increase arousal levels, thus acting as motivators to higher performance. Second, emotional labour recognizes that feelings can be part of a job's required behaviour. So, for instance, the ability to effectively manage emotions in leadership and sales positions may be critical to success in those positions.

What differentiates functional from dysfunctional emotions at work? While there is no precise answer to this, it's been suggested that the critical moderating variable is the complexity of the individual's task.[86] The more complex a task, the lower the level of arousal that can be tolerated without interfering with performance. While a certain minimal level of arousal is probably necessary for good performance, very high levels interfere with the ability to function, especially if the job requires calculative and detailed cognitive processes. Given that the trend is toward jobs becoming more complex, you can see why organizations are likely to go to considerable effort to discourage the overt display of emotions—especially intense ones—in the workplace.

# For You as an Individual

The summary above provides a number of ideas that are relevant to you as an individual, so we will focus on just a few issues here. First, the discussion of perception might be something to get you thinking about how you view the world. When we perceive someone as a troublemaker, for instance, this may only be a perception, and not a real characteristic of the other person. So sometimes it is good to question your perception, just to be sure that you are not reading something into a situation that is not there.

Our discussion of personality illustrates that personality differences affect behaviour. One important thing to consider when looking for a job is whether your personality will fit the organization to which you are applying. For instance, it may be a highly structured organization. If you, by nature, are much less formal, this may not be a good fit for you. The discussion of personalities may also help you understand that we sometimes have to identify ways to deal with the personality of others, so that we can get along. When working in groups, you may have sometimes noticed that personalities get in the way. You may want to see if you can figure out ways to get personality differences working in favour of group goals.

Finally, our discussion about emotions should make it clear that emotions need not always be suppressed in the workplace. While emotions can sometimes hinder performance, positive emotions can motivate you and those around you.

*ROADMAP*
*REMINDER*

Prior to this chapter we reviewed the changing nature of the Canadian workplace, and the importance of learning skills that would help us thrive in new and changing environments. In this chapter we considered the role of perception, to help you understand that what you perceive and what is "real" are not always the same. We also considered the role of personality in working with others. Both perception and personality are individual characteristics that affect our interactions with others. Finally, we considered how emotions can affect our behaviour in the workplace. In the next chapter we consider values and attitudes, which also influence our behaviour. The focus on these individual characteristics is to give you some insight into understanding yourself and others with whom you work or carry out tasks.

# For Review

1. Define perception.
2. What is attribution theory? What are its implications for explaining organizational behaviour?
3. How are our perceptions of our own actions different from our perceptions of the actions of others?
4. What is stereotyping? Give an example of how stereotyping can create perceptual distortion.
5. Give some positive results of using shortcuts when judging others.
6. What behavioural predictions might you make if you knew that an employee had (a) an external locus of control? (b) a low-mach score? (c) low self-esteem? (d) a Type A personality?
7. What are the personality dimensions of the Big Five Model?
8. Why might managers today pay more attention to the person-organization fit than the person-job fit?
9. What is emotional labour and why is it important to understanding OB?
10. What is emotional intelligence and why is it important?

# For Critical Thinking

1. How might the differences in experience of students and instructors affect their perceptions of students' written work and class comments?

2. An employee does an unsatisfactory job on an assigned project. Explain the attribution process that this person's manager will use to form judgments about this employee's job performance.

3. One day your boss comes in and he's nervous, edgy, and argumentative. The next day he is calm and relaxed. Does this behaviour suggest that personality traits aren't consistent from day to day?

4. What, if anything, can managers do to manage emotions?

5. Give some examples of situations where the overt expression of emotions might enhance job performance.

## LEARNING ABOUT YOURSELF EXERCISE #1

# Assess Your Locus of Control

**Instructions:** Read the following statements and indicate whether you agree more with choice A or choice B.

| A | B |
|---|---|
| 1. Making a lot of money is largely a matter of getting the right breaks. | 1. Promotions are earned through hard work and persistence. |
| 2. I have noticed that there is a direct connection between how hard I study and the grades I get. | 2. Many times, the reactions of teachers seem haphazard to me. |
| 3. The number of divorces indicates that more and more people are not trying to make their marriages work. | 3. Marriage is largely a gamble. |
| 4. It is silly to think that one can really change another person's basic attitudes. | 4. When I am right, I can convince others. |
| 5. Getting promoted is really a matter of being a little luckier than the next person. | 5. In our society, a person's future earning power is dependent upon his or her ability. |
| 6. If one knows how to deal with people, they are really quite easily led. | 6. I have little influence over the way other people behave. |
| 7. The grades I make are the result of my own efforts; luck has little or nothing to do with it. | 7. Sometimes I feel that I have little to do with the grades I get. |
| 8. People like me can change the course of world affairs if we make ourselves heard. | 8. It is only wishful thinking to believe that one can readily influence what happens in our society. |
| 9. A great deal that happens to me is probably a matter of chance. | 9. I am in control of my destiny. |
| 10. Getting along with people is a skill that must be practised. | 10. It is almost impossible to figure out how to please some people. |

Source: Adapted from J.B. Rotter, "External Control and Internal Control," *Psychology Today,* June 1971, p. 42. Copyright 1971 by the American Psychological Association. Adapted with permission.

*Scoring Key:* Give yourself 1 point for each of the following selections: 1B, 2A, 3A, 4B, 5B, 6A, 7A, 8A, 9B, and 10A. Scores can be interpreted as follows:

| | | |
|---|---|---|
| 8-10 | = | High internal locus of control |
| 6-7 | = | Moderate internal locus of control |
| 5 | = | Mixed |
| 3-4 | = | Moderate external locus of control |
| 1-2 | = | High external locus of control |

## *LEARNING ABOUT YOURSELF EXERCISE #2*

# How Machiavellian Are You?

**Instructions:** For each statement, circle the number that most closely resembles your attitude.

| Statement | Disagree | | | Agree | |
|---|---|---|---|---|---|
| | A Lot | A Little | Neutral | A Little | A Lot |
| 1. The best way to handle people is to tell them what they want to hear. | 1 | 2 | 3 | 4 | 5 |
| 2. When you ask someone to do something for you, it is best to give the real reason for wanting it rather than giving reasons that might carry more weight. | 1 | 2 | 3 | 4 | 5 |
| 3. Anyone who completely trusts anyone else is asking for trouble. | 1 | 2 | 3 | 4 | 5 |
| 4. It is hard to get ahead without cutting corners here and there. | 1 | 2 | 3 | 4 | 5 |
| 5. It is safest to assume that all people have a vicious streak, and it will come out when they are given a chance. | 1 | 2 | 3 | 4 | 5 |
| 6. One should take action only when it is morally right. | 1 | 2 | 3 | 4 | 5 |
| 7. Most people are basically good and kind. | 1 | 2 | 3 | 4 | 5 |
| 8. There is no excuse for lying to someone else. | 1 | 2 | 3 | 4 | 5 |
| 9. Most people more easily forget the death of their father than the loss of their property. | 1 | 2 | 3 | 4 | 5 |
| 10. Generally speaking, people won't work hard unless they're forced to do so. | 1 | 2 | 3 | 4 | 5 |

Source: R. Christie and F.L. Geis, *Studies in Machiavellianism*. (New York: Academic Press, 1970). Reprinted by permission.

*Scoring Key*: To obtain your mach score, add the number you have checked on questions 1, 3, 4, 5, 9, and 10. For the other 4 questions, reverse the numbers you have checked: 5 becomes 1, 4 is 2, 2 is 4, and 1 is 5. Total your 10 numbers to find your score. The higher your score, the more machiavellian you are. Among a random sample of American adults, the national average was 25.

# How's Your Self-Esteem?

**Instructions:** Answer each of the following questions *honestly*. Next to each question write a 1, 2, 3, 4, or 5 depending on which answer best describes you.

1 = Very often
2 = Fairly often
3 = Sometimes
4 = Once in a great while
5 = Practically never

_____ 1. How often do you have the feeling that there is nothing that you can do well?

_____ 2. When you talk in front of a class or group of people your own age, how often do you feel worried or afraid?

_____ 3. How often do you feel that you have handled yourself well at social gatherings?

_____ 4. How often do you have the feeling that you can do everything well?

_____ 5. How often are you comfortable when starting a conversation with people you don't know?

_____ 6. How often do you feel self-conscious?

_____ 7. How often do you feel that you are a successful person?

_____ 8. How often are you troubled with shyness?

_____ 9. How often do you feel inferior to most people you know?

_____ 10. How often do you feel that you are a worthless individual?

_____ 11. How often do you feel confident that your success in your future job or career is assured?

_____ 12. How often do you feel sure of yourself when among strangers?

_____ 13. How often do you feel confident that some day people will look up to you and respect you?

_____ 14. In general, how often do you feel confident about your abilities?

_____ 15. How often do you worry about how well you get along with other people?

_____ 16. How often do you feel that you dislike yourself?

_____ 17. How often do you feel so discouraged with yourself that you wonder whether anything is worthwhile?

_____ 18. How often do you worry about whether other people like to be with you?

_____ 19. When you talk in front of a class or a group of people of your own age, how often are you pleased with your performance?

_____ 20. How often do you feel sure of yourself when you speak in a class discussion?

Source: Developed by A.H. Eagly and adapted from J.R. Robinson and P.R. Shaver, *Measures of Social Psychological Attitudes* (Ann Arbor, MI: Institute of Social Research, 1973), pp. 79—80. With permission.

*Scoring Key:* Add up your score from the left column for the following 10 items: 1, 2, 6, 8, 9, 10, 15, 16, 17, and 18. For the other 10 items, reverse your scoring (that is, a 5 becomes a 1; a 4 becomes a 2). The higher your score, the higher your self-esteem.

## LEARNING ABOUT YOURSELF EXERCISE #4

# Are You a High Self-Monitor?

**Instructions:** Indicate the degree to which you think the following statements are true or false by circling the appropriate number. For example, if a statement is always true, circle the 5 next to that statement.

5 = Certainly, always true
4 = Generally true
3 = Somewhat true, but with exceptions
2 = Somewhat false, but with exceptions
1 = Generally false
0 = Certainly, always false

1. In social situations, I have the ability to alter my behaviour if I feel that something else is called for.　　5　4　3　2　1　0

2. I am often able to read people's true emotions correctly through their eyes.　　5　4　3　2　1　0

3. I have the ability to control the way I come across to people, depending on the impression I wish to give them.　　5　4　3　2　1　0

4. In conversations, I am sensitive to even the slightest change in the facial expression of the person I'm conversing with.　　5　4　3　2　1　0

5. My powers of intuition are quite good when it comes to understanding others' emotions and motives.　　5　4　3　2　1　0

6. I can usually tell when others consider a joke in bad taste, even though they may laugh convincingly.　　5　4　3　2　1　0

7. When I feel that the image I am portraying isn't working, I can readily change it to something that does.　　5　4　3　2　1　0

8. I can usually tell when I've said something inappropriate by reading the listener's eyes.　　5　4　3　2　1　0

9. I have trouble changing my behaviour to suit different people and different situations.　　5　4　3　2　1　0

10. I have found that I can adjust my behaviour to meet the requirements of any situation I find myself in.　　5　4　3　2　1　0

11. If someone is lying to me, I usually know it at once from that person's manner of expression.　　5　4　3　2　1　0

12. Even when it might be to my advantage, I have difficulty putting up a good front.　　5　4　3　2　1　0

13. Once I know what the situation calls for, it's easy for me to regulate my actions accordingly.　　5　4　3　2　1　0

Source: R.D. Lennox and R.N. Wolfe, "Revision of the Self-Monitoring Scale," *Journal of Personality and Social Psychology*, June 1984, p. 1361. Copyright 1984 by the American Psychological Association. Reprinted by permission.

*Scoring Key*: To obtain your score, add up the numbers circled, except reverse scores for questions 9 and 12. On those, a circled 5 becomes a 0, 4 becomes 1, and so forth. High self-monitors are defined as those with scores of 53 or higher.

## LEARNING ABOUT YOURSELF EXERCISE #5

# Are You a Risk-Taker?

**Instructions:** For each of the following situations, you will be asked to indicate the minimum odds of success you would demand before recommending that one alternative be chosen over another. Try to place yourself in the position of the adviser to the central person in each of the situations.

**1.** Mr. B, a 45-year-old accountant, has recently been informed by his physician that he has developed a severe heart ailment. The disease will be sufficiently serious to force Mr. B to change many of his strongest life habits—reducing his workload, drastically changing his diet, giving up favourite leisure-time pursuits. The physician suggests that a delicate medical operation could be attempted. If successful, the operation would completely relieve the heart condition. But its success cannot be assured, and, in fact, the operation might prove fatal.

Imagine that you are advising Mr. B. Listed below are several probabilities or odds that the operation will prove successful. Check the *lowest probability* that you would consider acceptable for the operation to be performed.

_____ Place a check mark here if you think that Mr. B should *not* have the operation, no matter what the probabilities.

_____ The chances are 9 in 10 that the operation will be a success.

_____ The chances are 7 in 10 that the operation will be a success.

_____ The chances are 5 in 10 that the operation will be a success.

_____ The chances are 3 in 10 that the operation will be a success.

_____ The chances are 1 in 10 that the operation will be a success.

**2.** Mr. D is the captain of University X's varsity football team. University X is playing its traditional rival, University Y, in the final game of the season. The game is in its final seconds, and Mr. D's team, University X, is behind in the score. University X has time to make one more play. Mr. D, the captain, must decide on a strategy. Would it be best to try a play that would be almost certain to work and try to settle for a tie score? Or, on the other hand, should he try a more complicated and risky play that would bring victory if it succeeded or defeat if it failed? Imagine that you are advising Mr. D. Listed below are several probabilities or odds that the risky play will work. Check the *lowest probability* that you would consider acceptable for the risky play to be attempted.

_____ Place a check mark here if you think that Mr. D should *not* attempt the risky play, no matter what the probabilities.

_____ The chances are 9 in 10 that the risky play will work.

_____ The chances are 7 in 10 that the risky play will work.

_____ The chances are 5 in 10 that the risky play will work.

_____ The chances are 3 in 10 that the risky play will work.

_____ The chances are 1 in 10 that the risky play will work.

**3.** Ms. K is a successful businesswoman who has participated in a number of civic activities of considerable value to the community. Ms. K has been approached by the leaders of her political party as a possible candidate in the next provincial election. Ms. K's party is a minority party in the district, though the party has won occasional elections in the past. Ms. K would like to hold political office, but to do so would involve a serious financial sacrifice, since the party has insufficient campaign funds. She would also have to endure the attacks of her political opponents in a hot campaign.

Imagine that you are advising Ms. K. Listed below are several probabilities or odds of Ms. K's winning the election in her district. Check the *lowest probability* that you would consider acceptable to make it worthwhile for Ms. K to run for political office.

_____ Place a check mark here if you think that Ms. K should *not* run for political office, no matter what the probabilities.

_____ The chances are 9 in 10 that Ms. K will win the election.

_____ The chances are 7 in 10 that Ms. K will win the election.

_____ The chances are 5 in 10 that Ms. K will win the election.

_____ The chances are 3 in 10 that Ms. K will win the election.

_____ The chances are 1 in 10 that Ms. K will win the election.

4.  Ms. L, a 30-year-old research physicist, has been given a 5-year appointment by a major university laboratory. As she contemplates the next 5 years, she realizes that she might work on a difficult long-term problem. If a solution to the problem could be found, it would resolve basic scientific issues in the field and bring high scientific honours. If no solution were found, however, Ms. L would have little to show for her 5 years in the laboratory, and it would be hard for her to get a good job afterward. On the other hand, she could, as most of her professional associates are doing, work on a series of short-term problems for which solutions would be easier to find. Those solutions, though, would be of lesser scientific importance.

Imagine that you are advising Ms. L. Listed below are several probabilities or odds that a solution will be found to the difficult long-term problem that Ms. L has in mind. Check the *lowest probability* that you would consider acceptable to make it worthwhile for Ms. L to work on the more difficult long-term problem.

_____ Place a check mark here if you think Ms. L should not choose the long-term, difficult problem, no matter what the probabilities.

_____ The chances are 9 in 10 that Ms. L will solve the long-term problem.

_____ The chances are 7 in 10 that Ms. L will solve the long-term problem.

_____ The chances are 5 in 10 that Ms. L will solve the long-term problem.

_____ The chances are 3 in 10 that Ms. L will solve the long-term problem.

_____ The chances are 1 in 10 that Ms. L will solve the long-term problem.

---

Source: Adapted from N. Kogan and M.A. Wallach, *Risk Taking: A Study in Cognition and Personality* (New York: Holt, Rinehart & Winston, 1964), pp. 256-261.

*Scoring Key*: These situations were based on a longer questionnaire. Your results are an indication of your general orientation toward risk rather than a precise measure. To calculate your risk-taking score, add up the chances you were willing to take and divide by four. For any of the situations in which you would not take the risk, regardless of the probabilities, give yourself a 10. The lower your number, the more risk-taking you are.

LEARNING ABOUT YOURSELF EXERCISE #6

# Are You a Type A?

**Instructions:** Circle the number on the scale below that best characterizes your behaviour for each trait.

| | | | | | | | | | |
|---|---|---|---|---|---|---|---|---|---|
| **1.** Casual about appointments | 1 | 2 | 3 | 4 | 5 | 6 | 7 | 8 | Never late |
| **2.** Not competitive | 1 | 2 | 3 | 4 | 5 | 6 | 7 | 8 | Very competitive |
| **3.** Never feel rushed | 1 | 2 | 3 | 4 | 5 | 6 | 7 | 8 | Always feel rushed |
| **4.** Take things one at a time | 1 | 2 | 3 | 4 | 5 | 6 | 7 | 8 | Try to do many things at once |
| **5.** Slow doing things | 1 | 2 | 3 | 4 | 5 | 6 | 7 | 8 | Fast (eating, walking, etc.) |
| **6.** Express feelings | 1 | 2 | 3 | 4 | 5 | 6 | 7 | 8 | "Sit on" feelings |
| **7.** Many interests | 1 | 2 | 3 | 4 | 5 | 6 | 7 | 8 | Few interests outside work |

Source: Adapted from R.W. Bortner, "Short Rating Scale as a Potential Measure of Pattern A Behavior," *Journal of Chronic Diseases,* June 1969, pp. 87-91. With permission.

*Scoring Key*: Total your score on the 7 questions. Now multiply the total by 3. A total of 120 or more indicates that you are a hard-core Type A. Scores below 90 indicate that you are a hard-core Type B. The following gives you more specifics:

| Points | Personality Type |
|---|---|
| 120 or more | A1 |
| 106-119 | A |
| 100-105 | A2 |
| 90-99 | B1 |
| Less than 90 | B |

LEARNING ABOUT YOURSELF EXERCISE #7

# What's Your EI at Work?

Evaluating the following 25 statements will allow you to rate your social skills and self-awareness, the components of emotional intelligence (EI).

EI, the social equivalent of IQ, is complex, in no small part because it depends on some pretty slippery variables—including your innate compatibility, or lack thereof, with the people who happen to be your co-workers. But if you want to get a rough idea of how your EI stacks up, this quiz will help.

As honestly as you can, estimate how you rate in the eyes of peers, bosses, and subordinates on each of the following traits, on a scale of 1-4, with 4 representing strong agreement, and 1 representing strong disagreement.

_____ I usually stay composed, positive, and unflappable even in trying moments.

*Continued on next page*

_____ I can think clearly and stay focused on the task at hand under pressure.

_____ I am able to admit my own mistakes.

_____ I usually or always meet commitments and keep promises.

_____ I hold myself accountable for meeting my goals.

_____ I'm organized and careful in my work.

_____ I regularly seek out fresh ideas from a wide variety of sources.

_____ I'm good at generating new ideas.

_____ I can smoothly handle multiple demands and changing priorities.

_____ I'm results-oriented, with a strong drive to meet my objectives.

_____ I like to set challenging goals and take calculated risks to reach them.

_____ I'm always trying to learn how to improve my performance, including asking advice from people younger than I am.

_____ I readily make sacrifices to meet an important organizational goal.

_____ The company's mission is something I understand and can identify with.

_____ The values of my team—or of our division or department, or the company—influence my decisions and clarify the choices I make.

_____ I actively seek out opportunities to further the overall goals of the organization and enlist others to help me.

_____ I pursue goals beyond what's required or expected of me in my current job.

_____ Obstacles and setbacks may delay me a little, but they don't stop me.

_____ Cutting through red tape and bending outdated rules are sometimes necessary.

_____ I seek fresh perspectives, even if that means trying something totally new.

_____ My impulses or distressing emotions don't often get the best of me at work.

_____ I can change tactics quickly when circumstances change.

_____ Pursuing new information is my best bet for cutting down on uncertainty and finding ways to do thing better.

_____ I usually don't attribute setbacks to a personal flaw (mine or someone else's.)

_____ I operate from an expectation of success rather than a fear of failure.

---

Source: A. Fisher, "Success Secret: A High Emotional IQ," *Fortune*, Ocober 26, 1998, p. 298.

*Scoring Key*: A score below 70 indicates very low EI. EI is not unimprovable. Says Dan Goleman, author of *Working With Emotional Intelligence*, "Emotional intelligence can be learned, and in fact we are each building it, in varying degrees, throughout life. It's sometimes called maturity. EQ is nothing more or less than a collection of tools that we can sharpen to help ensure our own survival."

## WORKING WITH OTHERS EXERCISE

# Evaluating Your Stereotypes

1. Your instructor will choose 4 volunteers willing to reveal an interesting true-life background fact about themselves. Examples of such background facts are:

   - I can perform various dances, such as polka, rumba, bossa nova, and waltz.

   - I am the youngest of four children and I attended Catholic high school.

   - Neither of my parents attended school beyond the eighth grade.

   - My mother is a homemaker and my father is an author.

2. The instructor will put the 4 facts on the board without revealing to which person each belongs, and the 4 students will remain in the front of the room for the first part of the group discussion below.

3. Students in the class should silently decide which person belongs to which fact.

4. Students should break into groups of about 5 or 6 and try to reach consensus about which person belongs to which fact. Meanwhile, the 4 students can serve as observers to group discussions, listening in on rationales for how students decide to link the facts with the individuals.

5. After 15 minutes of group discussion, several groups will be asked to present their consensus to the class, with justifications.

6. The classroom discussion will focus on perceptions, assumptions, and stereotyping that led to the decisions made.

7. At the end of the discussion, the instructor will reveal which student belongs to each fact.

## INTERNET SEARCH EXERCISES

1. Search for the most popular personality tests used in business firms for selection, placement, and promotion decisions. How were you able to conclude that these were the most popular?

2. Find 5 recent articles (published within the past 12 months) on emotional intelligence (EI). Summarize these articles. What, if any, criticism of the concept surfaced in your search?

## CASE INCIDENT

# Frank Stronach, Risk-Taker and Fair Enterprise Creator

When people describe the personality of Frank Stronach, chair of Toronto-based Magna International, they typically use such words as smart-aleck, obnoxious, canny, crazy, and arrogant. Stronach provides an excellent illustration of how an individual's personality shapes his or her behaviour.

Frank Stronach was born in Weiz, Austria, in 1932, the son of a Communist factory worker. He moved to Canada at the age of 22, with $200 in his pocket, plus his expertise as a tool-and-die maker. Within two years he had scraped together enough money to start Multimatic Investments Ltd., a small automotive tool-and-die shop, located in the east end of Toronto. In the 45 years since, he has built that shop into Magna—an auto-parts giant that employs 49 000 workers and has annual sales in excess of $12 billion. In 1998, he was paid $26.2 million for running Magna.

Stronach personifies the driven executive in terms of his various business acquisitions over the years. He has also taken a number of risks, some of which have resulted in huge failure. In 1990, for example, Magna reported a loss of $224.2 million, incredible by almost any standard. But Stronach turned the company around, got back to its roots, and between 1990 and 1994 share prices rose from $2.25 to $66-7/8. In October 1997, prices had risen to their highest yet, $101.50. However, Stronach had made a number of forays into other business ventures; and by late 1999, despite rising sales and a boom in the North American auto industry, shares were trading at $61.50. Stronach's new business venture? MI Entertainment, with interests in media, sports gaming, and online betting.

Stronach believes in "fair enterprise," including a universal charter of rights, and a fairer distribution of wealth. He criticizes socialist systems ("they stifle individualism"), totalitarianism ("benefits the few"), and even free enterprise ("from time-to-time self-destroying"). This may seem like a paradox from someone who earned $26.2 million in 1998 for heading Magna. However, as Hugh Segal, former chief of staff to Brian Mulroney and contender for leadership of the Progressive Conservative Party in 1998, explains, "If Frank were the kind of person for whom conventional orthodoxy mattered, he'd probably still be running a one-man machine shop on Dupont (in Toronto)," where he first started out in the mid-1950s.

Stronach created Magna's corporate philosophy to foster a "strong sense of ownership and entrepreneurial energy" among his employees. Ten percent of pre-tax profit is allocated to employees in the form of cash and share purchase plans, thus giving all employees a share in the profits of the company. Stronach insists that managers' salaries are to be pegged "below industry standards." At the same time, plant managers are given considerable autonomy over buying, selling, and hiring. Magna also tries to keep up with employee attitudes: Plant managers are required to meet with all their workers at least once a month, and employees return a comprehensive survey once a year.

# Questions

1. To what extent would you say that Frank Stronach's personality is reflected in his corporate policy?

2. What might our study of perceptions tell us about how different people might view Stronach's personality?

3. Are there people who might be unhappy working for Frank Stronach?

4. What are the pros and cons of being a manager who works under such a strong personality?

Sources: "Stronach's Pay Almost Matches Big 3 Combined," *Canadian Press Newswire*, October 31, 1997; B. Simon, "Work Ethic and the Magna Carta," *Financial Post Daily*, March 20, 1997, p. 14; "Magna in Overdrive: No Canadian Has Profited From Contracting Out as Much as Stronach," *Maclean's*, September 30, 1996, pp. 50-54; "Car and Striver (Will the World's Leading Auto-Parts Supplier Become the Globe's Newest Automaker?)," *Canadian Business*, September 1996, pp 92-94; "Magna-Mania: Resurrecting His on-the-Brink Auto Parts Empire Didn't Satisfy Frank Stronach Who Plans Growth and Monuments With Equal Flair," *Financial Post*, August 12/14, 1995, pp. 12-13; D. Steinhart, "Magna Moving Into Sports Gaming: Stock on Long Slide: Auto-Parts Giant Takes 17% Drop in Third-Quarter Profit," *Financial Post*, November 9, 1999, p. C3; D. Steinhart, "Market Remains Leery of Magna," *Financial Post*, November 5, 1999, pp. D1, D3; and D. Olive, "Some Canadian CEOS Did Better Than Their US Counterparts," *Financial Post*, June 14, 1999, p. C6.

# This Guy Never Quits

Mogens Smed, president and CEO of Calgary-based SMED International, has a charismatic personality. He can sweep people up in his enthusiasm, getting them to put high energy into helping develop his projects. He also isn't afraid of taking risks.

SMED specializes in building custom office interiors. In addition to upscale office furniture, the company designs floors and is the market leader in prefabricated movable walls. The new SMED factory in southeast Calgary is the largest manufacturing facility in Western Canada, with state-of-the-art manufacturing equipment, a large gym, and a huge brightly coloured cafeteria where employees gather for pep rallies. All of this building, however, has put SMED in a bad financial situation. In 1998 Mogens Smed had to lay off a lot of employees and try to figure out how to bring the company back to financial success.

SMED has some glamour clients, including Steven Spielberg's DreamWorks SKG in Los Angeles, the NFL Players' Union in New York City, Tommy Hilfiger Corp., and Calvin Klein. However, the company is really only a small player in the office-furniture industry, with about one percent of market share. Chief competitors are Herman Miller, which has 10 percent of market share, and Steelcase, which has 25 percent.

Smed has a reputation as an outstanding salesperson and a charismatic leader, and his leadership style doesn't allow him to fret about his small market share. SMED's motto is "Our only competition is conventional thinking." Smed explains that his company is different from the competition: "We do not play by the rules. There are no rules. We offer something completely different from them. We don't just make products and offer them to the customer. We ask the customer what they want and then make it for them."

Smed spares no expense for his clients. He built Falkridge, an alpine retreat, at a cost of $1.6 million. He brings clients to the retreat to woo them with gourmet dinners, fine wines, and Cuban cigars. At SMED, the rule has been that no expense is too great to impress a client.

Smed's charming personality may work well for his clients, but investors and market analysts are more critical of his style. SMED shares reached a peak of $32 in mid-1998, but after the large manufacturing facility was built in Calgary, a variety of factors sent the stock plummeting. In April 1999 it went as low as $5.50. And in early 2000 SMED faced a hostile takeover bid by Holland Landing, an Ontario-based office specialty company. SMED has now merged with Michigan-based Haworth Inc., a maker and marketer of office furniture and seating. SMED will keep its name and operate as an independent subsidiary. Shares were trading above $23 after the deal was announced. Whether Smed will still be able to be as flamboyant with his clients after the merger remains to be seen. He may find limits on what the parent corporation, Haworth Inc., will allow.

# Questions

1. How would you describe Mogens Smed's personality?

2. To what extent would you say that personality plays a role in how Mogens Smed runs SMED International?

3. Do you think Smed's personality causes him to take bigger risks than someone else leading SMED International might take? Why or why not?

Source: Based on "Turning Smed Around," *Venture 709*; aired January 19, 1999. Also see Mel Duvall, "New Plant Provides Impetus for SMED's Growth," *Financial Post Daily,* October 3, 1997, p. 19; Curtis Gillespie, "Selling Smed: Mogens Smed Is Passionate About Making SMED International a Global Player in Office Furniture," *Financial Post Magazine,* October 1997, pp. 70-81; S. Miles, "Smed Claws Its Way Back to Profitability," *Financial Post,* November 27, 1999, p. C3; P. Verburg, "His Party, Your Hangover," *Canadian Business,* August 27, 1999, pp. 36-39; D. Steinhart , "Hostile Move on Smed Could Trigger New Bids," *Financial Post,* December 22, 1999; and I. McKinnon, "Smed Gets $280M Bid From Haworth," *Financial Post,* January 26, 2000.

## CHAPTER 3

# Values, Attitudes, and Their Effects in the Workplace

Timothy Penner is president of Procter & Gamble Canada. He leads a company that values diversity in its workplace. Consider Procter & Gamble's statement on employee diversity:

> Developing and managing a strong, diverse organization is essential to achieving our business purpose. We value the different perspectives that the diversity of Procter & Gamble people bring to the business. At Procter & Gamble, we operate on the fundamental belief that these diverse viewpoints are needed for organization creativity which produces genuine competitive advantage.[1]

We expect that an organization's values, like those of an individual, will be reflected in corresponding behaviour and attitudes. If a company stated that they valued organizational diversity, and no behaviour flowed from that statement, we would question whether that value was really so important to the company. However, in Procter & Gamble's case, they back up their value statement with concrete policies

## Questions for Consideration

**What is the relationship between values and individual behaviour?**

**How do values differ across cultures?**

**How does job satisfaction affect one's behaviour in the workplace?**

and actions to show support for the value. For instance, they changed their recruiting practices to ensure diversity in their hiring. They broadened the number of universities from which they recruit, included French universities in Quebec in their recruiting, and targeted several campuses with high representation of visible minority students to ensure geographical, language, racial, and ethnic diversity. This resulted in a stronger and more diverse population at Procter & Gamble.

In this chapter, we look more carefully at how values influence an individual's behaviour and consider the relationship between values and attitudes. We then consider two specific issues that arise from our discussion of values and attitudes: workforce diversity and job satisfaction.

## Values

Is capital punishment right or wrong? How about racial or gender quotas in hiring—are they right or wrong? If a person likes power, is that good or bad? The answers to these questions are value-laden. Some might argue, for example, that capital punishment is right because it is an appropriate retribution for crimes such as murder. However, others might argue, just as strongly, that no government has the right to take anyone's life.

**Values** represent basic convictions about what is important to the individual. They contain a judgmental element in that they carry an individual's ideas as to what is right, good, or desirable. Values have both content and intensity attributes. The content attribute says that the value is *important*. The intensity attribute specifies *how important* it is. When we rank an individual's values in terms of their intensity, we obtain that person's **value system**. All of us have a hierarchy of values that forms our value system. This system is identified by the relative importance we assign to such values as freedom, pleasure, self-respect, honesty, obedience, and equality. Moreover, values are not fluid and flexible; rather they tend to be relatively stable and enduring.[2] A significant portion of the values we hold is established in our early years—from parents, teachers, friends, and others.

**values**
Basic convictions about what is important to the individual.

**value system**
A hierarchy based on a ranking of an individual's values in terms of their intensity.

**Procter & Gamble**
www.pg.com

**HR Around the World**
www.hroe.org/index.cfm?c=16&
lang=e&p=AL

**IBM**
www.ibm.ca

**power distance**
A national culture attribute describing the extent to which a society accepts that power in institutions and organizations is distributed unequally.

**individualism**
A national culture attribute describing a loosely knit social framework in which people emphasize only the care of themselves and their immediate family.

**collectivism**
A national culture attribute that describes a tight social framework in which people expect others in groups of which they are a part to look after them and protect them.

## Importance of Values

Values are important to the study of organizational behaviour because they lay the foundation for the understanding of attitudes and motivation, and because they influence our perceptions. Individuals enter an organization with preconceived notions of what "ought" and what "ought not" to be. Of course, these notions are not value-free. On the contrary, they contain interpretations of right and wrong. Furthermore, they imply that certain behaviours or outcomes are preferred over others. As a result, values cloud objectivity and rationality.

Values generally influence attitudes and behaviour.[3] Suppose that you enter an organization with the view that allocating pay on the basis of performance is right, whereas allocating pay on the basis of seniority is wrong or inferior. How will you react if you find that the organization you have just joined rewards seniority and not performance? You're likely to be disappointed—and this can lead to job dissatisfaction and the decision not to exert a high level of effort since "it's probably not going to lead to more money, anyway." Would your attitudes and behaviour be different if your values aligned with the organization's pay policies? Most likely. In this chapter's Learning About Yourself Exercise on page 117, you are given the opportunity to examine some of the things that you value.

# Values Across Cultures

Because values differ across cultures, an understanding of these differences should be helpful in explaining and predicting behaviour of employees from different countries. We will illustrate this point with a number of comparisons, starting first with differences in cultures within Canada. We will then compare American culture with Canadian and Japanese cultures.[4] This will be followed by a more general overview of some of the differences that researchers have found across other cultures. Additional insights are provided in this chapter's CBC Video Case on page 120.

## A Framework for Assessing Cultural Values

In Chapter 1, we described the new global village and said "managers have to become capable of working with people from different cultures." Before we look selectively at a variety of cultural value comparisons, it is helpful to know how cultures are examined. One of the most widely referenced approaches for analyzing variations among cultures has come from Geert Hofstede.[5] He surveyed more than 116 000 IBM employees in 40 countries about their work-related values. He found that managers and employees vary on five value dimensions of national culture. They are listed and defined as follows:

**Power distance.** The degree to which people in a country accept that power in institutions and organizations is distributed unequally. Ranges from relatively equal (low power distance) to extremely unequal (high power distance).

**Individualism** vs. **collectivism**. Individualism is the degree to which people in a country prefer to act as individuals rather than as members of groups. Collectivism is the equivalent of low individualism.

**quantity of life**
A national culture attribute describing the extent to which societal values are characterized by assertiveness and materialism.

**quality of life**
A national culture attribute that emphasizes relationships and concern for others.

**uncertainty avoidance**
A national culture attribute describing the extent to which a society feels threatened by uncertain and ambiguous situations, and tries to avoid them.

**long-term orientation**
A national culture attribute that emphasizes the future, thrift, and persistence.

**short-term orientation**
A national culture attribute that emphasizes the past and present, respect for tradition, and fulfilling social obligation.

**Quantity of life** vs. **quality of life.** Quantity of life is the degree to which values like assertiveness, the acquisition of money and material goods, and competition prevail. Quality of life is the degree to which people value relationships, and show sensitivity and concern for the welfare of others.[6]

**Uncertainty avoidance.** The degree to which people in a country prefer structured over unstructured situations. In countries that score high on uncertainty avoidance, people have an increased level of anxiety, which manifests itself in greater nervousness, stress, and aggressiveness.

**Long-term** vs. **short-term orientation.** People in cultures with long-term orientations look to the future and value thrift and persistence. A short-term orientation values the past and present, and emphasizes respect for tradition and fulfilling social obligations.

Exhibit 3-1 provides a summary of how a number of countries rate on Hofstede's five dimensions (power distance; individualism vs. collectivism; quantity of life vs. quality of life; uncertainty avoidance; and long-term vs. short-term orientation). Not surprisingly, most Asian countries are more collectivist than individualistic. On the other hand, the United States ranked highest on individualism among all countries surveyed.

Hofstede's findings are based on research that is nearly three decades old, and has been subject to some criticism, which he refutes.[7]

## Exhibit 3-1
## Examples of National Cultural Values

| Country | Power Distance | Individualism* | Quantity of Life** | Uncertainty Avoidance | Long-term Orientation*** |
|---------|----------------|----------------|--------------------|-----------------------|--------------------------|
| Canada | Moderate | High | High | Moderate | Low |
| China | High | Low | Moderate | Moderate | High |
| France | High | High | Moderate | High | Low |
| Germany**** | Low | High | High | Moderate | Moderate |
| Hong Kong | High | Low | High | Low | High |
| Indonesia | High | Low | Moderate | Low | Low |
| Japan | Moderate | Moderate | High | Moderate | Moderate |
| Mexico | High | Low | High | High | NA |
| Netherlands | Low | High | Low | Moderate | Moderate |
| Russia | High | Moderate | Low | High | Low |
| United States | Low | High | High | Low | Low |
| West Africa | High | Low | Moderate | Moderate | Low |

*A low score is synonymous with collectivism. **A low score is synonymous with high quality of life.
***A low score is synonymous with a short-term orientation. ****Includes only former West Germany.

Source: Adapted from G. Hofstede, "Cultural Constraints in Management Theories," *Academy of Management Executive*, February 1993, p. 91; G. Hofstede, "The Cultural Relativity of Organizational Practices and Theories," *Journal of International Business Studies*, 14, 1983, pp. 75–89. Mexico's scores were abstracted from G.K. Stephens and C.R. Greer, "Doing Business in Mexico: Understanding Cultural Differences," *Organizational Dynamics, Special Report*, 1998, pp. 43-59.

> **Do countries keep the same cultural values forever?**

It's important that you treat the ratings in Exhibit 3-1 as general guidelines that need to be modified over time to reflect that the world has changed since Hofstede conducted his study. Some examples: Communism has fallen in Eastern Europe; China has become significantly more open; Hong Kong is run by the Chinese rather than the British; Germany has become unified; South Africa has ended apartheid; Mexico has undergone significant economic development; and there has been a dramatic increase in the proportion of women in the labour force and in management positions in countries such as Canada and the United States. A recent follow-up to Hofstede's study confirmed many of the original findings but also found that transformational changes have made their way into various cultural values.[8] For instance, Mexico has moved in 30 years from an emphasis on collectivism to individualism. This is consistent with Mexico's economic development and the growth of capitalistic values. Similarly, in the United States, values have shifted from quantity of life to quality, which undoubtedly reflects the influence of women and younger entrants on the workforce. Our point here is that even though cultural values are generally stable and enduring, you need to be aware that Hofstede's classifications might, in some cases, need to be modified to include transformational changes within countries.

Below we examine some specific value issues across a variety of cultures, both within Canada and with some of Canada's trading partners: the parties of the North American Free Trade Agreement (NAFTA), and some of the Asian and Pacific Rim countries. In trying to understand the impact of cultural values on Canadian society, you should consider how multicultural Canada has become in recent years. For instance, in 1996, 42 percent of Metropolitan Toronto's population, 34.8 percent of Vancouver's and 18 percent of Montreal's were made up of immigrants. The 1991 Census found that 15.2 percent of Canada's population over age five spoke neither of the country's two official languages. Of those who did not speak either English or French, 28 percent spoke Chinese (either Mandarin or Cantonese, mainly), 15 percent spoke Italian, 11 percent spoke Portuguese, 6 percent spoke Spanish, and 5 percent spoke Punjabi.[9] These figures indicate the very different cultures that are part of the Canadian fabric of life.

In the discussion of values below, bear in mind that we present broad generalizations, and you should certainly avoid stereotyping individuals on the basis of these generalizations. Instead, you should try to understand how others might view things differently from you, even when they are exposed to the same situation.

## Canadian Social Values

In a recent book entitled *Sex in the Snow,* pollster Michael Adams attempted to identify the social values of today's Canadians.[10] He found that within three broad age groups of adult Canadians—those over 50 ("the elders"), baby boomers (born from the mid-1940s to the mid-1960s), and Generation X (born from the mid-1960s to the early 1980s)—there are at least 12 quite distinct "value tribes." We present some of the findings below. For further information and an opportunity to see where you might be classified in terms of your social values, visit the Environics Web site.

**Environics**
http://www.environics.net

**THE ELDERS** These individuals are characterized as "playing by the rules," and their core values are belief in order, authority, discipline, the

Judeo-Christian moral code, and the Golden Rule (do unto others as you would have others do unto you). About 80 percent of the elders resemble this description of traditional values, although there are variations within that 80 percent in the strength of fit.

**THE BOOMERS**  The view of boomers as a somewhat spoiled, hedonistic, rebellious group belies the four categories of boomers: autonomous rebels (25 percent), anxious communitarians (20 percent), connected enthusiasts (14 percent), and disengaged Darwinists (41 percent). So, unlike the elders, the boomers are a bit more fragmented in their views. Yet all but the disengaged Darwinists reflect, to some extent, the stereotypes of this generation: rejection of authority, scepticism regarding the motives of big business and government, a strong concern for the environment, and a strong desire for equality in the workplace and society. Of course, the disengaged Darwinists, the largest single group, do not fit this description as well. The Darwinists are characterized as being angry, intimidated by change, and anxious about their professional and financial futures.

**GENERATION X**  While this group is quite fragmented in its values, the research showed that the common values are experience-seeking, adaptability, and concern with personal image among peers. Despite these common values, Generation Xers can be divided into five tribes. Thrill-seeking materialists (25 percent) desire money and material possessions, as well as recognition, respect, and admiration. Aimless dependants (27 percent) seek financial independence, security, and stability. Social hedonists (15 percent) are experience-seeking, committed to their own pleasure, and seek immediate gratification. New Aquarians (13 percent) are experience-seeking, and also egalitarian and ecologically minded. Finally, autonomous post-materialists (20 percent) seek personal autonomy and self-fulfillment, and are concerned about human rights.

Beyond the differences in the three generational groups, it is safe to say that, overall, the values of Canadians have changed a lot in the last 10 years. Air Canada recently studied the core values of Canadians as part of an effort to develop its brand strategy.[11] Their results show that Canadians have become more confident and less nationalistic. They are also human, caring, and humble, while also seeking respect. Finally, the Air Canada results indicate that while there is a strong social conscience among Canadians, there is currently more emphasis on the individual than the collective than there was in the past.

Since Adams's book appeared, another generation has been identified by Don Tapscott, author of *Growing Up Digital: The Rise of the Net Generation*.[12] Tapscott says this generation, born between 1977 and 1997, are "creators, not recipients. And they are curious, contrarian, flexible, collaborative and high in self-esteem."[13]

## The Application of Canadian Values in the Workplace

An awareness of the overall value structure helps us to understand better how to manage and interrelate in the workplace. So, too, does an awareness of the very broad generalizations that characterize the differing values among the generational groups identified above. Senior management is often led by the elders, who have spent much of their careers working in hierarchical organizations. As boomers move into head offices, the "play-by-the-rules," "boss knows best" elders are being replaced by boomers who have a somewhat

> **Are Gen Xers really different from their elders?**

**Growing Up Digital**
www.growingupdigital.com

Vancouver-based Mainframe Entertainment, the company behind *Reboot* and *Beasties*, understands the values of its Generation X employees: experience, recognition, respect and admiration. Mainframe's animators get leadership opportunities, including the opportunity to direct shows, which they would not get at higher paying studios in Los Angeles. Mainframe has one of the lowest turnover rates in the animation business because of its emphasis on giving its young employees the opportunity to acquire new skills.

**Levi Strauss & Company**
www.levistrauss.com

more egalitarian view of the workplace. They dislike the command-and-control rules that were part of their parents' lives, although the boomers have also been described as workaholics. Meanwhile, the Generation Xers who enter the workplace are comfortable in adapting, but also want more experiences. They are not in awe of authority. And most important, they are not interested in copying the workaholic behaviour of their parents. Managing the expectations of each of these very different groups is not an easy task. It requires managers to be flexible, observant, and willing to adjust more to the individual needs of these different employees. The Net Generation will certainly change the face of the workplace in significant ways. They have mastered a communication and information system that many of their parents have yet to understand.

Organizations can mould their workplace by hiring people with similar values and/or aligning the jobs that people are given with their values. Studies have shown that when individual values align with organizational values, the results are positive. Individuals who have an accurate understanding of the job requirements and the organization's values adjust better to their jobs, and have greater levels of satisfaction and organizational commitment.[14] In addition, shared values between the employee and the organization lead to more positive work attitudes,[15] lower turnover,[16] and greater productivity.[17]

Robert Haas, chair and CEO of Levi Strauss & Company, has argued "that alignment between organizational values and personal values is the key driver of corporate success."[18] For instance, Toronto-based investment banking firm Griffiths McBurney & Partners Inc. hires people who are aggressive and risk-taking, because that is the kind of firm the partners have created. "Everyone starts the year with zero salary, zero draw, and no guarantees," and compensation is based on revenues.[19]

Asked to define the fundamentals that give National Bank Financial its edge, senior vice president and company director John Wells believes Montreal-based National Bank's financial edge comes from company management that is largely French Canadian. He argues that French Canadians treat their employees well, and will try to find *any* means of reducing expenses rather than lay off staff, in sharp contrast to the cost-cutting mechanisms of either English Canadian or American firms.

Some workplaces also try to change employee values through education or "propagandistic interventions."[20] Later in the chapter, for instance, we discuss how workplaces have attempted to introduce the value of cultural diversity. Interestingly enough, however, there is little research that shows that values can be changed successfully.[21] Values tend to be relatively stable, and thus more interventions are aimed at changing attitudes. After our discussion of attitudes below, we note some of these specific interventions with respect to cultural diversity in the workplace.

## Francophone and Anglophone Values

One of the larger issues that has confronted Canada in recent years is the question of Quebec separatism and anglophone-francophone differences. Consequently, it may be of interest to managers and employees in Canadian firms to be aware of some of the potential cultural differences when managing in various environments. A number of studies show that anglophones and francophones have distinctive value priorities. Francophones have been found to be more collectivist, or group-oriented, with a greater need for achievement, while anglophones were found to be more individualist, or I-centred.[22] Francophones have also been shown to be more concerned about the interpersonal aspects of the workplace than task competence.[23] Anglophones have been shown to take more risks.[24] Other studies have found that anglophone managers tended to value autonomy and intrinsic job values, such as achievement, and thus were more achievement-oriented, while francophone managers tended to value affiliation and extrinsic job values, such as technical supervision.[25]

A 1994 study conducted at the University of Ottawa and Laval University suggests that some of the differences reported in previous research may be decreasing.[26] For instance, that study reported that there were no significant differences in individualism and collectivism. While this is only one study, and thus needs further confirmation, the researchers suggest that some of the differences found in previous studies were a function of characteristics unrelated to whether a person was francophone or anglophone. Specifically, once the socio-economic status of the individuals is controlled, there are no differences due to linguistic background. The researchers also concluded that both francophone and anglophone managers today would have been exposed to more of the same types of organizational theories during their training in post-secondary school, which might also influence their outlooks as managers. Thus we would not expect to find large differences in the way that firms in francophone Canada are managed, compared with those in the rest of Canada. Throughout the textbook you will see a number of examples of Quebec-based businesses that support this conclusion.

## Canadian Aboriginal Values

| |
|---|
| **What can I learn about OB from Aboriginal culture?** |

**Aboriginal Business Map**
www.aboriginalmap.ic.gc.ca/

Entrepreneurial activity among Canada's Aboriginal people has been increasing at the same time that there are more partnerships and alliances between Aboriginal and non-Aboriginal businesses. Because of these business interactions, it is important to examine the types of differences one might observe in how each culture manages its businesses. "Aboriginal values are usually perceived (by non-aboriginals) as an impediment to economic development and organizational effectiveness."[27] These values include reluctance to compete, a time orientation different from the Western one, and an emphasis on consensus decision making.[28] Aboriginals do not necessarily agree that these values are business impediments, however.

Specifically, while Canadian businesses and government have historically assumed that "non-Native people must teach Native people how to run their own organizations," the First Nations of Canada are not convinced.[29] They believe that traditional culture, values, and languages do not have to be compromised to build a self-sustaining economy. Moreover, they believe that their cultural values may actually be a positive force in conducting business.[30]

To use Hofstede's framework to understand Aboriginal and non-Aboriginal cultures, we can rely on the research of Lindsay Redpath of Athabasca University.[31] Aboriginal cultures are more collectivist in orientation than non-Aboriginal cultures in either Canada or the United States. Aboriginal organizations are much more likely to reflect and advance the goals of the community. There is also a greater sense of family within the workplace, with greater affiliation and loyalty. Power distance in Aboriginal cultures is smaller than in non-Aboriginal cultures of Canada and the United States, and there is an emphasis on consensual decision making. Aboriginal cultures are lower on uncertainty avoidance than non-Aboriginal cultures in either Canada or the United States. Aboriginal organizations and cultures tend to have fewer rules and regulations. Each of these differences suggests that organizations created by Aboriginals will differ from non-Aboriginal businesses, and both research and anecdotal evidence support this conjecture.[32]

Certainly the opening ceremony for the First Nations Bank of Canada's head office branch in Saskatoon in September 1997 was different from many openings of Western businesses. The ceremony was accompanied by the

Prime Minister Jean Chrétien helped celebrate the opening of the Saskatoon head office of First Nations Bank of Canada. The Bank's opening ceremonies, as well as its operating procedures, emphasize a strong attachment to Aboriginal values.

burning of sweetgrass. "This is a blessing," Blaine Favel, chief of the Federation of Saskatchewan Indian Nations, said to a large outdoor gathering. "We are celebrating a great accomplishment by our people."[33]

Saskatoon-based Adam's Active Autowrecking is owned by Sandra Bighead, a member of the Beardy's and Okemasis First Nation. Her philosophy about running her business exhibits the family-value orientation that is more likely to be found in Aboriginal businesses. She believes in taking care of her staff: "For me, success is gaining personal satisfaction, self-confidence, and self-worth from the work I do," she said. "Part of that satisfaction comes from knowing that a lot of people and their families are depending on me."[34]

## Canadian Values and the Values of NAFTA Partners

**UNITED STATES** Pollster Michael Adams points out that compared with Canadians, "Americans have a greater faith in the family, the state (that is, 'America'), religion, and the market."[35] Americans are more comfortable with big business, probably because it means American big business, whereas in Canada big business means a foreign-owned, often American, business. The American business environment is characterized by intense competition, whereas Canada has historically had a more protectionist attitude in the market, as well as public-sector monopolies and private-sector oligopolies. While these "antimarket" forces are changing slowly, Canadian businesses are still adapting to the open markets that globalization has brought.

If we can talk about a national "personality," Canadians are more shy and deferential than Americans, as well as less violent and more courteous. There is more emphasis on being polite and following the rules. Canadians are more pragmatic, and less ideological. Canadians value peace, order, and equality, whereas Americans value individuality and freedom.[36] Movie marketing consultant Martin Rabinovitch, who recently moved to Vancouver to open Assiniboine Entertainment after working in Los Angeles for a number of years, notes that in Canada "there's a friendliness and innocence that you don't really find in the States."[37] Americans are thought to be more comfortable with the unknown, taking risks, and pushing the boundaries of creativity than Canadians. As one columnist notes, "ever since the late '50s, when singer Paul Anka couldn't record *Diana* in Canada but made it a hit in the U.S., there has been a perception that it is harder to take risks in

Hudson's Bay Co. hired two Americans after Canadian George Kossich retired from the CEO position in March 1997. Bill Fields was hired to head the parent corporation and a year later he hired Ira Pickell (shown here) to head the Bay stores. Pickell seemed to be everything the Bay was not: energetic, forceful, American. After share prices dropped from a high of about $38 soon after Fields started to a low of $14 in March 1999, both men were dismissed in early 1999. Canadians George Heller and Marc Chouinard replaced Fields and Pickell, respectively. Says Heller: "We know the shortcuts to what each other is thinking, we know what each of us can and can't do." That may be because they share common Canadian values.

Canada, the nation of life insurers."[38] Canadians also seem uncomfortable celebrating success, and even try to play it down. And Canada's broad social safety net makes it easier to fail in Canada than in the United States.

These differences in values and national personalities suggest that Canadian and American workplaces will likely look and operate somewhat differently. Canadians may be more suited to the teams that many organizations are creating, and more willing to work together than to be individual stars. They may follow the directives of their managers more, even as new organizational models suggest that both employees and managers need to take more responsibility to learn and share information. An awareness of these values will help you understand some of the differences you might observe in Canadian and American businesses.

**MEXICO** With the passage of the North American Free Trade Agreement (NAFTA), an understanding of Mexico's workplace issues and how they compare with those of Canada and the United States becomes increasingly important. Two researchers collected a variety of data from Mexican and American managers, as well as observing *maquiladora* manufacturing plants, during 1993 and 1994. We report a summary of their findings here.[39]

Mexico has a higher power distance than either Canada or the United States. However, while the Mexican managerial style is characterized as autocratic and paternalistic, managers do not rely exclusively on these traits. While Mexican workers defer more to their managers, they are less likely than Canadians or Americans to tolerate abrasiveness and insensitivity by their managers.

Mexico in general is characterized by a greater degree of uncertainty avoidance than either Canada or the United States. However, it would appear that Mexican managers are greater risk-takers than their counterparts in other North American countries. Because of the higher power distance and an autocratic style, managers in Mexico may feel freer to take risks than those in Canada and the United States. Both Canada and the United States are much more individualistic than Mexico. In part, this is reflected in the greater reliance on personal networks and relationships in Mexico. Mexican employees are also much more agreeable to teamwork, perhaps because of their greater need for affiliation. Mexico, Canada, and the United States score similarly high on quantity-of-life values.

All of these differences in values suggest that Mexican workplaces will look and operate differently than Canadian and American workplaces. Mexicans may be the most suited to teams, and much less likely to try to stand out individually. They are likely to defer to their managers more, but they also expect more respect from their managers. An awareness of these values will help you understand some of the differences you might observe in workplaces across North America.

## Japanese and American Values

American children are taught early the values of individuality and uniqueness.[40] In contrast, Japanese children are socialized to be "team players," to work within the group, and to conform. A significant part of American students' education is to learn to think, analyze, and question. Their Japanese counterparts are rewarded for recounting facts. These different socialization practices reflect different cultures and, not surprisingly, result in different types of employees. For example, the average US worker is more competitive and self-focused than the Japanese worker. Predictions of employee behaviour based on that of Canadian and US workers are likely to be off target when applied to a population of employees—such as the Japanese—who prefer and perform better in standardized tasks, as part of a work team, with group-based decisions and rewards.

From their earliest years, Japanese children are taught the value of working together. This socialization practice extends into the workplace, where employees work well as a team. The team of workers shown here at Japan's Yokogawa Electric, maker of industrial testing and measuring equipment, is able to make decisions about redesigning products in short periods of time while meeting the company's cost-cutting goals.

Dell Computer learned that Chinese work values differ from U.S. work values when it opened a computer factory in Xiamen, China. Chinese workers view the concept of a job for life. They expect to drink tea and read the papers on the job—and still keep their jobs. Dell China executives had to train employees so they understood that their jobs depended on their performance. To instill workers with a sense of ownership, managers gave employees stock options and explained to them how their increased productivity would result in higher pay.

**Asia Pacific Management Forum**
www.apmforum.com/survey/
guanxisurvey.htm

What do I need to know to set up a business in Asia?

### East and Southeast Asian Values

Professor Rosalie Tung of Simon Fraser University and her student Irene Yeung examined the importance of *guanxi* (personal connections with the appropriate authorities or individuals) for a sample of North American, European, and Hong Kong firms doing business with companies in Mainland China.[41] They suggest that their findings will also be relevant in understanding how to develop relationships with firms from Japan, South Korea, and Hong Kong.

"*Guanxi* refers to the establishment of a connection between two independent individuals to enable a bilateral flow of personal or social transactions. Both parties must derive benefits from the transaction to ensure the continuation of such a relationship."[42] *Guanxi* relations are based on reciprocation, unlike Western networked relationships, which may be characterized more by self-interest. *Guanxi* relationships are meant to be long-term and enduring, in contrast with the immediate gains sometimes expected in Western relationships. *Guanxi* also relies less on institutional law, and more on personal power and authority, than do Western relationships. And finally, *guanxi* relations are governed more by the notion of shame (that is, external pressures on performance), while Western relations often rely on guilt (that is internal pressures on performance) to maintain agreements. *Guanxi* is seen as extremely important for business success in China—more than such factors as right location, price or strategy, or product differentiation and quality. For Western firms wanting to do business with Asian firms, an understanding of *guanxi,* and an effort to build relationships, are important strategic advantages.

Our discussion about differences in cross-cultural values might suggest to you that understanding other cultures matters. When Canadian firms develop overseas operations or expand south of the Canadian border, the need to understand other cultures becomes important for employees transferred to foreign locations. Our Point/CounterPoint discussion on pages 100-101 investigates some of the pros and cons of cross-cultural training.

## Implications of Cultural Differences for OB

While Canadian researchers have contributed to the body of knowledge we call *organizational behaviour,* much of the theory we use in Canada has been developed by Americans using American subjects within domestic contexts.[43] What this means is that (1) not all OB theories and concepts are universally applicable to managing people around the world, especially in countries where work values are considerably different from those in either the United States or Canada; and (2) you should take into consideration cultural values when trying to understand the behaviour of people of different backgrounds within a country, as well as when you try to understand people in different countries.

In subsequent chapters we discuss such workplace practices as goal setting (Chapter 4), job enrichment (Chapter 13), quality circles (Chapter 6), and performance-based pay (Chapter 4). Researchers have noted that managerial interventions such as these have differed greatly in effectiveness among countries.[44] A recent theory—cultural self-presentation theory— suggests that worker responses to these interventions are affected by the individual's interpretation of the dominant social values.[45] For instance, the introduction of pay-for-performance, which rewards individual behaviour, is less likely to be welcomed by workers in a more collectivist culture, where the group is more important than any individual. This is relevant, for instance, in comparing Aboriginal firms and non-Aboriginal firms in Canada. It is also relevant for considering how to motivate and reward individuals from different cultural backgrounds who work in Canadian organizations. Although more empirical work needs to be done, cultural self-presentation theory seems to be able to account for the differential effectiveness of some of the most common workplace interventions. To find out more about working with others from different cultures, you might want to examine this chapter's Case Incident on page 119.

### Values and Workforce Diversity

Many organizations have attempted to incorporate workforce diversity initiatives into their workplaces. For example, Procter & Gamble's explicit statement about employment diversity, presented in the chapter opening, is representative of the types of statements that organizations often include in their annual reports and employee information packets. These statements signal corporate values to both employees and other people who might do business with the company. Some corporations choose to signal the value of diversity because they think it is an important strategic goal.

When companies design and then publicize statements about the importance of diversity, they are essentially producing value statements. The hope, of course, is that the statements will then change the attitudes of the members of the organization. But as noted above, values themselves do not often change. So the introduction of a company value statement is not likely, in and of itself, to change the values of organization members. The organization can

## POINT

# Cross-Cultural Training Doesn't Work

Academics seem to take it as a truism that the expanding global marketplace has serious implications for management practice. As a result, they have become strong advocates for the necessity of cross-cultural training. But most corporations don't provide cross-cultural training for employees. Studies indicate, for instance, that only 30 percent of managers who are sent on foreign assignments scheduled to last from one to five years receive any cross-cultural training before their departure.

Why don't most organizations provide their managers with cross-cultural training? We propose two possible explanations. One is that top managers believe that "managing is managing," so *where* it is done is irrelevant. The other explanation is that top management doesn't believe that cross-cultural training is effective.

Contrary to the evidence, many senior managers continue to believe that managerial skills are perfectly transferable across cultures. A good manager in Toronto or Vancouver, for instance, should be equally effective in Paris or Hong Kong. In organizations where this belief dominates, you won't find any concern with cross-cultural training. Moreover, there is likely to be little effort made to select candidates for foreign assignments based on their ability to fit into, or adapt to, a specific culture. Selection decisions for overseas postings in these organizations are primarily made using a single criterion: the person's domestic track record.

It's probably fair to say that most senior managers today recognize that cultural differences do affect managerial performance. But their organizations still don't provide cross-cultural training because these managers doubt the effectiveness of this training. They argue that people can't learn to manage in a foreign culture after only a few weeks or months of training. An understanding of a country's culture is something one assimilates over many years based on input from many sources. It is not something that lends itself to short-term learning, no matter how intensive a training program might be.

Given the previous arguments, it would be surprising to find organizations offering cross-cultural training. We submit that top executives of organizations typically take one of three approaches in dealing with the selection of managerial personnel for staff foreign assignments. One approach is to ignore cultural differences. They don't worry about them and make their selection decisions based solely on individuals' previous managerial records. Another approach is to hire nationals to manage foreign operations. Since cross-cultural training isn't effective, when a firm such as Xerox needs an executive to fill a key post in Italy, it might be best served by hiring an Italian. This solution has become even easier for North American firms in recent years as the number of foreigners in Canadian and American business schools has increased. For instance, there are now numbers of Italians, Arabs, Germans, Japanese, and other foreign nationals who have graduate business degrees from Canadian universities, understand Canadian business practices, and have returned to their homelands. The third solution to the problem is either to hire nationals or intensively train people to be expert advisers to management. AT&T, as a case in point, sent one executive and his family to Singapore for a lengthy stay to soak up the atmosphere and learn about the Singaporian way of doing business. He then returned to New York as the resident expert on Singapore. When problems involving that country arise, he is called upon to provide insight.

*Sources*: The evidence in this argument is drawn from J.S. Black and M. Mendenhall, "Cross-Cultural Training Effectiveness: A Review and a Theoretical Framework for Future Research," *Academy of Management Review*, January 1990, pp. 113–136; and A. Kupfer, "How to Be a Global Manager," *Fortune*, March 14, 1988, p. 52.

## COUNTERPOINT

# Cross-Cultural Training Is Effective

Yes, it's true that most corporations don't provide cross-cultural training. And that's a mistake! Clearly, the ability to adapt to the cultural differences in a foreign assignment is important to managerial success. Moreover, contrary to what many managers believe, cross-cultural training is very effective. Let's elaborate on this second point.

A comprehensive review of studies that specifically examined the effectiveness of cross-cultural training shows overwhelming evidence that this training fosters the development of cross-cultural skills and leads to higher performance. Training has been shown to improve an individual's relationships with host nationals, to allow that person to adjust more rapidly to a new culture, and to improve his or her work performance. In addition, training significantly reduces expatriate failure rates. For instance, in 1991 Mississauga, Ontario-based Northern Telecom (Nortel) discovered that some of its overseas employees were experiencing adjustment problems that affected their personal productivity and possibly the overall success of the business. In addition, the lack of preparation for being in a foreign country led to discontent that was manifested in demands for incentive pay, better housing and perquisites. It also showed up, in some cases, with negative employee attitudes. After Nortel introduced two training programs in 1993 and 1994, employees reported increased satisfaction with their overseas assignments.

Although these results are impressive, they don't say anything about the type of training the employee received. Does that make a difference?

There are a variety of training techniques available to prepare people for foreign work assignments. They range from documentary programs, which merely expose people to a new culture through written materials on the country's socio-political history, geography, economics, and cultural institutions, to intense interpersonal experience training, where individuals participate in role-playing exercises, simulated social settings, and similar experiences to "feel" the differences in a new culture.

One research study looked at the effectiveness of these two approaches on a group of North American

managers. These managers, who worked for an electronic products firm, were sent on assignment to Seoul, South Korea. Twenty of them received no training, 20 got only the documentary program, and 20 received only interpersonal experience training. The training activities were all completed in a three-day period. All participants, no matter which group they were in, received some language training, briefings covering company operations in South Korea, and a cursory three-page background description of the country. The results of this study confirmed the earlier evidence that cross-cultural training works. Specifically, the study found that managers who received either form of training were better performers and perceived less need to adjust to the new culture than those who received no such training. Additionally, neither method proved superior to the other.

In another study with civilian employees in a US military agency, participants were grouped so they received either a documentary orientation, experiential training, some combination of the two, or no training at all. Findings from this study again confirmed the value of cross-cultural training. Either type of training proved to be more effective than no training in improving cross-cultural knowledge and behavioural performance, and the combination approach was found to be the most effective. The findings of both of these studies are consistent with what Nortel found after introducing its cross-cultural training programs, which include, among other topics, training in cultural self-awareness, sensitization to culture shock and the adaptation process, and some basic language skills.

Sources: The evidence in this argument is drawn from J.S. Black and M. Mendenhall, "Cross-Cultural Training Effectiveness: A Review and a Theoretical Framework for Future Research," *Academy of Management Review*, January 1990, pp. 113–136; P.C. Earley, "Intercultural Training for Managers: A Comparison of Documentary and Interpersonal Methods," *Academy of Management Journal*, December 1987, pp. 685–698; S. Caudron, "Surviving Cross-Cultural Shock," *Industry Week*, July 6, 1992, pp. 35–38; J.S. Lublin, "Companies Use Cross-Cultural Training to Help Their Employees Adjust Abroad," *Wall Street Journal*, August 4, 1992, p. B1; J.K. Harrison, "Individual and Combined Effects of Behavior Modeling and the Cultural Assimilator in Cross-Cultural Management Training," *Journal of Applied Psychology*, December 1992, pp. 952–962; and S.R. Fishman, "Developing a Global Workforce: Assessment and Orientation Programs Help Employees Prepare for Successful International Assignments," *Canadian Business Review*, Spring, 1996, pp. 18–21.

attempt to change attitudes, but such change requires specially designed intervention programs. Below we discuss the importance of attitudes in the workplace, and then more specifically discuss attitudes towards diversity in the workplace.

## Attitudes

**attitudes**
Evaluative statements or judgments concerning objects, people, or events.

**Attitudes** are evaluative statements—either favourable or unfavourable—concerning objects, people, or events. They reflect how one feels about something. When I say "I like my job," I am expressing my attitude to work.

Attitudes are not the same as values, but the two are interrelated. In organizations, attitudes are important because they affect job behaviour. Workers may believe, for example, that supervisors, auditors, managers, and time-and-motion engineers are all conspiring to make employees work harder for the same or less money. It makes sense to try to understand how these attitudes were formed, their relationship to actual job behaviour, and how they might be changed. In From Concepts to Skills, we discuss whether it is possible to change someone's attitude, and how that might happen in the workplace.

## From CONCEPTS to SKILLS

# Changing Attitudes

Can you change unfavourable employee attitudes? Sometimes! It depends on who you are, the strength of the employee's attitude, the magnitude of the change, and the technique you choose to try to change the attitude.

People are most likely to respond to change efforts made by someone who is liked, credible, and convincing. If people like you, they're more apt to identify and adopt your message. Credibility implies trust, expertise, and objectivity. So you're more likely to change someone's attitude if that person views you as believable, knowledgeable about what you're talking about, and unbiased in your presentation. Finally, successful attitude change is enhanced when you present your arguments clearly and persuasively.

It's easier to change a person's attitude if he or she isn't strongly committed to it. Conversely, the stronger the belief in the attitude, the harder it is to change it. In addition, attitudes that have been expressed publicly are more difficult to change because it requires one to admit that he or she has made a mistake.

It's also easier to change attitudes when the change required isn't very significant. To get a person to accept a new attitude that varies greatly from his or her current position requires more effort. It may also threaten other deeply held attitudes and create increased dissonance.

All attitude-change techniques are not equally effective across situations. Oral persuasion techniques are most effective when you use a positive, tactful tone; present strong evidence to support your position; tailor your argument to the listener; use logic; and support your evidence by appealing to the person's fears, frustrations, and other emotions. But people are more likely to embrace change when they can experience it. The use of training sessions where employees share and personalize experiences, and practise new behaviours, can be powerful stimulants for change. Consistent with self-perception theory, changes in behaviour can lead to changes in attitudes.

## Types of Attitudes

A person can have thousands of attitudes, but OB focuses our attention on a very limited number of job-related attitudes. These job-related attitudes tap positive or negative evaluations that employees hold about aspects of their work environment. Most of the research in OB has been concerned with three attitudes: job satisfaction, job involvement, and organizational commitment.[46] Below we also consider attitudes towards diversity, because, as we noted in Chapter 1, Canadian workplaces are increasingly becoming multicultural environments. In this chapter's Working With Others Exercise on page 118, you have the opportunity to examine the attitudes that you and others hold toward the Canadian workplace.

**job satisfaction**
An individual's general attitude toward his or her job.

**JOB SATISFACTION**  The term **job satisfaction** refers to an individual's general attitude toward his or her job. A person with a high level of job satisfaction holds positive attitudes toward the job, while a person who is dissatisfied with his or her job holds negative attitudes toward the job. When people speak of employee attitudes, more often than not they mean job satisfaction. In fact, the two are frequently used interchangeably. Because of the high importance OB researchers have given to job satisfaction, we'll review this attitude in considerable detail later in this chapter.

**job involvement**
The degree to which a person identifies with his or her job, actively participates in it, and considers his or her performance important to self-worth.

**JOB INVOLVEMENT**  While there isn't complete agreement over what the term **job involvement** means, a workable definition does exist: Job involvement measures the degree to which a person identifies psychologically with his or her job, and considers his or her perceived performance level important to self-worth.[47] Employees with a high level of job involvement identify strongly with, and really care about, the kind of work they do.

High levels of job involvement have been found to be related to fewer absences and lower resignation rates.[48] However, it seems to predict turnover more consistently than absenteeism, accounting for as much as 16 percent of the variance in the former.[49]

**organizational commitment**
The degree to which an employee identifies with a particular organization and its goals, and wishes to maintain membership in the organization.

**ORGANIZATIONAL COMMITMENT**  The third job attitude we shall discuss is **organizational commitment**, which is defined as a state in which an employee identifies with a particular organization and its goals, and wishes to maintain membership in the organization.[50] So, high *job involvement* means identifying with one's specific job, while high *organizational commitment* means identifying with one's employing organization.

As with job involvement, the research evidence demonstrates that those with low organizational commitment engage in greater absenteeism and turnover.[51] The notion of organizational commitment has changed in recent years. Twenty years ago, employees and employers had an unwritten loyalty contract, with employees typically remaining with a single organization for most of their career. This notion has become increasingly obsolete. As such, "measures of employee-firm attachment, such as commitment, are problematic for new employment relations."[52] Canadian business consultant Barbara Moses notes that "40-somethings still value loyalty: they think people should be prepared to make sacrifices, to earn their way. The 20-somethings are saying, 'No, I want to be paid for my work; I have no belief in the goodness of organizations, so I'm going to be here as long as my work is meaningful.'"[53] This suggests that *organizational* commitment is probably less important as a job-related attitude than it once was. In its

**BBM Online**
www.bbmcareerdev.com/

place we might expect something akin to *occupational* commitment to become a more relevant variable because it better reflects today's fluid workforce.[54] The HR Implications feature for this chapter, on page 112, indicates ways that organizations can determine employee attitudes.

## Attitudes and Consistency

| Why do some people always seem to be changing their minds? |
| --- |

Did you ever notice how people change what they say so it doesn't contradict what they do? For instance, when going to an interview for a new job, a graduating student believes that the company conducting the interview is really good and that working there would be important. If the student doesn't get the job, however, the response might be, "That company isn't all it's cracked up to be, anyway!"

Research has generally concluded that people seek consistency among their attitudes and between their attitudes and their behaviour.[55] This means that individuals seek to reconcile divergent attitudes, and align their attitudes and behaviour so they appear rational and consistent. When there is an inconsistency, forces are initiated to return the individual to an equilibrium state where attitudes and behaviour are again consistent. This can be done by altering either the attitudes or the behaviour, or by developing a rationalization for the discrepancy.

**cognitive dissonance**
Any incompatibility between two or more attitudes or between behaviour and attitudes.

Can we also assume from this consistency principle that an individual's behaviour can always be predicted if we know his or her attitude to a subject? One theory helps to address this question. Leon Festinger, in the late 1950s, proposed the theory of **cognitive dissonance**.[56] Cognitive dissonance refers to any incompatibility that an individual might perceive between two or more of his or her attitudes, or between his or her behaviour and attitudes. Festinger argued that any form of inconsistency is uncomfortable and that individuals will attempt to reduce the dissonance and, hence, the discomfort. Therefore, individuals will seek a stable state where there is a minimum of dissonance.

Tobacco executives provide an example of how one deals with consistency and dissonance problems.[57] To cope with the ongoing barrage of data linking cigarette smoking and negative health outcomes, tobacco executives can deny that any clear causation between smoking and cancer has been established. They can brainwash themselves by continually articulating the benefits of tobacco. They can acknowledge the negative consequences of smoking, but they rationalize that people are going to smoke anyway and that tobacco companies merely promote freedom of choice. They can accept the research evidence and begin actively working to make healthier cigarettes, or at least to reduce the availability of cigarettes to more vulnerable groups, such as teenagers. Or tobacco executives can quit their jobs because the dissonance is too great.

What are the organizational implications of the theory of cognitive dissonance? It can help to predict the propensity to engage in attitude and behavioural change. For example, if individuals are required by the demands of their job to say or do things that contradict their personal attitude, they will tend to modify their attitude to make it compatible with the cognition of what they have said or done. Additionally, the greater the dissonance, the greater the pressures to reduce it.

The Law Courts

Tobacco executives have changed their attitudes about smoking. For years they argued that tobacco is not addictive, and they challenged scientific evidence of the health risks of smoking. But in lawsuits against tobacco firms, damaging documents emerged showing that the firms knew of the risks and intentionally marketed to minors. More recently they have admitted that smoking plays a role in causing cancer and that their marketing included teenage smokers. One executive said, "It is immoral, it is unethical, as well as illegal to market to people under age."

## Attitudes and Workforce Diversity

Organizations are increasingly having to face diversity concerns, both as they espouse commitment to diversity and as Canada's workplaces become more multicultural in nature. One of the intricacies of dealing with multicultural issues is determining how to accommodate the needs of employees with diverse responsibilities and affiliations. This chapter's Case Incident on page 119 gives an example of a situation where a workplace did not accommodate the needs of an employee.

Because of our multicultural workplace, managers are increasingly concerned with changing employee attitudes to reflect shifting perspectives on racial, gender, and other diversity issues. An ethnic joke or "flirtatious" remark that might have passed without comment 15 years ago can today become a career-limiting episode.[58] As such, organizations are investing in training to help reshape attitudes of employees. In our HR Implications starting on page 112, we present a variety of programs designed by organizations to change employee attitudes toward diversity.

Michael Adams's *Sex in the Snow* provides some information to help us understand how diversity initiatives to change attitudes might fare in the workplace in light of generational values. First, he notes that Generation Xers "eagerly embrace a number of egalitarian and pluralistic values."[59] This might suggest that as Generation Xers move through the workplace, some of the tensions currently surrounding the introduction of diversity initiatives might lessen. On the other hand, Adams also notes that there are 4.3 million boomers who belong to the disengaged Darwinist group, and many of these tend to be the younger boomers (that is, closer to their mid-30s than their mid-50s). This group, together with the rational traditionalists of the elders group (representing 3.5 million Canadians), tends to be very conservative. As Adams notes, "Among the men in this group are a large number of what have come to be known as 'angry white guys.'" They find that society has changed too much, too quickly, and for the worse. "They do not support the idea of women's equality or alternative family structures. They brand programs of affirmative action or employment equity for women or visible minorities as 'reverse discrimination.'"[60] As a result of these generational differences, it is not inconceivable that tensions in the workplace over diversity initiatives will remain for some time to come.

Diversity training at Harvard Pilgrim Health Care emphasizes practical conflict management. The organization uses real-life case studies of situations employees face daily. The training includes role-playing workshops to teach employees how to respond to differences among people with sensitivity and respect. Harvard Pilgrim serves a growing number of racial and ethnic minority customers and a large gay and lesbian population. Its diversity training helps employees in providing care to diverse customers who demand that health care workers are not judgmental.

## The Attitude of Job Satisfaction

We noted above that there are a variety of attitudes of concern to those who study organizational behaviour, including job involvement, organizational commitment, and job satisfaction. We briefly discussed each of these attitudes earlier in the chapter, and we will now examine job satisfaction at some length.

In 1997, the Angus Reid Group surveyed Canadians nationwide to find out their attitudes toward their jobs and their workplaces.[61] Almost half of Canadian workers (47 percent) are very satisfied with their jobs and an additional 39 percent are somewhat satisfied. Closer analysis of the positive findings indicated that they could largely be explained by the fact that jobs were generally meeting the primary needs of workers. Forty-four percent strongly agreed that their work was challenging and interesting, and another 27 percent somewhat agreed. About 75 percent responded that they were treated fairly at work.

Not everyone is happy, however. Almost 40 percent of employees would not recommend their company as a good place to work. Forty percent also believe they never see any of the benefits of their company making money. Almost 40 percent reported that red tape and bureaucracy are among the biggest barriers to job satisfaction. A majority of the workforce (55 percent) reported that they felt the "pressure of having too much to do."

In this section, we want to dissect the concept of job satisfaction more carefully. How do we measure job satisfaction? What determines job satisfaction? What is its effect on employee productivity, absenteeism, and turnover rates? We answer each of these questions in this section.

## Measuring Job Satisfaction

We've previously defined job satisfaction as an individual's general attitude toward his or her job. How, then, do we measure the concept?

The two most widely used approaches are a *single global rating* and a *summation score* made up of a number of job facets. The single global rating method is nothing more than asking individuals to respond to one question, such as "All things considered, how satisfied are you with your job?" Respondents then reply by circling a number between one and five that corresponds to answers from "highly satisfied" to "highly dissatisfied." It was this approach that the Angus Reid Group used in the findings reported above.

The other approach—a summation of job facets—is more sophisticated. It identifies key elements in a job and asks for the employee's feelings about each. Typical factors that would be included are the nature of the work, supervision, present pay, promotion opportunities, and relations with co-workers.[62] These factors are rated on a standardized scale and then added up to create an overall job satisfaction score. This approach, though not done explicitly in the Angus Reid survey, is represented by the additional workplace attitude items reported above. You may recall that even though Canadians reported overall satisfaction, there were a number of individual items with which they were dissatisfied.

Is one of the foregoing measurement approaches superior to the other? Intuitively, it would seem that summing up responses to a number of job factors would achieve a more accurate evaluation of job satisfaction. The research, however, doesn't support this intuition.[63] This is one of those rare instances in which simplicity does better than complexity. Comparisons of one-question global ratings with the more lengthy summation-of-job-factors method indicate that the former is as valid. The best explanation for this outcome is that the concept of job satisfaction is inherently so broad that the single question captures its essence.

## What Determines Job Satisfaction?

We now turn to the question "What work-related variables determine job satisfaction?" In Chapter 1 you read about the twenty-something employees who were organizing unions in their workplaces. The employees mentioned that they were dissatisfied with their jobs because they didn't get respect from their employer. Their report is not inconsistent with our knowledge of job satisfaction. An extensive review of the literature indicates that the more important factors conducive to job satisfaction are mentally challenging work, equitable rewards, supportive working conditions, and supportive colleagues.[64] Keeping in mind the results of the Angus Reid survey, we'll review these factors and consider their implications for the Canadian workplace.

**MENTALLY CHALLENGING WORK** Employees tend to prefer jobs that give them opportunities to use their skills and abilities, and offer a variety of tasks, freedom, and feedback on how well they are doing. These characteristics make work mentally challenging. Jobs that have too little challenge create boredom, but too much challenge creates frustration and feelings of failure. Under conditions of moderate challenge, most employees will experience pleasure and satisfaction.[65] As we noted above, 71 percent of Canadians do find their jobs challenging and rewarding. In Chapter 13, when we introduce job design, we will discuss factors that lead to more challenging jobs.

**EQUITABLE REWARDS** Employees want pay systems and promotion policies that they perceive as being just, unambiguous, and in line with their expectations. When pay is perceived as fair based on job demands, individual skill level, and community pay standards, satisfaction is likely to result. The Angus Reid study showed that 61 percent of workers feel their company offers fair or reasonable pay for the work done. In Chapter 4, we discuss further the need for equitable reward systems in the workplace.

Of course, not everyone seeks money. Many people willingly accept less money to work in a preferred location or in a less demanding job, or to have greater discretion in the work they do and the hours they work. But the key in linking pay to satisfaction is not the absolute amount one is paid; rather, it is the perception of fairness. Similarly, employees seek fair promotion policies and practices. Promotions provide opportunities for personal growth, more responsibilities, and increased social status. Individuals who perceive that promotion decisions are made in a fair and just manner, therefore, are likely to experience satisfaction from their jobs.[66]

**SUPPORTIVE WORKING CONDITIONS** Employees are concerned with their work environment for promoting both personal comfort and facilitating good job performance. Studies demonstrate that employees prefer physical surroundings that are not dangerous or uncomfortable. Temperature, light, noise, and other environmental factors should not be at either extreme—for example, workers should not have too much heat or too little light. Additionally, most employees prefer working relatively close to home, in clean and relatively modern facilities, and with adequate tools and equipment. Employees also want their organizations to respect a balance between work and the rest of one's life. In fact a recent study shows that Canadians rank this as the number one factor affecting their job satisfaction and commitment.[67] Level of pay was ranked fourth.

**SUPPORTIVE COLLEAGUES** People get more out of work than merely money or tangible achievements. For most employees, work also fills the need for social interaction. Not surprisingly, therefore, having friendly and supportive co-workers leads to increased job satisfaction. In the Angus Reid survey, 50 percent of the respondents reported that some of their good friends are their co-workers.

The behaviour of one's manager also is a major determinant of satisfaction. Studies generally find that employee satisfaction is increased when the immediate manager is understanding and friendly, offers praise for good performance, listens to employees' opinions, and shows a personal interest in them. This is a particular area where Canadian workplaces may not be doing enough for their employees. Only 44 percent said they received effective performance evaluations or feedback. In addition, only 44 percent of employees feel that they get any recognition for excelling at their jobs. At the organizational level, the feedback was not much better: Only 45 percent of employees said their company communicates corporate changes effectively.

Conditions in the workplace are another very important determinant of job satisfaction. But it is also critical to note that the fit of a person to a

Sears Canada's CEO Paul Walters believes it's employees who are the main reason the company has seen record sales in the last several years. "You can't grow by 25 percent without more and happier customers, and we think there's a definite link between employee satisfaction and customer satisfaction."

job, as well as disposition (some people are just inherently upbeat and positive about all things, including their job), will affect job satisfaction.[68]

## The Effect of Job Satisfaction on Employee Performance

Managers' interest in job satisfaction tends to centre on its effect on employee performance. Researchers have recognized this interest, so we find a large number of studies that have been designed to assess the impact of job satisfaction on employee productivity, absenteeism, and turnover. Let's look at the current state of our knowledge.

**SATISFACTION AND INDIVIDUAL PRODUCTIVITY** The evidence suggests that the link between an individual's job satisfaction and his or her productivity is slightly positive.[69] It turns out the productivity can be affected as much by external conditions as it is by job satisfaction. For instance, a stockbroker's productivity is largely constrained by the general movement of the stock market. When the market is moving up and volume is high, both satisfied and dissatisfied brokers will ring up lots of commissions. Conversely, when the market is in the doldrums, the level of broker satisfaction is not likely to mean much. Job level also seems to be an important moderating variable.

The relationship between job satisfaction and productivity is stronger when the employee's behaviour is not constrained or controlled by outside factors. An employee's productivity on machine-paced jobs, for instance, will be much more influenced by the speed of the machine than by his or her level of satisfaction.

The evidence also shows that the satisfaction–performance correlations are stronger for higher-level employees. Thus, we might expect the relationship to be more relevant for individuals in professional, supervisory, and managerial positions.

There is another complication in the satisfaction-productivity link. Some studies have found that productivity leads to satisfaction rather than the other way around.[70] If you do a good job, you intrinsically feel good about it. Additionally, assuming that the organization rewards productivity, your higher productivity should increase your verbal recognition, pay level, and probabilities for promotion. These rewards, in turn, increase your level of satisfaction with the job.

**SATISFACTION AND ORGANIZATIONAL PRODUCTIVITY** The link between satisfaction and productivity is much stronger when we look not at individuals, but at the organization as a whole.[71] When satisfaction and productivity data are gathered for the organization as a whole, rather than at the individual level, we find that organizations with more-satisfied employees tended to be more effective than organizations with less-satisfied employees. For instance, Paul Walters, chair and CEO of Toronto-based Sears Canada, thinks "there's a definite link between employee satisfaction and customer satisfaction. You can't have cranky employees and happy customers."[72]

*Fortune* magazine's 1998 list of the 100 Best Companies to Work for in America clearly shows a link between job satisfaction and productivity. "Of the 61 firms in the group that have been publicly traded for the past five years, 45 yielded higher returns to the shareholders than the Russell 3000, an index of large and small companies that mirrors our 100 Best. The 61 companies averaged annual returns of 27.5 percent, compared with 17.3 percent for the Russell 3000."[73] That's a substantial difference in return, all for having happy workers. Happy workers don't guarantee financial gains, however. Both Southwest Airlines and Nordstrom, which were included in the 100 Best list, had lower annual rates of return, but also faced very competitive economic climates.

The *Fortune* study identified four attitudes that, when taken together, correlated with higher profits: "workers feel they are given the opportunity to do what they do best every day; they believe their opinions count; they sense that other workers are committed to quality; and they've made a direct connection between their work and the company's mission."[74]

The *Fortune* study, coupled with previous research on organizational productivity, suggests that the reason we haven't received strong support for the *satisfaction-causes-productivity thesis* is twofold: Studies have focused on individuals rather than on the organization, and individual-level measures of productivity don't take into consideration all the interactions and complexities in the work process.

**SATISFACTION AND ABSENTEEISM**   We find a consistent negative relationship between satisfaction and absenteeism, but the correlation is moderate—usually less than −0.40.[75] While it certainly makes sense that dissatisfied employees are more likely to miss work, other factors have an impact on the relationship and reduce the correlation coefficient. For example, organizations that provide liberal sick leave benefits are encouraging all their employees—including those who are highly satisfied—to take days off. Also, as with productivity, outside factors can act to reduce the correlation.

**SATISFACTION AND TURNOVER**   Satisfaction is also negatively related to turnover, and the correlation is stronger than what we found for absenteeism.[76] Yet again, other factors such as labour market conditions, expectations about alternative job opportunities, and length of tenure with the organization are important constraints on the actual decision to leave one's current job.[77]

A person's general disposition toward life also moderates the satisfaction–turnover relationship.[78] Specifically, some individuals generally gripe more than others and such individuals, when dissatisfied with their jobs, are less likely to quit than those who are more positively disposed toward life. So if two workers report the same level of job dissatisfaction, the one most likely to quit is the one with the highest predisposition to be happy or satisfied in general.

Nevertheless, Vancouver-based Orca Bay and Pacific National Exhibition hired California consultant Matt Weinstein to help them develop programs to increase the satisfaction level of their employees.[79] Weinstein has promoted fun

**Exhibit 3-2**
**Responses to Job Dissatisfaction**

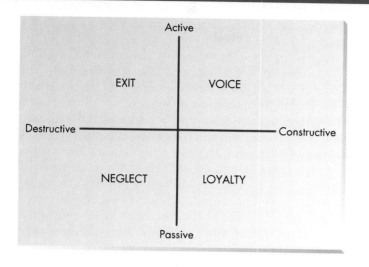

Source: C. Rusbult and D. Lowery, "When Bureaucrats Get the Blues," *Journal of Applied Social Psychology,* Vol. 15, No. 1(1985), p. 83. With permission.

**exit**
Dissatisfaction expressed through behaviour directed toward leaving the organization.

**voice**
Dissatisfaction expressed through active and constructive attempts to improve conditions.

**loyalty**
Dissatisfaction expressed by passively waiting for conditions to improve.

**neglect**
Dissatisfaction expressed through allowing conditions to worsen.

activities for employees, observing that happy workers will be more satisfied, more productive, and more likely to stay.

## How Employees Can Express Dissatisfaction

One final point before we leave the issue of job satisfaction: Employee dissatisfaction can be expressed in a number of ways.[80] For example, rather than quit, employees can complain, be insubordinate, steal organizational property, or shirk from a part of their work responsibilities. Exhibit 3-2 offers four responses that differ from one another along two dimensions: constructiveness/destructiveness and activity/passivity. They are defined as follows:[81]

- **Exit:** Behaviour directed toward leaving the organization, including looking for a new position, as well as resigning.

- **Voice:** Actively and constructively attempting to improve conditions, including suggesting improvements, discussing problems with superiors, and some forms of union activity.

- **Loyalty:** Passively but optimistically waiting for conditions to improve, including speaking up for the organization in the face of external criticism and trusting the organization and its management to "do the right thing."

- **Neglect:** Passively allowing conditions to worsen, including chronic absenteeism or lateness, reduced effort, and increased error rate.

Exit and neglect behaviours encompass our performance variables—productivity, absenteeism, and turnover. But this model expands employee response to include voice and loyalty—constructive behaviours that allow individuals to tolerate unpleasant situations or to revive satisfactory working conditions. It helps us to understand situations, such as those sometimes found among unionized workers, where low job satisfaction is coupled with low turnover.[82] Union members often express dissatisfaction through the grievance procedure or through formal contract negotiations. These voice mechanisms allow the union members to continue in their jobs while convincing themselves that they are acting to improve the situation.

## Job Satisfaction and OCB

We mentioned in Chapter 1 that organizations are looking for organizational citizenship behaviour (OCB). OCB is employee behaviour that goes above and beyond the call of duty, is not explicitly rewarded, is voluntary, and contributes to organizational effectiveness. Examples of such behaviour include helping one's colleagues with their workloads, taking only limited breaks, and alerting others to work-related problems.[83]

It seems logical to assume that job satisfaction should be a major determinant of an employee's organizational citizenship behaviour.[84] Satisfied employees would seem more likely to talk positively about an organization, help others, and go beyond the normal expectations in their job. Moreover, satisfied employees might be more prone to go beyond the call of duty because they want to reciprocate their positive experiences. Consistent with this thinking, early discussions of OCB assumed that it was closely linked with satisfaction.[85] More recent evidence, however, suggests that satisfaction does influence OCB, but through perceptions of fairness.

There is, then, a modest overall relationship between job satisfaction and OCB.[86] But satisfaction is unrelated to OCB when fairness is controlled for.[87] What does this mean? Basically, job satisfaction comes down to conceptions of fair outcomes, treatment, and procedures.[88] If you don't feel like your manager, the organization's procedures, or its pay policies are fair, your job satisfaction is likely to suffer significantly. However, when you perceive organizational processes and outcomes to be fair, trust is developed. And when you trust your employer, you're more willing to voluntarily engage in behaviours that go beyond your formal job requirements.

# HR Implications

# Attitude Surveys and Diversity Training

Our HR Implications considers two key facets of this chapter.

First, it is important for organizations to find out about the attitudes of employees. To do this, organizations sometimes conduct attitude surveys. Second, sometimes organizations want to try to change the attitudes of their employees. A number of firms have made this attempt with respect to diversity issues, trying to encourage employees to see that meeting employment equity targets is not about imposed quotas, but is rather an opportunity to increase the learning of the members of the organization by adding variation to the sources of information.

### Determining Attitudes: Attitude Surveys

How does management get information about employee attitudes? The most popular method is through the use of **attitude surveys.**[1]

Exhibit 3-3 illustrates what an attitude survey might look like. Typically, attitude surveys present the employee with a set of statements or questions. Ideally, the items are tailored to obtain the specific information that management desires. An attitude score is achieved by summing up responses to individual questionnaire items. These scores can then be averaged for job groups, departments, divisions, or the organization as a whole.

Results from attitude surveys can frequently surprise management.

For instance, managers at the Heavy-Duty Division of Springfield Remanufacturing thought everything was great.[2] Since employees were actively involved in division decisions and profitability was the highest within the entire company, management assumed morale was high. To confirm their beliefs, they conducted a short attitude survey. Employees were asked if they agreed or disagreed with the following statements: (1) At work, your opinions count; (2) those of you who want to be a leader in this company have the opportunity to become one; and (3) in the past six months someone has talked to you about your personal development. In the survey, 43 percent disagreed with the first statement, 48 percent with the second, and 62 percent with the third. Management was astounded. How could this be? The division had been holding shop floor meetings to review the numbers every week for more than 12 years. And most of the managers had come up through the ranks. Management responded by creating a committee made up of representatives from every department in the division and all three shifts. The committee quickly found that there were lots of little things the division was doing that were alienating employees. Out of this committee came a large number of suggestions which, after implementation, significantly improved employees' perception of their decision-making influence and their career opportunities in the division.

Using attitude surveys on a regular basis provides managers with valuable feedback on how employees perceive their working conditions. Policies and practices that management views as objective and fair may be seen as inequitable by employees in general or by certain groups of employees. That these distorted perceptions have led to negative attitudes toward the job and organization should be important to management. This is because employee behaviours are based on perceptions, not reality. Remember, the employee who quits because she believes she is underpaid—when, in fact, management has objective data to support that her salary is highly competitive—is just as gone as if she had actually been underpaid. The use of regular attitude surveys can alert management to potential problems and employees' intentions early so that action can be taken to prevent repercussions.[3]

## Modifying Attitudes: Diversity Training

Diversity training programs are generally intended to provide a vehicle for increasing awareness and examining stereotypes. Participants learn to value individual differences, increase their cross-cultural understanding, and confront stereotypes.[4]

Trevor Wilson, president of Toronto-based Omnibus Consulting, has presented employment equity programs to such clients as IBM Canada Ltd., Molson Co. Ltd., and National Grocers Co. Ltd. His approach has been popular because it supports a "no-guilt, no-blame, everybody's-not-the-same, business-friendly, all-inclusive" approach to equity, thus reducing the barriers that sometimes accompany equity training.[5] The core issues tackled in the actual training include the following: "that people tend to hire people like themselves; that we all harbour stereotypes; that cultural differences can lead you to misunderstand someone's qualifications; that continually talking to a colleague's breasts instead of her face is demeaning as well as illegal, and how would you like your wife or daughter to go through that?"[6]

---

### Exhibit 3-3
### Sample Attitude Survey

Please answer each of the following statements using the following rating scale:

| | | |
|---|---|---|
| 1 | = | Strongly agree |
| 2 | = | Agree |
| 3 | = | Undecided |
| 4 | = | Disagree |
| 5 | = | Strongly disagree |

**Statement**                                                                 **Rating**

1. This company is a pretty good place to work.  _____

2. I can get ahead in this company if I make the effort.  _____

3. This company's wage rates are competitive with those of other companies.  _____

4. Employee promotion decisions are handled fairly.  _____

5. I understand the various fringe benefits the company offers.  _____

6. My job makes the best use of my abilities.  _____

7. My workload is challenging but not burdensome.  _____

8. I have trust and confidence in my boss.  _____

9. I feel free to tell my boss what I think.  _____

10. I know what my boss expects of me.  _____

Maureen Geddes is team facilitator/workplace diversity at Chatham, Ontario-based Union Gas. She explains why the company sent all of its employees through diversity training, 25 employees at a time: "We certainly had some people who said we should be doing this because it's the right thing to do. Of course it's the right thing to do, but diversity training is a priority here today because it makes us more productive and competitive as an organization."[7]

What do these diversity programs look like, and how do they address attitude change?[8] They almost all include a self-evaluation phase. People are pressed to examine themselves and to confront ethnic and cultural stereotypes they might hold. Then participants typically take part in group discussions or panels with representatives from diverse groups. So, for instance, a Hmong man might describe his family's life in Southeast Asia and explain why they resettled in British Columbia; or a lesbian might describe how she discovered her sexual identity and the reaction of her friends and family when she "came out."

There are additional activities designed to change attitudes. These include arranging for people to do volunteer work in community or social service centres in order to meet face-to-face with individuals and groups from diverse backgrounds, and using exercises that let participants feel what it's like to be different. For example, when participants see the film *Eye of the Beholder*, where people are segregated and stereotyped according to their eye colour, participants realize what it's like to be judged by something over which they have no control.

The typical program lasts from half a day to three days and includes role-playing exercises, lectures, discussions, and group experiences. For example, in the United States, Xerox has worked with Cornell University's theatre department to create a set of short plays that increases awareness of work-related racial and gender conflicts. The show has been presented to more than 1300 Xerox managers.[9]

A training exercise at Hartford Insurance that sought to increase sensitivity to aging asked participants to respond to the following four questions:

(1) If you didn't know how old you are, how old would you guess you are? In other words, how old do you feel inside?

(2) When I was 18, I thought middle age began at age _____.

(3) Today, I think middle age begins at age _____.

(4) What would be your first reaction if someone called you an older worker?[10]

Answers to these questions were then used to analyze age-related stereotypes. In another program designed to raise awareness of the power of stereotypes, each participant was asked to write an anonymous paper detailing all groups—women, born-again Christians, Blacks, gays, men, etc.—to which they had attached stereotypes.[11] They were also asked to explain why they'd had trouble working with certain groups in the past. Based on responses, guest speakers were brought into the class to shatter the stereotypes directed at each group. This was followed by extensive discussion.

Sources:

[1] See, for example, B. Fishel, "A New Perspective: How to Get the Real Story From Attitude Surveys," *Training*, February 1998, pp. 91–94.

[2] J. Stack, "Measuring Morale," *INC.*, January 1997, pp. 29–30.

[3] T. Lammers, "The Essential Employee Survey," *INC.*, December 1992, pp. 159–161; and S. Shellenbarger, "Companies Are Finding It Really Pays to Be Nice to Employees," *Wall Street Journal*, July 22, 1998, p. B1.

[4] See, for example, M. Galen, "Diversity: Beyond the Numbers Game," *Business Week*, August 14, 1995, pp. 60–61.

[5] "Selling Equity," *Financial Post Magazine*, September 1994, pp. 20–25.

[6] "Selling Equity," *Financial Post Magazine*, September 1994, pp. 20–25.

[7] "Selling Equity," *Financial Post Magazine*, September 1994, pp. 20–25.

[8] This section is based on A. Rossett and T. Bickham, "Diversity Training: Hope, Faith and Cynicism," *Training*, January 1994, pp. 40–46.

[9] L.E. Wynter, "Theatre Program Tackles Issues of Diversity," *The Wall Street Journal*, April 18, 1991, p. B1.

[10] B. Hynes-Grace, "To Thrive, Not Merely Survive," in *Textbook Authors Conference Presentations* (Washington, DC: October 21, 1992), sponsored by the American Association of Retired Persons, p. 12.

[11] "Teaching Diversity: Business Schools Search for Model Approaches," *Newsline*, Fall 1992, p. 21.

# SUMMARY AND IMPLICATIONS

## For the Workplace

Why is it important to know an individual's values? Although they don't have a direct impact on behaviour, values strongly influence a person's attitudes. So knowledge of an individual's value system can provide insight into his or her attitudes.

An employee's performance and satisfaction are likely to be higher if his or her values fit well with those of the organization. For instance, the person who places high importance on imagination, independence, and freedom is likely to be poorly matched with an organization that seeks conformity from its employees. Managers are more likely to appreciate, evaluate positively, and allocate rewards to employees who "fit in," and employees are more likely to be satisfied if they perceive that they do fit. This argues for management to strive to find new employees who not only have the ability, experience, and motivation to perform, but also have a value system that is compatible with the organization's.

Managers should be interested in their employees' attitudes because attitudes give warnings of potential problems and because they influence behaviour. Satisfied and committed employees, for instance, have lower rates of turnover and absenteeism. Given that managers want to keep resignations and absences down—especially among their more productive employees—they will want to do those things that will generate positive job attitudes.

Managers should also be aware that employees will try to reduce cognitive dissonance. More important, dissonance can be managed. For example, employees may be required to engage in activities that appear inconsistent to them or that are at odds with their attitudes. If so, the pressures to reduce the resulting dissonance are lessened when the employee perceives that the dissonance is externally imposed and is beyond his or her control, or if the rewards are significant enough to offset the dissonance.

## For You as an Individual

Within the classroom, in various kinds of activities in which you participate, as well as in the workplace, you will encounter many people who have different values from you. We noted that values vary by both generation and culture, although they also vary within these groups. This chapter has encouraged you to try to understand value differences, and to figure out ways to work positively with people who are different from you.

In our discussion of attitudes, we focused on the specific attitude of job satisfaction. We indicated that many Canadians were satisfied with their jobs, and mentioned the sources of some of the satisfactions. We also identified areas in which people were dissatisfied with their jobs. This information may help you understand your own feelings about whether you're satisfied with your job. You may also be able to use some of the information on job satisfaction to help you when you're working on group projects. This is because some of the sources of satisfaction, such as challenging tasks, meaningful relationships with co-workers, and more open communication, are things that help make groups function better as well.

## ROADMAP REMINDER

With this chapter we conclude Part 1 of the text. We have examined the conditions within which organizations operate, the skills that managers and employees need to successfully navigate the transition to the 21st-century workplace, and the perceptions, values, and attitudes that influence how people get along in the workplace. In moving to Part 2 of the text, we are making a transition from describing the workplace to thinking about how to actually get people to work together positively—how they can accomplish tasks, and work in groups and teams. As a first step in understanding how to ensure that organizations are productive, we consider the subject of motivation. In the next chapter, you will learn about motivating both yourself and others.

## For Review

1. What are Hofstede's 5 value dimensions of national culture?

2. How might differences in generational values affect the workplace?

3. Compare Aboriginal and non-Aboriginal values.

4. How can managers get employees to more readily accept working with colleagues who are different from themselves?

5. Describe 3 job-related attitudes. What is their relevance to the workplace?

6. Are happy workers productive workers?

7. What is the relationship between job satisfaction and absenteeism? Job satisfaction and turnover? Which is the stronger relationship?

8. Contrast exit, voice, loyalty, and neglect as employee responses to job dissatisfaction.

## For Critical Thinking

1. "Thirty-five years ago, young employees we hired were ambitious, conscientious, hard-working, and honest. Today's young workers don't have the same values." Do you agree or disagree with this manager's comments? Support your position.

2. Do you think there might be any positive and significant relationship between the possession of certain personal values and successful career progression in organizations such as Merrill Lynch, the Canadian Union of Postal Workers (CUPW), and the City of Regina's police department? Discuss.

3. "Managers should do everything they can to enhance the job satisfaction of their employees." Do you agree or disagree? Support your position.

4. Discuss the advantages and disadvantages of using regular attitude surveys to monitor employee job satisfaction.

5. When employees are asked whether they would again choose the same work or whether they would want their children to follow in their footsteps, fewer than half typically answer in the affirmative. What, if anything, do you think this implies about employee job satisfaction?

## LEARNING ABOUT YOURSELF EXERCISE

# What Do You Value?

Following are 16 items. Rate how important each one is to you on a scale of 0 (not important) to 100 (very important). Write the number 0-100 on the line to the left of each item.

| Not important | | | Somewhat important | | | | | Very important | | |
|---|---|---|---|---|---|---|---|---|---|---|
| 0 | 10 | 20 | 30 | 40 | 50 | 60 | 70 | 80 | 90 | 100 |

_____ **1.** An enjoyable, satisfying job.

_____ **2.** A high-paying job.

_____ **3.** A good marriage.

_____ **4.** Meeting new people; social events.

_____ **5.** Involvement in community activities.

_____ **6.** My religion.

_____ **7.** Exercising, playing sports.

_____ **8.** Intellectual development.

_____ **9.** A career with challenging opportunities.

_____ **10.** Nice cars, clothes, home, and so on.

_____ **11.** Spending time with family.

_____ **12.** Having several close friends.

_____ **13.** Volunteer work for not-for-profit organizations, such as the Canadian Cancer Society.

_____ **14.** Meditation, quiet time to think, pray, and so on.

_____ **15.** A healthy, balanced diet.

_____ **16.** Educational reading, television, self-improvement programs, and so on.

Turn to page 632 for scoring directions and key.

Source: R.N. Lussier, *Human Relations in Organizations: A Skill Building Approach*, 2nd ed. (Homewood, IL: Richard D. Irwin, 1993). Used with permission.

## WORKING WITH OTHERS EXERCISE

# Assessing Work Attitudes

**Objective**

To compare attitudes of group members toward the workforce.

**Time**

Approximately 30 minutes.

**Procedure**

Choose the 1 best answer for each of the following 5 questions:

1. *Generally*, Canadian workers
   - _____ **a.** are highly motivated and hard-working
   - _____ **b.** try to give a fair day's effort
   - _____ **c.** will put forth effort if you make it worthwhile
   - _____ **d.** try to get by with a low level of effort
   - _____ **e.** are lazy and/or poorly motivated

2. The people *I have worked with*
   - _____ **a.** are highly motivated and hard-working
   - _____ **b.** try to give a fair day's effort
   - _____ **c.** will put forth effort if you make it worthwhile
   - _____ **d.** try to get by with a low level of effort
   - _____ **e.** are lazy and/or poorly motivated

3. *Compared with foreign workers*, Canadian workers are
   - _____ **a.** more productive
   - _____ **b.** equally productive
   - _____ **c.** less productive

4. *Over the past 20 years*, Canadian workers have
   - _____ **a.** improved in overall quality of job performance
   - _____ **b.** remained about the same in quality of job performance
   - _____ **c.** deteriorated in overall quality of job performance

5. If you have a low opinion of the Canadian workforce, give the 1 step (or action) that could be taken that would lead to the most improvement.

### Group Discussion

   **a.** Break into groups of 3-5 members each. Compare your answers to the 5 questions.

   **b.** For each question where 1 or more members disagree, discuss *why* each member chose his or her answer.

   **c.** After this discussion, members are free to change their original answers. Did any in your group do so?

   **d.** Your instructor will lead the class in discussing the implications or accuracy of these attitudes.

Source: Based on D.R. Brown, "Dealing with Student Conceptions and Misconceptions About Worker Attitudes and Productivity," *Journal of Management Education*, May 1991, pp. 259–264.

## INTERNET SEARCH EXERCISES

1. Find the best and latest data you can that describe the level of job satisfaction in (a) Canada, (b) the United States, and (c) Japan. What conclusions are you able to draw from these data?

2. Find the results from 3 different attitude surveys dealing with organizational attitudes such as job satisfaction, job involvement, or organizational commitment. What, if anything, did these surveys and/or their results have in common?

3. Marketers and others have developed instruments to determine your values based on your responses to various questions. For example, **http://www.future.sri.com/VALS/** is a site that explores American values, while **http://erg.environics.net/surveys/socialvalues/** looks at Canadian social values.

   Take the surveys on both sites and see whether they categorize you in consistent ways. Based on this exercise, what conclusions might you draw about differences in Canadian and American values?

## CASE INCIDENT

# "I Can't Work on Friday Nights"

Most Canadians understand that the Charter of Rights protects employees against discrimination based on gender or race bias. But most provincial human rights codes also prohibit discrimination on the basis of religion. Both the Canadian Union of Public Employees (CUPE) and the school board in the central Okanagan region of British Columbia didn't understand that they had a duty to accommodate an employee's need for a schedule change for religious reasons. As a result, a former employee brought a religious discrimination complaint against both of them.

The former employee, Larry S. Renaud, who is a Seventh-day Adventist, was terminated from his job at the Spring Valley Elementary School. He was terminated because the board and the union were unwilling to accommodate his request not to be scheduled to work on his church's Sabbath, which is from sundown Friday until sundown Saturday. Renaud had used his seniority to move to Spring Valley to work as a custodian. Under the collective agreement, he was the only custodian scheduled for the 3 p.m. to 11 p.m. shift during the week, including Friday night. Immediately upon moving to the new job, he requested that the board accommodate a schedule change, so that he wouldn't have to work on his Sabbath. The school board was willing to accommodate his request, but felt they needed the approval of his union. The union was unwilling to grant such an exception to the collective agreement, as they felt it would seriously violate the terms of the collective agreement. When the school board and CUPE failed to reach an agreement, the school board fired Renaud because of his inability to work the Friday-night shift.

After going through human rights tribunals and the lower courts, the case reached the Supreme Court of Canada, which ruled that both the school board and CUPE had a duty to accommodate Renaud's religious preferences, particularly when it would have been just as easy to allow him to clean the school on Sunday nights, rather than Friday nights. The school board was ordered to rehire Renaud, and both CUPE and the school board were ordered to pay Renaud $6250 for lost wages. Each was also responsible for paying him an additional $1000 for emotional distress.

This incident serves as a reminder to employers, especially in industries such as transportation, public safety, and retailing, where weekend work is often an expected part of the job. The courts have ruled that employers must "reasonably accommodate" requests to observe religious days unless the request would cause "undue hardship" to the business. The employees' religious beliefs are assumed to be sincerely held unless proven otherwise.

# Questions

1. Is there anything an employer could do at the time of hiring that could legally prevent this problem from occurring?

2. Why do you think gender and race bias in Canada have received more attention than religious bias?

3. How could training to reduce religious discrimination fit in as part of diversity training?

4. What might a training program look like that seeks to eliminate discrimination on the basis of religion? Be specific.

Source: This case is based on *Larry S. Renaud v. Board of School Trustees, School District No. 23 (Central Okanagan) and the Canadian Union of Public Employees, Local 523* [1992], S.C.J. No. 75.

# Managing in a Cross-Cultural World

Canadian workplaces are multicultural, and many Canadian companies also work in international contexts, increasing the chances that people working side by side do not share all of the same values, expectations, and beliefs about behaviour.

Understanding differences among people begins with basic awareness of different cultures and societies. For instance, Asian countries, such as China, Indonesia, and Japan, are lower on individualism than are Germany, the Netherlands, and the United States. Even within multicultural Canada, there are differences in how strongly individualistic vs. collectivist identities are balanced.

Part of understanding others is avoiding the assumption that everyone shares the same meanings about a situation. Sometimes "yes" does not mean "yes," but is a way of trying not to displease, rather than indicating strong agreement with a decision. People from some cultures are also much more low-key than in other cultures, but that does not mean that they are any less effective in doing a good job. For instance, in Dutch there is an expression that translates to "good wine doesn't need bragging."

The differences that we observe among individuals arise because of responses to one's environment, and each society and culture face different environments. Sometimes this makes it harder to understand the differences observed in other people, because what we are seeing is not part of our experience.

When working with people of different cultures, we may encounter responses to situations that seem different from our own. For instance, in Canada, individuals are more likely to express support for the law rather than friendship if a friend has broken the law and we have been asked to testify about the event. In Korea, however, individuals would be more likely to support their friend, rather than report that a friend had been driving 15 km above the speed limit. These differences suggest that working with people of other cultures means trying to understand the norms of that culture.

## Questions

1. To what extent might differences in values affect how individuals interact with one another?

2. How can organizations promote more understanding among workers from different cultures?

3. Should managers try to change the values of employees whose values differ from those of management?

Source: Based on "Cross-Culture," *Venture 552*; aired June 8, 1995.

# Rob Gareau: Background and Reflections on Developing a Business*

Rob Gareau is co-founder of Human Performance, a personal training and athletic development business with offices in Vancouver and Burnaby, BC. Gareau says that he's always had an entrepreneurial focus, and when the right opportunities came along, he merged a series of his activities under the Human Performance umbrella. The company's motto is "We train, you perform," which is captured well in the company logo.

Gareau formally started Human Performance with partners Dusan Benicky and Steve Ramsbottom in 1998. Prior to forming this company, he was running his own personal training business, Progressive Fitness, at Olympic Fitness in Vancouver. He was also one of the trainers on staff at the Performance Centre in Burnaby. In 1998, unhappy with some of the training arrangements at the Performance Centre, he decided to make the Centre's managers an offer to provide all of the training at the Centre under a lease agreement. When that offer was accepted, Gareau combined all of his training activities under the company name Human Performance. Gareau is still learning how to manage and grow his business. He was kind enough to describe some of his experiences and share with us some of his insights related to OB.

You should find this progressive case (which appears at the end of each Part of the book) valuable for at least two reasons. First, it will help you integrate many of the OB concepts introduced in this book. Unfortunately, textbooks have to be linear—moving sequentially through an artificially created set of independent chapters. The real world, however, is a juggling act of overlapping and highly interdependent activities. This progressive case will make this interdependence clearer and help demonstrate how individual, group, and organization-system factors overlap. Second, this progressive case will show you the applicability of OB concepts to actual management practice. Most textbook examples or cases are short and designed to illustrate only one or two points. As an integrated and progressive story, the Rob Gareau case will show you how one real-life manager-owner has dealt with dozens of OB issues faced on a daily basis.

In describing how he came to be one of the founders of Human Performance, Rob Gareau explains that he always thought that he would be in a career that combined health, fitness care, and training. He was inspired because of the work done with him by his own coaches when he was growing up: "They showed me how to train, and they took me from mediocre to great in what I was trying to accomplish." From those early experiences, he

---

**Robert Gareau**
Director of Human Performance
Strength and Conditioning Specialist

hUman PERFORMance
Burnaby and Vancouver, BC
http://www.u-perform.ca

## EMPLOYMENT HISTORY:

| | | |
|---|---|---|
| June 1997 | – present | **Director of U-Perform Athletics Ltd.; Strength and Conditioning Specialist** |
| August 1996 | – June 1997 | **Self Employed as Rehabilitation Consultant** |
| March 1995 | – August 1996 | **Senior Exercise Therapist** Canadian Back Institute |
| December 1994 | – March 1996 | **Rehabilitation Consultant** Maple Ridge Parks and Leisure |
| September 1994 | – March 1995 | **Childcare Worker** Share Community Services |

## EDUCATION:
Simon Fraser University (1990-1996), Burnaby, BC
- psychology honours degree
- kinesiology degree
- Health and Fitness Diploma

St. Thomas More Collegiate (1985-1990), Burnaby, BC

## ADDITIONAL CERTIFICATIONS:
- Certified Strength and Conditioning Specialist (National Strength and Conditioning Association)
- Professional Fitness and Lifestyle Consultant (Canadian Society of Exercise Physiology)
- NCCP level 1 Weight Lifting Coaching Certification
- Member of American College of Sports Medicine
- Member of National Strength and Conditioning Association

## PUBLICATION:
"Chronic Back Pain Patients: How To Recognize and Treat Their Biopsychosocial Symptoms,"
*Rehabilitation Review* (Spring '96 issue).

## ACTIVITIES AND INTERESTS:
Enjoy weight training, boxing, martial arts. Outdoor activities including skiing, mountain biking, and hiking.

## FAVOURITE BOOKS:
*Long Walk to Freedom*, Nelson Mandela; *Seven Habits of Highly Effective People*, Stephen R. Covey; *Words I Wish I Wrote*, Robert Fulghum; *The Autobiography of Malcolm X*

## FAVOURITE QUOTE:
To laugh often and much; to win the respect of intelligent people and the affection of children; to earn the appreciation of honest critics and endure the betrayal of false friends; to appreciate beauty; to leave the world a bit better whether by a healthy child, a garden patch or a redeemed social condition; to know even one life has breathed easier because you have lived. **This is to have succeeded.** (Ralph Waldo Emerson)

## BEST ADVICE ANYONE EVER GAVE ME:
Don't sweat it if you miss your bus because there'll be another coming around the corner.

## WHAT I HOPE TO BE DOING IN FIVE YEARS:
Succeeding (see favourite quote above).

**PART 1**

PROGRESSIVE CASE

*continued from page123*

understood the power of both motivation and coaching. Of course, Gareau did not realize in those early years of considering career possibilities that motivating and coaching are requisite skills for any great leader.

Gareau received a degree in kinesiology and psychology from Simon Fraser University (SFU) in 1995. This was followed by pursuing an honour's degree in psychology in 1996. He is one of the generation of "twenty-somethings" who are forging their way in an uncertain job market that is full of opportunities for those who know how to read the market and carve their own niche. He is justifiably proud of what he's accomplished in creating Human Performance, and of what he's accomplished at his age. Still, he acknowledges that to do all this he's had to be stubborn and tough, and thus expects others to be as strong as he is. And he confesses, "I am still trying to learn more about leadership."

Despite this, Gareau has no regrets about the path he has chosen, and feels he's been really lucky. He also has a good sense of balance—knowing where his strengths and weaknesses lie. He feels he leads best by having a peer relationship with his employees, leading by example, and trying to teach, rather than direct. He lets his employees have autonomy over a number of decisions. He realizes, however, that he does have high expectations sometimes, assuming that his employees are as tough as he is. And he acknowledges that sometimes, "perhaps I am a little too direct."

For Gareau, personality plays a large role in how he decides to add employees to his company. "Personality matters a lot." He looks for people who are happy, have a healthy lifestyle, and a "good personality." Of his own personality, he says he is "driven, focused, and balanced." He also characterizes himself as easygoing and not shy.

Employee values are another concern of Gareau's: "I always look for people of similar values. It's important that the people I hire value quality above everything else, and that they know not to compromise on quality." He is most concerned that his employees stay attuned to figuring out the best way to work with clients during each hour of training.

When asked about his philosophy of managing people, Gareau cites the Golden Rule: Do unto others, as you would have others do unto you. He dislikes what he calls "the typical bureaucratic corporate model," and favours instead an open and flexible style. His approach is client-driven, since much of his work is one on one with clients. But his openness extends to his employees. He doesn't micromanage, and instead aims to hire employees who love what they're doing.

Gareau's success at starting and growing Human Performance underscores the need for organizational behaviour skills. His background is in kinesiology and psychology, not in business. He certainly recognizes that "having good business skills" is an important part of running a business. But he also acknowledges the importance of being able to deal with people. Many times the people he deals with are under a lot of stress and personal pressures, and he has to help them cope with those pressures. He finds that personal development, knowledge of conflict-handling techniques and stress management, and expertise in how to deal with people are important parts of running any business. He also suggests that knowing what you like to do well and following through on that makes for a more pleasant work environment. And finally, he emphasizes the need to build a good management team to help him carry out his goals: "I focus on the things that I'm good at doing, and then surround myself with people who can help me do the things I know less about."

And if you were wondering how university or college life might compare with running a business, Gareau offers the following food for thought: "The pressure and stress of exam week is the real world in my business—the exams keep coming, in unexpected forms, when you're running your own business."

Gareau observes that running his own business is also very different from being an employee. A typical employee, he notes, is expected to do what he or she is told. Gareau again relates this to being "in school." In running his own business, however, he is faced with doing a wide variety of things, and must determine for himself the appropriate course of action for each problem. With the rise of an entrepreneurial model in Canada's business world, knowing how to lead yourself may be an important lesson to learn.

Gareau also underscores the need for mentoring and having a peer group if you are running your own business. He has recently become involved with the Young Entrepreneur's Program, and he said this has made a great deal of difference in his perspective. None of his own friends were making the same kinds of sacrifices he was in order to get his business up and running, so they weren't always sympathetic to what he was facing. Meeting with others who are also running their own businesses has helped him develop more insight into handling the various issues he faces.

Overall, if Gareau were to summarize how he sees his business right now, he would say, "The business is in the early stages of becoming what it has the potential to be. However, we are in a critical planning period because we did not anticipate success and opportunities at this pace." And when asked about the future, he says that he expects in five years he will be "working with an evolved form of Human Performance, consulting and spending more time educating people about health and athletic development."

## Questions:

1. In what ways does running your own business differ from being an employee?

2. Gareau makes a case for managers needing interpersonal skills at least as much as other business skills. To what extent do you agree with him?

3. What lessons might you learn from Gareau's observation that "I surround myself with people who can help me do the things I know less about?"

4. What challenges might you face if you followed Gareau's example and tried to start your own business?

# Stress at Work

**Celebrated clothing designer** and entrepreneur Linda Lundström, founder of Toronto-based Linda Lundström Ltd., knew she was under too much stress the day she started crying uncontrollably after she couldn't find a parking spot near her doctor's office.[1] "It was the proverbial last straw," she says about the parking incident. At the time, she was dealing with success, recognition, a growing business, and two small children. She had started to develop physical symptoms: skin rashes, intestinal disorders, neuralgia, and insomnia. That day, she walked into her doctor's office chanting over and over again, "I can't do it anymore."

While Lundström chose to go to her doctor, Pierre Lebrun chose another way to exhibit the stress he'd stored up from his workplace.[2] He took a hunting rifle to Ottawa-Carleton–based OC Transpo and killed four public transit co-workers on April 6, 1999, before turning the gun on himself. Lebrun felt that he had been the target of harassment by his co-workers for years because of his stuttering. While this may seem the unusual response of an irate employee, consider the circumstances at OC Transpo. "Quite apart from what's alleged or otherwise with Mr. Lebrun's situation, we know [OC Transpo's] had a very unhappy work environment for a long time," Al Loney, chair of Ottawa-Carleton's transit commission noted. A consultant's report produced the year before the shooting found a workplace with "rock-bottom morale and poor management." It was not uncommon for fights to break out in the unit where the four men were killed.

## Are We Overstressed?

Stress appears to be a major factor in the lives of many Canadians. A survey conducted by POLLARA in late 1997 found that Canadians experienced a great deal of stress, with those from Quebec topping the list.[3] The survey also found that women were more stressed than men. The inset "Stress Across the Country" reports the findings.

Among workers, stress is also a fact of life. An Angus Reid Group poll conducted in the fall of 1997 found that two-thirds of those surveyed said their job was either very or somewhat stressful.[4] Fifty-five percent of the workers said that their biggest problem was being asked to do too much in too little time. Juggling work and family demands created stress for 22 percent of those surveyed.

Front-line workers are not the only members of the organization who experience stress, however. In a 1997 study conducted by researchers Darren Larose and Bernadette Schell at Ontario's Laurentian University, 88 percent of the executives surveyed indicated elevated levels of stress and/or unhealthy personality traits.[5] They also had higher levels of predisposition to serious illnesses such as cancer and heart disease.

### The Most Stressful Jobs

How do jobs rate in terms of stress? The inset "The Most Stressful Jobs" shows how selected occupations ranked in an evaluation of 250 jobs. Among the criteria used in the rankings were overtime, quotas, deadlines, competitiveness, physical demands, environmental conditions, hazards encountered, initiative required, stamina required, win-lose situations, and working in the public eye.

Stress is not something that can be ignored in the workplace. It is likely responsible for the higher levels of absenteeism reported in 1997, compared with 1993. Statistics Canada reported that full-time workers took an average of 6.2 days off in 1997 for illness or disability.[6] This translates into the loss of an estimated 66 million workdays in 1997 alone. The report suggested that an aging workforce and increased workplace stress are responsible for the increase. "In the wake of years of fiscal downsizing, workers across all sectors are working harder and longer than ever while trying to balance family responsibilities," said Scott Morris, who heads the Calgary-based consulting firm Priority Management.[7]

Professor Daniel Ondrack, of the University of Toronto's The Rotman School of Management, notes that "one of the major reasons for absenteeism is the logistical problems workers face in just getting to work, including transporting children to school and finding daycare. Single parents, especially female, have to juggle all the daycare and family responsibilities, and that makes it extremely difficult for people to keep up with work demands."[8]

## What Is Stress?

Stress is usually defined in terms of a situation that creates excessive psychological or physiological demands on a person. Thus, the situation, often referred to as the stressor, and the response *together* create the stress that an individual experiences. This distinction is important because what is stressful to one person may be enjoyable, or at least neutrally viewed, by another. While almost anyone might feel stress if followed by a stranger in a dark alley, not everyone feels stressed when given the opportunity for public speaking.

Dr. Hans Selye, a Montreal-based researcher, pioneered the study of stress and its effects. His model, the general adaptation syndrome (GAS), suggests that stress

| Stress across the COUNTRY | |
| --- | --- |
| Region | Percentage (%) who reported they were as stressed as they could handle, or were on their way to being completely overwhelmed |
| Alberta | 38 |
| Atlantic Canada | 41 |
| British Columbia | 37 |
| Ontario | 39 |
| The Prairies | 32 |
| Quebec | 64 |

**Source:** "Stress Is Everywhere and Getting Worse, Survey Says," *Canadian Press Newswire*, December 17, 1997.

## The Most **STRESSFUL** Jobs

How do jobs rate in terms of stress? The following shows how selected occupations ranked in an evaluation of 250 jobs. Among the criteria used in the rankings were: overtime, quotas, deadlines, competitiveness, physical demands, environmental conditions, hazards encountered, initiative required, stamina required, win-lose situations, and working in the public eye.

| Rank | Score | Stress Score | Rank | Score | Stress Score |
|---|---|---|---|---|---|
| 1. | U.S. president | 176.6 | 47. | Auto salesperson | 56.3 |
| 2. | Firefighter | 110.9 | 50. | College professor | 54.2 |
| 3. | Senior executive | 108.6 | 60. | School principal | 51.7 |
| 6. | Surgeon | 99.5 | 103. | Market research analyst | 42.1 |
| 10. | Air traffic controller | 83.1 | 104. | Personnel recruiter | 41.8 |
| 12. | Public relations executive | 78.5 | 113. | Hospital administrator | 39.6 |
| 16. | Advertising account executive | 74.6 | 119. | Economist | 38.7 |
| 17. | Real estate agent | 73.1 | 122. | Mechanical engineer | 38.3 |
| 20. | Stockbroker | 71.7 | 124. | Chiropractor | 37.9 |
| 22. | Pilot | 68.7 | 132. | Technical writer | 36.5 |
| 25. | Architect | 66.9 | 149. | Retail salesperson | 34.9 |
| 31. | Lawyer | 64.3 | 173. | Accountant | 31.1 |
| 33. | General physician | 64.0 | 193. | Purchasing agent | 28.9 |
| 35. | Insurance agent | 63.3 | 229. | Broadcast technician | 24.2 |
| 42. | Advertising salesperson | 59.9 | 245. | Actuary | 20.2 |

**Source:** Reprinted by permission of *The Wall Street Journal*, © 1996 Dow Jones & Company, Inc. All rights reserved worldwide.

occurs in three stages: alarm, resistance, and exhaustion.[9] The alarm stage occurs when the body tries to meet the initial challenge of the stressor. The brain reacts by sending a message to the rest of the body's systems, causing such symptoms as increased respiration, raised blood pressure, dilated pupils, and tensed muscles.

The resistance stage occurs if the stressor continues. At this stage, one feels such symptoms as fatigue, anxiety, and tension due to the body's attempt to fight the stressor. The final stage is exhaustion, which occurs from prolonged and continual exposure to the same stressor. The important thing to remember about how GAS works is that it puts heavy demands on the body. The more that GAS is activated and the longer that it goes on, the more wear and tear your body experiences. Individuals who frequently go through alarm, resistance, and exhaustion cycles are more likely to be susceptible to fatigue, disease, aging, and other negative physical and psychological consequences.

Stress is not necessarily bad in and of itself. While stress is typically discussed in a negative context, it also has a positive value. Consider, for example, athletes or stage performers who use stress positively to rise to the occasion and perform at or near their maximum. On the other hand, students who put off studying for exams until the last moment, and then develop the flu, are not able to use their stress to perform at a maximum level.

While GAS explains the experience of stress, in the next section we try to answer the following questions: What causes stress? What are its consequences for individual employees? Why is it that the same set of conditions that creates stress for one person seems to have little or no effect on another person?

## Causes of Stress

A variety of sources of stress have been identified, including "work overload; role conflict; ineffective, hostile and incompetent bosses; lack of personal fit with a job; lack of recognition; lack of a clear job description or chain of command; fear, uncertainty, and doubt about career progress; and prejudice based on age, gender, ethnicity or religion."[10] However, a variety of changes in the workplace have resulted in additional causes of stress. We identify some of these key changes below:[11]

- **Competition and Change**: With globalization has come increasing pressure to compete and innovate, which has led to an increase in re-engineering and restructuring. Alicja Muszynski, a sociology professor at the University of Waterloo, notes that "As corporations, including universities, have been asked to tighten their belts, there are fewer jobs and people that are left have to take on more responsibility."[12] Meanwhile, she adds, "people are afraid to take on less in the workplace, or to complain, because they're afraid they're going to get downsized."

- **Technological Change**: Employees are often expected to learn new technologies without being given adequate training. Or they are not consulted when new technology is implemented. In addition, employees at all levels are flooded with information because of technological changes. As well, employees are frequently asked to be "on" for their jobs more hours

**OB** *on the Edge*

each day: pagers, voice mail, faxes, e-mail, the Internet, and intranets make it possible to stay in touch with the workplace 24 hours a day.

- **Increasingly Diverse Workforce:** "If diversity is not managed effectively it may lead to interpersonal stress, competition among different groups for attention and resources, and decreased interaction because of the perceived need for political correctness in speech, interaction, and recognition." In diverse groups individuals experience differences in beliefs and values; differences in role expectations, and differences in perceptions about fairness in procedures.

- **Downsizing:** With downsizing seemingly a routine procedure in many firms, even the threat of layoffs can be stressful. Moreover, after downsizing, firms often increase the workloads of those remaining, leading to additional stress.

- **Employee Empowerment and Teamwork:** Both empowerment and teamwork require greater decision-making responsibility and interaction skills from employees. While this alone is stressful, it is particularly stressful for individuals who "have little or no interest in empowerment or teamwork structures and processes. Many people do not function well in a group setting, and they and their work may suffer if forced into a team environment."

- **Work/Home Conflict:** Trying to balance work life and family life is difficult at the best of times, but more employees are finding that their jobs are demanding longer hours, either formally or informally. This makes it difficult to manage the nonwork parts of one's life. Families with children where both parents work, or where parents are raising children alone, often have the added stress of managing child-care arrangements.

About one in eight workers was responsible for providing some form of eldercare for aging parents in 1997, and this is expected to increase to one in four

## factbox [13]

- One in three Canadians between the ages of 25 and 44 claims to be a workaholic.

- 85% of married women who are employed full-time and have at least one child at home, and 75% of similarly situated men, say that weekdays are too short to accomplish what needs to get done.

- The financial cost to companies because employees are trying to balance work and family obligations is estimated to be at least $2.7 billion a year.

- 17% of employees who are offered promotions turn them down, and 25% who are offered transfers do the same, giving family-related reasons for doing so.

- 25% of white-collar workers and 40% of blue-collar workers had a stress-related absence in 1998. The cost of this to companies is $12 billion.

- The rate of physical or psychological assaults on women in the workplace is 19% higher in Canada than in the United States, and the rate of assaults on men is four times higher than in the US.

workers in 2000.[14] Being a caregiver is an additional stress both at home and work. Studies indicate that those who have difficulties finding effective child care or eldercare have lower work performance and increased absenteeism, decreased satisfaction, and lower physical and psychological well-being.[15]

A fact that tends to be overlooked when stressors are reviewed individually is that stress is an additive phenomenon.[16] Stress builds up. Each new and persistent stressor adds to an individual's stress level. A single stressor may seem relatively unimportant in and of itself, but if it is added to an already high level of stress, it can be "the straw that breaks the camel's back." You may recall that the final straw for Linda Lundström was not being able to find a parking space.

## Consequences of Stress

Stress manifests itself in a number of ways. For instance, an individual who is experiencing a high level of stress may develop high blood pressure, ulcers, irritability, difficulty in making routine decisions, loss of appetite, accident proneness, and the like. These symptoms can be placed under three general categories: physiological, psychological, and behavioural symptoms.[17]

- **Physiological Symptoms** Most of the research on stress suggests that it can create changes in metabolism, increase heart and breathing rates, increase blood pressure, cause headaches, and induce heart attacks. One of the interesting features of illness in today's workplace is the considerable change in how stress is manifested. In the past, sick leave, workers' compensation, and short- and long-term disability were claimed by an organization's older employees — most often in cases of catastrophic illness such as heart attacks, cancer, and major back surgeries. In recent years, however, it is not unusual for long-term disability programs to be filled with employees in their twenties, thirties, and forties. Employees are claiming illnesses that are either psychiatric (such as depression) or more difficult to diagnose (such as chronic fatigue syndrome or fibromyalgia, a musculoskeletal discomfort). The increase in disability claims may be the result of downsizing taking its toll on the psyches of those in the workforce.[18]

- **Psychological Symptoms** Job dissatisfaction is "the simplest and most obvious psychological effect" of stress.[19] However, stress also manifests itself in other psychological states — for instance, tension, anxiety, irritability, boredom, and procrastination.

The evidence indicates that when people are placed in jobs that make multiple and conflicting demands or in which there is a lack of clarity as to the incumbent's duties, authority, and responsibilities, both stress and dissatisfaction are increased.[20] Similarly, the less control that people have over the pace of their work, the greater the stress and dissatisfaction. While more research is needed to clarify the relationship, the evidence suggests that jobs that provide a low level of variety, significance, autonomy, feedback, and identity to incumbents create stress and reduce satisfaction and involvement in the job.[21]

- **Behavioural Symptoms** Behaviourally related stress symptoms include changes in productivity, absence, and turnover, as well as changes in eating habits, increased smoking or consumption of alcohol, rapid speech, fidgeting, and sleep disorders. More recently stress has been linked to aggression and violence in the workplace.

# Why Do Individuals Differ in Their Experience of Stress?

Some people thrive on stressful situations, while others are overwhelmed by them. What is it that differentiates people in terms of their ability to handle stress? What individual difference variables moderate the relationship between *potential* stressors and *experienced* stress? At least five variables — perception, job experience, social support, belief in locus of control, and hostility — have been found to be relevant moderators.

- **Perception** Individuals react in response to their *perception* of reality rather than to reality itself. Perception, therefore, will moderate the relationship

between a potential stress condition and an employee's reaction to it. One person's fear that he or she will lose his or her job because the company is laying off staff may be perceived by another as an opportunity to receive a large severance allowance and start a small business. Similarly, what one employee perceives as a challenging job may be viewed as threatening and demanding by others.[22] So the stress potential in environmental, organizational, and individual factors doesn't lie in their objective conditions. Rather, it lies in an employee's interpretation of those factors.

- **Job Experience** Experience is said to be a great teacher. It can also be a great stress reducer. Think back to your first date or your first few days in college or university. For most of us, the uncertainty and newness of those situations created stress. But as we gained experience, that stress disappeared or at least significantly decreased. The same phenomenon seems to apply to work situations. That is, experience on the job tends to be negatively related to work stress. Two explanations have been offered.[23] First, people who experience more stress on the job when they're first hired may be more likely to quit. Therefore, people who remain with the organization longer are those with more stress-resistant traits or those who are more resistant to the stress characteristics of their organization. Second, people eventually develop coping mechanisms to deal with stress. Because this takes time, senior members of the organization are more likely to be fully adapted and should experience less stress.

- **Social Support** There is increasing evidence that social support — that is, collegial relationships with co-workers or supervisors — can buffer the impact of stress.[24] The logic underlying this moderating variable is that social support helps to ease the negative effects of even high-strain jobs.

OB on the Edge

For individuals whose work associates are unhelpful or even actively hostile, social support may be found outside the job. Involvement with family, friends, and community can provide the support — especially for those with a high social need — that is missing at work, and this can make job stressors more tolerable.

- **Belief in Locus of Control**   The personality trait locus of control determines the extent to which individuals believe they have control over the things that happen in their lives. Those with an internal locus of control believe they control their own destiny. Those with an external locus believe their lives are controlled by outside forces. Evidence indicates that internals perceive their jobs to be less stressful than do externals.[25]

When internals and externals confront a similar stressful situation, the internals are likely to believe that they can have a significant effect on the results. They therefore act to take control of events. Externals are more likely to experience stress because they often act helpless, often by being passive and defensive, while feeling helpless.

- **Hostility**   Some people's personality includes a high degree of hostility and anger. These people are chronically suspicious and mistrustful of others. Recent evidence indicates that this *hostility* significantly increases a person's stress and risk for heart disease.[26] More specifically, people who are quick to anger, maintain a persistently hostile outlook, and project a cynical mistrust of others are more likely to experience stress in situations.

# How Do We Manage Stress?

Both the individual and the organization can take steps to help the individual manage stress. Below we discuss ways that individuals can manage stress, and then we examine programs that organizations are using to help employees manage stress.

## Individual Approaches

An employee can take personal responsibility for reducing his or her stress level. Individual strategies that have proven effective include implementing time management techniques, increasing physical exercise, relaxation training, and expanding the social support network.

- **Time Management**   Many people manage their time poorly. The things people have to accomplish in any given day or week are not necessarily beyond completion if they manage their time properly. The well-organized employee, like the well-organized student, can often accomplish twice as much as the person who is poorly organized. So an understanding and utilization of basic *time management* principles can help individuals better cope with tensions created by job demands.[27] A few of the more well-known time management principles are: (1) making daily lists of activities to be accomplished; (2) prioritizing activities by importance and urgency; (3) scheduling activities according to the priorities set; and (4) knowing your daily cycle and handling the most demanding parts of your job during the high part of your cycle when you are most alert and productive.[28]

- **Physical Activity**   Noncompetitive physical exercise, such as aerobics, walking, jogging, swimming, and riding a bicycle, has long been recommended by physicians as a way to deal with excessive stress levels. These forms of *physical exercise* increase heart capacity, lower at-rest heart rate, provide a mental diversion from work pressures, and offer a means to "let off steam."[29]

- **Relaxation Techniques**   Individuals can teach themselves to reduce tension through *relaxation techniques* such as meditation, hypnosis, and biofeedback. The objective is to reach a state of deep relaxation, where one feels physically relaxed, somewhat detached from the immediate environment, and detached from body sensations.[30] Fifteen or 20 minutes a day of deep relaxation releases tension and provides a person with a pronounced sense of peacefulness. Importantly, significant changes in heart rate, blood pressure, and other physiological factors result from achieving the deep relaxation condition.

## REDUCING stress in the workplace

- **Avoid electronic monitoring of staff.** Personal supervision generates considerably less stress.
- **Allow workers time to recharge** after periods of intense or demanding work.
- **Important information that significantly affects employees** is best transmitted face to face.
- **Encourage positive social interactions between staff** to promote problem-solving around work issues and increase emotional support.
- **Staff need balance between privacy and social interaction at work.** Extremes can generate stress.

**Source:** J. Lee, "How to Fight That Debilitating Stress in Your Workplace," *Vancouver Sun*, April 5, 1999, p. C3.

- **Building Social Supports** Having friends, family, or colleagues to talk to provides an outlet when stress levels become excessive. Expanding your *social support network*, therefore, can be a means for tension reduction. It provides you with someone to listen to your problems and to offer a more objective perspective on the situation. Research also demonstrates that social support moderates the stress-burnout relationship.[31] That is, high support reduces the likelihood that heavy work stress will result in job burnout.

## Organizational Approaches

Brampton, Ontario-based Nortel (Northern Telecom Limited) established Aralia Centre, a wellness centre, at its headquarters. Employees can enroll in a relaxation class, sign up for a social weekend, or take time out for a stretch break. These programs were specifically designed to help employees manage stress. In fact, Nortel's 3500 employees who work at corporate headquarters can choose from among 20 programs designed to improve and maintain their health. These programs include healthy eating, ulcer care, asthma management,

($360); lowering cholesterol from 240 to 190 mg ($1680); and slimming down from obese to normal weight ($248).[34] Husky does not fully measure the impact of its wellness program, but it has one of the best records on absenteeism in the industry. Its claims to the Workers' Compensation Board are also one of the lowest in the industry. Both of these are seen as related to the wellness program.[35]

So what else can organizations do to reduce employee stress? In general, strategies to reduce stress include improved processes for choosing employees, placement of employees in appropriate jobs, realistic goal setting, designing jobs with employee needs and skills in mind, increased employee involvement, improved organizational communication, and establishment of corporate wellness programs.

While certain jobs are more stressful than others, individuals also differ in their response to stress situations. We know, for example, that individuals with little experience or an external locus of control tend to be more prone to stress. *Selection and placement* decisions should take these facts into consideration. Obviously, while management shouldn't restrict hiring to only

**faceoff**

When organizations provide onsite daycare facilities, they are filling a needed role in parents' lives, and making it easier for parents to attend to their job demands rather than worry about child-care arrangements.

When employees expect organizations to provide child care, they are shifting their responsibilities to their employers, rather than keeping their family needs and concerns private. Moreover, it's unfair to give child-care benefits when not all employees have children.

motivation support, parenting classes, and family social events. There's also a fitness centre complete with aerobic studios and a workout area for cardiovascular and weight training.[32]

Similarly, Bolton, Ontario-based Husky Injection Molding Systems has a fully equipped state-of-the-art wellness centre to meet the health needs of more than 1200 employees. It houses a daycare centre, a fully equipped weight and training room, a library with health care books and videos, and offices for a variety of health care workers practising both regular and alternative medicine techniques.[33]

Organizations, of course, aren't altruistic. They expect a payoff from their investment in wellness programs. And most of those firms that have introduced wellness programs have found significant benefits. For instance, Johnson & Johnson calculated the following annual savings in insurance premiums when an employee exchanges bad habits for healthy ones: quitting smoking ($1550); starting to exercise

experienced individuals with an internal locus of control, such individuals may adapt better to high-stress jobs and perform those jobs more effectively.

Research shows that individuals perform better when they have specific and challenging goals and receive feedback on how well they are progressing toward these goals. The use of goals can reduce stress as well as provide motivation. Specific goals that are perceived as attainable clarify performance expectations. Additionally, goal feedback reduces uncertainties as to actual job performance. The result is less employee frustration, role ambiguity, and stress.

Creating jobs that give employees more responsibility, more meaningful work, more autonomy, and increased feedback can reduce stress because these factors give the employee greater control over work activities and lessen dependence on others. Of course, not all employees want jobs with increased responsibility. The right job for employees with a low need for growth might be less responsibility and increased specialization. If individuals prefer structure and routine, more structured jobs should also reduce uncertainties and stress levels.

When employees feel uncertain about goals, expectations, and methods of evaluation, this causes them stress. By giving employees a voice in decisions that directly affect their job performances, management can increase employee control and reduce stress. So managers should consider *increasing employee involvement* in decision making.[36]

Increasing formal *organizational communication* with employees reduces uncertainty by lessening role ambiguity and role conflict. Given the importance that perceptions play in moderating the stress-response relationship, management can also use effective communications as a means to shape employee perceptions. Remember that what employees categorize as demands, threats, or opportunities are merely interpretations, and those interpretations can be affected by the symbols and actions communicated by management.

Our final suggestion is to offer organizationally supported wellness programs, such as those provided by Nortel and Husky. These programs focus on the employee's total physical and mental condition.[37] For example, they typically provide workshops to help people quit smoking, control alcohol use, lose weight, eat better, and develop a regular exercise program. The assumption underlying most wellness programs is that employees need to take personal responsibility for their physical and mental health. The organization is merely a vehicle to facilitate this end.

## Research Exercises

1. Look for data on stress levels in other countries. How do these data compare with the Canadian data presented above? Are the sources of stress the same in different countries? What might you conclude about how stress affects people in different cultures?

2. Find out what 3 Canadian organizations in 3 different industries have done to help employees manage stress. Are there common themes in these programs? Did you find any unusual programs? To what extent would you say these programs are tailored to the needs of the employees in those industries?

## Your Perspective

1. Think of all of the technological changes that have happened in the workplace in recent years, including e-mail, faxes, intranets, etc. What are the positive benefits of all of this change? What are the downsides to this change? As an employee facing the demand to "stay connected" to your workplace, how would you try to maintain a balance in your life?

2. How much responsibility should individuals take for managing their own stress? To what extent should organizations become involved in the personal lives of their employees and in trying to help them manage stress? What are the pros and cons for whether employees or organizations take responsibility for managing stress?

## Want to Know More?

If you're wondering how stressed you are, go to **www.heartandstroke.ca** and take their test. The site also offers tips on how to relax and manage stress.

## Endnotes

1. Information in this paragraph based on S. McKay, "The Work-Family Conundrum," *The Financial Post Magazine*, December 1997, pp. 78-81.

2. Information in this paragraph based on B. Branswell, "Death in Ottawa: The Capital Is Shocked by a Massacre That Leaves Five Dead," *Maclean's*, April 19, 1999, p. 18; "Four Employees Killed by Former Co-Worker," *Occupational Health & Safety*, June 1999, pp. 14, 16; and "Preventing Workplace Violence," *Human Resources Advisor Newsletter Western Edition*, May/June 1999, pp. 1-2.

3. "Stress Is Everywhere and Getting Worse, Survey Says," *Canadian Press Newswire*, December 17, 1997.

4. S. Cordon, "Workers Underpaid, Overworked, Stressed: But Still Satisfied," *Canadian Press Newswire*, October 7, 1997.

5. R.B. Mason, "Taking Health Care to Factory Floor Proves Smart Move for Growing Ontario Company," *Canadian Medical Association Journal*, November 15, 1997, pp. 1423-1424.

6. N. Ayed, "Absenteeism Up Since 1993," *Canadian Press Newswire*, March 25, 1998.

7. N. Ayed, "Absenteeism Up Since 1993," *Canadian Press Newswire*, March 25, 1998.

8. N. Ayed, "Absenteeism Up Since 1993," *Canadian Press Newswire*, March 25, 1998.

9. H. Selye, *The Stress of Life* (New York: McGraw-Hill, 1976); and H. Selye, *Stress Without Distress* (Philadelphia, PA: J.B. Lippincott, 1974).

10. R. DeFrank and J.M. Ivancevich, "Stress on the Job: An Executive Update," *The Academy of Management Executive*, August 1998, pp. 55-66.

11. These key changes are taken from R. DeFrank and J.M. Ivancevich, "Stress on the Job: An Executive Update," *The Academy of Management Executive*, August 1998, pp. 55-66. All of the quotations in the list that follows derive from this source.

12. P. Demont and A.M. Tobin, "One in Three Canadians Say They're Workaholics," *Vancouver Sun*, November 10, 1999, pp. A1, A2.

13. Information for FactBox based on P. Demont and A.M. Tobin, "One in Three Canadians Say They're Workaholics," *Vancouver Sun*, November 10, 1999, pp. A1, A2; E. Beauchesne, "Lost Work Cost Placed At $10b: Growing Stress Levels Are Cited as a Leading Factor in the Rise in Absenteeism in Canada," *Vancouver Sun*, September 2, 1999, p. A3; L. Ramsay, "Caught Between the Potty and the PC," *National Post*, November 9, 1998, p. D9; T. Cole, "All the Rage: This Can't Be Happening. Work Stress Is Making Us Violent," *Report on Business Magazine*, February 1999, pp. 50-57.

14. S. McKay, "The Work-Family Conundrum," *The Financial Post Magazine*, December 1997, pp. 78-81.

15. L.T. Thomas and D.C. Ganster, "Impact of Family-supportive Work Variables on Work-Family Conflict and Strain: A Control Perspective," *Journal of Applied Psychology*, 80, 1995, pp. 6-15.

16. H. Selye, *The Stress of Life* (New York: McGraw-Hill, 1976).

17. R.S. Schuler, "Definition and Conceptualization of Stress in Organizations," *Organizational Behavior and Human Performance*, April 1980, p. 191; and R.L. Kahn and P. Byosiere, "Stress in Organizations," *Organizational Behavior and Human Performance*, April 1980, pp. 604-610.

18. KPMG Canada, *Compensation Letter*, July 1998.

19. B.D. Steffy and J.W. Jones, "Workplace Stress and Indicators of Coronary-Disease Risk," p. 687.

20. C.L. Cooper and J. Marshall, "Occupational Sources of Stress: A Review of the Literature Relating to Coronary Heart Disease and Mental Ill Health," *Journal of Occupational Psychology*, 49, no. 1, 1976, pp. 11-28.

21. J.R. Hackman and G.R. Oldham, "Development of the Job Diagnostic Survey," *Journal of Applied Psychology*, April 1975, pp. 159-170.

22. J.L. Xie and G. Johns, "Job Scope and Stress: Can Job Scope Be Too High?" *Academy of Management Journal*, October 1995, pp. 1288-1309.

23. S.J. Motowidlo, J.S. Packard, and M.R. Manning, "Occupational Stress: Its Causes and Consequences for Job Performance," *Journal of Applied Psychology*, November 1987, pp. 619-620.

24. See, for instance, J.J. House, *Work Stress and Social Support* (Reading, MA: Addison Wesley, 1981); S. Jayaratne, D. Himle, and W.A. Chess, "Dealing With Work Stress and Strain: Is the Perception of Support More Important Than Its Use?" *The Journal of Applied Behavioral Science*, 24, no. 2, 1988, pp. 191-202; R.C. Cummings, "Job Stress and the Buffering Effect of Supervisory Support," *Group & Organization Studies*, March 1990, pp. 92-104; C.L. Scheck, A.J. Kinicki, and J.A. Davy, "A Longitudinal Study of a Multivariate Model of the Stress Process Using Structural Equations Modeling," *Human Relations*, December 1995, pp. 1481-1510; and M.R. Manning, C.N. Jackson, and M.R. Fusilier, "Occupational Stress, Social Support, and the Cost of Health Care," *Academy of Management Journal*, June 1996, pp. 738-750.

25. See L.R. Murphy, "A Review of Organizational Stress Management Research," *Journal of Organizational Behavior Management*, Fall-Winter 1986, pp. 215-227.

26. R. Williams, *The Trusting Heart: Great News About Type A Behavior* (New York: Times Books, 1989).

27. T.H. Macan, "Time Management: Test of a Process Model," *Journal of Applied Psychology*, June 1994, pp. 381-391.

28. See, for example, M.E. Haynes, *Practical Time Management: How to Make the Most of Your Most Perishable Resource* (Tulsa, OK: PennWell Books, 1985).

29. J. Kiely and G. Hodgson, "Stress in the Prison Service: The Benefits of Exercise Programs," *Human Relations*, June 1990, pp. 551-572.

30. E.J. Forbes and R.J. Pekala, "Psychophysiological Effects of Several Stress Management Techniques," *Psychological Reports*, February 1993, pp. 19-27; and G. Smith, "Meditation, the New Balm for Corporate Stress," *Business Week*, May 10, 1993, pp. 86-87.

31. D. Etzion, "Moderating Effects of Social Support on the Stress-Burnout Relationship," *Journal of Applied Psychology*, November 1984, pp. 615-622; and S. Jackson, R. Schwab, and R. Schuler, "Toward an Understanding of the Burnout Phenomenon," *Journal of Applied Psychology* 71, no. 4, November 1986, pp. 630-640.

OB on the Edge

32. R. Waymen, "Wellness Workout: For Northern Telecom, A Business Case Was the Muscle Behind One of the Most Comprehensive Corporate Wellness Programs in Canada," *Benefits Canada*, January 1998, pp. 24-30.

33. R.B. Mason, "Taking Health Care to Factory Floor Proves Smart Move for Growing Ontario Company," *Canadian Medical Association Journal*, November 15, 1997, pp. 1423-1424.

34. S. Tully, "America's Healthiest Companies," *Fortune*, June 12, 1995, p. 104.

35. R.B. Mason, "Taking Health Care to Factory Floor Proves Smart Move for Growing Ontario Company," *Canadian Medical Association Journal*, November 15, 1997, pp. 1423-1424.

36. S.E. Jackson, "Participation in Decision Making as a Strategy for Reducing Job-Related Strain," *Journal of Applied Psychology*, February 1983, pp. 3-19; and P. Froiland, "What Cures Job Stress?" *Training*, December 1993, pp. 32-36.

37. See, for instance, R.A. Wolfe, D.O. Ulrich, and D.F. Parker, "Employee Health Management Programs: Review, Critique, and Research Agenda," *Journal of Management*, Winter 1987, pp. 603-615; D.L. Gebhardt and C.E. Crump, "Employee Fitness and Wellness Programs in the Workplace," *American Psychologist*, February 1990, pp. 262-272; and C.E. Beadle, "And Let's Save 'Wellness.' It Works," *New York Times*, July 24, 1994, p. F9.

# CHAPTER 4

# Motivating Self and Others

## Questions for Consideration

**What do theories tell us about motivating ourselves and others?**

**How do we motivate for specific organizational circumstances and/or individual differences?**

**Are rewards always necessary?**

M orton, Illinois, is the Pumpkin Capital of the World, supplying 80 percent of the canned pumpkin in the United States. In 1996, several of the local residents got together to build an entry for the 11ᵗʰ Annual World Champion Punkin' Chunkin' contest, held in Lewes, Delaware. The idea behind the contest is to hurl four- to five-kilogram pumpkins through the air, and determine which pumpkin goes farthest. Teams can build hurling devices of their choice, as long as they don't use explosives.

Matt Parker and several of the local Morton residents became inspired by the idea of building a better "punkin' chunker." As described in the *Wall Street Journal*:

> Soon (Parker) and some tinkering friends were swapping sketches on napkins in coffee shops. "It sounded kind of dumb at first," Parker says, "but pretty soon that's all we talked about." In a month's time, a group formed and built a machine largely from scrap parts, often working into the early morning at the shop of Rod Litwiller, a crew member. Friends and neighbors stopped in to help.

The team from Morton won the first time they entered the contest, setting a world distance

record by "flinging a pumpkin 900 metres at a velocity of more than 950 kilometres per hour." The distance they achieved was 18 metres farther than the record.

Fresh from success, the Morton team set themselves a more difficult task for the 1997 contest: hurling a pumpkin into the air at Mach I—the speed of sound. They finished second with their Aludium Q-36 Pumpkin Modulator, but their previous year's win had a big impact on the contest. The 1997 winner went 1239 metres, more than 330 metres beyond the record set the previous year. Morton's team hurled their pumpkin 1180 metres, which represented a 30 percent increase for the team's performance over the previous year. In 1998 the Morton team were declared the winner again, this time hurling their pumpkin 1227 metres, 188 metres more than the second-place team.

This story is interesting from an organizational behaviour perspective because it represents a group of people who got together on their own to make something that in many ways had no real practical application (except to hurl pumpkins). It may have been a silly idea—the people who committed to the task didn't even know if they would win, and they certainly weren't motivated by the rewards. But the idea of building the machine captured their imagination, they pulled together the resources they needed (materials, support of friends and neighbours), worked long hours, and didn't require supervision.

This story illustrates a rift in the motivation literature as to what motivates individuals to perform. On one side, a number of experts provide explicit guidance on the process of motivating individuals (for instance, through goal-setting theory or expectancy theory, described below). On the other side, scholars such as Alfie Kohn, in his book *Punished by Rewards*, argue that "the desire to do something, much less to do it well, simply cannot be imposed; in this sense, it is a mistake to talk about motivating other people. All we can do is set up certain conditions that will maximize the probability of their developing an interest in what they are doing and remove the conditions that function as constraints."[1]

In this chapter we explore both sides of the issue, examining theories of motivation but also exploring Kohn's notion of setting up the right conditions

**Punkin' Chunkin'**
www.punkinchunkin.com

**motivation**
The processes that account for an individual's intensity, direction, and persistence of effort toward obtaining a goal.

**Theory X**
The assumption that employees dislike work, are lazy, dislike responsibility, and must be coerced to perform.

**Theory Y**
The assumption that employees like work, are creative, seek responsibility, and can exercise self-direction.

**intrinsic motivators**
A person's internal desire to do something, due to such things as interest, challenge and personal satisfaction.

**extrinsic motivators**
Motivation that comes from outside the person, such as pay, bonuses, and other tangible rewards.

and encouraging individuals to motivate themselves. In this Chapter's Video Case, you'll learn about the problems organizations are facing today in trying to motivate individuals to work for them, rather than some other company.

## What Is Motivation?

We define **motivation** as the processes that account for an individual's intensity, direction, and persistence of effort toward attaining a goal.[2]

The three key elements in our definition are intensity, direction, and persistence. *Intensity* is concerned with how hard a person tries. This is the element most of us focus on when we talk about motivation. However, high intensity is unlikely to lead to favourable job-performance outcomes unless the effort is channelled in a *direction* that is beneficial. An intense gardener, for instance, trying to grow the perfect pumpkin, would probably not have been suited to the Morton team, who were looking to figure out better ways to hurl a pumpkin, not grow it. Finally, motivation has a *persistence* dimension. This is a measure of how long a person can maintain his or her effort. Motivated individuals stay with a task long enough to achieve their goal.

Many people incorrectly view motivation as a personal trait—that is, some have it and others don't. Along these lines, Douglas McGregor proposed two distinct views of human beings: one basically negative, labelled **Theory X**, and the other basically positive, labelled **Theory Y**.[3] Theory X suggests that employees dislike work, will attempt to avoid it, and must be coerced, controlled, or threatened with punishment to achieve goals. Theory Y suggests that employees will exercise self-direction and self-control if they are committed to the objectives.

Our knowledge of motivation tells us that neither theory alone fully accounts for employee behaviour. What we know is that motivation is the result of the interaction of the individual and the situation. Certainly, individuals differ in their basic motivational drive. But the same employee who is quickly bored when pulling the lever on his or her drill press may pull the lever on a slot machine in Casino Windsor for hours on end without the slightest hint of boredom. You may read a complete novel at one sitting, yet find it difficult to concentrate on a textbook for more than 20 minutes. It's not necessarily you—it's the situation. So as we analyze the concept of motivation, keep in mind that the level of motivation varies both between individuals and within individuals at different times.

You should also realize that the types of things that motivate individuals will also vary by both the individual and the situation. Motivation theorists talk about **intrinsic motivators** and **extrinsic motivators**. Extrinsic motivators come from outside the person and include such things as pay, bonuses, and other tangible rewards. Intrinsic motivators are a person's internal desire to do something, motivated by such things as interest, challenge, and personal satisfaction. We may be willing to drive our mother to a meeting an hour away, without any thought of compensation, because it will make us feel nice to do something for her, that is, we will be intrinsically motivated. Alternatively, if we have a love-hate relationship with our younger brother, we may insist that he buy us lunch for helping out. Lunch would then be an extrinsic motivator, something that came from outside yourself and motivated you to do the task. If you think money is a powerful motivator, you may be surprised to read an opposing viewpoint in this chapter's Point/CounterPoint feature on pages 140-141.

### Theories of Motivation

The main theories of motivation fall into one of two categories: needs theories and process theories. Needs theories describe the types of needs that must be met in order to motivate individuals, while process theories help us understand the actual ways by which we and others can be motivated.

## Needs Theories of Motivation

All needs theories of motivation, including Maslow's hierarchy of needs, Herzberg's two-factor theory (sometimes also called motivation-hygiene theory), Alderfer's ERG theory, and McClelland's theory of needs propose a similar idea: Individuals have needs that, when unsatisfied, will result in motivation. For instance, if you have a need to be praised, you may work harder at your task in order to receive recognition from your manager or other co-workers. Similarly, if you need money and you are asked to do something, within reason, that offers money as a reward, you will be motivated to complete the task in order to earn the money. Where needs theories differ is in the types of needs they consider, and whether they propose a hierarchy of needs (where some needs have to be satisfied before others) or simply a list of needs. Exhibit 4-1 illustrates the relationship of four needs theories to each other. While the theories use different names for the needs, and also have different numbers of needs, we can see that they are somewhat consistent in the types of needs addressed. The exhibit also indicates the contribution and empirical support for each theory.

After Highland copper mine closed down in May 1999, it took employees only three more months to accept a ground-breaking contract that will see their wages tied to the price of copper. If the price of copper goes up, wages go up. But if the price of copper drops below 68 cents US, which is the break-even point for the mine, wages will drop two percent for each one percent drop in price. The employees' decision indicated the importance of meeting their simplest needs first: having an income to clothe, house and feed themselves and their families.

## POINT

# Money Motivates!

The importance of money as a motivator has been consistently downgraded by most behavioural scientists. They prefer to point out the value of challenging jobs, goals, participation in decision making, feedback, cohesive work teams, and other nonmonetary factors as stimulants to employee motivation. We argue otherwise here—that money is *the* crucial incentive to work motivation. As a medium of exchange, it is the vehicle by which employees can purchase the numerous need-satisfying things they desire. Furthermore, money also performs the function of a scorecard, by which employees assess the value that the organization places on their services and by which employees can compare their value to others.[1]

Money's value as a medium of exchange is obvious. People may not work only for money, but remove the money and how many people would come to work? A recent study of nearly 2500 employees found that while these people disagreed over what was their primary motivator, they unanimously ranked money as their number two.[2] This study reaffirms that for the vast majority of the workforce, a regular paycheque is absolutely necessary in order to meet their basic physiological and safety needs.

As equity theory suggests, money has symbolic value in addition to its exchange value. We use pay as the primary outcome against which we compare our inputs to determine if we are being treated equitably. That an organization pays one executive $80 000 a year and another $95 000 means more than the latter's earning $15 000 a year more. It is a message from the organization to both employees, of how much it values the contribution of each.

In addition to equity theory, expectancy theory attests to the value of money as a motivator. Specifically, if pay is contingent on performance, it will encourage workers to generate high levels of effort. Consistent with expectancy theory, money will motivate to the extent that it is seen as being able to satisfy an individual's personal goals and is perceived as being dependent upon performance criteria.

The best case for money as a motivator is a review of studies done by Ed Locke at the University of Maryland.[3] Locke looked at four methods of motivating employee performance: money, goal setting, participation in decision making, and redesigning jobs to give workers more challenge and responsibility. He found that the average improvement from money was 30 percent; goal setting increased performance 16 percent; participation improved performance by less than one percent; and job redesign positively impacted performance by an average of 17 percent. Moreover, every study Locke reviewed that used money as a method of motivation resulted in some improvement in employee performance. Such evidence demonstrates that money may not be the *only* motivator, but it is difficult to argue that it *doesn't* motivate!

Sources:

[1] K.O. Doyle, "Introduction: Money and the Behavioral Sciences," *American Behavioral Scientist*, July 1992, pp. 641-657.

[2] S. Caudron, "Motivation? Money's Only No. 2," *Industry Week*, November 15, 1993, p. 33.

[3] E.A. Locke et al., "The Relative Effectiveness of Four Methods of Motivating Employee Performance," in K.D. Duncan, M.M. Gruneberg, and D. Wallis (eds.), *Changes in Working Life* (London: John Wiley, Ltd., 1980), pp. 363-383.

## COUNTERPOINT

# Money Doesn't Motivate Most Employees Today!

Money can motivate *some* people under *some* conditions, so the issue isn't really whether money *can* motivate. The answer to that is: "It can!" The more relevant question is this: Does money motivate most employees in the workforce today to higher performance? The answer to this question, we'll argue, is "no."[1]

For money to motivate an individual's performance, certain conditions must be met. First, money must be important to the individual. Second, money must be perceived by the individual as being a direct reward for performance. Third, the marginal amount of money offered for the performance must be perceived by the individual as being significant. Finally, management must have the discretion to reward high performers with more money. Let's take a look at each of these conditions.

Money is not important to all employees. High achievers, for instance, are intrinsically motivated. Money should have little impact on these people. Similarly, money is relevant to those individuals with strong lower-order needs; but for most of the workforce, lower-order needs are substantially satisfied.

Money would motivate if employees perceived a strong linkage between performance and rewards in organizations. Unfortunately, pay increases are far more often determined by levels of skills and experience, community pay standards, the national cost-of-living index, and the organization's current and future financial prospects than by each employee's level of performance.

For money to motivate, the marginal difference in pay increases between a high performer and an average performer must be significant. In practice, it rarely is. For instance, a high-performing employee who is currently earning $50 000 a year is given a $335-a-month raise. After taxes, that amounts to about $42 a week. But this employee's co-worker, who is an average performer and earns $50 000, is rarely passed over at raise time. Instead of getting an eight percent raise, the co-worker is likely to get half of that. The net difference in their weekly paycheques is little more than $20. How much motivation is there in knowing that if you work really hard you're going to end up with $20 a week more than someone who is doing just enough to get by? For a large number of people, not much! Research indicates that merit raises must be at least seven percent of base pay for employees to perceive them as motivating. Unfortunately, recent surveys find nonmanagerial employees averaging merit increases of only 4.9 percent.[2]

Our last point relates to the degree of discretion that managers have in being able to reward high performers. Where unions exist, that discretion is almost zero. Pay is determined through collective bargaining and is allocated by job title and seniority, not level of performance. In nonunionized environments, the organization's compensation policies will constrain managerial discretion. Each job typically has a pay grade. Thus, a Systems Analyst III can earn between $5350 and $6350 a month. No matter how good a job that analyst does, her boss cannot pay her more than $6350 a month. Similarly, no matter how poorly someone does in that job, he will earn at least $5350 a month. In most organizations, managers have a very small area of discretion within which they can reward their higher-performing employees. So money might be theoretically capable of motivating employees to higher levels of performance, but most managers aren't given enough flexibility to do much about it.

---

Sources:

[1] B. Filipczak, "Can't Buy Me Love," *Training*, January 1996, pp. 29-34.

[2] See A. Mitra, N. Gupta, and G.D. Jenkins, Jr., "The Case of the Invisible Merit Raise: How People See Their Pay Raises," *Compensation & Benefits Review*, May-June 1995, pp. 71-76.

## Exhibit 4-1
## Summarizing the Various Needs Theories

| Theory | Maslow | Herzberg | Alderfer | McClelland |
|---|---|---|---|---|
| **Needs** | *Physiological*: Includes hunger, thirst, shelter, sex, and other bodily needs. | *Hygiene Factors*: Those factors—such as company policy and administration, supervision and salary—that, when adequate in a job, placate workers. When these factors are adequate, workers will not be dissatisfied. | *Existence*: Concerned with providing our core basic material existence requirements. | |
| | *Safety*: Includes security and protection from physical and emotional harm. | | | |
| | *Social*: Includes affection, belongingness, acceptance, and friendship. | *Motivators*: Factors associated with the work itself or to outcomes directly derived from it, such as promotional opportunities, opportunities for personal growth, recognition, responsibility, and achievement. These are the characteristics that people find intrinsically rewarding. | *Relatedness*: The desire we have for maintaining important interpersonal relationships. | *Need for Affiliation*: The desire for friendly and close interpersonal relationships. |
| | *Esteem*: Includes internal esteem factors such as self-respect, autonomy, and achievement; and external esteem factors such as status, recognition, and attention. | | *Growth*: An intrinsic desire for personal development. | *Need for Achievement*: The drive to excel, to achieve in relation to a set of standards, to strive to succeed. |
| | *Self-Actualization*: The drive to become what one is capable of becoming; it includes growth, achieving one's potential, and self-fulfillment. | | | *Need for Power*: The desire to make others behave in a way that they would not otherwise have behaved. |

**Summarizing the Various Needs Theories** *Continued*

| Theory | Maslow | Herzberg | Alderfer | McClelland |
| --- | --- | --- | --- | --- |
| **View about hierarchy of needs** | Argues that lower-order needs must be satisfied before one progresses to higher-order needs. | Hygiene factors must be met if person is not to be dissatisfied. They will not lead to satisfaction, however. Motivators lead to satisfaction. | More than one need can be important at the same time. If a higher-order need is not being met, the desire to satisfy a lower-level need increases. | People vary in the types of needs they have. Their motivation and how well they perform in a work situation are related to whether they have a need for achievement, affiliation, or power. |
| **Theory's impact/ contribution** | Enjoys wide recognition among practising managers. Most managers are familiar with it. | The popularity of giving workers greater responsibility for planning and controlling their work can be attributed to his findings (see, for instance, the Job Characteristics Model in Chapter 13). Shows that more than one need may operate at the same time. | Notes that if the gratification of a higher-level need is stifled, the desire to satisfy a lower-level need increases. Seen as a more valid version of the need hierarchy. Tells us that achievers will be motivated by jobs that offer personal responsibility, feedback, and moderate risks. | Tells us that high need achievers do not necessarily make good managers, since high achievers are more interested in how they do personally. |
| **Empirical support/ criticisms** | Research does not generally validate the theory. In particular, there is little support for the hierarchical nature of needs. Criticized for how data were collected and interpreted. | Not really a *theory* of motivation: Assumes a link between satisfaction and productivity that was not measured or demonstrated. | Ignores situational variables. | Mixed empirical support, but theory is consistent with our knowledge of individual differences among people. Good empirical support, particularly on needs achievement. |

What can we conclude from the needs theories? We can safely say that individuals do have needs, and that they can be highly motivated to achieve those needs. The types of needs, and their importance, vary by individual, and probably vary over time for the same individual as well. When rewarding individuals, you should consider their specific needs. Obviously, in a workplace, it would be difficult to design a reward structure that could completely take into account the specific needs of each employee. To get some ideas about the factors that might motivate you in the workplace, you might want to have a look at this chapter's Learning About Yourself Exercise on page 191.

Golfers such as Prince Edward Island's Lorie Kane illustrate the effectiveness of the expectancy theory of motivation, where rewards are tied to effort and outcome. Players on the LPGA tour are paid strictly according to their performance, unlike members of professional team sports. Kane had her best season ever in 1997, ranking eleventh in money winnings and earning over $425 964, with eight top-10 finishes. In 1998 she ranked eight in money winnings and in 1999 she ranked fifth. As Kane has put more effort into her play, she has been increasing her earnings each year.

## Process Theories of Motivation

While needs theories address the different needs that individuals have that could be used for motivational purposes, process theories focus on the broader picture of how someone can set about motivating another individual. Within the process theories, we cover expectancy theory and goal-setting theory (and its application, management by objectives). We focus greater attention on these process theories to help you understand how you might actually motivate either yourself or someone else.

### Expectancy Theory

Currently, one of the most widely accepted explanations of motivation is Victor Vroom's **expectancy theory**.[4]

From a practical perspective, expectancy theory says that an employee will be motivated to exert a high level of effort when he or she believes that effort will lead to a good performance; that a good performance will lead to organizational rewards, such as a bonus, a salary increase, or a promotion; and that the rewards will satisfy the employee's personal goals. The theory, therefore, focuses on the three relationships illustrated in Exhibit 4-2:

- *Effort-performance relationship* (commonly referred to as expectancy): The probability perceived by the individual that exerting a given amount of effort will lead to performance. Employees are sometimes asked to do things for which they do not have the appropriate skills or training. When that is the case, they will be less motivated to try hard, because they already believe that they will not be able to accomplish the task that is expected of them.

**expectancy theory**
The strength of a tendency to act in a certain way depends on the strength of an expectation that the act will be followed by a given outcome and on the attractiveness of that outcome to the individual.

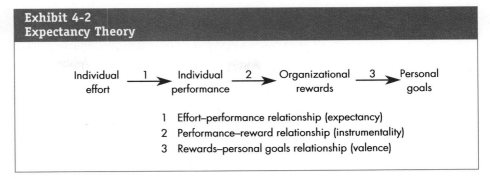

**Exhibit 4-2
Expectancy Theory**

1 Effort–performance relationship (expectancy)
2 Performance–reward relationship (instrumentality)
3 Rewards–personal goals relationship (valence)

- *Performance-reward relationship* (commonly referred to as instrumentality): The degree to which the individual believes that performing at a particular level will lead to the attainment of a desired outcome. In particular, will the performance be acknowledged by those who have the power to allocate rewards? In a 1997 study by the Angus Reid Group, only 44 percent of employees said that the workplace recognizes employees who excel at their job.[5] Therefore, one possible source of low employee motivation is the belief, of the employee, that no matter how hard he or she works, the likelihood of one's performance being recognized is low.

- *Rewards-personal goals relationship* (commonly referred to as valence): The degree to which organizational rewards satisfy an individual's personal goals or needs and the attractiveness of those potential rewards for the individual. Unfortunately, many managers are limited in the rewards they can distribute, which makes it difficult to individualize rewards. Moreover, some managers incorrectly assume that all employees want the same thing, thus overlooking the motivational effects of differentiating rewards. In either case, employee motivation is submaximized because the specific need the employee has is not being met through the reward structure.

In summary, the key to expectancy theory is the understanding of an individual's goals and the linkage between effort and performance, between performance and rewards, and, finally, between the rewards and individual goal satisfaction. As a contingency model, expectancy theory recognizes that there is no universal principle for explaining everyone's motivations. Additionally, just because we understand what needs a person seeks to satisfy does not ensure that the individual believes that high performance will lead to the satisfaction of these needs.

Does expectancy theory work? Although it has its critics,[6] most of the research evidence is supportive of the theory.[7] Some critics suggest that the theory tends to be more valid in situations where effort-performance and performance-reward linkages are clearly perceived by the individual.[8] A 1997 Angus Reid poll on workplace attitudes suggests that many individuals do not perceive a high correlation between performance and rewards in their jobs.[9] If organizations actually rewarded individuals for performance rather than according to such criteria as seniority, effort, skill level, and job difficulty, then the theory's validity might be considerably greater. However, rather than invalidating expectancy theory, this criticism can be used in support of the theory, for it explains why a significant segment of the workforce exerts low levels of effort in carrying out job responsibilities.

Exhibit 4-3 gives some suggestions for what a manager can do to increase the motivation of employees, using insights from expectancy theory.

**Why do some managers do a better job of motivating people than others?**

### Exhibit 4-3
### Steps to Increasing Motivation, Using Expectancy Theory

| Expectancy Theory Relationships | What Manager Can Do |
|---|---|
| Effort-performance relationship (expectancy) | • Make sure that employees have the skills required to do the task assigned.<br>• Provide training.<br>• Assign reasonable tasks and goals. |
| Performance-reward relationship (instrumentality) | • Be sure to actually observe or recognize performance.<br>• Be sure to deliver rewards as promised. |
| Rewards-personal goals relationship (valence) | • Determine from employees what kinds of rewards they value.<br>• Be sure that the rewards given are things that are valued. |

To more fully appreciate how expectancy theory might apply in the workplace, this chapter's Case Incident on page 195 has you consider what happens when expected rewards are withdrawn.

## Goal-Setting Theory

You've heard the phrase a number of times: "Just do your best. That's all anyone can ask for." But what does "do your best" mean? Do we ever know if we've achieved that vague goal? Might you have done better in your high school English class if your parents had said, "You should strive for 75 percent or higher on all your work in English" rather than telling you to "do your best"? The research on **goal-setting theory** addresses these issues, and the findings, as you will see, are impressive in terms of the effects of goal specificity, challenge, and feedback on performance.

**goal-setting theory**
The theory that specific and difficult goals lead to higher performance.

In the late 1960s, Edwin Locke proposed that intentions to work toward a goal are a major source of work motivation.[10] That is, goals tell an employee what needs to be done and how much effort will need to be expended.[11] The evidence strongly supports the value of goals. More to the point, we can say that specific goals increase performance; that difficult goals, when accepted, result in higher performance than do easy goals; and that feedback leads to higher performance than does nonfeedback.[12]

Goal-setting theory is not inconsistent with expectancy theory. The goals can be considered the effort-performance link, that is, the goals determine what must be done. Feedback can be considered the performance-reward relationship, where the individual's efforts are recognized. Goal setting does not explicitly address rewards or the worth of the rewards, although the implication is that the achievement of the goals will result in intrinsic satisfaction (and may of course be linked to external rewards).

**MANAGEMENT BY OBJECTIVES**  As a manager, how do you make goal setting operational? The best answer to that question is: Implement a management by objectives (MBO) program. **Management by objectives** (MBO) emphasizes participatively set goals that are tangible, verifiable, and measurable.

**management by objectives (MBO)**
A program that encompasses specific goals, participatively set, for an explicit time period, with feedback on goal progress.

MBO's appeal undoubtedly lies in its emphasis on converting overall organizational objectives into specific objectives for organizational units and individual members. As depicted in Exhibit 4-4, the organization's overall objectives are translated into specific objectives for each succeeding level (that is, divisional, departmental, individual) in the organization. Because individual employees and/or lower-unit managers jointly participate in setting their own goals, MBO works from the "bottom up" as well as from the "top down." The result is a hierarchy of objectives that links objectives at one level to those at the next level. And for the individual employee, MBO provides specific personal performance objectives.

There are four ingredients common to MBO programs. These are goal specificity, participative decision making, an explicit time period, and performance feedback.[13]

The objectives in MBO should be concise statements of specific accomplishments by the individual. It's not adequate, for example, to merely state a desire to cut costs, improve service, or increase quality. Such desires must be converted into tangible objectives that can be measured and evaluated. To cut departmental costs *by seven percent*, to improve service by ensuring that all telephone orders are processed *within 24 hours of receipt*, or to increase quality by keeping returns to *less than one percent of sales* are examples of specific objectives.

**Exhibit 4-4
Cascading of Objectives**

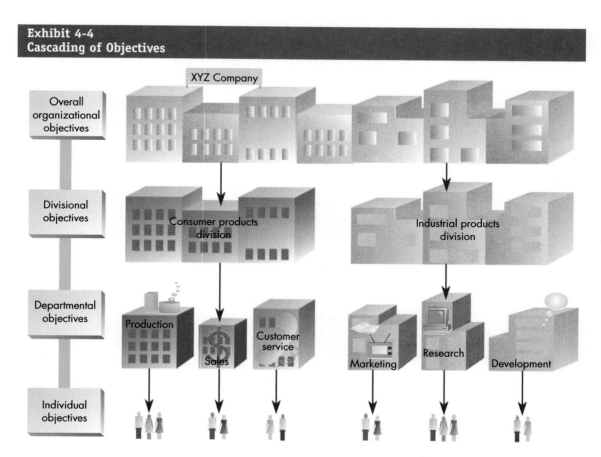

Why is it important for me to participate in goal setting with my manager?

Unlike in goal setting, the objectives in MBO are not unilaterally set by the manager and then assigned to employees. MBO replaces imposed goals with participatively determined goals. The manager and employee jointly choose the goals and agree on how they will be measured. The evidence is mixed regarding the superiority of participative over assigned goals.[14] In some cases, participatively set goals elicited superior performance, while in other cases, individuals performed best when assigned goals by their manager. But a major advantage of participation may be in increasing acceptance of the goal itself as a desirable one to work toward.[15] As we noted, resistance is greater when goals are difficult. If people participate in goal setting, they are more likely to accept even a difficult goal than if their boss arbitrarily assigns it.[16] The reason is that individuals are more committed to choices in which they have a part. Participative goals may have no superiority over assigned goals when acceptance is taken as a given. Allowing individuals to participate in goal setting also has the additional feature that the person is more likely to "buy in" to the goals, which may improve his or her overall commitment to the task.

Under MBO, each objective has a specific time period in which it is to be completed. Typically the time period is three months, six months, or a year. So managers and employees have specific objectives and stipulated time periods in which to accomplish them.

The final ingredient in an MBO program is feedback on performance. MBO seeks to give continuous feedback on progress toward goals. Ideally, this is accomplished by giving ongoing feedback to individuals so they can monitor and correct their own actions. This is supplemented by periodic managerial evaluations, when progress is reviewed. This applies at the top of the organization as well as at the bottom. The vice-president of sales, for instance, has objectives for overall sales and for each of his or her major products. He or she will monitor ongoing sales reports to determine progress toward the sales division's objectives. Similarly, district sales managers have objectives, as does each salesperson in the field. Feedback in terms of sales and performance data is provided to let these people know how they are doing. Formal appraisal meetings also take place at which managers and employers can review progress toward goals and further feedback can be provided.

You'll find MBO programs in many business, health care, educational, government, and nonprofit organizations.[17] MBO's popularity should not be construed to mean that it always works. There are a number of documented cases where MBO has been implemented but failed to meet management's expectations.[18] A close look at these cases, however, indicates that the problems rarely lie with MBO's basic components. Rather, the culprits tend to be factors such as unrealistic expectations regarding results, lack of flexibility when the situation or the environment changes, lack of top-management commitment, and an inability or unwillingness by management to allocate rewards based on goal accomplishment. Many of these problems can be resolved with realistic implementations of goal-setting theory.

Be aware that goal-setting theory and MBO programs are well adapted to countries such as Canada and the United States because the key components align reasonably well with North American cultures. These theories assume that employees will be reasonably independent (not too high a score on power distance), that managers and employees will seek challenging goals (low in uncertainty avoidance), and that performance is considered important by both (high in quantity of life). So don't expect goal setting and

MBO to necessarily lead to higher employee performance in countries such as Portugal or Chile, where the opposite conditions exist.

## Motivating for Specific Organizational Goals

**Ben Moss Jewellers**
www.benmoss.com

**National Post**
www.nationalpost.com

Thus far we have discussed the general framework for motivating individuals, using process theories as our guide. Let's now turn to specific practices in organizations, to see how organizations link their goals and individual performance to rewards. Below we examine three specific practices that organizations use (employee recognition, variable-pay programs, and stretch targets) to show how organizations motivate individuals to achieve organizational goals.

### Motivating to Show People Matter

Expectancy theory tells us that a key component of motivation is the link between performance and reward, that is, having one's behaviour recognized. In today's highly competitive global economy, most organizations are under severe cost pressures. That makes recognition programs particularly attractive. Recognizing an employee's superior performance often costs little or no money.

Employee recognition programs send a signal to employees that good performance is appreciated. In 1998, the *Financial Post* recognized Theresa Butcher, its head librarian, as an Unsung Hero for all of her help to reporters and editors over many years.

Employee recognition programs can take numerous forms. For example, *The Globe and Mail* gives the Stephen Godfrey Prize for Newsroom Citizenship. Virginia Galt won that award in 1998 for all of her work to improve relations among her colleagues. In addition to the prize, her accomplishments were printed in *The Globe and Mail*, giving her even more public recognition of her citizenship.[19] Brent Tepel, CEO of Winnipeg-based Ben Moss Jewellers, Ltd., which has 31 stores across Canada, and employs more than 290 people, phones his top-performing employees every Monday afternoon.[20] Other ways of recognizing performance include sending personal notes or e-mails for good performance, putting employees on prestigious committees or sending them for training, and giving someone an assistant for a day to help clear backlogs.

Employee recognition may reduce turnover in organizations, particularly that of good employees. When executives were asked the reasons why employees left for jobs with other companies, 34 percent said it was due to lack of recognition and praise, compared with 29 percent who mentioned low compensation, 13 percent who mentioned limited authority, and eight percent who cited personality problems.[21]

## Motivating for Improved Productivity

When organizations want to improve productivity, they can consider a variety of incentive schemes. Some of these are more individually based, and others rely on either team members or all of the organizational members to work together toward productivity goals. The rewards used are all forms of **variable-pay programs**. What differentiates these forms of compensation from more traditional programs is that they do not pay a person only for time on the job or seniority. Instead, a portion of an employee's pay is based on some individual and/or organizational measure of performance. Unlike more traditional base-pay programs, variable pay is not an annuity. There is no guarantee that just because you made $60 000 last year, you'll make the same amount this year. With variable pay, earnings fluctuate up and down with the measure of performance.[22]

According to a 1996 Conference Board of Canada report, roughly two-thirds of nonmanagement employees are affected by variable-pay plans, up from one-third in 1992. These programs are more predominant for nonunionized workers. As Conference Board's Prem Benimadhu notes, "Canadian unions have been very allergic to variable compensation."[23] Under variable-pay programs, individuals are not guaranteed specific annual wages, making their work experience a bit more risky. Union members, and others as well, may worry that they can't predict their wages ahead of time, thus leading to uncertainty. Union members are also concerned that factors out of their control might affect the extent to which bonuses are possible.

At Markham, Ontario-based Pillsbury Canada Limited, employees are eligible for the company's Value Incentive Plan, rewarding performance at three levels: corporate, team, and individual.[24] If the corporate financial target is met or exceeded, a percentage-of-pay bonus results. Employees can earn additional percentage-of-pay bonuses if teams meet their own goals, based on cost reduction, and quality and profit improvement are above the corporate plan. Finally, employees can earn an equivalent percentage-of-pay bonus if they meet two or three key individual objectives. While the theory behind individual, team, and company-wide variable incentive plans is similar, we review the programs separately to underscore the importance of linking rewards to the appropriate level of performance. Not all organizations have such comprehensive three-level programs as Pillsbury Canada. We briefly describe some examples of incentives at these different levels of the organization below.

**INDIVIDUAL-BASED INCENTIVES** Piece-rate wages are one of the earliest forms of individual performance pay. Piece-rates have long been popular as a means for compensating production workers. In **piece-rate pay plans**, workers are paid a fixed sum for each unit of production completed. When an employee gets no base salary and is paid only for what he or she produces, this is a pure piece-rate plan. People who work at baseball parks selling peanuts and soft drinks frequently are paid this way. They might get to keep 25 cents for every bag of peanuts they sell. If they sell 200 bags during a game, they make $50. If they sell only 40 bags, their take is a mere $10. Many organizations use a modified piece-rate plan, where employees earn a base hourly wage plus a piece-rate differential. So a legal typist might be paid $8.50 an hour plus 30 cents per page. Such modified plans provide a floor under an employee's earnings, while still offering a productivity incentive. When salespeople are paid commissions based on sales, this is another form of individual-based incentives.

**variable-pay programs**
A portion of an employee's pay is based on some individual and/or organizational measure of performance.

**Pillsbury**
www.pillsbury.com

**piece-rate pay plans**
Workers are paid a fixed sum for each unit of production completed.

**Molson**
www.iam.ca

Bonuses are another form of individual incentive, and these are becoming increasingly popular in Canada.[25] They are in use by such companies as Toronto-based Molson, Ontario Hydro, and the Bank of Montreal. In 1992, typical senior executives in Canada could expect bonuses equal to 9.7 percent of their salaries. In 1996, that had almost doubled to 18.5 percent. The growth rate in bonuses was even greater among hourly employees. The average bonus for an hourly worker during the same time period went from 1.1 percent of base pay to 5.8 percent.

Despite this evidence, incentive-based pay is more common in the United States than in Canada, both in terms of the proportion of employees covered and the size of the rewards.[26] This occurs because Canada has a more unionized economy, a relative lack of competition, and a large public sector. In Ottawa, until recently the only bonus for federal civil servants was $800 for those in bilingual jobs. More recently the federal and provincial governments have been introducing bonuses for public-sector workers. For instance, the Alberta government, which already had performance bonuses for senior administrators and for colleges and universities, introduced them for public school teachers and administrators in March 1999.[27] And in August 1999, federal executives were introduced to a new bonus plan, with their performance evaluated against business plans and corporate priorities of their departments. Their pay will also depend on their "leadership qualities, ethics, values and how they treat their staff."[28]

Federal executives and managers will be paid in a similar manner to the private sector starting in 2001. This is a radical change for these employees, who will only be eligible for performance pay—worth 10 to 20 percent of their salaries—if they meet or exceed the commitments and goals they specify each year in their performance contract. These will be lump-sum awards, and will have to be re-earned each year.

**gainsharing**
An incentive plan where improvements in group productivity determine the total amount of money that is allocated.

**Hydro-Quebec**
www.hydroquebec.com

**profit-sharing plans**
Organization wide programs that distribute compensation based on some established formula designed around a company's profitability.

**Avcorp Industries**
www.avcorp.com

**Town of Ajax**
www.townofajax.com

**IKEA**
www.ikea.ca/content

**employee stock ownership plans (ESOPs)**
Company-established benefit plans in which employees acquire stock as part of their benefits.

**Castek**
www.castek.com

**GROUP-BASED INCENTIVES** The variable-pay program that has received the most attention in recent years is undoubtedly **gainsharing**.[29] This is a formula-based group incentive plan. Improvements in group productivity—from one period to another—determine the total amount of money that is to be allocated. The division of productivity savings can be divided between the company and employees in any number of ways, but 50-50 is fairly typical.

Gainsharing differs from profit-sharing, discussed below. Gainsharing focuses on productivity gains rather than profits, and so it rewards specific behaviours that are less influenced by external factors. Employees in a gainsharing plan can receive incentive awards even when the organization isn't profitable. Gainsharing's popularity was initially limited to large unionized manufacturing companies,[30] such as Molson Breweries and Hydro-Québec. This has changed in recent years, with smaller companies, such as Delta, BC-based Avcorp Industries, and governments, such as Ontario's City of Ajax and Kingston Township, also introducing gainsharing.

**ORGANIZATIONAL-BASED INCENTIVES** **Profit-sharing plans** are organization-wide programs that distribute compensation based on some established formula designed around a company's profitability. These can be direct cash outlays or, particularly in the case of top managers, allocated as stock options. When you read about executives such as the CEO at Disney earning over $280 million in one year, almost all of this comes from cashing in stock options previously granted based on company profit performance. Profit-sharing is not confined to top executives only, however. IKEA divided every penny rung up in its 152 stores on October 8, 1999, among its 44 000 staffers in 28 countries. This amounted to $2500 for each employee.[31]

One thing to note about profit-sharing programs is that they focus on past financial results. They don't necessarily focus employees on the future. They also tend to ignore factors such as customer service and employee development, which may not be seen as having a direct link to profits. In addition, some industries, such as the financial services industry, have a somewhat cyclical nature, and during slumping economic periods such companies would offer few or no rewards. From an expectancy theory perspective, employees will be less motivated during these times because they know that the likelihood of receiving significant bonuses is low. This is consistent with expectancy theory, which argues that for employees to be motivated, performance must be directly linked to rewards.

One of the ways to induce employees to have values more like those of top management is to make them owners of their firms. **Employee stock ownership plans (ESOPs)**[32] are company-established benefit plans in which employees acquire stock as part of their benefits. Canadian companies lag far behind the United States in the use of ESOPs because Canada's tax environment is less conducive. Nevertheless, a recent survey of high-tech firms in Canada found that of those with ESOPs in place, 90 percent said the ESOPs helped attract employees, and 75 percent said the ESOPs helped retain employees. These firms also noted increased productivity, competitiveness, and employee interest, which they attributed to the ESOPs.[33]

Toronto-based Castek Software Factory Inc., an information technology firm specializing in the design and delivery of strategic business software, uses an ESOP.[34] Seventy-five percent of Castek's eligible employees are shareholders; turnover is under 10 percent, and employee satisfaction is 80 percent. Toronto-based Richardson Greenshields of Canada Ltd., an investment dealer to retail and institutional clients across Canada and around the world,

introduced an ESOP plan after the Canadian investment industry had suffered a loss of 35 percent of its employees in just four years (between 1989 and 1994). In the face of those losses, Richardson Greenshields wanted to move its organizational climate from one of survival to one of customer-centred service.[35] Since the introduction of this and other incentive plans, Richardson Greenshields's return on capital over the next five years consistently exceeded the industry average.

The research on ESOPs indicates that they increase employee satisfaction.[36] But their impact on performance is less clear. For instance, one study compared 45 ESOPs against 238 conventional companies.[37] The ESOPs outperformed the conventional firms both in terms of employment and sales growth. But other studies have shown disappointing results.[38]

ESOPs have the potential to increase employee job satisfaction and work motivation. But for this potential to be realized, employees need to psychologically experience ownership.[39] That is, in addition to merely having a financial stake in the company, employees need to be kept regularly informed on the status of the business and also have the opportunity to exercise influence over the business. The evidence consistently indicates that it takes ownership *and* a participative style of management to achieve significant improvements in an organization's performance.[40]

Pay-for-performance means that if you don't perform as well, you don't get paid as much. John Cleghorn, Chairman and CEO of Royal Bank, may have learned this the hard way. He took home $1.1 million less in 1998 than in 1997, because, as he says, "1998 was a good year, but 1997 was a phenomenal year." By permitting pay to drop when performance drops, the Royal Bank emphasizes that there is a clearcut link between performance and reward.

**LINKING PRODUCTIVITY-RELATED INCENTIVES TO MOTIVATION THEORIES** Variable pay is probably most compatible with expectancy theory predictions. Specifically, under these plans, individuals should perceive a strong relationship between their performance and the rewards they receive, and thus be more motivated. The evidence is consistent with the theory. For example, one study of 400 manufacturing firms found that those companies with wage incentive plans achieved 43 to 64 percent greater productivity than those without such plans.[41] Studies generally support that organizations with profit-sharing plans have higher levels of profitability than those without.[42] Similarly, gainsharing has been found to improve productivity in a majority of cases and often has a positive impact on employee attitudes.[43] An American Management Association study of 83 companies that used gainsharing also found, on average, that grievances dropped 83 percent, absences fell 84 percent, and lost-time accidents decreased by 69 percent.[44]

Among firms that haven't introduced performance-based compensation programs, common concerns tend to surface.[45] Managers worry over what should constitute performance and how it should be measured. They have to overcome the historical attachment to cost-of-living adjustments and the belief that they have an obligation to keep all employees' pay in step with inflation. Other barriers include salary scales keyed to what the competition is paying, traditional compensation systems that rely heavily on specific pay

**IBM Canada**
www.ibm.ca

grades and relatively narrow pay ranges, and performance appraisal practices that produce inflated evaluations and expectations of full rewards. Of course, from the employees' perspective, the major concern is a potential drop in earnings. Pay for performance means employees must share in the risks as well as the rewards of their employer's business. They are not guaranteed the same salary year in and year out under this system. After record profits in 1998, IBM Canada's employees received bonuses averaging 10 percent of their salary, which was considerably more than they received the previous year in bonuses. However, individual employees received more or less than 10 percent, depending on their own performance. Top performers in top units could receive as much as a 20 percent bonus.[46]

**WHAT ABOUT TEAMWORK?** Incentive pay, especially when it is awarded to individuals, can have negative effects in terms of group cohesiveness and productivity, and in some cases may not offer significant benefits to a company.[47] For example, Montreal-based National Bank of Canada offered a $5 employee bonus for every time employees referred clients for loans, mutual funds, or other bank products. But the bonus upset workers enough that the plan was abandoned after just three months.[48] The tellers complained that the bonus caused colleagues to compete against one another. Meanwhile, the bank could not determine whether the referrals actually generated new business.

**Canadian Labour Congress**
www.clc-ctc.ca

Organized labour is, in general, cool to the idea of pay-for-performance. Andrew Jackson, senior economist for the Canadian Labour Congress in Ottawa, explains that "it hurts co-operation in the workplace. It can lead to competition between workers, speeding up the pace of work. It's a bad thing if it creates a stressful work environment where older workers can't keep up."[49] Still, not all unions share that view, and the benefits and drawbacks on incentive plans must be carefully considered before implementation. In the HR Implications feature on pages 180-187, we examine the process of performance evaluation to illustrate the procedures organizations take in order to be able to link pay with productivity.

If an organization wants a group of individuals to function as a "team" (which will be defined in Chapter 6), emphasis needs to be on team-based rewards, rather than individual rewards. We will discuss the nature of team-based rewards in Chapter 6. Exhibit 4-5, which compares the strengths and weaknesses of variable pay, skill-based pay (discussed in more detail below), and team rewards, indicates some of the considerations to be addressed.

## Motivating for Other Types of Performance

In recent years, organizations have been paying for performances other than strict productivity. Compensation experts Patricia Zingheim and Jay Schuster note the following activities that merit additional compensation:[50]

- Commissions beyond sales: Commissions might be determined by customer satisfaction and/or sales team outcomes, such as meeting revenue or profit targets.
- Leadership effectiveness: This form of reward may include employee satisfaction, or measures of how the manager handles his or her employees.
- New goals: Rewards go to all employees who contribute to specific organizational goals, such as customer satisfaction, cycle time, or quality measures.

**Exhibit 4-5**
**Comparing Various Pay Programs**

| Approach | Strengths | Weaknesses |
|---|---|---|
| **Variable pay** | • Motivates for performance.<br>• Cost-effective.<br>• Makes a clear link between organizational goals and individual rewards. | • Individuals do not always have control over factors that affect productivity.<br>• Earnings vary from year to year.<br>• Can cause unhealthy competition among employees. |
| **Skill-based pay** | • Increases the skill levels of employees.<br>• Increases the flexibility of the workforce.<br>• Can reduce the number of employees needed. | • Employers may end up paying for unneeded skills.<br>• Employees may not be able to learn some skills, and thus feel demotivated. |
| **Team-based pay** | • Encourages individuals to work together effectively.<br>• Promotes goal of team-based work. | • Difficult to evaluate team performance sometimes.<br>• Equity problems could arise if all members paid equally. |

- Knowledge workers in teams: Pay is linked to the performance of knowledge workers and/or professional employees who work on teams.
- Competency and/or skills: This rewards abstract knowledge or competencies, for example, knowledge of technology, the international business context, customer service or social skills.

Below we address skill-based pay, to give you an idea of how these other forms of pay-for-performance might be implemented.

**skill-based pay**
Pay levels are based on how many skills employees have or how many jobs they can do.

**WHAT ARE SKILL-BASED PAY PLANS? Skill-based pay** is an alternative to job-based pay. Rather than having an individual's job title define his or her pay category, skill-based pay (also sometimes called competency-based pay) sets pay levels on the basis of how many skills employees have or how many jobs they can do.[51] The Shell Chemical Plant in Sarnia, Ontario (now part of Montell Canada Ltd.) has 10 knowledge clusters and 40 modules, each in specified specialty skill areas. Shift workers there earn increased pay when they demonstrate competence in one additional knowledge cluster and four skill modules in their chosen specialty area.[52] At Edmonton's Shell Canada complex, skill acquisition by team members is encouraged. Each operational team is organized so that it has the necessary skill sets and information to do the job. Each operator on a team is responsible for learning and using technical skills, leadership skills (particularly self-managing), and at least one specialty skill (which may include environment, safety, maintenance, or training) as required by the team. Pay is based on the level of skill mastered, and employees are required to reach the top level of pay for each skill.

Shell Canada holds teams responsible for developing and improving skills. Thus, the training system that helps employees acquire these skills was designed and is maintained by the operators and training specialists on each team.[53] At Polaroid Corporation, the highest pay a machine operator can earn is $14 an hour. However, because the company has a skill-based pay plan, machine operators have the chance to broaden their skills. If they master additional skills, such as material accounting, maintenance of equipment, and quality inspection, they can earn up to a 10 percent premium. If they can learn some of their manager's skills, they can earn even more.[54]

> **Should employees be paid on the basis of their skills?**

What's the appeal of skill-based pay plans? From management's perspective: flexibility. Filling staffing needs is easier when employee skills are interchangeable. This is particularly true today as many organizations cut the size of their workforce. Downsizing requires more generalists and fewer specialists. While skill-based pay encourages employees to acquire a broader range of skills, there are also other benefits. It facilitates communication across the organization because people gain a better understanding of others' jobs. It lessens dysfunctional "protection of territory" behaviour. Where skill-based pay exists, you're less likely to hear the phrase, "It's not my job!" The increased use of skills as a basis for pay appears particularly strong among organizations facing aggressive foreign competition and those companies with shorter product life cycles and speed-to-market concerns.[55] Also, skill-based pay is moving from the shop floor to the white-collar workforce, and sometimes as far as the executive suite.[56]

Skill-based pay additionally helps to meet the needs of ambitious employees who confront minimal advancement opportunities. These people can increase their earnings and knowledge without a promotion in job title. Finally, skill-based pay appears to lead to performance improvements. A number of studies have investigated the use and effectiveness of skill-based pay. The overall conclusion, based on these studies, is that skill-based pay is expanding and that it generally leads to higher employee performance and satisfaction. The Conference Board of Canada reported that about 10 percent of Canadian firms were using skill-based pay in 1996.[57] A broad-based survey of *Fortune 1000* firms found that 60 percent of those with skill-based pay plans rated their plans as successful or very successful in increasing organizational performance, while only six percent considered them unsuccessful or very unsuccessful.[58]

But what about the down side of skill-based pay? People can "top out"—learning all the skills the program calls for them to learn. This can frustrate employees after they've become challenged by an environment of learning, growth, and continual pay raises. Skills can become obsolete. When this happens, management should consider rewarding employees who learn appropriate new skills. There is the problem, however, created by paying people for acquiring skills for which there may be no immediate need. This happened at IDS Financial Services.[59] The company found itself paying people more money even though there was little immediate use for their new skills. IDS eventually dropped its skill-based pay plan and replaced it with one that equally balanced individual contribution and gains in work-team productivity. Finally, skill-based plans don't address level of performance. They deal only with the issue of whether someone can perform the skill. For some skills, such as checking quality or leading a team, level of performance may be equivocal. While it's possible to assess how well employees perform each of the skills and combine that with a skill-based plan, that is not an inherent part of skill-based pay.

**LINKING SKILL-BASED PAY PLANS TO MOTIVATION THEORIES** Skill-based pay plans are consistent with several motivation theories. Because they encourage employees to learn, expand their skills, and grow, they are consistent with needs theories. Among employees whose lower-order needs are substantially satisfied, the opportunity to experience growth can be a motivator.

Paying people to expand their skill levels is also consistent with research on the achievement need. High achievers have a compelling drive to do things better or more efficiently. By learning new skills or improving the skills they already hold, high achievers will find their jobs more challenging.

Skill-based pay may also have equity implications. When employees make their input-outcome comparisons, skills may provide a fairer input criterion for determining pay than factors such as seniority or education. To the degree that employees perceive skills as the critical variable in job performance, the use of skill-based pay may increase the perception of equity and help optimize employee motivation.

## Motivating for Organizational Change

**stretch target**
A virtually unachievable goal that forces an organization to significantly alter its processes.

We noted in Chapter 1 that Canadian organizations, as well as organizations throughout the world, are facing increasing pressure to make changes that accommodate doing business in the global environment. **Stretch targets** are a relatively new technique for improving organizational effectiveness.[60] Stretch targets are virtually unachievable goals that force organizations to significantly alter their processes. "The purpose of stretch targets is not only to allow employees to stretch their abilities to new levels, but also to change the organization's competitive position by dynamically altering its business processes."[61]

The purpose of stretch targets is to encourage employees to think beyond ordinary solutions to extraordinary solutions. With hard but achievable goals, employees tend to focus simply on working harder and longer. With stretch targets, employees have to look at ways to completely redesign the task. For example, Motorola used to take six weeks at the end of each year to close out its books, but wanted to reduce this time to less than a week, which seemed an impossible target when first set. However, with cross-divisional teams of employees, the time was reduced to four days. The team assigned to the task examined every part of the process, and then "made detailed process charts, developed strategies to speed processes, decided where to cut out unnecessary steps, and designed programs to standardize information flows."[62] 3M used stretch targets to increase the number and speed of new products introduced to the market after its sales growth increased only one percent in 1993. Previously, 25 percent of sales were generated by products introduced within the past five years. The stretch target raised this to 30 percent of sales to be generated by products introduced within the last four years.[63] Montreal-based Canadian National (CN) Railways' supply management department, GE, and Union Pacific Railroad are other examples of companies using stretch targets.

To some extent, stretch targets are inconsistent with what researchers in general have found about goal setting, that is, when goals are perceived as too difficult, individuals will not try to attain the goals. However, in the case of Motorola described above, as well as other examples of stretch targets, the "virtually impossible" goals were accomplished. A recent study

**What happens when people are faced with "impossible" tasks?**

**CN Railway**
www.cn.ca

explains the conditions under which stretch targets can work: autonomy, empowerment, structural accommodation, and bureaucratic immunity.[64]

Teams that successfully handle stretch targets need to be autonomous and empowered. *Autonomy* refers to the ability of the group working on the goal to control the situation themselves. Teams that were successful were also *empowered*, which meant that they had power over resources and power to propose and implement changes as necessary. When teams feel that they have autonomy and are empowered, they are more willing to accept stretch targets.[65]

Successful stretch-target teams must also know that top management supports them. Successful teams experienced the *structural accommodation* of their organizations, meaning they had unlimited access to information and the power to change organizational procedures if necessary. For instance, the Motorola team working on reducing end-of-year reporting time was allowed to change the reporting forms the various departments used so that they could simplify procedures. In essence, when organizations make structural accommodations to their teams, they are telling the teams to do whatever it takes to accomplish their tasks.

Successful teams with stretch targets were also given *bureaucratic immunity*. This meant that they were not subject to the bureaucratic review process of other projects, and reported only to top management. Therefore the "stretch" team is not subject to the power politics of other groups during the time that they are trying to accomplish their targets. "At Motorola, for example, the words 'if it looks feasible' or 'if we can get groups to agree, we will make the change' were never spoken."[66] Teams were told to do whatever it took, and they would be supported. This inspired their creativity and eliminated their fear of failure.

While any organization might be interested in achieving stretch targets, it must undergo important culture changes in order to provide the support that individuals need to achieve those targets. However, creating the environment that allows teams to work on stretch targets can result in significant changes in the way that processes within the organization are carried out. Teams that receive the structural support needed often do not require significant additional rewards because the actual process of working toward the goal is a major reward in itself.

## Motivating to Accommodate Individual Differences

Not everyone is motivated by money. Not everyone wants a challenging job. In order to maximize employees' motivation, employers must design work schedules, compensation plans, benefits, physical work settings, and the like to reflect employees' varied needs. For example, some employees are concerned with having an extended medical plan and enough life insurance to support a young family in the case of death. Other employees might not need extended medical and life insurance and might be more interested in extra vacation time and long-term financial benefits such as a tax-deferred savings plan. Or employees with family responsibilities might appreciate child and eldercare, flexible work hours, and job sharing. New immigrants might prefer flexible leave policies to make an extended return trip to their homelands. Other employees who are going to school might like to vary their work schedules from semester to semester. In the Working With Others

Exercise on page 192, you have the opportunity to consider how to apply flexible benefits in a variety of individual circumstances.

Some employees have also been willing to negotiate for job security in lieu of additional pay, particularly in the union sector. For Randy Somerville, a letter carrier in Saint John, New Brunswick, a reasonable assurance of stable employment is worth a lot more than a bigger paycheque. His contract provides only a one-percent pay increase per year, but it also contains a no-layoff clause and a guarantee that he will not be relocated outside a 40-kilometre radius. "The way most people look at it here," says Somerville, age 34, "we're just lucky to have a job."[67] Different types of jobs create additional motivational concerns for employees. For instance, motivating temporary workers is different from motivating professionals. Below we examine some of the unique problems faced in trying to motivate professional employees, contingent workers, low-skilled service workers, people doing highly repetitive tasks, and executives. We also look at the role that personality might play in determining appropriate rewards.

## One-Size Doesn't Fit All

**flexible benefits**
Employees tailor their benefit program to meet their personal needs by picking and choosing from a menu of benefit options.

**Flexible benefits** allow employees to choose a benefits package that is individually tailored to their own needs and situation. Such benefits replace the traditional "one-benefit-plan-fits-all" programs that have dominated organizations for more than 50 years.[68] Flexible benefits are consistent with expectancy theory's thesis that organizational rewards should be linked to each individual employee's goals. These benefits thus individualize rewards by allowing each employee to choose the compensation package that best satisfies his or her current needs.

In a flexible benefits plan, an organization sets up a flexible spending account for each employee, usually based on some percentage of his or her salary, and then a price tag is put on each benefit. Options might include extended medical plans with high deductibles; extended medical plans with low or no deductibles; hearing, dental, and eye coverage; vacation options; extended disability; a variety of savings and pension plans; life insurance; university tuition reimbursement plans; and extended vacation time. Employees then select benefit options until they have spent the dollar amount in their account.

At Richardson Greenshields, employees choose benefits that meet their needs. They can even transfer unused flex credits to a registered retirement savings plan (RRSP). This feature of the benefits program is particularly appealing to younger employees, who often have less need for more family-centred benefits. Instead, they can enjoy watching their retirement savings accumulate even faster.

Flexible benefits offer both benefits and drawbacks for the employees and employers involved. For employees, flexibility is attractive because they can tailor their benefits and levels of coverage to their own needs. The major drawback, from the employees' perspective, is that the costs of individual benefits often go up, so fewer total benefits can be purchased.[69] For example, low-risk employees keep the cost of medical plans low for everyone. As they are allowed to drop out, the high-risk population occupies a larger segment and the costs of medical benefits go up. From the organization's perspective, the good news is that flexible benefits often produce savings. The bad news for the organization is that these plans are more cumbersome for management to oversee and often more expensive to administer.

French computer services giant CAP Gemini Sogeti motivates its 17 000 software engineers and technicians by giving them the tools they need to tackle and solve challenging problems. The company's intranet, called Knowledge Galaxy, puts critical resources and expertise within every employee's reach, keeping the global workforce current on the latest technologies. CAP Gemini even installed an Internet café at its Paris headquarters, shown here, so employees can surf the Net during their breaks.

**Lucent**
www.lucent.ca

## Motivating Professionals

In contrast to a generation ago, the typical employee today is more likely to be a highly trained professional with a college or university degree than a blue-collar factory worker. These professionals receive a great deal of intrinsic satisfaction from their work. They tend to be well paid. So what, if any, special concerns should you be aware of when trying to motivate a team of engineers at Nortel, a software designer at Corel, or a group of accountants at Deloitte & Touche?

Carol Stephenson, president and CEO of Toronto-based Lucent Technologies Canada, describes the challenge that managing professionals presents. "I have very bright people in this company and I'm managing knowledge and intellectual capability. Knowledge workers like to be autonomous. They are more concerned with content of work rather than their place on the organization chart. If you manage by command and control, people will leave."[70]

What motivates professionals? Money and promotions typically are low on their priority list. Why? Because they tend to be well paid and they enjoy what they do. In contrast, job challenge tends to be ranked high. They like to tackle problems and find solutions. Their chief reward in their job is the work itself. Professionals also value support. They want others to think what they're working on is important. Although this may be true for all employees, professionals tend to be more focused on their work as their central life interest, while nonprofessionals typically have other interests outside of work that can compensate for needs not met on the job.

Here are a few guidelines to keep in mind if you're trying to motivate professionals. Provide them with ongoing challenging projects. Give them autonomy to follow their interests and allow them to structure their work in ways that they find productive. Reward them with educational opportunities—training, workshops, attending conferences—that allow them to keep current in their field. Also reward them with recognition, and ask questions and engage in other actions that demonstrate to them you're sincerely interested in what they're doing.

An increasing number of companies are creating alternative career paths for their professional/technical people, allowing employees to earn more money and status without assuming managerial responsibilities. At Merck & Co., IBM, and AT&T, the best scientists, engineers, and researchers gain titles such as research fellow and senior scientist. Their pay and prestige are comparable to those of managers but without the corresponding authority or responsibility.[71] At Montreal-based Advanced Bioconcept, head Lloyd Segal wants his scientists to have fun and avoid drudgery: "I reduce, wherever I can, the amount of hierarchy and bureaucracy and paperwork, because it's no fun. And it's not great leverage to have my best scientists spending half a day filling out expense forms."[72]

## Motivating Contingent Workers

One of the more comprehensive changes taking place in organizations is the addition of temporary or contingent employees. As downsizing has eliminated millions of "permanent" jobs, an increasing number of new openings are for part-time, contract, and other forms of temporary workers. The number of Canadians relying on temporary jobs grew by 24 percent—from 799 000 to 2.7 million—between 1989 and 1998.[73] Because these contingent employees lack the security or stability that permanent employees have, they don't always identify with the organization or display the commitment that other employees do. Temporary workers also are typically provided with no pension plans and few or no extended health-care benefits, such as dental care, prescription plans, and vision care, or similar benefits.[74]

There is no simple solution for motivating temporary employees. For those who prefer the freedom of a temporary status that permits them to attend school, care for their children, or have the flexibility to travel or pursue other interests, the lack of stability may not be an issue. For instance, in 1998, 68 percent of youths worked part-time because they were going to school, while 20 percent of adult women worked part-time to allow them the time to take care of children. However, about 23 percent of youths, 30 percent of adult women, and 44 percent of adult men working part-time would have preferred to work full-time in 1998.[75] The motivational challenge is in dealing with temporary employees who are in this status involuntarily.

What will motivate involuntarily temporary employees? An obvious answer is the opportunity for permanent status. In those cases where permanent employees are selected from the pool of temporaries, temporaries will often work hard in hopes of becoming permanent. A less obvious answer is the opportunity for training. The ability of a temporary employee to find a new job is largely dependent on his or her skills. If the employee sees that the job he or she is doing can help develop saleable skills, then motivation is increased. From an equity standpoint, there are repercussions from mixing permanent and temporary workers where pay differentials are significant.[76] When temps work alongside permanent employees who earn more, and get benefits too, for doing the same job, the performance of temps is likely to suffer. Separating such employees or converting all employees to a variable-pay or skill-based pay plan might help to lessen this problem.

## Motivating Low-Skilled Service Workers

For a variety of reasons, many young people are struggling to begin a career. Unemployment among 15- to 24-year-olds is around 14.4 percent across Canada, about twice the national average rate of unemployment. Service-sector jobs, which were once regarded as either a temporary after-school job or a stepping stone to a career, have become permanent positions for many young people. These jobs are often referred to as "McJobs." Pay levels are often little above minimum wage.

Here, then, is one of the most challenging motivation problems in industries such as retailing and fast food: How do you motivate individuals who are making very low wages and who have little opportunity to significantly increase their pay in either their current jobs or through promotions?

Starbucks' outlets in Vancouver discovered what can happen when they don't pay attention to the concerns of these workers.[77] In the summer of 1996, the company introduced an unpopular computerized scheduling system. Then management rolled back a 50-cent increase to the starting wage, to match the new BC provincial minimum of $7 an hour. Finally, management cut "T-shirt Fridays," the only day each week when staff could wear Starbucks T-shirts, rather than the regulation dress shirts. For Steve Emery, a then-26-year-old employee of the coffee giant, that was the last straw. "The taboo on T-shirts triggered us," explains Emery. In July 1997, 110 workers at nine Starbucks outlets in the Vancouver area joined the Canadian Auto Workers Union, an action they took to protest Starbucks' policies towards its workers.

We noted in Chapter 1 that many employees working in these low-skilled service jobs feel that they don't get the respect they deserve from their employers. In response to similar employee concerns, Taco Bell has tried to make some of its service jobs more interesting and challenging, but with limited results.[78] It has experimented with incentive pay and stock options for cashiers and cooks. These employees also have been given broader responsibility for inventory, scheduling, and hiring. But over a four-year period, this experiment has only reduced annual turnover from 223 percent to 160 percent.

What choices are left? Unless pay and benefits are significantly increased, high dissatisfaction is probably inevitable in these jobs. This can be somewhat offset by widening the recruiting net, making these jobs more appealing, and raising pay levels. Trying to understand the needs of these employees might help motivate them better. Nontraditional approaches might also be beneficial. To illustrate, Judy Wicks has found that celebrating employees' outside interests has dramatically reduced turnover among wait staff at her White Dog Café in Philadelphia.[79] For instance, to help create a close and family-like work climate, Wicks holds an annual event at which employees exhibit their art, read their poetry, explain their volunteer work, and introduce their new babies.

## Executive Compensation

> **Ever wonder what motivates executives?**

Throughout our discussion of motivation and compensation, we have shown that academic theory argues that rewards should be consistent with performance. In theory, the relationship between the pay given to heads of organizations and organizational performance should also be linked. A 1999 Conference Board of Canada survey of 276 Canadian companies found that 87 percent reported paying executives incentives based on performance in 1998. In addition, about 85 percent of the publicly traded companies in Canada offer long-term incentives, with stock options being the most popular.[80] "Yet, for the most part, academic researchers have been stymied in their search for a meaningful association between executive pay and firm performance."[81]

For instance, *Canadian Business* recently compared the total cash compensation (salary plus long-term bonus) of 154 executives of companies on the TSE 300 and correlated that with the sum of annual shareholder returns covering the three-year period from 1994 to 1996.[82] In doing this, the survey uncovered a number of executives who were overpaid (stock prices were mediocre at best, while pay was high), as well as a group who were underpaid (stock prices soared, while pay was modest). Exhibit 4-6 identifies executives in both groups. In general, the underpaid executives worked at relatively young mining and high-tech companies, while the overpaid often

### Exhibit 4-6
### Canada's Overpaid and Underpaid Chief Executives

| Rank | Executive | Company | Total Pay 1994-96 | Share Increase (%) | Relative Index* |
|------|-----------|---------|-------------------|--------------------|-----------------|
| **Top Overpaid Chief Executives** | | | | | |
| 1 | Donald Walker, president and CEO | Magna International Inc. | $7 918 000 | 22 | 0.46 |
| 2 | Michael Brown, president | Thomson Corp. | $7 219 000 | 114 | 0.61 |
| 3 | Richard Thomson, chair and CEO (now chair) | Toronto-Dominion Bank | $6 161 000 | 65 | 0.62 |
| 4 | Matthew Barrett, chair and CEO | Bank of Montreal | $6 200 000 | 73 | 0.63 |
| 5 | Ted Rogers, president and CEO | Rogers Communications Inc. | $3 227 000 | −53 | 0.63 |
| **Top Underpaid Chief Executives** | | | | | |
| 1 | Michael McInnis, president (now chair) | International Curator Resources Ltd. | $258 000 | 3972 | 210.6 |
| 2 | Eugene Melnyk, chair | Biovail Corp. International | $936 000 | 1801 | 42.8 |
| 3 | Grenville Thomas, president | Aber Resources Ltd. | $285 000 | 401 | 36.9 |
| 4 | Rubin Osten, president, CEO and chair | PC Docs Group International Inc. | $1 145 000 | 1151 | 17.8 |
| 5 | Greg Noval, president and CEO | Canadian 88 Energy Corp. | $428 000 | 216 | 12.6 |

* Relative Index = the sum of the value of $100 invested after one year, two years, and three years, divided by total pay, multiplied by 10 000.
Source: Adapted from David Berman, "Do They Deserve It?", *Canadian Business*, September 26, 1997, pp. 31-33.

headed the larger, more established companies of Canada. In the Ethical Dilemma Exercise on page 194, you can examine your own feelings about the amount of compensation executives receive. This lack of correspondence between executive compensation and firm performance applies as much to US as to Canadian firms.

Determining how to reward executives has been an issue of concern for many companies, researchers, and even executives. When the annual executive compensation lists are published each year in both Canada and the United States, discussion focuses on those leaders who are compensated well but who head companies that have performed poorly. As a result, in recent years boards of directors have moved more towards giving their executives less fixed salary and emphasizing more rewards linked to performance.

Many argue, however, that financial measures (for example, net earnings and return on investment) encourage short-term quick fixes rather than long-term strategic goals.[83] For instance, executives might forego risky strategic investment opportunities because these are more likely to have long-term payoffs, or they might reduce human resource expenditures aimed at developing a highly trained and productive workforce, concentrating instead on maximizing short-term profitability and shareholder wealth.[84]

Not everyone agrees, however, that the answer is to simply offer rewards based on nonfinancial measures. Some find that these measures, which might consider such factors as product quality and customer satisfaction, are far too subjective and can be easily manipulated by the CEO.

So which approach do companies prefer? In recent years, there has been a definite trend toward pay-for-performance, but not all companies pay that way. A recent study conducted in the United States assembled data from 317 large companies (annual sales ranging from $7.7 million to $32.1 billion). The researchers found that 36 percent of companies used nonfinancial measures. Those most likely to do so were companies pursuing strategies of innovation and new product development. Researchers have found that pay and performance are much more closely linked when firms have a dominant shareholder who can discipline top managers. Researchers have also discovered that executives of larger firms earn more than those working in smaller firms. This particular fact could provide the incentive for executives to diversify into areas that are not consistent with a firm's core competencies in order to increase the size of the firm.

In determining executive compensation, different firms will have different needs. For instance, a firm that values innovation should offer its executives incentives that reward investment in research and development. Exhibit 4-7 indicates some considerations for linking the strategy and performance of firms with executive compensation.

In looking at executive compensation, you might be interested to know that while stock options are commonly used in Canadian, US, and UK firms, these are not used worldwide to compensate executives. In fact, many European countries and Japan have had regulations that forbade offering stock options to executives. Consequently, executives in many other countries are paid on salary, with some very recent exceptions (changes in laws in Japan in 1997 and Germany in 1998 allowed some forms of stock options).

European executives, and even Canadian executives, are often paid considerably less than their American counterparts. For instance, in 1997, the average Canadian CEO received $500 000, while the average American CEO received $1 million.[85] The perks in some countries have often been higher, however: "European and Japanese companies have been very open-handed with executive perquisites—from $1-million golf-club memberships in Japan to chauffeured Rolls-Royces and lavish expense accounts in the U.K."[86] These perks do not necessarily compensate for the effect of stock options that many Canadian and American executives receive. For instance, Peter Munk, chair and fomer chief executive of Barrick Gold, exercised $33.6 million in stock options in 1998. That was an exceptionally high amount, by all accounts. However, in 1997 Northern Telecom's CEO, Jean Monty, exercised $12.298 million in options and David O'Brien, Canadian Pacific's CEO, exercised $3.39 million in options.[87]

**Northern Telecom**
www.nortelnetworks.com

> **Exhibit 4-7**
> **Strategies for Compensating Executives**
>
> - *Identify the firm's strategy and a decision-making horizon appropriate to it.* The appropriate decision-making horizon can be determined by identifying the key success factors necessary to achieve and sustain a competitive advantage. For example, high levels of current cash flow and operational efficiency are potentially key success factors for a cost leader. Long-term customer loyalty and innovation are probably key success factors for a firm pursuing a differentiation strategy.
>
> - *Identify an appropriate measure of firm performance.* If current cash flow and operational efficiency are key success factors, then accounting performance is probably the best measure. If innovation is a key factor, then market-based measures are probably most appropriate.
>
> - *Link CEO pay to the appropriate performance measure.* If short-term accounting performance is the goal, then firms might adopt an annual bonus scheme. If longer-term market performance is the objective, then a firm might grant restricted shares or stock options.
>
> - *Consider the timing of rewards.* A deferred compensation plan may be appropriate for companies pursuing intermediate- or long-term strategies.
>
> Source: David Berman, "Do They Deserve It?", *Canadian Business*, September 26, 1997, pp. 31-33.

These changes in executive compensation packages for executives outside of North America will present an interesting research comparison as these international firms switch from salaries for executives to performance-based compensation.

## Personality Differences and Motivation

Several consultants have recently suggested that managers should provide recognition and rewards that fit an employee's personality.[88] According to this notion, people can be divided into four distinct temperaments: Preservers, Strategists, Mavericks, and Energizers. These temperaments can be related to the types identified by the Myers-Briggs Type Indicator (MBTI), which we discussed in Chapter 2.

Exhibit 4-8 summarizes the values and needs of these four types, and suggests the kind of recognition each type prefers.

Preservers, who like to see their loyalty to the organization acknowledged, are best rewarded with direct thanks, such as letters of praise, copies of which are also forwarded to their managers and placed in the employees' file. They will also be motivated by such tangible awards as plaques or T-shirts acknowledging specific accomplishments. Strategists are the visionaries and change agents of the organization. They like autonomy, so giving them the opportunity to set their own work schedules and choose some of their assignments would motivate them. Also, providing opportunities to learn, through classes, journal subscriptions, and other activities, will motivate strategists. Mavericks like to negotiate and troubleshoot for the organization. Situations where they are allowed to negotiate their own

**Exhibit 4-8**
**Linking Rewards to Temperament**

| Temperament | Values | Like to be recognized for | How they like to be recognized |
|---|---|---|---|
| Preservers | Dependability Responsibility Stability | Follow-through Adherence to rules and policies Dedication and loyalty | Tangible thanks for steady work |
| Strategists | Intelligence and innovation Competence Tireless effort | Ideas Knowledge Competence | Freedom to learn, or explore a challenge |
| Mavericks | Great skill Grace under pressure Risk-taking action | Responsiveness Cleverness Ingenuity | Unusual reward for successful and risky action |
| Energizers | Commitment and passion Independent thinking Sincerity and kindness | Ideas Uniqueness Championing change | Social recognition for synergizing a team |

Source: B. Nelson, L. Good, and T. Hill, "Motivate Employees According to Temperament," *HR Magazine*, March 1997, p. 52.

reward are almost as important as the reward itself. Energizers are the "big-picture" people in the organization, and they are concerned with fairness and people issues. Personal notes and rewards that acknowledge interpersonal skills are most motivating to them.

Linking rewards to personality types is an intriguing idea, though there is little concrete empirical evidence that backs it up. However, the basic idea, that not every individual or employee will be motivated by the same rewards, allows managers to consider a range of rewards that are more appropriate to different employees.

## Responses to the Reward System

To a large extent, motivation theories are about rewards, in that the theories suggest that individuals have needs, and they will exert effort in order to have those needs met. The needs theories specifically identify those needs. Goal-setting and expectancy theories portray processes by which individuals act and then receive desirable rewards (intrinsic or extrinsic) for their behaviour. The extensive discussion of specific organizational goals and how rewards are linked to the goals helps you to see how these theories can be applied.

There are, however, additional factors to consider in the motivation process, specifically the issue of fairness in rewards. Equity theory suggests that individuals not only respond to rewards, but also evaluate and interpret them, which further complicates the motivation process. Fair process goes one step further, suggesting that employees are sensitive to a variety of fairness issues in the workplace that extend beyond the reward system but also affect employee motivation.

Organizations should also be careful in making sure that what they reward sends the right message to employees. As we'll see below, some organizations tell employees to do one thing but reward them for doing quite another. Employees respond to this mixed message by doing those things that are rewarded, not necessarily those things that are desired.

## Equity Theory

| How important is fairness? |
| :-- |

Jane Pearson graduated last year from university with a degree in accounting. After interviews with a number of organizations on campus, she accepted an articling position with one of the nation's largest public accounting firms and was assigned to their Edmonton office. Jane was very pleased with the offer she received: challenging work with a prestigious firm, an excellent opportunity to gain valuable experience, and the highest salary any accounting major at her university was offered last year—$4150 a month. But Jane was the top student in her class; she was ambitious and articulate, and fully expected to receive a commensurate salary.

Twelve months have passed since Jane joined her employer. The work has proved to be as challenging and satisfying as she had hoped. Her employer is

Because of the financial crisis in Russia, many firms do not have money to pay their employees. Instead of receiving a salary, employees get paid in goods the factories produce. Velta Company, a bicycle maker in Russia, gives workers one bicycle a month instead of a paycheck. Workers then have to sell their bike for cash or barter it for food. Some workers deal with the inequity of not getting a salary by using a different referent. "We are luckier than people over at the chemical plant," says one Velta employee. "At least our factory gives us something we can sell."

extremely pleased with her performance; in fact, she recently received a $200-a-month raise. However, Jane's motivational level has dropped dramatically in the past few weeks. Why? Her employer has just hired a new graduate from Jane's university, who lacks the one-year experience Jane has gained, for $4400 a month—$50 more than Jane now makes! It would be an understatement to describe Jane as irate. Jane is even talking about looking for another job.

**equity theory**
Individuals compare their job inputs and outcomes with those of others and then respond so as to eliminate any inequities.

Jane's situation illustrates the role that equity plays in motivation. **Equity theory** suggests that employees make comparisons of their job inputs (that is, effort, experience, education, competence) and outcomes (that is, salary levels, raises, recognition) relative to those of others. We perceive what we get from a job situation (outcomes) in relation to what we put into it (inputs), and then we compare our outcome-input ratio with the outcome-input ratio of relevant others. This is shown in Exhibit 4-9. If we perceive our ratio to be equal to that of the relevant others with whom we compare ourselves, a state of equity is said to exist. We perceive our situation as fair—that justice prevails. When we see the ratio as unequal, we experience this as inequity. For instance, consider you wrote a case analysis for your accounting professor and spent 18 hours researching and writing it up. Your classmate spent six hours preparing the same analysis. Each of you received a mark of 75 percent. It is likely that you would perceive this as unfair, as you worked considerably harder (that is, exerted more effort) than your classmate. J. Stacy Adams has proposed that those experiencing inequity are motivated to do something to correct it.[89] Thus, you might be inclined to spend considerably less time on your next assignment for your accounting professor.

In the case of the accounting assignment, the obvious referent is your classmate. However, in the workplace, the referent that an employee selects when making comparisons adds to the complexity of equity theory. Evidence indicates that the referent chosen is an important variable in equity theory.[90] There are four referent comparisons that an employee can use:

- *Self-inside*: An employee's experiences in a different position inside his or her current organization.

- *Self-outside*: An employee's experiences in a situation or position outside his or her current organization.

- *Other-inside*: Another individual or group of individuals inside the employee's organization.

- *Other-outside*: Another individual or group of individuals outside the employee's organization.

**Exhibit 4-9**
**Equity Theory**

| Ratio Comparisons* | Perception |
|---|---|
| $O/I_A < O/I_B$ | Inequity due to being under-rewarded |
| $O/I_A = O/I_B$ | Equity |
| $O/I_A > O/I_B$ | Inequity due to being over-rewarded |

*Where $O/I_A$ represents the employee; and $O/I_B$ represents relevant others.

Employees might compare themselves with friends, neighbours, co-workers, colleagues in other organizations, or past jobs they have had. Which referent an employee chooses will be influenced by the information the employee holds about referents, as well as by the attractiveness of the referent. This has led to focusing on four moderating variables—gender, length of tenure, level in the organization, and amount of education or professionalism.[91]

Research shows that both men and women prefer same-sex comparisons. Research also demonstrates that women are typically paid less than men in comparable jobs and have lower pay expectations than men for the same work. For instance, Statistics Canada reports that in 1996 the gap between the full-time wages of men and women was the lowest ever, with women earning, on average, 73 cents for every dollar earned by men.[92] So a woman who uses another woman as a referent tends to have a lower comparative standard for pay than a woman who uses a man as the referent. If women are to be paid equally to men in comparable jobs, the standard of comparison—as used by both employees and employers—needs to be expanded to include both sexes. Employees with short tenure in their current organizations tend to have little information about others inside the organization, so they rely on their own personal experiences. On the other hand, employees with long tenure rely more heavily on co-workers for comparison. Upper-level employees, those in the professional ranks, and those with more education, tend to be more cosmopolitan and have better information about people in other organizations. Therefore, these types of employees will make more other-outside comparisons.

| What can I do if my salary is "unfair"? |

Based on equity theory, when employees perceive an inequity, they can be predicted to make one of six choices:[93]

- *Change their inputs* (for example, don't exert as much effort)
- *Change their outcomes* (for example, individuals paid on a piece-rate basis can increase their pay by producing a higher quantity of units of lower quality)
- *Adjust perceptions of self* (for example, "I used to think I worked at a moderate pace but now I realize that I work a lot more slowly than everyone else.")
- *Adjust perceptions of others* (for example, "Mike's job isn't as desirable as I previously thought it was.")
- *Choose a different referent* (for example, "I may not make as much as my brother-in-law, but I'm doing a lot better than my Dad did when he was my age.")
- *Leave the field* (for example, quit the job)

The theory establishes the following propositions relating to inequitable pay:

- *Given payment by time, over-rewarded employees will produce more than will equitably paid employees.* Hourly and salaried employees will generate high quantity or quality of production in order to increase the input side of the ratio and bring about equity.
- *Given payment by quantity of production, over-rewarded employees will produce fewer, but higher-quality, units than will equitably paid employees.* Individuals paid on a piece-rate basis will increase their effort to achieve equity, which can result in greater quality or quantity.

However, increases in quantity will only increase inequity, since every unit produced results in further overpayment. Therefore, effort is directed toward increasing quality rather than increasing quantity.

- *Given payment by time, under-rewarded employees will produce less or poorer quality of output.* Effort will be decreased, which will bring about lower productivity or poorer-quality output than that of equitably paid subjects.
- *Given payment by quantity of production, under-rewarded employees will produce a large number of low-quality units in comparison with equitably paid employees.* Employees on piece-rate pay plans can bring about equity because trading off quality of output for quantity will result in an increase in rewards with little or no increase in contributions.

These propositions have generally been supported, with a few minor qualifications.[94] First, inequities created by overpayment do not seem to have a very significant impact on behaviour in most work situations. Apparently, people have a great deal more tolerance of overpayment inequities than of underpayment inequities, or are better able to rationalize them. Second, not all people are equity sensitive. For example, there is a small part of the working population who simply do not worry about how their rewards compare with those of others. Predictions from equity theory are unlikely to be very accurate with these individuals.

These propositions also suggest that when organizations reward only senior managers after a year of increased profitability and performance, lower-level employees receive a powerful message. They learn that only shareholders and senior management matter. This can lead to employees withholding effort and initiative.

It is important to note that while most research on equity theory has focused on pay, employees seem to look for equity in the distribution of other organizational rewards. For instance, it's been shown that the use of high-status job titles, as well as large and lavishly furnished offices, may function as outcomes for some employees in their equity equation.[95]

In conclusion, equity theory demonstrates that, for most employees, motivation is influenced significantly by relative rewards, as well as by absolute rewards, but some key issues are still unclear.[96] For instance, how do employees handle conflicting equity signals, such as when unions point to other employee groups who are substantially *better off*, while management argues how much things have *improved*? How do employees define inputs and outcomes? How do they combine and weigh their inputs and outcomes to arrive at totals? When and how do the factors change over time? Yet, regardless of these problems, equity theory continues to offer some important insights into employee motivation.

## Fair Process and Treatment

Recent research has been directed at expanding what is meant by equity or fairness.[97] Historically, equity theory focused on **distributive justice**, or the perceived fairness of the *amount* and *allocation* of rewards among individuals. But people also care about **procedural justice**—the perceived fairness of the *process* used to determine the distribution of rewards (for example, having a voice in a decision, finding accuracy in decision making). And they care, too, about **interactional justice**—the quality of the interpersonal

**distributive justice**
Perceived fairness of the amount and allocation of rewards among individuals.

**procedural justice**
The perceived fairness of the process used to determine the distribution of rewards.

**interactional justice**
The quality of the interpersonal treatment received from another.

treatment received from a manager (for example, being treated sensitively, being provided an explanation for decisions). The evidence indicates that distributive justice has a greater influence on employee satisfaction than procedural justice, while procedural and interactional justice tend to affect an employee's organizational commitment, trust in his or her boss, and intention to quit.[98] Researchers have found that when managers and employees believed that the company's processes were fair, they were more likely to show a high level of trust and commitment to the organization. Employees engaged in negative behaviour when they felt the process was unfair.[99]

For example, employees at Volkswagen's Puebla, Mexico, plant staged a lengthy walkout *after* being offered a 20 percent raise because their union leaders had agreed to work-rule concessions without consulting them. The employees, even though happy about the raise, did not believe that the process leading to the change in the work rules was fair. By contrast, when Siemens-Nixdorf Informationssysteme (SNI), the largest European supplier of information technology, needed to reduce the workforce from 52 000 to 35 000 in 1994, the CEO met with 11 000 employees to explain the difficulties that SNI faced and ask for their help in reducing costs. Many employees did volunteer, often working after hours without pay. Within a year, SNI was operating profitably, and employee satisfaction had almost doubled. These examples are consistent with the findings of Princeton University economist Alan Blinder. Blinder found that "Changing the way workers are *treated* may boost productivity more than changing the way they are *paid*."[100]

Managers should consider openly sharing information on how allocation decisions are made, following consistent and unbiased procedures, and engaging in similar practices to increase the perception of procedural justice. With increased procedural and interactional fairness, employees are likely to view their managers and the organization as positive, even if they're dissatisfied with pay, promotions, and other personal outcomes. Moreover, while low outcomes from an equity calculation might lead to low job satisfaction, Daniel Skarlicki at UBC has found that these relationships are often complex. According to Skarlicki, it is when unfavourable outcomes are combined with unfair procedures or poor interpersonal treatment that resentment and retaliation (for example, theft, bad-mouthing, sabotage) are most likely.[101]

## Beware the Signals That Are Sent by Rewards

> **Ever wonder why employees do some strange things?**

In 1998, Vancouver's bus drivers claimed, on average, 18.6 sick days. Victoria's bus drivers were only out about 16.6 days on average.[102] Are Vancouver's driver's more likely to catch cold than Victoria's? While we don't have all the evidence, it is unlikely. Rather, differences in the way that sick days are paid may account for the differences. Victoria's drivers get paid in full for six sick days, no matter how they're taken. But once they take their second "sick time," Vancouver's drivers aren't paid unless they're off more than three days for their illness. So it makes sense for them to stay home sick longer.

Or consider Peter Gorelkin, who worked as a tractor operator planting grain at a farm in Siberia in the former Soviet Union.[103] His supervisor was paid by the number of hectares Gorelkin was able to plant. While the grain was supposed to be planted at a depth of six centimetres to ensure it would germinate, Gorelkin's supervisor insisted that the grain be planted at a depth of only three centimetres. The supervisor knew that a tractor set to plant at six centimetres could only cover four hectares per day, whereas at a setting of three centimetres, 10 hectares could be planted. As Gorelkin reports, "The fact that we were able to plant more land meant nothing directly to us trainees, but not only did it mean more pay for our supervisor, it also meant the possibility of a bonus at the end of the job. The fact that most of the seeds might not survive the spring did not disturb him at all."

Perhaps more often than we'd like, organizations engage in what has been called "the folly of rewarding A, while hoping for B."[104] Organizations do this when they hope that employees will engage in one type of behaviour, but they reward for another type. Hoping for the behaviour you're not rewarding is not likely to make it get carried out to any great extent. In fact, as expectancy theory suggests, individuals will generally perform in ways to raise the probability of receiving the rewards offered.

Exhibit 4-10 provides further examples of common management reward follies. A recent survey suggests that three themes seem to account for some of the biggest obstacles to ending this folly.[105] First, individuals are unable to break out of old ways of thinking about reward and recognition practices. This is demonstrated in such things as emphasizing quantifiable behaviours, to the exclusion of nonquantifiable behaviours; employees having an entitlement mentality (that is, they don't support changing the reward system because they are comfortable with the current behaviours that are rewarded); and management being reluctant to change the existing performance system. A second factor is that organizations often don't look at the big picture of their performance system. Consequently, rewards are allocated at subunit levels, with the result that units often compete against each other.

### Exhibit 4-10
### Management Reward Follies

| We hope for ... | But we reward ... |
| --- | --- |
| Teamwork and collaboration | The best team members |
| Innovative thinking and risk-taking | Proven methods and not making mistakes |
| Development of people skills | Technical achievements and accomplishments |
| Employee involvement and empowerment | Tight control over operations and resources |
| High achievement | Another year's effort |
| Long-term growth; environmental responsibility | Quarterly earnings |
| Commitment to total quality | Shipping on schedule, even with defects |
| Candour; surfacing bad news early | Reporting good news, whether it's true or not; agreeing with the manager, whether or not (s)he's right |

Source: Constructed from S. Kerr, "On the Folly of Rewarding A, While Hoping for B," *Academy of Management Executive*, vol. 9, no. 1, 1995, pp. 7-14; "More on the Folly," *Academy of Management Executive*, vol. 9, no. 1, 1995, pp. 15-16.

Finally, both management and shareholders often focus on short-term results, rather than rewarding employees for planning for longer ranges.

Organizations would do well to ensure that they do not send the wrong message when offering rewards. When organizations outline an organizational objective of "team performance," for example, but reward each individual according to individual productivity, this does not send a message that teams are valued. Or when a retailer tells commissioned employees that they are responsible for monitoring and replacing stock as necessary, employees are likely to concentrate, particularly in the short-term, on making sales rather than stocking the floor. Employees motivated by the promise of rewards will do those things that earn them the rewards they value.

Our discussion of executive compensation illustrates two other examples of possible folly. In linking executive compensation to performance, two measures of performance have often been used for executives: accounting–based incentives and stock market–based incentives. Accounting–based incentives focus on the short-term, and many expenditures that might have long-term benefit are treated as expenses in determining current accounting earnings. To reduce expenses (and thus raise earnings, leading to greater compensation), executives may choose to reduce expenditures for "research and development that are necessary for product and process innovation, those for advertising and promotion aimed at developing new markets, and those for continuing employee education and development."[106] Thus, rewarding executives on the basis of accounting measures may encourage executives to forego long-term strategies to minimize costs.[107]

On the other hand, stock market–based incentives for executives can also result in a similar folly with respect to rewarding A while hoping for B. Many institutional investors, such as mutual funds, insurance companies, and pension plans, are interested in high levels of current performance because of their own short-term reward schemes. But stock prices are affected by many external conditions that have little to do with the executive's performance on a day-to-day level. As a result, executives may decide to cut back on the risks they can control, hoping to keep share prices high. For instance, they may cut back on risky projects or diversify a firm's portfolio of business units, both of which could have long-term payoffs.[108]

These examples indicate that the way executive compensation is determined may lead to longer-term negative impacts if not monitored carefully. As mentioned above, it is probably important for the compensation of executives to include a mix of factors that account for both short-term performance and longer-term strategic decision making.

## Caveat Emptor: Motivation Theories Are Culture-Bound

Reward strategies that have been used successfully in Canada and the United States do not always work successfully in other cultures. Take, for instance, a study comparing sales reps at a large electronics company in the United States with one in Japan. The study found that while Rolex watches, expensive dinners, and fancy vacations were appropriate rewards for star performers in the United States, taking the whole sales team bowling was more appreciated in Japan. The study's authors found that "being a member of a successful team with shared goals and values, rather than financial rewards, is what drives Japanese sales representatives to succeed."[109]

In the former Soviet Union, the effect of rewards was similar to North American findings, for the most part. At a cotton mill factory located 140 kilometres northwest of Moscow, a small group of employees were given either highly valued extrinsic rewards (North American T-shirts with logos, children's sweatpants, tapes of North American music, and a variety of other North American articles) or praise and recognition. Both types of rewards significantly increased worker productivity, with more top-grade fabric produced when rewards were delivered. Interestingly enough, however, the rewards did not increase the productivity very significantly for those who worked the Saturday shift. These findings illustrate that while rewards can be used to increase productivity in the former Soviet Union, the conditions of the work also affect productivity. Because the Soviet workers did not want to work the Saturday shift, the rewards had less impact on their productivity.[110] Expectancy theory would tell us that the workers did not value the rewards offered for Saturday work enough that the rewards increased their productivity. These findings show that the job context itself is an important motivator. We will explore this issue further in Chapter 13.

In China, the reward structure is undergoing a fundamental shift. During the Cultural Revolution (1966-1976), equal pay for everyone, regardless of productivity, was the rule. Since 1978, however, there has been more openness toward paying for productivity.[111] However, it is still the case that some companies pay everyone a bonus, regardless of individual productivity, and there is debate among Chinese workers about the standards set for performance. When Dell Computer Corporation went to Xiamen, China, in August 1998 to produce computers for the Chinese market, they offered employees 200 shares of Dell stock, which was then trading at $60.[112] Three months later, with shares trading at $110, each employee had a paper gain of $10 000, roughly a year's salary for the average Xiamen worker. But the Chinese workers had no idea what stock options were. Once these were explained to them, the productivity increased. Nevertheless, Dell has had to deal with the Chinese expectation of employment for life, even though that is no longer a guarantee. Dell executives say "that at first a little 'reeducation' was necessary in Xiamen so that workers understood that their jobs depended on their performance."

One final study of rewards in the international context may be of particular interest due to the impact of the North American Free Trade Agreement (NAFTA) on work arrangements in North America. In a study of a US-owned manufacturing plant in Mexico, a researcher noted that Mexican workers prefer immediate feedback on their work, and thus a daily incentive system with automatic payouts for production exceeding quotas is preferable.[113] This is equivalent to piece-rate wages paid daily. Employers often add extra incentives that are meaningful to the workers, including weekly food baskets, bonuses for quality, and free meals, bus service, and daycare.

Why do our motivation theories perform less well when we look at their implementation in countries beyond Canada and the United States? Most current motivation theories were developed in the United States and so take for granted the cultural norms of that country.[114] That may account for why Canada and the United States rely more heavily on extrinsic motivating factors than some other countries.[115] Japanese and German firms rarely make use of individual work incentives.[116]

Many of the social-psychological theories of motivation rely heavily on the notion of motivating the individual, through individual rewards.

**Dell Computer Corporation**
www.dell.ca

Therefore they emphasize, particularly in an organizational context, the meaning of pay, and give little attention to the informal rewards that come from group norms and prestige from peers.[117] In contrast, "large Japanese firms take a much more active role in shaping employee motivation. They do this in part by turning small work groups and company ideology into official reward mechanisms with powerful consequences for individual motivation."[118] In other words, Japanese organizations do not emphasize motivating each individual one at a time, but rely more heavily on group processes providing motivation to employees.

The motivation theories also assume some consistency in needs across society. For instance, Maslow's need hierarchy argues that people start at the physiological level and then move progressively up the hierarchy in this order: physiological, safety, social, esteem, and self-actualization. This hierarchy, if it has any application at all, aligns well with American culture and reasonably well with Canadian culture. However, in countries such as Japan, Greece, and Mexico, where uncertainty avoidance characteristics are strong, security needs would be at the top of the need hierarchy. Countries that score high on quality-of-life characteristics—Denmark, Sweden, Norway, the Netherlands, and Finland—would have social needs on top.[119] We would predict, for instance, that group work will motivate employees more when the country's culture scores high on the quality-of-life criterion.

Equity theory has gained a relatively strong following in Canada and the United States. That's not surprising, since their reward systems assume that workers are highly sensitive to equity in reward allocations, and expect pay to be tied closely to performance. However, recent evidence suggests that in collectivist cultures, especially in the former socialist countries of Central and Eastern Europe, employees expect rewards to reflect their individual needs as well as their performance.[120] Moreover, consistent with a legacy of Communism and centrally planned economies, employees exhibited an entitlement attitude—that is, they expected outcomes to be *greater* than their inputs.[121] These findings suggest that Canadian- and US-style pay practices may need modification, especially in Russia and former Communist countries, in order to be perceived as fair by employees.

The findings from these various countries support the need to examine the internal norms of a country in developing an incentive system, rather than simply importing one that is used effectively in Canada and the United States.

## Motivation in Practice: Perhaps Rewards Are Overrated

**cognitive evaluation theory** Allocating extrinsic rewards for behaviour that had been previously intrinsically rewarded tends to decrease the overall level of motivation.

All of the theories we've covered suggest that rewards can be used to motivate employees by offering ways to meet their needs in exchange for performing activities consistent with organizational goals. However, several researchers suggest that the introduction of extrinsic rewards, such as pay, for work effort that had been *previously rewarding intrinsically* will tend to decrease the overall level of motivation.[122] This proposal—which has come to be called **cognitive evaluation theory**—has been extensively researched, and a large number of studies have been supportive.[123] Alfie Kohn, often cited for his work on rewards, argues that people are actually punished by rewards, doing inferior work when they are enticed by money, grades, or other incentives. His extensive review of incentive studies concluded that

Calgary-based Nova Chemical needed to cut absenteeism after it started seeing an absenteeism rate of about 10 percent during the week, and as much as 20 percent on Fridays. They started a lottery, where those with perfect attendance can enter a draw to earn $5000. Brian Bickley (shown here), chair of the Construction Owner's Association, notes that the program is working, "but we've found it can work for a short time and then you have to change it to something else." What Bickley has observed is consistent with cognitive evaluation theory's claim that extrinsic rewards may not be very motivating over the long term.

"rewards usually improve performance only at extremely simple—indeed, mindless—tasks, and even then they improve only quantitative performance."[124]

Historically, motivation theorists have generally assumed that intrinsic motivators are independent of extrinsic motivators. That is, the stimulation of one would not affect the other. But cognitive evaluation theory suggests otherwise. It argues that when extrinsic rewards are used by organizations as payoffs for superior performance, the intrinsic rewards, which are derived from individuals doing what they like, are reduced. In other words, when extrinsic rewards are given to someone for performing an interesting task, it causes intrinsic interest in the task itself to decline. For instance, while a taxi driver expects to be paid if he or she takes your best friend to the airport, you do not expect your friend to pay you if you volunteer to drive her to the airport. In fact, the offer of pay might diminish your pleasure in doing a favour for your friend.

Why would such an outcome occur? The popular explanation is that the individual experiences a loss of control over his or her own behaviour when it is being rewarded by external sources. This causes the previous intrinsic motivation to diminish. Extrinsic rewards can produce a shift—from an internal to an external explanation—in an individual's perception of causation of why he or she works on a task. If you're reading a novel a week because your contemporary literature instructor requires you to, you can attribute your reading behaviour to an external source. If you stop reading novels the moment the course ends, this is more evidence that your behaviour was due to an external source. However, if you find yourself continuing to read a novel a week when the course ends, your natural inclination is to say, "I must enjoy reading novels because I'm still reading one a week!"

If cognitive evaluation theory is valid, it should have major implications for managerial practices. It has been a truism among compensation specialists for years that if pay or other extrinsic rewards are to be effective motivators, they should be made contingent on an individual's performance. But, cognitive evaluation theorists would argue, this will only tend to decrease the internal satisfaction that the individual receives from doing the job. We have substituted an external stimulus for an internal stimulus. In fact, if cognitive evaluation theory is correct, it would make sense to make an individual's pay noncontingent on performance in order to avoid decreasing intrinsic motivation.

Although further research is needed to clarify some of the current ambiguity, the evidence does lead us to conclude that the interdependence of extrinsic and intrinsic rewards is a real phenomenon.[125] A large body of research shows that large external rewards can undermine the positive performance of employees.[126] When employees work for a large reward, they will explain their behaviour through that reward—"I did it for the money." However, in the absence of large rewards, employees are more likely to reflect on the interesting nature of the work or the positive benefits of being an organizational member to explain their behaviour. For example, when the University of British Columbia redesigned its MBA Core program several years ago, the five members of the original design team (Nancy Langton, your Vancouver-based author, was one of those members) met for many hours each week, far exceeding the course release time they were offered for the task. The explanation for this behaviour was that the team was charged with designing and implementing a new program, and that carried with it a great deal of responsibility *and* excitement. When organizations provide employees with intrinsically interesting work, they will often work longer and harder than one might predict from the actual external rewards.

In studies dating back to the 1940s, employees have always ranked other items, such as being shown appreciation for work done, feeling "in" on things, and having interesting work as being more important to them than their salaries.[127] Employees at both Southwest Airlines and AES, an independent producer of electrical power with offices in the United States, Argentina, China, Hungary, and other countries, indicated that they appreciated the positive working climates of these organizations more than the specific financial rewards they received.[128]

In his 1998 book, *The Human Equation,* Jeffrey Pfeffer of Stanford University, one of the leaders in the field of organizational behaviour, encourages organizations to examine the messages they are sending to employees through the rewards they offer. Pfeffer argues that relying exclusively on financial incentives in organizations does not work and notes that people will work hard if the atmosphere is fun. As he points out, "At Apple Computer in its early days, employees didn't work 80 or 90 hours a week to maximize the expected value of some discounted stream of future earnings or to maximize shareholder wealth; they did it because the work was fun and challenging and because they were changing how the world viewed personal computers."[129]

Of course, organizations cannot simply ignore financial rewards. When people feel they are being treated unfairly in the workplace, pay often becomes a focal point of their concerns. If tasks are dull or unpleasant, extrinsic rewards will probably increase intrinsic motivation.[130] Even when a job is inherently interesting, there still exists a powerful norm for extrinsic payment.[131] But creating fun, challenging, and empowered workplaces may do more for motivation and performance than focusing simply on the compensation system.

## Can We Just Eliminate Rewards?

We opened this chapter describing the Morton team's efforts for the "Punkin' Chunkin'" contest. We conclude this chapter by raising a thought-provoking discussion about the possibility of eliminating rewards and concentrating more on the design of the workplace, to make the work experience itself more motivating.

The pumpkin story illustrates a point made by Alfie Kohn in his book *Punished by Rewards*. He argues that "the desire to do something, much less to do it well, simply cannot be imposed; in this sense, it is a mistake to talk about motivating other people. All we can do is set up certain conditions that will maximize the probability of their developing an interest in what they are doing and remove the conditions that function as constraints."[132]

The pumpkin story also illustrates the type of commitment that would benefit many organizations, even though it's seldom found there. People will work hard if the job captures their passion and their imagination. They will put in much more energy and devotion than they would if they were simply waiting to be rewarded every step of the way, and they generally do not require a lot of supervision in those situations.

Based on his research and consulting experience, Kohn proposes ways that organizations can create a motivating environment in their workplace:

- *Abolish incentives.* Pay people generously and fairly, make sure people don't feel exploited, and then make sure that pay is not on their minds. This way people will be more able to focus on the goals of the organization, rather than having as their main goal their paycheque.

- *Re-evaluate evaluation.* Rather than making performance appraisals look and feel like a punitive effort—who gets raises, who gets promoted, who is told they're performing poorly—the performance evaluation system might be structured more like a two-way conversation to trade ideas and questions, done continuously, not as a competition. And the discussion of performance should not be tied to compensation. "Providing feedback that employees can use to do a better job ought never to be confused or combined with controlling them by offering (or withholding) rewards."[133]

- *Create the conditions for authentic motivation.* A noted economist recently summarized the evidence about pay-for-productivity as follows: "Changing the way workers are *treated* may boost productivity more than changing the way they are *paid*."[134] There is some consensus about what these conditions might be: help employees rather than put them under surveillance; listen to their concerns and think about problems from their viewpoint; and provide plenty of informational feedback so they know what they've done right and what they need to improve.[135]

- *Collaboration.* People are more likely to perform better in well-functioning groups where they can get feedback and learn from each other.[136] Therefore, it is important to provide the necessary supports to create well-functioning teams.

- *Content.* People are generally the most motivated when their jobs give them an opportunity to learn new skills, provide variety in the tasks that are performed, and enable them to demonstrate competence. Some of this can be fostered by carefully matching people to their jobs, and giving them the opportunity to try new jobs. It is also possible to raise the meaningfulness of many jobs (which we will discuss in Chapter 13).

  But what about jobs that don't seem inherently interesting? One psychologist suggested that in cases where the jobs are fundamentally unappealing, the manager might acknowledge frankly that the task is not fun, give a meaningful rationale for why it must be done, and then give people as much choice as possible in how the task is completed.[137] One sociologist studying a group of garbage collectors in San Francisco discovered that they were quite satisfied with their work.[138] Their satisfaction came from the way the work and the company were organized: Relationships among the crew were important, the tasks and routes were varied to provide interest, and the company was set up as a cooperative, so that each worker owned a share of the company, and thus felt "pride of ownership."

- *Choice.* "We are most likely to become enthusiastic about what we are doing—and all else being equal, to do it well—when we are free to make decisions about the way we carry out a task."[139] Extrinsic rewards (and punishments too) actually remove choice, because they focus us on rewards, rather than on tasks or goals. A variety of research suggests that burnout, dissatisfaction, absenteeism, stress, and coronary heart disease are related to situations where individuals did not have enough control over their work situations.[140] By choice we do not propose lack of management, but rather, involving people in the decisions that are to be made. A number of case studies indicate that participative management, when it includes full participation by everyone, is successful.[141]

These steps represent an alternative to simply providing more and different kinds of incentives to try to induce people to work more effectively. They suggest that providing the proper environment may be more important than the reward structure. It would be difficult for many organizations to implement these ideas immediately and expect that they would work. It would require managers who were willing to relinquish control and instead take on the job of coaching. It would require employees who truly believed that their participation and input mattered, and that might require breaking down some of the suspicion that employees feel when managers give directives to employees, rather than seek collaborative input. Nevertheless, these steps, when implemented, can lead to quite a different workplace than what we often see. Moreover, these issues suggest that sometimes it is not the type or amount of rewards that makes a difference as much as whether the work itself is intrinsically interesting.

# HR Implications

# Performance Evaluation

This chapter has demonstrated that there are a variety of incentives to encourage employees to perform in accordance with an organization's goals. One of the roles of the HR specialist in an organization is to determine how to actually evaluate that performance. We remind you that the use of performance appraisals should be carefully considered, and care should also be used in ensuring that the purpose of performance appraisals is understood by employees. In some organizations performance appraisals are used as coaching and learning devices, while in others they are strictly tied to the reward program. A 1997 survey of 2004 Canadian workers from a variety of industrial sectors by Watson Wyatt Worldwide, an international consulting firm, found that many employees distrusted the performance appraisal process. Among the key findings:[1]

- Only 60 percent said that they understood the measures used to evaluate their performance.

- Only 57 percent thought that their performance was rated fairly.

- Only 47 percent said that their managers clearly expressed goals and assignments.

- Only 42 percent reported regular, timely performance reviews.

- Only 39 percent reported that their performance review was helpful in improving their on-the-job performance.

- Only 19 percent reported a clear, direct, and compelling linkage between their performance and their pay.

Below we describe the performance appraisal process, to illustrate ways that individual resistance might be lessened.

## Performance Evaluation and Motivation

A vital component of the expectancy model is performance, specifically the effort-performance and performance-reward linkages.

But what defines *performance*? In the expectancy model, it's the individual's performance evaluation.

To maximize motivation, people need to perceive that the effort they exert leads to a favourable performance evaluation, and that the favourable evaluation will lead to the rewards that they value.[3]

Following the expectancy model of motivation, we can expect individuals to work considerably below their potential under the following circumstances: 1) if the objectives that employees are expected to achieve are unclear; 2) if the criteria for measuring those objectives are vague; 3) if the employees lack confidence that their efforts will lead to a satisfactory appraisal of their performance; and/or 4) if employees believe that there will be an unsatisfactory payoff by the organization when their performance objectives are achieved.

## What Do We Evaluate?

The criteria or criterion that management chooses to evaluate when appraising employee performance will have a major influence on what employees do. Two examples illustrate this point.

In a public employment agency, which served workers seeking employment and employers seeking workers, employment interviewers were appraised by the number of interviews they conducted. Consistent with the thesis that the evaluating criteria influence behaviour, interviewers emphasized the *number* of interviews conducted rather than the *placements* of clients in jobs.[2]

A management consultant specializing in police research noticed that, in one community, officers would come on duty for their shift, proceed to get into their police cars, drive to the highway that cut through the town, and speed back and forth along that highway for their entire shift. Clearly this fast cruising had little to do with good police work, but this behaviour made considerably more sense once the consultant learned that the community's City Council used kilometrage on police vehicles as an evaluative measure of police effectiveness.[3]

These examples demonstrate the importance of criteria in performance evaluation. This, of course, begs the question: What should management evaluate? The three most popular sets of criteria are individual task outcomes, behaviours, and traits.

**Individual Task Outcomes** If ends count, rather than means, then management should evaluate an employee's task outcomes. Using task outcomes, a plant manager could be judged on criteria such as quantity produced, scrap generated, and cost per unit of production. Similarly, a salesperson could be assessed on overall sales volume in his or her territory, dollar increase in sales, and number of new accounts established.

**Behaviours** In many cases, it's difficult to identify specific outcomes that can be directly attributable to an employee's actions. This is particularly true of employees in staff positions, and individuals whose work assignments are intrinsically part of a group effort. In the latter case, the group's performance may be readily evaluated, but the contribution of each group member may be difficult or impossible to identify clearly. In such instances, it is not unusual for management to evaluate the employee's behaviour. Drawing on the previous examples, behaviours of a plant manager that could be used for performance evaluation purposes might include promptness in submitting his or her monthly reports, or the leadership style that the manager exhibits. Pertinent salesperson behaviours could be average number of contact calls made per day or sick days used per year.

**Traits** The weakest set of criteria, yet one that is still widely used by organizations, is individual traits.[4] We say they are weaker than either task outcomes or behaviours because they are farthest removed from the actual performance of the job itself. Traits such as having "a good attitude," showing "confidence," being "dependable" or "cooperative," "looking busy," or possessing "a wealth of experience" may or may not be highly correlated with positive task outcomes, but only the naive would ignore the reality that such traits are frequently used in organizations as criteria for assessing an employee's level of performance.

## Who Should Do the Evaluating?

Who should evaluate an employee's performance? The obvious answer would seem to be his or her immediate manager! By tradition, a manager's authority has typically included appraising employees' performances. The logic behind this tradition seems to be that since managers are held responsible for their employees' performances, it only makes sense that these managers evaluate that performance. But that logic may be flawed. Others may actually be able to do the job better.

**Immediate Manager** As we implied, about 95 percent of all performance evaluations at the lower and middle levels of the organization are conducted by the employee's immediate manager.[5] Yet a number of organizations are recognizing the drawbacks to using this source of evaluation. For instance, many managers feel unqualified to evaluate the unique contributions of each of their employees. Others resent being asked to "play God" with their employees' careers. Additionally, many of today's organizations are using self-managed teams, telecommuting, and other organizing devices that distance managers from their employees. For this reason, an employee's immediate manager may not be a reliable judge of that employee's performance.

**Peers** Peer evaluations are one of the most reliable sources of appraisal data. Why? First, peers are close to the action. Daily interactions provide them with a comprehensive view of an employee's job performance. Second, using peers as raters results in a number of independent judgments. A boss can offer only a single evaluation, but peers can provide multiple appraisals. And the average of several ratings is often more reliable than a single evaluation. On the downside, peer evaluations can suffer from co-workers' unwillingness to evaluate one another and from biases based on friendship or animosity.

**Self-Evaluation** Having employees evaluate their own performance is consistent with values such as self-management and empowerment. Self-evaluations get high marks from employees themselves; they tend to lessen employees' defensiveness about the appraisal process; and they make excellent vehicles for stimulating job performance discussions between employees and their managers. However, as you might guess, they suffer from overinflated assessment and self-serving bias. Moreover, self-evaluations are often low in agreement with managers' ratings.[6] Because of these serious drawbacks, self-evaluations are probably better suited to developmental uses than evaluative purposes. There is some evidence that women are more likely to underestimate their performance than men. In addition, with increasing diversity in the workplace, there are some cultural differences in how self-evaluation might be handled.

**Immediate Subordinates** A fourth judgment source is an employee's immediate subordinates. For instance, Datatec Industries, a maker of in-store computer systems, uses this form of appraisal.[7] The company's president says it's consistent with the firm's core values of honesty, openness, and employee empowerment.

Immediate subordinates' evaluations can provide accurate and detailed information about a manager's behaviour because the evaluators typically have frequent contact with the evaluatee. The obvious problem with this form of rating is fear of reprisal from managers given unfavourable evaluations. Therefore, respondent anonymity is crucial if these evaluations are to be accurate.

**The Comprehensive Approach: 360-Degree Evaluations** The latest approach to performance evaluation is the use of 360-degree evaluations.[8] They provide performance feedback from the full circle of daily contacts that an employee might have, ranging from mailroom workers to customers to managers to peers (see Exhibit 4-11). The number of appraisals can be as few as three or four evaluations, or as many as 25; most organizations collect five to 10 per employee. Hudson's Bay Company has used 360-degree evaluations with their managers who are sent to a three-week professional development course at the University of British Columbia.

What's the appeal of 360-degree evaluations? They fit well into organizations that have introduced teams, employee involvement, and Total Quality Management (TQM) programs. By relying on feedback from co-workers, customers, and employees, these organizations are hoping to give everyone more of a sense of participation in the review process and gain more accurate readings on employee performance.

The main concern with 360-degree evaluations is that it can be difficult to consolidate and make sense of the variety of information from all of the sources.[9] A related question is whether different evaluators should be asked to evaluate different aspects of the individual's performance, rather than all evaluators asked to evaluate the same things. Some research has shown that there can be inconsistencies across raters, when this appraisal system is used. [10]

## Methods of Performance Evaluation

The previous sections explained *what* we evaluate and *who* should do the evaluating. Now we ask: *How* do we evaluate an employee's performance? That is, what are the specific techniques for evaluation? This section reviews the major performance evaluation methods.

**Exhibit 4-11**
**360-Degree Evaluations**

The primary objective of the 360-degree performance evaluation is to pool feedback from all of the employee's customers

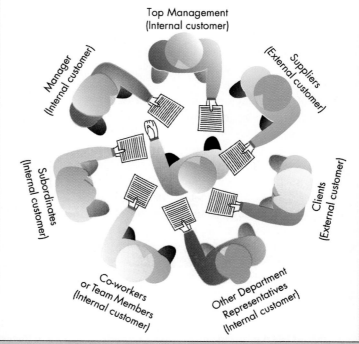

Top Management (Internal customer)

Manager (Internal customer)

Suppliers (External customer)

Subordinates (Internal customer)

Clients (External customer)

Co-workers or Team Members (Internal customer)

Other Department Representatives (Internal customer)

Source: J.F. Milliman, R.A. Zawacki, C. Norman, L. Powell, and J. Kirksey, "Companies Evaluate Employees From All Perspectives," *Personnel Journal*, November 1994, p.100.

**Written Essays** Probably the simplest method of evaluation is to write a narrative describing an employee's strengths, weaknesses, past performance, potential, and suggestions for improvement. The written essay requires no complex forms or extensive training to complete. But the results often reflect the ability of the writer. A good or bad appraisal may be determined as much by the evaluator's writing skill as by the employee's actual level of performance.

**Critical Incidents** Critical incidents focus the evaluator's attention on those behaviours that are key in making the difference between executing a job effectively and executing it ineffectively. That is, the appraiser writes down anecdotes that describe what the employee did that was especially effective or ineffective. The key here is that only specific behaviours, not vaguely defined personality traits, are cited. A list of critical incidents provides a rich set of examples from which the employee can be shown those behaviours that are desirable and those that call for improvement.

**Graphic Rating Scales** One of the oldest and most popular methods of evaluation is the use of graphic rating scales. In this method, a set of performance factors, such as quantity and quality of work, depth of knowledge, cooperation, loyalty, attendance, honesty, and initiative, is listed. The evaluator then goes down the list and rates each on incremental scales. The scales typically specify five points, so a factor like job knowledge might be rated 1 ("poorly informed about work duties") to 5 ("has complete mastery of all phases of the job").

Why are graphic ratings scales so popular? Though they don't provide the depth of information that essays or critical incidents do, they are less time-consuming to develop and administer. They also allow for quantitative analysis and comparison.

**Behaviourally Anchored Rating Scales** Behaviourally anchored rating scales (BARS) combine major elements from the critical incident and graphic rating scale approaches: The appraiser rates the employees based on items along a continuum, but the points are examples of actual behaviour on the given job rather than general descriptions or traits.

BARS specify definite, observable, and measurable job behaviour. Examples of job-related behaviour and performance dimensions are found by asking participants to give specific illustrations of effective and ineffective behaviour regarding each performance dimension. These behavioural examples are then translated into a set of performance dimensions, each dimension having varying levels of performance. The results of this process are behavioural descriptions, such as *anticipates, plans, executes, solves immediate problems, carries out orders*, and *handles emergency situations*.

**Multi-Person Comparisons** Multi-person comparisons evaluate one individual's performance against the performance of one or more others. They are a relative rather than an absolute measuring device. The three most popular comparisons are group order ranking, individual ranking, and paired comparisons.

The **group order ranking** requires the evaluator to place employees into a particular classification, such as top one-fifth or second one-fifth. This method is often used in recommending students to graduate schools. Evaluators are asked whether the student ranks in the top five percent of the class, the next five percent, the next 15 percent, and so forth. But when used by managers to appraise employees, managers deal with all their employees. Therefore, if a rater has 20 employees, only four can be in the top fifth and, of course, four must also be relegated to the bottom fifth.

The **individual ranking** approach rank-orders employees from best to worst. If the manager is required to appraise 30 employees, this approach assumes that the difference between the first and second employee is the same as that between the twenty-first and twenty-second. Even though some of the employees may be closely grouped, this approach allows for no ties. The result is a clear ordering of employees, from the highest performer down to the lowest.

The **paired comparison** approach compares each employee with every other employee and rates each as either the superior or the weaker member of the pair. After all paired comparisons are made, each employee is assigned a summary ranking based on the number of superior scores he or she achieved. This approach ensures that each employee is compared against every other, but it can obviously become unwieldy when many employees are being compared.

Multi-person comparisons can be combined with one of the other methods to blend the best from both absolute and relative standards. For example, in an effort to deal with grade inflation, Dartmouth College in the United States recently changed its transcripts to include not only a letter grade but also class size and class average.[11] So a prospective employer or graduate school can now look at two students who each got a B in their physical geology courses and draw considerably different conclusions about each. This is because next to one grade it says the average grade was a C, while next to the other it says the average grade was a B+. Obviously, the former student performed relatively better than did the latter.

## Potential Problems

While organizations may seek to make the performance evaluation process free from personal biases, prejudices, and idiosyncrasies, a number of potential problems can creep into the process. To the degree that the following factors are prevalent, an employee's evaluation is likely to be distorted.

**Single Criterion** The typical employee's job is made up of a number of tasks. An airline flight attendant's job, for example, includes welcoming passengers, seeing to their comfort, serving meals, and offering safety advice. If performance on this job were assessed by a single criterion measure—say, the time it took to provide food and beverages to 100 passengers—the result would be a limited evaluation of that job. More important, flight attendants whose performance evaluation included assessment on only this single criterion would be motivated to ignore the other tasks in their job. Similarly, if a football quarterback were appraised only on his percentage of completed passes, he would be likely to throw short passes and only in situations where he felt assured that they would be caught. Our point is that where employees are evaluated on a single job criterion, and where successful performance on that job requires good performance on a number of criteria, employees will emphasize the single criterion to the exclusion of other job-relevant factors.

**Recency Effect** A month before the annual performance appraisal, an employee has a spectacular sales success. Or an employee has the worst month of performance on record. Because these events happened shortly before the performance appraisal was due, some managers may give undue weight to these events. This is known as the recency effect, which means that undue weight is given to the most recent events that have occurred. While managers are supposed to give equal weight to the employee's performance during the entire year, it is often difficult for them to keep track of everything an employee does. Therefore, the manager may rely too heavily on recent events that may not even be representative of the employee's performance overall.

**Leniency Error** Every evaluator has his or her own value system that acts as a standard against which appraisals are made. Relative to the true or actual performance an individual exhibits, some evaluators mark high and others low. The former is referred to as positive leniency error, and the latter as negative leniency error. When evaluators are positively lenient in their appraisal, an individual's performance becomes overstated, that is, rated higher than it actually should be. This results in inflated evaluations, a problem widely acknowledged to exist in North American organizations.[12] A negative leniency error understates performance, giving the individual a lower appraisal than deserved.

If all individuals in an organization were appraised by the same person, there would be no problem. Although there would be an error factor, it would be applied equally to everyone. The difficulty arises when we have different raters with different leniency errors making judgments. For example, assume that Jones and Smith are performing the same job for different managers, but they have absolutely identical job performance. If Jones's manager tends to err toward positive leniency, while Smith's manager errs toward negative leniency, we might be confronted with two dramatically different evaluations.

**Halo Error** The halo effect or error, as we noted in Chapter 2, is the tendency for an evaluator to let the assessment of an individual on one trait influence his or her evaluation of that person on other traits. For example, if an employee tends to be dependable, we might become biased toward that individual to the extent that we will rate him or her high on many desirable attributes.[13]

People who design teaching appraisal forms for university students to fill out to evaluate the effectiveness of their instructors each semester must confront the halo error. Students tend to rate a faculty member as outstanding on all criteria when they are particularly appreciative of a few things he or she does in the classroom. Similarly, habits like being slow in returning papers or assigning an extremely demanding reading requirement might result in students' evaluating the instructor as "lousy" across the board.

**Similarity Error** When evaluators give special consideration to those qualities in other people that they perceive in themselves, they are making a similarity error. For example, evaluators who perceive themselves as aggressive may evaluate others by looking for aggressiveness. Those who demonstrate this characteristic tend to benefit, while others are penalized.[14]

Again, this error would tend to wash out if the same evaluator appraised all the people in the organization. However, interrater reliability obviously suffers when various evaluators are utilizing their own similarity criteria.

**Low Differentiation** It's possible that, regardless of whom the appraiser evaluates and what traits are used, the pattern of evaluation remains the same. It has been suggested that evaluators may be classified as (1) high differentiators, who use all or most of the scale; or (2) low differentiators, who use a limited range of the scale.[15]

Low differentiators tend to ignore or suppress differences, perceiving the universe as being more uniform than it really is. High differentiators, on the other hand, tend to utilize all available information to the utmost extent and thus are better able to perceptually define anomalies and contradictions than are low differentiators.[16]

This finding tells us that evaluations made by low differentiators need to be carefully inspected and that the people working for a low differentiator have a high probability of being appraised as being significantly more homogeneous than they really are.

**Forcing Information to Match Nonperformance Criteria** While rarely advocated, it is not an infrequent practice to find the formal evaluation taking place *following* the decision as to how the individual has been performing. This may sound illogical, but it merely recognizes that subjective, yet formal, decisions are often arrived at prior to the gathering of objective information to support those decisions.[17] For example, if the evaluator believes that the evaluation should not be based on performance, but rather on seniority, he or she may be unknowingly adjusting each "performance" evaluation so as to bring it into line with the employee's seniority rank. In this and other similar cases, the evaluator is increasing or decreasing performance appraisals to align with the nonperformance criteria actually being utilized.

## Overcoming the Problems

Just because organizations can encounter problems with performance evaluations, managers should not give up on the process. Some things can be done to overcome most of the problems we have identified.[18] Below we outline some of the most useful approaches.

**Use Multiple Criteria** Since successful performance on most jobs requires doing a number of things well, all those "things" should be identified and evaluated. The more complex the job, the more criteria that will need to be identified and evaluated. But everything need not be assessed. The critical activities that lead to high or low performance are the ones that need to be evaluated.

**Emphasize Behaviours Rather than Traits** Many traits often considered to be related to good performance may, in fact, have little or no performance relationship. For example, traits like loyalty, initiative, courage, reliability, and self-expression are intuitively appealing as desirable characteristics in employees. But the relevant question is this: Are individuals who are evaluated as high on those traits higher performers than those who rate low? We can't answer this question easily. We know that there are employees who rate high on these characteristics and are poor performers. We can find others who are excellent performers but do not score well on traits such as these. Our conclusion is that traits like loyalty and initiative may be prized by managers, but there is no evidence to support that certain traits will be adequate synonyms for performance in a large cross-section of jobs.

Another weakness of trait evaluation is the judgment itself. What is "loyalty"? When is an employee "reliable"? What you consider "loyalty," I may not. So traits suffer from weak interrater agreement.

**Document Performance Behaviours in a Diary** Keeping a diary of specific critical incidents for each employee tends to make evaluations more accurate.[19] Diaries, for instance, tend to reduce leniency and halo errors because they encourage the evaluator to focus on performance-related behaviours rather than traits. Appropriate documentation may also be useful for legal questions that may arise when an employee is dismissed due to poor performance. Most important, it is good to establish an ongoing routine to record behaviours at regular intervals.

**Use Multiple Evaluators** As the number of evaluators increases, the probability of attaining more accurate information increases. If rater error tends to follow a normal curve, an increase in the number of appraisers will tend to find the majority congregating about the middle. You see this approach being used in athletic competitions in such sports as diving and gymnastics. A set of evaluators judges a performance, the highest and lowest scores are dropped, and the final performance evaluation is made up from the cumulative scores of those remaining. The logic of multiple evaluators applies to organizations as well.

If an employee has had 10 managers, nine having rated her excellent and one poor, we can discount the value of the one poor evaluation. Therefore, by moving employees about within the organization so as to gain a number of evaluations or by using multiple assessors (as provided in 360-degree appraisals), we increase the probability of achieving more valid and reliable evaluations.

**Evaluate Selectively** It has been suggested that appraisers should evaluate in only those areas in which they have some expertise.[20] If raters make evaluations on only those dimensions on which they are in a good position to rate, we increase the interrater agreement and make the evaluation a more valid process. This approach also recognizes that different organizational levels often have different orientations toward ratees and observe them in different settings. In general, therefore, we would recommend that appraisers should be as close as possible, in terms of organizational level, to the individual being evaluated. Conversely, the more levels that separate the evaluator and evaluatee, the less opportunity the evaluator has to observe the individual's behaviour and, not surprisingly, the greater the possibility for inaccuracies.

The specific application of these concepts would result in having immediate managers, co-workers, employees, or some combination of these people provide the major input into the appraisal, and having them evaluate those factors they are best qualified to judge. For example, it has been suggested that when professors are evaluating secretaries within a university, they use such criteria as judgment, technical competence, and conscientiousness, whereas peers (other secretaries) use such criteria as job knowledge, organization, cooperation with co-workers, and responsibility.[21] Using both professors and peers as appraisers is a logical and reliable approach, since it results in having people appraise only those dimensions on which they are in a good position to make judgments.

**Train Evaluators** If you can't find good evaluators, the alternative is to make good evaluators. There is substantial evidence that training evaluators can make them more accurate raters.[22]

Common errors such as halo and leniency have been minimized or eliminated in workshops where managers practise observing and rating behaviours. These workshops typically run from one to three days, but allocating many hours to training may not always be necessary. One case has been cited where both halo and leniency errors were decreased immediately after exposing evaluators to explanatory training sessions lasting only five minutes.[23] But the effects of training do appear to diminish over time.[24] This suggests the need for regular refresher sessions.

**Provide Employees with Due Process** The concept of due process can be applied to appraisals to increase the perception that employees are treated fairly.[25] Three features characterize due process systems: (1) Individuals are provided with adequate notice of what is expected of them; (2) all relevant evidence to a proposed violation is aired in a fair hearing so individuals affected can respond; and (3) the final decision is based on the evidence and free from bias.

There is considerable evidence that evaluation systems often violate employees' due process by providing them with infrequent and relatively general performance feedback, allowing them little input into the appraisal process, and knowingly introducing bias into

performance ratings. However, where due process has been part of the evaluation system, employees report positive reactions to the appraisal process, perceive the evaluation results as more accurate, and express increased intent to remain with the organization.

Sources:

[1] T. Davis and M.J. Landa, "A Contrary Look at Employee Performance Appraisal," *Canadian Manager*, Fall 1999, pp. 18-19+.

[2] P.M. Blau, *The Dynamics of Bureaucracy*, rev. ed. (Chicago: University of Chicago Press, 1963).

[3] "The Cop-Out Cops," *National Observer*, August 3, 1974.

[4] A.H. Locher and K.S. Teel, "Appraisal Trends," *Personnel Journal*, September 1988, pp. 139-145.

[5] G.P. Latham and K.N. Wexley, *Increasing Productivity Through Performance Appraisal* (Reading, MA: Addison-Wesley, 1981), p. 80.

[6] See review in R.D. Bretz, Jr., G.T. Milkovich, and W. Read, "The Current State of Performance Appraisal Research and Practice: Concerns, Directions, and Implications," *Journal of Management*, June 1992, p. 326.

[7] "Appraisals: Reverse Reviews," *INC.*, October 1992, p. 33.

[8] See, for instance, J.F. Milliman, R.A. Zawacki, C. Norman, L. Powell, and J. Kirksey, "Companies Evaluate Employees From All Perspectives," *Personnel Journal*, November 1994, pp. 99-103; G. Yukl and R. Lepsinger, "How to Get the Most Out of 360-Degree Feedback," *Training*, December 1995, pp. 45-50; H. Lancaster, "Performance Reviews Are More Valuable When More Join In," *Wall Street Journal*, July 9, 1996, p. B1; and D. Antonioni, "Designing an Effective 360-Degree Appraisal Feedback Process," *Organizational Dynamics*, Autumn 1996, pp. 24-38.

[9] L.M. Sulsky and J.L. Keown, "Performance Appraisal in the Changing World of Work: Implications for the Meaning and Measurement of Work Performance," *Canadian Psychology*, 39:1-2, 1999, pp. 52-59.

[10] M.M. Harris and J. Schaubroeck, "A Meta-Analysis of Self-Supervisor, Self-Peer, and Peer-Supervisor Ratings," *Personnel Psychology*, 41, 1988, pp. 43-62.

[11] D. Goldin, "In a Change of Policy, and Heart, Colleges Join Fight Against Inflated Grades," *The New York Times*, July 4, 1996, p. Y-10.

[12] R.D. Bretz, Jr., G.T. Milkovich, and W. Read, "The Current State of Performance Appraisal Research and Practice: Concerns, Directions, and Implications," *Journal of Management*, June 1992, p. 333. See also J.S. Kanne, H.J. Bernardin, P. Villanova, and J. Peyrefitte, "Stability of Rater Leniency: Three Studies," *Academy of Management Journal*, August 1995, pp. 1036-1051.

[13] For a review of the role of halo error in performance evaluation, see W.K. Balzer and L.M. Sulsky, "Halo and Performance Appraisal Research: A Critical Evaluation," *Journal of Applied Psychology*, December 1992, pp. 975-985.

[14] See T.A. Judge and G.R. Ferris, "Social Context of Performance Evaluation Decisions," *Academy of Management Journal*, February 1993, pp. 80-105.

[15] A. Pizam, "Social Differentiation—A New Psychological Barrier to Performance Appraisal," *Public Personnel Management*, July-August 1975, pp. 244-247.

[16] A. Pizam, "Social Differentiation—A New Psychological Barrier to Performance Appraisal," *Public Personnel Management*, July-August 1975, pp. 245-246.

[17] See D.J. Woehr and J. Feldman, "Processing Objective and Question Order Effects on the Causal Relation Between Memory and Judgment in Performance Appraisal: The Tip of the Iceberg," *Journal of Applied Psychology*, April 1993, pp. 232-241.

[18] See, for example, W.M. Fox, "Improving Performance Appraisal Systems," *National Productivity Review*, Winter 1987-1988, pp. 20-27.

[19] See J. Greenberg, "Determinants of Perceived Fairness of Performance Evaluations," *Journal of Applied Psychology*, May 1986, pp. 340-342; and B.P. Maroney and M.R. Buckely, "Does Research in Performance Appraisal Influence the Practice of Performance Appraisal? Regretfully Not!" *Public Personnel Management*, Summer 1992, pp. 185-196.

[20] W.C. Borman, "The Rating of Individuals in Organizations: An Alternate Approach," *Organizational Behavior and Human Performance*, August 1974, pp. 105-124.

[21] W.C. Borman, "The Rating of Individuals in Organizations: An Alternate Approach," *Organizational Behavior and Human Performance*, August 1974, pp. 105-124.

[22] See, for instance, D.E. Smith, "Training Programs for Performance Appraisal: A Review," *Academy of Management Review*, January 1986, pp. 22-40; D.C. Martin and K. Bartol, "Training the Raters: A Key to Effective Performance Appraisal," *Public Personnel Management*, Summer 1986, pp. 101-109; and T.R. Athey and R.M. McIntyre, "Effect of Rater Training on Rater Accuracy: Levels-of-Processing Theory and Social Facilitation Theory Perspectives," *Journal of Applied Psychology*, November 1987, pp. 567-572.

[23] H.J. Bernardin, "The Effects of Rater Training on Leniency and Halo Errors in Student Rating of Instructors," *Journal of Applied Psychology*, June 1978, pp. 301-308.

[24] H.J. Bernardin, "The Effects of Rater Training on Leniency and Halo Errors in Student Rating of Instructors," *Journal of Applied Psychology*, June 1978, pp. 301-08; and J.M. Ivancevich, "Longitudinal Study of the Effects of Rater Training on Psychometric Error in Ratings," *Journal of Applied Psychology*, October 1979, pp. 502-508.

[25] M.S. Taylor, K.B. Tracy, M.K. Renard, J.K. Harrison, and S.J. Carroll, "Due Process in Performance Appraisal: A Quasi-Experiment in Procedural Justice," *Administrative Science Quarterly*, September 1995, pp. 495-523.

# SUMMARY AND IMPLICATIONS

## For the Workplace

We've looked at a lot of motivation theories in this chapter. How simple it would have been if, after presenting several theories, only one was found to be valid. But these theories are not all in competition with one another. In fact, many of the theories presented in this chapter are complementary. The challenge is now to tie these theories together to help you understand their interrelationships.[142]

We begin by explicitly recognizing that opportunities can aid or hinder individual effort. We should also remember that goals direct behaviour.

Needs theories suggest that motivation will be high to the degree that the rewards individuals receive for high performance satisfy their dominant needs. Expectancy theory predicts that an employee will exert a high level of effort if he or she perceives that there is a strong relationship between effort and performance, performance and rewards, and rewards and satisfaction of personal goals. Each of these relationships, in turn, is influenced by certain factors. For effort to lead to good performance, the individual must have the requisite ability to perform, and the performance appraisal system that measures the individual's performance must be perceived as being fair and objective. The performance-reward relationship will be strong if the individual perceives that it is performance (rather than seniority, being a personal favourite, or other criteria) that is rewarded. The final link in expectancy theory is the rewards-goals relationship.

In portraying these theories, we noted that their implementation is affected by the specific needs of the individual, as a given reward does not motivate all individuals similarly. We also noted that individuals look for fairness in the reward system. Moreover, individuals are responsive to the signals sent out by organizations, and if they determine that some activities are not valued, they may not engage in them, even when the firm expects employees to do so.

Finally, we raised the issue of whether rewards were always needed or beneficial. Our discussion of that topic should lead you to better understand that, in the right context, individuals often motivate themselves intrinsically and can achieve quite high levels of performance doing so.

While it's always dangerous to synthesize a large number of complex ideas into a few simple guidelines, the following suggestions summarize the essence of what we know about motivating employees in organizations.

**RECOGNIZE INDIVIDUAL DIFFERENCES**   Employees have different needs and shouldn't be treated alike. Managers should spend the time necessary to understand what's important to each employee and then align goals, level of involvement, and rewards with individual needs.

**USE GOALS AND FEEDBACK**   Employees should have hard, specific goals, as well as feedback on how well they are faring in pursuit of those goals.

**ALLOW EMPLOYEES TO PARTICIPATE IN DECISIONS THAT AFFECT THEM**   Employees can contribute to a number of decisions that affect them: setting work goals, choosing their own benefits packages, solving productivity and quality problems, and the like. This can increase employee productivity, commitment to work goals, motivation, and job satisfaction.

### WHEN GIVING REWARDS, BE SURE THAT THEY REWARD DESIRED PERFORMANCE

Rewards should be linked to the type of performance expected. It is important that employees perceive a clear linkage. How closely rewards are actually correlated to performance criteria is less important, then, than the perception of this relationship. If individuals perceive this relationship to be low, the results will be low performance, a decrease in job satisfaction, and an increase in turnover and absenteeism.

### CHECK THE SYSTEM FOR EQUITY

Rewards should be perceived by employees as equating with the inputs they bring to the job. At a simplistic level, this means that experience, skills, abilities, effort, and other obvious inputs should explain differences in performance and, hence, pay, job assignments, and other obvious rewards.

## For You as an Individual

With all of the theories presented in the chapter, it might be easy to conclude, particularly in the workplace, that motivation is something that someone (for example, the manager) should be doing for you. This is not your best conclusion, however. Motivation is actually something that we can do for ourselves. For instance, have you ever told yourself that when you finished reading a particularly long and dry chapter in a text you would take a snack break? Or promised yourself a new CD once that major accounting assignment was finished? These are examples of how you motivate yourself.

You also have the ability to motivate others, even if you haven't thought about this before. The people you interact with appreciate recognition. For example, Nancy Langton, your Vancouver-based author, is fortunate to work with a very good secretary. But because the author has absolutely no control over the reward structure at the University of British Columbia, she can't give her secretary a raise, merit pay, days off, or better benefits. Occasionally, however, she presents her secretary with brief notes on nice cards to mention a job well done and appreciated. Or she presents a basket of flowers. Sometimes just sending a pleasant, thankful e-mail is enough to make the person feel appreciated. All of these things are easy enough to do, and appreciated greatly by the recipient.

To take another example, you may be unhappy with the way a professor teaches. One of the challenges to yourself in learning about organizational behaviour is to think of ways that you might motivate the instructor to perform better. That is, you might consider giving positive, helpful feedback, and also participating more in class. This would convey interest in the course, which would be motivating to many instructors.

There are other small ways that you can engage in motivation practices yourself. In a new book, *The Psychology of Money*, authors Adrian Furnham and Michael Argyle report that waitresses receive bigger tips by drawing happy faces on the back of the bill (although this particular trick doesn't work for waiters, as it's viewed as gender-inappropriate).[143] The researchers also found that the size of the first smile that came from the waitperson was directly proportional to the amount of the tip received. So, don't think of motivation as something that should be done for you. Think about motivating others, and yourself, as well.

**ROADMAP REMINDER**

This chapter marked the entry into Part 2 of the text, Striving for Performance. We previously examined the context within which performance occurs in organizations: the changing face of Canada and the changing face of organizations. We explored how people's personality, perception, values, and attitudes influence their responses. Having done that, we now want to understand how we make it possible for people to work together. This chapter introduced the concept of motivation as part of the performance puzzle, and then looked more closely at using specific rewards to achieve specific types of performance. In many ways our emphasis was on motivating individuals, even though, for the most part, people do not work alone in organizations. It is now time for us to consider the crucial role that groups and teams play in organizations. In the following two chapters we explore the issues concerning working with others.

## For Review

1. What are the implications of Theories X and Y for motivation practices?
2. Identify the variables in expectancy theory.
3. Relate goal-setting theory to the MBO process. How are they similar? Different?
4. What are the pluses and minuses of variable-pay programs from an employee's viewpoint? From management's viewpoint?
5. What is an ESOP? How might it positively influence employee motivation?
6. How do stretch targets differ from what goal-setting theory suggests about goal difficulty?
7. What motivates professional employees?
8. What motivates contingent employees?
9. Explain cognitive evaluation theory. How applicable is it to management practice?
10. What can firms do to create more motivating environments for their employees?

## For Critical Thinking

1. Can an individual be too motivated, so that his or her performance declines as a result of excessive effort? Discuss.
2. Identify 3 activities you really enjoy (for example, playing tennis, reading a novel, going shopping). Next, identify 3 activities you really dislike (for example, visiting the dentist, cleaning the house, following a low-fat diet). Using the expectancy model, analyze each of your answers to assess why some activities stimulate your effort while others don't.
3. Identify 5 different criteria by which organizations can compensate employees. Based on your knowledge and experience, do you think performance is the criterion most used in practice? Discuss.

4. "Recognition may be motivational for the moment but it doesn't have any staying power. Why? Because they don't take recognition at Safeway or The Bay!" Do you agree or disagree? Discuss.

5. "Performance can't be measured, so any effort to link pay with performance is a fantasy. Differences in performance are often caused by the system, which means the organization ends up rewarding the circumstances. It's the same thing as rewarding the weather forecaster for a pleasant day." Do you agree or disagree with this statement? Support your position.

6. Your text argues for recognizing individual differences. It also suggests paying attention to members of diverse groups. Does this view contradict the principles of equity theory? Discuss.

## LEARNING ABOUT YOURSELF EXERCISE

# What Motivates You?

Circle the number that most closely agrees with how you feel. Consider your answers in the context of your current job or a past work experience.

| | Strongly Disagree | | | | Strongly Agree |
|---|---|---|---|---|---|
| **1.** I try very hard to improve on my past performance at work. | 1 | 2 | 3 | 4 | 5 |
| **2.** I enjoy competition and winning. | 1 | 2 | 3 | 4 | 5 |
| **3.** I often find myself talking to those around me about nonwork matters. | 1 | 2 | 3 | 4 | 5 |
| **4.** I enjoy a difficult challenge. | 1 | 2 | 3 | 4 | 5 |
| **5.** I enjoy being in charge. | 1 | 2 | 3 | 4 | 5 |
| **6.** I want to be liked by others. | 1 | 2 | 3 | 4 | 5 |
| **7.** I want to know how I am progressing as I complete tasks. | 1 | 2 | 3 | 4 | 5 |
| **8.** I confront people who do things I disagree with. | 1 | 2 | 3 | 4 | 5 |
| **9.** I tend to build close relationships with co-workers. | 1 | 2 | 3 | 4 | 5 |
| **10.** I enjoy setting and achieving realistic goals. | 1 | 2 | 3 | 4 | 5 |
| **11.** I enjoy influencing other people to get my way. | 1 | 2 | 3 | 4 | 5 |
| **12.** I enjoy belonging to groups and organizations. | 1 | 2 | 3 | 4 | 5 |
| **13.** I enjoy the satisfaction of completing a difficult task. | 1 | 2 | 3 | 4 | 5 |
| **14.** I often work to gain more control over the events around me. | 1 | 2 | 3 | 4 | 5 |
| **15.** I enjoy working with others more than working alone. | 1 | 2 | 3 | 4 | 5 |

Turn to page 632 for scoring directions and key.

Source: Based on R. Steers and D. Braunstein, "A Behaviorally Based Measure of Manifest Needs in Work Settings," *Journal of Vocational Behavior*, October 1976, p. 254; and R.N. Lussier, *Human Relations in Organizations: A Skill Building Approach* (Homewood, IL: Richard D. Irwin, 1990), p. 120.

## WORKING WITH OTHERS EXERCISE

# Rewards for Workforce Diversity

**Purpose:**    To learn about the different needs of a diverse workforce.

**Time:**    Approximately 40 minutes.

**Directions:**    Divide the class into groups of approximately size 6. Each group is assigned 1 of the following people and is to determine the best benefits package for that person.

- *Lise* is 28 years old. She is a divorced mother of 3 children, aged 3, 5, and 7. She is the department head. She earns $37 000 a year on her job and receives another $3600 a year in child support from her ex-husband.

- *Ethel* is a 72-year-old widow. She works 25 hours a week to supplement her $8000 annual pension. Including her hourly wage of $7.50, she earns $17 750 a year.

- *John* is a 34-year-old Black male born in Trinidad who is now a Canadian resident. He is married and the father of two small children. John attends college at night and is within a year of earning his bachelor's degree. His salary is $24 000 a year. His wife is an attorney and earns approximately $54 000 a year.

- *Sanjay* is a 26-year-old physically impaired Indo-Canadian male. He is single and has a master's degree in education. Sanjay is paralyzed and confined to a wheelchair as a result of an auto accident. He earns $29 000 a year.

- *Wei Mei* is a single 22-year-old immigrant. Born and raised in China, she came to Canada only three months ago. Wei Mei's English needs considerable improvement. She earns $18 000 a year.

- *Mike* is a 16-year-old white male in his 2nd year of high school. He works 15 hours a week after school and during vacations. He earns $6.25 an hour, or approximately $4875 a year.

**Background**    Our 6 participants work for a company that has recently installed a flexible benefits program. Instead of the traditional "one benefit package fits all," the company is allocating an additional 25 percent of each employee's annual pay to be used for discretionary benefits. Those benefits and their annual cost are listed below.

| Benefit | Yearly Cost |
| --- | --- |
| Extended medical care (for services such as private hospital room, eye glasses, and dental care that are not provided by the Medical Services Plan) for employee: | |
| Plan A (No deductible and pays 90%) | $3000 |
| Plan B ($200 deductible and pays 80%) | $2000 |
| Plan C ($1000 deductible and pays 70%) | $500 |
| Extended medical care for dependants (same deductibles and percentages as above): | |
| Plan A | $2000 |
| Plan B | $1500 |
| Plan C | $500 |

| Benefit | Yearly Cost |
|---|---|
| Supplementary dental plan | $500 |
| Life insurance: | |
| Plan A ($25 000 coverage) | $500 |
| Plan B ($50 000 coverage) | $1000 |
| Plan C ($100 000 coverage) | $2000 |
| Plan D ($250 000 coverage) | $3000 |
| Mental health plan | $500 |
| Prepaid legal assistance | $300 |
| Vacation | 2% of annual pay for each week, up to 6 weeks a year |
| Pension at retirement equal to approximately 50% of final annual earnings | $1500 |
| Four-day workweek during the three summer months | 4% of annual pay (available only to full-time employees) |
| Daycare services (after company contribution) | $2000 for all of an employee's children, regardless of number |
| Company-provided transportation to and from work | $750 |
| University tuition reimbursement | $1000 |
| Language class tuition reimbursement | $500 |

## The Task

1. Each group has 15 minutes to develop a flexible benefits package that consumes 25 percent (and no more!) of its character's pay.

2. After completing Step 1, each group appoints a spokesperson who describes to the entire class the benefits package the group has arrived at for its character.

3. The entire class then discusses the results. How did the needs, concerns, and problems of each participant influence the group's decision? What do the results suggest for trying to motivate a diverse workforce?

Source: Exercise developed by Steve Robbins, with special thanks to Professor Penny Wright (San Diego State University) for her suggestions during the development of this exercise. Exercise modified by Nancy Langton.

# Are Canadian CEOs Paid Too Much?

Critics have described the astronomical pay packages given to Canadian and American CEOs as "rampant greed." Consider the data in Exhibit 4-12.

**Exhibit 4-12**
**1998 Compensation of Canada's Five Best-Paid CEOs**

| CEO and Company | 1998 Total Compensation | % Change | |
| --- | --- | --- | --- |
| | | In Pay | In Profit |
| Peter Munk<br>Barrick Gold Corp. | $38 918 951 | +1 283.3 | +345.0 |
| Richard Currie<br>Loblaw Cos. Ltd. | $34 122 152 | +343.0 | +25.0 |
| Frank Stronach<br>Magna International Inc. | $26 154 250 | +.2 | −16.1 |
| Frank Hasenfratz<br>Linamar Corp. | $21 397 831 | +94.0 | −22.1 |
| Galen Weston<br>George Weston Ltd. | $15 226 858 | +99.0 | +216.8 |

In 1998, the average pretax compensation for the 100 highest-paid Canadian executives was $3.4 million, up 26 percent from $2.7 million in 1997. Meanwhile, earnings at Canada's 135 biggest companies that year slumped 18 percent.

How do you explain such large pay packages to CEOs? Some say this represents a classic economic response to a situation in which the demand is great for high-quality top-executive talent, and the supply is low. Other arguments in favour of paying executives $1 million a year or more are the need to compensate people for the tremendous responsibilities and stress that go with such jobs; the motivating potential that seven- and eight-figure annual incomes provide to senior executives and those who might aspire to be; and the influence of senior executives on the company's bottom line. (For example, research findings cited on page 434 of Chapter 10 attribute a 15-25 percent variation in profitability to the leadership quality of CEOs.)

Critics of executive pay practices in Canada and the United States argue that CEOs choose board members whom they can count on to support ever-increasing pay for top management. If board members fail to "play along," they risk losing their positions, their fees, and the prestige and power inherent in board membership.

In addition, it is not clear that executive compensation is tied to firm performance. For instance, KPMG found in one survey that for 40 percent of the respondents, there was no correlation between the size of the bonus and how poorly or well the company fared.

Is high compensation of chief executives a problem? If so, does the blame for the problem lie with CEOs or with the shareholders and boards that knowingly allow the practice? Are Canadian and American CEOs greedy? Are these CEOs acting unethically? Should their pay reflect more closely some multiple of their employees' wages? What do you think?

Source: M. MacKinnon, "Barrick's Munk Leads Pay Parade: $38.9m," *Canadian Press Newswire*, April 26, 1999; David Berman, "A Bad Place to Be Boss. Lesson #1 for Canadian CEOs: Learn to Live on a Lot Less Than Your International Peers," *Canadian Business*, July 1997, pp. 17-19; "Gimme Gimme: Greed, the Most Insidious of Sins, Has Once Again Embraced a Decade," *Financial Post*, September 28/30, 1996, pp 24-25; J.M. Pennings, "Executive Reward Systems: A Cross-National Comparison," *Journal of Management Studies*, March 1993, pp. 261-280; I. McGugan, "A Crapshoot Called Compensation," *Canadian Business*, July 1995, pp. 67-70; "50 Best-Paid CEOs," *Report on Business*, July 1999, pp. 125-126.

## INTERNET SEARCH EXERCISES

1. Choose a professional sport (hockey, basketball, baseball, etc.) and contrast the pay of the highest-paid professional athletes with their performance over the last year. Consider the implications of equity theory on your findings.

2. Contrast the pay of senior executives in the federal government (prime minister, minister of finance, etc.), your provincial government, and CEOs of a *Globe and Mail* Top 1000 that is headquartered in your community or region. What conclusions can you draw from your findings?

## CASE INCIDENT

## The Memo

The following memo was actually sent out three weeks before Christmas by the executive vice-president of a regional financial brokerage firm. For obvious reasons, the identity of the firm and the executive are disguised.

---

**December 4, 1999**

**To: LHI Retail Sales Group Employees**

**Re: Holiday Gifts for Nonexempt Employees**

I have received a number of questions regarding the possibility of a holiday cash gift. This year, Larson Hughes Inc. will not be providing a holiday gift for nonexempt employees (employees through Level 8), which includes many sales assistants, operations staff, and administrative assistants in Retail Sales Group.

As you may know, we paid all nonexempt employees a holiday gift in December 1996 and 1997. The gift was not dependent upon individual performance. Rather, as we explained at the time, the gift was a reflection of the exceptional earnings recorded at the Corporate Financial Group level.

RSG is having a very successful year, and CFG revenues are expected to hit record levels in 1999. The contributions of RSG's nonexempt employees certainly have played a role in both. However, CFG's overall profitability—the ultimate barometer of our performance—has not exceeded expectations this year.

This decision is not a reflection of the overall performance of our nonexempt employees nor the importance of their contributions to Larson Hughes. We highly value the work of all of our employees; you are our most valuable asset and our competitive advantage.

I deeply appreciate everyone's contributions in 1999. Your efforts continue to be important to our success now and in the future.

# Questions

1. Analyze this memo in terms of motivation concepts.

2. How would you respond if you received this memo?

3. What, if anything, would you have done differently if you were the executive vice-president and a number of your nonexempt employees asked you questions regarding the possibility of a holiday cash gift?

# Why Should I Work for You?

Thousands of large, medium, and small technology businesses across Canada are trying to hire and keep high-end, high-tech talent. In 1997 there were 20 000 job vacancies in the high-tech sector, and by late 1999, about 32 000 jobs needed filling. There's really no end in sight to the number of high-tech jobs that will need to be filled in Canada. The number is expected to increase to 50 000 jobs in the next few years alone.

Canada produces bright, technically educated individuals who can easily get jobs with six-figure salaries. However, there are not enough of them. A recent study by IDC (Canada) Ltd. found that 60 percent of large Canadian companies reported project delays due to a shortage of IT professionals.

Ken Miller, CEO of Richmond-based MDSI Mobile Data Solutions Inc., knows the hiring problem first-hand. MDSI could not fill three senior positions after posting them between 60 and 120 days in fall 1999.

Many Canadian companies are losing high-tech workers to American competitors who aggressively recruit Canadian employees. Canada offers an unequal economic playing field. Canada's maximum personal income-tax rate of 50 percent, applied to those who earn $63 000 or more, compares unfavourably with the top US rate of 43 percent, which doesn't affect individuals until they earn $379 000 or more. Canada's health system and the quality of life Canada's higher taxes support aren't enough to keep all of its best-trained employees here.

Companies are trying to lure good workers through a variety of techniques. Some offer current employees bonuses for referring qualified candidates who get hired. They also offer six-figure salaries, big bonuses tied to performance, and stock options. Often they offer an elaborate workplace, with gym, cappucino bars, even places to take a nap. But this so far has not been enough to win the hiring wars.

# Questions

1. Do motivation theories explain why high-tech Canadian firms are having so much difficulty hiring employees?

**2.** What additional things might firms do to retain valuable workers?

**3.** To what extent are the nonmonetary compensations an important motivation for these workers?

Source: Based on "Hiring Wars," *Venture 661*; aired September 23, 1997. See also S. McKay, "Hiring Line Blues: What's a Company to Do When Offering a Great Salary and Benefits Just Isn't Enough?" *National Post Business*, October 1999, pp. 52-58; and M. Anderson, "Ascent of the Nerd: Computer-Savvy Engineers Like Steven Wood Are Discovering Just How Much Companies Are Willing to Pay for Their Skills," *National Post Business,* October 1999, pp. 46-50.

## CHAPTER 5

# Foundations of Group Behaviour

I n April 1999, 54 students from Vancouver's St. Patrick Regional secondary school and their teacher, Tony Araujo, found themselves in Washington, DC, competing in the Festival of Gold, a competition for the best school choirs in the United States.[1] St. Pat's is a small Catholic high school, and this was the first time a Canadian choir had ever been invited to the competition.

## Questions for Consideration

**What are the stages of group development?**

**What makes groups work (or not work)?**

**How do we build a better work group?**

How did this group of young teens find themselves competing against 28 of the best choirs in the United States? They were no ordinary choir, that's for sure. Four years ago, the school didn't even have a choir, but Araujo was hired to start one. He was not your average choir director; in fact he was an English major. He knew nothing about choirs, much less directing them. To make matters worse, the kids under his direction didn't even want to be in the choir. Many of them couldn't take the business administration course that was their first choice. Moreover, as one student, speaking for the group, said, "Choir was for geeks."

As Pete McMartin, *Vancouver Sun* columnist noted, "But then, something like a miracle took place." The students and their teacher started working hard, developing a chemistry that pushed them to greater singing heights.

They first found out how good they were when they won a big competition in Southern California. From that came the invitation to the Festival of Gold.

Araujo spoke with the judges at the competition afterwards, and they told him two things stood out about the St. Pat's choir. First, the "choir did not look like any of the other choirs. These kids were Filipino and Chinese and Hispanic and Portuguese and German and Dutch and English, the usual cultural mishmash of Vancouver, and all the other choirs were so, well...white." Some of the choir are shown above, during their DC trip.

The other thing the judges commented on was the "soulfulness" of St. Pat's singing. One of the judges told Araujo that the St. Pat's singers were "the most musical choir" in the competition.

Araujo felt justifiably proud of his choir's performance: "The kids in the other choirs had auditioned; his kids had been conscripted. They had to feel their way into their music, had to discover it for themselves."

And how did St. Pat's do against those 28 American schools? The choirs were not ranked publicly, but in his conversations with the judges afterwards, Araujo learned that all three judges gave the kids marks in the 90s, and one gave them a 96. That was the top mark in the competition. The top eight choirs were invited to sing at the gala performance the next night, and St. Pat's led off the event.

The story of St. Patrick's choir is a story about how groups come together to perform tasks.

The behaviour of individuals in groups is something more than the sum total of each person acting in his or her own way. In other words, when individuals are in groups, they act differently than they do when they're alone. Even when the kids at St. Pat's had individually thought that choir was for "geeks," together they worked hard to make themselves one of the best secondary school choirs in North America.

St. Pat's choir is just one example of a group. As we show in this chapter, we encounter a number of formal and informal groups in our daily lives, and understanding how groups function is critical to explaining organizational behaviour.

# Defining Groups

**group**
Two or more individuals, interacting and interdependent, who have come together to achieve particular objectives.

A **group** is defined as two or more individuals, interacting and interdependent, who have come together to achieve particular objectives. The reasons for coming together can be quite varied, from serving on a committee or task force at work, to serving on the board of a daycare centre, to working together on a class project. Sometimes a group of people get together to do something socially as well, so groups don't always have work-related objectives.

There is no single reason why individuals join groups. Because most people belong to a number of groups, it's obvious that different groups provide different benefits to their members. Exhibit 5-1 summarizes the most popular reasons people have for joining groups. You too will be a member of groups throughout your life, both within and outside the workplace. We review in this chapter, then, the ways that groups function, how they can be made better, and what causes problems. Because most of you will work in student groups during your college and university days, you might want to think about applying the topics in this chapter to your own student groups. For some, the issue of working in groups is controversial. You may want to review the Point/CounterPoint discussion on page 202 to learn more of this controversy.

---

**Exhibit 5-1**
**Why Do People Join Groups?**

**Security**

By joining a group, individuals can reduce the insecurity of "standing alone." People feel stronger, have fewer self-doubts, and are more resistant to threats when they are part of a group.

**Status**

Inclusion in a group that is viewed as important by others provides recognition and status for its members.

**Self-Esteem**

Groups can provide people with feelings of self-worth. That is, in addition to conveying status to those outside the group, membership can also give increased feelings of worth to the group members themselves.

**Affiliation**

Groups can fulfill social needs. People enjoy the regular interaction that comes with group membership. For many people, these interactions are their primary way of satisfying their needs for affiliation.

**Power**

What cannot be achieved individually often becomes possible through group action. There is power in numbers.

**Goal Achievement**

There are times when it takes more than one person to accomplish a particular task: There is a need to pool talents, knowledge, or power in order to complete a job.

## Stages of Group Development

When people get together for the first time with the purpose of achieving some objective, they may not realize that acting as a group is not something simple, easy, or genetically programmed. Working in a group is often difficult, particularly in the initial stages, when people don't necessarily know each other. As it turns out, groups go through various stages over time, although the stages are not necessarily exactly the same for each group. In this section, we review the better-known five-stage model of group development, and then the more recently discovered punctuated-equilibrium model.

### The Five-Stage Model

From the mid-1960s, it was believed that groups passed through a standard sequence of five stages.[2] As shown in Exhibit 5-2, these five stages have been labelled forming, storming, norming, performing, and adjourning. Although we now know that not all groups pass through these stages in a linear fashion, the stages can still help in addressing your anxieties about working in groups.

Think about the first time you met with a new group that had been put together to accomplish some task. Do you remember how some people seemed silent and others felt confused about the task? Those feelings arise during the first stage of group development, know as **forming**. Forming is characterized by a great deal of uncertainty about the group's purpose, structure, and leadership. Members are "testing the waters" to determine what types of behaviour are acceptable. This stage is complete when members have begun to think of themselves as part of a group.

Do you remember how some people in your group just didn't seem to get along, and sometimes power struggles even emerged? These reactions are typical of the **storming** stage, which is one of intragroup conflict. Members accept the existence of the group, but resist the constraints that the group imposes on individuality. Furthermore, there is conflict over who will control the group. When this stage is complete, a relatively clear hierarchy of leadership will emerge within the group.

Some groups never really emerge from the storming stage, or they move back and forth through storming and the other stages. A group that remains forever planted in the storming stage may have less ability to complete the task because of all the interpersonal problems.

Many groups resolve the interpersonal conflict and reach the third stage, in which close relationships develop and the group demonstrates cohesiveness. There is now a strong sense of group identity and camaraderie.

**forming**
The first stage in group development, characterized by much uncertainty.

**storming**
The second stage in group development, characterized by intragroup conflict.

---

**Exhibit 5-2**
**Stages of Group Development**

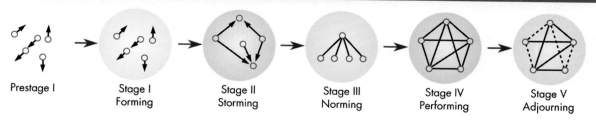

Prestage I → Stage I Forming → Stage II Storming → Stage III Norming → Stage IV Performing → Stage V Adjourning

# Designing Jobs Around Groups

It's time to take small groups seriously; that is, to use groups, rather than individuals, as the basic building blocks for an organization.[1] We should design organizations from scratch around small groups rather than the way we have traditionally done it—around individuals.

Why would management want to do such a thing? At least seven reasons can be identified. First, small groups seem to be good for people. They can satisfy important membership needs. They can provide a moderately wide range of activities for individual members. They can provide support in times of stress and crisis. They are settings in which people can learn not only cognitively, but also empirically, to be reasonably trusting and helpful to one another. Second, groups seem to be good problem-finding tools. They seem to be useful in promoting innovation and creativity. Third, in a wide variety of decision situations, groups make better decisions than individuals do. Fourth, groups are great tools for implementation. Groups gain commitment from their members so that group decisions are likely to be willingly carried out. Fifth, they can control and discipline individual members in ways that are often extremely difficult through impersonal quasi-legal disciplinary systems. Sixth, as organizations grow large, small groups appear to be useful mechanisms for fending off many of the negative effects of large size. They help to prevent communication lines from growing too long, the hierarchy from growing too steep, and the individual from getting lost in the crowd. There is also a seventh, but altogether different, kind of argument for taking groups seriously. Groups are natural phenomena and facts of organizational life. They can be created, but their spontaneous development cannot be prevented.

Operationally, how would an organization that was truly designed around groups function? One answer to this question is merely to take the things that organizations do with individuals and apply them to groups. The idea would be to raise the level from the atom to the molecule and select groups rather than individuals, train groups rather than individuals, pay groups rather than individuals, promote groups rather than individuals, fire groups rather than individuals, and so on down the list of activities that organizations have traditionally carried on in order to use human beings in their organizations.

In the past, the human group has primarily been used for patching and mending organizations that were built around the individual. The time has come for management to discard the notion that individuals are the basic building blocks of organizations and to redesign organizations around groups. Importantly, a number of organizations seem to be moving in this direction. Hundreds of major companies, including Honeywell, Toyota Canada, and Microsoft, have essentially designed their current operations around small groups.

Source:

[1] The argument presented here is based on H.J. Leavitt, "Suppose We Took Groups Seriously," in E.L. Cass and F.G. Zimmer (eds.), *Man and Work in Society* (New York: Van Nostrand Reinhold, 1975), pp. 67-77.

# Jobs Should Be Designed Around Individuals

The argument that organizations can and should be designed around groups might hold in a socialistic society, but not in capitalistic countries such as Canada, the United States, Australia, and the United Kingdom. Even though Canadians have a stronger orientation toward society as a whole than do Americans, many people here strongly value individual achievement, just as people in the United States and other capitalistic countries do. They praise competition. Even in team sports, they want to identify individuals for recognition. Sure, they enjoy group interaction. They like being part of a team, especially a winning team. But it is one thing to be a member of a work group while maintaining a strong individual identity, and another to sublimate one's identity to that of the group.

Many workers like a clear link between individual effort and a visible outcome. They are frustrated in job situations where their contribution is co-mingled and homogenized with the contributions of others.

Individuals want to be hired based on their individual talents. They want to be evaluated on their individual efforts. They also want to be rewarded with pay raises and promotions based on their individual performances. As we noted in Chapter 3 when we discussed values, Canadians believe in an authority and status hierarchy even more than Americans do. They accept a system where there are managers and employees. They are not completely comfortable accepting a group's decision on such issues as their job assignments and wage increases. It's hard to imagine, then, that they would be comfortable in a system where the sole basis for their promotion or termination would be the performance of their group.

One of the best examples of how fully the individual ethic has permeated the Canadian psyche is the general lack of enthusiasm that university students display toward group term papers. When students are offered the option to write term papers individually or as members of a small group, and the class must decide as a whole on a binding decision, the class almost always chooses individual term papers. This is really not all that surprising. It's consistent with someone who wants to rise or fall based on his or her own work performance. However, given this preference to do individual work, one might ask the following question: Are the students examples of future full-time employees who would be satisfied and reach their full productive capacities in a group-centred organization? Probably not!

**norming**
The third stage in group development, characterized by close relationships and cohesiveness.

**performing**
The fourth stage in group development, when the group is fully functional.

**adjourning**
The final stage in group development for temporary groups, characterized by concern with wrapping up activities rather than task performance.

**Honeywell**
www.honeywell.com

**Toyota Canada**
www.toyota.ca

**Microsoft**
www.microsoft.com

This **norming** stage is complete when the group structure solidifies, and the group has assimilated a common set of expectations of what defines correct member behaviour.

Finally, and you may have noticed this in some of your own group interactions, some groups just seem to come together well and start to do their work. This fourth stage, when significant task progress is being made, is called **performing**. The structure at this point is fully functional and accepted. Group energy has moved from getting to know and understand each other to performing the task at hand. When St. Pat's choir was singing its heart out in Washington, DC, it was performing.

For permanent work groups, performing is the last stage in their development. However, for temporary committees, teams, task forces, and similar groups that have a limited task to perform, there is an **adjourning** stage. In this stage, the group prepares for its disbandment. High task performance is no longer the group's top priority. Instead, attention is directed toward wrapping up activities. Group members' responses vary at this stage. Some members are upbeat, basking in the group's accomplishments. Others may be depressed over the loss of camaraderie and friendships gained during the work group's life.

Many interpreters of the five-stage model have assumed that a group becomes more effective as it progresses through the first four stages. While this assumption may be generally true, what makes a group effective is more complex than this model acknowledges. Under some conditions, high levels of conflict are conducive to high group performance, as long as the conflict is directed toward the task and not toward group members. So we might expect to find situations where groups in Stage II outperform those in Stages III or IV. Similarly, groups do not always proceed clearly from one stage to the next. Sometimes, in fact, several stages go on simultaneously, as when groups are storming and performing at the same time. Groups even occasionally regress to previous stages. Therefore, even the strongest proponents of this model do not assume that all groups follow the five-stage process precisely or that Stage IV is always the most preferable.

Another problem with the five-stage model, in terms of understanding work-related behaviour, is that it ignores organizational context.[3] For instance, a study of a cockpit crew in an airliner found that, within 10 minutes, three strangers assigned to fly together for the first time had become a high-performing group. What allowed for this speedy group development was the strong organizational context surrounding the tasks of the cockpit crew. This context provided the rules, task definitions, information, and resources needed for the group to perform. They didn't need to develop plans, assign roles, determine and allocate resources, resolve conflicts, and set norms the way the five-stage model predicts. Within the workplace, some group behaviour takes place within a strong organizational context, and it would appear that the five-stage development model might have limited applicability for those groups. However, there are a variety of situations in the workplace where groups are assigned to tasks, and the individuals do not know each other. They must therefore work out interpersonal differences at the same time that they work through the assigned tasks.

## The Punctuated-Equilibrium Model

Studies of more than a dozen field and laboratory task force groups confirmed that not all groups develop in a universal sequence of stages.[4]

> **Ever wonder what causes flurries of activity in groups?**

In particular, temporary groups with deadlines have their own unique sequencing of action (or inaction): (1) The first meeting sets the group's direction; (2) the first phase of group activity is one of inertia; (3) a transition takes place at the end of the first phase, which occurs exactly when the group has used up half its allotted time; (4) the transition initiates major changes; (5) a second phase of inertia follows the transition; and (6) the group's last meeting is characterized by markedly accelerated activity. This pattern is called the punctuated-equilibrium model, developed by Professor Connie Gersick of UCLA, and is shown in Exhibit 5-3.[5] It is important for you to understand these shifts in group behaviour, if for no other reason than when you're in a group that is not working well, you can start to think of ways to help the group move to a more productive phase.

As both a group member and possibly a group leader, it is important that you recognize that the first meeting sets the group's direction. A framework of behavioural patterns and assumptions through which the group will approach its project emerges in this first meeting. These lasting patterns can appear as early as the first few seconds of the group's life.

Once set, the group's direction becomes "written in stone" and is unlikely to be re-examined throughout the first half of the group's life. This is a period of inertia—that is, the group tends to stand still or become locked into a fixed course of action. Even if it gains new insights that challenge initial patterns and assumptions, the group is incapable of acting on these new insights in Phase 1. You may recognize that in some groups, during the early period of trying to get things accomplished, no one really did their assigned tasks. You may also recognize this phase as one where everyone carries out the tasks, but not in a very coordinated fashion.

At some point, however, the group moves out of the inertia stage and recognizes that work needs to get completed. One of the more interesting discoveries made in these studies was that each group experienced its transition at the same point in its calendar—precisely halfway between its first meeting and its official deadline. The similarity occurred despite the fact that some groups spent as little as an hour on their project while others spent six months. It was as if the groups universally experienced a mid-life crisis at this point. The midpoint appears to work like an alarm clock, heightening members' awareness that their time is limited and that they need to "get moving." When you work on your next group project, you might want to examine when your group starts to "get moving."

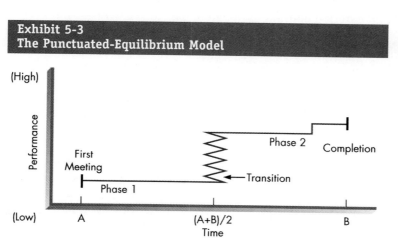

**Exhibit 5-3**
**The Punctuated-Equilibrium Model**

This transition ends Phase 1 and is characterized by a concentrated burst of changes, dropping of old patterns, and adoption of new perspectives. The transition sets a revised direction for Phase 2, which is a new equilibrium or period of inertia. In this phase, the group executes plans created during the transition period. The group's last meeting is characterized by a final burst of activity to finish its work.

We can use this model to describe some of your experiences with student teams created for doing group term projects. At the first meeting, a basic timetable is established. Members size up one another. They agree they have nine weeks to do their project. The instructor's requirements are discussed and debated. From that point, the group meets regularly to carry out its activities. About four or five weeks into the project, however, problems are confronted. Criticism begins to be taken seriously. Discussion becomes more open. The group re-assesses where it has been and aggressively moves to make necessary changes. If the right changes are made, the next four or five weeks find the group developing a first-rate project. The group's last meeting, which will probably occur just before the project is due, lasts longer than the others. In it, all final issues are discussed and details resolved.

In summary, the punctuated-equilibrium model characterizes groups as exhibiting long periods of inertia interspersed with brief revolutionary changes triggered primarily by their members' awareness of time and deadlines. To use the terminology of the five-stage group development model, the group begins by combining the forming and norming stages, then goes through a period of low performing, followed by storming, then a period of high performing, and, finally, adjourning. Keep in mind that this model is more appropriate for understanding temporary task groups that are working under a time-constrained deadline.

## What Makes Groups Work (or Not Work)?

Why are some group efforts more successful than others? The answer to that question is complex, but it includes variables such as the ability of the group's members, the size of the group, the level of conflict, and the internal pressures on members to conform to the group's norms. Exhibit 5-4 presents the major components that determine group performance and satisfaction.[6] It can help you sort out the key variables and their interrelationships. To help you think concretely about the group process and how various factors affect it, the Working With Others Exercise on page 234 has you observe a group in action and analyze various aspects of the process.

Perhaps the most important factor to consider is that work groups don't exist in isolation. They are part of a larger organization. A research team in Vancouver-based MacMillan Bloedel's forestry division, for instance, must live within the rules and policies dictated from the division's headquarters and MacBlo's corporate offices. So every work group is influenced by both internal *and* external conditions.

Internally, the work group has a distinct set of resources determined by its membership. This includes such things as the intelligence and motivation of members. It also has an internal structure that defines member roles and norms. These factors—group member resources and structure—determine interaction patterns and other processes within the group.

Finally, whether the group is able to perform, and also its

> **Can we build a better group?**

**Center for the Study of Work Teams**
www.workteams.unt.edu

**MacMillan Bloedel**
www.macblo.com

### Exhibit 5-4
### Group Behaviour Model

External conditions imposed on the group → Group member resources / Group structure → Group process → (Group task) → Performance and satisfaction

The new headquarters of SEI investments, a financial services firm, was designed to encourage group interaction. Al West, the firm's chief executive, asked architects to design a flexible work space in which employees could quickly and easily reconfigure their work areas to form groups. Coiled cables that drop from the ceiling contain telephone, computer, and electrical wiring. All office furniture is on wheels. By unplugging their cables and rolling their equipment to a new area, employees organize new work groups as their assignments change.

degree of satisfaction, are moderated by the type of task that the group is working on. In the following pages, we'll elaborate on each of the basic boxes identified in Exhibit 5-4.

## The Effects of the Workplace on the Group

**University of British Columbia MBA Program**
www.commerce.ubc.ca/mba

While all groups face interpersonal issues, groups are also affected by the organizational conditions that exist and the resources provided. For example, when the University of British Columbia (UBC) redesigned its MBA program several years ago, the faculty members who worked on the design teams were given some release time from their teaching responsibilities for their efforts. The extra time made it easier to plan meetings and carry out tasks. More recently, however, the faculty group assigned to evaluate the undergraduate program did not receive course release time. Clearly the committee working on the undergraduate issues faces more constraints in carrying out its tasks.

To begin understanding the behaviour of a work group, you need to view it as a subsystem embedded in a larger system.[7] That is, when we realize that groups are a subset of a larger organizational system, we can extract part of the explanation of the group's behaviour from an explanation of the organization to which it belongs.

**ORGANIZATIONAL STRATEGY** Many members of organizations observe that some groups within an organization get more attention than others. This treatment relates to organizational strategy. An organization's overall strategy, typically put in place by top management, outlines the organization's goals and the means for attaining these goals. The strategy that an organization is pursuing, at any given time, will influence the power of various work groups. That power will, in turn, determine the resources that the organization's top management is willing to allocate to the group for performing its tasks.

To illustrate, an organization that is retrenching through selling off or closing down major parts of its business will have work groups with a shrinking resource base, increased member anxiety, and the potential for heightened intragroup conflict.[8] Even in that situation, however, some groups will be allocated more resources to do their task than others. For instance, the group designated the task of determining how to carry out the downsizing effectively would likely receive more resources than the group assigned to a project likely to be cut in the downsizing.

**ORGANIZATIONAL INFRASTRUCTURE** Groups are constrained to work within the framework of an organization. Some organizations are more flexible than others, and the degree of flexibility will affect the ability of a group to carry out its tasks. Below we consider several elements of an organization's infrastructure that can affect group behaviour.

*Leadership.* When organizations create groups, they often designate some sort of hierarchy within the team. The person assigned the leadership role generally reports to management on behalf of the team and has authority that other group members don't have. This can sometimes cause problems, however, if a work group ends up being led by someone who emerges informally from within the group.

**McDonald's**
www.mcdonalds.com

*Rules.* All organizations have rules, although some have far fewer than others. The rules (or lack thereof) in an organization affect the ability of a group to function. For instance, because McDonald's has standard operating procedures for taking orders, cooking hamburgers, and filling soft-drink containers, the discretion of work-group members to set independent standards of behaviour is severely limited. The more formal regulations that the organization imposes on all its employees, the more the behaviour of work-group members will be consistent and predictable. The less formal the regulations, the more flexible and adaptable the group can be in responding to various situations.

*Resources.* Some organizations are large and profitable, with an abundance of resources. Their employees, for instance, will have modern, high-quality tools and equipment to do their jobs. Other organizations aren't as fortunate. When organizations have limited resources, so do their work groups. What a group actually accomplishes is, to a large degree, determined by what it is capable of accomplishing. The presence or absence of resources such as money, time, raw materials, and equipment—which are allocated to a group by an organization—has a large bearing on a group's behaviour.

*Evaluation and Rewards.* Another organization-wide variable that affects how groups perform is the performance evaluation and reward system.[9] Does the organization reward the accomplishment of individual or group objectives? Group members' behaviour will be influenced by how the organization evaluates performance and what behaviours are rewarded. For instance, students often act differently when their mark is based on individual contribution to the group project than when everyone receives the same mark, regardless of contribution. Because the assignment of marks

Electronic Arts-Canada, in Burnaby, BC, has a state of the art workplace: a fully-equipped gym, an outdoor basketball court, an entire soccer field. But walk through the company most afternoons, and employees are busy at their desks, putting out video games, not outdoors playing sports. EA-Canada president Glenn Wong believes in creating a climate and culture that gets everyone working together in groups. Employees know that everyone at EA-Canada is working together to win.

(or rewards) has some impact on individual behaviour, this is an important factor for organizations (and instructors) to think about.

**ORGANIZATIONAL CULTURE**  Beyond the ordinary infrastructure of the organization, every organization has an unwritten culture that defines standards of acceptable and unacceptable behaviour for employees. Within a few months, most employees understand their organization's culture. They know how to dress for work, whether rules are rigidly enforced, what kinds of questionable behaviours will get them into trouble and which ones are likely to be overlooked, the importance of honesty and integrity, and the like. Members of work groups must accept the standards implied in the organization's dominant culture if they are to remain in good standing. Because of an organization's culture, organizational members often know whether they have been assigned to a committee that is of importance to the organization. If they recognize that they have been assigned to one of the "unimportant" committees, they may not exert as much effort.

## The Effects of Group Members

While various organizational factors affect a group's performance, the group also depends on the resources that its members individually bring to the group. In this section, we will examine the resources that have received the greatest amount of attention: knowledge, skills and abilities, and personality characteristics. As you learn more in this section about the effects of group members on group performance, you may want to examine the Learning About Yourself Exercise on page 233, which helps you to assess how attracted you are to group work.

**KNOWLEDGE, SKILLS, AND ABILITIES**  Part of a group's performance can be predicted by assessing the knowledge, skills, and abilities of its individual members. It's true that we occasionally read about the athletic team composed of mediocre players who, because of excellent coaching, determination, and precision teamwork, beat a far more talented group of players. But such cases make the news precisely because they represent an aberration. While a group's performance is not merely the summation of its individual members' abilities, these abilities do limit what members can do and how effectively they will perform in a group.

What predictions can we make regarding ability and group performance? First, evidence indicates that individuals who hold crucial abilities for attaining the group's task tend to be more involved in group activity, generally contribute more, are more likely to emerge as the group leaders, and are more satisfied if their talents are effectively utilized by the group.[10] Second, intellectual ability and task-relevant ability have both been found to be related to overall group performance.[11] However, the correlation is not particularly high, suggesting that other factors, such as the size of the group, the type of tasks being performed, the actions of its leader, and level of conflict within the group, also influence performance.

A review of the evidence has found that interpersonal skills consistently emerge as important for high work-group performance.[12] These include conflict management and resolution, collaborative problem-solving, and communication. For instance, members need to be able to recognize the type and source of conflict confronting the group and to implement an appropriate conflict resolution strategy; to identify situations requiring participative group problem-solving, and to utilize the proper degree and type of participation; and to listen nonevaluatively and to appropriately use active listening techiques.

**PERSONALITY CHARACTERISTICS** You may remember that in Chapter 2 we discussed personality as it relates to individual performance. There has also been a great deal of research on the relationship between personality traits and group attitudes and behaviour. The general conclusion is that attributes that tend to have a positive connotation in our culture tend to be positively related to group productivity, morale, and cohesiveness. These include traits such as sociability, initiative, openness, and flexibility. In contrast, negatively evaluated characteristics, such as authoritarianism, dominance, and unconventionality, tend to be negatively related to the dependent variables.[13] These personality traits affect group performance by strongly influencing how the individual will interact with other group members.

Is any one personality characteristic a good predictor of group behaviour? The answer to that question is "no." The magnitude of the effect of any *single* characteristic is small, but taking personality characteristics *together*, the consequences for group behaviour are of major significance. This chapter's HR Implications starting on page 228 discusses some of the selection procedures that organizations use in order to hire employees. Selection is a key factor in having employees who will be able to work in groups, if that is what is important to the organization.

## The Effects of Group Structure

Work groups are not unorganized mobs. They have a structure that shapes the behaviour of members and makes it possible to explain and predict a large portion of individual behaviour within the group, as well as the performance of the group itself. What are some of these structural variables?

They include formal leadership, roles, norms, group status, group size, composition of the group, and the degree of group cohesiveness.

**FORMAL LEADERSHIP** Almost every work group has a formal leader. He or she is typically identified by titles such as unit or department manager, supervisor, foreperson, project leader, task force head, or committee chair. This leader can play an important part in the group's success—so much so, in fact, that we have devoted an entire chapter to the topic of leadership. In Chapter 10, we will review the research on leadership and the effect that leaders have on individual and group performance variables.

**ROLES** Shakespeare said, "all the world's a stage, and all the men and women merely players." Using the same metaphor, all group members are actors, each playing a **role**. By this term, we mean a set of expected behaviour patterns attributed to someone occupying a given position in a social unit. The understanding of role behaviour would be dramatically simplified if each of us chose one role and "played it out" regularly and consistently. Unfortunately, we are required to play a number of diverse roles, both on and off our jobs. As we will see, one of the tasks in understanding behaviour is grasping the role that a person is currently playing.

For example, Ira Schwartz is a plant manager with a large electrical equipment manufacturer in Saskatchewan. He has a number of roles that he fulfills on that job—for instance, employee, member of middle management, electrical engineer, and the primary company spokesperson in the community. Off the job, Ira Schwartz finds himself in still more roles: husband, father, Jew, tennis player, food bank volunteer, and coach of his son's softball team. Many of these roles are compatible; some create conflicts. For instance, how does his religious involvement influence his managerial decisions regarding meeting with clients during Sabbath? A recent offer of promotion requires Ira to relocate, yet his family very much want to stay in Saskatoon. Can the role demands of his job be reconciled with the demands of his roles as husband and father?

The issue should be clear: Like Ira Schwartz, we all are required to play a number of roles, and our behaviour varies with the role we are playing. Ira's behaviour when he attends synagogue on Friday evening is different from his behaviour on the tennis court the day before. Different groups impose different role requirements on individuals.

*Role identity.* There are certain attitudes and actual behaviours consistent with a role, and they create the **role identity**. People have the ability to shift roles rapidly when they recognize that the situation and its demands clearly require major changes. For instance, when union stewards were promoted to supervisory positions, it was found that their attitudes changed from pro-union to pro-management within a few months of their promotions. When these promotions had to be rescinded later because of economic difficulties in the firm, it was found that the demoted supervisors had once again adopted their pro-union attitudes.[14]

*Role perception.* One's view of how one is supposed to act in a given situation is a **role perception**. Based on an interpretation of how we believe we are supposed to behave, we engage in certain types of behaviour.

Where do we get these perceptions? We get them from stimuli all around us—friends, books, movies, television. Many current law enforcement

**role**
A set of expected behaviour patterns attributed to someone occupying a given position in a social unit.

**role identity**
Certain attitudes and behaviours consistent with a role.

**role perception**
An individual's view of how he or she is supposed to act in a given situation.

Watching a veteran employee on the housekeeping staff helped Lisa Jackson (left) learn her role as a housekeeper at a Marriott hotel. In addition to teaching on-the-job skills such as the proper way to make a bed, Jackson's apprenticeship training included observing how employees should react in stressful situations.

officers learned their roles from reading Joseph Wambaugh novels; while many of tomorrow's lawyers will be influenced by watching the actions of attorneys in *Ally McBeal* or *The Practice*. The primary reason that apprenticeship programs exist in many trades and professions is to allow beginners to watch an "expert," so that they can learn to act as they are supposed to.

**role expectations**
How others believe a person should act in a given situation.

*Role expectations.* **Role expectations** are defined as how others believe you should act in a given situation. How you behave is determined to a large extent by the role defined in the context in which you are acting. The role of a Supreme Court judge is viewed as having propriety and dignity, whereas a hockey coach is seen as being aggressive, dynamic, and inspiring to his players. In the same context, we might be surprised to learn that the neighbourhood priest moonlights during the week as a bartender because our role expectations of priests and bartenders tend to be considerably different. When role expectations are concentrated into generalized categories, we have role stereotypes.

In the workplace, it can be helpful to look at the topic of role expectations through the perspective of the **psychological contract**. There is an unwritten agreement that exists between employees and their employer. As Professor Sandra Robinson from the University of British Columbia and her colleagues note, this psychological contract sets out mutual expectations—what management expects from workers, and vice versa.[15] In effect, this contract defines the behavioural expectations that go with every role. Management is expected to treat employees justly, provide acceptable working conditions, clearly communicate what is a fair day's work, and give feedback on how well the employee is doing. Employees are expected to respond by demonstrating a good attitude, following directions, and showing loyalty to the organization.

**psychological contract**
An unwritten agreement that sets out what management expects from the employee, and vice versa.

What happens when role expectations as implied in the psychological contract are not met? If management is negligent in holding up its part of the bargain, we can expect negative repercussions on employee performance and satisfaction. When employees fail to live up to expectations, the result is usually some form of disciplinary action up to and including firing.

When Alex Campbell was in high school, he worked as a bagger in a local supermarket. That experience led him years later to open his own supermarket. He wanted to make sure his employees would be treated better than he had been at that unnamed market. At his Vancouver Island Thrifty Foods stores, the implicit psychological contract Campbell makes with his employees is that everyone will be treated fairly. Even new employees aren't expected to work the worst shifts all the time, i.e., every night and weekend.

The psychological contract should be recognized as a "powerful determiner of behaviour in organizations."[16] It points out the importance of accurately communicating role expectations. In Chapter 9, we discuss how organizations socialize employees in order to get them to play out their roles in the way management desires.

*Role conflict.* When an individual is confronted by divergent role expectations, the result is **role conflict**. It exists when an individual finds that compliance with one role requirement may make more difficult compliance with another.[17] At the extreme, it can include situations in which two or more role expectations are mutually contradictory.

Our previous discussion of the many roles Ira Schwartz had to deal with included several role conflicts—for instance, Ira's attempt to reconcile the expectations placed on him as a husband and father with those placed on him as a manager with his firm. The former, as you will remember, emphasizes stability and concern for the desire of his wife and children to remain in Saskatoon. His company, on the other hand, expects its employees to be responsive to its needs and requirements. Although it might be in Ira's financial and career interests to accept a relocation, the conflict comes down to choosing between family and career role expectations.

All of us have faced and will continue to face role conflicts. The critical issue, from our standpoint, is how conflicts imposed by divergent expectations within the organization impact behaviour. Certainly, they increase internal tension and frustration. There are a number of behavioural responses one may engage in. For example, one can give a formalized bureaucratic response. The conflict is then resolved by relying on the rules, regulations, and procedures that govern organizational activities. For example, a worker faced with the conflicting requirements imposed by the corporate controller's office and his own plant manager decides in favour of his immediate boss—the plant manager. Other behavioural responses may include withdrawal, stalling, negotiation, or, as we found in our discussion of dissonance in Chapter 3, redefining the facts or the situation to make them appear congruent.

**role conflict**
A situation in which an individual is confronted by divergent role expectations.

Informality reigns at PeopleSoft, where "having fun" is an official corporate goal. Casual dress and playful behaviour are the norm at PeopleSoft, which sells enterprise resource planning software. It's not unusual to see employees like Mark Hoernemann (centre) wearing a silly hat, shooting co-workers with a Nerf gun, or playing on a mini golf course that runs through the office. Industry analysts attribute PeopleSoft's financial success as much to the strength of the firms' fun-loving environment as to the high quality of its software.

**task-oriented roles**
Roles performed by group members to ensure that the tasks of the group are accomplished.

**maintenance roles**
Roles performed by group members to maintain good relations within the group.

**individual roles**
Roles performed by group members that are not productive for keeping the group on task.

**norms**
Acceptable standards of behaviour within a group that are shared by the group's members.

*Roles within groups.* The practical implication of our lengthy discussion on roles is to consider whether roles contribute to an understanding of group development and functioning. Within almost any group, two sets of role relationships need to be considered: **task-oriented roles** and **maintenance roles**. The task-oriented roles are performed by group members to ensure that the tasks of the group are accomplished. The maintenance roles are carried out to ensure that group members maintain good relations. Effective groups maintain some balance between task orientation and maintenance of relations. Occasionally within groups, you will see people take on **individual roles** that are not productive for keeping the group on task. When this happens, the individual is demonstrating more concern for himself or herself than the group as a whole. Exhibit 5-5 identifies a number of task-oriented and maintenance roles that you might find in a group. The Working With Others Exercise on page 234 gives you the opportunity to see how these roles actually apply in a group interaction.

**NORMS**  Have you ever noticed that golfers don't speak while their partners are putting on the green, or that employees don't criticize their bosses in public? Why? The answer is "norms!"

All groups have established **norms**, that is, acceptable standards of behaviour that are shared by the group's members. Norms tell members what they ought and ought not to do under certain circumstances. From an individual's perspective, they tell what is expected of you in certain situations. When agreed to and accepted by the group, norms act as a means of influencing the behaviour of group members with a minimum of external controls. Norms differ among groups, communities, and societies, but all of these entities have norms.[18]

**Exhibit 5-5**
**Roles Required for Effective Group Functioning**

|  | Function | Description | Example |
|---|---|---|---|
| **Roles that build task accomplishment** | Initiating | Stating the goal or problem, making proposals about how to work on it, setting time limits. | "Let's set up an agenda for discussing each of the problems we have to consider." |
|  | Seeking Information and Opinions | Asking group members for specific factual information related to the task or problem, or for their opinions about it. | "What do you think would be the best approach to this, Jack?" |
|  | Providing Information and Opinions | Sharing information or opinions related to the task or problems. | "I worked on a similar problem last year and found...." |
|  | Clarifying | Helping one another understand ideas and suggestions that come up in the group. | "What you mean, Sue, is that we could...?" |
|  | Elaborating | Building on one another's ideas and suggestions. | "Building on Don's idea, I think we could...." |
|  | Summarizing | Reviewing the points covered by the group and the different ideas stated so that decisions can be based on full information. | Appointing a recorder to take notes on a blackboard. |
|  | Consensus Testing | Periodic testing about whether the group is nearing a decision or needs to continue discussion. | "Is the group ready to decide about this?" |
| **Roles that build and maintain a group** | Harmonizing | Mediating conflict among other members, reconciling disagreements, relieving tensions. | "Don, I don't think you and Sue really see the question that differently." |
|  | Compromising | Admitting error at times of group conflict. | "Well, I'd be willing to change if you provided some help on...." |
|  | Gatekeeping | Making sure all members have a chance to express their ideas and feelings and preventing members from being interrupted. | "Sue, we haven't heard from you on this issue." |
|  | Encouraging | Helping a group member make his or her point. Establishing a climate of acceptance in the group. | "I think what you started to say is important, Jack. Please continue." |

Source: "Team Processes," in D. Ancona, T. Kochan, M. Scully, J. Van Maanen, D. E. Westney, *Managing for the Future* (Cincinnati, OH: South-Western College Publishing, 1996), p. 9.

Toronto-based NRG Group, a marketer of multimedia and consulting services across Canada, hires many employees from the Net Generation, Canada's youngest workers. Vicki Saunders, NRG co-founder, pairs up groups of young people assigned to develop products such as websites with an older more experienced coach to help them. The coach can help her young employees learn the norms of the work world when meeting with clients. As one client, who was delighted with the fresh perspective the NRG group gave noted, "it was sometimes difficult working with a young and inexperienced staff. They didn't always get the message that deadlines in the business world are real." NRG's training obviously pays off for its employees. Michael Furdyk, one of the partners in MyDestop.com, an online publishing company recently sold to Connecticut's internet.com LLC for more than $1 million (US), got his start at NRG.

Formalized norms are written up in organizational manuals setting out rules and procedures for employees to follow. By far, most norms in organizations are informal. You don't need someone to tell you that throwing paper airplanes or engaging in prolonged gossip sessions at the water cooler is an unacceptable behaviour when the "big boss from Toronto" is touring the office. Similarly, we all know that when we're in an employment interview discussing what we didn't like about our previous job, there are certain things we shouldn't talk about (difficulty in getting along with co-workers or our manager). At the same time, it's very appropriate to talk about other things (inadequate opportunities for advancement, or unimportant and meaningless work). Evidence suggests that even high school students recognize that certain answers are more socially desirable than others in such interviews.[19]

Norms for both work groups and organizations cover a wide variety of circumstances. Some of the most common norms have to do with performance (such as how hard to work, what kind of quality, levels of tardiness), appearance (personal dress, as well as norms about when to look busy, when to goof off, how to show loyalty), social arrangement (how the informal groups interact), and allocation of resources (pay, assignments, allocation of tools and equipment).

*The "how" and "why" of norms. How* do norms develop? *Why* are they enforced? A review of the research allows us to answer these questions.[20]

Norms typically develop gradually as group members learn what behaviours are necessary for the group to function effectively. Of course, critical events in the group might short-circuit the process and quickly prompt new norms. Most norms develop in one or more of the following four ways:

- *Explicit statements made by a group member*—often the group's supervisor or a powerful member. The group leader might, for instance, specifically say that no personal phone calls are allowed during working hours or that coffee breaks must be no longer than 10 minutes.

- *Critical events in the group's history.* These set important precedents. A bystander is injured while standing too close to a machine and, from that point on, members of the work group regularly monitor each other to ensure that no one other than the operator gets within two metres of any machine.
- *Primacy.* The first behaviour pattern that emerges in a group frequently sets group expectations. Groups of students who are friends often stake out seats near each other on the first day of class and become upset if an outsider takes "their" seats in a later class.
- *Carry-over behaviours from past situations.* Group members bring expectations with them from other groups of which they have been members. This can explain why work groups typically prefer to add new members who are similar to current ones in background and experience. This is likely to increase the probability that the expectations they bring are consistent with those already held by the group.

Groups don't establish or enforce norms for every conceivable situation, however. The norms that the group will enforce tend to be those that are important to it.[21] What makes a norm important?

- *It facilitates the group's survival.* Groups don't like to fail, so they seek to enforce those norms that increase their chances for success. This means that they'll try to protect themselves from interference from other groups or individuals.
- *It increases the predictability of group members' behaviours.* Norms that increase predictability enable group members to anticipate each other's actions and to prepare appropriate responses.
- *It reduces embarrassing interpersonal problems for group members.* Norms are important if they ensure the satisfaction of their members and prevent as much interpersonal discomfort as possible.
- *It allows members to express the central values of the group and clarify what is distinctive about the group's identity.* Norms that encourage expression of the group's values and distinctive identity help to solidify and maintain the group.

*Conformity.* As a group member, you desire acceptance by the group. Because of your desire for acceptance, you are susceptible to conforming to the group's norms. Considerable evidence shows that groups can place strong pressures on individual members to change their attitudes and behaviours to conform to the group's standard.[22]

Do individuals conform to the pressures of all the groups to which they belong? Obviously not, because people belong to many groups and their norms vary. In some cases, groups may even have contradictory norms. So what do people do? They conform to the important groups to which they belong or hope to belong. The important groups have been referred to as **reference groups** and are characterized as ones where the person is aware of the others in the group; the person defines himself or herself as a member, or would like to be a member; and the person feels that the group members are significant to him or her.[23] The implication, then, is that all groups do not impose equal conformity pressures on their members.

The impact that group pressures for **conformity** can have on an individual member's judgment and attitudes was demonstrated in the now classic studies by Solomon Asch.[24] Asch found that subjects gave answers that they knew were wrong but that were consistent with the replies of other group

**reference groups**
Important groups to which individuals belong or hope to belong and with whose norms individuals are likely to conform.

**conformity**
Adjusting one's behaviour to align with the norms of the group.

members about 35 percent of the time. The results suggest that certain group norms pressure us toward conformity. We desire to be one of the group and avoid being visibly different.

Recent research by UBC professor Sandra Robinson and a colleague indicates that conformity may explain why some work groups are more prone to antisocial behaviour than others.[25] Individuals who worked with others who exhibited antisocial behaviour at work were more likely to engage in antisocial behaviour themselves. Of course, not all conformity leads to negative behaviour. Other research has indicated that work groups can have more positive influences, leading to more prosocial behaviour in the workplace.[26]

Overall, research continues to indicate that conformity to norms is a powerful force in groups.

**status**
A socially defined position or rank given to groups or group members by others.

**STATUS** Status is a socially defined position or rank given to groups or group members by others, and it permeates all of society. We live in a class-structured society. Despite all attempts to make it more egalitarian, we have made little progress toward a classless society. Even the smallest group will develop roles, rights, and rituals to differentiate its members. Status is an important factor in understanding human behaviour because it is a significant motivator and has major behavioural consequences when individuals perceive a disparity between what they believe their status to be and what others perceive it to be.

*Status and norms.* Status has been shown to have some interesting effects on the power of norms and pressures to conform. For instance, high-status members of groups are often given more freedom to deviate from norms than are other group members.[27] High-status people are also better able to resist conformity pressures than their lower-status peers. An individual who is highly valued by a group but who doesn't much need or care about the social rewards the group provides is particularly able to pay minimal attention to conformity norms.[28]

The previous findings explain why many star athletes, famous actors, top-performing salespeople, and outstanding academics seem oblivious to appearance or social norms that constrain their peers. As high-status individuals, they're given a wider range of discretion. But this is true only as long as the high-status person's activities aren't severely detrimental to group goal achievement.[29]

*Status equity.* It is important for group members to believe that the status hierarchy is equitable. When inequity is perceived, it creates disequilibrium that results in various types of corrective behaviour.[30]

The concept of equity presented in Chapter 4 applies to status. People expect rewards to be proportionate to costs incurred. If Isaac and Anne are the two finalists for the head-nurse position in a hospital, and it is clear that Isaac has more seniority and better preparation for assuming the promotion, Anne will view the selection of Isaac to be equitable. However, if Anne is chosen because she is the daughter-in-law of the hospital director, Isaac will believe that an injustice has been committed. The trappings that go with formal positions are also important elements in maintaining equity. When we believe there is an inequity between the perceived ranking of an individual and the status rewards that the organization gives the person, we are experiencing status incongruence. Examples of this kind of incongruence are the more desirable office location being held by a lower-ranking individual, and paid country club memberships being provided by the company for division managers but not for vice-presidents. Pay incongruence has long been a problem in the insurance industry, where top sales agents often earn two to five times more than senior corporate executives. The result is that insurance companies find it difficult to entice successful agents into management positions. Our point is that employees expect the things an individual has and receives to be congruent with his or her status.

Groups generally agree within themselves on status criteria, and hence, there is usually high concurrence in group rankings of individuals. However, individuals can find themselves in conflict when they move between groups whose status criteria are different, or when they join groups whose members have heterogeneous backgrounds. For instance, business executives may use personal income or the growth rate of their companies as determinants of status. Government bureaucrats may use the size of their budgets. Professional employees and entrepreneurs may use the degree of autonomy that comes with their job assignment. Blue-collar workers may use years of seniority. In groups composed of heterogeneous individuals, or when heterogeneous groups are forced to be interdependent, status differences may initiate conflict as the group attempts to reconcile and align the differing hierarchies. As we'll see in the next chapter, this can be a particular problem when management creates teams composed of employees from across varied functions within the organization.

**STATUS AND CULTURE** Before we leave the topic of status, we should briefly address the issue of cross-cultural transferability. Do cultural differences affect status? The answer is a resounding "yes."[31]

The importance of status does vary between cultures. The French, for example, are highly status conscious. Additionally, countries differ on the critieria that create status. For instance, status for Latin Americans and Asians tends to be derived from family position and formal roles held in organizations. In contrast, while status is still important in countries like Canada, Australia, and the United States, it tends to be less "in your face." And it tends to be bestowed more through accomplishments than titles and family trees.

The message here is make sure you understand who and what holds status when interacting with people from a different culture than your own. An American manager who doesn't understand that office size is no measure of a Japanese executive's position, or who fails to grasp the importance that the British place on family genealogy and social class, is likely to unintentionally offend his or her Japanese or British counterpart. In so doing, the manager will lessen his or her interpersonal effectiveness.

**SIZE** Does the size of a group affect the group's overall behaviour? The answer to this question is a definite "yes," but the effect depends on what dependent variables you look at.[32]

The evidence indicates, for instance, that smaller groups are faster at completing tasks than are larger ones. However, if the group is engaged in problem-solving, large groups consistently get better marks than their smaller counterparts. Translating these results into specific numbers is a bit more hazardous, but we can offer some parameters. Large groups—with a dozen or more members—are good for gaining diverse input. So if the goal of the group is fact-finding, larger groups should be more effective. On the other hand, smaller groups are better at doing something productive with that input. Groups of approximately seven members, therefore, tend to be more effective for taking action.

One of the most important findings related to the size of a group has been labelled **social loafing**. Social loafing is the tendency for individuals to expend less effort when working collectively than when working individually.[33] It directly challenges the logic that the productivity of the group as a whole should at least equal the sum of the productivity of each individual in that group.

A common stereotype about groups is that the sense of team spirit spurs individual effort and enhances the group's overall productivity. In the late 1920s, a German psychologist named Max Ringelmann compared the results of individual and group performance on a rope-pulling task.[34] He expected that the group's effort would be equal to the sum of the efforts of individuals within the group. That is, three people pulling together should exert three times as much pull on the rope as one person, and eight people should exert eight times as much pull. Ringelmann's results, however, did not confirm his expectations. Groups of three people exerted a force only 2.5 times the average individual performance. Groups of eight collectively achieved less than four times the solo rate.

Replications of Ringelmann's research with similar tasks have generally supported his findings.[35] Increases in group size are inversely related to individual performance. More may be better in the sense that the total productivity of a group of four is greater than that of one or two people, but the individual productivity of each group member declines.

What causes this social loafing effect? It may be due to a belief that others in the group are not carrying their fair share. If you view others as lazy or inept, you can re-establish equity by reducing your effort. Another explanation is the dispersion of responsibility. Because the results of the group cannot be attributed to any single person, the relationship between an individual's input and the group's output is clouded. In such situations, individuals may be tempted to become "free riders" and coast on the group's efforts. In other words, there will be a reduction in efficiency when individuals believe that their contribution cannot be measured.

The implications for OB of this effect on work groups are significant. Where managers utilize collective work situations to enhance morale and teamwork, they must also provide means by which individual efforts can be identified. If this is not done, management must weigh the potential losses in productivity from using groups against any possible gains in worker satisfaction.[36] However, this conclusion has a Western bias. It's consistent with individualistic cultures that are dominated by self-interest, such as Canada and the United States. It is not consistent with collective societies where individuals are motivated by in-group goals. For instance, in studies comparing employees from the United States with employees from the People's Republic of China and Israel (both collectivist societies), the Chinese and Israelis showed no propensity to engage in social loafing. In fact, the Chinese and Israelis actually performed better in a group than when working alone.[37]

The research on group size leads us to two additional conclusions: (1) Groups with an odd number of members tend to be preferable to those with an even number; and (2) groups composed of five or seven members do a fairly good job of exercising the best elements of both small and large

**social loafing**
The tendency for individuals to expend less effort when working collectively than when working individually.

Ever notice that some group members don't seem to pull their weight?

groups.[38] Having an odd number of members eliminates the possibility of ties when votes are taken. And groups composed of five or seven members are large enough to form a majority and allow for diverse input, yet small enough to avoid the negative outcomes often associated with large groups, such as domination by a few members, development of subgroups, inhibited participation by some members, and excessive time taken to reach a decision.

**Why do some groups seem to get along with each other better than others?**

**COMPOSITION** Most group activities require a variety of skills and knowledge. Given this requirement, it would be reasonable to conclude that heterogeneous groups—those composed of dissimilar individuals—would be more likely to have diverse abilities and information, and should be more effective. Research studies generally substantiate this conclusion, especially on cognitive, creativity-demanding tasks.[39]

When a group is heterogeneous in terms of personalities, gender, age, education, functional specialization, and experience, there is an increased probability that the group will possess the needed characteristics to complete its tasks effectively and perform more effectively.[40] However, the group may be more conflict-laden and less expedient as diverse positions are introduced and assimilated, and individuals may express less cohesiveness and satisfaction about the group process. Essentially, diversity promotes conflict, which stimulates creativity and idea generation, which leads to improved decision making.

But what about diversity created by racial or national differences? The evidence is mixed.[41] Culturally heterogeneous groups have more difficulty in learning to work with each other and solving problems, in part because of cultural norms. Culturally diverse groups also report less cohesiveness and less satisfaction with the group process. The good news is that these difficulties seem to dissipate over time. Cultural diversity seems to be an asset on tasks that call for a variety of viewpoints. Newly formed culturally diverse groups may underperform newly formed culturally homogeneous groups, but the evidence on this is mixed.[42] At worst, the differences seem to disappear after about three months. It may take diverse groups a while to learn how to work through disagreements and different approaches to solving problems. In the Case Incident on page 237, you are asked to consider some of the interpersonal issues that arise when groups confront diversity considerations.

Some recent research on groups emphasizes the effect of friendship on group performance.[43] When groups were asked either to create models out of Tinkertoys or make decisions on ranking individuals, groups composed of friends performed better than those composed of acquaintances.

In a study examining the effectiveness of teams of strangers and teams of friends on bargaining, researchers found that teams of strangers gained greater profit than teams of friends, when teams reported to a supervisor.[44] However, teams of friends were more cohesive than teams of strangers. One potentially negative finding of this research is that teams of friends were more concerned about maintaining their relationship than were teams of strangers. In the workplace, the importance of maintaining relationships could lead to lower productivity.

Overall, the message to be drawn from research on friendships is not that organizations should hire friends, but that workplaces might do well to encourage environments that promote friendships among co-workers.

Can synergy and cohesiveness overcome the naysayers? Visit The Post Road Tea Room, located in the basement of the Uniacke Estate Museum Park in Mount Uniacke, just northwest of Halifax, and you'll see for yourself. Morgan Hicks, Carrie Donovan, Mary Middleton and Michael Sponagle were sure that the Uniacke Estate Museum could use a tea room. There were hiking trails there, which meant hungry, thirsty hikers. However, when the four first presented the idea as a business plan in their Grade 9 Maritime Studies class, their fellow students gave a resounding thumbs down to their idea, saying it was far-fetched. Unconvinced, the four friends made a presentation to the museum board, and then beat out at least one other bidder. The 1850's-style tearoom opened in the summer of 1995, and is still a growing business.

**cohesiveness**
Degree to which group members are attracted to each other and are motivated to stay in the group.

**COHESIVENESS**   Groups differ in their **cohesiveness**; that is, the degree to which members are attracted to each other and are motivated to stay in the group.[45] For instance, some work groups are cohesive because the members have spent a great deal of time together, the group's small size facilitates high interaction, or the group has experienced external threats that have brought members close together. Cohesiveness is important because it has been found to be related to the group's productivity.[46]

Studies consistently show that the relationship of cohesiveness and productivity depends on the performance-related norms established by the group. If performance-related norms are high (for example, high output, quality work, cooperation with individuals outside the group), a cohesive group will be more productive than will a less-cohesive group. If cohesiveness is high and performance norms are low, productivity will be low. If cohesiveness is low and performance norms are high, productivity increases but less than in the high cohesiveness–high norms situation. Where cohesiveness and performance-related norms are both low, productivity will tend to fall into the low-to-moderate range. These conclusions are summarized in Exhibit 5-6.

We consider how to increase group cohesion later in the chapter.

## Group Processes

The next component of our group behaviour model considers the processes that go on within a work group—the communication patterns used by members for information exchanges, group decision processes, leader behaviour, power dynamics, conflict interactions, and the like. Chapters 7 through 11 elaborate on many of these processes.

Why are processes important to understanding work group behaviour? One way to answer this question is to

**Exhibit 5-6**
**Relationship Between Group Cohesiveness, Performance Norms, and Productivity**

|                      |      | Cohesiveness | |
|----------------------|------|-------------|---------------------------|
|                      |      | High        | Low                       |
| **Performance norms** | High | High productivity | Moderate productivity |
|                      | Low  | Low productivity | Moderate to low productivity |

## Exhibit 5-7
## Effects of Group Processes

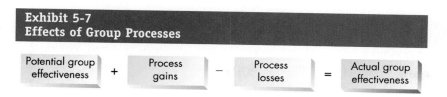

**synergy**
An action of two or more substances that results in an effect that is different from the individual summation of the substances.

return to the topic of social loafing. We've found that 1+1+1 doesn't necessarily add up to three. In group tasks where each member's contribution is not clearly visible, individuals tend to decrease their effort. Social loafing, in other words, illustrates a process loss as a result of using groups. But group processes can also produce positive results. That is, groups can create outputs greater than the sum of their inputs. Exhibit 5-7 illustrates how group processes can impact a group's actual effectiveness.[47]

**Synergy** is a term used in biology that refers to an action of two or more substances that results in an effect that is different from the individual summation of the substances. We can use the concept to better understand group processes.

Social loafing, for instance, represents negative synergy. The whole is less than the sum of its parts. On the other hand, research teams are often used in research laboratories because they can draw on the diverse skills of various individuals. In combining their skills, the researchers produce more meaningful research as a group than they could generate independently. That is, they produce positive synergy. Their process gains exceed their process losses.

Another line of research that helps us to better understand group processes is the social facilitation effect.[48] Have you ever noticed that performing a task in front of others can have a positive or negative effect on your performance? For instance, you privately practise a complex springboard dive at your home pool for weeks. Then you do the dive in front of a group of friends and you do it better than ever. Or you practise a speech in private and finally get it down perfectly, but you "bomb" when you have to give the speech in public.

**social facilitation effect**
The tendency for performance to improve or decline in response to the presence of others.

The **social facilitation effect** refers to this tendency for performance to improve or decline in response to the presence of others. While this effect is not entirely a group phenomenon—people can work in the presence of others and not be members of a group—the group situation is more likely to provide the conditions for social facilitation to occur. The research on social facilitation tells us that the performance of simple, routine tasks tends to be speeded up and made more accurate by the presence of others. Where the work is more complex, requiring closer attention, the presence of others is likely to have a negative effect on performance.[49] So what are the implications of this research in terms of managing process gains and losses? The implications relate to learning and training. People seem to perform better on a task in the presence of others if that task is very well learned, but poorly if it is not well learned. So process gains will be maximized by training people for simple tasks in groups, while training people for complex tasks in individual, private practice sessions.

## Group Tasks

Imagine, for a moment, that there are two groups at a major oil company. The job of the first is to consider possible location sites for a new refinery. The decision is going to affect people in many areas of the company—production, engineering, marketing, distribution, purchasing, real estate development, and the like—so key people from each of these areas will need to provide input into the decision. The job of the second group is to coordinate the building of the refinery after the site has been selected, the design finalized, and the financial arrangements completed. Research on group effectiveness tells us that management would be well advised to use a larger group for the first task than for the second.[50] The reason is that large groups facilitate pooling of information. The addition of a diverse perspective to a problem-solving committee typically results in a process gain. But when a group's task is coordinating and implementing a decision, the process loss created by each additional member's presence is likely to be greater than the process gain he or she makes. So the size-performance relationship is moderated by the group's task requirements.

The preceding conclusions can be extended: The impact of group processes on the group's performance and member satisfaction is also moderated by the tasks that the group is doing. The evidence indicates that the complexity and interdependence of tasks influence the group's effectiveness.[51]

Tasks can be generalized as either simple or complex. Complex tasks are ones that tend to be novel or nonroutine. Simple ones are routine and standardized. We would hypothesize that the more complex the task, the more the group will benefit from discussion among members on alternative work methods. If the task is simple, group members don't need to discuss such alternatives. They can rely on standardized operating procedures for doing the job. Similarly, if there is a high degree of interdependence among the tasks that group members must perform, they'll need to interact more. Effective communication and minimal levels of conflict, therefore, should be more relevant to group performance when tasks are interdependent.

These conclusions are consistent with what we know about information-processing capacity and uncertainty.[52] Tasks that have higher uncertainty—those that are complex and interdependent—require more information processing. This, in turn, puts more importance on group processes. So just because a group is characterized by poor communication, weak leadership, high levels of conflict, and the like, it doesn't necessarily mean that it will be low performing. If the group's tasks are simple and require little interdependence among members, the group still may be effective. This chapter's CBC Video Case illustrates further ways that groups can figure out the necessary tasks and then assign them, so that they get completed.

## Can We Build a Better Working Group?

Working in groups is probably an inevitable life experience, even for people who prefer to work alone. There are always student groups, task forces, and neighbourhood associations in addition to all of the workplace demands for working in a group. Therefore, it might be helpful to think a little about how to improve group performance and interaction. The From Concepts to Skills feature for this chapter gives guidelines for conducting a group meeting. These will help in many instances to keep discussions on track.

Beyond meetings, however, there are factors for both organizations and individuals to consider with respect to creating conditions that will lead groups to engage in higher productivity. These include the type of tasks assigned to a group, specific organizational supports, and ways that groups can increase their cohesiveness.

# From CONCEPTS to SKILLS

# Conducting a Group Meeting

Group meetings have a reputation for inefficiency. For instance, noted Canadian-born economist John Kenneth Galbraith has said, "Meetings are indispensable when you don't want to do anything."

When you're responsible for conducting a meeting, what can you do to make it more efficient and effective? Follow these 12 steps:

1. *Prepare a meeting agenda.* An agenda defines what you hope to accomplish at the meeting. It should state the meeting's purpose; who will be in attendance; what, if any, preparation is required of each participant; a detailed list of items to be covered; the specific time and location of the meeting; and a specific finishing time.

2. *Distribute the agenda in advance.* Participants should have the agenda sufficiently in advance so they can adequately prepare for the meeting.

3. *Consult with participants before the meeting.* An unprepared participant can't contribute to his or her full potential. It is your responsibility to ensure that members are prepared, so check with them ahead of time.

4. *Get participants to go over the agenda.* The first thing to do at the meeting is to have participants review the agenda, make any changes, then approve the final agenda.

5. *Establish specific time parameters.* Meetings should begin on time and have a specific time for completion. It is your responsibility to specify these time parameters and to hold to them.

6. *Maintain focused discussion.* It is your responsibility to give direction to the discussion; to keep it focused on the issues; and to minimize interruptions, disruptions, and irrelevant comments.

7. *Encourage and support participation of all members.* To maximize the effectiveness of problem-oriented meetings, each participant must be encouraged to contribute. Quiet or reserved personalities need to be drawn out so their ideas can be heard.

8. *Maintain a balanced style.* The effective group leader pushes when necessary and is passive when need be.

9. *Encourage the clash of ideas.* You need to encourage different points of view, critical thinking, and constructive disagreement.

10. *Discourage the clash of personalities.* An effective meeting is characterized by the critical assessment of ideas, not attacks on people. When running a meeting, you must quickly intercede to stop personal attacks or other forms of verbal insult.

11. *Be an effective listener.* You need to listen with intensity, empathy, and objectivity, and do whatever is necessary to get the full intended meaning from each participant's comments.

12. *Bring proper closure.* You should close a meeting by summarizing the group's accomplishments; clarifying what actions, if any, need to follow the meeting; and allocating follow-up assignments. If any decisions are made, you also need to determine who will be responsible for communicating and implementing them.

Source: S.P. Robbins and P.L. Hunsaker, *Training in Interpersonal Skills,* 2nd ed. (Upper Saddle River, NJ: Prentice Hall, 1996), pp. 168-184.

## Assigning Appropriate Tasks

Perhaps the first consideration for group effectiveness is the type of task that the group is asked to perform. Some tasks are simply more inspiring to groups than others, and therefore will result in a better work product. Richard Hackman (whose Hackman-Oldham model we will consider in Chapter 13) has outlined the following conditions under which we would expect groups to work "especially hard":[53]

- The group task requires members to use a variety of relatively high-level skills.

- The group task is a whole and meaningful piece of work with a visible outcome.

- The outcomes of the group's work on the task have significant consequences for other people (for example, other organization members or external clients).

- The task provides group members with substantial autonomy for deciding about how they do the work—in effect, the group "owns" the task and is responsible for the work outcomes.

- Work on the task generates regular, trustworthy feedback about how well the group is performing.

## Providing Organizational Support

Organizations can do a variety of things to provide support for groups to work together. These include the following:[54]

- *Assign appropriate people to the group.* Members of effective teams have the technical and interpersonal skills to function well together. It is often thought that having technical skills is enough, but for groups to work together they also need to trust each other. This trust leads to open and supportive relationships and a "we" feeling.

- *Provide appropriate group training.* Individuals do not necessarily know how to function well in a group. Therefore organizations should provide programs for all members to improve technical and interpersonal skills.

- *Provide adequate and timely information.* Managers should ensure that employees have the information they need to carry out their group tasks. When information is not available or forthcoming, managers should also explain this to the employees.

- *Give challenging, specific performance objectives.* We noted when discussing goal setting that individuals do well when faced with moderately difficult goals. The same is true for groups. Groups respond to the challenge of meeting deadlines, knowing what quality needs to be achieved, and so on. However, it is also important that the task be interesting and meaningful, as we noted above.

- *Give rewards for excellent performance.* We noted in Chapter 4 that people tend to engage in activities that are rewarded. The same is true for groups. The nature of the rewards can vary, from recognition to more specific tangible items. It is also the case, as we discussed in Chapter 4, that a motivating task is often a reward in itself.

- *Direct rewards and objectives to the group level.* If an organization wants a set of individuals to function as a group, then the activities and the rewards must be group-based. Organizational reward systems often focus on individuals, which creates an incentive for individuals to focus on their own needs, rather than those of the group.

## Building Group Cohesiveness

When teams function well, everyone is energized and works toward the task. Organizations can provide tasks that groups find challenging and motivating, and they can provide some of the structural support needed to do the task appropriately. But the group itself must create an internal climate that makes participating in the group worthwhile, both from an organizational and a personal perspective. Parker identifies 12 characteristics that he believes differentiate between effective and ineffective groups:[55]

- *Clear purpose.* The group has clear and jointly agreed-upon goals.
- *Participation.* Group members share information, and all contributions are respected and valued.
- *Civilized disagreement.* Conflict will naturally occur in most groups. Effective groups learn to manage the conflict and develop mechanisms to resolve it.
- *Open communications.* Group members communicate openly with each other, helping to build trust among group members. Group members use both formal and informal opportunities to communicate.
- *Listening.* Group members listen effectively—not only to understand the information presented, but also to achieve interpersonal understanding and empathy.
- *Informal climate.* The group operates in a comfortable and relaxed atmosphere. This leads to more open communication as well as flexibility.
- *Consensus decisions.* The group allows people to express opinions, reservations, disagreements, and then comes together for a solution that the entire group can support. Everyone does not necessarily have to agree on the solution itself, but they do need to agree that the solution is supported by the group as a whole. In other words, "A consensus is reached when all members can say they either agree with the decision or have had their 'day in court' and were unable to convince the others of their viewpoint. In the final analysis, everyone agrees to support the outcome."[56]
- *Clear roles and work assignments.* For the group to function there must be clear agreement about the roles, responsibilities, and assignments of group members. When these are unclear, conflict often occurs.
- *Shared leadership.* Members of the group work together, not burdening one person with all of the responsibility for how the team functions.
- *Style diversity.* Groups accept that there are differences in their members, and learn to use these differences in advantageous ways.
- *External relationships.* The group collects information from a variety of sources, rather than simply relying on its own resources.
- *Self-assessment.* Groups need to do periodic self-assessments to examine how well they are doing. This gives team members the opportunity to ask the following questions: "How well are we doing?" "What are we doing right?" "How can we improve our performance?" "Are there any interpersonal problems?" "Is everyone contributing adequately to the group's performance?"

By going through a checklist such as the above, groups have an opportunity to examine themselves as they work toward their goals. You might consider the items above when working in your next student group, so that you could improve your group's performance.

## HR Implications

# Selecting Organizational Members

This chapter focused on people working in groups and the problems they encounter. It also noted some of the pros and cons of diversity in organizations. One of the tasks of the HR manager is selecting (or hiring) the people who will work for the organization. While fit with groups already in the organization may not be the sole criterion used to hire a new employee, it is certainly one of the considerations. Below we describe the process of selection in the organization.

### Selection Practices

The objective of effective selection is to match individual characteristics (ability, experience, and so on) with the requirements of the job.[1] If the job also requires that the individual work closely as part of a team, then interpersonal characteristics may also become important. When management fails to get a proper match, both employee performance and satisfaction suffer.

### Selection Devices

Organizations can use application forms, interviews, employment tests, background checks, and reference letters to obtain information about a job applicant. This information can help the organization determine whether the applicant's skills, knowledge, and abilities are appropriate for the job in question. In this section, we review the more important of these selection devices—interviews, written tests, and performance simulation tests.

**Interviews** Do you know anyone who has received a job without at least one interview? You may have an acquaintance who got a part-time or summer job through a close friend or relative without having to go through an interview, but such instances are rare. Of all the selection devices that organizations use to differentiate candidates, the interview continues to be the most frequent.[2]

The interview also seems to carry a great deal of weight. That is, not only is it widely used, but its results also tend to have a disproportionate amount of influence on the selection decision. The candidate who performs poorly in the employment interview is likely to be cut from the applicant pool, regardless of his or her experience, test scores, or reference letters. Conversely, "all too often, the person most polished in job-seeking techniques, particularly those used in the interview process, is the one hired, even though he or she may not be the best candidate for the position."[3]

These findings are important because of the unstructured manner in which the selection interview is frequently conducted. The unstructured interview—short in duration, casual, and made up of random questions—has been proven to be an ineffective selection device.[4] The data gathered from such interviews are typically biased and often unrelated to future job performance. Without structure, a number of biases can distort results. These biases include interviewers tending to favour applicants who share their attitudes, giving unduly high weight to negative information, and allowing the order in which applicants are interviewed to influence evaluations.[5] By having interviewers use a standardized set of questions, providing interviewers with a uniform method of recording information, and standardizing the rating of the applicant's qualifications, the variability in results across applicants is reduced and the validity of the interview as a selection device is greatly enhanced.

The evidence indicates that interviews are most valuable for assessing an applicant's intelligence, level of motivation, and interpersonal skills.[6] When these qualities are related to job performance, the validity of the interview as a selection device is increased. For example, these qualities have demonstrated relevance for performance in upper managerial positions. This may explain why applicants for senior management positions typically undergo dozens of interviews with executive recruiters, board members, and other company executives before a final decision is made. It can also explain why organizations that design work around teams may similarly put applicants through an unusually large number of interviews.

**Written Tests** Typical written tests are tests of intelligence, aptitude, ability, interest, and integrity.

Long popular as selection devices, some concerns have arisen about them in recent years. Some tests have been characterized as discriminatory, and have not been validated as being job-related.

Tests in intellectual ability, spatial and mechanical ability, perceptual accuracy, and motor ability have shown to be moderately valid predictors for many semi-skilled and unskilled operative jobs in industrial organizations.[7] Intelligence tests have proven to be particularly good predictors for jobs that require cognitive complexity.[8] Japanese auto makers, when staffing plants in Canada and the United States, have relied heavily on written tests to predict candidates that will be high performers.[9] Getting a job with Toyota Canada, for instance, can take up to three days of testing and interviewing. Written tests typically focus on skills such as reading, mathematics, mechanical dexterity, and ability to work with others.

As ethical problems have increased in organizations, integrity tests have gained popularity. These are paper-and-pencil tests that measure factors such as dependability, carefulness, responsibility, and honesty. The evidence is impressive that these tests are powerful in predicting managerial ratings of job performance and counterproductive employee behaviour on the job, such as theft, discipline problems, and excessive absenteeism.[10]

**Performance Simulation Tests** What better way is there to find out if an applicant can do a job successfully than by having him or her do it? That's precisely the logic of performance simulation tests.

Performance simulation tests have increased in popularity during the past two decades. Undoubtedly the enthusiasm for these tests comes from the fact that they are based on job analysis data, and therefore, they more easily meet the requirement of job relatedness than do most written tests. Performance simulation tests are made up of actual job behaviours that the employee must perform.

The two best-known performance simulation tests are work sampling and assessment centres. The former is suited to routine jobs, whereas the latter is relevant for the selection of managerial personnel.

**Work sampling** is an effort to create a miniature replica of a job. Applicants demonstrate that they possess the necessary talents by actually doing the tasks. Employers choose a sample of behaviours that applicants must perform for a specific job, and the candidate then demonstrates his or her knowledge, skills, and abilities through the tasks given. For instance, a work sample for a job where the employee has to use computer spreadsheet software would require the applicant to actually solve a problem using a spreadsheet.

The results from work sample experiments are impressive. Studies almost consistently demonstrate that work samples yield validities superior to written aptitude and personality tests.[11]

A more elaborate set of performance simulation tests, specifically designed to evaluate a candidate's managerial potential, is administered in **assessment centres**. In assessment centres, line executives, managers, and/or trained psychologists evaluate candidates as they undergo two to four days of exercises that simulate real problems they would confront on the job. Based on a list of descriptive dimensions that the actual job incumbent has to meet, activities might include interviews, in-basket problem-solving exercises, group discussions, and business decision games. For instance, a candidate might be required to play the role of a manager who must decide how to respond to 10 memos in his or her in-basket within a two-hour period.

How valid is the assessment centre as a selection device? The evidence on the effectiveness of assessment centres is extremely impressive. They have consistently demonstrated results that predict later job performance in managerial positions.[12]

---

Sources:

1. See, for instance, C.T. Dortch, "Job-Person Match," *Personnel Journal*, June 1989, pp. 49-75; and S. Rynes and B. Gerhart, "Interviewer Assessments of Applicant 'Fit': An Exploratory Investigation," *Personnel Psychology*, Spring 1990, pp. 13-34.

2. R.L. Dipboye, *Selection Interviews: Process Perspectives* (Cincinnati: South-Western Publishing, 1992), p. 6; and J.E. Rigdon, "Talk Isn't Cheap," *Wall Street Journal*, February 27, 1995, p. R13.

3. T.J. Hanson and J.C. Balestreri-Spero, "An Alternative to Interviews," *Personnel Journal*, June 1985, p. 114.

4. See A.J. Huffcutt and W. Arthur Jr., "Hunter and Hunter (1984) Revisited: Interview Validity for Entry-Level Jobs," *Journal of*

*Applied Psychology*, April 1994, pp. 184-190; M.A. McDaniel, D.L. Whetzel, F.L. Schmidt, and S.D. Maurer, "The Validity of Employment Interviews: A Comprehensive Review and Meta-Analysis," *Journal of Applied Psychology*, August 1994, pp. 599-616; and J.M. Conway, R.A. Jako, and D.F. Goodman, "A Meta-Analysis of Interrater and Internal Consistency Reliability of Selection Interviews," *Journal of Applied Psychology*, October 1995, pp. 565-579.

5. R.L. Dipboye, *Selection Interviews: Process Perspectives* (Cincinnati: South-Western Publishing, 1992), pp. 42-44.

6. W.F. Cascio, *Applied Psychology in Personnel Management*, 4th ed. (Englewood Cliff, NJ: Prentice-Hall, 1991), p. 271.

7. E.E. Ghiselli, "The Validity of Aptitude Tests in Personnel Selection," *Personnel Psychology*, Winter 1973, p. 475.

8. R.J. Herrnstein and C. Murray, *The Bell Curve: Intelligence and Class Structure in American Life* (New York: Free Press, 1994); and

M.J. Ree, J.A. Earles, and M.S. Teachout, "Predicting Job Performance: Not Much More Than *g*," *Journal of Applied Psychology*, August 1994, pp. 518-524.

9. J. Flint, "Can You Tell Applesauce From Pickles?" *Forbes*, October 9, 1995, pp. 106-108.

10. D.S. Ones, C. Viswesvaran, and F.L. Schmidt, "Comprehensive Meta-Analysis of Integrity Test Validities: Findings and Implications for Personnel Selection and Theories of Job Performance," *Journal of Applied Psychology*, August 1993, pp. 679-703.

11. J.J. Asher and J.A. Sciarrino, "Realistic Work Sample Tests: A Review," *Personnel Psychology*, Winter 1974, pp. 519-533; and I.T. Robertson and R.S. Kandola, "Work Sample Tests: Validity, Adverse Impact and Application Reaction," *Journal of Occupational Psychology*, Spring 1982, pp. 171-182.

12. G.C. Thornton, *Assessment Centers in Human Resource Management* (Reading, MA: Addison-Wesley, 1992).

# *SUMMARY AND IMPLICATIONS*

## For the Workplace

We've covered a lot of territory in this chapter. Since we essentially organized our discussion around the group behaviour model in Exhibit 5-4, let's use this model to summarize our findings regarding performance and satisfaction. Then we'll look at the impact of group relations.

**PERFORMANCE** Any predictions about a group's performance must begin by recognizing that work groups are part of a larger organization and that factors such as the organization's strategy, authority structure, selection procedures, and reward system can provide a favourable or unfavourable climate for the group to operate within. For example, if an organization is characterized by distrust between management and workers, it is more likely that work groups in that organization will develop norms to restrict effort and output than will work groups in an organization where trust is high. So managers shouldn't look at any group in isolation. Rather, they should begin by assessing the degree of support external conditions provide the group. It is obviously a lot easier for any work group to be productive when the overall organization of which it is a part is growing, and the work group has both top management's support and abundant resources. Similarly, a group is more likely to be productive when its members have the requisite skills to do the group's tasks, along with the personality characteristics that facilitate working well together.

A number of structural factors show a relationship to performance. Among the more prominent are role perception, norms, status inequities, size of the group, its composition, the group's task, and its cohesiveness.

There is a positive relationship between role perception and an employee's performance evaluation.[57] The degree of congruence that exists between an employee and his or her boss in the perception of the employee's job influences the degree to which that employee will be judged as an effective performer by the boss. To the extent that the employee's role perception fulfills the boss's role expectations, the employee will receive a higher performance evaluation.

Norms control group-member behaviour by establishing standards of right and wrong. Knowing the norms of a given group can help managers to explain the behaviours of its members. Where norms support high output, managers can expect individual performance to be markedly higher than where group norms aim to restrict output. Similarly, acceptable standards of absenteeism will be dictated by the group norms.

Status inequities create frustration and can adversely influence productivity and the willingness to remain with an organization. Among those individuals who are equity sensitive, incongruence is likely to lead to reduced motivation and an increased search for ways to bring about fairness (that is, taking another job).

The impact of size on a group's performance depends upon the type of task in which the group is engaged. Larger groups are more effective at fact-finding activities. Smaller groups are more effective at action-taking tasks. Our knowledge of social loafing suggests that if management uses larger groups, efforts should be made to provide measures of individual performance within the group.

We also found that cohesiveness can play an important function in influencing a group's level of productivity. Whether or not it does depends on the group's performance-related norms.

The primary contingency variable moderating the relationship between group processes and performance is the group's tasks. The more complex and interdependent the tasks, the more that inefficient processes will lead to reduced group performance.

Group conflict can also affect performance. However, there is no reason to believe that all group conflict leads to problems. As you will see in Chapter 7, some minimal levels of conflict can facilitate critical thinking among group members, make a group more responsive to the need for change, and provide similar benefits that can enhance group and organizational performance.

**SATISFACTION** As with the role of the perception-performance relationship, high congruence between a boss and employee as to the perception of the employee's job shows a significant association with high employee satisfaction.[58] Similarly, role conflict is associated with job-induced tension and job dissatisfaction.[59]

Most people prefer to communicate with others at their own status level or a higher one rather than with those below them.[60] As a result, we should expect satisfaction to be greater among employees whose job minimizes interaction with individuals who are lower in status than themselves.

The group size-satisfaction relationship is what one would intuitively expect: Larger groups are associated with lower satisfaction.[61] As size increases, opportunities for participation and social interaction decrease, as does the ability of members to identify with the group's accomplishments. At the same time, having more members also prompts dissension, conflict, and the formation of subgroups, which all act to make the group a less pleasant entity of which to be a part.

## For You as an Individual

Many commerce and business courses require students to work in groups. So one of the first ways that you might use the lessons in this chapter is to think about how they might apply either to a group you are in now, or one you have participated in previously. In many groups, the task often gets in the way of building the foundation of group relationships that would make the group function more easily and more cohesively. Because students can be very goal-oriented (with good reason, since that's how higher grades are achieved), it becomes easy to focus on the group product rather than group relationships.

You may notice certain problems in poorly functioning groups. At the end of a project, when the group is trying to finish and the deadline is looming, the conflict among group members becomes stronger, and major difficulties arise in getting everyone to work together toward a shared goal. To try to avoid this situation, the group can work out the shared goals and norms in the early stages of group development, even if it seems like a waste of time at the beginning. The successful student groups agree to go out to dinner or otherwise celebrate after the team project is presented. The least-successful groups don't want to speak with each other after the project is over. As instructors, we have observed many examples of both kinds of groups. Managing the relationships during the development of the group project is something that might make your next group experience more positive. The chapter gives you several ideas about doing this. Two that might be especially helpful are Exhibit 5-5, to remind you of the kinds of roles you need within the group for both task and relationship success, and the section on group cohesiveness on page 227, which reminds you of effective behaviours by groups.

**ROADMAP REMINDER**

We arrived at our discussion of groups through the path of motivation. Much of our discussion of motivation was at the individual level, but the fact of the matter is that working in an organization is generally not an isolating experience. In general, within organizations are many shared activities that need to be done. In this chapter we've explored the functioning of groups, and how to build a better group. In the next chapter we move on to teams. Teams and groups are not synonymous, as you'll soon see. A team is meant to be a much higher-performing entity than a group.

## For Review

1. What might motivate you to join a group?

2. What is the relationship between a work group and the organization of which it is a part?

3. Describe the five-stage group-development model.

4. What is the difference between task-oriented roles and maintenance roles?

5. How do norms develop in a group?

6. What are the characteristics of important norms?

7. Explain the implications of the Asch experiments.

8. What can organizations do to provide support for groups?

9. What are the effects of group size on performance?

10. How do you build group cohesiveness?

## For Critical Thinking

1. How could you use the punctuated-equilibrium model to better understand group behaviour?

2. Identify 5 roles you play. What behaviours do they require? Are any of these roles in conflict? If so, in what way? How do you resolve these conflicts?

3. "High cohesiveness in a group leads to higher group productivity." Do you agree or disagree? Explain.

4. What effect, if any, do you expect that workforce diversity has on a group's performance and satisfaction?

## *LEARNING ABOUT YOURSELF EXERCISE*

# Are You Attracted to the Group?

Most of us have written a term paper. Some of these papers have been individual assignments. That is, the instructor expected each student to hand in a separate paper and your grade was determined solely by your own effort and contribution. But sometimes instructors assign group term papers, where students must work together on the project and share in the grade.

Think back to a recent experience in doing a group term paper. Now envision yourself at about the halfway point in the completion of that group assignment. Using your mind-set at this halfway point, answer the following 20 questions. This questionnaire measures your feelings about that work group.

|  | Agree |  |  |  |  |  |  | Disagree |  |
|---|---|---|---|---|---|---|---|---|---|
| **1.** I want to remain a member of this group. | 1 | 2 | 3 | 4 | 5 | 6 | 7 | 8 | 9 |
| **2.** I like my group. | 1 | 2 | 3 | 4 | 5 | 6 | 7 | 8 | 9 |
| **3.** I look forward to coming to the group. | 1 | 2 | 3 | 4 | 5 | 6 | 7 | 8 | 9 |
| **4.** I don't care what happens in this group. | 1 | 2 | 3 | 4 | 5 | 6 | 7 | 8 | 9 |
| **5.** I feel involved in what is happening in my group. | 1 | 2 | 3 | 4 | 5 | 6 | 7 | 8 | 9 |
| **6.** If I could drop out of the group now, I would. | 1 | 2 | 3 | 4 | 5 | 6 | 7 | 8 | 9 |
| **7.** I dread coming to this group. | 1 | 2 | 3 | 4 | 5 | 6 | 7 | 8 | 9 |
| **8.** I wish it were possible for the group to end now. | 1 | 2 | 3 | 4 | 5 | 6 | 7 | 8 | 9 |
| **9.** I am dissatisfied with the group. | 1 | 2 | 3 | 4 | 5 | 6 | 7 | 8 | 9 |
| **10.** If it were possible to move to another group at this time, I would. | 1 | 2 | 3 | 4 | 5 | 6 | 7 | 8 | 9 |

*Continued on next page*

| | | Agree | | | | | | | | Disagree |
|---|---|---|---|---|---|---|---|---|---|---|

*Exercise Continued*

**11.** I feel included in the group.　　　　　　　　　　1　2　3　4　5　6　7　8　9

**12.** In spite of individual differences, a feeling of unity exists in my group.　　1　2　3　4　5　6　7　8　9

**13.** Compared with other groups, I feel my group is better than most.　　1　2　3　4　5　6　7　8　9

**14.** I do not feel a part of the group's activities.　　1　2　3　4　5　6　7　8　9

**15.** I feel it would make a difference to the group if I were not here.　　1　2　3　4　5　6　7　8　9

**16.** If I were told my group would not meet today, I would feel bad.　　1　2　3　4　5　6　7　8　9

**17.** I feel distant from the group.　　1　2　3　4　5　6　7　8　9

**18.** It makes a difference to me how this group turns out.　　1　2　3　4　5　6　7　8　9

**19.** I feel my absence would not matter to the group.　　1　2　3　4　5　6　7　8　9

**20.** I would not feel bad if I had to miss a meeting of this group.　　1　2　3　4　5　6　7　8　9

Turn to page 633 for scoring directions and key.

Source: This questionnaire is reproduced from N.J. Evans and P.A. Jarvis, "The Group Attitude Scale: A Measure of Attraction to Group," *Small Group Behavior,* May 1986, pp. 203-216. Reprinted by permission of Sage Publications, Inc.

## WORKING WITH OTHERS EXERCISE

# Observing Group Processes

**Step 1**　Seven students will be chosen to participate in a role play. During the role play, group members will work to achieve consensus on how to rank order the list of the personal and professional qualifications they will use to select a department head. Each of the group members should rank order the criteria by him- or herself, before the group discussion to reach consensus begins.

**Selection Criteria to be Rank Ordered**

_____ Strong institutional loyalty

_____ Ability to give clear instructions

_____ Ability to discipline subordinates

_____ Ability to make decisions under pressure

_____ Ability to communicate

_____ Stable personality

_____ High intelligence

_____ Ability to grasp the overall picture

_____ Ability to get along with people

_____ Familiarity with office procedures

_____ Professional achievement

_____ Ability to develop subordinates

**Step 2**　Students who are not part of the role play will be divided into 2 groups. One group will observe group processes related to the entire group, using the Group Process Observation Guide. The other group will observe individual behaviours that occur in the role play, using the Individual Role Observation Guide.

**Step 3**　Your instructor will lead you in a discussion of what you observed.

**Step 4**　What did the group do well? What recommendations might you make for how this group could improve its performance?

## Group Process Observation Guide

**Instructions:** Observe the group behaviour in the following dimensions. Prepare notes for feedback.

| Group Behaviours | Description (What did you see?) | What Was the Impact on the Group? |
|---|---|---|
| **Stages of Development:** How did the group get started? How did their interactions change over time? | | |
| **Group Goal:** Were group goals clearly defined? | | |
| **Leadership:** Did a leader emerge? | | |
| **Group Norms:** Observe the degrees of cohesiveness, compatibility, and conformity. | | |
| **Group Composition:** What would you say about the membership of this group in terms of age, gender, ethnicity, etc.? | | |
| **Other Behaviour:** Is there any other behaviour that influences the group process? | | |

## Individual Role Observation Guide

**Instructions:** Before the role play begins, choose 1 committee member to observe. Keep a count of the behaviours listed below that he or she exhibits as the group carries out its discussion.

| | |
|---|---|
| **Initiating Ideas:** Initiates or clarifies ideas and issues. | **Confusing Issues:** Confuses others by bringing up irrelevant issues or by jumping to other issues. |
| **Seeking Information and Opinions:** Asks for specific factual information related to task, or for opinions about it. | **Mismanaging Conflicts:** Avoids or suppresses conflict, or creates "win-or-lose" situations. |

*Continued on next page*

*Observing Group Processes Exercise Continued*

| | |
|---|---|
| **Providing Information and Opinions:** Shares information or opinions related to task. | **Forcing Others:** Gives orders or forces others to agree. |
| **Clarifying:** Helping one another understand ideas and suggestions that come up in the group | **Example:** "What you mean, Sue, is that we could...?" |
| **Elaborating:** Builds on others' ideas and suggestion. | **Rejecting Others:** Deflates or antagonizes others. |
| **Summarizing:** Reviews the points covered by the group. | **Showing Indifference:** Does not listen or brushes off others. |
| **Consensus Taking:** Checks to see whether the group is close to a decision or needs more time. | **Self-Serving Behaviour:** Exhibits behaviour that is self-serving. |
| **Harmonizing:** Mediates conflicts, reconciles disagreements, relieves tensions. | |
| **Compromising:** Admits error at times of conflict, or offers to meet halfway. | |
| **Gatekeeping:** Makes sure all members have a chance to express their ideas, and prevents members from being interrupted. | |
| **Encouraging:** Helps a group member make his or her point. Establishes a climate of acceptance in the group. | |

Source: This exercise was adapted from K.H. Chung and L.C. Megginson, *Organizational Behavior* (New York: Harper & Row, 1981), pp. 241-244. The descriptions in the left-hand column of the Individual Role Observation Guide come from Exhibit 5-5, which is adapted from "Team Processes," in D. Ancona, T. Kochan, M. Scully, J. Van Maanen, and D.E. Westney, *Managing for the Future* (Cincinnati, OH: South-Western College Publishing, 1996), p. 9.

## INTERNET SEARCH EXERCISES

1. Find a situation in which there is evidence that someone engaged in a behaviour that was very much counter to his or her normal behaviour, and in which at least some of the explanation for this behaviour was group pressure. Analyze your findings in terms of concepts described in this chapter.

2. Find data comparing Canadians and Japanese in terms of their preference for group work. What do your findings suggest?

## CASE INCIDENT

# The Law Offices of Dickinson, Stilwell, and Gardner (DSG)

James Dickinson and Richard Stilwell opened their Richmond, British Columbia, law office in 1963. It has since grown to employ 25 people. Dickinson is now deceased and Stilwell is semi-retired. The firm's senior managing partner is now Charles Gardner. Gardner has been with the firm for more than 20 years.

Today, the law office of DSG has five partners and 12 full-time associates. Additionally, the firm employs an administrative manager (Linda Chan) and an assistant administrative manager, a receptionist, four secretaries, and two legal interns who work 20 hours a week doing research.

Richmond has a large Chinese community. For various reasons, DSG has historically not done a very effective job of hiring and keeping Chinese-Canadian employees. Until very recently, only two of the associates, and none of the partners, were Chinese Canadians. Five months ago, the firm lured a prominent Chinese lawyer, Richard Lee, away from a competitor. Lee was brought in as a partner, at a base salary higher than any other DSG employee earned, with the exception of Charles Gardner.

The hiring of Lee has created a number of interpersonal issues at DSG. Many of the associates are unhappy. They feel the company hired Lee solely because he was one of the few big-name Chinese lawyers in Richmond and could open doors for the firm into the Chinese community. The associates were also concerned that the hiring of a new partner from the outside would lower the likelihood that they would become partners in the firm.

It was also clear that a clique was forming within the firm. This clique was made up of Richard Lee, Linda Chan, the two Chinese associates, and one of the secretaries (all of the clique are Chinese by background). Morale has suffered in recent months. Privately, several employees have made complaints to Gardner, such as "Linda gives favoured treatment to Richard and the Chinese associates," "the Chinese associates are suddenly working on the most visible and important cases within the firm," and "there's no future around here if you're not Chinese."

# Questions

**1.** What do you think you can learn from this case about diversity and group behaviour?

**2.** What should Gardner do to deal with this dilemma?

**3.** In what ways might group cohesiveness be increased at DSG?

# Ready, Set, Action (Plan)

One of the most difficult tasks groups face is trying to come up with an action plan so that everyone contributes to the overall success of a project. Consultant David Talbott developed the "Business Huddle," a computer-augmented business meeting, to show clients how to work more effectively in groups. He developed his idea based on athletes huddled with their coach or manager, making plans together. He believes that people in business should also come together to plan, because planning makes a big difference.

Talbott is helping Home Products to launch a new product, Merlin, a motion sensor for garden lights, which has to get to market in six weeks. He meets with the people responsible for getting the product to market. The steps he takes in helping the group formulate its plans would be useful to any group trying to complete a project.

The management of Home Products comes together to build the plan. They start by looking ahead to a critical date in the future, and then determining what needs to be done by that date to achieve success. The group states its objectives, visualizing the big picture.

Next, all of the team members get to see all of the information presented in the discussion of goals and objectives because Talbott displays this information through a computer and video monitor. This helps everyone to pay attention to the task at hand. Group members are also provided with minutes of the meetings.

Once the group members have identified the objectives, they are asked to outline all of the obstacles they face. This gives everyone the opportunity to speak up and express concerns. All of these concerns will also be addressed during the ensuing discussion.

The group then develops an action plan that includes all of the tasks needing to be completed, the date by which completion is expected, and the name of the person who will be responsible for the task. The purpose of this step is to get everyone in the group to accept responsibility for some part of the project, to agree to the milestone dates, and to commit to actually meeting the dates. To help with this commitment, each person is given a detailed action plan in writing so that everyone's responsibilities are clear.

# Questions

1. What are the benefits of the "Business Huddle" for group members trying to make a deadline?

2. How might you apply the lessons of the "Business Huddle" to a project group of your own?

3. What role do you think the action plan plays in ensuring that people get jobs done? How would you use this in a group of your own?

Source: Based on "Business Huddle," *Venture 589*; aired May 5, 1996. See also the online case at http://www.tv.cbc.ca/venture/archives/business_huddle_960505/two.html.

**CHAPTER 6**

# Developing Teamwork

## Questions for Consideration

**What's the difference between a group and a team?**

**Are teams always the right answer?**

**How can we ensure that teams work effectively?**

Walk into Toronto-based Willow Manufacturing and you'll find that everyone who works there, even president Dennis Wild, wears the same-style uniform.[1] That's one way the company conveys that everyone at Willow is part of the team, and equally important.

Willow, which manufactures a variety of precision components, used to have seven levels of management, and its inefficient processes caused lost time and money. The plant was dirty, noisy, and smoky, and employee morale was so poor that employees were fighting among each other. On the brink of bankruptcy, Willow decided to redesign the company from the ground up. It hauled out 40 tons of physical garbage, cleaned out the emotional skeletons in the closets, resolved conflicts, and got the employees working together again, this time as a team.

As Wild reports, "We looked at the old procedures...and threw it all out and said this has never really worked." The staff were split up into teams. In the first week, each team redesigned its own ISO procedures. The next week, the team's procedures were examined by another team, streamlining procedures even further. Each team served as an auditor to the other team.

In an unbelievably short 120 days, Willow ended up with very simplified procedures for many of its tasks, thereby achieving ISO 9002 certification. The overhaul happened because Willow's employees and management believed it could.

During the time Willow went through its redesign process, the improvement teams met daily, to sum up the day's accomplishments and map out the next day's strategies.

When asked what he thought of the hour-by-hour action planning, Dennis Wild said, "I loved it! It allowed us to implement improvements and make progress before we even had time to create barriers to the ideas. The key was the involvement of all employees, so that the processes we documented were sound and accepted by the people who had to use them."

Adds Linda Snow, Willow's vice-president, "We would not have had the success we did without the intensity and adrenaline rush of the approach. It was a self-imposed test in which we began to believe in our ability as a team and see how far we could stretch the improvement envelope in a short time."

Willow now relies on teams for everything. Employees are consulted before a new piece of equipment is purchased, and they decide themselves which hours they will work. Wild believes that his teams are the secret to Willow's success. "We've got a great group of people and they are the ones that are driving all of these changes, not me. It's the team that's driving the system. That is what all manufacturers need to do if they want to stay in business."

Olive Alvaro, Willow's office manager, sums up the value of the new approach. "We'd had manufacturing work cells in place for at least two years, but change didn't really happen until we added teamwork. You can't change people, but if you change the environment around them, it removes the roadblocks and allows them to start working as a team."

Willow's experience highlights the key idea of this chapter: Teams, when used well, can make a big difference in the workplace. Business organizations have traditionally been organized around individuals. That's no longer true. Teams have increasingly become the primary means for organizing work in contemporary business firms. As you read through this chapter,

**Willow Manufacturing**
www.willowcnc.com

be aware of some of the important things Willow did right: Everyone's input was sought and valued, everyone was totally immersed in the project, old ways were discarded readily, an environment for team contribution was created, and employees believed in what they were doing.

## Teams vs. Groups: What's the Difference?

**work group**
A group that interacts primarily to share information and to make decisions to help each other perform within his or her area of responsibility.

Groups and teams are not the same thing.[2] In the last chapter, we defined a *group* as two or more individuals, interacting and interdependent, who have come together to achieve particular objectives. A **work group** is a group that interacts primarily to share information and to make decisions to help each member perform within his or her area of responsibility.

Work groups have no need or opportunity to engage in collective work that requires joint effort. So their performance is merely the sum of each group member's individual contribution. There is no positive synergy that would create an overall level of performance that is greater than the sum of the inputs.

**work team**
A group whose individual efforts result in a performance that is greater than the sum of those individual inputs.

A **work team** generate positive synergy through coordinated effort. The individual efforts result in a level of performance that is greater than the sum of those individual inputs. Exhibit 6-1 highlights the differences between a group and a team.

**Zellers**
www.hbc.com/zellers/home.asp
**Motorola**
www.motorola.ca
**3M Canada**
www3.3m.com/intl/CA/english
**Johnson & Johnson**
www.johnsonandjohnson.com
**London Life**
www.londonlife.com

## Why Have Teams Become So Popular?

Pick up almost any business periodical today and you'll read how teams have become an essential part of the way business is being done in companies such as Zellers, Xerox, Sears Canada, General Electric, AT&T, Hewlett-Packard, Motorola, Apple Computer, DaimlerChrysler AG, 3M Co., Australian Airlines, Johnson & Johnson, and London Life. A 1994 Conference Board of Canada report found that over 80 percent of its 109 respondents used teams in the workplace.[3] This compares with 78 percent of US organizations.[4]

**total quality management (TQM)**
A philosophy of management that's driven by the constant attainment of customer satisfaction through the continuous improvement of all organizational processes.

The reason that so many organizations have recently restructured work processes around teams is that management is looking for the positive synergy coming from teams. It is this synergy that will allow their organization to increase performance. One of the biggest pushes for teams in organizations is **total quality management** (TQM), a philosophy of management that's driven by the constant attainment of customer satisfaction through the continuous improvement of all organizational processes. We discuss TQM in greater detail in Chapter 13.

The extensive use of teams creates the *potential* for an organization to generate greater outputs with no increase in inputs. Notice, however, we said "potential." There is nothing inherently magical in the creation of teams that ensures the achievement of this positive synergy. Merely calling a *group* a *team* doesn't automatically increase its performance. As we will show later in this chapter, successful, or high-performing, teams have certain common characteristics. If management hopes to gain increases in organizational performance through the use of teams, it must ensure that its teams possess these characteristics.

Do teams work? The evidence suggests that teams typically outperform individuals when the tasks being done require multiple skills, judgment, and experience.[5] As organizations have restructured themselves to compete more effectively and efficiently, they have turned to teams as a way to better utilize employee talents. Management has found that teams are more flexible

**Exhibit 6-1**
**Teams and Work Groups: It Pays to Know the Difference**

Managers tend to label every working group in an organization a "team," whether it's a roomful of customer service operators or a string of assemblers on a manufacturing line. But employees quickly lose motivation and commitment when they're assigned to a team that turns out to be a single-leader work group. If executives want to spark energy and commitment on the front lines they must know how a team differs from a single-leader work group, and when to create one or the other.

| | Team | Single-leader Work Group |
|---|---|---|
| **Run by:** | the members of the team best-suited to lead the tasks at hand; the leadership role shifts among the members | one person, usually the senior member, who is formally designated to lead |
| **Goals and agenda set by:** | the group, based on dialogue about purpose; constructive conflict and integration predominate | the formal leader, often in consultation with a sponsoring executive; conflict with group members is avoided, and the leader integrates |
| **Performance evaluated by:** | the members of the group, as well as the leader and sponsor | the leader and the sponsor |
| **Work style determined by:** | the members | the leader's preference |
| **Success defined by:** | the members' aspirations | the leader's aspirations |
| **Most appropriate business context:** | a complex challenge that requires people with various skill sets working together much of the time | a challenge in which time is of the essence and the leader already knows best how to proceed; the leader is the primary integrator |
| **Speed and efficiency:** | low until the group has learned to function as a team; afterward, however, the team is as fast as a single-leader group | higher than that of teams initially, as the members need no time to develop commitment or to learn to work as a team |
| **Primary end-products:** | largely collective, requiring several team members to work together to produce results | largely individual and can be accomplished best by each person working on his or her own |
| **Accountability characterized by:** | "We hold one another mutually accountable for achieving the goals and performance of the team." | "The leader holds us individually accountable for our output." |

Source: Jon R. Katzenback and Jason A. Santamaria, "Firing Up the Front Line," *Harvard Business Review*, May-June, 1999, p. 114.

and responsive to changing events than are traditional departments or other forms of permanent groupings. Teams have the capability to quickly assemble, deploy, refocus, and disband.

Teams are not necessarily appropriate in every situation, however. Read this chapter's Point/CounterPoint on the next pages for a debate on the positives and negatives of teams.

# Teams: The Way to Go

The value of teams is now well-known. Let's summarize the primary benefits that experts agree can result from the introduction of work teams.

*Increased employee motivation.* Work teams enhance employee involvement. They typically make jobs more interesting. They help employees meet their social needs. They also create social pressures on slackers to exert higher levels of effort in order to remain in the team's good graces.

*Higher levels of productivity.* Teams have the potential to create positive synergy. In recent years, the introduction of teams in most organizations has been associated with cuts in staff. What management has done is to use the positive synergy to get the same or greater output from fewer people.

*Increased employee satisfaction.* Employees have a need for affiliation. Working in teams can help meet this need by increasing worker interactions and creating camaraderie among team members.

*Common commitment to goals.* Teams encourage individuals to sublimate their individual goals for those of the group. The process of developing a common purpose, of committing to that purpose, and of agreeing upon specific goals—combined with the social pressures exerted by the team—results in a high unity of commitment to team goals.

*Improved communication.* Self-managed teams create interpersonal dependencies that require members to interact considerably more than when they work on jobs alone.

*Expanded job skills.* The implementation of teams almost always comes with expanded training building employees' technical and interpersonal skills.

*Organizational flexibility.* Teams focus on processes rather than functions. They encourage cross-training, so members can do each other's jobs, and expansion of skills. It's not unusual for compensation on teams to be based on the number of skills a member has acquired. This expansion of skills increases organizational flexibility.

Does the introduction of teams *always* achieve these benefits? No! For instance, a study by Ernst & Young found that forming teams to investigate and improve products and processes led to measurable improvement only in organizations that were performing poorly in their markets in terms of profit, productivity, and quality.[1] In medium-performing companies, the study found, bottom-line results were unaffected by team activities. In high-performing companies, the introduction of new team-based work systems actually lowered performance.

There are obviously contingency factors that influence the acceptance and success of teams. Some examples might be tasks that benefit from combining multiple skills; when the market will pay a premium for improved quality or innovation; with employees who value continual learning and enjoy complex tasks; and where management-employee relations already have a strong basis of mutual trust. Nevertheless, the team movement currently has tremendous momentum and reflects management's belief that teams can be successful in a wide range of settings.

Source:

[1] R. Zemke, "Rethinking the Rush to Team Up," *Training*, November 1993, p. 56.

## COUNTERPOINT

# Teams Are Not Always the Answer

Beliefs about the benefits of teams have achieved an unquestioned place in the study of organizations. But teams are no panacea. Let's take a critical look at four of the assumptions that seem to underlie this team ideology.

*Mature teams are task-oriented and have successfully minimized the negative influences of other group forces.* Task-oriented teams still experience antitask behaviour, and indeed have much in common with other types of groups. For instance, they often suffer from infighting over assignments and decision outcomes, low participation rates, and member apathy.

*Individual, group, and organizational goals can all be integrated into common team goals.* Contrary to what team advocates assume, people are not so simply motivated by the sociability and self-actualization supposedly offered by work teams. These teams suffer from competitiveness, conflict, and hostility. Additionally, contrary to the notion that teams increase job satisfaction, the evidence suggests that individuals experience substantial and continuing stress as team members. Rarely is the team experience satisfying. Moreover, certain types of workers and certain types of work are better suited to solitary work situations. For the hard-driving, competitive person who thrives on individual achievement, the cult of the team player is likely to produce only frustration and stress.

*Participative or shared leadership is always effective.* The team ideology oversimplifies the requirement for leadership. It downplays the importance of leadership by suggesting that high-performing teams can dispense with, or ignore, leadership concerns. Group process theorists are unanimous that all groups will experience phases of identifying with, rejecting, and working through relations with authority. This

process cannot be eliminated simply by eliminating leaders from groups. The abdication of leadership can, in effect, paralyze teams.

*The team environment drives out the subversive forces of politics, power, and conflict that divert groups from doing their work efficiently.* Recipes for effective teams rate them on the quality of decision making, communication, cohesion, clarity and acceptance of goals, acceptance of minority views, and other criteria. Such recipes betray the fact that teams are composed of people with self-interests who are prepared to make deals, reward favourites, punish enemies, and engage in similar behaviours to further those self-interests. Neither training nor organizational actions will alter the intrinsically political nature of teams.

The argument here has been that the team ideology, under the banner of benefits for all, ignores that teams are frequently used to camouflage coercion under the pretence of maintaining cohesion; conceal conflict under the guise of consensus; convert conformity into a semblance of creativity; delay action in the supposed interests of consultation; legitimize lack of leadership; and disguise expedient arguments and personal agendas. Teams do not necessarily provide fulfillment of individual needs, nor do they necessarily contribute to individual satisfaction and performance or organizational effectiveness. On the contrary, it's likely that the infatuation with teams and making every employee part of a team results in organizations not getting the best performance from many of their members.

Source: Based on A. Sinclair, "The Tyranny of a Team Ideology," *Organization Studies*, vol. 13, no. 4 (1992), pp. 611-626.

# Types of Teams

Teams can be classified based on their objective. The four most common forms of teams you're likely to find in an organization are problem-solving (or process-improvement) teams, self-managed (or self-directed) teams, cross-functional teams, and virtual teams. The types of relationships that members within each team have to each other is shown in Exhibit 6-2.

## Problem-Solving Teams

If we look back 20 years or so, teams were just beginning to grow in popularity, and most of these teams took a similar form. These were typically composed of five to 12 hourly employees from the same department who met for a few hours each week to discuss ways of improving quality, efficiency, and the work environment.[6] We call these **problem-solving**, or **process-improvement**, **teams**.

In problem-solving teams, members share ideas or offer suggestions on how to improve work processes and methods. Rarely, however, are these teams given the authority to unilaterally implement any of their suggested actions. Montreal-based Clairol Canada Inc. is an exception, giving employees more problem-solving ability. When a Clairol employee identifies a problem, he or she has the authority to call together an ad hoc group to investigate, and then define and implement solutions. Clairol presents GOC Awards (Group Operating Committee) to teams for their efforts.

One of the most widely practised applications of problem-solving teams is the quality circle, which became quite popular in North America and Europe during the 1980s.[7] The quality circle concept is often mentioned as one of the techniques that Japanese firms use to allow them to make high-quality products at low costs. However, quality circles originated in the United States and were exported to Japan in the 1950s.[8]

A **quality circle** is a work group of eight to 10 employees and managers who share an area of responsibility. They meet regularly—typically once a week, on company time and on company premises—to discuss their quality problems, investigate causes of the problems, recommend solutions, and take corrective actions. They assume responsibility for solving quality problems, and generate and evaluate their own feedback. But management typically retains control over the final decision regarding implementation of recommended solutions. Of course, it is not presumed that employees inherently have the ability to analyze and solve quality problems. Therefore, part of the quality circle concept includes teaching participating employees group communication skills, various quality strategies, and measurement and problem

**problem-solving teams/ process-improvement teams**
Groups of five to 12 employees from the same department who meet for a few hours each week to discuss ways of improving quality, efficiency, and the work environment.

**quality circle**
A work group of employees who meet regularly to discuss their quality problems, investigate causes, recommend solutions, and take corrective actions.

---

### Exhibit 6-2
### Four Types of Teams

  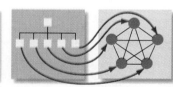 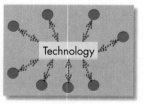

**Problem solving**   **Self-managed**   **Cross-functional**   **Virtual**

**Exhibit 6-3**
**How a Typical Quality Circle Operates**

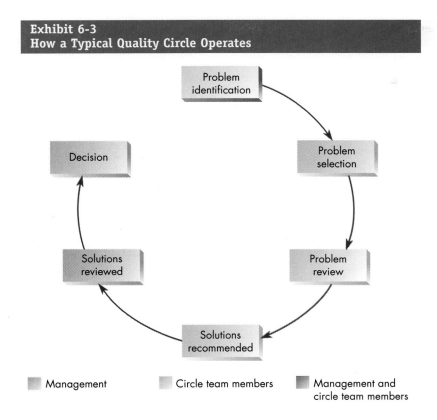

- Management
- Circle team members
- Management and circle team members

**Canadian Autoworkers Union**
www.caw.ca

**DaimlerChrysler AG**
www.daimlerchrysler.com

analysis techniques. Exhibit 6-3 describes a typical quality circle process.

Do quality circles improve employee productivity and satisfaction? A review of the evidence indicates that they are much more likely to positively affect productivity. They tend to show little or no effect on employee satisfaction, and while many studies report positive results from quality circles on productivity, these results are by no means guaranteed.[9] The failure of many quality circle programs to produce measurable benefits has also led to the discontinuation of a large number of them.

The Canadian Auto Workers Union (CAW) has not been entirely pleased with changes introduced at DaimlerChrysler AG plants, where workers have been asked to assume more responsibility for work through quality circles. Ken Lewenza, president of a Windsor-area CAW local, explains, "A key change has been to transfer responsibility for monitoring and resolving quality problems at the minivan and truck plants from management employees to teams of unionized workers."[10] But he adds that the union "is resisting company efforts to establish Japanese-style cells of assembly workers because of concerns that the concept could lead to job losses through increased efficiency."

One author, J.L. Cotton, suggests that while quality circles were the management fad of the 1980s, they've "become a flop."[11] He points out that little time is spent in quality circles in places that use them, and quality circles were often viewed as a simple device that could be added on to the organization with few changes required outside the program itself.

However, failure does not have to be inevitable for quality circles. A case in point involves Montreal-based CAE Electronics Ltd., which showed that a company can overcome some of the failures associated with quality circles.[12] CAE's success with quality circles indicates that they can work even where they have previously failed if management introduces the proper supports. White Rock, British Columbia-based Toyota Captin, a wheel-manufacturing plant, has also used quality circles for a number of years with good results.

## Self-Managed Work Teams

Problem-solving teams were on the right track, but they didn't go far enough in involving employees in work-related decisions and processes. This led to experiments with truly autonomous teams that could not only solve problems but also implement solutions and assume responsibility for outcomes.

Many employees are asked to work in teams in order to accomplish their tasks. In a self-managed work team, such as the one from Xerox shown here, members make decisions about how to manage and schedule production, and also monitor the quality of their output.

**self-managed work teams/self-directed work teams**
Groups of 10 to 15 people who take on responsibilities of their former managers.

**Self-managed**, or **self-directed**, **work teams** are groups of employees (typically 10 to 15 in number) who perform highly related or interdependent jobs and take on many of the responsibilities of their former managers.[13] Typically, this includes planning and scheduling of work, assigning tasks to members, collectively controlling the pace of work, making operating decisions, and taking action on problems. Fully self-managed work teams even select their own members and have the members evaluate each other's performance. As a result, managerial positions take on decreased importance and may even be eliminated.

Toyota Canada's Toronto parts distribution centre reorganized its workforce into work teams in 1995. Workers have a team-focused mission statement, and employees are divided into six work teams, each with its own leader. Teams rotate through shift and work assignment schedules, making their own adjustments as necessary. At the Honeywell Ltd. plant in Scarborough, Ontario, unionized workers have been known to shut down the production line, not for more money, but to correct a production line defect.[14] According to the Conference Board of Canada, self-directed work teams are found in a variety of manufacturing (such as the auto industry, chemicals, equipment repair) and service environments (such as hotels, banks and airlines).[15] The Case Incident for this chapter on page 269 gives you the opportunity to determine some of the opportunities and challenges of introducing self-managed teams in the workplace.

It should be noted that some organizations have been disappointed with the results from self-managed teams, and the overall research on the effectiveness of self-managed work teams has not been uniformly positive.[16] For example, individuals on these teams tend to report higher levels of job satisfaction. However, counter to conventional wisdom, employees on self-managed work teams seem to have higher absenteeism and turnover rates than do employees working in traditional work structures. The specific reasons for these findings are unclear, which implies a need for additional research.

In some cases, the introduction of these teams is viewed negatively by workers who fear that increasing use of teams will lead to layoffs. Their concerns may be well founded. At Honeywell's Scarborough plant, one-third of the 75 salaried positions were eliminated between 1991 and 1994 as a result of the shift to self-managed teams. The plant now runs with 40 percent fewer workers, with no drop in production.

## Cross-Functional Teams

**cross-functional teams/project teams**
Employees from about the same hierarchical level, but from different work areas, who come together to accomplish a task.

**task force**
A temporary cross-functional team.

**committee**
Group composed of members from across departmental lines.

**Nissan Canada**
www.nissancanada.com

**BMW**
www.bmw.com

The Boeing Company used the latest application of the team concept to develop its 777 jet. This application is called **cross-functional**, or **project**, **teams**. These teams are made up of employees from about the same hierarchical level, but from different work areas, who come together to accomplish a task.[17]

Many organizations have used horizontal, boundary-spanning groups for years. For example, IBM created a large task force in the 1960s—made up of employees from across departments in the company—to develop the highly successful System 360. And a **task force** is really nothing other than a temporary cross-functional team. Similarly, **committees** composed of members from across departmental lines are another example of cross-functional teams.

But the popularity of cross-discipline work teams exploded in the late 1980s. All the major automobile manufacturers—including Toyota, Honda, Nissan, BMW, GM, Ford, and DaimlerChrysler AG—have turned to this form of team to coordinate complex projects. The 1998 Chrysler Intrepid and its elegant cousin, the Concorde, both produced at Chryslers Bramalea, Ontario, assembly plant, were developed in record time through the teamwork of staff from design, engineering, manufacturing, marketing, and finance. Markham, Ontario-based AMP of Canada Ltd., manufacturer of electrical connectors and interconnection systems, puts together teams who may or may not be employees to bring a project to completion.

In summary, cross-functional teams are an effective means for allowing people from diverse areas within an organization (or even between organizations) to exchange information, develop new ideas and solve problems, and coordinate complex projects. Of course, cross-functional teams are no picnic to manage.[18] Their early stages of development are often very time-consuming as members learn to work with diversity and complexity. It takes time to build trust and teamwork, especially among people from different backgrounds, with different experiences and perspectives. Later in this chapter, we'll discuss ways managers can help facilitate and build trust among team members. In our HR Implications feature on page 262, we discuss further things that organizations can do to turn individuals into team players.

## Virtual Teams

**virtual teams**
Teams that use computer technology to tie together physically dispersed members in order to achieve a common goal.

The previous types of teams do their work face to face. **Virtual teams** use computer technology to tie together physically dispersed members in order to achieve a common goal.[19] They allow people to collaborate online—using communication links like wide-area networks, video conferencing, or e-mail—whether they're only a room away or continents apart.

Sheila Goldgrab coaches virtual teams from the comfort of her home in Toronto. She can do that coaching via teleconference, videoconference or e-mail. She gets hired as a consultant to help virtual teams work together more smoothly. As one recipient of her coaching said, "Sheila was the rudder of the planning group. While we were going at high speed in different directions, she ensured there was a link among the group that kept us focused on the task at hand."

Virtual teams can do all the things that other teams do—share information, make decisions, complete tasks. And they can include members from the same organization or link an organization's members with employees from other organizations (that is, suppliers and joint partners). They can convene for a few days to solve a problem, a few months to complete a project, or exist permanently.[20] Often they can be more efficient at tasks as well, because of the ease of sharing information through e-mail and voice mail.

There has been some concern that virtual teams lack the face-to-face interaction that helps to build trust among individuals. However, a recent study[21] examining how virtual teams work on projects indicates that virtual teams can develop close interaction and trust; these qualities simply evolve differently than in face-to-face groups. In face-to-face groups, trust comes from direct interaction, over time. In virtual teams, trust is either established at the outset or it generally doesn't develop. The researchers found that initial electronic messages set the tone for how interactions occurred throughout the entire project. In one team, for instance, when the appointed leader sent an introductory message that had a distrustful tone, the team suffered low morale and poor performance throughout the duration of the project. The researchers suggest that virtual teams should start with an electronic "courtship," where members provide some personal information. Then the teams should assign clear roles to members, helping members to identify with each other. Finally, the researchers noted that teams that had the best attitude (eagerness, enthusiasm, and intense action orientation in messages) did considerably better than teams that had one or more pessimists among them. S.L. Jarvenpaa et al.'s article about team struggle, cited in endnote 21 for this chapter, provides more detail on this subject. You might find the team experience reported there interesting.

## Beware! Teams Aren't Always the Answer

Teamwork takes more time and often more resources than individual work. Teams, for instance, have increased communication demands, conflicts to be managed, and meetings to be run. So the benefits of using teams have to exceed the costs. And that's not always the case. In the excitement to enjoy the benefits of teams, some managers have introduced them into situations where the work is better done by individuals. So before you rush to implement teams, you should carefully assess whether the work requires or will benefit from a collective effort.

How do you know if the work of your group would be better done in teams? It's been suggested that three tests be applied to see if a team fits the situation:[22]

- Can the work be done better by more than one person? Simple tasks that don't require diverse input are probably better left to individuals.

- Does the work create a common purpose or set of goals for the people in the group that is more than the aggregate of individual goals? For instance, many new-car dealer service departments have introduced teams that link customer service personnel, mechanics, parts specialists, and sales representatives. Such teams can better manage collective responsibility for ensuring that customer needs are properly met.

- Are the members of the group interdependent? Teams make sense where there is interdependence between tasks; where the success of the whole depends on the success of each one *and* the success of each one depends on the success of the others. Soccer, for instance, is an obvious *team* sport because of the interdependence of the players. Swim teams, by contrast, are not really teams, but groups of individuals whose total performance is merely the sum of the individual performances.

Others have outlined the conditions under which organizations would find teams more useful: "when work processes cut across functional lines; when speed is important (and complex relationships are involved); when the organization mirrors a complex, differentiated and rapidly changing market environment; when innovation and learning have priority; when the tasks that have to be done require online integration of highly interdependent performers."[23] In this Chapter's CBC Video Case on page 270, you will have the opportunity to view further discussion about some of the downsides of using teams in the workplace.

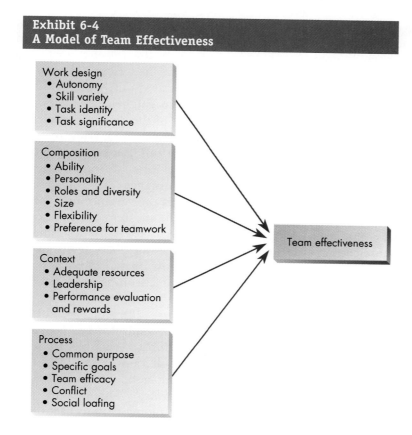

**Exhibit 6-4**
**A Model of Team Effectiveness**

Work design
- Autonomy
- Skill variety
- Task identity
- Task significance

Composition
- Ability
- Personality
- Roles and diversity
- Size
- Flexibility
- Preference for teamwork

Context
- Adequate resources
- Leadership
- Performance evaluation and rewards

Process
- Common purpose
- Specific goals
- Team efficacy
- Conflict
- Social loafing

Team effectiveness

# Creating Effective Teams

There is no shortage of efforts at trying to identify factors related to team effectiveness.[24] However, recent studies have taken what was once a "veritable laundry list of characteristics"[25] and organized them into a relatively focused model.[26] Exhibit 6-4 summarizes what we currently know about what makes teams effective, assuming a situation demands a team. As you'll see, the model builds on many of the group concepts introduced in the previous chapter.

The key components making up effective teams can be subsumed into four general categories. The first category is *work design*. The second relates to the team's *composition*. Third is the resources and other *contextual* influences that make teams effective. Finally, *process* variables represent those things that go on in the team that influence how effective the team is. When measuring effectiveness, one might consider objective measures of the team's productivity, managers' ratings of the team's performance, and aggregate measures of member satisfaction.

## Work Design

Effective teams need to work together and take collective responsibility to complete significant tasks. They must be more than a "team-in-name-only."[27] The work-design category includes variables like freedom and autonomy, the opportunity to utilize different skills and talents, the ability to complete a whole and identifiable task or product, and the participation in a task or project that has a substantial impact on others. The evidence indicates that these characteristics enhance member motivation and increase team effectiveness.[28] These work design characteristics motivate because they increase members' sense of responsibility and ownership over the work, and because they make the work more interesting to perform.[29]

## Composition Considerations

The most effective teams are neither very small (under four or five) nor very large (over a dozen).[30] Very small teams are likely to lack for diversity of views. But when teams have more than about 10 to 12 members, it becomes difficult to get much done. Group members have trouble interacting constructively and agreeing on much. Large numbers of people can't usually develop the cohesiveness, commitment, and mutual accountability necessary to achieve high performance. So in designing effective teams, managers should keep them to under a dozen people. If a natural working unit is larger and you want a team effort, consider breaking the group into subteams.

Teams have different needs, and people should be selected for the team on the basis of their personalities and preferences, as well as the team needs for diversity and roles to be filled. We demonstrated in Chapter 2 that personality has a significant influence on individual employee behaviour. This can also be extended to team behaviour. Many of the dimensions identified in the Big Five Personality Model have been shown to be relevant to team effectiveness. Specifically, teams that rate higher in mean levels of extroversion, agreeableness, conscientiousness, and emotional stability tend to receive higher managerial ratings for team performance.[31]

Very interestingly, the evidence indicates that the variance in personality characteristics may be more important than the mean.[32] So, for example, while higher mean levels of conscientiousness on a team are desirable, mixing both conscientious and not-so-conscientious members tends to lower performance. Including just one person who is low on agreeableness, conscientiousness, or extroversion can result in strained internal processes and decreased overall performance.[33]

To perform effectively, a team requires three different types of skills. First, it needs people with *technical expertise*. Second, it needs people with the *problem-solving* and *decision-making skills* to be able to identify problems, generate alternatives, evaluate those alternatives, and make competent choices. Finally, teams need people with good listening, feedback, conflict resolution, and other *interpersonal skills*.[34] This chapter's From Concepts to Skills discusses the importance of building trust as part of team-building activities.

> Ever wonder whether having a team built just from people who are friends is desirable?

# From CONCEPTS to SKILLS

## Building Trust

Team leaders have a significant impact on a team's trust climate. As a result, team leaders need to build trust between themselves and team members. The following summarizes ways to build team trust.

*Demonstrate that you're working for others' interests as well as your own.* All of us are concerned with our own self-interest, but if others see you using them, your job, or the organization for your personal goals to the exclusion of your team's, department's, and organization's interests, your credibility will be undermined.

*Be a team player.* Support your work team both through words and actions. Defend the team and team members when they're attacked by outsiders. This will demonstrate your loyalty to your work group.

*Practise openness.* Mistrust comes as much from what people don't know as from what they do know. Openness leads to confidence and trust. So keep people informed, explain your decisions, be candid about problems, and fully disclose relevant information.

*Be fair.* Before making decisions or taking actions, consider how others will perceive them in terms of objectivity and fairness. Give credit where it's due, be objective and impartial in performance evaluations, and pay attention to equity perceptions in reward distributions.

*Speak your feelings.* Managers and leaders who convey only hard facts come across as cold and dis-tant. By sharing your feelings, you will encourage others to view you as real and human. They will know who you are and will increase their respect for you.

*Show consistency in the basic values that guide your decision making.* Mistrust comes from not knowing what to expect. Take the time to think about your values and beliefs. Then let them consistently guide your decisions. When you know your central purpose, your actions will follow accordingly, and you'll project a consistency that earns trust.

*Maintain confidences.* You trust those you can confide in and rely on. So if people tell you something in confidence, they need to feel assured that you won't discuss it with others or betray that confidence. If people perceive you as someone who "leaks" personal confidences or someone who can't be depended upon, you won't be perceived as trustworthy.

*Demonstrate competence.* Develop the admiration and respect of others by demonstrating technical and professional ability and good business sense. Pay particular attention to developing and displaying your communication, team-building, and other interpersonal skills.

Teams should approach their own development as part of a search for continuous improvement.

Sources: Based on F. Bartolome, "Nobody Trusts the Boss Completely—Now What?" *Harvard Business Review*, March-April 1989, pp. 135-142; and P. Pascarella, "15 Ways to Win People's Trust," *Industry Week*, February 1, 1993, pp. 47-51.

No team can achieve its performance potential without developing all three types of skills. The right mix is crucial. Too much of one at the expense of others will result in lower team performance. But teams don't need to have all the complementary skills in place at their beginning. It's not uncommon for one or more members to take responsibility to learn the skills in which the group is deficient, thereby allowing the team to reach its full potential.

We can identify nine potential team roles that successful teams need filled (see Exhibit 6-5).[35] On many teams, there are individuals who will be flexible enough to play multiple roles and/or complete each other's tasks. This is an obvious plus to a team because it greatly improves its adaptability and makes it less reliant on any single member.[36] Selecting members who themselves value flexibility, and then cross-training them to be able to do each other's jobs, should lead to higher team performance over time. Not every employee is a team player, though. Given the option, many employees

**Exhibit 6-5**
**Key Roles on Teams**

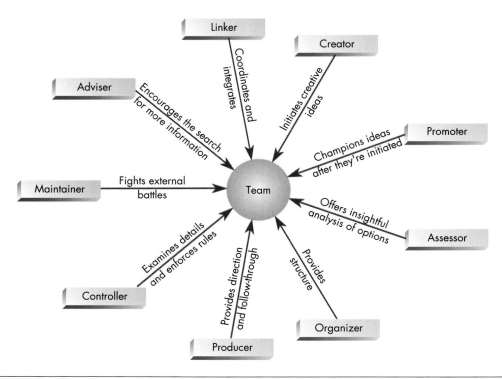

Based on C. Margerison and D. McCann, *Team Management: Practical New Approaches* (London: Mercury Books, 1990).

will select themselves *out* of team participation. When people who would prefer to work alone are required to team up, there is a direct threat to the team's morale.[37] This suggests that, when selecting team members, individual preferences should be considered, as well as abilities, personalities, and skills. High-performing teams are likely to be composed of people who prefer working as part of a group.

Managers need, then, to understand the individual strengths that each person can bring to a team, select members with their strengths in mind, and allocate work assignments that fit with members' preferred styles. By matching individual preferences with team role demands, managers increase the likelihood that the team members will work well together. This chapter's Working With Others Exercise on page 268 examines the issue of team building by asking you to build a paper tower with teammates, and then analyze how the team performed.

## Context

The three contextual factors that appear to be most significantly related to team performance are the presence of adequate resources, effective leadership, and a performance evaluation and reward system that reflects team contributions.

**RESOURCES** All work teams rely on resources outside the group to sustain them. And a scarcity of resources directly reduces the ability of a team to

Randy Powell, president of Toronto-based specialty coffee retailer Second Cup Limited, creates teams that people want to be a part of. As a leader, Powell realizes the importance of setting a direction, giving his people the freedom to do their work, providing the appropriate resources and removing any barriers to the team's success.

perform its job effectively. As one set of researchers concluded, after looking at 13 factors potentially related to group performance, "perhaps one of the most important characteristics of an effective work group is the support the group receives from the organization."[38] This includes such support as timely information, technology, adequate staffing, encouragement, and administrative assistance. Teams must receive the necessary support from management and the larger organization if they are going to succeed in achieving their goals.

**LEADERSHIP AND STRUCTURE**  Team members must agree on who is to do what, and ensure that all members contribute equally in sharing the workload. Additionally, the team needs to determine how schedules will be set, what skills need to be developed, how the group will resolve conflicts, and how the group will make and modify decisions. Agreeing on the specifics of work and how they fit together to integrate individual skills requires team leadership and structure. This, incidentally, can be provided directly by management or by the team members themselves as they fulfill promoter, organizer, producer, maintainer, and linker roles (refer back to Exhibit 6-5).

Leadership, of course, isn't always needed. For instance, the evidence indicates that self-managed work teams often perform better than teams with formally appointed leaders.[39] And leaders can obstruct high performance when they interfere with self-managing teams.[40] On self-managed teams, team members absorb many of the duties typically assumed by managers.

On traditionally managed teams, we find that two factors seem to be important in influencing team performance—the leader's expectations and his or her mood. Leaders who expect good things from their team are more likely to get them! For instance, military platoons under leaders who held high expectations performed significantly better in training than control platoons.[41] Additionally, studies have found that leaders who exhibit positive mood get better team performance and lower turnover.[42]

**APPROPRIATE PERFORMANCE EVALUATION**  How do you get team members to be both individually and jointly accountable? The traditional individually oriented evaluation must be modified to reflect team performance.[43] At Imperial Oil, team members provide feedback to each other in three critical areas: team results, team functioning/effectiveness, and personal effectiveness. Exhibit 6-6 illustrates the behaviours expected of team members at Imperial Oil. This type of appraisal reminds members of their responsibilities to their team. Teams should not rely solely on the formal performance appraisal process, however. To manage the team process more effectively, they might encourage presentations of work in progress to get feedback from other members and/or outsiders on quality and completeness of work. Sitting down together informally and reviewing both individual and team behaviour helps keep the team on track.

**Imperial Oil**
www.imperialoil.ca

## Exhibit 6-6
## Team Behaviour at Imperial Oil

Individuals are asked to assess team members in three major areas. Behaviours related to these areas are indicated.

| **Team Results** | **Team Functioning** | **Personal Effectiveness** |
|---|---|---|
| Effort | Sustaining morale and team spirit | Giving personal support |
| Achieving individual role requirements | Recognizing others' contributions and opinions | Giving recognition |
| Collaborating with others toward achieving common goals | Listening | Giving clear and useful feedback |
| Smoothing relationships with customers/suppliers | Solving problems without taking total ownership | Enthusiasm |
| Adhering to standards | Resolving conflict but maintaining everyone's dignity | Understanding or priorities |
| Realizing tactical plans | Helping the team carry out strategic long-term thinking and planning | Skill expansion |
| | Living up to company principles, values, and ethics | Understanding of roles and behaviours |
| | Building trust by meeting commitments and keeping agreements | Growth and development |
| | | Mentoring |
| | | Understanding interpersonal relationships |
| | | Pointing out opportunities and risks regarding career development |

Source: Extracted from P. Booth, *Challenge and Change: Embracing the Team Concept*, Report 123-94, Conference Board of Canada, 1994.

**Canadian Tire**
www.canadiantire.com

> Should someone be paid for their "teamwork" or their individual performance?

**REWARD SYSTEMS THAT ACKNOWLEDGE TEAM EFFORT**   A Conference Board of Canada study of teams in the workplace found that the most commonly used incentive to acknowledge teamwork was recognition, including "small financial rewards, plaques, ceremonies, publicity in company newspapers, and celebrations of success at company gatherings," used by well over half of the companies surveyed.[44] Other forms of team reward were found less often, with the most common of those being the use of team cash bonus plans by 25 percent of the surveyed companies and gainsharing by 17 percent of the companies.[45]

Companies across Canada are using team rewards. For example, Canadian Tire offers team incentives to employees of its gas bars. "Secret" retail shoppers visit the outlets on a regular basis, and score them on such factors as cleanliness, manner in which the transaction was processed, and the type of products offered, using a 100-point scoring system. Scores above a particular threshold provide additional compensation that is shared by the team. Xerox Canada has its XTRA program, which rewards districts for achieving profit and customer satisfaction targets. Everyone in the district shares equally in the bonuses.

Do these team rewards make a difference to team performance? The evidence addressing this question is mixed. Certainly, there is a belief that if you want team commitment and cooperation, then it does not make sense to focus on individual behaviour. And there is evidence that small group rewards, where there are clear links between the group's performance and the reward, do motivate group members.[46] However, others argue that neither goal-setting nor expectancy theory's conditions are satisfied when there are group incentives. Specifically, group incentives can make it harder for individuals to see that goals are achievable, and individuals may be less likely to see the link between performance and outcomes. Group incentives can lead to feelings of inequity as well if some members of the group do not carry their weight. A field study of 150 teams found that when groups worked on tasks, it was the degree of interdependence of the tasks that related to cooperation, helping, job satisfaction, and the quality of the group process. The type of reward system (individual *or* group) had no effect on these factors. Team rewards may also lead to competition *between* teams, and decrease the flow of information across teams.[47] At the moment, more research on this issue needs to be conducted, particularly because studies on group incentives and performance conducted in the field have been less conclusive than those conducted in the laboratory.[48]

One additional consideration when deciding whether and how to reward team members is effect of pay dispersion on team performance. Research by Nancy Langton shows that when there is a large discrepancy in wages among group members, collaboration is lowered.[49] A study of baseball player salaries also found that teams where players were paid more similarly often outperformed teams with highly paid "stars" and lowly paid "scrubs."[50] This finding accounts for why the New York Yankees, the San Diego Padres, and the Cleveland Indians, who have very little pay difference among the players on their teams, had a great season in 1999. The Florida Marlins and the Arizona Diamondbacks, both very poor teams in 1999, had large gaps in salaries between so-called stars and other players. The Montreal Expos also had a poor 1999 season, and their players receive fairly uniform salaries. However, the Expos players' salaries are also very low by league standards. In the case of the Expos, then, the low salaries may have a greater impact than the similarity in pay across team members.

## Process

The final category related to team effectiveness are process variables. These include member commitment to a common purpose, establishment of specific team goals, team efficacy, a managed level of conflict, and a system of accountability.

**A COMMON PURPOSE** Effective teams have a common and meaningful purpose that provides direction, momentum, and commitment for members.[51] This purpose is a vision. It's broader than specific goals.

The New Brunswick government's Department of Economic Development and Tourism illustrates how a common purpose can empower employees. The department's vision statement, which includes the mandates "Help create jobs for our fellow New Brunswickers" and "Do things well or not at all," inspired some of its employees to develop strategies to attract telemarketing firms to New Brunswick. When the provincial government agreed to provide the employees with only half of the anticipated $100 000 needed to implement their strategy, the employees didn't give up. Instead, they successfully approached NB Tel for the other $50 000. Less than a year

**Major League Baseball**
www.majorleaguebaseball.com

**New Brunswick Tourism**
www.tourismnbcanada.com

**NB Tel**
www.nbtel.nb.ca

This Hot Wheels® model is one of the latest designs by the Mattel toy design team. Most toy cars take 18 months to perfect.

later, telemarketing and call centres became the fastest-growing sector in New Brunswick.[52]

Members of successful teams put a tremendous amount of time and effort into discussing, shaping, and agreeing upon a purpose that belongs to them both collectively and individually. This common purpose, when accepted by the team, becomes the equivalent of what celestial navigation is to a ship captain—it provides direction and guidance under any and all conditions.

**SPECIFIC GOALS** Successful teams translate their common purpose into specific, measurable, and realistic performance goals. Just as we demonstrated in Chapter 4 how goals lead individuals to higher performance, goals also energize teams. These specific goals facilitate clear communication. They also help teams maintain their focus on achieving results.

Consistent with the research on individual goals, team goals should be challenging. Difficult goals have been found to raise team performance on those criteria for which they're set. So, for instance, goals for quantity tend to raise quantity, goals for speed tend to raise speed, goals for accuracy raise accuracy, and so on.[53]

Along with goals, teams should be encouraged to develop milestones—tangible steps toward completion of the project. This allows teams to focus on their goal and evaluate progress toward the goal. The milestones should be sufficiently important and readily accomplished so that teams can celebrate some of their accomplishments along the way.

**TEAM EFFICACY** Effective teams have confidence in themselves. They believe they can succeed. We call this *team efficacy*.[54]

Success breeds success. Teams that have been successful raise their beliefs about future success which, in turn, motivates them to work harder.

What, if anything, can management do to increase team efficacy? Two possible options are helping the team to achieve small successes and skill training. Small successes build team confidence. As a team develops an increasingly stronger performance record, it also increases the collective belief that future efforts will lead to success. In addition, managers should consider providing training to improve members' technical and interpersonal skills. The greater the abilities of team members, the greater the likelihood that the team will develop confidence and the capability to deliver on that confidence.

**CONFLICT LEVELS** Conflict on a team isn't necessarily bad. As we'll elaborate in Chapter 7, teams that are completely void of conflict are likely to become apathetic and stagnant. Some types of conflict can actually improve team effectiveness.[55] Relationship conflicts—those based on interpersonal incompatibilities, tension, and animosity toward others—are almost always dysfunctional. However, on teams performing nonroutine activities, disagreements among members about task content (called task conflicts) is not detrimental. In fact, it is often beneficial because it lessens the likelihood of groupthink. Task conflicts stimulate discussion, promote critical assessment of problems and options, and can lead to better team decisions. So effective teams will be characterized by an appropriate level of conflict.

**ACCOUNTABILITY** We learned in the previous chapter that individuals can hide inside a group. They can engage in social loafing and coast on the group's effort because their individual contributions can't be identified. High-performing teams undermine this tendency by holding themselves accountable at both the individual and team level.

Successful teams make members individually and jointly accountable for the team's purpose, goals, and approach.[56] They clearly define what they are individually responsible for and what they are jointly responsible for. For example, joint responsibility led the New Brunswick government's Department of Economic Development and Tourism to gamble their jobs on a new tourism strategy. In 1992, the department developed a three-year $750 000 tourism strategy. Realizing the provincial government might be reluctant to approve such a request, the department guaranteed Cabinet that

Goals are important for high team performance. This team from a Motorola plant in Tianjin, China, won the grand prize award at the Motorola employee's total customer satisfaction team competition. The team was recognized for its success at achieving three supplier-related goals: providing increased support for existing suppliers, relocating high-tech support to China, and developing new local suppliers.

if their strategy didn't result in a 10 percent increase in tourism to the province, they would return the money and pay a matching penalty. Before presenting this high-risk measure to Cabinet, the tourism group polled the team to confirm each individual's commitment to this possibly risky strategy. After all, failure to achieve their goal would certainly involve loss of jobs for many of the employees. However, so confident were the team members of the unit who had done the research, that they gave unanimous approval to the proposal to return the money and pay the penalty if their strategy failed. Within only one year, the program had realized 60 percent of its goal.[57] Tourism has continued to increase in New Brunswick since then.

## Developing Trust

Many Canadian and US organizations have been suffering from a lack of trust by their employees, who faced massive layoffs throughout much of the 1990s. A 1998 survey of Canadian workers concluded that three out of four Canadians do not trust the people for whom they work.[58]

Lack of trust in an organization is a serious problem. Professors Linda Duxbury of the Carleton University School of Business and Christopher Higgins of the University of Western Ontario's Richard Ivey School of Business found that employees who work in environments characterized by trust and respect report less stress and greater productivity than those who work in environments where trust is lacking.[59]

Trust is a positive expectation (or belief) that another will not—through words, actions, or decisions—act opportunistically.[60] Trust involves making oneself vulnerable as when, for example, we disclose intimate information or rely on another's promises.[61] By its very nature, trust provides the opportunity for disappointment or to be taken advantage of.[62] So when I trust someone, I expect that they will not take advantage of me.

What are the key dimensions that underlie the concept of trust? Recent evidence has identified five: integrity, competence, consistency, loyalty, and openness.[63] These are illustrated in Exhibit 6-7. These are listed below in their order of importance in determining one's trustworthiness.

- *Integrity*: Honesty and truthfulness. Of all five dimensions, this one seems to be most critical when someone assesses another's trustworthiness. "Without a perception of the other's 'moral character' and 'basic honesty,' other dimensions of trust [are] meaningless."[64]

- *Competence*: Technical and interpersonal knowledge and skills. Does the person know what he or she is talking about? You're unlikely to listen to or depend upon someone whose abilities you don't respect. You need to believe that the person has the skills and abilities to carry out what he or she says they will do.

- *Consistency*: Reliability, predictability, and good judgment in handling situations. "Inconsistencies between words and action decrease trust."[65] Individuals quickly notice if one does not practise what one preaches.[66]

- *Loyalty*: Willingness to protect and save face for another person. Trust requires that you can depend on someone not to act opportunistically.

- *Openness*: Willingness to share ideas and information freely. Can you rely on the person to give you the full truth?

**Exhibit 6-7
Dimensions of Trust**

Wainwright Industries is a team-oriented company, and its teams played a critical role in the company winning a Malcolm Baldrige National Quality Award. Wainwright's teams are small (about six members plus a team leader), so members can easily share ideas and implement improvements. The company's owners believe that teams help create an environment in which employees take more ownership in each other and in the company.

High-performance teams are characterized by high mutual trust among members. That is, members believe in the integrity, character, and ability of each other. But as you know from personal relationships, trust is fragile. It takes a long time to build, can be easily destroyed, and is hard to regain.[67] Also, since trust begets trust and distrust begets distrust, maintaining trust requires careful attention by leaders and team members. As trust is one issue in accountability, you may want to look at the Learning About Yourself Exercise on page 268 to gain a sense of whether others would view you as trustworthy.

## Teams and Workforce Diversity

Managing diversity on teams is a balancing act (see Exhibit 6-8). Diversity typically provides fresh perspectives on issues but it makes it more difficult to unify the team and reach agreements.

### Exhibit 6-8
### Advantages and Disadvantages of Diversity

| Advantages | Disadvantages |
|---|---|
| Multiple perspectives | Ambiguity |
| Greater openness to new ideas | Complexity |
| Multiple interpretations | Confusion |
| Increased creativity | Miscommunication |
| Increased flexibility | Difficulty in reaching a single agreement |
| Increased problem-solving skills | Difficulty in agreeing on specific actions |

Source: N.J. Adler, *International Dimensions of Organizational Behavior*, 2nd ed. (Cincinnati, OH: South-Western College Publishing, 1991). Used by permission.

The strongest case for diversity on work teams is when these teams are engaged in problem-solving and decision-making tasks.[68] Heterogeneous teams bring multiple perspectives to the discussion, thus increasing the likelihood that these teams will identify creative or unique solutions. Additionally, the lack of a common perspective usually means diverse teams spend more time discussing issues, which decreases the possibility that a weak alternative will be chosen. As we pointed out in the previous chapter, diverse groups have more difficulty working together and solving problems, *but this dissipates with time* as the members come to know each other. Expect the value-added component of diverse teams to increase as members become more familiar with each other and the team becomes more cohesive.

Studies tell us that members of cohesive teams have greater satisfaction, lower absenteeism, and lower attrition from the group.[69] Yet cohesiveness is likely to be lower on diverse teams.[70] So here is a potential negative of diversity: It is detrimental to group cohesiveness. But again, referring to the last chapter, we found that the relationship between cohesiveness and group productivity was moderated by performance-related norms. We suggest that if the norms of the team are supportive of diversity, then a team can maximize the value of heterogeneity while also achieving the benefits of high cohesiveness.[71] This makes a strong case for team members to participate in diversity training.

Honeywell Ltd. in Scarborough, Ontario, which has a large number of employees for whom English is a second language, uses a "Learning for Life" program to help employees cope in a diverse workforce. Employees take courses at the workplace during and after hours to learn about empowerment, conflict resolution, and working in teams. Honeywell's training program looks for practical solutions to address conflicts arising from differences in race, age, gender, religion, values, and cultural norms. The company also tries to help employees understand that conflict resolution varies by culture.[72]

## HR Implications

# Turning Individuals Into Team Players

In this chapter we've made a strong case for the value and growing popularity of teams. But many people are not inherently team players. Instead, they're loners or people who want to be recognized for their individual achievements. There are also many organizations that have historically nurtured individual accomplishments. These companies have created competitive work environments where only the strong survive. If these organizations now introduce a team-based structure, what do they do about the selfish "I-got-to-look-out-for-me" employees that they've

created? Finally, as we discussed in Chapter 3, countries differ in terms of how they rate on individualism and collectivism. Teams fit well with countries that score high on collectivism.[1]

But what if an organization wants to introduce teams into a work population that is composed largely of individuals born and raised in a highly individualistic society, such as Canada, the United States, the United Kingdom, or Australia? James Mitchell, president of Steelcase Canada Ltd., sums up the difficulties of introducing teams to the workplace: "People talk about

As part of her training to become an astronaut, Roberta Bondar worked with other NASA astronauts to become a team player. Members of shuttle crews have to work harmoniously with other crew members to achieve the mission's goals. By stressing that the mission's success depends on teamwork, NASA teaches astronauts how to compromise and make decisions that benefit the entire team.

teams, but very few operate in a pure team sense. They tend to think that if they get cross-functional groups together— a person out of marketing, one out of sales, one out of product development, another out of engineering— somehow they've got a team-based organization. But they haven't. They have a committee."[2]

## The Challenge

The previous points are meant to highlight two substantial barriers to using work teams: individual resistance and management resistance.

When an employee is assigned to a team, his or her success is no longer defined in terms of individual performance. To perform well as team members, individuals must be able to communicate openly and honestly, to confront differences and resolve conflicts, and to sublimate personal goals for the good of the team. For many employees, this is a difficult, if not impossible, task. The challenge of creating team players will be greatest where (1) the national culture is highly individualistic and (2) the teams are being introduced into an established organization that has historically valued individual achievement. This describes, for instance, what faced managers at AT&T, Ford, Motorola, and other large Canadian- and US-based companies. These firms prospered by hiring and rewarding corporate stars, and they bred a competitive climate that encouraged individual achievement and recognition. Employees in these types of firms can be jolted by this sudden shift to the importance of team play.[3] A veteran employee of a large company, who had done well working alone, described the experience of joining a team: "I'm learning my lesson. I just had my first negative performance appraisal in 20 years."[4]

On the other hand, the challenge for management is less demanding when teams are introduced where employees have strong collectivist values— such as in Japan or Mexico—or in new organizations that use teams as their initial form for structuring work. For example, when Toyota opened plants in Canada, the working environment was designed around teams from the inception. Employees were hired with the knowledge that they would be working in teams. The ability to be a good team player was a basic hiring qualification that all new employees had to meet.

While it might seem easy enough to blame individual resistance as the cause of team failure, in many organizations there is no genuine infrastructure created to build teams. When organizations focus their rewards at the individual level, employees have no incentive to operate within a team structure. In some situations, managers are quite reluctant to give up their power and, in fact, share power with the other team members. This also makes it difficult for a real team to develop. As we mentioned in our extensive discussion of incentive programs in Chapter 4, organizations must align their incentives with their goals. If team behaviour is important to the organization, the incentive system must reflect this objective.

Below we discuss some individual and organizational factors that can be carried out through the human resources function of the organization to improve team performance.

NASA knows that turning individuals into team players takes time and training. Astronauts (such as Canadian Roberta Bondar) are high-achieving individuals who undergo an extremely competitive selection process to become astronauts. But when they become part of a shuttle crew, they must work harmoniously with other crew members to achieve their mission's goal. NASA shapes astronauts into team players by training them to work together—including brushing their teeth together—every day for a year or two before their shuttle mission. By stressing that the mission's success depends on teamwork, NASA teaches astronauts to compromise and make decisions that benefit the entire team.

## Shaping Team Players

The following summarizes the primary options managers have for trying to turn individuals into team players.

**Selection**  Some people already possess the interpersonal skills to be effective team players. When hiring team members, managers naturally look for people with the technical skills required to fill the job. But managers also need to ensure that candidates can fulfill their team roles, as well as the technical requirements.[5]

Many job candidates don't have team skills. This is especially true for those socialized around individual contributions. When faced with such candidates, managers have three options. The candidates can undergo training to "make them into team players." If this isn't possible or doesn't work, the other two options are to transfer the individual to another unit within the organization, without teams (if this possibility exists); or not to hire the candidate. In established organizations that decide to redesign jobs around teams, it

should be expected that some employees will resist being team players and may be untrainable. Unfortunately, such people typically become casualties of the team approach.

**Training**  On a more optimistic note, a large proportion of people raised on the importance of individual accomplishment can be trained to become team players. To develop team-related skills, Markham, Ontario-based AMP of Canada Ltd. put all 40 of its management people through a one-year team and project management training program of about 500 hours in 1991. They were taught how to manage commitments to each other, make specific promises and requests, and manage projects together. During 1994, the 260 people in the company underwent an intensive six-week team and project management training program called People in Action.[6]

In other companies, training specialists conduct exercises that allow employees to experience the satisfaction that teamwork can provide. They typically offer workshops to help employees improve their problem-solving, communication, negotiation, conflict-management, and coaching skills. Employees also learn the five-stage group development model described in Chapter 5. At Bell Atlantic, for example, trainers focus on how a team goes through various stages before it finally gels. And employees are reminded of the importance of patience—because teams take longer to make decisions than if employees were acting alone.[7]

**Performance evaluation**  Performance evaluation concepts have been almost exclusively developed with only individual employees in mind. This reflects the historical belief that individuals are the core building block around which organizations are built. But as we've described throughout this book, more and more organizations are restructuring themselves around teams. In those organizations using teams, how should they evaluate performance? Four suggestions have been offered for designing a system that supports and improves the performance of teams.[8]

1. *Tie the team's results to the organization's goals.* It's important to find measurements that apply to important goals that the team is supposed to accomplish.

2. *Begin with the team's customers and the work process that the team follows to satisfy customers' needs.* The final product the customer receives can be evaluated in terms of the customer's requirements. The transactions between teams can be evaluated based on delivery and quality. And the process steps can be evaluated based on waste and cycle time.

3. *Measure both team and individual performance.* Define the roles of each team member in terms of accomplishments that support the team's work process. Then assess each member's contribution and the team's overall performance.

4. *Train the team to create its own measures.* Having the team define its objectives and those of each member ensures everyone understands his or her role on the team and helps the team develop into a more cohesive unit.

**Rewards**  The reward system should be reworked to encourage cooperative efforts rather than competitive ones. For instance, Hallmark Cards, Inc. added an annual bonus based on achievement of team goals to its basic individual-incentive system. Imperial Oil adjusted its system to reward both individual goals and team behaviours.

If companies value teamwork, then promotions, pay raises, and other forms of recognition should be given to individuals for how effectively they work as a collaborative team member. This doesn't mean individual contribution is ignored; rather, it is balanced with selfless contributions to the team. Examples of behaviours that should be rewarded include training new colleagues, sharing information with teammates, helping to resolve team conflicts, and mastering new skills that the team needs but in which it is deficient.

However, Canadian organizations that use teams have been slow to link team performance to rewards in a clear way. The Conference Board of Canada reported that only 10 percent of respondents assessed contribution to team performance as part of the regular performance appraisal. Of the 45 companies that evaluated contributions to team performance as part of an employee's performance appraisal, only 19 included peer review as part of the appraisal system, with 10 more reporting that they were considering implementing it.[9]

Although explicit links between team performance and extrinsic rewards are important, don't forget the intrinsic rewards that employees can receive from teamwork. Teams provide camaraderie. It's exciting and satisfying to be an integral part of a successful team. The opportunity to engage in personal development and to help teammates grow can also be a very satisfying and rewarding experience for employees. For instance, at Steelcase Canada, teams are invited to conferences to present their successes to delegates and top company management. Teams are encouraged to celebrate when they reach their goals, including designing the celebration themselves.

Sources:

[1] See, for instance, B.L. Kirkman and D.L. Shapiro, "The Impact of Cultural Values on Employee Resistance to Teams: Toward a Model of Globalized Self-Managing Work Team Effectiveness," *Academy of Management Review*, July 1997, pp. 730-757.

[2] D.B. Harrison and H.P. Conn, "Mobilizing Abilities Through Teamwork," *Canadian Business Review*, Autumn 1994, p. 21.

[3] T.D. Schellhardt, "To Be a Star Among Equals, Be a Team Player," *Wall Street Journal*, April 20, 1994, p. B1.

[4] T.D. Schellhardt, "To Be a Star Among Equals, Be a Team Player," *Wall Street Journal*, April 20, 1994, p. B1.

[5] See, for instance, J. Prieto, "The Team Perspective in Selection and Assessment," in H. Schuler, J.L. Farr, and M. Smith (eds.), *Personnel Selection and Assessment: Industrial and Organizational Perspectives* (Hillsdale, NJ: Erlbaum, 1994); and R. Klimoski and R.G. Jones, "Staffing for Effective Group Decision Making: Key Issues in Matching People and Teams," in R.A. Guzzo and E. Salas (eds.), *Team Effectiveness and Decision Making in Organizations* (San Francisco: Jossey-Bass, 1995), pp. 307-326.

[6] D.B. Harrison and H.P. Conn, "Mobilizing Abilities Through Teamwork," *Canadian Business Review*, Autumn 1994, p. 21.

[7] T.D. Schellhardt, "To Be a Star Among Equals, Be a Team Player," *Wall Street Journal*, April 20, 1994, p. B1.

[8] J. Zigon, "Making Performance Appraisal Work for Teams," *Training*, June 1994, pp. 58-63.

[9] P. Booth, Challenge and Change: Embracing the Team Conflict. Report 123-94, Conference Board of Canada, 1994, p. 7.

## SUMMARY AND IMPLICATIONS

## For the Workplace

Few trends have influenced employee jobs as much as the massive movement to introduce teams into the workplace. The shift from working alone to working on teams requires employees to cooperate with others, share information, confront differences, and sublimate personal interests for the greater good of the team.

Effective teams have been found to have common characteristics. The work that members do should provide freedom and autonomy, the opportunity to utilize different skills and talents, the ability to complete a whole and identifiable task or product, and the belief that the task will have a substantial impact on others. The teams require individuals with technical expertise, as well as problem-solving, decision making, and interpersonal skills; and high scores on the personality characteristics of extroversion, agreeableness, conscientiousness, and emotional stability. Effective teams are neither too large nor too small—typically they range in size from five to 12 people. They have members who fill role demands, are flexible, and who prefer to be part of a group. They also have adequate resources, effective leadership, and a performance evaluation and reward system that reflects team contributions. Finally, effective teams have members committed to a common purpose and specific team goals; as well as members who believe in the team's capabilities, and tolerate a managable level of conflict and a minimal degree of social loafing.

Because individualistic organizations and societies attract and reward individual accomplishment, it is more difficult to create team players in these environments. To make the conversion, management should try to select individuals with the interpersonal skills to be effective team players, provide training to develop teamwork skills, and reward individuals for cooperative efforts.

Once teams are mature and performing effectively, management's job isn't over. This is because mature teams can become stagnant and complacent. Managers must support mature teams with advice, guidance, and training if these teams are to continue to improve.

## For You as an Individual

You will be asked to work on teams and groups both during your undergraduate years and later on in life. A team experience is often a more intense experience than working in a group, because team experiences require more interdependent work. This chapter gave a number of ideas about how to get teams to perform better. Many of those examples related ways that the team itself had to pull together, develop trust, and build cohesion. You might want to use some of those suggestions as you are working to build a team. You might also want to refer to some of those suggestions when a team on which you are working seems to be suffering difficulties.

**ROADMAP**
*REMINDER*

In the previous chapter, we discussed the concept of groups and explained how groups developed and formed norms. In this chapter, we moved to a discussion of teams, indicating that many collections of individuals form groups, not teams, and that a requirement of teams was higher participation levels. We indicated a variety of ways that teams could improve their performance. In the next chapter, we move to the topic of interaction. Now that we have discussed how to motivate individuals and have them work together, we want to consider how to improve communication among individuals in the workplace. The chapter on interacting with others also opens Part 3, The Uneasy Sides of Interaction.

## For Review

1. How can teams increase employee motivation?
2. Contrast *self-managed* and *cross-functional* teams.
3. List and describe 9 team roles.
4. How do high-performing teams minimize social loafing?
5. How do high-performing teams minimize groupthink?
6. What are the 5 dimensions that underlie the concept of trust?
7. Under what conditions will the challenge of creating team players be greatest?
8. Contrast the pros and cons of having diverse teams.

## For Critical Thinking

1. Don't teams create conflict? Isn't conflict bad? Why, then, would management support the concept of teams?
2. Are there factors in Japanese society that make teams more acceptable in the workplace than in Canada or the United States? Explain.
3. How do you think member expectation might affect team performance?
4. Would you prefer to work alone or as part of a team? Why? How do you think your answer compares with that of others in your class?

# Do Others See Me as Trustworthy?

To get some insight into how others may view your trustworthiness, complete this questionnaire. First, however, identify the person that will be evaluating you (that is, a colleague, friend, manager, team leader).

Use the following scale to score each question:

**Strongly Disagree**    1    2    3    4    5    6    7    8    9    10    **Strongly Agree**

**Score**

**1.** I can be expected to play fair.    _____

**2.** You can confide in me and know I will keep what's told
to me in confidence.    _____

**3.** I can be counted on to tell the truth.    _____

**4.** I would never intentionally misrepresent my point
of view to others.    _____

**5.** If I promise to do a favour, I can be counted on
to carry out that promise.    _____

**6.** If I have an appointment with someone, I can be counted
on to show up promptly.    _____

**7.** If I'm lent money, I can be counted on to pay it back
as soon as possible.    _____

Turn to page 633 for scoring directions and key.

---

Source: Based on C. Johnson-George and W.C. Swap, "Measurement of Specific Interpersonal Trust: Construction and Validation of a Scale to Assess Trust in a Specific Other," *Journal of Personality and Social Psychology*, December 1982, pp. 1306-1317.

# The Paper Tower Exercise

**Step 1**    Each group will receive 20 index cards, 12 paper clips, and 2 marking pens. Groups have 10 minutes to plan a paper tower that will be judged on the basis of three criteria: height, stability, and beauty. No physical work (building) is allowed during this planning period.

**Step 2**    Each group has 15 minutes for the actual construction of the paper tower.

**Step 3**    Each tower will be identified by a number assigned by your instructor. Each student is to individually examine all the paper towers. Your group is then to come to a consensus as to which tower is the winner (5 minutes). A spokesperson from your group should report its decision and the criteria the group used in reaching it.

**Step 4** In your small groups, discuss the following questions (your instructor may choose to have you discuss only a subset of these questions):

  **a.** What percent of the plan did each member of your group contribute on average?

  **b.** Did your group have a leader? Why or why not?

  **c.** How did the group generally respond to the ideas that were expressed during the planning period?

  **d.** To what extent did your group follow the five-step group development model?

  **e.** List specific behaviours exhibited during the planning and building sessions that you felt were helpful to the group. Explain why you found them to be helpful.

  **f.** List specific behaviours exhibited during the planning and building sessions that you felt were dysfunctional to the group. Explain why you found them dysfunctional.

---

Source: This exercise is based on *The Paper Tower Exercise: Experiencing Leadership and Group Dynamics* by Phillip L. Hunsaker and Johanna S. Hunsaker, unpublished manuscript. A brief description is included in "Exchange," *The Organizational Behavior Teaching Journal*, 4(2), 1979, p. 49. Reprinted by permission of the authors. The materials list was suggested by Sally Maitlis, Faculty of Commerce, UBC.

## *INTERNET SEARCH EXERCISES*

**1.** Identify 3 new and/or current trends in terms of team building, team facilitation, and/or team development. Why have these trends emerged? What are the benefits of the tools on which these trends are based? How easy would it be for managers to implement these new tools?

**2.** Find 3 organizations that are using virtual teams. Describe how they are using these teams and any evidence of their effectiveness.

## *CASE INCIDENT*

# XEL Communications

XEL Communications is a small fish in a big pond. The company employs 180 people and manufactures custom circuit boards. It competes against the likes of Nortel and AT&T.

Bill Sanko and his partners bought the company from GTE Corp. GTE is its major customer, but Sanko wants to reduce its dependence on GTE. He needs to sell more to the regional phone companies and to big industrial customers that operate their own phone systems.

Sanko's problem is that to compete successfully for new business he has to dramatically improve XEL's agility. He wants lightning turnaround of orders, more quickly than any big company could manage. He wants speedy response to customer needs. And he wants all of this done with close attention to cost. Unfortunately, XEL is not designed for speed or flexibility. Its costs are also too high to give the firm a competitive advantage.

For example, on the shop floor, it takes XEL eight weeks to get a product through the production cycle—from start-up to finished product. This ties up a lot of money in inventory and frustrates customers who want quick delivery. Sanko believes that high-performing teams could cut this down to four days or fewer. The company's structure is also burdensome. Line workers report to supervisors, who report to unit or departmental managers, who report on up the ladder to Sanko and a crew of top executives. This high vertical structure delays decision making and increases expenses. "If a hardware engineer needs some software help, he goes to his manager," Sanko says. "The manager says, 'Go write it up.' Then the hardware manager takes the software manager to lunch and they talk about it."

Sanko has decided to reorganize his company around self-managed teams. He believes that a well-designed team structure can help him better satisfy his customers by cutting cycle time from eight weeks to four days, significantly improving quality, cutting assembly costs by 25 percent, and reducing inventory costs by 50 percent. Ambitious goals? You bet! But Sanko thinks it's possible. Moreover, achieving these goals might be necessary if his company is to survive.

## Questions

**1.** Describe, in detail, the steps you think Sanko should take in planning and implementing self-managed teams.

**2.** What problems should Sanko watch for?

Source: Based on J. Case, "What the Experts Forgot to Mention," *INC.*, September 1993, pp. 66-78.

# Another Team? Oh No!

Jaime looks forward to going to this morning's meeting. Her team is developing a new product, and this morning they're meeting to talk about the best way to market it. She likes how everyone interacts together, so different from her last experience, when one self-acknowledged "star" tried to derail the work of everyone else.

Or consider Kingston-based ESG Canada, started by five friends who created a monitoring system to be used in underground mines. The five try to make all decisions together, with each considered an equal partner, but it's not always easy. The teamwork bogs them down, and takes a lot of effort. They have started wondering whether a team approach is the best way to run their company.

Many Canadian companies started moving to teamwork in the 1980s, for at least some of the work performed. Companies that did so often claimed that the benefits of successful teams were numerous. They cited such benefits as increased productivity, better communication, greater creativity and problem-solving, and higher-quality decisions.

Teamwork is not always perfect, however. Peter Drucker, a leading management guru, once advised companies that they had to have teams. Now he preaches that leaders are everything. And researchers at the Massachusetts Institute of Technology (MIT) who used to advocate teamwork are now saying that there isn't proof of better performance from teams.

Almost everyone has been on a team that didn't work well. For instance, sometimes no one on the team takes responsibility for the project, or no one takes a leadership role, so that roles and responsibilities are unclear. Other times, for a variety of reasons, some or all of the team members don't get along.

Management and researchers are starting to realize that getting individuals to work together on a team takes more than just assigning people to the team. And a team might not even be the right way to do a job.

## Questions

1. What can be done to improve working relationships on a team?

2. What can be done when a team member acts like a star, claiming that his or her work is better than everyone else's and/or redoing others' work?

3. What are the advantages and disadvantages of ESG's team management approach?

Source: Based on "The Trouble With Teams," *Venture 703*; aired October 28, 1998.

# Rob Gareau: Managing and Inspiring Individuals and Teams

Human Performance has a team-based structure on a variety of fronts. First, the co-owners work as a team. Rob Gareau, Dusan Benicky, and Steve Ramsbottom each own one-third of the Burnaby operation. Gareau owns all of the Vancouver operation, although he is looking toward having Ramsbottom as a partner for that part of the business.

How did this team come together? It turned out that they were all working in the same place, the Burnaby Performance Centre, at the same time, and all three of them were unhappy with the management structure in place there. Benicky was prepared to leave, and it was obvious to both Gareau and Ramsbottom that if he did so, the Centre was likely to fold and they would be looking for new jobs. Gareau offered to take over the management of the training program at the Centre in September 1998, in anticipation of getting a lease agreement in January 1999 to provide all of the Centre's training.

In putting together the co-founders as a team, Gareau said that he was looking for complementarity among the individuals. There were a variety of skills needed for Human Performance to be successful. Together, the three fit the bill: Gareau had the necessary business savvy, Benicky brought both credibility and contacts, and Ramsbottom was a hard worker.

The owners of Human Performance also try to create a team atmosphere with their employees. The trainers work in a small space, and it's important for everyone to get along. Gareau encourages the trainers to help one another and to offer support to each other. Sometimes trainers have to substitute for each other as well, making it even more important that everyone works as a team.

When asked how he motivates his employees, Gareau notes that in part he motivates just through his own general enthusiasm. He shows employees the behaviours that he wants them to carry out. He also says that he gives personal, meaningful rewards to his employees. These might include giving a bonus to someone who has been doing well and needs the money, or paying for a course that another employee wants to take. He also writes notes to thank staff for jobs well done. He gives them flexibility too in choosing their work schedules. Gareau believes in intermittent reinforcement, and thinks extrinsic motivation works best when it's unexpected.

Because Human Performance is a relatively young, though growing, company, the extrinsic rewards to employees may be fewer than in larger, established corporations. Employees are paid a flat rate per contact hour with clients, with senior trainers paid more than novice trainers. Trainers' rates increase when they've done really well, and Gareau reviews their rates every six months. Understandably, raises are "dependent on money in the bank." But as the company grows, he will consider profit sharing and gain sharing for his staff.

Though Gareau believes that extrinsic motivation is an important aspect of getting employees to perform appropriately, he also emphasizes the need for intrinsic motivation. He wants people to be internally motivated. As he explains, because the company has two locations, he's not always present to manage day-to-day issues. He wants employees to try to figure out resolutions to problems they are having, and he encourages them when they solve issues on their own.

Gareau illustrates how much he values staff who are self-starters when he describes his "best hire." This person was also Human Performance's first administrator. She took the new position and set the tempo for carrying out the work. She implemented new systems and developed a policy manual. Her energy and enthusiasm were an inspiration for other employees.

Gareau spends a lot of time dealing with motivation issues, and trying to understand what motivates people, because it's not just his staff who may be in need of motivation. As a personal trainer, he also has to motivate his clients. He has learned that the best way to do this is to work with both the personalities and needs of his clients. In other words, Gareau does not adhere to a "one size fits all" theory of motivation. With his youngest clients, the seven-, eight-, and nine-year-olds, he finds that sometimes they can be *too* motivated. He often needs to simply calm their energies, and get them to learn more awareness of basic body mechanics, because these children still have growing bodies. With his adult clients who are not athletes, Gareau first meets with them to find out their goals and expectations. Sometimes he has to help them set more realistic goals.

While motivating clients is an exciting part of his job, Gareau admits that occasionally a client can be difficult to motivate. Sometimes his clients have so much going on in their personal lives that they get stuck at a particular level in their training, and it's difficult to get them to move on to the next level. He notes that for the most part "if clients just show up rested and ready to be there, that is much of the battle for advancing through a training program." Yet some are just so busy with their lives that they can't even do this. Consequently, Gareau has had to convince the occasional client that it would be best to discontinue training.

While Gareau does have a regular "performance appraisal" system for his clients, he is still working on an appraisal system for his staff. He meets with his clients every three months to discuss past goals, set new goals, and consider any new factors in clients' aspirations. He also does fitness assessments for his clients every six months. This way clients have an objective set of measures to gauge their performance. By meeting with clients and setting quarterly goals, he also makes sure that the training program meets the their individual needs.

Gareau realizes he also needs an appraisal system for his staff, and he is still trying to figure out the best way to implement this. He knows that there is a lot of variation among his trainers, and he wants to have a clearer way of evaluating and rewarding performance. However, he recognizes that for the performance appraisal system to work, he has to involve his employees in developing the system. He wants them to agree to the mechanism and get their buy-in. He also wants the appraisal process to be used as a way of improving employee performance.

# Questions:

1. What theories could help explain Gareau's motivation techniques with his clients? With his employees?

2. What advice would you give to Gareau about motivating his employees? Keep in mind that Human Performance is still young and the owners have to keep an eye on the bottom line.

3. To what extent do you think the team spirit that Gareau tries to foster allows for instrinsic motivation? Are there other things he might do to improve intrinsic motivation?

4. What advice might you give Gareau about developing a performance appraisal system for his employees?

# PART 3
## The Uneasy Sides of Interaction

**ROADMAP**



# CHAPTER 7
# Interacting With Others

The Vancouver Police Board fired Chief Constable Bruce Chambers (at right) in June 1999, in part because of conflict between Chambers and his police force.[1] Chambers noted a communication breakdown that was "due to a lack of support for me personally and for what I hope(d) to communicate." Chambers illustrated this problem through the example of his relationship with a deputy chief constable with whom he barely spoke: "The only exception was when I confronted him about an issue or when he needed something from me."

In firing Chambers, the board clearly felt that conflict among the chief and some of the officers was bad for the police force. Despite the conflict, however, not all performance was affected. Chambers, by all accounts, had done an outstanding job of reducing crime in Vancouver: "a 25 percent reduction in property crime, a 43-percent reduction in commercial break-and-enters and a 22 percent drop in residential break-ins." However, Vancouver mayor Phillip Owen, chair of the police board, noted that the city's crime rate was only one factor to be considered in Chambers' performance. He also noted that "there was a leadership style that

*Questions for Consideration*

**How can we improve communication?**

**How do we manage conflict?**

**How do we negotiate?**

some people liked, some didn't. And we had to consider all [the] factors."

How do breakdowns in communication happen? Chambers offered a glimpse into this process: "The breakdown of communication...is in part my responsibility. Equal responsibility also rests with the Board and the Deputies. I believe these communication problems flow from the climate of mistrust that prevails among us." Establishing trust is not always easy. Chambers was hired from outside the Vancouver Police Force, and many officers felt that an insider should have been promoted to chief. One police board member noted that "It's very difficult for anybody from the outside to come into a paramilitary situation—be it the police or the fire service—and take control. He should have been aware of these problems and he should have taken them into consideration."

Research indicates that poor communication is probably the most frequently cited source of interpersonal conflict.[2] Individuals spend nearly 70 percent of their waking hours communicating—writing, reading, speaking, listening—which means that they have many opportunities in which to engage in poor communication. It is also likely that one of the most inhibiting forces to successful group performance is a lack of effective communication. In 1997, a WorkCanada survey of 2039 Canadians in six industrial and service categories explored the state of communication in Canadian businesses.[3] The survey found that 61 percent of senior executives believed that they did a good job of communicating with employees. However, those who worked below the senior executives failed to share this feeling; only 33 percent of the managers and department heads believed that senior executives were effective communicators. The report of communication was even lower for those in nonmanagerial positions: Only 22 percent of hourly workers, 27 percent of clerical employees, and 22 percent of professional staff reported that senior executives did a good job of communicating with them.

Both Chief Constable Chambers' problems with his police force and the survey of communication practices in the Canadian workplace point to the same reality: that communication is an important problem and consideration for organizations and individuals alike. Communication is a foundation for

Communication at Home Depot is designed to give employees information, build their morale, and provide a release for the emotional expression of their feelings. Company founders Bernard Marcus and Arthur Blank spend about 40 percent of their time in stores talking with employees, who are encouraged to express their opinions without fear of being fired or demoted. During a closed-circuit television program called *Breakfast With Bernie and Art*, Marcus (shown here) and Blank speak to employees from one of their stores, updating them on corporate news, sharing sales and profits results, and answering their questions.

**City of Vancouver Police Department**
www.city.vancouver.bc.ca/police

**Home Depot**
www.homedepot.com

**communication**
The transference and understanding of meaning.

**encoding**
Converting a communication message to symbolic form.

**decoding**
Retranslating a sender's communication message.

many things that happen among groups and within the workplace—from motivating, to providing information, to controlling behaviour, to expressing emotion. Poor communication can lead to conflicts, while good communication builds trust, and allows parties to engage in various negotiations to get tasks done. So important is communication that Vancouver-based Seagate Software, which employs many high-tech workers, looks for "people with strong personal skills rather than specific technical skills, [because] communication skills...are the most important qualities for success," according to president and CEO Greg Kerfoot.[4]

In this chapter we explore the foundations of communication, and then consider the effects of communication on conflict and negotiation. The first of the two CBC Video Cases for this chapter, "Small Talk," also gives you tips for building trust in communication.

## The Communication Process

No group can exist without **communication**: the transference of meaning among its members. Communication can be thought of as a process, or flow, as shown in Exhibit 7-1. The model indicates that *both* the sender *and* the receiver are part of the communication process, with the sender establishing a message, **encoding** the message, and choosing the channel to send it, and the receiver **decoding** the message and providing feedback to the sender. Communication problems occur when something disrupts the flow during encoding, channel selection, decoding, or feedback.

Four factors have been described that affect how the message is encoded by the sender and decoded by the receiver: skill, attitudes, knowledge, and the social-cultural system. For example, our success in communicating to you depends upon our writing skills and your reading skills. Communicative success also includes speaking, listening, and reasoning skills. Clearly, the amount of knowledge the source and receiver hold about the subject will affect the clarity of the message that is transferred. As we discussed in Chapter 3, our interactions with others are affected by our attitudes, values,

**Exhibit 7-1**
**The Communication Process Model**

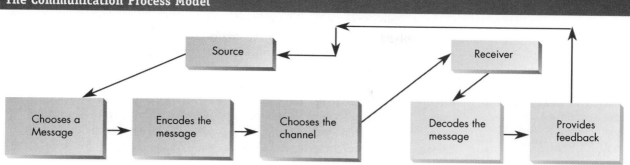

and beliefs. Thus, the attitudes of the sender and receiver toward each other will affect how the message is transmitted. Finally, our position in the social-cultural system in which we exist affects our ability to successfully engage in communication. Messages sent and received by people in equal positions are sometimes interpreted differently than messages sent and received by people in very different positions.

**message**
What is communicated.

The **message** is the actual physical product from the source encoding. "When we speak, the speech is the message. When we write, the writing is the message. When we paint, the picture is the message. When we gesture, the movements of our arms, the expressions on our face are the message."[5] Our message is affected by the code, or group of symbols, we use to transfer meaning, the content of the message itself, and the decisions that we make in selecting and arranging both codes and content. The poor choice of symbols, and confusion in the content of the message, can cause problems.

The new national political party Canadian Alliance learned in its infancy that one can easily communicate unintended messages. The party's first choice of name, Canadian Conservative Reform Alliance Party, caused quite a stir for its acronym (CCRAP). People across the country wondered what the new party was trying to communicate about its objectives.

**channel**
The medium through which a communication message travels.

The **channel** is the medium through which the message travels. It is selected by the source, who must determine which channel is formal and which one is informal. Formal channels are established by the organization and transmit messages that pertain to the job-related activities of members. They traditionally follow the authority network within the organization.

Other forms of messages, such as personal or social messages, follow the informal channels in the organization. Examples of channels are formal memos, voice mail, e-mail, meetings, and so on. The channel can distort a communication if a poor one is selected or if the noise level is high.

Why do people choose one channel of communication over another; for instance, a phone call instead of a face-to-face talk? One answer might be anxiety! An estimated five to 20 percent of the population[6] suffer from debilitating **communication apprehension** or anxiety. We all know people who dread speaking in front of a group, but some people may find it extremely difficult to talk with others face to face or become extremely anxious when they have to use the telephone. As a result, they may rely on memos, letters, or e-mail to convey messages when a phone call would not only be faster but also more appropriate.

But what about the 80 to 95 percent of the population who don't suffer from this problem? Is there any general insight we might be able to provide regarding choice of communication channel? The answer is a qualified "yes." A model of media richness has been developed to explain channel selection among managers.[7]

Recent research has found that channels differ in their capacity to convey information. Some are rich in that they have the ability to (1) handle multiple cues simultaneously, (2) facilitate rapid feedback, and (3) be very personal. Others are lean in that they score low on these three factors. As Exhibit 7-2 illustrates, face-to-face talk scores highest in terms of **channel richness** because it provides for the maximum amount of information to be transmitted during a communication episode. That is, it offers multiple information cues (words, postures, facial expressions, gestures, intonations), immediate feedback (both verbal and nonverbal), and the personal touch of "being there." Impersonal written media such as bulletins and general reports rate lowest in richness.

The choice of one channel over another depends on whether the message is routine or nonroutine. The former types of messages tend to be straightforward and have a minimum of ambiguity. The latter are likely to be complicated and have the potential for misunderstanding. Managers can communicate routine messages efficiently through channels that are lower in richness. However, they can communicate nonroutine messages effectively only by selecting rich channels. Evidence indicates that high-performing managers tend to be more media-sensitive than low-performing managers.[8] That is, they're better able to match appropriate media richness with the ambiguity involved in the communication.

It is not just coincidence that more and more senior managers have been using meetings to facilitate communication and are regularly leaving the isolated sanctuary of their executive offices to manage by walking around. Effective executives are relying on richer channels of communication to transmit the more ambiguous nonroutine messages they need to convey about closing facilities, imposing large layoffs, restructuring, merging, consolidating, and introducing new products and services at an accelerated pace.

---

**communication apprehension**
Undue tension and anxiety about oral communication, written communication, or both.

**channel richness**
The amount of information that can be transmitted during a communication episode.

---

## Exhibit 7-2
## Hierarchy of Channel Richness

| Channel richness | Type of message | Information medium |
|---|---|---|
| Richest | Nonroutine, ambiguous | Face-to-face talk |
| | | Telephone |
| | | Electronic mail |
| | | Memos, letters |
| Leanest | Routine, clear | Flyers, bulletins, general reports |

**feedback loop**
The final link in the communication process; puts the message back into the system as a check against misunderstandings.

The final link in the communication process is a **feedback loop**. Feedback lets us know whether understanding has been achieved. If the feedback loop is to succeed in preventing miscommunication, the receiver needs to give feedback and the sender needs to check for it.

## Barriers to Effective Communication

A number of factors have been identified as barriers to communication. Below we review some of the more prominent.

**filtering**
A sender's manipulation of information so that it will be seen more favourably by the receiver.

**FILTERING** **Filtering** refers to a sender manipulating information so that the receiver will view it more favourably. For example, when a manager tells a senior executive what the manager feels the executive wants to hear, the manager is filtering information. Does this happen much in organizations? Sure! As information is passed up to senior executives, employees must condense and synthesize it so that those on top don't become overloaded with information. The personal interests and perceptions of what is important by those doing the synthesizing will result in filtering.

How disastrous is filtering? Eckhard Pfeiffer, CEO of Houston-based Compaq Computer Corp., was dismissed in April 1999. Interestingly, some of his former employees say that Pfeiffer refused to hear bad news, listening only to selected senior vice-presidents. If the selected vice-presidents "didn't say it to him, he didn't give it much weight." Meanwhile Eckhard did not get "the information he needed to make the decisions he had to make. [Hans] Gutsch and [Earl] Mason [favoured senior vice presidents] would not let [negative] information through."[9]

The major determinant of filtering is the number of levels in an organization's structure. The more vertical levels in an organization's hierarchy, the more opportunities there are for filtering.

**SELECTIVE PERCEPTION** Receivers in the communication process selectively see and hear based on their needs, motivations, experience, background, and other personal characteristics. Receivers also project their interests and expectations into communications as they decode them. For example, the employment interviewer who believes that young people are more interested in spending time on leisure and social activities than working extra hours to further their careers is likely to apply that stereotype to all young job applicants. As we discussed in Chapter 2, we don't see reality; rather, we interpret what we see and call it "reality."

Selective perception worked against C. Richard Cowan (in photo), founder and president of Power Lift, a distributor of fork lift trucks. After a year in business, Cowan bought a competitor, where most employees had worked at least 15 years. Perceiving their new boss as young and inexperienced, 40 of the 200 employees quit their jobs, which caused rumours that Power Lift had financial problems. Cowan blamed the situation on poor communication, admitting that he should have met with his new employees to reassure them of the importance of their roles at Power Lift and of the firm's financial soundness. Now Cowan has made communication his top priority, talking personally with each employee to learn about his or her concerns.

**Compaq Canada**
www.compaq.ca

**The Alanis Morissette
Lyric Generator**
www.brunching.com/toys/
toy-alanislyrics.html

**DEFENSIVENESS** When people feel that they're being threatened, they tend to react in ways that reduce their ability to achieve mutual understanding. That is, they become defensive—engaging in behaviours such as verbally attacking others, making sarcastic remarks, being overly judgmental, and questioning others' motives. So when individuals interpret another's message as threatening, they often respond in ways that hinder effective communication.

**LANGUAGE** Words mean different things to different people. "The meanings of words are not in the words; they are in us."[10] Age, education, and cultural background are three of the more obvious variables that influence the language a person uses and the definitions he or she gives to words. For instance, when Alanis Morissette sang "Isn't It Ironic?", middle-aged English professors complained that she completely misunderstood the meaning of "irony"—but the millions who bought her CD understood what she meant.

In an organization, employees usually come from diverse backgrounds and, therefore, have different patterns of speech. Additionally, the grouping of employees into departments creates specialists who develop their own jargon or technical language. In large organizations, members are also frequently widely dispersed geographically—even operating in different countries—and individuals in each locale will use terms and phrases that are unique to their area. The existence of vertical levels can also cause language problems. The language of senior executives, for instance, can be mystifying to operative employees who are unfamiliar with management jargon.

The point is that even with a common language, such as English, our usage of that language is far from uniform. Senders tend to assume that the words and terms they use mean the same to the receiver as they do to them. This, of course, is often incorrect, thus creating communication difficulties. The multicultural environment of many of today's workplaces makes communication issues even more complex. Many of us interact, or will interact, with colleagues for whom English is a second language. This means that even more opportunities arise for confusion about meaning. It is therefore important to be aware that your understanding of the particular meaning of a word or phrase may not be shared similarly. For more about effective listening skills, refer to the From Concepts to Skills feature on pages 281-282.

## Communication Flows in Organizations

Communication can flow vertically (upward or downward), laterally, or through networks in organizations.[11] We will explore each of these directional flows and their implications.

### Downward

Communication that flows from one level of a group or organization to a lower level is a downward communication.

When we think of managers communicating with employees, the downward pattern is the one we usually think of. Group leaders and managers use this approach to assign goals, provide job instructions, inform employees of policies and procedures, identify problems that need attention, and offer feedback about performance. The complex issues associated with performance feedback are discussed in more detail in our HR Implications feature on page 313. But downward communication doesn't have to involve

# From CONCEPTS to SKILLS

## Effective Listening

Too many people take listening skills for granted. They confuse hearing with listening.

What's the difference? Hearing is merely picking up sound vibrations. Listening is making sense out of what we hear. That is, listening requires paying attention, interpreting, and remembering sound stimuli.

The average person normally speaks at a rate of 125 to 200 words per minute. However, the average listener can comprehend up to 400 words per minute. This leaves a lot of time for idle mind-wandering while listening. For most people, it also means they've acquired a number of bad listening habits to fill in the "idle time."

The following eight behaviours are associated with effective listening skills. If you want to improve your listening skills, look to these behaviours as guides:

1. *Make eye contact.* How do you feel when somebody doesn't look at you when you're speaking? If you're like most people, you're likely to interpret this behaviour as aloofness or lack of interest. We may listen with our ears, but others tend to judge whether we're really listening by looking at our eyes.

2. *Exhibit affirmative head nods and appropriate facial expressions.* The effective listener shows interest in what is being said. How? Through nonverbal signals. Affirmative head nods and appropriate facial expressions, when added to good eye contact, convey to the speaker that you're listening.

3. *Avoid distracting actions or gestures.* The other side of showing interest is avoiding actions that suggest your mind is somewhere else. When listening, don't look at your watch, shuffle papers, play with your pencil, or engage in similar distractions. They make the speaker feel you're bored or uninterested. Maybe more important, they indicate that you aren't fully attentive and may be missing part of the message that the speaker wants to convey.

4. *Ask questions.* The critical listener analyzes what he or she hears and asks questions. This behaviour provides clarification, ensures understanding, and assures the speaker that you're listening.

5. *Paraphrase.* Paraphrasing means restating what the speaker has said in your own words. The effective listener uses phrases like: "What I hear you saying is. . ." or "Do you mean . . . ?" Why rephrase what's already been said? Two reasons! First, it's an excellent control device to check on whether you're listening carefully. You can't paraphrase accurately if your mind is wandering or if you're thinking about what you're going to say next. Second, it's a control for accuracy. By rephrasing what the speaker has said in your own words and feeding it back to the speaker, you verify the accuracy of your understanding.

6. *Avoid interrupting the speaker.* Let the speaker complete his or her thought before you try to respond. Don't try to second-guess where the speaker's thoughts are going. When the speaker is finished, you'll know it!

7. *Don't overtalk.* Most of us would rather voice our own ideas than listen to what someone else says. Too many of us listen only because it's the price we have to pay to get people to let us talk. While talking may be more fun and silence may be uncomfortable, you can't talk and listen at the same time. The good listener recognizes this fact and doesn't overtalk.

8. *Make smooth transitions between the roles of speaker and listener.* When you're a student sitting in a lecture hall, you find it relatively easy to get into an effective listening frame of mind. Why? Because communication is essentially one-way: The teacher talks and you listen. But the teacher-student dyad is atypical. In most work situations, you're continually shifting back and forth between the roles of speaker and listener. The effective listener, therefore, makes transitions smoothly from speaker to listener and back to speaker.

From a listening perspective, this means concentrating on what a speaker has to say and practising not thinking about what you're going to say as soon as you get an opportunity.

Sources: Based on S.P. Robbins and P.L. Hunsaker, *Training in Interpersonal Skills: TIPs for Managing People at Work*, 2nd ed. (Upper Saddle River, NJ: Prentice Hall, 1996), Chapter 3; and data in R.C. Huseman, J.M. Lahiff, and J.M. Penrose, *Business Communication: Strategies and Skills* (Chicago: Dryden Press, 1988), pp. 380 and 425.

verbal or face-to-face contact. For example, when management sends notices or e-mails to employees to advise them of the organization's new sick-leave policy, it is using downward communication.

## Upward

Upward communication flows to a higher level in the group or organization.

Some organizational examples of upward communication are performance reports prepared by lower management for review by middle and top management, suggestion boxes, employee attitude surveys, grievance procedures, manager-employee discussions, and informal sessions where employees have the opportunity to identify and discuss problems with their direct manager or representatives of higher management. For example, at Vancouver-based heavy-equipment dealer Finning International, employees complete climate surveys and reviews of management. Finning notes that the attention management gives to these surveys has led to improved employee satisfaction and safety. At British Columbia-based A&W Food Services of Canada, management encourages employee feedback through regular open and honest discussions. Similarly, at Xerox Canada, the annual employee attitude survey includes a section on management practices and behaviour, to elicit feedback on management performance separate from the objective numbers of production. And if managers want additional feedback on their management styles, they may also conduct a "management practices" survey at any time during the year.[12] Ontario-based Teranet Land Information Services Inc. encourages its employees to "bitch up," that is, complain to someone above them who can solve their problem, rather than simply complaining to other co-workers.

Despite these examples, however, in general few Canadian firms rely on upward communication. In their study of 375 Canadian organizations, David Saunders, Dean of the Faculty of Management at the University of Calgary, and Joanne Leck of École des Hautes Études Commerciales found that unionized organizations were more likely to use upward communication. Seventy percent of unionized firms had grievance procedures, compared with six percent of nonunionized firms. Committees and meetings were the next most frequent upward communication technique (33 percent for nonunionized, 44 percent for unionized). Less than 15 percent of either type of firm used suggestion programs.[13] It is important to note that simply collecting information from employees but then not acting on it, even if only to inform employees that their concerns are being considered, will have a negative effect on employees overall. Most workers do not appreciate solicitation of information if it will not be used for some purpose.

**Finning International**
www.finning.ca

**Teranet Land Information Systems**
www.teranet.on.ca

## Lateral

When communication occurs among members of the same work group, among members of work groups at the same level, among managers at the same level, or among any horizontally equivalent employees, we describe it as lateral (or horizontal) communication.

Why would there be a need for horizontal communications if a group's or organization's vertical communications are effective? The answer is that horizontal communications are often necessary to save time and facilitate coordination. In some cases, these lateral relationships are formally sanctioned. Often, they are informally created to short-circuit the vertical hierarchy and expedite action. So lateral communications can, from management's perspective, be good or bad. Since strict adherence to the formal vertical structure for all communications can impede the efficient and accurate transfer of information, lateral communications can be beneficial. In such cases, they occur with the knowledge and support of managers. But they can create dysfunctional conflicts when the formal vertical channels are breached, when members go above or around their managers to get things done, or when employers find out that actions have been taken or decisions made without their knowledge.

## Networks

**communication networks**
Channels by which information flows.

**formal networks**
Task-related communications that follow the authority chain.

**informal network**
Communications that flow along social and relational lines.

**Communication networks** define the channels by which information flows. These channels are one of two varieties—either formal or informal. **Formal networks** are typically vertical, follow the authority chain, and are limited to task-related communications. In contrast, the **informal network**—usually better known as the grapevine—is free to move in any direction, skip authority levels, and is as likely to satisfy group members' social needs as it is to facilitate task accomplishments.

**FORMAL SMALL-GROUP NETWORKS** Exhibit 7-3 illustrates three common small-group networks. These are the chain, wheel, and all-channel. The chain rigidly follows the formal chain of command. The wheel relies on the leader to act as the central conduit for all the group's communication. The all-channel network permits all group members to communicate actively with each other. As Exhibit 7-4 demonstrates, the effectiveness of each network depends on the dependent variable you are concerned about. For instance,

### Exhibit 7-3
### Three Common Small-Group Networks

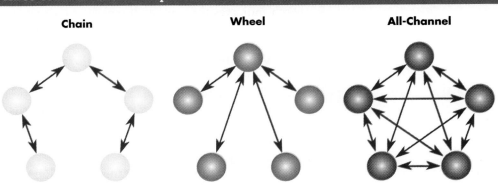

| Chain | Wheel | All-Channel |

Exhibit 7-4
Small-Group Networks and Effectiveness Channels

| Criteria | Networks | | |
| --- | --- | --- | --- |
| | Chain | Wheel | All-Channel |
| Speed | Moderate | Fast | Fast |
| Accuracy | High | High | Moderate |
| Emergence of a leader | Moderate | High | None |
| Member satisfaction | Moderate | Low | High |

the structure of the wheel facilitates the emergence of a leader, the all-channel network is best if you are concerned with having high member satisfaction, and the chain is best if accuracy is most important. Exhibit 7-4 leads us to the conclusion that no single network will be best for all occasions.

**THE INFORMAL NETWORK**  The previous discussion of networks emphasized formal communication patterns, but the formal system is not the only communication system in a group or between groups.

Now let's turn our attention to the **grapevine**—the organization's informal communication network. Is the grapevine important as a source for information? Absolutely. For instance, a recent survey found that 75 percent of employees hear about matters first through rumours on the grapevine.[14] The grapevine has three main characteristics.[15] First, it is not controlled by management. Second, it is perceived by most employees as being more believable and reliable than formal communiqués issued by top management. Third, it is largely used to serve the self-interests of those people within it.

Is the information that flows along the grapevine accurate? The evidence indicates that about 75 percent of what is carried is accurate.[16] But what conditions foster an active grapevine? What gets the rumour mill rolling?

It is frequently assumed that rumours start because they make titillating gossip. However, this is rarely the case. Rumours have at least four purposes: (1) to structure and reduce anxiety; (2) to make sense of limited or fragmented information; (3) to serve as a vehicle to organize group members, and possibly outsiders, into coalitions; and (4) to signal a sender's status ("I'm an insider and, with respect to this rumour, you're an outsider") or power ("I have the power to make you into an insider").[17] Research indicates that rumours emerge as a response to situations that are important to us, where there is ambiguity, and under conditions that arouse anxiety.[18] Work situations frequently contain these three elements, which explains why rumours flourish in organizations. The secrecy and competition that typically prevail in large organizations around such issues as the appointment of new senior managers, the relocation of offices, and the re-alignment of work assignments create conditions that encourage and sustain rumours on the grapevine. A rumour will persist either until the wants and expectations creating the uncertainty underlying the rumour are fulfilled or until the anxiety is reduced.

What can we conclude from this discussion? Certainly the grapevine is an important part of any group's or organization's communication network

**grapevine**
The organization's informal communication network.

---

**Exhibit 7-5**
**Suggestions for Reducing the Negative Consequences of Rumours**

**1.** Announce timetables for making important decisions.

**2.** Explain decisions and behaviours that may appear inconsistent or secretive.

**3.** Emphasize the downside, as well as the upside, of current decisions and future plans.

**4.** Openly discuss worst-case possibilities—these are almost never as anxiety-provoking as the unspoken fantasy.

Source: Adapted from L. Hirschhorn, "Managing Rumors," in L. Hirschhorn (ed.), *Cutting Back* (San Francisco: Jossey-Bass, 1983), pp. 54-56. With permission.

---

and well worth understanding.[19] It identifies for managers those confusing issues that employees consider important and anxiety-provoking. It acts, therefore, as both a filter and a feedback mechanism, picking up the issues that employees consider relevant. Perhaps more important, again from a managerial perspective, it seems possible to analyze grapevine information and to predict its flow, given that only a small set of individuals (around 10 percent) actively pass on information to more than one other person. By assessing which liaison individuals will consider a given piece of information to be relevant, we can improve our ability to explain and predict the pattern of the grapevine.

Can management entirely eliminate rumours? No! What management should do, however, is minimize the negative consequences of rumours by limiting their range and impact. Exhibit 7-5 offers a few suggestions for minimizing those negative consequences.

## Creating Effective Mechanisms for Communication

**How can we ensure better communication?**

How many of us have been told, "If you have any problems, just let us know?" Or we might have been told by a professor, "Class participation is important in this course, so please speak up in class." In both of these instances, the person giving the message may genuinely want information or participation, but often the listener is not inspired to act on that request. For instance, the request for feedback about problems does not really inform the listener about how to advise the speaker of the problems. And the request for more class participation does not necessarily convey how to participate.

Jim Collins, co-author of the best-selling management book *Built to Last*,[20] notes the importance of creating effective **mechanisms**, "the practices that bring what you stand for to life and stimulate change."[21] Mechanisms can be used to support the messages that managers and organizations are trying to convey. For instance, Collins cites the example of Granite Rock Co., which wanted to signal to customers its commitment to quality and customer service. To make this clear to customers, each Granite Rock invoice contains the following guarantee: "If you're not satisfied with something, don't pay us for it. Simply scratch out the related line item and send your cheque for the remaining balance." By doing this, Granite Rock is not simply claiming a strategy of good customer service, but it is also putting in place a mechanism so that if a customer is dissatisfied, he or she

**mechanisms**
Practices designed to reinforce your message and enable people to carry it out.

knows what to do. And the company clearly receives the message that there's a problem when a line item is crossed off the invoice by the customer and less money is received than expected.

When Collins was a professor at the Stanford Graduate School of Business, he wanted to ensure that students who had an important insight to share with the class had the opportunity to be heard. He also knew, however, that with 66 students in his class, some very important insights might go unnoticed. So he created a mechanism to guarantee students that when they had something really important to say, they would have the opportunity to speak up. At the beginning of the term he gave each student a sheet of bright red paper and told them, "This is your red flag. You get to raise it only one time in a quarter, but when you do—no matter what's going on—the world will stop for you. So when you have your best contribution to make, your key insight or challenge or story, that's your red-flag point. You're the only screen. Raise the flag, and the floor is yours."

In the workplace, Collins notes that most executives try to solve problems with initiatives and memos, rather than creating mechanisms that signal how people are to act. He suggests that an executive facing the problem of getting people to share their important ideas might have come into Collins's classroom and addressed the students by saying, "It's come to my attention that people may not be getting their comments in. I really want to emphasize again that if you have something important to say, make sure you get heard." However, this would not have conveyed what students could do to ensure that they were heard. Organizations and managers can improve communication by providing mechanisms to employees, customers, and clients so that they know specifically the action they are to take.

## Current Issues in Communication

How important is nonverbal communication? Why do men and women often have difficulty communicating with each other? How can individuals improve their cross-cultural communications? And how is electronics changing the way people communicate with each other in organizations? We address each of these issues below.

### Nonverbal Communication

Anyone who has ever paid a visit to a singles bar or a nightclub is aware that communication need not be verbal in order to convey a message. A glance, a stare, a smile, a frown, a provocative body movement—they all convey meaning. This example illustrates that no discussion of communication would be complete without a discussion of **nonverbal communications**. This includes body movements, facial expressions, and the physical distance between the sender and receiver.

The academic study of body motions has been labeled **kinesics**. It refers to gestures, facial configurations, and other movements of the body. It is a relatively new field, and it has been subject to far more conjecture and popularizing than the research findings support. Hence, while we acknowledge that body movement is an important segment of the study of communication and behaviour, conclusions must be guarded. Recognizing this qualification, let us briefly consider the ways in which body motions convey meaning.

**nonverbal communications**
Messages conveyed through body movements, facial expressions, and the physical distance between the sender and receiver.

**kinesics**
The study of body motions, such as gestures, facial configurations, and other movements of the body.

You can tell from his body language that David Weinberg likes his employees. Rather than talking down to them, he crouches to talk face-to-face with them. His smile is genuine. Weinberg is co-chairman of Fel-Pro, a Skokie, Illinois, manufacturer of auto parts. Fel-Pro is well known in the business world as a company that treats its employees exceptionally well. It gives employees profit sharing, above-market wages, $1,000 Treasury bonds when they have a new baby, and $3,500-a-year scholarship for children's college tuition. Weinberg's nonverbal messages are in sync with his verbal messages. Both express his sincere concern for employees.

**Does body language really make a difference?**

It has been argued that every body movement has a meaning and that no movement is accidental.[22] For example, through body language, we can say such things as, "Help me, I'm confused," or "Leave me alone, I'm really angry." And rarely do we send our messages consciously. We act out our state of being with nonverbal body language. We lift one eyebrow for disbelief. We rub our noses for puzzlement. We clasp our arms to isolate ourselves or to protect ourselves. We shrug our shoulders for indifference, wink one eye for intimacy, tap our fingers for impatience, slap our forehead for forgetfulness.[23] Babies and young children provide another good illustration of effective use of nonverbal communication. Although they lack developed language skills, they often use fairly sophisticated body language to communicate their physical and emotional needs. Such a use of body language underscores its importance in communicating needs throughout life.

While we may disagree with the specific meaning of these movements, body language adds to and often complicates verbal communication. For instance, if you read the verbatim minutes of a meeting, you do not grasp the impact of what was said in the same way you would if you had been there or had seen the meeting on video. Why? There is no record of nonverbal communication. The *intonations,* or emphasis, given to words or phrases is missing.

The *facial expression* of a person also conveys meaning. A snarling face says something different from a smile. Facial expressions, along with intonations, can show arrogance, aggressiveness, fear, shyness, and other characteristics that would never be communicated if you read a transcript of the meeting.

The way individuals space themselves in terms of *physical distance* also has meaning. What is considered proper spacing is largely dependent on cultural norms. For example, what is considered to be businesslike distance in some European countries would be viewed as intimate in many parts of North America. If someone stands closer to you than expected according to your cultural norms, you may interpret the action as an expression of aggressiveness or sexual interest. However, if the person stands farther away than you expect, you might think he or she is displeased with you or uninterested. Someone whose cultural norms differ from yours might be very surprised by your interpretation.

It is important for the receiver to be alert to these nonverbal aspects of communication. You should look for nonverbal cues as well as listen to the literal meaning of a sender's words. You should particularly be aware of contradictions between the messages. The manager may say that she is free to talk to you about that raise you have been seeking, but you may see nonverbal signals that suggest that this is not the time to discuss the subject. Regardless of what is being said, an individual who frequently glances at her watch is giving the message that she would prefer to end the conversation. We misinform others when we express one emotion verbally, such as trust, but nonverbally communicate a contradictory message that reads, "I don't have confidence in you." These contradictions often suggest that "actions speak louder (and more accurately) than words."

## Communication Barriers Between Women and Men

Research by Deborah Tannen provides us with some important insights into the differences between men and women in terms of their conversational styles.[24] In particular, Tannen has been able to explain why gender often creates oral communication barriers. Her research does not suggest that *all* men or *all* women behave as a gendered class in their communication, rather she illustrates some important generalizations.

The essence of Tannen's research is that men use talk to emphasize status, while women use it to create connection. Tannen states that communication is a continual balancing act, juggling the conflicting needs for intimacy and independence. Intimacy emphasizes closeness and commonalities. Independence emphasizes separateness and differences. Consequently, women speak and hear a language of connection and intimacy; men speak and hear

Michele Wong (right) supports Tannen's thesis that women speak and hear a language of connection and intimacy. Wong, president of software firm Synergex, fosters open communication. She shares the company's monthly financial statements with employees and holds biweekly open forums where employees can inform, thank, and question one another. She sponsors learning-at-lunch programs where employees share what they do with workers from other departments. Wong also publishes a newsletter on the company's intranet that keeps employees informed about Synergex products and people.

a language of status and independence. So, for many men, conversations are primarily a means to preserve independence and maintain status in a hierarchical social order. For many women, however, conversations are negotiations for closeness in which people try to seek and give confirmation and support. The following examples will illustrate Tannen's thesis.

Men frequently complain that women talk on and on about their problems. Women criticize men for not listening. What's happening is that when men hear a problem, they frequently assert their desire for independence and control by offering solutions. Many women, on the other hand, view telling a problem as a means to promote closeness. The women present the problem to gain support and connection, not to get the male's advice. Mutual understanding, as sought by women, is symmetrical. But giving advice is asymmetrical—it sets up the (male) advice giver as more knowledgeable, more reasonable, and more in control. This contributes to distancing men and women in their efforts to communicate.

In conversation, women and men tend to approach points of conflict in different ways. A woman might say, "Have you looked at the marketing department's research on that point?" (the implication being that the report will show the error). Rather than simply relying on her own knowledge or beliefs, she presents the supporting evidence. A man might say, "I think you're wrong on that point," and may not even provide documented evidence. These lead to gendered interpretations of the communication. Men frequently view female indirectness as "covert" or "sneaky," and they also interpret weakness when women won't take definitive stands, whereas women interpret male directness as an assertion of status and one-upmanship. Neither position is correct. It is helpful, though, to begin to understand the ways that females and males sometimes interpret the same dialogue differently.

Finally, men often criticize women for seeming to apologize all the time. Men tend to see the phrase "I'm sorry" as a weakness because they interpret the phrase to mean the woman is accepting blame. However, women typically use "I'm sorry" to express empathy: "I know you must feel bad about this; I probably would too in the same position."

While Tannen has received wide acknowledgment of her work, some suggest that it is anecdotal and/or based on faulty research. Goldsmith and Fulfs argue that men and women have more similarities than differences as communicators, although they acknowledge that when communication difficulties do appear, it is appealing to attribute them to gender.[25] Despite this, Nancy Langton, your Vancouver-based author, has noted, based on evidence from role plays, that men and women make requests for raises differently; and men are more likely to state that men were more effective at making requests, while women are more likely to indicate that it was women who handled the interaction more favourably.[26]

## Cross-Cultural Communication

| Are there special difficulties in communicating cross-culturally? |

Effective communication is difficult under the best of conditions. Cross-cultural factors clearly create the potential for increased communication problems. This is illustrated in Exhibit 7-6. A gesture that is well understood and acceptable in one culture can be meaningless or lewd in another.[27]

One author has identified some specific problems related to language difficulties in cross-cultural communications.[28] First, there are *barriers*

**Exhibit 7-6**
**Hand Gestures Mean Different Things in Different Countries**

| The A-OK Sign | "V" for Victory Sign | Finger-Beckoning Sign |
|---|---|---|
|  |  |  |

In the United States and Canada, this is just a friendly sign for "All right!" or "Good going." In Australia and Islamic countries, it is equivalent to what generations of high school students know as "flipping the bird."

In many parts of the world, this means "victory" or "peace." In England, if the palm and fingers face inward, it means "Up yours!" especially if executed with an upward jerk of the fingers.

This sign means "come here" in the United States and Canada. In Malaysia, it is used only for calling animals. In Indonesia and Australia, it is used for beckoning "ladies of the night."

Source: "What's A-O.K. in the U.S.A. Is Lewd and Worthless Beyond," *New York Times*, August 18, 1996, p. E7. From Roger E. Axtell, *Gestures: The Do's and Taboos of Body Language Around the World*. Copyright © 1991. This material is used by permission of John Wiley & Sons, Inc.

*caused by semantics*. As we've noted previously, words mean different things to different people. This is particularly true for people from different national cultures. Some words, for instance, don't translate between cultures. Understanding the word *sisu* will help you in communicating with people from Finland, but this word is untranslatable into English. It means something akin to "guts" or "dogged persistence." Similarly, the new capitalists in Russia may have difficulty communicating with their Canadian or British counterparts because English terms such as *efficiency*, *free market*, and *regulation* cannot be directly translated into Russian.

Second, there are *barriers caused by word connotations*. Words imply different things in different languages. The Japanese word *hai* translates as "yes," but its connotation may be "yes, I'm listening," rather than "yes, I agree." Western executives may be hampered in their negotiations if they don't understand this connotation.

Third are *barriers caused by tone differences*. In some cultures, language is formal, in others it's informal. In some cultures, the tone changes depending on the context: People speak differently at home, in social situations, and at work. Using a personal, informal style in a situation where a more formal style is expected can be embarrassing and off-putting.

When communicating with people from a different culture, what can you do to reduce misperceptions, misinterpretations, and misevaluations? Following these four rules can be helpful:[29]

- *Assume differences until similarity is proven*. Most of us assume that others are more similar to us than they actually are. But people from different countries often are very different from us. So you are far less likely to make an error if you assume others are different from you rather than assuming similarity until difference is proven.

- *Emphasize description rather than interpretation or evaluation*. Interpreting or evaluating what someone has said or done, in contrast with

Ottawa-based Donna Cona made history when it designed and installed the computer network for the government of the new Nunavut territory. Two-thirds of the firm's software engineers are aboriginal. Peter Baril, Nunavut's director of information technology operations, notes: "Donna Cona's quiet and knowledgeable approach was perhaps the most important skill brought to our project. No other style could have worked in this predominantly aboriginal environment." Donna Cona's president, John Bernard, is shown above.

describing, is based more on the observer's culture and background than on the observed situation. As a result, delay judgment until you've had sufficient time to observe and interpret the situation from the differing perspectives of all the cultures involved.

- *Practise empathy.* Before sending a message, put yourself in the recipient's shoes. What are his or her values, experiences, and frames of reference? What do you know about his or her education, upbringing, and background that can give you added insight? Try to see the other person as he or she really is.

- *Treat your interpretations as a working hypothesis.* Once you've developed an explanation for a new situation or think you empathize with someone from a foreign culture, treat your interpretation as a hypothesis that needs further testing rather than as a certainty. Carefully assess the feedback provided by recipients to see if it confirms your hypothesis. For important decisions or communiqués, you can also check with other foreign and home-country colleagues to ensure that your interpretations are on target.

## Electronic Communications

Since the early 1980s, we've been subjected to an onslaught of new electronic technologies that are largely reshaping the way we communicate in organizations.[30] These include pagers, fax machines, videoconferencing, electronic meetings, e-mail, cellular phones, voice messaging, and palm-sized personal communicators.

Electronic communications no longer make it necessary for you to be at your workstation or desk to be "available." Pagers, cellular phones, and personal communicators allow you to be reached when you're in a meeting, during your lunch break, while visiting in a customer's office across town, in the middle of watching a movie in a crowded theatre, or during a golf game on Saturday morning. The line between an employee's work and nonwork life is no longer distinct. In the electronic age, all employees can theoretically be "on call" 24 hours a day.

Organizational boundaries become less relevant as a result of electronic communications. Why? Because networked computers—that is, computers that are interlinked to communicate with each other—allow employees to jump vertical levels within the organization, work full-time at home or someplace other than "the office," and carry ongoing communications with people in other organizations. For example, the market researcher who wants to discuss an issue with the vice-president of marketing, who is three levels up in the hierarchy, can bypass the people in between and send an e-mail message directly. And as a result, the traditional status hierarchy, largely determined by level and access, becomes essentially negated. Or that same market

Investment bank Morgan Stanley distributes data and information to employees at its 37 offices around the world on the company's intranet. For example, the global network allows traders in Japan to receive up-to-the-minute information on securities transactions from colleagues in New York. Morgan Stanley has also connected its "hoot-and-holler" worldwide voice-messaging system to its intranet, allowing salespeople to receive messages from their workstation speakers on the trading floor.

**Morgan Stanley**
www.msdw.com

Ever notice that communicating via e-mail can be particularly sticky?

researcher may choose to live in the Cayman Islands and work at home via telecommuting rather than do his or her job in the company's Halifax office. And when an employee's computer is linked to suppliers' and customers' computers, the boundaries separating organizations become further blurred.

Although the telephone allows people to transmit verbal messages instantly, only recently has this same speed become available for the written word. In the mid-1960s, organizations were almost completely dependent on interoffice memos for internal, on-site messages, and on wire services and the post office for external messages. Then came overnight express delivery and fax machines. Today, almost all organizations have introduced e-mail, and an increasing number are providing their employees with access to the Internet.

A number of companies have even set up intranets for their employees as a way of increasing the communication flow within an organization. These are the equivalent of an internal Internet, accessible only to employees of the firm. Although intranets are not currently used to their full capacity, they can be used to store information centrally and easily exchange ideas among employees. Intranets can also bring together teams of people to discuss ideas through online forums. They can be used to provide faster problem-solving mechanisms, and give greater access to those who have the expertise to solve a particular problem. Employees can also be encouraged to share ideas about how to do work more efficiently on the intranet.

While electronic communications have revolutionized both the ability to access other people and to reach them almost instantaneously, this access and speed have come with some costs. E-mail, for instance, doesn't provide either the verbal or nonverbal nuances that a face-to-face meeting does. There has been some attempt to remedy this through the development of "emoticons" (for example, the smiley face :-)) to indicate a friendly tone; symbols (for example, <vbg> for very big grin) to indicate that one is telling a joke; and abbreviations (for example, IMHO, "in my humble opinion") to indicate that a person is respectfully trying to convey his or her own viewpoint.

Videoconferences and electronic meetings have similar drawbacks to e-mail. It's been noted that meetings have historically served two distinct purposes: fulfilling a need for group affiliation and serving as a forum for completing work tasks.[31] Videoconferences and electronic meetings do a good job at supporting tasks but don't address affiliation needs. For people with a high need for social contact, a heavy reliance on electronic communications is likely to lead to lower job satisfaction.

As electronic interaction becomes more widespread and more accepted, it will no doubt have a profound impact on how communication is conducted. For example, while working on this textbook, Nancy Langton, your Vancouver-based author, interacted with numerous people from Pearson Education Canada, some of whom she's never met, many of whom she worked with for over a year before meeting face to face or talking to on the telephone, and most of whom work across the country in Toronto. In fact, contract negotiations for the book were done almost exclusively by e-mail and fax. Additionally, it has been her experience that one can conduct entire friendships via e-mail.

A 1999 study at Boston University revealed that managers found it easier to deliver bad news (layoffs, promotion denials, and negative feedback) via e-mail, and that the messages were delivered more accurately this way. However, this does not mean that sending negative information through e-mail is always recommended. Sussman, one of the co-authors of the study, noted that "offering negative comments face-to-face is often taken as a sign that the news is important and the deliverer cares about the recipient."[32]

Despite many advantages to e-mail, it is important to realize that it is virtually indestructible once it gets backed up on your company's server. And its very speed and accessibility often lend themselves to miscommunication and misdirected messages. With these issues in mind, consider the following tips for writing and sending e-mail:[33] (1) Don't write anything that you don't want anyone other than the intended receiver to see; (2) be careful in addressing your e-mail—a simple typo can send your e-mail to the wrong person; (3) think about the e-mail you're sending, and perhaps wait an hour before you do send it off; and (4) be careful when forwarding e-mail that you are not circulating something that is untrue. You should also consider whether the originator of the message would approve of your copying it to others, especially to co-workers and managers.

Employees should also be aware that e-mail is not necessarily private, and companies often take the position that they have the right to scrutinize your e-mail. For example, the Canadian Auto Workers Union (CAW) expressed outrage in early 1998 when they discovered that Montreal-based Canadian National Railway Co. (CN) was reading employees' e-mail messages.[34] "Our people feel violated. You're given an e-mail address and you have a password, and it's yours. It's personal," is the view of Abe Rosner, a national CAW representative. CN, however, disagrees: "E-mail is to be used for CN business-approved activities only. Flowing from this is that any communication exchanged on the system is viewed as company property," explains Mark Hallman, a CN spokesperson.

Ann Cavoukian, head of the Information and Privacy Commission of Ontario, notes that "employees deserve to be treated like adults and companies should limit surveillance to rare instances, such as when there is suspicion of criminal activity or harassment."[35] She suggests that employers use respect and courtesy when dealing with employees' e-mail, and she likens e-mail to office phone calls, which generally are not monitored by the employer. It is clearly important, in any event, that employees be aware of their company's policy on e-mail. For further discussion of e-mail privacy, see the Ethical Dilemma Exercise "Employee Monitoring: How Far Is Too Far?" in Chapter 12.

**McCain Foods**
www.mccain.com

**Maple Leaf Foods International**
www.mlfi.com

# How Communication Breakdown Leads to Conflict

In our opening vignette we noted that communication had broken down between Chief Constable Chambers and his officers. This led to suspicion between the two groups, and the spread of rumours that made it into the city newspapers. But the Vancouver Police Force is not an isolated example of conflict in organizations.

For 37 years, Wallace McCain and his older brother Harrison shared command of McCain Foods Ltd., the New Brunswick-based french-fry empire they had built together.[36] In August 1993, however, that partnership came to an end, much to the surprise of the public. The brothers started McCain Foods in 1956 and "one brother never made a decision without consulting the other." What brought these two brothers down was a conflict, which had simmered quietly for 20 years, over who would succeed the brothers to run the family business. Harrison convinced other family members that Wallace and his sons would not share the business with the other McCains. The dispute ended up in a New Brunswick arbitration court, where Wallace McCain was ousted as co-CEO. In 1995, Wallace left McCain Foods and moved to Toronto to become chair of Maple Leaf Foods Ltd. Ultimately the brothers could not resolve their conflict, and more than four years after the feud went public, Harrison acknowledged, "There are still strained relations in our family holding company. I wish I could say the bitterness is all gone, but that would be an overstatement."

Conflict can be a serious problem in *any* organization. It might not lead to co-CEOs going after each other in court, as happened at McCain's, or even lead to dismissal, as was the case with Chief Constable Chambers, but it can certainly hurt an organization's performance and lead to the loss of good employees. Despite this, not all conflicts are bad. Conflict has positive sides and negative sides. For more on this debate, refer to the Point/CounterPoint discussion on pages 296-297.

Several common themes underlie most definitions of conflict.[37] Conflict must be *perceived* by the parties to it; if no one is aware of a conflict, then it is generally agreed that no conflict exists. Conflict also involves opposition or incompatibility, and some form of interaction.[38] These factors set the conditions that determine the beginning point of the conflict process. We can define **conflict**, then, as a process that begins when one party perceives that another party has negatively affected, or is about to negatively affect, something that the first party cares about.[39]

This definition is deliberately broad. It describes that point in any ongoing activity when an interaction "crosses over" to become an interparty conflict. It encompasses the wide range of conflicts that people experience in groups and organizations — incompatibility of goals, differences over interpretations of facts, disagreements based on behavioural expectations, and the like. Finally, our definition is flexible enough to cover the full range of conflict levels — from overt and violent acts to subtle forms of disagreement.

**conflict**
A process that begins when one party perceives that another party has negatively affected, or is about to negatively affect, something that the first party cares about.

## Sources of Conflict

As we've seen, communication can be a source of conflict through semantic difficulties, misunderstandings, and "noise" in the communication channels. But, of course, poor communication is certainly not the source of all conflicts. For simplicity's sake, the conditions (which also may be looked at as causes or sources of conflict) that lead to conflict have been condensed into three general categories. Besides communication, the categories include structure and personal variables.[40]

**STRUCTURE**  Consider the following vignette: Charlotte and Teri both work at a large discount-furniture retailer. Charlotte is a salesperson on the floor and she does a great job. But most of her sales are made on credit. Teri is the company credit manager, and her job is to ensure that the company minimizes credit losses. She regularly has to turn down the credit application of a customer for whom Charlotte has just closed a sale. It's nothing personal between Charlotte and Teri — the requirements of their jobs just bring them into conflict.

The two women have known each other for years and have much in common. If Charlotte and Teri had different jobs they might be best friends; instead, they are constantly fighting battles with each other. The conflicts between Charlotte and Teri are structural in nature; that is, they are a consequence of jobs rather than personality. The term *structure* in this context includes variables such as size, degree of specialization in the tasks assigned to group members, jurisdictional clarity, member-goal compatibility, leadership styles, reward systems, and the degree of dependence between groups.

A review of the conditions that can lead to conflict suggests that:

- Size, specialization, and composition of the group act as forces to stimulate conflict. The larger the group and the more specialized its activities, the greater the likelihood of conflict. The potential for conflict tends to be greatest where group members are younger and where turnover is high.

- The greater the ambiguity in precisely defining where responsibility for actions lies, the greater the potential for conflict to emerge. Such jurisdictional ambiguities increase intergroup fighting for control of resources and territory.

- The diversity of goals among groups is a major source of conflict. When groups within an organization seek diverse ends, some of which — such as sales and credit at the discount-furniture retailer — are inherently at odds, there are increased opportunities for conflict. If a group is dependent on another group (in contrast to the two being mutually independent), or if interdependence allows one group to gain at another's expense, opposing forces are stimulated.

- Too much reliance on participation may also stimulate conflict. Research tends to confirm that participation and conflict are highly correlated, apparently because participation encourages the promotion of differences.

- Reward systems create conflict when one member's gain is at another's expense.

**PERSONAL VARIABLES**  Have you ever met people to whom you take an immediate dislike? You disagree with most of their opinions. The sound of their voice, their smirk when they smile, and their personality annoy you. We've all met people like that. When you have to work with such individuals, there is often the potential for conflict.

Our last category of potential sources of conflict is personal variables. As indicated, they include the individual value systems that each person has, and the personality characteristics that account for individual idiosyncrasies and differences.

# Conflict Is Good for an Organization

We've made considerable progress in the last 25 years toward overcoming the negative stereotype given to conflict. Most behavioural scientists and an increasing number of practising managers now accept that the goal of effective management is not to eliminate conflict. Rather, it's to create the right intensity of conflict so as to reap its functional benefits.

Since conflict can be good for an organization, it is only logical to acknowledge that there may be times when managers will purposely want to increase its intensity. Let's briefly review how stimulating conflict can provide benefits to the organization.

- *Conflict is a means by which to bring about radical change.* It's an effective device by which management can drastically change the existing power structure, current interaction patterns, and entrenched attitudes.

- *Conflict facilitates group cohesiveness.* While conflict increases hostility between groups, external threats tend to cause a group to pull together as a unit. Intergroup conflicts raise the extent to which members identify with their own group and increase feelings of solidarity, while, at the same time, internal differences and irritations dissolve.

- *Conflict improves group and organizational effectiveness.* The stimulation of conflict initiates the search for new means and goals and clears the way for innovation. The successful solution of a conflict leads to greater effectiveness, to more trust and openness, to greater attraction of members for each other, and to depersonalization of future conflicts. In fact, it has been found that as the number of minor disagreements increases, the number of major clashes decreases.

- *Conflict brings about a slightly higher, more constructive level of tension.* This enhances the chances of solving the conflicts in a way satisfactory to all parties concerned. When the level of tension is very low, the parties are not sufficiently motivated to do something about a conflict.

These points are clearly not comprehensive. As noted in the chapter, conflict provides a number of benefits to an organization. However, groups or organizations devoid of conflict are likely to suffer from apathy, stagnation, groupthink, and other debilitating diseases. In fact, more organizations probably fail because they have *too little* conflict rather than too much. Take a look at a list of large organizations that have failed or suffered serious financial setbacks over the past decade or two. You see names like Olympia and York Developments, Consumers Distributing, Eaton's, and General Motors. The common thread through these companies is that they stagnated. Their management became complacent and unable or unwilling to facilitate change. These organizations could have benefited by having had more conflict—the functional kind.

Source: The points presented here were influenced by E. Van de Vliert, "Escalative Intervention in Small-Group Conflicts," *Journal of Applied Behavioral Science*, Winter 1985, pp. 19-36.

# All Conflicts Are Dysfunctional!

It may be true that conflict is an inherent part of any group or organization. It may not be possible to eliminate it completely. However, just because conflicts exist is no reason to deify them. All conflicts are dysfunctional, and it is one of management's major responsibilities to keep conflict intensity as low as humanly possible. A few points will support this case.

- *The negative consequences from conflict can be devastating.* The list of negatives associated with conflict is awesome. The most obvious are increased turnover, decreased employee satisfaction, inefficiencies between work units, sabotage, labour grievances and strikes, and physical aggression.

- *Effective managers build teamwork.* A good manager builds a coordinated team. Conflict works against such an objective. A successful work group is like a successful sports team; each member knows his or her role and supports his or her teammates. When a team works well, the whole becomes greater than the sum of the parts. Management creates teamwork by minimizing internal conflicts and facilitating internal coordination.

- *Competition is good for an organization, but not conflict.* Competition and conflict should not be confused with each other. Conflict is behaviour directed against another party, whereas competition is behaviour aimed at obtaining a goal without interference from another party. Competition is healthy; it's the source of organizational vitality. Conflict, on the other hand, is destructive.

- *Managers who accept and stimulate conflict don't survive in organizations.* The whole argument on the value of conflict may be moot as long as most senior executives in organizations view conflict traditionally. In the traditional view, any conflict will be seen as bad. Since the evaluation of a manager's performance is made by higher-level executives, those managers who do not succeed in eliminating conflicts are likely to be appraised negatively. This, in turn, will reduce opportunities for advancement. Any manager who aspires to move up in such an environment will be wise to follow the traditional view and eliminate any outward signs of conflict. Failure to follow this advice might result in the premature departure of the manager.

Positive emotions played a key role in shaping perceptions when a new member joined the world-famous Tokyo String Quartet. The chemistry among the original members, all Japanese musicians, was incredibly strong, as they had practised and performed together for decades. When one of the original artists left the group, remaining members Kazukide Isomura, Sadao Harada, and Kikuei Ikeda asked Canadian violinist Peter Oundjian to take his place. With an outsider's perspective, Oundjian began questioning everything the ensemble did, from musical selections to tour destinations. Rather than perceiving the new violinist's ideas in a negative way, the other members framed the conflict as a potential win-win situation. They took a positive approach, viewing the situation as an opportunity to make the group more creative and innovative.

The evidence indicates that certain personality types — for example, individuals who are highly authoritarian and dogmatic, and who demonstrate low esteem — lead to potential conflict. Most important, and probably the most overlooked variable in the study of social conflict, is differing value systems. For example, value differences are the best explanation of such diverse issues as prejudice, disagreements over one's contribution to the group and the rewards one deserves, and assessments of whether this particular book is any good. That John dislikes Indo-Canadians and Dana believes John's position indicates his ignorance, that an employee thinks he is worth $60 000 a year but his manager believes him to be worth $55 000, and that Ann thinks this book is interesting to read while Jennifer views it as garbage are all value judgments. And differences in value systems are important sources for creating the potential for conflict.

## From Potential to Actual Conflict

While conditions arise that may lead to conflict, it does not necessarily follow that conflict will occur. For instance, you may notice something about someone's behaviour that bothers you, but you may also choose to ignore that behaviour, thus avoiding the conflict. The way a conflict is defined goes a long way toward establishing the sort of outcomes that might settle it. For instance, if I define our budget disagreement as a zero-sum situation — that is, if you receive the increase in your budget you want, there will be just that amount less for me — I will be far less willing to compromise than if I frame the conflict as a potential win-win situation (that is, the dollars in the budget pool might be increased so that both of us could get the added resources we want). So the definition of a conflict is important, for it typically delineates the set of possible settlements. In a potential conflict situation, one progresses through stages, from perceiving and evaluating the situation,

### Exhibit 7-7
### How Conflict Builds

Conflict-handling intentions
- Competing
- Collaborating
- Compromising
- Avoiding
- Accommodating

→ Behaviour →

Outcomes
- Functional: increased performance
- Dysfunctional: decreased group performance

to forming intentions, engaging in behaviour, and achieving an outcome. The process is diagrammed in Exhibit 7-7.

**intentions**
Decisions to act in a given way in a situation.

**INTENTIONS Intentions** intervene between people's perceptions and emotions and their overt behaviour. These intentions are decisions to act in a given way.[41] Why are intentions important? Many conflicts are escalated merely by one party attributing the wrong intentions to the other party. Additionally, there is typically a great deal of slippage between intentions and behaviour, so that behaviour does not always accurately reflect a person's intentions.

Exhibit 7-8 represents one author's effort to identify the primary conflict-handling intentions. Using two dimensions — *cooperativeness* (the degree to which one party attempts to satisfy the other party's concerns) and *assertiveness* (the degree to which one party attempts to satisfy his or her own concerns) — five conflict-handling intentions can be identified: *competing* (assertive and uncooperative), *collaborating* (assertive and cooperative), *avoiding* (unassertive and uncooperative), *accommodating* (unassertive and cooperative), and *compromising* (mid-range on both assertiveness and cooperativeness).[42] Exhibit 7-9 describes these behaviours and gives examples of each.

**Exhibit 7-8**
**Dimensions of Conflict-Handling Intentions**

Source: K.W. Thomas, "Conflict and Negotiation Processes in Organizations," in M.D. Dunnette and L.M. Hough (eds.), *Handbook of Industrial and Organizational Psychology*, 2nd ed., vol. 3 (Palo Alto, CA: Consulting Psychologists Press, 1992), p. 668. With permission.

**Exhibit 7-9**
**Understanding Conflict-Handling Intentions**

| Description | Examples | When Best Used |
|---|---|---|
| **COMPETING** When one person seeks to satisfy his or her own interests, regardless of the impact on the other parties to the conflict, he or she is competing. | Intending to achieve your goal at the sacrifice of the other's goal; attempting to convince another that your conclusion is correct and his or hers is mistaken; and trying to make someone else accept blame for a problem. | When quick, decisive action is vital (in emergencies); on important issues, where unpopular actions need implementing (in cost-cutting, enforcing unpopular rules, discipline); on issues vital to the organization's welfare when you know you're right; and against people who take advantage of noncompetitive behaviour. |
| **COLLABORATING** When the intention of the parties is to solve the problem by clarifying differences rather than by accommodating various points of view, they are collaborating for mutually beneficial outcome. | Attempting to find a win-win solution that allows both parties' goals to be completely achieved; seeking a conclusion that incorporates the valid insights of both parties. | To find an integrative solution when both sets of concerns are too important to be compromised; when your objective is to learn; to merge insights from people with different perspectives; to gain commitment by incorporating concerns into a consensus; and to work through feelings that have interfered with a relationship. |

*Continued on next page*

**Exhibit 7-9**
**Understanding Conflict-Handling Intentions** *continued*

| Description | Examples | When Best Used |
|---|---|---|
| **AVOIDING** A person may recognize that a conflict exists and want to withdraw from it or suppress it. | Trying to just ignore a conflict; avoiding others with whom you disagree. | When an issue is trivial, or more important issues are pressing; when you perceive no chance of satisfying your concerns; when potential disruption outweighs the benefits of resolution; to let people cool down and regain perspective; when gathering information supersedes immediate decision; when others can resolve the conflict more effectively; and when issues seem tangential or symptomatic of other issues. |
| **ACCOMMODATING** One party seeks to appease an opponent by placing the opponent's interests above his or her own. | Willingness to sacrifice your goal so the other party's goal can be attained; supporting someone else's opinion despite your reservations about it; forgiving someone for an infraction and allowing subsequent ones. | When you find you're wrong and to allow a better position to be heard, to learn, and to show your reasonableness; when issues are more important to others than yourself, and to satisfy others and maintain cooperation; to build social credits for later issues; to minimize loss when you are outmatched and losing; when harmony and stability are especially important; and to allow others to develop by learning from mistakes. |
| **COMPROMISING** When each party to the conflict seeks to give up something, sharing occurs, resulting in a compromised outcome. In compromising, there is no clear winner or loser, and each party intends to give up something. | Willingness to accept a raise of $1.50 an hour rather than the $2 desired and the $1 initially offered by the employer; acknowledging partial agreement with a specific viewpoint; taking partial blame for an infraction. | When goals are important but not worth the effort of potential disruption of more assertive approaches; when opponents with equal power are committed to mutually exclusive goals; to achieve temporary settlements to complex issues; to arrive at expedient solutions under time pressure; and as a backup when collaboration or competition is unsuccessful. |

Source: K.W. Thomas, "Toward Multidimensional Values in Teaching: The Example of Conflict Behaviors," *Academy of Management Review*, July 1977, p. 487.

Intentions provide general guidelines for parties in a conflict situation. They define each party's purpose. Yet people's intentions are not fixed and can alter in reaction to changes in the situation or behaviour of the other individual. However, research does indicate that people have an underlying disposition to handle conflicts in certain ways.[43] That is, when confronting a conflict situation, some people want to win it all at any cost, some want to find an optimum solution, some want to run away, others want to be obliging, and still others want to "split the difference." This chapter's Learning

About Yourself Exercise on page 319 gives you the opportunity to discover your own conflict-handling style. And the second CBC Video Case for the chapter, on page 323, gives you a unique perspective on handling conflicts through the use of masks.

**behaviours**
Statements, actions, and reactions by an individual.

**BEHAVIOURS**  Conflict **behaviours** (statements, actions, and reactions made by the conflicting parties) are usually overt attempts to carry out each party's intentions. However, overt behaviours sometimes deviate from original intentions.[44]

At some point conflict can result in interaction between the two parties. For example, you make a demand on me; I respond by arguing; you threaten me; I threaten you back; and so on. Exhibit 7-10 provides a way of visualizing conflict behaviour. All conflicts exist somewhere along this continuum. At the lower part of the continuum, we have conflicts characterized by subtle, indirect, and highly controlled forms of tension. An illustration might be a student questioning in class a point the instructor has just made. Conflict intensities escalate as they move upward along the continuum, until they become highly destructive. Strikes and lockouts, riots, and wars clearly fall in this upper range. For the most part, you should assume that conflicts that reach the upper ranges of the continuum are almost always dysfunctional. Functional conflicts are typically confined to the lower range of the continuum.

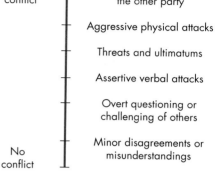

**Exhibit 7-10
Conflict Intensity Continuum**

Annihilatory conflict — Overt efforts to destroy the other party

— Aggressive physical attacks

— Threats and ultimatums

— Assertive verbal attacks

— Overt questioning or challenging of others

No conflict — Minor disagreements or misunderstandings

Source: Based on S.P. Robbins, *Managing Organizational Conflict: A Nontraditional Approach* (Upper Saddle River, NJ: Prentice Hall, 1974), pp. 93–97; and F. Glasl, "The Process of Conflict Escalation and the Roles of Third Parties," in G.B.J. Bomers and R. Peterson (eds.), *Conflict Management and Industrial Relations* (Boston: Kluwer-Nijhoff, 1982), pp. 119-140.

**conflict management**
The use of resolution and stimulation techniques to achieve the desired level of conflict.

If a conflict is dysfunctional, what can the parties do to de-escalate it? Or, conversely, what options exist if conflict is too low and needs to be increased? This brings us to **conflict management** techniques. Exhibit 7-11 lists the major resolution and stimulation techniques that allow managers to control conflict levels. Notice that several of the resolution techniques were earlier described as conflict-handling intentions. This, of course, shouldn't be surprising. Under ideal conditions, a person's intentions should translate into comparable behaviours.

**OUTCOMES**  The action-reaction interplay between the conflicting parties results in consequences. As Exhibit 7-12 demonstrates, these outcomes may be functional in that the conflict results in an improvement in the group's performance, or dysfunctional in that it hinders group performance. We see that there is an optimal level of conflict that results in the highest productivity.

**functional conflict**
Conflict that supports the goals of the group and improves its performance.

**dysfunctional conflict**
Conflict that hinders group performance.

One should not label all conflict as either good *or* bad. Rather, some conflicts support the goals of the group and improve its performance; these are **functional**, or constructive, forms of conflict. Additionally, there are conflicts that hinder group performance; these are **dysfunctional**, or destructive, forms of conflict. The conflict between brothers Harrison and Wallace McCain, reported above, was clearly in the dysfunctional category. In the case of the Vancouver police force, the conflict was accompanied by mixed results: The improvement in crime statistics coincided with weakening morale.

**Exhibit 7-11**
**Conflict Management Techniques**

**Conflict Resolution Techniques**

| | |
|---|---|
| *Problem-solving* | Face-to-face meeting of the conflicting parties for the purpose of identifying the problem and resolving it through open discussion. |
| *Superordinate goals* | Creating a shared goal that cannot be attained without the cooperation of each of the conflicting parties. |
| *Expansion of resources* | When a conflict is caused by the scarcity of a resource — say, money, promotion opportunities, office space — expansion of the resource can create a win-win solution. |
| *Avoidance* | Withdrawal from, or suppression of, the conflict. |
| *Smoothing* | Playing down differences while emphasizing common interests between the conflicting parties. |
| *Compromise* | Each party to the conflict gives up something of value. |
| *Authoritative command* | Management uses its formal authority to resolve the conflict and then communicates its desires to the parties involved. |
| *Altering the human variables* | Using behavioural change techniques such as human relations training, to alter attitudes and behaviours that cause conflict. |
| *Altering the structural variables* | Changing the formal organization structure and the interaction patterns of conflicting parties through job redesign, transfers, creation of coordinating positions, and the like. |

**Conflict Stimulation Techniques**

| | |
|---|---|
| *Communication* | Using ambiguous or threatening messages to increase conflict levels. |
| *Bringing in outsiders* | Adding employees to a group whose backgrounds, values, attitudes, or managerial styles differ from those of present members. |
| *Restructuring the organization* | Realigning work groups, altering rules and regulations, increasing interdependence, and making similar structural changes to disrupt the status quo. |
| *Appointing a devil's advocate* | Designating a critic to purposely argue against the majority positions held by the group. |

Source: Based on S.P. Robbins, *Managing Organizational Conflict: A Nontraditional Approach* (Upper Saddle River, NJ: Prentice Hall, 1974), pp. 59-89.

Of course, it is one thing to argue that conflict can be valuable for the group, and another to be able to tell whether a conflict is functional or dysfunctional.[45] The demarcation between functional and dysfunctional is neither clear nor precise. No one level of conflict can be regarded as acceptable or unacceptable under all conditions. The type and level of conflict that creates healthy and positive involvement toward one group's goals today may, in another group or in the same group at another time, be highly dysfunctional. The criterion that differentiates functional from dysfunctional conflict, however, is group performance.

**Exhibit 7-12
Conflict and Unit Performance**

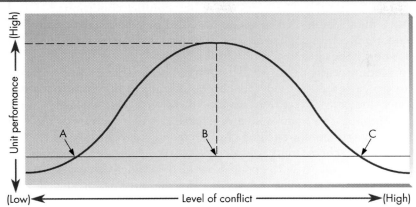

| Situation | Level of conflict | Type of conflict | Unit's internal characteristics | Unit performance outcome |
|---|---|---|---|---|
| A | Low or none | Dysfunctional | Apathetic Stagnant Nonresponsive to change Lack of new ideas | Low |
| B | Optimal | Functional | Viable Self-critical Innovative | High |
| C | High | Dysfunctional | Disruptive Chaotic Uncooperative | Low |

**FUNCTIONAL OUTCOMES** How might conflict act as a force to increase group performance? It is hard to visualize a situation where open or violent aggression could be functional. Not surprisingly, then, people often find it difficult to think of instances where conflict can be constructive. But conflict *is* constructive when it improves the quality of decisions, stimulates creativity and innovation, encourages interest and curiosity among group members, provides the medium through which problems can be aired and tensions released, and fosters an environment of self-evaluation and change. The evidence suggests that conflict can improve the quality of decision making by allowing all points, particularly the ones that are unusual or held by a minority, to be weighed in important decisions.[46] Conflict is an antidote for groupthink. It doesn't allow the group passively to "rubber-stamp" decisions that may be based on weak assumptions, inadequate consideration of relevant alternatives, or other debilities. Conflict challenges the status quo and therefore supports the creation of new ideas, promotes reassessment of group goals and activities, and increases the probability that the group will respond to change.

Many of the problems that faced both Eaton's and IBM Canada as they entered the 1990s can be traced to a lack of functional conflict. They hired and promoted individuals who were loyal to the organization to the point of never questioning company actions. Managers for the most part resisted change — they preferred looking back to past successes rather than forward to new challenges. Moreover, both firms kept their senior executives sheltered in headquarters' offices, protected from hearing anything they didn't want to hear, and a world away from the changes that were dramatically altering the retailing and computer industries. Eaton's, for instance, ignored such signs of trouble as losses endured by its in-store drug sections in competition with Shoppers Drug Mart, as well as the drain on profits of its small-town stores.[47] Eaton's did not survive while IBM Canada managed to turn its fortunes around.

Research studies in diverse settings confirm the functionality of conflict, particularly as it relates to productivity. For instance, it was demonstrated that among established groups, performance tended to improve more when conflict occurred among members than when there was fairly close agreement. The investigators observed that when groups analyzed decisions that

**Shoppers Drug Mart**
www.shoppersdrugmart.ca

had been made by the individual members of that group, the average improvement among the high-conflict groups was 73 percent greater than was that of those groups characterized by low-conflict conditions.[48] Others have found similar results: Groups composed of members with different interests tend to produce higher-quality solutions to a variety of problems than do homogeneous groups.[49]

The preceding leads us to predict that the increasing cultural diversity of the workforce should provide benefits to organizations. And that's what the evidence indicates. Research demonstrates that heterogeneity among group and organization members can increase creativity, improve the quality of decisions, and facilitate change by enhancing member flexibility.[50] For example, US researchers compared decision-making groups composed entirely of Anglo individuals with groups that also included Asians, Hispanics, and African Americans. The ethnically diverse groups produced more effective and more feasible ideas, and the unique ideas they generated tended to be of higher quality than the unique ideas produced by the purely Anglo groups.

Similarly, studies of professionals — systems analysts, and research and development scientists — support the constructive value of conflict. An investigation of 22 teams of systems analysts found that the more incompatible groups were likely to be more productive.[51] Research and development scientists have been found to be most productive where a certain amount of intellectual conflict exists.[52] These findings might suggest that conflict within a group indicates strength rather than weakness.

If managers accept the view that conflict can have positive value, what can they do to encourage functional conflict in their organizations?[53] There seems to be general agreement that creating functional conflict is a tough job, particularly in large corporations. As one consultant put it, "A high proportion of people who get to the top are conflict avoiders. They don't like hearing negatives, they don't like saying or thinking negative things. They frequently make it up the ladder in part because they don't irritate people on the way up." Another suggests that at least seven out of 10 people in business hush up when their opinions are at odds with those of their managers, allowing managers to make mistakes even when they know better. Such anticonflict cultures might have been tolerable in the past but not in today's fiercely competitive global economy. Organizations that don't encourage and support dissent may not survive long into the 21st century.

One common ingredient in organizations that successfully create functional conflict is that they reward dissent and punish conflict avoiders. Hewlett-Packard rewards dissenters by recognizing go-against-the-grain types, or people who stay with the ideas they believe in even when those ideas are rejected by management. The president of Innovis Interactive Technologies fired a top executive who refused to dissent. His explanation: "He was the ultimate yes-man. In this organization, I can't afford to pay someone to hear my own opinion."

**DYSFUNCTIONAL OUTCOMES** The destructive consequences of conflict upon a group's or organization's performance are generally well-known. A reasonable summary might state the following: Uncontrolled opposition breeds discontent, which acts to dissolve common ties and eventually leads to the destruction of the group. And, of course, there is a substantial body of literature to document how conflict — the dysfunctional variety — can reduce group effectiveness.[54] Among the more undesirable consequences are a retarding of communication, reductions in group cohesiveness, and subordination of group goals to the primacy of infighting between members. At the extreme, conflict can bring group functioning to a halt and potentially threaten the group's survival.

Canada Post is a classic example of a company facing dysfunctional conflict. Canada experienced a 15-day postal strike just before the Christmas 1997 holiday season because of a labour conflict at the Crown corporation. As federal Public Works Minister Alphonso Gagliano commented after the strike ended, "Labour-management relations are not the way you and I would like them to be. There is a historical mistrust here," he added. "Management is the enemy. Worker is the enemy."[55]

This discussion returns us to the issue of what is functional and what is dysfunctional. Research on conflict has yet to clearly identify those situations where conflict is more likely to be constructive than destructive. However, there is growing evidence that the source of the conflict is a significant factor determining functionality.[56] **Cognitive conflict**, which is task-oriented and occurs because of differences in perspectives and judgments, can often result in identifying potential solutions to problems. Thus it would be regarded as functional conflict. **Affective conflict**, which is emotional, and aimed at a person rather than an issue, tends to be dysfunctional conflict. One study of 53 teams found that cognitive conflict, because it generates more alternatives, led to better decisions, more acceptance of the decisions, and ownership of the decisions. Teams experiencing affective conflict, where members had personality incompatibilities and disputes, had poorer decisions and lower levels of acceptance of the decisions.[57] Because conflict can involve our emotions in a variety of ways, it can also lead to stress. You may want to refer to the OB on the Edge on pages 126-135 to get some ideas of how to manage the stress that might arise from conflicts you experience.

**cognitive conflict**
Conflict related to differences in perspectives and judgments.

**affective conflict**
Emotional conflict aimed at a person rather than an issue.

## Conflict Management and Teams

Kathleen Eisenhardt of the Stanford Graduate School of Business and her colleagues studied top management teams to understand how they manage conflict.[58] The researchers observed the interactions of 12 teams in technology-based companies. Each team consisted of five to nine executives. Four teams had little conflict to observe. Four teams experienced considerable conflict, but reported their interactions as "open," "fun," and "productive." As one member of one of these teams noted: "We scream a lot, then laugh, and then resolve the issue." Four other teams had a lot of conflict, which included interpersonal conflict. They were more likely to describe each other as "manipulative," "secretive," and "political."

> Do you ever think it's possible to reduce team conflict?

Before we examine the findings regarding the teams that successfully negotiated conflict, you might want to think about group situations you have been in that were characterized by conflict. In which cases did the conflict spill over into interpersonal relationships? Were there other situations where you felt the conflict was resolved without harming the relationships of the people involved in the conflict?

Eisenhardt and her colleagues' research identified six tactics that helped teams successfully manage the interpersonal conflict that can accompany group interactions. By handling the interpersonal conflict well, these groups were able to achieve their goals without letting conflict get in the way. The six tactics that helped reduce conflict were as follows:[59]

- Team members worked with more, rather than less, information, and debated on the basis of facts.
- Team members developed multiple alternatives to enrich the level of debate.
- Team members shared commonly agreed-upon goals.
- Team members injected humour into the decision process.
- Team members maintained a balanced power structure.
- Team members resolved issues without forcing consensus.

Whenever people work together on important strategic issues, or even if the task is completing a class project, it is not surprising, nor even necessarily bad, that conflict occurs. Groups need mechanisms by which they can manage the conflict, however. From the research reported above, one could conclude that sharing information and goals, and striving to be open and get along are helpful strategies for negotiating one's way through the maze of conflict. A sense of humour, and a willingness to understand the points of others without insisting that everyone agree on all points, are also important. Group members should try to focus too on the issues, rather than on personalities, and strive to achieve fairness and equity in the group process.

Groups should not try to avoid conflict, although many individuals prefer to avoid conflict whenever possible. Eisenhardt and her colleagues found that groups that didn't have conflict were generally less effective, with the members becoming withdrawn and only superficially harmonious. Often, if there was no conflict, the alternative was not agreement, but apathy and disengagement. Conflict also has an effect on performance. Those teams that avoided conflict tended to have lower performance levels, forgot to consider key issues, or were unaware of important aspects of their situation. They also did not take the opportunity to question assumptions or consider enough alternatives. You might want to review the Case Incident on page 321 to help you determine situations where conflict needs to be reduced or increased.

# Negotiation

When parties are potentially in conflict, they may choose to negotiate a resolution. Negotiation permeates the interactions of almost everyone in groups and organizations: Labour bargains with management; managers negotiate with employees, peers, and senior management; salespeople negotiate with customers; purchasing agents negotiate with suppliers; employees agree to answer a colleague's phone for a few minutes in exchange for some past or future benefit. In today's team-based organizations, negotiation skills become critical so that teams can work together effectively.

**negotiation**
A process in which two or more parties exchange goods or services and attempt to agree upon the exchange rate for them.

We define **negotiation** as a process in which two or more parties who exchange goods or services attempt to agree upon the exchange rate for them.[60] Note that we use the terms *negotiation* and *bargaining* interchangeably.

## Bargaining Strategies

There are two general approaches to negotiation — *distributive bargaining* and *integrative bargaining*.[61] These are compared in Exhibit 7-13.

**Exhibit 7-13**
**Distributive vs. Integrative Bargaining**

| Bargaining Characteristic | Distributive Bargaining | Integrative Bargaining |
|---|---|---|
| Available resources | Fixed amount of resources to be divided | Variable amount of resources to be divided |
| Primary motivations | I win, you lose | I win, you win |
| Primary interests | Opposed to each other | Convergent or congruent with each other |
| Focus of relationships | Short-term | Long-term |

Source: Based on R.J. Lewicki and J.A. Litterer, *Negotiation* (Homewood, IL: Irwin, 1985), p. 280.

**distributive bargaining**
Negotiation that seeks to divide up a fixed amount of resources; a win-lose situation.

**DISTRIBUTIVE BARGAINING** The negotiating strategy known as **distributive bargaining** operates under zero-sum conditions. That is, any gain I make is at your expense, and vice versa. Probably the most widely cited example of distributive bargaining is in labour-management negotiations over wages. Typically, labour representatives come to the bargaining table determined to get as much money as possible out of management. Since every cent more that labour negotiates increases management's costs, each party bargains aggressively and treats the other as an opponent who must be defeated.

When engaged in distributive bargaining, a party focuses on trying to get the opponent to agree to a specific target point, or to get as close to it as possible. Examples of such tactics are persuading your opponent of the impossibility of reaching his or her target point and the advisability of accepting a settlement near yours; arguing that your target is fair, while your opponent's isn't; and attempting to get your opponent to feel emotionally generous toward you and thus accept an outcome close to your target point.

**integrative bargaining**
Negotiation that seeks one or more settlements that can create a win-win solution.

**INTEGRATIVE BARGAINING** In contrast to distributive bargaining, **integrative bargaining** operates under the assumption that there exists one or more settlements that can create a win-win solution. In terms of intraorganizational behaviour, all things being equal, integrative bargaining is preferable to distributive bargaining. Why? Because the former builds long-term relationships and facilitates working together in the future. It bonds negotiators and allows each to leave the bargaining table feeling that he or she has achieved a victory. Distributive bargaining, on the other hand, leaves one party a loser. It tends to build animosities and deepen divisions when people must work together on an ongoing basis.

For examples of effective approaches to conflict resolution through negotiation in Canadian businesses, see this chapter's HR Implications feature on pages 313-316.

## How to Negotiate

**BATNA**
The best alternative to a negotiated agreement; the lowest acceptable value to an individual for a negotiated agreement.

In any negotiation, each party assesses its goals, considers the other party's goals and interests, and develops a strategy. In determining goals, parties are well advised to consider their "target and resistance" points, as well as their "best alternative to a negotiated agreement (**BATNA**)."[62] Exhibit 7-14

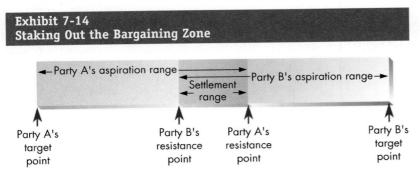

**Exhibit 7-14**
**Staking Out the Bargaining Zone**

**Daewoo Leganza**
www.dm.co.kr/english/
showroom/leganza.htm

illustrates this notion. Parties A and B represent two negotiators. Each has a *target point* that defines what he or she would like to achieve. Each also has a *resistance point*, which marks the lowest outcome that is acceptable — the point below which each would break off negotiations rather than accept a less favourable settlement. The area between these two points makes up each negotiator's aspiration range. As long as there is some overlap between A's and B's aspiration ranges, there exists a settlement range where each one's aspirations can be met.

One's BATNA represents the alternative that will be faced if negotiations fail. For instance, suppose you are interested in buying *either* a Ford Contour or a Daewoo Leganza. You are already comfortable with the price that the dealer has offered for the Contour, so you know that if the negotiations don't go well with the Leganza salesperson, you will buy the Contour. Thus your BATNA, when speaking to the Leganza dealer, is the Ford Contour. On the other hand, suppose your heart is set on the Contour, your own car has broken down, and you need a car to go on holiday in two days. Your BATNA is no car, which may encourage you to negotiate less strenuously with the Ford salesperson. To understand more about participating in negotiations, turn to the Working With Others Exercise on page 320.

To improve your negotiating skills, you might consider the following:[63]

- *Begin with a positive overture.* Studies on negotiation show that concessions tend to be reciprocated and lead to agreements. As a result, begin bargaining with a positive overture — perhaps a small concession — and then reciprocate your opponent's concessions.

- *Address problems, not personalities.* Concentrate on the negotiation issues, not on the personal characteristics of your opponent. When negotiations get tough, avoid the tendency to attack your opponent. It's your opponent's ideas or position that you disagree with, not him or her personally. Separate the people from the problem, and don't personalize differences.

- *Pay little attention to initial offers.* Treat an initial offer as merely a point of departure. Everyone has to have an initial position. These initial offers tend to be extreme and idealistic. Treat them as such.

- *Emphasize win-win solutions.* Inexperienced negotiators often assume that their gain must come at the expense of the other party. But assuming a zero-sum game means missed opportunities for trade-offs that could benefit both sides. If conditions are supportive, look for an integrative solution. Frame options in terms of your opponent's interests and look for solutions that can allow your opponent, as well as yourself, to declare a victory.

- *Create an open and trusting climate.* Skilled negotiators are better listeners, ask more questions, focus their arguments more directly, are less defensive, and have learned to avoid words and phrases that can irritate an opponent (that is, "generous offer," "fair price," "reasonable arrangement"). In other words, they are better at creating the open and trusting climate necessary for reaching an integrative settlement.

## Issues in Negotiation

We conclude our discussion of negotiation by reviewing three contemporary issues in negotiation: gender differences in negotiating, the effect of cultural differences on negotiating styles, and the use of third parties to help resolve differences.

### Gender Differences in Negotiations

Do men and women negotiate differently? The answer appears to be "it depends."[64] It is difficult to generalize about gender differences in negotiating styles, because the research yields many opinions, but few reliable conclusions. One review of a number of studies found no overall difference in effectiveness of men and women leaders in negotiation, although the study also indicated that men performed better when the negotiations were over male-stereotypical tasks (for example, negotiating for airplanes, turboengine parts), whereas women did better when the negotiations were over female-stereotypical tasks (for example, negotiations involving child care, caretaker issues).[65] Moreover, a 1999 review of 53 studies suggest that women receive lower gains than men after a negotiation process.[66] Let's look at some of the interesting and relevant differences that have been found.

> Ever wonder if men and women communicate differently?

Kolb and Coolidge found four basic areas of difference.[67] The first difference was that women are more inclined to be concerned with feelings and perceptions, and thus take a longer-term view. Men are more inclined to focus on resolving the matter at hand. Bill Forbes, president of Edmonton-based career management firm CDR Associates, observes that women assume they're not going to earn as much as men. They focus "on getting a position that utilizes their skills and gives them some challenge. When presented with the compensation range for their job classification, women generally aren't worried if they end up in the bottom half, whereas males might often be concerned if they're not in the top."[68] Unfortunately, employers may take advantage of these differing expectations to offer women lower wages when they first negotiate salary. This may be changing in more recent times, however. For example, University of Waterloo psychology professor Serge Desmarais found that the narrowest pay gap between men and women existed with those who had graduated from university since 1992. The difference in wages for those men and women was only six percent.[69]

A second gender difference in bargaining identified by Kolb and Coolidge is that men view the bargaining session as a separate event, whereas women view it as part of the overall relationship with the individual. A third finding was that women tend to want all parties in the negotiation to be empowered, whereas men are more likely to use power as part of the bargaining strategy. Finally, the researchers reported differences in dialogue. Men more often used dialogue to persuade other parties in the negotiation, whereas women were more likely to use dialogue to achieve understanding. Desmarais, whose work we noted above, suggests that men are socialized to be more aggressive negotiators, which would then result in some of the observed differences in men's and women's styles.[70] One important thing to note is that even if a difference in style of negotiation exists, one style may not always be preferable to the other. The best style may, in fact, depend on the situation. For instance, in situations where trust, openness, and long-term relationships are critical, a woman's style may be more useful. However, when conflict, competition, and self-interest are an important part of the agenda, a man's style may be more effective.[71]

There is another thing worth noting: The belief that women are nicer than men in negotiations may well result not from gender, but from the lack of power typically held by women in most large organizations. The research indicates that low-power managers, regardless of gender, attempt to placate their opponents and tend to use softly persuasive tactics rather than direct confrontation and threats. Where women and men have similar power bases, there may be less significant differences in their negotiation styles. There is still work to be done in this area, however. A recent study by two economists found that women were more likely to share some of the $10 they were given by researchers (53 percent to 40 percent), and women were also more likely to give away a larger portion ($1.60 vs. .82)[72]

Women's attitudes toward negotiation and toward themselves as negotiators also appear to be quite different from men's. Managerial women demonstrate less confidence in anticipation of negotiating and are less satisfied with their performance after the process is complete, despite the fact that their performance and the outcomes they achieve are similar to men's. This latter conclusion suggests that women may unduly penalize themselves by failing to engage in negotiations when such action would be in their best interests.

The outcomes of negotiations for women and men also seem to differ. One researcher found that when women negotiated to buy a car, the opening offer by the salesperson was higher than it was for men.[73] In a study of salary offers, researchers found that men were offered higher starting salaries in a negotiating process than were women.[74] While in each of these instances the opening offers were just that, offers to be negotiated, women also fared less well than men at the end of the negotiating process, even when they used the same negotiating tactics as men.

The results of these studies may shed some light on the pay and promotion discrepancies between men and women, which we discuss in Chapter 10. If women negotiate even slightly lower starting salaries, then over time, with raises based on percentages of salaries, the gap between men's and women's salaries can grow quite substantially.

Chris Brough, President of Sextant Entertainment Group in Vancouver, finds the negotiating style of Canadians much more pleasant than that of Americans. He particularly appreciates their softness and self-deprecation.

## Cultural Differences in Negotiations

Although there appears to be no significant direct relationship between an individual's personality and negotiation style, cultural background does seem to be relevant. Negotiating styles clearly do vary across national cultures.[75]

The French, for instance, like conflict. They frequently gain recognition and develop their reputations by thinking and acting against others. As a result, the French tend to take a long time in negotiating agreements and they aren't overly concerned about whether their opponents like or dislike them.[76] The Chinese also draw out negotiations, but that's because they believe negotiations never end. Just when you think you've pinned down every detail and reached a final solution with a Chinese executive, that executive might smile and start the process all over again. Like the Japanese, the Chinese negotiate to develop a relationship and a commitment to work together rather than to tie up every loose end.[77] Americans are known around the world for their impatience and their desire to be liked. Astute negotiators from other countries often turn these characteristics to their advantage by dragging out negotiations and making friendship conditional on the final settlement.

The cultural context of the negotiation significantly influences the amount and type of preparation for bargaining, the relative emphasis on task vs. interpersonal relationships, the tactics used, and even the place where the negotiation should be conducted. Chris Brough, President of Vancouver-based Sextant Entertainment Group, speaks about negotiating differences based on his experiences working in both Los Angeles and Vancouver: "There is a wonderful softness and self-deprecation about Canadians that I have come to enjoy. When you do a deal in Canada, very often you can extend a handshake and there is a firm belief the deal is solid. In Los Angeles, on the other hand, you can have a signed contract and it is still based on the idea of 'Okay, you're not happy, sue me.'"[78]

To further illustrate some of these differences, let's look at two studies comparing the influence of culture on business negotiations. The first study compared North Americans, Arabs, and Russians.[79] Among the factors looked at were the groups' negotiating styles, their responses to an opponent's arguments, their approaches to making concessions, and their handling of negotiating deadlines. North Americans tried to persuade by relying on facts and appealing to logic. They countered opponents' arguments with objective facts. They made small concessions early in the negotiation to establish a relationship, and usually reciprocated opponents' concessions. North Americans treated deadlines as very important. The Arabs, however, tried to persuade by appealing to emotion. They countered opponents' arguments with subjective feelings. They made concessions throughout the bargaining process and almost always reciprocated opponents' concessions. The Arabs also approached deadlines very casually. The Russians based their arguments on asserted ideals. They made few, if any, concessions. Any concession offered by an opponent was viewed as a weakness and almost never reciprocated. Finally, the Russians tended to ignore deadlines.

The second study looked at verbal and nonverbal negotiation tactics exhibited by North Americans, Japanese, and Brazilians during half-hour bargaining sessions.[80] Some of the differences were particularly interesting. For instance, the Brazilians on average said "no" 83 times, compared with five times for the Japanese and nine times for the North Americans. The Japanese displayed more than five periods of silence lasting longer than 10 seconds during the 30-minute sessions. North Americans averaged 3.5 such periods; the Brazilians had none. The Japanese and North Americans interrupted their opponent about the same number of times, but the Brazilians interrupted 2.5 to 3 times more often than the North Americans and the Japanese. Finally, while the Japanese and the North Americans had no physical contact with their opponents during negotiations except for handshaking, the Brazilians touched each other almost five times every half-hour.

## Third-Party Negotiations

Occasionally, individuals or group representatives reach a stalemate and are unable to resolve their differences through direct negotiations. In such cases, they may turn to alternative dispute resolution (ADR) where a third party

**mediator**
A neutral third party who facilitates a negotiated solution by using reasoning, persuasion, and suggestions for alternatives.

**Syncrude Canada**
www.syncrude.com

**arbitrator**
A third party to a negotiation who has the authority to dictate an agreement.

**conciliator**
A trusted third party who provides an informal communication link between the negotiator and the opponent.

helps both sides find a solution. ADR encompasses a variety of strategies, including mediation, arbitration, conciliation, and consultation.[81]

A **mediator** is a neutral third party who facilitates a negotiated solution by using reasoning and persuasion, suggesting alternatives, and the like. Mediators are widely used in labour-management negotiations and in civil-court disputes. In Vancouver, where there has been a "leaky condo crisis" in recent years, owners and builders can insist upon mediation with the aid of an independent mediator. BC's Motor Vehicle Branch uses mediation to help settle accident claims. In Ontario, all disputes between companies and employees now go to mediation within 100 days. Pilot projects found that over 60 percent of the disputes were partially or fully resolved within 60 days after the start of the mediation session.[82]

Alberta-based Syncrude Canada Ltd. successfully used mediation in the case against its maintenance company for a fire at the Fort McMurray, Alberta, oil-sands plant in August 1984. Syncrude's example indicates the savings that a mediated decision can yield. The case did not reach the court until 1992, after tens of millions of dollars in legal fees had been spent. While the court case was underway, Syncrude and the maintenance company met on the side with mediator Yves Fortier, a lawyer with Ogilvy Renault of Montreal. Two years later, the two sides achieved a mediated solution while the court had heard just one side of the case. The total cost of mediation was less than $200 000.[83]

The overall effectiveness of mediated negotiations is fairly impressive. The settlement rate is approximately 60 percent, with negotiator satisfaction at about 75 percent. But the situation is the key to whether mediation will succeed; the conflicting parties must be motivated to bargain and resolve their conflict. Additionally, conflict intensity cannot be too high; mediation is most effective under moderate levels of conflict. Finally, perceptions of the mediator are important; to be effective, the mediator must be perceived as neutral and noncoercive.

An **arbitrator** is a third party with the authority to dictate an agreement. Arbitration can be voluntary (requested) or compulsory (forced on the parties by law or contract).

The authority of the arbitrator varies according to the rules set by the negotiators. For instance, the arbitrator might be limited to choosing one of the negotiator's last offers or to suggesting an agreement point that is nonbinding. Or the arbitrator might be free to choose and make any judgment that he or she wishes.

The big advantage of arbitration over mediation is that it always results in a settlement. Whether or not there is a negative side depends on how "heavy-handed" the arbitrator appears. If one party is left feeling overwhelmingly defeated, that party is certain to be dissatisfied and unlikely to accept the arbitrator's decision graciously. Therefore, the conflict may resurface at a later time.

A **conciliator** is a trusted third party who provides an informal communication link between the negotiator and the opponent. Conciliation is used extensively in international, labour, family, and community disputes. Comparing its effectiveness with that of mediation has proven difficult because the two overlap a great deal. In practice, conciliators typically act as more than mere communication conduits. They also engage in fact-finding, interpreting messages, and persuading disputants to develop agreements.

In February 1998, talks between Canadian National Railway Co. (CN) and the Canadian Auto Workers (CAW), as well as talks between Canadian

**Canadian Pacific Railway**
www.cpr.ca/internet/cprportal.asp

**Brotherhood of Maintenance
of Way Employees**
www.bmwe.org

**consultant (as negotiator)**
An impartial third party, skilled
in conflict management, who
attempts to facilitate creative
problem-solving through
communication and analysis.

Pacific Railway Co. (CP) and the Brotherhood of Maintenance of Way Employees, used the services of federal conciliators. In both cases the unions were hoping to resolve outstanding issues with the railway companies. The Brotherhood of Maintenance of Way Employees signed an agreement with both CN and CP in May 1998.

Conciliation did not work between CN and CAW, however, and the CN-CAW conciliator, Akivah Starkman, resigned from his position. In September 1998 CAW finally reached an agreement with CN, without the help of a conciliator.[84]

A **consultant** is a skilled and impartial third party who attempts to facilitate problem-solving through communication and analysis, aided by his or her knowledge of conflict management. The consultant's role is to improve relations between the conflicting parties so that they can reach a settlement themselves. Instead of putting forward specific solutions, the consultant tries to help the parties learn to understand and work with each other. Therefore, this approach has a longer-term focus: to build new and positive perceptions and attitudes between the conflicting parties.

## HR Implications

# Providing Performance Feedback and Dealing With Unions

In a chapter that emphasizes communication, conflict, and negotiation, it's not surprising that the implications for human resource practices are large. One area that provides a great deal of conflict for managers in particular and individuals in general is providing performance feedback. Another area that causes stress in organizations is having to negotiate with unions. Below we discuss each of these topics to give you some idea of how conflict, communication, and negotiation are applied in the workplace.

### Providing Performance Feedback

For many managers, few activities are more unpleasant than providing performance feedback to employees.[1] In fact, unless pressured by organizational policies and controls, managers are likely to ignore this responsibility.[2]

Why the reluctance to give performance feedback? There seem to be at least three reasons. First, managers are often uncomfortable discussing performance weaknesses directly with employees. Given that almost every employee could undoubtedly improve in

some areas, managers fear a confrontation when presenting negative feedback. This apparently applies even when people give negative feedback to a computer! Bill Gates reports that Microsoft recently conducted a project requiring users to rate their experience with a computer. "When we had the computer the users had worked with ask for an evaluation of its performance, the responses tended to be positive. But when we had a second computer ask the same people to evaluate their encounters with the first machine, the people were significantly more critical. Their reluctance to criticize the first computer 'to its face' suggested that they didn't want to hurt its feelings, even though they knew it was only a machine."[3]

Second, many employees tend to become defensive when their weaknesses are pointed out. Instead of accepting the feedback as constructive and a basis for improving performance, some employees challenge the evaluation by criticizing the manager or redirecting blame to someone else.

Finally, employees tend to have an inflated assessment of their own performance. Statistically speaking,

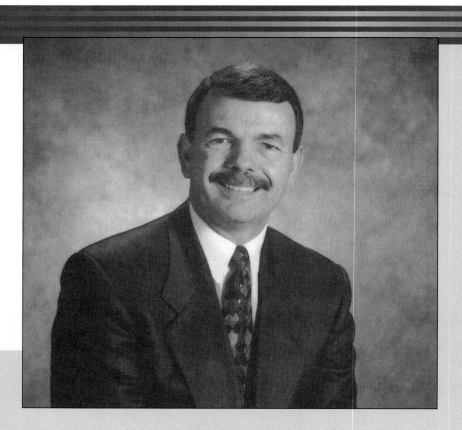

Receiving feedback from superiors, co-workers and subordinates, as happens with 360-degree feedback, can be an unsettling experience. Claude Norfolk, VP with Ottawa-based Bank of Nova Scotia, finds that sometimes it hurts. "I was really surprised, for example, to find out that I needed to work on my listening skills, because I thought I was a pretty good listener." Turns out his wife agreed with Norfolk's colleagues. Still, he found value in the exercise.

half of all employees must be below-average performers. But the evidence indicates that the average employee's estimate of his or her own performance level generally falls around the 75th percentile.[4] So even when managers are providing good news, employees are likely to perceive it as not good enough!

The solution to the performance feedback problem is not to ignore it, but to train managers in how to conduct constructive feedback sessions. An effective review in which the employee perceives the appraisal as fair, the manager as sincere, and the climate as constructive can result in the employee leaving the interview in an upbeat mood. The employee will be informed about the performance areas in which he or she needs to improve, and determined to correct the deficiencies.[5] In addition, the performance review should be designed more as a counselling activity than a judgmental process. This can best be accomplished by allowing the review to evolve out of the employee's own self-evaluation.

Performance reviews can also include feedback from sources other than just one's manager. For example, the Toronto-Dominion Bank uses a Customer Service Index to measure service and quality, in addition to sales. The results are posted for each branch monthly, so that it can compare itself with other branches. The results are also linked directly to TD's performance appraisal system.[6]

Toronto-based Consumers Gas has gone one step farther with its performance appraisal feedback, using one of the newest management trends—360-degree feedback assessment.[7] In this system, not just your manager, but also your colleagues, employees, customers, and other people with whom you deal regularly are part of the evaluation process. Millar Western Industries, a family-owned forestry company based in Edmonton, introduced 360-degree feedback for its 250 supervisory and managerial staff in 1995, and has been working toward using it for all of its employees.

The 360-degree feedback can cause anxiety in employees at first, as they learn perhaps more than they ever wanted to know about what others think of them. However, Millar's human resources manager found that employees actually liked knowing where they stood and how they were doing. A variety of companies, including Ciba-Geigy Canada, Hudson's Bay, Maclean-Hunter, IBM, Disney, and Federal Express use 360-degree feedback. This feedback system emphasizes the importance of communication to all levels of employees, not just the manager. It also shows customers and suppliers that they have a voice in the company.

A recent issue of *Leadership Quarterly* devoted to 360-degree feedback indicates that the jury is not in on its utility.[8] The use of 360-degree feedback as simple feedback results in different ratings from employees and peers than when it is used as evidence for performance evaluation.[9] Moreover, others have found that when managers received lower ratings, they tended to discount the feedback,[10] which might suggest that those most likely to need feedback will be least likely to pay attention to it.

## Resolving Union-Management Conflict

Conflict in the workplace arises for a variety of reasons, but one major conflict that occurs in many of Canada's businesses is conflict between labour and management. A number of unions and businesses are trying to figure out ways to resolve that conflict so that both sides work together more effectively. We present several examples below, to give you some indications of ways that management and unions can work together.

Ville d'Anjou–based Transport Provost Inc. and the Communications, Energy and Paperworkers Union of Canada (CEP) decided to form a partnership in 1992 to try to resolve some of the many conflicts that had arisen between them. Transport Provost introduced a two-year conflict prevention program costing $276 000 to teach communication skills, problem-solving, and effective conflict management. Representatives of both management and the union attended the workshops. At first union members were somewhat suspicious of the introduction of this program, worrying that it was a way of co-opting the union. However, after some experience with the program, Joel Nerome, former president of the local union, noted that "most of the employees see more positives in it than negatives."[11]

The workers and management at Leaside, Ontario-based Alcatel Canada Wire Inc. were facing the prospect of plant closure in the late 1980s, partly due to severe management-union conflict. In 1990, they started to realize that the world was changing and the company was going to have to become more profitable to survive. Kevin Corrigan, then president of the local union, decided that perhaps the union should extend an olive branch to management. An independent facilitator was brought in to help the two

sides discover the common goals that would allow them to work together. Corrigan reports that the facilitator "got us feeling positive about the process and what might need to be done. After the first two-day session, a joint communiqué of common goals and objectives was drafted." Not everything has been perfect among union and management at Alcatel, but relations have been better as a result of both sides working together to understand and help determine the company goals.[12]

At Alberta-based AGT, the union asked managers to attend a two-day training seminar on mutual gains bargaining (MGB) in 1990. Management agreed, as they recognized the need to foster better relations. Before the training sessions, management and the union generally engaged in win-lose bargaining. Under the new process, both sides look to see the mutual gains in bargaining. Thus, each side shifts its focus to finding things that will work for the other side. Former business manager of the local, Tom Panelli notes that MGB has resulted in "less stressful negotiations, less concurrent turmoil at work sites and faster, more cost-effective use of management and union time."[13] Engaging in mutual gains bargaining has not resolved all of the problems of union and management at AGT, but it has helped their bargaining process considerably.

These examples show just a few of the ways that groups that might naturally have conflicting interests can choose to work towards a more positive environment. In some cases the union extended the olive branch; in others, it was management. The mechanisms for addressing conflict ranged from formal programs, such as a conflict prevention program or consultation through an independent facilitator, to a short-term training seminar on MGB. In all of the instances described, the relationships did not become perfect after agreement was made to work together. But each side did agree that the relationship was considerably better.

These examples, which come from the union-management perspective, do not have to be confined to that sector. In any conflict situation, it is helpful if at least one of the sides takes the opportunity to try to resolve the conflict by making an offer to work together.

Sources:

[1] J.S. Lublin, "It's Shape-up Time for Performance Reviews," *Wall Street Journal*, October 3, 1994, p. B1.

[2] Much of this section is based on H.H. Meyer, "A Solution to the Performance Appraisal Feedback Enigma," *Academy of Management Executive*, February 1991, pp. 68-76.

[3] B. Gates, *The Road Ahead* (New York: Viking, 1995), p. 86.

[4] R.J. Burke, "Why Performance Appraisal Systems Fail," *Personnel Administration*, June 1972, pp. 32-40.

[5] B.R. Nathan, A.M. Mohrman, Jr., and J. Milliman, "Interpersonal Relations as a Context for the Effects of Appraisal Interviews on Performance and Satisfaction: A Longitudinal Study," *Academy of Management Journal*, June 1991, pp. 352-369.

[6] Material in this paragraph based on "A Jury System for Jobs," *Maclean's*, August 5, 1996, p. 45.

[7] P. Booth, *Challenge and Change: Embracing the Team Concept.* Report 123-94, Conference Board of Canada, 1994, p. 10.

[8] L. Atwater and D. Waldman, "360 Degree Feedback and Leadership Development," *Leadership Quarterly*, 9(4), 1998, pp. 423-426.

[9] D.A. Waldman, L.E. Atwater, and D. Antonioni, "Has 360 Degree Feedback Gone Amok?" *Academy of Management Executive*, 12(2), 1998, pp. 86-94.

[10] C.L. Facteau, J.D. Facteau, L.C. Schoel, J.E.A. Russell, and M.L Poteet, "Reactions of Leaders to 360-Degree Feedback From Subordinates and Peers," *Leadership Quarterly*, 9(4), 1998, pp. 427-448.

[11] "An Industrial Transportation Company Counts on Conflict Prevention to Deal With a Changing Market," in *Labour Management Innovation in Canada*, Ottawa: Minister of Supply and Services, 1994, pp. 38-41.

[12] "Plugging In: Dialogue at a Wire and Cable Plant," in *Labour Management Innovation in Canada*, Ottawa: Minister of Supply and Services, 1994, pp. 42-45.

[13] "Mutual Gains Bargaining Means Less Strain and More Gain," in *Labour Management Innovation in Canada*, Ottawa: Minister of Supply and Services, 1994, pp. 96-99.

# SUMMARY AND IMPLICATIONS

## For the Workplace

A careful review of this chapter finds a common theme regarding how effective communication can improve satisfaction, productivity, and interpersonal dynamics. We noted for instance that distortions, ambiguities, and incongruities all increase uncertainty, and hence, they have a negative impact on satisfaction.[85]

The less distortion that occurs in communication, the more that goals, feedback, and other messages will be received as they were intended.[86] This, in turn, should reduce ambiguities and clarify the group's task. Extensive use of vertical, lateral, and informal channels will increase communication flow, reduce uncertainty, and improve group performance and satisfaction. We should also expect incongruities between verbal and nonverbal communiqués to increase uncertainty and to reduce satisfaction.

Findings in the chapter further suggest that the goal of perfect communication is unattainable. Yet there is evidence that demonstrates a positive relationship between effective communication (which includes factors such as perceived trust, perceived accuracy, desire for interaction, top-management receptiveness, and upward information requirements) and worker productivity.[87] Choosing the correct channel, being an effective listener, and utilizing feedback may, therefore, make for more effective communication. But the human factor generates distortions that can never be fully eliminated. The communication process represents an exchange of messages, but the outcome is meanings that may or may not approximate those that the sender intended. Whatever the sender's expectations, the decoded message in the mind of the receiver represents his or her reality. And this "reality" will determine performance, along with the individual's level of motivation and degree of satisfaction.

Communication breakdown can lead to conflict. Many people automatically assume that conflict is related to lower group and organizational performance. This chapter has demonstrated that this assumption is frequently incorrect. Conflict can be either constructive or destructive to the functioning of a group or unit. As we saw in Exhibit 7-12, levels of conflict can be too high or too low. Either extreme hinders performance. An optimal level is where there is enough conflict to encourage communication, prevent stagnation, stimulate creativity, allow tensions to be released, and initiate the seeds for change, yet not so much as to be disruptive or deter coordination of activities.

Inadequate or excessive levels of conflict can hinder the effectiveness of a group or an organization, resulting in reduced satisfaction of group members, increased absence and turnover rates, and, eventually, lower productivity. On the other hand, when conflict is at an optimal level, complacency and apathy should be minimized, motivation should be enhanced through the creation of a challenging and questioning environment with a vitality that makes work interesting, and there should be the amount of turnover needed to rid the organization of misfits and poor performers.

What advice can we give managers faced with excessive conflict and the need to reduce it? Don't assume that one conflict-handling intention will always be best! You should select an intention appropriate for the situation. Exhibit 7-9 helps you to understand how to choose appropriate intentions.

Negotiation was shown to be an ongoing activity in groups and organizations. Distributive bargaining can resolve disputes, but it often negatively affects one or more negotiators' satisfaction because it is focused on the short-term and because it is confrontational. Integrative bargaining, in contrast, tends to provide outcomes that satisfy all parties and that build lasting relationships.

## For You as an Individual

Communication difficulties occur as often outside the workplace as they do inside. As a result, it may be helpful to think about interactions you have had where the communication did not work, and to try to assess your contribution to the breakdown. In general, when two people are having difficulty communicating, each of them is contributing something to that breakdown. This tends to be the rule even if you are inclined to believe that the other person is the more responsible party.

The chapter identifies a number of barriers to communication of which you might want to be aware. Often either selective perception or defensiveness gets in the way of communication. As you work in your groups on student projects, you may want to observe communication flows more critically to help you understand ways that communication can be improved and dysfunctional conflict avoided.

Conflict is something that you will experience in a variety of situations throughout your life. Some people like to avoid all conflict, feeling that it is an unpleasant process. However, we pointed out that avoiding conflict does not necessarily have a positive outcome (for instance, it caused major problems for Eaton's, leading to its demise, as well as for McCain Foods).

When you work in your student groups to accomplish tasks, it will not be unusual for conflict to arise. You may have disagreements about how to proceed on a project, or there may be conflicts over meeting times, as different people in your group have different needs they are trying to accommodate. The chapter gives you a variety of ideas about how to resolve these conflicts, including ways to negotiate differences so that each of the people involved in the conflict can learn to accommodate the needs of the others.

**ROADMAP**
**REMINDER**

In the two previous chapters we examined group and team behaviour, and how to get people to work together on important goals. In this chapter we focused on communication, which is a large factor in determining how well people will get along. We want you to be aware of the factors that lead both to better and worse communication. We also discussed how communication can lead to conflict, and then explored other mechanisms that generated conflict. We considered the resolution of conflict, including negotiation. In the next chapter we consider power and politics. Both represent additional ways that interaction can be very uneasy in an organization.

## For Review

1. Describe the communication process and identify its key components. Give an example of how this process operates with both oral and written messages.
2. Identify 3 common small-group networks and give the advantages of each.
3. What conditions stimulate the emergence of rumours?
4. List 3 specific problems related to language difficulties in cross-cultural communication.
5. What are the managerial implications from the research contrasting male and female communication and negotiation styles?
6. What is the difference between functional and dysfunctional conflict? What determines functionality?
7. How could a manager stimulate conflict in his or her department?
8. What defines the settlement range in distributive bargaining?
9. Why isn't integrative bargaining more widely practised in organizations?
10. How can you improve your negotiating effectiveness?

## For Critical Thinking

1. "Ineffective communication is the fault of the sender." Do you agree or disagree? Discuss.
2. How might managers use the grapevine for their benefit?
3. Using the concept of channel richness, give examples of messages best conveyed by e-mail, by face-to-face communication, and on the company bulletin board.

4. Why do you think so many people are poor listeners?

5. Assume one of your co-workers had to negotiate a contract with someone from China. What problems might he or she face? If the co-worker asked for advice, what suggestions would you make to help facilitate a settlement?

6. From your own experience, describe a situation you were involved in where the conflict was dysfunctional. Describe another example, from your experience, where the conflict was functional. Now analyze how other parties in both conflicts might have interpreted the situation in terms of whether the conflicts were functional or dysfunctional.

## *LEARNING ABOUT YOURSELF EXERCISE*

# What Is Your Primary Conflict-Handling Intention?

Indicate how often you rely on each of the following tactics by circling the number that you feel is most appropriate.

| | Rarely | | | | Always |
|---|---|---|---|---|---|
| **1.** I argue my case with my co-workers to show the merits of my position. | 1 | 2 | 3 | 4 | 5 |
| **2.** I negotiate with my co-workers so that a compromise can be reached. | 1 | 2 | 3 | 4 | 5 |
| **3.** I try to satisfy the expectations of my co-workers. | 1 | 2 | 3 | 4 | 5 |
| **4.** I try to investigate an issue with my co-workers to find a solution acceptable to us. | 1 | 2 | 3 | 4 | 5 |
| **5.** I am firm in pursuing my side of the issue. | 1 | 2 | 3 | 4 | 5 |
| **6.** I attempt to avoid being put on the spot and try to keep my conflict with my co-workers to myself. | 1 | 2 | 3 | 4 | 5 |
| **7.** I hold on to my solution to a problem. | 1 | 2 | 3 | 4 | 5 |
| **8.** I use give-and-take so that a compromise can be made. | 1 | 2 | 3 | 4 | 5 |
| **9.** I exchange accurate information with my co-workers to solve a problem together. | 1 | 2 | 3 | 4 | 5 |
| **10.** I avoid open discussion of my differences with my co-workers. | 1 | 2 | 3 | 4 | 5 |
| **11.** I accommodate the wishes of my co-workers. | 1 | 2 | 3 | 4 | 5 |
| **12.** I try to bring all our concerns out in the open so that the issues can be resolved in the best possible way. | 1 | 2 | 3 | 4 | 5 |
| **13.** I propose a middle ground for breaking deadlocks. | 1 | 2 | 3 | 4 | 5 |
| **14.** I go along with the suggestions of my co-workers. | 1 | 2 | 3 | 4 | 5 |
| **15.** I try to keep my disagreements with my co-workers to myself in order to avoid hard feelings. | 1 | 2 | 3 | 4 | 5 |

Turn to page 633 for scoring directions and key.

Source: This is an abbreviated version of a 35-item instrument described in M.A. Rahim, "A Measure of Styles of Handling Interpersonal Conflict," *Academy of Management Journal*, June 1983, pp. 368-376.

# A Negotiation Role Play

This role play is designed to help you develop your negotiating skills. The class is to break into pairs. One person will play the role of Terry, the department supervisor. The other person will play Dale, Terry's boss.

**The Situation:**  Terry and Dale work for Bauer. Terry supervises a research laboratory. Dale is the manager of research and development. Terry and Dale are former skaters who have worked for Bauer for more than 6 years. Dale has been Terry's boss for 2 years.

One of Terry's employees has greatly impressed Terry. This employee is Lisa Roland. Lisa was hired 11 months ago. She is 24 years old and holds a master's degree in mechanical engineering. Her entry-level salary was $52 500 a year. She was told by Terry that, in accordance with corporation policy, she would receive an initial performance evaluation at 6 months and a comprehensive review after 1 year. Based on her performance record, Lisa was told she could expect a salary adjustment at the time of the 1-year evaluation.

Terry's evaluation of Lisa after 6 months was very positive. Terry commented on the long hours Lisa was working, her cooperative spirit, the fact that others in the lab enjoyed working with her, and her immediate positive impact on the project she had been assigned. Now that Lisa's 1st anniversary is coming up, Terry has again reviewed Lisa's performance. Terry thinks Lisa may be the best new person the R&D group has ever hired. After only a year, Terry has ranked Lisa as the number-three performer in a department of 11.

Salaries in the department vary greatly. Terry, for instance, has a basic salary of $93 800, plus eligibility for a bonus that might add another $7000 to $11 000 a year. The salary range of the 11 department members is $42 500 to $79 000. The lowest salary is a recent hire with a bachelor's degree in physics. The two people that Terry has rated above Lisa earn base salaries of $73 800 and $78 900. They're both 27 years old and have been at Bauer for 3 and 4 years, respectively. The median salary in Terry's department is $65 300.

**Terry's Role:**  You want to give Lisa a big raise. While she's young, she has proven to be an excellent addition to the department. You don't want to lose her. More important, she knows in general what other people in the department are earning and she thinks she's underpaid. The company typically gives 1-year raises of 5 percent, although 10 percent is not unusual and 20 to 30 percent increases have been approved on occasion. You'd like to get Terry as large an increase as Dale will approve.

**Dale's Role:**  All your supervisors typically try to squeeze you for as much money as they can for their people. You understand this because you did the same thing when you were a supervisor, but your boss wants to keep a lid on costs. He wants you to keep raises for recent hires generally in the range of 5 to 8 percent. In fact, he's sent a memo to all managers and supervisors stating this objective. However, your boss is also very concerned with equity and paying people what they're worth. You feel assured that he will support any salary recommendation you make, as long as it can be justified. Your goal, consistent with cost reduction, is to keep salary increases as low as possible.

**The Negotiation:**  Terry has a meeting scheduled with Dale to discuss Lisa's performance review and salary adjustment. Take a couple of minutes to think through the facts in this exercise and to prepare a strategy. Then you have up to 15 minutes to conduct your negotiation. When your negotiation is complete, the class will compare the various strategies used and pair outcomes.

## INTERNET SEARCH EXERCISES

1. Find a Canadian manufacturing firm, a German company, and a government agency (in any country) that have recently resolved a labour negotiation. What were the initial positions of management and the union? What were the final resolutions? Can you explain any significant differences you found among the 3?

2. Find (a) an organization whose recent performance was in some way hindered as a result of having too much conflict and (b) an organization whose performance was hindered as a result of having too little conflict. Explain how you arrived at your assessment of each.

## CASE INCIDENT

# Not Your Dream Team

Mallory Murray hadn't had much experience working as part of a team. A recent graduate of the University of Saskatchewan, she had taken a business program focused primarily on individual projects and accomplishments. What little exposure she had had to teams was in her organizational behaviour, marketing research, and strategy formulation courses. When she interviewed with ThinkLink, an educational software firm, she didn't give much thought to the fact that ThinkLink made extensive use of cross-functional teams. During on-site interviews, she told interviewers and managers alike that she had limited experience on teams. But she did tell them that she worked well with people and thought that she could be an effective team player. Unfortunately, Mallory Murray didn't realize that working on a team is generally more complicated than simply working one-on-one with other people.

Mallory joined ThinkLink as an assistant marketing manager for the company's high school core programs. These are essentially software programs designed to help students learn algebra and geometry. Mallory's manager is Lin Chen (marketing manager). Other members of her team include Todd Schlotsky (senior programmer); Laura Willow (advertising); Sean Traynor (vice-president for strategic marketing); Joyce Rothman (co-founder of ThinkLink, who now only works part-time in the company; formerly a high school math teacher; the formal leader of this project); and Harlow Gray (educational consultant).

After her first week on the job, Mallory was seriously considering quitting. "I never imagined how difficult it would be working with people who are so opinionated and competitive. Every decision seems to be a power contest. Sean, Joyce, and Harlow are particularly troublesome. Sean thinks his rank entitles him to the last word. Joyce thinks her opinions should carry more weight because she was instrumental in creating the company. And Harlow views everyone as less knowledgeable than he is. Because he consults with a number of software firms and school districts, Harlow's a 'know-it-all.' To make things worse, Lin is passive and quiet. He rarely speaks up in meetings and appears to want to avoid any conflicts.

"What makes my job particularly difficult," Mallory continued, "is that I don't have any specific job responsibilities. It seems that someone else is always interfering with what I'm doing or telling me how to do it. Our team has seven members — six chiefs and me!"

The project team that Mallory is working on has a deadline to meet that is only six weeks away. Currently the team is at least two weeks behind schedule. Everyone is aware that there's a problem, but no one seems able to solve it. What is especially frustrating to Mallory is that neither Lin Chen nor Joyce Rothman is showing any leadership. Lin is preoccupied with a number of other projects, and Joyce can't seem to control Sean's and Harlow's strong personalities.

## Questions

1. Discuss the situation that has created the conflict.

2. What techniques or procedures might help reduce the conflict in this particular situation?

3. If you were Mallory, could you do anything to lessen the conflict on the core project? Elaborate.

# Small Talk

Is it enough to know about corporate finances, international trade, and the latest accounting methods as you set off for your first job? Perhaps not!

How to interact with others is another important piece of the workplace puzzle. Recruiters often make an assessment of how suitable you'll be for a job within the first four minutes of your first interview. They're looking for a confident first impression, a good handshake, and your ability to establish rapport.

Knowing how to make "small talk" is one of the important parts of effective communication. "Small talk leads to big talk," says corporate image expert Roz Usheroff. "The key is to find commonality with people."

So what are the tips for making appropriate small talk? Avoid topics like religion and politics. Know about current events happening both nationally and internationally, but keep the conversation positive. You can always ask people about shows they've seen, books they've read, or foreign places they've visited.

So why does small talk make a difference? The more people find in common with one another, the more they trust one another. This leads to better interaction, better teamwork, and an easier time at negotiating when there are differences.

## Questions

1. What have been your most successful experiences in engaging in small talk with strangers?

2. What kinds of situations create anxiety for you in trying to communicate with others?

3. What can people do to make others feel at ease when communicating?

Source: Based on "Small Talk," *Venture* 726, aired October 26, 1999. For even more of Roz Usheroff's tips, try her etiquette quiz: http://tv.cbc.ca/venture/onventure/100698.html. Also visit her Web site at http://www.usheroff.com/usheroff.

**VIDEO CASE**

# Go Ahead! Make My Day

Conflict arises in all kinds of situations, but knowing how to deal with that conflict and getting the other person to hear our side is not always easy. Barb Matthews, a Toronto-based consultant, runs her Make-a-Face seminar to teach people how to deal with conflict. Seminar participants wear masks to help them learn how to deal with their conflicts at work.

The point of the Make-a-Face seminar is to get people to learn how to react better in difficult situations. Matthews says that behind a mask an individual feels safer, and is thus more willing to take risks and try new reactions. The mask helps people to get in touch with their real feelings, without trying to personalize the situation.

Matthews is trying to encourage her clients to learn a new mode for dealing with conflict. Many people use either the Mouse or the Lion mode, either running away from conflict or coming on far too strong. The better alternative, Matthews says, is the Freedom mode, where the person is confident, calm, and comfortable in dealing with conflict. She suggests that to remain calm, individuals take on a role or use their imagination to diffuse some of the conflict.

# Questions

1. Would wearing a mask help you to deal more effectively with conflict?

2. Discuss alternative ways of dealing with conflict.

3. How effective are different ways of handling conflict?

Source: Based on "Make-A-Face," *Venture 661*; aired September 23, 1997.

## CHAPTER 8

# Power and Politics

## Questions for Consideration

### What is power? How does one get it?

### What does it mean to empower employees?

### How can we be effective at office politics?

The Whitbread Book of the Year Award in 1999 featured a showdown of two fictional characters: a young wizard against a monster-slaying warrior.[1] The controversy? Whether Nobel laureate Seamus Heaney's *Beowulf* or J.K. Rowling's *Harry Potter and the Prisoner of Azkaban* would win the honour and its £23 000 prize (about $52 000 in Canadian dollars). During the meeting to decide the award, committee members almost broke into a brawl over the decision, and one member even threatened it would be "over my dead body" if his choice didn't win.

Why the controversy? Before the committee even met to make a decision, spokespeople for the rival Booker Prize had already criticized the Whitbread organizers for "dumbing down" the award by appointing Jerry Hall, model and ex-wife of Mick Jagger, as one of the judges. The English literary establishment mocked Hall's appointment to the prestigious award panel, especially when, in response to a question about her qualifications for the task, she responded, "I love reading and I love reading to my children." Other nonacademic appointees included actor Imogen Stubbs and Sandi Toksvig, a comic.

*The Prisoner of Azkaban* was also criticized for being a lightweight choice as a finalist for the prize. Even though over 30 million Harry Potter books have been sold worldwide, London's *Evening Standard* wrote: "Rowling is a brilliant writer of children's books but only readers who refuse to grow up demand that Harry Potter should be treated as a masterpiece for adults too."

By contrast, Seamus Heaney (shown above) is an Irish poet whose international stature was confirmed when he was awarded the Nobel Prize for Literature in 1995. He was a previous Whitbread winner in 1996 for his collection *The Spirit Level*. *Beowulf*, his translation of a thousand-year-old Anglo-Saxon epic, has been widely praised for restoring a dusty classic to modern readers through a vivid, colloquial style.

During the meeting to decide the winner, Anthony Holden, a biographer and one of nine judges, threatened to walk out and dissociate himself from the enterprise if *The Prisoner of Azkaban* won the Book of the Year Award. Three of the other judges, including Hall and Stubbs, said they would walk out with him.

Holden said letting Harry Potter win "would be a 'national humiliation' and would send out the wrong message about a serious literary competition." Robert Harris, also one of the judges and the author of the bestselling thrillers *Fatherland* and *Enigma*, accused Holden of blackmailing the other committee members. After a brief shouting match between the two, Dr. Eric Anderson, the chair of judges, called for a vote in the hopes of restoring order.

Even the announcement of the final decision was fraught with controversy: At first, Dr. Anderson announced that *Beowulf* had won by a clear margin. The next day, another judge said that the 90-minute meeting of judges had been tense and the final vote was five to four.

What makes some people able to influence others? To what extent do individuals try to manipulate how they are perceived by others? These are questions that this chapter tries to address as it looks at power and politics in organizations. The 1999 Whitbread Awards contain elements of power, politics, and impression management. Judge Holden tried to use his power as a well-known author to intimidate others on the committee to vote for

**Whitbread Book Awards**
www.whitbread-bookawards.
co.uk

**The Booker Prize**
www.bookerprize.co.uk

**power**
A capacity that A has to
influence the behaviour of B
so that B acts in accordance
with A's wishes.

**dependency**
B's relationship to A when A
possesses something that B
requires.

*Beowulf*. The Booker Prize organizers tried to increase the prestige of their own award by suggesting that the Whitbread organizers were dumbing down the selection process. And Jerry Hall, criticized for being a lightweight judge, might have felt obligated to choose *Beowulf*, just to appease her detractors. Even the first announcement that Beowulf was a *clear* winner was an attempt to manage the impression that there was considerable agreement on the winning book.

Organizational behaviour researchers have learned a lot in recent years about how people gain and use power in organizations. Part of using power in organizations is engaging in organizational politics.

A major theme throughout this chapter is that power and politics are a natural process in any group or organization. Thus, you need to know how power is acquired and exercised, and how to engage in effective political behaviour. Although you might have heard the phrase "power corrupts, and absolute power corrupts absolutely," power is not always bad. It's a reality of organizational life, and it's not going to go away. Moreover, it is increasingly shared by managers and employees through the process of empowerment.

## A Definition of Power

**Power** refers to a capacity that A has to influence the behaviour of B, so that B acts in accordance with A's wishes.[2] This definition implies a *potential* that need not be actualized to be effective and a *dependency* relationship. In addition, power may exist but not be used. It is, therefore, a capacity or potential. One can have power but not impose it.

Probably the most important aspect of power is that it is a function of **dependency**. The greater B's dependence on A, the greater is A's power in the relationship. Dependence, in turn, is based on the alternatives that B perceives and the importance that B places on the alternative(s) that A controls. A person can have power over you only if he or she controls something you desire. For example, you may want a post-secondary degree and have to pass a certain course to get it. If your current instructor is the only faculty member who teaches that course, he or she has power over you. Your alternatives are highly limited, and you place a high degree of importance on obtaining a passing grade. Similarly, if you're attending college or university on funds totally provided by your parents, you probably recognize the power that your parents hold over you. You're dependent on them for financial support. But once you are out of school, have a job, and are making a good income, your parents' power is reduced significantly. Who among us, though, has not known or heard of the rich relative who is able to control a large number of family members merely through the implicit or explicit threat of "writing them out of the will"?

## Contrasting Leadership and Power

A careful comparison of our description of power with our description of leadership in Chapter 10 reveals that the two concepts are closely intertwined. Leaders use power as a means of attaining group goals. Leaders achieve goals, and power is a means of facilitating their achievement.

What differences are there between the two terms? One main difference relates to goal compatibility. Power does not require goal compatibility, merely dependence. Leadership, on the other hand, requires some congruence between the goals of the leader and those being led.

## Bases of Power

Where does power come from? What is it that gives an individual or a group influence over others? The answer to these questions is a five-category classification scheme identified by French and Raven.[3] They proposed that there were five bases or sources of power: coercive, reward, legitimate, expert, and referent (see Exhibit 8-1).

### Coercive Power

**coercive power**
Power that is based on fear.

The **coercive power** base is defined by French and Raven as being dependent on fear. One reacts to this power out of fear of the negative results that might occur if one failed to comply. It rests on the application, or the threat of the application, of physical sanctions such as the infliction of pain, the generation of frustration through restriction of movement, or the controlling by force of basic physiological or safety needs. When Anthony Holden, one of the Whitbread Award judges, threatened to walk out of the meeting, he was using a form of coercion. He was trying to intimidate the others, making them fear that if the meeting ended in disarray, all would be embarrassed.

Of all the bases of power available, the power to hurt others is possibly the most often used, most often condemned, and most difficult to control: The state relies on its military and legal resources to intimidate nations, or even its own citizens; businesses rely upon the control of economic resources; and schools and universities rely upon their rights to deny students formal education, while religious institutions threaten individuals with dire consequences in the afterlife if they do not conduct themselves properly in this life.

---

**Exhibit 8-1**
**Measuring Bases of Power**

Does a person have one or more of the five bases of power? Affirmative responses to the following statements can answer this question:

- The person can make things difficult for people, and you want to avoid getting him or her angry. [coercive power]

- The person is able to give special benefits or rewards to people, and you find it advantageous to trade favours with him or her. [reward power]

- The person has the right, considering his or her position and your job responsibilities, to expect you to comply with legitimate requests. [legitimate power]

- The person has the experience and knowledge to earn your respect, and you defer to his or her judgment in some matters. [expert power]

- You like the person and enjoy doing things for him or her. [referent power]

---

Source: G. Yukl and C.M. Falbe, "Importance of Different Power Sources in Downward and Lateral Relations," *Journal of Applied Psychology*, June 1991, p. 417. With permission.

Microsoft chair Bill Gates' power comes from a variety of sources. He has *legitimate* power within Microsoft because he co-founded the company and was until recently its CEO. His *expert* power is recognized throughout the world. It is based on his software development expertise and his reputation for building a first-rate company. Gates also has *referent* power, because many people look up to him and admire his incredible accomplishments. Unfortunately, the US government was not persuaded by his referent power and has used its *coercive* power to try to break up what the government views as Gates' monopolistic hold on the computer world.

**reward power**
Power that achieves compliance based on the ability to distribute rewards that others view as valuable.

**legitimate power**
The power a person receives as a result of his or her position in the formal hierarchy of an organization.

At the personal level, individuals exercise coercive power through a reliance upon physical strength, verbal facility, or the ability to grant emotional support or withhold emotional support from others. These bases provide the individual with the means to physically harm, bully, humiliate, or deny love to others.[4]

At the organizational level, A has coercive power over B if A can dismiss, suspend, or demote B, assuming that B values his or her job. Similarly, if A can assign B work activities that B finds unpleasant or treat B in a manner that B finds embarrassing, A possesses coercive power over B.

## Reward Power

The opposite of coercive power is **reward power**. People comply with the wishes or directives of another because doing so produces positive benefits; therefore, one who can distribute rewards that others view as valuable will have power over those others. These rewards can be anything that another person values. In an organizational context, we think of money, favourable performance appraisals, promotions, interesting work assignments, friendly colleagues, important information, and preferred work shifts or sales territories. Coercive power and reward power are actually counterparts of each other. If you can remove something of positive value from another or inflict something of negative value upon him or her, you have coercive power over that person. If you can give someone something of positive value or remove something of negative value, you have reward power over that person. Again, as with coercive power, you don't have to be a manager to be able to exert influence through rewards. Rewards such as friendliness, acceptance, and praise are available to everyone in an organization. To the degree that an individual seeks such rewards, your ability to give or withhold them gives you power over that individual.

## Legitimate Power

In formal groups and organizations, probably the most frequent access to one or more of the power bases is one's structural position. This is called **legitimate power**. It represents the power a person receives as a result of his or her position in the formal hierarchy of an organization.

Positions of authority include coercive and reward powers. Legitimate power, however, is broader than the power to coerce and reward. Specifically, it includes acceptance by members of an organization of the authority of a position. When school principals, bank presidents, or army captains speak (assuming that their directives are viewed to be within the authority of their positions), teachers, tellers, and lieutenants listen and usually comply. You will note in Exhibit 8-2 that one of the men in the meeting identifies himself as the rule maker, which means that he has legitimate power. Similarly, when

**Exhibit 8-2**

"*I was just going to say 'Well, I don't make the rules.' But, of course, I do make the rules.*"

Source: Drawing by Leo Cullum in *The New Yorker.* Copyright © 1986 *The New Yorker Magazine.* Reprinted by permission.

Dr. Eric Anderson, chair of the Whitbread Award judges, called for a vote, hoping to end the hostility between the warring judges, he was using his legitimate power as chair to end the debate.

## Expert Power

**expert power**
Influence based on special skills or knowledge.

**Expert power** is influence wielded as a result of expertise, special skill, or knowledge. Expertise has become one of the most powerful sources of influence as the world has become more technologically oriented. As jobs become more specialized, we become increasingly dependent on experts to achieve goals. So, while it is generally acknowledged that physicians have expertise and hence expert power — most of us follow the advice that our doctor gives us — you should also recognize that computer specialists, tax accountants, economists, industrial psychologists, and other specialists are able to wield power as a result of their expertise. When judge Anthony Holden, a biographer, said that letting *Harry Potter* win the Whitbread Award "would be a 'national humiliation' and would send out the wrong message about a serious literary competition," he was trying to use his influence as a literary expert to persuade others to vote for *Beowulf*.

## Referent Power

**referent power**
Influence based on possession by an individual of desirable resources or personal traits.

The last category of influence that French and Raven identified was **referent power**. Its base is identification with a person who has desirable resources or personal traits. If I admire you and identify with you, you can exercise power over me because I want to please you.

**Roots Canada**
www.roots.com

**Deborah Cox**
www.deborahcoxonline.com

Referent power develops out of admiration of another and a desire to be like that person. In a sense, then, it is a lot like charisma. If you admire someone to the point of modelling your behaviour and attitudes after him or her, that person possesses referent power over you. Referent power explains why celebrities are paid millions of dollars to endorse products in commercials. Marketing research shows that people such as Elvis Stojko can influence your choice of breakfast drinks or your choice of computer printers. And advertisers such as Toronto-based Roots Canada Ltd. have developed advertising themes around popular Canadians such as "bad boy" Olympic gold-medallist and snowboarder Ross Rebagliati, Canadian R&B diva Deborah Cox, and Toronto-based rapper Maestro to convince people to buy specific products.[5] With a little practice, you and I could probably deliver as smooth a sales pitch as these celebrities, but the buying public doesn't identify with you and me. In organizations, if you are articulate, domineering, physically imposing, or charismatic, you hold personal characteristics that may be used to get others to do what you want.

## Evaluating the Bases of Power

Are some forms of power more effective than others?

A review of the research on the effectiveness of these forms of power finds that they differ in their ability to improve a person's performance.[6] Coercive power tends to result in negative performance responses from individuals, decreases satisfaction, increases mistrust, and creates fear. Legitimate power does not have a negative effect, but does not generally stimulate employees to *improve* their attitudes or performance, and it does not generally result in increased commitment. In other words, legitimate power does not inspire individuals to act beyond the basic level.

Reward power may improve performance in a variety of situations if the rewards are consistent with what the individuals want as rewards. Reward power can also lead to unethical behaviour, however. For instance, former Sears Roebuck chair Edward A. Brennan instituted a compensation program aimed at encouraging increased sales. Two years later, Sears' Tire and Auto Centers were accused of overcharging customers an average of $235 for unnecessary repairs, the result of unreasonably high quotas, commission-based compensation, and attractive incentives for top sellers.[7] Even if reward power does not always lead to unethical behaviour, you may remember from the discussion in Chapter 4 that extrinsic rewards can lead to demotivated behaviour when they replace intrinsic rewards. Ironically, the least effective power bases—coercive, legitimate, and reward — are the ones most likely to be used by managers, perhaps because they are the easiest to implement.

By contrast, effective leaders use referent and/or expert power.[8] These are forms of power derived from the person's position. Referent and expert powers are thus "personal" forms of influence and are achieved through interpersonal interactions and relationships with employees. When people identify with someone because of referent or expert power, their respect and admiration make them more likely to copy the performance of that individual.

Expert power relies on trust that all relevant information is given out honestly and completely. Of course, since knowledge is power, the more that information is shared, the less expert power a person has. Thus, some individuals try to protect their power by withholding information.[9] This tactic

**Sears Roebuck**
www.sears.com

can result in poor-quality performance by those who need the information.[10] The Working With Others Exercise on page 365 gives you the opportunity to explore the effectiveness of different power bases in changing someone's behaviour.

## Dependency: The Key to Power

Earlier in this chapter, you read that probably the most important aspect of power is that it is a function of dependence. In this section, we show how an understanding of dependency is central to furthering your understanding of power itself.

### The General Dependency Postulate

Let's begin with a general postulate: *The greater B's dependency on A, the greater the power A has over B.* When you possess anything that others require but that you alone control, you make them dependent upon you and, therefore, you gain power over them.[11] Dependency, then, is inversely proportional to the alternative sources of supply. If something is plentiful, possession of it will not increase your power. If everyone is intelligent, intelligence gives no special advantage. Similarly, in the circles of the superrich, money does not result in power. But, as the old saying goes, "In the land of the blind, the one-eyed man is king!" If you can create a monopoly by controlling information, prestige, or anything that others crave, they become dependent on you. Conversely, the more that you can expand your options, the less power you place in the hands of others. This explains, for example, why most organizations develop multiple suppliers rather than give their business to only one. It also explains why so many of us aspire to financial independence. Financial independence reduces the power that others can have over us.

Roots hired Ross Rebagliati as a spokesperson after his controversial gold medal performance in the 1998 Winter Olympics. The Toronto-based company was relying on Rebagliati's *referent* power with teens and twenty-somethings to increase sales.

## What Creates Dependency?

Dependency is increased when the resource you control is important, scarce, and nonsubstitutable.[12]

**IMPORTANCE** If nobody wants what you've got, there is no dependency. To create dependency, the thing(s) you control must be perceived as being important. It's been found, for instance, that organizations actively seek to avoid uncertainty.[13] We should therefore expect that those individuals or groups who can absorb an organization's uncertainty will be perceived as controlling an important resource. At organizations such as Intel, which are heavily technologically oriented and highly dependent on their engineers to maintain products' technical advantages and quality, engineers are clearly a powerful group. At Procter & Gamble, marketing is the name of the game, and marketers are the most powerful occupational group. These examples support not only the view that the ability to reduce uncertainty increases a group's importance, and hence its power, but also that what's important is situational. It varies among organizations and undoubtedly also varies over time within any given organization.

**SCARCITY** As noted previously, if something is plentiful, possession of it will not increase your power. A resource must be perceived as being scarce to create dependency.

This can help to explain how low-ranking members in an organization who have important knowledge not available to high-ranking members gain power. Possession of a scarce resource — in this case, important knowledge — makes the high-ranking member dependent on the low-ranking member. This also helps to make sense out of behaviours of low-ranking members that otherwise might seem illogical, such as destroying the procedure manuals

The location of power varies among organizations. At Walt Disney Co., enormous power is held by high-tech scientists in the research and development group of Disney Imagineering, a division created by Walt Disney in 1952 to create Disneyland. Today, the company is relying on Bran Ferren (upper left), who heads the R&D unit, and his highly skilled and creative staffers to develop cyberland fantasies like virtual-reality theme parks, Web sites for kids, and smart TV sets that learn viewers' programming preferences and automatically record programs they forget to watch.

that describe how a job is done, refusing to train people in their jobs or even to show others exactly what they do, creating specialized language and terminology that inhibit others from understanding their jobs, or operating in secrecy so an activity will appear more complex and difficult than it really is. The use of knowledge and the power it brings will become increasingly important in organizations of the 21st century. One of the major tasks of organizations is to figure out ways to handle the volume of information that is available. Individuals who acquire excellent information-handling abilities will have more power in their organizations.

The scarcity-dependency relationship can further be seen in the power of occupational categories. Individuals in occupations in which the supply of human resources is low relative to demand can negotiate compensation and benefit packages that are far more attractive than can individuals in occupations where candidates abound. For example, college and university administrators have no problem today finding English instructors. There are more individuals who have degrees enabling them to work as English instructors than there are positions available in Canada. The market for corporate finance professors, by contrast, is extremely tight, with the demand high and the supply limited. The result is that the bargaining power of finance faculty allows them to negotiate higher salaries, lighter teaching loads, and other benefits.

**Steve Jobs**
www.apple.com/pr/bios/jobs.html

**NONSUBSTITUTABILITY** The more that a resource has no viable substitutes, the more power control over that resource provides. In the case of Apple Computer, most observers, as well as the board, believed that no one other than Steve Jobs could turn the company around. When a union goes on strike, and management is not permitted to replace the absent employees, the union has considerable control over the organization's ability to carry out its tasks.

## Identifying Where the Power Is

How do you determine where the power is in an organization at any given point in time? We can answer this question from both the department and individual manager levels.

At the department level, answers to the following questions will give you a good idea of how powerful that department is: What proportion of the organization's top-level managers came up through the department? Is the department represented on important interdepartmental teams and committees? How does the salary of the senior manager in the department compare with that of others at his or her level? Is the department located in the headquarters building? What's the average size of offices for people working in the department compared with that of offices in other departments? Has the department grown in number of employees relative to other departments? How does the promotion rate for people in the department compare with that of other units? Has the department's budget allocation been increasing relative to that of other departments?[14]

At the level of the individual manager, there are certain symbols you should be on the lookout for that suggest that a manager has power.[15] These include the ability to intercede favourably on behalf of someone in trouble in the organization, to get approval for expenditures beyond the budget, to get items on the agenda at major meetings, and to get fast access to top decision makers in the organization.

# Power Tactics

power tactics
Ways in which individuals translate power bases into specific actions.

**Have you ever wondered how you might get power?**

This section is a logical extension of our previous discussions. We've reviewed where power comes from. Now we move to the topic of **power tactics** to learn how employees translate their power bases into specific actions. Recent research indicates that there are standardized ways by which powerholders attempt to get what they want.[16]

One particular study identified seven tactical dimensions, or strategies, that managers and employees use: [17]

- *Reason*: Using facts and data to make a logical or rational presentation of ideas;
- *Friendliness*: Using flattery, creating goodwill, acting humble, and being friendly prior to making a request;
- *Coalition*: Getting the support of other people in the organization to back up the request;
- *Bargaining*: Using negotiation through the exchange of benefits or favours;
- *Assertiveness*: Using a direct and forceful approach, such as demanding compliance with requests, repeating reminders, ordering individuals to do what is asked, and pointing out that rules require compliance;
- *Higher authority*: Gaining the support of higher levels in the organization to back up requests;
- *Sanctions*: Using organizationally derived rewards and punishments, such as preventing or promising a salary increase, threatening to give an unsatisfactory performance evaluation, or withholding a promotion.

You may want to review the opening vignette to see whether you can identify examples of most of these power tactics used by participants in the Whitbread Award discussions.

Researchers found that employees do not rely on the seven tactics equally. However, as shown in Exhibit 8-3, the most popular strategy was the use of reason, regardless of whether the influence was directed upward or downward. Additionally, the researchers uncovered four contingency variables that affect the selection of a power tactic: the manager's relative power; the manager's objectives for wanting to influence; the manager's expectation of the target person's willingness to comply; and the organization's culture.

A manager's relative power affects the selection of tactics in two ways. First, managers who control resources that are valued by others or who are perceived to be in positions of dominance use a greater variety of tactics than do those with less power. Second, managers with power use assertiveness with greater frequency than do those with less power. Initially, we can expect that most managers will attempt to use simple requests and reason. Assertiveness is a back-up strategy, used when the target of influence refuses or appears reluctant to comply with the request. Resistance leads to managers using more directive strategies. Typically, they shift from using simple requests to insisting that their demands be met. The manager with relatively little power is more likely to stop trying to influence others when he or she encounters resistance because he or she perceives the costs associated with assertiveness as unacceptable.

Managers vary their power tactics in relation to their objectives. When managers seek benefits from a more senior manager, they tend to rely on kind words and the promotion of pleasant relationships; that is, they use

**Exhibit 8-3**
**Popularity of Power Tactics**

| | When Managers Influenced Superiors* | When Managers Influenced Employees |
|---|---|---|
| Most Popular ↑ | Reason | Reason |
| | Coalition | Assertiveness |
| | Friendliness | Friendliness |
| | Bargaining | Coalition |
| | Assertiveness | Bargaining |
| | Higher authority | Higher authority |
| Least Popular ↓ | | Sanctions |

*The dimension of sanctions is omitted in the scale that measures upward influence.

Source: Reprinted, by permission of the publisher, from D. Kipnis et al.,"Patterns of Managerial Influence: Shotgun Managers, Tacticians, and Bystanders," in *Organizational Dynamics,* Winter 1984, p. 62. © 1984 Periodicals Division, American Management Association, New York. All rights reserved.

friendliness. In comparison, managers attempting to persuade top management to accept new ideas usually rely on reason. This matching of tactics to objectives also holds true for downward influence. For example, managers use reason to sell ideas to employees and friendliness to obtain favours.

Managers' expectations of success guide their choice of tactics. When past experience indicates a high probability of success, managers use simple requests to gain compliance. Where success is less predictable, managers are more tempted to use assertiveness and sanctions to achieve their objectives.

Finally, we know that organizational cultures differ markedly. For example, some are warm, relaxed, and supportive; others are formal and conservative. The organizational culture in which managers work, therefore, will have a significant bearing on defining which tactics are considered appropriate. Some cultures encourage the use of friendliness; some encourage reason; and still others rely on sanctions and assertiveness. The organization itself will influence which subset of power tactics managers will view as acceptable for use.

## Empowerment:  Giving Power to Employees

Thus far our discussion has implied, at least to some extent, that power is something that is more likely to reside in the hands of management, to be used as part of their interaction with employees. However, in today's workplace, there is a movement toward sharing more power with employees by putting them in teams and also by making them responsible for some of the decisions regarding their jobs. Organizational specialists refer to this increasing responsibility as empowerment. We briefly mention in Chapter 10 that one of the current trends in leadership is empowering workers. Between 1995 and 1999, nearly 30 000 articles about empowerment have appeared in the print media.[18]

Ellen Wessel (right) is founder and president of Moving Comfort, a manufacturer of women's athletic wear. She has created a corporate culture that encourages the use of kind words and friendliness. The environment at Moving Comfort is warm and relaxed because Wessel is supportive in empowering employees to make decisions. She views employees as goodwill ambassadors for her company and attributes the company's rapid growth to giving employees the freedom to make things happen.

**Moving Comfort**
www.movingcomfort.com

**Patriot Computers**
canada.patriot.com

**job content**
The tasks and procedures necessary for carrying out a particular job.

**job context**
The reason for the job and the setting in which it is done.

Unfortunately, the definition of empowerment is not agreed upon by either managers or researchers. Quinn and Spreitzer, in their work with a Fortune 50 manufacturing company, found that executives were split about 50-50 in their definition.[19] One group of executives "believed that empowerment was about delegating decision making within a set of clear boundaries." Empowerment would start at the top, specific goals and tasks would be assigned, responsibility would be delegated, and people would be held accountable for their results. The other group believed that empowerment was "a process of risk taking and personal growth." This type of empowerment starts at the bottom, considering the employees' needs, showing them what empowered behaviour looks like, building teams, encouraging risk-taking, and demonstrating trust in employees' ability to perform.

Much of the press on empowerment has been positive, with both executives and employees applauding the ability of front-line workers to make and execute important decisions.[20] However, not all reports are favourable. One management expert noted that much of the talk about empowerment is simply lip service,[21] with organizations telling employees that they have decision-making responsibility, but not giving them the authority to carry out their decisions. In order for an employee to be fully empowered, he or she needs access to the information required to make decisions; rewards for acting in appropriate, responsible ways; and authority to make the necessary decisions. Empowerment means that the employee understands how his or her job fits into the organization and is able to make decisions regarding job action in light of the organization's purpose and mission. This chapter's CBC Video Case, on page 368, shows you the extent to which Patriot Computers empowers its employees.

The concept of empowerment has caused much cynicism in many workplaces. Employees are told that they are empowered, and yet they do not feel that they have the authority to act, or they feel that their manager still micromanages their performance. Some managers are reluctant to empower their employees, because this means sharing or even relinquishing their own power. Other managers worry that empowered workers may decide to work on goals and jobs that are not as closely aligned to the organizational goals. Some managers, of course, do not fully understand how to go about empowering their employees.

One study that helps us to understand the degrees of empowerment looks at jobs in terms of both their context and their content.[22] The **content** of a job represents the tasks and procedures necessary for carrying out a particular job. The **context** of a job is the reason for the job being done and reflects the organizational mission, objectives, and setting. The context of the job would also include the organization's structure, culture, and reward systems.

When employees are empowered, as we noted above, they are given decision-making authority over some aspect of their job. In Chapter 11 we will describe the steps of the decision-making model as identifying the problem, discovering alternative solutions, evaluating the alternatives, making a

Even though Ken Funk was a 1999 nominee for Entrepreneur of the Year, Pacific Region, he doesn't take the credit for his success. He is CEO of Golden Valley Foods, based in Abbotsford, BC, producer of jam, salsa and pasta sauce for such customers as Safeway Overwaitea, and IGA. He credits his staff: "I am extremely pleased I have the opportunity to be involved with good people—and that's the key. You have to empower them to make decisions, let them have the responsibility, let them do their work, and get the hell out of the way."

choice, and then carrying out the choice. We can use this same decision-making model to understand the degree of empowerment an employee has. Exhibit 8-4 links the steps of the decision-making model to job content and job context decisions.

As shown on the horizontal grid of Exhibit 8-4, an employee's (or team's) decision-making authority over job content increases as he or she is permitted to complete more of the steps. At the very left the employee has little power, and at the very right, the employee has a great deal of power. On the vertical axis, an employee's (or team's) decision-making authority over job context increases similarly. On the very bottom an employee has very little power, while at the very top the employee has a great deal of power.

Exhibit 8-4 indicates five particular points on the grid, representing stages of employee power, including no discretion, task setting, participatory empowerment, mission defining, and self-management. The five types of power and their effects on employees are the following:[23]

- *No Discretion* (Point A) is the typical assembly-line job — highly routine and repetitive. The worker is assigned the task, given no discretion, and most likely monitored by a supervisor. When employees have no power, they are less likely to be satisfied with their jobs. They can also be less productive because the lack of discretion may cause a "rule mentality" where the employee chooses to operate strictly by the rules, rather than showing initiative.

- *Task Setting* (Point B) is typical of most workers who have been empowered today. The worker can determine how the job gets done but has no discretion in determining what jobs get done. Management defines the general tasks, giving the employee discretion over the timing

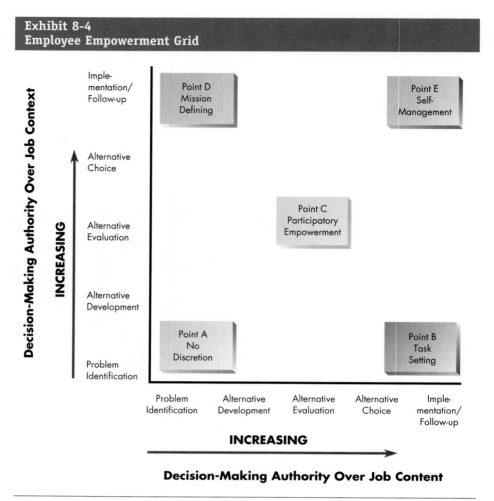

**Exhibit 8-4**
**Employee Empowerment Grid**

Source: R.C. Ford and M.D. Fottler, "Empowerment: A Matter of Degree," *Academy of Management Executive*, August 1995, p. 24.

and procedures for completing the task. Employees who are granted task-setting power may become more energized about their work, as they look to find new ways to do the work, and they may develop new skills to help them do the work in a better fashion. Consequently, many workers will feel more motivated and satisfied when they have task-setting power, leading them to do higher-quality work.

- *Participatory Empowerment* (Point C) represents the situation of autonomous work groups that are given some decision-making authority over both job content and job context. There is some evidence of higher job satisfaction and productivity in such groups.[24] One of the best-known success stories of autonomous work groups is the Saturn plant of General Motors in Spring Hill, Tennessee.

- *Mission Defining* (Point D) represents a more unusual situation in the workplace, although not an impossible one. It is not unusual for a design team, for instance, to set out the broad goals of a project, but not be responsible for carrying out the tasks of that project. For instance, in a number of business schools in recent years, design teams have tried to restructure MBA programs. Often the design team set out the broad goals of what a new program would look like, but the actual implementation was left to a set of instructors who found it more difficult to implement the design.

- *Self-Management* (Point E) represents employees who have total decision-making power for both job content and job context. Granting an employee this much power requires considerable faith on the part of management that the employee will carry out the goals and mission of the organization in an effective manner. Generally this sort of power is reserved for those in top management, although it is also sometimes granted to high-level salespeople. Obviously this kind of power can be very rewarding to those who hold it.

When employees are empowered, it means that they are expected to act, at least in a small way, as owners of the company, rather than just employees. Ownership is not necessary in the financial sense, but in terms of identifying with the goals and mission of the organization. For employees to be empowered, however, and have an ownership mentality, four conditions need to be met, according to Professor Dan Ondrack at the University of Toronto's Rotman School of Management: 1) There must be a clear definition of the values and mission of the company; 2) the company must help employees acquire the relevant skills; 3) employees need to be supported in their decision making, and not criticized when they try to do something extraordinary; and 4) workers need to be recognized for their efforts.[25] Exhibit 8-5 outlines what two researchers discovered in studying the characteristics of empowered workers.

Does empowerment work? Researchers have shown that at both the individual level[26] and the team level,[27] empowerment leads to greater productivity. Two British Columbia firms have discovered the bottom-line rewards of empowering their employees.[28] Vancouver-based Dominion Directory, which publishes *The Yellow Pages*, cut customer complaints by 40 percent in three years. They also reduced the time it takes to fix complaints from 27 days

---

**Exhibit 8-5**
**Characteristics of Empowered People**

Robert E. Quinn and Gretchen M. Spreitzer, in their research on the characteristics of empowered people (through both in-depth interviews and survey analysis), found four characteristics that most empowered people have in common:

- Empowered people have a sense of *self-determination* (this means that they are free to choose how to do their work; they are not micromanaged).

- Empowered people have a sense of *meaning* (they feel that their work is important to them; they care about what they are doing).

- Empowered people have a sense of *competence* (this means that they are confident about their ability to do their work well; they know they can perform).

- Empowered people have a sense of *impact* (this means that people believe they can have influence on their work unit; others listen to their ideas).

Source: R.E. Quinn and G.M. Spreitzer, "The Road to Empowerment: Seven Questions Every Leader Should Consider," *Organizational Dynamics*, Autumn 1997, pp. 41.

Workers at Redwood Plastics in Langley, British Columbia, have been cross-trained so that they know the jobs that other employees do. This training is part of Redwood Plastics' aim to empower its workers and reach 100 percent on-time delivery.

down to 48 hours. Not ready to rest on this accomplishment, however, they are aiming for same-day complaint resolution. Dominion reports that their employee-empowerment efforts also led to revenues that have grown 40 percent during the past six years and an annual employee turnover that is the lowest in the business at 5.27 percent.

Similarly, Langley-based Redwood Plastics has increased its on-time deliveries from 60 percent of the time to 92 percent. The company is hoping to reach 100 percent on-time delivery. To improve procedures, Redwood's vice-president Dan Pearce said the company "asked people on the line what we could do to eliminate problems and we did a lot of cross-training. Salespeople would make some parts and floor people would watch the people in the office. All of that caused a huge coming-together of the business and it has increased our quality exponentially."

Doug Martin, executive director of the Quality Council of British Columbia, summarizes what he believes is the importance of empowering employees: "You really need to involve anybody who is in a position where they can influence how the business works. If people aren't relying on a hierarchy to fix problems, they can take action right where it counts." He points out that this has a bottom-line positive outcome.

## Power in Groups: Coalitions

**coalition**

Two or more individuals who combine their power to push for or support their demands.

Those "out of power" and seeking to be "in" will first try to increase their power individually. Why share the rewards if one doesn't have to? If this proves ineffective, the alternative is to form a **coalition**—an informal group bound together by the active pursuit of a single issue.[29] There is often strength in numbers.

The natural way to gain influence is to become a powerholder. Therefore, those who want power will attempt to build a personal power base, but in many instances this may be difficult, risky, costly, or impossible. In such cases, efforts will be made to form a coalition of two or more "outs" who, by joining together, can combine their resources to increase rewards for themselves.[30] For instance, Whitbread Award judges Jerry Hall and actor Imogen Stubbs, together with shadow home secretary Ann Widdecombe, sided with biographer Anthony Holden. By threatening to walk out with him if *Beowulf* lost, they were forming a coalition intent on swaying the views of the others.

Successful coalitions have been found to contain fluid membership and are able to form swiftly, achieve their target issue, and quickly disappear.[31]

What predictions can we make about coalition formation?[32] First, coalitions in organizations often seek to maximize their size. In political science theory, coalitions move the other way — they try to minimize their size. They tend to be just large enough to exert the power necessary to achieve their objectives. But legislatures are different from organizations. Specifically, decision making in organizations does not end just with selection from among a set of alternatives. The decision must also be implemented. In organizations, the implementation of and commitment to the decision is at least as important as the decision itself. It's necessary, therefore, for coalitions in organizations to seek a broad constituency to support the coalition's objectives. This means expanding the coalition to encompass as many interests as possible. This coalition expansion to facilitate consensus building, of course, is more likely to occur in organizational cultures where cooperation, commitment, and shared decision making are highly valued. In autocratic and hierarchically controlled organizations, however, this search for maximizing the coalition's size is less likely to be sought.

Another prediction about coalitions relates to the degree of interdependence within the organization. More coalitions will likely be created where there is a great deal of task and resource interdependence. In contrast, there will be less interdependence among subunits and less coalition formation activity where subunits are largely self-contained or resources are abundant.

Finally, coalition formation will be influenced by the actual tasks that workers do. The more routine the task of a group, the greater the likelihood that coalitions will form. The more that the work that people do is routine, the greater their substitutability for each other, and thus the greater their dependence. To offset this dependence, they can be expected to resort to a coalition.

> Can coalitions help us understand why labour unions are more prevalent among factory workers?

**Sears Canada**
www.sears.ca

**Human Resources Development Canada — Labour Standards**
info.load-otea.hrdc-drhc.gc.ca/~lsweb/harassen.htm

## The Abuse of Power: Harassment in the Workplace

People who engage in harassment in the workplace are typically abusing their power position. Some categories of harassment have long been held to be illegal, including those based on race, religion, and national origin, as well as sexual harassment. Unfortunately, some types of harassment that occur in the workplace are not deemed illegal, even if they create problems for employees and managers. We focus here on sexual harassment because it is currently the most publicized form of harassment. Yet many of us are also aware, anecdotally, of managers who harass employees, demanding overtime without pay or excessive work performance. And some of the recent stories of workplace violence have reportedly been the result of an employee feeling intimidated at work.

### Sexual Harassment

The issue of sexual harassment has received increasing attention by corporations and the media because of the growing ranks of female employees, especially in nontraditional work environments, and because of a number of high-profile cases. For example, the Canadian Armed Forces was subject to intense media scrutiny during 1998 for alleged cover-ups of sexual harassment. Similarly, Sears Canada had a notorious incident that led to the death of two employees. (This case is discussed in more detail in the HR Implications starting on page 359.) Sexual harassment has also generated much discussion at several universities in recent years, including the University of British Columbia and Simon Fraser University. Moreover, the extensive debate about what happened between US president Bill Clinton and White House intern Monica Lewinsky increased the spotlight on sexual harassment in both Canada and the United States.

**sexual harassment**
Unwelcome behaviour of a
sexual nature in the workplace
that negatively affects the work
environment or leads to
adverse job-related
consequences for the employee.

The Supreme Court of Canada defines **sexual harassment** as unwelcome behaviour of a sexual nature in the workplace that negatively affects the work environment or leads to adverse job-related consequences for the employee. Despite the legal framework for defining sexual harassment, there continues to be disagreement as to what *specifically* constitutes sexual harassment. Sexual harassment includes unwanted physical touching, recurring requests for dates when it is made clear the person isn't interested, and coercive threats that a person will lose her or his job if she or he refuses a sexual proposition. The problems of interpreting sexual harassment often surface around some of its more subtle forms — unwanted looks or comments, off-colour jokes, sexual artifacts such as nude calendars in the workplace, sexual innuendo, or misinterpretations of where the line between "being friendly" ends and "harassment" begins. The Case Incident starting on page 367, "Damned If You Do; Damned If You Don't," illustrates how these problems can make people feel uncomfortable in the workplace. Most studies confirm that the concept of power is central to understanding sexual harassment.[33] This seems to be true whether the harassment comes from a manager, a co-worker, or even an employee.

The manager-employee relationship best characterizes an unequal power relationship, where position power gives the manager the capacity to reward and coerce. Managers give employees their assignments, evaluate their performance, make recommendations for salary adjustments and promotions, and even decide whether employees retain their job. These decisions give a manager power. Since employees want favourable performance reviews, salary increases, and the like, it's clear that managers control the resources that most employees consider important and scarce. It's also worth noting that individuals who occupy high-status roles (such as management positions) sometimes believe that sexually harassing employees is merely an extension of their right to make demands on lower-status individuals. Because of power inequities, sexual harassment by one's manager typically creates the greatest difficulty for the person being harassed. If there are no witnesses, it is the manager's word against the employee's word. Are there others whom this manager has harassed, and if so, will they come forward? Because of the manager's control over resources, many of those who are harassed are afraid of speaking out for fear of retaliation by the manager.

Although co-workers don't have position power, they can have influence and use it to sexually harass peers. In fact, although co-workers appear to engage in somewhat less severe forms of harassment than do managers, co-workers are the most frequent perpetrators of sexual harassment in organizations. How do co-workers exercise power? Most often it's by providing or withholding information, cooperation, and support. For example, the effective performance of most jobs requires interaction and support from co-workers. This is especially true nowadays as work is assigned to teams. By threatening to withhold or delay providing information that's necessary for the successful achievement of your work goals, co-workers can exert power over you.

One of the places where there has been a dramatic increase in the number of sexual harassment complaints is at university campuses across Canada, according to Paddy Stamp, sexual harassment officer at the University of Toronto.[34] However, agreement on what constitutes sexual harassment, and how it should be investigated, is no clearer for universities than for industry.

While nonconsensual sex between professors and students is rape and subject to criminal charges, it is harder to evaluate apparently consensual relationships that occur outside the classroom. There is some argument over whether truly consensual sex is ever possible between students and professors. In an effort to underscore the power discrepancy and potential for abuse of it by professors, Yale University recently decided that there could be no sexual relations between students and professors. Most universities have been unwilling to adopt such an extreme stance. However, this issue is certainly one of concern, as the power distance between professors and students is considerable. Similar issues were raised with the alleged consensual sexual relationship between US president Bill Clinton and White House intern Monica Lewinsky. The main question asked by some is whether an unpaid intern should be considered an equal to the president in agreeing to "consensual" sex. The issue of defining consensual sex when there are power differences among the participants is not confined to the university or the White House, however. It also arises in the factory and the office.

In concluding this discussion, we would like to point out that sexual harassment is about power. It's about an individual controlling or threatening another individual. It's wrong. Moreover, it's illegal. You can understand how sexual harassment surfaces in organizations if you analyze it in power terms. We should also point out that sexual harassment is not something that is only done by men, to women. There have been several cases of males reporting harassment by male managers; for example, in May 1999 the U.S. Equal Employment Opportunity Commission ordered a Ford car dealership in Boston, Massachusetts, to pay $125 000 US to four salesmen who claimed they were sexually harassed by their male sales manager.[35] While there have been no media reports of women sexually harassing either men or women in Canada, under the framework of the law, it is certainly feasible. This chapter's HR Implications starting on page 359 explores further issues of sexual harassment in the workplace.

**U.S. Equal Employment Opportunity Commission**
www.eeoc.gov

## Sexual Harassment in an International Context

Policies governing sexual harassment are not uniformly agreed upon around the world. While Canada and the United States have relatively similar policies, significant differences arise in other countries. For example, though the North American automobile industry is still predominantly male (as we note in the HR Implications feature), a North American firm would not print and distribute a calendar of nude women to its clients, as is done by tiremaker Pirelli SpA of Italy.[36]

**Pirelli SpA**
www.it.pirelli.com/it/index.html

**Mitsubishi Motors**
www.mitsubishicars.com

Italy is not alone in its differences from North America in this regard. Japan, for instance, does not have laws regarding sexual harassment. Mayumi Makita, an editor of *Femin*, a Japanese magazine published by the rights group Women's Democratic Club, says that "Japanese companies do not treat women as proper workers and they do not care about sexual harassment."[37] This has led to problems when Japanese companies have set up business in North America. For instance, Mitsubishi Motors Corp. of America settled one lawsuit with 27 women in August 1997. A second well-publicized sexual harassment suit, filed in April 1996 and involving about 300 women, was settled in June 1998 for US $34 million, more than three times the amount of any other harassment case ever settled in the United States. The women who are part of the claim will receive payments according to the extent of the

**Husky Oil**
www.husky-oil.com

harassment suffered. Those who suffered the most extensive harassment could receive up to US $300 000.

Closer to home, a report in *Canadian Business* suggested that Calgary-based Husky Oil Company's problems with sexual harassment stem from the mixed cultures of being based in Canada with a more progressive and relatively democratic culture, but being run by CEO John Chin-Sung Lau, a Hong Kong native who governs with a more "Chinese, paternalistic, and strictly authoritarian" style.[38] Consequently, when women from Husky first complained of sexual harassment in the workplace, Lau ignored them, as sexual harassment does not receive the same legal sanctions in Hong Kong. Lower management simply followed his cue and also ignored the complaints. Eventually, after more complaints of sexual harassment arose in the mid-1990s, the management structure was changed, says CEO Lau. "All the previous difficulties are gone, Husky is different now. We have to treat humans right. World standards are changing. If we don't do it, we'll be out of style."[39] Both the Husky and Mitsubishi examples illustrate the problems of doing business in other countries, where values may be different from one's own.

## Politics: Power in Action

When people get together in groups, power will be exerted. People want to carve out a niche from which to exert influence, to earn awards, and to advance their careers.[40] When employees in organizations convert their power into action, we describe them as being engaged in politics. Those with good political skills have the ability to use their bases of power effectively.[41] Political skills aren't confined to adults, of course. When your Vancouver author's six-year-old nephew wanted Game Boy Color knowing full well his parents didn't approve, he waged a careful, deliberate campaign to wear them down, explaining how he would use the toy only at assigned times, etc. His politicking paid off: within six weeks he succeeded in getting the toy.

### Definition

There has been no shortage of definitions for organizational politics. One clever definition of politics comes from Tom Jakobek, Toronto's former budget chief, who said "In politics, you may have to go from A to C to D to E to F to G and then to B."[42]

**political behaviour**
Those activities that are not required as part of one's formal role in the organization, but that influence, or attempt to influence, the distribution of advantages and disadvantages within the organization.

For our purposes, we will define **political behaviour** in organizations as those activities that are not required as part of one's formal role in the organization, but that influence, or attempt to influence, the distribution of advantages and disadvantages within the organization.[43]

This definition encompasses key elements from what most people mean when they talk about organizational politics. Political behaviour is *outside* one's specified job requirements. The behaviour requires some attempt to use one's *power* bases. Additionally, our definition encompasses efforts to influence the goals, criteria, or processes used for *decision making* when we state that politics is concerned with "the distribution of advantages and disadvantages within the organization." Our definition is broad enough to include such varied political behaviours as withholding key information from decision makers, whistleblowing, spreading rumours, leaking confidential information about organizational activities to the media, exchanging favours with others in the organization for mutual benefit, and lobbying on behalf of or against a particular individual or decision alternative. Exhibit 8-6 provides a quick measure to help you assess how political your workplace is.

A final comment relates to what has been referred to as the "legitimate-illegitimate" dimension in political behaviour.[44] **Legitimate political behaviour** refers to normal everyday politics — complaining to your manager, bypassing the chain of command, forming coalitions, obstructing organizational policies or decisions through inaction or excessive adherence to rules, and developing contacts outside the organization through one's professional activities.

**legitimate political behaviour**
Normal everyday politics.

---

### Exhibit 8-6
### A Quick Measure of How Political Your Workplace Is

How political is your workplace? Answer the 12 questions using the following scale:

SD = Strongly disagree
D = Disagree
U = Uncertain
A = Agree
SA = Strongly agree

1. Managers often use the selection system to hire only people who can help them in their future. _____

2. The rules and policies concerning promotion and pay are fair; it is how managers carry out the policies that is unfair and self-serving. _____

3. The performance ratings people receive from their managers reflect more of the managers' "own agenda" than the actual performance of the employee. _____

4. Although a lot of what my manager does around here appears to be directed at helping employees, it is actually intended to protect my manager. _____

5. There are cliques or "in-groups" that hinder effectiveness around here. _____

6. My co-workers help themselves, not others. _____

7. I have seen people deliberately distort information requested by others for purposes of personal gain, either by withholding it or by selectively reporting it. _____

8. If co-workers offer to lend some assistance, it is because they expect to get something out of it. _____

9. Favouritism rather than merit determines who gets ahead around here. _____

10. You can usually get what you want around here if you know the right person to ask. _____

11. Overall, the rules and policies concerning promotion and pay are specific and well-defined. _____

12. Pay and promotion policies are generally clearly communicated in this organization. _____

This questionnaire taps the three salient dimensions that have been found to be related to perceptions of politics: manager behaviour; co-worker behaviour; and organizational policies and practices. To calculate your score for items 1-10, give yourself 1 point for Strongly disagree; 2 points for Disagree; and so forth (through 5 points for Strongly agree). For items 11 and 12, reverse the score (that is, 1 point for Strongly agree, etc.). Sum up the total: the higher the total score, the greater degree of perceived organizational politics.

Source: G.R. Ferris, D.D. Frink, D.P.S. Bhawuk, J. Zhou, and D.C. Gilmore, "Reactions of Diverse Groups to Politics in the Workplace," *Journal of Management,* vol. 22, no. 1, 1996, pp. 32-33.

**illegitimate political behaviours**
Extreme political behaviours that violate the implied rules of the game.

On the other hand, there are also **illegitimate political behaviours** that violate the implied rules of the game. Those who pursue such extreme activities are often described as individuals who "play hardball." Illegitimate activities include sabotage, whistleblowing, and symbolic protests, such as wearing unconventional clothes or protest buttons, and groups of employees simultaneously calling in sick.

The vast majority of all organizational political actions are of the legitimate variety. The reasons are pragmatic: The extreme illegitimate forms of political behaviour pose a very real risk of loss of organizational membership or extreme sanctions against those who use them and then fall short in having enough power to ensure that they work. Now that you have learned a bit about political behaviour, you may want to assess your own political behaviour in our Learning About Yourself Exercise on page 364.

## The Reality of Politics

Politics is a fact of life inside organizations. People who ignore this fact of life do so at their own peril. Why, you may wonder, must politics exist? Isn't it possible for an organization to be politics free? It's *possible*, but most unlikely. Organizations are made up of individuals and groups with different values, goals, and interests.[45] This sets up the potential for conflict over resources. Departmental budgets, space allocations, project responsibilities, and salary adjustments are just a few examples of the resources about whose allocation organizational members will disagree.

Resources in organizations are also limited, which often turns potential conflict into real conflict. If resources were abundant, then all the various constituencies within the organization could satisfy their goals. Because they are limited, not everyone's interests can be provided for. Furthermore, whether true or not, gains by one individual or group are often *perceived* as being at the expense of others within the organization. These forces create a competition among members for the organization's limited resources.

Maybe the most important factor leading to politics within organizations is the realization that most of the "facts" that are used to allocate the limited resources are open to interpretation. What, for instance, is *good* performance? What's an *adequate* improvement? What constitutes an *unsatisfactory* job? One person's view that an act is a "selfless effort to benefit the organization" is seen by another as a "blatant attempt to further one's interest."[46] The manager of any major law firm knows that a legal secretary who types 100 words a minute is a high performer and one who types 35 words a minute is a poor performer. But what if you have to choose between a legal secretary who types 100 words a minute and one who types 90 words a minute? Then other factors — less objective ones — come into play: attitude, potential, ability to perform under pressure, loyalty to the firm, and so on. More managerial decisions resemble choosing between a 90-word and a 100-word typist than deciding between a 35-word and a 100-word typist. It is in this large and ambiguous middle ground of organizational life — where the facts *don't* speak for themselves — that politics flourish.

Finally, because most decisions must be made in a climate of ambiguity — where facts are rarely fully objective, and thus are open to interpretation — people within organizations will use whatever influence they can to taint the facts to support their goals and interests. That, of course, creates the activities we call *politicking*. For more about how one engages in politicking, see the From Concepts to Skills feature.

# From CONCEPTS to SKILLS

# Politicking

Forget, for a moment, the ethics of politicking and any negative impressions you may have of people who engage in organizational politics. If you wanted to be more politically adept in your organization, what could you do? The following eight suggestions are likely to improve your political effectiveness.

1. *Frame arguments in terms of organizational goals.* Effective politicking requires camouflaging your self-interest. No matter that your objective is self-serving; all the arguments you marshal in support of it must be framed in terms of the benefits that will accrue to the organization. People whose actions appear to blatantly further their own interests at the expense of the organization's are almost universally denounced, are likely to lose influence, and often suffer the ultimate penalty of being expelled from the organization.

2. *Develop the right image.* If you know your organization's culture, you understand what the organization wants and values from its employees — in terms of dress; associates to cultivate, and those to avoid; whether to appear risk-taking or risk-aversive; the preferred leadership style; the importance placed on getting along well with others, and so forth. Then you are equipped to project the appropriate image. Because the assessment of your performance is not a fully objective process, both style and substance must be addressed.

3. *Gain control of organizational resources.* The control of organizational resources that are scarce and important is a source of power. Knowledge and expertise are particularly effective resources to control. They make you more valuable to the organization and, therefore, more likely to gain security, advancement, and a receptive audience for your ideas.

4. *Make yourself appear indispensable.* Because we're dealing with appearances rather than objective facts, you can enhance your power by appearing to be indispensable. That is, you don't have to really be indispensable as long as key people in

the organization believe that you are. If the organization's prime decision makers believe there is no ready substitute for what you are giving the organization, they are likely to go to great lengths to ensure that your desires are satisfied.

5. *Be visible.* Because performance evaluation has a substantial subjective component, it's important that your manager and those in power in the organization be made aware of your contribution. If you are fortunate enough to have a job that brings your accomplishments to the attention of others, it may not be necessary to take direct measures to increase your visibility. But your job may require you to handle activities that are low in visibility, or your specific contribution may be indistinguishable because you're part of a team endeavour. In such cases — *without appearing to be tooting your own horn or creating the image of a braggart* — you'll want to call attention to yourself by highlighting your successes in routine reports, having satisfied customers relay their appreciation to senior executives in your organization, being seen at social functions, being active in your professional associations, developing powerful allies who speak positively about your accomplishments, and similar tactics. Of course, the skilled politician actively and successfully lobbies to get those projects that will increase his or her visibility.

6. *Develop powerful allies.* It helps to have powerful people in your camp. Cultivate contacts with potentially influential people above you, at your own level, and in the lower ranks. They can provide you with important information that may not be available through normal channels. Additionally, there will be times when decisions will be made in favour of those with the greatest support. Having powerful allies can provide you with a coalition of support if and when you need it.

7. *Avoid "tainted" members.* In almost every organization, there are fringe members whose status is questionable. Their performance and/or loyalty is

suspect. Keep your distance from such individuals. Given the reality that effectiveness has a large subjective component, your own effectiveness might be called into question if you're perceived as being too closely associated with tainted members.

8. *Support your manager.* Your immediate future is in the hands of your current manager. Since he or she evaluates your performance, you will typically want to do whatever is necessary to have your manager on your side. You should make every effort to help your manager succeed, make her look good, support her if she is under siege, and spend the time to find out what criteria she will be using to assess your effectiveness. Don't undermine your manager, and don't speak negatively of her to others.

Source: S.P. Robbins and P.L. Hunsaker, *Training in Interpersonal Skills: Tips for Managing People at Work*, 2<sup>nd</sup> ed. (Upper Saddle River, NJ: Prentice Hall, 1996), pp. 131-134.

Therefore, to answer the earlier question of whether it is possible for an organization to be politics free, we can say "yes" if all members of that organization hold the same goals and interests, if organizational resources are not scarce, and if performance outcomes are completely clear and objective. However, that doesn't describe the organizational world that most of us live in! The debate about the importance of politics continues in this chapter's Point/CounterPoint feature on pages 350-351. Politics can also cross organizational boundaries.

## Factors Contributing to Political Behaviour

| Why do some people seem to engage in politics more than others? |

Not all groups or organizations are equally political. In some organizations, for instance, politicking is overt and rampant, while in others, politics plays a small role in influencing outcomes. Why is there this variation? Recent research and observation have identified a number of factors that appear to encourage political behaviour. Some are individual characteristics, derived from the unique qualities of the people the organization employs; others are a result of the organization's culture or internal environment. Exhibit 8-7 illustrates how both individual and organizational factors can increase political behaviour and provide favourable outcomes (increased rewards and averted punishments) for both individuals and groups in the organization.

**INDIVIDUAL FACTORS** At the individual level, researchers have identified certain personality traits, needs, and other factors that are likely to be related to political behaviour. In terms of traits, we find that employees who are high self-monitors, who possess an internal locus of control, and who have a high need for power are more likely to engage in political behaviour.[47]

The high self-monitor is more sensitive to social cues, exhibits higher levels of social conformity, and is more likely to be skilled in political behaviour than the low self-monitor. Individuals with an internal locus of control, because they believe they can control their environment, are more prone to take a proactive stance and attempt to manipulate situations in their favour. You may remember our discussion of machiavellianism in Chapter 2. Not surprisingly, the machiavellian personality — which is char-

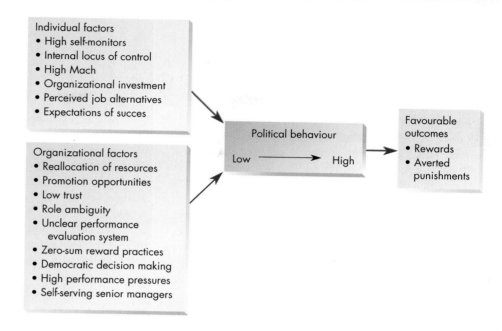

**Exhibit 8-7**
**Factors Influencing Political Behaviour**

Individual factors
- High self-monitors
- Internal locus of control
- High Mach
- Organizational investment
- Perceived job alternatives
- Expectations of succes

Organizational factors
- Reallocation of resources
- Promotion opportunities
- Low trust
- Role ambiguity
- Unclear performance evaluation system
- Zero-sum reward practices
- Democratic decision making
- High performance pressures
- Self-serving senior managers

Political behaviour

Low ⟶ High

Favourable outcomes
- Rewards
- Averted punishments

acterized by the will to manipulate and the desire for power — is comfortable using politics as a means to further his or her self-interest.

Additionally, an individual's investment in the organization, perceived alternatives, and expectations of success will influence the degree to which he or she will pursue illegitimate means of political action.[48] The more that a person has invested in the organization in terms of expectations of increased future benefits, the more a person has to lose if forced out and the less likely he or she is to use illegitimate means. The more alternative job opportunities an individual has — due to a favourable job market or the possession of scarce skills or knowledge, a prominent reputation, or influential contacts outside the organization — the more likely he or she is to risk illegitimate political actions. Finally, if an individual has a low expectation of success in using illegitimate means, it is unlikely that he or she will attempt to do so. High expectations of success in the use of illegitimate means are most likely to be the province of both experienced and powerful individuals with polished political skills and inexperienced and naive employees who misjudge their chances.

**ORGANIZATIONAL FACTORS** Political activity is probably more a function of the organization's characteristics than of individual difference variables. Why? Many organizations have a large number of employees with the individual characteristics we listed, yet the extent of political behaviour varies widely.

Although we acknowledge the role that individual differences can play in fostering politicking, the evidence more strongly supports that certain situations and cultures promote politics. More specifically, when an organization's resources are declining, when the existing pattern of resources is changing, and when there is opportunity for promotions, politics is more likely to surface.[49] In addition, cultures characterized by low trust, role ambiguity, unclear

# POINT

# It's a Political Jungle Out There!

Nick is a talented television camera operator. He has worked on a number of popular television shows over a 10-year period, but he has had trouble keeping those jobs. While most other camera operators and production employees are rehired from one season to the next, Nick seems never to be called back for a second year. It isn't that Nick isn't competent. Quite the contrary, his technical knowledge and formal education are typically more impressive than those of the directors he works for. Nick's problem is that he frequently disagrees with the camera angles that directors want him to set up, and he has no qualms about expressing his displeasure to those directors. He also feels some need to offer unsolicited suggestions to directors and producers on how to improve camera placements and shots.

Ellen is also a camera operator. Like Nick, Ellen sees directors and producers regularly making decisions that she doesn't agree with. But Ellen holds her tongue and does what she's told. She recently finished her third straight year as the lead camera operator on one of Canada's most successful comedies.

Ellen gets it. Nick doesn't. Nick has failed to recognize the reality that organizations are political systems. While Ellen is secure in her job, Nick's career continues to suffer because of his political naivete.

It would be nice if all organizations or formal groups within organizations could be described as supportive, harmonious, objective, trusting, collaborative, or cooperative. A nonpolitical perspective can lead one to believe that employees will always behave in ways consistent with the interests of the organization, and that competence and high performance will always be rewarded. In contrast, a political view can explain much of what may seem to be irrational behaviour in organizations. It can help to explain, for instance, why employees withhold information, restrict output, attempt to "build empires," publicize their successes, hide their failures, distort performance figures to make themselves look better, and engage in similar activities that appear to be at odds with the organization's desire for effectiveness and efficiency.

For those who want tangible evidence that "it's a political jungle out there" in the real world, let's look at two studies. The first analyzed what it takes to get promoted fast in organizations. The second addressed the performance appraisal process.

Fred Luthans and his associates[1] studied more than 450 managers. They found that these managers engaged in four managerial activities: traditional management (decision making, planning, and controlling), communication (exchanging routine information and processing paperwork), human resource management (motivating, disciplining, managing conflict, staffing, and training), and networking (socializing, politicking, and interacting with outsiders). Those managers who were promoted fastest spent 48 percent of their time networking. The average managers spent most of their efforts on traditional management and communication activities, and only 19 percent of their time networking. We suggest that this provides strong evidence of the importance that social and political skills play in getting ahead in organizations.

Longenecker and his associates[2] held in-depth interviews with 60 upper-level executives to find out what went into performance ratings. They found that executives frankly admitted to deliberately manipulating formal appraisals for political purposes. Accuracy was not a primary concern of these executives. Rather, they manipulated the appraisal results in an intentional and systematic manner to get the outcomes they wanted.

Sources

[1] F. Luthans, R.M. Hodgetts, and S.A. Rosenkrantz, *Real Managers* (Cambridge, MA: Ballinger, 1988).

[2] C.O. Longenecker, D.A. Gioia, and H.P. Sims, Jr., "Behind the Mask: The Politics of Employee Appraisal," *Academy of Management Executive*, August 1987, pp. 183-194.

# Corporate Politics:
# What You See Is What You Get!

Organizational behaviour currently appears to be undergoing a period of fascination with workplace politics. Proponents argue that politics is inevitable in organizations — that power struggles, alliance formations, strategic manoeuvrings, and cutthroat actions are as endemic to organizational life as work schedules and meetings. But is organizational politics inevitable? Maybe not. The existence of politics may be a perceptual interpretation.[1]

A recent study suggests that politics are more myth and interpretation than reality.[2] In this study of 180 experienced managers, 92 men and 88 women completed questionnaires. They analyzed a series of decisions and indicated the degree to which they thought the decisions were influenced by politics. They also completed a measure that assessed political inevitability. This included items such as "Politics is a normal part of any decision making process," and "Politics can have as many helpful outcomes for the organizations as harmful ones." Additionally, the questionnaire asked respondents their beliefs about power and control in the world at large. Finally, respondents provided data on their income, job responsibilities, and years of managerial experience.

The study found that beliefs about politics affected how respondents perceived organizational events. Those managers who held strong beliefs in the inevitability of politics tended to see their own organization and the decision situations in the questionnaire in highly political terms. Moreover, there was evidence suggesting that these beliefs encompass not only beliefs about politics but also about power and control in the world at large. Managers who viewed the world as posing difficult and complex problems and ruled by luck also tended to perceive events as highly politicized. That is, they perceived organizations as part of a disorderly and unpredictable world where politics is inevitable.

Interestingly, not *all* managers viewed organizations as political jungles. It was typically the inexperienced managers, with lower incomes and more limited responsibilities, who held this view. The researchers concluded that because junior managers often lack clear understandings of how organizations really work, they tend to interpret events as irrational. It's through their attempts to make sense of their situations that these junior managers may come to make political attributions.

This study attempted to determine whether the corporate political jungle is myth, reality, or a matter of interpretation. The popular press often presents the political jungle as the dominant corporate reality where gamesmanship and manipulation are key to survival. However, the findings of this study suggest that a manager's political reality is somewhat mythical in nature, partially constructed through his or her beliefs about politics' inevitability and about power and control in the world. More specifically, it's the inexperienced managers — those who are likely to hold the fewest and least accurate interpretations of organizational events — who perceive the extent of organizational politics to be greatest.

So if there is a corporate political jungle, it appears to be mostly in the eyes of the young and inexperienced. Because they tend to have less understanding of organizational processes and less power to influence outcomes, they are more likely to see organizations through a political lens. More experienced and higher-ranking managers, on the other hand, are more likely to see the corporate political jungle as a myth.

Sources:

[1] See, for instance, C.P. Parker, R.L. Dipboye, and S.L. Jackson, "Perceptions of Organizational Politics: An Investigation of Antecedents and Consequences," *Journal of Management*, vol. 21, no. 5, 1995, pp. 891-912; and G.R. Ferris, D.D. Frink, M.C. Galang, J. Zhou, K.M. Kacmar, and J.L. Howard, "Perceptions of Organizational Politics: Prediction, Stress-Related Implications, and Outcomes," *Human Relations*, February 1996, pp. 233-266.

[2] Cited in C. Kirchmeyer, "The Corporate Political Jungle: Myth, Reality, or a Matter of Interpretation," in C. Harris and C.C. Lundberg (eds.), *Proceedings of the 29th Annual Eastern Academy of Management* (Baltimore, 1992), pp. 161-164.

performance evaluation systems, zero-sum reward allocation practices, democratic decision making, high pressures for performance, and self-serving senior managers will create breeding grounds for politicking.[50]

When organizations downsize to improve efficiency, such as happened throughout much of the 1990s, reductions in resources have to be made. Threatened with the loss of resources, people may engage in political actions to safeguard what they have. Any changes, especially those that imply significant reallocation of resources within the organization, are likely to stimulate conflict and increase politicking.

Promotion decisions have consistently been found to be one of the most political arenas in organizations. The opportunity for promotions or advancement encourages people to compete for a limited resource and to try to positively influence the decision outcome.

The less trust there is within the organization, the higher the level of political behaviour and the more likely that the political behaviour will be of the illegitimate kind. High trust should suppress the level of political behaviour in general and inhibit illegitimate actions in particular.

Role ambiguity means that the prescribed behaviours of the employee are unclear. There are fewer limits, therefore, to the scope and functions of the employee's political actions. Since political activities are defined as those not required as part of one's formal role, the greater the role ambiguity, the more one can engage in political activity with little chance of it being visible.

The practice of performance evaluation is far from a perfected science. The more that organizations use subjective criteria in the appraisal, emphasize a single outcome measure, or allow significant time to pass between the time of an action and its appraisal, the greater the likelihood that an employee can get away with politicking. Subjective performance criteria create ambiguity. The use of a single outcome measure encourages individuals to do whatever is necessary to "look good" on that measure, but often at the expense of performing well on other important parts of the job that are not being appraised. The amount of time that elapses between an action and its appraisal is also a relevant factor. The longer the time period, the more unlikely that the employee will be held accountable for his or her political behaviours.

President and CEO Aris Kaplanis of Toronto-based Teranet Land Information Services, a high-tech firm, discourages negative office politics by his employees. The company employs the golden rule of "do unto others as you would have others do unto you." He tells his employees, "If you're here to play a game, you're in the wrong business."

The more that an organization's culture emphasizes the zero-sum or win-lose approach to reward allocations, the more employees will be motivated to engage in politicking. The zero-sum approach treats the reward "pie" as fixed so that any gain one person or group achieves has to come at the expense of another person or group. If I win, you must lose! If $10 000 in annual raises is to be distributed among five employees, then any employee who receives more than $2000 takes money away from one or more of the others. Such a practice encourages making others look bad and increasing the visibility of what you do.

In the last 25 years, there has been a general move in North America and among most developed nations toward making organizations less autocratic. Managers in these organizations are being asked to behave more democratically. They're told that they should allow employees to advise them on decisions and that they should rely more on group input into the decision process. Such moves toward democracy, however, are not necessarily embraced by all individual managers. Many managers sought their positions in order to have legitimate power so as to be able to make unilateral decisions. They fought hard and often paid high personal costs to achieve their influential positions. Sharing their power with others runs directly against their desires. The result is that managers, especially those who began their careers in the 1960s and 1970s, may use the required committees, conferences, and group meetings in a superficial way, as arenas for manoeuvring and manipulating.

The more pressure that employees feel to perform well, the more likely they are to engage in politicking. When people are held strictly accountable for outcomes, this puts great pressure on them to "look good." If a person perceives that his or her entire career is riding on next quarter's sales figures or next month's plant productivity report, there is motivation to do whatever is necessary to ensure that the numbers come out favourably.

Finally, when employees see the people on top engaging in political behaviour, especially when they do so successfully and are rewarded for it, a climate is created that supports politicking. Politicking by top management, in a sense, gives permission to those lower in the organization to play politics by implying that such behaviour is acceptable.

## Making Office Politics Work

**Fast Company Magazine**
www.fastcompany.com

The reason that office politics occurs is that people with different interests are trying to get their interests heard, in the hopes that their view will win. We discussed different negotiation strategies in Chapter 7, including a "win-lose" strategy, which means if I win, you lose, and a "win-win" strategy, which means creating situations where both of us can win. Suppose you have something that you would like to see carried out in your organization. Is there an effective way to engage in office politics that is less likely to be disruptive or negative? *Fast Company*, an online business magazine, identifies several rules that may help to improve the climate of the organization while negotiating through the office politics maze: [51]

- *Nobody wins unless everybody wins.* The most successful proposals look for ways to acknowledge, if not include, the interests of others. This requires building support for your ideas across the organization. "Real political skill isn't about campaign tactics," says Lou Di Natale, a veteran political consultant at the University of Massachusetts. "It's about pulling people toward your ideas and then pushing those ideas through to other people." When ideas are packaged to look like they're best for the organization as a whole and will help others, it is harder for others to counteract your proposal.

- *Don't just ask for opinions — change them.* It is helpful to find out what people think and then, if necessary, set out to change their opinions so that they can see what you want to do. It is also important to seek out the opinions of those you don't know well, or who are less

General Electric wants its managers to share their power with employees. GE is breaking down autocratic barriers between labour and management that "cramp people, inhibit creativity, waste time, restrict visions, smother dreams, and above all, slow things down." GE expects managers to behave more democratically by fostering teamwork and rewarding employees who suggest ideas for improvement. This photo illustrates GE's move toward democracy, as a manager at the company's plant in Louisville, Kentucky, and an employee work together to improve the plant's profitability.

**General Electric Canada**
www.ge.com/canada

likely to agree with you. Gathering together people who always support you is often not enough to build an effective coalition.

- *Everyone expects to be paid back.* In organizations, as in life, we develop personal relationships with those around us. And it is those personal relationships that affect much of the behaviour in organizations. By building good relationships with colleagues, supporting them in their endeavours, and showing appreciation for what they accomplish, you are building a foundation of support for your own ideas.

- *Success can create opposition.* As part of the office politics, success can be viewed as a "win-lose" strategy, which we identified above. Some people may feel that your success either gets you a higher profile, or that it means a project of theirs will be received less favourably. You have to be prepared to deal with this opposition.

## Impression Management

We know that people and organizations have an ongoing interest in how others perceive and evaluate them. For example, North Americans spend billions of dollars on diets, health-club memberships, cosmetics, and plastic surgery — all intended to make them more attractive to others.[52] Organizations spend billions on getting people to believe they are more socially conscious, more ethical, more quality concerned than their competitors. You should return to the opening vignette to see if you can identify possible impression management behaviours by the participants in the Whitbread Award story.

Being perceived positively by others should have benefits for people in organizations. It might, for instance, help them initially to get the jobs they want in an organization and, once hired, to get favourable evaluations, superior salary increases, and more rapid promotions. In a political context, it might help sway the distribution of advantages in their favour.

This process by which individuals attempt to control the impression others form of them is called **impression management (IM)**.[53]

Impression management is more likely to be used by high self-monitors than low self-monitors.[54] Low self-monitors tend to present images of themselves that are consistent with their personalities, regardless of the beneficial or detrimental effects for them. In contrast, high self-monitors are skilled at reading situations and moulding their appearances and behaviour to fit each situation.

Given that you want to control the impression others form of you, what techniques could you use? Exhibit 8-8 summarizes some of the more popular IM techniques and provides an example of each.

Keep in mind that IM does not imply that the impressions people convey are necessarily false (although, of course, they sometimes are).[55] Excuses and acclamations, for instance, may be offered with sincerity. Referring to the examples used in Exhibit 8-8, you can *actually* believe that ads contribute little to sales in your region or that you are the key to the tripling of your division's sales. But misrepresentation can have a high cost. If the image claimed is false, you may be discredited.[56] If you "cry wolf" once too often, no one is likely to believe you when the wolf really comes. The impression manager must be cautious not to be perceived as insincere or manipulative.[57]

Are there *situations* where individuals are more likely to misrepresent themselves or more likely to get away with it? Yes — situations that are characterized by high uncertainty or ambiguity.[58] These situations provide relatively little information for challenging a fraudulent claim and reduce the risks associated with misrepresentation.

A number of studies have examined the effectiveness of IM techniques in a variety of work situations. Studies show that IM behaviour is positively associated with job-interview success.[59]

For instance, one study found that recent university graduates who used more self-promotion tactics got higher evaluations by interviewers and more follow-up job-site visits, even after adjusting for grade point average, gender, and job type.[60] Other studies have found that those using IM techniques received better performance evaluations from their managers,[61] were liked more by their managers,[62] and criticized less.[63] IM effects seem to work more strongly when the measures of performance are subjective, however, than when they can be measured more objectively.[64] For instance those using IM techniques were rated more highly for interpersonal effectiveness, but they could be more negatively evaluated on their business competence.[65] Overall, the findings of these studies suggest that there is some advantage to engaging in IM, as long as the person delivers on the objective measures of performance as well. And for those who intend to become leaders, engaging in impression management techniques makes it more likely that you will be chosen.[66]

---

**impression management**
The process by which individuals attempt to control the impression others form of them.

---

Have you wondered whether impression management works?

---

**Exhibit 8-8**
**Impression Management (IM) Techniques**

**Conformity**

Agreeing with someone else's opinion in order to gain his or her approval.

*Example:* A manager tells his boss, "You're absolutely right on your reorganization plan for the western regional office. I couldn't agree with you more."

**Excuses**

Explanations of a predicament-creating event aimed at minimizing the apparent severity of the predicament.

*Example:* Sales manager to boss, "We failed to get the ad in the paper on time, but no one responds to those ads anyway."

**Apologies**

Admitting responsibility for an undesirable event and simultaneously seeking to get a pardon for the action.

*Example:* Employee to boss, "I'm sorry I made a mistake on the report. Please forgive me."

**Acclamations**

Explanation of favourable events to maximize the desirable implications for oneself.

*Example:* A salesperson informs a peer, "The sales in our division have nearly tripled since I was hired."

**Flattery**

Complimenting others on their virtues in an effort to make oneself appear perceptive and likeable.

*Example:* New sales trainee to peer, "You handled that client's complaint so tactfully! I could never have handled that as well as you did."

**Favours**

Doing something nice for someone to gain that person's approval.

*Example:* Salesperson to prospective client, "I've got two tickets to the theatre tonight that I can't use. Take them. Consider it a thank you for taking the time to talk with me."

**Association**

Enhancing or protecting one's image by managing information about people and things with which one is associated.

*Example:* A job applicant says to an interviewer, "What a coincidence. Your boss and I were roommates in university."

---

Sources: Based on B.R. Schlenker, *Impression Management* (Monterey, CA: Brooks/Cole, 1980); W.L. Gardner and M.J. Martinko, "Impression Management in Organizations," *Journal of Management,* June 1988, p. 332; and R.B. Cialdini, "Indirect Tactics of Image Management: Beyond Basking," in R.A. Giacalone and P. Rosenfeld (eds.), *Impression Management in the Organization* (Hillsdale, NJ: Lawrence Erlbaum Associates, 1989), pp. 45-71.

## Managing Emotions

Impression management focuses on how individuals strategically manage the impressions formed of them. But sometimes what individuals manage is actually their emotions. For instance, you may be very angry with a co-worker or manager, but you may choose to suppress that anger in the interest of keeping the peace and/or your job. You may also decide not to kiss a co-worker in a moment of overwhelming exuberance, to make sure that your intentions are not misinterpreted. Though the management of emotions in the workplace has only recently been studied, it is clear that organizations have a vested interest, at least sometimes, in making sure that their employees manage their emotions.

**emotional labour**
The requirement to express particular emotions at work to maximize organizational productivity.

As we have seen in Chapter 2, Arlie Hochschild first coined the term **emotional labour** to refer to the requirement to express particular emotions at work (for instance, enthusiasm or loyalty) to maximize organizational productivity.[67] Studies of emotional labour have explored how smiling flight attendants, cheerful grocery clerks, gossipy hairdressers, and nasty bill collectors are expected to control their emotional expression to improve productivity, customer satisfaction, efficiency, and even profitability.[68] As these studies show, however, managing emotions can take a toll when there is a discrepancy between the outward behaviour the person is required to display as part of his or her job and the inward feelings that the person has.

We may conclude from our discussion of impression management and emotional labour that these practices have positive implications within the workplace, at least under certain conditions. Yet they can also have negative personal consequences when a person consistently hides real emotions behind a work "face."[69] Flight attendants use the phrase "go robot" to describe how they separate their private feelings from their public behaviour.[70] Other researchers have discussed both the individual effects of emotional labour, such as distancing, burnout, and phoniness,[71] and the organizational effects, such as suppressed disagreements, reduced upward information flow, and loss of "voice".[72] A Vancouver Safeway employee described her company's requirement to smile at all shoppers: "My personal opinion is, they're expecting us not to be human. I just can't walk around with a smile on my face all day."[73]

## The Ethics of Behaving Politically

In Chapter 7 we described 360-degree feedback, noting that this was a method of providing feedback to an employee from a variety of people who had contact with that employee. However, this method of feedback can be affected by politics. For instance, one employee can say to another, "Give me high marks, and I'll give you high marks." Or, a person wanting to get even with someone else for some reason, may decide to retaliate through the 360-degree feedback. There are numerous other situations in the workplace where politics can affect outcomes as well.

We conclude our discussion of politics by providing some ethical guidelines for political behaviour. While there are no clear-cut ways to differentiate ethical from unethical politicking, there are some questions you should consider.

Exhibit 8-9 illustrates a decision tree to guide ethical actions.[74] This tree is built on the three ethical decision criteria—utilitarianism, rights, and justice—presented in Chapter 11. The first question you need to answer addresses self-interest vs. organizational goals. Ethical actions are consistent with the organization's goals. Spreading untrue rumours about the safety of a new product introduced by your company in order to make that product's design team look bad is unethical. However, there may be nothing unethical if a department head exchanges favours (for instance, offering to help with a report) with the division's purchasing manager in order to get a critical contract processed quickly.

The second question concerns the rights of other parties. If the department head described in the previous paragraph went down to the mailroom

## Exhibit 8-9
## Is a Political Action Ethical?

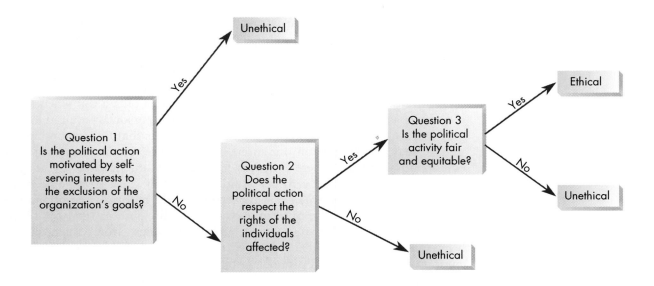

at lunch and read through the mail directed to the purchasing manager — with the intent of "getting something" that would force the purchasing manager to expedite the contract — the department head would be acting unethically, having violated the purchasing manager's right to privacy.

The final question that needs to be addressed relates to whether the political activity conforms to standards of equity and justice. The department head who inflates the performance evaluation of a favoured employee and deflates the evaluation of a disfavoured employee — and then uses these evaluations to justify giving the former a big raise and nothing to the latter — has treated the disfavoured employee unfairly.

Unfortunately, the answers to the questions in Exhibit 8-9 are often argued in ways to make unethical practices seem ethical. Powerful people, for example, can become very adept at explaining self-serving behaviours in terms of the organization's best interests. Similarly, they can persuasively argue that unfair actions are really fair and just. Our point is that immoral people can justify almost any behaviour. Those who are powerful, articulate, and persuasive are the most likely to be able to get away with unethical practices successfully. When faced with an ethical dilemma regarding organizational politics, try to answer the questions in Exhibit 8-9 truthfully. If you have a strong power base, recognize the ability of power to corrupt. Remember, it's a lot easier for the powerless to act ethically, if for no other reason than they typically have very little political discretion to exploit.

## HR Implications

# Dealing With Sexual Harassment in the Workplace

The Ontario Human Rights Commission reported in March 1998 that sexual harassment complaints have more than doubled over the past 10 years, from 106 complaints to 225.[1] In a poll conducted in British Columbia in April 1998, 39 percent of 400 women and 14 percent of 400 men said they'd experienced sexual harassment at work.[2] Below we review the legal aspects of sexual harassment, and then discuss how organizations are dealing with it in their workplaces.

### Sexual Harassment and Canadian Law

The Supreme Court of Canada defines **sexual harassment** as unwelcome behaviour of a sexual nature in the workplace that negatively affects the work environment or leads to adverse job-related consequences for the employee. In 1987, the Court ruled that employers will be held responsible for harassment by their employees. The Court also said the employer is in the best position to stop harassment and should promote a workplace that is free of it. The Court recommended that employers have clear guidelines to prevent harassment, which included procedures to investigate complaints.

Protection from sexual harassment is governed by human rights legislation, which prohibits discrimination on the basis of sex (and age, ethnic origin, race, disability, religion, and sexual orientation, among other things). At both the provincial/territorial and federal levels, these laws have been widely interpreted to mean both quid pro quo harassment involving exchange of sexual acts for job-related benefits, and a range of behaviours that create a hostile work environment for the person to whom the attention is directed. The Canadian Human Rights Act is currently under review, and one of the issues it will consider is overhauling the way it deals with these complaints, given that sexual harassment is still so prevalent in the workplace.[3] Typically sexual harassment complaints that are not resolved in the workplace are heard by a provincial or territorial human rights tribunal. However, in an effort to provide more venues for hearing sexual harassment complaints, the Ontario Labour Relations Board conceded in August 1997 that sexual harassment is a health and safety issue, and thus could be addressed by that board.[4] This may lead to other provinces making similar moves.

### Dealing With Sexual Harassment in the Workplace

Examples of several recent cases of sexual harassment can be used to illustrate procedures that organizations need to lessen its prevalence in the workplace. For instance, researchers representing Women in Trades and Technology interviewed a number of women who worked on the Hibernia offshore oil project based in Bull Arm, Newfoundland, in 1995. The women interviewed expressed concerns ranging from "not being allowed to do the heavy work they were trained and hired to do" to "degrading and sexual remarks made by male co-workers." The women reported being uncomfortable bringing the problems to their unions or management, and they received little support or help when they did. The researchers made a number of recommendations for both the Hibernia project, which has since been completed, as well as for future projects, such as the Terra Nova offshore oil development and the Voisey Bay nickel discovery in Labrador. These recommendations include the following:[5]

- developing formal avenues to consult with women about integrating into nontraditional jobs;
- planning work camps with the needs of women in mind;
- providing better on-site education about sexual harassment;
- creating an employment equity plan covering recruitment, training, and promotion.

In another example, Markham, Ontario-based Magna International Inc. is facing a sexual harassment suit in the United States, brought by a former saleswoman in the parts maker's Detroit sales office.[6] The woman alleges that she faced harassment in the office, and that her male co-workers regularly entertained customers at area strip clubs. One of the allegations in the complaint is that a Magna sales manager spent $23 000 in 1996 entertaining customers at strip joints and other bars and restaurants. Magna denies the charges and has issued a memo to customers and employees in the Detroit area that the company "does not tolerate any form of sexual discrimination or harassment."

However, auto industry executives and observers agree that the auto business remains male-dominated, and that some purchasing executives are entertained at strip clubs. Scott Upham, president of Providata Inc., an analyst firm located in Southgate, Michigan, said that entertaining this way "is less prevalent than it used to be. I used to work at suppliers where this sort of conduct was commonplace. There are certain customers who want to be entertained that way, just like some like to go to the ball game."

The Magna example raises questions for both employers and employees about appropriate client and customer relationships, particularly with both more women in the workplace and more women in the roles of clients and customers. Behaviour that might have once been tolerated because it was restricted to interactions between males is less tolerated in today's working environment.

Sears Canada faced a sexual harassment issue that turned into a murder-suicide at a Sears store in Chatham, Ontario. Theresa Vince, a human resources supervisor, was killed by her store manager, Russell Davis, on June 2, 1996. Davis, who'd been sexually harassing her, then turned the gun on himself. Davis was infatuated with Vince and continuously gave her praise and compliments. Vince complained to her regional human resources manager and confronted Davis with her objections. Though he apologized, the situation persisted. Even co-workers noticed the abnormal attention Davis paid to Vince. However, Vince rejected Sears Canada's recommendation that Davis be transferred, instead requesting that Sears Canada

not pursue Davis further. Sears honoured Vince's wishes. However, the harassment did not stop, and Vince decided to retire. She was killed on her last day on the job. This example raises the question of when and how an employer should become involved in a sexual harassment complaint.

A coroner's inquest into the murder-suicide released recommendations in December 1997 to various groups involved in dealing with sexual harassment in Ontario. These recommendations could equally apply to the other provinces and territories in Canada:[7]

*Employers*: Should have effective workplace harassment and discrimination policies and procedures in place. Confidential sources of help should be offered.

*Ontario Human Rights Commission*: Should develop an advertising campaign, encouraging victims to come forward with their complaints. The commission's services should be periodically reviewed by an outside audit.

*Ontario Ministry of Labour*: Should make a priority of the ongoing study of sexual harassment as a health and safety issue, so an informed decision about including it under labour legislation can be made.

*Province*: Should make funds available to the Human Rights Commission, allowing it to increase its investigation capabilities and "prevent cases from falling through the cracks.'"

Though sexual harassment is defined by the law, and there are procedures for dealing with it through human rights tribunals, organizations are still trying to define their own policies and procedures. Vancouver-based lawyer Heather MacKenzie notes that: "Companies have a direct financial interest in ensuring they have a comprehensive policy in place. The courts have said you also have to educate all members of the organization about how the policy works."[8]

Sources:

[1] J. Goddu, "Sexual Harassment Complaints Rise Dramatically," *Canadian Press Newswire*, March 6, 1998.

[2] M. Jimenez, "Sexual Harassment at Work Prevalent in B.C., Poll Shows," *Vancouver Sun*, May 4, 1998, pp. A1, A2.

[3] J. Tibbets, "Human Rights Agency Says Protection Laws at Standstill," *Canadian Press Newswire*, March 24, 1998; and C. Wittmeier, "Oppression Is Everywhere: The Canadian Human Rights Commission Targets New Forms of Discrimination," *British Columbia Report*, September 13, 1999, p. 42.

⁴ P. Arab, "Sexual Harassment Ruled a Workplace Safety Hazard," *Canadian Press Newswire*, August 22, 1997.

⁵ "Female Workers Mistreated at Hibernia, Study Says," *Plant*, September 2, 1996, p. 4.

⁶ Information in this paragraph based on I. Jack, "Magna Suit Spotlights Auto Industry Practices," *Financial Post Daily*, September 10, 1997, p. 1.

⁷ "Harassment Inquest Doesn't Go Far Enough, Say Critics," *Canadian Press Newswire*, December 2, 1997.

⁸ M. Jiminez, "Sexual Harassment at Work Prevalent in B.C., Poll Shows," *Vancouver Sun*, May 4, 1998, pp. A1, A2.

# *SUMMARY AND IMPLICATIONS*

## For the Workplace

If you want to get things done in a group or organization, it helps to have power. To maximize your power, you will want to increase others' dependence on you. You can, for instance, increase your power in relation to your employer by developing knowledge or a skill that he or she needs and for which there is no ready substitute. However, power is a two-way street. You will not be alone in attempting to build your power bases. Others, particularly employees and peers, will be seeking to make you dependent on them. The result is a continual battle. While you seek to maximize others' dependence on you, you will be seeking to minimize your dependence on others. And, of course, others you work with will be trying to do the same.

Few employees relish being powerless in their job and organization. It has been argued, for instance, that when people in organizations are difficult, argumentative, and temperamental, it may be because they are in positions of powerlessness where the performance expectations placed on them exceed their resources and capabilities.[75]

There is evidence that people respond differently to the various power bases.[76] Expert and referent power are derived from an individual's personal qualities. In contrast, coercion, reward, and legitimate power are essentially organizationally derived. Since people are more likely to enthusiastically accept and commit to an individual whom they admire or whose knowledge they respect (rather than someone who relies on his or her position to reward or coerce them), the effective use of expert and referent power should lead to higher employee performance, commitment, and satisfaction. Evidence indicates, for instance, that employees working under managers who use coercive power are unlikely to be committed to the organization and more likely to resist the managers' attempts at influence.[77] In contrast, expert power has been found to be the most strongly and consistently related to effective employee performance.[78] For example, in a study of five organizations, knowledge was the most effective base for getting others to perform as desired.[79] Competence appears to offer wide appeal, and its use as a power base results in high performance by group members. The message here for managers seems to be this: Develop and use your expert power base!

The power of your boss may also play a role in determining your job satisfaction. "One of the reasons many of us like to work for and with people who are powerful is that they are generally more pleasant — not because it is their native disposition, but because the reputation and reality of being powerful permits them more discretion and more ability to delegate to others."[80]

The effective manager accepts the political nature of organizations. By assessing behaviour in a political framework, you can better predict the actions of others and use this information to formulate political strategies that will gain advantages for you and your work unit.

We can only speculate at this time on whether or not organizational politics is positively related to *actual* performance. However, there seems to be ample evidence that good political skills are positively related to high performance evaluations and, hence, to salary increases and promotions.[81] We can comment more confidently on the relationship between politics and employee satisfaction.

In terms of office politics, we can report that the more political employees perceive an organization to be, the lower their satisfaction.[82] However, this conclusion must be moderated to reflect the employees' level in the organization.[83] Lower-ranking employees, who lack the power base and the means of influence needed to benefit from the political game, perceive organizational politics as a source of frustration and indicate lower satisfaction. But higher-ranking employees, who are in a better position to handle political behaviour and benefit from it, don't tend to exhibit this negative attitude.

A final thought on organizational politics: Regardless of level in the organization, some people are just significantly more "politically astute" than are others. Although there is little evidence to support or negate the following conclusion, it seems reasonable that the politically naive or inept are likely to exhibit lower job satisfaction than their politically astute counterparts. The politically naive and inept tend to feel continually powerless to influence those decisions that most affect them. They look at actions around them and are perplexed at why they are regularly "shafted" by colleagues, bosses, and "the system."

## For You as an Individual

Power and politics reveal themselves in a variety of ways, and not just in the workplace. Within volunteer organizations, and even in informal groups, some people seem to have more power than others. We identified some of the factors that lead to differences in power, including the amount of information one has, the kind of role one plays, and the scarcity of resources. In other words, there are ways to increase your power. In particular, you could acquire more knowledge about a situation and then use that information to help your group perform better on one of its projects.

We also discussed politicking, which involves getting others to understand and appreciate your ideas. We presented positive ways of doing this that may make you a more effective team member. In particular, building coalitions where everyone feels that decisions will be "win-win" creates a more productive environment than one where some people become upset at the thought that they have lost something.

**ROADMAP** *REMINDER*

In the previous chapter we considered communication, how firms can let employees know what is important, and how individuals can improve their communication. We also looked at conflict and negotiation. In this chapter we looked at the notion of power. Conflict is often the result of power struggles, and negotiation is part of the process of politics. We reminded you that leaders have power, but they are not the only people in the organization who hold power. The secretary to the president also wields considerable power, as he or she determines who will actually get to speak or meet with the boss. In the next chapter, we move towards a new theme, Part 4: Sharing the Organizational Vision, as we consider the topic of organizational culture.

## For Review

1. What is power? How do you get it?
2. Contrast power tactics with power bases. What are some of the key contingency variables that determine which tactic a power holder is likely to use?
3. Which of the 5 power bases lie with the individual? Which are derived from the organization?
4. State the general dependency postulate. What does it mean?
5. What creates dependency? Give an applied example.
6. What is a coalition? When is it likely to develop?
7. How are power and politics related?
8. Define political behaviour. Why is politics a fact of life in organizations?
9. What factors contribute to political activity?
10. Define sexual harassment. Who is most likely to harass an employee: A boss, a co-worker, or a subordinate?

## For Critical Thinking

1. Based on the information presented in this chapter, what would you do as a recent university graduate entering a new job to maximize your power and accelerate your career progress?
2. "Politics isn't inherently bad. It it merely a way to get things accomplished within organizations." Do you agree or disagree? Defend your position.
3. You're a sales representative for an international software company. After 4 excellent years, sales in your territory are off 30 percent this year. Describe 3 impression management techniques you might use to convince your manager that your sales record is better than one could hope under the circumstances.
4. "Sexual harassment should not be tolerated at the workplace." "Workplace romances are a natural occurrence in organizations." Are both of these statements true? Can they be reconciled?
5. Which impression management techniques have you used? What ethical implications, if any, are there in using impression management?

## LEARNING ABOUT YOURSELF EXERCISE

# How Political Are You?

To determine your political tendencies, please review the following statements. Check the answer that best represents your behaviour or belief, even if that particular behaviour or belief is not present all the time.

|  | True | False |
|---|---|---|
| 1. You should make others feel important through an open appreciation of their ideas and work. | _____ | _____ |
| 2. Because people tend to judge you when they first meet you, always try to make a good first impression. | _____ | _____ |
| 3. Try to let others do most of the talking, be sympathetic to their problems, and resist telling people that they are totally wrong. | _____ | _____ |
| 4. Praise the good traits of the people you meet and always give people an opportunity to save face if they are wrong or make a mistake. | _____ | _____ |
| 5. Spreading false rumours, planting misleading information, and backstabbing are necessary, if somewhat unpleasant, methods to deal with your enemies. | _____ | _____ |
| 6. Sometimes it is necessary to make promises that you know you will not or cannot keep. | _____ | _____ |
| 7. It is important to get along with everybody, even with those who are generally recognized as windbags, abrasive, or constant complainers. | _____ | _____ |
| 8. It is vital to do favours for others so that you can call in these IOUs at times when they will do you the most good. | _____ | _____ |
| 9. Be willing to compromise, particularly on issues that are minor to you but major to others. | _____ | _____ |
| 10. On controversial issues, it is important to delay or avoid your involvement if possible. | _____ | _____ |

Turn to page 634 for scoring directions and key.

Source: J.F. Byrnes, "The Political Behavior Inventory." With permission.

## WORKING WITH OTHERS EXERCISE

# Understanding Power Bases

**Step 1:** Your instructor will divide the class into groups of about 5 or 6 (making sure there are at least 5 groups). Each group will be assigned 1 of the following bases of power: (1) coercive; (2) reward; (3) legitimate; (4) expert; and (5) referent. Refer to your text for discussion of these terms.

**Step 2:** Each group is to develop a role play that highlights the use of the power assigned. The role play should be developed using the following scenario:

> You are the leader of a group that is trying to develop a Web site for a new client. One of your group members, who was assigned the task of researching and analyzing the Web sites of your client's competition, has twice failed to bring the analysis to scheduled meetings, even though the member knew the assignment was due. Consequently, your group is falling behind in getting the Web site developed. As leader of the group, you have decided to speak with this team member, and to use your specific brand of power to influence the individual's behaviour.

**Step 3:** Each group should select 1 person to play the group leader, and another to play the member who hasn't done the assignment. You have 10 minutes to prepare an influence plan.

**Step 4:** Each group will conduct its role play. In the event of multiple groups assigned the same power base, 1 of the groups may be asked to volunteer. While you are watching the other groups' role plays, try to put yourself in the place of the person being influenced, to see whether that type of influence would cause you to change your behaviour.

> Immediately after each role play, while the next one is being set up, you should pretend that you were the person being influenced, and then record your reaction using the questionnaire below. To do this, take out a sheet of paper and tear it into 5 pieces. At the top of each piece of paper write the type of influence that was used. Then write the letters A, B, C, and D in a column, and indicate which number on the scale reflects the influence attempt.

---

### REACTION TO INFLUENCE QUESTIONNAIRE

---

For each role play, think of yourself on the receiving end of the influence attempt described, and record your own reaction.

Type of power used _____

---

**A.** As a result of the influence attempt, I will ....

**definitely not comply**     1     2     3     4     5     **definitely comply**

---

**B.** Any change that does come about will be ....

**temporary**     1     2     3     4     5     **long-lasting**

*Continued on next page*

**C.** My own personal reaction is ....

resistant     **1**     **2**     **3**     **4**     **5**     acceptant

**D.** As a result of this influence attempt, my relationship with my group leader will probably be ....

worse     **1**     **2**     **3**     **4**     **5**     better

**Step 5:** For each influence type, 1 member of each group will take the pieces of paper from group members and calculate the average group score for each of the 4 questions. For efficiency, this should be done while the role plays are being conducted.

**Step 6:** Your instructor will collect the summaries from each group, and then lead a discussion based on these results.

**Step 7:** Discussion.

1. Which kind of influence is most likely to immediately result in the desired behaviour?

2. Which will have the most long-lasting effects?

3. What effect will using a particular base of power have on the ongoing relationship?

4. Which form of power will others find most acceptable? Least acceptable? Why?

5. Are there some situations where a particular type of influence strategy might be more effective than others?

This exercise was inspired by one in found in Judith R. Gordon, *Organizational Behavior,* 2nd ed. (Englewood Cliffs, NJ: Prentice Hall, 1992), pp. 499-502.

## INTERNET SEARCH EXERCISES

1. Locate a manufacturing company and a service-oriented company that have introduced empowerment into the workplace (do not use companies that are already identified in your text). Are there differences in either the way these companies introduced the technique, or in its outcome?

2. Review the makeup of the boards of directors in the current top 20 on the *Report on Business* list of corporations. Identify individuals who appear on 2 or more boards. Thinking in terms of power, explain why these specific individuals might have been chosen by their boards.

## CASE INCIDENT

# Damned If You Do; Damned If You Don't

Fran Gilson has spent 15 years with the Thompson Grocery Company, starting out as a part-time cashier and rising up through the ranks of the grocery store chain.* Today, at 34, she is a regional manager, overseeing seven stores and earning nearly $110 000 a year. About five weeks ago, she was contacted by an executive-search firm inquiring about her interest in the position of vice-president and regional manager for a national drugstore chain. The position would be responsible for more than 100 stores in five provinces. After two meetings with top executives at the drugstore chain, she was notified two days ago that she was one of two finalists for the job.

The only person at Thompson who knows this news is Fran's good friend and colleague, Ken Hamilton. Ken is director of finance for the grocery chain. "It's a dream job, with a lot more responsibility," Fran told Ken. "The pay is almost double what I earn here and I'd be their only female vice-president. The job would allow me to be a more visible role model for young women and give me a bigger voice in opening up doors for women and ethnic minorities in retailing management."

Since Fran wanted to keep the fact that she was looking at another job secret, she asked Ken, whom she trusted completely, to be one of her references. He promised to write a great recommendation for her. Fran made it very clear to the recruiter that Ken was the only person at Thompson who knew she was considering another job. She knew that if anyone heard she was talking to another company, it might seriously jeopardize her chances for promotion. It's against this backdrop that this morning's incident became more than just a question of sexual harassment. It became a full-blown ethical and political dilemma for Fran.

Jennifer Chung has been a financial analyst in Ken's department for five months. Fran met Jennifer through Ken and her impression of Jennifer is quite positive. In many ways, Jennifer strikes Fran as a lot like she was 10 years ago. This morning, Jennifer came into Fran's office. It was immediately evident that something was wrong. Jennifer was very nervous and uncomfortable, which was most unlike her. Jennifer said that about a month after she joined Thompson, Ken began making off-colour comments to her when they were alone. And from there the behaviour escalated further. Ken would leer at her, put his arm over her shoulder when they were reviewing reports, even pat her bum. Every time one of these occurrences happened, Jennifer would ask him to stop and not do it again, but it fell on deaf ears. Yesterday, Ken reminded Jennifer that her six-month probationary review was coming up. "He told me that if I didn't sleep with him that I couldn't expect a very favourable evaluation."

Jennifer said that she had come to Fran because she didn't know what to do or to whom to turn. "I came to you, Fran, because you're a friend of Ken's and the highest-ranking woman here. Will you help me?" Fran had never heard anything like this about Ken before, but neither did she have any reason to suspect that Jennifer was lying.

# Questions

1. Analyze Fran's situation in a purely legal sense.

2. Analyze Fran's dilemma in political terms.

3. Analyze Fran's situation in an ethical sense. What is the ethically right thing for her to do? Is that also the politically right thing to do?

4. If you were Fran, what would you do?

\* The identity of this organization and the people described are disguised for obvious reasons.

# You've Got the Power

Markham, Ontario-based Patriot Computer, founded in 1991 by twin brothers Mark and John Durst and Rob Chernenko, illustrates the changing nature of organizations in the 21st century. Patriot, calling itself "Canada's computer company," is a $50-million business—manufacturing everything from custom-designed personal computers to satellite television receivers.

Patriot thrives on a program of employee empowerment and mutual respect. As president and CEO Mark Durst notes, "If you treat your employees like dirt, you'll lose them." "At Patriot, employees are encouraged to think and act like entrepreneurs, and have fun," explains vice-president of sales John Durst.

Patriot's employee purchase plan was developed by one of Patriot's employees, who informed the twins that they could make more sales if their customers could prequalify for loans to purchase computers. Though the twins were sceptical that a financial backer could be found for such a plan, the employee was encouraged to see his plan through. As Mark Durst notes, it was the employee's initiative that made this happen, not the work of the Durst twins.

In 1995 two other Patriot employees created Aegis Manufacturing out of their idea to expand Patriot's assembly work to do the same for other firms. For the fiscal year ending in June 1997, Aegis had revenue of US $58 million, which was expected to double the following year. When the two employees approached the Durst twins about their idea, they were told that they could run the show if their idea worked. Patriot gave them 40 percent ownership in the new business.

Patriot's founders believe that employees must be involved if companies are to get ahead. John Durst notes, "Unless we're changing, we're going to be left behind. Innovate, and you survive."

One of Patriot's most recent endeavours is linking up with Mattel corporation to create trendy computers based on Barbie and Hot Wheels themes. These would be entry-level computers for children. Patriot sells the computers exclusively via the Internet. As a sign of its innovativeness, the company was the first manufacturer to build a PC with children in mind.

Employee ideas are what lead to change. Patriot's employees note that the founders are not afraid of ideas, and find it easy to support and encourage their employees when they bring new ideas to the table. They also rely on their employees to make sure that there is strict quality control, orders are filled as they are placed, and inventory expenses are kept low with just-in-time delivery. As Durst notes, "Part of focusing on profits is not only making money on the sale, but also ensuring your business is run efficiently, allowing you to keep the money."

# Questions

1. Describe the empowerment techniques used at Patriot Computer.

2. What kind of personal attributes do you think would be needed to work for a company such as Patriot?

3. How readily do you think most people will come up with new ideas and take them to their employer? Discuss.

Source: Based on "Patriot Computers," *Venture 585*; aired July 4, 1996. See also "The Definitive Guide to Understanding Business Cycles for Growing Companies [Advertising Supplement], *Profit: The Magazine for Canadian Entrepreneurs,* June 1999, pp. Insert 1-27; and J. Schofield, "Microsoft's Darkest Hour: Rivals Cheer an Antitrust Case Against the Software Giant," *Maclean's,* June 1, 1998, p. 42.

# Rob Gareau: Communication, Conflict, and Politics

Communication is an important part of the business of Human Performance. All employees work closely, and often individually, with clients. Thus it is important that all of them have good communication skills. The employees must have good listening skills, they need to know how to give feedback to clients, and they need to effectively explain to their clients the activities they expect them to carry out during their sessions.

When asked how he gives feedback, Rob Gareau distinguished between positive and negative feedback. With positive feedback he generally writes notes, gives on the spot compliments, and also gives positive feedback at group meetings. Negative feedback is almost always done one on one, unless the problem is a "group issue." Then, at a meeting, he will outline the problem, and ask employees to give suggestions for how to fix the problem. He tries to involve employees in fixing problems wherever possible.

In order to keep the lines of communication open among staff and owners, Human Performance holds a monthly staff meeting. Meanwhile, all three owners meet once a week, together with the administrator and the bookkeeper (who also manages the front desk). Human Performance has just started a quarterly newsletter for staff and clients as another means of improving communication. Gareau notes that e-mail is primarily used only by the managers. He prefers face-to-face contact with his staff.

Gareau illustrates the importance of good communication by relating an experience at a previous workplace: "The clinical manager would come into our clinic to substitute for other clinicians and to check on the quality of our work. I would be so frustrated when she came on site because she would reprimand me for 'mistakes' which I had no idea were mistakes. I was frequently on the defence for actions which I thought were fine, and her reaction to mistakes was very demeaning. Had I known her precise certain expectations they would have been met. But she would never tell us what these were. I also did not need to be reprimanded, I needed information on the process for meeting her expectations."

Despite being easygoing, Gareau has faced difficult situations that have required clear and concise communication. He illustrates this with an example. "I had an employee who just wasn't working out. I met with her once, and tried to explain what the problem was. Then I waited about two months, while she was 'on probation,' hoping the problem would change, or maybe even go away. It didn't. And meanwhile I was getting negative feedback from other staff members about her behaviour, and I knew I had to do something about it."

Gareau was obviously uncomfortable in reporting the difficulty of dealing with this employee. Giving negative feedback is not easy, and he did not want to pretend that he had all of the answers. While it might have been easier simply to tell her on the spot that she was being dismissed, he really wanted to do what he thought was the right thing. So, he sat down with the employee and described to her the problems he had observed. He requested that she explain the situation to him, so that he could be sure that he wasn't leaping to an unwarranted conclusion. And he was willing to consider that there was an acceptable explanation for the problem behaviour. In the end, there was not, and Gareau did dismiss the employee, as he had intended. But he spent the time to communicate fully with the employee, because he wanted it to be a learning experience for her. He really wanted her to understand why her behaviour had been a problem, and why, finally, his only alternative was to dismiss her. That way he hoped she would learn from the experience and be more effective at her next job.

Gareau explains that while he tries to avoid conflict, he is not afraid of it. When conflict does arise, he tries to do "good background work first," to make sure he understands the issues and how to resolve the conflict. When faced with one-on-one conflict, he is very clear that he does not want things to get emotional. He tries to focus on the issue and/or behaviours, rather than the person. He tries to insist that there are no raised voices.

Gareau explains why he takes this approach: "I think my style of not raising my voice and not getting emotional evolved from my 'do unto others' philosophy. I have learned to resolve conflicts quickly from numerous experiences in the past few years where small problems grew to large issues when they were allowed to fester. I also know that if I become aware of a problem that my staff are experiencing, and if I don't at least acknowledge the problem, I risk losing their respect."

Because Human Performance is a relatively small firm, Gareau reports there is not much "office politics." The family environment he tries to create amongst staff may also keep politics to a minimum. He says too that because of the company's small size, it is generally not necessary for the owners to engage in power plays. Gareau considers himself the "quality control person" within the management team. If he finds quality isssues, he is quick to simply assert "this just can't happen," but fortunately he does not have to exercise this form of power very often.

When asked about how power is distributed across the management team, Gareau notes that because of their complementary skills, there is no one person who has all of the power. Gareau, Ramsbottom, and Bernicky have their own areas of expertise. Thus each owner plays a larger role in decisions in which he has the greatest expertise. Gareau does not feel that this expertise power causes a problem, however. "We respect each other's expertise, respect what each other knows."

# Questions:

1. Evaluate Gareau's effectiveness at handling communication. What changes might you suggest to possibly improve communication among managers, staff, and clients?

2. What do you think of Gareau's conflict-handling style?

3. What advice would you give to Gareau about handling power more effectively?

4. Evaluate Gareau's assertion that Human Performance's small size makes politics less likely. Are there other conditions that might reduce the need for politics at Human Performance?

# The Toxic Workplace

## It's not unusual to find

the following employee behaviours in today's workplace:

Answering the phone with a "yeah," neglecting to say thank you or please, using voice mail to screen calls, leaving a half cup of coffee behind to avoid having to brew the next pot, standing uninvited but impatiently over the desk of someone engaged in a telephone conversation, dropping trash on the floor and leaving it for the maintenance crew to clean up, and talking loudly on the phone about personal matters.[1]

And some employers or managers fit the following descriptions:

In the months since [the new owner of the pharmacy] has been in charge [he] has made it clear that he is at liberty to fire employees at will ... change their positions, decrease their bonus percentages, and refuse time-off and vacation choices.

Furthermore, he has established an authoritarian work structure characterized by distrust, cut-backs on many items deemed essential to work comfort, disrespect, rigidity and poor-to-no-communication.[2]

He walked all over people. He made fun of them; he intimidated them. He criticized work for no reason, and he changed his plans daily.[3]

# What's Happening in Our Workplaces?

Workplaces today are receiving highly critical reviews, at one end being called uncivil while at the other end they are referred to as toxic.

Lynne Anderson and Christine Pearson, two management professors from St. Joseph's University and the University of North Carolina respectively, note that "Historians may view the dawn of the twenty-first century as a time of thoughtless acts and rudeness: we tailgate, even in the slow lane; we dial wrong numbers and then slam the receiver on the innocent respondent; we break appointments with nonchalance."[4] The workplace has often been seen as one of the places where civility still ruled, with co-workers treating each other with a mixture of formality and friendliness, distance and politeness. However, with downsizing, re-engineering, budget cuts, pressures for increased productivity, autocratic work environments, and the use of part-time employees, there has been an increase in "uncivil and aggressive workplace behaviours."[5]

What does civility in the workplace mean? A simple definition of workplace civility is behaviour "involving politeness and regard for others in the workplace, within workplace norms for respect."[6] Workplace incivility then "involves acting with disregard for others in the workplace, in violation of workplace norms for respect."[7] Of course, different workplaces will have different norms for what determines mutual respect. For instance, in most restaurants, if the staff were rude to you when you were there for dinner, you would be annoyed, and perhaps even complain to the manager. However, at Elbow Room Cafe in downtown Vancouver, if customers complain they are in a hurry, they might be told the following by manager Patrick Savoie: "If you're in a hurry, you should have gone to McDonald's."[8] And that behaviour is acceptable to the diners at Elbow Room Cafe.

Most work environments are not expected to be marked by such rudeness, however, although this has been changing in recent years. Robert Warren, a University of Manitoba marketing professor, notes that "simple courtesy has gone by the board."[9]

While there is documented evidence of the rise of violence and threats of violence at work,[10] little research has been done on less extreme forms of negative interaction, such as rudeness, thoughtlessness, or negative gestures.[11] However, several studies have found that there is persistent negative behaviour in the workplace that is not of a violent nature.[12] For instance, a

survey of 603 Toronto nurses found that 33 percent had experienced verbal abuse during the five previous days of work.[14]

Another recent study found that 78 percent of employees interviewed think that workplace incivility has increased in the past 10 years.[15] The researchers found that men are mostly to blame for this change: "Although men and women are targets of disrespect and rudeness in equal numbers...men instigate the rudeness 70 percent of the time."[16]

Not all rude behaviour is confined to men, however. Professor Andrée Roberge at Laval University suggests that some of the rudeness is generational. He finds that "young clerks often lack both knowledge and civility. Employers are having to train young people in simple manners because that is not being done at home."[17] Professor Warren backs this up: "One of the biggest complaints I hear from businesses when I go to talk about graduates is the lack of interpersonal skills."[18]

Rudeness isn't the only offensive behaviour in the workplace, however. Recently, researchers have suggested that incivility may be a precursor to more negative behaviours in the workplace, including aggression and violence.[19] No Canadian statistics on violence and anger at work are available.[20] However, a 1996 Gallup poll conducted in the United States found that 25 percent of those working adults surveyed reported that they were "generally at least somewhat angry at work."[21] This may underreport the full extent of anger at work, though, as 49 percent say that they felt "at least 'a little angry' at work."[22]

## factbox [13]

- In 2000, only 49% of working Canadians say they are committed to their employer. In 1991, the level of commitment was 62%.
- More Americans report commitment to their employers than Canadians: 55% of Americans vs. 49% of Canadians.
- Only 52% of Canadians are satisfied with their supervisors.
- Employees over the age of 55 express the highest degree of commitment to their employers.
- Top performers show greater commitment to their employers than average performers.

# What Causes Incivility (and Worse) in the Workplace?

If employers and employees are acting with less civility towards each other, what is causing this to happen?

Managers and employees often have different views of the employee's role in the organization. Jeffrey Pfeffer, a professor at Stanford's Graduate School of Business, notes that many companies don't really value their employees: "Most managers, if they're being honest with

## Do You Have a TOXIC Manager?

Below are some of the toxic behaviours of managers and the workplace cultures that allow these behaviours to thrive.

| Managerial Toxic Behaviour | Workplace Culture that Fosters this Behaviour |
|---|---|
| *Actor Behaviour*: These managers act out anger rather than discuss problems. They slam doors, sulk and make it clear they're angry, but refuse to talk about it. | *Macho Culture*: People don't discuss problems. The emphasis is to "take it like a man." |
| *Fragmentor Behaviour*: These managers see no connection between what they do and the outcome, and take no responsibility for their behaviour. | *Specialist Culture*: Employees who are technically gifted or great in their fields don't have to consider how their behaviour or work impacts anyone. |
| *Me-First Behaviour*: These managers make decisions based on their own convenience. | *Elitist Culture*: Promotes and rewards not according to work but to who your buddies are. |
| *Mixed-Messenger Behaviour*: These managers present themselves one way, but their behaviour doesn't match what they say. | *Office-Politics Culture*: Promotes and rewards based on flattery and positioning. |
| *Wooden-Stick Behaviour*: These managers are extremely rigid and controlling. | *Change-Resistant Culture*: Upper management struggles to maintain the status quo regardless of the outcome. |
| *Escape-Artist Behaviour*: These managers don't deal with reality, often lying, or at the extreme, escaping through drugs or alcohol. | *Workaholic Culture*: Forces employees to spend more time at the office than necessary. |

**Source:** L. McClure, *Risky Business*, (Binghamton, NY: Haworth Press, 1996).

themselves, will admit it: When they look at their people, they see costs, they see salaries, they see benefits, they see overhead. Very few companies look at their people and see assets."[23]

Most employees, however, like to think that they are assets to the organization. The realization that one is simply a cost and not a valued member of an organization can cause frustration to employees.

In addition, "employers' excessive demands and top-down style of management are contributing to the rise of 'work rage,'" claims Gerry Smith, of Toronto-based Warren Shepell Consultants.[24] He is the author of the recently released *Work Rage*.[25] Smith worries about the consequences of these demands: "If you push people too hard, set unrealistic expectations and cut back their benefits, they're going to strike back."[26]

Smith's work supports the findings of a recent study that reported the most common cause of anger is the actions of supervisors or managers.[27] Other common causes of anger identified by the researchers include lack of productivity by co-workers and others, tight deadlines, heavy workload, interaction with the public, and bad treatment.

Some researchers have looked at this frustration in terms of a breakdown of the psychological contract formed between employees and employers. Psychological contracts begin to develop between employers and employees as they are first introduced to each other in the hiring process.[28] They continue over time as the employer and the employee come to understand each other's expectations about the amounts and quality of work to be performed and the types of rewards to be given. For instance, when an employee is continually asked to work late and/or be available at all hours through pagers and e-mail, the employee may assume that doing so will result in greater rewards or faster promotion down the line. The employer may have had no such intention, and may even be thinking that the employee should be grateful simply to have a job. Later, when the employee does not get expected (though never promised) rewards, he or she is disappointed.

Sandra Robinson, an OB professor at the University of British Columbia, and her colleagues have found that when a psychological contract is violated (perceptually or actually), the relationship between the employee and the employer is damaged. This can result in the loss of trust.[29] The breakdown in trust can cause employees to be less ready to accept decisions or obey rules.[30] The erosion of the trust can also lead employees to take revenge on the employer. So they don't carry out their end of a task. Or they refuse to pass on messages. They engage in any number of subtle and not so subtle behaviours that affect the way work gets done—or prevents work from getting done.

## The Toxic Organization

Jeffrey Pfeffer of Stanford suggests that companies have become "toxic places to work."[31] He notes that companies, particularly in Silicon Valley, ask their employees

OB on the Edge

## faceoff

**Manners are an over-romanticized concept. The big issue isn't that employees need to be concerned about their manners. Rather employers should be paying better wages.**

**The Golden Rule, "to do unto others as others do unto you," should still have a role in today's workplace. Being nice pays off.**

to sign contracts on the first day of work indicating the employee's understanding that the company has the right to fire at will and for any reason. Some employers also ask their employees to choose between having a life and having a career. Pfeffer relates a joke people used to tell about Microsoft: "We offer flexible time—you can work any 18 hours you want."[32]

What does it mean to be a toxic organization? Peter Frost, a professor at UBC, notes that there will always be pain in organizations, but that sometimes it becomes too intense or too prolonged and conditions within the organization begin to break down. In other words, the situation becomes toxic. This is not dissimilar to what the liver or kidneys do when toxins become too intense in a human body.[33]

What causes organizations to be toxic? Like Pfeffer, UBC's Peter Frost and Sandra Robinson identify a number of factors. Downsizing and organizational change are two main factors, particularly in recent years. Sometimes organizations experience unexpected events, which then lead to toxicity, including the sudden death of a key manager, an unwise move by senior management, strong competition from a start-up company. Other organizations are toxic throughout their system, however, due to policies and practices that create distress. Such factors as unreasonable stretch goals or performance targets, or unrelenting internal competition, can create toxicity. There are also toxic managers who lead through insensitivity, vindictiveness, and failure to take responsibility, or they are control freaks or are unethical. The inset "Do You Have a Toxic Manager?" lists some of the types of toxic managers and the cultures that inspire their behaviour.

## What Are the Effects of Incivility and Toxicity in the Workplace?

Twelve percent of those who experience rudeness quit their jobs in response, 22 percent decreased their work effort, and 52 percent lost work time worrying about it.[34] In general, researchers have found that the effects of workplace anger are sometimes subtle: a hostile work environment and the tendency to do only enough work to get by.

Those who feel chronic anger in the workplace are more likely to report "feelings of betrayal by the organiza-

tion, decreased feelings of loyalty, a decreased sense that respondent values and the organization's values are similar, a decreased sense that the employer treated the respondent with dignity and respect, and a decreased sense that employers had fulfilled promises made to respondents."[35] So do these feelings make a difference? Apparently so. Researchers have found that those who felt angry with their employers were less likely to put forth their best effort, more likely to be competitive towards other employees, and less likely to suggest "a quicker and better way to do their job."[36] All of these actions would tend to decrease the productivity possible in the workplace.

It is not just those who work for an organization who are affected by incivility and toxicity. Poor service, from indifference to rudeness to outright hostility, characterizes many transactions in Canadian businesses. "Across the country, better business bureaus, provincial government consumer-help agencies and media ombudsmen report a lengthening litany of complaints about contractors, car dealers, repair shops, moving companies, airlines and department stores."[37] This suggests that customers and clients may well be feeling the impact of internal workplace dynamics.

## The Toxic Handler

Employees of toxic organizations suffer pain from their experiences in a toxic environment. In some organizations, mechanisms, often informal, are set up to deal with some of the problems toxicity causes.

Peter Frost and Sandra Robinson identified a special role that some employees play in trying to relieve the toxicity within an organization: the toxic handler. This person tries to mitigate this pain by softening the blow of downsizing, or change, or the behaviour of the toxic leader. Essentially the toxic handler helps others around him or her deal with the strains of the organization, by counselling, advising, shielding employees from the wrath of angry managers, reinterpreting the managers' messages to make them less harsh, etc.

So who takes on this role? Certainly no organization to date has a line on its organizational chart for "the toxic handler." Often the role emerges as part of one's position in an organization, for instance a manager in the human resources department. In many cases, however, the handler is pulled into the role "bit by bit—by their colleagues, who turn to them because they are trustworthy, calm, kind and nonjudgmental."[38]

Frost and Robinson, in profiling these individuals, suggest that toxic handlers are predisposed to say yes, have a high tolerance for pain, a surplus of empathy, and when they notice people in pain, they have a need to make the situation right. However, these are not individuals who thrive simply on dealing with the emotional needs of others. Quoting one of the managers in their study, Frost and Robinson cite the full range of activities of most toxic handlers: "These people are usually relentless in their drive to accomplish organizational targets and rarely lose focus on business issues. Managing emotional pain is one of their means."[39]

The inset "How Toxic Handlers Alleviate Organizational Pain" identifies the many tasks that toxic handlers take on in an organization. Frost and Robinson suggest that these tasks will probably need to be handled forever, and they recommend that organizations take steps to actively support people performing this role.

## How Toxic Handlers Alleviate ORGANIZATIONAL Pain

- They listen empathically
- They suggest solutions
- They work behind the scenes to prevent pain
- They carry the confidences of others
- They reframe difficult messages

**Source:** P. Frost and S. Robinson, "The Toxic Handler: Organizational Hero—and Casualty," *Harvard Business Review*, July-August 1999, p. 101, (Reprint 99406).

## Research Exercises

1. Look for data on violence and anger in the workplace in other countries. How do these data compare with the Canadian and American data presented here? What might you conclude about how violence and anger in the workplace are expressed in different cultures?

2. Identify 3 Canadian organizations that are attempting to foster better and/or less toxic environments for their employees. What kind of effect is this having on the organizations' bottom lines?

## Your Perspective

1. Is it reasonable to suggest, as some researchers have, that young people today have not learned to be civil to others, or don't place a high priority on doing so? Do you see this as one of the causes of incivility in the workplace?

2. What should be done about managers who create toxicity in the workplace while being rewarded because they do achieve bottom-line results? Should bottom-line results justify their behaviour?

## Want to Know More?

If you'd like to read more on this topic, see P. Frost and S. Robinson, "The Toxic Handler: Organizational Hero — and Casualty," *Harvard Business Review*, July-August 1999, pp. 96-106 (Reprint 99406); and A.M. Webber, "Danger: Toxic Company," *Fast Company*, November 1998, pp. 152-157. You can find the latter article at http://www.fastcompany.com/online/19/toxic.html. It contains an interview with Jeffrey Pfeffer, Professor of Organizational Behavior at Stanford University, who discusses examples of toxic organizations.

## Endnotes:

1. L.M. Anderson and C.M. Pearson, "Tit for Tat? The Spiraling Effect of Incivility in the Workplace," *Academy of Management Review*, 24:3, 1999, pp. 453.

2. The source of this quote is N. Giarrusso, "An Issue of Job Satisfaction," unpublished undergraduate term paper, Concordia University, Montreal, 1990. It is cited in B.E. Ashforth, "Petty Tyranny in Organizations: A Preliminary Examination of Antecedents and Consequences," *Canadian Journal of Administrative Sciences*, 14(2), 1997, pp. 126-140.

3. P. Frost and S. Robinson, "The Toxic Handler: Organizational Hero — and Casualty," *Harvard Business Review*, July-August 1999, p. 101, (Reprint 99406).

4. L.M. Anderson and C.M. Pearson, "Tit for Tat? The Spiraling Effect of Incivility in the Workplace," *Academy of Management Review*, 24:3, 1999, pp. 452-471.

5. L.M. Anderson and C.M. Pearson, "Tit for Tat? The Spiraling Effect of Incivility in the Workplace," *Academy of Management Review*, 24:3, 1999, pp. 452-471. For further discussion of this, see R.A. Baron and J.H. Neuman, "Workplace Violence and Workplace Aggression: Evidence on Their Relative Frequency and Potential Causes," *Aggressive Behavior*, 22, 1996, pp. 161-173; C.C. Chen and W. Eastman, "Towards a Civic Culture for Multicultural Organizations," *Journal of Applied Behavioral Science*, 33, 1997, pp. 454-470; J.H. Neuman and R.A. Baron, "Aggression in the Workplace," in R.A. Giacalone and J. Greenberg (eds.), *Antisocial Behavior in Organizations* (Thousand Oaks, CA: Sage, 1997), pp. 37-67.

6. L.M. Anderson and C.M. Pearson, "Tit for Tat? The Spiraling Effect of Incivility in the Workplace," *Academy of Management Review*, 24:3, 1999, pp. 452-471.

**OB** *on the Edge*

7.  L.M. Anderson and C.M. Pearson, "Tit for Tat? The Spiraling Effect of Incivility in the Workplace," *Academy of Management Review*, 24:3, 1999, pp. 452-471.

8.  R. Corelli, "Dishing Out Rudeness: Complaints Abound as Customers Are Ignored, Berated," *Maclean's*, January 11, 1999, p. 44.

9.  R. Corelli, "Dishing Out Rudeness: Complaints Abound As Customers Are Ignored, Berated," *Maclean's*, January 11, 1999, p. 44.

10. See, for example, Northwestern National Life Insurance Company, *Fear and Violence in the Workplace*, research report (Minneapolis, MN. 1993); C. Romano, "Workplace Violence Takes a Deadly Turn," *Management Review*, 83(7), 1994, p. 5; J.A. Segal, "When Charles Manson Comes to the Workplace," *HRMagazine*, 39(6), 1994, pp. 33-40.

11. J.H. Neuman and R.A. Baron, "Aggression in the Workplace," in R.A. Giacalone and J. Greenberg (eds.), *Antisocial Behavior in Organizations* (Thousand Oaks, CA: Sage, 1997), pp. 37-67.

12. R.A. Baron and J.H. Neuman, "Workplace Violence and Workplace Aggression: Evidence on Their Relative Frequency and Potential Causes," *Aggressive Behavior*, 22, 1996, pp. 161-173; K. Bjorkqvist, K. Osterman, and M. Hjelt-Back, "Aggression Among University Employees," *Aggressive Behavior*, 20, 1986, pp. 173-184; and H.J. Ehrlich and B.E.K. Larcom, *Ethnoviolence in the Workplace* (Baltimore, MD: Center for the Applied Study of Ethnoviolence, 1994).

13. Information for the Fact Box based on "Breeding Loyalty Pays for Employers," *Vancouver Sun*, April 22, 2000, p. D14.

14. J. Graydon, W. Kasta, and P. Khan, "Verbal and Physical Abuse of Nurses," *Canadian Journal of Nursing Administration*, November-December 1994, pp. 70-89.

15. C. M. Pearson and C. L. Porath, "Workplace Incivility: The Target's Eye View," paper presented at the annual meetings of The Academy of Management, Chicago, IL, August 10, 1999.

16. "Men More Likely to Be Rude in Workplace, Survey Shows," *Vancouver Sun*, August 16, 1999, p. B10.

17. R. Corelli, "Dishing Out Rudeness: Complaints Abound as Customers Are Ignored, Berated," *Maclean's*, January 11, 1999, p. 44.

18. R. Corelli, "Dishing Out Rudeness: Complaints Abound as Customers Are Ignored, Berated," *Maclean's*, January 11, 1999, p. 44.

19. R.A. Baron and J.H. Neuman, "Workplace Violence and Workplace Aggression: Evidence on Their Relative Frequency and Potential Causes," *Aggressive Behavior*, 22, 1996, pp. 161-173; C. MacKinnon, *Only Words* (New York: Basic Books), 1994; J. Marks, "The American Uncivil Wars," *U.S. News & World Report*, April 22, 1996, pp. 66-72; and L.P. Spratlen, "Workplace Mistreatment: Its Relationship to Interpersonal Violence," *Journal of Psychosocial Nursing*, 32(12), 1994, pp. 5-6.

20. D. Flavelle, "Managers Cited for Increase in 'Work Rage,'" *Vancouver Sun*, April 11, 2000, pp. D1, D11.

21. E. Girardet, "Office Rage Is on the Boil," *National Post*, August 11, 1999, p. B1.

22. D.E. Gibson and S.G. Barsade, "The Experience of Anger at Work: Lessons From the Chronically Angry," paper presented at the annual meetings of The Academy of Management, Chicago, IL, August 11, 1999.

23. A.M. Webber, "Danger: Toxic Company," *Fast Company*, November 1998, pp. 152-157.

24. D. Flavelle, "Managers Cited for Increase in 'Work Rage,'" *Vancouver Sun*, April 11, 2000, pp. D1, D11.

25. G. Smith, *Work Rage*, (Toronto, ON: Harper Collins Canada, 2000).

26. D. Flavelle, "Managers Cited for Increase in 'Work Rage,'" *Vancouver Sun*, April 11, 2000, pp. D1, D11.

27. D.E. Gibson and S.G. Barsade, "The Experience of Anger at Work: Lessons From the Chronically Angry," paper presented at the annual meetings of The Academy of Management, Chicago, IL, August 11, 1999.

28. H. Levinson, *Emotional Health in the World of Work* (Boston: South End Press, 1964); E. Schein, *Organizational Psychology* (Englewood Cliffs, NJ: Prentice Hall, 1980).

29. E.W. Morrison and S.L. Robinson, "When Employees Feel Betrayed: A Model of How Psychological Contract Violation Develops," *Academy of Management Journal*, 22, 1997, pp. 226-256; S.L. Robinson, "Trust and Breach of the Psychological Contract," *Administrative Science Quarterly*, 41, 1996, pp. 574-599; and S.L. Robinson, M.S. Kraatz, and D.M. Rousseau, "Changing Obligations and the Psychological Contract: A Longitudinal Study," *Academy of Management Journal*, 37, 1994, pp. 137-152.

30. T.R. Tyler and P. Dogoey, "Trust in Organizational Authorities: The Influence of Motive Attributions on Willingness to Accept Decisions," in R.M. Kramer and T.R. Tyler (eds.), *Trust in Organizations* (Thousand Oaks, CA: Sage Publications, 1996), pp. 246-260.

31. A.M. Webber, "Danger: Toxic Company," *Fast Company*, November 1998, pp. 152-157.

32. A.M. Webber, "Danger: Toxic Company," *Fast Company*, November 1998, pp. 152-157.

33. Private communication with Peter Frost, April 25, 2000.

34. "Men More Likely to be Rude in Workplace, Survey Shows," *Vancouver Sun*, August 16, 1999, p. B10.

35. D.E. Gibson and S.G. Barsade, "The Experience of Anger at Work: Lessons From the Chronically Angry," paper presented at the annual meetings of The Academy of Management, Chicago, IL, August 11, 1999.

36. D.E. Gibson and S.G. Barsade, "The Experience of Anger at Work: Lessons From the Chronically Angry," paper presented at the annual meetings of The Academy of Management, Chicago, IL, August 11, 1999.

37. R. Corelli, "Dishing Out Rudeness: Complaints Abound as Customers Are Ignored, Berated," *Maclean's*, January 11, 1999, p. 44.

38. P. Frost and S. Robinson, "The Toxic Handler: Organizational Hero — and Casualty," *Harvard Business Review*, July-August 1999, p. 101, (Reprint 99406).

39. P. Frost and S. Robinson, "The Toxic Handler: Organizational Hero — and Casualty," *Harvard Business Review*, July-August 1999, p. 101, (Reprint 99406).

**CHAPTER 9**

# Organizational Culture

## Questions for Consideration

**What is organizational culture?**

**When is organizational culture functional? Dysfunctional?**

**How do employees learn about the culture of their organization?**

I n 1997, when John Wetmore took over as the new head of Markham, Ontario-based IBM Canada Inc., it was a good time to be leading an IBM subsidiary.[1] Profits were up and no layoffs were in sight. This had not been the case five years earlier, when IBM worldwide was facing eroding profits, questionable product directions, and numerous layoffs. IBM Canada first realized it had a problem in the spring of 1991, when the company discovered that it would not reach the revenue and profit plans for that year. Gaye Emery, vice-president and general manager of marketing for IBM Canada, attributed the problems to maintaining the status quo due to four decades of unparalleled growth. Specifically, she noted that IBM Canada had stopped listening to the customer and neglected to watch the competition.

IBM Canada recognized immediately that it needed a culture change. As Emery reported, "What we found was a culture that included many wonderful traits: confidence, loyalty, perseverance, and an admirable work ethic. But we also found a degree of arrogance, a sense of entitlement, and an entrenched aversion to risk." Canadian-born Bill Etherington, currently an IBM senior vice-president with the parent organization, introduced some of

the culture change at IBM Canada through a change in the IBM dress code in 1993. No more dark blue suit, white shirt, conservative tie, and dark socks that could not bunch at the ankles. Now it was time to dress so the customer felt comfortable.

Over the next several years, IBM Canada set out to change more of that culture and, among other things, trained its managers and professionals in leadership skills, teamwork, empowerment, and risk-taking. This encouraged managers to function more as coaches and employees to work better as team members. And IBM's advertising campaign in 1995 managed to change its corporate image from Big Blue to Cool Blue, in the eyes of customers and employees alike.

Has that culture change paid off? Wetmore, after finishing his first full fiscal year at the top, probably thinks so. In 1998 his firm saw domestic revenue increase by 17 percent to $4.8 billion. The employees probably think so too. After 1998's great performance, all employees received bonuses, based on their performances. Bonuses averaged 10 percent of salary, and totalled 25 percent of IBM's profits for the year. IBM continued its successful performance through 1999, reporting record revenues for the fifth straight year in a row.

Culture provides stability to an organization and gives employees a clear understanding of "the way things are done around here." Unfortunately, culture can also be a major barrier to change, as it was at IBM Canada for many years. Culture sets the tone for how organizations operate and how individuals within the organization interact. You might have noticed in stopping at the main reception desk at a large organization that in some places you are told "Ms. Dettweiler" will be with you in a moment, while at another organization, the receptionist will tell you that "Emma" will be available as soon as she gets off the phone. These two ways of referring to individuals convey different meanings to you — in one organization the rules are more formal than the other.

Because culture sets the tone for how people interact within the organization, it also has an impact on the employees who work for the firm. Thus, as you start to think about different organizations where you might work, you will want to think about their cultures. An organization that has a culture

**IBM Canada**
www.ibm.ca

where employees are expected to work 15 hours a day may not be one in which you would like to work. For instance, television ads for Unisys (Unisys Canada is based in Fredricton, NB) show their employees at parties where their bodies are present, but their minds are elsewhere, trying to solve business problems. The voiceover brags that at Unisys, "we eat, drink and sleep this stuff." Perhaps this is nice for the client, but consider the poor employees. (If you want to see Unisys' justification for its "monitor head" employees who work all the time, visit http://www.unisys.com/unisys/thinkers/default.asp.) An understanding of culture might help you discover the firm's expectations before you accept a job or might help you understand why you like (or don't like) the current college or university you attend.

In this chapter we show that every organization has a culture. We examine how that culture is manifested and the impact it has on the attitudes and behaviours of members of that organization. To help you think more about culture and its impact on you, you may want to complete the Learning About Yourself Exercise for this chapter, on page 411, which assesses the extent to which you would be more comfortable in either a formal, rule-oriented culture or a more informal, flexible culture.

## Institutionalization: A Forerunner of Culture

**Richard Ivey School of Business**
www.ivey.uwo.ca

The idea of viewing organizations as cultures — where there is a system of shared meaning among members — is a relatively recent phenomenon. Until the mid-1980s, organizations were, for the most part, simply thought of as rational means by which to coordinate and control a group of people. They had vertical levels, departments, authority relationships, and so forth, but organizations are more than this. They have personalities too, just like individuals. They can be rigid or flexible, unfriendly or supportive, innovative or conservative. For example, Bombardier's offices and people *are* different from the offices and people at IBM Canada. The University of Western Ontario's Richard Ivey School of Business and the University of British Columbia's Faculty of Commerce are in the same business — education — but each has a unique feeling and character beyond its structural characteristics. Organizational theorists now acknowledge this by recognizing the important role that culture plays in the lives of organization members. Interestingly, though, the origin of culture as a phenomenon that affects an employee's attitudes and behaviour can be traced back more than 50 years ago to the notion of **institutionalization**.[2]

**institutionalization**
The process whereby an organization takes on a life of its own, apart from any of its members, and acquires immortality.

When an organization becomes institutionalized, it takes on a life of its own, apart from its founders or any of its members. For example, Disney Corporation founder Walt Disney died in 1966, but the company has continued to thrive despite his death. Birks, the Hudson's Bay Corporation, and Sony Canada are examples of organizations that have existed beyond the life of their founder or any one member. Additionally, when an organization becomes institutionalized, it becomes valued for itself, not merely for the goods or services it produces. It acquires immortality. If its original goals are no longer relevant, it doesn't go out of business. Rather, it redefines itself. For example, when the demand for Timex's watches declined, Timex Corp. merely redirected itself into the consumer electronics business — making, in addition to watches, clocks, computers, and health-care products such as digital thermometers and blood-pressure testing devices. Timex took on an existence that went beyond its original mission to manufacture low-cost mechanical watches.

**Disney**
disney.go.com

**Birks**
www.birks.com

**Hudson's Bay Corporation**
www.hbc.com

Institutionalization operates to produce common understandings among members about what is appropriate and fundamentally meaningful behaviour.[3] So when an organization takes on institutional permanence, acceptable modes of behaviour become largely self-evident to its members. As we'll see, this is essentially the same thing that organizational culture does. An understanding of what makes up an organization's culture and how it is created, sustained, and learned will enhance our ability to explain and predict the behaviour of people at work.

## What Is Organizational Culture?

When Henry Mintzberg, professor at McGill University, was asked to compare organizational structure and corporate culture, he said: "Culture is the soul of the organization — the beliefs and values, and how they are manifested. I think of the structure as the skeleton, and as the flesh and blood. And culture is the soul that holds the thing together and gives it life force."[4] Mintzberg's culture metaphor provides a clear image of how to think about culture. In this section, we propose a specific definition and review several peripheral issues that revolve around this definition. From Concept to Skills on the next page tells you how to read an organization's culture.

### A Definition

**organizational culture**
A system of shared meaning and common perception held by members of an organization, which distinguishes it from other organizations.

There seems to be wide agreement that **organizational culture** refers to a system of shared meaning, held by organization members, that distinguishes the organization from other organizations.[5] This system of shared meaning is, on closer examination, a set of key characteristics that the organization values. Research suggests that seven primary characteristics, in aggregate, capture the essence of an organization's culture.[6]

- *Innovation and risk-taking*: The degree to which employees are encouraged to be innovative and take risks.
- *Attention to detail*: The degree to which employees are expected to exhibit precision, analysis, and attention to detail.
- *Outcome orientation*: The degree to which management focuses on results, or outcomes, rather than on the techniques and processes used to achieve these outcomes.
- *People orientation*: The degree to which management decisions take into consideration the effect of outcomes on people within the organization.
- *Team orientation*: The degree to which work activities are organized around teams rather than individuals.
- *Aggressiveness*: The degree to which people are aggressive and competitive rather than easygoing.
- *Stability*: The degree to which organizational activities emphasize maintaining the status quo in contrast to growth.

Each of these characteristics exists on a continuum from low to high. Appraising the organization on these seven characteristics, then, gives a composite picture of the organization's culture. This picture becomes the basis for feelings of shared understanding that members have about the organization, how things are done in it, and the way members are supposed to

## From CONCEPTS to SKILLS

# How to "Read" an Organization's Culture

The ability to read and assess an organization's culture can be a valuable skill. If you're looking for a job, you'll want to choose an employer whose culture is compatible with your values and in which you'll feel comfortable. If you can accurately assess a prospective employer's culture before you make your decision, you may be able to save yourself a lot of grief and reduce the likelihood of making a poor choice. Similarly, you'll undoubtedly have business transactions with numerous organizations during your professional career. You'll be trying to sell a product or service, negotiate a contract, arrange a joint venture, or you may merely be seeking out which individual in an organization controls certain decisions. The ability to assess another organization's culture can be a definite plus in successfully completing these pursuits.

For the sake of simplicity, we'll approach the problem of reading an organization's culture from that of a job applicant. We'll assume you're interviewing for a job. Here's a list of things you can do to help learn about a potential employer's culture:

- Observe the physical surroundings. Pay attention to signs, pictures, style of dress, length of hair, degree of openness between offices, and office furnishings and arrangements.

- With whom did you meet? Just the person who would be your immediate manager? Or potential colleagues, managers from other departments, or senior executives? And based on what they revealed, to what degree do people other than the immediate manager have input into the hiring decision?

- How would you characterize the style of the people you met? Formal? Casual? Serious? Jovial?

- Does the organization have formal rules and regulations printed in a human resources policy manual? If so, how detailed are these policies?

- Ask questions of the people with whom you meet. The most valid and reliable information tends to come from asking the same questions of many people (to see how closely their responses align) and by talking with boundary spanners. Boundary spanners are employees whose work links them to the external environment and includes jobs such as human resources interviewer, salesperson, purchasing agent, labour negotiator, public relations specialist, and company lawyer. Questions that will give you insights into organizational processes and practices might include the following:

- What is the background of the founders?

- What is the background of current senior managers? What are their functional specializations? Were they promoted from within or hired from outside?

- How does the organization integrate new employees? Is there an orientation program? Training? If so, could you describe these features?

- How does your boss define his or her job success? (Amount of profit? Serving customers? Meeting deadlines? Acquiring budget increases?)

- How would you define fairness in terms of reward allocations?

- Can you identify some people here who are on the "fast track"? What do you think has put them on the fast track?

- Can you identify someone who seems to be considered a deviant in the organization? How has the organization responded to this person?

- Can you describe a decision that someone made here that was well received?

- Can you describe a decision that didn't work out well? What were the consequences for the decision maker?

- Could you describe a crisis or critical event that has occurred recently in the organization? How did top management respond? What was learned from this experience?

Source: Ideas in this box were influenced by A.L. Wilkins, "The Culture Audit: A Tool for Understanding Organizations," *Organizational Dynamics*, Autumn 1983, pp. 24–38; H.M. Trice and J.M. Beyer, *The Cultures of Work Organizations* (Englewood Cliffs, NJ: Prentice Hall, 1993), pp. 358–362; H. Lancaster, "To Avoid a Job Failure, Learn the Culture of a Company First," *Wall Street Journal*, July 14, 1998, p. B1; and M. Belliveau, "4 Ways to Read a Company," *Fast Company*, October 1998, p. 158.

## Exhibit 9-1
## Contrasting Organizational Cultures

### Organization A

This organization is a manufacturing firm. Managers are expected to fully document all decisions, and "good managers" are those who can provide detailed data to support their recommendations. Creative decisions that incur significant change or risk are not encouraged. Because managers of failed projects are openly criticized and penalized, they try not to implement ideas that deviate much from the status quo. One lower-level manager quoted an often-used phrase in the company: "If it ain't broke, don't fix it."

There are extensive rules and regulations in this firm that employees are required to follow. Managers supervise employees closely to ensure there are no deviations. Management is concerned with high productivity, regardless of the impact on employee morale or turnover.

Work activities are designed around individuals. There are distinct departments and lines of authority, and employees are expected to minimize formal contact with other employees outside their functional area or line of command. Performance evaluations and rewards emphasize individual effort, although seniority tends to be the primary factor in the determination of pay raises and promotions.

### Organization B

This organization is also a manufacturing firm. Here, however, management encourages and rewards risk-taking and change. Decisions based on intuition are valued as much as those that are well rationalized. Management prides itself on its history of experimenting with new technologies and its success in regularly introducing innovative products. Managers or employees who have a good idea are encouraged to "run with it," and failures are treated as "learning experiences." The company prides itself on being market driven and rapidly responsive to the changing needs of its customers.

There are few rules and regulations for employees to follow, and supervision is loose because management believes that its employees are hardworking and trustworthy. Management is concerned with high productivity, but believes that this comes through treating its people right. The company is proud of its reputation as being a good place to work.

Job activities are designed around work teams and team members are encouraged to interact with people across functions and authority levels. Employees talk positively about the competition between teams. Individuals and teams have goals, and bonuses are based on achievement of these outcomes. Employees are given considerable autonomy in choosing the means by which the goals are attained.

behave. Exhibit 9-1 demonstrates how these characteristics can be mixed to create highly diverse organizations. To help you understand some of the characteristics of culture, you may want to look at the Working With Others Exercise on page 412, which asks you to rate your classroom culture.

## Culture Is a Descriptive Term

Organizational culture is concerned with how employees perceive the characteristics of an organization's culture, not with whether they like them. That is, it is a descriptive term. This is important because it differentiates this concept from that of job satisfaction.

Research on organizational culture has sought to measure how employees view their organization: Does it encourage teamwork? Does it reward innovation? Does it stifle initiative?

In contrast, job satisfaction seeks to measure affective responses to the work environment. It is concerned with how employees feel about the organization's expectations, reward practices, and the like. Although the two terms undoubtedly have overlapping characteristics, keep in mind that the term *organizational culture* is descriptive, while *job satisfaction* is evaluative.

## Strong vs. Weak Cultures

**strong culture**
Culture where the core values are intensely held and widely shared.

It has become increasingly popular to differentiate between strong and weak cultures.[7] In a **strong culture**, the organization's core values are both intensely held and widely shared.[8] The more members who accept the core values and the greater their commitment to those values is, the stronger the culture is. Consistent with this definition, a strong culture will have a great influence on the behaviour of its members because the high degree of sharedness and intensity creates an internal climate of high behavioural control. For example, Seattle-based retailer Nordstrom has developed one of the strongest service cultures in the retailing industry. Nordstrom employees know what is expected of them and these expectations go a long way in shaping their behaviour.

St. Joseph's Printing, located in Concord, Ontario, and one of the fastest-growing printing companies in Canada, illustrates some benefits of strong culture. St. Joseph's culture is strongly family-oriented (it's been owned by the Gagliano family for over 40 years), and also emphasizes learning by encouraging employees to "play" with the new equipment. These aspects of the culture translate into employee enthusiasm. For example, when the company introduced its new press in 1997 (only the second of its type installed in Canada at that time), employees had it up to speed three months ahead of what management had expected.[9]

One specific result of a strong culture should be lower employee turnover. A strong culture demonstrates high agreement among members about what the organization stands for. Such unanimity of purpose builds cohesiveness, loyalty, and organizational commitment. These qualities, in turn, lessen employees' propensity to leave the organization.[10] This chapter's HR Implications feature starting on page 406 illustrates specific types of strong cultures, including a family-friendly culture, a culture of diversity, and a culture of innovation.

## Do Organizations Have Uniform Cultures?

Organizational culture represents a common perception held by the organization's members. This was made explicit when we defined culture as a system of *shared* meaning. We should expect, therefore, that individuals with different backgrounds or at different levels in the organization will tend to describe the organization's culture in similar terms.[11]

Acknowledgment that organizational culture has common properties does not mean, however, that there cannot be subcultures within any given culture. Most large organizations have a dominant culture and numerous sets of subcultures.[12]

**dominant culture**
A system of shared meaning that expresses the core values shared by a majority of the organization's members.

**subcultures**
Minicultures within an organization, typically defined by department designations and geographical separation.

A **dominant culture** expresses the core values that are shared by a majority of the organization's members. When we talk about an *organization's* culture, we are referring to its dominant culture. It is this macro view of culture that gives an organization its distinct personality.[13] **Subcultures** tend to develop in large organizations to reflect common problems, situations, or experiences that members face. These subcultures are likely to be defined by department designations and geographical separation. The purchasing department, for example, can have a subculture that is uniquely shared by

**core values**
The primary, or dominant, values that are accepted throughout the organization.

members of that department. It will include the **core values** of the dominant culture, plus additional values unique to members of the purchasing department. Similarly, an office or unit of the organization that is physically separated from the organization's main operations may take on a different personality. Again, the core values are essentially retained but modified to reflect the separated unit's distinct situation. If organizations had no dominant culture and were composed only of numerous subcultures, the value of organizational culture as an independent variable would be significantly lessened. This is because there would be no uniform interpretation of what represented appropriate and inappropriate behaviour. It is the "shared meaning" aspect of culture that makes it such a potent device for guiding and shaping behaviour. That's what allows us to say that Microsoft's culture values aggressiveness and risk-taking;[14] and then to use that information to better understand the behaviour of Microsoft executives and employees. But we cannot ignore the reality that many organizations also have subcultures that can influence the behaviour of members.

## Culture vs. Formalization

> **Is culture the same as rules?**

A strong organizational culture increases behavioural consistency. In this sense, we should recognize that a strong culture can act as a substitute for formalization.

Some companies develop strict rules, and regulations act to govern employee behaviour. This is known as formalization, which will be discussed further in Chapter 12. Formalization creates predictability, orderliness, and consistency. A strong culture achieves the same end without the need for written documentation. Therefore, we should view formalization and culture as two different roads to a common destination. The stronger an organization's culture, the less management need be concerned with developing formal rules and regulations to guide employee behaviour. Those guides will be internalized in employees when they accept the organization's culture.

MGI Packers Inc. in Kitchener, Ontario, illustrates how a strong organizational culture can be used to communicate the internal values of a firm to the external world. MGI, which is owned by four non-Muslims, exports *halal* (food prepared according to the rules of the Koran) beef to the Muslim world, from Egypt to Indonesia. To prepare *halal* meat, MGI must ensure that animals are killed according to Islamic law, which means the slaughtering must be done without anger or violence, and must show compassion for the life that is ending. The Islamic Society of North America is responsible for certifying meat as *halal*. The society's director for Canadian operations, Mohammad Ashraf, was asked if he ever conducted surprise inspections of MGI's plant to ensure compliance with Islamic slaughtering rules. Ashraf replied that the non-Muslim owners seemed like honest people, and he believed he could rely on MGI's Muslim employees to alert him to problems at the plant. Ashraf's confidence arises from MGI's strong cultural norms for providing a quality product to the Muslim community.[15]

## Organizational Culture vs. National Culture

Throughout this book we've argued that national differences — that is, national cultures — must be taken into account if accurate predictions are to be made about organizational behaviour in different countries. It seems

Japan's electronic giant Matsushita Electric Company recognizes that national culture has a greater impact on employees than does organizational culture. Matsushita tries to accommodate national cultural values in managing its 150 plants in 38 countries throughout Southeast Asia, North America, Europe, the Middle East, Latin America, and Africa. At its plants in Malaysia, the company offers special ethnic food in its cafeterias for Muslim Malays, Chinese, and Indian employees and accommodates Muslim religious customs by providing special prayer rooms at each plant and allowing two prayer sessions per shift.

**Olivetti**
www.olivetti.com

**Ventra Group Inc.**
www.ventra.com

**Harvey's**
www.harveys.ca

**Wendy's**
www.wendys.com

appropriate at this point, then, to ask the question: Does national culture override an organization's culture? Is an IBM facility in Germany, for example, more likely to reflect German ethnic culture or IBM's corporate culture?

The research indicates that national culture has a greater impact on employees than does their organization's culture.[16] German employees at an IBM facility in Munich, therefore, will be influenced more by German culture than by IBM's culture. This means that as influential as organizational culture is to understanding the behaviour of people at work, national culture is even more influential.

The preceding conclusion must be further qualified to reflect the self-selection that goes on at the hiring stage. IBM, for example, may be less concerned with hiring the "typical Italian" for its Italian operations than with hiring an Italian who fits within the IBM way of doing things.[17] Historically, Italians who have a high need for autonomy are more likely to go to Olivetti than IBM. Why? Olivetti's organizational culture is informal and nonstructured. It has tended to allow employees considerably more freedom than IBM does.[18] In fact, Olivetti seeks to hire individuals who are impatient, risk-taking, and innovative — qualities in job candidates that IBM's Italian operations historically sought to exclude in new hires.

Some organizations do try to import organizational cultures from other countries, however. A number of elements of Japanese organizational culture, including *keiretsu* (where companies form partnerships with one another, rather than strictly hierarchical relationships) and *kaizen* (Japanese techniques of continuous improvements in manufacturing), have been introduced in North America. For example, in Chapter 13 we describe how Oakville, Ontario-based Ventra introduced *kaizen* into its workplace.

In mainland China, Zhang Ruimin, president and chair of Haier Group, the state-owned maker of white goods such as towels and sheets, stands out as one of the few managers to receive star status in a country that tends to celebrate the proletariat rather than management. He explained his success by noting that he has been importing culture. "From the Japanese, we have learned about teamwork and the Americans have shown how to encourage innovation, creativity."[19]

## What Does Culture Do?

We've alluded to organizational culture's impact on behaviour. We've also explicitly argued that a strong culture should be associated with reduced turnover. In this section, we will more carefully review the positive functions that culture performs. We will also note that sometimes culture can be a liability for an organization. To help you put this discussion in focus, consider the five big burger chains in Canada. McDonald's is known for consistency and kids' toy tie-ins; Burger King is know for flame broiling its meat and custom service ("have it your way"); Harvey's claims it has the best-tasting burger; Wendy's is less kid-friendly and offers more variety; and A&W tries to appeal to aging baby boomers. As you enter each of these different establishments, you notice right away their differences. Our discussion of culture should help you understand how these differences across organizations occur.

## Culture's Functions

| Does culture do anything important? |
| --- |

Culture performs a number of functions within an organization. First, it has a boundary-defining role; that is, it creates distinctions between one organization and others. Second, it conveys a sense of identity for organization members. Third, culture facilitates the generation of commitment to something larger than one's individual self-interest. Fourth, it enhances social-system stability. Culture is the social glue that helps to hold the organization together by providing appropriate standards for what employees should say and do. Finally, culture serves as a sense-making and control mechanism that guides and shapes the attitudes and behaviour of employees. It is this last function that is of particular interest to us.[20] As the following quotation makes clear, culture defines the rules of the game:

> Culture by definition is elusive, intangible, implicit, and taken for granted. But every organization develops a core set of assumptions, understandings, and implicit rules that govern day-to-day behaviour in the workplace. Until newcomers learn the rules, they are not accepted as full-fledged members of the organization. Transgressions of the rules on the part of high-level executives or front-line employees result in universal disapproval and powerful penalties. Conformity to the rules becomes the primary basis for reward and upward mobility.[21]

The role of culture in influencing employee behaviour appears to be increasingly important in today's workplace.[22] As organizations have widened spans of control, flattened structures, introduced teams, reduced formalization, and empowered employees, the *shared meaning* provided by a strong culture ensures that everyone is pointed in the same direction. Geoffrey Relph, IBM's director of services marketing, compared the culture of his previous company (G.E. Appliances in Louisville, Kentucky) with that of IBM Canada: "The priorities in G.E. are: 'Make the financial commitments. Make the financial commitments. Make the financial commitments.' At IBM, the company's attention is divided among customer satisfaction, employee morale, and positive financial results."[23] These two cultures give employees and managers different messages about where they should direct their attention.

Culture can also influence people's ethical behaviour. When lower-level employees see their managers padding expense reports, this sends a signal that the firm tolerates this dishonest behaviour. As another example, firms that emphasize individual sales records may encourage unhealthy competition among sales staff, including "misplacing" phone messages, and not being helpful to someone else's client. Toronto-based Griffith McBurney & Partners, on the other hand, emphasizes a teamwork culture. Founding partner Brad Griffith notes that "the corporate culture is to make an environment where everybody feels they're involved. We want to be successful, but not at the expense of the individual."[24] (For further discussion of the effect of culture on ethical behaviour, see this chapter's Ethical Dilemma Exercise, "Cultural Factors and Unethical Behaviour," on page 412.)

As we show later in this chapter, who receives a job offer to join the organization, who is appraised as a high performer, and who gets the promotion are strongly influenced by the individual-organization "fit"—that is, whether the applicant's or employee's attitudes and behaviour are compatible with the culture.

## Culture as a Liability

Are there any downsides to culture?

We are treating culture in a nonjudgmental manner. We haven't said that it is good or bad, only that it exists. Many of its functions, as outlined, are valuable for both the organization and the employee. Culture enhances organizational commitment and increases the consistency of employee behaviour. These are clearly benefits to an organization. From an employee's standpoint, culture is valuable because it reduces ambiguity. It tells employees how things are done and what's important. However, we shouldn't ignore the potentially dysfunctional aspects of culture, especially of a strong culture, on an organization's effectiveness. We consider specifically culture's impact on change, diversity, and mergers and acquisitions. The Point-Counterpoint feature on pages 390-391 gives you further ideas about whether cultures can change or not.

**BARRIER TO CHANGE** Culture is a liability when the shared values are not in agreement with those that will further the organization's effectiveness. This is most likely to occur when the organization's environment is dynamic. When the environment is undergoing rapid change, the organization's entrenched culture may no longer be appropriate. Consistency of behaviour is an asset to an organization when it faces a stable environment. However, it may burden the organization and make it difficult to respond to changes in the environment. For many organizations with strong cultures, practices that led to previous successes can lead to failure when those practices no longer match up well with environmental needs.[25]

**Atomic Energy of Canada Limited**
www.aecl.ca

That's what happened at Ontario Hydro. Former Hydro president Allan Kupcis described how the nuclear division went from being one of the best in the world in the 1970s and 1980s to operating at a minimally acceptable level in 1997.[26] "The problems in Ontario Hydro's nuclear division began when nuclear-plant workers started believing they were the best in the world and became complacent. Back in the 1970s and 1980s, our CANDU system was unique in the world and Hydro was continually setting records for nuclear efficiency. But when people stop looking outside to see what others are doing in terms of getting better, you tend to forget that the target is raised every time someone sets a record." The difficulties of cultural change at Canada Post are discussed in detail in this chapter's Case Incident on page 413.

**BARRIER TO DIVERSITY** Hiring new employees who, because of race, gender, disability, or other differences, are not like the majority of the organization's members creates a paradox.[27] Management wants the new employees to accept the organization's core cultural values. Otherwise, these employees are unlikely to fit in or be accepted. But at the same time, management wants to openly acknowledge and demonstrate support for the differences that these employees bring to the workplace.

Strong cultures put considerable pressure on employees to conform. They limit the range of values and styles that are acceptable. It's not a coincidence that employees at Disney theme parks appear to be almost universally attractive, clean, and wholesome looking, with bright smiles. That's the image Disney seeks. The company selects employees who will maintain that image. And once on the job, a strong culture, supported by formal rules and regulations, ensures that Disney theme-park employees will act in a relatively uniform and predictable way.

A strong culture that condones prejudice can even undermine formal corporate diversity policies. A widely publicized example is the Texaco case in the United States, where senior managers made disparaging remarks about minorities and, as a result of legal action on behalf of 1400 employees, paid a settlement of $246 million.[28] Organizations seek out and hire diverse individuals because of the alternative strengths that these people bring to the workplace. Yet these diverse behaviours and strengths are likely to diminish in strong cultures as people attempt to fit in. Strong cultures, therefore, can be liabilities when they effectively eliminate the unique strengths that people of different backgrounds bring to the organization. Moreover, strong cultures can also be liabilities when they support institutional bias or become insensitive to people who are different.

**BARRIER TO MERGERS AND ACQUISITIONS** Historically, the key factors that management looked at in making merger or acquisition decisions were related to financial advantages or product synergy. In recent years, cultural compatibility has become the primary concern.[29] While a favourable financial statement or product line may be the initial attraction of an acquisition candidate, whether the acquisition actually works seems to have more to do with how well the two organizations' cultures match up.

A number of mergers consummated in the 1990s already have failed, and the primary cause is conflicting organizational cultures.[30] For instance, many Canadian banks are dealing with culture problems these days. After deregulation in 1987, most of the chartered banks bought large brokerage firms: Royal Bank of Canada acquired Dominion Securities Inc.; Bank of Montreal got Nesbitt Burns Inc.; and Scotiabank bought McLeod Young Weir. Banks and investment houses have historically had two different cultures. Banks are hierarchical, with fixed reporting relationships and career paths; whereas investment bankers can be prima donnas, with much more flamboyant styles. The Canadian Imperial Bank of Commerce's (CIBC) problems after merging with Wood Gundy in 1988 are representative of what happens when a company tries to merge two cultures after an acquisition. Initially CIBC kept the two cultures somewhat separate, but by 1995, there was more push to unite Wood Gundy's operations with CIBC's. In the first six months of 1996, more than 25 top-ranked individuals left Toronto-based CIBC Wood Gundy to move to more entrepreneurial brokerage firms. Many of the brokers did not like the new compensation scheme, where bonuses above $50 000 were paid over three years, rather than all at once. When Richard Dufresne, who worked at Gundy for four years, left for Nesbitt Burns Inc. in Montreal, he explained the difficulties of the merger: "You're marrying two cultures, so you can expect it's not going to work well for everybody."[31] Another possible culture clash to consider is that of the 1999 merger of Montreal-based Lévesque Beaubien Geoffrion with Toronto-based First Marathon. As some observers note, "First Marathon has a reputation as aggressive, young and ambitious, while Lévesque is known as cautious, conservative, and old-school."[32]

# Organizational Culture Doesn't Change

That an organization's culture is made up of relatively stable characteristics would imply that culture is very difficult for management to change. Such a conclusion would be correct.

An organization's culture develops over many years and is rooted in deeply held values to which employees are strongly committed. In addition, there are a number of forces continually operating to maintain a given culture. These would include written statements about the organization's mission and philosophy, the design of physical spaces and buildings, the dominant leadership style, hiring criteria, past promotion practices, entrenched rituals, popular stories about key people and events, the organization's historical performance evaluation criteria, and the organization's formal structure.

Selection and promotion policies are particularly important devices that work against cultural change. Employees chose the organization because they perceived their values to be a "good fit" with those of the organization. They become comfortable with that fit and will strongly resist efforts to disturb the equilibrium. The terrific difficulties that organizations such as General Motors, MacMillan Bloedel, and Canada Post have had in trying to reshape their cultures attest to this dilemma. These organizations historically tended to attract individuals who desired and flourished in situations that were stable and highly structured.

Those in control in organizations will also select senior managers who will continue the current culture. Even attempts to change a culture by going outside the organization to hire a new chief executive are unlikely to be effective. The evidence indicates that the culture is more likely to change the executive than the other way around. Why? It's too entrenched, and change becomes a potential threat to member self-interest. In fact, a more pragmatic view of the relationship between an organization's culture and its chief executive would be to note that the practice of filling senior-level management positions from current managerial employees ensures that those who run the organization have been fully indoctrinated in the organization's culture. Promoting from within provides stability and lessens uncertainty. When Exxon's board of directors selects as a new chief executive officer an individual who has spent 30 years in the company, it virtually guarantees that the culture will continue unchanged.

Our argument, however, should not be viewed as saying that culture can never be changed. In the unusual case when an organization confronts a survival-threatening crisis — a crisis that is universally acknowledged as a true life-or-death situation — members of the organization will be responsive to efforts at cultural change. For instance, it was only when IBM Canada's and General Motors' executives were able to successfully convey to employees the crises faced from competitors that these organizations' cultures began to show signs of adaptation. However, anything less than a crisis is unlikely to be effective in bringing about cultural change.

**COUNTERPOINT**

# How to Change an Organization's Culture

Changing an organization's culture is extremely difficult, but cultures *can* be changed. For example, Lee Iacocca came to Chrysler Corp. in 1978, when the company appeared to be only weeks away from bankruptcy. It took him about five years, but in what is now a well-worn story, he took Chrysler's conservative, inward-looking, and engineering-oriented culture and changed it into an action-oriented, market-responsive culture.

The evidence suggests that cultural change is most likely to occur when most or all of the following conditions exist:

*A dramatic crisis*. This is the shock that undermines the status quo and calls into question the relevance of the current culture. Examples of these crises might be a surprising financial setback, the loss of a major customer, or a dramatic technological breakthrough by a competitor. Calgary-based Suncor hired Richard George as president and CEO in 1992 to take it from a downsizing to a growth culture, and experienced a dramatic turnaround in three years. The results have continued. Profits reached a record high in 1997, following five years of reporting profits. Executives at Pepsi-Cola and Ameritech even admit to creating crises in order to stimulate cultural change in their organizations.[1]

*Turnover in leadership*. New top leadership, which can provide an alternative set of key values, may be perceived as more capable of responding to the crisis. This would definitely be the organization's chief executive but also might need to include all senior management positions. The hiring of outside CEOs at MacMillan Bloedel (Tom Stephens) and IBM (Louis Gerstner) illustrates attempts to introduce new leadership.

*Young and small organization*. The younger the organization is, the less entrenched its culture will be. Similarly, it's easier for management to communicate its new values when the organization is small. This again

helps to explain the difficulty that multi-billion-dollar corporations have in changing their cultures.

*Weak culture*. The more widely held a culture is and the higher the agreement among members on its values, the more difficult it will be to change. Conversely, weak cultures are more amenable to change than strong ones.

If conditions support cultural change, you should consider the following suggestions:

1. Have top-management people become positive role models, setting the tone through their behaviour.

2. Create new stories, symbols, and rituals to replace those currently in vogue.

3. Select, promote, and support employees who espouse the new values that are sought.

4. Redesign socialization processes to align with the new values.

5. Change the reward system to encourage acceptance of a new set of values.

6. Replace unwritten norms with formal rules and regulations that are tightly enforced.

7. Shake up current subcultures through transfers, job rotation, and/or terminations.

8. Work to get peer group consensus through utilization of employee participation and creation of a climate with a high level of trust.

Implementing most or all of these suggestions will not result in an immediate or dramatic shift in the organization's culture. For, in the final analysis, cultural change is a lengthy process — measured in years rather than months. But we *can* ask the question "Can culture be changed?" And the answer is "Yes!"

Source:

[1] B. Dumaine, "Times Are Good? Create a Crisis," *Fortune*, June 28, 1993, pp. 123-130.

## Creating and Sustaining Culture

An organization's culture doesn't pop out of thin air. Once established, it rarely fades away. What forces influence the creation of a culture? What reinforces and sustains these forces once they are in place? We answer both of these questions in this section.

### How a Culture Begins

An organization's current customs, traditions, and general way of doing things are largely due to what it has done before and the degree of success it has had with those endeavours. This leads us to the ultimate source of an organization's culture: its founders.[33]

The founders of an organization traditionally have a major impact on that organization's early culture. They have a vision of what the organization should be. They are unconstrained by previous customs or ideologies. The small size that typically characterizes new organizations further facilitates the founders' imposition of their vision on all organizational members.

The process of culture-creation occurs in three ways.[34] First, founders only hire and keep employees who think and feel the way they do. Second, they indoctrinate and socialize these employees to their way of thinking and feeling. And finally, the founders' own behaviour acts as a role model that encourages employees to identify with them and thereby internalize their beliefs, values, and assumptions. When the organization succeeds, the founders' vision becomes seen as a primary determinant of that success. At that point, the founders' entire personality becomes embedded in the culture of the organization.

How important is vision? In 1990, at the age of 64, Andree Beaulieu-Green walked away from tenure and an annual salary of $75,000 at the Université du Québec à Montréal to start her own interactive-technology training centre. "She envisioned giving artists the tools they needed to produce more attractive 2-D and 3-D animation, cartoon animation and interactive multimedia without them having to go to Toronto or Vancouver. But she knew nothing about business. She was simply passionate about her dream." Today, her Montreal-based school, ICARI, teaches about 160 students a year and the students are wildly successful in Canada's animation industry.

**Rogers Communications**
www.rogers.com

**Magna International**
www.magnaint.com

Microsoft's culture is largely a reflection of its co-founder and former CEO, Bill Gates. Gates is personally aggressive, competitive, and highly disciplined. Those are the same characteristics often used to describe the software giant he founded. Other contemporary examples of founders who have had an immeasurable impact on their organizations' cultures are Akio Morita at Sony, Ted Rogers at Toronto-based Rogers Communications, Frank Stronach of Toronto-based Magna International, Mary Kay at Mary Kay Cosmetics, and Richard Branson at the Virgin Group.

## Keeping a Culture Alive

Once a culture is in place, there are human resource practices within the organization that act to maintain it by giving employees a set of similar experiences.[35] For example, the selection process, performance evaluation criteria, training and career development activities, and promotion procedures ensure that those hired fit in with the culture, reward those who support it, and penalize (and even expel) those who challenge it. Three forces play a particularly important part in sustaining a culture: selection practices, the actions of top management, and socialization methods. Let's take a closer look at each.

The core value of enhancing people's lives through sports and fitness is intensely held and widely shared by Nike employees. Nike founder Philip Knight has created a strong sports-oriented culture and promotes it through company practices such as paying employees extra for biking to work instead of driving. Nike is recognized worldwide as an athlete's company that hires former varsity, professional, and Olympic athletes to design and market its shoes and clothing for sports enthusiasts. Nike headquarters in Beaverton, Oregon, is a large campus with walking and jogging trails and buildings named for sports heroes, such as the Joan Benoit Samuelson Center, the Bo Jackson Fitness Center, and the Joe Paterno Day Care Center.

**SELECTION**  The explicit goal of the selection process is to identify and hire individuals who have the knowledge, skills, and abilities to perform the jobs within the organization successfully. Typically, more than one candidate will be identified who meets any given job's requirements. The final decision as to who is hired is significantly influenced by the decision maker's judgment of how well each candidate will fit into the organization. This attempt to ensure a proper match, either deliberately or inadvertently, results in the hiring of people who have values essentially consistent with those of the organization, or at least a good portion of those values.[36]

Additionally, the selection process provides information to applicants about the organization. Candidates learn about the organization, and if they perceive a conflict between their values and those of the organization, they can self-select themselves out of the applicant pool. Selection, therefore, becomes a two-way street, allowing the employer or applicant to look elsewhere if there appears to be a mismatch. In this way, the selection process sustains an organization's culture by selecting out those individuals who might attack or undermine its core values.

Applicants for entry-level positions in brand management at Procter & Gamble (P&G) experience an exhaustive application and screening process. Their interviewers are part of an elite cadre who have been selected and trained extensively via lectures, videotapes, films, practice interviews, and role plays to identify applicants who will successfully fit in at P&G. Applicants are interviewed in depth for such qualities as their ability to "turn out high volumes of excellent work," "identify and understand problems," and "reach thoroughly substantiated and well-reasoned conclusions that lead to action." P&G values rationality and seeks applicants who think that way. University and college applicants receive two interviews and a general-knowledge test on

Markham, Ontario-based InSystems Technologies wants to be known as a high-performance culture and a hip place to work. Founder and CEO Michael Egan appears in one of his company's recruiting pamphlets atop his Harley-Davidson. To ensure that new hires will fit into the culture, he offers bonuses to his employees for recommending a successful hire. Recruits who meet the technical requirements for the job go through five to seven interviews "because the cultural fit is key."

campus before being flown back to head office for three more one-on-one interviews and a group interview at lunch. Each encounter seeks corroborating evidence of the traits that the firm believes correlate highly with "what counts" for success at P&G.[37]

Similarly, applicants for positions at Compaq Computer are carefully chosen for their ability to fit into the company's teamwork-oriented culture. As one executive put it, "We can find lots of people who are competent. The No. 1 issue is whether they fit into the way we do business."[38] At Compaq, that means job candidates who are easy to get along with and who feel comfortable with the company's consensus management style. To increase the likelihood that loners and those with big egos get screened out, it's not unusual for an applicant to be interviewed by 15 people, who represent all departments of the company and a variety of seniority levels.[39]

**TOP MANAGEMENT** The actions of top management also have a major impact on the organization's culture.[40] Through what they say and how they behave, senior executives establish norms that filter down through the organization as to whether risk-taking is desirable; how much freedom managers should give their employees; what is appropriate dress; what actions will pay off in terms of pay raises, promotions, and other rewards; and the like.

New management can also try to change the culture of an organization, although this is not an easy task. When John Cruickshank took over as editor-in-chief for *The Vancouver Sun* in September 1995, he wanted to demonstrate quickly and definitively that the old culture of the newspaper was being replaced.[41] Three quick moves signalled his intent. He met with representatives of the Newspaper Guild, the union that represents *Sun* staffers; instituted a daily post-mortem of the paper; and rejected the large corner suite with a built-in boardroom in favour of an office with a wall of windows that overlooks the newsroom. Cruickshank, in replacing previous editor-in-chief Ian Hayson, who was widely viewed as remote, was signalling that he would be working hands-on with his reporters to improve the newspaper's quality. "In much the same way that a new chief executive seeks to shape a corporate culture when taking the helm, new editors put their mark on a newspaper, and Cruickshank lost no time in remaking *The Vancouver Sun*. By week two of his tenure, the newspaper had a new look." While the jury is still out on how successful these changes have been, one small indicator is improved circulation. Only four of the country's largest newspapers increased their circulation in 1997: *The Vancouver Sun* was one of them.[42] *The Vancouver Sun's* circulation was up even more in 1998. We would not want to leave you with the impression that changing culture is easy, however. In fact, it is a difficult process. We discuss the process of changing culture in greater detail in Chapter 14.

**SOCIALIZATION** No matter how effectively the organization recruits and selects new employees, they are not fully indoctrinated in the organization's culture when they start their job. Maybe most important, because they are unfamiliar with the organization's culture, new employees are potentially likely to disturb the beliefs and customs that are in place. The organization will, therefore, want to help new employees adapt to its culture. This adaptation process is called **socialization**.[43] Sometimes employees are not fully socialized. For instance, you will note in Exhibit 9-2 that the employees of that organization had learned they were supposed to wear checkerboard caps to work, but they clearly hadn't been told why.

Xerox Canada shares with its American parent a corporate vision to be the leader in the global document market. It's up to Kevin Francis, president and CEO of Xerox Canada since February 1998, to ensure that the vision gets carried out in Canada. To accomplish this, "New employees must take a week-long course where, among other things, they are taught the customer must come first; and how to operate as part of a team."[44]

Similarly, new Sanyo employees undergo an intensive five-month training program (trainees eat and sleep together in company-subsidized dorms and are required to vacation together at company-owned resorts) where they learn the Sanyo way of doing everything — from how to speak to managers to proper grooming and dress.[45] The company considers this program essential for transforming young employees, fresh out of school, into dedicated *kaisha senshi*, or corporate warriors. Starbucks, the rapidly growing gourmet-coffee chain, doesn't go to the extreme that Sanyo does, but it seeks the same outcome.[46] All new employees go through 24 hours of training. Just for an entry-level job in a retail store making coffee? Yes! Classes cover everything necessary to transform new employees into brewing consultants. They learn the Starbucks philosophy, the company jargon (including phrases such as "half-decaf double tall almond skim mocha"), and even how to help customers make decisions about beans, grind, and espresso machines. The result is employees who understand Starbucks' culture and who project an enthusiastic and knowledgeable interface with customers.

**socialization**
The process that adapts employees to the organization's culture.

Exhibit 9-2

*"I don't know how it started, either. All I know is that it's part of our corporate culture."*

Drawing by Mick Stevens in *The New Yorker*, October 3, 1994. Copyright © 1994 by The New Yorker Magazine, Inc. Reprinted by permission.

As we discuss socialization, keep in mind that the most critical socialization stage occurs at the time of entry into the organization. This is when the organization seeks to mould the outsider into an employee "in good standing." Those employees who fail to learn the essential or pivotal role behaviours risk being labelled "nonconformists" or "rebels," which often leads to expulsion. Moreover, the organization will be socializing every employee, though maybe not as explicitly, throughout his or her career in the organization. This further contributes to sustaining the culture.

Socialization can be conceptualized as a process composed of three stages: prearrival, encounter, and metamorphosis.[47] The first stage encompasses all the learning that occurs before a new member joins the organization. In the second stage, the new employee sees what the organization is really like and confronts the possibility that expectations and reality may diverge. In the third stage, the relatively long-lasting changes take place. The new employee masters the skills required for his or her job, successfully performs his or her new roles, and makes the adjustments to his or her work group's values and norms.[48] This three-stage process has an impact on the new employee's work productivity, commitment to the organization's objectives, and eventual decision to stay with the organization. Exhibit 9-3 depicts this process.

**prearrival stage**
The period of learning in the socialization process that occurs before a new employee joins the organization.

The **prearrival stage** explicitly recognizes that each individual arrives with a set of values, attitudes, and expectations. These cover both the work to be done and the organization. For instance, in many jobs, particularly professional work, new members will have undergone a considerable degree of prior socialization in training and in school. One major purpose of a business school, for example, is to socialize business students to the attitudes and behaviours that business firms want. If business executives believe that successful employees value the profit ethic, are loyal, will work hard, and desire to achieve, they can hire individuals out of business schools who have been premoulded in this pattern. But prearrival socialization goes beyond the specific job. The selection process is used in most organizations to inform prospective employees about the organization as a whole. In addition, as noted previously, the selection process also acts to ensure the inclusion of the "right type" — those who will fit in. "Indeed, the ability of the individual to present the appropriate face during the selection process determines his or her ability to move into the organization in the first place. Thus, success depends on the degree to which the aspiring member has correctly anticipated the expectations and desires of those in the organization in charge of selection."[49]

**Exhibit 9-3**
**A Socialization Model**

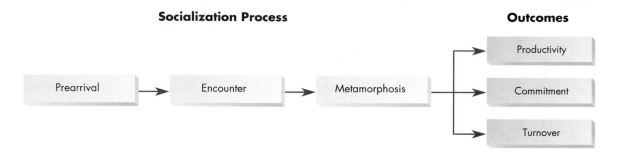

Socialization Process      Outcomes

Prearrival → Encounter → Metamorphosis → Productivity / Commitment / Turnover

**encounter stage**
The stage in the socialization process in which a new employee sees what the organization is really like and confronts the possibility that expectations and reality may diverge.

Upon entry into the organization, the new member enters the **encounter stage**. Here the individual confronts the possible dichotomy between expectations — of the job, co-workers, boss, and the organization in general — and reality. If the employee's expectations prove to have been more or less accurate, the encounter stage merely provides a reaffirmation of the perceptions gained earlier. However, this is often not the case. Where expectations and reality differ, the socialization period for the new employee should be designed to help him or her detach from previous assumptions and replace them with another set that the organization deems desirable. Of course, not all organizations actively socialize their members such that the adoption of a new set of assumptions is perfectly completed. At the extreme, new members may become totally disillusioned with the realities of their job and resign. Proper selection should significantly reduce the probability of the latter occurrence.

**metamorphosis stage**
The stage in the socialization process in which a new employee adjusts to his or her work group's values and norms.

Finally, the new member must work out any problems discovered during the encounter stage. This may mean going through changes — hence, we call this the **metamorphosis stage**. The options presented in Exhibit 9-4 are alternatives designed to bring about the desired metamorphosis. Note, for example, that the more management relies on socialization programs that are formal, collective, fixed, serial, and emphasize divestiture, the greater the likelihood that newcomers' differences and perspectives will be stripped away and replaced by standardized and predictable behaviours. Careful selection by management of newcomers' socialization experiences can — at the extreme — create conformists who maintain traditions and customs, or inventive and creative individualists who consider no organizational practice sacred.

---

**Exhibit 9-4**
**Entry Socialization Options**

**Formal vs. Informal** The more a new employee is segregated from the ongoing work setting and differentiated in some way to make explicit his or her newcomer's role, the more formal socialization is. Specific orientation and training programs are examples. Informal socialization puts the new employee directly into his or her job, with little or no special attention.

**Individual vs. Collective** New members can be socialized individually. This describes how it's done in many professional offices. They can also be grouped together and processed through an identical set of experiences, as in military boot camp.

**Fixed vs. Variable** This refers to the time schedule in which newcomers make the transition from outsider to insider. A fixed schedule establishes standardized stages of transition. This characterizes rotational training programs. It also includes probationary periods, such as the eight- to 10-year "associate" status used by accounting and law firms before deciding on whether or not a candidate is made a partner. Variable schedules give no advanced notice of their transition timetable. Variable schedules describe the typical promotion system, where one is not advanced to the next stage until he or she is "ready."

**Serial vs. Random** Serial socialization is characterized by the use of role models who train and encourage the newcomer. Apprenticeship and mentoring programs are examples. In random socialization, role models are deliberately withheld. The new employee is left on his or her own to figure things out.

**Investiture vs. Divestiture** Investiture socialization assumes that the newcomer's qualities and qualifications are the necessary ingredients for job success, so these qualities and qualifications are confirmed and supported. Divestiture socialization tries to strip away certain characteristics of the recruit. Fraternity and sorority "pledges" go through divestiture socialization to shape them into the proper role.

---

Source: Based on J. Van Maanen, "People Processing: Strategies of Organizational Socialization," *Organizational Dynamics,* Summer 1978, pp. 19-36; and E.H. Schein, "Organizational Culture," *American Psychologist,* February 1990, p. 116.

We can say that metamorphosis and the entry socialization process is complete when the new member has become comfortable with the organization and his or her job. The new employee has internalized the norms of the organization and the work group and understands and accepts these norms. The new member feels accepted by his or her peers as a trusted and valued individual, is self-confident that he or she has the competence to complete the job successfully, and understands the system — not only his or her own tasks, but also the rules, procedures, and informally accepted practices. Finally, the new employee understands how he or she will be evaluated, that is, what criteria will be used to measure and appraise his or her work. He or she knows what is expected and what constitutes a job "well done." As Exhibit 9-3 shows, successful metamorphosis should have a positive impact on the new employee's productivity and his or her commitment to the organization, and it should reduce the propensity to leave the organization.

Some people, of course, do not fit well with the company culture. Doug Hobbes, director of product marketing for Globe Information Services, lasted just four months at Ontario-based GlobeStar Systems Inc.[50] In his words, "It was a culture thing." He didn't enjoy going out for hamburgers after work or working late, "even though the organization's key people often stayed till 9 or 10 p.m." Because his work habits were different from theirs, his co-workers viewed him as unenterprising and aloof. His story serves as a reminder to make sure that you fit with the organization's culture when you accept a job.

## How Cultures Form

Exhibit 9-5 summarizes how an organization's culture is established and sustained. The original culture is derived from the founder's philosophy. This, in turn, strongly influences the criteria used in hiring. The actions of the current top management set the general climate of what is acceptable behaviour and what is not. How employees are to be socialized will depend both on the degree of success achieved in matching new employees' values to those of the organization's in the selection process and on top management's preference for socialization methods.

Bolton, Ontario-based Husky Injection Molding Systems Ltd. illustrates how a company forms and maintains its culture. Robert Schad, the company's 68-year-old founder, believes in a competitive, ecologically friendly, healthy, and humane workplace.[51] Through employee councils, workers at head office meet with Schad monthly and are able to voice any concerns they have, which has led to better lighting in the parking lot, speed bumps on access roads, tightened security, a fitness centre on site, and a performance-review process that has received no complaints since 1995. Husky's cafeteria serves hot organic vegetarian meals, which are subsidized by the company. There are free herbal teas, but no candy, doughnuts, or vending machines on the premises. The firm believes in egalitarianism, and thus executives and employees share the parking lot, dining room, and washrooms. Employees

**Exhibit 9-5
How Organizational Cultures Form**

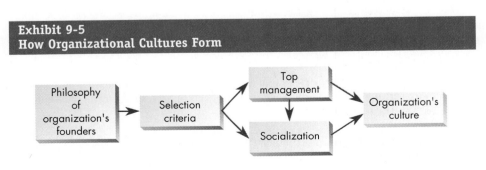

To make sure that new employees are socialized into Vancouver-based Creo's corporate culture, employees are introduced to a buddy on the first day of work. Rather than relying on formal systems and policies, the high-tech manufacturer for the graphic arts industry has buddies explain how everything works informally. The Creo culture is based on a philosophy of self-management and creativity, with everyone accountable to the organization and to one another. Creo has 4200 employees globally, and information is openly shared, decisions are made by consensus, and people work in teams, where both team leaders and peers evaluate performance.

receive an annual report and monthly newsletter that provide them with financial information about the company. They also receive salaries at the high end of the industry scale. The salaries, together with Husky's benefits package, allow the company to attract and retain the very brightest technical people, according to Husky's former director of human resources David Alcock. Employees serve on the hiring committee as well, to evaluate and recommend potential employees. When the committee is divided over a candidate, often the person is not hired, because it is not clear that he or she fits in with Husky's culture.

## How Employees Learn Culture

Culture is transmitted to employees in a number of forms, the most potent being stories, rituals, material symbols, and language. You can observe some of the ways Wal-Mart taught its culture to Canadian employees in this chapter's CBC Video Case on page 414.

### Stories

During the days when Henry Ford II was chairman of the Ford Motor Co., one would have been hard-pressed to find a manager who hadn't heard the story about Mr. Ford's reminder to his executives. When they became too arrogant, Ford reminded the executives that "it's my name that's on the building." The message was clear: Henry Ford II ran the company!

For many years, Ford Motor Co. has paid attention to women car buyers. One company anecdote about senior designer Mimi Vandermolen, a Canadian who headed the interior-design team of the Taurus, reminds employees of the extent to which they should go to consider all of their customers' needs. "Vandermolen decreed that every member of her team, both male and female, would wear their fingernails long in order to better understand the needs of women drivers."[52] Her team obliged, and the car became one of the best-selling sedans in North America.

Nordstrom employees are fond of the following story, which strongly conveys the company's policy toward customer returns: When this specialty retail chain was in its infancy, a customer came in and wanted to return a set of automobile tires. The salesperson was a bit uncertain how to handle the problem. As the customer and salesperson spoke, Mr. Nordstrom walked by and overheard the conversation. He immediately interceded,

**Nordstrom's**
www2.nordstrom.com/shop/

asking the customer how much he had paid for the tires. Mr. Nordstrom then instructed the salesperson to take the tires back and provide a full cash refund. After the customer had received his refund and left, the perplexed salesperson looked at the boss. "But, Mr. Nordstrom, we don't sell tires!" "I know," replied the boss, "but we do whatever we need to do to make the customer happy. I mean it when I say we have a no-questions-asked return policy." Nordstrom then picked up the telephone and called a friend in the auto-parts business to see how much he could get for the tires.

Stories such as these circulate through many organizations. They typically contain a narrative of events about the organization's founders, rule breaking, rags-to-riches successes, reductions in the workforce, relocation of employees, reactions to past mistakes, and organizational coping.[53] These stories anchor the present in the past and provide explanations and legitimacy for current practices.[54]

## Rituals

**rituals**
Repetitive sequences of activities that express and reinforce the key values of the organization, what goals are most important, which people are important, and which are expendable.

**Rituals** are repetitive sequences of activities that express and reinforce the key values of the organization, what goals are most important, which people are important, and which ones are expendable.[55] College and university faculty members undergo a lengthy ritual in their quest for permanent employment — tenure. Typically, the faculty member is on probation for six years. At the end of that period, the member's colleagues must make one of two choices: extend a tenured appointment or issue a one-year terminal contract. What does it take to obtain tenure? It usually requires satisfactory teaching performance, service to the department and university, and scholarly activity. Of course, what satisfies the requirements for tenure in one department at one university may be appraised as inadequate in another. The key is that the tenure decision, in essence, asks those who are tenured to assess whether the candidate has demonstrated, based on six years of performance, whether he or she fits in. Colleagues who have been socialized

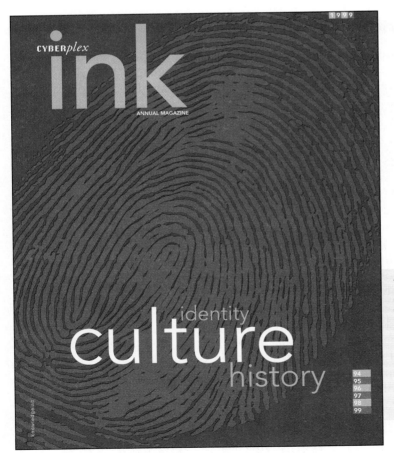

Toronto-based Cyberplex Inc. makes its money developing websites and e-commerce for others. Yet, when it wanted to make sure that its employees knew their company's culture, it decided to publish it in a glossy magazine. *Ink*, a full-colour magazine, tells the company's story and introduces the employees who work there. The magazine is intended to make employees and potential hires think "this is the place I want to be."

properly will have proved themselves worthy of being granted tenure. Every year, hundreds of faculty members at colleges and universities are denied tenure. In some cases, this action is a result of poor performance across the board. More often, however, the decision can be traced to the faculty member's not doing well in those areas that the tenured faculty believe are important. The instructor who spends dozens of hours each week preparing for class and achieves outstanding evaluations by students but neglects research and publication activities may be passed over for tenure. What has happened, simply, is that the instructor has failed to adapt to the norms set by the department. The astute faculty member will assess early on in the probationary period what attitudes and behaviours his or her colleagues want and will then proceed to give them what they want. By demanding certain attitudes and behaviours, the tenured faculty have made significant strides toward standardizing tenure candidates.

One of the best-known corporate rituals is Mary Kay Cosmetics' annual award meeting.[56] Looking like a cross between a circus and a Miss America Pageant, the meeting takes place over two days in a large auditorium, on a stage in front of a large, cheering audience, with all the participants dressed in glamorous evening clothes. Saleswomen are rewarded with an array of flashy gifts — gold and diamond pins, fur stoles, pink Cadillacs — based on success in achieving sales quota. This "show" acts as a motivator by publicly recognizing outstanding sales performance. In addition, the ritual aspect reinforces Mary Kay's personal determination and optimism, which enabled her to overcome personal hardships, found her own company, and achieve material success. It conveys to her salespeople that reaching their sales quota is important and that, through hard work and encouragement, they too can achieve success.

## Material Symbols

The layout of corporate headquarters, the types of automobiles top executives are given, and the presence or absence of corporate aircraft are a few examples of material symbols. Others include the size of offices, the elegance of furnishings, executive perks, and dress attire.[57] These material symbols convey to employees who is important, the degree of egalitarianism desired by top management, and the kinds of behaviour (for example, risk-taking, conservative, authoritarian, participative, individualistic, social) that are appropriate. For instance, Sony Music Canada's ending statement to its mission statement — "our success is in our attitude" — is reflected in the layout of its Toronto head office. Rick Camilleri, Sony's CEO, spent $60 million to create a "state-of-the-art, one-stop, funky playhouse for adults, replete with writing, editing, and recording studios,...a Main Street thoroughfare, gourmet cafeteria,...and floor-to-ceiling murals." Camilleri describes both head office and Sony Canada as follows: "We want to be irreverent, to be renegades, to be different. Successful companies are not followers."[58]

The design of General Motors Canada's corporate office in Oshawa reflects the values of Maureen Kempston Darkes, president and general manager of General Motors of Canada since 1994. The office is functional, modest, and almost spartan; she doesn't even have her own formal office — just a desk at the end of a row of desks. Not surprisingly, her friends describe her as "direct, solid, rooted and without airs — the antithesis of flash."[59]

Her headquarters conveys to employees that Kempston Darkes values openness, equality, creativity, and flexibility.

The president and chief executive officer of Ford Canada, Bobbie Gaunt, has the same huge desk in her office in Toronto as does Ford Motor Co. CEO Jacques Nassar and every other Ford divisional head. The design of the office buildings for each of these heads is also the same (although the size may differ). This corporate decision reflects the continuing influence of Henry Ford, who believed it was more efficient that way.[60] Ontario-based St. Joseph's Printing uses its office layout to encourage an atmosphere of friendliness among its employees. The building has a large atrium, an art gallery displaying local artists' work, and a gym with lunchtime aerobics classes.[61]

Corporations differ in how much separation they want to make between their executives and employees, and this plays out in how material benefits are distributed to executives. Some corporations provide their top executives with chauffeur-driven limousines and, when they travel by air, unlimited use of the corporate jet. Others may not get to ride in limousines or private jets, but they might still get a car and air transportation paid for by the company (only the car is a Chevrolet with no driver, and the jet seat is in the economy section of a commercial airliner). As mentioned earlier in this chapter, at Bolton, Ontario-based Husky Injection Molding Systems, a more egalitarian culture is favoured. Employees and management share the parking lot, dining room, and even washrooms.

The shared meaning provided by Yahoo! Inc.'s strong corporate culture is stated in the company's motto—"Do what's crazy, but not stupid." The motto guides employees as they develop entertaining programs and services that grab the attention of today's Internet users. Employee creativity is key to keeping Yahoo! the leading search engine on the Internet. Yahoo! hires young Net enthusiasts who thrive in an informal setting where there are few rules and regulations to stifle the creative process.

## Language

Many organizations and units within organizations use language as a way to identify members of a culture or subculture. By learning this language, members attest to their acceptance of the culture and, in so doing, help to preserve it.

At the Saint John headquarters of New Brunswick Telephone Co. Ltd. (before it merged with the three other major Atlantic Canada telephone companies to form Aliant in March 1999), "Gerryisms," named for Gerry Pond, the former president and CEO, abounded. The Gerryisms served as mantras for NBTel and staffers, who referred to the company's vision with such catchphrases as "electronic service integration," "LivingLAB," or "NB First."[62] At St. Joseph's Printing, a large poster hangs in the plant, declaring, "Let's all make learning a process that never ends."[63]

If you're a new employee at Boeing, you'll find yourself learning a whole unique vocabulary of acronyms, including BOLD (Boeing online data); CATIA (computer-graphics-aided three-dimensional interactive application); MAIDS (manufacturing assembly and installation data system); POP (purchased outside production); and SLO (service level objectives).[64]

Over time, organizations often develop unique terms to describe equipment, offices, key staff, suppliers, customers, or products that relate to its business. New employees are frequently overwhelmed with acronyms and jargon that, after six months on the job, have become fully part of their language. Once assimilated, this terminology acts as a common denominator that unites members of a given culture or subculture.

## Matching People With Cultures

There is now a substantive body of evidence to demonstrate that organizations attempt to select new members who fit well with the organization's culture.[65] And most job candidates similarly try to find organizations where their values and personality will fit in.

Recent research by Goffee and Jones provides some interesting insights on different organizational cultures and guidance for prospective employees.[66] They have identified four distinct cultural types. Let's take a look at their cultural framework and how you can use it to select an employer where you'll best fit in.

Goffee and Jones argue that two dimensions underly organizational culture. The first they call *sociability*. This is a measure of friendliness. High sociability means people do kind things for one another without expecting something in return and relate to each other in a friendly, caring way. In terms of the characteristics of organizational culture presented at the beginning of this chapter, sociability is consistent with a high people orientation, high team orientation, and focus on processes rather than outcomes. The second is *solidarity*. It's a measure of task-orientation. High solidarity means people can overlook personal biases and rally behind common interests and common goals. Again, referring back to our earlier discussion of the characteristics of culture, solidarity is consistent with high attention to detail and high aggressiveness. Exhibit 9-6 illustrates a matrix with these two dimensions rated as either high or low. They create four distinct culture types:

- *Networked culture* (high on sociability; low on solidarity). These organizations view members as family and friends. People know and like each other. People willingly give assistance to others and openly share information. The major negative associated with this culture is that the focus on friendships can lead to a tolerance for poor performance and creation of political cliques.

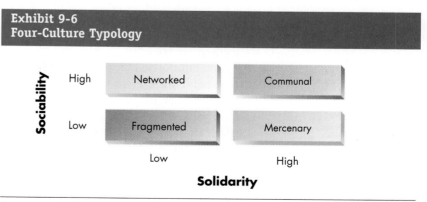

**Exhibit 9-6
Four-Culture Typology**

Source: Adapted from R. Goffee and G. Jones, *The Character of Corporation: How Your Company's Culture Can Make or Break Your Business* (New York: HarperBusiness, 1998), p. 21.

> **Do you wonder what kind of culture would work best for you?**

- *Mercenary culture* (low on sociability; high on solidarity). These organizations are fiercely goal-focused. People are intense and determined to meet goals. They have a zest for getting things done quickly and a powerful sense of purpose. Mercenary cultures aren't just about winning; they're about destroying the enemy. This focus on goals and objectivity also leads to a minimal degree of politicking. The downside of this culture is that it can lead to an almost inhumane treatment of people who are perceived as low performers.

- *Fragmented culture* (low on sociability; low on solidarity). These organizations are made up of individualists. Commitment is first and foremost to individual members and their job tasks. There is little or no identification with the organization. In fragmented cultures, employees are judged solely on their productivity and the quality of their work. The major negatives in these cultures are excessive critiquing of others and an absence of collegiality.

- *Communal culture* (high on sociability; high on solidarity). This final category values both friendship and performance. People have a feeling of belonging but there is still a ruthless focus on goal achievement. Leaders of these cultures tend to be inspirational and charismatic, with a clear vision of the organizations' future. The downside of these cultures is that they often consume one's total life. Their charismatic leaders frequently look to create disciples rather than followers, resulting in a work climate that is almost "cult-like."

Unilever and Heineken are examples of networked cultures. Heineken, for example, has over 30 000 employees but retains the feeling of friendship and family that is more typical among small firms. The company's highly social culture produces a strong sense of belonging and often a passionate identification with its product. Are you cut out for a networked culture? You are if you possess good social skills and empathy; you like to forge close, work-related friendships; you thrive in a relaxed and convivial atmosphere; and you're not obsessed with efficiency and task performance.

Mars, Campbell Soup, and Japanese heavy-equipment manufacturer Komatsu are classic mercenary cultures. At Mars, for instance, meetings are almost totally concerned with work issues. There's little tolerance for socializing or small talk. You're well matched to a mercenary culture if you're goal-oriented; thrive on competition; like clearly structured work tasks; enjoy risk-taking; and are able to deal openly with conflict.

Most top-tier universities and law firms take on the properties of fragmented cultures. Professors at major universities, for instance, are judged on their research and scholarship. Senior professors with big reputations don't need to be friendly to their peers or attend social functions to retain their status. Similarly, law partners who bring in new clients and win cases need to expend little energy getting to know co-workers or being visible in the office. You're likely to fit in well in a fragmented culture if you are independent; have a low need to be part of a group atmosphere; are analytical rather than intuitive; and have a strong sense of self that is not easily undermined by criticism.

Examples of communal cultures would include Hewlett-Packard, Johnson & Johnson, and consulting firm Bain & Co. Hewlett-Packard is large and very goal focused. Yet it has a strong family feel. The "HP Way" is a set

**Hewlett-Packard**
www.hp.com

of values the company has enumerated that govern how people should behave and interact with each other. The HP Way's value of trust and community encourages loyalty to the company. And the company returns that loyalty to employees as long as they perform well. Who fits into communal cultures? You might if you have a strong need to identify with something bigger than yourself; enjoy working in teams; and are willing to put the organization above family and personal life.

How important is this culture-person fit? In a recent study of accounting firms, new employees whose personalities meshed with the company were 20 percent less likely to leave their jobs in the first three years than those who did not fit as well.[67] This chapter's From Concepts to Skills on page 382 gives you some idea of factors that you might consider when trying to determine an organization's culture.

## Changing Organizational Culture

Trying to change the culture of an organization is quite difficult, and requires that many aspects of the organization change at the same time, especially the reward structure. Organizations often undergo cultural change as the result of a crisis. For instance, in the early 1980s AT&T, a monopoly phone system in the United States, had to get its people to change from the attitude "we are a monopoly and have time to do things the way we think best" to "we have to compete in the market and pay attention to our customers and the competition — and do so rapidly."[68]

After GM experienced huge losses in market share, the automaker established its Saturn subsidiary. To overcome GM's bureaucracy and be competitive, Saturn started from scratch, creating new structures, new technologies, and new relationships, both between workers and managers and between dealers and customers. Saturn's culture has in fact spread to car owners themselves. Greg Parker of Hamilton, Ontario, recently co-authored the *Saturn Owners Cookbook*, "a different kind of cookbook for the owners of a different kind of car."[69]

To change a culture, the everyday policies, practices, procedures, and routines have to change. For instance, AT&T had to stop certain practices (like relying on "readiness" to introduce new products) and start new practices (like requiring less paperwork to take a discovery to market). When Saturn decided to sell its cars at a fixed price, the company had to change the way it rewarded and supported dealers so that they would not feel threatened by the loss of possibly bigger commissions that could be gained through negotiations with customers. Saturn also had to make sure that customers really believed they were getting the "best" price when there was no negotiation between salesperson and customer.

Chapter 14, which is about organizational change, specifically addresses the topic of culture change. To help you begin to think about these ideas, you might want to consult the Point/CounterPoint discussion on pages 390-391, which gives you two views on the ease with which culture can be changed. For a specific example of the difficulties of culture change, you should read this chapter's Case Incident on page 413, which examines culture change attempts at Canada Post.

# HR Implications

# Examples of Organizational Cultures

Organizations can introduce specific cultures that represent important values to the organization. For instance, culture can be used to signal that a company values families through its family-friendly policy, values diversity through an emphasis on diversity throughout the firm, or values innovation through a culture of innovation. We examine these three examples of cultures in turn.

## Family-Friendly Workplaces

In today's diverse workforce, more and more employees are females, single parents, step-parents, individuals responsible for aging relatives, or members of two-career households. These employees have different needs than the traditional stereotype of a working dad with a stay-at-home wife and two kids. An increasing number of organizations are responding to their diverse workforce by creating family-friendly workplaces.

So what's a **family-friendly workplace**? The term refers to an umbrella of work/family programs, such as on-site daycare, child-care and eldercare referrals, flexible hours, compressed workweeks, job sharing, telecommuting, temporary part-time employment, and relocation assistance for employees' family members.[1]

Creating a family-friendly work climate was initially motivated by management's concern to improve employee morale and productivity and to reduce absenteeism. At Quaker Oats, for instance, 60 percent of employees admitted being absent at least three days a year because of children's illnesses, and 56 percent said they were unable to attend company-related functions or work overtime because of child-care problems.[2] However, the overall evidence indicates that the major benefit to creating a family-friendly workplace is that it makes it easier for employers to recruit and retain first-class workers.[3]

For many parents, the ultimate determinant of whether they are able to work is the availability of child care. Ontarians faced a crisis in the fall of 1997 when teachers went out on strike. Some large employers, such as Toronto-based law firm McMillan Binch and several branches of the Royal Bank of Canada, set up temporary daycare facilities for younger children.[4] Ottawa-based Mitel did even more. They established resources for their employees' children to continue studying at Mitel. The parents referred to this as "Mitel High," and it made it easier for parents to cope with the strike. Mitel also kept about 65 high-school students busy each day, offering them résumé-writing and job-hunting seminars.

Husky Injection Molding Systems, the world's third-largest firm in the plastics industry, is a model of what a company can do for the children of its employees.[5] Husky built Copper House, a 1600-square-metre child-care centre that cost $5 million to develop. According to Valerie Nease, director of Copper House, "no expense was spared to build and equip" the centre. Staff have at least a diploma, though many have degrees in early childhood education. The child-staff ratio is well below legal requirements. Nease says: "There are other companies that have implemented child-care centres. But in 20 years of working, I've never seen anything done to this degree."

As the population ages, an increasing number of employees find themselves responsible for caring for parents or grandparents.[6] Employees who spend time worrying about eldercare have less time for, and are less focused on, work-related issues. Therefore many organizations are widening child-care concerns to cover all dependants, including elderly family members.

One of the more interesting findings related to family-friendly workplaces is their appeal to both sexes. The common assumption is that family-friendly programs are used mostly by women, but the evidence suggests that this is not the case. Workers of both sexes make trade-offs for family; and men are as likely as women to seek these programs.[7] Similarly, men are increasingly rejecting relocation, overnight travel, and overtime to spend more time with their families. For instance, at Du Pont, 41 percent of men in management or professional jobs told their supervisors they weren't available for relocation; and 19 percent told their bosses they would not accept a job that required extensive travel. Among those in manufacturing jobs at Du Pont, 39 percent of men refused to work overtime in order to spend more time with family.[8]

## Organizations That Value Diversity

Some organizations have been more proactive than others in indicating the need to promote more inclusive environments where employees from various cultures and races could work easily side by side. We noted in Chapter 3 that Procter & Gamble Canada explicitly values diversity in the workplace. Another example to consider is GM Canada.

Maureen Kempston Darkes (president and general manager of General Motors Canada) believes in emphasizing the importance of promoting ethnic, gender, and racial diversity for GM. "Unless we can create a culture where everyone can contribute," she says, "we'll never be very successful." Long before she arrived at her post in Canada, she had been promoting diversity initiatives at GM. In the early 1980s, she spearheaded the creation of GM's women's advisory council to deal with such issues as employment equity and networking opportunities. She's also worked to make improvements to GM's flextime hours and telecommuting programs, to make them more family friendly. At GM Canada she has initiated a Diversity Strategy Team with a goal "to create a workforce that mirrors the multinational character of customers in the showrooms."[9]

## The Culture of Innovation

What does it take to be an innovative company? Several of Canada's most well-known companies fit the bill. Montreal-based Bank of Montreal, Bombardier, and forestry giant Avenor Inc., Brampton, Ontario-based Northern Telecom Ltd. (Nortel), Vancouver-based zinc producer Cominco Ltd., Ottawa-based software developer Corel Corp., and Calgary-based ABB Vetco Gray Inc., (a company that invented a spill-free system to retrieve oil from the ocean floor) have all been cited for their innovative actions.[10]

Jean Monty, CEO of Northern Telecom Ltd. (Nortel) from 1992 to 1997, took a company with demoralized employees and stagnant revenue and built it into one of Canada's few high-tech multinationals, creating an innovative organization at the same time. Monty replaced Paul Stern, who had "chopped R&D spending, alienated customers and obliterated employee morale"

according to a *Report on Business* story.[11] Monty's vision was to have world-class research and development happening at Nortel, because the rapid pace in technology required that Nortel stay ahead. Therefore, he says, "We invested massively, particularly in R&D, and we didn't try to shrink ourselves to greatness."[12] He also wanted to improve both employee morale and customer relations. To do this, he spent many hours communicating his vision directly to his employees and tying customer satisfaction levels to managers' pay. "He's an outstanding field commander who inspires his troops with strong leadership," says Lynton "Red" Wilson, chair and chief executive of BCE Inc., which owns 51.6 percent of Nortel.[13]

While Monty managed to return Nortel to innovative status after the company had suffered under Paul Stern, many companies are still trying to achieve a similar turnaround. Typically an organization stimulates organizational innovation through its culture. How does it do this? The standard toward which many organizations strive is that achieved by the 3M Co.[14] It has developed a reputation for being able to stimulate innovation over a long period of time. 3M has a stated objective that 30 percent of its sales are to come from products less than four years old. In 1995, the figure was 32 percent. In one recent year alone, 3M launched more than 200 new products.

Innovative organizations tend to have similar cultures. They encourage experimentation. They reward both successes and failures. They celebrate mistakes. At Hewlett-Packard, for instance, CEO Lewis Platt has successfully built a corporate culture that supports people who try something that doesn't work out.[15] Platt himself protects people who stick their neck out, fearful that to do otherwise would stifle the risk-taking culture he encourages among his managers. Unfortunately, in too many organizations, people are rewarded for the absence of failures rather than for the presence of successes. Such cultures extinguish risk-taking and innovation. People will suggest and try new ideas only where they feel such behaviours exact no penalties. Managers in innovative organizations recognize that failures are a natural by-product of venturing into the unknown. When Babe Ruth set his record for home runs in one season, he also led the league in strikeouts. He is remembered for the former, not the latter!

Companies that believe in creating the future for themselves are also likely to be more innovative. That certainly describes Nortel's moves under Monty, with its increased budget for research and development. The Bank of Montreal's introduction of mbanx in October 1996 came about when former CEO Matthew Barrett and his senior team sat down and asked, "What about those people who are too busy to go to the bank?" according to Bryan Smith of Toronto-based Innovation Associates.[16] Mbanx is a virtual banking division of the Bank of Montreal and is viewed as a new form of banking.

Within the human resources category, innovative organizations actively promote the training and development of their members so that they keep current; offer high job security so employees don't fear getting fired for making mistakes; and encourage individuals to become champions of change. Once a new idea is developed, idea champions actively and enthusiastically promote the idea, build support, overcome resistance, and ensure that the innovation is implemented.[17] The evidence indicates that champions have common personality characteristics: extremely high self-confidence, persistence, energy, and a tendency to take risks. Idea champions also display characteristics associated with transformational leadership. They inspire and energize others with their vision of the potential of an innovation and through their strong personal conviction in their mission. They are also good at gaining the commitment of others to support their mission. In addition, idea champions have jobs that provide considerable decision-making discretion. This autonomy helps them introduce and implement innovations in organizations.[18]

Given the status of 3M as a premier product innovator, we would expect it to have most of the properties we've identified. And it does. The company is so highly decentralized that it has many of the characteristics of small, organic organizations. The structure relies on extensive redundancy. For instance, every division, department, and product group has its own labs — many of which are deliberately duplicating the work of others. Consistent with the need for cross-fertilization of ideas, the company holds internal trade shows where divisions will show their technologies to employees of other divisions. All of 3M's scientists and managers are challenged to "keep current." Idea champions are created and encouraged by allowing scientists and engineers to spend up to 15 percent of their time on projects of their own choosing. And if a 3M scientist comes up with a new idea but finds resistance within the researcher's own division, he or she can apply for a $70 000 grant from an internal venture-capital fund to further develop the idea.

The company encourages its employees to take risks — and rewards the failures as well as the successes. And 3M's management has the patience to see ideas through to successful products. It invests nearly seven percent of company sales revenue (more than $1.4 billion a year) in research and development, yet management tells its R&D people that *not everything will work*. It also fosters a culture that allows people to defy their managers. For instance, each new employee and his or her manager take a one-day orientation class where, among other things, stories are told of victories won by employees despite the opposition of their boss. Finally, while 3M incurred its first layoffs in decades during 1995, the company still continues to be a model of corporate stability. The average tenure for company officers is 31 years, and the overall annual turnover rate within the company is a minuscule three percent.

Sources:

[1] See, for instance, A. Saltzman, "Family Friendliness," *U.S. News & World Report*, February 22, 1993, pp. 59-66; M. Galen, "Work & Family," *Business Week*, June 28, 1993, pp. 80-88; S. Hand and R.A. Zawacki, "Family-Friendly Benefits: More Than a Frill, *HR Magazine*, October 1994, pp. 79-84; S. Nelton, "Adjusting Benefits for Family Needs," *Nation's Business*, August 1995, pp. 27-28; L.T. Thomas and D.C. Ganster, "Impact of Family-Supportive Work Variables on Work-Family Conflict and Strain: A Control Perspective," *Journal of Applied Psychology*, February 1995, pp. 6-15; and K.H. Hammonds, "Balancing Work and Family," *Business Week*, September 16, 1996, pp. 74-80.

[2] Cited in M.A. Verespej, "People-First Policies," *Industry Week*, June 21, 1993, p. 20.

[3] S. Shellenbarger, "Data Gap," *Wall Street Journal*, June 21, 1993, p. R6.

[4] D. Jenish, "Going to the Wall: A Power Struggle Hits Two Million Ontario Children," *Maclean's*, November 10, 1997, p. 18.

[5] Information on Husky based on B. Livesey, "Provide and Conquer," *Report on Business Magazine*, March 1997, pp. 34-44.

[6] S. Shellenbarger, "The Aging of America Is Making 'Elder Care' a Big Workplace Issue," *Wall Street Journal*, February 16, 1994, p. A1.

7 See S.J. Lambert, "An Investigation of Workers' Use and Appreciation of Supportive Workplace Policies," in D.P. Moore (ed.), *Academy of Management Best Paper Proceedings* (Vancouver, BC, 1995), pp. 136-140; and T. Lewin, "Workers of Both Sexes Make Trade-offs for Family, Study Shows," The *New York Times*, October 29, 1995, p. Y14.

8 Cited in T. Lewin, "Workers of Both Sexes Make Trade-offs for Family, Study Shows," *The New York Times*, October 29, 1995, p. Y14.

9 M. Posner, "The 28 Billion Dollar Woman," *Chatelaine*, December 1997, pp. 70-75.

10 A. Walmsley, "Smart Company," *Report on Business Magazine*, April 1997, pp. 24-29.

11 B. Livesey, "Tag Team," *Report on Business Magazine*, July 1997, pp. 39-46.

12 B. Livesey, "Tag Team," *Report on Business Magazine*, July 1997, p. 40.

13 "Northern Exposure: For His Outstanding Turnaround at Northern Telecom, Jean Monty is Canada's CEO of the Year," *Financial Post*, June 28/30, 1997, p. 8.

14 Discussion of the 3M Co. is based on K. Labich, "The Innovators," *Fortune*, June 6, 1988, p. 49; R. Mitchell, "Masters of Innovation," *Business Week*, April 10, 1989, p. 58; K. Kelly, "The Drought Is Over at 3M," *Business Week*, November 7, 1994, pp. 140-141; T.A. Stewart, "3M Fights Back," *Fortune*, February 5, 1996, pp. 94-99; and T.D. Schellhardt, "David in Goliath," *Wall Street Journal*, May 23, 1996, p. R14.

15 J.H. Sheridan, "Lew Platt: Creating a Culture for Innovation," *Industry Week*, December 19, 1994, pp. 26-30.

16 A. Walmsley, "Smart Company," *Report on Business Magazine*, April 1997, p. 26.

17 J.M. Howell and C.A. Higgins, "Champions of Change," *Business Quarterly*, Spring 1990, pp. 31-32; and D.L. Day, "Raising Radicals: Different Processes for Championing Innovative Corporate Ventures," *Organization Science*, May 1994, pp. 148-172.

18 J.M. Howell and C.A. Higgins, "Champions of Change," *Business Quarterly*, Spring 1990, pp. 31-32.

# SUMMARY AND IMPLICATIONS

## For the Workplace

Employees form an overall subjective perception of an organization based on such factors as degree of risk tolerance, team emphasis, and support of people. This overall perception becomes, in effect, the organization's culture or personality. The favourable or unfavourable perception then affects employee performance and satisfaction, with the impact being greater in organizations with stronger cultures.

Just as people's personalities tend to be stable over time, so too do strong cultures. This makes strong cultures difficult for managers to change. When a culture becomes mismatched to its environment, management will want to change it. But as the Point/CounterPoint debate on page 388 demonstrates, changing an organization's culture is a long and difficult process. The result, at least in the short term, is that managers should treat their organization's culture as relatively fixed.

One of the more important managerial implications of organizational culture relates to selection decisions. Hiring individuals whose values don't align with those of the organization is likely to lead to employees who lack motivation and commitment, and who are dissatisfied with their jobs and the organization.[70] Not surprisingly, employee "misfits" have considerably higher turnover rates than do individuals who perceive a good fit.[71]

We should also not overlook the influence socialization has on employee performance. An employee's performance depends to a considerable degree on knowing what he or she should or should not do. Understanding the right way to do a job indicates proper socialization. Furthermore, the appraisal of an individual's performance includes how well the person fits into the organization. Can he or she get along with co-workers? Does he or she have acceptable work habits and demonstrate the right attitude? These qualities differ between jobs and organizations. For instance, on some jobs employees will be evaluated more favourably if they are aggressive and outwardly indicate that they are ambitious. On another job, or on the same job in another organization, such an approach may be evaluated negatively. As a result, proper socialization becomes a significant factor in influencing both actual job performance and how others perceive it.

## For You as an Individual

The culture of an organization has a strong impact on how you will feel about working for that organization. The same is true for how the culture of your college or university might affect you. In both cases, the organization offers particular expectations about behaviours, and you, as the employee or student, are expected to follow the norms. You will feel more comfortable in cultures that share your values and expectations. This might be as simple as being in classes where participation is valued, if you enjoy participating. If the classroom culture is one of participation and you like to remain passive, however, that class might make you feel less comfortable.

When you work in groups on student projects, the groups create mini-cultures of their own. You will probably observe this if you pay attention to the other groups in the class. Some will be quite cohesive, and others will look as if the members hardly know each other. These outcomes occur, in part, because of the cultures that the groups create.

In the two previous chapters, we examined the uneasy sides of interaction: conflict, negotiation, power and politics. Starting with this chapter we have moved from studying interaction to understanding how organizations set and communicate vision. Specifically, we addressed what culture was and how it formed. The culture of an organization can influence how much politicking goes on, and the degree to which there is conflict and negotiation. In the next chapter we will examine leadership to understand more fully how organizations transmit visions to their employees.

## For Review

1. What is the difference between job satisfaction and organizational culture?
2. Can an employee survive in an organization if he or she rejects its core values? Explain.
3. How can an outsider assess an organization's culture?
4. What defines an organization's subcultures?
5. Contrast organizational culture with national culture.
6. How can culture be a liability to an organization?
7. How does a strong culture affect an organization's efforts to improve diversity?
8. What benefits can socialization provide for the organization? For the new employee?

9. How is language related to organizational culture?
10. Describe 4 cultural types and the characteristics of employees who fit best with each.

# For Critical Thinking

1. Contrast individual personality and organizational culture. How are they similar? How are they different?
2. Is socialization brainwashing? Explain.
3. If management sought a culture characterized as innovative and autonomous, what might its socialization program look like?
4. Can you identify a set of characteristics that describes your college's or university's culture? Compare them with several of your peers. How closely do they agree?
5. "We should be opposed to the manipulation of individuals for organizational purposes, but a degree of social uniformity enables organizations to work better." Do you agree or disagree with this statement? What are its implications for organizational culture? Discuss.

## *LEARNING ABOUT YOURSELF EXERCISE*

# What Kind of Organizational Culture Fits You Best?

For each of the following statements, circle the level of agreement or disagreement that you personally feel:

SA = Strongly Agree
A = Agree
U = Uncertain
D = Disagree
SD = Strongly disagree

| | SA | A | U | D | SD |
|---|---|---|---|---|---|
| 1. I like being part of a team and having my performance assessed in terms of my contribution to the team. | SA | A | U | D | SD |
| 2. No person's needs should be compromised in order for a department to achieve its goals. | SA | A | U | D | SD |
| 3. I like the thrill and excitement from taking risks. | SA | A | U | D | SD |
| 4. If a person's job performance is inadequate, it's irrelevant how much effort he or she made. | SA | A | U | D | SD |
| 5. I like things to be stable and predictable. | SA | A | U | D | SD |
| 6. I prefer managers who provide detailed and rational explanations for their decisions. | SA | A | U | D | SD |
| 7. I like to work where there isn't a great deal of pressure and where people are essentially easygoing. | SA | A | U | D | SD |

Turn to page 634 for scoring direction and key

## WORKING WITH OTHERS EXERCISE

# Rate Your Classroom Culture

Listed here are 10 statements. Score each statement by indicating the degree to which you agree with it. If you strongly agree, give it a 5. If you strongly disagree, give it a 1.

1. My classmates are friendly and supportive.  _____

2. My instructor is friendly and supportive.  _____

3. My instructor encourages me to question and challenge him or her as well as other classmates.  _____

4. My instructor clearly expresses his or her expectations to the class.  _____

5. I think the grading system used by my instructor is based on clear standards of performance.  _____

6. My instructor's behaviour during examinations demonstrates his or her belief that students are honest and trustworthy.  _____

7. My instructor provides regular and rapid feedback on my performance.  _____

8. My instructor uses a strict bell curve to allocate grades.  _____

9. My instructor is open to suggestions on how the course might be improved.  _____

10. My instructor makes me want to learn.  _____

Add up your score for all the statements except number 8. For number 8, reverse the score (strongly agree=1; strongly disagree=5) and add it to your total. Your score will fall between 10 and 50.

A high score (37 or above) describes an open, warm, human, trusting, and supportive culture. A low score (25 or below) describes a closed, cold, task-oriented, autocratic, and tense culture.

Form groups of 5-7 members each. Compare your scores. How closely do they align? Discuss and resolve discrepancies.

## ETHICAL DILEMMA EXERCISE

# Cultural Factors and Unethical Behaviour

An organization's culture socializes people. It subtly conveys to members that certain actions are acceptable, even though they may be illegal. For instance, when executives at General Electric, Westinghouse, and other manufacturers of heavy electrical equipment illegally conspired to set prices in the early 1960s, the defendants invariably testified that they came new to their jobs, found price fixing to be an established way of life, and simply entered into it as they did into other aspects of their job. One GE manager noted that every one of his bosses had directed him to meet with the competition: "It had become so common and gone on for so many years that I think we lost sight of the fact that it was illegal."[1]

The strength of an organization's culture has an influence on the ethical behaviour of its managers. A strong culture will exert more influence on managers than a weak one. If the culture is strong and supports high ethical standards, it should have a very powerful positive influence on a manager's ethical behaviour. However, in a weak culture, managers are more likely to rely on subculture norms to guide their behaviour. Work groups and departmental standards will more strongly influence ethical behaviour in organizations that have weak overall cultures.

It is also generally acknowledged that the content of a culture affects ethical behaviour. Assuming this is true, what would a culture look like that would shape high ethical standards? What could top management do to strengthen that culture? Do you think it's possible for a manager with high ethical standards to uphold those standards in an organizational culture that tolerates, or even encourages, unethical practices?

Source:

[1] As described in P.C. Yeager, "Analyzing Corporate Offenses: Progress and Prospects," in W.C. Frederick and L.E. Preston (eds.), *Business Ethics: Research Issues and Empirical Studies* (Greenwich, CT: JAI Press, 1990), p. 174.

## INTERNET SEARCH EXERCISES

1. Identify a merger or acquisition that has run into trouble (or been dissolved) in the past year and in which the primary problem identified was incompatible cultures. Describe and discuss what specific elements of the cultures led to the problem.

2. Provide examples of jargon used at 2 Canadian, 2 US, and 2 Australian firms (that is, 6 firms in all). In each case, describe how that jargon helps members of these organizations to learn their culture.

## CASE INCIDENT

# The Difficulty of Culture Change at Canada Post

Canada's postal service has been faced with labour troubles for much of the past 50 years. Many trace the problems back to extensive hiring of returning veterans after the Second World War. This created a garrison culture. "The paramilitary environment [created at Canada Post at that time] spawned some of the most aggressive and self-centred unions in Canadian history," says Michael Warren, who served as president of Canada Post in the early 1980s. That culture has been difficult to change.

Canada Post needs to change its culture because it is under pressure from the federal government to cut about $200 million from its operating costs. Critics contend that the Crown corporation refuses to implement cost-cutting efficiencies that a truly private enterprise would be forced to undertake. In the private sector, when companies have to cut costs, they downsize and/or make changes in the labour process. However, the Canadian Union of Postal Workers' (CUPW) collective agreement makes it difficult for Canada Post to impose cost-saving work rules. The union rarely wants to go along with the proposals by management for changing work procedures.

One example of a cost-saving measure that Canada Post is trying to introduce is to shave 10 minutes off every route in the country. The company plans to examine how many steps a letter carrier should be taking to deliver the mail. In the private sector this would be done as part of a re-engineering process. "What we're doing is looking at their whole day and how we can make productive time out of unproductive time," Canada Post spokesperson John Caines said. "No one will be working any longer than they are now and nobody will be losing any salary." He also said that Canada Post can save $2 million for every minute cut from the routes.

But CUPW's president Darrell Tingley notes, "Basically every minute cut from the routes means 32 jobs lost. If they are successful in getting 10 minutes out, it equates to between 300 and 400 jobs." Tingley believes that Canada Post is just trying to give already-overworked postal workers an even heavier load. "I don't know how much you can get from a stone, but postal workers already work hard and they're just trying to squeeze a lot of orange from the juice."

Canada Post's Caines characterizes the dispute between the two parties as "boiling down to the fundamental issue of who is going to control the workplace — management or the union." The clearer issue, however, is, how do you change a culture that is so entrenched, with each of the parties unwilling to see what the other side wants?

## Questions

**1.** Describe Canada Post's current culture.

**2.** How might cultural change efforts be different in public-sector organizations than in for-profit business firms?

**3.** What suggestions would you have for top management that could help it enlist the unions in the cultural change efforts?

**4.** Discuss the specific suggestions you would make to top management that could help it succeed in changing Canada Post's culture into one that was more friendly.

Sources: Based on B. Came, "Handle With Care: Canada Post Tries to Avert a Nationwide Postal Strike," *Maclean's*, November 17, 1997, p. 86; J. Ditchburn, "Canada Post, Union Return to Bargaining Table," *Canadian Press Newswire*, August 19, 1997; G. McIntosh, "Canada Post Says Carriers Should do the Quick Step," *Canadian Press Newswire*, April 4, 1997.

# Wal-Mart's Culture Comes to Canada

In early 1994, Wal-Mart started its move into Canada, transforming Woolco stores and turning Woolco employees into Wal-Mart associates. Wal-Mart faced resistance, however, as Canadians were aware that the giant retailer had often caused local businesses to be eliminated, had refused to buy any of Woolco's unionized stores, and had even sent English-only flyers to potential customers in Quebec.

So, how has Wal-Mart managed its move into Canada? By bringing its corporate culture with it. Wal-Mart has a strong culture, replete with slogans, posters, and socialization practices. The company even introduced its culture using cheerleading techniques more readily identified with Americans than Canadians, with workers and trainers shouting "We are family!" and "Who's number one? The customer, always."

Wal-Mart's office space is covered with posters, including "Eight Steps to Building Your Business," "Corporate Beliefs," and "The Top 10 Principles of Success." The Wal-Mart operation is fuelled by slogans such as "Pride Through Performance."

Employees also understand the importance of these slogans. As one employee reports, after mentioning some of the slogans ("respect for individual," "meet the needs of the customer," "be the best in all we do"), "The slogans are what we do."

As Wal-Mart moved into Canada, it understood the importance of introducing its corporate culture to Canadian workers. The company wanted to ensure that Woolco employees would adopt the mindset of Wal-Mart Associates. It even hired a "morning kicker" to help employees get into the spirit.

Wal-Mart has been successful in making its northern move. Although there have been some rumblings about unionization, these have not resulted in successful campaigns. In the fall of 1997, the second unionization attempt Wal-Mart faced was turned down by Nelson, British Columbia, workers. The first unionization attempt, in Windsor, Ontario, was also rebuffed, although the Ontario Labor Relations Board certified the union anyway. However, in the late spring of 1998, the Windsor workers appealed the Ontario Board's ruling, indicating that they preferred to be decertified.

By late 1999 Wal-Mart had doubled its sales since arriving in Canada, and had 56 percent of the $10.6-billion discount department store market. Canadians ranked Wal-Mart first, ahead of Zellers, the Bay, Sears, and the now-closed Eaton's, in value for money, variety and selection, and customer service. Eighty-five percent of Canadian consumers say they shop at Wal-Mart, up from 62 percent in 1995. Its success has particularly hurt sales at Zeller's.

What accounts for Wal-Mart's success in Canada? Spokesperson Andrew Pelletier, representing the Mississauga, Ontario-based Wal-Mart Canada, Inc., notes that "Wal-Mart doesn't use a cookie-cutter approach to business, it adapts to the markets it operates in." Wal-Mart has even received calls from communities in New Brunswick and British Columbia, asking for stores to come to their towns.

# Questions

1. Describe how Wal-Mart's slogans reinforce its culture.

2. What difficulties might you have anticipated in bringing Wal-Mart's "American culture" into Canada?

3. Do you think everyone would be interested in working for a company with a strong culture such as Wal-Mart's? Why or why not?

Source: Based on "Wal-Martization of Canada," *Venture 508*; aired February 10, 1994. See also "Wal-Mart's Growth a Wake-Up Call: Study," *Vancouver Sun*, December 24, 1998, p. D7; and Z. Olijnyk, "Wal-Mart Takes Premier Rank in Market Share in Five Years: Sales Soar to 5.9b," *Financial Post*, November 30, 1999, p. C5.

# CHAPTER 10

# Leadership

C an one person make a difference in an organization's performance? Apple Computer thinks so. After years of underperforming under the leadership of both Michael Spindler and Gil Amelio, Apple Computer is once again headed by Steve Jobs, its legendary co-founder who was ousted from his original leadership position in 1985.[1]

Despite undergoing two massive restructurings, firing thousands of employees, replacing entire groups of senior executives, and discontinuing several unprofitable products under Amelio, Apple faced red ink every quarter except one in the 18 months of Amelio's leadership. In December 1996, Apple brought Jobs back in an advisory role and expanded his role further when Amelio was dismissed in July 1997. Jobs has led a remarkable turnaround since he returned as "interim CEO" in 1997; 1998 was Apple's first profitable fiscal year since 1965, and saw the launch of the colourful iMac computer, its most successful product in about five years. In January 2000, to the delight of Apple shareholders, Jobs announced he was dropping "interim" from his title.

## Questions for Consideration

### Why is leadership associated with both supervision and vision?

### Can anyone be a leader?

### How important are followers in understanding leadership?

Steve Jobs is what is known as a charismatic leader. He can inspire those around him to do more than they might have considered doing on their own. He is not without his critics, however. A 1998 book about him (*Apple: The Inside Story of Intrigue, Egomania, and Business Blunders* by Jim Carlton) describes Jobs as mercurial, arrogant, and having a rather large ego.[2]

Despite these possible flaws, those who have watched Jobs perform his turn-around note that he is different from his predecessors in an important way: he's not afraid to make tough decisions quickly. "He's not afraid to make a call," says analyst Louis Mazzuchelli of Gerard Klauer Mattison and Co.

As Steve Jobs is demonstrating once again at Apple, leaders can make a difference. In this chapter, we examine the various studies on leadership to determine what makes an effective leader. Understanding leadership is important because, in many of today's organizations, leadership occurs at all levels: from the top, of course, but also within work groups, where leadership might be more informal, and from individuals who take on projects for their organizations because they see new ways of doing things. Leading is no longer just for supervisors and CEOs. Thus learning about leadership helps you relate better to different leadership styles and enables you to take on the role of leader if necessary. Let's first take a look at the differences between managers and leaders.

## Are Managers and Leaders the Same?

Leadership and management are two terms that are often confused. What is the difference between them?

John Kotter of the Harvard Business School argues that managers bring about order and consistency by drawing up formal plans, designing rigid

**Apple Canada**
www.apple.com/ca

organizational structures, and monitoring results against the plans.[3] Leaders, in contrast, establish direction by developing a vision of the future; then they align people by communicating this vision and inspiring them to overcome hurdles. Robert House of the Wharton School at the University of Pennsylvania basically concurs when he says that managers use the authority inherent in their designated formal rank to obtain compliance from organizational members.[4]

Although Kotter and House provide separate definitions of managers and leaders, both researchers and practising managers frequently make no such distinctions. However, as Professor Rabindra Kanungo at McGill notes, there is a growing consensus emerging "among management scholars that the concept of 'leadership' must be distinguished from the concept of 'supervision/management.'"[5] Exhibit 10-1 illustrates Professor Kanungo's distinctions between management and leadership. Leaders provide vision and strategy; management implements that vision and strategy, coordinates and staffs the organization, and handles day-to-day problems.

### Exhibit 10-1
### Distinguishing Leadership From Managership

| Managership | Leadership |
|---|---|
| 1. Engages in day-to-day caretaker activities: Maintains and allocates resources | Formulates long-term objectives for reforming the system: Plans strategy and tactics |
| 2. Exhibits supervisory behaviour: Acts to make others maintain standard job behaviour | Exhibits leading behaviour: Acts to bring about change in others congruent with long-term objectives |
| 3. Administers subsystems within organizations | Innovates for the entire organization |
| 4. Asks how and when to engage in standard practice | Asks what and why to change standard practice |
| 5. Acts within established culture of the organization | Creates vision and meaning for the organization |
| 6. Uses transactional influence: Induces compliance in manifest behaviour using rewards, sanctions, and formal authority | Uses tranformational influence: Induces change in values, attitudes, and behaviour using personal examples and expertise |
| 7. Relies on control strategies to get things done by subordinates | Uses empowering strategies to make followers internalize values |
| 8. Status Quo supporter and stabilizer | Status Quo challenger and change creator |

Source: R.N. Kanungo, "Leadership in Organizations: Looking Ahead to the 21st Century," *Canadian Psychology*, 39(1-2), 1998, p. 77.

When Rick George, president and CEO of Calgary-based Suncor Energy Inc., arrived in 1991, Suncor was one of the highest-cost oil producers, and had just suffered a devastating fire at its oilsands plant at Fort McMurray. Today Suncor is one of the country's leading stock-market performers. George did this by balancing the competing demands that face any leader. He determined new strategies for the company, and led his employees well. He believes in leading by example and keeping Suncor "feeling like a small company with the right values and beliefs."

**Suncor**
www.suncor.com

## The New Leadership Demands in Organizations

Traditional notions of leadership have operated from the assumption that employees in organizations are divided into two camps: those who manage or lead and those who follow. This view suggests that there is no overlap in the two roles. However, there are many more opportunities to be a leader in today's organization.

To understand how the leadership role has expanded, it is necessary to understand the variety of tasks that get carried out in a successful organization. Robert Quinn, Kim Cameron, and their colleagues categorized these tasks in a model known as the "Competing Values Framework."[6] As Exhibit 10-2 indicates, the tasks are divided along two dimensions: an internal-external focus and a flexibility-control focus.

The internal-external dimension refers to the extent that the focus is either inwards (toward employee issues and/or production processes) or outwards (toward the marketplace, government regulations, and the changing social, environmental, and technological conditions of the future). For example, during the 1980s and 1990s, almost without exception, Eaton's was more focused internally on maintaining its established system of retailing than on looking outwards toward the marketplace to anticipate what demands lay ahead. As a consequence, 1999 saw the closure of this distinctly Canadian institution.

The flexibility-control dimension refers to the competing demands of staying focused on doing what has been done in the past versus being more flexible in orientation and outlook. Some organizations are more stable, maintaining the status quo and exhibiting less change. McDonald's, for instance, emphasizes stability with its successfully developed assembly-line process to produce fast food. Other organizations are more flexible and dynamic, allowing more teamwork, participation, and innovation from their employees, and/or seeking new opportunities for products and services.

**Exhibit 10-2**
**The Competencies and the Leadership Roles in the Competing Values Framework**

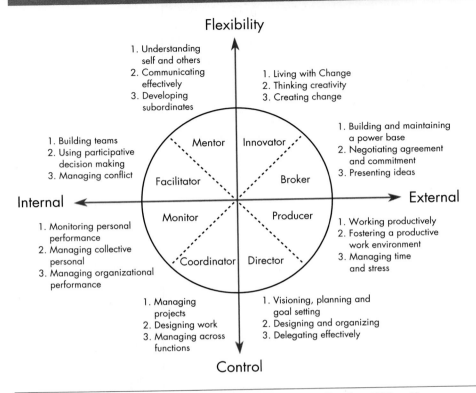

Source: R.E. Quinn, *Beyond Rational Management* (San Francisco: Jossey-Bass Inc., 1988), p. 48.

Exhibit 10-2 outlines the variety of roles, including innovator, broker, producer, director, coordinator, monitor, facilitator, and mentor, that a leader must adopt today. As organizations increasingly cut layers, reducing the number of managers, while relying more on the use of teams in the workplace, and expecting employees to take on more responsibility themselves, these skills become important to everyone.

In developing our discussion of leadership below, we will focus on two major tasks of those who lead in organizations: managing those around them to get the day-to-day tasks done and inspiring others to do the extraordinary. It will become clear that successful leaders rely on a variety of interpersonal skills in order to encourage others to perform at their best. And it will also become clear that, no matter what your place in the hierarchy, from CEO to team leader, the skills to inspire and carry out a vision may rest with you.

## Leadership as Supervision

In this section we discuss theories of leadership that were developed prior to about 1980. These theories focused on the supervisory nature of leadership, that is, how one managed the day-to-day functioning of employees. The theories took different approaches in understanding how best to lead in a supervisory capacity, and the three general themes that emerged were as follows: 1) Are there a particular set of traits that all leaders have, making them different from nonleaders? 2) Are there particular behaviours that

Randy Jones ranks high in the traits associated with leadership. His ambition, energy, desire to lead, self-confidence, intelligence, and knowledge of publishing increase the likelihood of his success as the leader in establishing *Worth* as a new financial management magazine. Jones is also a high self-monitor, taking the lead in promoting his new product, whether it's participating in event marketing (shown here), dining with influential political and media people, or working with his sales reps in making presentations to woo advertisers.

*Worth* Magazine
www.worth.com

**trait theories of leadership**
Theories that sought personality, social, physical, or intellectual traits that differentiated leaders from nonleaders.

make for better leaders? 3) How much impact does the situation have on leaders? When you think about these theories, remember that although they have been considered "theories of leadership," they rely on an older understanding of what "leadership" means, and they don't convey Professor Kanungo's distinction between leadership and supervision.

## Are Leaders Different From Others?

Have you ever wondered whether there's some fundamental personality difference that makes some people "born leaders"? The dominant research on leadership up until the 1940s was the trait approach, where researchers looked to find universal personality traits that leaders were more likely to have than nonleaders.[7] Trait theory was also revisited for a time in the late 1980s.[8] Trait theory emerged in the hope that if it were possible to identify the traits of leaders, it would be easier to select people to fill leadership roles.

The media have long been believers in **trait theories of leadership.** They identify people such as Nelson Mandela, Richard Branson of Virgin, and Steve Jobs of Apple as leaders, and then describe them in terms such as *charismatic, enthusiastic, decisive,* and *courageous.* The media aren't alone. The search for personality, social, physical, or intellectual attributes that would describe leaders and differentiate them from nonleaders goes back to research done by psychologists in the 1930s.

Until recently, research efforts at isolating leadership traits resulted in a number of dead ends.[9] The bulk of the studies considered one of three main categories of traits: "physical traits, such as physique, height, and appearance; abilities, such as intelligence and fluency of speech; and personality characteristics, such as conservatism, introversion-extroversion, and self-confidence."[10] It is still the case that researchers have not found a set of traits that would *always* differentiate leaders from followers and effective from ineffective leaders. However, six traits have been identified that are consistently associated with leadership: 1) ambition and energy; 2) the desire to lead; 3) honesty and integrity; 4) self-confidence; 5) intelligence; and 6) job-relevant knowledge.[11] Additionally, recent research provides strong evidence that people who are high self-monitors — that is, are highly flexible in adjusting their behaviour in different situations — are much more likely to emerge as leaders in groups than low self-monitors.[12] Overall, the cumulative findings from more than half a century of research lead us to conclude that some traits increase the likelihood of success as a leader, but none of the traits *guarantees* success.[13]

## Do Leaders Behave in Particular Ways?

The inability to strike "gold" in the trait "mines" led researchers to look at the behaviours that specific leaders exhibited. They wondered if there was something unique in the way that effective leaders behave. Trait theory, had

**behavioural theories of leadership**
Theories proposing that specific behaviours differentiate leaders from nonleaders.

**initiating structure**
The extent to which a leader is likely to define and structure his or her role and those of employees in the search for goal attainment.

**consideration**
The extent to which a leader is likely to have job relationships characterized by mutual trust, respect for employees' ideas, and regard for their feelings.

**employee-oriented leader**
A leader who emphasizes interpersonal relations.

**production-oriented leader**
A leader who emphasizes technical or task aspects of the job.

**Managerial Grid**
A nine-by-nine matrix outlining 81 different leadership styles.

it been successful, would have provided a basis for *selecting* the "right" people to assume formal positions in groups and organizations requiring leadership. In contrast, behavioural theories tried to identify critical behavioural determinants of leadership, in the hope that we could *train* people to be leaders.

The three most well-known **behavioural theories of leadership** are the Ohio State University studies conducted beginning in the late 1940s,[14] the University of Michigan studies conducted at about the same time, and Blake and Mouton's Managerial Grid, which reflects the behavioural definitions of both the Ohio and Michigan studies. All three approaches consider two main dimensions by which managers can be characterized: attention to production and attention to people.

In the Ohio State studies, these two dimensions are known as *initiating structure* and *consideration*. **Initiating structure** refers to the extent to which a leader is likely to define and structure his or her role and those of employees in the search for goal attainment, and includes behaviour that attempts to organize work, work relationships, and goals. **Consideration** is described as the extent to which a person is likely to have job relationships that are characterized by mutual trust, respect for employees' ideas, and regard for their feelings. He or she shows concern for followers' comfort, well-being, status, and satisfaction.

The Michigan group also developed two dimensions of leadership behaviour that they labelled **employee oriented** and **production oriented**.[15] Leaders who were employee oriented were described as emphasizing interpersonal relations. They took a personal interest in the needs of their subordinates and accepted individual differences among members. The production-oriented leaders, in contrast, tended to emphasize the technical or task aspects of the job. Their main concern was in accomplishing their group's tasks, and the group members were a means to that end.

A graphic portrayal of a two-dimensional view of leadership style was developed by Blake and Mouton.[16] They proposed a **Managerial Grid** based on the styles of "concern for people" and "concern for production," which essentially represent the Ohio State dimensions of consideration and initiating structure, or the Michigan dimensions of employee oriented and production oriented.

The grid, depicted in Exhibit 10-3, has nine possible positions along each axis, creating 81 different positions in which the leader's style may fall. The grid does not show results produced but, rather, the dominating factors in a leader's thinking with respect to getting results.

Each of the three behavioural approaches received some empirical support for the idea that being people oriented was an important behaviour of leaders, although there were also exceptions in each case. In the Ohio studies, leaders who were production oriented (that is, high on initiating structure) experienced greater rates of grievances, absenteeism, and turnover, and lower levels of job satisfaction from workers performing routine tasks. In the Michigan studies, employee-oriented leaders were associated with higher group productivity and higher job satisfaction. Production-oriented leaders tended to be associated with low group productivity and lower job satisfaction.

The results based on the findings of Blake and Mouton are consistent with those of the Ohio and Michigan studies. Managers were found to perform best under a 9,9 (team management style), as contrasted, for example, with a 9,1 (authority-obedience) or 1,9 (country club) style.[17] However,

**Exhibit 10-3**
**The Managerial Grid**

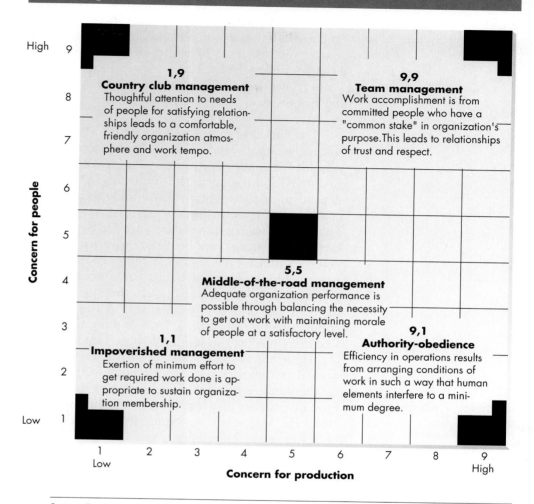

Source: Reprinted by permission of *Harvard Business Review:* An exhibit from "Breakthrough in Organization Development" by R.R. Blake, J.S. Mouton, L.B. Barnes, and L.E. Greiner (November-December 1964). Copyright © 1964 by the President and Fellows of Harvard College; all rights reserved.

there is little substantive evidence to support the conclusion that a 9,9 style is most effective in all situations.[18]

Early on in the development of the Ohio studies, inconsistent results were noted. Similar problems arose with both the Michigan studies and the Managerial Grid. Thus, starting in the 1960s, leadership theories began to examine the situational factors that affect the leader's ability to act. To understand the role of situation, consider changes that occurred at Eaton's before it ultimately failed. For the first 127 years of Eaton's existence, members of the Eaton family provided the leadership. However, by the late 1980s it became increasingly obvious that the leadership style that had kept Eaton's so successful for much of the century no longer worked. And even a change in leadership in 1997 did nothing to halt the demise of a once-great Canadian institution. In other words, the situation for Eaton's had changed and the once-successful leadership no longer worked. Unfortunately, the behavioural approaches don't recognize the impact that situations have on one's ability to lead.

Have you ever wondered if there was one *right way* to lead?

## Considering the Situation

It became increasingly clear to those who were studying the leadership phenomenon that predicting leadership success was more complex than simply isolating a few traits or preferable behaviours. The failure to obtain consistent results led to a focus on situational influences. For instance, Apple brought Steve Jobs back as leader in 1996 despite having dismissed him 11 years earlier. It is unlikely that his leadership skills changed that much during his absence, but the circumstances at Apple were quite different upon his return than when he left.

The relationship between leadership style and effectiveness suggests that under condition *a*, style *x* would be appropriate, while style *y* would be more suitable for condition *b*, and style *z* for condition *c*. But what are the conditions *a*, *b*, *c*, and so forth? It is one thing to say that leadership effectiveness is dependent on the situation and another to be able to isolate those situational conditions. Moreover leaders may oversee employees *and* report to someone above. For instance, in publicly traded organizations, leaders answer to a board of governors or a board of directors. So, just as there is pressure from below to adjust leadership style, there can be pressure from above. Therefore, when thinking about leadership, you should be aware that leaders face multiple situations simultaneously, including the types of employees, the environment of the organization, as well as the demands of the board when a company is publicly traded. Each of these alone, and certainly several factors working together, can seriously affect a leader's ability to lead.

There has been no shortage of studies attempting to isolate critical situational factors that affect leadership effectiveness. The volume is illustrated by the number of moderating variables that researchers have identified in their discussions of **situational, or contingency, theories**. These variables include the degree of structure in the task being performed, the quality of leader–member relations, the leader's position power, employees' role clarity, group norms, information availability, employee acceptance of leader's decisions, and employee maturity.[19]

We consider four situational theories below: the Fiedler contingency model, Hersey and Blanchard's situational theory, the path-goal theory, and substitutes for leadership.

**FIEDLER CONTINGENCY MODEL**  The first comprehensive contingency model for leadership was developed by Fred Fiedler.[20] The Fiedler contingency model proposes that effective group performance depends upon the proper match between the leader's style and the degree to which the situation gives control to the leader.

Fiedler created the *least preferred co-worker (LPC) questionnaire* to determine whether individuals were primarily interested in good personal relations with co-workers, and thus *relationship oriented*, or primarily interested in productivity, and thus *task oriented*. Fiedler assumed that an individual's leadership style is fixed. Therefore, if a situation requires a task-oriented leader and the person in that leadership position is relationship oriented, either the situation has to be modified or the leader must be removed and replaced for optimum effectiveness is to be achieved.

Fiedler identified three contingency dimensions that together define the situation a leader faces:

- **Leader–member relations:** The degree of confidence, trust, and respect members have in their leader.

**situational, or contingency, theories**
Theories that note the importance of considering the context within which leadership occurs.

**Fiedler contingency model**
Model proposing that effective group performance depends upon the proper match between the leader's style and the degree to which the situation gives control to the leader.

Rhonda Fryman is a team leader at Toyota Motor Manufacturing's plant in Georgetown, Kentucky. She exemplifies Toyota's philosophy of striving to create a warm, caring atmosphere with a high degree of respect for employees, which leads to their high levels of motivation and productivity. Consistent with the contingency models, Fryman is an effective leader because she assists her team in meeting their daily production goals and provides direction and support in achieving Toyota's quality goals.

- **Task structure:** The degree to which the job assignments are procedurized (that is, structured or unstructured).

- **Position power:** The degree of influence a leader has over power variables such as hiring, firing, discipline, promotions, and salary increases.

Fiedler stated that the better the leader–member relations, the more highly structured the job, and the stronger the position power, the more control the leader has. He suggested that task-oriented leaders perform best in situations of high and low control, while relationship-oriented leaders perform best in moderate control situations.[21]

**HERSEY AND BLANCHARD'S SITUATIONAL THEORY** Paul Hersey and Ken Blanchard have developed a leadership model that has gained a strong following among management development specialists.[22] This model—called **situational leadership theory (SLT)**—has been incorporated into leadership training programs at over 400 of the Fortune 500 companies; and over one million managers a year from a wide variety of organizations are being taught its basic elements.[23]

SLT essentially views the leader-follower relationship as analogous to that between a parent and child. Just as a parent needs to relinquish control as a child becomes more mature and responsible, so too should leaders. Hersey and Blanchard identify four specific leader behaviours—from highly directive to highly laissez-faire. The most effective behaviour depends on a follower's ability and motivation. So SLT says if a follower is *unable* and *unwilling* to do a task, the leader needs to give clear and specific directions (in other words, be highly directive). If a follower is *unable* but *willing*, the leader needs to display high task orientation to compensate for the follower's lack of ability, and high relationship orientation to get the follower to "buy into" the leader's desires (in other words, "sell" the task). If the follower is *able* but *unwilling*, the leader needs to use a supportive and participative style. Finally, if the employee is both *able* and *willing*, the leader doesn't need to do much (in other words, a laissez-faire approach will work).

**situational leadership theory (SLT)**
Theory essentially views the leader-follower relationship as analogous to that between a parent and a child.

While both the Fiedler model and Hersey and Blanchard's situational theory have some intuitive appeal, they have received far less empirical support for their approaches, and are more difficult to apply in the work situation, than the next theory we consider, the path-goal model.[24]

**path-goal theory**
The theory that a leader's behaviour is acceptable to employees insofar as they view it as a source of either immediate or future satisfaction.

**PATH-GOAL THEORY** Currently, one of the most respected approaches to leadership is the **path-goal theory**. Developed by University of Toronto professor Martin Evans in the late 1960s, it was subsequently expanded upon by Robert House (formerly at the University of Toronto, but now at the Wharton School of Business). Path-goal theory is a contingency model of leadership that extracts key elements from the Ohio State leadership research on initiating structure and consideration, and from the expectancy theory of motivation.[25]

The essence of the theory is that it is the leader's job to assist followers in attaining their goals and to provide the necessary direction and/or support to ensure that their goals are compatible with the overall objectives of the group or organization. The term *path-goal* derives from the belief that effective leaders clarify the path to help their followers get from where they are to the achievement of their work goals, and to make the journey along the path easier by reducing roadblocks and pitfalls.

Path-goal theory identifies four leadership behaviours that might be used in different situations. The *directive leader* lets followers know what is expected of them, schedules work to be done, and gives specific guidance as to how to accomplish tasks. This closely parallels the Ohio State dimension of initiating structure. The *supportive leader* is friendly and shows concern for the needs of followers. This is essentially synonymous with the Ohio State dimension of consideration. The *participative leader* consults with followers and uses their suggestions before making a decision. The *achievement-oriented leader* sets challenging goals and expects followers to perform at their highest level. House assumes that leaders are flexible and can display any or all of these behaviours depending on the situation.

As Exhibit 10-4 illustrates, path-goal theory proposes two types of contingency variables that affect the leadership behaviour–outcome relationship: environmental variables that are outside the control of the employee and variables that are part of the personal characteristics of the employee. The theory proposes that employee performance and satisfaction are likely to be positively influenced when the leader compensates for things lacking in either the employee or the work setting. However, the leader who spends time explaining tasks when those tasks are already clear or when the employee has the ability and experience to handle them without interference is likely to be ineffective because the employee will see such directive behaviour as redundant or even insulting.

The following are some examples of hypotheses that have evolved out of path-goal theory:

- *Directive leadership:*
  — leads to greater satisfaction when tasks are ambiguous or stressful than when they are highly structured and well laid out;
  — is likely to be perceived as redundant among employees with high perceived ability or with considerable experience;
  — leads to higher employee satisfaction when there is substantive conflict within a work group;
  — will lead to greater satisfaction when employees have an external locus of control.

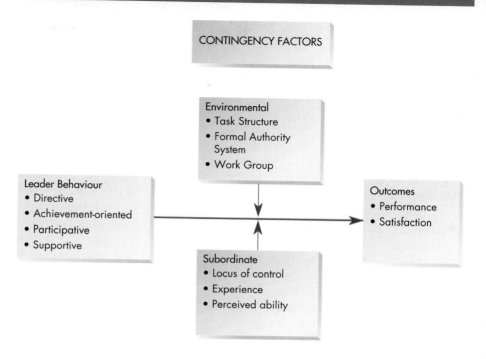

**Exhibit 10-4
The Path-Goal Theory**

- *Supportive leadership:*
  - results in high employee performance and satisfaction when employees are performing structured tasks;
  - is needed when there are clear and bureaucratic formal authority relationships.
- *Participative leadership:*
  - will lead to greater satisfaction when employees have an internal locus of control (they believe they control their own destiny).
- *Achievement-oriented leadership:*
  - is effective when tasks are ambiguously structured.

The research evidence generally supports the path-goal theory.[26]

One question that arises from these theories is whether leaders can actually adjust their behaviour to various situations. As we know, individuals differ in their behavioural flexibility. Some people show considerable ability to adjust their behaviour to external, situational factors; they are adaptable. Others, however, exhibit high levels of consistency regardless of the situation. High self-monitors are generally able to adjust their leadership style to suit changing situations better than low self-monitors.[27] Clearly, if an individual's leadership style range is very narrow and he or she can't or won't adjust (that is, the person is a low self-monitor), that individual will only be successful in very specific situations suitable to his or her style. To find out more about your style of leadership, see the Learning About Yourself Exercise on page 453.

**SUBSTITUTES FOR LEADERSHIP** The previous three theories argue that leaders are needed, but that leaders should consider the situation in determining the style of leadership to take. However, numerous studies collectively

## POINT

# Leaders Make a Real Difference!

There can be little question that the success of an organization, or any group within an organization, depends largely on the quality of its leadership. Whether in business, government, education, medicine, or religion, the quality of an organization's leadership determines the quality of the organization itself. Successful leaders anticipate change, vigorously exploit opportunities, motivate their followers to higher levels of productivity, correct poor performance, and lead the organization toward its objectives.

The importance relegated to the leadership function is well-known. Rarely does a week go by that we don't hear or read about some leadership concern: "Premier Fails to Provide the Leadership Canada Needs!" "The Conservative Party Searches for New Leadership!" "Finally Steve Jobs Removes 'Interim' From His CEO Title at Apple." A review of the leadership literature led two academics to conclude that the research shows "a consistent effect for leadership explaining 20 to 45 percent of the variance on relevant organizational outcomes."[1]

Why is leadership so important to an organization's success? The answer lies in the need for coordination and control. Organizations exist to achieve objectives that are either impossible or extremely inefficient to achieve if done by individuals acting alone. The organization itself is a coordination and control mechanism. Rules, policies, job descriptions, and authority hierarchies are illustrations of devices created to facilitate coordination and control. But leadership, too, contributes toward integrating various job activities, coordinating communication between organizational subunits, monitoring activities, and controlling deviations from standard. No amount of rules and regulations can replace the experienced leader who can make rapid and firm decisions.

The importance of leadership is not lost on those who staff organizations. Corporations, government agencies, school systems, and institutions of all shapes and sizes cumulatively spend billions of dollars every year to recruit, select, evaluate, and train individuals for leadership positions. The best evidence, however, of the importance that organizations place on leadership roles is exhibited in salary schedules. Leaders are routinely paid 10, 20, or more times the salary of those in nonleadership positions. For example, the head of General Motors earns more than $1.5 million annually. The highest-skilled auto worker, in contrast, earns under $50 000 a year. The president of this auto worker's union makes better than $100 000 a year. Police officers typically earn $30 000 to $45 000 a year. Their boss probably earns 25 percent more, and his or her boss another 25 percent. The pattern is well-established. The more responsibility a leader has, as evidenced by his or her level in the organization, the more he or she earns. Would organizations voluntarily pay their leaders so much more than their nonleaders if they didn't strongly believe that leaders make a real difference?

Source:

[1] D.V. Day and R.G. Lord, "Executive Leadership and Organizational Performance: Suggestions for a New Theory and Methodology," *Journal of Management*, Fall 1988, pp. 453-464.

# Leaders Don't Make a Difference!

Given the resources that have been spent on studying, selecting, and training leaders, you'd expect there would be overwhelming evidence supporting the positive effect of leadership on organizational performance, but that's not the case!

Currently, the two most popular approaches to leadership are contingency models and the study of charisma. For the most part, both operate under the naive assumption that through selection and/or training, leaders can learn to exhibit certain behaviours that, when properly matched to the situation, will result in improved employee and organizational performance. There are a number of flaws in this assumption.

First, leaders exist in a social system that constrains their behaviour. They have to live with role expectations that define behaviours that are acceptable and unacceptable. Pressures to conform to the expectations of peers, employees, and superiors all limit the range of behaviours that a leader can exhibit.

Second, organizational rules, procedures, policies, and historical precedents all act to limit a leader's unilateral control over decisions and resources. Hiring decisions, for instance, must be made according to procedures. And budget allocations are typically heavily influenced by previous budget precedents.

Third, there are factors outside the organization that leaders can't control but that have a large bearing on organizational performance. For example, consider the executive in a home-construction firm. Costs are largely determined by the operations of the commodities and labour markets, and demand is largely dependent on interest rates, availability of mortgage money, and economic conditions that are affected by governmental policies over which the executive has little control. Or consider the case of school superintendents. They have little control over birth rates and community economic development, both of which profoundly affect school system budgets. While a leader may react to problems as they arise or attempt to forecast and anticipate external changes, he or she has little influence over the environment. On the contrary, the environment typically puts significant limits and constraints on the leader.

Finally, the trend in recent years is toward leaders playing a smaller and smaller role in organizational activities. Important decisions are increasingly made by committees, not individuals. Additionally, the widespread popularity of employee involvement programs, the empowerment movement, and self-managed work teams has contributed to reducing any specific leader's influence.

There is a basic myth associated with leadership. We believe in attribution — when something happens, we believe something has *caused* it. Leaders play that role in organizations, and the fact that leaders earn higher pay than nonleaders is a symbolic gesture that organizations have created to further add to the impression that leaders make a difference. So while leaders may not really matter, the *belief* in leadership does. Although leaders take the credit for successes and the blame for failures, a more realistic conclusion would probably be that, except in times of rapid growth, change, or crisis, leaders don't make much of a difference in an organization's actual performance. However, people want to believe that leadership is the cause of performance changes, particularly at the extremes.

Sources: Ideas in this argument came from J. Pfeffer, "The Ambiguity of Leadership," *Academy of Management Review*, January 1977, pp. 104-111; A.B. Thomas, "Does Leadership Make a Difference to Organizational Performance?" *Administrative Science Quarterly*, September 1988, pp. 388-400; C.C. Manz and H.P. Sims, Jr., "SuperLeadership: Beyond the Myth of Heroic Leadership," *Organizational Dynamics*, Spring 1991, pp. 18-35; and G. Gemmill and J. Oakley, "Leadership: An Alienating Social Myth?" *Human Relations*, February 1992, pp. 113-129.

**Exhibit 10-5**
**Substitutes and Neutralizers for Leadership**

| Defining Characteristics | Relationship-Oriented Leadership | Task-Oriented Leadership |
|---|---|---|
| Individual | | |
| Experience/training | No effect on | Substitutes for |
| Professionalism | Substitutes for | Substitutes for |
| Indifference to rewards | Neutralizes | Neutralizes |
| Job | | |
| Highly structured task | No effect on | Substitutes for |
| Provides its own feedback | No effect on | Substitutes for |
| Intrinsically satisfying | Substitutes for | No effect on |
| Organization | | |
| Explicit formalized goals | No effect on | Substitutes for |
| Rigid rules and procedures | No effect on | Substitutes for |
| Cohesive work groups | Substitutes for | Substitutes for |

Source: Based on S. Kerr and J.M. Jermier, "Substitutes for Leadership: Their Meaning and Measurement," *Organizational Behavior and Human Performance,* December 1978, p. 378.

demonstrate that, in many situations, leaders' actions are irrelevant. Certain individual, job, and organizational variables can act as *substitutes* for leadership or *neutralize* the leader's ability to influence his or her followers.[28]

If employees have appropriate experience, training, or "professional" orientation, or if employees are indifferent to organizational rewards, the effect of leadership can be replaced or neutralized. Experience and training, for instance, can replace the need for a leader's support or ability to create structure and reduce task ambiguity. Jobs that are inherently unambiguous and routine or that are intrinsically satisfying may place fewer demands on the leadership variable. Organizational characteristics such as explicit formalized goals, rigid rules and procedures, and cohesive work groups can replace formal leadership (see Exhibit 10-5).

For more discussion of when leadership is necessary and when it is less important, you might want to examine this chapter's Point/CounterPoint feature on the previous pages.

## Leading With Vision

The theories reported above were developed at a time when most organizations were organized in traditional hierarchies where there were classic lines of command. While this form still dominates in Canada's "Most Respected Corporations,"[29] there are organizations trying to be more innovative, faster moving, and more responsive to employees who are highly educated and intelligent, and who want more say in the workplace. Thus new styles of leadership are evolving to meet the demands of these organizations. The more recent approaches to leadership move away from the supervisory tasks of leaders and focus on vision-setting activities. These theories try to explain how certain leaders can achieve extraordinary levels from their followers, and they stress symbolic and emotionally appealing leadership behaviours.[30]

## From Transactional to Transformational Leadership

Most of the leadership theories presented thus far in this chapter have concerned **transactional leaders**. These kinds of leaders guide or motivate their followers in the direction of established goals by clarifying role and task requirements. In some styles of transactional leadership, the leader uses rewarding and recognizing behaviour. This results in performance that meets expectations, though rarely does one see results that exceed performance.[31] In other styles of transactional leadership, the leader emphasizes correction and possibly punishment rather than rewards and recognition. This style "results in performance below expectations, and discourages innovation and initiative in the workplace."[32] Of course, leaders should not ignore poor performance, but effective leaders emphasize how to achieve expectations, rather than dwell on mistakes.

Some leaders inspire followers to transcend their own self-interests for the good of the organization, and have a profound and extraordinary effect on their followers. These are **transformational leaders**, such as Matthew Barrett, CEO of Barclays PLC, Britain's second-largest bank and former CEO of Bank of Montreal, Frank Stronach of Toronto-based Magna International, Bobbie Gaunt at Ford Canada, and Mogens Smed of Calgary-based SMED International, the subject of this chapter's Case Incident on page 455. Some other Canadians who have frequently been cited as being charismatic leaders include René Lévesque, Lucien Bouchard, Governor General Adrienne Clarkson, Robert Chisolm, Nova Scotia's former NDP leader, and Craig Kielburger (the Canadian teenager who founded Free the Children to promote children's rights and combat exploitation of child labour). What links these individuals is that they pay attention to the concerns and developmental needs of individual followers; they change followers' awareness of issues by helping them to look at old problems in new ways; and they are able to excite, arouse, and inspire followers to exert extra effort to achieve group goals. This chapter's CBC Video Case on page 457 features Richard Branson, of the Virgin Group, who is another example of a charismatic leader.

Transformational leadership is sometimes identified separately from **charismatic leadership** in the literature, although McGill's Kanungo notes that the two formulations are not different. Relying on his judgment, we use the two notions interchangeably. As Kanungo notes, the charismatic leader "critically examines the status quo with a view to developing and articulating future strategic goals or vision for the organization and then leading organizational members to achieve these goals through empowering strategies."[33]

Transactional and transformational leadership should not be viewed as opposing approaches to getting things done.[34] Transformational leadership is built *on top of* transactional leadership — it produces levels of employee effort and performance that go beyond what would occur with a transactional approach alone. Exhibit 10-6 outlines the difference between transactional and transformational (or charismatic) leaders. Would you be able to be a charismatic leader? We give you tips in this chapter's From Concepts to Skills feature on page 432.

**transactional leaders**
Leaders who guide or motivate their followers in the direction of established goals by clarifying role and task requirements.

**transformational leaders**
Leaders who provide individualized consideration and intellectual stimulation, and who possess charisma.

**Frank Stronach**
www.magnaint.com/Magna.nsf/Pages/M2-Founder

**Ford Canada**
www.fordcanada.com

**Craig Kielburger**
freethechildren.org/ftccraig.html

**charismatic leadership**
Leadership that critically examines the status quo with a view to developing and articulating future strategic goals or vision for the organization, and then leading organizational members to achieve these goals through empowering strategies.

## From CONCEPTS to SKILLS

# Practising to Be Charismatic

In order to be charismatic in your leadership style, you need to engage in the following behaviours:

1. *Project a powerful, confident, and dynamic presence.* This has both verbal and nonverbal components. Use a captivating and engaging voice tone. Convey confidence. Talk directly to people, maintain direct eye contact, and hold your body posture in a way that says you're sure of yourself. Speak clearly, avoid stammering, and avoid sprinkling your sentences with noncontent phrases such as "ahhh" and "you know."

2. *Articulate an overarching goal.* You need to share a vision for the future, an unconventional way of achieving the vision, and to have the ability to communicate the vision to others.

   The vision is a clear statement of where you want to go and how you're going to get there. You need to persuade others how the achievement of this vision is in the others' self-interest.

   You need to look for fresh and radically different approaches to problems. The road to achieving your vision should be seen as novel but also appropriate to the context.

Charismatic individuals not only have a vision, but they're also able to get others to buy into it. The real power of Martin Luther King, Jr., was not that he had a dream, but that he could articulate it in terms that made it accessible to millions.

3. *Communicate high-performance expectations and confidence in others' ability to meet these expectations.* You need to demonstrate your confidence in people by stating ambitious goals for them individually and as a group. You then convey absolute belief that they will achieve their expectations.

4. *Be sensitive to the needs of followers.* Charismatic leaders get to know their followers individually. You need to understand their individual needs and develop intensely personal relationships with each. This is done through encouraging followers to express their points of view, being approachable, genuinely listening to and caring about followers' concerns, and asking questions so that followers can learn what is really important to them.

Source: Based on J.M. Howell and P.J. Frost, "A Laboratory Study of Charismatic Leadership," *Organizational Behavior and Human Decision Processes*, April 1989, pp. 243-269.

Several authors have attempted to identify personal characteristics of the charismatic leader.[35] The most comprehensive analysis of charismatic leadership, however, has been completed by Jay Conger and Rabindra Kanungo.[36] They validated their measures with managers from Canada, the United States, and India, and identified five dimensions that characterize charismatic leadership. Among their conclusions, they propose that charismatic or transformational leaders articulate a strategic vision, are sensitive to the environment, are sensitive to member needs, engage in personal risk in carrying out their vision, and are perceived as unconventional in their behaviour. Exhibit 10-7 summarizes their findings on the key characteristics that appear to differentiate charismatic leaders from noncharismatic ones.

Perhaps one of the key components of charismatic leadership is the ability to articulate a vision. A review of various definitions finds that a vision differs from other forms of direction setting in several ways:

A vision has clear and compelling imagery that offers an innovative way to improve, which recognizes and draws on traditions, and connects to actions that people can take to realize change. Vision taps people's emotions and energy. Properly articulated, a vision creates the enthusiasm that people have for sporting events and other leisure time activities, bringing the energy and commitment to the workplace.[37]

**Exhibit 10-6**
**Characteristics of Transactional and Transformational Leaders**

**Transactional Leader**

*Contingent Reward:* Contracts exchange of rewards for effort, promises rewards for good performance, recognizes accomplishments.

*Management by Exception* (active): Watches and searches for deviations from rules and standards, takes corrective action.

*Management by Exception* (passive): Intervenes only if standards are not met.

*Laissez Faire*: Abdicates responsibilities, avoids making decisions.

**Transformational Leader**

*Charisma:* Provides vision and sense of mission, instills pride, gains respect and trust.

*Inspiration:* Communicates high expectations, uses symbols to focus efforts, expresses important purposes in simple ways.

*Intellectual Stimulation:* Promotes intelligence, rationality, and careful problem-solving.

*Individualized Consideration:* Gives personal attention, treats each employee individually, coaches, advises.

Source: B.M. Bass, "From Transactional to Transformational Leadership: Learning to Share the Vision," *Organizational Dynamics*, Winter 1990, p. 22. Reprinted by permission of the publisher. *American Management Association*, New York. All rights reserved.

**Exhibit 10-7**
**Key Characteristics of Charismatic Leaders**

1. *Vision and articulation*. Has a vision—expressed as an idealized goal—that proposes a future better than the status quo; and is able to clarify the importance of the vision in terms that are understandable to others.

2. *Personal risk*. Willing to take on high personal risk, incur high costs, and engage in self-sacrifice to achieve the vision.

3. *Environmental sensitivity*. Able to make realistic assessments of the environmental constraints and resources needed to bring about change.

4. *Sensitivity to follower needs*. Perceptive of others' abilities and responsive to their needs and feelings.

5. *Unconventional behaviour*. Engages in behaviours that are perceived as novel and counter to norms.

Source: Based on J.A. Conger and R.N. Kanungo, *Charismatic Leadership in Organizations* (Thousand Oaks, CA: Sage, 1998), p. 94.

This chapter's Case Incident on page 455 describes how Mogens Smed shares his vision with his employees. The key properties of a vision seem to be inspirational possibilities that are value-centred and realizable, with superior imagery and articulation.[38] Visions should be able to create possibilities that are inspirational and unique, and offer a new order that

Mogens Smed, president and CEO of Calgary-based SMED International, has a reputation as a charismatic leader. He believes his upscale office-furniture making company differs from the competitors' because "We do not play by the rules. There are no rules."

**Onvia.com**
www.onvia.com

**Gulf Canada**
www.gulf.ca

**Manulife Financial**
www.manulife.com

can produce organizational distinction. A vision is likely to fail if it doesn't offer a view of the future that is clearly and demonstrably better for the organization and its members. Desirable visions fit the times and circumstances and reflect the uniqueness of the organization. Visions that have clear articulation and powerful imagery are more easily grasped and accepted. In November 1999, Onvia.com, whose Canadian headquarters are in Vancouver, revealed its corporate vision when it formally unveiled its new name (formerly MegaDepot.com) and Canadian Web site. Onvia's vision is "to be the right arm of small businesses, available to help with any purchasing, financing, and information issues that come up when starting and running a business." It plans to do this through its Web site.[39] Glenn Ballman, Onvia's CEO and founder, feels that small businesses in Canada don't get enough support. That's why he thinks his company will make a difference, and he's driving everyone in his company to work to help small business in Canada.

Do vision and charismatic leadership really make a difference? In a survey of 1500 senior leaders (870 of them CEOs from 20 different countries) to determine the key traits or talents desirable for a CEO in the year 2000, 98 percent rated a "strong sense of vision" as "most important."[40] Another study contrasted 18 visionary companies with 18 comparable nonvisionary firms over a 65-year period.[41] The visionary companies were found to have outperformed the comparison group by six times on standard financial criteria and their stocks outperformed the general market by 15 times. An unpublished study by Robert House and some colleagues of 63 US and 49 Canadian companies (including Nortel, Molson, Gulf Canada, and Manulife) found that "between 15 and 25 percent of the variation in profitability among the companies was accounted for by the leadership qualities of their CEO."[42] That is, charismatic leaders led more profitable companies. This may explain the high compensation packages for CEOs that we discussed in Chapter 4.

An increasing body of research shows that people working for charismatic leaders are motivated to exert extra work effort and, because they like their leaders, they express greater satisfaction.[43] One of the most cited studies of the effects of charismatic leadership was done at the University of British Columbia in the early 1980s by Jane Howell (now at the Richard Ivey School of Business at the University of Western Ontario) and Peter Frost (at the University of British Columbia).[44] Their study compared the charismatic leadership style with structuring (that is, task-oriented) and considerate (that is, employee-oriented) styles, and found that those who worked under a charismatic leader generated more ideas and reported higher job satisfaction than those working under structuring leaders. Charismatic leaders also produced better results than considerate leaders, with employees performing at a higher level. Those working under charismatic leaders also showed higher job satisfaction and stronger bonds of loyalty. Howell, in summarizing these results, says, "While it is true that considerate leaders make people feel good, that doesn't necessarily translate into increased productivity. In contrast, charismatic leaders know how to inspire people to think in new directions."[45]

The evidence supporting the superiority of transformational leadership over the transactional variety is overwhelmingly impressive. For instance, a number of studies with US, Canadian, and German military officers found, at every level, that transformational leaders were evaluated as more effective than their transactional counterparts.[46] Managers at Federal Express who were rated by their followers as exhibiting more transformational leadership were evaluated by their immediate supervisors as higher performers and more promotable.[47] And Howell and her colleagues found in a study of 250 executives and managers at a major financial-services company that "transformational leaders had 34 percent higher business unit performance results than other types of leaders."[48] In summary, the overall evidence indicates that transformational leadership is more strongly correlated than transactional leadership with lower turnover rates, higher productivity, and higher employee satisfaction.[49]

> **So how do you become a transformational leader?**

For those who want to move toward a more transformational style, Howell and her colleagues recommend that leaders develop an awareness of how often they use the five behaviours of visioning, inspiring, stimulating, coaching, and team building.[50] Leaders could then set goals for themselves for working on areas where they need improvement. It is important to note, however, that organizations themselves must be encouraging and supportive of transformational leadership in order for leaders to be able to work toward the goal of becoming a more transformational leader. Performance appraisals that measure and reward transformational behaviours are one element crucial to changing behaviour. Cultures that encourage creative ideas, risk-taking, and change are also more supportive of transformational leadership. To learn more about how to be transformational/charismatic yourself, see the Working With Others Exercise on page 454.

One last comment on this topic: Charismatic leadership may not always be needed to achieve high levels of employee performance. It may be most appropriate when the follower's task has an ideological component.[51] This may explain why, when charismatic leaders surface, it is more likely to be in politics or religion, during wartime, or when a business firm is introducing a radically new product or facing a life-threatening crisis. Thus when Canada Post and Royal Trustco faced major turnaround opportunities in the 1980s, charismatic leaders emerged to take on the task. Don Lander, president and CEO of Canada Post from 1986 to 1993, is credited with transforming the corporation from an inefficient government department to a sleeker profitable Crown corporation. His success with Canada Post is viewed as a classic case of corporate culture change.[52]

Be aware that charismatic leaders may become a liability to an organization once the crisis is over and the need for dramatic change subsides.[53] Why? Because then the charismatic leader's overwhelming self-confidence often becomes a liability. He or she is unable to listen to others, becomes uncomfortable when challenged by aggressive employees, and begins to hold an unjustifiable belief in his or her "rightness" on issues.

To conclude, let's return to the subject of the chapter-opening vignette for a good example of how charismatic leadership can sometimes become a liability. Steve Jobs achieved unwavering loyalty and commitment from the technical staff he oversaw at Apple Computer during the late 1970s and early 1980s. He did so by articulating a vision of personal computers that would dramatically change the way people lived. By 1985 he was forced out of Apple when the board of directors felt that Apple needed a leadership change. Jobs's style, a sort of "my-way-or-the-highway," had been effective in the entrepreneurial days of the firm. However, in the mid 1980s, that style didn't work for building a stable corporation. But in 1996, with Apple doing so poorly, Jobs was brought back to Apple because of his vision and charisma, in the hope of restoring Apple to some of its former glory.

## Dispersed Leadership: Spreading Leadership Throughout the Organization

> **Can anyone be a leader?**

Transformational leadership theory focuses on heroic leaders, leaders at the top echelons of the organization, and also on individuals rather than teams. The theories addressed below aim to explain how leadership can be spread throughout the organization. Even if you are not a manager or someone thinking about leadership in a corporate situation, this discussion offers important insights into how you can take on a leadership role in an organization. Moreover, in today's flatter organizations, you may well be expected to show leadership characteristics, even if you are not a formal leader.

As you consider the ways that organizations are spreading leadership throughout the organization, be aware that not all organizations engage in this practice, and even within organizations, not all managers are happy with the notion of sharing power or leadership. Gifted leaders often recognize that they actually have more power if they share power. That is, sharing power enables them to build coalitions and teams that work together for the overall good of the organization. There are other managers, though, who fear the loss of any power.

### Turning Constituents Into Leaders

Several researchers have developed the idea that good leaders develop the leadership skills of their employees.[54] One set of researchers actually refer to this as superleadership, which they view as the leadership design of the future.[55] A major feature of superleadership is the emphasis on "leading others to lead themselves," so that the followers also become leaders.[56] This view is not inconsistent with the transformational view of leadership, although superleadership places more emphasis on how leaders can get followers to lead themselves. Leaders do this by developing leadership capacity in others and nurturing employees so that they do not feel the need to depend on formal leaders. Further, leaders liberate employees so that they will use their own abilities to lead themselves.

### Providing Team Leadership

Leadership is increasingly taking place within a team context. As teams grow in popularity, the role of the leader in guiding team members takes on heightened importance.[57] Also, because of its more collaborative nature, the role of team leader is different from the traditional leadership role performed by first-line supervisors.

Many leaders are not equipped to handle the change to teams. As one prominent consultant noted, "Even the most capable managers have trouble making the transition because all the command-and-control type things they were encouraged to do before are no longer appropriate. There's no reason to have any skill or sense of this."[58] This same consultant estimated that "probably 15 percent of managers are natural team leaders; another 15 percent could never lead a team because it runs counter to their personality. [They're unable to sublimate their dominating style for the good of the team.] Then there's that huge group in the middle: team leadership doesn't come naturally to them, but they can learn it."[59]

Effective team leaders need to build commitment and confidence, remove obstacles, create opportunities, and be part of the team.[60] They have to learn skills such as the patience to share information, the willingness to trust others, the ability to give up authority, and an understanding of when to intervene. New team leaders may try to retain too much control at a time when team members need more autonomy, or they may abandon their teams at times when the teams need support and help.[61]

A recent study of 20 organizations that reorganized themselves around teams found certain common responsibilities that all leaders had to assume. These included coaching, facilitating, handling disciplinary problems, reviewing team/individual performance, training, and communication.[62] Many of these responsibilities apply to managers in general. A more meaningful way to describe the team leader's job is to focus on two priorities: managing the team's external boundary and facilitating the team process.[63] We've divided these priorities into four specific roles.

- Team leaders are *liaisons with external constituencies*. These include upper management, other internal teams, customers, and suppliers. The leader represents the team to other constituencies, secures needed resources, clarifies others' expectations of the team, gathers information from the outside, and shares this information with team members.

- Team leaders are *troubleshooters*. When the team has problems and asks for assistance, team leaders sit in on meetings and try to help resolve the problems. This rarely relates to technical or operational issues because the team members typically know more about the tasks being done than does the team leader. The leader contributes by asking penetrating questions, by helping the team discuss problems, and by getting needed resources from external constituencies. For instance, when a team in an aerospace firm found itself short-handed, its team leader took responsibility for getting more staff. He presented the team's case to upper management and got the approval through the company's human resources department.

- Team leaders are *conflict managers*. When disagreements surface, team leaders help process the conflict. What's the source of the conflict? Who is involved? What are the issues? What resolution options are available? What are the advantages and disadvantages of each? By getting team members to address questions such as these, the leader minimizes the disruptive aspects of intrateam conflicts.

- Team leaders are *coaches*. They clarify expectations and roles, teach, offer support, cheerlead, and do whatever else is necessary to help team members improve their work performance.

## Leading Through Empowerment

Over the past decade, an important trend has developed that has immense implications for leadership. That trend is for managers to embrace **empowerment**. More specifically, managers are being advised that effective leaders share power and responsibility with their employees.[64] The empowering leader's role is to show trust, provide vision, remove performance-blocking barriers, offer encouragement, motivate, and coach employees.

The list of companies that have jumped on the "empowerment bandwagon" includes such world-famous corporations as General Electric, Intel, Ford, Saturn, Scandinavian Airline Systems, Harley-Davidson, Goodyear, and Conrail. They also include smaller Canadian corporations such as Vancouver-based Dominion Directory and Langley, British Columbia-based Redwood Plastics. (The empowerment strategies of both Dominion Directory and Redwood Plastics are discussed further in Chapter 8.) Many other organizations have introduced empowerment as part of their corporate-wide efforts to implement total quality management.[65] Because of factors such as downsizing, higher employee skills, commitment of organizations to continuous training, implementation of total quality management programs, and introduction of self-managed teams, there seems to be no doubt that an increasing number of situations call for a more empowering approach to leadership. But it might not work in *all* situations! Blanket acceptance of empowerment, or *any* universal approach to leadership, is inconsistent with the best and most current evidence we have on the subject.[66]

**empowerment**
Giving employees responsibility for what they do.

**Intel**
www.intel.com

**Scandinavian Airline Systems**
www.scandinavian.net

**Harley-Davidson**
www.harley-davidson.com/home.asp

**Goodyear**
www.goodyear.com

---

### Exhibit 10-8

**THE FAR SIDE**   By GARY LARSON

© 1991 FarWorks, Inc./Dist. by Universal Press Syndicate

"Well, what d'ya know! . . . *I'm* a follower, too!"

## Leading One's Self

Thus far we have discussed the role of leadership as if it were mainly a one-way street: Leadership is something someone at the top does, and hopefully, those at the bottom, the followers, follow. However, we would like to raise two provocative issues for you to consider when thinking about leadership. The first is your role as a follower. The second is the issue of self-leadership, or taking responsibility for your own actions, and learning how to be a leader, even if only in small areas of your situation.

### Can You Be a Better Follower?

When someone was once asked what it took to be a great leader, he responded: Great followers! While the response might have seemed sarcastic, it had some truth. We have long known that many managers can't lead a horse to water. But, then again, many employees can't follow a parade. Only recently have we begun to recognize that in addition to having leaders who can lead, successful organizations need followers who can follow.[67] In fact, it's probably fair to say that all organizations have far more followers than leaders, so ineffective followers may be more of a handicap to an organization than ineffective leaders. The *Far Side* cartoon shown in Exhibit 10-8 gives you some indication of what can happen when someone finally realizes that he or she is "a follower, too."

What qualities do effective followers have? One writer focuses on four.[68]

- *They manage themselves well.* They are able to think for themselves. They can work independently and without close supervision.

- *They are committed to a purpose outside themselves.* Effective followers are committed to something — a cause, a product, a work team, an organization, an idea — in addition to the care of their own lives. Most people like working with colleagues who are emotionally, as well as physically, committed to their work.

- *They build their competence and focus their efforts for maximum impact.* Effective followers master skills that will be useful to their organizations, and they hold higher performance standards than their job or work group requires.

- *They are courageous, honest, and credible.* Effective followers establish themselves as independent, critical thinkers whose knowledge and judgment can be trusted. They hold high ethical standards, give credit where credit is due, and aren't afraid to own up to their mistakes.

## Self-Management

| How do I manage myself? |
|---|

A growing trend in organizations is the focus on self-management. We saw this in Chapter 6 when we discussed self-managed teams. With reduced levels of supervision, offices in the home, teamwork, and growth in service and professional employment where individuals are often required to make decisions on the spot, individuals are increasingly being called upon to self-manage. Following from our discussion above on substitutes for leadership, self-management can be a substitute or neutralizer for leadership from others.

Despite the lack of studies of self-management techniques in organizational settings, self-management strategies have been shown to be successful in nonorganizational settings.[69] Those who practise self-management look for opportunities to be more effective in the workplace and improve their career success. Their behaviour is self-reinforced, that is, they provide their own sense of reward and feedback after carrying out their accomplishments. Moreover, self-reinforced behaviour is often maintained at a higher rate than behaviour that is externally regulated.[70]

What does self-management look like? Though "individuals in organizations are regularly taught how to manage subordinates, groups, and even organizations, they rarely receive instruction on how to manage themselves."[71] Few empirical studies of this kind have been carried out in the workplace,[72] but a 1999 study of 305 managers at a large retailing organization in the Midwestern United States identified four behaviours that can be considered self-management: planning, access management, catch-up activities, and emotions management.[73] Exhibit 10-9 describes these behaviours in greater detail.

**Exhibit 10-9**
**Self-management Practices**

In order to determine their self-management initiative, managers were asked to rate each of the following items, from 1 ("never do this") to 7 ("always do this"). Higher scores meant a higher degree of self-management.

**Planning**
- I plan out my day before beginning to work
- I try to schedule my work in advance
- I plan my career carefully
- I come to work early to plan my day
- I use lists and agendas to structure my workday
- I set specific job goals on a regular basis
- I set daily goals for myself
- I try to manage my time

**Access management**
- I control the access subordinates have to me in order to get my work done
- I use a special place at work where I can work uninterrupted
- I hold my telephone calls when I need to get things done

**Catch-up activities**
- I come in early or stay late at work to prevent distractions from interfering with my work
- I take my work home with me to make sure it get done
- I come in on my days off to catch up on my work

**Emotions management**
- I have learned to manage my aggressiveness with my subordinates
- My facial expression and conversational tone are important in dealing with subordinates
- It is important for me to maintain a "professional" manager-subordinate relationship
- I try to keep my emotions under control

Source: M. Castaneda, T.A. Kolenko, and R.J. Aldag, "Self-Management Perceptions and Practices: A Structural Equations Analysis," *Journal of Organizational Behavior*, 20, 1999, pp. 114-115.

## Leading Without Authority

Thus far in this section we have discussed how to be a follower, and how to manage yourself, but what if your goal is to be a leader, even if you don't have the authority (or formal appointment) to be one? For instance, what if you wanted to convince the dean of your school to introduce new business courses that were more relevant, or you wanted to convince the president of the company where you work that she should start thinking about more effective environmentally friendly strategies in dealing with waste? How do you effectively lead in a student group, when everyone is a peer?

Leadership at the grassroots level in organizations does happen. Rosabeth Moss Kanter, in her book *The Change Masters,*[74] discusses examples of people who saw something in their workplace that needed changing and took the responsibility to do so upon themselves. Employees were more likely to do this when organizations permitted initiative at all levels of the organization, rather than making it a tool of senior executives only.

Leading without authority simply means exhibiting leadership behaviour even though you do not have a formal position or title that might encourage others "to obey." Neither Martin Luther King nor Mahatma Gandhi operated from a position of authority, yet each was able to inspire many to follow them in the quest for social justice. The workplace can be an opportunity for leading without authority as well. As Heifetz notes, "leadership means taking responsibility for hard problems beyond anyone's expectations."[75] It also means not waiting for the coach's call.[76]

What are the benefits of leading without authority? Heifetz has identified three:[77]

- *Latitude for creative deviance.* Because one does not have authority, and the trappings that go with authority, it is easier to raise harder questions and look for less traditional solutions.
- *Issue focus.* Leading without authority means that one can focus on a single issue, rather than be concerned with the myriad issues that those in authority face.
- *Frontline information.* Leading without authority means that one is closer to the detailed experiences of some of the stakeholders. Thus more information is available to this kind of leader.

Not all organizations will support this type of leadership, and some have been known to actively suppress it. Still others will look aside, not encouraging, but not discouraging either. Nevertheless, you may want to reflect on the possibility of engaging in leadership behaviour, because you see a need, rather than because you are required to act.

# Contemporary Issues in Leadership

Is emotional intelligence an essential element of leadership? Do men and women rely on different leadership styles, and if so, is one style inherently superior to the other? How does one lead in a workplace now characterized by telecommuting, contracting out, and globalization, where workers and leaders may not even occupy the same physical location? How does national culture affect the choice of leadership style? Is there a moral dimension to leadership?

In this section, we briefly address these contemporary issues in leadership.

## Emotional Intelligence and Leadership

We introduced emotional intelligence (EI) in our discussion of emotions in Chapter 2. Recent studies indicate that EI—more than IQ, expertise, or any other single factor—is the best predictor of who will emerge as a leader.[78]

As our trait research demonstrated, leaders need basic intelligence and job-relevant knowledge. But IQ and technical skills are "threshold capabilities." They're necessary but not sufficient requirements for leadership.

**Royal Canadian Mint**
www.rcmint.ca/home.html

It's the possession of the five components of emotional intelligence—self-awareness, self-management, self-motivation, empathy, and social skills—that allows an individual to become a star performer. Without EI, a person can have outstanding training, a highly analytical mind, a long-term vision, and an endless supply of terrific ideas, but still not make a great leader. This is especially true as individuals move up in an organization. The evidence indicates that the higher the rank of a person considered to be a star performer, the more that EI capabilities surface as the reason for his or her effectiveness. Specifically, when star performers were compared with average ones in senior management positions, nearly 90 percent of the difference in their effectiveness was attributable to EI factors rather than basic intelligence.

EI has been shown to be positively related to job performance at all levels. But it appears to be especially relevant in jobs that demand a high degree of social interaction. And of course, that's what leadership is all about. Great leaders demonstrate their EI by exhibiting all five of its key components.

The recent evidence makes a strong case for concluding that EI is an essential element in leadership effectiveness. As such, it should probably be added to our earlier list of traits associated with leadership.

## Gender: Do Males and Females Lead Differently?

**HOW MANY WOMEN MAKE IT TO THE TOP?**  In August 1999, 13 of the country's largest companies had women as CEOs. Nine of those reported to US parent companies, three worked for Canadian owners (Markham, Ontario-based Extendicare Ltd., Montreal-based Telemedia Communications, and Alberta-based ATCO Ltd.), and the 13th ran the Royal Canadian Mint, a Crown corporation.[79] The United States, by comparison, had just seven women in comparable positions, with the largest firm being Hewlett-Packard Corp., led by Carly Fiorina. Overall, only two percent of the *Financial Post*

Emmie Wong Leung, founder and CEO of International Paper Industries Ltd. (IPI) of North Vancouver, which collects, processes and sells waste paper to offshore buyers, has been exporting to the United States, Hong Kong, Japan, China, the Philippines, India and Indonesia for over 20 years. She says: "I think an old-boys' network operates all over the world, but you can get them to accept you."

*500* were headed by female CEOs in 2000.

Regardless of the industry, a woman may be senior vice-president of human resources or corporate communications, but she is very rarely the president or CEO. To further illustrate this point, in 2000 just 6.1 percent of all directors in Canada's top corporations were women. Professor Ronald Burke of York University's Schulich School of Business notes that women have made little progress in both Canada and the United States in making it to the top. While he expects the percentage of women directors to rise, he doesn't expect it will happen soon.[80] Women have greatest representation among the entrepreneurial ranks, where they are starting businesses at three to four times the rate of men.[81] To put these numbers in perspective, women make up 15 percent of senior managers, 34 percent of managers and administrators,

45 percent of the labour force, 57 percent of graduate degree holders, and 51 percent of the Canadian population.

Environics Communications recently surveyed more than 650 affluent Canadian women (that is, those with annual household incomes of more than $137 000), most of whom had careers.[82] Sixty-nine percent said the opportunities offered to women are more limited than those offered to men. Apparently, it is not just Canadian women who feel that corporate opportunities are sometimes limited. In surveys conducted worldwide in both 1997 and 1998, IBM's female employees reported that the most difficult barrier they faced was the "male-dominated culture" of the organization.[83] Other top barriers identified were difficulty in balancing work and personal responsibilities, lack of networking and mentors, access to key positions, and a "culture that doesn't take risks with women." Maria Ferris, manager of global workforce diversity initiatives at IBM, notes that "the top five [barriers] are the top five in every single geography."

A study by the Center for Creative Leadership found that there were some differences, as well as many similarities, in the promotion processes for men and women.[84] The promotions of 16 men and 13 women to middle and upper management were examined through discussions with the person promoted, that person's promoting supervisor, the promoting supervisor's supervisor, and an HR representative. The researchers discovered that for both men and women, "credentials, experience, track record, skills, work ethic, ability to work on a team, interpersonal skills, and growth potential" were important. The differences underlying promotion were more subtle. The men's supervisors mentioned in 75 percent of the cases that they felt comfortable with the candidate at an interpersonal level, and that's what led to their promotions. This was cited in only 23 percent of the women's cases. For women, it was more important that they exhibited personal strength and a willingness to take risks and accept responsibility. For women's promotions, continuity with the job (that is, moving up along the same career track) was cited in 38 percent of the promotions, whereas this was cited in only six percent of the men's cases. This suggests that men are more likely to be promoted into new opportunities, whereas women are more likely to be promoted in areas where they can continue using their existing knowledge. To illustrate the significance of this point, in one case a supervisor waited to promote a woman until an opportunity appeared in the plant where she worked. The supervisor "thought it would be easier for the woman to succeed in a new job in a location where she already had credibility." The woman would have preferred to take a similar opportunity elsewhere sooner and "felt restricted by having to wait for the right opportunity to open up" in her own plant.

While it is heartening to note that on many dimensions men and women are evaluated similarly with respect to promotion opportunities, the study above also indicates that more work needs to be done to ensure that women and men have the same promotion opportunities. Part of the problem is that men and women do not even agree on what is happening in today's workplace. In 1997, Linda Duxbury, a professor in the School of Business at Carleton University, produced a study looking at differences in perceptions of men and women at work.[85] She found that 86 percent of men surveyed said that organizations actively communicate with employees, but only 65 percent of women agreed. Women were also less likely to state that their companies had established a policy of inclusion, with 44 percent of the women and 73 percent of the men agreeing with this statement.

> **Do men and women get promoted differently?**

**Kraft**
www.kraftfoods.com

**General Mills**
www.generalmills.com

Lorna Rosenstein, general manager of Lotus Development Canada Ltd., accounts for some of the difficulties women face in reaching the top: "Women have to be smarter, more creative, more focused, more bottom-line oriented, simply better than men overall if they want to rise as far. And they still get just 70 cents on the dollar in earnings compared with their male counterparts."[86]

It has become common to refer to women "hitting the glass ceiling," meaning that they reach a point beyond which they don't seem able to be promoted. Canada has women at the top of some large organizations, including GM Canada, Ford Canada, Motorola Canada, EDS, Kraft Canada, General Mills Canada, and Home Depot Canada. However, this does not mean that women are making it to the top as easily as men. When Fiorina said that she thought her appointment to the top job at Hewlett-Packard demonstrated that the glass ceiling had been broken, women at the top in Canada strongly disagreed, including Bobbie Gaunt at Ford Canada and Joy Calkin at Extendicare.[87] Sheelagh Whittaker, president and CEO of EDS Canada Ltd., notes: "I've always said that we'll have true equality when we have as many incompetent women in positions as we have incompetent men."[88] And Diane McGarry, former chair, CEO, and president of Xerox Canada, and now a vice-president with the parent corporation, refers not to the glass ceiling, but rather the "plastic ceiling" in corporations "because plastic is even harder to break than glass."[89]

More than 800 American female executives and CEOs were recently asked what they saw as the primary strategies for the successful advancement of women. The four that stood out were consistently exceeding performance expectations (cited as critical by 77 percent); developing a style with which male managers are comfortable (61 percent); seeking out difficult or challenging assignments (50 percent); and having influential mentors (37 percent).[90]

Low representation of women in management's highest places is not limited to Canada and the United States, of course. In Japan, for instance, "It's almost impossible for women to keep their full-time jobs as soon as they have children, because there is virtually no corporate support," according to Yuko Fukawa of the women's bureau of the labour ministry.[91]

**SIMILARITIES AND DIFFERENCES IN WOMEN'S AND MEN'S LEADERSHIP STYLES** Do men and women lead differently? An extensive review of the literature suggests two conclusions.[92] First, the similarities between men and women tend to outweigh the differences. Second, what differences there are seem to be that women fall back on a more democratic leadership style, while men feel more comfortable with a directive style.

The similarities among men and women leaders shouldn't be completely surprising. Almost all the studies looking at this issue have used managerial positions as being synonymous with leadership. As such, gender differences apparent in the general population don't tend to be as evident because of career self-selection and organization selection. Just as people who choose careers in law enforcement or civil engineering have a lot in common, individuals who choose managerial careers also tend to have commonalities. People with traits associated with leadership — such as intelligence, confidence, and sociability — are more likely to be perceived as leaders and encouraged to pursue careers where they can exert leadership. This is true regardless of gender. Similarly, organizations tend to recruit and promote people into

Bobbie Gaunt, president of Ford Motor Co. of Canada, believes that women who run businesses view them more holistically and are more willing to make long-term investments in the company.

leadership positions who project leadership attributes. The result is that, regardless of gender, those who achieve formal leadership positions in organizations tend to be more alike than different.

Despite the previous conclusion, studies indicate some differences in the inherent leadership styles between women and men. Women tend to adopt a style of shared leadership. They encourage participation, share power and information, and attempt to enhance followers' self-worth. They prefer to lead through inclusion and rely on their charisma, expertise, contacts, and interpersonal skills to influence others. Men, on the other hand, are more likely to use a directive command-and-control style. They rely on the formal authority of their position for their influence base. Exhibit 10-10 summarizes the views of several women who have headed major corporations in Canada on whether gender makes a difference for leadership. Their views are consistent with the research evidence we've noted here.

Given that men have historically held the great majority of leadership positions in organizations, it's tempting to assume that the existence of the differences noted between men and women would automatically work to favour men. It doesn't. In today's organizations, flexibility, teamwork, trust, and information sharing are replacing rigid structures, competitive individualism, control, and secrecy. The best managers listen, motivate, and provide support to their people. And many women seem to do those things better than men. As a specific example, the expanded use of cross-functional teams in organizations means that effective managers must become skilled negotiators. The leadership styles women typically use can make them better at negotiating, as they are less likely to focus on wins, losses, and competition, as do men. They tend to treat negotiations in the context of a continuing relationship — trying hard to make the other party a winner in his or her own and others' eyes. Chapter 7 discussed differences between men's and women's negotiating styles in greater detail. In this chapter's HR Implications feature on page 449, in addition to discussing how to improve the leadership skills of all employees, we also consider some specific ways for organizations to prepare women for more leadership opportunities.

**Exhibit 10-10**
**Do Men and Women Lead Differently? What Women at the Top Say**

**Sheelagh Whittaker,** president and CEO of EDS Canada Ltd., one of the country's leading providers of information technology services: "Women in business are less preoccupied with status, if only because they have been granted so little in corporate life."

**Peggy Witte,** founder, former president and CEO of Royal Oak Mines Inc.: While she might be more inclined than a man to consider the social effects of her actions, "at the end of the day, the hard decisions are probably exactly the same."

**Carol Stephenson,** president and CEO of Lucent Technologies Canada: "Women by nature tend to possess better interpersonal skills and are more suited than men to the task of consensus-building."

**Bobbie Gaunt,** president and CEO of Ford Motor Co. of Canada (and corporate vice-president): "Women tend to view their businesses holistically: not only are they more mindful of employees, but they are more aware of their company's image in the eyes of customers and investors — and willing to make long-term investments to improve it."

**Maureen Kempston Darkes,** president and general manager of General Motors of Canada Ltd., may be the dissenting voice in the group: "The challenges that confront chief executives are the same whether they are men or women. Once you get to the CEO spot, you're focused on the same kinds of issues that men would focus on."

Source: D. Maley, "Canada's Top Women CEOs," *Maclean's*, October 20, 1997.

## Leading From a Distance

Organizations are facing more telecommuting by workers (which we discuss in Chapter 13), more contracting out, more mergers, and increasing globalization. It is becoming more common, then, that the person doing the leading is not necessarily in the same building, let alone the same organization or country, as the person being led. Leaders must increasingly develop ways to carry out "long-distance" leading that do not involve face-to-face contact.

Jane Howell at the Richard Ivey School of Business and one of her students, Kate Hall-Merenda, have considered the issues of leading from a distance.[93] They note that physical distance can create many potential problems, with employees feeling isolated, forgotten, and perhaps not cared about. This may result in lowered productivity. Their study of 109 business leaders and 371 followers in a large financial institution found that physical distance makes it more difficult for managers and employees to develop high-quality relationships.

Brian Augur, telework coordinator for the Bank of Canada, notes that "managers often like to have staff members in the office, just because they're not quite sure all of what they should be doing, but they're happy to see them doing *something*."[94] The Bank of Canada held a half-day workshop for its managers to learn how to manage their teleworking employees, including "requesting weekly status reports, defining time sensitive projects for delivery and agreeing on the logistics of daily communication—by phone, e-mail or intranet."[95] Employees who telework should consider making these same sorts of arrangements with their managers.

Howell and Hall-Merenda suggest that some of the same characteristics of transformational leaders are appropriate for long-distance managing. In particular, they emphasize the need to articulate a compelling vision to employees and to communicate that vision in an inspiring way. Encouraging employees to think about ways to strive toward that vision is another important task of the leader. Their research also indicates that communication does not have to be done face to face, as long as the vision is communicated clearly in some fashion.

## Cross-Cultural Leadership

One general conclusion that surfaces from our discussion of leadership is that effective leaders don't use any single style. They adjust their style to the situation. While not mentioned explicitly in any of the theories we presented, certainly national culture is an important situational factor determining which leadership style will be most effective.[96] It can help explain, for instance, why executives at the highly successful Asia Department Store in central China blatantly brag about practising "heartless" management, require new employees to undergo two to four weeks of military training with units of the People's Liberation Army in order to increase their obedience, and conduct the store's in-house training sessions in a public place where employees can openly suffer embarrassment from their mistakes.[97]

One way that national culture affects leadership style is by the cultural expectations and norms of followers. Leaders, particularly when they are working in international situations, are constrained by the cultural conditions that their followers have come to expect. Consider the following: Korean leaders are expected to be paternalistic toward employees.[98] Arab leaders who show kindness or generosity without being asked to do so are seen by other Arabs as weak.[99] Japanese leaders are expected to be humble and speak infrequently.[100] And Scandinavian and Dutch leaders who single out individuals for public praise are likely to embarrass those individuals rather than energize them.[101]

Remember that most leadership theories were developed in the United States using US subjects, so they have an American bias. They emphasize follower responsibilities rather than rights; assume hedonism rather than commitment to duty or altruistic motivation; rely on a democratic value orientation and the centrality of work in followers' lives; and stress rationality rather than spirituality, religion, or superstition.[102] These theories generally do apply in the Canadian workplace, but bear in mind the cultural differences between Canadians and Americans noted in Chapter 3. And be aware, too, that the theories do not always apply outside of North America in quite the same way.

As a guide for adjusting your leadership style, you might consider the various dimensions of national culture presented in Chapter 3. For example, a manipulative or autocratic style is compatible with high power distance, and we find high power distance scores in Arab, Far Eastern, and Latin countries. Power distance rankings should also be good indicators of employee willingness to accept participative leadership. Participation is likely to be most effective in such low power distance cultures as exist in Norway, Finland, Denmark, and Sweden. Not incidentally, this may explain (a) why a number of leadership theories (for example, the University of Michigan behavioural studies) implicitly favour the use of a participative or people-oriented style; (b) the emergence of development-oriented leader behaviour found by Scandinavian researchers; and (c) the recent enthusiasm in North America for empowerment. Remember that most leadership theories were developed by North Americans, using North American subjects; and the United States, Canada, and Scandinavian countries all rate below average on power distance.

In 1997, Joseph Di Stefano and one of his students, Nick Bontis, both of the Richard Ivey School of Business at the University of Western Ontario, studied differences in leadership styles across cultures.[103] They were particularly interested in the behaviours that were used to generate exceptional performance by employees. In general, they reported that there were quite a lot of similarities in managers from the United States, Northern Europe, Southern Europe, Latin America, the Far East, and Commonwealth countries, including Canada. In order to achieve exceptional performance from employees, leaders from all of these countries used visioning, coaching, and stimulating (encouraging new ideas) behaviours similarly, and as their chief strategies. US leaders reported they were more likely to correct employees' behaviour than did Far Eastern or Latin managers. Americans also used team building more often than did Asian managers. Far Eastern managers were less likely to include recognition as part of how they encouraged their employees' exceptional performance than were Southern European leaders. These findings suggest that there are some minor differences in how leaders throughout the world achieve exceptional performance from their employees. However, they also suggest a great degree of similarity in what it takes to get high-performing employees.

## Is There a Moral Dimension to Leadership?

The topic of leadership and ethics has surprisingly received little attention. Only very recently have ethicists and leadership researchers begun to consider the ethical implications in leadership.[104] Why now? One reason may be the growing general interest in ethics throughout the field of management. Another reason may be the discovery by probing biographers that some of our past leaders suffered from ethical shortcomings. Regardless, no contemporary discussion of leadership is complete without addressing its ethical dimension.

Ethics touches on leadership at a number of junctures. Transformational leaders, for instance, have been described by one authority as fostering moral virtue when they try to change the attitudes and behaviours of followers.[105] Charisma, too, has an ethical component. Unethical leaders are more likely to use their charisma to enhance power over followers, directed toward self-serving ends. Ethical leaders are considered to use their charisma in a socially constructive way to serve others.[106] There is also the issue of abuse of power by leaders, for example, when they give themselves large salaries and bonuses while also seeking to cut costs by laying off long-time employees.

Gerald Chamales (center), president of Omni Computer Products, provides a good example of moral leadership. A key part of his corporate strategy is giving hard-to-employ people an opportunity to succeed in the workplace. Chamales hires people with drug and alcohol addiction problems and uses the principles of recovery programs in managing them. Chamales's rehabilitating mission includes providing in-house mentors who counsel new employees on basic social and workplace skills. Tolerant of their personal struggles, he helps them handle legal, health, and family problems caused by their addiction. Chamales views his recovering employees as long-term investments who have helped him build his start-up firm into a $28 million company.

Leadership effectiveness needs to address the *means* that a leader uses in trying to achieve goals as well as the content of those goals. GE's Jack Welch, for instance, is consistently described as a highly effective leader because he has succeeded in achieving outstanding returns for shareholders. But Welch is also widely regarded as one of the world's toughest managers. He is regularly listed high on *Fortune*'s annual list of the most hated and reviled executives. Similarly, Bill Gates's success in leading Microsoft to domination of the world's software business has been achieved by means of an extremely demanding work culture. Microsoft's culture demands long work hours by employees and is intolerant of individuals who want to balance work and their personal life. Additionally, ethical leadership must address the content of a leader's goals. Are the changes that the leader seeks for the organization morally acceptable? Is a business leader effective if he or she builds an organization's success by selling products that damage the health of their users? This question might be asked of tobacco executives. Or is a military leader successful by winning a war that should not have been fought in the first place?

Leadership is not value-free. Before we judge any leader to be effective, we should consider both the means used by the leader to achieve his or her goals and the moral content of those goals.

## HR Implications

# Developing Leadership Potential

One of the challenges of the human resources function in organizations is to identify the skill and learning needs of employees, and help employees get appropriate training. We have previously discussed in Chapter 2 the importance of learning and training with respect to developing employee skills. It is also important to ensure that those in management and leadership positions are considered for educational opportunities. This is especially important now as many executives are looking for better ways to lead their companies as they face challenges such as continual change, flatter corporate structures that have removed the familiar hierarchical leadership, and the demands of globalization. As a consequence, many executives are returning to the classroom. Below we discuss general management training, and then we follow that with some specific examples of what has been done to promote women's leadership skills and abilities.

## General Management Training

There are a variety of programs that executives can take. Some opt to go for their master of business administration degrees. "The executive MBA is the ultimate in self-improvement," says Don Nightingale, executive director of the executive MBA programs at Queen's University's School of Business.[1]

An MBA isn't the only educational option executives have, however. Senior and middle managers are taking everything from four- or five-day programs on specific topics to five- to six-week executive programs. They study such issues as managing change, strategic decision making, leadership, global management, and teamwork.

While management development courses have traditionally been almost exclusively in budgeting, planning, and managing, there is increasingly an emphasis on "personal development" courses, where those who attend are encouraged to learn more about themselves to help them become better people. As an example of this new trend, Vancouver-based Fletcher Challenge Canada has sent some of its employees to a course called "The Seven Habits of Highly Effective People," offered by the Covey Leadership Center, headquartered in Utah. Lois Nahirney, one of Fletcher Challenge's employees, found the course extremely useful, partly because it gave her time to reflect on her own goals in life: "It's very much about personal vision, personal mastery," she says. Fletcher Challenge believes programs such as these benefit both the individual and the company, and over 600 employees have been through such courses as leadership, communication, and facilitation.

The Hongkong Bank of Canada sends two or three executives a year to external courses, often university-based. BCTV has sent senior managers to the Covey course. BC Hydro, Coast Hotels, and A&W have also sent managers to various programs. Vancouver-based A&B Sound has sent more than a dozen people to Seattle's Pacific Institute "affirmation" program.

All of these companies believe that courses help their managers. For example, BC Hydro's Gary Rodford says course participants come back to work "better managers and better people." Lois Nahirney at Fletcher Challenge agrees: "The better you understand who you are and who you want to be, the better you can approach your job and the people you

do it with. A company which helps its people do that is going to be more successful."[2]

## Efforts to Develop Women's Leadership Capabilities

Some corporations have become increasingly aware that women do not seem to be making it into higher management positions as rapidly as men. As a result, some have started tying compensation directly to senior executives' identification and promotion of "high potential" women. Burnaby-based B.C. Tel has been doing this since 1994.[3] "We're not simply encouraging people to ensure we have the appropriate representation of women within the organization, we're requiring that by putting their variable compensation at risk," says Paul Smith, the company's senior vice-president of human resources. To accomplish this objective, 20 percent of a manager's variable compensation is tied to the "people issues" on the manager's performance appraisal. For 1998, every senior executive at B.C. Tel was required to have a career-development strategy in place for women. "Everyone [had] to participate in that in order to maximize their variable pay," says Smith. B.C. Tel also identified managers who were not prepared to support the new women-friendly environment and they have been encouraged to look for jobs elsewhere.

When Anthony Comper, now CEO of the Bank of Montreal (BMO), became its president in 1990, he was determined to find out why 75 percent of the bank's employees were women but only nine percent of women had made it into the executive ranks. He created a task force to investigate the problems and develop action plans for change. The task force's report, submitted in November 1991, found that women were held back by stereotypical attitudes, myths, and "conventional wisdoms." The following fictions and facts, highlighted in the report, illustrate some of those conventional wisdoms:[4]

*Fiction:* Women were less committed to their work, less educated than men, and tended to turn in weaker job performances.

*Fact:* Women in the bank turned out to be at least as fully qualified as men in every respect — just as educated and just as dedicated.

*Fiction:* Women had not been in the pipeline long enough.

*Fact:* Women had put in longer service than men at every level, except senior management, where their presence was a recent development.

*Fiction:* Child-rearing women tend to quit, and ergo, were not committed to their careers.

*Fact:* Ninety-eight percent of women returned to the company after giving birth.

*Fiction:* Time will take care of gender imbalances.

*Fact:* If the bank relied on time solving the problem, women's representation at executive and senior management levels would have risen to only 18 percent and 22 percent respectively by the year 2000.

The task force also determined that more direct involvement to promote women was necessary. The bank's women employees were well educated, had received better performance appraisals than men at all levels, and wanted advancement as much as the men did, but they weren't making it. Comper recognized that simply waiting for things to right themselves wouldn't work. In light of that fact, the task force concluded that the bank needed to act aggressively to move women up the ranks. In order to do that, they tied performance appraisals and compensation of managers to the promotion of women. The bank also created a more family-friendly environment to help their employees manage the stress of work and home, and introduced such things as flex work arrangements and people-care days to the workplace. By late 1998, women held 25 percent of all executive positions at BMO. Comper would still like to see 50 percent of the top offices held by women by the year 2007.

While it might seem obvious from the examples of both B.C. Tel and the Bank of Montreal that senior management needs to be involved in the training and development of women to ensure that they have the same access as men to leadership positions in organizations, this is not always an accepted view. Maria Ferris, manager of global workforce diversity initiatives at IBM, notes that in three European countries she visited she "found that some women feel (IBM's diversity initiatives are) about women getting something they don't deserve. But when you can show that the goal is removing a disadvantage—just creating a level playing field, not granting special rights—everyone can understand."[5]

Even when companies have good policies in place, they can't simply relax their vigilance. Linda Scherr, a software engineer who has been with IBM for 26 years and chairs the IBM Women in Technology Steering Committee, notes that "while the vast majority of our managers both recognize and endorse the value of these programs," not all do. She adds, "we must be relentless until every manager is supportive."[6]

Sources:

[1] Johanna Powell, "Forging Fearless Leaders," *Financial Post Daily*, March 13, 1997, pp. 14,16.

[2] "Camp Overhaul: Where BC Companies Send Their Best and Brightest for Management Development," *B.C. Business Magazine*, February, 1995, pp. 27-30.

[3] Information on B.C. Tel and Bank of Montreal based on Jennifer Wells, "Stuck on the Ladder: Not Only Is the Glass Ceiling Still in Place, But Men and Women Have Very Different Views of the Problem," *Maclean's*, October 20, 1997, p. 60.

[4] Jennifer Wells, "Stuck on the Ladder; Not only Is the Glass Ceiling Still in Place, But Men and Women Have Very Different Views of the Problem," *Maclean's,* October 20, 1997, p. 60; and Matthew Barrett, "Workplace Equality: Pursuing a Goal That Makes the Best of Business Sense," *CMA Management Accounting Magazine*, September, 1993, p. 11.

[5] M.B. White, "Women of the World: Diversity Goes Global at IBM," *Diversity Factor*, Summer 1999, pp. 13-16.

[6] M.B. White, "Women of the World: Diversity Goes Global at IBM," *Diversity Factor*, Summer 1999, pp. 13-16.

# *SUMMARY AND IMPLICATIONS*

## For the Workplace

Leadership plays a central part in understanding group behaviour, for it's the leader who usually provides the direction toward goal attainment. Therefore, a more accurate predictive capability of who makes a good leader, or what conditions affect leadership ability, should be valuable in improving group performance.

In this chapter, we differentiated between management/supervision and leadership.

A major breakthrough in our understanding of leadership came when we recognized the need to include situational factors. We can now explain under what conditions a given approach (such as task oriented or people oriented) is likely to lead to high employee performance and satisfaction.

In addition, the study of leadership has expanded to include more transformational approaches to leadership. As we learn more about the personal characteristics that followers attribute to charismatic, transformational leaders, and about the conditions that facilitate their emergence, we should be better able to predict when followers will exhibit extraordinary commitment and loyalty to their leaders and to those leaders' goals.

Effective team leaders were found to perform four roles: They act as liaisons with external constituencies; they are troubleshooters; they manage conflict; and they coach team members. Empowered leadership was shown to be increasingly popular, providing individuals with the responsibility necessary to carry out their tasks. We also considered the importance of self-management and leading without authority.

Finally, we addressed a number of contemporary issues in leadership. We learned, for instance, that male and female leadership styles have some similarities, but that women's propensity to rely on shared leadership is more in line with organizational needs in 2000 and beyond than the directive style often preferred by men. Also, consistent with the contingency approach, managers should be sure to consider national culture as an important variable in choosing a leadership style. Finally, we propose that leadership is not value-free. We should look at the moral content of a leader's goals and the means he or she uses to achieve those goals.

## For You as an Individual

It is easy to imagine that theories of leadership are more important to those who are leaders or who plan in the near future to become leaders. However, this attitude would be a mistake. As the chapter suggests in outlining the new approaches to leadership, more emphasis is being placed on individuals either learning to lead themselves or being good followers. In other words, regardless of your role in an organization, you are being asked to contribute more.

Understanding leadership is also important beyond the workplace. Most of you will work on teams doing class projects over the next few years. In addition, you may serve on committees, student groups, or even neighbourhood or volunteer groups. In all of these instances, you will need to know enough about leadership to understand how to relate to the leader, to take on the role of leader if necessary, and to be an effective team player.

*ROADMAP*
*REMINDER*

In the previous chapter we considered ways that the organization shares its vision with its members through culture. In this chapter we consider the role of leadership in sharing the vision, and note that the most recent theories of leadership have increased the emphasis on communicating vision and getting individuals more involved with the vision. In the next chapter we consider decision making, ethics, and creativity. These topics describe the difficulties sometimes involved in making decisions, and also encourage you in ways to expand your creativity.

# For Review

1. Trace the development of leadership research.
2. Describe the strengths and weaknesses in the trait approach to leadership.
3. What is the Managerial Grid?
4. When might leaders be irrelevant?
5. Describe the strengths and weaknesses of a charismatic leader.
6. What are the differences among transactional, transformational, and laissez-faire leaders?
7. What is dispersed leadership? What are some examples of dispersed leadership?
8. Why do you think effective female and male managers often exhibit similar traits and behaviours?
9. What characteristics define an effective follower?
10. What is moral leadership?

# For Critical Thinking

1. Develop an example where you apply path-goal theory.
2. Reconcile path-goal theory and substitutes for leadership.
3. What kind of activities could a full-time college or university student pursue that might lead to the perception that he or she is a charismatic leader? In pursuing those activities, what might the student do to enhance this perception of being charismatic?
4. Based on the low representation of women in upper management, to what extent do you think that organizations should actively promote women into the senior ranks of management?

## LEARNING ABOUT YOURSELF EXERCISE

# Are You a Charismatic Leader?

Instructions: The following statements refer to the possible ways in which you might behave toward others when you are in a leadership role. Please read each statement carefully and decide to what extent it applies to you. Then circle the appropriate number.

| To little or no extent | 1 |
| To a slight extent | 2 |
| To a moderate extent | 3 |
| To a considerable extent | 4 |
| To a very great extent | 5 |

**You ...**

| | | | | | |
|---|---|---|---|---|---|
| 1. Pay close attention to what others say when they are talking | 1 | 2 | 3 | 4 | 5 |
| 2. Communicate clearly | 1 | 2 | 3 | 4 | 5 |
| 3. Are trustworthy | 1 | 2 | 3 | 4 | 5 |
| 4. Care about other people | 1 | 2 | 3 | 4 | 5 |
| 5. Do not put excessive energy into avoiding failure | 1 | 2 | 3 | 4 | 5 |

| | | | | | |
|---|---|---|---|---|---|
| **6.** Make the work of others more meaningful | 1 | 2 | 3 | 4 | 5 |
| **7.** Seem to focus on the key issues in a situation | 1 | 2 | 3 | 4 | 5 |
| **8.** Get across your meaning effectively, often in unusual ways | 1 | 2 | 3 | 4 | 5 |
| **9.** Can be relied on to follow through on commitments | 1 | 2 | 3 | 4 | 5 |
| **10.** Have a great deal of self-respect | 1 | 2 | 3 | 4 | 5 |
| **11.** Enjoy taking carefully calculated risks | 1 | 2 | 3 | 4 | 5 |
| **12.** Help others feel more competent in what they do | 1 | 2 | 3 | 4 | 5 |
| **13.** Have a clear set of priorities | 1 | 2 | 3 | 4 | 5 |
| **14.** Are in touch with how others feel | 1 | 2 | 3 | 4 | 5 |
| **15.** Rarely change once you have taken a clear position | 1 | 2 | 3 | 4 | 5 |
| **16.** Focus on strengths, of yourself and others | 1 | 2 | 3 | 4 | 5 |
| **17.** Seem most alive when deeply involved in some project | 1 | 2 | 3 | 4 | 5 |
| **18.** Show others that they are all part of the same group | 1 | 2 | 3 | 4 | 5 |
| **19.** Get others to focus on the issues you see as important | 1 | 2 | 3 | 4 | 5 |
| **20.** Communicate feelings as well as ideas | 1 | 2 | 3 | 4 | 5 |
| **21.** Let others know where you stand | 1 | 2 | 3 | 4 | 5 |
| **22.** Seem to know just how you "fit" into a group | 1 | 2 | 3 | 4 | 5 |
| **23.** Learn from mistakes, do not treat errors as disasters, but as learning | 1 | 2 | 3 | 4 | 5 |
| **24.** Are fun to be around | 1 | 2 | 3 | 4 | 5 |

Turn to page 634 for scoring directions and key.

Source: M. Sashkin and W.C. Morris, *Experiencing Management,* (Addison-Wesley Publishing Company, Inc., 1987).

## *WORKING WITH OTHERS EXERCISE*

# Practising to Be Charismatic

The From Concepts to Skills box on page 432 indicates how one goes about being charismatic. In this exercise, you will use that information to practise projecting charisma.

**a.** The class should break into pairs.

**b.** Student A's task is to "lead" Student B through a new-student orientation to your college or university. The orientation should last about 10 to 15 minutes. Assume Student B is new to your college or university and is unfamiliar with the campus. Remember, Student A should attempt to project himself or herself as charismatic.

**c.** Roles now reverse and Student B's task is to "lead" Student A in a 10- to 15-minute program on how to study more effectively for college or university exams. Take a few minutes to think about what has worked well for you, and assume that Student A is a new student interested in improving his or her study habits. Again remember that Student B should attempt to project himself or herself as charismatic.

**d.** When both role plays are complete, each pair should assess how well they did in projecting charisma and how they might improve.

Source: This exercise is based on J.M. Howell and P.J. Frost, "A Laboratory Study of Charismatic Leadership," *Organizational Behavior and Human Decision Processes,* April 1989, pp. 243-269.

## INTERNET SEARCH EXERCISES

**1.** Find 5 companies whose CEOs have left for reasons other than normal retirement in the past 12 months. Assess each company's performance following the CEO's departure. Was the organization's stock price affected? Why might a CEO's departure affect company performance?

**2.** Find 5 retail or manufacturing companies that proclaim trust is an important element in their interactions with customers and/or employees. Describe this proclamation. Can you find any substantiation for this claim, or do you think it's merely saying what is politically correct?

## CASE INCIDENT

# Mogens Smed: Charismatic Leader of SMED International

Mogens Smed is the 54-year-old president and CEO of Calgary-based SMED International, which specializes in building custom office interiors. In addition to upscale office furniture, the company designs floors and is the market leader in pre-fabricated movable walls. At 69 675 square metres, SMED's new factory in southeast Calgary is the largest manufacturing facility in Western Canada. Besides state-of-the-art manufacturing equipment, there is a large gym and a huge, brightly coloured cafeteria where employees gather for pep rallies.

SMED, founded in 1982, has 49 marketing offices in seven countries and has clients in over 40 countries. Some of its most well-known clients include Steven Spielberg's DreamWorks SKG in Los Angeles, the NFL Players' Union in New York City, the Royal Bank, the Toronto-Dominion Bank, the Canadian Imperial Bank of Commerce, Fox Television, Penthouse Magazine, Coca-Cola Co., Tommy Hilfiger Corp., and Calvin Klein.

SMED's competitors include American giants such as Herman Miller, Steelcase, and Knoll, all of which are larger than SMED. SMED is really only a small player in the office-furniture industry, with about one percent of market share. Chief competitors are Herman Miller, which has 10 percent of market share, and Steelcase, which has 25 percent.

Smed himself has a reputation as an outstanding salesperson and a charismatic leader, and his leadership style doesn't allow him to fret about his small market share. SMED's motto is "Our only competition is conventional thinking." Smed explains that SMED is different from the competition: "We do not play by the rules. There are no rules. We offer something completely different from them. We don't just make products and offer them to the customer. We ask the customer what they want and then make it for them."

SMED's vision is that the customer is always first. To remind everyone of this, brochures, magazines, and books supporting this philosophy are evident in both the foyer and other parts of the organization. These publications include *Culture Shift* and *The Employee Handbook of New Work Habits for a Radically Changing World* by Price Pritchett, and *The Customer-Driven Company* by Richard Whiteley. And in fact, the heart of SMED's marketing campaign is actually an alpine retreat. Smed built Falkridge at a cost of $1.6 million, so that he and his staff could woo clients with gourmet dinners, fine wines, and Cuban cigars. At SMED, no expense is too great to impress a client.

Like all charismatic leaders, Smed has truly inspired his employees. In fact, industry analysts have commented on the nearly messianic fervour of the company. "In some ways, SMED is like a cult," says James David, an analyst at HSBC James Capel Canada Inc. in Montreal. "Mogens Smed displays a great deal of charisma and enthusiasm, and that carries down through the ranks. The people around him are so much on the same page, it's scary."

Characteristic of charismatic leaders, Smed interacts personally with both employees and clients. He is willing to go anywhere, any time, if he thinks it will clinch a sale. For instance, Smed has taken clients for a seven-day excursion to an exclusive fishing lodge in BC's Queen Charlotte Islands where guests caught 14-kilogram chinook salmon and watched killer whales frolic in the ocean. He can do this because, like many charismatic leaders, he makes all the major decisions but leaves the day-to-day operations to his executive vice-presidents.

Smed's vision and charisma may work well for his clients, but investors and market analysts are more critical of his style. SMED shares reached a peak of $32 in mid-1998, before it consolidated its six plants into the large manufacturing facility in Calgary, but a variety of factors sent the stock plummeting. In April 1999 it fell as low as $5.50. Some in the financial community "question whether the company is going overboard, needlessly sacrificing profit for feel-good schmoozing." SMED's share prices did increase in early 2000, after Holland Landing, Ontario-based Office Specialty began a hostile takeover bid. Outraged, Smed looked for a white knight, which it found in Holland, Michigan-based Haworth Inc., a maker and marketer of office furniture and seating. The deal will make Haworth the second-largest office furniture maker in the world behind Steelcase Inc. SMED will keep its name and operate as an independent subsidiary. Shares were trading above $23 after the deal was announced. What impact the union of the two companies will have on Smed's charismatic style remains to be seen.

## Questions

1. Describe how Smed can be classified as a charismatic leader.

2. What situational variables do you think explain Smed's success?

3. How might Smed's charismatic nature affect his business decisions?

4. Would you want to work for a charismatic leader such as Smed? Why or why not?

Sources: Based on Mel Duvall, "New plant provides impetus for SMED's growth," *Financial Post Daily*, October 3, 1997, p. 19; Curtis Gillespie, "Selling Smed: Mogens Smed is passionate about making SMED International a global player in office furniture," *Financial Post Magazine*, October 1997, pp. 70-81; S. Miles, "Smed claws its way back to profitability," *Financial Post*, November 27, 1999, p. C3; P. Verburg, "His Party, Your Hangover," *Canadian Business*, August 27, 1999, pp. 36-39; D. Steinhart, "Hostile move on Smed could trigger new bids," *Financial Post*, December 22, 1999; and I. McKinnon, "Smed gets $280M bid from Haworth," *Financial Post*, January 26, 2000.

# Richard Branson

Richard Branson, CEO of Virgin Group Ltd., Britain's largest private company, leads a conglomerate that encompasses more than 120 companies, including Virgin Airlines, Virgin Records, and Virgin Cola. He's even created a beachhead in Canada, establishing Virgin Records in Vancouver in December 1996. How does he maintain responsibility for so many companies? By delegating.

Branson is free-spirited, innovative, and irreverent, and his company is just like him. He relishes the opportunity to be different, and he enjoys a challenge. He has repeatedly gone after the industry giants, believing he sees how to do things better than them.

Branson doesn't believe in micromanaging organizations. He has only a thin corporate structure beneath him, no bureaucracy, and no corporate headquarters. All of his small companies (none have more than 20 percent of market share in an area) are headed by managing directors who run them. The directors have lots of freedom to make decisions. They also have a stake in the companies, so they can run the companies as if they were their own.

Branson says, "My job is empowering people and helping them to get up and go, and then leave them to do it." This is evidence of his charismatic leadership: He can trust that those he's empowered will successfully run the Virgin companies. Branson's style of management ensures also that he will not be spread too thin, as those running the companies are responsible for making decisions.

Branson's charisma is demonstrated outside of the workplace as well. He has enormous personal popularity in Britain. In a 1997 survey asking Londoners to name their choice for mayor, he was the hands-down winner. An impressive approval rating indeed for a free spirit in a country known for its conformity.

# Questions

1. How does charisma make it possible for Richard Branson to run the 120 or so businesses of Virgin Group Ltd.?

2. Why is it possible for Branson to have almost no bureaucracy in his company?

3. What kinds of limitations might be associated with Branson's leadership style?

Source: Based on "Richard Branson," *Venture 613*; aired October 20, 1996.

**CHAPTER 11**

# Decision Making, Creativity, and Ethics

When Irene Rosenfeld moved to Canada in 1996 to become president of Kraft Canada Inc., she believed there was food on everyone's table.[1] After living here for a year, however, she came to realize "that beneath the surface appearance of prosperity lies 'an awful lot of need.'" In fact, the number of people relying on food banks has doubled since 1989.

Even before Rosenfeld arrived, Kraft Canada was already involved in two formal programs with the Canadian Association of Food Banks (CAFB). Under the "Breakage Donation" program, damaged cases of food from Kraft's warehouses in Cobourg, ON, and Moncion, PQ, are taken to a local food bank warehouse where food that is still acceptable is then distributed to those in need.

Kraft has also spearheaded the "National Product Return Program." When a retailer refuses five or fewer cases of product, for whatever reason (for example, shipping error or damage), the refused goods are automatically donated to a CAFB food bank in that area. This is actually more cost-effective than shipping product back to Montreal from Vancouver, for instance.

Since Rosenfeld arrived, attention to food bank needs has become more visible. For instance,

## Questions for Consideration

**Who should make decisions: individuals or groups?**

**How does one increase creativity in organizations?**

**How difficult is it to make ethical decisions?**

Kraft Canada has incorporated the CAFB into its marketing promotions, thus raising funds for CAFB and raising Kraft's profile as a socially responsible corporation. The company's "I Love KD Tour" and contest is a notable example. Crews visited cities across the country to videotape Canadians of all ages explaining their love for Kraft Dinner, with the footage to be used in future TV commercials. For every "audition," Kraft donated one box of Kraft Dinner to the CAFB, more than 25 000 boxes in total.

Rosenfeld summed up Kraft's strategy of social responsibility this way: "We really believe we can do well by doing good."

The activities of Kraft Canada reflect decisions that the organization has made with respect to its core values, which include social responsibility. Kraft Canada is not alone in making these kinds of decisions. The Body Shop, Kellogg Canada, Pfizer Canada, and Hewlett-Packard also have campaigns to make positive changes in Canada. CIBC spent more than $8 million in 1998 to help Canadian youth through Youthvision, a collection of hundreds of programs supported by the bank.

In this chapter, we'll describe how decisions in organizations are made, as well as how creativity is linked to decision making. We'll also look at the ethical and socially responsible aspects of decision making as part of our discussion. But first, we discuss perceptual processes and show how they are linked to individual decision making.

## The Link Between Perception and Individual Decision Making

Individuals in organizations make decisions. That is, they make choices from among two or more alternatives. For instance, top managers such as Irene Rosenfeld at Kraft Canada and John Hunkin, chair and CEO of CIBC, determine their organization's goals, what products or services to offer, how best to finance operations, or where to locate a new high-tech

**decisions**
The choices made from among two or more alternatives.

**problem**
A discrepancy between some current state of affairs and some desired state.

research and development facility. Exhibit 11-1 illustrates some of the difficult **decisions** CEOs made in fiscal year 1998. Middle- and lower-level managers also make decisions. They determine production schedules, select new employees, and decide how pay raises are to be allocated. Of course, making decisions is not the sole province of managers. Nonmanagerial employees also make decisions that affect their jobs and the organizations they work for. The more obvious of these decisions might include whether to come to work on any given day, how much effort to put forward once at work, and whether to comply with a request made by the manager. In addition, an increasing number of organizations in recent years have been empowering their nonmanagerial employees with job-related decision-making authority that was historically reserved for managers alone. Individual decision making, therefore, is an important part of organizational behaviour. But how individuals in organizations make decisions and the quality of their final choices are largely influenced by their perceptions.

Decision making occurs as a reaction to a **problem**. That is, there is a discrepancy between some *current* state of affairs and some *desired* state, requiring consideration of alternative courses of action. So if your car breaks down and you rely on it to get to school, you have a problem that requires a decision on your part. Unfortunately, most problems don't come neatly packaged with the label "problem" clearly displayed on them. Moreover, one person's *problem* can be another person's *satisfactory state of affairs*. One manager may view her division's two percent decline in quarterly sales to be a serious problem requiring immediate action on her part. In contrast, her counterpart in another division of the same company, who also had a

**Westcoast Energy**
www.westcoastenergy.com

**Placer Dome**
www.placerdome.com

**A&W Food Services**
www.aw.ca

---

**Exhibit 11-1**
**CEOs Describe Difficult Decisions of 1998**

**Michael E. J. Phelps**, *Chair and CEO, Westcoast Energy*: "To sell Centra Gas Manitoba, an asset which we held for close to 10 years. It was sold in order to free up opportunities for some higher growth projects. It was an asset that had worked out quite well, where we were close to the people on an emotional level."

**John Willson**, *President and CEO, Placer Dome*: "The decision to enter South Africa."

**Jeff Mooney**, *President and CEO, A&W Food Services of Canada*: "The most difficult decision of 1998 was firing Drew Carey as our advertising spokesperson. We had used him in our ads for the 1998 campaign. His TV show had gained in popularity and we were about to start shooting the 1999 commercials when he did a theme highlighting a competitor in one of his shows. Some might have chosen to overlook it, but great companies and great brands, like A&W, are built on trust. Carey had broken trust with us and our customers."

**Gerry Rasmussen**, *President and CEO, ISM Information Systems Management (BC) Corp*.: "In 1998 the toughest decision was to walk away from a very large international opportunity which could have transformed our company, when it became apparent that we were unlikely to get the necessary internal support without jeopardizing the relationships on which we depend."

**Frank Barker**, *President and CEO, Canlan Investment Corp"*: "Downsizing personnel."

---

Source: N. Hulsman, "For the Record," *BCBusiness*, July 1999, pp. 72-73.

two percent sales decrease, may consider that percentage quite acceptable. So the awareness that a problem exists and that a decision must be made is a perceptual issue.

Additionally, every decision requires interpretation and evaluation of information. Data are typically received from multiple sources, and they need to be screened, processed, and interpreted. Which data, for instance, are relevant to the decision and which are not? The perceptions of the decision maker will answer that question. Alternatives will be developed, and the strengths and weaknesses of each will need to be evaluated. Again, because alternatives don't come with "red flags" identifying them as such, or with their strengths and weaknesses clearly marked, the individual decision maker's perceptual process will have a large bearing on the final outcome.

# How Should Decisions Be Made?

Let's begin by describing how individuals should behave in order to maximize or optimize a certain outcome. We call this the *rational decision-making process*.

## The Rational Decision-Making Process

**rational**
Refers to choices that are consistent and value maximizing.

**rational decision-making model**
A decision-making model that describes how individuals should behave in order to maximize some outcome.

The optimizing decision maker is **rational**. That is, he or she makes consistent, value-maximizing choices within specified constraints.[2] These choices are made following a six-step **rational decision-making model**.[3] Moreover, specific assumptions underlie this model.

**THE RATIONAL MODEL** The six steps in the rational decision-making model are listed in Exhibit 11-2.

The model begins by *defining the problem*. As noted previously, a problem exists when a discrepancy occurs between an existing and a desired state of affairs.[4] If you calculate your monthly expenses and find you're spending $50 more than you allocated in your budget, you have defined a problem. Many poor decisions can be traced to the decision maker overlooking a problem or defining the wrong problem.

Once a decision maker has defined the problem, he or she needs to *identify the decision criteria* that will be important in solving the problem. In this step, the decision maker determines what is relevant in making the decision. This step brings the decision maker's interests, values, and similar personal preferences into the process. Identifying criteria is important

---

**Exhibit 11-2**
**Steps in the Rational Decision-Making Model**

1. Define the problem.
2. Identify the decision criteria.
3. Allocate weights to the criteria.
4. Develop the alternatives.
5. Evaluate the alternatives.
6. Select the best alternative.

When CIBC received a request from the Girl Guides of Canada to sponsor the national cookie campaign, the bank had to decide whether doing so met its corporate objectives. After reviewing the proposal, the bank concluded that the Guides' key mission, to help prepare young women to become successful leaders and reach their full potential, mirrored CIBC's own objective of helping kids reach their full potential. Their sponsorship includes running the CIBC SmartStart logo on all Girl Guide cookie boxes during 2000 and 2001.

because what one person thinks is relevant, another person may not. Also keep in mind that any factors not identified in this step are considered irrelevant to the decision maker.

To understand the type of criteria that might be used to make a decision, consider the many sponsorship requests Toronto-based Canadian Imperial Bank of Commerce receives each year. In making a decision about whether or not to support the request, the bank considers the following criteria:[5]

- Strategic fit with CIBC's overall goals and objectives;
- Ability to achieve youth customer segment marketing objectives;
- Tangible and intangible benefits of the proposal, such as goodwill, reputation and cost/potential revenue;
- Organizational impact;
- Business risks (if any).

If the proposals do not meet these criteria, they are not funded.

The criteria identified are rarely all equal in importance. So the third step requires the decision maker to *weight the previously identified criteria* in order to give them the correct priority in the decision.

The fourth step requires the decision maker to *generate possible alternatives* that could succeed in resolving the problem. No attempt is made in this step to appraise these alternatives, only to list them.

Once the alternatives have been generated, the decision maker must critically analyze and evaluate each one. This is done by *rating each alternative on each criterion*. The strengths and weaknesses of each alternative become evident as they are compared with the criteria and weights established in the second and third steps.

The final step in this model requires *computing the optimal decision*. This is done by evaluating each alternative against the weighted criteria and selecting the alternative with the highest total score.

**ASSUMPTIONS OF THE MODEL** The rational decision-making model we just described contains a number of assumptions.[6] Let's briefly outline those assumptions.

- *Problem clarity*. The problem is clear and unambiguous. The decision maker is assumed to have complete information regarding the decision situation.
- *Known options*. It is assumed the decision maker can identify all the relevant criteria and can list all the viable alternatives. Furthermore, the decision maker is aware of all the possible consequences of each alternative.
- *Clear preferences*. Rationality assumes that the criteria and alternatives can be ranked and weighted to reflect their importance.
- *Constant preferences*. It's assumed that the specific decision criteria are constant and that the weights assigned to them are stable over time.

- *No time or cost constraints*. The rational decision maker can obtain full information about criteria and alternatives because it is assumed that there are no time or cost constraints.
- *Maximum payoff*. The rational decision maker will choose the alternative that yields the highest perceived value.

## How Are Decisions Actually Made in Organizations?

> **Do individuals really follow the rational model when they make decisions?**

But are decision makers in organizations rational? Do they carefully assess problems, identify all relevant criteria, use their creativity to identify all viable alternatives, and painstakingly evaluate every alternative to find an optimizing choice? When decision makers are faced with a simple problem with few alternative courses of action, and when the cost of searching out and evaluating alternatives is low, the rational model provides a fairly accurate description of the decision process.[7] However, such situations are the exception. Most decisions in the real world don't follow the rational model. For instance, people are usually content to find an acceptable or reasonable solution to their problem rather than an optimizing one. As such, decision makers generally make limited use of their creativity. Choices tend to be confined to the neighbourhood of the problem symptom and to the neighbourhood of the current alternative. As one expert in decision making recently concluded: "Most significant decisions are made by judgment, rather than by a defined prescriptive model."[8]

In the following sections we indicate areas where the reality of decision making conflicts with the rational model.[9]

### Problem Identification

Problems don't come with flashing neon lights to identify themselves. And one person's *problem* is another person's *acceptable status quo*. So how do decision makers identify and select problems?

Problems that are visible tend to have a higher probability of being selected than ones that are important.[10] Why? We can offer at least two reasons. First, it's easier to recognize visible problems. They are more likely to catch a decision maker's attention. This explains why politicians are more likely to talk about the "crime problem" than the "illiteracy problem." Second, remember we're concerned with decision making in organizations. Decision makers want to appear competent and "on top of problems." This motivates them to focus attention on problems that are visible to others.

Don't ignore the decision maker's self-interest. If a decision maker faces a conflict between selecting a problem that is important to the organization and one that is important to the decision maker, self-interest tends to win out.[11] This also ties in with the issue of visibility. It's usually in a decision maker's best interest to attack high-profile problems. It conveys to others that things are under control. Moreover, when the decision maker's performance is later reviewed, the evaluator is more likely to give a high rating to someone who has been aggressively attacking visible problems than to someone whose actions have been less obvious.

## Bounded Rationality in Considering Alternatives

When you considered which university or college to attend, did you look at *every* viable alternative? Did you carefully identify all the criteria that were important in your decision? Did you evaluate each alternative against the criteria in order to find the optimum school? The answer to these questions is probably "no." But don't feel bad, because few people selected their educational institution this way.

Since the capacity of the human mind for formulating and solving complex problems is far too small to meet the requirements for full rationality, individuals operate within the confines of **bounded rationality**. That is, they construct simplified models that extract the essential features from problems without capturing all their complexity.[12] Individuals can then behave rationally within the limits of the simple model.

How does bounded rationality work for the typical individual? Once a problem is identified, the search for criteria and alternatives begins, but the list of criteria is likely to be far from exhaustive. The decision maker will identify a limited list of the more conspicuous choices. In most cases, they will represent familiar criteria and previously tried-and-true solutions. Once this limited set of alternatives is identified, the decision maker will review it. But this review will not be comprehensive—not all the alternatives will be carefully evaluated. Instead, the decision maker will begin with alternatives that differ only in a relatively small degree from the choice currently in effect. Following along familiar and well-worn paths, the decision maker proceeds to review alternatives only until he or she identifies an alternative that is "good enough"—one that meets an acceptable level of performance. The first alternative that meets the "good enough" criterion ends the search. So decision makers choose a final solution that **satisfices** rather than optimizes; that is, they seek solutions that are both satisfactory and sufficient.

One of the more interesting aspects of bounded rationality is that the order in which alternatives are considered is critical in determining which alternative is selected. Remember, in the fully rational decision-making model, all alternatives are eventually listed in a hierarchy of preferred order. Because all alternatives are considered, the initial order in which they are evaluated is irrelevant. Every potential solution would receive a full and complete evaluation. But this isn't the case with bounded rationality. Assuming that a problem has more than one potential solution, the satisficing choice will be the first *acceptable* one the decision maker encounters. Since decision makers use simple and limited models, they typically begin by identifying alternatives that are obvious, ones with which they are familiar, and those not too far from the status quo. Those solutions that depart least from the status quo and meet the decision criteria are most likely to be selected. A unique and creative alternative may present an optimizing solution to the problem; however, it is unlikely to be chosen because an acceptable solution will be identified well before the decision maker is required to search very far beyond the status quo.

## Intuition

Jessie Lam has just committed her corporation to spend in excess of $40 million to build a new plant in New Westminster, British Columbia, to manufacture electronic components for satellite communication equipment. A vice-president of operations for her firm, Lam had before her a compre-

---

**bounded rationality**
Individuals make decisions by constructing simplified models that extract the essential features from problems without capturing all their complexity.

**satisfice**
A decision model that relies on solutions that are both satisfactory and sufficient.

hensive analysis of five possible plant locations developed by a site-location consulting firm she had hired. This report ranked the New Westminster location third among the five alternatives. After carefully reading the report and its conclusions, Lam decided against the consultant's recommendation. When asked to explain her decision, Lam said, "I looked the report over very carefully. Despite its recommendation, I felt that the numbers didn't tell the whole story. Intuitively, I just sensed that New Westminster would prove to be the best bet over the long run."

Intuitive decision making, like that used by Jessie Lam, has recently come out of the closet and gained some respectability. Experts no longer automatically assume that using intuition to make decisions is irrational or ineffective.[13] There is growing recognition that rational analysis has been overemphasized and that, in certain instances, relying on intuition can improve decision making.

What do we mean by intuitive decision making? There are a number of ways to conceptualize intuition.[14] For instance, some consider it a form of extrasensory power or sixth sense, and some believe it is a personality trait that a limited number of people are born with. For our purposes, we define **intuitive decision making** as a subconscious process created out of distilled experience. It doesn't necessarily operate independently of rational analysis; rather, the two complement each other.

Research on chess playing provides an excellent example of how intuition works.[15] Novice chess players and grandmasters were shown an actual, but unfamiliar, chess game with about 25 pieces on the board. After five or 10 seconds, the pieces were removed and each player was asked to reconstruct the pieces by position. On average, the grandmaster could put 23 or 24 pieces in their correct squares, while the novice was able to replace only six. Then the exercise was changed. This time the pieces were placed randomly on the board. Again, the novice placed only about six correctly, but so did the grandmaster! The second exercise demonstrated that the grandmaster didn't have any better memory than the novice. What he or she did have, however, was the ability, based on the experience of having played thousands of chess games, to recognize patterns and clusters of pieces that occur on chessboards in the course of games. Studies further show that chess professionals can play 50 or more games simultaneously, where decisions often must be made in only seconds, and they can exhibit only a moderately lower level of skill than when playing one game under tournament conditions, where decisions take half an hour or longer. The expert's experience allows him or her to recognize the pattern in a situation and draw upon previously learned information associated with that pattern to arrive quickly at a decision choice. The result is that the intuitive decision maker can decide rapidly with what appears to be very limited information.

When are people most likely to use intuitive decision making? Eight conditions have been identified: (1) when a high level of uncertainty exists; (2) when there is little precedent to draw on; (3) when variables are less scientifically predictable; (4) when "facts" are limited; (5) when facts don't clearly point the way to go; (6) when analytical data are of little use; (7) when there are several plausible alternative solutions to choose from, with good arguments for each; and (8) when time is limited and there is pressure to come up with the right decision.[16]

Although intuitive decision making has gained respectability, don't expect people—especially in North America, Great Britain, and other cultures where rational analysis is the expected way of making decisions—to

**intuitive decision making**
A subconscious process created out of distilled experience.

acknowledge they are using it. People with strong intuitive abilities don't usually tell their colleagues how they reached their conclusions. Since rational analysis is considered more socially desirable, intuitive ability is often disguised or hidden. As one top executive commented, "Sometimes one must dress up a gut decision in 'data clothes' to make it acceptable or palatable, but this fine-tuning is usually after the fact of the decision."[17]

So what does all of this discussion about making decisions tell us? Based on our discussion above, you should consider the following when making decisions:

- Make sure that you define the problem as best you can.
- Be clear on the factors that you will use to make your decision.
- Be sure to collect enough alternatives that you can clearly differentiate among them.

> So why is it that we sometimes make bad decisions?

## Constraints Affecting the Decision Choice

When a person finally reaches the point of making a decision, various internal and external factors affect how the final decision is made. We review a few of the common constraints and influences, including judgment shortcuts, individual decision-making styles, and organizational barriers.

### Judgment Shortcuts

Two eminent psychologists, Daniel Kahneman and Amos Tversky, discovered that even when people are trying to be coldly logical, they give radically different answers to the same question when posed in different ways.[18] For instance, consider choices A and B in scenario 1 in Exhibit 11-3. Most people come to opposite conclusions when faced with these two problems, even though they're identical. The only difference is that the first states the problem in terms of lives saved, while the second states it in terms of lives lost. On the basis of his research in decision making, Kahneman concluded that "we can't assume our judgments are good building blocks for decisions because the judgments themselves may be flawed."[19]

**framing**
Error in judgment arising from the selective use of perspective (that is, the way in which a set of ideas, facts, or information is presented) that alters the way one views a situation in forming a decision.

The judgment error described above is referred to as **framing**, and refers to how the selective use of perspective alters the way one might view a situation in formulating a decision. In examining the ways that people make decisions, the two psychologists discovered that individuals often rely on additional **heuristics**, or judgment shortcuts, to simplify the decision process, rather than going through all of the steps of the rational decision-making model.[20]

**heuristics**
Judgment shortcuts in decision making.

Framing is one of the errors people make, but others are also made. For instance, sometimes people make judgments using **statistical regression to the mean**. This heuristic may be of particular interest to those trying to decide whether rewards or punishments work better with employees, colleagues, children, and even friends. Although many studies indicate that rewards are a more effective teaching tool than punishment, Kahneman was once faced with a student who begged to differ on this point. "I've often praised people warmly for beautifully executed manoeuvres, and the next time they almost always do worse. And I've screamed at people for badly executed manoeuvres, and by and large the next time they improve." What the student failed to recognize is that generally an exceptional performance is followed by a

**statistical regression to the mean**
The statistical observation that either very good performances or very poor performances are followed by their opposite, resulting in a record of average performance over time.

> ### Exhibit 11-3
> ### Examples of Decision Biases
>
> **Scenario 1: Answer part A *before* reading part B.**
>
> **A:** Threatened by a superior enemy force, the general faces a dilemma. His intelligence officers say his soldiers will be caught in an ambush in which 600 of them will die unless he leads them to safety by one of two available routes. If he takes the first route, 200 soldiers will be saved. If he takes the second, there's a one-third chance that 600 soldiers will be saved and a two-thirds chance that none will be saved. Which route should he take?
>
> **B:** The general again has to choose between two escape routes. But this time his aides tell him that if he takes the first, 400 soldiers will die. If he takes the second, there's a one-third chance that no soldiers will die, and a two-thirds chance that 600 soldiers will die. Which route should he take?
>
> **Scenario 2:**
>
> Linda is 31, single, outspoken, and very bright. She majored in philosophy in university. As a student, she was deeply concerned with discrimination and other social issues and participated in antinuclear demonstrations. Which statement is more likely:
>
> **a.** Linda is a bank teller.
>
> **b.** Linda is a bank teller and active in the feminist movement.
>
> Source: K. McKean, "Decisions, Decisions," *Discover*, June, 1985, pp. 22-31.

lesser performance, while a poorer performance is more likely followed by a better performance. This happens because each person has an average performance level, so the highs and the lows balance out. The rewards and punishments had little effect on the short-term performance being observed. Rather, improvements happen over the long term. Thus, in this example, it would be helpful to realize that screaming is less likely to result in long-term improvements in behaviour and also tends to damage the relationship between the two parties.

Consider another example of a judgment shortcut. Many more people suffer from fear of flying than from fear of driving in a car. The reason is that many people think flying is more dangerous. It isn't, of course. If flying on a commercial airline were as dangerous as driving, the equivalent of two 747s filled to capacity would have to crash every week, killing all aboard, to match the risk of being killed in a car accident. Because the media give a lot more attention to air accidents, we tend to overstate the risk in flying and understate the risk in driving.

**availability heuristic**
The tendency for people to base their judgments on information that is readily available to them.

This illustrates an example of the **availability heuristic**, which is the tendency for people to base their judgments on information that is readily available to them. Events that evoke emotions, that are particularly vivid, or that have occurred more recently tend to be more available in our memory. As a result, we tend to be prone to overestimating unlikely events like an airplane crash. The availability heuristic can also explain why managers, when doing annual performance appraisals, tend to give more weight to recent behaviours of an employee than to those behaviours of six or nine months ago.

**representative heuristic**
Assessing the likelihood of an occurrence by drawing analogies and seeing identical situations where they don't exist.

Many youngsters in Canada dream of playing hockey in the National Hockey League (NHL) when they grow up. In reality, they have a better chance of becoming medical doctors than they do of playing in the NHL, but these kids are suffering from a **representative heuristic**. They tend to assess the likelihood of an occurrence by trying to match it with a pre-existing category. They hear about a boy from their neighbourhood 10 years ago who went on to play professional hockey, or they watch NHL games on television and think that those players are like them. We all are guilty of using this heuristic at times. Managers, for example, frequently predict the performance of a new product by relating it to a previous product's success. Or if three graduates from the same university were hired and turned out to be poor performers, managers might predict that a current job applicant from the same university would not be a good employee. Scenario 2 in Exhibit 11-3 gives an additional example of representativeness. In that case, Linda is assumed to be a bank teller and a feminist, given her concerns about social issues, even though the probability of both situations being true is much less than the probability of just being a bank teller.

**ignoring the base rate**
Error in judgment that occurs when someone ignores the statistical likelihood of an event when making a decision.

Yet another biasing error that people make is **ignoring the base rate**. For instance, if you were planning to become an entrepreneur, and we were to ask you whether your business would succeed, you would almost undoubtedly respond with a resounding "yes." This is no different from venture capitalists funding new ventures even when the failure rate of new businesses is quite high. Each individual believes that he or she will beat the odds, even when, in the case of founding a business, the failure rate is close to 90 percent.

**escalation of commitment**
An increased commitment to a previous decision despite negative information.

Finally, the last bias we will discuss is the common tendency by decision makers to escalate commitment to a failing course of action.[21] **Escalation of commitment** is an increased commitment to a previous decision despite negative information. For example, a friend had been dating a man for about four years. Although she admitted that things weren't going too well in the relationship, she was determined to marry the man. When asked to explain this seemingly nonrational choice of action, she responded: "I have a lot invested in the relationship!"

It has been well documented that individuals escalate commitment to a failing course of action when they view themselves as responsible for the failure. That is, they "throw good money after bad" to demonstrate that their initial decision wasn't wrong and to avoid having to admit they made a mistake. Escalation of commitment is also congruent with evidence that people try to appear consistent in what they say and do. Increasing commitment to previous actions conveys consistency.

Escalation of commitment has obvious implications for managerial decisions. Many organizations have suffered large losses because a manager was determined to prove his or her original decision was right by continuing to commit resources to what was a lost cause from the beginning. Additionally, consistency is a characteristic often associated with effective leaders. As a result, many managers, in an effort to appear effective, may be motivated to be consistent when, in fact, it may be more appropriate to adopt a new course of action. In actuality, effective managers are those who are able to differentiate between situations in which persistence will pay off and situations in which it will not.

When making decisions you should consider whether you are falling into any of the judgment traps described above. In particular, understanding the base rates, and making sure that you collect information beyond that which is immediately available to you, will provide you with more alternatives from which to frame a decision. In addition, it is useful to consider whether you are sticking with a decision simply because you have invested time in that particular alternative, even though it may not be wise to continue.

## Individual Differences: Decision-Making Styles

Research on decision styles has identified four different individual approaches to making decisions.[22] This model was designed to be used by managers and aspiring managers, but its general framework can be used with any individual decision maker.

The basic foundation of the model is the recognition that people differ along two dimensions. The first is their way of *thinking*. Some people are logical and rational, processing information serially. In contrast, some people are intuitive and creative, perceiving things as a whole. Note that these differences are above and beyond general human limitations such as we described regarding bounded rationality. The other dimension addresses a person's *tolerance for ambiguity*. Some people have a high need to structure information in ways that minimize ambiguity, while others are able to deal better with uncertainty. When these two dimensions are diagrammed, they form four styles of decision making (see Exhibit 11-4). These are directive, analytic, conceptual, and behavioural.

People using the *directive* style have low tolerance for ambiguity and seek rationality. They are efficient and logical, but their efficiency concerns result in decisions made with minimal information and with few alternatives assessed. Directive types make decisions fast and they focus on the short run.

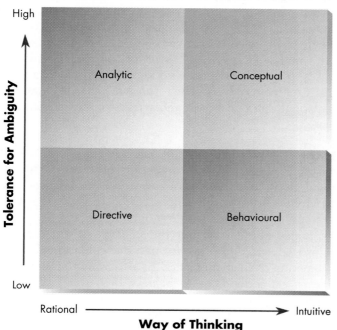

**Exhibit 11-4
Decision-Style Model**

Tolerance for Ambiguity (High / Low)

Analytic | Conceptual

Directive | Behavioural

Way of Thinking (Rational → Intuitive)

Source: A.J. Rowe and J.D. Boulgarides, *Managerial Decision Making*, © 1992 Prentice Hall, Upper Saddle River, NJ, p. 29.

The *analytic* types have a much greater tolerance for ambiguity than do directive decision makers. This leads to the desire for more information and consideration of more alternatives than is true for directives. Analytic managers would be best characterized as careful decision makers with the ability to adapt to or cope with new situations.

Individuals with a *conceptual* style tend to be very broad in their outlook and consider many alternatives. Their focus is long range and they are adept at finding creative solutions to problems.

The final category—the *behavioural* style—characterizes decision makers who work well with others. They're concerned with the achievement of peers and those working for them, and are receptive to suggestions from others, relying heavily on meetings for communicating. This type of manager avoids conflict and seeks acceptance.

Although these four categories are distinct, most managers have characteristics that fall into more than one. It's probably best to think in terms of a manager's dominant style and his or her back-up styles. Some managers rely almost exclusively on their dominant style; more flexible managers can make shifts depending on the situation.

Business students, lower-level managers, and top executives tend to score highest in the analytic style. That's not surprising given the emphasis that formal education, particularly business education, gives to developing rational thinking. For instance, courses in accounting, statistics, and finance all stress rational analysis. To learn more about your style of decision making, refer to the Learning About Yourself Exercise on page 498.

In addition to providing a framework for looking at individual differences, focusing on decision styles can be useful for helping you to understand how two equally intelligent people, with access to the same information, can differ in the ways they approach decisions and the final choices they make.

## Organizational Constraints

The organization itself constrains decision makers. Managers, for instance, shape their decisions to reflect the organization's performance evaluation and reward system, to comply with the organization's formal regulations, and to meet organizationally imposed time constraints. Previous organizational decisions also act as precedents to constrain current decisions.

**PERFORMANCE EVALUATION** Managers are strongly influenced in their decision making by the criteria by which they are evaluated. For example, if a division manager believes that the manufacturing plants under his or her responsibility are operating best when nothing negative is heard, we shouldn't be surprised to find plant managers spending a good part of their time ensuring that negative information doesn't reach the division boss.

**REWARD SYSTEMS** The organization's reward system influences decision makers by suggesting to them what choices are preferable in terms of personal payoff. For example, if the organization rewards risk aversion, managers are more likely to make conservative decisions. For instance, from the 1930s through the mid-1980s, General Motors consistently awarded promotions and bonuses to those managers who kept a low profile, avoided controversy, and were good team players. The result was that GM managers became very adept at dodging tough issues and passing controversial decisions on to committees.

**PROGRAMMED ROUTINES** Amir Jadeep, a shift manager at a McDonald's restaurant in the Maritimes, describes the constraints he faces on his job: "I've got rules and regulations covering almost every decision I make—from how long to cook the french fries to how often I need to clean the washrooms. My job doesn't come with much freedom of choice."

Jadeep's situation is not unique. All but the smallest of organizations create rules, policies, procedures, and other formalized regulations in order to standardize the behaviour of their members. By programming decisions, organizations are able to get individuals to achieve high levels of performance without paying for the years of experience that would be necessary in the absence of regulations. Amir Jadeep, for instance, earns about $29 000 a year, but he's only 20 years old and has no university exposure. To get the same quality of decisions from someone in Jadeep's job without providing him or her with extensive operations manuals to follow, McDonald's would need to hire managers with considerably more work experience and training—and probably have to pay them $40 000 or more per year.

**SYSTEM-IMPOSED TIME CONSTRAINTS** Organizations impose deadlines on decisions. For instance, department budgets need to be completed by next Friday; or the report on new-product development must be ready for the executive committee to review by the first of the month. A host of decisions must be made quickly to stay ahead of the competition and keep customers satisfied. And almost all important decisions come with explicit deadlines. These conditions create time pressures on decision makers and often make it difficult, if not impossible, to gather all the information they might like to have before making a final choice. The rational model ignores the reality that, in organizations, decisions come with time constraints.

**HISTORICAL PRECEDENTS** Decisions aren't made in a vacuum. They have a context. In fact, as noted at the beginning of this chapter, individual decisions are more accurately characterized as points in a stream of decisions.

Decisions made in the past are ghosts that continually haunt current choices. For instance, past commitments may constrain current options. To use a social situation as an example, the decision you might make after meeting "Mr. or Ms. Right" is more complicated if you're married than if you're single. Prior commitments—in this case, having chosen to get married—constrain your options. The auto industry was caught short in the late 1970s because consumers had exhibited a preference for larger cars, until soaring gas prices made smaller calls more desirable. The industry was slow to move away from its commitment to producing larger cars.

## Cultural Differences

> Do decisions get made the same way around the world?

The rational model makes no acknowledgment of cultural differences. However, Canadians don't necessarily make decisions the same way that people from other backgrounds do. Therefore, we need to recognize that the cultural background of the decision maker can have significant influence on his or her selection of problems, the depth of analysis, the importance placed on logic and rationality, or whether organizational decisions should be made autocratically by an individual manager or collectively in groups.[23]

Cultures, for example, differ in terms of time orientation, the importance of rationality, and preference for collective decision making. Differences in time orientation help us understand why managers in Egypt will make decisions at a much slower and more deliberate pace than their North American counterparts. While rationality is valued in North America, that's not the case everywhere in the world. As discussed earlier in the chapter, a North American manager might make an important decision intuitively, but he or she knows that it is important to appear to proceed in a rational fashion. In countries where intuition, tradition, deference to authority, or other values play a greater role in decision making, strictly and exclusively logical justifications for decisions may not be as important. Finally, decision making by Japanese managers is much more group-oriented than in Canada and the United States. The Japanese value conformity and cooperation. Before Japanese CEOs make an important decision, they collect a large amount of information, which they then use in consensus-forming group decisions.

Molly Mak was chosen President of a national information technology solutions provider, Onward Computer Systems, by other partners in the firm after she showed that she had the vision and determination to lead the company to greater growth and profits. She says that consensus is not always possible, especially when it is important to get things accomplished under tight time constraints.

# Group Decision Making

While a variety of decisions in both life and organizations are made at the individual level, the belief—characterized by juries—that two heads are better than one has long been accepted as a basic component of North American and many other countries' legal systems. This belief has expanded to the point that, today, many decisions in organizations are made by groups, teams, or committees. In this section, we will review group decision making and compare it with individual decision making.

## Groups vs. the Individual

Decision-making groups may be widely used in organizations, but does that imply that group decisions are preferable to those made by an individual alone? The answer to this question depends on a number of factors. Let's begin by looking at the strengths and weaknesses of group decision making.[24]

**STRENGTHS OF GROUP DECISION MAKING** Groups generate *more complete information and knowledge*. By aggregating the resources of several individuals, groups bring more input into the decision process. In addition to more input, groups can bring heterogeneity to the decision process. They offer *increased diversity of views*. This offers the opportunity to consider more approaches and alternatives. The evidence indicates that a group will almost always outperform even the best individual. So groups generate *higher-quality decisions*. Finally, groups lead to *increased acceptance of a solution*. Many decisions fail after the final choice is made because people don't accept the solution. Group members who participated in making a decision are likely to enthusiastically support the decision and encourage others to accept it.

**WEAKNESSES OF GROUP DECISION MAKING** Despite the advantages noted, group decisions involve certain drawbacks. First, they're *time-consuming*. They typically take more time to reach a solution than would be the case if an individual were making the decision alone. Second, there are *conformity pressures* in groups. The desire by group members to be accepted and considered an asset to the group can result in squashing any overt disagreement. Third, group discussion can be *dominated by one or a few members*. If this dominant coalition is composed of low- and medium-ability members, the group's overall effectiveness will suffer. Finally, group decisions suffer from *ambiguous responsibility*. In an individual decision, it's clear who is accountable for the final outcome. In a group decision, the responsibility of any single member is watered down.

**EFFECTIVENESS AND EFFICIENCY** Whether groups are more effective than individuals depends on the criteria you use for defining effectiveness. In terms of *accuracy*, group decisions will tend to be more accurate. The evidence indicates that, on the average, groups make better-quality decisions than individuals.[25] However, if decision effectiveness is defined in terms of *speed*, individuals are superior. If *creativity* is important, groups tend to be more effective than individuals. Finally, if effectiveness means the degree of *acceptance* the final solution achieves, the nod again goes to the group.[26]

Effectiveness, however, cannot be considered without also assessing efficiency. In terms of efficiency, groups almost always stack up as a poor second to the individual decision maker. With few exceptions, group decision making consumes more work hours than an individual who is tackling the same problem alone. The exceptions tend to be those instances where, to achieve comparable quantities of diverse input, the single decision maker must spend a great deal of time reviewing files and talking to people. Because groups can include members from diverse areas, the time spent searching for information can be reduced. However, as we noted, these advantages in efficiency tend to be the exception. Groups are generally less efficient than individuals. In deciding whether to use groups, then, consideration should be given to assessing whether the increases in effectiveness are sufficient to offset the losses in efficiency.

In summary, groups offer an excellent vehicle for performing many of the steps in the decision-making process. They are a source of both breadth and depth of input for information gathering. If the group is composed of individuals with diverse backgrounds, the alternatives generated should be more extensive and the analysis more critical than what an individual alone could achieve. When the final solution is agreed upon, there are more people in a group decision to support and implement it. These advantages, however, can be more than offset by the time consumed by group decisions, the internal conflicts they create, and the pressures they generate toward conformity.

## Groupthink and Groupshift

Two byproducts of group decision making have received a considerable amount of attention by researchers in OB. As we'll show, these two phenomena have the potential to affect the group's ability to appraise alternatives objectively and arrive at quality decision solutions.

**groupthink**
Phenomenon in which the norm for consensus overrides the realistic appraisal of alternative courses of action.

**GROUPTHINK** Have you ever felt like speaking up in a meeting, classroom, or informal group, but decided against it? One reason may have been shyness. On the other hand, you may have been a victim of **groupthink**, the phenomenon that occurs when group members become so enamoured with seeking agreement that the norm for consensus overrides the realistic appraisal of alternative courses of action and the full expression of deviant, minority, or unpopular views. It describes a deterioration in an individual's mental efficiency, reality testing, and moral judgment as a result of group pressures.[27]

We have all seen the symptoms of the groupthink phenomenon: [28]

- *Illusion of invulnerability*: Group members become overconfident among themselves, allowing them to take extraordinary risks.

- *Assumption of morality*: Group members believe highly in the moral rightness of the group's objectives and do not feel the need to debate the ethics of their actions.

- *Rationalized resistance.* Group members rationalize any resistance to the assumptions they have made. No matter how strongly the evidence may contradict their basic assumptions, members behave so as to reinforce those assumptions continually.
- *Peer pressure.* Members apply direct pressures on those who momentarily express doubts about any of the group's shared views or who question the validity of arguments supporting the alternative favoured by the majority.
- *Minimized doubts.* Those members who have doubts or hold differing points of view seek to avoid deviating from what appears to be group consensus by keeping silent about misgivings and even minimizing to themselves the importance of their doubts.
- *Illusion of unanimity.* If someone doesn't speak, it's assumed that he or she is in full accord. In other words, abstention becomes viewed as a "Yes" vote.

As the Bre-X scandal was unfolding in early 1997, many people who possibly should have known better refused to accept the initial evidence that there might not be any gold at Busang. Because investors and the companies involved had convinced themselves that they were sitting on the gold find of the 20th century, they were reluctant to challenge their beliefs when the first evidence of tampered core samples was produced.

Groupthink appears to be closely aligned with the conclusions Solomon Asch drew in his experiments with a lone dissenter, which we described in Chapter 5. Individuals who hold a position that is different from that of the dominant majority are under pressure to suppress, withhold, or modify their true feelings and beliefs. As members of a group, we find it more pleasant to be in agreement—to be a positive part of the group—than to be a disruptive force, even if disruption is necessary to improve the effectiveness of the group's decisions.

Does groupthink attack all groups? No. It seems to occur most often where there is a clear group identity, where members hold a positive image of their group, which they want to protect, and where the group perceives a collective threat to this positive image.[29] So groupthink is less a dissenter-suppression mechanism than a means for a group to protect its positive image.

What can managers do to minimize groupthink?[30] One thing they can do is encourage group leaders to play an impartial role. Leaders should actively seek input from all members and avoid expressing their own opinions, especially in the early stages of deliberation. Another thing is to appoint one group member to play the role of devil's advocate. This member's role is to overtly challenge the majority position and offer divergent perspectives. Still another suggestion is to utilize exercises that stimulate active discussion of diverse alternatives without threatening the group and intensifying identity protection. One such exercise is to have group members talk about dangers or risks involved in a decision and delaying discussion of any potential gains. By requiring members to first focus on the negatives of a decision alternative, the group is less likely to stifle dissenting views and more likely to gain an objective evaluation.

Despite considerable anecdotal evidence indicating the negative implications of groupthink in organizational settings, there has not been much actual empirical work conducted in organizations on this matter.[31] In fact, groupthink has been criticized for suggesting that its effect is uniformly negative[32] and for overestimating the link between the decision-making process

**Second Cup**
www.secondcup.com

**Campbell Soup Co.**
www.campbellkitchen.com

and its outcome.[33] A 1999 study of groupthink using 30 teams from five large corporations suggests that elements of groupthink may affect decision making differently. For instance, the illusion of vulnerability, belief in inherent group morality and the illusion of unanimity were positively associated with team performance.[34]

The most recent research suggests that one should be aware of groupthink conditions that are leading to poor decisions, while realizing that not all groupthink symptoms harm decision making. As Randy Powell, president of Toronto-based Second Cup, cautions, "Groupthink can happen, and what the senior person says tends to rule. I have always believed I should speak for what I believe to be true."[35] Powell's first test with overcoming groupthink happened at a previous position with Campbell Soup Co., just one month after he'd been hired. At a presentation to senior executives, Campbell's CEO, David Clark, told the group that Prego's spaghetti sauce was a poor performer and outlined the reasons why. Powell believed he knew the product better than the CEO. After some hesitation, he pointed this out: "It took every ounce of courage I had but I said, 'David, I beg to differ.'" After the meeting, Powell's immediate supervisor approached him and admitted, "I wanted to say that, but I just didn't have the courage to step in front of David." Powell was congratulated for speaking up, and in his own words says, "That established my reputation at Campbell's, without a doubt." In this case, speaking up really did make a difference.

**groupshift**
The phenomenon in which the initial positions of individual members of a group are exaggerated toward a more extreme position.

**GROUPSHIFT** Evidence suggests that there are differences between the decisions groups make and the decisions that might be made by individual members within the group.[36] In some cases, the group decisions are more conservative than the individual decisions. More often, the shift is toward greater risk.[37] In either case, participants have engaged in groupshift, a tendency where one's initial position becomes exaggerated because of the interactions of the group.

What appears to happen in groups is that the discussion leads to a significant shift in the positions of members toward a more extreme position in the direction in which they were already leaning before the discussion. So conservative types become more cautious and more aggressive types assume more risk. The group discussion tends to exaggerate the initial position of the group.

Groupshift can be viewed as a special case of groupthink. The group's decision reflects the dominant decision-making norm that develops during the group's discussion. Whether the shift in the group's decision is toward greater caution or more risk depends on the dominant prediscussion norm.

The greater occurrence of the shift toward risk has generated several explanations for the phenomenon.[38] It's been argued, for instance, that the discussion creates familiarization among the members. As they become more comfortable with each other, they also become more bold and daring. Another argument is that our society values risk, that we admire individuals who are willing to take risks, and that group discussion motivates members to show that they are at least as willing as their peers to take risks. The most plausible explanation of the shift toward risk, however, seems to be that the group diffuses responsibility. Group decisions free any single member from accountability for the group's final choice. Greater risk can be taken because even if the decision fails, no one member can be held wholly responsible.

How should you use the findings on groupshift? You should recognize that group decisions exaggerate the initial position of the individual members, that the shift has been shown more often to be toward greater risk, and that whether a group will shift toward greater risk or caution is a function of the members' prediscussion inclinations.

## Group Decision-Making Techniques

**interacting groups**
Typical groups, where members interact with each other face to face.

The most common form of group decision making takes place in **interacting groups**. In these groups, members meet face to face and rely on both verbal and nonverbal interaction to communicate with each other. But as our discussion of groupthink demonstrated, interacting groups often censor themselves and pressure individual members toward conformity of opinion. Brainstorming, the nominal group technique, and electronic meetings have been proposed as ways to reduce many of the problems inherent in the traditional interacting group.

**brainstorming**
An idea-generation process that specifically encourages any and all alternatives, while withholding any criticism of those alternatives.

**Brainstorming** is meant to overcome pressures for conformity in the interacting group that retard the development of creative alternatives.[39] It achieves this by utilizing an idea-generation process that specifically encourages any and all alternatives, while withholding any criticism of those alternatives.

In a typical brainstorming session, a half-dozen to a dozen people sit around a table. The group leader states the problem in a clear manner so that all participants understand it. Members then "free-wheel" as many alternatives as they can in a given period of time. No criticism is allowed, and all the alternatives are recorded for later discussion and analysis. With one idea stimulating others and judgments of even the most bizarre suggestions withheld until later, group members are encouraged to "think the unusual."

**Food in Canada**
www.foodincanada.com

How successful can a brainstorming session be? You may have noticed in one of your recent visits to a fast-food restaurant something called a "wrap."[40] *Food in Canada* rated wraps as the hot trend for 1997-1998. What you might not know is that the wrap was the result of a brainstorming session by four twenty-something Californians who developed the concept while vacationing in Mexico in 1993. Will Weisman, now executive director of marketing with World Wrapp Inc., and one of the four, explains how the wrap came about: "The four of us started doing a lot of brainstorming about what was going on in the restaurant industry with food trends, and we wanted to do something with the burrito concept." The results of the four's brainstorming session have also reached Canada. Both Mr. Submarine, a Canadian franchise, and the Red Robin restaurant, which has locations in British Columbia and Alberta, now sell wraps. A number of wrap outlets have opened across Canada, including That's A Wrapp in downtown Calgary and Bad Ass Jack's Subs and Wraps in Edmonton. In downtown Vancouver there is Wrap City Burritos and Wrap Zone. And on Bloor Street in Toronto you'll find Wrap N Roll.

**Mr. Submarine**
www.mrsub.ca

**Wrap N Roll**
www.wrapnroll.com

A more recent variant of brainstorming is electronic brainstorming, which is done by people interacting on computers to generate ideas. For example, Calgary-based Jerilyn Wright and Associates uses electronic brainstorming to help clients design their workspaces through software that has been adapted for office-space design; Calgary-based Tarragon Oil and Gas was one of Wright's clients.[41]

Queen's University's Executive Decision Centre is "one of the first electronic [decision making] facilities in North America and the first to be made accessible to the public."[42] Professor Brent Gallupe and another facilitator at the Centre have conducted over 600 decision-making sessions with a va-

**Glaxo Wellcome**
www.glaxowellcome.co.uk

**DuPont**
www.dupont.com

**Department of National Defence**
www.dnd.ca

**United Way Canada**
www.uwc-cc.ca

**nominal group technique**
A group decision-making method in which individual members meet face to face to pool their judgments in a systematic but independent fashion.

**electronic meeting**
A meeting where members interact on computers, allowing for anonymity of comments and aggregating of votes.

riety of North American organizations, including Glaxo Wellcome, Bombardier, DuPont, Imperial Oil, the Department of National Defence, the Canadian Security and Intelligence Service, and the United Way. The strength of Queen's system is that participants simultaneously interact via computer terminals, all responses are anonymous, and the speed allows for generating numerous ideas in a short time. Mississauga, Ontario-based DuPont Canada uses the system regularly for focused creativity sessions with both employees and customers. Whitby, Ontario-based McGraw-Hill Ryerson Canada became a regular user after finding that one of its divisions experienced a surge in sales after visiting the Queen's Centre. "They came up with a better, more soundly developed strategy, with more commitment on the part of the people. People feel very committed to the outcomes of the process because they don't feel like they've been strong-armed into the outcomes. They've had a voice in it," says John Dill, McGraw-Hill Ryerson's president and CEO.

However, brainstorming isn't always the right strategy to use. For example, President and CEO Terry Graham of Scarborough, Ontario-based Image Processing Systems Inc., which won Canada's 1997 Export Award, saw brainstorming backfire when doing business in China. He says that meetings with Chinese business people "are definitely not for brainstorming. We learned this lesson the hard way. Our team thought we could show our creativity by placing fresh alternatives in front of an important manager. It was two years before the company would talk to us again."[43]

Brainstorming, we should also note, is merely a process for generating ideas. The following two techniques go further by offering methods of actually arriving at a preferred solution.[44]

The **nominal group technique** restricts discussion or interpersonal communication during the decision-making process, hence, the term *nominal*. Group members are all physically present, as in a traditional committee meeting, but members operate independently. Specifically, a problem is presented and then the following steps take place:

- Members meet as a group, but before any discussion takes place, each member independently writes down his or her ideas on the problem.

- After this silent period, each member presents one idea to the group. Each member takes his or her turn, presenting a single idea until all ideas have been presented and recorded. No discussion takes place until all ideas have been recorded.

- The group then discusses the ideas for clarity and evaluates them.

- Each group member silently and independently ranks the ideas. The idea with the highest aggregate ranking determines the final decision.

The chief advantage of the nominal group technique is that it permits the group to meet formally but does not restrict independent thinking, as does the interacting group.

The most recent approach to group decision making blends the nominal group technique with sophisticated computer technology.[45] It's called the computer-assisted group, or **electronic meeting**. Once the technology is in place, the concept is simple. Up to 50 people sit around a horseshoe-shaped table, which is empty except for a series of computer terminals. Issues are presented to participants and they type their responses onto their computer monitors. Individual comments, as well as aggregate votes, are displayed on a projection screen in the room.

**Exhibit 11-5**
**Evaluating Group Effectiveness**

| Effectiveness Criteria | Type of Group | | | |
|---|---|---|---|---|
| | Interacting | Brainstorming | Nominal | Electronic |
| Number of ideas | Low | Moderate | High | High |
| Quality of ideas | Low | Moderate | High | High |
| Social pressure | High | Low | Moderate | Low |
| Money costs | Low | Low | Low | High |
| Speed | Moderate | Moderate | Moderate | High |
| Task orientation | Low | High | High | High |
| Potential for interpersonal conflict | High | Low | Moderate | Low |
| Feelings of accomplishment | High to low | High | High | High |
| Commitment to solution | High | Not applicable | Moderate | Moderate |
| Develops group cohesiveness | High | High | Moderate | Low |

Source: Based on J.K. Murnighan, "Group Decision Making: What Strategies Should You Use?" *Management Review*, February 1981, p. 61.

The major advantages of electronic meetings are anonymity, honesty, and speed. Participants can anonymously type any message they want and it flashes on the screen for all to see at the push of a participant's board key. It also allows people to be brutally honest without penalty. And it's fast because chit-chat is eliminated, discussions don't digress, and many participants can "talk" at once without stepping on one another's toes. The future of group meetings undoubtedly will include extensive use of this technology.

Each of these four group decision techniques offers its own strengths and weaknesses. The choice of one technique over another will depend on what criteria you want to emphasize and the cost-benefit trade-off. For instance, as Exhibit 11-5 indicates, the interacting group is effective for building group cohesiveness; brainstorming keeps social pressures to a minimum; the nominal group technique is an inexpensive means for generating a large number of ideas; and electronic meetings process ideas quickly.

## The Influence of the Leader on Group Decision Making

You're the head of your own business, or you're the manager of your division at work, and you're trying to decide whether you should make a decision yourself, or involve the members of your team in the decision. Is there anything that informs you about whether it is better for the leader to make the decision, or to get everyone involved in the decision-making process?

Julia Levy, president of Vancouver-based QLT PhotoTherapeutics Inc., a biotech firm that develops and markets light-activated drugs used to treat diseases such as cancer and arthritis, regards herself as a team leader, not the sole decision maker in her company. She enjoys brainstorming with her other managers to come up with the best solutions, and then getting everyone to agree on key decisions. She doesn't mind being the tie-breaker though.

**leader-participation model**
A leadership theory that provides a set of rules to determine the form and amount of participative decision making in different situations.

Back in 1973, Victor Vroom and Phillip Yetton developed a **leader-participation model** to account for various actions the leader might take with respect to the decision-making processes of the group he or she led.[46] Vroom and Yetton's model was normative—it provided a sequential set of rules that should be followed for determining the form and amount of participation desirable by the manager or group leader in decision making, as dictated by different types of situations. The model was a complex decision tree incorporating seven contingencies (whose relevance could be identified by making "Yes" or "No" choices) and five alternative leadership styles.

More recent work by Vroom and Arthur Jago has resulted in a revision of this model.[47] The new model retains the same five alternative leadership styles but expands the contingency variables to 12, 10 of which are answered along a five-point scale. Exhibit 11-6 lists the 12 variables.

The model assumes that any of five possible behaviours that leaders could use might be feasible in a given situation—Autocratic I (AI), Autocratic II (AII), Consultative I (CI), Consultative II (CII), and Group II (GII). Thus the group leader or manager has the following alternatives from which to choose when deciding how involved he or she should be with decisions that affect a work group.

**AI:** You solve the problem or make a decision yourself using whatever facts you have at hand.

**AII:** You obtain the necessary information from employees and then decide on the solution to the problem yourself. You may or may not tell them about the nature of the situation you face. You seek only relevant facts from them, not their advice or counsel.

**CI:** You share the problem with relevant employees one-on-one, getting their ideas and suggestions. However, the final decision is yours alone.

**Exhibit 11-6**
**Contingency Variables in the Revised Leader-Participation Model**

**QR: Quality Requirement**
How important is the technical quality of this decision?

| 1 | 2 | 3 | 4 | 5 |
|---|---|---|---|---|
| No Importance | Low Importance | Average Importance | High Importance | Critical Importance |

**CR: Commitment Requirement**
How important is subordinate commitment to the decision?

| 1 | 2 | 3 | 4 | 5 |
|---|---|---|---|---|
| No Importance | Low Importance | Average Importance | High Importance | Critical Importance |

**LI: Leader Information**
Do you have sufficient information to make a high-quality decision?

| 1 | 2 | 3 | 4 | 5 |
|---|---|---|---|---|
| No | Probably No | Maybe | Probably Yes | Yes |

**ST: Problem Structure**
Is the problem well structured?

| 1 | 2 | 3 | 4 | 5 |
|---|---|---|---|---|
| No | Probably No | Maybe | Probably Yes | Yes |

**CP: Commitment Probability**
If you were to make the decision by yourself, is it reasonably certain that your subordinates would be committed to the decision?

| 1 | 2 | 3 | 4 | 5 |
|---|---|---|---|---|
| No | Probably No | Maybe | Probably Yes | Yes |

**GC: Goal Congruence**
Do subordinates share the organizational goals to be attained in solving this problem?

| 1 | 2 | 3 | 4 | 5 |
|---|---|---|---|---|
| No | Probably No | Maybe | Probably Yes | Yes |

**CO: Subordinate Conflict**
Is conflict among subordinates over preferred solutions likely?

| 1 | 2 | 3 | 4 | 5 |
|---|---|---|---|---|
| No | Probably No | Maybe | Probably Yes | Yes |

**SI: Subordinate Information**
Do subordinates have sufficient information to make a high-quality decision?

| 1 | 2 | 3 | 4 | 5 |
|---|---|---|---|---|
| No | Probably No | Maybe | Probably Yes | Yes |

**TC: Time Constraint**
Does a critically severe time constraint limit your ability to involve subordinates?

| 1 | 5 |
|---|---|
| No | Yes |

**GD: Geographical Dispersion**
Are the costs involved in bringing together geographically dispersed subordinates prohibitive?

| 1 | 5 |
|---|---|
| No | Yes |

**MT: Motivation — Time**
How important is it to you to minimize the time it takes to make the decision?

| 1 | 2 | 3 | 4 | 5 |
|---|---|---|---|---|
| No Importance | Low Importance | Average Importance | High Importance | Critical Importance |

**MD: Motivation — Development**
How important is it to you to maximize the opportunities for subordinate development?

| 1 | 2 | 3 | 4 | 5 |
|---|---|---|---|---|
| No Importance | Low Importance | Average Importance | High Importance | Critical Importance |

Source: V.H. Vroom and A.G. Jago (eds.), *The New Leadership: Managing Participation in Organizations,* ©1988. Reprinted with permission of Prentice Hall, Inc., Upper Saddle River, NJ.

**CII:** You share the problem with your employees as a group, collectively obtaining their ideas and suggestions. Then you make the decision, which may or may not reflect your employees' influence.

**GII:** You share the problem with your employees as a group. Your goal is to help the group concur on a decision. Your ideas are not given any greater weight than those of others.

Vroom and Jago have developed a computer program that cuts through the complexity of the new model. But managers can still use decision trees to select their leader style if there are no shades of grey (that is, when the status of a variable is clear-cut so that a "Yes" or "No" response will be accurate), there are no critically severe time constraints, and employees are not geographically dispersed. Exhibit 11-7 illustrates one of these decision trees. To help you become more familiar with using one of these decision trees, the Working With Others Exercise on page 499 presents several cases for you to analyze.

Research testing of the original leader-participation model was very encouraging.[48] We have every reason to believe that the revised model provides an excellent guide to help managers choose the most appropriate leadership style in different situations.

## Exhibit 11-7
### The Revised Leadership-Participation Model (Time-Driven Decision Tree Group Problems)

| | | |
|---|---|---|
| QR | Quality requirement: | How important is the technical quality of this decision? |
| CR | Commitment requirement: | How important is subordinate commitment to the decision? |
| LI | Leader's information: | Do you have sufficient information to make a high-quality decision? |
| ST | Problem structure: | Is the problem well structured? |
| CP | Commitment probability: | If you were to make the decision by yourself, is it reasonably certain that your subordinate(s) would be committed to the decision? |
| GC | Goal congruence: | Do subordinates share the organizational goals to be attained in solving this problem? |
| CO | Subordinate conflict: | Is conflict among subordinates over preferred solutions likely? |
| SI | Subordinate information: | Do subordinates have sufficient information to make a high-quality decision? |

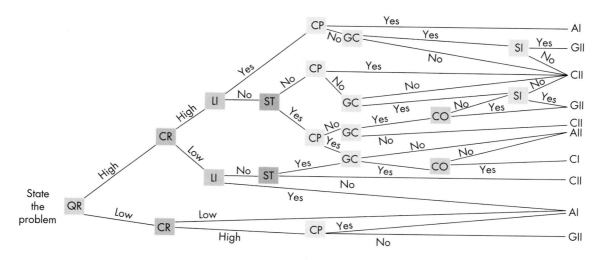

Creativity and the bottom-line can go hand-in-hand. In fact, at Vancouver-based Big House Communications, creativity rules. Big House develops communications, including websites, for other companies. They are known for giving clients several alternatives: traditional, wacky and fun. The company must be doing something right. They're 10 years old, which makes them *really* old for their business.

One last point before we move on. The revised leader-participation model is very sophisticated and complex, which makes it impossible to describe in detail in a basic OB textbook. However, the variables identified in Exhibit 11-6 provide you with some solid insights about when you as a leader should participate in a group decision, make the decision yourself, or delegate to someone else.

## Creativity in Organizational Decision Making

Creativity is another important aspect of decision making in organizations. A survey conducted in the mid-1990s by the Toronto- and Montreal-based law firm Goodman Phillips and Vineberg found that both large public companies and entrepreneurs recognize a link between creative thinking within the organization and having a competitive edge.[49] "It [creative thinking] will not necessarily spell the difference between success and failure. But it is one of those tangential issues that can add a few cents per share profit," noted the head of an Ontario agriproducts company, who was not identified by the survey.

The study interviewed 100 CEOs of public companies and 100 entrepreneurs across Canada. Of those surveyed, 58 percent believe that the results of a creative thinking process are important to their company's overall success. Many *Fortune 500* companies, such as DuPont, Monsanto, Royal Bank, Disney, Thomson Corporation, Bell, Hewlett-Packard, Bank of Montreal, and CIBA Vision are training their employees specifically to "think outside the box"; that is, to think creatively.[50] To do this, the companies either bring in creativity experts to train their people or they attempt to guide thinking along more creative routes during planning sessions.

Before we discuss decision-making issues, let's consider what we mean by creativity in organizations. A variety of definitions exist for the concept of creativity, with some viewing it as a characteristic of a person, while others view it as a process.[51] Most contemporary researchers and theorists use a definition that addresses either the product or the outcome of the product development process.[52] In our discussion below, we consider **creativity** as the process of creating products, ideas, or procedures that are novel or original, and are potentially relevant or useful to an organization.[53]

**Thomson Corporation**
www.thomcorp.com

**Bell Canada**
www.bell.ca

**CIBA Vision**
www.cvworld.com

**creativity**
The process of creating products, ideas, or procedures that are novel or original, and are potentially relevant or useful to an organization.

## Factors That Affect Individual Creativity

**Why are some people more creative than others?**

People differ in their inherent creativity. Albert Einstein, Marie Curie, Thomas Edison, Pablo Picasso, and Wolfgang Amadeus Mozart were individuals of exceptional creativity. In more recent times, Emily Carr, Garth Drabinsky, and Michael Jordan have been noted for the creative contributions they made to their fields. Not surprisingly, exceptional creativity is scarce. For example, a study of lifetime creativity of 461 men and women found that less than one percent were exceptionally creative.[54] But 10 percent were highly creative and about 60 percent were somewhat creative. This suggests that most of us have creative potential, if we can learn to unleash it.

A large body of literature has examined the personal attributes associated with creative achievement.[55] In general, "these studies have demonstrated that a stable set of core personal characteristics, including broad interests, attraction to complexity, intuition, aesthetic sensitivity, toleration of ambiguity, and self-confidence, relate positively and consistently to measures of creative performance across a variety of domains."[56]

While personality and cognitive skills are linked to creativity,[57] the task itself plays an important role. Individuals are more creative when they are motivated by intrinsic interest, challenge, task satisfaction, and self-set goals.[58] Those who are extrinsically motivated are more likely to look for the most efficient solution to a problem, in order to receive the desired rewards. Those who are intrinsically motivated may take more time exploring issues and situations, which gives them the opportunity to see things in different lights.[59] The setting also makes a difference, and those settings that provide opportunities, absence of constraints,[60] and rewards[61] encourage creativity.

There is some evidence that the brain is set up to think linearly, rather than laterally, and yet lateral thinking is needed for creative thinking. Edward De Bono, a leading authority on creative and conceptual thinking for over 25 years, has written a number of books on this topic, including *Six Thinking Hats* and *The Mechanism of Mind*.[62] He has identified various tools for helping one use more lateral thinking. One such tool is called provocation, where people create a crazy idea and then transform it into a workable new concept. Toronto-based real estate firm Cambridge Shopping Centres used provocation to identify ways to build more cost-efficient office towers.[63] The provocation exercise of the cross-functional planning team was to imagine that there was no air conditioning in the towers. This led the team to the idea "that in multi-towered projects, excess air conditioning capacity from existing buildings could be used to cool adjoining towers," which was a radical new concept.

De Bono's "six thinking hats" concept is a simple yet powerful tool that is intended to change the way people think. He suggests that innovative and creative problem-solving can develop from working through decisions using each of the frameworks represented by one of the hats. The hats are metaphors to represent different kinds of thinking.[64]

- The *white hat* represents impartial thinking, focusing strictly on the facts.

- The *red hat* represents expression of feelings, passions, intuitions, emotions.

- The *black hat* stands for a critical, deliberate, evaluating outlook.

- The *yellow hat* represents an optimistic, upbeat, positive outlook.
- The *green hat* represents creativity, inspiration, imagination, and the free flow of new concepts.
- The *blue hat* represents control, an overall "managerial" perspective of the process.

Each hat has its own place in the decision-making process. De Bono suggests that we use all six in order to fully develop our capacity to think more creatively. Toronto-based Royal Trust used this framework to collect ideas from employees across Canada on how to generate revenue and reduce costs.[65] The company received numerous ideas and discovered that the creativity process helped to remove barriers between senior management and front-line employees.[66]

## Organizational Factors That Affect Creativity

In two decades of research analyzing the links between work environment and creativity, six general categories have been found:[67]

- *Challenge:* When people are matched up with the right assignments, their expertise and skills can be brought to the task of creative thinking. Individuals should be stretched, but not overwhelmed.
- *Freedom:* To be creative, once a person is given a project, he or she needs the autonomy to determine the process. In other words, let the person decide how to tackle the problem. This heightens intrinsic motivation.
- *Resources:* Time and money are the two main resources that affect creativity. Thus, managers need to allot these resources carefully.
- *Work-Group Features:* Our discussion of group composition and diversity concluded that heterogeneous groups were likely to come up with more creative solutions. In addition to ensuring a diverse group of people, team members need to share excitement over the goal, must be willing to support each other through difficult periods, and must recognize each other's unique knowledge and perspective.
- *Supervisory Encouragement:* To sustain passion, most people need to feel that what they are doing matters to others. Managers can reward, collaborate, and communicate to nurture the creativity of individuals and teams.
- *Organizational Support:* Creativity-supporting organizations reward creativity, and also make sure that there is information sharing and collaboration. They make sure that negative political problems do not get out of control.

Five organizational factors have been found that can block your creativity at work: (1) expected evaluation—focusing on how your work is going to be evaluated; (2) surveillance—being watched while you're working; (3) external motivators—emphasizing external, tangible rewards; (4) competition—facing win-lose situations with peers; and (5) constrained choice—being given limits on how you can do your work.[68] This chapter's CBC Video Case on page 502 features Eureka Ranch, where companies go for help with developing creative ideas.

## What About Ethics in Decision Making?

No contemporary discussion of decision making would be complete without the inclusion of ethics because ethical considerations should be an important criterion in organizational decision making. In this final section, we present three ways to ethically frame decisions and examine the factors that shape an individual's ethical decision-making behaviour. We also examine organizational responses to the demand for ethical behaviour, as well as consideration of ethical decisions when doing business in other cultures. To learn more about your ethical decision-making approach, see the Ethical Dilemma Exercise on page 500.

### Three Ethical Decision Criteria

An individual can use three different criteria in making ethical choices.[69] The first is the *utilitarian* criterion, in which decisions are made solely on the basis of their outcomes or consequences. The goal of **utilitarianism** is to provide the greatest good for the greatest number. This view tends to dominate business decision making. It is consistent with goals such as efficiency, productivity, and high profits. By maximizing profits, for instance, a business executive can argue that he or she is securing the greatest good for the greatest number—as he or she hands out dismissal notices to 15 percent of employees.

Another ethical criterion is to focus on *rights*. This calls on individuals to make decisions consistent with fundamental liberties and privileges as set forth in documents such as the Charter of Rights and Freedoms. An emphasis on rights in decision making means respecting and protecting the basic rights of individuals, such as the right to privacy, to free speech, and to due process.

**utilitarianism**
Decisions are made so as to provide the greatest good for the greatest number.

Stewart Leibl, President of Perth's, a Winnipeg drycleaning chain, is a founding sponsor of the Koats for Kids program. The company's outlets are a drop off point for no-longer-needed children's coats, and Perth's cleans the coats free of charge before they're distributed to children who don't have winter coats. Leibl is going beyond utilitarian criteria when he says, "We all have a responsibility to contribute to the society that we live in." He is also looking at social justice.

For instance, use of this criterion would protect whistleblowers when they report unethical or illegal practices by their organization to the media or to government agencies on the grounds of their right to free speech.

A third criterion is to focus on *justice*. This requires individuals to impose and enforce rules fairly and impartially so there is an equitable distribution of benefits and costs. Union members typically favour this view. It justifies paying people the same wage for a given job, regardless of performance differences, and using seniority as the primary determination in making layoff decisions.

Each of these three criteria has advantages and liabilities. A focus on utilitarianism promotes efficiency and productivity, but it can result in ignoring the rights of some individuals, particularly those with minority representation in the organization. The use of rights as a criterion protects individuals from injury and is consistent with freedom and privacy, but it can create an overly legalistic work environment that hinders productivity and efficiency. A focus on justice protects the interests of the under-represented and less powerful, but it can encourage a sense of entitlement that reduces risk-taking, innovation, and productivity.

Decision makers, particularly in for-profit organizations, tend to feel safe and comfortable when they use utilitarianism. Many questionable actions can be justified when framed as being in the best interests of "the organization" and stockholders. But many critics of business decision makers argue that this perspective should change.[70] Increased concern in society about individual rights and social justice suggests the need for managers to develop ethical standards based on nonutilitarian criteria. This presents a solid challenge to today's managers because making decisions using criteria such as individual rights and social justice involves far more ambiguities than using utilitarian criteria, such as effects on efficiency and profits. Raising prices, selling products with questionable effects on consumer health, closing down plants, laying off large numbers of employees, moving production to other countries to cut costs, and similar decisions can be justified in utilitarian terms. However, that may no longer be the single criterion by which good decisions should be judged.

## Factors Influencing Ethical Decision-Making Behaviour

What accounts for unethical behaviour in organizations? Is it immoral individuals or work environments that promote unethical activity? The answer is *both*! The evidence indicates that ethical or unethical actions are largely a function of both the individual's characteristics and the environment in which he or she works.[71]

**stages of moral development**
An assessment of a person's capacity to judge what is morally right.

Exhibit 11-8 presents a model for explaining ethical or unethical behaviour. **Stages of moral development** assess a person's capacity to judge what is morally right.[72] The higher one's moral development, the less dependent he or she is on outside influences and, hence, the more he or she will be predisposed to behave ethically. For instance, most adults are at a midlevel of moral development—they're strongly influenced by peers and will follow an organization's rules and procedures. Those individuals who have progressed to the higher stages place increased value on the rights of others, regardless of the majority's opinion, and are likely to challenge organizational practices they personally believe are wrong.

Research indicates that people with an external *locus of control* (that is, what happens to them in life is due to luck or chance) are less likely to take

## Exhibit 11-8
## Factors Affecting Ethical Decision-Making Behaviour

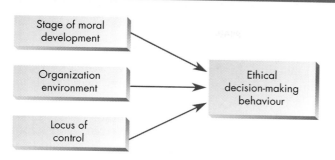

responsibility for the consequences of their behaviour and are more likely to rely on external influences. Those with an internal locus of control (who believe they are responsible for what happens), on the other hand, are more likely to rely on their own internal standards of right or wrong to guide their behaviour.

The *organizational environment* refers to an employee's perception of organizational expectations. Does the organization encourage and support ethical behaviour by rewarding it or discourage unethical behaviour by punishing it? Written codes of ethics, high moral behaviour by senior management, realistic performance expectations, performance appraisals that evaluate means as well as ends, visible recognition and promotions for individuals who display high moral behaviour, and visible punishment for those who act unethically are some examples of an organizational environment that is likely to foster high ethical decision making.

In summary, people who lack a strong moral sense are much less likely to make unethical decisions if they are constrained by an organizational environment that frowns on such behaviours. Conversely, very righteous individuals can be corrupted by an organizational environment that permits or encourages unethical practices.

## Organizational Response to Demands for Ethical Behaviour and Social Responsibility

As the demand for ethical behaviour has increased in recent years, Canadian organizations have responded in a variety of ways to signal their concern for members of the organization acting ethically, as well as for the organization

United Parcel Service Canada, based in Fredericton, New Brunswick, wants to make sure that its employees approach ethical dilemmas with the confidence to make the right decision. Therefore, the company conducts an ethics training program for all of its employees, from senior managers right down to the delivery truck drivers.

itself acting socially responsible. Below we consider organizational developments along both of these fronts. There is further information about the types of ethical policies that organizations implement in this chapter's HR Implications feature on page 495.

**ETHICS**  During the 1990s, one could say an ethics explosion occurred in Canada and the United States. In Canada, more than 120 ethics specialists now offer services as in-house moral arbitrators, mediators, watchdogs, and listening posts. Some work at Canada's largest corporations, including the Canadian Imperial Bank of Commerce, Canada Post, Magna International, The Royal Bank of Canada, Nortel (Northern Telecom), and McDonald's Restaurants of Canada. These corporate ethics officers hear about issues such as colleagues making phone calls on company time, managers yelling at their employees, product researchers being asked to fake data to meet a deadline, or a company wanting to terminate a contract because the costs are higher than anticipated. University of British Columbia ethics professor Wayne Norman believes that ethics officers are a positive trend, noting, "all sorts of studies show the companies that take ethics seriously tend to be more successful."[73]

Many corporations are also developing ethics codes. For example, about 66 percent of Canada's largest 1000 corporations have them,[74] while about 90 percent of the companies on the *Fortune 500* index have them. Twenty percent of the top 300 Canadian organizations employ ethics specialists, compared with 30 percent of the *Fortune 500* companies in the United States. Unlike the United States, however, Canada does not legally require companies to create an ethical culture. In the United States, when a company is sued for illegal practices, financial damages may be reduced considerably if the company has a fully functioning ethics program in place.

Saint Laurent, Quebec-based telecommunications producer Nortel (Northern Telecom) is one company that has developed a code of business conduct. Because Nortel wanted its employees to feel committed to the code, Nortel involved them in the process of revising the code through participation in 36 focus groups around the world. They gave all employees opportunities to comment on early drafts that were available on Nortel's intranet. A copy of Nortel's business conduct code is also available on the Internet.

Having a corporate ethics policy is not enough; employees must be instructed in how to follow the policy. Yet only about 27 percent of Canadian firms were providing training in ethical decision making in 1999, although this was up six percent from 1997. And more companies had instituted policies to protect employees who reported ethical or legal violations, 38 percent in 1999, compared with 22 percent in 1997.[75] United Parcel Services Canada Ltd. (UPS) launched its ethics training program in July 1999. As David Cole, vice-president of human resources at UPS noted, "We want to make sure that as people approach ethical dilemmas, they understand there is a support structure in place."[76]

A small group of companies is even starting a new trend in monitoring ethical practices, hiring an ethical auditor, much like they would hire a financial auditor. The ethical auditor is hired to "double-check an organization's perception of its own morals."[77] VanCity Credit Union, Bell Canada, TetraPak, British Telecom, the University of Toronto, and The Body Shop have all brought in ethical auditors.

Vancouver-based VanCity Credit Union is "far and away the leader" in championing an ethical culture, according to Larry Colero, an ethics specialist

**United Parcel Service**
www.ups.com

**The Body Shop**
www.bodyshop.ca

Halifax-based Nova Scotia Power wants its employees to be active in helping their communities. To encourage them to invest their time, the company started a Good Neighbour funding program. Employees apply to the Good Neighbour committee to receive up to $1000 for capital costs for a community project.

with Vancouver-based Crossroads Group.[78] The 38-branch, $5-billion-asset credit union emphasizes a full range of proactive educational ethical programs. The company does not have an ethics officer, although it has considered the possibility of hiring one. Mark Lee, VanCity's manager of corporate responsibility, explains that there are "worries that the existence of an ethics officer might offload the responsibility that the 1400-employee credit union feels to build ethics into every aspect of operations."[79]

**SOCIAL RESPONSIBILITY** A number of Canadian corporations are beginning to acknowledge the need to accept responsibilities beyond those of the shareholder. The Imagine Campaign, for instance, is an effort by the Canadian Centre for Philanthropy to promote charitable giving by Canadian corporations. As a result of a campaign designed in 1997 by Allan Taylor, retired chair of the Royal Bank of Canada, 436 firms pledged to donate one percent of their pretax profits to charity.

Not everyone agrees with the position of organizations assuming social responsibility, however. For example, economist Milton Friedman remarked in *Capitalism and Freedom* that "few trends could so thoroughly undermine the very foundations of our free society as the acceptance by corporate officials of a social responsibility other than to make as much money for their stockholders as possible."[80] Not all Canadian companies agree with Friedman, however. Both Vancouver-based VanCity Credit Union and Bolton, Ontario-based Husky Injection Molding Systems Ltd. have "taken comprehensive steps to include customer, employee, community and environmental concerns in both long-term planning and day-to-day decision making."[81] In June 1999, VanCity's electronic banking arm, Citizens Bank, went even farther, announcing a new "Ethical Policy," which states, for instance, that the bank is against excessive environmental harm, and will not do business with companies that either violate the fundamental rights of children or are involved in weapons.[82] For more on the debate about social responsibility vs. concentrating on the bottom line, see this chapter's Point/CounterPoint feature starting on the next page.

## POINT

# Organizations Should Just Stick to the Bottom Line

The major goals of organizations are and should be efficiency, productivity, and high profits. By maximizing profits, businesses ensure that they will survive and thus make it possible to provide employment. Doing so is in the best interests of the organization, employees, and stockholders. Moreover, it is up to individuals to show that they are concerned about the environment through their investment and purchasing activities, not for corporations to lead the way. Let's examine some of the reasons why it is not economically feasible to place all of the burden of protecting the environment on the shoulders of big business.

Shareholder demands necessitate avoiding environmental regulations if possible. For instance, Toronto-based Noranda Inc., Canada's largest resource conglomerate, announced in 1997 that it was selling off its forestry, oil, and gas subsidiaries to focus on the more profitable metals and mining sector. Craig Campbell, the partner in charge of the forest industry group at Price Waterhouse in Montreal, notes, "It's all being driven by shareholders [who are] ...demanding higher share value. The cost of logging is increasing rapidly because of environmental pressures. Companies now have to completely clean up a site when they've finished logging.... These kind of expenditures didn't have to be paid before."[1]

Studies show that environmental regulations are too costly. The Conference Board of Canada suggested that environmental regulations cost Canadian companies $580 to $600 million a year.[2] Finally, the Fraser Institute in Vancouver reported that all regulations, including those designed to protect the environment, cost Canadian industry $85 billion a year.[3]

Environmental regulations can also be harmful to jobs. Consider the case of MacMillan Bloedel (MacBlo), British Columbia's largest forest firm, whose then pres-ident and CEO, Thomas Stephens, announced January 21, 1998, that he would fire 2700 of the firm's 13 000 employees by the end of the year. Stephens criticized BC's Forest Practices Code as part of the problem MacBlo had experienced in recent years. The two-year-old Forest Practices Code is said to have added $1 billion a year to harvesting costs in British Columbia. Stumpage fees are three times higher than those in Ontario and Quebec.

While businesses are concerned with the high cost that results from environmental regulations, the general public are not completely supportive of protecting the environment either, particularly if it will inconvenience them.[4]

Companies would be better off sticking to the bottom line, and governments should stay away from imposing costly environmental regulations on business. Stringent environmental standards cause trade distortions, and governments rarely consider the cost of complying with regulations. Companies should be allowed to take their lead from shareholders and customers. If these constituencies want businesses to pay for environmental protection, they will indicate this by investing in firms that do so. Until they do, the cost of environmental legislation is simply too high.

---

Sources:

[1] M. MacDonald, "Noranda to Restructure Operations," *Canadian Press Newswire*, November 18, 1997.

[2] A. Howatson, *Lean Green: Benefits From a Streamlined Canadian Environmental Regulatory System* (Ottawa: The Conference Board of Canada, April 1996).

[3] F. Mihlar, *Regulatory Overkill: The Cost of Regulation in Canada* (Vancouver: The Fraser Institute, September 1996).

[4] R. Brunet, "To Survive and Thrive: Bled Dry by the NDP, BC Business Plots a New Course for the 21st Century," *British Columbia Report*, February 9, 1998, pp. 18-22.

## COUNTERPOINT

# Environmental Responsibility Is Part of the Bottom Line

Going green makes good economic sense. The studies reported in the *Point* argument tend to overstate the cost of environmental regulations.[1] They do not consider the benefits to society of those regulations.

Companies are starting to see the value of protecting the environment on their bottom line. During the last five years, a number of companies have conducted environmental audits, including Ottawa-based E.B. Eddy; Toronto-based Noranda; Scarborough, Ontario-based Consumers Gas; Hamilton, Ontario-based Dofasco; Montreal-based Avenor; and Calgary-based Shell. At least some private-sector firms are finding that focusing on the environment saves costs, is a competitive strategy, and has social benefits.

A closer look at a few companies that have devoted efforts to being more environmentally friendly will illustrate the benefits of this approach. John Grant, CEO of Quaker Oats Canada from 1967 to 1994, reports that Quaker Oats started working towards a "greener" work environment in 1987. One of the plants, located in Peterborough, Ontario, saved over $1 million in three years through various environmental initiatives. Grant reports that employees responded with pride to the environmental culture and the best university graduates wanted to work at a company that had strong environmental values. Grant also believes that shareholders receive a value in their shares that goes beyond the quarterly earnings and annual reports when a company commits itself to improving the environment. Moreover, suppliers and customers, the public, and consumers also respond favourably to products designed and produced in an environmentally friendly manner. Grant summarizes his views on why business should be concerned with the environment: "Environmental stewardship goes hand-in-hand with improved efficiency, productivity, profitability, and world competitiveness. To achieve a healthy economy requires environmental stewardship. The two are mutually interdependent and it is not a choice of one or the other."[2]

Inco Ltd., for example, has worked to repair the environmental abuse of past generations at its Sudbury,

Ontario, operations. Inco spent $600 million to change the way it produces nickel in order to be less devastating to the local environment. Its new smelting process is the most energy efficient and environmentally friendly process in the world. At the same time, Inco continues to work to restore the appearance of Sudbury. Trees have grown back, the wildlife has returned, and the air is clean. Sudbury has even been listed as one of the 10 most desirable places to live in Canada. While Inco invested a lot of money to change its production process, Doug Hamilton, controller at Inco's Ontario division in Sudbury, says, "Our Sulphur Dioxide Abatement Program was an awesome undertaking. Not only did this investment allow us to capture 90 percent of the sulphur in the ore we mine, but the new processes save the company $90 million a year in production costs. That strikes me as a pretty smart investment."[3]

London, Ontario-based 3M Canada Inc. started a Pollution Prevention Pays (3P) program over 20 years ago. The program emphasizes stopping pollution at the source to avoid the expense and effort of cleaning it up or treating it after the fact. The recycling program at 3M Canada's tape plant in Perth, Ontario, reduced their waste by 96 percent and saved the company about $650 000 annually. The capital cost for the program was only $30 000.

The examples of Quaker Oats, Inco, and 3M show that companies that are environmentally friendly have an advantage over their competitors. If organizations control their pollution costs better than their competitors, they will use their resources more efficiently and therefore increase profitability.

Sources:

[1] G. Gallon, "Bunk Behind the Backlash: Highly Publicized Reports Exaggerate the Costs of Environmental Regulation, *Alternatives*, Fall 1997, pp. 14-15.

[2] J.K. Grant, "Whatever Happened to Our Concern About the Environment?" *Canadian Speeches*, April 1997, pp. 37-42.

[3] "The Business of Being Green," Advertising Supplement, *Canadian Business*, January 1996, pp. 41-56.

In recognition of the changes occurring in the Canadian workforce, the *Financial Post* singled out several firms for corporate social responsibility in 1997.[83] Vancouver-based Viceroy Resource Corp., a gold mining firm, was chosen for its environmental responsibility. The firm follows the most rigorous environmental and reclamation standards in its Castle Mountain Mine in California. Viceroy has been praised by both environmentalists and regulators alike and won numerous environmental awards in the 1990s, including being designated as a model mine in 1995 by the U.S. Bureau of Land Management. Similarly, Winnipeg-based The North West Co., Inc., a clothing, food, and general merchandise retailer with 160 stores in Northern Canada, was cited for its commitment to Aboriginal people. The company is the largest private-sector employer of Aboriginal people in Canada, and much of its donation budget goes towards the northern communities and national Aboriginal and northern issues. Montreal-based Tembec Inc. was cited for its community contribution. Tembec is a forest-products company that, among other things, gives its employees five paid days off per year to volunteer for the nonprofit group of their choice. And Xerox Canada was cited for its women-friendly policies.

All of the companies noted above are not only contributing to the well-being of Canada, but are also contributing to the well-being of their shareholders—illustrating that being profitable while acting in a socially responsible manner is possible. Exhibit 11-9 identifies additional companies that are committed to social responsibility in Canada. The Case Incident on page 501 examines the practice of ethical investing.

## What About National Culture?

We have already shown that there are differences between Canada and the United States in the legal treatment of ethics violations and the creation of an ethical corporate culture. However, it is important to note that what is considered unethical in one country may not be viewed similarly in another country. The reason is that there are no global ethical standards. Contrasts between Asia and the West provide an illustration.[84] In Japan, people doing business together often exchange gifts, even expensive ones. This is part of Japanese tradition. When North American and European companies started doing business in Japan, most North American executives weren't aware of the Japanese tradition of exchanging gifts and wondered whether this was a form of bribery. Most have come to accept this tradition now and have even set different limits on gift giving in Japan than in other countries.[85]

In another instance illustrating the differences between Asia and North America, a manager of a large US company that operates in China caught an employee stealing. Following company policy, she fired the employee and turned him over to the local authorities for his act. Later she discovered, much to her horror, that the former employee had been executed for his deed.[86] These examples indicate that standards for ethical behaviour and the consequences of particular acts are not universally similar. This presents a variety of problems for those doing business in other countries.

Companies operating branches in foreign countries are faced with tough decisions about how to conduct business under different ethical standards from those in Canada. For instance, Canadian companies must decide whether they want to operate in countries such as China, Burma, and Nigeria,

**Exhibit 11-9**
**Corporate Responsibility, 1997: The Financial Post's**
**Top 50 Canadian Corporations** [1]

| | |
|---|---|
| Alcan Aluminum Ltd. | National Bank of Canada |
| Archer Resources Ltd. | NewTel Enterprises Ltd. |
| Ault Foods Ltd. | Noranda Inc. |
| Bank of Montreal | PanCanadian Petroleum Ltd. |
| BCE Inc. | Petro-Canada |
| BCE Mobile Comm's Inc. | Petromet Resources Ltd. |
| BC TELECOM Inc. | Phoenix Int'l Life Sciences Inc. |
| Bruncor Inc. | Renaissance Energy Ltd. |
| Canadian Airlines Corp. | Royal Bank of Canada |
| Canadian Tire Corp., Ltd. | Shaw Communications Inc. |
| Chieftain International, Inc. | Stampeder Exploration Ltd. |
| CIBC | Summit Resources Ltd. |
| Dominion Textile Inc. | Talisman Energy Inc. |
| DuPont Canada Inc. | TELUS Corp. |
| Emco Ltd. | Tembec Inc. |
| Geac Computer Corp. Ltd. | The Bank of Nova Scotia |
| Great-West Lifeco Inc. | The North West Co. Inc. |
| G.T.C. Transcontinental Group Ltd. | The Toronto-Dominion Bank |
| Hudson's Bay Co. | Torstar Corp. |
| Investors Group Inc. | TransAlta Corp. |
| Le Groupe Vidéotron Ltée | TransCanada PipeLines Ltd. |
| London Insurance Group Inc. | Transwest Energy Inc. |
| Maritime Tel. and Tel. Co. Ltd. | Viceroy Resources Corp. |
| Merfin International Inc. | Wascana Energy Inc. |
| Moore Corp. | Xerox Canada Inc. |

[1] List arranged in alphabetical, not ranked, order. Companies for the analysis were limited to those on the TSE in late November 1996.

Source: R. Walker and S. Flanagan, "The ethical imperative: if you don't talk about a wider range of values, you may not have a bottom line," *Financial Post 500*, 1997, p. 31.

which abuse human rights. Although the Canadian government permits investing in these countries, it also encourages companies to act ethically.

Because bribery is commonplace in countries such as Nigeria, Bolivia, Russia, and Mexico, a Canadian working in these countries might face this dilemma: Should I pay a bribe to secure business if it is an accepted part of

**Bata Shoes**
www.bata.com

that country's culture? The Bata shoe empire decided in October 1997 to sell its business holdings in Nigeria because of corruption by officials there. Sonja Bata, president of Bata Ltd., explained this decision: "The corruption killed us. Telephone lines were cut, power was cut, products couldn't get through customs. We decided not to play along and finally moved out. It's heartbreaking."[87] Facing the dilemma of bribery is a common feature of doing business for many organizations. A 1997 World Bank survey of 3600 businesses found that 40 percent of them were paying bribes in 69 countries.[88] Some have estimated that bribery accounts for 10 to 20 percent of contract amounts worldwide, which means that bribery is costing companies billions of dollars.

While ethical standards may seem ambiguous in the West, criteria defining right and wrong are actually much clearer in the West than in Asia. Few issues are black and white there; most are grey. John B. McWilliams, senior vice-president and general counsel for Calgary-based Canadian Occidental Petroleum Ltd., notes that requests for bribes are not necessarily direct: "Usually, they don't say, 'Give me X thousands of dollars and you've got the deal.' It's a lot more subtle than that."[89] Michael Davies, vice-president and general counsel for Toronto-based General Electric Canada Inc., describes it as "a payment made to an administrative official to do the job that he's supposed to do. In other words, you pay a fellow over the counter $10 when you're in the airport in Saudi Arabia to get on the flight you're supposed to get on, because, otherwise, he's going to keep you there for two days."[90]

The need for global organizations to establish ethical principles for decision makers in countries such as India and China may be critical if high standards are to be upheld and if consistent practices are to be achieved. In December 1997, "all 29 members of the OECD signed an anticorruption convention that commits them to criminalizing the bribing of foreign officials."[91] Prior to that, only the United States had taken that step. Canada only passed The Corruption of Foreign Public Officials Act in December 1998. The World Bank has ordered random audits of projects, barred corrupt firms from bidding on contracts, and requested no-bribery pledges from companies that bid on public-sector contracts. Other organizations that have adopted declarations, reports, and conventions against bribery include the United Nations, the International Chamber of Commerce, the Organization of American States, and the European Union.

Canada's need for legislation in this area was considerable. It ranks 11th on a scale of 12 countries most disposed to offering bribes, according to Transparency International, an international agency that investigates and tries to stop bribery. Belgium/Luxembourg scored in first place, France second, and Japan ranked 12th.[92] The United States did not appear on the list. It also has the most stringent anti-bribery law in the world: the U.S. Foreign Corrupt Practices Act (FCPA).

It's clear that despite Canada's domestic record of ethical concern, we have a long way to go when it comes to international dealings.

# HR Implications

# Developing Corporate Ethics Policies

Canadian corporations have chosen a variety of ways to implement ethics programs. These include developing training sessions, writing out explicit codes, making more general principles, or developing a culture of ethics. In the examples below, we indicate companies that have chosen one or more of these ways of developing their ethics approach.[1]

Northern Telecom hired a senior ethics adviser to help the company get its 68 000 employees around the world to agree on a definition of right and wrong. Megan Barry, who is based in Nashville, Tennessee, started interviewing employees in 1994, and the process was still going on in late 1997. Her job is to understand how Nortel employees think about ethical issues at the same time that she also trains them about Nortel's policy. Nortel developed its code of ethics in 1994 and believes that it has resulted in improved employee morale and better relations with customers and suppliers.

To introduce its code, Northern Telecom distributed copies to its employees globally and also placed the code on its intranet and Internet sites.[2] Posting it on the Internet has alerted those outside Nortel to the importance the company places on corporate ethics. Nortel includes ethics training modules as part of its new employee training, and newly promoted managers receive ethics modules. Nortel produces the modules locally, so that the relevant business examples are provided in the proper cultural context.

In 1995, the Canadian Department of Defence appointed a team headed by Rosalie Bernier to develop a statement of ethics that would apply across all ranks and divisions of the department, both military and bureaucratic. Bernier, who now serves as manager of the defence ethics program at the Department of Defence, noted that the team tried to take a positive approach by establishing a set of values rather than rules. The core values are loyalty, honesty, courage, diligence, fairness, and responsibility. There are also three principles to frame the values: "to respect the dignity of all persons; to serve Canada before self; and to obey and support lawful authority."

At the Bank of Montreal, Glenn Higginbotham, vice-president, corporate compliance, has chosen to avoid the "corporate-cop" approach to ethical behaviour, and instead rely on people to be guided by their conscience. "If you have a good ethical culture, people will be making the right decisions," he says. The Bank of Montreal has chosen to encourage a strong ethical culture among its employees, and so far, that approach has worked well for the bank.

Glaxo Wellcome Inc. used to leave ethical issues to the judgment of its employees. However, following the 1995 takeover of Burroughs Wellcome, the company decided to rebuild its corporate culture due to the merging of employees from the two different companies. The company is still working on a comprehensive document covering a range of moral issues. It will also include specific examples for situations where there often is no right or wrong answer.

John Zych, ethics officer for Imperial Oil, believes he must work hard just to keep his company's code of ethics current. The company's original document was written 30 years ago, and it has been revised four times in the last 10 years. Imperial Oil's code of ethics has been in place longer than that of most Canadian companies. Imperial takes its ethics responsibilities seriously and in 1997 was ranked by EthicScan Canada near the top of a recent survey of ethical corporations.

It should be obvious from these examples that there is no one right way to introduce ethics to employees, and that it also takes some realistic planning to do so.

Sources:

[1] Information about these companies is based, except where noted below, on John Greenwood, "The Guardians: Six Portraits in the Emerging Discipline of Playing Watchdog Over a Company's Code of Conduct," *Financial Post 500*, 1997, pp. 40–50.

[2] Information in this paragraph based on N. Richardson and M. Barry, "Minding Your Ps and Qs at Nortel," *CMA Management Accounting Magazine*, May 1997, pp. 20–22.

## SUMMARY AND IMPLICATIONS

### For the Workplace

We described the rational decision-making process and then discussed how it is often difficult to implement because of time and information constraints. Yet organizations could improve the decisions made by employees by ensuring, where possible, that people have the information they need to make the decisions.

Organizations that use teams face additional problems and synergies with respect to decision making. We described instances where teams make better decisions than individuals, including when problems are sufficiently complex that no one person has all of the relevant information. The leader participation model can also be used to determine the extent to which managers should be involved in team decision making.

We also examined the process of creativity in organizations and noted that when organizations reward for not making mistakes, employees are less likely to feel free to look for creative solutions that might include better ways of getting something done. We also indicated conditions under which creativity is more likely to occur.

What can we conclude regarding ethics? Managers should seek to convey high ethical standards to employees through the actions taken. By what managers say, do, reward, punish, and overlook, they set the ethical tone for their employees. When hiring new employees, managers have an opportunity to weed out ethically undesirable applicants. The hiring process—for instance, interviews, tests, and background checks—should be viewed as an opportunity to learn about an individual's level of moral development and locus of control. This can then be used to identify individuals whose ethical standards might be in conflict with those of the organization or who are particularly vulnerable to negative external influences.

We also noted that organizations are trying to become more socially responsible. One outlet for this is the Imagine Campaign's idea to contribute one percent of pretax corporate earnings to social causes.

### For You as an Individual

Individuals think and reason before they act. It is because of this that an understanding of how people make decisions can be helpful for explaining and predicting their behaviour.

In some decision situations, you might follow the rational decision-making model. But in many cases, this is probably more the exception than the rule. Given the evidence we've described on how decisions are actually made, what can be done to improve decision making? We offer four suggestions.

First, analyze the situation. Make sure you understand the complexities of the decision to be made.

Second, be aware of biases. We all bring biases to the decisions we make. If you understand the biases influencing your judgment, you can begin to change the way you make decisions to reduce those biases.

Third, combine rational analysis with intuition. These are not conflicting approaches to decision making. By using both, you can actually improve your decision-making effectiveness. As you gain experience, you should feel increasingly confident in imposing your intuitive processes on top of your rational analysis.

Finally, use creativity-stimulation techniques. You can improve your overall decision-making effectiveness by searching for innovative solutions to problems. This can be as basic as telling yourself to think creatively and to look specifically for unique alternatives. Additionally, you can practise the attribute listing and lateral thinking techniques described in this chapter.

We also considered ethics in this chapter and provided an overview of ways to decide whether a decision was ethical. We noted the complexity of making ethical decisions when working in other countries. Individuals would do well first to understand their own ethical limits, and then seek to understand how these match with employers' ethical demands.

*ROADMAP*
*REMINDER*

In the previous chapter we considered leadership and how leaders can inspire organizational members to perform. In this chapter, we considered decision making, mindful that one of the most important jobs of leaders is making decisions. We examined how one makes decisions and then explored creativity and ethics in decision making. With the next chapter we move to the final part of the textbook, Towards Reorganizing the Workplace. We begin in the next chapter with examining how workplaces are structured.

## For Review

1. What is the rational decision-making model? Under what conditions is it applicable?
2. Describe organizational factors that might constrain decision makers.
3. What role does intuition play in effective decision making?
4. Describe the 3 criteria individuals can use in making ethical decisions.
5. What is *groupthink*? What is its effect on decision-making quality?
6. What is *groupshift*? What is its effect on decision-making quality?
7. Identify factors that block creativity.
8. Are unethical decisions more a function of the individual decision maker or the decision maker's work environment? Explain.

## For Critical Thinking

1. "For the most part, individual decision making in organizations is an irrational process." Do you agree or disagree? Discuss.
2. What factors do you think differentiate good decision makers from poor ones? Relate your answer to the 6-step rational decision-making model.
3. Have you ever increased your commitment to a failed course of action? If so, analyze the follow-up decision to increase your commitment and explain why you behaved as you did.
4. If group decisions consistently achieve better-quality outcomes than those achieved by individuals, how did the phrase "a camel is a horse designed by a committee" become so popular and ingrained in our culture?

## LEARNING ABOUT YOURSELF EXERCISE

# Decision-Making Style Questionnaire

Circle the response that comes closest to how you usually feel or act. There are no right or wrong responses to any of these items.

1. I am more careful about
   a. people's feelings          **b.** their rights

2. I usually get along better with
   **a.** imaginative people      **b.** realistic people

3. It is a higher compliment to be called
   **a.** a person of real feeling    **b.** a consistently reasonable person

4. In doing something with other people, it appeals more to me
   a. to do it in the accepted way   **b.** to invent a way of my own

5. I get more annoyed at
   a. fancy theories              **b.** people who do not like theories

6. It is higher praise to call someone
   **a.** a person of vision       **b.** a person of common sense

7. I more often let
   a. my heart rule my head       **b.** my head rule my heart

8. I think it is a worse fault
   a. to show too much warmth     **b.** to be unsympathetic

9. If I were a teacher, I would rather teach
   **a.** courses involving theory    **b.** factual courses

Which word in the following pairs appeals to you more? Circle a or b.

10. **a.** Compassion      **b.** Foresight
11. **a.** Justice         **b.** Mercy
12. a. Production          **b.** Design
13. **a.** Gentle          **b.** Firm
14. **a.** Uncritical      **b.** Critical
15. a. Literal             **b.** Figurative
16. **a.** Imaginative     **b.** Matter-of-fact

Turn to page 635 for scoring directions and key.

Sources: Based on a personality scale developed by D. Hellriegel, J. Slocum, and R.W. Woodman, *Organizational Behavior*, 3rd ed. (St. Paul, MN: West Publishing, 1983), pp. 127-141, and reproduced in J.M. Ivancevich and M.T. Matteson, *Organizational Behavior and Management*, 2nd ed. (Homewood, IL: BPI/Irwin, 1990), pp. 538-539.

## WORKING WITH OTHERS EXERCISE

# Individual or Group Decision Making

1. Read each of the cases below, and using the Revised Leadership-Participation Model in Exhibit 11-7 on page 481, select the appropriate decision style for each case.

2. Your instructor will divide the class into small groups where you will be asked to reach a consensus about the appropriate decision style.

3. A group spokesperson will be asked to present the group's response and the rationale for this decision.

### Case 1

Assume that you are a production manager and one of your responsibilities is to order the materials used by your employees to manufacture wheels. A large stockpile of material sitting idle is costly, but having idle workers because there are not enough materials also costs money. Based on past records, you have been able to determine with considerable accuracy which materials employees will need a few weeks in advance. The purchase orders are written up by the Purchasing Office, not by your employees.

How would you decide how much material you should order? Specifically, would you tell the Purchasing Office how much to order, or would you first ask your employees what they think? Why?

### Case 2

Assume that you are the vice-president for production in a small computer-assembly company. Your plant is working close to capacity to fill current orders. You have just been offered a contract to assemble 25 computers for a new customer. If the customer is pleased with the way you handle this order, additional orders are likely and the new customer could become one of your company's largest clients. You are confident that your production supervisors can handle the job, but it would impose a heavy burden on them in terms of rescheduling production, hiring extra workers, and working extra hours.

How would you decide whether to accept the new contract? Specifically, would you make the decision yourself or would you ask others for help? Why?

### Case 3

Assume that you have been appointed the chair of a committee formed to coordinate the interdependent activities of the marketing, production, and design departments in the company. Coordination problems have interfered with the flow of work, causing bottlenecks, delays, and wasted effort. The coordination problems are complex, and solving them requires knowledge of ongoing events in the different departments. Even though you are the designated chair, you have no formal authority over the other members, who are not your employees. You depend on committee members to return to their respective departments and implement the decisions made by the committee. You are pleased that most members appear to be sincerely interested in improving coordination among departments.

How would you make decisions about coordination? Specifically, would you decide how best to coordinate amongst the departments yourself, or would you ask others for help? Why?

Your instructor will discuss with you possible answers to these cases.

## ETHICAL DILEMMA EXERCISE

# Five Ethical Decisions: What Would You Do?

Assume you're a middle manager in a company with about 1000 employees. How would you respond to each of the following situations?

1. You're negotiating a contract with a potentially very large customer whose representative has hinted that you could almost certainly be assured of getting his business if you gave him and his wife an all-expenses-paid cruise to the Caribbean. You know the representative's employer wouldn't approve of such a "payoff," but you have the discretion to authorize such an expenditure. What would you do?

2. You have the opportunity to steal $100 000 from your company with absolute certainty that you would not be detected or caught. Would you do it?

3. Your company policy on reimbursement for meals while travelling on company business is that you will be repaid for your out-of-pocket costs, which are not to exceed $50 a day. You don't need receipts for these expenses—the company will take your word. When travelling, you tend to eat at fast-food places and rarely spend in excess of $15 a day. Most of your colleagues submit reimbursement requests in the range of $40 to $45 a day regardless of what their actual expenses are. How much would you request for your meal reimbursements?

4. You want to get feedback from people who are using one of your competitor's products. You believe you'll get much more honest responses from these people if you disguise the identity of your company. Your boss suggests you contact possible participants by using the fictitious name of the Consumer Marketing Research Corporation. What would you do?

5. You've discovered that one of your closest friends at work has stolen a large sum of money from the company. Would you do nothing? Go directly to an executive to report the incident before talking about it with the offender? Confront the individual before taking action? Make contact with the individual with the goal of persuading that person to return the money?

Sources: Several of these scenarios are based on D.R. Altany, "Torn Between Halo and Horns," *Industry Week*, March 15, 1993, pp. 15-20.

## INTERNET SEARCH EXERCISES

1. Find 3 articles or Web sites that describe ways to develop creative thinking skills. Do all of the techniques seem valid? How easy would it be for managers to help their employees develop creative thinking skills using these techniques?

2. Find comprehensive data that characterize the degree of ethical behaviour exhibited by (a) college students and (b) employees at work. How do you interpret these findings?

## CASE INCIDENT

# Ethical Investing and Profit Making

Ethical Funds, Canada's largest family of "green" mutual funds, has a dilemma. How does it decide whether a company is one "good enough" in which to invest?

Ethical Funds invests only in companies that can pass its ethical screens. The mutual fund company gives high marks for harmonious labour relations and generous charitable contributions. Firms that manufacture tobacco products and nuclear power are not considered. Even with these rules, however, deciding which companies to invest in is not an easy task.

Michael Jantzi, who heads MJRA, a firm that tracks the ethical records of publicly traded companies, admits that sometimes these ethical mutual funds must "settle for the least-bad actors." For instance, ethical funds typically favour stocks in the financial services industry, because companies in this industry are nonpolluting. However, it is the rare bank that has never made a loan to a natural-resource firm or a defence contractor. Natural-resource firms are often off limits for ethical investors, particularly in the United States. However, this screen is not applied so vigorously in Canada, where resource companies comprise more than 40 percent of the Toronto Stock Exchange. If these companies were eliminated from investment consideration, it would considerably reduce the ability of the funds to be diversified.

Another area that poses a dilemma is tobacco. Ethical funds generally avoid tobacco companies. However, what about a firm that manufactures packaging for tobacco companies? David Shuttleworth, vice-president, marketing and sales, for Ethical Funds, says he would invest in the packaging company "if less than 20 percent of its business is making tobacco packaging." How does he arrive at the 20 percent figure? "Well, that's just the cutoff point we set."

Some of the information gathered by the analysts for ethical funds may also be questionable. In particular, not all of the information gathered comes from independent or neutral sources. The analysts also send questionnaires to companies, and review the annual reports and other published information about each company. This can lead to problems, however. For instance, The Body Shop International has come under scrutiny for having stated goals and achievements in their public documents that were not always consistent with their practices.

Do ethical funds make a difference to society? Jantzi argues that companies respond to the negative publicity of not being considered for these ethical mutual funds so he believes that the funds can, over time, affect corporate behaviour. But John Bishop, a professor at Trent University, believes that with ethical investing accounting "for less than one percent of the market, the impact is negligible, like taking a bucket of water out of the shallow end of a swimming pool and emptying it into the deep end."

Moreover, the funds must produce decent returns, or even investors who want to support ethical considerations may be unwilling to invest. "The bottom line is still money," Shuttleworth says. "We have to make a profit for our investors." Ethical Funds must be doing something right, though. In November 1998, it was managing $2.1 billion in assets, up from $803 million in 1996.

# Questions

**1.** What dilemmas do ethical fund companies face in choosing firms in which to invest?

**2.** Are these funds striking a compromise with their ethics?

**3.** Is it possible to reconcile making a profit with ethical decisions?

**4.** Analyze this case in terms of decision-making styles.

---

Source: Based on P.C. Judge, "In Search of Saintly Stock Picks," *Report on Business,* October 1995, p. 45; and S. Heinrich, "Campaign Targets Complacent Investors: Ethical Funds Inc Is Now Managing $2.1b in Assets, Compared With $80m Two Years Ago, Thanks to Its Aggressive and Emotional Advertising Strategies," *Financial Post*, December 5, 1998, p. D10.

# Get Your Creativity Here

What does a company do when it wants to develop new products? Molson, Lipton Canada, Nike, Disney, and Procter & Gamble turn to Doug Hale, president of Eureka Ranch, in Cincinnati, Ohio. At Eureka, Hale conducts product-storming sessions, helping companies to create new ideas. Clients come to the ranch to think and have their creativity flow.

Tyson Foods is one of Eureka's clients. Tyson is the world's largest chicken producer and the company wants to develop new chicken ideas. Hale has created a "chicken for lunch" three-day session for Tyson executives, so that they can develop at least a dozen new food concepts to take back to head office. During their brainstorming session some of the ideas the executives come up with include chicken pudding, chicken drinks, and crunchy chicken feet.

At Eureka, brainstorming is key. And no idea is to be killed. As Hale says, "Newborn ideas are sacred. It takes no courage to kill an idea. It takes courage to take an idea that's absolutely ridiculous and do something with it." Hale teaches his clients to get the killing feeling for new ideas out of their system by having them engage in a miniwar. Here, they can expend their "killing energies" and have fun at the same time. Then they can get down to the business at hand: loving everyone's ideas as they're presented, so that every idea has a chance.

Hale notes that at the ranch, executives have to think creatively, something they're not used to doing. Usually they spend about three percent of their time thinking and creating. He hopes to expand this to 30 percent of their time while they're at the ranch.

Not all of the brainstorming session is "work," however. Play is very much a part of thinking creatively. Clients take play breaks so that they can get away from the work for a bit, refocus, and then go back to work ready to brainstorm some more.

Creativity can bring out tensions as well. Not everyone gets along all the time, and not everyone remembers to love every idea that comes out. Hale keeps the group on track, however. Even with a passionate discussion of ideas, people are encouraged to be respectful of each other's contributions. Hale views his work as simply helping people to get a vision. The company can develop the product once the vision is there. But getting that vision can be difficult—which is the reason for Doug Hale and Eureka Ranch.

## Questions

**1.** Describe the brainstorming process at Eureka Ranch.

**2.** Why would play help brainstorming develop more effectively?

**3.** How might you use brainstorming in a group in which you are a member?

Source: Based on "Eureka Ranch," *Venture 679*; aired March 3, 1998.

# Rob Gareau: Organizational Culture, Leadership, and Decision Making

Developing the kind of culture in which he wanted to work was very important to Rob Gareau. He had previously worked for several other organizations, and he was committed to creating an environment at Human Performance that he and the others would enjoy. In order to create this kind of culture, Gareau has organized trips and other events in which all members of staff participate. From the very first staff meeting, he has insisted that dinner be part of the monthly staff meeting, so that the staff can see both the business side and the personal side of everyone with whom they work. "I think this is really important. It's after doing things like this together that the staff are more likely to help each other and see the other person more as a person, rather than as a fellow employee."

Human Performance strives for a family-friendly culture on two levels: the employee level and the client level. First, a family-like atmosphere is created amongst employees and owners. Staff members get along, and are expected and encouraged to do things together. The monthly staff meetings may be preceded by a skiing trip or other athletic activity. It is not unusual for everyone on the staff to go out together at least once during the week. This creates an atmosphere where everyone gets along.

So important is getting along that Gareau notes that one of his worst hires was not someone with performance problems, but someone who ended up in a lot of conflict with other employees. This particular employee showed disrespect for others, which created a huge backlash amongst other employees. They were concerned because one of their fellow staff members was not conducting herself appropriately in the workplace. In the end, the employee was fired because of the difficulties she created in relations with other staff members, even though her on-the-job performance had not been questioned.

The need for a family-like environment is important, particularly at the Performance Centre in Burnaby. Here the staff train young elite athletes ranging in age from six or seven up to 30, with most clients between 12 and 20 years of age. Parents of these young clients want to be assured that they will be trained in an appropriate atmosphere.

New employees learn about the culture of Human Performance, and the expectations for employees, through a five-day training program they go through when first hired. During the training program they learn about the Centre, and about how training is carried out in that environment. Gareau is planning to put together a policies and procedures manual to help codify more of the expectations and norms of the business.

When asked to describe his leadership style, Gareau says that primarily he leads by example. He tries always to do "the right thing," and he wants his employees to follow suit. He allows his staff considerable autonomy in making decisions, and he encourages them to pursue personal development activities.

It is very important to Gareau that his employees "feel free to do what they think is right." They are dealing with clients, usually for an hour at a time, and it is important for them to figure out what is the best thing that can be done for that client in that hour. Often that is an "on the spot" decision, and Gareau trusts his employees to do the right thing for the client. On any given day this might mean "giving nutrition instruction for the hour, or doing some weight training, or finding out what is going on in the client's life and helping him or her with stress management." Gareau does not believe he can or should create a template for these activities. He thus tries to create an environment where the trainers feel empowered to make the appropriate decisions regarding clients.

One of the leadership issues faced by Gareau is that most of his employees are around the same age as he is, although he notes that one of the other owners, Benicky, is older than the rest. As a result of this age distribution, Gareau has to tread a fine line between being a peer and being a leader. While all of the staff are encouraged to socialize together, he understands that he is the person responsible for running the business, and he needs to convey both a professional demeanour and a friendly one. He is aware of his leadership role with his staff, and considers the repercussions that would occur if he simply yielded to peer pressure, rather than remembering that he is also an owner of the business.

When asked to describe his decision style, Gareau says: "When I make decisions, I bank on conscience and follow my heart. I've learned that when I follow myself in making decisions, it works, and when I follow others, it often backfires." Among the three owners, there is often a division of labour regarding decisions. Each is expected to make the decisions in his own area of expertise. Nevertheless, the norm among the owners is to find out whether others want to be a part of the decision making for a specific issue. And before a final decision is implemented, every attempt is made to ensure that all three owners are on side.

Gareau says that though he makes decisions "following his heart," he also feels that his decisions are rational. He is interested in determining what "feels" right, but is also interested in the *intent* of the decision. That way he achieves more clarity in understanding the decision to be made.

Perhaps the most difficult decision Gareau faces right now is how big and how fast to grow his business. He acknowledges that he's had the opportunity to take on more clients than he has so far, but didn't because he couldn't deliver the quality that was at the heart of his business. He says that while it's easy to focus on quantity, "at Human Performance, we tend to downplay quantity in favour of quality." He elaborates: "That's where I think a lot of businesses in my field fall down, because of that conflict between quality and quantity. It is very easy to focus on quantity because of the growing industry and the growing market." For him, the right decision is to focus on quality.

Gareau sees what he's doing as partly a lifestyle decision—he wants to be in this field, and he wants to enjoy his work. He does not believe this attitude will limit his business, however. "If we do things right, if we focus on the right things, the money will come. We already have a good clientele base, but we want to have a stronger foundation before we grow any bigger."

When asked about taking his company public, which seems to be the big thing to do by almost any small and growing firm, Gareau simply says, "Not yet. We are not ready for it. We have to establish more procedures—we need to have our system more established, and that is what we are focusing on right now. Those are the objectives for the next year. Maybe the next year, or the year after that, we will think about going public. But that is definitely not an objective at all this year."

## Questions:

1. Gareau notes that many of his employees are the same age as him. What leadership challenges might this pose?

2. What do you think Gareau means when he says that employees must "feel free to do what they think is right"? What kind of work environment is needed for this to happen?

3. What role would you say intuition plays when Gareau makes decisions?

4. Does supplementing intuition with a rational approach to decision making suggest that intuition is not a valuable means for making decisions?

## CHAPTER 12

# Organizational Variety

Lisette (Lee) McDonald won the 1997 Canadian Woman Entrepreneur of the Year Award for International Competitiveness and the Business Women's Network 1998 Leadership Award for her business, Southmedic Inc. The Barrie, Ontario-based organization, founded in 1982, manufactures and distributes surgical instruments for hospital operating rooms. The company has a staff of 41 and markets in 45 countries. McDonald says her growth rate has been in excess of 50 percent a year, mainly because of her custom manufacturing division. "We are one of the few companies in North America able to take a prototype from design to packaging in the short time of six weeks. The big companies can do it but not at my speed."[1]

What makes Southmedic run so effectively? It may be the company's organizational structure. McDonald believes she's succeeded in the all-male world of medical supply because she listens to people and does not believe in hierarchy. "I believe in a horizontal management team. There are no pyramids here. I couldn't structure the company as if the world depended on me. My managers have a lot of autonomy." McDonald chose this flattened, more participative structure for Southmedic to accommodate her own needs.

## Questions for Consideration

**What are the key elements of organizational structure?**

**How do traditional organizational designs compare with newer organizational structures?**

**Why do organizational structures differ?**

Because of the business, she has a heavy travel schedule. More important, she has three young children at home. "I have to be able to come and go without this place falling apart," she says.

Deciding how to organize the people who work in a company into positions is the task of those who design the organization's structure. The structure can represent a tall pyramid or it can be relatively flat. For instance, Exhibit 12-1 shows a pyramidal organization with five layers (and some organizations can have even more), while Exhibit 12-2 shows a flatter organization, with only three layers. The organizational structure can also be something intermediate between pyramid and flat. Among other things, the structure determines the reporting relationships of people. Thus, in a flat organization, if you have a problem, you can talk to the person at the top of the organization. In a pyramidal structure, you would talk to your manager, who might talk to his or her manager, who might talk to the manager above, until finally, if the message did actually reach the top of the organization, it might be very different from the original message you told your manager.

The actual structure of an organization is chosen for a variety of reasons. In the case of Lee McDonald and Southmedic, she wanted a structure that would suit her travelling and family needs. Consequently, she gives her managers a lot of freedom to make decisions. Because the managers are positioned horizontally, they share power in making organizational decisions. McDonald does not place herself ahead of the others in the organization; thus, to some extent, she also shares power with her managers.

Not all organizations are flat like Southmedic. When Paul Tellier became president and CEO of Montreal-based Canadian National Railway (CN), he eliminated five vice-presidents and reduced the number of layers of management. When he arrived at CN, in some cases there were 10 layers of authority between the president and any line employee. Now there are no more than five. Even though five layers is flatter than 10, CN's structure comprises a lot more layers than Southmedic's, which is closer to just two layers. CN is a much larger organization than Southmedic, however, which means that it would be much more difficult to operate it with the same organizational structure as Southmedic's.

**Exhibit 12-1
Pyramidal Organizational Structure**

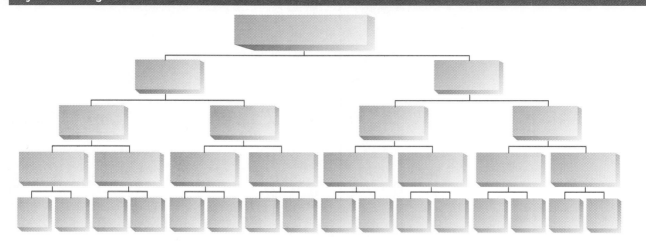

**Exhibit 12-2
Flat Organizational Structure**

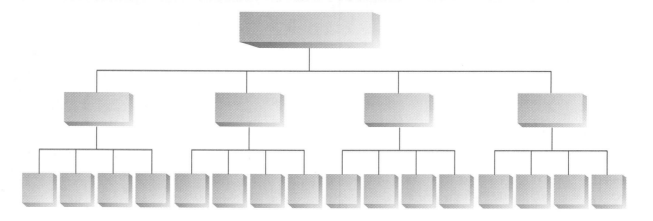

**Southmedic**
www.southmedic.on.ca

The theme of this chapter is that organizations have different structures, generally determined by their strategies, and that these structures have a bearing on employee attitudes and behaviour. Moreover, as we noted in Chapter 1, today's companies are becoming more team-oriented. Workers are becoming more empowered because managers are being asked to share power, and organizations are becoming more globally focused. All of these factors cause organizations to think more carefully about the best way to organize how people in the organization are connected to each other. These connections form the basis for organizational structure.

In the following pages, we define the key components that comprise an organization's structure, present six structural design factors from which organizations choose, identify the contingency factors that make certain structural designs preferable in varying situations, and conclude by considering the different effects that various organizational designs have on employee behaviour. Because this is a textbook on organizational behaviour, we are particularly interested in how structure affects behaviour. Some organizational structures that allow only limited freedom in choosing how to do your job, such as an assembly-line process, might cause you extreme dissatisfaction.

On the other hand, a very flat structure, such as Southmedic's, might make you feel as though you could contribute more to the organization. Bear in mind, however, that individuals differ in their reactions to organizational structure, so you should not assume that everyone will respond the same way you might respond.

## What Is Organizational Structure?

**organizational structure**
How job tasks are formally divided, grouped, and coordinated.

An **organizational structure** defines how job tasks are formally divided, grouped, and coordinated. There are six key elements that managers need to address when they design their organization's structure. These are work specialization, departmentalization, chain of command, span of control, centralization and decentralization, and formalization.[2] Exhibit 12-3 presents each of these elements as answers to an important structural question. The following sections describe these six elements of structure.

### Work Specialization

Early in this century, Henry Ford became rich and famous by building automobiles on an assembly line. Every Ford worker was assigned a specific, repetitive task. For instance, one person would just put on the right-front wheel, and someone else would install the right-front door. By breaking jobs up into small standardized tasks that could be performed over and over again, Ford was able to produce cars at the rate of one every 10 seconds, while using employees who had relatively limited skills.

**work specialization**
The degree to which tasks in the organization are subdivided into separate jobs.

Ford demonstrated that work can be performed more efficiently if employees are allowed to specialize. Today we use the term **work specialization**, or *division of labour,* to describe the degree to which tasks in the organization are subdivided into separate jobs.

The essence of work specialization is that, rather than an entire job being completed by one individual, it is broken down into a number of steps, with each step being completed by a separate individual. In essence, individuals specialize in doing part of an activity rather than the entire activity.

---

**Exhibit 12-3**
**Six Key Questions That Managers Need to Answer in Designing the Proper Organizational Structure**

| The Key Question | The Answer Is Provided By |
|---|---|
| 1. To what degree are tasks subdivided into separate jobs? | *Work specialization* |
| 2. On what basis will jobs be grouped together? | *Departmentalization* |
| 3. To whom do individuals and groups report? | *Chain of command* |
| 4. How many individuals can a manager efficiently and effectively direct? | *Span of control* |
| 5. Where does decision-making authority lie? | *Centralization and decentralization* |
| 6. To what degree will there be rules and regulations to direct employees and managers? | *Formalization* |

> **Wouldn't it be better if each person just did his or her same job over and over again?**

In most organizations, some tasks require highly developed skills; others can be performed by the untrained. If all workers were engaged in each step of, say, an organization's manufacturing process, all would have to have the skills necessary to perform both the most demanding and least demanding jobs. The result would be that, except when performing the most skilled or highly complex tasks, employees would be working below their skill levels. And since skilled workers are paid more than unskilled workers and their wages tend to reflect their highest level of skill, it represents an inefficient usage of organizational resources to pay highly skilled workers to do easy tasks.

Specialization can be efficient. Employee skills at performing a task successfully increase through repetition. Less time is spent in changing tasks, in putting away one's tools and equipment from a prior step in the work process, and in preparing for another. It is easier and less costly to find and train workers to do specific and repetitive tasks. This is especially true of highly sophisticated and complex operations. For example, could Montreal-based Bombardier produce even one CRJ plane a year if one person had to build the entire plane alone? Not likely! Finally, work specialization increases efficiency and productivity by encouraging the creation of special inventions and machinery.

Specialization did generate higher productivity in the first half of the 20th century. But by the 1960s, some jobs had reached a point where the human diseconomies from specialization — which surfaced as boredom, fatigue, stress, low productivity, poor quality, increased absenteeism, and high turnover — more than offset the economic advantages (see Exhibit 12-4). In such cases, giving employees a variety of activities to do, allowing them to do a whole and complete job, and putting them into teams with interchangeable skills result in significantly higher output and increased employee satisfaction.

Organizations today exhibit a range of specialization. You'll find, for example, high work specialization being used by McDonald's to make and sell hamburgers and fries efficiently, and by medical specialists in hospitals. On the other hand, companies such as Saturn Corporation have had success by broadening the scope of jobs and reducing specialization.

**Saturn Cars**
www.saturncanada.com

**INDIVIDUAL RESPONSES TO WORK SPECIALIZATION** The evidence generally indicates that *work specialization* contributes to higher employee productivity but at the price of reduced job satisfaction. However, this statement ignores individual differences and the type of job tasks people do.

As we noted previously, productivity begins to suffer when the human diseconomies of doing repetitive and narrow tasks overtake the economies of specialization. As the workforce has become more highly educated and desirous of jobs that are intrinsically rewarding, the point where productivity begins to decline seems to be reached more quickly than in decades past.

However, some individuals want work that makes minimal intellectual demands and provides the security of routine. For these people, high work specialization is a source of job satisfaction.

**Exhibit 12-4**
**Economies and Diseconomies of Work Specialization**

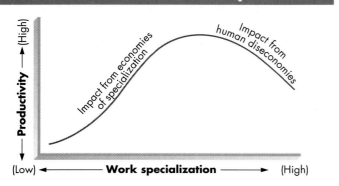

Until the mid-1990s, Montreal-based Hydro-Quebec had been organized geographically, with each territory having its own business units responsible for production, transmission and distribution for a total of 40 business units. However, they've recently decided that being organized functionally made more sense. Now they have only three business units. They expect this change in structure will lead to greater growth in business both inside and outside Quebec.

## Departmentalization

Once you've divided up jobs through work specialization, you need to group together these jobs so that common tasks can be coordinated. The basis on which jobs are grouped together is called **departmentalization**.

One of the most popular ways to group activities is by *functions* performed. For example, a manufacturing manager might separate engineering, accounting, manufacturing, human resources, and purchasing specialists into common departments. Similarly, a hospital might have departments devoted to research, patient care, accounting, and so forth. The major advantage to functional groupings is obtaining efficiencies from putting together people with common skills and orientations into common units. Exhibit 12-5 illustrates how Composites Atlantic of Nova Scotia, which designs and manufactures advanced composites for aerospace and defence, organizes its departments by function.

Tasks can also be departmentalized by the type of *product* the organization produces. Estée Lauder, which produces the Clinique, Prescriptives, and Origins lines, in addition to Canadian-created MAC cosmetics and its own original line of Estée Lauder products, operates each of these products as a distinct company. The major advantage to this type of grouping is increased accountability for product performance, since all activities related to a specific product are under the direction of a single manager. If an organization's activities are service- rather than product-related, each service would be grouped autonomously. For instance, many of the big accounting firms, such as KPMG, now call themselves "professional services firms" to reflect the variety of services that they offer, including tax, management consulting, auditing, and the like. Each of the different services is under the direction of a product or service manager. Exhibit 12-6 illustrates Northern Telecom's (Nortel) four separate businesses, which are organized by product lines to make it easier to service customers.

**departmentalization**
The basis on which jobs are grouped together.

**Estée Lauder**
www.esteelauder.com

**KPMG**
www.kpmg.ca

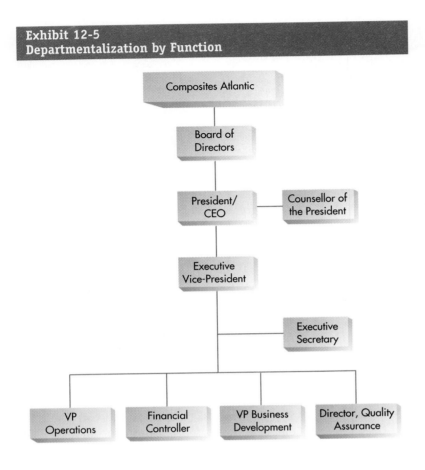

**Exhibit 12-5**
**Departmentalization by Function**

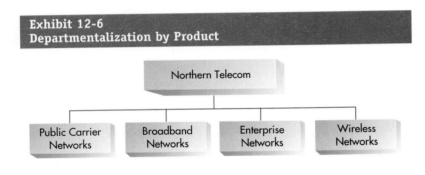

**Exhibit 12-6**
**Departmentalization by Product**

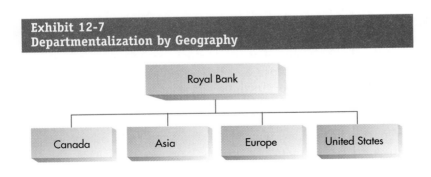

**Exhibit 12-7**
**Departmentalization by Geography**

Another way to departmentalize is on the basis of *geography*, or territory. The sales function, for instance, may be divided regionally with departments for British Columbia, the Prairies, Central Canada, and Atlantic Canada. Each of these regions is, in effect, a department organized around geography. If an organization's customers are scattered over a large geographic area and have similar needs based on their location, then this form of departmentalization can be valuable. Exhibit 12-7 illustrates how Royal Bank organizes itself by regional units (not all of its regional units are included in the exhibit, however).

At a Reynolds Metals aluminum-tubing plant in upstate New York, production is organized into five departments: casting; press; tubing; finishing; and inspecting, packing, and shipping. This is an example of *process* departmentalization because each department specializes in one specific phase in the production of aluminum tubing. Since each process requires different skills, this method offers a basis for the homogeneous categorizing of activities.

Process departmentalization can be used for processing customers as well as products. For example, in some provinces, to get a driver's licence, you may go through a series of steps handled by several departments before receiving your licence: (1) validation by motor-vehicles division; (2) processing by the licensing department; and (3) payment collection by the treasury department.

A final category of departmentalization is to use the particular type of *customer* the organization seeks to reach. The sales activities in an office supply firm, for instance, can be broken down into three departments to service retail, wholesale, and government customers. A large law office can segment its staff on the basis of whether they service corporate or individual clients. The assumption underlying customer departmental-

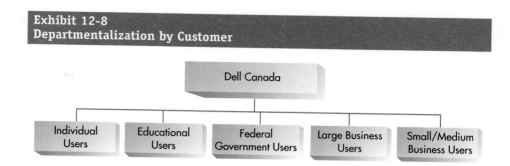

**Exhibit 12-8**
**Departmentalization by Customer**

Dell Canada

- Individual Users
- Educational Users
- Federal Government Users
- Large Business Users
- Small/Medium Business Users

ization is that customers in each department have a common set of problems and needs that can best be met by having specialists for each. Exhibit 12-8 illustrates how Dell Canada is divided into sales marketing units, according to the type of customer serviced.

Large organizations may use all of the forms of departmentalization that we've described. A major Japanese electronics firm, for instance, organizes each of its divisions along functional lines and its manufacturing units around processes; it departmentalizes sales around seven geographic regions, and divides each sales region into four customer groupings. Two general trends, however, seem to be gaining momentum. First, many organizations have given greater emphasis to customer departmentalization. Second, rigid, functional departmentalization is being increasingly complemented by teams that cross over traditional departmental lines. As we described in Chapter 6, as tasks have become more complex, and more diverse skills are needed to accomplish those tasks, management has turned to cross-functional teams.

Organizations may choose to go a step further than departmentalization and actually turn departments into divisions that are separate profit centres. For instance, within Estée Lauder's product-based departmentalization (discussed earlier), the Clinique, Prescriptives, and MAC lines are each separate profit centres, responsible for setting their own strategic goals.

## Chain of Command

**chain of command**
The unbroken line of authority that extends from the top of the organization to the lowest echelon and clarifies who reports to whom.

The **chain of command** is an unbroken line of authority that extends from the top of the organization to the lowest echelon and clarifies who reports to whom. It answers questions for employees such as, "To whom do I go if I have a problem?" and "To whom do I report?"

Twenty-five years ago, the chain-of-command concept was a basic cornerstone in the design of organizations. Today's workplace is substantially different. Because of computer technology, low-level employees can access information in seconds that 25 years ago was available only to top managers, and communicate with anyone else without going through formal channels. Operating employees are being empowered to make decisions that previously were reserved for management. Add to this the popularity of self-managed and cross-functional teams, along with the creation of new structural designs that include multiple bosses, and the unity-of-command concept takes on less relevance. There are, of course, still many organizations that find they can be most productive by enforcing the chain of command. There just seem to be fewer of them nowadays. This chapter's From Concepts to Skills feature on page 514 presents strategies that management uses to effectively delegate authority.

## From CONCEPTS to SKILLS

# Delegating Authority

If you're a manager and want to delegate some of your authority to someone else, how do you go about it? The following summarizes the primary steps you need to take.

1. *Clarify the assignment.* The place to begin is to determine what is to be delegated and to whom. You need to identify the person most capable of doing the task, then determine if he or she has the time and motivation to do the job.

   Assuming you have a willing and able employee, it is your responsibility to provide clear information on what is being delegated, the results you expect, and any time or performance expectations you hold.

   Unless there is an overriding need to adhere to specific methods, you should delegate only the end results. That is, get agreement on what is to be done and the end results expected, but let the employee decide on the means.

2. *Specify the employee's range of discretion.* Every act of delegation comes with constraints. You're delegating authority to act, but not *unlimited* authority. What you're delegating is authority to act on certain issues and, on those issues, within certain parameters. You need to specify what those parameters are so employees know, in no uncertain terms, the range of their discretion.

3. *Allow the employee to participate.* One of the best sources for determining how much authority will be necessary to accomplish a task is the employee who will be held accountable for that task. If you allow employees to participate in determining what is delegated, how much authority is needed to get the job done, and the standards by which they'll be judged, you increase employee motivation, satisfaction, and accountability for performance.

4. *Inform others that delegation has occurred.* Delegation should not occur in a vacuum. Not only do you and the employee need to know specifically what has been delegated and how much authority has been granted, but anyone else who may be affected by the delegation act also needs to be informed.

5. *Establish feedback controls.* The establishment of controls to monitor the employee's progress increases the likelihood that important problems will be identified early and that the task will be completed on time and to the desired specifications. For instance, agree on a specific time for completion of the task, and then set progress dates when the employee will report back on how well he or she is doing and any major problems that have surfaced. This can be supplemented with periodic spot checks to ensure that authority guidelines are not being abused, organization policies are being followed, and proper procedures are being met.

## Span of Control

**span of control**
The number of employees a manager can efficiently and effectively direct.

How many employees can a manager efficiently and effectively direct? This question of **span of control** is important because, to a large degree, it determines the number of levels and managers an organization has. All things being equal, the wider or larger the span, the more efficient the organization. An example can illustrate the validity of this statement.

Assume that we have two organizations, both of which have approximately 4100 operative-level employees. As Exhibit 12-9 illustrates, if one has a uniform span of four and the other a span of eight, the wider span would have two fewer levels and approximately 800 fewer managers. If the average manager earned $56 000 a year, the wider span would save $45 million a year in management salaries! Obviously, wider spans are more

Computer technology is increasing sales managers' span of control at Owens-Corning, a building-supply manufacturer and retailer. The company has equipped its salespeople with computers loaded with software that provides up-to-date information about products, customers, and marketplace trends. The information empowers salespeople to manage their territory by making on-the-spot decisions on their own. Regional sales manager Charles Causey (left) expects the computer system to increase his span of control from nine salespeople to 15.

efficient in terms of cost. However, at some point wider spans reduce effectiveness. That is, when the span becomes too large, employee performance suffers because managers no longer have the time to provide the necessary leadership and support.

Narrow or small spans have their advocates. By keeping the span of control to five or six employees, a manager can maintain close control.[3] For instance, the Ethical Dilemma Exercise on page 544 illustrates several instances of close employee monitoring. But narrow spans pose three major drawbacks. First, as already described, they're expensive because they add levels of management. Second, they make vertical communication in the organization more complex. The added levels of hierarchy slow down decision making and tend to isolate upper management. Third, narrow spans of control encourage overly tight supervision and discourage employee autonomy.

The trend in recent years has been toward wider spans of control, in part because of downsizing and the move to teamwork in some organizations.[4] Wider spans of control are also consistent with recent efforts by companies to reduce costs, cut overhead, speed up decision making, increase flexibility, get closer to customers, and empower employees. However, to ensure that performance doesn't suffer because of these wider spans, organizations have been investing heavily in employee training. Managers recognize that they can handle a wider span when employees know their jobs inside and out or can turn to their co-workers when they have questions.

**INDIVIDUAL RESPONSES TO SPAN OF CONTROL**  A review of the research indicates that it is probably safe to say that there is no evidence to support a relationship between *span of control* and employee performance. While it is intuitively attractive to argue that large spans might lead to higher employee performance because they provide more distant supervision and more opportunity for personal initiative, the research fails to support this notion. At this point it is impossible to state that any particular span of control is best for producing high performance or high satisfaction among employees. The reason is, again, probably individual differences. That is, some people like to be left alone, while others prefer the security of a boss who is quickly available at all times. Consistent with several of the contingency theories of leadership discussed in Chapter 10, we would expect factors such as employees' experiences and abilities, and the degree of structure in their tasks, to explain when wide or narrow spans of control are likely to contribute to employees' performance and job satisfaction. However, there is some evidence to indicate that a *manager's* job satisfaction increases as the number of employees he or she supervises increases.

## Exhibit 12-9
## Contrasting Spans of Control

**Members at each level**

| (Highest) | Assuming span of 4 | Assuming span of 8 |
|---|---|---|
| 1 | 1 | 1 |
| 2 | 4 | 8 |
| 3 | 16 | 64 |
| 4 | 64 | 512 |
| 5 | 256 | 4096 |
| 6 | 1024 | |
| 7 | 4096 | |

Organizational level

Span of 4:
Operatives = 4096
Managers (Levels 1–6) = 1365

Span of 8:
Operatives = 4096
Managers (Levels 1–4) = 585

## Centralization and Decentralization

**centralization**
The degree to which decision making is concentrated at a single point in the organization.

**decentralization**
Decision discretion is pushed down to lower-level employees.

**Dilbert Zone**
www.unitedmedia.com/comics/
dilbert

**Rogers Cantel**
www.rogers.com

The term **centralization** refers to the degree to which decision making is concentrated at a single point in the organization. The concept includes only formal authority, that is, the rights inherent in one's position. Typically, it's said that if top management makes the organization's key decisions with little or no input from lower-level employees, then the organization is centralized. In contrast, the more that lower-level employees provide input or are actually given the discretion to make decisions, the more **decentralization** there is. As Dilbert points out in Exhibit 12-10, however, some organizations do not seem able to decide upon an appropriate level of decentralization.

An organization characterized by centralization is an inherently different structural animal from one that is decentralized. In a decentralized organization, action can be taken more quickly to solve problems, more people provide input into decisions, and employees are less likely to feel alienated from those who make the decisions that affect their work lives. Decentralized departments make it easier to address customer concerns as well. Toronto-based Rogers Cantel's CEO Charles Hoffman began decentralizing Cantel's business a month after he assumed the top post in January 1998. One of his

**Exhibit 12-10**

Source: S. Adams, *Dogbert's Big Book of Business*, DILBERT reprinted by permission of United Feature Syndicate, Inc.

When Surrey, BC RCMP decentralized their offices, the results were positive. Merchants, local politicians and police in Surrey, BC say they are happy with the results. Some crime statistics have dropped, and the police feel that they are closer to the people they serve. The RCMP split its force into five units operating at regional stations, rather than out of one headquarters opposite Surrey's city hall. The advantage is that "regional offices can concentrate on the unique problems of the various areas."

first moves was to eliminate the top executive floor at Toronto headquarters, and move the executives to offices on the same floor as their departments. He believes that "wireless companies have to build their markets locally, and so centralized processes and procedures rarely make sense — especially when competition is intense."[5] In 1998, the RCMP unit in Surrey, BC, decentralized, splitting its force into five districts, with officers working out of regional stations, rather than out of detachment headquarters. A year later, merchants, local politicians, and police speak favourably of the change. "The real benefit of the decentralization," according to Chief Superintendent Terry Smith, "is the force's ability now to work with the community."[6]

Consistent with recent management efforts to make organizations more flexible and responsive, there has been a marked trend toward decentralizing decision making. A survey of 100 international corporations found that 36 percent of them are centrally structured today, compared with 53 percent in 1990.[7] The reason for decentralization in large companies is that lower-level managers are closer to "the action" and typically have more detailed knowledge about problems than do top managers. Big retailers such as The Bay and Sears have given their store managers considerably more discretion in choosing what merchandise to stock. This allows those stores to compete more effectively against local merchants. Similarly, the Bank of Montreal grouped its 1164 branches into 236 "communities," or groups of branches within limited geographical areas.[8] Each community is led by a community area manager, who typically works within a 20-minute drive of the other branches. These area managers can respond more quickly and more intelligently to problems in their communities than could some senior executive located in Montreal.

**INDIVIDUAL RESPONSES TO CENTRALIZATION** We find fairly strong evidence linking *centralization* and job satisfaction. In general, organizations that are less centralized have a greater amount of participative decision making. And the evidence suggests that participative decision making is positively related to job satisfaction. But, again, individual differences surface. The decentralization-satisfaction relationship is strongest with employees who have low self-esteem. Because individuals with low self-esteem have less confidence in their abilities, they place a higher value on shared decision making, which means that they're not held solely responsible for decision outcomes.

## Formalization

**formalization**
The degree to which jobs within the organization are standardized.

**Formalization** refers to the degree to which jobs within the organization are standardized. If a job is highly formalized, there are explicit job descriptions, lots of organizational rules, and clearly defined procedures covering work processes in organizations. Employees can be expected always to handle the same input in exactly the same way, resulting in a consistent and uniform output where there is high formalization. Where formalization is low, job behaviours are relatively nonprogrammed, and employees have a great deal of freedom to exercise discretion in their work. Since an individual's discretion on the job is inversely related to the amount of behaviour in that job that is preprogrammed by the organization, the greater the standardization, the less input the employee has into how his or her work is to be done. Standardization not only eliminates the possibility of employees engaging in alternative behaviours, but it also removes the need for employees to consider alternatives.

The degree of formalization can vary widely between organizations and within organizations. Certain jobs, for instance, are well-known to have little formalization. University textbook sellers — the representatives of publishers who call on professors to inform them of their company's new publications — have a great deal of freedom in their jobs. They have no standard sales "spiel," and the extent of rules and procedures governing their behaviour may be little more than the requirement that they submit a weekly sales report and some suggestions on what to emphasize for the various new titles. At the other extreme, there are clerical and editorial positions in the same publishing houses where employees are required to "clock in" at their workstations by 8 a.m. or be docked a half-hour's pay and, once at that workstation, to follow a set of precise procedures dictated by management.

Employees' jobs at McDonald's restaurants are highly formalized. To provide customers with consistent product quality and fast service, workers are expected to follow defined food-preparation procedures. Learning these procedures is an important part of employee training at McDonald's Hamburger University training centre, shown here.

McDonald's is an example of a company where employee routines are highly formalized. Employees are instructed in such things as how to greet the customer (smile, be sincere, make eye contact), ask for and receive payment (state amount of order clearly and loudly, announce the amount of money customer gives to the employee, count change out loud and efficiently), and thank the customer (give a sincere thank you, make eye contact, ask customer to come again). McDonald's includes this information in training and employee handbooks, and managers are given a checklist of these behaviours so that they can observe their employees to ensure that the proper procedures are followed.[9]

# Common Organizational Designs

In the previous section, we described six elements of organizational structure. If you think of these as design decisions that an owner or CEO makes about his or her organization, you begin to realize that a variety of organizational forms might emerge based on individual responses to each of the structural questions. Management in some firms may choose a highly formalized and centralized structure, while others might choose a structure that is looser and more amorphous. A variety of other designs exist somewhere between these two extremes.

Exhibit 12-11 presents two extreme models of organizational design. One extreme we'll call the **mechanistic model**. It has extensive departmentalization, high formalization, a limited information network (mostly downward communication), and little participation by low-level members in decision making. Historically, government bureaucracies have tended to operate at a more mechanistic level. At the other extreme is the **organic model**. This model is flat, uses cross-hierarchical and cross-functional teams, has low formalization, possesses a comprehensive information network (utilizing lateral and upward communication, as well as downward), and involves high participation in decision making.[10] High-tech firms, particularly those in their early years, operate in a more organic fashion, with individuals collaborating on many of the tasks.

**INDIVIDUAL RESPONSES TO ORGANIZATIONAL STRUCTURE** As we review the different design possibilities of organization, you might want to think about how organizational design would affect you. Your response to organizational design will be affected by factors such as your experience, personality, and the work task. For simplicity's sake, it might help to keep in mind that individuals with a high degree of bureaucratic orientation (see the Learning About Yourself Exercise on page 541) tend to place a heavy reliance on higher authority, prefer formalized and specific rules, and prefer formal relationships with others on the job. These people seem better suited to mechanistic structures. Individuals with a low degree of bureaucratic orientation would probably fit better in organic structures. Additionally, cultural background influences preference for structure. Thus, employees from high power distance cultures, such as those found in Greece, France, and most of Latin America, will be much more accepting of mechanistic structures

**mechanistic model**
A structure characterized by extensive departmentalization, high formalization, a limited information network, and centralization.

**organic model**
A structure that is flat, uses cross-hierarchical and cross-functional teams, has low formalization, possesses a comprehensive information network, and relies on participative decision making.

## Exhibit 12-11
## Mechanistic vs. Organic Models

**The mechanistic model**

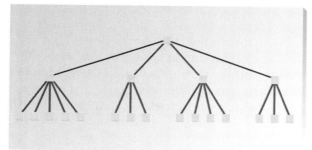

**The organic model**

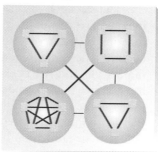

- High specialization
- Rigid departmentalization
- Clear chain of command
- Narrow spans of control
- Centralization
- High formalization

- Cross-functional teams
- Cross-hierarchical teams
- Free flow of information
- Wide spans of control
- Decentralization
- Low formalization

than will employees who come from low power distance countries. So you need to consider cultural differences along with individual differences when making predictions on how structure will affect employee performance and satisfaction. These same factors should be considered if you are ever in the position to design a new organization, for instance, if you choose to become an entrepreneur. You may want to explore your feelings about different structures in this chapter's Working With Others Exercise on page 542.

## Traditional Designs

With the extremes of mechanistic and organic models in mind, we now turn to describing some of the more common organizational designs found in use: the *simple structure*, the *bureaucracy*, and the *matrix structure*. We follow this with a discussion of some of the newer design options in use: the *team structure*, the *modular* and *virtual organization*, and the *boundaryless organization*.

### The Simple Structure

**simple structure**
A structure characterized by a low degree of departmentalization, wide spans of control, authority centralized in a single person, and little formalization.

What do a small retail store, a start-up electronics firm run by a hard-driving entrepreneur, a new Planned Parenthood office, and an airline in the midst of a companywide pilot's strike have in common? They probably all utilize the **simple structure**.

The simple structure is said to be characterized most by what it is not rather than what it is. The simple structure is not elaborated.[11] It has a low degree of departmentalization, wide spans of control, authority centralized in a single person, and little formalization. The simple structure is a "flat" organization; it usually has only two or three vertical levels, a loose body of employees, and one individual in whom the decision-making authority is centralized.

The simple structure is most widely practised in small businesses in which the manager and the owner are one and the same. Langley, British-Columbia-based Sepp's Gourmet Foods Ltd. represents an example of a simple structure for head office. There is no secretary or reception area there, and CEO Tom Poole, CFO James Pratt, and John Wallace, director of corporate development, take turns answering the phone.[12]

The strength of the simple structure lies in its simplicity. It's fast, flexible, inexpensive to maintain, and accountability is clear. One major weakness is that it's difficult to maintain in anything other than small organizations. It becomes increasingly inadequate as an organization grows because its low formalization and high centralization tend to create information overload at the top. As size increases, decision making typically becomes slower and can eventually come to a standstill as the single executive tries to continue making all the decisions. This often proves to be the undoing of many small businesses. When an organization begins to employ 50 or 100 people, it's very difficult for the owner-manager to make all the choices. If the structure isn't changed and made more elaborate, the firm often loses momentum and can eventually fail. This chapter's CBC Video Case on page 546 gives you the opportunity to see how a simple organizational structure may not be sufficient as a business starts to grow more rapidly. The simple structure's other weakness is that it's risky — everything depends on one person. One serious illness can literally destroy the organization's information and decision-making centre.

## The Bureaucracy

Standardization! That's the key concept that underlies all bureaucracies. Take a look at the bank where you keep your chequing account, the department store where you buy your clothes, or the government offices that collect your taxes, enforce health regulations, or provide local fire protection. They all rely on standardized work processes for coordination and control.

The **bureaucracy** is characterized by highly routine operating tasks achieved through specialization, very formalized rules and regulations, tasks that are grouped into functional departments, centralized authority, narrow spans of control, and decision making that follows the chain of command.

The primary strength of the bureaucracy lies in its ability to perform standardized activities in a highly efficient manner. Putting together similar specialties in functional departments results in economies of scale, minimum duplication of staff and equipment, and employees who have the opportunity to talk "the same language" with their peers. Furthermore, bureaucracies can get by nicely with less talented — and, hence, less costly — middle- and lower-level managers. The pervasiveness of rules and regulations substitutes for managerial discretion. Standardized operations, coupled with high formalization, allow decision making to be centralized. There is little need, therefore, for innovative and experienced decision makers below the level of senior executives.

One of the major weaknesses of a bureaucracy, however, is that it can create subunit conflict. For instance, the production department believes that it has the most important role in the organization because nothing happens until something is produced. Meanwhile, the research and development department may believe that designing something is far more essential than producing it. At the same time, the marketing department views its role as selling the product, and believes that is the most important task in the organization. Finally, the accounting department sees itself in the central role of tallying up the results. Thus each department focuses more on what it perceives as its own value and contribution to the organization, and fails to understand how the departments are really interdependent on each other, with each having to perform well for the company as a whole to survive. The conflict that can happen among functional units means that sometimes functional unit goals can override the overall goals of the organization.

In thinking about the possible conflicts that can arise in a bureaucracy, you might want to refer to Chapter 8, which discussed the relationship of dependency to power. That chapter pointed out that importance, scarcity, and nonsubstitutability will all affect the degree of power an individual or unit has. We also noted that the amount of power that an engineering department has, for instance, will vary, depending upon the specific organization and its overall goals.

The other major weakness of a bureaucracy is something we've all experienced at one time or another when dealing with people who work in these organizations: obsessive concern with following the rules. When cases arise that don't precisely fit the rules, there is no room for modification. The bureaucracy is efficient only as long as employees confront problems that they have previously encountered and for which programmed decision rules have already been established.

**bureaucracy**
A structure with highly routine operating tasks achieved through specialization, very formalized rules and regulations, tasks that are grouped into functional departments, centralized authority, narrow spans of control, and decision making that follows the chain of command.

## The Matrix Structure

**matrix structure**
A structure that creates dual lines of authority; combines functional and product departmentalization.

Another popular organizational design option is the **matrix structure**. You'll find it being used in advertising agencies, aerospace firms, research and development laboratories, construction companies, hospitals, government agencies, universities, management consulting firms, and entertainment companies.[13] Ideally, the matrix combines the benefits of two forms of departmentalization—functional and product—without their drawbacks. Specifically, functional departmentalization groups similar specialists, which minimizes the number necessary, while it allows the pooling and sharing of specialized resources across products. Product departmentalization facilitates coordination among specialties to achieve on-time completion and meet budget targets. Furthermore, it provides clear responsibility for all activities related to a product, but with duplication of activities and costs.

The most obvious structural characteristic of the matrix is that it breaks the unity-of-command concept. Employees in the matrix have two bosses — their functional department managers and their product managers. Therefore, the matrix has a dual chain of command.

Exhibit 12-12 shows the matrix form as used in a faculty of business administration. The academic departments of accounting, economics, marketing, and so forth are functional units. Additionally, specific programs (that is, products) are overlaid on the functions. In this way, members in a matrix structure have a dual assignment — to their functional department, and to their product groups. For instance, a professor of accounting who is teaching an undergraduate course reports to the director of undergraduate programs, as well as to the chair of the accounting department.

The strength of the matrix lies in its ability to facilitate coordination when the organization has a multiplicity of complex and interdependent activities. As an organization becomes larger, its information-processing capacity can become overloaded. In a bureaucracy, complexity results in increased formalization. The direct and frequent contact between different specialties in the matrix can result in improved communication and more flexibility. Information permeates the organization and more quickly reaches those people who need to take account of it. Furthermore, the matrix

**Exhibit 12-12**
**Matrix Structure for a Faculty of Business Administration**

| Programs  Academic departments | Undergraduate | Master's | PhD | Research | Executive development | Community service |
|---|---|---|---|---|---|---|
| Accounting | | | | | | |
| Administrative studies | | | | | | |
| Finance | | | | | | |
| Information and decision sciences | | | | | | |
| Marketing | | | | | | |
| Organizational behaviour | | | | | | |
| Quantitative methods | | | | | | |

reduces "bureaupathologies." The dual lines of authority reduce tendencies of departmental members to become so busy protecting their little worlds that the organization's overall goals become secondary.

The matrix offers another fundamental advantage: It facilitates the efficient allocation of specialists. When individuals with highly specialized skills are lodged in one functional department or product group, their talents are monopolized and underutilized. The matrix achieves the advantages of economies of scale by providing the organization with both the best resources and an effective way of ensuring their efficient deployment.

The major disadvantages of the matrix lie in the confusion it creates, its propensity to foster power struggles, and the stress it places on individuals.[14] For example, it's frequently unclear who reports to whom, and it is not unusual for product managers to fight over getting the best specialists assigned to their products. Confusion and ambiguity also create the seeds of power struggles. Bureaucracy reduces the potential for power grabs by defining the rules of the game. When those rules are "up for grabs," power struggles between functional and product managers result. For individuals who desire security and absence from ambiguity, this work climate can produce stress. Reporting to more than one manager introduces role conflict, and unclear expectations introduce role ambiguity. The comfort of bureaucracy's predictability is absent, replaced by insecurity and stress.

Toronto Hydro has tried to solve some of the problems of a matrix organization by adopting a "soft matrix" structure to help it go through an organizational change process. The soft matrix retains the functional structure of one-employee, one-manager while introducing flexibility through temporary, time-sensitive project or task teams with people drawn from a variety of functions. The teams do not have the authority to make sweeping cross-departmental decisions or changes, only to develop recommendations to present to higher management. For Toronto Hydro, the advantage is that the day-to-day delivery of product occurs with minimal disruption, while the project teams make recommendations for change.[15]

> **What happens when you report to two bosses?**

## New Design Options

Since the early 1980s, senior managers in a number of organizations have been working to develop new structural options that can better help their firms compete effectively. All of these options involve breaking down the boundaries of the organization in some fashion, either internally, externally, or a combination of the two. In this section, we'll describe four such structural designs: the *team structure*, which modifies internal boundaries; the *modular* and *virtual organizations*, which modify external organizational boundaries; and the *boundaryless organization*, which attempts to break down both internal and external boundaries.[16]

### Breaking the Boundaries Internally

**THE TEAM STRUCTURE** As described in Chapter 6, teams have become an extremely popular means around which to organize work activities. Forty-two percent of 109 Canadian companies surveyed reported widespread team-based activity and an almost equal number indicated that teams operated among certain employee groupings or in specific areas.[17] When

**team structure**
The use of teams as the central device to coordinate work activities.

**Boeing**
www.boeing.com

management uses teams as its central coordination device, you have a **team structure**. The primary characteristics of the team structure are that it breaks down departmental barriers and decentralizes decision making to the level of the work team. Team structures also require employees to be generalists as well as specialists.[18]

In smaller companies, the team structure can define the entire organization. For instance, Toyota Canada's parts distribution centre in Toronto reorganized its workforce into work teams in 1995. Workers have a team-focused mission statement, and the staff are split into six work teams, each with its own leader. Among larger organizations, such as Xerox Canada and GM Canada, the team structure often complements what is typically a bureaucratic structure. This allows the organization to achieve the efficiency of bureaucracy's standardization, while gaining the flexibility that teams provide.

Teams generally consist of three to 20 people who work together for a common purpose on either a short-term or permanent basis. Project teams usually work on a functional or cross-functional project with an explicit set of goals and objectives. For instance, when companies such as Boeing or Hewlett-Packard need to design new products or coordinate major projects, they'll structure activities around cross-functional teams. Projects can be short-term or longer-term in duration, and the teams disband once the project is completed. Quality-oriented, problem-solving, and process-improvement teams generally operate parallel to the organizational structure.

Two consultants have recently described a model for team-based organizations that indicates what is needed for forming this type of structure, getting the needed parts in place, and building the support system.[19] Their model is shown in Exhibit 12-13, which shows the seven different spheres of concern for team-based organizations; the Keys, which represent the focal points of attention and action to master for the sphere; and the Offkeys, which describe what happens when a given sphere is not handled effectively. The spheres also show the qualities that result to the organization when that sphere is handled properly.

The model is not meant to indicate stages of team-based performance, as all of the spheres need to be handled constantly to achieve high performance. The various elements are in play all of the time within an organization, although which ones are in the immediate foreground may vary from time to time. When starting a team-based organization from scratch, however, the elements do follow the sequence that might be taken:[20]

- *Formation:* Assembling the necessary pieces to create an organizational system.

- *Dependability:* Connecting the pieces and managing the space between them.

- *Focus:* This is what the organization wants to do.

- *Buy-in:* The decision by members to do what needs to be done to reach the organizational goals.

- *Coordination:* How the organization builds momentum

- *Impact:* Occurs when the organization reaches its goal. Does it make an impression, or simply fade away?

- *Vitality:* Has to do with getting ready for the next destination (goal), as well as making sure the organization doesn't burn itself out.

## Exhibit 12-13
## Team-Based Organization Performance Model

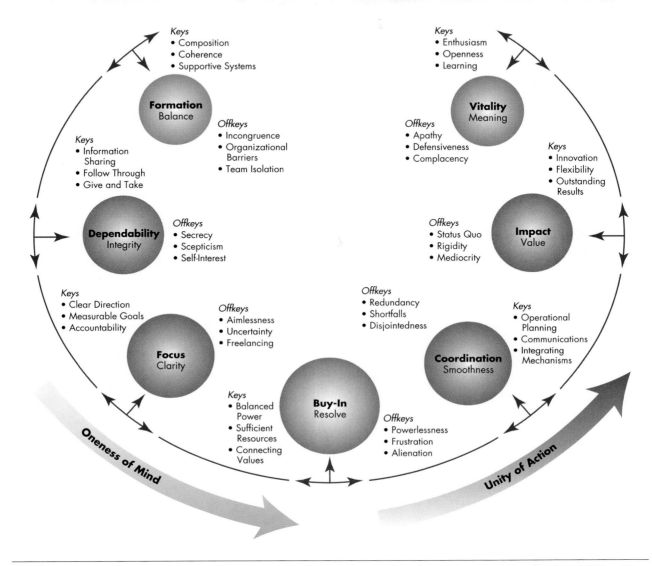

Source: R. Forrester and A.B. Drexler, "A Model for Team-Based Organization Performance," *Academy of Management Executive*, August 1999, p. 38.

The model is not intended to suggest that all organizations should become team-based. Rather, it suggests what to do once an organization decides to be team-based.

This chapter's Case Incident on page 545 allows you to examine additional considerations related to the team structure of an organization.

## Breaking the Boundaries Externally

**modular organization**
A small core organization that outsources major business functions.

**THE MODULAR ORGANIZATION** Why do it all when sometimes someone else can do it better? That question captures the essence of the **modular organization**, which is typically a small core organization that outsources major business functions.[21]

**Palmer Jarvis**
www.palmerjarvisddb.com

**Nike**
www.nike.com

**Liz Claiborne**
www.lizclaiborne.com

**Bauer**
www.bauer.com

Vancouver-based Palmer Jarvis Communications represents the modular structure at its best, able to flexibly meet the needs of clients. Traditional large advertising agencies of the past were huge, vertically integrated full-service corporations. Committed to full service, they would often refuse to do a single brochure, an annual report, or a public relations program. Palmer Jarvis set out to deliver advertising differently, however, building a strong network of people and resources that successfully serves clients regionally, nationally, and internationally. The modular corporation concept allows Palmer Jarvis to use its various strengths independently or in concert. The agency's primary responsibility is seamlessly integrating all of the elements of advertising, design, strategic planning, public relations, promotions, direct marketing, media, or research. This structural form allows each project to be staffed with the talent most suited to its demands, rather than just choosing from among those people whom the studio employs. It minimizes bureaucratic overhead since fewer functions are done in-house. And it lessens long-term risks and their costs because often there is no "long-term"— a team is assembled for a finite period and then disbanded. Finally, as in Palmer Jarvis's case, the modular corporation allows the company to respond to clients as individuals, devising solutions that are imaginative, appealing to both consumers and clients.[22]

Companies such as Nike, Reebok, Liz Claiborne, Emerson Radio, and Dell Computer are just a few of the thousands of companies that have found that they can do hundreds of millions of dollars in business without owning manufacturing facilities. Dell Computer, for instance, owns no plants and merely assembles computers from outsourced parts. Both Nike and Reebok succeed by concentrating on designing and marketing high-tech fashionable footwear. The two companies contract out almost all of their production to suppliers in Taiwan, South Korea, and other low-cost-labour countries.

What's going on here? A quest for maximum flexibility. These organizations have created networks of relationships that allow them to contract out manufacturing, distribution, marketing, or any other business function where management believes that others can do it better or more cheaply. The modular organization stands in sharp contrast to the typical bureaucracy that has many vertical levels of management and where control is sought through ownership. In such organizations, research and development are done in-house, production occurs in company-owned plants, and sales and marketing are performed by the company's own employees. To support all this, management must employ extra staff, including accountants, human resource specialists, and lawyers. The modular organization, however, outsources many of these functions and concentrates on what it does best. For many Canadian firms, that means focusing on design or marketing. Montreal-based Bauer Inc., designer and manufacturer of hockey and performance skates, decided to outsource the manufacture of certain products to maintain competitiveness and flexibility, while continuing to work on design and marketing.[23] Making the decision to contract out, however, does not necessarily come without other costs, particularly when the decision is made to manufacture overseas. Nike and several other companies have come under attack for relying on low-paid, exploited labourers, many of whom are children. These organizations are having to make decisions about the trade-offs between low-cost production strategies and criticisms from potential customers who are concerned about human rights.

**Exhibit 12-14**
**Modular Structure**

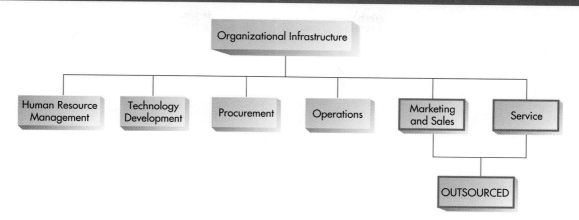

Exhibit 12-14 shows a modular organization in which management outsources the marketing, sales, and service functions of the business. Top management oversees directly the activities that are done in-house and coordinates relationships with the other organizations that perform the sales, marketing, and service functions for the modular organization. Managers in modular structures spend some of their time coordinating and controlling external relations, typically by way of computer network links.

There are several advantages to modular organizations. Organizations can devote their technical and managerial talent to their most critical activities. They can respond more quickly to environmental changes, and there is increased focus on customers and markets. The primary drawback to this structure is that it reduces management's control over key parts of its business. The organization is forced to rely on outsiders, which decreases operational control.

**virtual organization**
A continually evolving network of independent companies — suppliers, customers, even competitors — linked together to share skills, costs, and access to one another's markets.

**United Airlines**
www.ual.com

**THE VIRTUAL ORGANIZATION**  The **virtual organization** "is a continually evolving network of independent companies — suppliers, customers, even competitors — linked together to share skills, costs, and access to one another's markets."[24] In a virtual organization, units of different firms join together in an alliance to pursue common strategic objectives. While control in the modular structure remains with the core organization (such as Nike, Dell Computer, and Bauer), in the virtual organization participants relinquish some of their control and act more interdependently. Virtual organizations may not have a central office, an organizational chart, or a hierarchy. Typically, the organizations come together to exploit specific opportunities or attain specific strategic objectives.

In May 1997, Air Canada founded star alliance with UAL Corp.'s United Airlines, Lufthansa AG, Scandinavian Airlines Systems, and Thai Airways International Co. Varig Brazilian Airlines came on board later, bringing the alliance's combined revenues to about $63 billion. Airlines code-share so that travellers can buy a single ticket for a trip, although it may involve boarding several different airlines' planes to reach a destination. En route, travellers will collect frequent flyer points redeemable for flights on the home airline and even relax in the partners' lounges on a "seamless" journey. Airlines are also integrating their services and operations. The airlines say the alliances can increase consumer choice. For instance, Air Canada and United Airlines were able to launch a Montreal-Chicago route, which neither airline believed that it could launch alone, offering airline travellers an alternative to American Airlines.

Bruce Brown (wearing hat) operates a virtual organization. He publishes an on-line newsletter, BugNet, that provides subscribers with solutions for fixing computer bugs. Brown and employees are shown here at the firm's headquarters in Sumas, Washington. But most functions are outsourced to people throughout the country and as far away as London. They're managed through an intranet that contains editorial guidelines, deadlines, contact information, and photos. Brown has never met most of these people, including a senior editor in Cleveland who he has worked with for five years.

**ING Direct**
www.ingdirect.ca

Canadian firms are actively seeking domestic and foreign alliance partners and are taking part in various forms of interfirm cooperative agreements. About one in nine Canadian companies has some sort of arrangement of this type. These alliances take many forms, ranging from precompetitive consortia to coproduction, cross-equity arrangements, and equity joint ventures with separate legal entities.[25] Exhibit 12-15 illustrates a possible virtual structure where the reference firm is responsible for technology development, and then works together with the alliance partners to complete the other functions. Another example of a virtual structure is ING Direct, a Dutch-owned virtual bank. Canadian Tire joined forces with ING Direct in the spring of 1998, installing ATMs in five Canadian Tire stores in London, Ontario.

There are several advantages to virtual organizations. They allow organizations to share costs and skills, provide access to global markets, and increase market responsiveness. However, there are also distinct disadvantages. The boundaries between companies become blurred due to interdependence.

**Exhibit 12-15**
**Virtual Structure**

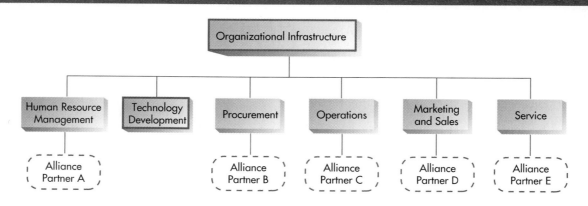

In order to work together, companies must relinquish operational and strategic control. This form of organization also requires new managerial skills. Managers must build relations with other companies, negotiate "win-win" deals, find compatible partners in terms of values and goals, and then develop appropriate communication systems to keep everyone informed.[26]

## Breaking the Boundaries Externally and Internally

**boundaryless organization**
An organization that seeks to eliminate the chain of command, have limitless spans of control, and replace departments with empowered teams.

**THE BOUNDARYLESS ORGANIZATION** Both the modular organization and the virtual organization break down external boundaries of the organization without generally affecting the internal workings of each of the cooperating organizations. Some organizations, however, strive to break down *both* the internal and external boundaries. General Electric Chairman Jack Welch coined the term **boundaryless organization** to describe his idea of what he wanted GE to become. Welch wanted to turn his company into a "$60 billion family grocery store."[27] That is, despite its monstrous size, he wanted to eliminate *vertical* and *horizontal* boundaries within GE and break down *external* barriers between the company and its customers and suppliers. The boundaryless organization seeks to eliminate the chain of command, have limitless spans of control, and replace departments with empowered teams. And because it relies so heavily on information technology, some have turned to calling this structure the *T-form* (or technology-based) organization.[28]

Can an organization really have no boundaries?

Although GE hasn't yet achieved this boundaryless state — and probably never will — it has made significant progress toward this end. So have other companies such as Hewlett-Packard, AT&T, and Motorola. Let's explore what a boundaryless organization would look like and what some firms are doing to make it a reality.[29]

**Motorola**
www.motorola.ca

The boundaryless organization breaks down barriers internally, much the way we described, by flattening the hierarchy, creating cross-hierarchical teams (which include top executives, middle managers, supervisors, and operative employees), and using participative decision-making practices and 360-degree performance appraisals (where peers and others above and below the employee evaluate his or her performance).

The boundaryless organization also breaks down barriers to external constituencies (suppliers, customers, regulators, etc.) and barriers created by geography. Globalization, strategic alliances, supplier-organization and customer-organization linkages, and telecommuting are all examples of practices that reduce external boundaries. Many organizations are blurring the line between themselves and their suppliers. Companies such as AT&T and TWA are allowing customers to perform functions that previously were done by management. For instance, some AT&T units are receiving bonuses based on customer evaluations of the teams that serve them. TWA's Royal Ambassador frequent flyers get "Something Good" coupons to give to outstanding TWA employees. Recipients can turn the coupons in for prizes and will be featured in company ads. This practice, in essence, allows TWA's customers to participate in employee appraisals.

The one common technological thread that makes the boundaryless organization possible is networked computers. They allow people to communicate across intraorganizational and interorganizational boundaries.[30] Electronic mail, for instance, enables hundreds of employees to share information simultaneously and allows rank-and-file workers to communicate directly with senior executives. Additionally, many large companies, including Federal

Express, AT&T, and 3M, are developing private nets, or intranets. Using the infrastructure and standards of the Internet and the World Wide Web, these private nets are internal communication systems, protected from the public Internet by special software. And interorganizational networks now make it possible for Wal-Mart suppliers such as Procter & Gamble (P&G) to monitor inventory levels of laundry soap, because P&G's company computer system is networked to Wal-Mart's system.

One of the drawbacks is that boundaryless organizations are difficult to manage. It is difficult to overcome the political and authority boundaries inherent in many organizations. It can also be time-consuming and difficult to manage the coordination necessary with so many different stakeholders. That said, the well-managed boundaryless organization offers the best talents of employees across several different organizations; enhances cooperation across functions, divisions, and external groups; and potentially offers much quicker response time to the environment.

## Why Do Structures Differ?

With an understanding of the various structures possible, we are now prepared to address the following questions: What are the forces that influence the design that is chosen? Why are some organizations structured along more mechanistic lines while others follow organic characteristics? In the following pages, we present the major forces that have been identified as causes, or determinants, of an organization's structure.[31]

### Strategy

An organization's structure is a means to help management achieve its objectives. Since objectives are derived from the organization's overall strategy, it is only logical that the structure should support the strategy.[32]

Most current strategy frameworks focus on three strategy dimensions — innovation, cost minimization, and imitation — and the structural design that works best with each.[33]

**innovation strategy**
A strategy that emphasizes the introduction of major new products and services.

To what degree does an organization introduce major new products or services? An **innovation strategy** does not mean a strategy merely for simple or cosmetic changes from previous offerings, but rather one for meaningful and unique innovations. Obviously, not all firms pursue innovation. This strategy may appropriately characterize 3M Co., but it certainly is not a strategy pursued by McDonald's.

**cost-minimization strategy**
A strategy that emphasizes tight cost controls, avoidance of unnecessary innovation or marketing expenses, and price cutting.

An organization that is pursuing a **cost-minimization strategy** tightly controls costs, refrains from incurring unnecessary innovation or marketing expenses, and cuts prices in selling a basic product. This would describe the strategy pursued by Wal-Mart or the sellers of generic grocery products.

**imitation strategy**
A strategy that seeks to move into new products or new markets only after their viability has already been proven.

Organizations following an **imitation strategy** try to capitalize on the best of both of the previous strategies. They seek to minimize risk and maximize opportunity for profit. Their strategy is to move into new products or new markets only after viability has been proven by innovators. They take the successful ideas of innovators and copy them. Manufacturers of mass-marketed fashion goods that are "rip-offs" of designer styles follow the imitation strategy. This label also probably characterizes such well-known firms as IBM and Caterpillar. They essentially follow their smaller and more innovative competitors with superior products, but only after their competitors have demonstrated that the market is there.

> ## Exhibit 12-16
> ## The Strategy-Structure Thesis
>
> | Strategy | Structural Option |
> |---|---|
> | **Innovation** | **Organic:** A loose structure; low specialization, low formalization, decentralized |
> | **Cost-minimization** | **Mechanistic:** Tight control; extensive work specialization, high formalization, high centralization |
> | **Imitation** | **Mechanistic and organic:** Mix of loose with tight properties; tight controls over current activities and looser controls for new undertakings |

**Humungous Bank**
www.humungous.com

Exhibit 12-16 describes the structural option that best matches each strategy. Innovators need the flexibility of the organic structure, while cost minimizers seek the efficiency and stability of the mechanistic structure. Imitators combine the two structures. They use a mechanistic structure in order to maintain tight controls and low costs in their current activities, while at the same time they create organic subunits in which to pursue new undertakings.

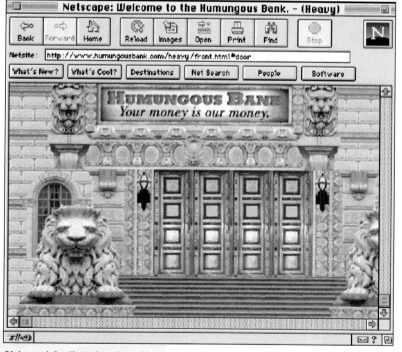

Richmond Credit Union, based in British Columbia, wants customers to know that smaller is better. They criticize the large "Humungous Bank" for being impersonal and inflexible.

## Organization Size

There is considerable evidence to support the idea that an organization's size significantly affects its structure.[34] For instance, large organizations — those typically employing 2000 or more people — tend to have more specialization, more departmentalization, more vertical levels, and more rules and regulations than do small organizations. However, the relationship isn't linear. Rather, size affects structure at a decreasing rate. The impact of size becomes less important as an organization expands. Why is this? Essentially, once an organization has around 2000 employees, it's already fairly mechanistic. An additional 500 employees will not have much impact. On the other hand, adding 500 employees to an organization that has only 300 members is likely to result in a shift toward a more mechanistic structure.

As an illustration of the effects of size, Greater Vancouver Area's Richmond Credit Union, which is small compared with the national banks, claims that its size enables it to be far more responsive to consumer needs than the big banks, such as Bank of Montreal and the Canadian Imperial Bank of Commerce. Consumers have responded particularly well to Richmond Credit Union's "humungous bank" ads, which take a jab at the large banks. The chapter's Point/CounterPoint discussion on the next page gives further illustrations of the positives and negatives of large organizational size.

## POINT

# Small Is Beautiful

The Davids are beating up on the Goliaths. Big corporations are going the way of the dinosaurs because they're overly rigid, technologically obsolete, and too bureaucratic. They're being replaced by small, agile companies. These small organizations are the technology innovators, able to respond quickly to changing market opportunities, and have become the primary job generators in almost all developed countries.[1]

In almost every major industry, the smaller and more agile firms are outperforming their larger competitors. Among steel producers, Regina-based IPSCO is outperforming Ontario-based Dofasco and Stelco. CanWest's Global Television Network has taken on CBC and CTV with impressive results, winning a large pile of awards at the 1998 Geminis, and sharing top honours with the CBC in several instances.[2] Greater Vancouver Area's VanCity Credit Union and Richmond Credit Union have been far more responsive to consumers than big banks such as the Bank of Montreal and Canadian Imperial Bank of Commerce. Consumers have particularly responded well to Richmond Credit Union's "humungous bank" ads, which take a jab at the large banks. Winnipeg-based McNally Robinson Booksellers Ltd. made plans to open the first Canadian mega-bookstore while Canada's two largest booksellers, Smith Books and Coles Book Stores, were too busy negotiating the merger that eventually led to the creation of their own superstore, Chapters. In a cross-Canada bookstore study conducted in March 1997, the Winnipeg superstore outshone Chapters in terms of customer service and product selection, illustrating that a small independent retailer can beat a bigger player at its own game.[3]

What's going on? The law of economies of scale is being repealed! The law of economies of scale argued that larger operations drove out smaller ones because with large size came greater efficiency. Fixed costs, for instance, could be spread over more units. Large companies could use standardization and mass production to produce the lowest-cost products. But that no longer applies because of market fragmentation, strategic alliances, and technology.

Niche markets have removed the advantages of large size. Southwest can compete successfully against American and United because it doesn't try to match the larger airlines' full-service strategy. It doesn't use hubs, it doesn't transfer baggage, it doesn't compete in every market, it doesn't offer meals, and it provides no reserved seats.

Strategic alliances offer small firms the opportunity to share others' expertise and development costs, allowing little companies to compete with big ones. For example, many small North American book publishers don't have the money to develop marketing operations and sales staffs in Australia or Asia. By joining forces with publishers in those countries to market their books, they can behave like the "big guys."

Technology is also taking away a lot of the advantage that used to go to size. Computer and satellite linkage and flexible manufacturing systems are examples of such technology. Quick & Reilly can execute orders as efficiently as Merrill Lynch through computer links to exchanges, even though it's a fraction of Merrill's size.

In today's increasingly dynamic environment, large size has become a serious handicap. It restricts the creativity to develop new products and services. It also limits job growth. More specifically, it's the small organizations that innovate and create jobs. For instance, Statistics Canada reports that between 1979 and 1995, small business (that is, those under 50 employees) created 755 000 new jobs; medium companies (those between 50 and 499 employees) created 515 000 new jobs; and large companies (those with more than 500 employees) created 227 000 jobs.[4]

Big companies are getting the message. They're laying off tens of thousands of employees. They're selling businesses that don't fit with their core competencies. And they're restructuring themselves to be more agile and responsive.

Sources:

[1] This argument is based on J. Case, "The Disciples of David Birch," *INC.*, January 1989, pp. 39-45; T. Peters, "Rethinking Scale," *California Management Review*, Fall 1992, pp. 7-28; G. Gendron, "Small Is Beautiful! Big Is Best!" *INC.*, May 1995, pp. 39-49.

[2] D. Saunders, "Global the Big Surprise at the Geminis," *The Globe and Mail*, March 2, 1998, p. A1.

[3] B. Hutchinson, "Merchants of Boom. Take Hard-as-Nails Consumers. Add Murderous Competition. What Do You Get? Some Sizzling Opportunities for Radical Retailers," *Canadian Business*, May 1997, pp. 38-41+.

[4] C. Harris, "Prime Numbers: A Statistical Look at the Trends and Issues That Will Dominate Our Future," *Financial Post*, November 15/17, 1997, p. P13.

## COUNTERPOINT

# "Small Is Beautiful" Is a Myth!

It's now become the "conventional wisdom" to acknowledge that large organizations are at a disadvantage in today's dynamic environment. Their large size limits their agility. Additionally, competitive and technological forces have ganged up to take away the economies that derived from scale. Well, the conventional wisdom is wrong![1] The hard evidence shows that the importance of small businesses as job generators and as engines of technological dynamism has been greatly exaggerated. Moreover, large organizations have discovered how to become less rigid, more entrepreneurial, and less hierarchical while still maintaining the advantages that accrue to large size. Moreover, small businesses may not be the best place to work. While they win high marks for providing a pleasant work environment and effective decision making, they get low marks for job opportunities and financial rewards.[2]

The research showing that small companies have been the prime job generators in recent years is flawed. The early data that were used exaggerated the incidence of start-ups and covered too short a period. The research failed to recategorize companies once they grew or shrunk, which systematically inflated the relative importance of small firms. While it is the case that businesses with fewer than 50 employees accounted for 97 percent of the 928 000 firms in Canada in 1996, fewer than five percent of these firms accounted for 45 percent of the job growth. Many of the remaining firms were really individuals creating jobs for themselves because of losing a job to downsizing. These firms were not creating jobs for others. The vast majority of job creation over time is contributed by a tiny fraction of new firms.

The job creation statistics also fail to consider that many new small businesses fail, and the failure rate is largely dependent on the economy. For instance, from 1990 through 1994, there were 706 000 small business births and 686 000 deaths, for a net gain of 20 000 firms over the period. This contrasts with a net gain of 110 000 firms from 1986 through 1990, when 763 000 firms were started. So, many of the firms creating jobs at one period

in time are responsible for lost jobs when the firms fail. Overall, small business accounts for only about one-third of the jobs in Canada, while big business' share is over 40 percent. The same arguments about employment levels holds internationally: In Germany, Japan, and the United States, large businesses have been the big net-job producers.

It's true that the typical organization is becoming smaller. The average Canadian and American business establishment has shrunk dramatically during the last 25 years. But what these numbers don't reveal is that these smaller establishments are increasingly part of a large multi-location firm with the financial and technological resources to compete in a global marketplace. In other words, these smaller organizations are de facto part of the large enterprise, and this practice is going on throughout the world.

Technology favours the big guys. Studies demonstrate that small firms turn out to be systematically backward when it comes to technology. For example, on every continent, the big companies are far more likely than the small ones to invest in computer-controlled factory automation.

Everyone agrees with the fact that large organizations are improving their flexibility by increasing their use of strategic alliances, interorganizational networks, and similar devices. This worldwide trend, coupled with efforts to widen spans of control, decentralize decision making, cut vertical levels, and sell off or close operations that don't fit with the organization's primary purpose, has made large firms increasingly agile and responsive.

Sources:

[1] This argument is based on B. Harrison, *Lean and Mean: The Changing Landscape of Corporate Power in the Age of Flexibility* (New York: Basic Books, 1994). See also M.J. Mandel, "Land of the Giants," *Business Week*, September 11, 1995, pp. 34-35; and C. Harris, "Prime Numbers: A Statistical Look at the Trends and Issues that Will Dominate our Future," *Financial Post*, November 15/17, 1997, p. P13.

[2] C. Winn, "FP/COMPAS Poll: An Exclusive Survey of CEOs and Canadians at Large. This Week: Small Is Beautiful, Sort Of," *Financial Post*, November, 15/17 1997, p. P17.

## Technology

The term **technology** refers to the way in which an organization transfers its inputs into outputs. Every organization has at least one technology for converting financial, human, and physical resources into products or services. The Ford Motor Co., for instance, predominantly uses an assembly-line process to make its products. On the other hand, universities may use a number of instruction technologies — the ever-popular formal lecture method, the case-analysis method, the experiential exercise method, the programmed learning method, and so forth. In this section we want to show that organizational structures adapt to their technology.

Numerous studies have been carried out on the technology-structure relationship.[35] The details of those studies are quite complex, so we'll go straight to "the bottom line" and attempt to summarize what we know.

The common theme that differentiates technologies is their *degree of routineness*. By this we mean that technologies tend toward either routine or nonroutine activities. The former are characterized by automated and standardized operations, such as an assembly line, where one might affix a car door to a car at set intervals. Nonroutine activities are customized. They include such varied operations as furniture restoring, custom shoemaking, and genetic research.

What relationships have been found between technology and structure? Although the relationship is not overwhelmingly strong, we find that routine tasks are associated with taller and more departmentalized structures. The relationship between technology and formalization, however, is stronger. Studies consistently show routineness to be associated with the presence of rule manuals, job descriptions, and other formalized documentation. Finally, an interesting relationship has been found between technology and centralization. It seems logical that routine technologies would be associated with a centralized structure, whereas nonroutine technologies, which rely more heavily on the knowledge of specialists, would be characterized by delegated decision authority. This position has met with some support. However, a more generalizable conclusion is that the technology-centralization relationship is moderated by the degree of formalization. Both formal regulations and centralized decision making are control mechanisms, and management can substitute one for the other. Routine technologies should be associated with centralized control if there is a minimum of rules and regulations. However, if formalization is high, routine technology can be accompanied by decentralization. So, we would predict that routine technology would lead to centralization, but only if formalization is low.

## Environment

An organization's **environment** is composed of those institutions or forces outside the organization that potentially affect the organization's performance. These typically include suppliers, customers, competitors, government regulatory agencies, public pressure groups, and the like.

Why should an organization's structure be affected by its environment? The answer is environmental uncertainty. Some organizations face relatively static environments — few forces in their environment are changing. There are, for example, no new competitors, no new technological breakthroughs by current competitors, or little activity by public pressure groups to influence the organization. Other organizations face very dynamic environments — rapidly changing government regulations affecting their business, new competitors, difficulties in acquiring raw materials, continually changing product preferences by customers, and so on. Static environments create significantly less uncertainty for managers than do dynamic ones. And since uncertainty is a threat to an organization's effectiveness, management will try to minimize it. One way to reduce environmental uncertainty is through adjustments in the organization's structure.[36]

Recent research has helped clarify what is meant by environmental uncertainty. It's been found that there are three key dimensions to any organization's environment: capacity, volatility, and complexity.[37]

The *capacity* of an environment refers to the degree to which it can support growth. Rich and growing environments generate excess resources, which can buffer the organization in times of relative scarcity. Abundant capacity, for example, leaves room for an organization to make mistakes, while scarce capacity does not. In 2000, firms operating in the multimedia software business had relatively abundant environments, whereas those in the full-service brokerage business faced relative scarcity.

The degree of instability in an environment is captured in the *volatility* dimension. Where there is a high degree of unpredictable change, the environment is dynamic. This makes it difficult for management to predict accurately the probabilities associated with various decision alternatives. At the other extreme is a stable environment. The recent turmoil in Asian financial markets caught many by surprise and created a lot of instability in the late 1990s, particularly in resource industries. Canada's resource exports suffered as demand shrank in Asia. This led to widespread layoffs in the BC lumber industry, and Japan's steel producers demanded a cut in the price they pay for Canadian coal. The instability is not limited to the resource sector, however. Small manufacturers were also hit. In summer 1996, Viceroy Homes Ltd. of Toronto opened a plant in Vancouver to produce prefabricated houses for the Asian market. Initially, Japan accounted for as much as 62 percent of Viceroy's sales until the yen fell, the market collapsed, and profits fell 30 percent in the first six months of 1997.[38]

The experience of the recent Asian crisis is a valuable reminder to all organizations that they are operating in a global environment.

Finally, the environment needs to be assessed in terms of *complexity*; that is, the degree of heterogeneity and concentration among environmental elements. Simple environments are homogeneous and concentrated. This might describe the tobacco industry, since there are relatively few players. It's easy for firms in this industry to keep a close eye on the competition. In contrast, environments characterized by heterogeneity and dispersion are called complex. This sums up the current environment for firms competing in the Internet connection business. Every day, there seems to be another "new kid on the block" with whom current Internet service providers must deal.

Exhibit 12-17 summarizes our definition of the environment along its three dimensions. The arrows in this figure are meant to indicate movement toward higher uncertainty. Organizations that operate in environments characterized as scarce, dynamic, and complex face the greatest degree of uncertainty. Why? They have little room for error, high unpredictability, and a diverse set of elements in the environment to monitor constantly.

---

**So what is meant by the term "technology"?**

**Exhibit 12-17**
**Three-Dimensional Model of the Environment**

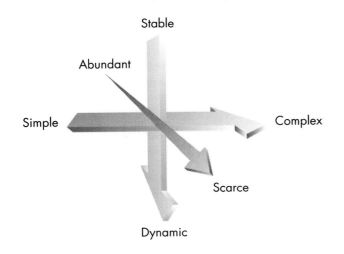

Given this three-dimensional definition of environment, we can offer some general conclusions. There is evidence that relates the degrees of environmental uncertainty to different structural arrangements. Specifically, the more scarce, dynamic, and complex the environment, the more organic a structure should be. The more abundant, stable, and simple the environment, the more the mechanistic structure will be preferred.

## Structural Changes Over Time

We've shown that four variables — strategy, size, technology, and environment — are the primary forces that determine whether an organization is mechanistic or organic. Now let's use our previous analysis to explain the evolution of structural designs throughout this century.

The Industrial Revolution encouraged economies of scale and the rise of the modern, large corporation. As companies grew from their original simple structures, they took on mechanistic characteristics and became bureaucracies. The rise of bureaucracy to become the dominant structure in industrialized nations from the 1920s through the 1970s can be largely explained by three facts. First, the environment was relatively stable and certain over this period. The monopoly power of the large corporations, coupled with little international competition, kept environmental uncertainty to a minimum. Second, economies of scale and minimal competition allowed these corporations to introduce highly routine technologies. And third, most of these large corporations chose to pursue cost minimization or imitation strategies — leaving innovation to the smaller operators. Combine these strategies with large size, routine technologies, and relatively abundant, stable, and simple environments, and you have a reasonably clear explanation for the rise and domination of the bureaucracy.

Things began to change in the late 1970s, when the environment became significantly more uncertain. Interest rates soared in 1979 and then again in 1981. Advances in computer technology — especially the availability of increasingly powerful systems at dramatically falling prices — began to lessen the advantage that accrued to large size. And, of course, competition moved to the global arena. To compete effectively, top management responded by restructuring their organizations. Some went to the matrix to give their companies increased flexibility. Some added team structures so they could respond more rapidly to change. Today, senior managers in most large corporations are "debureaucratizing" their organizations — making them more organic by reducing staff, cutting vertical levels, decentralizing authority, and the like — primarily because the environment continues to be uncertain. Despite the profound impact restructuring has on employees (discussed in detail in this chapter's HR Implications feature on the next page), managers realize that in a dynamic and changing environment, inflexible organizations end up as bankruptcy statistics.

## HR Implications

# The Effects of Restructuring on Employees

Nearly every day, it seems, companies throughout the world announce that they are "restructuring" and laying off their employees. In November 1999, for instance, the following companies were among those who made such announcements (size of layoff in parentheses): Ottawa-based Newbridge (10 percent of workforce); Peterborough, Ontario-based General Electric (85 employees, after announcements in August and September of similar layoffs); Toronto-based Royal Bank (between 3000 and 6000 employees); Halifax-based High Liner Foods (50 employees); Japan's Nissan (14 percent reduction by 2003) and NTT (16 percent reduction by 2003); and Germany's Phillipp Holzmann AG (3000 employees). Restructuring often goes by various names, including downsizing, rightsizing, and delayering, but all of these terms are really euphemisms for layoffs.

Restructuring happens in a variety of ways. Sometimes organizations decide to engage in work redesign. Whole divisions or business units might be combined, or disaggregated, or even spun off. Sometimes business functions, such as engineering, operations, and distribution, might be joined together. Or some of these functions might be contracted out. Delayering is another restructuring technique, which means that the organization reduces the number of layers, or hierarchical levels. Finally, restructuring can also involve downsizing, or layoffs.

While structural changes and work redesign may be a more planned approach to workforce change, generally the intent behind layoffs is not some planned approach to a new organizational structure. Rather it serves as an attempt to increase shareholder well-being.[1] Consider, for instance, the case of AT&T Corp. In December 1995, AT&T announced that it would cut 40 000 employees from its rolls. Several months later, chair Robert Allen said the job cuts would be closer to 10 000. However, the impact of announcing that 40 000 jobs would be lost was that AT&T's stock price jumped $9.[2]

AT&T is not unique in the relationship of layoffs to increased earnings. The statistics for 1995 show that General Motors Canada reported a record profit

for any Canadian company in 1995 ($1.39 billion) and fired 2500 of its workers. Canada's largest banks — Royal Bank, Toronto-Dominion, Bank of Montreal, Nova Scotia, and CIBC — announced record collective profits from 1995 through 1998, and laid off thousands of people while doing so. It is estimated the banks are planning additional layoffs of about 10 000 employees between 2000 and 2003.[3] Bell Canada enjoyed a healthy profit in 1995 and dismissed 3200 of its employees. Similar stories happened at Inco, Imperial Oil, Petro-Canada, Maritime Telephone and Telegraph, CP Rail, and Shell Canada, among others.

Industry minister John Manley worries about the impact of these cuts for society: "I think it's part of my job to push the corporate sector and urge them to take into account the enormous damage it does when you cast people aside instead of retraining them."[4] Canadian citizens are also concerned about the impact of layoffs and the responsibilities of corporations. When the Maclean's/CBC News 1996 year-end poll asked respondents about the acceptability of profitable corporations laying off workers, 58 percent did not find this acceptable.[5] Negative reactions to downsizing are even higher in the regions experiencing the most difficult economic times, with Quebec (64 percent) and the Atlantic provinces (66 percent) giving the most unfavourable views. In Alberta, where the economy has been booming, fewer people were reluctant to criticize companies for layoffs (49 percent).

Len Brooks, executive director of the Clarkson Centre for Business Ethics at the University of Toronto, says laying off employees to maximize profit and improve cash flow "is really a dumb idea. Only a third of its practitioners achieve their financial objectives while paying a huge price as employee morale craters."[6] Study after study shows that after downsizing "surviving employees become narrow-minded, self-absorbed, and risk averse. Morale sinks, productivity drops, and survivors distrust management."[7]

Brooks's views are supported by a study conducted by the American Management Association (AMA) in 1995. The AMA surveyed 700 companies that had downsized between 1989 and 1994 and found that these actions do not necessarily pay off over the long term, even if there are short-term gains.[8] For instance, productivity fell in 30 percent of the cases, while rising in 34 percent of the cases. Profits fell 30 percent of the time, and rose 51 percent of the time. Employee morale fell in 83 percent of the companies, so the biggest gain in downsizing is an increase in employee ill will, which may not be good for the company overall.

Lloyd Cooper, in charge of career management at Watson Wyatt Worldwide, explains some of the reasons for low morale after downsizing. He notes that many companies have been cutting jobs to cut payroll costs. "But they haven't been downsizing the workload. They just went on with more, faster, quicker but without thinking: 'What are we actually doing?'"[9]

If there is any consolation to the downsizing/shareholder dilemma, it may be that the emphasis on shareholder value is less in Canada than in the United States. A survey in 1994 found that 69 percent of executives in the United States consider shareholder value a "critical" issue.[10] In Canada, the figure was 43 percent, while in Europe it was only 25 percent.

There are several options that the human resources department can recommend to senior executives as alternatives to downsizing.[11] A number of Canadian corporations have developed options such as job sharing, voluntarily reduced work time, and phased-in retirement as ways to avoid downsizing. These companies have chosen this option as a way of preserving employee morale.

Professor Ronald Burke of the Schulich School of Business at York University and his co-author Debra Nelson proposed a three-stage guide for managing revitalization efforts:[12]

- *Initiation: Planning and preparing for the transition*: During this stage, develop concrete goals, communicate the strategy clearly, look for alternatives to and criteria for downsizing, and develop timetables.

- *Implementation: Moving towards change*: During this stage, involve the employees, communicate extensively, give support, and watch for stress.

- *Institutionalization: Healing and refocusing*: During this stage focus on why changes are needed, celebrate accomplishments, retrain employees as needed, and maintain individual and organizational health.

They note that how managers treat employees during downsizing and restructuring makes a large difference in the results. For instance, telling employees that they are lucky to have survived the cuts does not necessarily instill good will.

Sources:

[1] R.W. Keidel, "Rethinking Organizational Design," *Academy of Management Executive*, 8, 1994, pp. 12-30.

[2] "Haves & Have-nots: Canadians Look for Corporate Conscience," *Maclean's*, December 30, 1996/January 6, 1997, pp. 26, 37.

[3] K. Macklem, "More Than 10,000 Jobs Lost in Banks," *Financial Post*, November 19, 1999, pp. C1, C5.

[4] "Haves & Have-nots: Canadians Look for Corporate Conscience," *Maclean's*, December 30, 1996/January 6, 1997, pp. 26, 37.

[5] "Haves & Have-nots: Canadians Look for Corporate Conscience," *Maclean's*, December 30, 1996/January 6, 1997, pp. 26, 37.

[6] "Haves & Have-nots: Canadians Look for Corporate Conscience," *Maclean's*, December 30, 1996/January 6, 1997, pp. 26, 37.

[7] W.F. Cascio, "Downsizing: What Do We Know? What Have We Learned?" *Academy of Management Executive*, 7, 1993, p. 100.

[8] "Shareholders Versus Job Holders. Do Corporations Have an Obligation to Provide Work? Or, Are They Solely Economic Units That Have No Social Function?" *Canada and the World Backgrounder*, October, 1996, pp. 11-13.

[9] "Mistake to Downsize Just for Profit, Experts Say," *Canadian Press Newswire*, May 9, 1996.

[10] "Shareholders Versus Job Holders: Do Corporations Have an Obligation to Provide Work? Or, Are They Solely Economic Units That Have No Social Function?" *Canada and the World Backgrounder*, October, 1996, pp. 11-13.

[11] "Work Option Plans Can Soften Blows of Layoffs," *Financial Post*, May 4/6, 1996, p. 37.

[12] D.L. Nelson and R.J. Burke, "Lessons Learned," *Canadian Journal of Administrative Sciences*, 15(4), 1998, pp. 372-381.

# SUMMARY AND IMPLICATIONS

## For the Workplace

The theme of this chapter has been that an organization's internal structure contributes to explaining and predicting behaviour. That is, in addition to individual and group factors, the structural relationships in which people work have an important bearing on employee attitudes and behaviour.

What's the basis for the argument that structure has an impact on both attitudes and behaviour? A well-defined structure reduces ambiguity for the employees and clarifies such concerns as "What am I supposed to do?" "How am I supposed to do it?" "To whom do I report?" and "To whom do I go if I have a problem?" By doing so, structure can shape employee attitudes, facilitate performance, and motivate employees to higher levels. Of course, structure also constrains employees to the extent that it limits and controls what they do. For example, organizations structured around high levels of formalization and specialization, strict adherence to the chain of command, limited delegation of authority, and narrow spans of control give employees little autonomy. Controls in such organizations are tight, and behaviour will tend to vary within a narrow range. In contrast, organizations that are structured around limited specialization, low formalization, wide spans of control, and the like provide employees with greater freedom and, thus, will be characterized by greater behavioural diversity.

Exhibit 12-18 visually summarizes what we've discussed in this chapter. Strategy, size, technology, and environment determine the type of structure an organization will have. For simplicity's sake, we can classify structural designs around one of two models: mechanistic or organic. The specific effect of structural designs on performance and satisfaction is moderated by employees' individual preferences and cultural norms.

## For You as an Individual

Our discussion of structure was meant to get you to think about two things. The first is to consider the type of organization in which you might like to work, trying to determine for yourself whether you're a person who prefers

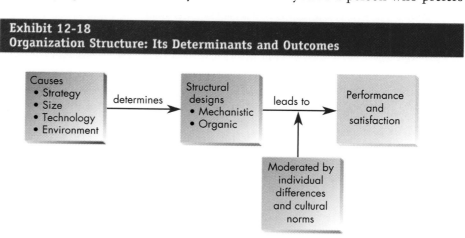

**Exhibit 12-18**
**Organization Structure: Its Determinants and Outcomes**

a more formalized mechanistic structure or a highly organic organizational structure. Each of us differs in our reactions to these two types, and of course some organizations fall in between these extremes. Part of choosing a job that is a good fit for you is to understand how the structure of the organization will affect you.

Another thing that you might be considering is becoming an entrepreneur. If you start your own company, you will need to determine, among other things, how much responsibility you want to take for yourself compared with how much you are willing to share with other managers or employees. We saw in the case of Lee McDonald of Southmedic that she preferred to share more of the responsibility of running the organization with her managers. This suited both her travel schedule and her personal needs. A knowledge of the different organizational considerations can help you create an organization that meets your needs as both a business person and a person with additional interests.

## *ROADMAP* REMINDER

In arriving at this chapter, we moved away from some of the internal dynamics of the organization to consider how employees and managers are grouped into units that relate to the various tasks, responsibilities, and goals of the organization. We noted that some designs may have more conflict embedded in them than others. This would happen, for example, if each functional unit viewed itself as "the most important" in the organization. As mentioned previously, structure relates to organizing the major units of the organization. It is also necessary to organize the major tasks that need to be done within the organization. Therefore, in the next chapter we will consider job design, which informs us about how to group the various tasks of a job into different configurations.

## For Review

1. Why isn't work specialization an unending source of increased productivity?
2. All things being equal, which is more efficient, a wide or narrow span of control? Why?
3. In what ways can management departmentalize?
4. What is a matrix structure? When would management use it?
5. Contrast the virtual organization with the boundaryless organization.
6. What type of structure works best with an innovation strategy? A cost-minimization strategy? An imitation strategy?
7. Summarize the size-structure relationship.
8. Define and give an example of what is meant by the term *technology*.
9. Summarize the environment-structure relationship.
10. Explain the importance of the statement: "Employees form implicit models of organizational structure."

## For Critical Thinking

1. How is the typical large corporation of today organized in contrast with how that same organization was probably organized in the 1960s?

2. Do you think most employees prefer high formalization? Support your position.
3. If you were an employee in a matrix structure, what pluses do you think the structure would provide? What about minuses?
4. What could management do to make a bureaucracy more like a boundaryless organization?
5. What behavioural predictions would you make about people who worked in a "pure" boundaryless organization (if such a structure were ever to exist)?

## LEARNING ABOUT YOURSELF EXERCISE

# Bureaucratic Orientation Test

Instructions: For each statement, check the response (either mostly agree or mostly disagree) that best represents your feelings.

|  | Mostly Agree | Mostly Disagree |
|---|---|---|
| **1.** I value stability in my job. | _____ | _____ |
| **2.** I like a predictable organization. | _____ | _____ |
| **3.** The best job for me would be one in which the future is uncertain. | _____ | _____ |
| **4.** The federal government would be a nice place to work. | _____ | _____ |
| **5.** Rules, policies, and procedures tend to frustrate me. | _____ | _____ |
| **6.** I would enjoy working for a company that employed 85 000 people worldwide. | _____ | _____ |
| **7.** Being self-employed would involve more risk than I'm willing to take. | _____ | _____ |
| **8.** Before accepting a job, I would like to see an exact job description. | _____ | _____ |
| **9.** I would prefer a job as a freelance house painter to one as a clerk for the Department of Motor Vehicles. | _____ | _____ |
| **10.** Seniority should be as important as performance in determining pay increases and promotion. | _____ | _____ |
| **11.** It would give me a feeling of pride to work for the largest and most successful company in its field. | _____ | _____ |
| **12.** Given a choice, I would prefer to make $70 000 per year as a vice-president in a small company than $85 000 as a staff specialist in a large company. | _____ | _____ |
| **13.** I would regard wearing an employee badge with a number on it as a degrading experience. | _____ | _____ |
| **14.** Parking spaces in a company lot should be assigned on the basis of job level. | _____ | _____ |
| **15.** If an accountant works for a large organization, he or she cannot be a true professional. | _____ | _____ |
| **16.** Before accepting a job (given a choice), I would want to make sure that the company had a very fine program of employee benefits. | _____ | _____ |

*Continued on next page*

*Bureaucratic Orientation Test Continued*

|  | Mostly Agree | Mostly Disagree |
|---|---|---|
| **17.** A company will probably not be successful unless it establishes a clear set of rules and procedures. | _____ | _____ |
| **18.** Regular working hours and vacations are more important to me than finding thrills on the job. | _____ | _____ |
| **19.** You should respect people according to their rank. | _____ | _____ |
| **20.** Rules are meant to be broken. | _____ | _____ |

Turn to page 636 for scoring directions and key.

Source: Adapted from A.J. DuBrin, *Human Relations: A Job Oriented Approach,* 5ᵗʰ edition, 1992. Reprinted with permission of Prentice Hall, Inc., Upper Saddle River, NJ.

## WORKING WITH OTHERS EXERCISE

# Words-in-Sentences Company

| | |
|---|---|
| **Overview:** | You are a small company that |
| | 1) manufactures words; and |
| | 2) packages them into meaningful English-language sentences. |
| | Market research has established that sentences of at least 3 words but not more than 6 words are in demand. Therefore, packaging, distribution, and sales should be set up for **3- to 6-word sentences**. |
| **Time:** | Approximately 30 minutes. (Note: A production run takes 10 minutes. While the game is more effective if 2 [or more] production runs are completed, even 1 production run will generate effective discussion about how organizational structure affects performance.) |
| **Group Task:** | Your group must design and participate in running a WIS company. You will be competing with other companies in your industry. The success of your company will depend on (a) your objectives, (b) planning, (c) organization structure, and (d) quality control. You should design your organization to be as efficient as possible during each 10-minute production run. After the first production run, you will have an opportunity to reorganize your company if you want. |
| **Raw Materials:** | For each production run you will be given a "**raw material phrase.**" The letters found in the phrase serve as the raw materials available to produce new words in sentences. For example, if the raw material phrase is "organizational behaviour is fun," you could produce the words and sentence "Nat ran to a zoo." One way to think of your raw material phrase is to take all the letters appearing in the phrase and write them down as many times as they appear in the phrase. Thus, for the phrase "organizational behaviour is fun" you have: a-4; b-1; c-0; d-0; e-1; f-1; g-1; h-1; i-4; j-0; k-0; l-1; m-0; n-3; o-3; p-0; q-0; r-2; s-1; t-1; u-2; v-1; w-0; x-0; y-0; z-1 for a total of 28 raw material letters. |
| **Production Standards:** | There are several rules that have to be followed in producing "words-in-sentences." **If these rules are not followed, your output will not meet production specifications and will not pass quality-control inspection.** |

1. A letter may appear only as often in a manufactured word as it appears in the raw material phrase; for example, "organizational behaviour is fun" has one l and one e. Thus "steal" is legitimate, but not "teller." It has too many l's and e's.

2. Raw material letters can be used again in different manufactured words.

3. A manufactured **word** may be used only **once** during a production run; once a word — for example, "the" — is used in a sentence, it is out of stock for the rest of the production run. No other sentence may use the word "the."

4. A new word may not be made by adding "s" to form the plural of an already used manufactured word.

5. Sentences must make grammatical and logical sense.

6. All words must be in the English language.

7. Names and places are acceptable.

8. Slang is not acceptable.

9. Writing must be legible. Any illegible sentence will be disqualified.

10. Only sentences that have a minimum of 3 words and a maximum of 6 words will be considered.

## Directions

**Step 1:** Design your organization using as many group members as you see fit to produce your "words-in-sentences."

**Step 2:** Production Run 1. The instructor will place a raw material phrase on the board or overhead. When the instructor announces "Begin production," you are to manufacture as many words as possible and package them in sentences for delivery to the Quality Control Review Board. You will have 10 minutes.

**Step 3:** When the instructor announces "Stop production," you will have 30 seconds to deliver your output to the Quality Control Review Board. Output received after 30 seconds does not meet the delivery schedule and will not be counted. You may use up to 2 sheets of paper and each sheet of paper must identify your group.

**Step 4:** Your output should be delivered by your quality control representative, who will work with the other representatives to evaluate the performance of each of the groups.

**Measuring Performance:** The output of your WIS company is measured by the total number of acceptable words that are packaged in sentences of 3-6 words only.

**Quality Control:** If any word in a sentence does not meet the standards set forth above, all the words in the sentence will be rejected. The Quality Control Review Board (composed of 1 member from each company) is the final arbiter of acceptability. In the event of a tie vote on the Review Board, a coin toss will determine the outcome.

**Step 5:** While the output is being evaluated, you should make plans for organizing the 2nd production run.

**Step 6:** Production Run 2.

**Step 7:** The results are presented.

**Step 8:** Discussion.

---

Source: The source of this exercise is unknown.

## ETHICAL DILEMMA EXERCISE

# Employee Monitoring: How Far Is Too Far?

When does management's effort to control the actions of others become an invasion of privacy? Consider 3 cases.[1]

> At call centres in New Brunswick, managers monitor almost all aspects of their employees' work, from taping calls and analyzing them with the employee, to calculating the length of calls and determining why some employees are on the phone longer than others.

> In December 1996, a physicist working for Canada's Department of National Defence was arrested and charged with possessing and distributing child pornography. The evidence was contained in his office computer, with files downloaded from the World Wide Web.

> The law firm of Fasken Campbell Godfrey in Toronto periodically monitors employee e-mails. Employees are notified that this may happen occasionally.

Are any of these cases — monitoring calls, computer activities, or e-mail — an invasion of privacy? When does management overstep the bounds of decency and privacy by silently (even covertly) scrutinizing the behaviour of its employees or associates?

Managers defend these practices in terms of ensuring quality, productivity, and proper employee behaviour. For instance, silent surveillance of telephone calls can be used to help employees perform their jobs better. Surveillance can also prevent employees from taking unauthorized looks at the tax returns of friends, neighbours, or celebrities, or examining their health or financial records.

In banking, insurance, telecommunications, and travel, as many as 80 percent of employees may be subject to some level of monitoring.[2] While it is an offence under the Criminal Code in Canada to intercept private communications, the law is less clear about how privacy may be applied in the workplace. Unionized employees may have a bit more security. The Canada Labour Code requires employers operating under a collective agreement to disclose information about plans for technological change. This might provide unions an opportunity to bargain over electronic surveillance.

**Questions for Discussion:**

1. When does management's need for information about employee performance cross over the line and interfere with a worker's right to privacy?

2. Should employees be notified in advance that they will be monitored?

3. Does management's right to protect its interests extend to electronic monitoring of every place a worker might be — for example, washrooms and locker rooms?

---

Sources:

[1] J. Markoff, "The Snooping Mayor," *New York Times*, May 4, 1990, p. B1; G. Bylinsky, "How Companies Spy on Employees," *Fortune*, November 4, 1991, pp. 131-140; D. Warner, "The Move to Curb Worker Monitoring," *Nation's Business*, December 1993, pp. 37-38; and M. Picard, "Working Under an Electronic Thumb," *Training*, February 1994, pp. 47-51.

[2] A. Gahtan, "Title: Big Brother or Good Business?", *WebWorld*, March 1997, p. 24.

## INTERNET SEARCH EXERCISES

1. Find 3 companies (not mentioned in your text) that are in some way monitoring their employees via computer controls. Describe each.

2. Contrast the organization structures of 3 companies—1 each from (a) a resource-based industry (for example, mining, forestry); (b) a large retail chain; and (c) a large software developer. What contingency variables do you think best explain each company's structure?

**CASE INCIDENT**

# Motorola Inc.: What Went Wrong?

If ever there was an organization that exemplified the challenges of managing in rapidly changing times, it's Motorola Inc. In the mid-1980s, Motorola teams achieved technological breakthroughs in miniaturizing pagers and cellular phones—just before those markets took off. As recently as 1995, the company was the world leader in pagers and cell phones—and generating record-breaking growth rates in sales and earnings. By 1999, however, the company was struggling.

Motorola stumbled badly when it failed to anticipate the industry's switch to digital cell phones from the long-dominant analog devices. It then overestimated its capability to get digital equipment to market. A major player in Japan and Southeast Asia, Motorola has seen the collapse of consumer demand for its products as a result of the economic downturn in Asia. And it now has serious problems in marketing, timely delivery of products, and the quality of its wireless networks. While it still holds on, although weakly, to its No. 1 spot in the US market for wireless phones, its share has fallen by about 30 percent between 1996 and 1999, to just above one-third of the industry's sales. Its worldwide share of wireless network systems has dropped sharply over the same period, to below one-third.

What was once hailed as one of Motorola's competitive advantages—its heavy reliance on teams and group sectors as an organizing device—is now seen by many as a negative. The original idea was to create tribes that would compete internally for funding and support from headquarters. This tribal approach would weed out weak ideas and identify the strongest products. Critics now blame the "warring tribes" for much of Motorola's problems. This approach has impeded the company's ability to work with outside partners to provide critical components that the company is unable to produce internally, as well as creating internal conflicts. In one memorable incident, top managers visiting Hungary were shaken when a telecommunications minister flung Motorola business cards at them from a dozen different Motorola divisions. "Which of these people am I supposed to talk to?" the minister demanded.

The company's current CEO, Christopher Galvin, took over in January 1997. The grandson of Motorola's founder, he follows in the footsteps of his father, who led the company in its glory days. Galvin, 48, knows the business. He grew up in it. But some wonder if he's up to the job. He'll need to replace many senior managers in the near future. Two-thirds of the company's top managers are currently 57 or older.

Some critics suggest that Galvin may be too nice to run a company in crisis. For instance, he shows no willingness to hold his executives accountable. He recently announced an "amnesty" for "past mistakes and judgments so we can move forward."

Still others criticize Galvin for his willingness to think big. He seems open to practically anything. He regularly holds executive meetings where he and others brainstorm about the future. He talks, for instance, about going after markets for chip implants for human ears that could be hooked up to cell-phone networks, and developing semiconductors that could be placed in trees to help timber firms monitor growth. Acknowledging that such ideas may sound silly, he points out that the company's early investment in transistors was also considered a long shot. "I don't know what the next business will be in 2003," he adds.

## Questions:

1. How would you classify Motorola's structure? Defend your choice.

2. Is Motorola's problem one of poor leadership or inadequate structural design? Explain.

3. If you were a consultant advising Galvin, what would you suggest?

Source: Q. Hardy, "Motorola, Broadsided by the Digital Era, Struggles for a Footing," *Wall Street Journal*, April 22, 1998, p. A1.

# Growing Big Can Be Hard to Do

DCB Productions, headed by Debra Belinsky and Cheryl Benson-Guanci, has hit it big with its business of sports entertainment. The "two girls from Winnipeg" produce shows and entertainment for audiences of the Calgary Flames, as well as for a number of US organizations, including the Disney Sports organization, the NHL teams Mighty Ducks, Tampa Bay Lightning, Calgary Flames, and Carolina Hurricanes, the pro-basketball team the L.A. Clippers, and the major league baseball team the Anaheim Angels.

The two women started their business on a shoestring. After producing one game for the Winnipeg Jets, they borrowed $6000 from their parents and approached the Disney Corporation about doing the entertainment for the Mighty Ducks. How could these women market a successful proposal to Disney, home of entertainment in the United States? The Disney entertainers didn't know hockey, and their Mighty Ducks productions weren't working with the fans. They were happy to hire someone who knew how to reach hockey audiences.

The business has grown fairly rapidly, but Cheryl is based in Anaheim, California, while Deb is based in Calgary, so getting together for business meetings is full of complications. They are starting to feel some of the pains of expanding rapidly, a situation many entrepreneurs face as their businesses grow. Whereas at one time they used to be able to put out their business fires, now they're having more difficulty doing so. Moreover, their clients only want either Deb or Cheryl to run the show, but the two women know they can't be everywhere all the time. They've already acknowledged that they need to hire a business manager to run the organizational affairs. So the challenge these two women from Winnipeg face is this: How do they get away from the daily grind of the business so that they can grow as fast as the sports entertainment business is growing?

# Questions

1. Describe the organizational structure of DCB Productions.

2. In what ways might this structure have helped the organization grow successfully in a short period of time?

3. In what ways does the organizational structure need to be changed to meet the growing demands placed on Deb and Cheryl by their clients?

Source: Based on "Duck Ladies," *Venture 593*; aired June 2, 1996.

CHAPTER 13

# Work Design

E ver wonder whether diligence, teamwork, and innovation could characterize an automotive plant? Ingersoll, Ontario-based CAMI Automotive Inc. may fit the bill. In re-engineering its work processes, it has reduced inventory by 40 percent, and increased the space used on its inbound supply trucks by about 85 to 90 percent.[1]

## Questions for Consideration

**How can we use job design to increase an individual's motivation to perform?**

**How is technology changing the organization of the workplace?**

**What kinds of flexible work arrangements are available in the workplace?**

CAMI, a joint venture between General Motors of Canada Ltd. and Suzuki Motors Corp., manufactures a truck about every two minutes, without having any excess inventory on site. Parts arrive just-in-time (JIT) and then get distributed to assembly lines where employees build and paint Chevrolet Metros and Trackers, and Suzuki Swifts and Vitaras.

Several years ago CAMI formed a partnership with Cambridge, Ontario-based Transfreight to get supplies to the assembly lines on a daily basis. Transfreight sends trucks several times a day to more than 200 of CAMI's suppliers, doing a sort of "milk run" to pick up supplies as needed. Trucks travel to several suppliers, returning when the truck is full. This ensures a good mix of supplies on each shipment, improves efficiency, minimizes costs, and increases integration with suppliers.

To make sure that supplies are ordered properly, CAMI moved the material planners from the offices above the plant to spaces right on the production floor. "Before, they were up in the office and they just looked at a screen and didn't know what was happening on the floor. As a matter of fact, they never came to the floor. When product ran out, the planners were always the last to know," Phil Williams, manager of logistics and material handling explains. Moving the planners to the floor created better communication, and the planners now feel more responsible when there are too many parts, or not enough.

Employees on the floor are also responsible for making sure that the shop floor stays organized and uncluttered. They do this by rebuilding racks for temporary storage as needed. This has speeded up the assembly lines by 50 percent and freed up 30 to 35 percent of CAMI's storage area.

Williams's next goal is to bring the suppliers and the production workers together, at the assembly line. "The idea is to make suppliers more understanding of the needs of the plant workers," Williams explains. He also wants to send a team of CAMI employees to the suppliers' companies. He hopes that the meetings between the suppliers and the CAMI employees will lead to improvements in both CAMI's and the vendors' operations.

Summing up CAMI's operations, Williams says his plant is "always evolving."

CAMI's employees are part of the new world of work expectations: employees who are responsible for managing the workflow, flexible about changing needs, and able to think up new processes to improve production and efficiency. Of course, not everyone is completely comfortable with these kinds of changes.

In this chapter we explore how organizations arrange work tasks into jobs. Jobs can be limited in activity, such as painting passenger-car doors for an entire shift, or they can include a large variety of tasks. Organizations try to identify optimum levels of variety in employees' jobs, because jobs themselves can cause people to be either motivated or unmotivated. When companies arrange tasks into jobs, they are engaging in job design. To understand the complexities of job design, we begin this chapter by considering the

**General Motors**
www.gm.com

**Suzuki Motors Corp.**
www.suzuki.com

factors that affect how people view their jobs. We then discuss the various ways that organizations arrange jobs, as well as the new ways of arranging jobs that have been occurring in the workplace. This chapter's CBC Video Case on page 583 features telemarketing, giving you the opportunity to think about job design for a high turnover position.

## Conceptual Frameworks for Analyzing How People Respond to Their Work Tasks

For some employees, when an organization starts changing the work process, there is an excitement and energy. For others, however, the change is unwelcome. They may even leave to work for another employer. These different actions by people doing the same job acknowledge basic facts we all know: (1) People's preferences for jobs are different; (2) jobs themselves are different; and (3) some jobs are more interesting and challenging than others. These facts have not gone unnoticed by OB researchers. They have responded by developing a number of **task characteristics theories** that seek to identify task characteristics of jobs, how these characteristics are combined to form different jobs, and the relationship of these task characteristics to employee motivation, satisfaction, and performance.

There are at least seven task characteristics theories that explain why some people like some jobs better than others.[2] Below, we review two task characteristics theories —the job characteristics model and the social information processing model.

**task characteristics theories**
Seek to identify task characteristics of jobs, how these characteristics are combined to form different jobs, and their relationship to employee motivation, satisfaction, and performance.

### The Job Characteristics Model

Today the dominant framework for defining task characteristics and understanding their relationship to employee motivation, performance, and satisfaction is the Hackman and Oldham **job characteristics model (JCM)**.[3]

**job characteristics model (JCM)**
Identifies five job characteristics and their relationship to personal and work outcomes.

At Vancouver-based Great Little Box Company (GLBC), which designs and manufactures corrugated containers, employees are given the freedom to do whatever they feel is necessary and appropriate to make customers happy. If a customer is dissatisfied with the product, the employee can say "OK, I'll bring this product back and re-run it for you," without having to get prior authorization. The job characteristics model suggests that GLBC's employees would have a high motivation potential score (MPS) because their jobs have task identity, autonomy and feedback.

**skill variety**
The degree to which the job requires a variety of different activities.

**task identity**
The degree to which the job requires completion of a whole and identifiable piece of work.

**task significance**
The degree to which the job has a substantial impact on the lives or work of other people.

**autonomy**
The degree to which the job provides substantial freedom and discretion to the individual in scheduling the work and in determining the procedures to be used in carrying it out.

**feedback**
The degree to which carrying out the work activities required by a job results in the individual obtaining direct and clear information about the effectiveness of his or her performance.

According to the JCM, any job can be described in terms of five core job dimensions, defined as follows:

**Skill variety:** The degree to which the job requires a variety of different activities so the worker can use a number of different skills and talents.

**Task identity:** The degree to which the job requires completion of a whole and identifiable piece of work.

**Task significance:** The degree to which the job has a substantial impact on the lives or work of other people.

**Autonomy:** The degree to which the job provides substantial freedom, independence, and discretion to the individual in scheduling the work and in determining the procedures to be used in carrying it out.

**Feedback:** The degree to which carrying out the work activities required by the job results in the individual obtaining direct and clear information about the effectiveness of his or her performance.

Exhibit 13-1 offers examples of job activities that rate high and low for each characteristic.

---

**Exhibit 13-1
Examples of High and Low Job Characteristics**

**Skill Variety**

| High variety | The owner-operator of a garage who does electrical repair, rebuilds engines, does body work, and interacts with customers |
| Low variety | A body shop worker who sprays paint eight hours a day |

**Task Identity**

| High identity | A cabinet maker who designs a piece of furniture, selects the wood, builds the object, and finishes it to perfection |
| Low identity | A worker in a furniture factory who operates a lathe solely to make table legs |

**Task Significance**

| High significance | Nursing the sick in a hospital intensive care unit |
| Low significance | Sweeping hospital floors |

**Autonomy**

| High autonomy | A telephone installer who schedules his or her own work for the day, makes visits without supervision, and decides on the most effective techniques for a particular installation |
| Low autonomy | A telephone operator who must handle calls as they come according to a routine, highly specified procedure |

**Feedback**

| High feedback | An electronics factory worker who assembles a radio and then tests it to determine if it operates properly |
| Low feedback | An electronics factory worker who assembles a radio and then routes it to a quality control inspector who tests it for proper operation and makes needed adjustments |

Source: Adapted from G. Johns, *Organizational Behavior: Understanding and Managing Life at Work,* 4th ed. Copyright © 1981 by HarperCollins College Publishers. Reprinted by permission of Addison-Wesley Educational Publishers, Inc.

## Exhibit 13-2
## The Job Characteristics Model

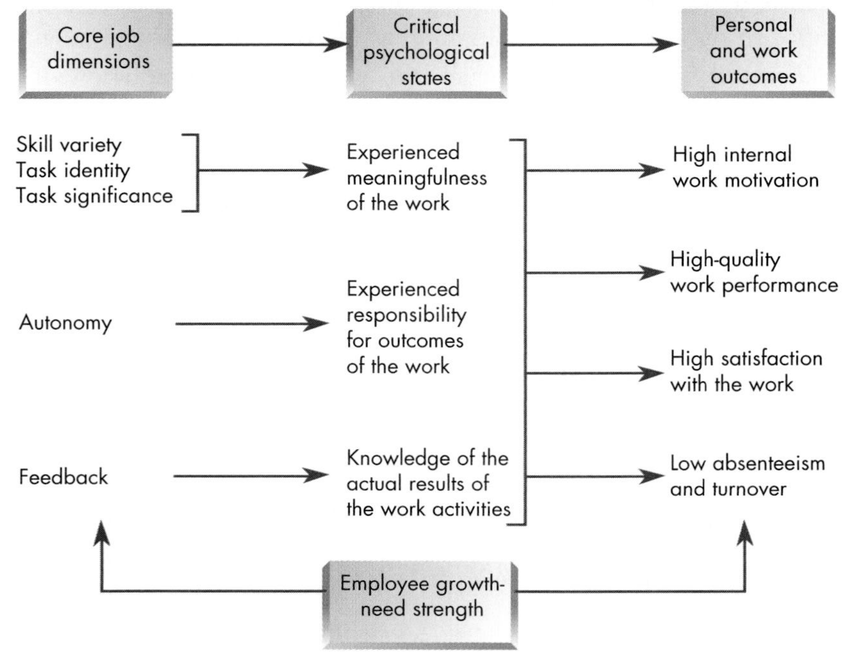

Source: J.R. Hackman, G.R. Oldham, *Work Design* (excerpted from pages 78-80.) © 1980 by Addison-Wesley Publishing Co., Inc. Reprinted by permission of Addison-Wesley Longman Inc.

Exhibit 13-2 presents the job characteristics model. Notice how the first three dimensions — skill variety, task identity, and task significance — combine to create meaningful work. That is, if these three characteristics exist in a job, we can predict that the employee will view the job as being important, valuable, and worthwhile. Notice, too, that jobs that possess autonomy give employees a feeling of personal responsibility for the results and that, if a job provides feedback, employees will know how effectively they are performing. From a motivational perspective, the model says that internal rewards are obtained by individuals when they learn (knowledge of results) that they personally (experienced responsibility) have performed well on a task that they care about (experienced meaningfulness).[4] The more that these three psychological states are present, the greater will be employees' motivation, performance, and satisfaction, and the lower their absenteeism and likelihood of leaving the organization. As Exhibit 13-2 shows, the links between the job dimensions and the outcomes are moderated or adjusted by the strength of the individual's growth need; that is, by the employee's desire for self-esteem and self-actualization. This means that individuals with a high growth need are more likely to experience the critical psychological states when their jobs are enriched than are their counterparts with a low growth need. Moreover, they will respond more positively to the psychological states when they are present than will individuals with a low growth need.

The job characteristics model can be viewed as a model of how to create jobs in the workplace that will motivate employees. The core job dimensions can be combined into a single predictive index, called the **motivating potential score (MPS)**. Its computation is shown in Exhibit 13-3. This chapter's From Concepts to Skills feature on page 553 provides specific guidelines on the kinds of changes that help increase the motivating potential of jobs.

**motivating potential score (MPS)**

A predictive index suggesting the motivation potential in a job.

## Exhibit 13-3
## Computing a Motivating Potential Score

$$\text{Motivating Potential Score (MPS)} = \left[ \frac{\text{Skill variety} + \text{Task identity} + \text{Task significance}}{3} \right] \times \text{Autonomy} \times \text{Feedback}$$

# From CONCEPTS to SKILLS

## Designing Enriched Jobs

How does management enrich an employee's job? The following suggestions, based on the job characteristics model, specify the types of changes in jobs that are most likely to lead to improving their motivating potential.

1. Combine tasks. Managers should seek to take existing and fractionalized tasks and put them back together to form a new and larger module of work. This increases skill variety and task identity.

2. Create natural work units. The creation of natural work units means that the tasks an employee does form an identifiable and meaningful whole. This increases employee "ownership" of the work and improves the likelihood that employees will view their work as meaningful and important rather than as irrelevant and boring.

3. Establish client relationships. The client is the user of the product or service that the employee works on (and may be an "internal customer" as well as someone outside the organization).

Wherever possible, managers should try to establish direct relationships between workers and their clients. This increases skill variety, autonomy, and feedback for the employee.

4. Expand jobs vertically. Vertical expansion gives employees responsibilities and control that were formerly reserved for management. It seeks to partially close the gap between the "doing" and the "controlling" aspects of the job, and it increases employee autonomy.

5. Open feedback channels. By increasing feedback, employees not only learn how well they are performing their jobs, but also whether their performance is improving, deteriorating, or remaining at a constant level. Ideally, this feedback about performance should be received directly as the employee does the job, rather than from management on an occasional basis.

Source: J.R. Hackman, "Work Design," in J.R. Hackman and J.L. Suttle (eds.), *Improving Life at Work* (Santa Monica, CA: Goodyear, 1977), pp. 132-133.

Jobs that are high on motivating potential must be high on at least one of the three factors that lead to experienced meaningfulness, and they must be high on both autonomy and feedback. If jobs score high on motivating potential, the model predicts that motivation, performance, and satisfaction will be positively affected, while the likelihood of absence and turnover will be lessened.

The job characteristics model has been well researched. Most of the evidence supports the general framework of the theory — that is, there is a multiple set of job characteristics and these characteristics impact behavioural outcomes.[5] But there is still considerable debate around the five specific core dimensions in the JCM, the multiplicative properties of the MPS, and the validity of growth-need strength as a moderating variable.

There is some question as to whether task identity adds to the model's predictive ability,[6] and there is evidence suggesting that skill variety may be redundant with autonomy.[7] Furthermore, a number of studies have found that by adding all the variables in the MPS, rather than adding some and multiplying by others, the MPS becomes a better predictor of work outcomes.[8] Finally, the strength of an individual's growth needs as a meaningful moderating variable has been called into question.[9] Other variables, such as the presence or absence of social cues, perceived equity with comparison groups, and propensity to assimilate work experience,[10] may be more valid in moderating the job characteristics-outcome relationship. The first part of the Working With Others Exercise on page 581 provides an opportunity for you to apply the job characteristics model to a chosen job. You will also calculate its motivating potential score.

So where does the discussion of the job characteristics model leave us? Given the current state of evidence, we can make the following statements with relative confidence: (1) People who work on jobs with high core job dimensions are generally more motivated, satisfied, and productive than are those who do not. (2) Job dimensions operate through the psychological states in influencing personal and work outcome variables rather than influencing them directly.[11] A recent survey of college and university students who will graduate in 2001 highlights the underlying theme of the job characteristics model. When the students were asked about what was most important to them as they thought about their careers, their top four answers were (1) having idealistic and committed co-workers (very important to 68 percent of the respondents); (2) doing work that helps others (very important to 65 percent); (3) doing work that requires creativity (very important to 47 percent); and (4) having a lot of responsibility (very important to 39 percent).[12] Salary and prestige ranked lower in importance than these four job characteristics.

## Social Information Processing Model

Have you ever noticed that if you go into a coffee shop or a restaurant some employees seem to love their jobs, while others, doing the same work, seem unhappy? This suggests to us that people don't respond to the objective jobs themselves, but rather as they perceive them. This is the central thesis of the **social information processing (SIP) model.**[13]

**social information processing (SIP) model**
Employees adopt attitudes and behaviours in response to the social cues provided by others with whom they have contact.

While the JCM argues that it is the elements of the job itself that affect an individual's response to a job, the SIP model takes a different approach. The SIP model argues that employees may adopt attitudes and behaviours towards their jobs in response to the social cues provided by others with whom they have contact. These others can be co-workers, managers, friends, family members, or customers. For instance, Gary Ling got a summer job working in a BC sawmill. Since jobs were scarce and this one paid particularly well, Gary arrived on his first day of work highly motivated. Two weeks later, however, his motivation was quite low. What happened was that his co-workers consistently bad-mouthed their jobs. They said that the work was boring, that having to clock in and out proved management didn't trust them, and that supervisors never listened to their opinions. The objective characteristics of Gary's job had not changed in the two-week period; rather, Gary had reconstructed reality based on messages he had received from others.

A number of studies generally confirm the validity of the SIP model.[14] For instance, it has been shown that employee motivation and satisfaction can be manipulated by such subtle actions as a co-worker or manager commenting on the existence or absence of job features such as difficulty, challenge, and autonomy. At the Dartmouth, Nova Scotia, Imperial Oil refinery, a former employee observed that before the Joint Industrial Council (which for decades had governed relations between management and wage earners in Dartmouth's nonunion shop) was disbanded, "You had guys with

[a] high school [education] earning $65 000 a year, who did nothing but complain about being asked to work."[15]

The SIP model tells us that managers should give as much (or more) attention to employees' attitudes about and perceptions of their jobs as to the actual characteristics of those jobs. They might spend more time telling employees how interesting and important their jobs are. And managers should also not be surprised that newly hired employees and people transferred or promoted to a new position are more likely to be receptive to social information than are those with greater seniority.

## Work Redesign Options

Why might a manager want to redesign jobs, and what are some of the options that managers have at their disposal if they want to redesign or change the composition of employees' jobs? Consider the organization at Canada Post's South Central Toronto letter-processing plant. The work is divided into such specific jobs that one employee's entire daily job is to take bag after bag of unopened mail from a conveyor belt, and just place it into a shallow moving bucket. John Wozney, a manager at the plant, notes that under these circumstances, "if a couple of key people call in sick, you're behind the eight ball." The South Central management is currently examining how to redesign both the plant and jobs.[16]

> **When might job redesign be most appropriate?**

Several factors affect the decision to redesign jobs. From a simple human resources perspective, the manager may note that employees seem less motivated, they are absent more, satisfaction is low, and/or turnover is high. These factors suggest that employees are having negative reactions to their jobs. From a strategic level, managers may need to redesign jobs because technology in the industry is changing or head office has requested increased and/or more efficient production by employees. To understand how to address these workplace issues, we begin with the simplest case of job redesign, where the concern is with an individual worker or group of workers. We identify four options for redesign: job rotation, job enlargement, job enrichment, and team-based designs. Later in the chapter we will discuss redesigns that result from technology or productivity improvements. In these cases the jobs of the whole organization are redesigned, incorporating a variety of elements from job rotation, job enlargement, job enrichment, and teams.

### Job Rotation

**job rotation**
The periodic shifting of a worker from one task to another.

You may remember our discussion about job specialization in the previous chapter. If employees suffer from overroutinization of their work because of specialization, one alternative is to use **job rotation** (or what many now call cross-training). When an activity is no longer challenging, the employee is rotated to another job at the same level that has similar skill requirements.[17] This happens, for instance, at McDonald's as a way to make sure that the new employees learn all of the tasks associated with making, packaging, and serving hamburgers and other items.

G.S.I. Transcomm Data Systems Inc. in Pittsburgh uses job rotation to keep its staff of 110 people from becoming bored.[18] Over one two-year period, nearly 20 percent of Transcomm's employees made lateral job switches. Management believes that the job rotation program has been a major contributor to cutting employee turnover from 25 percent to less than seven percent a year. Brazil's Semco SA makes extensive use of job rotation. "Practically no one," says Semco's president, "stays in the same position for more than two or three years. We try to motivate people to move their areas completely from time to time so they don't get stuck to the technical solutions, to ways of doing things in which they have become entrenched."[19]

The strengths of job rotation are that it reduces boredom and increases motivation through diversifying the employee's activities. Of course, it can also have indirect benefits for the organization since employees with a wider range of skills give management more flexibility in scheduling work, adapting to changes, and filling vacancies. On the other hand, job rotation has drawbacks. Training costs are increased, and productivity is reduced by moving a worker into a new position just when his or her efficiency at the prior job was creating organizational economies. Job rotation also creates disruptions. Members of the work group must adjust to the new employee. The manager may also have to spend more time answering questions and monitoring the work of the recently rotated employee. Finally, job rotation can demotivate intelligent and ambitious trainees who seek specific responsibilities in their chosen specialty.

## Job Enlargement

**job enlargement**
The horizontal expansion of jobs.

More than 35 years ago, the idea of expanding jobs horizontally, or what we call **job enlargement**, grew in popularity. Increasing the number and variety of tasks that an individual performed resulted in jobs with more diversity. Instead of only sorting the incoming mail by department, for instance, a mail sorter's job could be enlarged to include delivering the mail to the various departments or running outgoing letters through the postage meter.

Efforts at job enlargement have sometimes met with less than enthusiastic results.[20] As one employee who experienced such a redesign on his job remarked, "Before I had *one* lousy job. Now, through enlargement, I have three!" However, there have been some successful applications of job enlargement. For example, GM Canada's Synchronous Administration through Managerial Excellence (SAME) system ensures that all of the employees in a work unit can perform each of the tasks of any of the individuals in the unit. The system significantly reduces the need for meetings, halves the cost of office equipment, and allows job continuity when workers leave the company or go on holiday.[21] The Candour unit of Montreal-based Bombardier's aerospace group moved to job enlargement to get away from having a large number of highly specialized manufacturing jobs.[22] Serge Perron, vice-president and general manager of operations, notes that the move gave Bombardier more flexibility, with workers installing several types of parts instead of just one, and also led to productivity improvements.

While job enlargement attacks the lack of diversity in overspecialized jobs, it does little to add challenge or meaningfulness to a worker's activities. Job enrichment was introduced to deal with the shortcomings of enlargement.

## Job Enrichment

**job enrichment**
The vertical expansion of jobs.

**Job enrichment**, an application of the JCM, refers to the vertical expansion of jobs. It increases the degree to which the worker controls the planning, execution, and evaluation of his or her work. An enriched job organizes tasks so as to allow the worker to do a complete activity, increases the em-

Control over the production line is not restricted to the non-union environment. At the Honeywell Ltd. plant in Scarborough, Ontario, unionized workers have the authority to shut down the production line to correct production defects. The work team meets to review the schedule and check quality as part of its daily responsibilities. This enriches the workers' jobs over many assembly line jobs.

**First Chicago Corporation**
www.bankone.com

ployee's freedom and independence, increases responsibility, and provides feedback, so an individual will be able to assess and correct his or her own performance.[23] THE JCM gives relatively clear advice concerning how managers can enrich the jobs of employees. You might want to complete the Learning About Yourself Exercise on page 580 to find out your own preferences with respect to job characteristics.

Lawrence Buettner enriched the jobs of employees in his international trade banking department at First Chicago Corporation.[24] His department's chief product is commercial letters of credit — essentially a bank guarantee to stand behind huge import and export transactions. When he took over the department of 300 employees, he found paperwork crawling along a document "assembly line," with errors creeping in at each handoff. And employees did little to hide the boredom they were experiencing in their jobs. Buettner replaced the narrow, specialized tasks that employees were doing with enriched jobs. Each clerk is now a trade expert who can handle a customer from start to finish. After 200 hours of training in finance and law, the clerks became full-service advisers who could turn around documents in a day while advising clients on such arcane matters as bank procedures in Turkey and US munitions' export controls. And the results? Productivity has more than tripled, employee satisfaction has soared, and transaction volume has risen more than 10 percent a year. Additionally, increased skills have translated into higher pay for the employees who are performing the enriched jobs. These trade service representatives, some of whom had come to the bank directly out of high school, now earn from $52 000 to $90 000 a year.

The First Chicago example shouldn't be taken as a blanket endorsement of job enrichment, however. The overall evidence generally shows that job enrichment reduces absenteeism and turnover costs and increases satisfaction, but on the critical issue of productivity, the evidence is inconclusive.[25] In some situations, such as at First Chicago, job enrichment increases productivity; in others, it decreases it. However, even when productivity goes down, there does seem to be consistently more conscientious use of resources and a higher quality of product or service.

### Team-Based Work Designs Revisited

Increasingly, people are doing work in groups and teams. What, if anything, can we say about the design of group-based work to try to improve employee performance in those groups? The best work in this area offers two sets of suggestions.[26]

First, the JCM recommendations seem to be as valid at the group level as they are at the individual level. Managers should expect a group to perform at a high level when (1) the group task requires members to use a variety of relatively high-level skills; (2) the group task is a whole and meaningful piece of work, with a visible outcome; (3) the outcomes of the group's work on the task have significant consequences for other people; (4) the task provides group members with substantial autonomy for deciding how they do the work; and (5) work on the task generates regular, trustworthy feedback about how well the group is performing.

Second, group composition is critical to the success of the work group. Consistent with findings described in Chapter 6, managers should try to ensure that the following four conditions are met: (1) Individual members have the necessary task-relevant expertise to do their work; (2) the group is large enough to perform the work; (3) members possess interpersonal as well as task skills; and (4) membership is moderately diverse in terms of talents and perspectives. In the second part of the Working With Others Exercise on page 581, you can determine different ways to redesign jobs to show how you might increase their motivation potential.

## Technology and New Work Designs

We introduced the term *technology* in the previous chapter's discussion of why structures differ. We said technology was how an organization transfers its inputs into outputs. In recent years, the term has become widely used by economists, managers, consultants, and business analysts to describe machinery and equipment that utilize sophisticated electronics and computers to produce those outputs.

The common theme among new technologies in the workplace is that they substitute machinery for human labour in transforming inputs into outputs. This substitution of capital for labour has been going on essentially nonstop since the Industrial Revolution began in the mid-1800s. But it's been the computerization of equipment and machinery in the last 25 years that has been the prime mover in reshaping the contemporary workplace. Automated teller machines, for example, have replaced tens of thousands of human tellers in banks. Auto-guided vehicles at Pacific Press (publisher of *The Vancouver Sun* and *The Province*) pick up and deliver 1500-kg rolls of newsprint, replacing the fork-lift operators who used to do this task. IBM has built a plant in Austin, Texas, that can produce laptop com-

Exhibit 13-4

THE WALL STREET JOURNAL

"Cool! A keyboard that writes without a printer."

Source: *Wall Street Journal*, October 11, 1995. With permission from Cartoon Features Syndicate.

puters without the help of a single worker. Everything — from the time parts arrive at the IBM plant to the final packing of finished products — is completely automated. And an increasing number of companies, small and large alike, are turning to multimedia and interactive technology for employee training. Exhibit 13-4 gives a humorous perspective on just how extensive some of the technological changes have been during the 20th century.

Below we examine three ways that organizations are redesigning their entire operation (or large parts of it) by using total quality management (TQM) and continuous improvement processes, re-engineering, and flexible manufacturing systems. Each of these processes builds from the original job design methods of job rotation, job enlargement, job enrichment, and work production in teams.

## Continuous Improvement Processes

**total quality management (TQM)**
A philosophy of management that is driven by the constant attainment of customer satisfaction through the continuous improvement of all organizational processes.

**Total quality management (TQM)** is a philosophy of management that's driven by the constant attainment of customer satisfaction through the continuous improvement of all organizational processes.[27] Exhibit 13-5 summarizes the key features of TQM for you. Managers in many organizations, especially in North America, have been criticized for accepting a level of performance that is below perfection. TQM, however, argues that good isn't good enough! To dramatize this point, it's easy to assume that 99.9 percent error-free performance represents the highest standards of excellence. Yet it doesn't look so impressive when you recognize that this standard would result in Canada Post's South Central Toronto letter processing plant losing 6000 pieces of mail per day, or US doctors performing 500 incorrect surgical operations per week, or two plane crashes occurring each day at O'Hare Airport in Chicago![28]

TQM programs seek to achieve continuous process improvements so that variability in the quality of the output is constantly reduced. When you

### Exhibit 13-5
### What Is Total Quality Management

1. *Intense focus on the customer.* The customer includes not only outsiders who buy the organization's products or services but also internal customers (such as shipping or accounts payable staff) who interact with and serve others in the organization.

2. *Concern for continuous improvement.* TQM is a commitment to never being satisfied. "Very good" is not good enough. Quality can always be improved.

3. *Improvement in the quality of everything the organization does.* TQM uses a very broad definition of quality. It relates not only to the final product but also to how the organization handles deliveries, how rapidly it responds to complaints, how politely the phones are answered, and the like.

4. *Accurate measurement.* TQM uses statistical techniques to measure every critical performance variable in the organization's operations. These performance variables are then compared against standards or benchmarks to identify problems, the problems are traced to their roots, and the causes are eliminated.

5. *Empowerment of employees.* TQM involves the people on the line in the improvement process. Teams are widely used in TQM programs as empowerment vehicles for finding and solving problems.

eliminate variations, you increase the uniformity of the product or service. This, in turn, results in lower costs and higher quality. For instance, when Winnipeg-based Reimer Express Lines wanted to improve its delivery rates, it adopted a TQM approach. The movement of freight can be divided into eight major steps, from city pickup through transfer to a highway unit to delivery. Workers at Reimer were led through seminars on each of the eight steps, so that they learned about the entire process, how their jobs fit into the process, and how to do the other steps. At a minimum, the changes at Reimer involved job rotation, in that individuals learned how to perform each step. However, at Reimer, employees did more than just rotate through the tasks. Their jobs were enriched because they had to make decisions about the best way to route things through the freight-movement steps.

Continuous improvement runs counter to the more historical North American management approach of seeing work projects as being linear — with a beginning and an end. For example, Canadian and US managers traditionally viewed cost cutting as a short-term project. They set a goal of cutting costs by 20 percent, achieved it, and then said: "Whew! Our cost cutting is over." The Japanese, on the other hand, have regarded cost control as an ongoing endeavour. The search for continuous improvement creates a race without a finish line. This chapter's Case Incident on page 582 describes how Oakville, Ontario-based Ventra introduced *kaizen* — that is, Japanese techniques of continuous improvements in manufacturing. The quest for never-ending improvement requires a circular rather than a linear approach. This is illustrated in the Plan-Do-Check-Act (PDCA) cycle shown in Exhibit 13-6.[29] Management plans a change, does it, checks the results, and, depending on the outcome, acts to standardize the change or begin the cycle of improvement again with new information. This cycle treats all organizational processes as being in a constant state of improvement.

Toronto-based NRI Industries Inc., which takes tires and waste rubber and turns them into parts for the automotive industry, has been using the PDCA cycle for continuous improvement for several years. The company has achieved an average of zero defective parts per million (ppm) for four of its five largest customers, and its ppm for its fifth-largest customer, Daimler-Chrysler AG, is 28, even though DaimlerChrysler only requires it to be 150. But NRI's good performance does not prevent it from looking for more ways to reduce defects. "What's good enough today in the auto business is not good enough tomorrow," says Greg Bavington, vice-president of operations.[30] NRI recently sent 15 of its middle managers to a training course to help them identify additional areas of improvement in their plant.

Total quality management has been successfully introduced not only in the private sector, but also in the public sector. A commitment to TQM brought the province of New Brunswick a balanced budget in 1994. University of Alberta Hospitals and North York, Ontario's school board also successfully introduced total quality management programs.[31]

Overall, the results of TQM have been mixed. There have been a number of successful implementations, but there have also been notable failures. When accounting for some of the failures of TQM, authors have suggested that sometimes firms were not actually performing TQM, they were just calling it that.[32] Other researchers have suggested that managers had unrealistic expectations of what could be accomplished with TQM, with managers "expecting to do in a year or two what it took some of the leading Japanese companies 30 years to achieve."[33] Other failures occurred because the

**kaizen**
Japanese techniques of continuous improvements in manufacturing.

**Exhibit 13-6
The PDCA Cycle**

programs did not assure employees' job security, did not provide adequate training,[34] or did not appreciate the complexity of changes involved.[35]

A 1997 study looking at successful and unsuccessful implementations of TQM among US suppliers of components to automobile manufacturers found that the managerial attitude toward TQM explained much of the success or lack thereof of TQM initiatives.[36] In particular, managers who viewed TQM as a tool for increasing the firm's business introduced the most widespread and successful implementations of TQM. Managers who introduced TQM because customers requested it, and who focused on the importance of customer needs, initiated less extensive TQM programs. These firms were more likely to introduce TQM in a piecemeal fashion and to seek the publicity that accompanied having a TQM program, rather than being fully committed to TQM as an overall business strategy. Workers in these firms were also less likely to see the value of TQM or to find that it was not introduced as a coherent strategy.

The researchers also identified a group of managers who were reluctant to introduce TQM and therefore only did it under great pressure from customers. These firms had the least successful implementation of TQM. The researchers concluded that those firms that introduced TQM as a tool for expanding the business were more likely to have programs that were quite successful. They noted that the decision to introduce it just to please customers was not necessarily a wise strategic decision, because "if all firms conform to customers' specifications, conformance provides no competitive advantage."[37]

As literally tens of thousands of organizations introduce TQM and continuous process improvement, what does it mean for employees and their jobs? Probably the most significant implication of TQM for employees is that management looks to them as the prime source for improvement ideas. The essence of TQM is process improvement, and employee involvement is the linchpin of process improvement. In other words, TQM requires management to encourage employees to share ideas and act on what they suggest. It means they're no longer able to rest on their previous accomplishments

> **When is TQM most likely to be successfully implemented?**

At Toronto-based NRI Industries Inc., which takes tires and waste rubber and makes parts for the auto industry, workers play with Lego to get a feeling for how continuous process improvement works. The company, which is already a stellar performer for its low rate of defective parts, does not want to rest on its laurels. So it engages in continuous improvement to make sure that it will still be stellar in the years to come.

and successes. Some people are likely to lose their jobs. Therefore, employees may experience increased stress from a work climate that no longer accepts complacency with the status quo. A race with no finish line means a race that's never over, which creates constant tension. While this tension may be positive for the organization (remember functional conflict from Chapter 7), the pressures from an unrelenting search for process improvements can create anxiety and stress in some employees. Therefore it is important for companies that introduce TQM programs to examine the impact of those programs on their employees. In this chapter's HR Implications on page 577, we discuss the performance appraisal implications of TQM.

**TEAMS AND TOTAL QUALITY MANAGEMENT** Teams provide the natural vehicle for employees to share ideas and to implement improvements. As stated by Gil Mosard, a TQM specialist at McDonnell Douglas: "When your measurement system tells you your process is out of control, you need teamwork for structured problem solving. Not everyone needs to know how to do all kinds of fancy control charts for performance tracking, but everybody does need to know where their process stands so they can judge if it is improving."[38]

To understand how teams are being used in TQM programs, let's consider two examples.[39] Montreal-based Cartier Group Ltd., an engineering firm, adopted its TQM program in 1989. Members of project teams are expected to assume full responsibility for quality and to be proactive rather than reactive. Team members seek out the information they need to complete assignments and, when needed, suggest changes.

Ford Motor Co. began its TQM efforts in the early 1980s with teams as the primary organizing mechanism. "Because this business is so complex, you can't make an impact on it without a team approach," noted one Ford manager. In designing its quality problem-solving teams, Ford's management identified five goals. The teams should (1) be small enough to be efficient and effective; (2) be properly trained in the skills their members will need; (3) be allocated enough time to work on the problems they plan to address; (4) be given the authority to resolve the problems and implement corrective action; and (5) each have a designated "champion" whose job it is to help the team get around roadblocks that arise.

Successful TQM requires not just the formation of teams, but also training and development to help team members learn how to work together. Successful Canadian implementation of TQM has been achieved at Pratt and Whitney, AMP, Steelcase, and Cargill, all of which provide teams with clear goals and recognition for achieving those goals. Pratt and Whitney, for instance, uses a portion of savings resulting from improvements to reward team, rather than individual, efforts.[40] In this team based approach, individuals often share parts of their jobs. For an interesting discussion about whether jobs are becoming obsolete, see this chapter's Point/CounterPoint discussion on pages 564-565.

## Re-engineering Work Processes

**re-engineering**
Reconsiders how work would be done and the organization structured if they were being created from scratch.

In times of rapid and dramatic change, it's sometimes necessary to approach improving quality and productivity from the perspective of "How would we do things around here if we were starting over from scratch?" That, in essence, is the approach of **re-engineering**. It asks managers to reconsider how work would be done and their organization structured if they were

Top management at Union Carbide's industrial chemicals division led the drive to re-engineer work processes in plant and equipment maintenance, which accounted for 30 percent of costs. Directed to work in teams and to set ambitious cost-cutting goals, employees (shown here) worked out the details of their new work process by developing new repair and maintenance procedures. The re-engineering effort saved Union Carbide $38 million, 50 percent more than management's target. Companywide, Union Carbide has used re-engineering to cut $560 million out of fixed costs over a recent three-year period.

**Union Carbide**
www.unioncarbide.com

starting over.[41] To illustrate the concept of re-engineering, consider a manufacturer of roller skates. The product is essentially a leather boot with shoelaces, attached to a steel platform that holds four wooden wheels. If our manufacturer took a continuous improvement approach to change, he or she would look for small incremental improvements to be introduced to the product. For instance, he or she might consider adding hooks to the upper part of the boot for speed lacing; or changing the weight of leather used for improved comfort; or using different ballbearings to make the wheels spin more smoothly. In-line skates represent a re-engineering approach to roller skates. The goal was to develop a skating device that could improve skating speed, mobility, and control. In-line skates fulfilled those goals in a completely different type of shoe. The upper was made of injected plastic, which was made popular in skiing. Laces were replaced by easy-close clamps. And the four wooden wheels, set in pairs of two, were replaced by four to six in-line plastic wheels. The re-engineered result, which didn't look much like the traditional roller skate, proved universally superior. The rest, of course, is history. In-line skates have revolutionized the roller-skate business.

The term re-engineering comes from the historical process of taking apart an electronics product and designing a better version. Michael Hammer coined the term for organizations. When he found that companies were using computers simply to automate outdated processes, rather than finding fundamentally better ways of doing things, he realized the same re-engineering principles could be applied to business. So, as applied to organizations, re-engineering means management should start with a clean slate — rethinking and redesigning those processes by which the organization creates value and does work, ridding itself of operations that have become antiquated in the computer age.[42]

**KEY ELEMENTS OF RE-ENGINEERING** Three key elements of re-engineering are identifying an organization's distinctive competencies, assessing core processes, and reorganizing horizontally by process.

**POINT**

# The Notion of Jobs Is Becoming Obsolete

Prior to 1800, very few people had a job. People worked hard raising food or making things at home. They had no regular hours, no job descriptions, no bosses, and no employee benefits. Instead, they put in long hours on shifting clusters of tasks, in a variety of locations, on a schedule set by the sun and the weather and the needs of the day. It was the Industrial Revolution and the creation of large manufacturing companies that brought about the concept of what we have come to think of as jobs. But the conditions that created "the job" are disappearing. Customized production is pushing out mass production; most workers now handle information, not physical products; and competitive conditions are demanding rapid response to changing markets. Although economists and social analysts continue to talk about the disappearance of jobs in certain countries or industries, they're missing a more relevant point: What's actually disappearing is the job itself.

In a fast-moving economy, jobs are rigid solutions to an elastic problem. We can rewrite a person's job description occasionally, but not every week. When the work that needs doing changes constantly — which increasingly describes today's world — organizations can't afford the inflexibility that traditional jobs bring.

In the near future, very few people will have jobs as we have come to know them. In place of jobs, there will be part-time and temporary work situations. Organizations will be transformed from a structure built out of jobs into a field of work needing to be done. These organizations will be essentially made up of "hired guns" — contingent employees (temporaries, part-timers, consultants, and contract workers) who join project teams created to complete a specific task. When that task is finished, the team disbands. People will work on more than one team at a time, keeping irregular hours, and maybe never meeting their co-workers face to face. Computers, pagers, cellular phones, modems, and the like will allow people to work for multiple employers, at the same time, in locations throughout the world. Few of these employees will be working nine to five at specific work spots, and they'll have little of the security that their grandfathers had, who worked for IBM Canada, MacMillan Bloedel, General Motors, Sears, Bank of Montreal, or similar large bureaucracies. In place of security and predictability, they'll have flexibility and autonomy. They'll be able to put together their own place-time combinations to support their diverse work, family, lifestyle, and financial needs.

---

Source: This argument is based on W. Bridges, *JobShift* (Reading, MA: Addison-Wesley, 1994).

# Jobs Are the Essence of Organizational Life

The central core to any discussion of work or organizational behaviour is the concept of a job. It is the aggregation of tasks that defines an individual's duties and responsibilities.

When an organization is created, managers have to determine what tasks need to be accomplished for the organization to achieve its goals and who will perform those tasks. These decisions precede the hiring of a workforce. Remember, it's the tasks that determine the need for people, not the other way around. Job analysis is the formal process managers use to define the jobs within the organization and the behaviours that are necessary to perform those jobs. For instance, what are the duties of a purchasing specialist, grade 3, who works for International Paper? What minimal knowledge, skills, and abilities are necessary for adequate performance of a grade 3 purchasing specialist's job? How do the requirements for a purchasing specialist, grade 3, compare with those for a purchasing specialist, grade 2, or a purchasing analyst? These are questions that job analysis can answer.

Can you conceive of an organization without jobs? No more than you can conceive of a car without an engine. There are no doubt changes taking place in organizations that are requiring managers to redefine what a job is. For instance, today's jobs often include extensive customer interaction as well as team respon-

sibilities. In many cases, organizations are having to make job descriptions more flexible to reflect the more dynamic nature of work today. Because it's inefficient to rewrite job descriptions on a weekly basis, managers are rethinking what makes up a job and defining jobs in more fluid terms. But the concept of jobs continues to be at the core of any work design effort and a fundamental cornerstone to understanding formal work behaviour in organizations.[1]

For those who believe that the concept of jobs is on the wane, all they need to do is look to the trade union movement and its determination to maintain clear job delineations. Labour unions have a vested interest in the status quo and will fight hard to protect the security and predictability that traditional jobs provide. Moreover, if it looked like the jobless society was to become a widespread reality, politicians would be under strong pressure to create legislation to outlaw it. A world of part-time and temporary employment is a threat to the stability of our society. Working people want stability and predictability, and they will look to their elected representatives to protect that. Those politicians who ignore this desire face the wrath of the electorate.

Source:

[1] See J. Mays, "Why We Haven't Seen 'the End of Jobs' or the End of Pay Surveys," *Compensation & Benefits Review*, July-August 1997, pp. 25-29.

**distinctive competencies**
Defines what an organization delivers better than its competition.

An organization's **distinctive competencies** define what that organization delivers better than its competition. Examples might include superior store locations, a more efficient distribution system, higher-quality products, more knowledgeable salespeople, or superior technical support. Dell Computer, for instance, differentiates itself from its competitors by emphasizing high-quality hardware, comprehensive service and technical support, and low prices. Why is identifying distinctive competencies so important? Because it guides decisions regarding which activities are crucial to the organization's success.

Management also needs to assess the core processes that clearly add value to the organization's distinctive competencies. These are the processes that transform materials, capital, information, and labour into products and services that the customer values. When the organization is viewed as a series of processes, ranging from strategic planning to after-sales customer support, management can determine to what degree each adds value. Not surprisingly, this **process value analysis** typically uncovers many activities that add little or nothing of value and whose only justification is "we've always done it this way."

**process value analysis**
Determination to what degree each organizational process adds value to the organization's distinctive competencies.

Re-engineering requires management to reorganize around horizontal processes. This means cross-functional and self-managed teams. It means focusing on processes rather than functions. So, for instance, the vice-president of marketing might become the "process owner of finding and keeping customers."[43] And it also means eliminating levels of middle management. As Hammer pointed out, "Managers are not value-added. A customer never buys a product because of the calibre of management. Management is, by definition, indirect. So if possible, less is better. One of the goals of re-engineering is to minimize the necessary amount of management."[44]

The story of Imperial Oil's Dartmouth, Nova Scotia, refinery illustrates how successful process re-engineering can be. In July 1991, Dartmouth refinery manager Ken Ball received a report card showing that his refinery placed in the bottom quartile of 116 other North American refineries. With that news, Ball knew that the refinery was in danger of being closed. In an effort to prevent his refinery from being sold or closed, in January 1992 Ball presented his plan to turn things around at Dartmouth to head office in Toronto. On February 4, 1992, Imperial Oil gave him until year-end to go from among the worst-performing refineries to among the best.

Ball had less than a year to turn things around, and faced a workforce "where people were interested more in their job descriptions than the refinery's margin on a barrel of crude. A culture in which a mechanic who found a way to help an electrician would have to convince up to four supervisors the idea was worthwhile."[45]

Ball faced a difficult task, one made easier only because the employees realized that remaining with the status quo would certainly mean plant closure. Facing that, the employees adopted Ball's unilateral moves to improve processes. Almost immediately, Ball disbanded the Joint Industrial Council (JIC) that had governed employee-management relations for years, eliminated seniority rights, emphasized individual performance, and instituted a team approach to work. Each of the four main work teams, composed of 40 to 50 workers per team, now took responsibility for an entire chunk of the plant's operation. By early 1993, costs had fallen 30 percent in the plant, and most believed the refinery would remain open. In fact, in February 1998, Dartmouth was still operating, with about 240 employees, the same number as in 1993.

**RE-ENGINEERING VS. TQM** Is re-engineering just another term for TQM? No! They do have some common characteristics, though.[46] They both, for instance, emphasize processes and satisfying the customer. After that, they diverge radically. This is evident in their goals and the means they use for achieving their goals.

TQM seeks incremental improvements, while re-engineering looks for quantum leaps in performance. That is, the former is essentially about improving something that is basically okay; the latter is about taking something that is irrelevant, discarding it, and starting over. And the means that the two approaches use are totally different. TQM relies on bottom-up, participative decision making in both the planning of a TQM program and its execution. Re-engineering, on the other hand, is initially driven by top management. When re-engineering is complete, the workplace is largely self-managed. But getting there is a very autocratic, nondemocratic process. Re-engineering's supporters argue that it must be this way because the level of change that the process demands is highly threatening to people and they aren't likely to accept it voluntarily. When top management commits to re-engineering, employees have no choice. As Hammer is fond of saying, "You either get on the train, or we'll run over you with the train."[47] Of course, autocratically imposed change is likely to face employee resistance. While there is no easy solution to the resistance that top-down change creates, some of the techniques presented in Chapter 14 in our discussion of overcoming resistance to change can be helpful. A study of Canadian companies suggests that the most significant factor leading to a positive re-engineering experience is top management support (78%), followed by keeping lines of communication open (44%), a strong project management team (41%), and appropriate leadership (41%).[48]

**DOES RE-ENGINEERING WORK?** University of Waterloo professor Howard Armitage and his graduate student Neil Chandler studied 324 Canadian organizations with 1995 net sales over $100 million and found that Canadian companies reported higher success rates of completed projects than those reported by American firms. Ninety-four percent of Canadian firms were at least moderately successful, compared with Ernst & Young's survey of US companies, which reported a success rate of only 54 percent.[49] However, in terms of measurable success, the Canadian findings raise some interesting questions. Of the companies that had completed a project, 32 percent experienced increased competitive advantage, 17 percent experienced increased profits, and 18 percent experienced an increase in the quality of their products and/or services. The value of a company's stock increased for only four percent of the respondents.[50] Based on this Canadian study, the re-engineering efforts do not appear to improve shareholder value. And there have been some notable failures in re-engineering. In 1995, after several years and an investment of several million dollars, SaskTel wound down its re-engineering project due to widespread negative reactions from management and employees alike. Almost half of the 20 employees involved in the re-engineering team ended up on stress leave.[51]

**IMPLICATIONS FOR EMPLOYEES** Re-engineering is rapidly gaining momentum in business and industry.[52] A 1995 survey by Ernst & Young and *CFO Magazine* conducted among top financial officers at 80 major North American corporations, including eight from Canada, found that 50 percent of respondents were conducting re-engineering projects and 88 percent had them in the works.[53]

**Petro-Canada**
www.petro-canada.ca

**Volkswagen**
www.vw.com

**Amex Canada**
home3.americanexpress.com/ca
nada/index.html

**Crayola**
www.crayola.com

Some of the companies that have implemented re-engineering in at least some of their divisions include Petro-Canada, Abitibi-Price, Canadian Tire, Sears, Volkswagen Canada, Amex Canada, Banca di America e di Italia, Siemens, and KPMG Peat Marwick. Re-engineering's popularity isn't surprising. In today's highly competitive global marketplace, companies are finding that they're forced to re-engineer their work processes if they're going to survive. And employees will "have to get on the train."

Many people will lose their jobs as a direct result of re-engineering efforts. Just how many depends on the pace at which organizations adopt the new techniques. Staff support jobs, especially those of middle managers, will be most vulnerable. So, too, will clerical jobs in service industries. For instance, one knowledgeable observer predicted that re-engineering would reduce employment in commercial banks and thrift institutions by 30 to 40 percent during the 1990s.[54]

In 1992, after Binney & Smith Canada's Lindsay, Ontario-based Crayola Crayon factory re-engineered its production process and trained its employees to work in teams, it faced a string of successes. The plant received its first-ever crayon order for the American market. The improvements had allowed the Lindsay plant to double its productions in just several months, and it met the American order on time and with perfect quality. The plant won the contract to produce a fabric paint product for the Sears Wish Book. By 1994, it was producing UPC/Item/Article number stickers for Costco and Price Club's membership customers. All these success stories were linked to the re-engineering of the Lindsay plant. Then, in February 1997, Binney & Smith announced that it was moving Lindsay's crayon, paint, and modelling-compound operations to Easton, Pennsylvania. This resulted in a loss of almost 50 jobs at the Lindsay plant, although the marker, activity kit, and plastic moulding operations for the Canadian market were to remain at Lindsay.[55] However, just one month later, Binney & Smith Canada launched a new product, Crayola IQ, a new line of crayons, pencils, and markers for the tween market (eight- to 12-year-olds). This line was so successful that the company's US parent brought out its own tween product line in 1998.[56] Once again, Binney & Smith Canada had turned itself around, in part due to its overall re-engineering efforts.

Employees who keep their jobs after re-engineering will find that the jobs are no longer the same. These new jobs will typically require a wider range of skills, include more interaction with customers and suppliers, offer greater challenge, contain increased responsibilities, and provide higher pay. However, the three- to five-year period involved in implementing re-engineering is usually tough on employees. They suffer from uncertainty and anxiety associated with taking on new tasks and having to discard long-established work practices and formal social networks.

## Flexible Manufacturing Systems

When customers were willing to accept standardized products, fixed assembly lines made sense. But nowadays, flexible technologies are increasingly necessary to compete effectively.

**flexible manufacturing system** Integration of computer-aided design, engineering, and manufacturing to produce low-volume products at mass-production costs.

The unique characteristic of **flexible manufacturing systems** is that by integrating computer-aided design, engineering, and manufacturing, they can produce low-volume products for customers at a cost comparable to what had been previously possible only through mass production. Flexible manufacturing systems are, in effect, repealing the laws of economies of scale.

A flexible manufacturing system at IBM's plant in Charlotte, North Carolina, can produce 27 different computer products at the same time. The automated assembly lines are controlled by computer instructions that vary based on diverse customer needs. The computers also give employees assembly instructions. This flexible system brings efficiency to IBM's manufacturing process and helps the company deliver products to customers more quickly than competitors.

**Pratt & Whitney Canada**
www.pwc.ca

Management no longer must mass-produce thousands of identical products to achieve low per-unit production costs. With flexible manufacturing, when management wants to produce a new part, it doesn't change machines — it just changes the computer program.

Some automated plants can build a wide variety of flawless products and switch from one product to another on cue from a central computer. Pratt & Whitney Canada Inc.'s Halifax facility, for instance, produces 1600 engines a year across 127 models without plant shutdowns for retooling. Before the onset of flexible manufacturing, it was producing 3000 engines a year but only 20 different models. While the automated technology of the Halifax facility attracts a lot of attention, plant manager Peter Wressel believes the true key to the plant's success lies in its motivated workforce. There are only six managers, including Wressell, for close to 450 workers. Employees work in teams and are involved in all aspects of plant administration including pay, benefits, job rotation, and community relations. They have even established a work schedule of five days on and five days off.[57] Similarly, National Bicycle Industrial Co., which sells its bikes under the Panasonic brand, uses flexible manufacturing to produce any of 11 231 862 variations on 18 models of racing, road, and mountain bikes in 199 colour patterns and an almost unlimited number of sizes. This allows Panasonic to provide almost customized bikes at mass-produced prices.[58]

What do flexible manufacturing systems mean for the people who work within them? They require a different breed of industrial employee.[59] At Halifax's Pratt & Whitney operation, employees are hired for their high-tech skills, initiative, and ability to thrive in a self-managing environment. In addition to greater skills, workers in flexible manufacturing plants also need more training. This is because there are fewer employees, so each must be able to do a greater variety of tasks. In addition to higher skills, employees in flexible plants are typically organized into teams and given considerable decision-making discretion. Consistent with the objective of high flexibility, these plants tend to have organic structures. They decentralize authority into the hands of the operating teams.

## Job Redesign in the Canadian Context: The Role of Unions

But don't unions just get in the way?

**Communications, Energy and Paperworkers Union of Canada**
www.cep.ca

Until recently, labour unions have been largely resistant to participating in discussions with management over job-design issues. As noted above, these redesigns often result in loss of jobs, and labour unions try to protect workers' jobs. Union head offices, however, can sometimes be at odds with their membership on the acceptance of job redesign. Some members value the opportunity for skill development and more interesting work. During the 1990s, at least some of the larger unions became more open to discussions about job redesign. This was reflected, for instance, in the position taken by the Communications, Energy and Paperworkers Union of Canada (CEP).[60] The CEP asserts that unions should be involved in the decisions and share in the benefits of work redesign. It calls for negotiated workplace changes, with greater union input into the conception, development, and implementation of work reorganization initiatives. The union also believes that basic wages, negotiated through a collective agreement, must remain the primary form of compensation, although they are open to other forms of compensation as long as they do not detract from basic wages determined through collective bargaining. While managers may regard job redesign as more difficult under a collective agreement, the reality is that for change to be effective in the workplace, management must gain employees' acceptance of the plan whether or not they are unionized.

As a case in point, in 1990 Lac-Megantic, Quebec-based Bestar Inc., a furniture maker, joined with its union, the National Brotherhood of Carpenters, Joiners, Foresters and Industrial Workers, to try to save the plant from serious financial difficulties.[61] Bestar wanted to introduce some quality programs, and it required convincing both management and union members that it was in everyone's best interest to work together. Not all of the managers supported employee participation, however. Sylvain Roy, then-president of the union at Bestar, recalled that "the least adaptable managers, who did not want to accept worker involvement, either left the company of their own accord or were let go." This signalled to both management and union members that everyone needed to work together on quality initiatives. Roy also noted that once the workers were encouraged to become more involved, they were "more conscious of losses and mistakes" and realized that their job survival depended on focusing on quality. The Lac-Megantic plant has continued to thrive. In December 1997, it announced a three-year, $10-million expansion at the plant. And in April 1998, it announced record profits and sales for the first quarter of 1998. The company continues to thrive.

Although there are union-management success stories in gaining changes in the workplace, there have been a number of difficulties as well. The Case Incident in Chapter 9 highlights evidence of the difficulties that Canada Post and the Canadian Union of Postal Workers (CUPW) have had in working together for workplace change. While CUPW has resisted most attempts at change, the Bestar example indicates that management can also be resistant to change.

**Canadian Union of Postal Workers (CUPW)**
www.cupw-sttp.org

## Flexible Work Arrangements

Historically, most people worked an eight-hour day, five days a week. They started at a fixed time and left at a fixed time. However, a recent survey of work arrangements found that only 39 percent of employed Canadians have "normal" schedules in which they work Monday to Friday at regular starting times.[62] A number of organizations have introduced flexible work schedule options, including job sharing, telecommuting, compressed workweeks, and flextime as a way to improve employee motivation, productivity, and satisfaction. About 24 percent of employees have some sort of flexible work arrangements.

These arrangements also help employees ease the stress of juggling family needs alongside work demands. Gay Bank, vice-president of human resources at Royal Bank of Canada, notes that "it is estimated that as many as three in four working Canadians have responsibility for caring for children or aging parents."[63]

A 1998 survey of Royal Bank and Royal Trust employees shows strong support for flextime arrangements:[64]

- 94 percent of flex workers are very satisfied with their work arrangements.

- 70 percent of flex workers reported less stress.

- 81 percent of flex workers said they were more effective at balancing work and their outside lives.

- 63 percent of managers would highly recommend flex work arrangements. (This is notable because a similar survey conducted in 1994 found that only 34 percent of managers would have highly recommended flex work at that time).

- 37 percent of managers reported that flex work led to an increase in employee efficiency.

- 48 percent of employees use flex work to deal with family responsibilities and child care and/or eldercare.

- 36 percent of employees said they would leave the company if flex work were not available.

- 78 percent of employees on flexwork said their opportunities for advancement were the same or better than when they worked a traditional schedule.

Do employees really like flexible arrangements?

## Compressed Workweek

**compressed workweek**
A four-day week, with employees working 10 hours a day.

There are two common forms of **compressed workweek**: the four 10-hour days per week plan (known as the 4-40 program) and the nine days over two weeks plan, where workers get either a Friday or Monday off once every two weeks in exchange for working slightly longer hours the other days. These compressed workweek programs were conceived to allow workers more leisure time and shopping time, and to permit them to travel to and from work outside of rush hour. Supporters suggest that such a program can increase employee enthusiasm, morale, and commitment to the organization; increase productivity and reduce costs; reduce machine downtime in manufacturing; reduce overtime, turnover, and absenteeism; and make it easier for the organization to recruit employees.

These programs can also have a positive impact on the environment, with fewer cars involved in rush-hour gridlock, as well as providing additional support for managing work and family conflicts. For instance, Burnaby-based BCTel (now Telus) pilot-tested compressed workweeks in 1998 as a way to provide service and remain competitive without increasing staff or overtime.

**Amoco**
www.bpamoco.com

**BC Hydro**
eww.bchydro.bc.ca

**Canada Customs and Revenue Agency**
www.ccra-adrc.gc.ca

**Coca-Cola**
www.cocacola.com

Calgary-based Amoco offered compressed workweeks to all employees in head office two years ago, with the result that 85 percent take off every second Friday and work slightly longer hours on the other days. Other Canadian companies that offer flexible workweeks include BC Hydro, Air Canada, Revenue Canada, Hewlett-Packard, IBM, Xerox, Johnson and Johnson, and Coca-Cola. Companies vary in their way of determining an appropriate flexible workweek schedule, however. For instance, while Royal Bank also has a compressed workweek, because of concerns about possible reduced customer service, very few employees are offered a four-day week as an option.

Proponents argue that the compressed workweek may positively affect productivity in situations in which the work process requires significant start-up and shutdown periods.[65] When start-up and shutdown times are a major factor, productivity standards take these periods into consideration in determining the time required to generate a given output. Consequently, in such cases, the compressed workweek will increase productivity even though worker performance is not affected, simply because the improved work scheduling reduces nonproductive time. Not all employers agree that a compressed week is beneficial to performance, however.

The evidence on the impact of compressed workweek schedules on employees is generally positive.[66] In one study, for instance, when employees were asked whether they wanted to continue their 4-40 program, which had been in place for six months, or go back to a traditional five-day week, 78 percent wanted to keep the compressed workweek.[67] However, some employees complain of fatigue near the end of the day, and about the difficulty of coordinating their jobs with their personal lives — the latter posing a problem especially for working mothers. A 1996 Statistics Canada study reported more stress for women working a compressed week than those working a traditional week (30 percent compared to 21 percent).[68] However, these findings may not indicate that the compressed workweek itself causes stress. Rather, those who opt to take the compressed workweek option are more likely to be doing so to balance out work and family conflicts, and thus these employees have more stress in their lives in general.

## Flextime

**flextime**
Employees work during a common core time period each day but have discretion in forming their total workday from a flexible set of hours outside the core.

**Flextime** is short for flexible work hours. It allows employees some discretion over when they arrive at and leave work. Employees must work a specific number of hours a week, but they are free to vary the hours of work within certain limits. As shown in Exhibit 13-7, each day consists of a common core, usually six hours, with a flexibility band surrounding the core. For example, exclusive of a one-hour lunch break, the core may be 9 a.m. to 3 p.m., with the office actually opening at 6 a.m. and closing at 6 p.m. All employees are required to be at their jobs during the common core period, but they are allowed to accumulate their other two hours before and/or after the core time. Some flextime programs allow extra hours to be accumulated and turned into a free day off each month.

**Exhibit 13-7
Example of a Flextime Schedule**

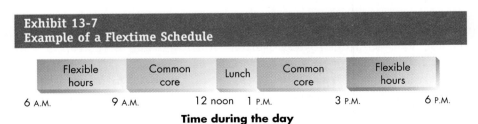

**CCH Canadian Ltd.**
www.ca.cch.com

Flextime has become an extremely popular scheduling option, although in Canada women are less likely than men to have flexible work schedules. About 30 percent of women have flexible work schedules, compared with 40 percent of men.[69] This compares with nearly 28 percent of the US full-time workforce who have flexibility in their daily arrival and departure times.[70] But flextime isn't available to all employees equally. More managers (42.4 percent) enjoy the freedom of flextime than do manufacturing workers (23.3 percent).[71] Levi Strauss & Co. Canada, Bank of Montreal, and Toronto-based legal publishers CCH Canadian Ltd. are examples of companies that offer flextime to their workers.

Most of the performance evidence stacks up favourably. Flextime tends to reduce absenteeism and frequently improves worker productivity and satisfaction,[72] probably for several reasons. Employees can schedule their work hours to align with personal demands, thus reducing tardiness and absences, and employees can adjust their work activities to those hours in which they are individually more productive. Other research on the impact of flextime on the Canadian workplace has found that employees have positive attitudes and view it as their most preferred option;[73] managers were favourable;[74] and women with flextime suffered less stress.[75]

Flextime's major drawback is that it's not applicable to every job. It works well with clerical tasks where an employee's interaction with people outside his or her department is limited. It is not a viable option for receptionists, salespeople in retail stores, or similar jobs where comprehensive service demands that people be at their workstations at predetermined times.

## Job Sharing

**job sharing**
The practice of having two or more people split a 40-hour-a-week job.

A recent work scheduling innovation is **job sharing**. It allows two or more individuals to split a traditional 40-hour-a-week job. So, for example, one person might perform the job from 8 a.m. to noon, while another performs the same job from 1 p.m. to 5 p.m.; or the two could work full, but alternate, days. In 1995, about eight percent of all part-time paid workers in Canada shared a job with someone.[76] About 48 percent of larger Canadian organizations offer this option.[77]

The Royal Bank is one organization that offers job sharing.[78] Kim Beitel handles loans and mortgages in a downtown Regina branch of the bank. She shares her job with another employee. Each employee works one week on, one week off. The two leave notes for each other about the status of loan applications so that each will know what has happened during the week off. Neither employee knew the other when the two started the job sharing, but Beitel reports that the arrangement is working well. Calgary-based Phillips Petroleum Resources and Gulf Canada Resources also offer job-sharing arrangements for some of their employees.

Job sharing allows the organization to draw upon the talents of more than one individual in a given job. A bank manager who oversees two job sharers describes it as an opportunity to get two heads, but "pay for one."[79] It also opens up the opportunity to acquire skilled workers — for instance, women with young children, retirees, and others desiring flexibility — who might not be available on a full-time basis.[80] Consequently, it can increase motivation and satisfaction for those for whom a 40-hour-a-week job is just not practical. The major difficulty of job sharing is finding compatible pairs of employees who can successfully coordinate the intricacies of one job.[81]

## Telecommuting

**telecommuting**
Employees do their work at
home on a computer that is
linked to their office.

It might be close to the ideal job for many people. No commuting, flexible hours, freedom to dress as you please, and little or no interruptions from colleagues. It's called **telecommuting** and refers to employees who do their work at home at least two days a week on a computer that is linked to their office.[82] (A closely related term—*the virtual office*—is increasingly being used to describe employees who work out of their home on a relatively permanent basis).

Telecommuting is on the rise in Canada. In 1988-1989, 11 percent of organizations surveyed indicated they offered a work-at-home or telecommuting arrangement with employees. At the end of 1995, that number had increased to 28 percent of companies reporting work-at-home or telecommuting arrangements with employees.[83] Statistics Canada projects that by 2001, 1.5 million Canadians will be telecommuting.[84] The US Department of Transportation predicts that the number of US telecommuters may reach 15 million, representing over 10 percent of the workforce, by 2002.[85] The concept is also catching on worldwide, although more slowly. In Great Britain and France, there are currently 563 000 and 215 000 telecommuters, respectively.[86]

Brampton, Ontario-based Northern Telecom (Nortel) operates one of the biggest telecommuting programs in Canada.[87] Nearly 30 percent of its workforce telecommutes to some extent. Some employees, including 60 percent of those in the Ottawa office who telecommute, do so part-time, maintaining offices both at home and work. The rest work entirely from home, showing up at the office occasionally for mail. About two-thirds of the telecommuters are male, mostly thirty-somethings. Nortel sets up home offices with regulation office furniture and equipment, makes sure there is a secure computer line connecting the home to the office, and requires telecommuters to attend some meetings and lunches in the office, so that employees can maintain contact. Nortel's telecommuters reported in a recent survey that they were "overwhelmingly happier, less stressed out and more productive than when they used to come to the office."

The Bank of Canada introduced a pilot project for telecommuting in 1997, and by the end of 1999 telecommuting had become part of the bank's corporate culture. IBM Canada initiated a telecommuting program in the early 1990s and currently about 2500 of its employees are involved in the program.[88] Telecommuters do not always work from home, however. In one BCTel (now Telus) program, for example, workers avoid up to three hours a day commuting to and from downtown Vancouver by reporting for work at a specially established satellite office in suburban Langley, nearer to their homes. Telecommuting does, however, typically mean that employees are remote from their managers.

BCTel's arrangement shows that telecommuting employees can be more productive than they had previously been because of the reduced commute and fewer disruptions. [89]

In order to telecommute, firms have to make appropriate arrangements to facilitate working away from the office. At North Vancouver, BC-based law firm Ratcliff & Co., one lawyer occasionally works from Bowen Island, while two others work from Vancouver Island. When they need documents typed, they e-mail their dictated audio files to their support staff.[90]

Telecommuting is not just for staff, either. Liz Codling, a senior manager at Bank of Montreal in Toronto, manages her staff from the United Kingdom.[91] After running the bank's staff education centre for four years and overseeing a team of eight people, she decided to return home to the United Kingdom with her husband. But Codling's bosses didn't want to lose her, so she became the bank's first transatlantic telecommuter. Although separated from her staff by five time zones and more than 4828 kilometres, she is able to manage her team by relying on communication technology—phone, fax, computer, modem, e-mail, voice mail, videoconferencing, and the Internet. Some adjustments were needed. For instance, Codling has had to adjust her workday to align with Toronto hours, and her colleagues have had to learn to schedule meetings in the mornings so she can be included. But after more than two years, this long-distance telecommute seems to be a success.

What kinds of jobs lend themselves to telecommuting? Three categories have been identified as most appropriate: routine information-handling tasks, mobile activities, and professional and other knowledge-related tasks.[92] Writers, attorneys, analysts, and employees who spend the majority of their time on computers or the telephone are natural candidates for telecommuting. For instance, telemarketers, customer-service representatives, reservation agents, and product-support specialists spend most of their time on the phone. As telecommuters, they can access information on their computer screens at home as easily as on the company screen in any office.

A recent Ekos Research study found that 55 percent of Canadians want to telecommute, and 43 percent would leave their current jobs if offered one where telecommuting were a possibility. Thirty-three percent of those surveyed said they would choose the opportunity to telecommute rather than a 10 percent raise. Other researchers looking at teleworking in Canada have found that it results in increased productivity,[93] decreased stress,[94] and better customer service to customers and clients.[95] Telecommuting has been found to reduce turnover[96] and decrease absenteeism.[97]

Not all employees embrace the idea of telecommuting, however. Some workers complain that they miss out on important meetings and informal interactions that lead to new policies and ideas. They also miss the social contacts that occur at work. Teleworking can decrease commitment to the organization,[98] and increase feelings of isolation[99] and burnout.[100] Telecommuters may be less likely to function as team players as well.[101]

The long-term future of telecommuting depends on some questions for which we don't yet have definitive answers. For instance, will employees who do their work at home be at a disadvantage in office politics? Might they be less likely to be considered for salary increases and promotions? Is being out of sight equivalent to being out of mind? Will nonwork-related distractions, such as children, neighbours, and the close proximity of the television and refrigerator, significantly reduce productivity for those without superior willpower and discipline? We also do not know the effects on individuals working in somewhat isolated circumstances day after day, if they do most of their work away from the office. Experts agree that home telecommuters in particular should come into the central office at least once a week. As Ernie Gauvreau, law firm Ratcliff & Co.'s chief operating officer, explains, it is unlikely that Ratcliff's lawyers will work from home every day. "We need to bounce ideas off each other. And if you're at home, that doesn't exist."[102]

> **If I wanted to telecommute, what kind of job should I consider?**

## Hotelling

One of the latest trends in reducing office space is **hotelling**, where no one "owns" a workspace anymore. Instead, desks, offices, and conference rooms are booked for the time required.[103] At the main Toronto office of Deloitte & Touche Canada, the 1600 employees lost their permanent workspaces in June 1999. People now sit in different places each day, and portable filing cabinets and phones are provided. Deloitte predicts an annual saving of $6 million from this move by 2003.[104] Pricewaterhouse Coopers, Andersen Consulting, and Ernst and Young employees face similar arrangements.

The concept of hotelling is so new to Canada that no statistics are available on its use to date. It is more common in the United States, where it is used in the management-consulting, financial, and high-tech sectors. Often, organizations have extra space in these industries because employees work from home or are on the road. To save building costs, they have moved to hotelling. In Canada, it is frequently used among the smaller and newer boutique advertising agencies, and it is being considered for the federal public service.

Larry Haiven, of the College of Commerce at the University of Saskatchewan, suggests that hotelling, like re-engineering, rightsizing, and other restructuring techniques, "ends up damaging organizations."[105] It also changes the way work is done. For example, at the Mississauga, Ontario, office of Revenue Canada, 250 auditors compete for desks on a first-come, first-served basis. The results, according to a *Report on Business* article, are "a bullpen of tension, frayed nerves — even fistfights — in a profession not known for excitability." Seventy-five percent of the auditors have filed grievances against Revenue Canada through the collective bargaining process. The resulting tensions and grievances suggest that the auditors may have difficulty performing their jobs effectively. Ralph Herman, a spokesperson for the union that represents the auditors (Professional Institute of the Public Service of Canada), says that hotelling "hurts productivity because it eliminates the informal socializing and learning among employees sitting next to each other."

Michael Brill, a professor of architecture at the University of Buffalo and a leading advocate of hotelling, notes that "it is not designed to increase job performance or job satisfaction." Actually, its main savings are in overhead costs to firms.[106] At Chiat/Day's Toronto office, hotelling had to be modified, after the company realized that "you can't take personal space away from people."[107]

The strategies for work redesign that we've described have already had a profound impact on the ways Canadians perform and think about their jobs. Some even argue that "jobs" as we know them are becoming obsolete — that demands by employers and workers alike for greater flexibility and autonomy will result in the development of a contingent workforce with very little resemblance to jobholders of the past. A critical debate about the future of jobs is set out in this chapter's Point/CountPoint feature on pages 564-565.

At the Mississauga, ON office of Revenue Canada, auditors do not have designated work spaces. Instead, they compete for desks on a first-come, first-served basis every day. Revenue Canada's arrangement with its auditors represents hotelling.

## HR Implications

# Performance Appraisals Under Total Quality Management (TQM)

The effective implementation of TQM requires that employees work together, and develop, with management, systems that help to increase productivity. As a result, the performance of any particular individual is tied more heavily to how the system operates, including other members of the team, as well as whatever processes are installed to aid the quality programs. In fact, W.E. Deming, one of the major writers on TQM, argues that in a TQM system, 85 percent of performance variance across individuals is actually due to the system, and only 15 percent is due to person factors.[1] Ordinary performance evaluation programs that consider the role of the individual as the primary source of performance are not adequate for evaluating individuals working in a more team-based environment.

Deming suggests the elimination of performance appraisal, or at least a reduction in it. However, many organizations might find that an extreme approach. Because the TQM system that is implemented is largely responsible for differences in outcome, one approach to performance appraisal would be to use it to detect large differences among individuals (that is, those meeting expectations, those exceeding expectations, and those underperforming).[2] Those who are exceeding expectations could be groomed for promotion and those who were underperforming could receive remedial training or be reassigned. If a company were interested in developing more of its employees, then a finer grading of categories could be used.

When those who work in TQM systems are evaluated, what gets evaluated may well be different from areas covered in the more usual performance appraisal system. (We reviewed regular performance appraisal systems in HR Implications in Chapter 4.) Team-orientation, flexibility, continuous learning, and organizational citizenship are important characteristics for TQM. It may be especially helpful to use self-rating mechanisms under TQM, as the individual in these systems is expected to be more aware of how the system could be improved, and his or her role in that improvement. Rating team effort is similarly important.

Sources:

[1] W.E. Deming, *Out of the Crisis* (Cambridge: MIT Institute for Advanced Engineering Study, 1986).

[2] R.L. Cardy, G.H. Dobbins, and K.P. Carson, "TQM and HRM: Improving Performance Appraisal Research, Theory and Practice," *Canadian Journal of Administrative Sciences*, 12, pp. 106-115.

## SUMMARY AND IMPLICATIONS

### For the Workplace

An understanding of work design can help managers design jobs that positively affect employee motivation. For instance, jobs that score high in motivating potential increase an employee's control over key elements in his or her work. Therefore, jobs that offer autonomy, feedback, and similar complex task characteristics help to satisfy the individual goals of those employees who desire greater control over their work. Of course, consistent with the social information processing model, the perception that task characteristics are complex is probably more important in influencing an employee's motivation than the objective task characteristics themselves. The key, then, is to provide employees with cues that suggest that their jobs score high on factors such as skill variety, task identity, autonomy, and feedback.

Technology is changing people's jobs and their work behaviour. TQM and its emphasis on continuous process improvement can increase employee stress as individuals find that performance expectations are constantly being increased. Re-engineering is eliminating millions of jobs and completely reshaping the jobs of those that remain. Flexible manufacturing systems require employees to learn new skills and accept increased responsibilities. And technology is making many job skills obsolete and shortening the life span of almost all skills — technical, administrative, and managerial.

Alternative work schedule options such as the compressed workweek, shorter workweeks, flextime, job sharing, and telecommuting have grown in popularity in recent years. They have become an important strategic tool as organizations try to increase the flexibility their employees need in a changing workplace.

## For You as an Individual

Our discussion on job design gives you some insight into how jobs are arranged in the workplace, both in terms of the tasks done (from very specialized, to being responsible for a variety of tasks) and the arrangement of workplace hours. These are factors that you may want to consider when you begin your job search, as the studies reviewed indicate that job satisfaction is related to types of jobs, as well as the ability to have a flexible schedule.

Should you ever decide to become an entrepreneur, you will have to make decisions about how to allocate tasks to people, and the job characteristics model should give you some indication of the motivation potential of various arrangements. As an entrepreneur, you might also want to consider what kinds of hours your employees will be assigned if you want to help them manage their jobs and families.

*ROADMAP*
*REMINDER*

In the previous chapter we examined the structure of organizations: that is, how the different individuals who are employed by the organization are arranged into work units. In this chapter we considered work arrangement at the individual level: What are the tasks that are assigned to each individual employee? Both the structural arrangement and the job design in an organization affect employees' motivation and job satisfaction. In the next, and final, chapter we consider how organizational change occurs, looking specifically at how cultural change can be enacted.

# For Review

1. Describe 3 jobs that score high on the JCM. Describe 3 jobs that score low.
2. What are the implications of the social information processing model for predicting employee behaviour?
3. What are the implications for employees of a continuous improvement program?
4. What are the implications for employees of a re-engineering program?
5. What are flexible manufacturing systems?
6. What can you do through work design to improve employee performance on teams?
7. What are the advantages of flextime from an employee's perspective? From management's perspective?
8. What are the advantages of job sharing from an employee's perspective? From management's perspective?
9. From an employee's perspective, what are the pros and cons of telecommuting?

# For Critical Thinking

1. Re-engineering needs to be autocratically imposed in order to overcome employee resistance. This runs directly counter to the model of a contemporary manager who is a good listener, a coach, someone who motivates through employee involvement and who possesses strong team support skills. Can these two positions be reconciled?
2. How has technology changed the manager's job over the past 20 years?
3. Would you want a full-time job telecommuting? How do you think most of your friends would feel about such a job? Do you think telecommuting has a future?
4. What can management do to improve employees' perceptions that their jobs are interesting and challenging?
5. How might communication in an organization be affected by telecommuting, job sharing, and other work arrangements where employees are less often in the workplace?

## LEARNING ABOUT YOURSELF EXERCISE

# Is an Enriched Job for You?

**INSTRUCTIONS**  People differ in what they like and dislike in their jobs. Listed below are 12 pairs of jobs. For each pair, indicate which job you would prefer. Assume that everything else about the jobs is the same — pay attention only to the characteristics actually listed for each pair of jobs. If you would prefer the job in Column A, indicate how much you prefer it by putting a checkmark in a blank to the left of the Neutral point. If you prefer the job in Column B, check 1 of the blanks to the right of Neutral. Check the Neutral blank only if you find the 2 jobs equally attractive or unattractive. Try to use the Neutral blank rarely.

**Column A**

1. A job that offers little or no challenge.

   Strongly prefer A   Neutral   Strongly prefer B

   A job that requires you to be completely isolated from co-workers.

2. A job that pays well.

   Strongly prefer A   Neutral   Strongly prefer B

   A job that allows considerable opportunity to be creative and innovative.

3. A job that often requires you to make important decisions.

   Strongly prefer A   Neutral   Strongly prefer B

   A job in which there are many pleasant people to work with.

4. A job with little security in a somewhat unstable organization.

   Strongly prefer A   Neutral   Strongly prefer B

   A job in which you have little or no opportunity to participate in decisions that affect your work.

5. A job in which greater responsibility is given to those who do the best work.

   Strongly prefer A   Neutral   Strongly prefer B

   A job in which greater responsibility is given to loyal employees who have the most seniority.

6. A job with a manager who sometimes is highly critical.

   Strongly prefer A   Neutral   Strongly prefer B

   A job that does not require you to use much of your talent.

7. A very routine job.

   Strongly prefer A   Neutral   Strongly prefer B

   A job in which your co-workers are not very friendly.

8. A job with a manager who respects you and treats you fairly.

   Strongly prefer A   Neutral   Strongly prefer B

   A job that provides constant opportunities for you to learn new and interesting things.

9. A job that gives you a real chance to develop yourself personally.

   Strongly prefer A   Neutral   Strongly prefer B

   A job with excellent vacation and fringe benefits.

10. A job in which there is a real chance you could be laid off.

    Strongly prefer A   Neutral   Strongly prefer B

    A job with very little chance to do challenging work.

11. A job with little freedom and independence to do your work in the way you think best.

    Strongly prefer A   Neutral   Strongly prefer B

    A job with poor working conditions.

12. A job with very satisfying teamwork.

    Strongly prefer A   Neutral   Strongly prefer B

    A job that allows you to use your skills and abilities to the fullest extent.

**Column B**

Turn to page 636 for scoring directions and key.

Source: J.R. Hackman and G.R. Oldham, *The Job Diagnostic Survey: An Instrument for the Diagnosis of Jobs and the Evaluation of Job Redesign Projects*. Technical Report No. 4 (New Haven, CT: Yale University, Department of Administrative Sciences, 1974). Reprinted with permission.

# Analyzing and Redesigning Jobs

Break into groups of 5-7 members each. Each student should describe the worst job he or she has ever had. Use any criteria you want to select 1 of these jobs for analysis by the group.

Members of the group will analyze the job selected by determining how well it scores on the job characteristics model. Use the following scale for your analysis of each job dimension:

7 = Very high

6 = High

5 = Somewhat high

4 = Moderate

3 = Somewhat low

2 = Low

1 = Very low

Following are sample questions that can guide the group in its analysis of the job in question:

- *Skill variety:* Describe the different identifiable skills required to do this job. What is the nature of the oral, written, and/or quantitative skills needed? Physical skills? Does the jobholder get the opportunity to use all of his or her skills?

- *Task identity:* What is the product that the jobholder creates? Is he or she involved in its production from beginning to end? If not, is he or she involved in a particular phase of its production from beginning to end?

- *Task significance:* How important is the product? How important is the jobholder's role in producing it? How important is the jobholder's contribution to the people he or she works with? If the jobholder's job were eliminated, how inferior would the product be?

- *Autonomy:* How much independence does the jobholder have? Does he or she have to follow a strict schedule? How closely is he or she supervised?

- *Feedback:* Does the jobholder get regular feedback from his or her manager? From peers? From his or her staff? From customers? How about intrinsic performance feedback when doing the job?

Using the formula in Exhibit 13-3, calculate the job's motivating potential. Then using the suggestions offered in the chapter for redesigning jobs, describe specific actions management could take to increase this job's motivating potential.

Calculate the costs to management of redesigning the job in question. Do the benefits exceed the costs?

Conclude the exercise by having a representative of each group share his or her group's analysis and redesign suggestions with the entire class. Possible topics for class discussion might include similarities in the jobs chosen, problems in rating job dimensions, and the cost-benefit assessment of design changes.

---

Source: This exercise is based on W.P. Ferris, "Enlivening the Job Characteristics Model," in C. Harris and C.C. Lundberg (eds.), *Proceedings of the 29th Annual Eastern Academy of Management Meeting*, Baltimore, MD, May 1992, pp. 125-128.

**1.** Find the latest data indicating the popularity of flextime and telecommuting.

**2.** Find 3 companies that had introduced process re-engineering but were disappointed with its results. What factors led to this disappointment?

# CASE INCIDENT

# Continuous Improvement Through *Kaizen* at Ventra Group

*Kaizen* is the Japanese term for the techniques of continuous manufacturing improvements. It can include such things as tagging unproductive equipment for removal, colour-coding the shop floor to represent different parts of the manufacturing process, altering routine maintenance on a production line, or moving to just-in-time delivery of parts. In Canadian assembly plants for such Japanese automakers as Honda Motor Co. Ltd., Toyota Motor Corp., and Suzuki Motor Corp., there are clear incentives to adopt *kaizen* techniques.

Oakville, Ontario-based auto-parts company Ventra Group Inc. has been using *kaizen* techniques since 1988. When it acquired Seeburn, a leading maker of car jacks, there was talk of developing a third plant, because Seeburn was at overcapacity. However, through *kaizen*, the need for a third plant was eliminated. In 1993, Seeburn had $45 million in annual sales, but *kaizen* allowed it to move to $70 million in 1995, with room for another $30 million, without having to build a new plant.

Former president Frank Legate brought more *kaizen* culture to Ventra's Chatham, Ontario, plastics plant after the plant lost a big contract to supply Ford's Mustang with tail-light lenses in spring 1995. The contract had accounted for about 25 percent of the plant's output. Significant layoffs resulted when the contract was lost. "The loss of the Mustang contract is an incentive to make change to the organization. It highlights to people if we don't do things right, this is what the customer is going to do to us. Our jobs are at risk," noted Legate at the time. One major *kaizen* improvement was freeing up 900 square metres of space and reducing the need for a costly warehouse. To do this, hourly workers attached a red tag to every piece of equipment they felt was not needed. Management then took action, based on the red tags.

The next *kaizen* activity is to improve the Chatham plant's layout. Gary Nettleton, the plant's manufacturing manager, believes this will increase productivity significantly. He estimates that his hourly workers waste about 75 percent of their work time on such things as "getting presses ready for production runs, moving tools between presses and double handling of material." In other words, workers are preparing to work, rather than working.

The adjustment to *kaizen* procedures has not been completely smooth, however. Plant manager Steve Hackney notes that "the problem is that the plant is 60 percent different on Thursday than Monday. The rate of change is schizophrenic here. There are just too many things to do in a day." Hackney at least tries to adjust to the changes. He reports that some of the hourly workers, whom he calls hardliners, resist change at all costs. Legate, however, doesn't view the hardliners as a problem. "The hardliners are the most valuable. On the face of it, they're the most negative, but their bitches are really suggestions. The trick is to harness those suggestions."

Ventra's *kaizen* methods seem to be working. For the first six months of fiscal 1999, Ventra reported record revenue and earnings.

## Questions

1. Identify the *kaizen* activities at Ventra. Would you have expected them to be as successful as they appear to have been?

**2.** What do you think it would be like to work in a plant that was engaged in "a continuous improvement process"?

**3.** Why might some of the "hardliners" be resistant to the changes going on at Ventra?

Sources: "The Kaizen Advantage: Japanese Term for the Unglamorous Techniques You Use to Get Continuous Manufacturing Improvements," *Financial Post*, October 21/23, 1995, pp. 10-11; "Performance 500 Top 10," *Canadian Business 500*, June 1997, pp. 137-146; "Ventra Logs Record Results," *Financial Post*, May 14, 1999, p. C2.

# Hold Those Phones

Dread that telemarketing call that interrupts your dinner? Imagine working for a telemarketing firm, sitting in a room all evening with a large number of people who are all making the same phone calls across the country.

Telemarketing is the new assembly-line job — highly routinized, very little worker flexibility, specific expectations for hourly production. It is also a growing business in Canada, where there are more than 6000 of these centres. Provincial governments often view them as key job creators rather than places for low-skilled labour. For instance, New Brunswick has had 43 calling centres open there since 1992, creating 6000 new jobs in a province with a workforce of 315 000.

Sitel Corporation's telemarketing campaign for Tracker Corporation shows just what a telemarketer does. The job starts with learning the script for the product. Telephone service representatives (TSRs) undergo rigorous training to get the script right, practising with each other possible responses to a contact's refusals to listen to the sales pitch. During the three-hour calling session, managers try to motivate the TSRs through encouragement, back rubs, and even little contests where they can earn $10 bonuses for making the first sale of the time period.

The training can be demoralizing, however. As we see in the video, one TSR shows fatigue and dismay at not being able to field all of the negative responses given by her role-playing partner. The TSRs are also carefully monitored. A computer tracks the number of calls they've made, along with the number of sales, and both the client and managers have ready access to this information. TSRs are told their sales goals, and those at Sitel are expected to make three sales per hour. After three days, however, TSRs on the Tracker project are averaging closer to one sale per hour. On the fourth day of the project, four of six TSRs call in sick.

So, the next time you pick up the phone and hear a sales pitch, imagine the telemarketer and his or her job conditions.

# Questions

**1.** Describe the job design of telemarketing work.

**2.** How might you improve the working conditions of the telemarketer without doing a complete job redesign?

**3.** How would you use the Hackman-Oldham model to propose a possible redesign of the telemarketer's job? How might your proposed design affect sales?

Source: Based on "Telemarketing," *Venture 584;* aired March 31, 1996; see http://www.tv.cbc.ca/venture/archives/telemarketing_960331/two.html for a CBC case presentation.

# CHAPTER 14

# Organizational Change

## Questions for Consideration

**What forces create the need for organizational change?**

**What kinds of changes do organizations make? Can organizations stop changing?**

**What causes resistance to change? How can it be overcome?**

S tephen Bachand, CEO of Toronto-based Canadian Tire Corp. Ltd., created a remarkable turnaround between taking over in 1994 and announcing his resignation in 2000.[1] While Eaton's liquidated and Marks and Spencer closed its Canadian stores in 1999, Canadian Tire turned in a record profit of $167 million in 1998, a 3000 percent improvement over five years. Between 1994 and late 1999, Canadian Tire's stock price quadrupled. The picture for 1999 was not quite as rosy due to some unusual expenses, but total retail sales were up 7.7 percent over 1998, following an increase of 7.5 percent in 1998 over 1997.

During his tenure, Bachand worked to change both the employees and the stores. Canadian Tire wanted improvements in both customer service and employee training. To do this, the company "outlined core company values—like honesty, respect and responsibility—and established a long-term training program for employees to develop leadership and customer relationship skills."

To make sure that the changes to the stores were right, Canadian Tire built a 4645-square-metre lab in north Toronto, complete with all the features of a real store, except the customers. All changes are tested there, from product shelving to new fixtures and layout, before being introduced into other stores.

Why did Canadian Tire's change strategy worked? Bachand would say that it's because the company set out to "make adapting to change part of its corporate culture." Employees were asked to help define and solve problems, and change was not seen as a one-time effort. Canadian Tire faces a new set of challenges as it enters 2001. Bachand announced in early 2000 that he would be stepping down within the year. His announcement sent the stock downward immediately, from $34.50 prior to the announcement, to $31.80 just two days afterwards. By late May 2000, Canadian Tire stock was trading at around $21.

So was Canadian Tire's makeover only as good as its CEO? At the time of his announced resignation, most analysts suggested that Bachand did a remarkable job while at the helm, and some suggested that he would be difficult to replace. However, one analyst suggested that Canadian Tire was ready for someone with fresh ideas for growth, and who would bring a stronger e-commerce profile to the corporation. "It's a short-term negative, but in the long run the way it is being done is very positive," said the analyst.

Canadian Tire is just one of the many organizations that need to reinvent themselves often if they are to survive in a challenging business environment. Engaging in any kind of change in an organization is not easy. Below we examine the forces for change and consider how organizational change comes about.

## Forces for Change

A 1999 study of 309 human resource executives across a variety of industries found that 100 percent of them were going through at least one of the following changes: mergers, acquisitions, divestitures, global competition, management and/or organizational structure.[2]

Throughout this text we noted many opportunities that organizations have to engage in change. For instance, we noted the importance of motivating employees and discussed a variety of programs that could be used to

**Canadian Tire**
www.canadiantire.ca

motivate individuals for specific outcomes. We also talked about the increasing emphasis on working on teams in organizations. We suggested that organizations are moving toward more ethically and socially responsible positions. We also discussed the new leadership challenges of sharing power with employees, as well as the need for employees to be good followers in some instances. We discussed reorganizing the workplace, noting how recent changes in organizational structure have, in some instances, led to more flattened organizations, as well as more interconnections with other organizations. We described job redesign as a way of motivating employees and indicated that increasing factors such as autonomy and feedback generally increased satisfaction. We also noted that the culture of the organization was like the glue that held the organization together, and that sometimes, the entire culture of the organization needed to be changed in order to effect change.

As we discussed the workplace in this textbook, and talked about possible change, we might have implied that change happened easily, perhaps overnight, and did not require careful thought or planning. This implication occurred because we did not discuss how these changes actually happened in the workplace, what one needed to do in order to effect change, and how difficult change actually was. We wanted you to understand what changes were possible before we actually discussed how to carry out that change.

In this chapter we consider the process of organizational change, and examine organizations whose processes and structures might have worked in the 1980s and 1990s but need changing to survive in the 21st century. We discuss what it takes to become more productive in an era of globalization, changing technology, and demands for efficiency. In exploring change we also consider resistance to change.

## Types of Organizational Change

When we discuss change in this chapter, we're concerned with activities that are proactive and purposeful; that is, change as an intentional, goal-oriented activity. We refer to this as **planned change**.

**planned change**
Change as an intentional and goal-oriented activity.

What are the goals of planned change? Essentially there are two. First, it seeks to improve the ability of the organization to adapt to new factors in its environment. Second, it seeks to modify employee behaviour.

**first-order change**
Change that is linear and continuous.

**second-order change**
Change that is multidimensional, multilevel, discontinuous, and radical.

You might find it helpful to think of planned change in terms of order of magnitude.[3] **First-order change** is linear and continuous. It implies no fundamental shifts in the assumptions that organizational members hold about the world or how the organization can improve its functioning. In contrast, **second-order change** is a multidimensional, multilevel, discontinuous, radical change involving reframing of assumptions about the organization and the world in which it operates. Mikio Kitano, director of all production engineering at Toyota, introduced first-order change in his company.[4] He pursued slow, subtle, incremental changes in production processes to improve the efficiency of Toyota's plants. On the other hand, Boeing's top executives committed themselves to radically reinventing their company.[5] Responding to a massive airline slump, aggressive competition from Airbus, and the threat of Japanese competitors, this second-order change process at Boeing included slashing costs by up to 30 percent, reducing the time it takes to make a 737 from 13 months to six months, dramatically cutting inventories, putting the company's entire workforce through a four-day course in "competitiveness," and bringing customers and suppliers into the once-secret process of designing new planes.

If an organization is to survive, it must respond to changes in its environment. When competitors introduce new products or services, government agencies enact new laws, important sources of supply go out of business, or similar environmental changes take place, the organization must adapt. Efforts to stimulate innovation, empower employees, and introduce work teams are examples of second-order planned change activities directed at responding to changes in the environment. Organizations have also had to change where they manufacture goods in response to public criticism, as happened to Nike when some criticized its use of exploited labour in the Third World.

Since an organization's success or failure is essentially due to the things that its employees or managers may do or fail to do, planned change also is concerned with changing the behaviour of individuals and groups within the organization. In this chapter we review techniques that organizations can use to get people to behave differently in the tasks they perform and in their interactions with others.

## What Do Organizations Change?

Organizational change affects five aspects of a company: its culture, structure, technology, physical setting, and people.[6] This is illustrated in Exhibit 14-1. Changing *culture* may well be the most profound of the changes an organization makes because it requires changing the underlying values and goals of the organization. We referred earlier to culture as the glue that holds the organization together, which is why culture change is the most dramatic, as we saw for IBM Canada in Chapter 9. Changing *structure* involves altering authority relations, coordination mechanisms, job redesign, or similar structural variables. Changing *technology* encompasses modifications in the way work is processed and in the methods and equipment used. Changing the *physical setting* covers altering the space and layout arrangements in the workplace. Changing *people* refers to changes in employee skills, expectations, and/or behaviour. Below we examine each of these changes in turn, reserving our discussion of culture change to the end because of its complex and wide-ranging impact.

### Changing Structure

In Chapter 12 we discussed structural issues such as work specialization, span of control, and various organizational designs. However, organizational structures are not set in concrete. Changing conditions demand structural changes. As a result, organizations sometimes modify their structure.

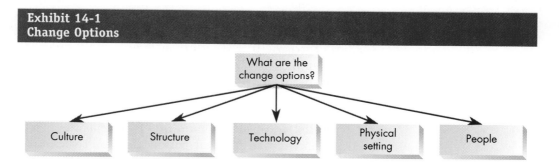

**Exhibit 14-1**
**Change Options**

When Paul Tellier took over as President and CEO of Montreal-based Canadian National Railway, his major focus was to turn it into a profitable company. Among the changes Tellier undertook was structural change, reducing the number of management layers and increasing the ease of communication. He also instituted regularly scheduled departures and a customer bill of rights. CN is viewed as the most improved railroad in North America.

So what would a change in organizational structure look like?

An organization's structure is defined by how tasks are formally divided, grouped, and coordinated. Organizations can alter one or more of the key elements in their design. For instance, departmental responsibilities can be combined, vertical layers removed, and spans of control widened to make the organization flatter and less bureaucratic. More rules and procedures can be implemented to increase standardization. An increase in decentralization can be made to speed up the decision-making process.

Organizations can also introduce major modifications in the actual structural design. This might include a shift from a simple structure to a team-based structure or the creation of a matrix design. Organizations might consider redesigning jobs or work schedules. Job descriptions can be redefined, jobs enriched, or flexible work hours introduced. Still another option is to modify the organization's compensation system. Motivation could be increased by, for example, introducing performance bonuses or profit-sharing.

Paul Tellier, president and CEO of Montreal-based Canadian National Railway (CN), had to make major changes to the railway after taking the helm. In order to transform CN into a profitable company that would be responsive to customer needs, Tellier "reduced the number of layers of management and abolished five vice-president posts, so that where formerly there were sometimes 10 layers of authority between the president and any line employee, there are now no more than five."[7] Managers were given more breadth of command, and communication became clearer as there were fewer communication channels through which messages had to travel. While these are not the only changes CN undertook, they do illustrate the types of structural changes organizations might make. The changes that CN started in the early 1990s and continued through the decade were very successful. By March 1998, CN was two years ahead of schedule in efficiency improvements, as measured by its operating ratio (the percentage of each dollar of revenue needed to run the railway).[8] And for third quarter 1999, CN posted an operating ratio of 71 percent, the best of any major North American railroad for that period. Tellier's structural change program resulted in a much more profitable railroad operation.

**Delta Lloyd**
www.deltalloyd.nl

When Amsterdam-based Delta Lloyd decided to implement teamwork to speed up its insurance processing, it asked all 268 of its managers to reapply for their jobs. Only 58 percent of them won jobs in the new organization; they were not sure the rest would support the move to teamwork. In this instance Delta Lloyd was signalling to managers and employees alike that teamwork was an important component of the new work process, and if you couldn't function in a team, you might not have a job with the company. The team process worked, and files that were taking two to three weeks to complete are now finished the same day in 70 to 80 percent of the cases.[9]

## Changing Technology

Most of the early studies in management and organizational behaviour dealt with efforts aimed at technological change. At the turn of the century, for example, scientific management sought to implement changes based on time-and-motion studies that would increase production efficiency. Today, major technological changes usually involve the introduction of new equipment, tools, methods, automation, or computerization.

Competitive factors or innovations within an industry often require organizations to introduce new equipment, tools, or operating methods. For example, steel makers today are building small, mini-mills rather than sprawling manufacturing complexes. The former are built to make specific products and are much more efficient than their larger counterparts.

Automation is a technological change that replaces people with machines. It began in the Industrial Revolution and continues as a change option today. Examples of automation are the introduction of automatic mail sorters by Canada Post and robots on automobile assembly lines.

As noted in previous chapters, the most visible technological change in recent years has been expanding computerization. Most organizations now have sophisticated management information systems that link the organizations' employees regardless of where they're located. The office of 2001 is dramatically different from its counterpart of 1981, predominantly because of computerization. This is typified by desktop microcomputers that can run hundreds of business software packages and network systems that allow these computers to communicate with one another.

In 1996, executives at West Coast Energy's Chatham, Ontario-based Union Gas Ltd. and Willowdale, Ontario-based Centra Gas units requested that their regional managers install a new computerized financial system project by an ambitious January 1, 1997, deadline. The response from the regional managers was, "Forget it, buster."[10] The executives were planning to have the computers shipped in the fall, but what they had failed to realize is that September to December is the "light-up" season, "when customer service departments are pushed to their limits serving customers who want their furnaces started, checked, and repaired."[11]

While employees are often resistant to change, the above story illustrates a failure on the part of senior management to plan for a major change to be introduced at an appropriate time. Senior management was surprised by the resistance and hired change management specialists from Price Waterhouse to talk to the financial system project team and employees who would be using the system. The change specialists discovered that there was not a lot of support for the introduction of the new technology. How did Union and Centra deal with the resistance? They hired Price Waterhouse to join the project team and help with the transition. "Plans were explained to the staff, training plans were put in place, and employees from all over the field who were informal champions of the new technology were recruited to help turn the situation around."[12] One of the critical changes made to the schedule was to install all of the computers in a six-week period during the summer. Training was also done during summer months, so that when light-up season started, the whole system was up and running.

Union's and Centra's experiences with introducing change are not unique. However, the companies did a number of things correctly to ensure that change occurred in as smooth a manner as possible. First, they listened to their employees about the causes of their resistance. Second, they hired a consulting agency to further identify sources of resistance. Third, they brought together a team that could help inspire the change, including bringing Price Waterhouse onto the team, and also recruiting supportive employees who would help encourage their peers. Finally, they scheduled the change for a time that would be less likely to induce stress for the employees. Ken Kawall, director of information technology for Union Gas and Centra Gas, also offers a piece of advice: "Make sure people issues are included as a major part of the planning exercise."[13]

**PriceWaterhouseCoopers Canada**
www.pwcglobal.com/ca

Do organizations really change their physical settings?

## Changing the Physical Setting

Workplace layout should not be set up piecemeal or at random. Typically, management thoughtfully considers work demands, formal interaction requirements, and social needs when making decisions about space configurations, interior design, equipment placement, and the like. For example, by eliminating walls and partitions and opening up an office design, it becomes easier for employees to communicate with each other. Similarly, management can change the quantity and types of lights, the level of heat or cold, the levels and types of noise, and the cleanliness of the work area, as well as interior design aspects, such as furniture, decorations, and colour schemes.

Trimark Financial Corp. moved its 700 employees from its downtown Toronto headquarters to a new headquarters 10 km away in North York so that the company could change both the physical layout for employees and the employee culture. Employees were consulted about their needs for having a productive and creatively stimulating environment, and the office layout was planned. There's a fitness club, a great cafeteria, an internet café and a reading room, so that employees can relax and interact with each other, while working on their projects. Everything Trimark did was to foster the culture of their employees. Says Bradeau, the president: "We have to give to the individual before the individual can give to us."

Cobourg, Ontario-based Rusco Canada Ltd., a manufacturer of vinyl windows, steel entrance doors, and steel security screens, redesigned its plant in 1996 after its largest client said to "deliver on time or lose our orders."[14] Rusco had been struggling with getting orders out on time because no one seemed to have all the information to know when an order would be completed or where it was once it was shipped. Faced with losing its biggest client, the company engaged in a variety of changes. One such change involved the physical layout of the plant. The company "moved all the machines and production equipment into a new layout during the peak business period—...expanding and redesigning production into a progressive, straight-line configuration over a few weekends and after shifts." Among other things, this configuration made it possible for line workers to see the progress of products along the line and into shipping, which helped everyone have a better sense of when products would be ready for shipping.

Rusco's redesign of its plant was done in a way to minimize the disruption on production. Much of the move was done during a few weekends and after shifts. The redesign paid off. Within six weeks, the company was having trouble keeping up with new orders. In early 1997, CEO Bob Young reported, "We have gone up to 369 windows a period with 8 workers from 200 with 14 people, and now we are vertically integrating."

## Changing People

Organizations can also help individuals and groups within to work more effectively together. This category typically involves changing the attitudes and behaviours of organizational members through the processes of communication, decision making, and problem-solving.

When Gilles Pansera purchased Lac-Megantic, Quebec-based Industries Manufacturières Mégantic Inc. (IMMI) in 1990 and became its president, the operation had been losing money for the previous 10 years.[15] Pansera believed, however, that it could be profitable, if the company retargeted the market and upgraded machinery. Pansera decided to concentrate on "doorskin" plywood, which requires a much more labour-intensive production process, needing the careful involvement of employees. Pansera realized that to improve productivity, he would have to modify employees' habits. He quickly discovered that this was "a much harder proposal than expected." While the employees were generally good, they had not been offered responsibility under the previous owners, and therefore there were employees who had worked for the company for 20 years yet knew nothing about the other end of the plant.

Pansera shut down the plant for two hours after he bought it, discussing the situation with the employees, and showing the books to them. He discussed the problems with the company and outlined what he intended to do about it. He repeats these sessions every quarter, because he believes that employees should know everything about the company. IMMI is unionized, and the employees appreciated his openness. After their first meeting, they agreed to renegotiate their collective agreement in return for ending the private deals that the previous owners had made with favoured employees.

Dealing with the union turned out to be one of Pansera's easier problems, as it turned out. In 1992, he wanted to establish a total quality management program and produced an employee manual describing the changes and procedures. That was when he discovered that 30 percent of his employees did not know how to read. He scrapped the manual and, with the support of the local school board, started a program to teach literacy and basic mathematics to workers. IMMI spends $200 000 a year on staff training, and Pansera believes that it is a worthwhile investment. He notes, "Everybody has what it takes to learn more complex tasks, and above all to assimilate the programs" that need to be implemented.

In the case of IMMI, change worked for two main reasons. First, Pansera communicated openly with employees. Second, when he discovered that they lacked the skills to implement the changes he had in mind, he helped them to acquire those skills. This made it less likely they would resist the change, because they had the skills to confront new demands. This chapter's HR Implications feature starting on page 613 gives you further examples of how to deal with people issues in the management of change.

## Changing the Culture of the Organization

So how would someone change the organizational culture?

Culture sets the tone for how employees interact with each other, what things are valued by the organization, and what the expectations for managers and employees are. Often, changing just the structure, or the technology, or the people may not be enough to achieve fundamental change in the organization. That is because culture often represents the mindset of the employees and managers. In this section we consider several examples of culture change and how they were accomplished.

When Brian Groff bought Waterloo, Ontario-based Sutherland-Schultz Inc., a construction company, in 1996, the company had lost money for the previous four years.[16] Moreover, it was characterized by infighting among the 400 workers spread across 13 divisions. The divisions represented such things as electrical and mechanical contracting, as well as pipefitting, and thus traditional trade rivalries plagued the company. The divisions were unwilling to work together, and Groff characterized the company as a war zone. "Even worse, long-time customers doing business with one division didn't realize there were other divisions they might use. Relations had so deteriorated that, given the chance, staff would often recommend competitors."

Groff recognized that in order to resolve this kind of infighting, an organization needed more than just a simple structural change — it needed a cultural change as well. Two months after taking over, he closed two small divisions and fired five key division managers. He then replaced these managers with five experienced individuals from outside the company. This gave Groff an aggressive, knowledgeable, team-oriented management group to help him turn the culture around.

Groff believed that his employees needed more knowledge about each other, how each division operated, and how to work as a team. To do this, he set up a training program aimed at management and field supervisors that would cover everything from teamwork to problem-solving skills. Employees were initially quite resistant about devoting time to learning, although gradually they came to understand the value of the training. An added benefit was that by bringing together the managers from all the divisions in one room for training, they came to know more about each other's problems and could learn to work together. Eventually employees came to realize that there were major advantages to acting as a multitrade organization, rather than trying to protect the turf of individual trades, as they had done in the past. After just one year under Groff's culture change program, Sutherland-Schultz doubled its sales to $105 million and produced its first profitable year since 1992.

Groff's success at turning around the culture of Sutherland-Schultz occurred in part because of the extensive training provided for employees. This gave them the opportunity to learn about the other divisions and how they could work together, rather than referring business outside the company. Had Groff simply replaced the five division managers he fired and not engaged in extensive training, the change might not have occurred as successfully, because he would have had difficulty getting the other employees to understand the changes that needed to be made.

As the 1990s began, Calgary-based Suncor Energy, Inc. underwent major downsizing, suffered a major fire at one of its plants, had operating groups that did not communicate with each other, and experienced a decline in profits.[17] In facing these problems, Suncor recognized that it needed to change its culture and did so. By 1996, Suncor had turned itself around, making its oil sands business into a success story, seeing its Resources Group breaking all of its production and reserve replacement records, and developing efficient refinery and retail businesses.

To change its culture, Suncor started with a vision statement. Suncor's senior executives determined that the company's core purpose was to "consistently deliver outstanding achievements in Canadian petroleum and related businesses." To achieve this core purpose, the company outlined a number of related activities, which are identified in Exhibit 14-2. Suncor also moved from a command-and-control system "to a more flexible, more innovative environment that is open to ideas and focuses on individual initiative." In making the changes, Suncor strove to inform employees that they were a valuable part of the organization, because the changes required enormous commitment on the part of the employees. Suncor also kept employees informed of changes, even in one case stopping trading on its stock for an hour so that it could inform employees directly of imminent downsizing, rather than having them find out about it in the news. Peter Spelliscy, former senior vice-president, human resources and communication at Suncor, states that this action "earned [Suncor] a level of trust and commitment that made the turnaround happen quickly and professionally."

**Suncor**
www.suncor.com

**Exhibit 14-2
Elements of Suncor's Vision Statement**

- Seize opportunities that we identify or create in the rapidly changing business environment.

- Capitalize on the existing core assets and businesses.

- Ensure excellence in execution in all aspects of our business.

- Earn exceptional loyalty in relationships with our customers by consistently providing quality, cost-effective products and services.

- Set and attain progressive standards in health, safety, environment, workforce diversity, business ethics, and community involvement.

- Encourage individual and collective contribution to these achievements to create the opportunity for personal growth, reward, and satisfaction.

Source: P. Spelliscy, "Changing the Corporate Culture from Downsizing to Growth," *Canadian Speeches*, June 1996, pp. 45-50.

Are there appropriate ways to carry out change in organizations? At Suncor, Spelliscy developed ABCs of change that would be relevant to any organization undergoing a major change in its workplace:

A is to achieve awareness that things must change. You have to create a compelling case for change and convince people the need is real. Too often we fail to share information and involve people in the business issues. If people don't feel a sense of personal involvement and ownership, they just don't care.

B is to build belief among employees that they are part of the change. There's nothing more frustrating than realizing you are being changed. It is necessary for individuals to contribute to and control their destiny.

Once people know change needs to happen, and they understand that it is possible, then and only then can you expect to achieve C, a commitment to change. If you don't get everyone involved in the changes, they either won't happen or they won't be effective.

## Organizational Learning

In order to understand the change process, it is helpful to know a little about how organizations learn, that is, the processes by which organizations acquire knowledge and change behaviour.

Theories about organizational learning can be classified into two major approaches: the **adaptive learning perspective** and the **knowledge development perspective**.[18] The adaptive learning perspective views organizations as learning by feedback, that is, organizations repeat behaviours that have been successful in the past and avoid those behaviours that failed in the past.[19] The knowledge development perspective views organizations as collecting information, interpreting it, and then acting on the interpretations, possibly in entirely new ways.[20]

The adaptive learning approach views learning as a process of adjusting in response to one's experience. Thus it emphasizes experiential learning. "Organizational learning is assumed to be based on trial and error, where successful behaviour is repeated and unsuccessful behaviour is not."[21] The research indicates that adaptive learning works better in some situations than others. For instance, adaptive learning makes sense when environmental and performance feedback signals are clear. Adaptive learning is less possible to implement in the presence of ambiguity about either the environment or how well performance is doing, because there is not enough information to know how to act. Organizations that learn from experience also have difficulty dealing with environmental change because they will not have experienced the new situation before. This is problematic because "environmental change makes adaptation essential, but it also makes learning from experience difficult."[22] Organizations that only engage in adaptive learning, therefore, will have difficulty in managing major change that is dictated by shifts in their environment.

The knowledge development perspective considers that organizations and organizational members share knowledge, impressions, beliefs, and thus transfer knowledge to one another. Organizations using this perspective to learn "allow valid information to be exposed, confrontations aired, viewpoints challenged, and choices informed and freely made."[23] These organizations are less likely to rely on traditional methods, and more apt to look for entirely new processes and procedures to carry out tasks.

**adaptive learning perspective**
Organizations learn by feedback based on previous behaviour.

**knowledge development perspective**
Organizations collect, interpret, and then act upon information.

Organizations that try to learn simply through experience are less likely to be prepared to face new challenges for which they have no experience. To be a truly learning organization, then, it is important to take a knowledge development approach to learning, where one gathers new information and tries to use it in new ways.

## Organizational Learning in Practice

Organizations are starting to develop processes that encourage their employees and managers to learn. Several Canadian and US companies have established corporate universities, although they are much more predominant in the United States, where about 1200 US companies now offer such facilities.[24] For example, the Bank of Montreal has an Institute of Learning in suburban Toronto, while the Canadian Imperial Bank of Commerce (CIBC) has a Leadership Centre in King City, located about an hour north of Toronto, where employees learn such skills as empowerment, entrepreneurship, and creativity. The banks are trying to turn employees from all levels into "continuous learners" who can both recognize and adapt to changes in customer demands, technology, economic conditions, and competitive threats. "A learning organization reacts much more quickly to dramatic change than a non-learning organization," says James Rush, senior vice-president and executive director of the Bank of Montreal's Institute of Learning. "If we can unleash the creativity and knowledge of our workers, we will be able to weather the storms."[25]

Hamilton, Ontario-based steel manufacturer Dofasco sends groups of employees on a three-day course at a ski resort located 165 kilometres north of the city. They participate in team building and other exercises intended to foster communication among employees. Not all teaching is done in such exotic settings, however, nor is all teaching done from a top-down position. For example, unionized workers at DaimlerChrysler AG Canada's minivan plant in Windsor, Ontario, teach quality awareness programs to managers.

## Roadblocks to Organizational Learning

Holger Kluge, former president of CIBC, notes that "Wealth, success and security will go to firms that can constantly adapt, firms where creativity and innovation belong to the many rather than the few, firms that are organized to exploit change, from whatever source, at a moment's notice—firms that recognize that just because something works today is no reason to assume it will work tomorrow."[26]

Unfortunately, organizations are not always so ready to give up on what works today to go out searching for something that might work tomorrow. Peter Senge, author of one of the landmark books on organizational learning, *The Fifth Discipline*, identifies a number of thought patterns that are roadblocks to learning, including:[27]

- *I am my position.* People often become so loyal to their jobs that they confuse their jobs with their identities. This becomes evident when people are asked what they do, and they can describe their duties, but not the *purpose* of the greater enterprise. When people focus on their positions, they take little responsibility for the results that occur when all the positions interact together.

- *The enemy is out there.* When things go wrong in the organization, blame is always placed somewhere else in the organization. Individuals

**Dofasco**
www.dofasco.ca

Ever wonder why organizations (and people) get stuck?

do not like to see that their actions may have contributed to the problem. For many Canadian companies the enemy might be viewed as foreign competition, labour unions, government regulations, or customers that chose to go elsewhere. This sort of thinking makes it more difficult to figure out how to turn challenges into opportunities.

- *The fixation of events.* We often see life as a series of events, and we try to attribute one obvious cause to each event. Consequently, we don't take time to find out the longer-term patterns of change related to those events. For instance, it is not uncommon to read a sentence like the following in the *Financial Post*: "The TSE average dropped 16 points today, because low fourth-quarter profits were announced yesterday." While those two events might be linked in a very real way, they tell us nothing about why fourth-quarter profits are low. The news also suggests that there was no way of knowing about the low profits until just yesterday, when in fact longer-term things are related to the drop in profits.

- *The parable of the boiled frog.* If you place a frog in boiling water, it will immediately jump out. However, if you place a frog in a pot of cold water on the stove and slowly bring it to the boil, the frog will eventually be boiled to death, without ever doing anything to react. The frog does this because it is geared to sense sudden changes in the environment, not slow, gradual changes. It is important to slow down enough to see the gradual processes that will eventually lead to threats, rather than waiting until the threats simply present themselves.

These roadblocks to learning may suggest to you why many companies never do make the changes they need to come out of the crisis situations they face. Below we examine the process of organizational change, which takes as its premise that organizations have engaged in enough learning that they know they want to do something differently.

## Managing Organizational Change

### A General Overview of the Process: Lewin's Three-Step Model

Assuming that an organization has uncovered a need for change, how does it engage in the change process? Kurt Lewin argued that successful change in organizations should follow three steps, which are illustrated in Exhibit 14-3: **unfreezing** the status quo, **moving** to a new state, and **refreezing** the new change to make it permanent.[28] The value of this model can be seen in the following example where the management of a large company decided to reorganize its marketing function in Western Canada.

The oil company had three divisional offices in the West, located in Winnipeg, Calgary, and Vancouver. The decision was made to consolidate the

**unfreezing**
Change efforts to overcome the pressures of both individual resistance and group conformity.

**moving**
Efforts to get employees involved in the change process.

**refreezing**
Stabilizing a change intervention by balancing driving and restraining forces.

**Exhibit 14-3**
**Lewin's Three-Step Change Model**

Unfreezing → Moving → Refreezing

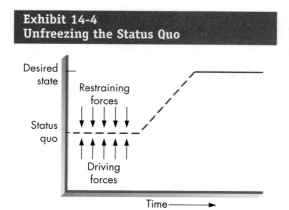

**Exhibit 14-4**
**Unfreezing the Status Quo**

Desired state

Restraining forces

Status quo

Driving forces

Time

**driving forces**
Forces that direct behaviour away from the status quo.

**restraining forces**
Forces that hinder movement away from the status quo.

divisions into a single regional office to be located in Calgary. The reorganization meant transferring over 150 employees, eliminating some duplicate managerial positions, and instituting a new hierarchy of command. As you might guess, a move of this magnitude was difficult to keep secret. The rumour of its occurrence preceded the announcement by several months. The decision itself was made unilaterally. It came from the executive offices in Toronto. Those people affected had no say whatsoever in the choice. For those in Vancouver or Winnipeg, who might have disliked the decision and its consequences — the problems inherent in transferring to another city, pulling youngsters out of school, making new friends, having new co-workers, undergoing the reassignment of responsibilities — their only recourse was to quit. In actuality, fewer than 10 percent did.

The status quo can be considered to be an equilibrium state. To move from this equilibrium — to overcome the pressures of both individual resistance and group conformity — unfreezing is necessary. Exhibit 14-4 shows that unfreezing can occur in one of three ways. The **driving forces**, which direct behaviour away from the status quo, can be increased. The **restraining forces,** which hinder movement from the existing equilibrium, can be decreased. A third alternative is to *combine the first two approaches.*

The company's management could expect employee resistance to the consolidation. To deal with that resistance, management could use positive incentives to encourage employees to accept the change. For instance, increases in pay can be offered to those who accept the transfer. Very liberal moving expenses can be paid by the company. Management might offer low-cost mortgage funds to allow employees to buy new homes in Calgary. Of course, management might also consider unfreezing acceptance of the status quo by removing restraining forces. Employees could be counselled individually. Each employee's concerns and apprehensions could be heard and specifically clarified. Assuming that most of the fears are unjustified, the counsellor could assure the employees that there was nothing to fear and then demonstrate, through tangible evidence, that restraining forces are unwarranted. If resistance is extremely high, management may have to resort to both reducing resistance and increasing the attractiveness of the alternative if the unfreezing is to be successful.

Once the consolidation change has been implemented, if it is to be successful, the new situation must be refrozen so that it can be sustained over time. Unless this last step is taken, there is a very high chance that the change will be short-lived and that employees will attempt to revert to the previous equilibrium state. The objective of refreezing, then, is to stabilize the new situation by balancing the driving and restraining forces.

How could the oil company's management refreeze its consolidation change? It could systematically replace temporary forces with permanent ones. For instance, management might impose a new bonus system tied to the specific changes desired. The formal rules and regulations governing behaviour of those affected by the change should also be revised to reinforce the new situation. Over time, of course, the work group's own norms will evolve to sustain the new equilibrium. But until that point is reached, management will have to rely on more formal mechanisms. The Working With Others Exercise on page 618 gives you the opportunity to identify driving and restraining forces for another company experiencing problems with change, and to make some recommendations for change. This chapter's first CBC Video Case, on page 620, takes a look at CP Railway's move to Alberta, and shows some of the responses given by managers and employees.

A key feature of Lewin's three-step model is its conception of change as an episodic activity. For a debate about whether change can continue to be implemented as an activity with a beginning, a middle, and an end, or whether the structure of the 21st century workplace will require change to occur as an ongoing if not chaotic process, see this chapter's Point/Counter-Point feature starting on page 600.

## Communicating Effectively When Undergoing Change

As we've noted throughout this book, organizations around the world are restructuring in order to reduce costs and improve competitiveness. Almost all *Fortune 100* companies, for instance, have scaled back the size of their labour force in the last five years or so through attrition and layoffs. Many Canadian companies have done the same.

A recent study examined employee communications programs in 10 leading companies that had successfully undertaken major restructuring programs.[29] The companies in the study were chosen because they had developed reputations for having excellent internal communication programs. The authors were interested in seeing whether common factors determined the effectiveness of these firms' employee communications. The authors specifically chose companies that had undergone restructuring and reorganizations because they believed that the true test of a firm's communication effectiveness was how well it worked in times of major organizational change.

The authors identified eight factors that were related to the effectiveness of employee communications during times of organizational change in these 10 firms: (1) CEO commitment to communication; (2) matching actions and words; (3) commitment to two-way communication; (4) emphasis on face-to-face communication; (5) shared responsibility for employee communication; (6) positive ways of dealing with bad news; (7) shaping messages for intended audience; and (8) treating communication as an ongoing process. Since the companies studied came from a variety of industries and organizational settings, the authors propose that these eight characteristics should apply to many types of organizations.

Let's look at these eight factors because they provide some research-based guidance to managers in helping decide how best to communicate with employees.

### The CEO Must Be Committed to the Importance of Communication

The most significant factor in a successful employee-communications program is the chief executive's leadership. That is, he or she must be philosophically and behaviourally committed to the notion that communicating with employees is essential to the achievement of the organization's goals. If the organization's senior executive is committed to communication through his or her words and actions, this message "trickles down" to the rest of the organization.

In addition to espousing a philosophical commitment to employee communications, the CEO must be a skilled and visible communications role model, and be willing to personally deliver key messages. The CEOs in this study spent a significant amount of their time talking with employees, responding to questions, listening to their concerns, and conveying their vision of the company. Importantly, they tended to do this "in person" and didn't delegate the task to other managers. By personally championing the cause of good communication, they lessen employee fears about changes that are being implemented and set the precedent for other managers to follow.

## Managers Match Actions and Words

Closely related to CEO support and involvement is managerial action. As we've noted previously, actions speak louder than words. When the implicit messages that managers send contradict the official messages as conveyed in formal communications, the managers lose credibility with employees. Employees will listen to what management has to say regarding changes being made and where the company is going, but these words must be supported by matching actions.

## Commitment to Two-Way Communication

Ineffective programs are dominated by downward communication. Successful programs balance downward and upward communication.

How does a firm promote upward communication and stimulate employee dialogue? The company that displayed the highest commitment to two-way communication used interactive television broadcasts that allowed employees to call in questions and get responses directly from top management. Company publications offered question-and-answer columns and employees were encouraged to submit questions. The company developed a grievance procedure that processed complaints quickly. Managers were trained in feedback techniques and then were rewarded for using them.

General Electric and Hallmark are two companies that have perfected two-way communication. General Electric, for instance, launched a company-wide town meeting effort in the late 1980s. Managers credit these meetings for "uncovering all kinds of crazy stuff we were doing."[30] And Hallmark regularly selects 50 to 100 nonmanagement employees at random for a 90-minute face-to-face discussion with the company's CEO.[31]

## Emphasis on Face-to-Face Communication

In times of uncertainty and change—which characterize major restructuring efforts—employees have many fears and concerns. Is their job in jeopardy? Will they have to learn new skills? Will their work group be disbanded? Consistent with our previous discussion of channel richness, these messages are nonroutine and ambiguous. The maximum amount of information can be transmitted through face-to-face conversation. Because the firms in this study were all undergoing significant changes, their senior executives personally carried their messages to operating employees. Candid, open, face-to-face communication with employees presents executives as living, breathing people who understand workers' needs and concerns.

**General Electric**
www.ge.com

**Hallmark**
www.hallmark.com

## POINT

# Change Is an Episodic Activity

With very few exceptions, the study of planned organizational change has been viewed as an episodic activity. That is, it starts at some point, proceeds through a series of steps, and culminates in some outcome that those involved hope is an improvement over the starting point. When change is viewed as an episodic activity, it has a beginning, a middle, and an end.

Lewin's three-step model follows this perspective. Change is seen as a break in the organization's equilibrium. The status quo has been disturbed, and change is necessary to establish a new equilibrium state. The objective of refreezing is to stabilize the new situation by balancing the driving and restraining forces. Action research begins with a diagnostic assessment in which problems are identified. These problems are then analyzed and shared with those who are affected, solutions are developed, and action plans are initiated. The process is brought to closure by an evaluation of the action plan's effectiveness. Even though supporters of action research recognize that the cycle may need to go through numerous iterations, the process is still seen as a cycle with a beginning and an end.

Some experts have argued that organizational change should be thought of as balancing a system made up of five interacting variables within the organization — people, tasks, technology, structure, and strategy. A change in any one variable has repercussions on one or more of the others. Again, this perspective is episodic in that it treats organizational change as essentially an effort to sustain an equilibrium. A change in one variable begins a chain of events that, if properly managed, requires adjustments in the other variables to achieve a new state of equilibrium.

Another way to conceptualize the episodic way of looking at change is to think of managing change as analogous to captaining a ship. The organization is like a large ship travelling across the calm Mediterranean Sea to a specific port. The ship's captain has made this exact trip hundreds of times before with the same crew. Every once in a while, however, a storm will appear, and the crew has to respond. The captain will make the appropriate adjustments — that is, implement changes — and, having manoeuvred through the storm, will return to calm waters. Managing an organization should therefore be seen as a journey with a beginning and an end, and implementing change as a response to a break in the status quo, needed only in occasional situations.

## COUNTERPOINT

# Change Is an Ongoing Activity

The episodic approach may be the dominant paradigm for handling planned organizational change, but it has become obsolete. It applies to a world of certainty and predictability. The episodic approach was developed in the 1950s and 1960s, and it reflects the environment of those times. It treats change as the occasional disturbance in an otherwise peaceful world. However, this paradigm has little resemblance to the 1990s environment of constant and chaotic change.

If you want to understand what it's like to manage change in today's organizations, think of it as equivalent to permanent white-water rafting. The organization is not a large ship, but more akin to a 12-metre raft. Rather than sailing a calm sea, this raft must traverse a raging river made up of an uninterrupted flow of permanent white-water rapids. To make things worse, the raft is manned by 10 people who have never worked together or travelled the river before; much of the trip is in the dark; the river is dotted with unexpected turns and obstacles; the exact destination of the raft is not clear; and at irregular intervals the raft needs to pull to shore, where some new crew members are added and others leave. Change is a natural state, and managing change is a continuous process. That is, managers never get the luxury of escaping the white-water rapids.

To get a feeling for what managers are facing, think of what it would be like to attend a college or university that had the following structure: Courses vary in length. When you sign up for a course, you don't know how long it will last. It may go for two weeks or 30. Furthermore, the instructor can end a course any time he or she wants, with no prior warning. If that isn't frustrating enough, the length of the class changes each time it meets — sometimes it lasts 20 minutes, while other times it runs for three hours — and determination of when the next class meeting will take place is set by the instructor during the previous class. And one more thing: The exams are all unannounced, so you have to be ready for a test at any time.

A growing number of managers are coming to accept that their jobs are much like what a student would face in such a university or college. The stability and predictability of the episodic perspective don't exist. Nor are disruptions in the status quo only occasional, temporary, and followed by a return to an equilibrium state. Managers today face constant change, bordering on chaos. They are being forced to play a game they've never played before, governed by rules that are created as the game progresses. To manage in this dynamic arena, they are moving toward creating learning organizations.

Source: This perspective is based on P.B. Vaill, *Managing as a Performing Art: New Ideas for a World of Chaotic Change* (San Francisco: Jossey-Bass, 1989).

## Shared Responsibility for Employee Communications

Top management provides the "big picture" of where the company is going. Supervisors link the big picture to their work group and to individual employees. Every manager has some responsibility in ensuring that employees are well informed, with the implications for changes becoming more specific as they flow down the organization hierarchy.

People prefer to hear about the changes that might affect them from their manager, not from their peers or through the grapevine. This requires top management to keep middle and lower managers fully apprised of planned changes. And it means that middle- and lower-level managers must quickly share information with their work group to minimize ambiguity.

## Dealing With Bad News

Organizations with effective employee communications aren't afraid to confront bad news. In fact, they typically have a high bad-news to good-news ratio. This doesn't mean that these firms have more problems; rather that they don't penalize the "bearer of bad news."

Increasingly, many corporations are using their company publications to keep employees current on setbacks as well as upbeat news. Allied-Signal's *Horizons* magazine, for instance, carried a recent article by the company's president on the loss of a major bid from Northrop.[32]

All organizations will, at times, experience product failures, delivery delays, customer complaints, or similar problems. The issue is how comfortable people feel in communicating those problems. When bad news is candidly reported, a climate is created in which people aren't afraid to be truthful and good news gains increased credibility.

## The Message Is Shaped for Its Intended Audience

Different people in the organization have different information needs. What is important to supervisors may not be so to middle managers. Similarly, what is interesting information to someone in product planning may be irrelevant to someone in accounting.

What information do individuals and groups want to know? When do they need to know it? What is the best way for them to receive it (at home, newsletter, e-mail, team meeting)? Employees vary in the type of information they need and the most effective way for them to receive it. Managers must recognize this distinction and design their communication program accordingly.

## Treat Communication as an Ongoing Process

These leading companies viewed employee communications as a critical management process. This is illustrated by five common activities in which these firms engaged.

**MANAGERS CONVEY THE RATIONALE UNDERLYING DECISIONS** As change occurs more frequently, and their future becomes less certain, employees increasingly want to know the rationale underlying the decisions and changes that are being made. Why is this occurring? How will it affect me?

**Allied-Signal**
www.alliedsignal.com

As the historical psychological contract that traded employee loyalty for job security has eroded, employees have new expectations from management. In times of permanent employment, comprehensive explanations of management decisions weren't as critical for employees because no matter what the changes, their jobs were relatively secure. But under the new covenant, with workers assuming much greater responsibility for their own careers, employees feel a need for more information so they can make intelligent career decisions. Employees are looking for something from management to make up the difference between what they used to have guaranteed and what they have now. One of those things is information. Even confidential financial information, generally off limits to employees, is now made accessible to workers in companies that practise open-book management.

**TIMELINESS IS VITAL** It's important for managers to communicate what they know, when they know it. Employees don't want to be treated as children, parcelled out bits of information piece by piece or kept from information for fear that it might be misconstrued. They want the facts as soon as they become available. This lessens the power of the grapevine and increases management's credibility. The cost of not communicating in a timely manner is disaffection, anger, and loss of trust.

New technologies make speedy communications possible. Federal Express (FedEx), as a case in point, has built a $10-million internal television network so it can communicate quickly with employees. For example, when FedEx purchased Flying Tigers, the company's chief executive was on the air with the announcement just minutes after the news hit the financial wires.[33]

**COMMUNICATE CONTINUOUSLY** Communication should be continuous, particularly during periods of change or crisis. When employees need information and it's not forthcoming, they'll fall back on informal channels to fill the void, even if those channels provide only unsubstantiated rumours. In those organizations where management strives to keep the information continuously flowing, employees are also more forgiving of the occasional error or omission.

**Irving Forest Discovery Network**
www.ifdn.com

**LINK THE "BIG PICTURE" WITH THE "LITTLE PICTURE"** Truly effective communication does not occur until employees understand how the "big picture" affects them and their jobs. Changes in the economy, among competitors in the industry, or in the organization as a whole must be translated into implications for each location, department, and employee. This responsibility falls most directly on employees' direct managers. In 1997, Saint John, New Brunswick-based Irving Paper was able to sign a six-year contract with its two locals of the Communication, Energy and Paperworkers (CEP) union, in part because it chose to share more information with its employees about its financial status. Instead of simply giving the information to union leaders, management erected information bulletin boards and production boards to ensure that all employees knew how much money the company was making and whether productivity quotas were being met. Management also took union members to visit other mills to show them what change might look like, and to make them more comfortable with engaging in the change process at Irving.[34] Similarly, Winnipeg-based Pollard Bank Note Ltd., a lottery ticket printing company with plants in Kamloops, British Columbia, and Barrhead, Alberta, as well as Winnipeg, set up a joint planning committee of management and employees to ensure that employees have access to the company's information.[35] The committee meets regularly, and critical numbers, such as sales and profits, are open to scrutiny.

**DON'T DICTATE THE WAY PEOPLE SHOULD FEEL ABOUT THE NEWS** Employees don't want to be told how they should interpret and feel about change. Trust and openness are not enhanced by claims such as "These new changes are really exciting!" or "You're going to like the way that the department is being restructured!" More often than not, these attempts to sway opinion only provoke antagonistic responses.

It's more effective to communicate "who, what, when, where, why, and how" and then let employees draw their own conclusions. Although this study looked at companies undergoing change, the recommendations for effective communication apply to organizations at any time, and not just during the change process.

Communication, of course, is not the only process that organizations must be concerned about when carrying out change. In From Concepts to Skills on page 605, you will see an outline of the processes that successful organizations have used to implement change.

## Resistance to Change

| Am I the only one who dislikes change? |
| --- |

One of the most well-documented findings from studies of individual and organizational behaviour is that organizations and their members resist change. In a sense, this is positive. It provides a degree of stability and predictability to behaviour. If there weren't some resistance, organizational behaviour would take on characteristics of chaotic randomness. Resistance to change can also be a source of functional conflict. For example, resistance to a reorganization plan or a change in a product line can stimulate a healthy debate over the merits of the idea and result in a better decision. However, there is a definite downside to resistance to change: It hinders adaptation and progress. You can see the effects of resistance to change in this chapter's second CBC Video Case, on page 621, which shows one young entrepreneur's struggle with deciding how and whether to grow.

Resistance to change doesn't necessarily surface in standardized ways. Resistance can be overt, implicit, immediate, or deferred. It is easiest for management to deal with resistance when it is overt and immediate. For instance, a change is proposed, and employees respond immediately by voicing complaints, engaging in a work slowdown, threatening to go on strike, or the like. The greater challenge is managing resistance that is implicit or deferred. Implicit resistance efforts are more subtle — loss of loyalty to the organization, loss of motivation to work, increased errors or mistakes, increased absenteeism due to "sickness" — and hence more difficult to recognize. Similarly, deferred actions cloud the link between the source of the resistance and the reaction to it. A change may produce what appears to be only a minimal reaction at the time it is initiated, but then resistance surfaces weeks, months, or even years later. Or a single change that in and of itself might have little impact becomes the straw that breaks the camel's back. Reactions to change can build up and then explode in some response that seems totally out of proportion to the change action it follows. The resistance, of course, has merely been deferred and stockpiled. What surfaces is a response to an accumulation of previous changes.

## From CONCEPTS to SKILLS

# Carrying Out Organizational Change

In their 1997 review of three US organizations that have effectively undergone major changes recently (Sears, Roebuck & Company; Royal Dutch Shell; and the US Army), three organizational change consultants used the US Army's *After Action Review* to summarize how an effective change process can be carried out in both business and the military. The *After Action Review* is a nonhierarchical team debriefing to help participants understand performance. The consultants identified seven disciplines embedded in the *After Action Review* that help create effective change:

- *Build an intricate understanding of the business.* Organizational members need to have the big picture revealed to them so they know why change is needed and what is happening in the industry. Let organizational members know what is expected of them as the change proceeds.

- *Encourage uncompromising straight talk.* Communication cannot be based on hierarchy, but must allow everyone to contribute freely to the discussion.

- *Manage from the future.* Rather than setting goals that are directed toward a specific future point in time (and thus encouraging everyone to stop when the goal is achieved), manage from the perspective of always looking toward the future and future needs.

- *Harness setbacks.* When things do not go as planned, and there are setbacks, it is natural to blame one's self, others, or bad luck. Instead, teach everyone to view setbacks as learning opportunities and opportunities for improvement.

- *Promote inventive accountability.* While employees know what the specific targets and goals are, they should also be encouraged in the change process to look to being inventive and taking initiative when new opportunities arise.

- *Understand the quid pro quo.* When organizations undergo change processes, this puts a lot of stress and strain on employees. Organizations must ensure that employees are rewarded for their efforts. To build appropriate commitment, organizations must develop four levels of incentives:

  a) reward and recognition for effort;

  b) training and skill development that will make the employee marketable;

  c) meaningful work that provides intrinsic satisfaction;

  d) communication about where the organization is going and some say in the process for employees.

- *Create relentless discomfort with the status quo.* People are more willing to change when the current situation looks less attractive than the new situation.

These points indicate that effective change is a comprehensive process, requiring a lot of commitment from both the organization's leaders and its members.

Source: R. Pascale, M. Millemann, and L. Gioja, "Changing the Way We Change," *Harvard Business Review*, November-December 1997, pp. 127-139. The actual names of the points based on the *After Action Review* are taken from the article, although the summaries are provided by the authors of this textbook.

Let's look at the sources of resistance. For analytical purposes, we've categorized them by individual and organizational sources. In the real world, the sources often overlap.

### Individual Resistance

Individual sources of resistance to change reside in basic human characteristics such as perceptions, personalities, and needs. The following summarizes

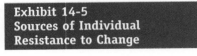

**Exhibit 14-5
Sources of Individual
Resistance to Change**

five reasons why individuals may resist change. These are shown in Exhibit 14-5.

**HABIT**  Every time you go out to eat, do you try a different restaurant? Probably not. If you're like most people, you find a couple of places you like and return to them on a somewhat regular basis.

As human beings, we're creatures of habit. Life is complex enough; we don't need to consider the full range of options for the hundreds of decisions we have to make every day. To cope with this complexity, we all rely on habits or programmed responses. But when confronted with change, we tend to respond in our accustomed ways and this becomes a source of resistance. So when your department is moved to a new office building across town, it means you're likely to have to change many habits: waking up 10 minutes earlier, taking a new set of streets to work, finding a new parking place, adjusting to a new office layout, developing a new lunchtime routine, and so on.

**SECURITY**  People with a high need for security are likely to resist change because it threatens their feelings of safety. For example, when CTV announces it is laying off thousands of people or Ford introduces new robotic equipment, many employees at these firms may fear that their jobs are in jeopardy.

**ECONOMIC FACTORS**  Another source of individual resistance is concern that changes will lower one's income. Changes in job tasks or established work routines also can arouse economic fears if people are concerned that they won't be able to perform the new tasks or routines to their previous standards, especially when pay is closely tied to productivity.

**FEAR OF THE UNKNOWN**  Changes substitute ambiguity and uncertainty for the known. The transition from high school to university is typically such an experience. By the time we've completed our high-school years, we understand how things work. You might not have liked high school, but at least you understood the system. Then you move on to college or university and face a whole new and uncertain system. You have traded the known for the unknown and the fear or insecurity that accompanies it.

Employees in organizations hold the same dislike for uncertainty. If, for example, the introduction of TQM means production workers will have to learn statistical process control techniques, some may fear they'll be unable to do so. They may, therefore, develop a negative attitude toward TQM or behave dysfunctionally if required to use statistical techniques.

**SELECTIVE INFORMATION PROCESSING**  As we learned in Chapter 2, individuals shape their world through their perceptions. Once they have created this world, it resists change. Individuals are guilty of selectively processing information in order to keep their perceptions intact. They hear what they want to hear. They ignore information that challenges the world they've created. To return to the production workers who are faced with the introduction of TQM, they may ignore the arguments their managers make in explaining why a knowledge of statistics is necessary or the potential benefits that the change will provide them.

**CYNICISM**  In addition to simple resistance to change, employees often feel cynical about the change process, particularly if they have been through

**Exhibit 14-6**

Source: Dilbert by Scott Adams. August 3, 1996. DILBERT reprinted by permission of United Feature Syndicate, Inc.

several rounds of change, and nothing appears (to them) to have changed. In a 1997 study, three researchers from Ohio State University identified sources of cynicism in the change process of a large unionized manufacturing plant.[36] The major elements contributing to the cynicism were:

- feeling uninformed about what was happening;
- lack of communication and respect from one's manager;
- lack of communication and respect from one's union representative;
- lack of opportunity for meaningful participation in decision making.

The researchers also found that employees with negative personalities were more likely to be cynical about change. While organizations might not be able to change an individual's personality, they certainly have the ability to provide greater communication and respect, as well as opportunities to participate in decision making. The researchers found that cynicism about change led to such outcomes as lower commitment, less satisfaction, and reduced motivation to work hard. Exhibit 14-6 illustrates why some employees, particularly Dilbert, may have reason to feel cynical about organizational change. You can discover more about how comfortable you are with change by taking the "Managing-in-a-Turbulent-World Tolerance Test" in this chapter's Learning About Yourself Exercise on page 616.

## Organizational Resistance

Organizations, by their very nature, are conservative.[37] They actively resist change. You don't have to look far to see evidence of this phenomenon. Government agencies want to continue doing what they have been doing for years, whether the need for their service changes or remains the same. Organized religions are deeply entrenched in their history. Attempts to change church doctrine require great persistence and patience. Educational institutions, which exist to open minds and challenge established ways of thinking, are themselves extremely resistant to change. Most school systems are using essentially the same teaching technologies today as they were 50 years ago. Similarly, most business firms appear highly resistant to change. Half of the 309 human resources executives of Canadian firms rated their company's ability to manage change as "fair."[38] One-third of them said that their ability to manage change was their weakest skill, and only 25 percent of the companies make a strong effort to train leaders in the change process.

**Exhibit 14-7
Sources of Organizational
Resistance to Change**

Threat to established resource allocations

Structural inertia

Threat to established power relationships

Organizational Resistance

Limited focus of change

Threat to expertise

Group inertia

Six major sources of organizational resistance have been identified.[39] They are shown in Exhibit 14-7.

**STRUCTURAL INERTIA** Organizations have built-in mechanisms to produce stability. For example, the selection process systematically selects certain people in and certain people out. Training and other socialization techniques reinforce specific role requirements and skills. Formalization provides job descriptions, rules, and procedures for employees to follow.

The people who are hired into an organization are chosen for fit; they are then shaped and directed to behave in certain ways. When an organization is confronted with change, this structural inertia acts as a counterbalance to sustain stability.

**LIMITED FOCUS OF CHANGE** Organizations are composed of a number of interdependent subsystems. You can't change one without affecting the others. For example, if management changes the technological processes without simultaneously modifying the organization's structure to match, the change in technology is unlikely to be accepted. So limited changes in subsystems tend to be nullified by the larger system.

**GROUP INERTIA** Even if individuals want to change their behaviour, group norms may act as a constraint. An individual union member, for instance, may be willing to accept changes in his or her job suggested by management. But if union norms dictate resisting any unilateral change made by management, he or she is likely to resist.

**THREAT TO EXPERTISE** Changes in organizational patterns may threaten the expertise of specialized groups. The introduction of decentralized personal computers, which allow managers to gain access to information directly from a company's mainframe, is an example of a change that was strongly resisted by many information systems departments in the early 1980s. Why? Decentralized end-user computing posed a threat to the specialized skills held by those in the centralized information systems departments.

**THREAT TO ESTABLISHED POWER RELATIONSHIPS** Any redistribution of decision-making authority can threaten long-established power relationships within the organization. The introduction of participative decision making or self-managed work teams is the kind of change that supervisors and middle managers often view as threatening.

**THREAT TO ESTABLISHED RESOURCE ALLOCATIONS** Those groups in the organization that control sizable resources often view change as a threat. They tend to be content with the status quo. Will the change, for instance, mean a reduction in their budgets or a cut in their staff size? Those that most benefit from the current allocation of resources often feel threatened by changes that may affect future allocations.

## Overcoming Resistance to Change

Six tactics have been suggested for use by organizations dealing with resistance to change.[40] Let's review them briefly.

**Esprit**
www.esprit.com

**EDUCATION AND COMMUNICATION** Resistance can be reduced through communicating with employees to help them see the logic of a change. This tactic basically assumes that the source of resistance lies in misinformation or poor communication; that is, if employees receive the full facts and any misunderstandings are cleared up, resistance will be decreased. Communication can be achieved through one-on-one discussions, memos, group presentations, or reports. Does this approach work? It does, provided that the source of resistance is inadequate communication and that management-employee relations are characterized by mutual trust and credibility. If these conditions don't exist, the change is unlikely to succeed.

**PARTICIPATION** It's difficult for individuals to resist a change decision in which they participated. Prior to making a change, those opposed can be brought into the decision process. Assuming that the participants have the expertise to make a meaningful contribution, their involvement can reduce resistance, obtain commitment, and increase the quality of the change decision. However, against these advantages are the negatives: potential for a poor solution and great time consumption.

**FACILITATION AND SUPPORT** Organizations undergoing change can offer a range of supportive efforts to reduce resistance. When employee fear and anxiety are high, employee counselling and therapy, new-skills training, or a short paid leave of absence may facilitate adjustment. The drawback of this tactic is that, as with the others, it is time-consuming. It is also expensive, and its implementation offers no assurance of success.

**NEGOTIATION** Another way for organizations to deal with potential resistance to change is to exchange something of value for a lessening of the resistance. For instance, if the resistance is centred in a few powerful individuals, a specific reward package can be negotiated that will meet their individual needs. Negotiation as a tactic may be necessary when resistance comes from a powerful source. Yet one cannot ignore its potentially high costs. Additionally, there is the risk that once senior management in an organization negotiates with one party to avoid resistance, he or she is open to the possibility of being beleaguered by other individuals in positions of power.

**MANIPULATION AND COOPTATION** Manipulation refers to covert influence attempts. Twisting and distorting facts to make them appear more attractive, withholding undesirable information, and creating false rumours to get employees to accept a change are all examples of manipulation. If corporate management threatens to close down a particular manufacturing plant if that plant's employees fail to accept an across-the-board pay cut, and if the threat is actually untrue, management is using manipulation. Cooptation, on the other hand, is a form of both manipulation and participation. It seeks to "buy off" the leaders of a resistance group by giving them a key role in the change decision. The leaders' advice is sought, not to seek a better decision, but to receive their endorsement. Both manipulation and cooptation are relatively inexpensive and easy ways to gain the support of adversaries, but the tactics can backfire if the targets become aware that they are being tricked or used. Once the tactics are discovered, management's credibility may drop to zero.

**COERCION** Last on the list of tactics is coercion; that is, the application of direct threats or force upon the resisters. If the corporate management mentioned in the previous discussion is determined to close a manufacturing plant if employees don't acquiesce to a pay cut, then coercion would be the label attached to its change tactic. Other examples of coercion are threats of transfer, loss of promotions, negative performance evaluations, and a poor letter of recommendation. The advantages and drawbacks of coercion are approximately the same as those mentioned for manipulation and cooptation.

## The Politics of Change

No discussion of resistance to change would be complete without a brief mention of the politics of change. Politics suggests that the impetus for change is more likely to come from employees who are new to the organization (and have less invested in the status quo) or managers who are slightly removed from the main power structure. Those managers who have spent their entire careers with a single organization and eventually achieve a senior position in the hierarchy are often major impediments to change. Change itself is a very real threat to their status and position. Yet they may be expected to implement changes to demonstrate that they're not merely caretakers. By trying to bring about change, they can symbolically convey to various constituencies — stockholders, suppliers, employees, customers — that they are on top of problems and adapting to a dynamic environment. Of course, as you might guess, when forced to introduce change, these long-time power holders tend to implement first-order changes. Radical change is too threatening. This, incidentally, explains why boards of directors that recognize the imperative for the rapid introduction of second-order change in their organizations frequently turn to outside candidates for new leadership.[41]

You may remember that we discussed politics in Chapter 8 and gave some suggestions for how to more effectively encourage people to go along with your ideas. That chapter also indicated how individuals acquire power, which provides further insight into the ability of some individuals to resist change.

## Caveats on Undergoing Change

We have presented numerous examples of organizational change in this chapter and discussed how one goes about conducting effective organizational change. However, should all organizations set out to restructure? A consulting firm in Massachusetts studied several dozen *Fortune 500* companies to address this question. Their investigation suggests that continued bouts of reorganization were more likely to lead to poorer rather than improved performance. The study of 41 of these companies found that "90 percent of the companies whose financial performance had improved (during the 1980s) rarely embarked on major reorganization programs. By contrast, 90 percent of those that had lost market value had undergone frequent and difficult reorganization efforts."[42]

Why would change lead to poor results in so many cases? Sometimes reorganizing the structure of an organization seems easier than identifying the root problem of the organization. Hartmax Corporation, a US apparel manufacturer, underwent several unsuccessful reorganizations in the 1980s. Finally, it realized that its problems were strategic, not structural. Sometimes the kinds of changes implemented may not be completely appropriate for the organization, as in this chapter's Case Incident on page 619, where measures more suitable to the private sector were applied in an effort to reduce costs and increase efficiency at a Toronto hospital. Another reason to carefully consider the decision to undergo change is that all reorganizations put the company into a form of shock, which can lead to lower efficiency, learning, and productivity.

## National Culture and Change

A number of change issues we've discussed are culture bound. To illustrate, let's briefly look at five questions: (1) Do people believe change is possible? (2) If it is possible, how long will it take to bring it about? (3) Is resistance to change greater in some cultures than in others? (4) Does culture influence how

These Chinese couples prefer Western-style dancing over *t'ai chi*, the traditional meditative morning exercise. But in the workplace, Chinese workers are more resistant to change, holding fast to their past traditions. Significant cultural differences challenge foreign companies operating in China. They face China's rigid hierarchical structure, where the idea of younger managers telling older workers what to do is unheard of and employees work in state-controlled companies that provide no incentives for advancement.

change efforts will be implemented? (5) Do successful idea champions do things differently in different cultures?

Do people believe change is possible? Remember that cultures vary in terms of beliefs about their ability to control their environment. In cultures where people believe that they can dominate their environment, individuals will take a proactive view of change. This would describe Canada and the United States. In many other countries, people see themselves as subjugated to their environment and thus will tend to take a passive approach toward change.

If change is possible, how long will it take to bring it about? A culture's time orientation can help us answer this question. Societies that focus on the long-term, such as Japan, will demonstrate considerable patience while waiting for positive outcomes from change efforts. In societies with a short-term focus, such as the United States and Canada, people expect quick improvements and will seek change programs that promise fast results.

Is resistance to change greater in some cultures than in others? Resistance to change will be influenced by a society's reliance on tradition. Italians, as an example, focus on the past, while Americans emphasize the present. Italians, therefore, should generally be more resistant to change efforts than their American counterparts.

Does culture influence how change efforts will be implemented? Power distance can help with this issue. In high power distance cultures, such as the Philippines or Venezuela, change efforts will tend to be autocratically implemented by top management. In contrast, low power distance cultures value democratic methods. We'd predict, therefore, a greater use of participation in countries such as Denmark and Israel.

Finally, do successful idea champions do things differently in different cultures? The evidence indicates that the answer is "yes."[43] People in collectivist cultures, in contrast with those in individualistic cultures, prefer appeals for cross-functional support for innovation efforts. People in high power distance cultures prefer champions to work closely with those in authority to approve innovative activities before work is conducted on them; and the higher the uncertainty avoidance of a society, the more champions should work within the organization's rules and procedures to develop the innovation. These findings suggest that effective managers will alter their organization's championing strategies to reflect cultural values. So, for instance, while idea champions in the United States might succeed by ignoring budgetary limitations and working around confining procedures, champions in Venezuela, Greece, Italy, or other cultures high in uncertainty avoidance will be more effective by closely following budgets and procedures.

A 1997 study of the turnaround at Micron Corporation, one of the two largest semiconductor producers in Russia, provides first-hand evidence of how the change process differs in North America compared with Russia. The researchers noted Russian culture differs in that the power to lay off employees and managers alike was considerably more restricted than in North American organizations. The researchers observed that Russian managers are less oriented towards the market, and more toward the collective good. Russian firms were also more likely to cut research and development spending in times of change. Micron did carry out a turnaround that has been somewhat successful, though less profitable than desired. The culture differences may be a partial explanation for Micron's outcome. Because of many years of communism and an emphasis on a collectivist society, it will take some time for Russian managers to adjust to a market orientation.

# HR Implications

# Managing Change in a Unionized Environment

Canada's workplace is more likely to be unionized than is the workplace in the United States, and this has led to some complications in accomplishing change in some organizations. In Chapter 13 we noted some of the difficulties that both MacMillan Bloedel and Canada Post had in dealing with a unionized environment, and in both Chapters 9 and 13 we discussed how the *Vancouver Sun* worked with its unions to change its printing process. In Chapter 13 we also noted that some of the management of Bestar's Lac-Megantic plant did not want the union involved in quality programs if it meant that managers had to share their power. On the other hand, there are numerous examples of successful changes in a unionized environment. We discussed in Chapter 7 that part of the reason for New Brunswick-based Irving Paper's success in dealing with its union was the company's willingness to communicate openly with the members. We will present two additional examples of working with unions, and then we will discuss the factors that make it easier to manage change in a unionized environment.

Earlier in this chapter we looked at some of the changes that have occurred at Canadian National Railway (CN) under Paul Tellier. CN's employees are covered by the Brotherhood of Maintenance of Way Employees, the International Brotherhood of Electrical Workers, Rail Canada Traffic Controllers, and the Canadian Auto Workers. Tellier brought to CN a philosophy of employees and change: "Managing change is first and foremost influencing mentalities: not the mentality of your customers so that they appreciate what you are trying to do, but the mentality of your employees so that they conform to the realities the customer must face."[1]

One of the mentalities Tellier had to change was the practice of "featherbedding."[2] Upon his arrival he discovered that because of union contracts, CN was paying 2000 employees whose jobs had been abolished and who therefore did not even report to work. Previous union contracts had guaranteed pay until age 65 for anyone who had worked at CN for eight years and whose job had disappeared. Union contracts also made it impossible to transfer employees against their will.

The result of this was that CN was hiring new workers in Edmonton even though there were employees who were not needed in Moncton but who refused to move. CN changed these rules after a 1995 strike. Under the new agreement, employees would receive 90 percent of their pay for six years, and workers who refused to be transferred would receive only 65 percent of their pay for two years. Also under the new contract, train conductors and engineers had to work longer shifts — up to 12 hours. This has reduced the number of shift changes required on routes like those from Sarnia, Ontario, to Halifax, Nova Scotia, from six to three.

Not all CN workers are happy, of course. Cliff Hamilton, a CN train engineer, says, "I think it's a crime what's going on. They're taking money out of the pockets of Canadian workers and putting it in the hands of American shareholders." And CN does not have a completely easy time with the unions. In 1995, CN faced strikes and lockouts for nine days before Ottawa legislated the unions back to work. However, in August 1998 contract negotiations ended successfully without any strikes. Nevertheless, as we noted earlier in this chapter, CN has managed a remarkable turnaround while operating in a unionized environment.

In a similar case, when Hollis Harris took over at Air Canada in 1993, after the company had posted consecutive unprofitable quarters straight back to 1989, one of his tasks was to get five unions to accept wage concessions and guarantee productivity improvements. In working through these concessions, the unions give Harris a lot of credit for his frank and open negotiating style. When he was in discussions with the Canadian Air Line Pilots Association (CALPA), Harris agreed to have Air Canada's financial books inspected by an outside consultant hired by CALPA. "When the consultants reported that the situation was indeed as desperate as Harris had been claiming, the pilots agreed to a five percent wage rollback."[3] Harris also earned the pilots' respect for this action.

Two consultants who have worked with a number of Canadian organizations in recent years note four essential elements for managing change in a unionized environment:[4]

- *An effective system for resolving day-to-day issues.* Employees should feel that they do not have to go through the formal grievance process in order to be heard. Instead, the workplace should be open to hearing workers' issues, as this will underscore a commitment to participation and empowerment.

- *A jointly administered business education process.* Union leaders and their members become uneasy about the future, particularly as Canadian organizations have gone through prolonged periods of downsizing. An education process that allows employees to understand the financial statements of the company and understand how their performance affects the bottom line helps them better understand the decisions the company makes.

- *A jointly developed strategic vision for the organization.* When union members are involved in setting the vision, they are more likely to focus on how change can be made, rather than whether it should be made. The vision "should describe performance expectations, work design, organizational structure, the supply chain, governance, pay and rewards, technology, education and training, operating processes, employee involvement, employment security, and union-management roles and relations."[5]

- *A nontraditional problem-solving method of negotiating collective agreements.* It is important to promote an atmosphere of tolerance and willingness to listen, where issues are problems to be solved rather than victories to be claimed. It is also helpful to expand the traditional scope of bargaining to include complex issues such as strategic plans. Generally management does not want to bargain over these issues, but when they do, it signals further commitment to working jointly with unionized employees.

Sources:

[1] P. Tellier, "Turning CN Around," *Canadian Business Review*, Spring 1995, pp. 31-32+.

[2] Featherbedding discussion based on "Back on the Rails: Years of Cutting Have Produced a Leaner and Meaner CN," *Maclean's*, January 13, 1997, pp. 36-38.

[3] "Tough Guys Don't Cuss. Air Canada's Employees Didn't Quite Know What to Make of Hollis Harris," *Canadian Business,* February 1995, pp. 22-28.

[4] J.R. Stepp and T.J. Schneider, "Fostering Change in a Unionized Environment," *Canadian Business Review*, Summer 1995, pp. 13-16.

[5] J.R. Stepp and T.J. Schneider, "Fostering Change in a Unionized Environment," *Canadian Business Review*, Summer 1995, pp. 13-16.

## SUMMARY AND IMPLICATIONS

## For the Workplace

The need for change has been implied throughout this text. "A casual reflection on change should indicate that it encompasses almost all our concepts in the organizational behaviour literature. Think about leadership, motivation, organizational environment, and roles. It is impossible to think about these and other concepts without inquiring about change."[44]

If environments were perfectly static, if employees' skills and abilities were always up-to-date and incapable of deteriorating, and if tomorrow were always exactly the same as today, organizational change would have little or no relevance to managers. But the real world is turbulent, requiring organizations and their members to undergo dynamic change if they are to perform at competitive levels.

Managers are the primary introducers of change in most organizations. By the decisions they make and their role-modelling behaviours, they shape the organization's change culture. For instance, management decisions related to structural design, cultural factors, and human resource policies largely determine the level of innovation within the organization. Similarly, management decisions, policies, and practices will determine the degree to which the organization learns and adapts to changing environmental factors.

## For You as an Individual

Given the speed of change happening in today's world, it is unlikely that you will escape some type of organizational restructuring during your lifetime, and probably you will encounter this more than once. Many people are resistant to change, but one of the messages of this book is to encourage individuals to continue learning throughout their lifetime. Engaging in continuous learning means change does not have to be so upsetting, because you will have the skills you need to either work in the restructured organization or land yourself a new position. For example, you may want to view yourself as "self-employed" even when you are employed by an organization. This will encourage you to continue to upgrade your skills, giving you the opportunity to "sell" these skills to your existing employer or transfer these skills to a new employer elsewhere.

*ROADMAP*
*REMINDER*

With this chapter we conclude our discussion of organizational behaviour, but we do not believe you should end your study of organizational behaviour here. For all of your life you will be working with others in a variety of situations and the lessons of organizational behaviour will continue to apply.

## For Review

1. What are the types of planned change?
2. What are the different parts of the organization that can be changed?
3. What is the knowledge development process of organizational learning?
4. What is the adaptive learning process for organizational learning?
5. What are the roadblocks to organizational learning?
6. How does Lewin's 3-step model of change deal with resistance to change?
7. What does the *After Action Review* tell us about conducting change?
8. What is the difference between driving forces and restraining forces?
9. What are the factors that lead individuals to resist change?
10. What are the factors that lead organizations to resist change?

# For Critical Thinking

1. How have changes in the workforce during the past 20 years affected organizational policies?
2. "Managing today is easier than at the start of the 20th century because the years of real change took place between Confederation and World War I." Do you agree or disagree? Discuss.
3. What is meant by the phrase "we live in an age of discontinuity"?
4. "Resistance to change is an irrational response." Do you agree or disagree? Explain.

## LEARNING ABOUT YOURSELF EXERCISE

# Managing-in-a-Turbulent-World Tolerance Test

**Instructions**

Listed below are some statements a 37-year-old manager made about his job at a large, successful corporation. If your job had these characteristics, how would you react to them? After each statement are 5 letters, A to E. Circle the letter that best describes how you think you would react according to the following scale:

A *I would enjoy this very much: It's completely acceptable.*

B *This would be enjoyable and acceptable most of the time.*

C *I'd have no reaction to this feature one way or another, or it would be about equally enjoyable and unpleasant.*

D *This feature would be somewhat unpleasant for me.*

E *This feature would be very unpleasant for me.*

1. I regularly spend 30 to 40 percent of my time in meetings.    A  B  C  D  E

2. A year and a half ago, my job did not exist, and I have been essentially inventing it as I go along.    A  B  C  D  E

3. The responsibilities I either assume or am assigned consistently exceed the authority I have for discharging them.    A  B  C  D  E

4. At any given moment in my job, I have on the average about a dozen phone calls to be returned.    A  B  C  D  E

5. There seems to be very little relation in my job between the quality of my performance and my actual pay and fringe benefits.    A  B  C  D  E

6. About 2 weeks a year of formal management training is needed in my job just to stay current.    A  B  C  D  E

7. Because we have very effective equal employment opportunity in my company, and because it is thoroughly multinational, my job consistently brings me into close working contact at a professional level with people of many races, ethnic groups, and nationalities and of both sexes.    A  B  C  D  E

8. There is no objective way to measure my effectiveness.    A  B  C  D  E

9. I report to 3 different bosses for different aspects of my job, and each has an equal say in my performance appraisal.    A   B   C   D   E

10. On average, about a third of my time is spent dealing with unexpected emergencies that force all scheduled work to be postponed.    A   B   C   D   E

11. When I must have a meeting of the people who report to me, it takes my secretary most of a day to find a time when we are all available, and even then, I have yet to have a meeting where everyone is present for the entire meeting.    A   B   C   D   E

12. The university degree I earned in preparation for this type of work is now obsolete, and I probably should go back for another degree.    A   B   C   D   E

13. My job requires that I absorb 100 to 200 pages per week of technical materials.    A   B   C   D   E

14. I am out of town overnight at least 1 night per week.    A   B   C   D   E

15. My department is so interdependent with several other departments in the company that all distinctions about which departments are responsible for which tasks are quite arbitrary.    A   B   C   D   E

16. I will probably get a promotion in about a year to a job in another division that has most of these same characteristics.    A   B   C   D   E

17. During the period of my employment here, either the entire company or the division I worked in has been reorganized every year or so.    A   B   C   D   E

18. Although there are several possible promotions I can see ahead of me, I have no real career path in an objective sense.    A   B   C   D   E

19. Although there are several possible promotions I can see ahead of me, I think I have no realistic chance of reaching the top levels of the company.    A   B   C   D   E

20. Although I have many ideas about how to make things work better, I have no direct influence on either the business policies or the personnel policies that govern my division.    A   B   C   D   E

21. My company has recently put in an "assessment centre" where I and all other managers will be required to go through an extensive battery of psychological tests to assess our potential.    A   B   C   D   E

22. My company is a defendant in an antitrust suit, and if the case comes to trial, I will probably have to testify about some decisions that were made a few years ago.    A   B   C   D   E

23. Advanced computer and other electronic office technology is continually being introduced into my division, necessitating constant learning on my part.    A   B   C   D   E

24. The computer terminal and screen I have in my office can be monitored in my bosses' offices without my knowledge.    A   B   C   D   E

Turn to page 636 for scoring directions and key.

Source: From P.B. Vaill, *Managing as a Performing Art: New Ideas for a World of Chaotic Change* (San Francisco: Jossey-Bass, 1989), pp. 8–9. Reproduced with permission of the publisher.

# The Beacon Aircraft Company

## Objectives

1. To illustrate how forces for change and stability must be managed in organizational change programs.
2. To illustrate the effects of alternative change techniques on the relative strength of forces for change and forces for stability.

## The Situation

The marketing division of the Beacon Aircraft Company has undergone two reorganizations in the past two years. Initially, its structure changed from a functional to a matrix form. But the matrix structure did not satisfy some functional managers. They complained that the structure confused the authority and responsibility relationships.

In reaction to these complaints, the marketing manager revised the structure to the functional form. This new structure maintained market and project groups, which were managed by project managers with a few general staff members, but no functional specialists were assigned to these groups.

After the change, some problems began to surface. Project managers complained that they could not obtain adequate assistance from functional staff members. It not only took more time to obtain necessary assistance, but it also created problems in establishing stable relationships with functional staff members. Since these problems affected their services to customers, project managers demanded a change in the organizational structure — probably again toward a matrix structure. Faced with these complaints and demands from project managers, the vice-president is pondering another reorganization. He has requested an outside consultant to help him in the reorganization plan.

## The Procedure

1. Divide yourselves into groups of 5-7 and take the role of consultants.
2. Each group identifies the driving and resisting forces found in the firm. List these forces in the spaces provided.

| The Driving Forces | The Resisting Forces |
| --- | --- |
| _____ | _____ |
| _____ | _____ |
| _____ | _____ |
| _____ | _____ |
| _____ | _____ |

3. Each group develops a set of strategies for increasing the driving forces and another set for reducing the resisting forces.
4. Each group prepares a list of changes it wants to introduce.
5. The class reassembles and hears each group's recommendations.

Source: Adapted from K.H. Chung and L.C. Megginson, *Organizational Behavior,* Copyright © 1981 by K.H. Chung and L.C. Megginson. Reprinted by permission of Harper Collins Publishers, Inc.

1. Find 5 companies whose primary business is helping organizations to manage change. What common characteristics, if any, did you find in the programs these companies offer?
2. Find 3 companies that have gone through major organizational changes in the last 3 years. What kinds of changes did they undertake? How would you evaluate the effectiveness of these changes?

**CASE INCIDENT**

# Organizational Change at St. Michael's Hospital

Dr. Philip Berger found out how tightly his new employer, St. Michael's Hospital in downtown Toronto, watches costs when he went to use the photocopy machine for the first time. He discovered that he was supposed to bring his own paper. Berger, chief of family and community medicine, says he now appreciates the policy because "it makes every employee individually responsible for how they spend the public's money."

For St. Michael's Hospital, after close to a decade of provincial funding cutbacks, plus the hospital's own financial problems, there have been other cutbacks as well. Volunteers bring supplies to the wards. On weekends, intensive care sometimes runs out of intravenous bags, bandages, and gauze.

In 1998, the hospital prepared for more problems as Ontario shut some of the other hospitals in the city. Many employees, including doctors and administrators, are wondering how much harder and faster they can work before they compromise health care. "Maybe we have to back up a bit on efficiency and spend more time per patient," admits Michael Heilbronn, chief financial officer at St. Michael's.

Due to a variety of causes, the hospital's debt reached $63 million in 1991, the largest total at any hospital in Canadian history. Jeff Lozon, now Ontario's deputy minister of health, was recruited as president and, thanks to his cuts and to $15 million in loans forgiven by the Sisters of St. Joseph, who operate the hospital, and the government of Ontario, the debt was paid off. To do this, the hospital re-engineered — changing every job in the hospital, collapsing job classifications, and streamlining admissions.

The hospital uses a just-in-time delivery system for all of its medical supplies. As a result, inventory was slashed from $900 000 to about $200 000, but it doesn't always work. Steve Lobsinger, an intensive care nurse who heads the nurses' local bargaining unit, says, "The big joke at the hospital is that often just in time is a day late."

In six years at St. Michael's, Lozon has cut staff from 2900 to 2200 employees. At the same time, inpatient admissions have jumped to 19 000 from 18 000, and outpatient visits have increased to 290 000 from 200 000.

A study looking at the University of Toronto's 11 teaching hospitals has found cost per patient at St. Michael's to be the lowest. At the same time, St. Michael's trains more medical students per patient than the other hospitals and puts more of its nursing resources to direct patient care. This represents quite an accomplishment for the hospital.

However, another study of 12 Ontario hospitals, released in the fall of 1997 by the Richard Ivey School of Business at the University of Western Ontario, raises questions about how well St. Michael's is really performing. In 400 interviews, front-line workers, middle managers, senior executives, and board members pointed to declines in service, including "less nursing time per patient, less palatable food, lower levels of cleanliness in facilities, high employee stress, slow recording of patient data, and reduced patient supervision."

Even Heilbronn admits, "If you look at the numbers, we have probably taken it a little too lean and can back off a little bit," and agrees that there is a limit to applying private-sector efficiency to a hospital. "You've got to be sensitive that the core business is patient care. In the private sector, if you make a lousy product you get an unsatisfied customer. At a hospital, your patient is dead. So you've got to be sensitive and balance it out."

# Questions

1. "Hospitals simply can't be run as business organizations." Do you agree with this statement?

2. Was Lozon trying to implement too much change too fast? Support your position.

3. Do you think the hospital can continue to run a just-in-time supply system with increased patient numbers? Explain your position.

Source: Based on P. Kuitenbrouwer, "St. Efficiency's Caring Ways: Toronto's St Michael's Hospital Is a Lean, Cost Efficient Machine. But Staff Is Harried and Administrators Are Beginning to Wonder About Quality of Patient Care," *Financial Post*, February 7/9, 1998, pp. 8,9.

# Do I Have to Move?

In 1996, CP Rail packed up its corporate offices and moved from Montreal to Calgary, accomplishing the largest corporate makeover in Canadian history. The task for the year was to downsize, change cities, and make the old company new again. At the same time, the company planned an internal restructure, cutting 1500 employees and saving $125 million by the year's end.

CP Rail's top management imposed the change on its employees, trying to convince employees that the company needed to re-establish a culture focusing on performance and personal accountability. Employees who were not downsized were told that they had to move to Calgary or accept buy-out packages. Tensions ran high as preparations for the move got underway.

In trying to impose the new order on management and employees, top management signalled that it was not interested in excuses to avoid moving towards new goals. As one senior executive instructed managers, "We don't want to hear why it didn't work [in the past]. It's irrelevant." This was a clear signal that managers were not to focus on the past, but instead concentrate their energies on a radically new future.

Independent of workplace changes, the CP Rail move could be expected to be hard on the families of the 730 slated to be transferred to Calgary from Montreal, Vancouver, Toronto, Minneapolis, and Albany, NY. To make this adjustment easier, CP Rail arranged a two-day session to answer questions about Alberta, and real estate agents, counsellors for spouses, and other services were supplied to try to create an easier transition. Even the Alberta Francophone Society was brought in to help Quebecers who wanted to continue French-language instruction for their children, and maintain ties to the francophone community after their move.

Despite what appears to be a pretty gruelling move, CP Rail ended 1996 on a high note, producing a profit of $405 million, compared with a loss of $592 million in 1995.

# Questions

1. To what extent does Lewin's "Unfreezing, Moving, and Refreezing" model apply to CP Rail's move?

**2.** Why might you expect CP Rail's mid-level managers to be resistant to the move to Calgary?

**3.** What suggestions might you make to a company planning a similar move in the future to make things easier on its employees?

Source: Based on "CP Move," *Venture 586;* aired April 14, 1996; and "Relocating Employees Involves Intensive Planning," *Financial Post,* February 10/12, 1996, p. 35.

# Should I Grow or Should I Stay?

Sue Klabunde has spent 10 years running Spots Pots, a pottery business in Halifax. Some years she's been very successful. But in general, Klabunde has taken Spots Pots from a small-sized to a medium-sized struggling business, faced with historical debt problems.

Klabunde has no trouble coming up with creative ideas for her pots, but profitability has been another issue. And she finds running a business much like trying to organize a massive dinner party where different foods need different preparation times. She's also had trouble with some of her suppliers, who have not met deadlines or have shipped poor-quality product.

Klabunde has found a new supplier, Jim Gimeon, in Tatamagouche, NS, two hours away from Halifax. He's encouraging Klabunde to relocate her business to his site. But she's not sure this is the right move. Klabunde has several reservations. She's been running her business by herself all these years, and she's reluctant to move to a new town. As part of the move, Gimeon has suggested that he will be in charge of production, and she will be in charge of design. But Klabunde is afraid of surrendering control to someone else, particularly someone she doesn't know well.

Though it's obvious Klabunde has been struggling for years, she doesn't seem able to make a decision about whether to make the big move and perhaps have the opportunity to really grow her business. She notes that change is hard, the decision is not obvious, and it will involve a lot of risks. If she doesn't make some decision soon, however, she is going to have to fire some or all of her employees, because she doesn't have enough business to keep them working. But she's reluctant to give up control too.

## Questions

**1.** Klabunde's business is obviously struggling. What factors do you think prevent her from moving ahead?

**2.** How might Klabunde's personality be reflected in the current state of Spots Pots?

**3.** What recommendations might you make to Klabunde to help her make a decision about what to do with her company?

Source: Based on "The Reluctant Entrepreneur," *Venture 708;* aired January 12, 1999. Visit the Spots Pots Web site at www.spotspots.com.

# Rob Gareau: Creating an Organization to Suit the Times

In looking at the organizational structure of Human Performance, it becomes apparent that there is some specialization of labour. Each of the three owners has his own areas of operation. Rob Gareau is the manager, and his primary responsibilities are business systems, hiring, developing business plans, and budgeting. Dusan Benicky is the program coordinator. He conducts research and does assessments, as well as working with the professional athletes and promoting the Burnaby Centre. Steve Ramsbottom is the senior trainer, and is responsible for supervising and scheduling the other trainers. The Centre also has one full-time administrator who provides clerical and secretarial support, a part-time bookkeeper, and at any given time six to 10 trainers, most of whom work part-time. The trainers report to whomever is at the Centre when they are on duty, though specific training questions are handled by Gareau and Ramsbottom. These two also develop the overall training programs administered at Human Performance. Clinical issues and questions are handled by Benicky. The administrator and the bookkeeper/receptionist report to Gareau.

In terms of staff responsibilities, most of the remaining staff are trainers. While they do have some flexibility in choosing their schedules, once they are linked up with clients they have to keep to the agreed schedules. The consistency of training and the rapport with clients are very important features of Human Performance. Even when doing training in small groups, as Gareau does with his athlete clients, it's important that the same people are training these groups.

Human Performance has experienced tremendous growth in a short time. During 1999, the company went from three employees to 10 in just eight months. This growth occurred due to more doors opening and more opportunity: "In a short period of time we went from hoping to get enough business to having too much business for our staff size." As Gareau observes, "Human Performance is starting to be recognized as the prototype of athletic training in BC, and is setting the benchmarks." The company has already been asked to coach professional athletes and to go overseas to work with some professional hockey players, creating training camps, "So we know we are doing the right things, and all the opportunities are coming."

Though he is clearly pleased with this initial success, Gareau notes that the owners do not celebrate this success. "These good things are the beginning, not the end of where we're going."

For the most part, the owner-managers have been able to deal with this fast-paced growth, even professing some lack of surprise. They had studied the market before they started the company, so they had some idea of what to expect. Nevertheless, while really enthusiastic about the growth, "we are also concerned about quality," Gareau says.

Because Human Performance is growing so rapidly, and because Gareau is in the business of personal training and development, we asked him whether his staff felt the stresses of the business. And we also asked whether he could recommend ways of dealing with stress. For the most part, the stress on the staff has been of a positive sort. While it takes more energy to manage growth, they are also enthusiastic about the changes that are occurring, and this serves to reduce the negative effects of stress that sometimes occur when one faces more demands.

Gareau noted that it's important to recognize the warning signs of stress, and then to engage in stress management. While acknowledging that specific techniques for managing stress can depend on the individual, he noted that during stressful times it is important to get more rest, and to engage in hobbies and other releases to get away from the stress. For Gareau these hobbies include exercise, skiing, and snowboarding. He also slips in an occasional trip with a group of his buddies from school, where they all can relax and enjoy each other's company.

Gareau has made changes in his own life to manage the stresses of coping with a young and growing business. When Human Performance first started, he invested almost all of his free time in the business. More recently, however, he is starting to take his own advice, and working towards a bit more balance. He realized he needed to do this when he began regretting some of the things he was missing because of all of the time he spent with his business. Gareau is clear that he wants balance in his life: "I was willing to make a lot of sacrifices in the beginning to make sure that Human Performance would be an ongoing part of my life. But I want it to be a balanced life as well, which I can do now, because I've gotten the company to the stage where I needed it to be at this point."

Gareau feels confident that he's found a formula that will keep Human Performance on a successful track. From the beginning, all three owners were intent on managing their ambitions and growing with the business, rather than getting ahead of themselves, and perhaps in over their heads. As he points out, "we took out no loans, and simply used our own money." But this has helped them go from opening their doors in early 1999, to having nearly 15 people working in the business just 18 months later.

As Gareau looks back, he identifies the most important problems he's faced in the last 18 months:

- completing a partnership agreement that satisfied the needs of all parties;

- learning how to best train staff and delegate responsibility once they're trained;

- dealing with a high volume of business while developing our policies and systems.

It is clear that many of the issues he faced had OB implications and resolutions.

And in looking forward, Gareau expects that his biggest personal challenge will be this: "Balancing my business opportunities and goals with my personal goals. I do not want to wake up and realize I have been swept up in a business at the expense of my personal relationships and plans."

# Questions:

1. To what extent do you think that the staff at Human Performance can handle the stress of growth? At what point would you anticipate that growth might become more difficult for the company?

2. Human Performance has a relatively flat structure at this point in time. Can you anticipate the need for a hierarchical structure? If Gareau wants to keep this flatter structure, what issues must he keep in mind if the company continues to grow?

3. How might Gareau use the Hackman-Oldham Job Characteristics Model to make sure his staff continues feeling motivated as they carry out their daily tasks?

4. To what extent do you think the culture Gareau has tried to create at Human Performance might have an impact on the company's ability to grow? What recommendations would you make about whether he can continue this sort of culture as Human Performance gets larger?

# Working in a Dot-Com World

Richard Howard quit his job as an Amazon.com customer service representative in early 1998.[1] Perhaps the last straw was being admonished by his supervisor for holding a three-to-four-minute phone conversation to help a customer looking for Civil War-era fiction.

How could this happen? Amazon prides itself on speed. "If it's hard for you to go fast, it can be hard for you here," said Jane Slade, until recently Amazon's customer service director. "If you like things comfortable, it can be a difficult place to be."

Nevertheless, being admonished for giving "prolonged" customer service seems odd for a company that claims it wants to be "Earth's most customer-centric company." One former customer service representative commented: "We're supposed to care deeply about customers, provided we can care deeply about them at an incredible rate of speed."

Add to this the tensions between stock-option millionaires and low-wage co-workers and Amazon's internal dynamics may not seem as bright as its dot-com reputation.

After all, many of Amazon's employees spend their working time doing rather mundane tasks: boxing books and answering e-mails. A stellar Amazon representative is one who responds to 12 e-mails in an hour. Answering fewer than 7.5 e-mails an hour for an extended period, however, can result in probation or termination.

To the outsider, Amazon, the company created by Jeff Bezos (at left), looks like a trailblazer, the original dot-com company. But internally are Amazon, and other e-commerce businesses, more like traditional companies, or do these organizations represent a new organizational form with a new way of managing and leading employees?

Certainly Amazon's customer service centres have many of the same problems one might find in an old-style manufacturing plant: tensions "between gung-ho managers and disaffected employees; speedy machines and mortal paces; even union and anti-union interests, a high-tech industry rarity."[2]

E-commerce has taken the world by storm, or so it seems. It's not unusual for companies and executives to be told that they have to jump on the train, or risk going under. Richard Oliver, a business professor at Vanderbilt University, argues that "executives who don't make the move on e-commerce will find themselves fired. And companies that refuse to adapt will lose their more forward-thinking talent."[3]

And yet there is some concern about whether Canada will keep up with the demand for e-commerce. Canada's share of global electronic commerce was about seven percent in 1999, but it is projected to drop to four percent by 2003 if Canadian businesses do not move more quickly.[4] Some suggest that if Canada doesn't start to narrow its gap with the United States' dominance of e-commerce, "Canadians could feel their standard of living fall more than it has."[5] Knowing how to manage in an e-commerce world may help close that gap.

## Does OB Have Anything to Say to E-Commerce?

Much of organizational behaviour theory was developed amidst employees working in larger, manufacturing organizations. What can OB say to the new world of work: dominated by the Internet, speed, and youthful employees willing to bet their futures on dreams of stock-option payoffs? Consider, for instance, Epinions, the company that developed a Web site to gather together reviewers' opinions on any subject (www.epinions.com). Founder Naval Ravikant, together with five others who had experience working for Yahoo!, @Home, and Netscape, took the company from idea stage to Web site launch in just 13 weeks.[6] In doing so, Ravikant gathered together 31 people to work at Epinions as well as $8-million (US) in seed financing from venture capitalists.

It wasn't that long ago that two years to build an Internet company seemed fast. In today's world, taking two years would probably leave a company in the dust.

Organizational behaviour can address some of the issues that these Internet companies face as effectively as it has addressed the issues of more traditional organizations in the past. We identify below some of the key issues to consider in an e-commerce world, specifically organizational structure, leadership, decision making, and motivation, and show how OB can help us understand these issues.

## Organizational Structure

The Internet hasn't changed the fact that businesses need to be concerned about customer service, cashflow management, inventory control, distribution, and human resources. But it has also opened up new avenues for expanding business and making connections with other businesses. As Marty Lippert, chief information officer and vice-chair at Royal Bank, says, "The Net is tearing down the barriers that kept small businesses from challenging their largest competitors."[7]

It's remarkably easier to set up new businesses these days, and also to compete nationally and internationally. "Today's companies are fast," Lippert says. "They can charge into this new world by using the Internet to offer a new customer experience, a wide selection of products and services, satisfy customers, control costs and manage inventory without the legacy of old business problems."[8]

Organizational structure determines how quickly an organization can act. Mechanistic, bureaucratic structures usually result in a slower pace of operation, particularly in a dynamic environment. Nonetheless, some business-to-consumer e-commerce businesses

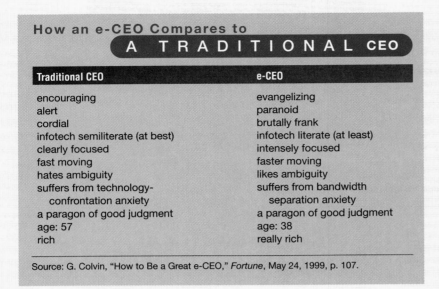

## How an e-CEO Compares to A TRADITIONAL CEO

| Traditional CEO | e-CEO |
| --- | --- |
| encouraging | evangelizing |
| alert | paranoid |
| cordial | brutally frank |
| infotech semiliterate (at best) | infotech literate (at least) |
| clearly focused | intensely focused |
| fast moving | faster moving |
| hates ambiguity | likes ambiguity |
| suffers from technology-confrontation anxiety | suffers from bandwidth separation anxiety |
| a paragon of good judgment | a paragon of good judgment |
| age: 57 | age: 38 |
| rich | really rich |

Source: G. Colvin, "How to Be a Great e-CEO," *Fortune*, May 24, 1999, p. 107.

simply repeat the traditional arrangements of many corporations: Orders come in over the Web, and products need to be shipped. These companies merely carry a traditional structure to a different environment.

However, in other e-commerce businesses, the structure will be very different from the typical organizations of the 20th century. A **modular organization** is typically a small, core organization that outsources major business functions.[9] This closely reflects the organizational structure of San Francisco-based Cisco Systems Inc. Cisco has a business model based almost exclusively on partnering: It outsources any business function that is not considered a core competency. While Cisco provides sophisticated networking technology, it does not manufacture any of its hardware products. Rather, it specializes in customer relationships and marketing integrated customer solutions. Then it works with distributors, original equipment manufacturers (OEMs), and suppliers to get the customer what he or she wants.

Why is a modular style effective for e-commerce businesses? Traditional companies often have sophisticated infrastructures that have enabled them to interact with loyal customers, established business partners, and their distribution channels. Dot-com companies are less likely to be burdened with established organizational structures. Moreover, they need to be nimble, flexible and innovative. A modular structure allows for maximum flexibility because organizations create networks of relationships that allow them to contract out any business function that management believes others can do better or more cheaply. The modular organization stands in sharp contrast with the typical bureaucracy that has many vertical levels of management and where control is sought through ownership.

Other e-commerce businesses take on a structure that resembles a **virtual organization**. A virtual organization "is a continually evolving network of independent companies — suppliers, customers, even competitors — linked together to share skills, costs, and access to one another's markets."[10] For example, the auto industry has joined together with parts suppliers to form this type of structure. Parts suppliers can keep track of demand more easily, as well as being able to suggest innovations in design.

## Building Teamwork

When management uses teams as its central coordination device, you have a **team structure**. The primary characteristics of the team structure are that it breaks down departmental barriers and decentralizes decision making to the level of the work team. Team structures also require employees to be generalists as well as specialists.[11]

The culture of e-commerce businesses is particularly suited to teamwork. "There is more need for creative qualities and a tendency to define staff roles less, resulting in a fundamental change in a company's culture," says Bob Scott, director of global e-commerce at IT group Cap Gemini.[12] "Bubbling enthusiasms, hard work and fun environment" applies to most young Internet companies.[13]

To create this "hard work *and* fun environment" Internet firms may rely more on building teams and establishing team relationships than traditional companies. After all, many dot-com employees work very long hours. "We still pull all-nighters," says Shawn Thomas, co-founder of Vancouver-based Mindquake Software Inc. "It's a badge of honour at Mindquake pulling an all-nighter. It's not because someone is behind you. It's because you get into the flow and there are times when you have so much creative energy doing what you are doing, you just go straight through the night."[14] Thomas notes that for people in e-commerce "there's no difference between work and play," which suggests that individuals have to get along even better than they might in a traditional company.

# What Does It Take to Be a Leader in an E-Commerce World?

The Competing Values Framework suggests that leaders have two sets of balancing acts: internal and external demands of the firm, and the needs for both flexibility and control.[15] The internal-external dimension refers to

*OB on the Edge*

the extent that the focus is either inwards (toward employee issues and/or production processes) or outwards (toward the marketplace, government regulations, and the changing social, environmental, and technological conditions of the future). The flexibility-control dimension refers to the competing demands of staying focused on doing what has been done in the past vs. being more flexible in orientation and outlook.

In an e-commerce world, leaders may have to emphasize change and innovation over control. There is also a greater demand for an external focus. Businesses engaged in e-commerce need to design and build "strategic, co-operative relationships with partners, suppliers and customers, while also cultivating trust."[16]

The new structures of e-commerce businesses also demand a new style of leadership. When companies are joined in modular or virtual structures, each individual company relinquishes some operational and strategic control. Managers in these new structures need the skills to build relations with other companies, negotiate "win-win" deals, find compatible partners in terms of values and goals, and then develop appropriate communication systems to keep everyone informed.[17]

Ensuring that external relationships work does not mean that internal concerns won't also arise. Leaders in an e-commerce world need to be prepared to "abandon the command-and-control corporate model in favor of team-based leadership" when dealing with their employees and managers.[18] They need to learn to share leadership with others around them. The two inset boxes on pages 625 and 626 give additional insights about being an e-CEO.

# Decision Making in a World of Constant Change

Of course, e-commerce CEOs must also face many of the same things mainstream CEOs face: making fast decisions with limited information, understanding technology and brands, having faith. But the pace they face is much, much faster than anything experienced by CEOs

## factbox [19]

- In 1999 the United States led the world in revenues from e-commerce, at $71 400 million (US). Canada's revenues, by contrast, were $2780 million (US). Germany, Japan, and the United Kingdom were all ahead of Canada, though far behind the United States.

- Only 20% of Canadian businesses have established extensive e-businesses.

- 70% of Canadian businesses believe that e-commerce will transform their companies.

- 80% of Canadian business leaders do not believe that e-commerce represents a serious business threat.

- In 1999 there were only four Internet IPOs on the Toronto Stock Exchange, compared with 165 on the US Nasdaq exchange.

- Canadian knowledge workers earn 26% less than their American counterparts.

before. Companies can be built in 13 weeks, like Epinions, but they can also be decimated in five months, or even overnight, as stock market fluctuations in April 2000 demonstrated.

Working in an e-commerce world means making decisions faster than you've ever made them before. "You're driving too fast—you feel the exhilaration and the threat—you must turn left and right at death-defying speeds without blinking—never blink—if you go up and down with the news, you'll never make it," says Roger Siboni, CEO of Epiphany.[20] His company creates software to help e-corporations use their customer data efficiently.

The rational decision-making model suggests that individuals consider all their options, weight them, and select and implement the best decision. E-commerce firms are often making decisions so quickly that they rely more on both intuition and risk-taking to make decisions. For instance, when the *Vancouver Sun* invests in a new printing press, the employees don't expect that next month, or even next year, the newspaper will enter the fashion industry. The newspaper, with its capital investments, simply couldn't make such radical changes that quickly or easily. However, with an Internet company the primary capital equipment is brainpower. Employees can start pursuing new strategies at any moment. They can target new niche groups at almost a moment's notice. As Doug McCuaig, senior VP at Ernst & Young notes, companies have to be ready to "transform or die." He says the winners in e-commerce will be those firms that are open to change.[21]

In fact, one of the biggest problems facing most decision makers will be their ability to deal with change rapidly and effectively. "The hardest thing to deal with has to be change, but learning how to do that is essential, as new competitors are coming out of nowhere and becoming household names," says Rick Broadhead, a Toronto-based consultant.[22]

Thus the e-CEO and/or the leadership team have to be ready to evaluate new ideas at a moment's notice. As Kevin O'Connor, CEO of DoubleClick notes, "Strategy is half deciding what to do and half what not to do.

You have to be able to say no to $10 million."[23] Fortunately, e-commerce businesses are most likely to appeal to risk-takers, those who are willing to move fast, even without clear rewards, while still willing to put in long, long hours.

Decision making also gets pushed down lower into the organization with e-business. Staff have more access to data, and this empowers them to make more decisions more quickly.

# Motivation

When Freddy Nager joined Iz.com in fall 1999, the Los Angeles online entertainment startup offered him 5000 stock options that he could purchase at 51 cents (US). The founders told him that after the initial public offering (IPO), Nager would be wealthy. The reality was far less rosy. The IPO never happened, and in March 2000 Iz.com was bought by Popmail.com. Nager was laid off. He was allowed to keep only 1000 of his options. So he had paid $2550 (US) for stock options when he was hired, but the value of his investment was about $1400

when his friends interview with pre-IPO companies, "they always hear talk about options, but their eyes glaze over."[26]

Bill Lessard, co-author of *Net Slaves: True Tales of Working the Web,*[27] points out the harsh reality of working for many of today's dot-com companies: "Most Internet careers are nasty, brutish and short."[28] When the Nasdaq hit its bumpy ride in spring 2000, new companies were struggling with both cash problems and talent problems. Fewer individuals were willing to bet their time on IPOs that might not happen.

The lure of stock options may be hard for some to understand as a motivational tool. There is much risk, particularly if most or all of your "salary" is given in options. Unlike a real paycheque, which arrives weekly or monthly, stock-option value may never appear. Or the options could result in relatively quick wealth. Expectancy theory suggests that individuals are motivated to the extent they believe that their effort will lead to performance, and the performance will result in a rather certain probability that the valued reward will materialize. When individuals were signing on to new dot-coms in the hopes of stratospheric payoffs through stock options, they were betting that there would be a sure and certain payoff. With the collapse of stock prices for many dot-coms in early 2000, and some flight away from employment with these companies, employees are signalling

## faceoff

E-commerce is so important to the development of business opportunities that expecting employees to work "all hours" to meet demands makes good business sense. Moreover, the promise of stock options will encourage employees' extra effort.

Employees in some dot-com businesses are expected to take too much risk through the use of stock options as incentives. A dot-com business can only be successful over the long run if it manages its employees the same as regular businesses do.

when he was laid off. Meanwhile he had worked for Iz.com for nearly six months, on that promise of becoming wealthy.[24]

In 1999 it seemed that many wanted to work for one of the new dot-com firms. The lure of stock options that would make one wealthy convinced potential employees that the risk of working for little or no pay would pay off tremendously when the dot-com went public. And many companies did become overnight sensations. But over time, reality has sunk in. For instance in mid-April 2000, Amazon.com's shares were trading at $46.78 (US), down from a 52-week high of $113 (US). Business professor Edward Lawler of the University of Southern California noted that "Amazon is at significant risk right now in terms of losing employees."[25] Nager notes that now

that receiving tangible rewards for efforts does affect their behaviour.

Some dot-com employees do not expect to reach the stratosphere in earnings, however. At Mindquake, with projected sales in excess of $5 million for 2000, some employees earn $75 000. The partners of the private company (which has no outside investors and no debt) pay themselves in the $45 000 a year range. How can the partners be motivated when they're earning less than their employees? "We pay ourselves what we need and everything else is invested in the company. There is more to life than money," says Mindquake's Thomas.[29]

# OB on the Edge

Thomas notes that it is the challenge that keeps his partners and employees motivated, not money. "As long as there is a challenge, that's what keeps me going. There's always a goal, raising the bar. It's about growing something and giving it a life of its own."[30] Thomas's argument shows the importance of intrinsic motivation in achieving high effort.

Dot-coms are not immune from engaging in poor motivational practices, however. Since 1999, Amazon.com has been faced with a union-organizing campaign, a rare event in the high-tech sector. Customer service employees at Amazon complain of overcrowding (up to four people sharing cubicles), low wages, and "a top-down management style."[31]

Amazon may have brought these union problems on itself. For the 1998 holiday season, Amazon's customer service managers announced a new holiday bonus program so "everyone will feel energized to work as efficiently as possible."[32]

Employees at a specified level who worked at least 50 hours in a given week while answering an average of 10 e-mails an hour and "maintaining a consistently high level of quality" were offered a choice between a $50 taxable cash bonus or four paid hours of time off. Employees were further told that the bonus would end after the holiday season, but "these productivity expectations will continue into next year." In other words, work extra hard for a bonus now, but you'll be expected to work just as hard for no bonus next month.

Amazon's productivity bonus defies almost anything that motivational theories might suggest. Small bonuses for greatly increased work are hardly an incentive. Customer service vice-president Bill Price now says that Amazon's approach was a mistake. "I wouldn't do that again, and I wouldn't do it it now," he said.[33]

From these examples it should be clear that organizational behaviour speaks as much to the "Old Economy" as to the "New Economy," and can even help those starting up their own e-commerce businesses from setting up environments that lead to the employee complaints that Amazon.com has faced.

## Research Exercises

1. Look for data on companies that have created Internet businesses while maintaining their "bricks and mortar" businesses. Are the two forms of organization managed differently? Should they be?
2. What kinds of compensation are dot-com companies offering their employees? To what extent is this compensation tied to expectations about company performance?

## Your Perspective

1. What kinds of skills do you think employees need to be successful in an e-commerce world?
2. The risks and opportunities available to e-commerce business mean that creativity, enthusiasm, and motivation are in high demand. What would motivate you to join an e-commerce employer? How would you keep up with the new skills demanded in these jobs?

## Want to Know More?

For news and information about business-to-business (B2B) e-commerce, you might want to have a look at E-Commerce Times: www.ecommercetimes.com, Yahoo!: fullcoverage.yahoo.com/fc/Tech/Electronic-Commerce, and Canadian E-Business Opportunities Roundtable: www.bcg.com/roundtable/mission.asp.

If you're thinking about how you might move into e-commerce, you might begin by finding out about Web sales and marketing in industries of interest. Electric Library Canada at http://www.elibrary.ca charges an annual subscription fee. For US data you can go to Northern Light at http://www.nlsearch.com, which charges by the article. Or you can go to search engines like Yahoo! at http://www.yahoo.com to get the information you need.

## Endnotes:

1. Information in this vignette based on M. Leibovich, "At Amazon.com, Service Workers Without a Smile," *Washington Post*, November 22, 1999, p. A01.

2. M. Leibovich, "At Amazon.com, Service Workers Without a Smile," *Washington Post*, November 22, 1999, p. A01.

3. G. Shaw, "Business Advised to Hop Aboard E-commerce Train," *Vancouver Sun*, March 14, 2000, pp. D1-D2.

4. G. Shaw, "IBM Boss Preaching Gospel of E-Business," *Vancouver Sun*, April 8, 2000, p. D16.

5. G. Shaw, "IBM Boss Preaching Gospel of E-Business," *Vancouver Sun*, April 8, 2000, p. D16.

6. P. Bronson, "Silicon Valley: The Next Generation," *National Post*, July 17, 1999, p. B3. (Reprinted from *The New York Times Magazine*.)

7. "The Definitive Guide to E-Commerce for Small Business: How to Profit From the Internet" [Advertising supplement], *Profit: The Magazine for Canadian Entrepreneurs*, October 1999, pp. Insert 1-23.

8. "The Definitive Guide to E-Commerce for Small Business: How to Profit From the Internet" [Advertising supplement], *Profit: The Magazine for Canadian Entrepreneurs*, October 1999, pp. Insert 1-23.

9. See, for instance, E.A. Gargan, "'Virtual' Companies Leave the Manufacturing to Others," *New York Times,* July 17, 1994, p. F5; D.W. Cravens, S.H. Shipp, and K.S. Cravens, "Reforming the Traditional Organization: The Mandate for Developing Networks," *Business Horizons,* July-August 1994, pp. 19-27; R.T. King, Jr., "The Virtual Company," *Wall Street Journal,* November 14, 1994, p. 85; R.E. Miles and C.C. Snow, "The New Network Firm: A Spherical Structure Built on Human Investment Philosophy," *Organizational Dynamics,* Spring 1995, pp. 5-18; G.G. Dess, A.M.A. Rasheed, K.J. McLaughlin, and R.L. Priem, "The New Corporate Architecture," *Academy of Management Executive,* August 1995, pp. 7-20; D. Morse, "Where's the Company?" *Wall Street Journal,* May 21, 1998, p. R19; and G. Hamel and J. Sampler, "The e-Corporation," *Fortune,* December 7, 1998, pp. 80-92.

10. G.G. Dess, A.M.A. Rasheed, K.J. McLaughlin, and R. Priem, "The New Corporate Architecture," *Academy of Management Executive*, August 1995, pp. 7-18.

11. M. Kaeter, "The Age of the Specialized Generalist," *Training*, December 1993, pp. 48-53.

12. T. Foremski, "Creating a New Class of Worker," *Financial Post*, March 6, 2000, p. E3.

13. A. Daniels, "Internet Firm Treats Employees Royally," *Vancouver Sun*, January 31, 2000, p. B6.

14. A. Daniels, "Mindquake Makes Most of Work, Play," *Vancouver Sun*, February 14, 2000, p. D10.

15. K. Cameron and R.E. Quinn, *The Competing Values Framework*; R.E. Quinn, S.R. Faerman, M.P. Thompson, and M.R. McGrath, *Becoming a Master Manager: A Competency Framework* (New York: John Wiley and Sons, 1990); K. Cameron and R.E. Quinn, *Diagnosing and Changing Organizational Culture: Based on the Competing Values Framework*, 1st ed. (Reading, MA: Addison Wesley Longman Inc., 1999).

16. D. Ticoll and N. Klym, "The Real Bottom Line of the Virtual Company," *The Financial Post Magazine*, November 1998, p. 136.

17. G.G. Dess, A.M.A. Rasheed, K.J. McLaughlin, and R. Priem, "The New Corporate Architecture," *Academy of Management Executive*, August 1995, p. 13. See also P. Lorange and J. Roos, "Why Some Strategic Alliances Succeed and Why Others Fail," *Journal of Business Strategy*, January/February 1991, 25-30; and G. Slowinski, "The Human Touch in Strategic Alliances," *Mergers and Acquisitions*, July/August 1992, pp. 44-47.

18. D. Ticoll and N. Klym, "The Real Bottom Line of the Virtual Company," *The Financial Post Magazine*, November 1998, p. 136.

19. Information for this Fact Box comes from P. Demont, "E-Comm's Time Has Come in Canada, Study Says," *Vancouver Sun*, March 10, 2000, p. F1; "The Definitive Guide to E-Commerce for Small Business: How to Profit From the Internet" [Advertising supplement], *Profit: The Magazine for Canadian Entrepreneurs*, October 1999, pp. Insert 1-23; P. Demont, "Shift Into E-commerce High Gear, Business Told," *Vancouver Sun*, January 18, 2000, p. D1.

20. G. Colvin, "How to Be a Great e-CEO," *Fortune*, May 24, 1999, p. 107.

21. C. Mulroney, "E-commerce Experts Dispense Their Advice," *The Globe and Mail*, September 24, 1999, p. R9.

22. C. Mulroney, "E-commerce Experts Dispense Their Advice," *The Globe and Mail*, September 24, 1999, p. R9.

23. G. Colvin, "How to Be a Great e-CEO," *Fortune*, May 24, 1999, p. 107.

24. C. Piller, "Dot.Com Careers Fast Losing Their Lustre," *Vancouver Sun*, April 17, 2000, pp. A1, A8.

25. C. Piller, "Dot.Com Careers Fast Losing Their Lustre," *Vancouver Sun*, April 17, 2000, pp. A1, A8.

26. C. Piller, "Dot.Com Careers Fast Losing Their Lustre," *Vancouver Sun*, April 17, 2000, pp. A1, A8.

27. B. Lessard and S. Baldwin, *Net Slaves: True Tales of Working the Web* (McGraw-Hill, 1999).

28. C. Piller, "Dot.Com Careers Fast Losing Their Lustre," *Vancouver Sun*, April 17, 2000, pp. A1, A8.

29. A. Daniels, "Mindquake Makes Most of Work, Play," *Vancouver Sun*, February 14, 2000, p. D10.

30. A. Daniels, "Mindquake Makes Most of Work, Play," *Vancouver Sun*, February 14, 2000, p. D10.

31. M. Leibovich, "At Amazon.com, Service Workers Without a Smile," *Washington Post*, November 22, 1999, p. A01.

32. M. Leibovich, "At Amazon.com, Service Workers Without a Smile," *Washington Post*, November 22, 1999, p. A01.

33. M. Leibovich, "At Amazon.com, Service Workers Without a Smile," *Washington Post*, November 22, 1999, p. A01.

# APPENDIX

## SCORING KEYS FOR "LEARNING ABOUT YOURSELF" EXERCISES

### Chapter 1: The Competing Values Framework: Identifying Your Interpersonal Skills

These skills are taken from the Competing Values Framework, and are shown in Exhibit 1-2. Below, you will see how the individual skills relate to various managerial roles. Using the skills you identified as strongest, identify which roles you feel especially prepared for right now. Then, using the skills you identified as weakest, identify areas in which you might want to gain more skill. You should also use this information to determine whether you are currently more internally or externally focused, or oriented more towards flexibility or control.

| | |
|---|---|
| Director: 1, 2, 3 | Mentor: 13, 14, 15 |
| Producer: 4, 5, 6 | Facilitator: 16, 17, 18 |
| Coordinator: 7, 8, 9 | Innovator: 19, 20, 21 |
| Monitor: 10, 11, 12 | Broker: 22, 23, 24 |

### Chapter 3: What Do You Value?

Transfer the numbers for each of the 16 items to the appropriate column; then add up the 2 numbers in each column.

| | Professional | Financial | Family | Social |
|---|---|---|---|---|
| | 1. _____ | 2. _____ | 3. _____ | 4. _____ |
| | 9. _____ | 10. _____ | 11. _____ | 12. _____ |
| Totals | _____ | _____ | _____ | _____ |
| | Community | Spiritual | Physical | Intellectual |
| | 5. _____ | 6. _____ | 7. _____ | 8. _____ |
| | 13. _____ | 14. _____ | 15. _____ | 16. _____ |
| Totals | _____ | _____ | _____ | _____ |

The higher the total in any value dimension, the higher the importance you place on that value set. The closer the numbers are in all 8 dimensions, the more well rounded you are.

### Chapter 4: What Motivates You?

To determine your dominant needs—and what motivates you—place the number 1 through 5 that represents your score for each statement next to the number for that statement.

|  | Achievement | Power | Affiliation |
|--|-------------|-------|-------------|
|  | 1. _____ | 2. _____ | 3. _____ |
|  | 4. _____ | 5. _____ | 6. _____ |
|  | 7. _____ | 8. _____ | 9. _____ |
|  | 10. _____ | 11. _____ | 12. _____ |
|  | 13. _____ | 14. _____ | 15. _____ |
| Totals: | _____ | _____ | _____ |

Add up the total of each column. The sum of the numbers in each column will be between 5 and 25 points. The column with the highest score tells you your dominant need.

## Chapter 5: Are You Attracted to the Group?

Add up your scores for items 4, 6, 7, 8, 9, 10, 14, 17, 19, and 20. Obtain a corrected score by subtracting the score for each of the remaining questions from 10. For example, if you marked 3 for item 1, you would obtain a corrected score of 7 (10 – 3). Add the corrected scores together with the total obtained on the 10 items scored directly. The higher your score, the more positive are your feelings about the group.

## Chapter 6: Do Others See Me as Trustworthy?

Add up your total score for the 7 statements. The following provides general guidelines for interpreting your score.

57 – 70 points = You're seen as highly trustworthy.

21 – 56 points = You're seen as moderately trustworthy.

7 – 20 points = You're rated low on this characteristic.

## Chapter 7: What Is Your Primary Conflict-Handling Intention?

To determine your primary conflict-handling intention, place the number 1 through 5 that represents your score for each statement next to the number for that statement. Then total up the columns.

| | Competing | Collaborating | Avoiding | Accommodating | Compromising |
|--|-----------|---------------|----------|---------------|--------------|
| | 1. ___ | 4. ___ | 6. ___ | 3. ___ | 2. ___ |
| | 5. ___ | 9. ___ | 10. ___ | 11. ___ | 8. ___ |
| | 7. ___ | 12. ___ | 15. ___ | 14. ___ | 13. ___ |
| Totals | ___ | ___ | ___ | ___ | ___ |

Your primary conflict-handling intention is the category with the highest total. Your fall-back intention is the category with the second-highest total.

## Chapter 8: How Political Are You?

According to the author of this instrument, a complete organizational politician will answer "true" to all 10 questions. Organizational politicians with fundamental ethical standards will answer "false" to questions 5 and 6, which deal with deliberate lies and uncharitable behaviour. Individuals who regard manipulation, incomplete disclosure, and self-serving behaviour as unacceptable will answer "false" to all or almost all of the questions.

## Chapter 9: What Kind of Organizational Culture Fits You Best?

For items 5 and 6, score as follows:

$$
\begin{array}{rcl}
\text{Strongly agree} & = & +2 \\
\text{Agree} & = & +1 \\
\text{Uncertain} & = & 0 \\
\text{Disagree} & = & -1 \\
\text{Strongly disagree} & = & -2
\end{array}
$$

For items 1, 2, 3, 4, and 7, reverse the score (Strongly agree = –2, and so on). Add up your total. Your score will fall somewhere between +14 and –14.

What does your score mean? The higher your score (positive), the more comfortable you'll be in a formal, mechanistic, rule-oriented, and structured culture. This is often associated with large corporations and government agencies. Negative scores indicate a preference for informal, humanistic, flexible, and innovative cultures, which are more likely to be found in research units, advertising firms, high-tech companies, and small businesses.

## Chapter 10: Are You a Charismatic Leader?

The questionnaire measures each of the 6 basic behaviour leader patterns, as well as a set of emotional responses. Each question is stated as a measure of the extent to which you engage in the behaviour, or elicit the feelings. The higher your overall score, the more you demonstrate charismatic leader behaviours. The indices outline a variety of traits associated with charismatic behaviour. For each index, add up the scores you gave to the relevant questions. Your score on each index can range from 4 to 20.

*Index 1: Management of Attention* (1, 7, 13, 19). Your score _____. You pay especially close attention to people with whom you are communicating. You are also "focused in" on the key issues under discussion and help others to see clearly these key points. They have clear ideas about the relative importance or priorities of different issues under discussion.

*Index 2: Management of Meaning* (2, 8, 14, 20). Your score _____. This set of items centres on your communication skills, specifically your ability to get the meaning of a message across, even if this means devising some quite innovative approach.

*Index 3: Management of Trust* (3, 9, 15, 21). Your score _____. The key factor is your perceived trustworthiness as shown by your willingness to follow through on promises, avoidance of "flip-flop" shifts in position, and willingness to take a clear position.

*Index 4: Management of Self* (4, 10, 16, 22). Your score _____. This index concerns your general attitudes toward yourself and others, that is, your overall concern for others and their feelings, as well as for "taking care of" feelings about yourself in a positive sense (e.g., self-regard).

*Index 5: Management of Risk* (5, 11, 17, 23). Your score _____. Effective charismatic leaders are deeply involved in what they do, and do not spend excessive amounts of time or energy on plans to "protect" themselves against failure. These leaders are willing to take risks, not on a hit-or-miss basis, but after careful estimation of the odds of success or failure.

*Index 6: Management of Feelings* (6, 12, 18, 24). Your score _____. Charismatic leaders seem to consistently generate a set of feelings in others. Others feel that their work becomes more meaningful and that they are the "masters" of their own behaviour; that is, they feel competent. They feel a sense of community, a "we-ness" with their colleagues and their co-workers.

## Chapter 11: Decision-Making Style Questionnaire

Mark each of your responses on the following scales. Then use the point value column to arrive at your score. For example, if you answered a to the first question, you would check 1a in the feeling column. This response receives zero points when you add up the point value column. Instructions for classifying your scores are indicated following the scales.

| Sensation | Point Value | Intuition | Point Value | Thinking | Point Value | Feeling | Point Value |
|-----------|-------------|-----------|-------------|----------|-------------|---------|-------------|
| 2b __X__ | 1 | 2a _____ | 2 | 1b __X__ | 1 | 1a _____ | 0 |
| 4a _____ | 1 | 4b __X__ | 1 | 3b _____ | 2 | 3a __X__ | 1 |
| 5a _____ | 1 | 5b __X__ | 1 | 7b __X__ | 1 | 7a _____ | 1 |
| 6b _____ | 1 | 6a __X__ | 0 | 8a _____ | 0 | 8b __X__ | 1 |
| 9b _____ | 2 | 9a __X__ | 2 | 10b _____ | 2 | 10a __X__ | 1 |
| 12a _____ | 1 | 12b __X__ | 0 | 11a __X__ | 2 | 11b _____ | 1 |
| 15a _____ | 1 | 15b __X__ | 1 | 13b _____ | 1 | 13a __X__ | 1 |
| 16b _____ | 2 | 16a __X__ | 0 | 14b _____ | 0 | 14a __X__ | 1 |
| | 1 | | 5 | | 4 | | 5 |
| Maximum Point Value | (10) | | (7) | | (9) | | (7) |

Write *intuition* if your intuition score is equal to or greater than your sensation score. Write *sensation* if your sensation score is greater than your intuition score. Write *feeling* if your feeling score is greater than your thinking score. Write *thinking* if your thinking score is greater than your feeling score.

A high score on *intuition* indicates you see the world in holistic terms. You tend to be creative. A high score on *sensation* indicates that you are realistic and see the world in terms of facts. A high score on *feeling* means you make decisions based on gut feeling. A high score on *thinking* indicates a highly logical and analytical approach to decision making.

## Chapter 12: Bureaucratic Orientation Test

Give yourself 1 point for each statement for which you responded in the bureaucratic direction:

| | | | |
|---|---|---|---|
| 1. | Mostly agree | 11. | Mostly agree |
| 2. | Mostly agree | 12. | Mostly disagree |
| 3. | Mostly disagree | 13. | Mostly disagree |
| 4. | Mostly agree | 14. | Mostly agree |
| 5. | Mostly disagree | 15. | Mostly disagree |
| 6. | Mostly disagree | 16. | Mostly agree |
| 7. | Mostly agree | 17. | Mostly disagree |
| 8. | Mostly agree | 18. | Mostly agree |
| 9. | Mostly disagree | 19. | Mostly agree |
| 10. | Mostly agree | 20. | Mostly disagree |

A very high score (15 or over) suggests that you would enjoy working in a bureaucracy. A very low score (5 or lower) suggests that you would be frustrated by working in a bureaucracy, especially a large one.

## Chapter 13: Is an Enriched Job for You?

This questionnaire taps the degree to which you have a strong vs. weak desire to obtain growth satisfaction from your work. Each item on the questionnaire yields a score from 1 to 7 (that is, "Strongly prefer A" is scored 1; "Neutral" is scored 4; and "Strongly prefer B" is scored 7). To obtain your individual growth need strength score, average the 12 items as follows:

Numbers 1, 2, 7, 8, 11, 12 (direct scoring)
Numbers 3, 4, 5, 6, 9, 10 (reverse scoring)

Average scores for typical respondents are close to the midpoint of 4.0. Research indicates that if you score high on this measure, you will respond positively to an enriched job. Conversely, if you score low, you will tend *not* to find enriched jobs satisfying or motivating.

You can use this questionnaire to identify areas where you can improve your interview skills. If you scored 3 or less on any statement, you should consider what you can do to improve that score.

## Chapter 14: Managing-in-a-Turbulent-World Tolerance Test

Score 4 points for each A, 3 for each B, 2 for each C, 1 for each D, and 0 for each E. Compute the total, divide by 24, and round to one decimal place.

While the results are not intended to be more than suggestive, the higher your score, the more comfortable you seem to be with change. The test's author suggests analyzing scores as if they were grade-point averages. In this way, a 4.0 average is an A, a 2.0 is a C, and scores below 1.0 flunk.

Using replies from nearly 500 MBA students and young managers, the range of scores was found to be narrow—between 1.0 and 2.2. The average score was between 1.5 and 1.6—equivalent to a D+/C- grade! If these scores are generalizable to the work population, clearly people are not very tolerant of the kind of changes that come with a turbulent environment. However, this sample is now nearly a decade old. We should expect average scores today to be higher as people have become more accustomed to living in a dynamic environment.

# ENDNOTES

## Chapter 1

1. B. Evenson, "Canadian Psychiatrist Tries to Keep the Hotshots Out of Space," *The National Post*, August 16, 1999, p. A1.

2. D. Milbank, "Managers Are Sent to 'Charm Schools' to Discover How to Polish Up Their Acts," *Wall Street Journal*, December 14, 1990, p. B1.

3. The Conference Board of Canada, *Employability Skills Profile*, 1998.

4. S. Sherman, "Are You as Good as the Best in the World?", *Fortune*, December 13, 1993, p. 96. This point is elaborated in J. Pfeffer, "Producing Sustainable Competitive Advantage Through the Effective Management of People," *Academy of Management Executive*, February 1995, pp. 55-69.

5. M. Rothman, "Into the Black," *INC.*, January 1993, p. 59.

6. C. Hymowitz, "Five Main Reasons Why Managers Fail," *Wall Street Journal*, May 2, 1988, p. 25.

7. D. Milbank, "Managers Are Sent to 'Charm Schools' to Discover How to Polish Up Their Acts," *Wall Street Journal*, December 14, 1990, p. B1.

8. Cited in A. Fisher, "Don't Blow Your New Job," *Fortune*, June 22, 1998, p. 159.

9. Cited in A. Fisher, "Don't Blow Your New Job," *Fortune*, June 22, 1998, p. 160.

10. S.A. Waddock, "Educating Tomorrow's Managers," *Journal of Management Education*, February 1991, pp. 69-96; and K.F. Kane, "MBAs: A Recruiter's-Eye View," *Business Horizons*, January-February 1993, pp. 65-71.

11. C. Taylor, "Gaming Glory," *Financial Post*, July 26, 1999, p. C3.

12. "New Boss Sets Goals of Opening Up CIBC," *Vancouver Sun*, June 29, 1999, p. D. 13.

13. See, for instance, J.E. Garcia and K.S. Keleman, "What Is Organizational Behavior Anyhow?", paper presented at the 16th Annual Organizational Behavior Teaching Conference, Columbia, MO, June 1989.

14. C. Harris, "Prime Numbers: A Statistical Look at the Trends and Issues That Will Dominate Our Future," *Financial Post*, 10, no. 46, November 15/17, 1997, p. P13.

15. *StatsCan Daily*, January 27, 1999.

16. J. McCallum, "New Managers, Same Old Skills," *Financial Post*, November 22/24, 1997, pp. P4-P6.

17. C.R. Farquhar and J.A. Longair, "Creating High-Performance Organizations With People," Conference Board of Canada, 1996, Report #R164-96.

18. C.R. Farquhar and J.A. Longair, "Creating High-Performance Organizations With People," Conference Board of Canada, 1996, Report #R164-96.

19. "People Power," *Canadian Business Review*, Spring 1996, p. 42.

20. V. Smith, "Money Talks," *Report on Business Magazine*, April 1998, pp. 97-100.

21. J.D. Costa, "Getting It," *Report on Business Magazine*, April 1998, pp. 102-105. Other studies that also discuss the ill effects of downsizing include T. Mroczkowski and M. Hanaoka, "Effective Rightsizing Strategies in Japan and America: Is There a Convergence of Employment Practices?", *Academy of Management Executive*, 11, no. 2, 1997, pp. 57-67; and S.S. Roach, "The Hollow Ring of Productivity Revival," *Harvard Business Review*, November-December 1996, pp. 81-89.

22. J.D. Costa, "Getting It," *Report on Business Magazine*, April 1998, pp. 102-105.

23. P. Demont, "Employees Find It Hard to Be Loyal to Their Firm," *Vancouver Sun*, June 18, 1999, p. H1.

24. "'Haves and Have-Nots' Canadians Look for Corporate Conscience," *Maclean's*, December 30, 1996/January 6, 1997, pp. 26, 37.

25. J.D. Costa, "Getting It," *Report on Business Magazine*, April 1998, pp. 102-105.

26. J.D. Costa, "Getting It," *Report on Business Magazine*, April 1998, pp. 102-105.

27. G. Crone, "Ontario Hydro Moves into Hiring Mode Again," *Financial Post*, April 11, 1998, p. 4.

28. "FP/COMPAS Poll: An Exclusive Survey of CEOs and Canadians at Large: This Week: New Burdens for Managers," *Financial Post*, November 22/24, 1997, p. 17.

29. "FP/COMPAS Poll: An Exclusive Survey of CEOs and Canadians at Large: This Week: New Burdens for Managers," *Financial Post*, November 22/24, 1997, p. 17.

30. Angus Reid Group, *Workplace 2000: Working Toward the Millennium*, Fall 1997.

31. C. Thompson, "State of the Union," *Report on Business Magazine*, April 1998, pp. 73-82.

32. C. Thompson, "State of the Union," *Report on Business Magazine*, April 1998, pp. 73-82.

33. E. Beauchesne, "Brain Drain a Worse Problem Than Originally Thought, Report Suggests," *Vancouver Sun*, February 11, 2000, p. A12.

34. Taken from "Controlling Sky-High Absenteeism," *Occupational Health & Safety*, January/February 1996, p. 54, and "Expensive Absenteeism," *Wall Street Journal*, July 29, 1986, p. 1.

35. M. Mercer, "Turnover: Reducing the Costs," *Personnel*, December 1988, pp. 36-42; and R. Darmon, "Identifying Sources of Turnover Cost," *Journal of Marketing*, April 1990, pp. 46-56.

36. See, for example, D.R. Dalton and W.D. Todor, "Functional Turnover: An Empirical Assessment," *Journal*

of *Applied Psychology*, December 1981, pp. 716-721; G.M. McEvoy and W.F. Cascio, "Do Good or Poor Performers Leave? A Meta-Analysis of the Relationship Between Performance and Turnover," *Academy of Management Journal*, December 1987, pp. 744-762; and D. Gilbertson, "Why Do People Quit Their Jobs? Because They Can," *New York Times*, February 1, 1998, p. BU 12.

37. Cited in "You Often Lose the Ones You Love," *Industry Week*, November 21, 1988, p. 5.

38. H.J. Leavitt, *Managerial Psychology*, rev. ed. (Chicago: University of Chicago Press, 1964), p. 3.

39. Cited in "You Often Lose the Ones You Love," *Industry Week*, November 21, 1988, p. 5.

40. B. Dumaine, "The New Non-Manager Managers," *Fortune*, February 22, 1993, pp. 80-84.

41. "Wanted: Teammates, Crew Members, and Cast Members: But No Employees," *Wall Street Journal*, April 30, 1996, p. A1.

42. M. Sashkin, "Participative Management Is an Ethical Imperative," *Organizational Dynamics*, Spring 1984, pp. 5-22.

43. See, "What Self-Managing Teams Manage," *Training*, October 1995, p. 72.

44. S. Ross, "U.S. Managers Fail to Fit the Bill in New Workplace: Study," *Reuters News Agency*, November 19, 1999.

45. M. Adam, "Law Firms Follow Merger Trend: Borden and Elliot Joins Forces With Scott and Aylen," *Financial Post*, June 16, 1999, p. C5.

46. P. Demont, "First on Planet, Canada Post Says," *Vancouver Sun*, November 27, 1999, p. D3.

47. M. Kaeter, "The Age of the Specialized Generalist," *Training*, December 1993, pp. 48-53; and N. Templin, "Auto Plants, Hiring Again, Are Demanding Higher-Skilled Labor," *Wall Street Journal*, March 11, 1994, p. A1.

48. J. Lee, "Family Business Has Nerves of Steel," *Vancouver Sun*, December 22, 1997, pp. D1, D3.

49. J.H. Eggers, "The Dynamics of Asian Business, Culture," *The Globe and Mail*, March 13, 1998, p. C5.

50. See, for instance, R.R. Thomas Jr., "From Affirmative Action to Affirming Diversity," *Harvard Business Review*, March-April 1990, pp. 107-117; B. Mandrell and S. Kohler-Gray, "Management Development That Values Diversity," *Personnel*, March 1990, pp. 41-47; J. Dreyfuss, "Get Ready for the New Work Force," *Fortune*, April 23, 1990, pp. 165-181; and I. Wielawski, "Diversity Makes Both Dollars and Sense," *Los Angeles Times*, May 16, 1994, p. II-3.

51. See, for instance, E.E. Kossek and S.A. Lobel (eds.), *Managing Diversity* (Cambridge, MA: Blackwell, 1996); J.A. Segal, "Diversify for Dollars," *HRMagazine*, April 1997, pp. 134-140; and "Strength Through Diversity for Bottom-Line Success," *Working Women*, March 1999, pp. 67-77.

52. C. Thompson, "State of the Union," *Report on Business Magazine*, April 1998, pp. 73-82.

53. B. Livesey, "Making Nice," *Report on Business Magazine*, March 1998, pp. 96-104.

54. R. McQueen, "Companies That Raise the Bar: The Standards for Becoming One of the 50 Best Gets Higher Each Year," *Financial Post*, December 13/15, 1997, p. 11.

55. R.B. Lieber, "Why Employees Love These Companies," *Fortune*, January 12, 1998, pp. 72-74.

56. A. Fisher, "100 Best Companies to Work for in America," *Fortune*, January 12, 1998, pp. 68-70.

57. R.T. Mowday, L.W. Porter, and R.M. Steers, *Employee Organization Linkages: The Psychology of Commitment, Absenteeism, and Turnover* (New York: Academic Press, 1982).

58. D.W. Organ, *Organizational Citizenship Behavior: The Good Soldier Syndrome* (Lexington, MA: Lexington Books, 1988), p. 4.

59. See, for example, P.M. Podsakoff and S.B. MacKenzie, "Organizational Citizenship Behavior and Sales Unit Effectiveness," *Journal of Marketing Research,* August 1994, pp. 351-363; and P.M. Podsakoff, M. Ahearne, and S.B. MacKenzie, "Organizational Citizenship Behavior and the Quantity and Quality of Work Group Performance," *Journal of Applied Psychology,* April 1997, pp. 262-270.

60. See, for example, M.J. Driver, "Cognitive Psychology: An Interactionist View," R.H. Hall, "Organizational Behavior: A Sociological Perspective," and C. Hardy, "The Contribution of Political Science to Organizational Behavior," all in J.W. Lorsch (ed.), *Handbook of Organizational Behavior* (Englewood Cliffs, NJ: Prentice Hall, 1987), pp. 62-108.

61. R. Weinberg and W. Nord, "Coping with 'It's All Common Sense'", *Exchange,* 7, no. 2, 1982, pp. 29-33; R.P. Vecchio, "Some Popular (But Misguided) Criticisms of the Organizational Sciences," *Organizational Behavior Teaching Review*, 10, no. 1, 1986-87, pp. 28-34; and M.L. Lynn, "Organizational Behavior and Common Sense: Philosophical Implications for Teaching and Thinking," paper presented at the 14th Annual Organizational Behavior Teaching Conference, Waltham, MA, May 1987.

62. S.R. Rhodes and R.M. Steers, *Managing Employee Absenteeism* (Reading, MA: Addison-Wesley, 1990). For a full review of the direct and indirect costs of absenteeism, see D.A. Harrison and J.J. Martocchio, "Time for Absenteeism: A 20-Year Review of Origins, Offshoots, and Outcomes," *Journal of Management*, vol. 24, no. 3, 1998, pp. 305-350.

63. Angus Reid Group, *Workplace 2000: Working Toward the Millennium*, Fall 1997.

64. Angus Reid Group, *Workplace 2000: Working Toward the Millennium*, Fall 1997.

65. Angus Reid Group, *Workplace 2000: Working Toward the Millennium*, Fall 1997.

66. J.H. Eggers, "The Dynamics of Asian Business, Culture," *The Globe and Mail*, Friday, March 13, 1998, p. C5.

## Chapter 2

1. Based on P. Kuitenbrouwer, "New Boss in Sharp Contrast: F Anthony Comper. Incoming Bank of Montreal Chief Opposite of Flashy Barrett," *Financial Post,* February 24, 1999, p. C4; K. Noble and J. Nicol, "Barrett Takes His Exit: The Bank of Montreal's Charismatic CEO Turns Down Two More Years at the Helm," *Maclean's*, March 8, 1999, p. 34; and J. Nicol, "The Man Who Must Plot a New Course," *Maclean's,* March 8, 1999, p. 36.

2. T. Cole, "Who Loves Ya?", *Report on Business Magazine*, April 1999, pp. 44-60.

3. H.H. Kelley, "Attribution in Social Interaction," in E. Jones et al. (eds.), *Attribution: Perceiving the Causes of Behavior* (Morristown, NJ: General Learning Press, 1972).

4. See L. Ross, "The Intuitive Psychologist and His Shortcomings," in L. Berkowitz (ed.), *Advances in Experimental Social Psychology,* 10 (Orlando, FL: Academic Press, 1977), pp. 174-220; and A.G. Miller and T. Lawson, "The Effect of an Informational Option on the Fundamental Attribution Error," *Personality and Social Psychology, Bulletin,* June 1989, pp. 194-204.

5. S. Nam, *Cultural and Managerial Attributions for Group Performance*, unpublished doctoral dissertation, University of Oregon. Cited in R.M. Steers, S.J. Bischoff, and L.H. Higgins, "Cross-Cultural Management Research," *Journal of Management Inquiry*, December 1992, pp. 325-326.

6. B. McKenna, "Modern Suicides Hold Little Glory," *The Globe and Mail*, June 2, 1998, p. A14.

7. D.C. Dearborn and H.A. Simon, "Selective Perception: A Note on the Departmental Identification of Executives," *Sociometry*, June 1958, pp. 140-144. Some of the conclusions in this classic study have recently been challenged in J.P. Walsh, "Selectivity and Selective Perception: An Investigation of Managers' Belief Structures and Information Processing," *Academy of Management Journal*, December 1988, pp. 873-896; M.J. Waller, G.P. Huber, and W.H. Glick, "Functional Background as a Determinant of Executives' Selective Perception," *Academy of Management Journal*, August 1995, pp. 943-974; and J.M. Beyer, P. Chattopadhyay, E. George, W.H. Glick, D.T. Ogilvie, and D. Pugliese, "The Selective Perception of Managers Revisited," *Academy of Management Journal*, June 1997, pp. 716-737.

8. S.E. Asch, "Forming Impressions of Personality," *Journal of Abnormal and Social Psychology*, July 1946, pp. 258-290.

9. J.S. Bruner and R. Tagiuri, "The Perception of People," in E. Lindzey (ed.), *Handbook of Social Psychology* (Reading, MA: Addison-Wesley, 1954), p. 641.

10. See, for example, C.M. Judd and B. Park, "Definition and Assessment of Accuracy in Social Stereotypes," *Psychological Review*, January 1993, pp. 109-128.

11. See, for example, S.T. Fiske, D.N. Beroff, E. Borgida, K. Deaux, and M.E. Heilman, "Use of Sex Stereotyping Research in Price Waterhouse vs. Hopkins," *American Psychologist*, 1991, pp. 1049-1060; G.N. Powell, "The Good Manager: Business Students' Stereotypes of Japanese Managers Versus Stereotypes of American Managers," *Group & Organizational Management*, 1992, pp. 44-56; and K.J. Gibson, W.J. Zerbe, and R.E. Franken, "Job Search Strategies for Older Job Hunters: Addressing Employers' Perceptions," *Canadian Journal of Counseling*, 1992, pp. 166-176.

12. See, for example, E.C. Webster, *Decision Making in the Employment Interview* (Montreal: McGill University, Industrial Relations Center, 1964).

13. See, for example, R.D. Bretz Jr., G.T. Milkovich, and W. Read, "The Current State of Performance Appraisal Research and Practice: Concerns, Directions, and Implications," *Journal of Management*, June 1992, pp. 323-324; and P.M. Swiercz, M.L. Icenogle, N.B. Bryan, and R.W. Renn, "Do Perceptions of Performance Appraisal Fairness Predict Employee Attitudes and Performance?", in D.P. Moore (ed.), *Proceedings of the Academy of Management* (Atlanta: Academy of Management, 1993), pp. 304-308.

14. G.W. Allport, *Personality: A Psychological Interpretation* (New York: Holt, Rinehart & Winston, 1937), p. 48.

15. Reported in R.L. Hotz, "Genetics, Not Parenting, Key to Temperament, Studies Say," *Los Angeles Times*, February 20, 1994, p. A1.

16. See D.T. Lykken, T.J. Bouchard Jr., M. McGue, and A. Tellegen, "Heritability of Interests: A Twin Study," *Journal of Applied Psychology*, August 1993, pp. 649-661; R.D. Arvey and T.J. Bouchard Jr., "Genetics, Twins, and Organizational Behavior," in B.M. Staw and L.L. Cummings, *Research in Organizational Behavior*, 16 (Greenwich, CT: JAI Press, 1994), pp. 65-66; and D. Lykken and A. Tellegen, "Happiness Is a Stochastic Phenomenon," *Psychological Science*, May 1996, pp. 186-189; and W. Wright, *Born That Way: Genes, Behavior, Personality* (New York: Knopf, 1998).

17. See B.M. Staw and J. Ross, "Stability in the Midst of Change: A Dispositional Approach to Job Attitudes," *Journal of Applied Psychology*, August 1985, pp. 469-480; and B.M. Staw, N.E. Bell, and J.A. Clausen, "The Dispositional Approach to Job Attitudes: A Lifetime Longitudinal Test," *Administrative Science Quarterly*, March 1986, pp. 56-77.

18. R.C. Carson, "Personality," in M.R. Rosenzweig and L.W. Porter (eds.), *Annual Review of Psychology,* 40 (Palo Alto, CA: Annual Reviews, 1989), pp. 228-229.

19. L. Sechrest, "Personality," in M.R. Rosenzweig and L.W. Porter (eds.), *Annual Review of Psychology,* 27 (Palo Alto, CA: Annual Reviews, 1976), p. 10.

20. W. Mischel, "The Interaction of Person and Situation," in D. Magnusson and N.S. Endler (eds.), *Personality at the Crossroads: Current Issues in Interactional Psychology* (Hillsdale, NJ: Erlbaum, 1977), pp. 166-207.

21. See A.H. Buss, "Personality as Traits," *American Psychologist*, November 1989, pp. 1378-1388; and D.G. Winter, O.P. John, A.J. Stewart, E.C. Klohnen, and L.E. Duncan, "Traits and Motives: Toward an Integration of

Two Traditions in Personality Research," *Psychological Review*, April 1998, pp. 230-250.

22. R.B. Catell, "Personality Pinned Down," *Psychology Today*, July 1973, pp. 40-46.

23. See R.R. McCrae and P.T. Costa Jr., "Reinterpreting the Myers-Briggs Type Indicator from the Perspective of the Five Factor Model of Personality," *Journal of Personality*, March 1989, pp. 17-40; and C. Fitzgerald and L.K. Kirby, (eds.), *Developing Leaders: Research and Applications in Psychological Type and Leadership Development* (Palo Alto, CA: Davies-Black Publishing, 1997).

24. G.N. Landrum, *Profiles of Genius* (New York: Prometheus, 1993).

25. See, for example, J.M. Digman, "Personality Structure: Emergence of the Five-Factor Model," in M.R. Rosenzweig and L.W. Porter (eds.), *Annual Review of Psychology*, 41 (Palo Alto, CA: Annual Reviews, 1990), pp. 417-440; R.R. McCrae and O.P. John, "An Introduction to the Five-Factor Model and Its Applications," *Journal of Personality*, June 1992, pp. 175-215; L.R. Goldberg, "The Structure of Phenotypic Personality Traits," *American Psychologist*, January 1993, pp. 26-34; P.H. Raymark, M.J. Schmit; R.M. Guion, "Identifying Potentially Useful Personality Constructs for Employee Selection," *Personnel Psychology*, Autumn 1997, pp. 723-736; and O. Behling, "Employee Selection: Will Intelligence and Conscientiousness Do the Job?", *Academy of Management Executive*, 12, 1998, pp. 77-86.

26. See, for instance, M.R. Barrick and M.K. Mount, "The Big Five Personality Dimensions and Job Performance: A Meta-Analysis," *Personnel Psychology*, 44 (1991), pp. 1-26; R.P. Tett, D.N. Jackson, and M. Rothstein, "Personality Measures as Predictors of Job Performance: A Meta-Analytic Review, *Personnel Psychology*, Winter 1991, pp. 703-742; T.A. Judge, J.J. Martocchio, and C.J. Thoresen, "Five-Factor Model of Personality and Employee Absence," *Journal of Applied Psychology*, October 1997, pp. 745-755; and O. Behling, "Employee Selection: Will Intelligence and Conscientiousness Do the Job?", *Academy of Management Executive*, February 1998, pp. 77-86; and F.S. Switzer III and P.L. Roth, "A Meta-Analytic Review of Predictors of Job Performance for Salespeople," *Journal of Applied Psychology*, August 1998, pp. 586-597.

27. See, for instance, S.L. Kichuk and W.H. Wiesner, "Work Teams: Selecting Members for Optimal Performance," *Canadian Psychology*, 39(1-2), 1999, pp. 23-32; M.R. Barrick and M.K. Mount, "The Big Five Personality Dimensions and Job Performance: A Meta-Analysis," *Personnel Psychology*, 44 (1991), pp. 1-26; D. Ones, C. Viswesvaran, and F. Schmidt, "Meta-Analysis of Integrity Test Validities: Findings and Implications for Personnel Selection and Theories of Job Performance [Monograph]," *Journal of Applied Psychology*, 47(1), 1993, pp. 147-156; and R.T. Hogan, J. Hogan, and B.W. Roberts, "Personality Measurement and Employment Decisions: Questions and Answers, *American Psychologist*, 51(5), 1996, pp. 469-477.

28. P. Thoms, "The Relationship Between Self-Efficacy for Participating in Self-Managed Work Groups and the Big Five Personality Dimensions," *Journal of Applied Psychology*, 82, 1996, pp. 472-484; R.A. Guzzo, P.R. Yost, R.J. Campbell, and G.P. Shea, "Potency in Groups: Articulating a Construct," *British Journal of Social Psychology*, 32, 1993, pp. 87-106; G.A. Neuman and J. Wright, "Team Effectiveness: Beyond Skills and Cognitive Ability," *Journal of Applied Psychology*, 84, 1999, pp. 376-389. See also S.L. Kichuk and W.H. Wiesner, "Work Teams: Selecting Members for Optimal Performance," *Canadian Psychology*, 39(1-2), 1999, pp. 23-32, who summarize a wide body of literature on this topic. You might also be interested in B. Barry and G.L. Stewart, "Compositions, Process and Performance in Self-Managed Groups: The Role of Personality," *Journal of Applied Psychology*, 82, 1997, pp. 62-78, for an opposing look at the conscientiousness-performance link.

29. D.W. Organ, "Personality and Organizational Citizenship Behavior," *Journal of Management*, Summer 1994, pp. 465-478; D.W. Organ and K. Ryan, "A Meta-Analytic Review of Attitudinal and Dispositional Predictors of Organizational Citizenship Behavior," *Personnel Psychology*, Winter 1995, pp. 775-802; and M.A. Konovsky and D.W. Organ, "Dispositional and Contextual Determinants of Organizational Citizenship Behavior," *Journal of Organizational Behavior*, May 1996, pp. 253-266.

30. J.B. Rotter, "Generalized Expectancies for Internal Versus External Control of Reinforcement," *Psychological Monographs,* 80, no. 609 (1966).

31. J.B. Rotter, "Generalized Expectancies for Internal Versus External Control of Reinforcement," *Psychological Monographs,* 80, no. 609 (1966).

32. R.T. Keller, "Predicting Absenteeism from Prior Absenteeism, Attitudinal Factors, and Nonattitudinal Factors," *Journal of Applied Psychology*, August 1983, pp. 536-540.

33. P.E. Spector, "Behavior in Organizations as a Function of Employee's Locus of Control," *Psychological Bulletin*, May 1982, p. 493.

34. R.G. Vleeming, "Machiavellianism: A Preliminary Review," *Psychological Reports*, February 1979, pp. 295-310.

35. R. Christie and F.L. Geis, *Studies in Machiavellianism* (New York: Academic Press, 1970), p. 312; and N.V. Ramanaiah, A. Byravan, and F.R.J. Detwiler, "Revised Neo Personality Inventory Profiles of Machiavellian and Non-Machiavellian People," *Psychological Reports*, October 1994, pp. 937-938.

36. R. Christie and F.L. Geis, *Studies in Machiavellianism* (New York: Academic Press, 1970).

37. Based on J. Brockner, *Self-Esteem at Work* (Lexington, MA: Lexington Books, 1988), Chapters 1-4; and N. Branden, *Self-Esteem at Work* (San Francisco: Jossey-Bass, 1998).

38. See M. Snyder, *Public Appearances/Private Realities: The Psychology of Self-Monitoring* (New York: W.H. Freeman, 1987).

39. See M. Snyder, *Public Appearances/Private Realities: The Psychology of Self-Monitoring* (New York: W.H. Freeman, 1987).

40. M. Kilduff and D.V. Day, "Do Chameleons Get Ahead? The Effects of Self-Monitoring on Managerial Careers," *Academy of Management Journal*, August 1994, pp. 1047-1060.

41. R.N. Taylor and M.D. Dunnette, "Influence of Dogmatism, Risk-Taking Propensity, and Intelligence on

Decision-Making Strategies for a Sample of Industrial Managers," *Journal of Applied Psychology*, August 1974, pp. 420-423.

42. I.L. Janis and L. Mann, *Decision Making: A Psychological Analysis of Conflict, Choice, and Commitment* (New York: Free Press, 1977).

43. N. Kogan and M.A. Wallach, "Group Risk Taking as a Function of Members' Anxiety and Defensiveness," *Journal of Personality*, March 1967, pp. 50-63.

44. M. Friedman and R.H. Rosenman, *Type A Behavior and Your Heart* (New York: Alfred A. Knopf, 1974), p. 84 (emphasis in original).

45. M. Friedman and R.H. Rosenman, *Type A Behavior and Your Heart* (New York: Alfred A. Knopf, 1974), pp. 84-85.

46. K.A. Matthews, "Assessment of Type A Behavior, Anger, and Hostility in Epidemiological Studies of Cardiovascular Disease," in A.M. Ostfield and E.D. Eaker (eds.), *Measuring Psychological Variables in Epidemiologic Studies of Cardiovascular Disease*, 1985 (NIH Publication No. 85-2270), Washington, DC: U.S. Department of Health and Human Services.

47. M. Friedman and R.H. Rosenman, *Type A Behavior and Your Heart* (New York: Alfred A. Knopf, 1974), p. 86.

48. D.C. Ganster, W.E. Sime, and B.T. Mayes, "Type A Behavior in the Work Setting: A Review and Some New Data," in A.W. Siegman and T.M. Dembroski (eds.), *In Search of Coronary-Prone Behavior: Beyond Type A* (Hillsdale, NJ: Erlbaum, 1989), pp. 117-118; and B.K. Houston, "Cardiovascular and Neuroendocrine Reactivity, Global Type A, and Components of Type A," In B.K. Houston & C.R. Snyder (eds.), *Type A Behavior Pattern: Research, Theory, and Intervention* (New York: Wiley, 1988), pp. 212-253.

49. J. Schaubroeck, D.C. Ganster, and B.E. Kemmerer, "Job Complexity, 'Type A' Behavior, and Cardiovascular Disorder," *Academy of Management Journal*, April 1994 (37), pp. 426-439.

50. F. Kluckhohn and F.L. Strodtbeck, *Variations in Value Orientations* (Evanston, IL: Row Peterson, 1961).

51. J.L. Holland, *Making Vocational Choices: A Theory of Vocational Personalities and Work Environments*, 2nd ed. (Englewood Cliffs, NJ: Prentice Hall, 1985); see also R. Hogan and R.J. Blake, "Vocational Interests: Matching Self-Concept with the Work Environment," in K.R. Murphy (ed.), *Individual Differences and Behavior in Organizations* (San Francisco: Jossey-Bass, 1996), pp. 89-144.

52. See, for example, A.R. Spokane, "A Review of Research on Person-Environment Congruence in Holland's Theory of Careers," *Journal of Vocational Behavior*, June 1985, pp. 306-343; D. Brown, "The Status of Holland's Theory of Career Choice," *Career Development Journal*, September 1987, pp. 13-23; J.L. Holland and G.D. Gottfredson, "Studies of the Hexagonal Model: An Evaluation (or, The Perils of Stalking the Perfect Hexagon)," *Journal of Vocational Behavior*, April 1992, pp. 158-170; and T.J. Tracey and J. Rounds, "Evaluating Holland's and Gati's Vocational-Interest Models: A Structural Meta-Analysis," *Psychological Bulletin*, March 1993, pp. 229-246.

53. See B. Schneider, "The People Make the Place," *Personnel Psychology*, Autumn 1987, pp. 437-453; D.E. Bowen, G.E. Ledford, Jr., and B.R. Nathan, "Hiring for the Organization, Not the Job," *Academy of Management Executive*, November 1991, pp. 35-51; B. Schneider, H.W. Goldstein, and D.B. Smith, "The ASA Framework: An Update," *Personnel Psychology*, Winter 1995, pp. 747-773; A.L. Kristof, "Person-Organization Fit: An Integrative Review of Its Conceptualizations, Measurement, and Implications," *Personnel Psychology*, Spring 1996, pp. 1-49; and J. Schaubroeck, D.C. Ganster, and J.R. Jones, "Organization and Occupation Influences in the Attraction-Selection-Attrition Process," *Journal of Applied Psychology*, December 1998, pp. 869-891.

54. Based on T.A. Judge and D.M. Cable, "Applicant Personality, Organizational Culture, and Organization Attraction," *Personnel Psychology*, Summer 1997, pp. 359-394.

55. S. Thorne, "Five Dead in Transit Shooting," *Canadian Press Newswire*, April 6, 1999; and N. Ayed, "Lebrun Had History of Trouble at Work," *Canadian Press Newswire*, April 7, 1999.

56. J.M. George, "Trait and State Affect," in K.R. Murphy (ed.), *Individual Differences and Behavior in Organizations* (San Francisco: Jossey-Bass, 1996), p. 145.

57. See N.H. Frijda, "Moods, Emotion Episodes and Emotions," in M. Lewis and J.M. Haviland (eds.), *Handbook of Emotions* (New York: Guildford Press, 1993), pp. 381-403.

58. H.M. Weiss and R. Cropanzano, "Affective Events Theory," in B.M. Staw and L.L. Cummings, *Research in Organizational Behavior*, vol. 18 (Greenwich, CT: JAI Press, 1996), pp. 17-19.

59. N.H. Frijda, "Moods, Emotion Episodes and Emotions," in M. Lewis and J.M. Haviland (eds.), *Handbook of Emotions* (New York: Guildford Press, 1993), p. 381.

60. H.M. Weiss and R. Cropanzano, "Affective Events Theory," in B.M. Staw and L.L. Cummings, *Research in Organizational Behavior*, vol. 18 (Greenwich, CT: JAI Press, 1996), pp. 20-22.

61. A. Hochschild, *The Managed Heart: The Commercialization of Human Feeling* (Berkeley, CA: University of California Press, 1983); R.I. Sutton and A. Rafaeli, "Untangling the Relationship Between Displayed Emotions and Organizational Sales: The Case of Convenience Stores," *Academy of Management Journal*, 31, pp. 461-487, 1988; A. Rafaeli, "When Cashiers Meet Customers: An Analysis of the Role of Supermarket Cashiers," *Academy of Management Journal*, 32, pp. 245-273, 1989; A. Rafaeli and R.I. Sutton, "The Expression of Emotion in Organizational Life," in L.L. Cummings and B.M. Staw (eds.), *Research in Organizational Behavior*, 11, pp. 1-42, Greenwich, CT: JAI Press, 1989; A. Rafaeli and R.I. Sutton, "Busy Stores and Demanding Customers: How Do They Affect the Display of Positive Emotion?" *Academy of Management Journal*, 33, pp. 623-637, 1990; A. Rafaeli and R.I. Sutton, "Emotional Contrast Strategies as Means of Social Influence: Lessons from Criminal Interrogators and Bill Collectors," *Academy of Management Journal*, 34, pp. 749-775, 1991; R.I. Sutton, "Maintaining Norms About Expressed Emotions: The Case of Bill Collectors," *Administrative Science Quarterly*, 36, pp. 245-268, 1991; and J.A. Morris and D.C. Feldman, "The Dimensions, Antecedents, and Consequences of Emotional Labor," *Academy of Management Review*, October 1996, pp. 986-1010.

62. A.R. Hochschild, "Emotion Work, Feeling Rules, and Social Structure," *American Journal of Sociology*, November 1979, pp. 551-575.

63. B.M. DePaulo, "Nonverbal Behavior and Self-Presentation," *Psychological Bulletin*, March 1992, pp. 203-243.

64. C.S. Hunt, "Although I Might Be Laughing Loud and Hearty, Deep Inside I'm Blue: Individual Perceptions Regarding Feeling and Displaying Emotions at Work," paper presented at the Academy of Management National Conference, Cincinnati, OH, August 1996, p. 3.

65. See J.K. Salminen, S. Saarijanvi, E. Aairela, and T. Tamminen, "Alexithymia: State or Trait? One-Year Follow-Up Study of General Hospital Psychiatric Consultation Outpatients," *Journal of Psychosomatic Research*, July 1994, pp. 681-685.

66. K. Deaux, "Sex Differences," in M.R. Rosenzweig and L.W. Porter (eds.), *Annual Review of Psychology*, vol. 26 (Palo Alto, CA: Annual Reviews, 1985), pp. 48-82; M. LaFrance and M. Banaji, "Toward a Reconsideration of the Gender-Emotion Relationship," in M. Clark (ed.), *Review of Personality and Social Psychology*, vol. 14 (Newbury Park, CA: Sage, 1992), pp. 178-197; and A.M. Kring and A.H. Gordon, "Sex Differences in Emotion: Expression, Experience, and Physiology," *Journal of Personality and Social Psychology*, March 1998, pp. 686-703.

67. L.R. Brody and J.A. Hall, "Gender and Emotion," in M. Lewis and J.M. Haviland (eds.), *Handbook of Emotions* (New York: Guilford Press, 1993), pp. 447-460; and M. Grossman and W. Wood, "Sex Differences in Intensity of Emotional Experience: A Social Role Interpretation," *Journal of Personality and Social Psychology*, November 1992, pp. 1010-1022.

68. J.A. Hall, *Nonverbal Sex Differences: Communication Accuracy and Expressive Style* (Baltimore: Johns Hopkins Press, 1984).

69. N. James, "Emotional Labour: Skill and Work in the Social Regulations of Feelings," *Sociological Review*, February 1989, pp. 15-42; A. Hochschild, *The Second Shift* (New York: Viking, 1989); and F.M. Deutsch, "Status, Sex, and Smiling: The Effect of Role on Smiling in Men and Women," *Personality and Social Psychology Bulletin*, September 1990, pp. 531-540.

70. A. Rafaeli, "When Clerks Meet Customers: A Test of Variables Related to Emotional Expression on the Job," *Journal of Applied Psychology*, June 1989, pp. 385-393; and M. LaFrance and M. Banaji, "Toward a Reconsideration of the Gender-Emotion Relationship," in M.S. Clark (ed.), *Emotion and Social Behavior: Review of Personality and Social Psychology*, vol. 14 (Newbury Park, CA: Sage Publications, 1992), pp. 178 and 201.

71. L.W. Hoffman, "Early Childhood Experiences and Women's Achievement Motives," *Journal of Social Issues*, vol. 28, no. 2, 1972, pp. 129-155.

72. This section is based on Daniel Goleman, *Emotional Intelligence* (New York: Bantam, 1995); J.D. Mayer and G. Geher, "Emotional Intelligence and the Identification of Emotion," *Intelligence*, March-April 1996, pp. 89-113; J. Stuller, "EQ: Edging Toward Respectability," *Training*, June 1997, pp. 43-48; R.K. Cooper, "Applying Emotional Intelligence in the Workplace," *Training & Development*, December 1997, pp. 31-38; "HR Pulse: Emotional Intelligence," *HRMagazine*, January 1998, p. 19; M. Davies, L. Stankov, and R.D. Roberts, "Emotional Intelligence: In Search of an Elusive Construct," *Journal of Personality and Social Psychology*, October 1998, pp. 989-1015; and D. Goleman, *Working with Emotional Intelligence* (New York: Bantam, 1999).

73. H. Schachter, "Programmed for Obsolescence?" *Canadian Business*, June 25/July 9 1999, pp. 49-51.

74. D. Goleman, *Working with Emotional Intelligence* (New York: Bantam, 1999).

75. R. McQueen, "New CEO Brings Fresh Style to BMO: Tony Comper Slowly Stepping out of the Shadows," *Financial Post*, November 10, 1999, p. C3.

76. See, for example, K. Fiedler, "Emotional Mood, Cognitive Style, and Behavioral Regulation," in K. Fiedler and J. Forgas (eds.), *Affect, Cognition, and Social Behavior* (Toronto: Hogrefe International, 1988), pp. 100-119; A.M. Isen, "Positive Affect and Decision Making," in M. Lewis and J.M. Haviland (eds.), *Handbook of Emotions* (New York: Guilford, 1993), pp. 261-277; and M. Luce, J. Bettman, and J.W. Payne, "Choice Processing in Difficult Decisions," *Journal of Experimental Psychology: Learning, Memory, and Cognition*, vol. 23, 1997, pp. 384-405.

77. B.E. Ashforth and R.H. Humphrey, "Emotion in the Workplace: A Reappraisal," *Human Relations*, February 1995, p. 110.

78. J.M. George, "Trait and State Affect," in K.R. Murphy (ed.), *Individual Differences and Behavior in Organizations* (San Francisco: Jossey-Bass, 1996), p. 162.

79. B.E. Ashforth and R.H. Humphrey, "Emotion in the Workplace: A Reappraisal," *Human Relations*, February 1995, p. 116.

80. S.L. Robinson and R.J. Bennett, "A Typology of Deviant Workplace Behaviors: A Multidimensional Scaling Study," *Academy of Management Journal*, April 1995, p. 556.

81. S.L. Robinson and R.J. Bennett, "A Typology of Deviant Workplace Behaviors: A Multidimensional Scaling Study," *Academy of Management Journal*, April 1995, pp. 555-572.

82. Based on A.G. Bedeian, "Workplace Envy," *Organizational Dynamics*, Spring 1995, p. 50.

83. A.G. Bedeian, "Workplace Envy," *Organizational Dynamics*, Spring 1995, p. 54.

84. S. Nelton, "Emotions in the Workplace," *Nation's Business*, February 1996, p. 25.

85. H.M. Weiss and R. Cropanzano, "Affective Events Theory," in B.M. Staw and L.L. Cummings, *Research in Organizational Behavior*, vol. 18 (Greenwich, CT: JAI Press, 1996), p. 55.

86. The Yerkes-Dodson law is described in R.M. Yerkes and J. Dodson, "The Relation of Strength of Stimulus to Rapidity of Habit Formation," *Journal of Comparative Neurology and Psychology*, November 1908, pp. 459-482. Selye (H. Selye, *The Stress of Life*. [New York: McGraw-Hill, 1956]) first used the clinical studies from Yerkes and Dodson (1908) to posit that stressors and performance are related by an inverted U-shaped function.

## Chapter 3

1. Taken from the Web site of Procter & Gamble: www.pg.com.

2. M. Rokeach and S.J. Ball-Rokeach, "Stability and Change in American Value Priorities, 1968-1981," *American Psychologist*, May 1989, pp. 775-784.

3. See, for instance, P.E. Connor and B.W. Becker, "Personal Values and Management: What Do We Know and Why Don't We Know More?", *Journal of Management Inquiry*, March 1994, p. 68.

4. See, for instance, D.A. Ralston, D.H. Holt, R.H. Terpstra, and Y. Kai-cheng, "The Impact of Culture and Ideology on Managerial Work Values: A Study of the United States, Russia, Japan, and China," in D.P. Moore (ed.), *Academy of Management Best Paper Proceedings* (Vancouver, BC: August 1995), pp. 187-191.

5. G. Hofstede, *Culture's Consequences: International Differences in Work Related Values* (Beverly Hills, CA: Sage, 1980); G. Hofstede, *Cultures and Organizations: Software of the Mind* (London: McGraw-Hill, 1991); and G. Hofstede, "Cultural Constraints in Management Theories," *Academy of Management Executive*, February 1993, pp. 81-94.

6. G. Hofstede called this dimension masculinity versus femininity, but we've changed his terms because of their strong sexist connotation.

7. The five usual criticisms and Hofstede's responses (in parentheses) are: 1. Surveys are not a suitable way to measure cultural differences (answer: they should not be the only way); 2. Nations are not the proper units for studying cultures (answer: they are usually the only kind of units available for comparison); 3. A study of the subsidiaries of one company cannot provide information about entire national cultures (answer: what was measured were differences among national cultures. Any set of functionally equivalent samples can supply information about such differences); 4. The IBM data are old and therefore obsolete (answer: the dimensions found are assumed to have centuries-old roots; they have been validated against all kinds of external measurements; recent replications show no loss of validity); 5. Four or five dimensions are not enough (answer: additional dimensions should be statistically independent of the dimensions defined earlier; they should be valid on the basis of correlations with external measures; candidates are welcome to apply). See A. Harzing and G. Hofstede, "Planned Change in Organizations: The Influence of National Culture," in P.A. Bamberger, M. Erez, and S.B. Bacharach (eds.), *Research in the Sociology of Organizations*, Volume 14: *Cross Cultural Analysis of Organizations* (Greenwich, CN: JAI Press, 1996), pp. 297-340.

8. D. Fernandez, D.S. Carlson, L.P. Stepina, and J.D. Nicholson, "Hofstede's Country Classification 25 Years Later," *Journal of Social Psychology*, February 1997, pp. 43-54.

9. Figures for this paragraph are derived from "Canada: a Nation of Immigrants," *Canada and the World Backgrounder*, January 1998, Insert, pp. 1-28.

10. The material presented in this section is based on the work of Michael Adams, *Sex in the Snow* (Toronto: Penguin Books, 1997).

11. G. Chiasson, "I Am Not a Seat Number, I Am a Person," *EnRoute*, March 1998, pp. 5-9.

12. D. Tapscott, *Growing Up Digital: The Rise of the Net Generation* (New York: McGraw-Hill), 1998.

13. "Get Used to It: The Net Generation Knows More Than Its Parents," *Financial Post*, February 8, 2000, p. C10.

14. B. Meglino, E.C. Ravlin, and C.L. Adkins, "A Work Values Approach to Corporate Culture: A Field Test of the Value Congruence Process and Its Relationship to Individual Outcomes," *Journal of Applied Psychology*, 74, 1989, pp. 424-432.

15. B.Z. Posner, J. M. Kouzes, and W.H. Schmidt, "Shared Values Make a Difference: An Empirical Test of Corporate Culture," *Human Resource Management*, 24, 1985, pp. 293-310; A.L. Balazas, "Value Congruency: The Case of the 'Socially Responsible' Firm," *Journal of Business Research*, 20, 1990, pp. 171-181.

16. C.A. O'Reilly, J. Chatman, and D. Caldwell: 1991, "People and Organizational Culture: A Q-sort Approach to Assessing Person-Organizational Fit," *Academy of Management Journal*, 34, 1991, pp. 487-516.

17. C. Enz and C.K. Schwenk, "Performance and Sharing of Organizational Values," paper presented at the annual meeting of the Academy of Management, Washington, D.C., 1989.

18. K. Howard, "Values Make the Company: An Interview with Robert Haas," *Harvard Business Review*, September-October 1990, pp. 132-144.

19. R. McQueen, "Bad Boys Make Good," *The Financial Post*, April 4, 1998, p. 6.

20. R.A. Roe and P. Ester, "Values and Work: Empirical Findings and Theoretical Perspective," *Applied Psychology: An International Review*, 48, 1999, pp. 1-21.

21. R.A. Roe and P. Ester, "Values and Work: Empirical Findings and Theoretical Perspective," *Applied Psychology: An International Review*, 48, 1999, pp. 1-21.

22. R.N. Kanungo and J.K. Bhatnagar, "Achievement Orientation and Occupational Values: A Comparative Study of Young French and English Canadians," *Canadian Journal of Behavioural Science*, 12, 1978, pp. 384-392; M.W. McCarrey, S. Edwards, and R. Jones, "The Influence of Ethnolinguistic Group Membership, Sex and Position Level on Motivational Orientation of Canadian Anglophone and Francophone Employees," *Canadian Journal of Behavioural Science*, 9, 1977, pp. 274-282; M.W. McCarrey, S. Edwards, and R. Jones, "Personal Values of Canadian Anglophone and Francophone Employees and Ethnolinguistic Group Membership, Sex and Position Level," *Journal of Psychology*, 104, 1978, pp. 175-184; S. Richer and P. Laporte, "Culture, Cognition and English-French Competition," in D. Koulack and D. Perlman (eds.), *Readings in Social Psychology: Focus on Canada* (Toronto, ON: Wiley & Sons, 1973); L. Shapiro and D. Perlman, "Value Differences Between English and French Canadian High School Students," *Canadian Ethnic Studies*, 8, 1976, pp. 50-55.

23. R.N. Kanungo and J.K. Bhatnagar, "Achievement Orientation and Occupational Values: A Comparative Study of Young French and English Canadians," *Canadian Journal of Behavioural Science*, 12, 1978, pp. 384-392.

24. R.N. Kanungo and J.K. Bhatnagar, "Achievement Orientation and Occupational Values: A Comparative Study of Young French and English Canadians," *Canadian Journal of Behavioural Science*, 12, 1978, pp. 384-392.

25. H.C. Jain, J. Normand, and R.N. Kanungo, "Job Motivation of Canadian Anglophone and Francophone Hospital Employees," *Canadian Journal of Behavioural Science*, April 1979, pp. 160-163; R.N. Kanungo, G.J. Gorn, and H.J. Dauderis, "Motivational Orientation of Canadian Anglophone and Francophone Managers," *Canadian Journal of Behavioural Science*, April 1976, pp. 107-121.

26. M. Major, M. McCarrey, P. Mercier, and Y. Gasse, "Meanings of Work and Personal Values of Canadian Anglophone and Francophone Middle Managers," *Canadian Journal of Administrative Sciences*, September 1994, pp. 251-263.

27. L. Redpath and M.O. Nielsen, "A Comparison of Native Culture, Non-Native Culture and New Management Ideology," *Canadian Journal of Administrative Sciences*, 14(3), 1997, p. 327.

28. G.C. Anders and K.K. Anders, "Incompatible Goals in Unconventional Organizations: The Politics of Alaska Native Corporations," *Organization Studies*, 7, 1986, pp. 213-233; G. Dacks, "Worker-Controlled Native Enterprises," A Vehicle for Community Development in Northern Canada?", *The Canadian Journal of Native Studies*, 3, 1983, pp. 289-310; L.P. Dana, "Self-Employment in the Canadian Sub-Arctic: An Exploratory Study," *Canadian Journal of Administrative Sciences*, 13, 1996, pp. 65-77.

29. L. Redpath and M.O. Nielsen, "A Comparison of Native Culture, Non-Native Culture and New Management Ideology," *Canadian Journal of Administrative Sciences*, 14(3), 1997, p. 327.

30. R.B. Anderson, "The Business Economy of the First Nations in Saskatchewan: A Contingency Perspective," *Canadian Journal of Native Studies*, 2, 1995, pp. 309-345.

31. Discussion based on L. Redpath and M.O. Nielsen, "A Comparison of Native Culture, Non-Native Culture and New Management Ideology," *Canadian Journal of Administrative Sciences*, 14(3), 1997, pp. 327-339.

32. Discussion based on L. Redpath, M.O. Nielsen, "A Comparison of Native Culture, Non-Native Culture and New Management Ideology," *Canadian Journal of Administrative Sciences*, 14(3), 1997, pp. 327-339.

33. J. Paulson, "First Nations Bank Launches First Branch with Sweetgrass Ceremony," *Canadian Press Newswire*, September 23, 1997.

34. "Autowrecker Defies Stereotypes, Blazes Trail," *Windspeaker*, February 1997, p. 28.

35. The material presented in this section is based on the work of M. Adams, *Sex in the Snow* (Toronto: Penguin Books, 1997).

36. The material presented in this section is based on the work of M. Adams, *Sex in the Snow* (Toronto: Penguin Books, 1997).

37. K. Monk, "Rabinovitch's Marketing Mojo Comes Home," *Vancouver Sun*, July 2, 1999, p. C8.

38. A. Cohen, "So You Wanna Live the Dream," *Report on Business Magazine*, July 1999, pp. 75-78.

39. G.K. Stephens and C.R. Greer, "Doing Business in Mexico: Understanding Cultural Differences," *Organizational Dynamics, Special Report*, 1998, pp. 43-59.

40. See, for instance, D.A. Ralston, D.H. Holt, R.H. Terpstra, and Y. Kai-cheng, "The Impact of Culture and Ideology on Managerial Work Values: A Study of the United States, Russia, Japan, and China, in D.P. Moore (ed.), *Academy of Management Best Paper Proceedings* (Vancouver, BC: August 1995), pp. 187-191.

41. I.Y.M. Yeung and R.L. Tung, "Achieving Business Success in Confucian Societies: The Importance of Guanxi (Connections)," *Organizational Dynamics, Special Report*, 1998, pp. 72-83.

42. I.Y.M. Yeung and R.L. Tung, "Achieving Business Success in Confucian Societies: The Importance of Guanxi (Connections)," *Organizational Dynamics, Special Report*, 1998, p. 73.

43. N.J. Adler, "Cross-Cultural Management Research: The Ostrich and the Trend," *Academy of Management Review*, April 1983, pp. 226-232.

44. R.A. Roe and P. Ester, "Values and Work: Empirical Findings and Theoretical Perspective," *Applied Psychology: An International Review*, 48, 1999, pp. 1-21.

45. M. Erez and P.C. Earley, *Culture, Self-Identity and Work* (Oxford: Oxford University Press, 1993).

46. P.P. Brooke Jr., D.W. Russell, and J.L. Price, "Discriminant Validation of Measures of Job Satisfaction, Job Involvement, and Organizational Commitment," *Journal of Applied Psychology*, May 1988, pp. 139–145; and R.T. Keller, "Job Involvement and Organizational Commitment as Longitudinal Predictors of Job Performance: A Study of Scientists and Engineers," *Journal of Applied Psychology*, August 1997, pp. 539-545.

47. Based on G.J. Blau and K.R. Boal, "Conceptualizing How Job Involvement and Organizational Commitment Affect Turnover and Absenteeism," *Academy of Management Review*, April 1987, p. 290. See also S. Rabinowitz and D.T. Hall, "Organizational Research in Job Involvement," *Psychological Bulletin*, March 1977, pp. 265-288; G.J. Blau, "A Multiple Study Investigation of the Dimensionality of Job Involvement," *Journal of Vocational Behavior*, August 1985, pp. 19-36; and N.A. Jans, "Organizational Factors and Work Involvement," *Organizational Behavior and Human Decision Processes*, June 1985, pp. 382-396.

48. G.J. Blau, "Job Involvement and Organizational Commitment as Interactive Predictors of Tardiness and Absenteeism," *Journal of Management*, Winter 1986, pp. 577-584; and K.R. Boal and R. Cidambi, "Attitudinal Correlates of Turnover and Absenteeism: A Meta Analysis," paper presented at the meeting of the American Psychological Association, Toronto, Canada, 1984.

49. G. Farris, "A Predictive Study of Turnover," *Personnel Psychology*, Summer 1971, pp. 311-328.

50. G.J. Blau and K.R. Boal, "Conceptualizing How Job Involvement and Organizational Commitment Affect Turnover and Absenteeism," *Academy of Management Review*, April 1987, p. 290.

51. See, for instance, P.W. Hom, R. Katerberg, and C.L. Hulin, "Comparative Examination of Three Approaches to the Prediction of Turnover," *Journal of Applied*

*Psychology*, June 1979, pp. 280-290; H. Angle and J. Perry, "Organizational Commitment: Individual and Organizational Influence," *Work and Occupations*, May 1983, pp. 123-146; and J.L. Pierce and R.B. Dunham, "Organizational Commitment: Pre-Employment Propensity and Initial Work Experiences," *Journal of Management*, Spring 1987, pp. 163-78.

52. D.M. Rousseau, "Organizational Behavior in the New Organizational Era," in J.T. Spence, J.M. Darley, and D.J. Foss (eds.), *Annual Review of Psychology*, vol. 48 (Palo Alto, CA: Annual Reviews, 1997), p. 523.

53. "Do As I Do," *Canadian Business*, March 12, 1999, p. 35.

54. D.M. Rousseau, "Organizational Behavior in the New Organizational Era," in J.T. Spence, J.M. Darley, and D.J. Foss (eds.), *Annual Review of Psychology*, vol. 48 (Palo Alto, CA: Annual Reviews, 1997), p. 523.

55. See, for instance, A.J. Elliot and P.G. Devine, "On the Motivational Nature of Cognitive Dissonance: Dissonance as Psychological Discomfort," *Journal of Personality and Social Psychology*, September 1994, pp. 382-394.

56. L. Festinger, *A Theory of Cognitive Dissonance* (Stanford, CA: Stanford University Press, 1957).

57. See R. Rosenblatt, "How Do Tobacco Executives Live with Themselves?" *The New York Times Magazine*, March 20, 1994, pp. 34-41.

58. M. Crawford, "The New Office Etiquette," *Canadian Business*, May 1993, pp. 22-31.

59. M. Adams, *Sex in the Snow* (Toronto: Penguin Books, 1997), p. 102.

60. M. Adams, *Sex in the Snow* (Toronto: Penguin Books, 1997), p. 102.

61. "Workplace 2000: Working Toward the Millennium," *Angus Reid Group*, Fall 1997.

62. See J.L. Price and C.W. Mueller, *Handbook of Organizational Measurement* (Marshfield, MA: Pitman Publishing, 1986), pp. 223-227.

63. V. Scarpello and J.P. Campbell, "Job Satisfaction: Are All the Parts There?", *Personnel Psychology*, Autumn 1983, pp. 577-600.

64. E.A. Locke, "The Nature and Causes of Job Satisfaction," in M.D. Dunnette (ed.), *Handbook of Industrial and Organizational Psychology* (Chicago: Rand McNally, 1976), pp. 1319-328.

65. R.A. Katzell, D.E. Thompson, and R.A. Guzzo, "How Job Satisfaction and Job Performance Are and Are Not Linked," in C.J. Cranny, P.C. Smith, and E.F. Stone (eds.), *Job Satisfaction* (New York: Lexington Books, 1992), pp. 195-217.

66. L.A. Witt and L.G. Nye, "Gender and the Relationship Between Perceived Fairness of Pay or Promotion and Job Satisfaction," *Journal of Applied Psychology*, December 1992, pp. 910-917.

67. R. Laver, "The Best & Worst Jobs," *Maclean's*, May 31, 1999, pp. 18-23.

68. See, for example, D.C. Feldman and H.J. Arnold, "Personality Types and Career Patterns: Some Empirical Evidence on Holland's Model," *Canadian Journal of Administrative Science*, June 1985, pp. 192-210. For the data on this issue, see Staw, Bell, and Clausen, "The Dispositional Approach to Job Attitudes"; R.D. Arvey, T.J.

Bouchard, Jr., N.L. Segal, and L.M. Abraham, "Job Satisfaction: Environmental and Genetic Components," *Journal of Applied Psychology*, April 1989, pp. 187-192; B. Gerhart, "How Important Are Dispositional Factors as Determinants of Job Satisfaction? Implications for Job Design and Other Personnel Programs," *Journal of Applied Psychology*, August 1987, pp. 366-373; R.D. Arvey, G.W. Carter, and D.K. Buerkley, "Job Satisfaction: Dispositional and Situational Influences," in C.L. Cooper and I.T. Robertson (eds.), *International Review of Industrial and Organizational Psychology*, vol. 6 (Chichester, England: John Wiley, 1991), pp. 359-383; T.J. Bouchard, Jr., R.D. Arvey, L.M. Keller, and N.L. Segal, "Genetic Influences on Job Satisfaction: A Reply to Cropanzano and James," *Journal of Applied Psychology*, February 1992, pp. 89-93; T.A. Judge, "Dispositional Perspective in Human Resources Research," in G.R. Ferris and K.M. Rowland (eds.), *Research in Personality and Human Resources Management*, vol. 10 (Greenwich, CT: JAI Press, 1992); R.D. Arvey and T.J. Bouchard, Jr., "Genetics, Twins, and Organizational Behavior," in B.M. Staw and L.L. Cummings (eds.), *Research in Organizational Behavior*; T.A. Judge and S. Watanabe, "Another Look at the Job Satisfaction-Life Satisfaction Relationship," *Journal of Applied Psychology*, December 1993, pp. 939-948; and R.D. Arvey, B.P. McCall, T.J. Bouchard, Jr., and P. Taubman, "Genetic Influences on Job Satisfaction and Work Values," *Personality and Individual Differences*, July 1994, pp. 21-33.

69. A.H. Brayfield and W.H. Crockett, "Employee Attitudes and Employee Performance," *Psychological Bulletin*, September 1955, pp. 396-428; F. Herzberg, B. Mausner, R.O. Peterson, and D.F. Capwell, *Job Attitudes: Review of Research and Opinion* (Pittsburgh: Psychological Service of Pittsburgh, 1957); V.H. Vroom, *Work and Motivation* (New York: John Wiley, 1964); G.P. Fournet, M.K. Distefano, Jr., and M.W. Pryer, "Job Satisfaction: Issues and Problems," *Personnel Psychology*, Summer 1966, pp. 165-183.

70. C.N. Greene, "The Satisfaction-Performance Controversy," *Business Horizons*, February 1972, pp. 31-41; E.E. Lawler III, *Motivation in Organizations* (Monterey, CA: Brooks/Cole, 1973); and M.M. Petty, G.W. McGee, and J.W. Cavender, "A Meta-Analysis of the Relationship Between Individual Job Satisfaction and Individual Performance," *Academy of Management Review*, October 1984, pp. 712-721.

71. C. Ostroff, "The Relationship Between Satisfaction, Attitudes, and Performance: An Organizational Level Analysis," *Journal of Applied Psychology*, December 1992, pp. 963-974.

72. "Sears Chief Sees 'Definite Link' Between Employee and Customer Satisfaction," *Financial Post*, May 4, 1999, p. C5.

73. L. Grant, "Happy Workers, High Returns," *Fortune*, January 12, 1998, p. 81.

74. L. Grant, "Happy Workers, High Returns," *Fortune*, January 12, 1998, p. 81.

75. E.A. Locke, "The Nature and Causes of Job Satisfaction," p. 1331; S.L. McShane, "Job Satisfaction and Absenteeism: A Meta-Analytic Re-Examination," *Canadian Journal of Administrative Science*, June 1984, pp. 61-77; R.D. Hackett and R.M. Guion, "A Reevaluation of the

Absenteeism-Job Satisfaction Relationship," *Organizational Behavior and Human Decision Processes*, June 1985, pp. 340-381; K.D. Scott and G.S. Taylor, "An Examination of Conflicting Findings on the Relationship Between Job Satisfaction and Absenteeism: A Meta-Analysis," *Academy of Management Journal*, September 1985, pp. 599-612; R.D. Hackett, "Work Attitudes and Employee Absenteeism: A Synthesis of the Literature," paper presented at 1988 National Academy of Management Conference, Anaheim, CA, August 1988; and R.P. Steel and J.R. Rentsch, "Influence of Cumulation Strategies on the Long-Range Prediction of Absenteeism," *Academy of Management Journal*, December 1995, pp. 1616-1634.

76. A.H. Brayfield and W.H. Crockett, "Employee Attitudes and Employee Performance," *Psychological Bulletin*, 52, 1955, pp. 396-424; V.H. Vroom, *Work and Motivation* (New York: Wiley, 1964); J. Price, *The Study of Turnover* (Ames: Iowa State University Press, 1977); and W.H. Mobley, R.W. Griffeth, H.H. Hand, and B.M. Meglino, "Review and Conceptual Analysis of the Employee Turnover Process," *Psychological Bulletin*, May 1979, pp. 493-522.

77. See, for example, C.L. Hulin, M. Roznowski, and D. Hachiya, "Alternative Opportunities and Withdrawal Decisions: Empirical and Theoretical Discrepancies and an Integration," *Psychological Bulletin*, July 1985, pp. 233-250; and J.M. Carsten and P.E. Spector, "Unemployment, Job Satisfaction, and Employee Turnover: A Meta-Analytic Test of the Muchinsky Model," *Journal of Applied Psychology*, August 1987, pp. 374-381.

78. T.A. Judge, "Does Affective Disposition Moderate the Relationship Between Job Satisfaction and Voluntary Turnover?" *Journal of Applied Psychology*, June 1993, pp. 395-401.

79. M. Kane, "Are We Having Fun Yet?", *Vancouver Sun*, May 28, 1999, p. H5.

80. S.M. Puffer, "Prosocial Behavior, Noncompliant Behavior, and Work Performance Among Commission Salespeople," *Journal of Applied Psychology*, November 1987, pp. 615-621; J. Hogan and R. Hogan, "How to Measure Employee Reliability," *Journal of Applied Psychology*, May 1989, pp. 273-279; and C.D. Fisher and E.A. Locke, "The New Look in Job Satisfaction Research and Theory," in C.J. Cranny, P.C. Smith, and E.F. Stone (eds.), *Job Satisfaction* (New York: Lexington Books, 1992), pp. 165-194.

81. S.M. Puffer, "Prosocial Behavior, Noncompliant Behavior, and Work Performance Among Commission Salespeople," *Journal of Applied Psychology*, November 1987, pp. 615-21; J. Hogan and R. Hogan, "How to Measure Employee Reliability," *Journal of Applied Psychology*, May 1989, pp. 273-79; and C.D. Fisher and E.A. Locke, "The New Look in Job Satisfaction Research and Theory," in C.J. Cranny, P.C. Smith, and E.F. Stone (eds.), *Job Satisfaction* (New York: Lexington Books, 1992), pp. 165-194.

82. R.B. Freeman, "Job Satisfaction as an Economic Variable," *American Economic Review*, January 1978, pp. 135-141.

83. D.W. Organ, *Organizational Citizenship Behavior: The Good Soldier Syndrome* (Lexington, MA: Lexington Books, 1988); C.A. Smith, D.W. Organ, and J.P. Near, "Organizational Citizenship Behavior: Its Nature and Antecedents," *Journal of Applied Psychology*, 1983, pp. 653-663.

84. P.E. Spector, *Job Satisfaction: Application, Assessment, Causes, and Consequences* (Thousand Oaks, CA: Sage, 1997), pp. 57-58.

85. See T.S. Bateman and D.W. Organ, "Job Satisfaction and the Good Soldier: The Relationship Between Affect and Employee 'Citizenship,'" *Academy of Management Journal*, December 1983, pp. 587-595; C.A. Smith, D.W. Organ, and J.P. Near, "Organizational Citizenship Behavior: Its Nature and Antecedents," *Journal of Applied Psychology*, October 1983, pp. 653-663; and A.P. Brief, *Attitudes in and Around Organizations* (Thousand Oaks, CA: Sage, 1998), pp. 44-45.

86. D.W. Organ and K. Ryan, "A Meta-Analytic Review of Attitudinal and Dispositional Predictors of Organizational Citizenship Behavior," *Personnel Psychology*, Winter 1995, p. 791.

87. J. Fahr, P.M. Podsakoff, and D.W. Organ, "Accounting for Organizational Citizenship Behavior: Leader Fairness and Task Scope Versus Satisfaction," *Journal of Management*, December 1990, pp. 705-722; R.H. Moorman, "Relationship Between Organizational Justice and Organizational Citizenship Behaviors: Do Fairness Perceptions Influence Employee Citizenship?", *Journal of Applied Psychology*, December 1991, pp. 845-855; and M.A. Konovsky and D.W. Organ, "Dispositional and Contextual Determinants of Organizational Citizenship Behavior," *Journal of Organizational Behavior*, May 1996, pp. 253-266.

88. D.W. Organ, "Personality and Organizational Citizenship Behavior," *Journal of Management*, Summer 1994, p. 466.

## Chapter 4

1. A. Kohn, *Punished by Rewards* (Boston: Houghton Mifflin Company, 1993), p. 181.

2. See, for instance, T.R. Mitchell, "Matching Motivational Strategies With Organizational Contexts," in L.L. Cummings and B.M. Staw (eds.), *Research in Organizational Behavior*, vol. 19 (Greenwich, CT: JAI Press, 1997), pp. 60-62.

3. D. McGregor, *The Human Side of Enterprise* (New York: McGraw-Hill, 1960). For an updated analysis of Theory X and Theory Y constructs, see R.J. Summers and S.F. Cronshaw, "A Study of McGregor's Theory X, Theory Y and the Influence of Theory X, Theory Y Assumptions on Causal Attributions for Instances of Worker Poor Performance," in S.L. McShane (ed.), *Organizational Behavior*, ASAC 1988 Conference Proceedings, vol. 9, Part 5, Halifax, NS, 1988, pp. 115-123.

4. V.H. Vroom, *Work and Motivation* (New York: John Wiley, 1964).

5. "Workplace 2000: Working Toward the Millennium," Angus Reid Group, Fall 1997, p. 14.

6. See, for example, H.G. Heneman III and D.P. Schwab, "Evaluation of Research on Expectancy Theory Prediction of Employee Performance," *Psychological Bulletin*, July 1972, pp. 1-9; T.R. Mitchell, "Expectancy Models of Job Satisfaction, Occupational Preference and Effort: A Theoretical, Methodological and Empirical Appraisal," *Psychological Bulletin*, November 1974, pp. 1053-1077; and L. Reinharth and M.A. Wahba, "Expectancy Theory as a Predictor of Work Motivation, Effort Expenditure,

and Job Performance," *Academy of Management Journal*, September 1975, pp. 502-537.

7. See, for example, L.W. Porter and E.E. Lawler III, *Managerial Attitudes and Performance* (Homewood, IL: Richard D. Irwin, 1968); D.F. Parker and L. Dyer, "Expectancy Theory as a Within-Person Behavioral Choice Model: An Empirical Test of Some Conceptual and Methodological Refinements," *Organizational Behavior and Human Performance*, October 1976, pp. 97-117; H.J. Arnold, "A Test of the Multiplicative Hypothesis of Expectancy-Valence Theories of Work Motivation," *Academy of Management Journal*, April 1981, pp. 128-141; and W. Van Eerde and H. Thierry, "Vroom's Expectancy Models and Work-Related Criteria: A Meta-Analysis," *Journal of Applied Psychology*, October 1996, pp. 575-586.

8. R.J. House, H.J. Shapiro, and M.A. Wahba, "Expectancy Theory as a Predictor of Work Behavior and Attitudes: A Re-evaluation of Empirical Evidence," *Decision Sciences*, January 1974, pp. 481-506.

9. "Workplace 2000: Working Toward the Millennium," Angus Reid Group, Fall 1997, p. 14.

10. E.A. Locke, "Toward a Theory of Task Motivation and Incentives," *Organizational Behavior and Human Performance*, May 1968, pp. 157-189.

11. P.C. Earley, P. Wojnaroski, and W. Prest, "Task Planning and Energy Expended: Exploration of How Goals Influence Performance," *Journal of Applied Psychology*, February 1987, pp. 107-114.

12. G.P. Latham and G.A. Yukl, "A Review of Research on the Application of Goal Setting in Organizations," *Academy of Management Journal*, December 1975, pp. 824-845; E.A. Locke, K.N. Shaw, L.M. Saari, and G.P. Latham, "Goal Setting and Task Performance," *Psychological Bulletin*, January 1981, pp. 125-152; A.J. Mento, R.P. Steel, and R.J. Karren, "A Meta-Analytic Study of the Effects of Goal Setting on Task Performance: 1966-1984," *Organizational Behavior and Human Decision Processes*, February 1987, pp. 52-83; M.E. Tubbs, "Goal Setting: A Meta-Analytic Examination of the Empirical Evidence," *Journal of Applied Psychology*, August 1986, pp. 474-483; P.C. Earley, G.B. Northcraft, C. Lee, and T.R. Lituchy, "Impact of Process and Outcome Feedback on the Relation of Goal Setting to Task Performance," *Academy of Management Journal*, March 1990, pp. 87-105; and E.A. Locke and G.P. Latham, *A Theory of Goal Setting and Task Performance* (Englewood Cliffs, NJ: Prentice Hall, 1990).

13. See, for instance, S.J. Carroll and H.L. Tosi, *Management by Objectives: Applications and Research* (New York, Macmillan, 1973); and R. Rodgers and J.E. Hunter, "Impact of Management by Objectives on Organizational Productivity," *Journal of Applied Psychology*, April 1991, pp. 322-336.

14. See, for example, G.P. Latham, M. Erez, and E.A. Locke, "Resolving Scientific Disputes by the Joint Design of Crucial Experiments by the Antagonists: Application to the Erez-Latham Dispute Regarding Participation in Goal Setting," *Journal of Applied Psychology*, November 1988, pp. 753-772; and T.D. Ludwig and E.S. Geller, "Assigned Versus Participative Goal Setting and Response Generalization: Managing Injury Control Among Professional Pizza

Deliverers," *Journal of Applied Psychology*, April 1997, pp. 253-261.

15. M. Erez, P.C. Earley, and C.L. Hulin, "The Impact of Participation on Goal Acceptance and Performance: A Two-Step Model," *Academy of Management Journal*, March 1985, pp. 50-66.

16. K.R. Thompson, W.A. Hochwarter, and N.J. Mathys, "Stretch Targets: What Makes Them Effective?", *Academy of Management Executive*, 11, no. 3 (1997), pp. 48-60; J. Hollenbeck and H. Klein, "Goal Commitment and the Goal-Setting Process: Problems, Prospects, and Proposals for Future Research," *Journal of Applied Psychology*, 72, no. 2 (1987), 212-220; G. Latham and E. Locke, "Self-Regulation Through Goal Setting," *Organizational Behavior and Human Decision Processes*, 50, no. 2 (1991), 212-247; E. Locke, K. Shaw, L. Saari, and G. Latham, "Goal Setting and Task Performance: 1969-1980," *Psychological Bulletin*, 85, 1981, 125-152.

17. See, for instance, R.C. Ford, F.S. MacLaughlin, and J. Nixdorf, "Ten Questions About MBO," *California Management Review*, Winter 1980, p. 89; T.J. Collamore, "Making MBO Work in the Public Sector," *Bureaucrat*, Fall 1989, pp. 37-40; G. Dabbs, "Nonprofit Businesses in the 1990s: Models for Success," *Business Horizons*, September-October 1991, pp. 68-71; R. Rodgers and J.E. Hunter, "A Foundation of Good Management Practice in Government: Management by Objectives," *Public Administration Review*, January-February 1992, pp. 27-39; and T.H. Poister and G. Streib, "MBO in Municipal Government: Variations on a Traditional Management Tool," *Public Administration Review*, January/February 1995, pp. 48-56.

18. See, for instance, C.H. Ford, "MBO: An Idea Whose Time Has Gone?", *Business Horizons*, December 1979, p. 49; R. Rodgers and J.E. Hunter, "Impact of Management by Objectives on Organizational Productivity," *Journal of Applied Psychology*, April 1991, pp. 322-336; and R. Rodgers, J.E. Hunter, and D.L. Rogers, "Influence of Top Management Commitment on Management Program Success," *Journal of Applied Psychology*, February 1993, pp. 151-155.

19. W. Thorsell, "Globe Awards Reward the Seen and Unseen," *The Globe and Mail*, February 28, 1998, p. A2.

20. "Clear Visions: The Top 40 Under 40," *Financial Post Magazine*, April, 1997 pp. 16-30.

21. "Praise Beats Raise as Best Motivator, Survey Shows," *Vancouver Sun*, September 10, 1994.

22. Based on S.E. Gross and J.P. Bacher, "The New Variable Pay Programs: How Some Succeed, Why Some Don't," *Compensation & Benefits Review,* January-February 1993, p. 51; and J.R. Schuster and P.K. Zingheim, "The New Variable Pay: Key Design Issues," *Compensation & Benefits Review,* March-April 1993, p. 28.

23. "Hope for Higher Pay: The Squeeze on Incomes Is Gradually Easing Up," *Maclean's*, 109, no. 48, November 25, 1996, pp. 100-101.

24. P. Booth, *Challenge and Change: Embracing the Team Concept.* Report 123-94, Conference Board of Canada, 1994, p. 18.

25. "Bonus Pay in Canada," *Manpower Argus*, September 1996, p. 5.

26. "Risk and Reward: More Canadian Companies Are Experimenting with Variable Pay," *Maclean's*, January 8, 1996, pp. 26-27.

27. C. Mandel, "Cash by the Numbers: The Vogue for 'Performance Incentives' Spreads to Primary Schools," *Alberta Report*, March 29, 1999, p. 33.

28. K. May, "New Pay Scheme Intended to Help Retain Canada's Top Bureaucrats," *Vancouver Sun*, August 3, 1999, pp. A5.

29. See, for instance, S.C. Hanlon, D.G. Meyer, and R.R. Taylor, "Consequences of Gainsharing," *Group & Organization Management*, March 1994, pp. 87-111; J.G. Belcher, Jr., "Gainsharing and Variable Pay: The State of the Art," *Compensation & Benefits Review*, May-June 1994, pp. 50-60; and T.M. Welbourne and L.R. Gomez Mejia, "Gainsharing: A Critical Review and a Future Research Agenda," *Journal of Management*, 21, no. 3, 1995, pp. 559-609.

30. D. Beck, "Implementing a Gainsharing Plan: What Companies Need to Know," *Compensation & Benefits Review*, January-February 1992, p. 23.

31. M. Byfield, "Ikea's Boss Gives Away the Store for a Day," *Report Newsmagazine*, October 25, 1999, p. 47.

32. See K.M. Young (ed.), *The Expanding Role of ESOPs in Public Companies* (New York: Quorum, 1990); J.L. Pierce and C.A. Furo, "Employee Ownership: Implications for Management," *Organizational Dynamics*, Winter 1990, pp. 32-43; J. Blasi and D.L. Druse, *The New Owners: The Mass Emergence of Employee Ownership in Public Companies and What It Means to American Business* (Champaign, IL: Harper Business, 1991); F.T. Adams and G.B. Hansen, *Putting Democracy to Work: A Practical Guide for Starting and Managing Worker-Owned Businesses* (San Francisco: Berrett-Koehler, 1993); and A.A. Buchko, "The Effects of Employee Ownership on Employee Attitudes: An Integrated Causal Model and Path Analysis," *Journal of Management Studies*, July 1993, pp. 633-656.

33. P. Phillips, "The Business of ESOPs: Canada Lags Behind When It Comes To Employee Share Ownership Plans," *Benefits Canada*, 23(4), pp. 8-9.

34. P. Phillips, "The Business of ESOPs: Canada Lags Behind When It Comes To Employee Share Ownership Plans," *Benefits Canada*, 23(4), pp. 8-9.

35. "Tracking Success: Is Competency-Based Human Resources Management an Effective Strategy or Simply the Flavor of the Month?" *Benefits Canada*, 20, no. 5, May 1996, pp. 71-73.

36. A.A. Buchko, "The Effects of Employee Ownership on Employee Attitudes: An Integrated Causal Model and Path Analysis," *Journal of Management Studies*, July 1993, pp. 633-656.

37. C.M. Rosen and M. Quarrey, "How Well Is Employee Ownership Working?" *Harvard Business Review*, September-October 1987, pp. 126-132.

38. W.N. Davidson and D.L. Worrell, "ESOP's Fables: The Influence of Employee Stock Ownership Plans on Corporate Stock Prices and Subsequent Operating Performance," *Human Resource Planning*, 1994, pp. 69-85.

39. J.L. Pierce and C.A. Furo, "Employee Ownership: Implications for Management," *Organizational Dynamics*, Winter 1990, pp. 32-43; and S. Kaufman, "ESOPs' Appeal on the Increase," *Nation's Business*, June 1997, p. 43.

40. See data in D. Stamps, "A Piece of the Action," *Training*, March 1996, p. 66.

41. M. Fein, "Work Measurement and Wage Incentives," *Industrial Engineering*, September 1973, pp. 49-51. For an updated review of the effect of pay on performance, see G.D. Jenkins Jr., N. Gupta, A. Mitra, and J.D. Shaw, "Are Financial Incentives Related to Performance? A Meta-Analytic Review of Empirical Research," *Journal of Applied Psychology*, October 1998, pp. 777-787.

42. C.G. Hanson and W.D. Bell, *Profit Sharing and Profitability: How Profit Sharing Promotes Business Success* (London: Kogan Page Ltd., 1987); and M. Magnan and S. St-Onge, "Profit-Sharing and Firm Performance: A Comparative and Longitudinal Analysis," paper presented at the 58th Annual Meeting of the Academy of Management San Diego, CA, August 1998.

43. See E.M. Doherty, W.R. Nord, and J.L. McAdams, "Gainsharing and Organizational Development: A Productive Synergy," *Journal of Applied Behavioral Science*, August 1989, pp. 209-230; and T.C. McGrath, "How Three Screw Machine Companies Are Tapping Human Productivity Through Gainsharing," *Employment Relations Today*, vol. 20, no. 4, 1994, pp. 437-447.

44. M. Fein, "Work Measurement and Wage Incentives," *Industrial Engineering*, September 1973, pp. 49-51. For an updated review of the effect of pay on performance, see G.D. Jenkins Jr., N. Gupta, A. Mitra, and J.D. Shaw, "Are Financial Incentives Related to Performance? A Meta-Analytic Review of Empirical Research," *Journal of Applied Psychology*, October 1998, pp. 777-787.

45. Cited in "Pay for Performance," *Wall Street Journal*, February 20, 1990, p. 1.

46. D. Steinhart, "IBM to Dish Out $1.6b in Cash Bonuses: Bonuses Amount to 25% of Company's 1998 Profit," *Financial Post*, February 1, 1999, pp. C1, C6.

47. J. Pfeffer and N. Langton, "The Effects of Wage Dispersion on Satisfaction, Productivity, and Working Collaboratively: Evidence From College and University Faculty," *Administrative Science Quarterly*, 38, no. 3, 1983, pp. 382-407.

48. "Risk and Reward: More Canadian Companies Are Experimenting With Variable Pay," *Maclean's*, January 8, 1996, pp. 26-27.

49. "Risk and Reward: More Canadian Companies Are Experimenting With Variable Pay," *Maclean's*, January 8, 1996, pp. 26-27.

50. P.K. Zingheim and J.R. Schuster, "Introduction: How Are The New Pay Tools Being Deployed?", *Compensation and Benefits Review*, July-August 1995, pp. 10-11.

51. G.E. Ledford, Jr., "Paying for the Skills, Knowledge, and Competencies of Knowledge Workers," *Compensation & Benefits Review*, July-August 1995, pp. 55-62.

52. Human Resources Development Canada, "Moving Parts and Moving People: Sociotechnical Design of a New Plant," in *Labour Management Innovations in Canada*, 1994, pp. 72-76.

53. P. Booth, *Challenge and Change: Embracing the Team Concept*. Report 123-94, Conference Board of Canada, 1994, p. 14.

54. M. Rowland, "For Each New Skill, More Money," *New York Times*, June 13, 1993, p. F16.

55. E.E. Lawler III, G.E. Ledford, Jr., and L. Chang, "Who Uses Skill-Based Pay, and Why," *Compensation & Benefits Review*, March-April 1993, p. 22.

56. M. Rowland, "It's What You Can Do That Counts," *New York Times*, June 6, 1993, p. F17.

57. N.B. Carlyle, *Compensation Planning Outlook 1997*, Ottawa: Conference Board, 1996.

58. E.E. Lawler III, G.E. Ledford, Jr., and L. Chang, "Who Uses Skill-Based Pay, and Why," *Compensation & Benefits Review*, March-April 1993, p. 22.

59. "Tensions of a New Pay Plan," *New York Times*, May 17, 1992, p. F5.

60. S. Sherman, "Stretch Goals: The Dark Side of Asking for Miracles," *Fortune*, 132, no. 10, 1995, pp. 231-232; A.V. Feigenbaum, "Quality Leadership in the Global Economy," *Journal of Quality and Participation*, 17, no. 2, 1994, pp. 36-41; S. Tully, "Why Go for Stretch Targets," *Fortune*, 130, no. 10, 1994, 145-158.

61. K.R. Thompson, W.A. Hochwarter, and N.J. Mathys, "Stretch Targets: What Makes Them Effective?" *Academy of Management Executive*, 11, no. 3, 1997, pp. 48-60. See also F. Hume, "Developing Technology to Increase Competitiveness," *Industry Week*, 241, no. 21, 1992, p. 35; A.V. Roth and C.A. Giffi, "Critical Factors for Achieving World Class Manufacturing: Benchmarking North American Manufacturing Strategies," *Operations Management Review*, 11, no. 2, 1995, 79-84.

62. K.R. Thompson, W.A. Hochwarter, and N.J. Mathys, "Stretch Targets: What Makes Them Effective?" *Academy of Management Executive*, 11, no. 3, 1997, pp. 48-60.

63. S. Tully, "Why Go for Stretch Targets," *Fortune*, 130(10), 1994, pp. 145-158.

64. K.R. Thompson, W.A. Hochwarter, and N.J. Mathys, "Stretch Targets: What Makes Them Effective?", *Academy of Management Executive*, 11, no. 3, 1997, pp. 48-60.

65. L.E. Parker and R. H. Price, "Empowered Managers and Empowered Workers: The Effects of Managerial Support and Managerial Perceived Control on Workers' Sense of Control over Decision Making," *Human Relations*, 47, no. 8, 1994, pp. 911-928; S. Wernick, "Self-Directed Work Teams and Empowerment," *Journal of Quality and Participation*, 17, no. 4, 1994, pp. 34-36, E.E. Lawler III, "Total Quality Management and Employee Involvement: Are They Compatible?", *Academy of Management Executive*, 8, no. 1, 1994, pp. 68-76.

66. K.R. Thompson, W.A. Hochwarter, and N.J. Mathys, "Stretch Targets: What Makes Them Effective?", *Academy of Management Executive*, 11, no. 3, 1997, pp. 48-60.

67. "Hope for Higher Pay: The Squeeze on Incomes Is Gradually Easing Up," *Maclean's*, 109, no. 48, November 25, 1996, pp. 100-101.

68. See, for instance, "When You Want to Contain Costs and Let Employees Pick Their Benefits: Cafeteria Plans," *INC.*, December 1989, p. 142; "More Benefits Bend with Workers' Needs," *Wall Street Journal*, January 9, 1990, p.

B1; R. Thompson, "Switching to Flexible Benefits," *Nation's Business*, July 1991, pp. 16-23; and A.E. Barber, R.B. Dunham, and R.A. Formisano, "The Impact of Flexible Benefits on Employee Satisfaction: A Field Study," *Personnel Psychology*, Spring 1992, pp. 55-75.

69. H. Bernstein, "New Benefit Schemes Can Be Deceiving," *Los Angeles Times*, May 14, 1991, p. D3.

70. "One Smooth Operator: This Former Bell Canada Part-Timer Has Come a Long Way," *Computing Canada*, January 23, 1997, p. 11.

71. See, for example, B. Geber, "The Flexible Work Force," *Training*, December 1993, pp. 23-30; M. Barrier, "Now You Hire Them, Now You Don't," *Nation's Business*, January 1994, pp. 30-31; J. Fierman, "The Contingency Work Force," *Fortune*, January 24, 1994, pp. 30-36; and D.C. Feldman, H.I. Doerpinghaus, and W.H. Turnley, "Managing Temporary Workers: A Permanent HRM Challenge," *Organizational Dynamics*, Autumn 1994, pp. 49-63.

72. R. Bingham, "Rebels with a Business Plan," *Report on Business Magazine*, November 1998, p. 82.

73. "Temporary Jobs Replacing Careers, Study Finds: Canadian Council for Social Development," *Canadian Press Newswire*, February 25, 1996.

74. G. Fuchsberg, "Parallel Lines," *Wall Street Journal*, April 21, 1993, p. R4; and A. Penzias, "New Paths to Success," *Fortune*, June 12, 1995, pp. 90-94.

75. *StatsCan Daily*, January 27, 1999.

76. B. Filipczak, "Managing a Mixed Work Force," *Training*, October 1997, pp. 96-103.

77. K. Damsell, "Service with No Smile: Blame It on Looser Labor Laws and a Newly Cynical Young Workforce. From Waiters to Video Clerks, BC's Service Industry Employees Are Flocking to Unions," *Financial Post*, August 23/25, 1997, p. 14.

78. D. Hage and J. Impoco, "Jawboning the Jobs," *U.S. News & World Report*, August 9, 1993, p. 53.

79. M.P. Cronin, "One Life to Live," *INC.*, July 1993, pp. 56-60.

80. G. Crone, "More Firms Link CEO Pay to Performance: Canada Following US," *Financial Post*, September 14, 1999, pp. C4.

81. W. Grossman and R.E. Hoskisson, "CEO Pay at the Crossroads of Wall Street and Main: Toward the Strategic Design of Executive Compensation," *Academy of Management Executive*, 12, no. 1, 1998, pp. 43. See also M.C. Jensen and K.J. Murphy, "Performance and Top Management Incentives," *Journal of Political Economy*, 98, 1990, pp. 225-264.

82. D. Berman, "Do They Deserve It?", *Canadian Business*, September 26, 1997, pp. 31-33.

83. A. Rappaport, "Executive Incentives vs. Corporate Growth," *Harvard Business Review*, July-August 1978, pp. 81-88; C.W.L. Hill, M.A. Hitt, and R.E. Hoskisson, "Declining U.S. Competitiveness: Reflections on a Crisis," *Academy of Management Executive*, 2, pp. 151-160.

84. W. Grossman and R.E. Hoskisson, "CEO Pay at the Crossroads of Wall Street and Main: Toward the Strategic Design of Executive Compensation," *Academy of Management Executive*, 12, no. 1, 1998, pp. 43-57.

85. M. MacKinnon, "Barrick's Munk Leads Pay Parade: $38.9m," *Canadian Press Newswire*, April 26, 1999.

86. L. Kroll, "Catching Up," *Forbes*, May 19, 1997.

87. D. Francis, "CEOs Doing Nicely, Thank You: Pay Hikes for Top Management Far Outstrip Their Companies' Stock Performance over the Past 10 Years," *Financial Post*, January 16, 1999, p. D8.

88. This section is based on information from B. Nelson, L. Good, and T. Hill, "Motivate Employees According to Temperament," *HR Magazine*, March 1997, pp. 51-56.

89. J.S. Adams, "Inequity in Social Exchanges," in L. Berkowitz (ed.), *Advances in Experimental Social Psychology* (New York: Academic Press, 1965), pp. 267-300.

90. P.S. Goodman, "An Examination of Referents Used in the Evaluation of Pay," *Organizational Behavior and Human Performance*, October 1974, pp. 170-195; S. Ronen, "Equity Perception in Multiple Comparisons: A Field Study," *Human Relations*, April 1986, pp. 333-346; R.W. Scholl, E.A. Cooper, and J.F. McKenna, "Referent Selection in Determining Equity Perception: Differential Effects on Behavioral and Attitudinal Outcomes," *Personnel Psychology*, Spring 1987, pp. 113-127; and T.P. Summers and A.S. DeNisi, "In Search of Adams' Other: Reexamination of Referents Used in the Evaluation of Pay," *Human Relations*, June 1990, pp. 497-511.

91. C.T. Kulik and M.L. Ambrose, "Personal and Situational Determinants of Referent Choice," *Academy of Management Review*, April 1992, pp. 212-237.

92. K. Torrance, "Robbing Peter to Pay Paula: Rising Female Wages Come Out of the Pockets of Men," *British Columbia Report*, April 13, 1998, p. 39.

93. See, for example, E. Walster, G.W. Walster, and W.G. Scott, *Equity: Theory and Research* (Boston: Allyn & Bacon, 1978); and J. Greenberg, "Cognitive Reevaluation of Outcomes in Response to Underpayment Inequity," *Academy of Management Journal*, March 1989, pp. 174-184.

94. P.S. Goodman and A. Friedman, "An Examination of Adams' Theory of Inequity," *Administrative Science Quarterly*, September 1971, pp. 271-288; R.P. Vecchio, "An Individual-Differences Interpretation of the Conflicting Predictions Generated by Equity Theory and Expectancy Theory," *Journal of Applied Psychology*, August 1981, pp. 470-481; J. Greenberg, "Approaching Equity and Avoiding Inequity in Groups and Organizations," in J. Greenberg and R.L. Cohen (eds.), *Equity and Justice in Social Behavior* (New York: Academic Press, 1982), pp. 389-435; E.W. Miles, J.D. Hatfield, and R.C. Huseman, "The Equity Sensitive Construct: Potential Implications for Worker Performance," *Journal of Management*, December 1989, pp. 581-588; and R.T. Mowday, "Equity Theory Predictions of Behavior in Organizations," in R. Steers and L.W. Porter (eds.), *Motivation and Work Behavior*, 5th ed. (New York: McGraw-Hill, 1991), pp. 111-131.

95. J. Greenberg and S. Ornstein, "High Status Job Title as Compensation for Underpayment: A Test of Equity Theory," *Journal of Applied Psychology*, May 1983, pp. 285-297; and J. Greenberg, "Equity and Workplace Status: A Field Experiment," *Journal of Applied Psychology*, November 1988, pp. 606-613.

96. P.S. Goodman, "Social Comparison Process in Organizations," in B.M. Staw and G.R. Salancik (eds.), *New Directions in Organizational Behavior* (Chicago: St. Clair, 1977), pp. 97-132; and J. Greenberg, "A Taxonomy of Organizational Justice Theories," *Academy of Management Review*, January 1987, pp. 9-22.

97. See, for instance, J. Greenberg, *The Quest for Justice on the Job* (Thousand Oaks, CA: Sage, 1996).

98. See, for example, R.C. Dailey and D.J. Kirk, "Distributive and Procedural Justice as Antecedents of Job Dissatisfaction and Intent to Turnover," *Human Relations*, March 1992, pp. 305-316; D.B. McFarlin and P.D. Sweeney, "Distributive and Procedural Justice as Predictors of Satisfaction with Personal and Organizational Outcomes," *Academy of Management Journal*, August 1992, pp. 626-637; and M.A. Korsgaard, D.M. Schweiger, and H.J. Sapienza, "Building Commitment, Attachment, and Trust in Strategic Decision-Making Teams: The Role of Procedural Justice," *Academy of Management Journal*, February 1995, pp. 60-84.

99. The remainder of this paragraph is based on W. Chan Kim and R. Mauborgne, "Fair Process: Managing in the Knowledge Economy," *Harvard Business Review*, July-August 1997, pp. 65-76.

100. A.S. Blinder, "Introduction," in A.S. Blinder (ed.), *Paying for Productivity: A Look at the Evidence* (Washington, D.C.: Brookings Institution, 1990), p. 30.

101. D.P. Skarlicki and R. Folger, "Retaliation in the Workplace: The Roles of Distributive, Procedural and Interactional Justice," *Journal of Applied Psychology*, 82, 1997, pp. 434-443.

102. H. Munro, "Transit Drivers Taking Fewer Sick Days," *Vancouver Sun*, June 2, 1999, p. B3.

103. Story based on M. Gorelkin, "Sowing Seeds of Discontent Back in the U.S.S.R." *Vancouver Sun*, June 9, 1990, pp. D3-4.

104. S. Kerr, "On the Folly of Rewarding A, While Hoping for B," *Academy of Management Executive*, vol. 9, no. 1, 1995, pp. 7-14.

105. "More on the Folly," *Academy of Management Executive*, vol. 9, no. 1, 1995, pp. 15-16.

106. W. Grossman and R.E. Hoskisson, "CEO Pay at the Crossroads of Wall Street and Main: Toward the Strategic Design of Executive Compensation," *Academy of Management Executive*, 12, no. 1, 1998, p. 47.

107. A. Rappaport, "Executive Incentives vs. Corporate Growth," *Harvard Business Review*, July-August 1978, pp. 81-88.

108. Y. Amihud and B. Lev, "Risk Reduction as a Managerial Motive for Conglomerate Mergers," *Bell Journal of Economics*, 12, pp. 605-617.

109. J.A. Ross, "Japan: Does Money Motivate?", *Harvard Business Review*, September-October 1997. See also R. Bruce Money and John L. Graham, "Salesperson Performance, Pay, and Job Satisfaction: Tests of a Model Using Data Collected in the U.S. and Japan," *Working Paper*, University of South Carolina, 1997.

110. D.H.B. Welsh, F. Luthans, and S.M. Sommer, "Managing Russian Factory Workers: The Impact of U.S.-Based Behavioral and Participative Techniques," *Academy of Management Journal*, 36, no. 1, 1993, pp. 58-79.

111. S.K. Saha, "Managing Human Resources: China vs. the West," *Canadian Journal of Administrative Sciences*, 10(2), 1998, pp. 167-177; Chao C. Chen, "New Trends in Reward Allocation Preference: A Sino/U.S. Comparison," *Academy of Management Journal*, 38(2), 1995, pp. 408-492.

112. N. Chowdhury, "Dell Cracks China," *Fortune*, June 21, 1999, pp. 120-124.

113. M.E. de Forest, "Thinking of a Plant in Mexico?", *Academy of Management Executive*, 8, no. 1, 1994, pp. 33-40.

114. N.J. Adler, *International Dimensions of Organizational Behavior*, 3rd ed. (Cincinnati, OH: Southwestern, 1997), p. 158.

115. A. Kohn, *Punished by Rewards* (Boston: Houghton Mifflin Company, 1993).

116. W.G. Ouchi, *Theory Z* (New York: Avon Books, 1982); "Bosses' Pay," *The Economist*, February 1, 1992, pp. 19-22; W. Edwards Deming, *Out of the Crisis* (Cambridge: MIT Center for Advanced Engineering Study, 1986).

117. J. Pfeffer, *The Human Equation: Building Profits by Putting People First* (Boston, Massachusetts: Harvard Business School Press, 1998).

118. T.L. Besser, "Reward and Organizational Goal Achievement: A Case Study of Toyota Motor Manufacturing in Kentucky," *Journal of Management Studies* 32, 1995, p. 387.

119. G. Hofstede, "Motivation, Leadership, and Organization: Do American Theories Apply Abroad?" *Organizational Dynamics*, Summer 1980, p. 55.

120. J.K. Giacobbe-Miller, D.J. Miller, and V.I. Victorov, "A Comparison of Russian and U.S. Pay Allocation Decisions, Distributive Justice Judgments, and Productivity Under Different Payment Conditions," *Personnel Psychology*, Spring 1998, pp. 137-163.

121. S.L. Mueller and L.D. Clarke, "Political-Economic Context and Sensitivity to Equity: Differences Between the United States and the Transition Economies of Central and Eastern Europe," *Academy of Management Journal*, June 1998, pp. 319-329.

122. R. de Charms, *Personal Causation: The Internal Affective Determinants of Behavior* (New York: Academic Press, 1968).

123. E.L. Deci, *Intrinsic Motivation* (New York: Plenum, 1975); R.D. Pritchard, K.M. Campbell, and D.J. Campbell, "Effects of Extrinsic Financial Rewards on Intrinsic Motivation," *Journal of Applied Psychology*, February 1977, pp. 9-15; E.L. Deci, G. Betly, J. Kahle, L. Abrams, and J. Porac, "When Trying to Win: Competition and Intrinsic Motivation," *Personality and Social Psychology Bulletin*, March 1981, pp. 79-83; and P.C. Jordan, "Effects of an Extrinsic Reward on Intrinsic Motivation: A Field Experiment," *Academy of Management Journal*, June 1986, pp. 405-412. See also J.M. Schrof, "Tarnished Trophies," *U.S. News & World Report*, October 25, 1993, pp. 52-59.

124. A. Kohn, *Punished by Rewards* (Boston: Houghton Mifflin Company, 1993).

125. J.B. Miner, *Theories of Organizational Behavior* (Hinsdale, IL: Dryden Press, 1980), p. 157.

126. A. Kohn, *Punished by Rewards* (Boston: Houghton Mifflin Company, 1993).

127. B. Nelson, "Dump the Cash, Load on the Praise," *Personnel Journal*, 75, July 1996, pp. 65-66.

128. J. Pfeffer, *The Human Equation: Building Profits by Putting People First* (Boston, Massachusetts: Harvard Business School Press, 1998).

129. J. Pfeffer, *The Human Equation: Building Profits by Putting People First* (Boston, Massachusetts: Harvard Business School Press, 1998).

130. B.J. Calder and B.M. Staw, "Self-Perception of Intrinsic and Extrinsic Motivation," *Journal of Personality and Social Psychology*, April 1975, pp. 599-605; J. Pfeffer, *The Human Equation: Building Profits by Putting People First* (Boston, Massachusetts: Harvard Business School Press, 1998), p. 217.

131. B.M. Staw, "Motivation in Organizations: Toward Synthesis and Redirection," in B.M. Staw and G.R. Salancik (eds.), *New Directions in Organizational Behavior* (Chicago: St. Clair, 1977), p. 76.

132. A. Kohn, *Punished by Rewards* (Boston: Houghton Mifflin Company, 1993), p. 181.

133. A. Kohn, *Punished by Rewards* (Boston: Houghton Mifflin Company, 1993), p. 186; see also Peter R. Scholtes, "An Elaboration of Deming's Teachings on Performance Appraisal," in Gary N. McLean, Susan R. Damme, and Richard A. Swanson (eds.), *Performance Appraisal: Perspectives on a Quality Management Approach* (Alexandria, VA: American Society for Training and Development, 1990); H.H. Meyer, E. Kay, and J.R.P French, Jr., "Split Roles in Performance Appraisal," 1965, excerpts reprinted in "HBR Retrospect," *Harvard Business Review,* January-February 1989, p. 26; W.-U. Meyer, M. Bachmann, U. Biermann, M. Hempelmann, F.-O. Ploeger, and H. Spiller, "The Informational Value of Evaluative Behavior: Influences of Praise and Blame on Perceptions of Ability," *Journal of Educational Psychology*, 71, 1979, pp. 259-268; A. Halachmi and M. Holzer, "Merit Pay, Performance Targetting, and Productivity," *Review of Public Personnel Administration*, 7, 1987, pp. 80-91.

134. A.S. Blinder, "Introduction," in A.S. Blinder (ed.), *Paying for Productivity: A Look at the Evidence* (Washington, D.C.: Brookings Institution, 1990).

135. A. Kohn, *Punished by Rewards* (Boston: Houghton Mifflin Company, 1993), p. 187.

136. D. Tjosvold, *Working Together to Get Things Done: Managing for Organizational Productivity* (Lexington, MA: Lexington Books, 1986); P.R. Scholtes, *The Team Handbook: How to Use Teams to Improve Quality* (Madison, WI: Joiner Associates, 1988); A. Kohn, *No Contest: The Case Against Competition*, rev. ed. (Boston: Houghton Mifflin, 1992).

137. E.L. Deci, "Applications of Research on the Effects of Rewards," in M.R. Lepper and D. Green (eds.), *The Hidden Costs of Rewards: New Perspectives on the Psychology of Human Motivation* (Hillsdale, NJ: Erlbaum, 1978).

138. S.E. Perry, *San Francisco Scavengers: Dirty Work and the Pride of Ownership* (Berkeley: University of California Press, 1978).

139. A. Kohn, *Punished by Rewards* (Boston: Houghton Mifflin Company, 1993), p. 192.

140. T.H. Naylor, "Redefining Corporate Motivation, Swedish Style," *Christian Century*, May 30-June 6, 1990, pp. 566-570; Robert A. Karasek, Tores Thorell, Joseph E. Schwartz, Peter L. Schnall, Carl F. Pieper, and John L. Michela, "Job Characteristics in Relation to the Prevalence of Myocardial Infarction in the US Health Examiniation Survey (HES) and the Health and Nutrition Examination Survey (HANES)," *American Journal of Public Health*, 78, 1988, pp. 910-916; D.P. Levin, "Toyota Plant in Kentucky Is Font of Ideas for the U.S.," *New York Times*, May 5, 1992, pp. A1, D8.

141. M. Bosquet, "The Prison Factory," reprinted from *Le Nouvel Observateur* in *Working Papers for a New Society*, Spring 1973, pp. 20-27; J. Holusha, "Grace Pastiak's 'Web of Inclusion,'" *New York Times*, May 5, 1991, pp. F1, F6; J. Simmons and W. Mares, *Working Together: Employee Participation in Action* (New York: New York University Press, 1985); D.I. Levine and L. D'Andrea Tyson, "Participation, Productivity, and the Firm's Environment," in A.S. Blinder (ed.), *Paying for Productivity: A Look at the Evidence* (Washington, DC: Brookings Institution, 1990); W.F. Whyte, "Worker Participation: International and Historical Perspectives," *Journal of Applied Behavioral Science*, 19, 1983, pp. 395-407.

142. For other examples of models that seek to integrate motivation theories, see H.J. Klein, "An Integrated Control Theory Model of Work Motivation," *Academy of Management Review*, April 1989, pp. 150-172; and E.A. Locke, "The Motivation Sequence, the Motivation Hub, and the Motivation Core," *Organizational Behavior and Human Decision Processes*, December 1991, pp. 288-299.

143. B. Ward, "Smiley Face Wins Tips for Waitresses," *Vancouver Sun*, April 25, 1998, p. B11.

## Chapter 5

1. Based on P. McMartin, "Singers from St. Pat's School Overwhelm Judges at Festival," *The Vancouver Sun*, May 15, 1999, pp. A1, A2.

2. B.W. Tuckman, "Developmental Sequences in Small Groups," *Psychological Bulletin*, June 1965, pp. 384-399; B.W. Tuckman and M.C. Jensen, "Stages of Small-Group Development Revisited," *Group and Organizational Studies*, December 1977, pp. 419-427; and M.F. Maples, "Group Development: Extending Tuckman's Theory," *Journal for Specialists in Group Work*, Fall 1988, pp. 17-23.

3. R.C. Ginnett, "The Airline Cockpit Crew," in J.R. Hackman (ed.), *Groups That Work (and Those That Don't)* (San Francisco: Jossey-Bass, 1990).

4. C.J.G. Gersick, "Time and Transition in Work Teams: Toward a New Model of Group Development," *Academy of Management Journal*, March 1988, pp. 9-41; C.J.G. Gersick, "Marking Time: Predictable Transitions in Task Groups," *Academy of Management Journal*, June 1989, pp. 274-309; E. Romanelli and M.L. Tushman, "Organizational Transformation as Punctuated Equilibrium: An Empirical Test," *Academy of Management Journal*, October 1994, pp. 1141-1166; B.M. Lichtenstein, "Evolution or Transformation: A Critique and Alternative

to Punctuated Equilibrium," in D.P. Moore (ed.), *Academy of Management Best Paper Proceedings* (National Academy of Management Conference; Vancouver, BC, 1995), pp. 291-295; and A. Seers and S. Woodruff, "Temporal Pacing in Task Forces: Group Development or Deadline Pressure?", *Journal of Management*, vol. 23, no. 2, 1997, pp. 169-187.

5. C.J.G. Gersick, "Time and Transition in Work Teams: Toward a New Model of Group Development," *Academy of Management Journal*, March 1988, pp. 9-41.

6. This model is based on the work of P.S. Goodman, E. Ravlin, and M. Schminke, "Understanding Groups in Organizations," in L.L. Cummings and B.M. Staw (eds.), *Research in Organizational Behavior*, 9 (Greenwich, CT: JAI Press, 1987), pp. 124-128; J.R. Hackman, "The Design of Work Teams," in J.W. Lorsch (ed.), *Handbook of Organizational Behavior* (Englewood Cliffs, NJ: Prentice Hall, 1987), pp. 315-342; G.R. Bushe and A.L. Johnson, "Contextual and Internal Variables Affecting Task Group Outcomes in Organizations," *Group and Organization Studies*, December 1989, pp. 462-482; and M.A. Campion, G.J. Medsker, and A.C. Higgs, "Relations Between Work Group Characteristics and Effectiveness: Implications for Designing Effective Work Groups," *Personnel Psychology*, Winter 1993, pp. 823-850.

7. F. Friedlander, "The Ecology of Work Groups," in J.W. Lorsch (ed.), *Handbook of Organizational Behavior*, (Englewood Cliffs, NJ: Prentice Hall, 1987), pp. 301-314; P.B. Paulus and D. Nagar, "Environmental Influences on Groups," in P. Paulus (ed.), *Psychology of Group Influence*, 2nd ed. (Hillsdale, NJ: Erlbaum, 1989); and E. Sundstrom and I. Altman, "Physical Environments and Work-Group Effectiveness," in L.L. Cummings and B.M. Staw (eds.), *Research in Organizational Behavior*, 11 (Greenwich, CT: JAI Press, 1989), pp. 175-209.

8. See, for example, J. Krantz, "Group Processes Under Conditions of Organizational Decline," *The Journal of Applied Behavioral Science*, 21, no. 1 (1985), pp. 1-17.

9. J.R. Hackman, "The Design of Work Teams," in J.W. Lorsch (ed.), *Handbook of Organizational Behavior* (Englewood Cliffs, NJ: Prentice Hall, 1987), pp. 325-326.

10. Cited in A.D. Szilagyi, Jr., and M.J. Wallace, Jr., *Organizational Behavior and Performance*, 4th ed. (Glenview, IL: Scott, Foresman, 1987), p. 223.

11. See M. Hill, "Group Versus Individual Performance. Are N+1 Heads Better Than One?" *Psychological Reports*, April 1982, pp. 517-539; and A. Tziner and D. Eden, "Effects of Crew Composition on Crew Performance: Does the Whole Equal the Sum of Its Parts?" *Journal of Applied Psychology*, February 1985, pp. 85-93.

12. M.J. Stevens and M.A. Campion, "The Knowledge, Skill, and Ability Requirements for Teamwork: Implications for Human Resource Management," *Journal of Management*, Summer 1994, pp. 503-530.

13. M.E. Shaw, *Contemporary Topics in Social Psychology* (Morristown, NJ: General Learning Press, 1976), pp. 350-351; and and D.C. Kinlaw, *Developing Superior Work Teams: Building Quality and the Competitive Edge* (San Diego, CA: Lexington, 1991).

14. S. Lieberman, "The Effects of Changes in Roles on the Attitudes of Role Occupants," *Human Relations*, November 1956, pp. 385-402.

15. See S.L. Robinson, M.S. Kraatz, and D.M. Rousseau, "Changing Obligations and the Psychological Contract: A Longitudinal Study," *Academy of Management Journal*, February 1994, pp. 137-152; and D.M. Rousseau, *Psychological Contracts in Organizations: Understanding Written and Unwritten Agreements* (Thousand Oaks, CA: Sage, 1995).

16. E.H. Schein, *Organizational Psychology*, 3rd ed. (Englewood Cliffs, NJ: Prentice Hall, 1980), p. 24.

17. See M.F. Peterson et al., "Role Conflict, Ambiguity, and Overload: A 21-Nation Study," *Academy of Management Journal*, April 1995, pp. 429-452.

18. For a recent review of the research on group norms, see J.R. Hackman, "Group Influences on Individuals in Organizations," in M.D. Dunnette and L.M. Hough (eds.), *Handbook of Industrial & Organizational Psychology*, 2nd ed., vol. 3 (Palo Alto, CA: Consulting Psychologists Press, 1992), pp. 235-250.

19. A. Harlan, J. Kerr, and S. Kerr, "Preference for Motivator and Hygiene Factors in a Hypothetical Interview Situation: Further Findings and Some Implications for the Employment Interview," *Personnel Psychology*, Winter 1977, pp. 557-566.

20. D.C. Feldman, "The Development and Enforcement of Group Norms," *Academy of Management Journal*, January 1984, pp. 47-53; and K.L. Bettenhausen and J.K. Murnighan, "The Development of an Intragroup Norm and the Effects of Interpersonal and Structural Challenges," *Administrative Science Quarterly*, March 1991, pp. 20-35.

21. D.C. Feldman, "The Development and Enforcement of Group Norms," *Academy of Management Journal*, January 1984, pp. 47–53; and K.L. Bettenhausen and J.K. Murnighan, "The Development of an Intragroup Norm and the Effects of Interpersonal and Structural Challenges," *Administrative Science Quarterly*, March 1991, pp. 20–35.

22. C.A. Kiesler and S.B. Kiesler, *Conformity* (Reading, MA: Addison-Wesley, 1969).

23. C.A. Kiesler and S.B. Kiesler, *Conformity* (Reading, MA: Addison-Wesley, 1969), p. 27.

24. S.E. Asch, "Effects of Group Pressure upon the Modification and Distortion of Judgments," in H. Guetzkow (ed.), *Groups, Leadership and Men* (Pittsburgh: Carnegie Press, 1951), pp. 177-190.

25. S.L. Robinson and A.M. O'Leary-Kelly, "Monkey See, Monkey Do: The Influence of Work Groups on the Antisocial Behavior of Employees," *Academy of Management Journal*, 41, 1998, pp. 658-672.

26. J.M. George, "Personality, Affect and Behavior in Groups," *Journal of Applied Psychology*, 78, 1993, pp. 798-804; and J.M. George and L.R. James, "Personality, Affect, and Behavior in Groups Revisited: Comment on Aggregation, Levels of Analysis, and a Recent Application of Within and Between Analysis," *Journal of Applied Psychology*, 78, 1993, pp. 798-804.

27. Cited in J.R. Hackman, "Group Influences on Individuals in Organizations," in M.D. Dunnette and L.M. Hough (eds.), *Handbook of Industrial & Organizational Psychology*, 2nd ed., vol. 3 (Palo Alto, CA: Consulting Psychologists Press, 1992), p. 236.

28. O.J. Harvey and C. Consalvi, "Status and Conformity to Pressures in Informal Groups," *Journal of Abnormal and Social Psychology*, Spring 1960, pp. 182-187.

29. J.A. Wiggins, F. Dill, and R.D. Schwartz, "On 'Status-Liability,'" *Sociometry*, April-May 1965, pp. 197-209.

30. J. Greenberg, "Equity and Workplace Status: A Field Experiment," *Journal of Applied Psychology*, November 1988, pp. 606-613.

31. This section is based on P.R. Harris and R.T. Moran, *Managing Cultural Differences*, 4th ed. (Houston: Gulf Publishing, 1996).

32. E.J. Thomas and C.F. Fink, "Effects of Group Size," *Psychological Bulletin*, July 1963, pp. 371-384; A.P. Hare, *Handbook of Small Group Research* (New York: Free Press, 1976); and M.E. Shaw, *Group Dynamics: The Psychology of Small Group Behavior*, 3rd ed. (New York: McGraw-Hill, 1981).

33. See D.R. Comer, "A Model of Social Loafing in Real Work Groups," *Human Relations*, June 1995, pp. 647-667.

34. W. Moede, "Die Richtlinien der Leistungs-Psychologie," *Industrielle Psychotechnik*, 4 (1927), pp. 193-207. See also D.A. Kravitz and B. Martin, "Ringelmann Rediscovered: The Original Article," *Journal of Personality and Social Psychology*, May 1986, pp. 936-941.

35. See, for example, J.A. Shepperd, "Productivity Loss in Performance Groups: A Motivation Analysis," *Psychological Bulletin*, January 1993, pp. 67-81; and S.J. Karau and K.D. Williams, "Social Loafing: A Meta-Analytic Review and Theoretical Integration," *Journal of Personality and Social Psychology*, October 1993, pp. 681-706.

36. S.G. Harkins and K. Szymanski, "Social Loafing and Group Evaluation," *Journal of Personality and Social Psychology*, December 1989, pp. 934-941.

37. See P.C. Earley, "Social Loafing and Collectivism: A Comparison of the United States and the People's Republic of China," *Administrative Science Quarterly*, December 1989, pp. 565-581; and P.C. Earley, "East Meets West Meets Mideast: Further Explorations of Collectivistic and Individualistic Work Groups," *Academy of Management Journal*, April 1993, pp. 319-348.

38. E.J. Thomas and C.F. Fink, "Effects of Group Size," *Psychological Bulletin*, July 1963, pp. 371-384; A.P. Hare, *Handbook of Small Group Research* (New York: Free Press, 1976); M.E. Shaw, *Group Dynamics: The Psychology of Small Group Behavior*, 3rd ed. (New York: McGraw-Hill, 1981); and P. Yetton and P. Bottger, "The Relationships Among Group Size, Member Ability, Social Decision Schemes, and Performance," *Organizational Behavior and Human Performance*, October 1983, pp. 145-159.

39. See, for example, P.S. Goodman, E.C. Ravlin, and L. Argote, "Current Thinking About Groups: Setting the Stage for New Ideas," in P.S. Goodman and Associates, *Designing Effective Work Groups* (San Francisco: Jossey-Bass, 1986), pp. 15-16; R.A. Guzzo and G.P. Shea, "Group Performance and Intergroup Relations in Organizations," in M.D. Dunnette and L.M. Hough (eds.), *Handbook of Industrial & Organizational Psychology*, 2nd ed., vol. 3 (Palo Alto, CA: Consulting Psychologists Press, 1992), pp. 288-290; and S.E. Jackson, K.E. May, and

K. Whitney, "Understanding the Dynamics of Diversity in Decision-Making Teams," in R.A. Guzzo and E. Salas (eds.), *Team Effectiveness and Decision Making in Organizations* (San Francisco: Jossey-Bass, 1995), pp. 204-261; and K.Y. Williams and C.A. O'Reilly III, "Demography and Diversity in Organizations: A Review of 40 Years of Research," in B.M. Staw and L.L. Cummings (eds.), *Research in Organizational Behavior*, vol. 20 (Greenwich, CT: JAI Press, 1998), pp. 77-140.

40. D.C. Thomas, E.C. Ravlin, and A.W. Wallace, "Effect of Cultural Diversity in Work Groups," *Research in the Sociology of Organizations*, 14, 1996, pp. 1-33.

41. W.E. Watson, K. Kumar, and L.K. Michaelsen, "Cultural Diversity's Impact on Interaction Process and Performance: Comparing Homogeneous and Diverse Task Groups," *Academy of Management Journal*, June 1993, pp. 590-602; D.C. Thomas, E.C. Ravlin, and A.W. Wallace, "Effect of Cultural Diversity in Work Groups," *Research in the Sociology of Organizations*, 14, 1996, pp. 1-33.

42. D.C. Thomas, E.C. Ravlin, and A.W. Wallace, "Effect of Cultural Diversity in Work Groups," *Research in the Sociology of Organizations*, 14, 1996, pp. 1-33, found no indication of lower performance in culturally diverse groups, while W.E. Watson, K. Kumar, and L.K. Michaelsen, "Cultural Diversity's Impact on Interaction Process and Performance: Comparing Homogeneous and Diverse Task Groups," *Academy of Management Journal*, June 1993, pp. 590-602, did find evidence of lower performance in the short-run.

43. K. Jehn and P.P. Shah, "Interpersonal Relationships and Task Performance: An Examination of Mediating Processses in Friendship and Acquaintance Groups," *Journal of Personality and Social Psychology*, 72, 1997, pp. 775-790.

44. E. Peterson, "Negotiation Teamwork: The Impact of Information Distribution and Accountability on Performance Depends on the Relationship Among Team Members," *Organizational Behavior and Human Decision Processes*, 72, 1997, pp. 364-384.

45. For some of the controversy surrounding the definition of cohesion, see J. Keyton and J. Springston, "Redefining Cohesiveness in Groups," *Small Group Research*, May 1990, pp. 234-254.

46. C.R. Evans and K.L. Dion, "Group Cohesion and Performance: A Meta-Analysis," *Small Group Research*, May 1991, pp. 175-186; B. Mullen and C. Cooper, "The Relation Between Group Cohesiveness and Performance: An Integration," *Psychological Bulletin*, March 1994, pp. 210–227; S.M. Gully, D.J. Devine, and D.J. Whitney, "A Meta-Analysis of Cohesion and Performance: Effects of Level of Analysis and Task Interdependence," *Small Group Research*, 1995, pp. 497-520; and P.M. Podsakoff, S.B. MacKenzie, and M. Ahearne, "Moderating Effects of Goal Acceptance on the Relationship Between Group Cohesiveness and Productivity," *Journal of Applied Psychology*, December 1997, pp. 974-983.

47. I.D. Steiner, *Group Process and Productivity* (New York: Academic Press, 1972).

48. R.B. Zajonc, "Social Facilitation," *Science*, March 1965, pp. 269-274.

49. C.F. Bond, Jr., and L.J. Titus, "Social Facilitation: A Meta-Analysis of 241 Studies," *Psychological Bulletin*, September 1983, pp. 265-292.

50. V.F. Nieva, E.A. Fleishman, and A. Rieck, "Team Dimensions: Their Identity, Their Measurement, and Their Relationships." Final Technical Report for Contract No. DAHC 19-C-0001 (Washington, DC: Advanced Research Resources Organizations, 1978).

51. See, for example, J.R. Hackman and C.G. Morris, "Group Tasks, Group Interaction Process and Group Performance Effectiveness: A Review and Proposed Integration," in L. Berkowitz (ed.), *Advances in Experimental Social Psychology* (New York: Academic Press, 1975), pp. 45-99; and R. Saavedra, P.C. Earley, and L. Van Dyne, "Complex Interdependence in Task-Performing Groups," *Journal of Applied Psychology*, February 1993, pp. 61-72.

52. J. Galbraith, *Organizational Design* (Reading, MA: Addison-Wesley, 1977).

53. Quoted from Richard Hackman, "The Design of Work Teams," in J.W. Lorsch (ed.), *Handbook of Organizational Behavior* (Englewood Cliffs, NJ: Prentice-Hall, 1987), pp. 315-339.

54. While the specific subject points are taken from Richard Hackman, "The Design of Work Teams," in J.W. Lorsch (ed.), *Handbook of Organizational Behavior* (Englewood Cliffs, NJ: Prentice-Hall, 1987), pp. 315-339, the discussion of the individual items is developed separately.

55. G.M. Parker, *Team Player and Teamwork: The Competitive Business Strategy* (Jossey-Bass, San Francisco, 1990).

56. G.M. Parker, *Team Player and Teamwork: The Competitive Business Strategy* (Jossey-Bass, San Francisco, 1990), p. 44.

57. T.P. Verney, "Role Perception Congruence, Performance, and Satisfaction," in D.J. Vredenburgh and R.S. Schuler (eds.), *Effective Management: Research and Application*, Proceedings of the 20th Annual Eastern Academy of Management, Pittsburgh, PA, May 1983, pp. 24-27.

58. T.P. Verney, "Role Perception Congruence, Performance, and Satisfaction," in D.J. Vredenburgh and R.S. Schuler (eds.), *Effective Management: Research and Application*, Proceedings of the 20th Annual Eastern Academy of Management, Pittsburgh, PA, May 1983, pp. 24-27.

59. M. Van Sell, A.P. Brief, and R.S. Schuler, "Role Conflict and Role Ambiguity: Integration of the Literature and Directions for Future Research," *Human Relations*, January 1981, pp. 43-71; and A.G. Bedeian and A.A. Armenakis, "A Path-Analytic Study of the Consequences of Role Conflict and Ambiguity," *Academy of Management Journal*, June 1981, pp. 417-424.

60. M.E. Shaw, *Group Dynamics: The Psychology of Small Group Behavior*, 3rd ed. (New York: McGraw-Hill, 1981).

61. B. Mullen, C. Symons, L. Hu, and E. Salas, "Group Size, Leadership Behavior, and Subordinate Satisfaction," *Journal of General Psychology*, April 1989, pp. 155-170.

## Chapter 6

1. B. Wheatley, "Innovation in ISO Registration [Kaizen blitz]," *CMA Management Accounting Magazine*, June 1998, p. 23; C. McLean, "Reinventing a Clean, Lean Manufacturing Machine: Willow Pulls Together as a Team

to Survive in the Competitive Metal Working Industry," *Plant*, September 27, 1999, p. 13.

2. This section is based on J.R. Katzenbach and D.K. Smith, *The Wisdom of Teams* (Boston: Harvard Business School Press, 1993), pp. 21, 45, and 85; and D.C. Kinlaw, *Developing Superior Work Teams* (Lexington, MA: Lexington Books, 1991), pp. 3-21.

3. P. Booth, *Challenge and Change: Embracing the Team Concept*, Report 123-94, Conference Board of Canada, 1994.

4. *Training Magazine*, October 1995, Lakewood Publications, Minneapolis, MN.

5. See, for example, D. Tjosvold, *Team Organization: An Enduring Competitive Advantage* (Chichester, England: Wiley, 1991); J. Lipnack and J. Stamps, *The TeamNet Factor* (Essex Junction, VT: Oliver Wight, 1993); J.R. Katzenbach and D.K. Smith, *The Wisdom of Teams* (Boston: Harvard Business School Press, 1993); and S.A. Mohrman, S.G. Cohen, and A.M. Mohrman, Jr., *Designing Team-Based Organizations* (San Francisco: Jossey-Bass, 1995).

6. J.H. Shonk, *Team-Based Organizations* (Homewood, IL: Business One Irwin, 1992); and M.A. Verespej, "When Workers Get New Roles," *Industry Week*, February 3, 1992, p. 11.

7. M.L. Marks, P.H. Mirvis, E.J. Hackett, and J.F. Grady, Jr., "Employee Participation in a Quality Circle Program: Impact on Quality of Work Life, Productivity, and Absenteeism," *Journal of Applied Psychology*, February 1986, pp. 61-69; T.R. Miller, "The Quality Circle Phenomenon: A Review and Appraisal," *SAM Advanced Management Journal*, Winter 1989, pp. 4-7; and E.E. Adams, Jr., "Quality Circle Performance," *Journal of Management*, March 1991, pp. 25-39.

8. See, for example, G.W. Meyer and R.G. Stott, "Quality Circles: Panacea or Pandora's Box?", *Organizational Dynamics*, Spring 1985, pp. 34-50; M.L. Marks, P.H. Mirvis, E.J. Hackett, and J.F. Grady, Jr., "Employee Participation in a Quality Circle Program: Impact on Quality of Life, Productivity, and Absenteeism," *Journal of Applied Psychology*, February 1986, pp. 61-69; E.E. Lawler III and S.A. Mohrman, "Quality Circles: After the Honeymoon," *Organizational Dynamics*, Spring 1987, pp. 42-54; R.P. Steel and R.F. Lloyd, "Cognitive, Affective, and Behavioral Outcomes of Participation in Quality Circles: Conceptual and Empirical Findings," *Journal of Applied Behavioral Science*, 24, no. 1 (1988), pp. 1-17; T.R. Miller, "The Quality Circles Phenomenon: A Review and Appraisal," *SAM Advanced Management Journal*, Winter 1989, pp. 4-7; K. Buch and R. Spangler, "The Effects of Quality Circles on Performance and Promotions," *Human Relations*, June 1990, pp. 573-582; P.R. Liverpool, "Employee Participation in Decision-Making: An Analysis of the Perceptions of Members and Nonmembers of Quality Circles," *Journal of Business and Psychology*, Summer 1990, pp. 411-422; and E.E. Adams, Jr., "Quality Circle Performance," *Journal of Management*, March 1991, pp. 25-39.

9. J.L. Cotton, *Employee Involvement* (Newbury Park, CA: Sage, 1993), p. 76.

10. "Corporate Culture Club: Companies Are Focusing on Employee Morale and Training to Boost the Bottom Line," *Maclean's*, December 12, 1994, pp. 42-43.

11. J.L. Cotton, *Employee Involvement* (Newbury Park, CA: Sage, 1993), p. 76.

12. J.L. Cotton, *Employee Involvement* (Newbury Park, CA: Sage, 1993), p. 3.

13. See, for example, C.C. Manz and H.P. Sims, Jr., *Business Without Bosses: How Self-Managing Teams Are Building High Performance Companies* (New York: Wiley, 1993); J.R. Barker, "Tightening the Iron Cage: Concertive Control in Self-Managing Teams," *Administrative Science Quarterly*, September 1993, pp. 408-437; and S.G. Cohen, G.E. Ledford, Jr., and G.M. Spreitzer, "A Predictive Model of Self-Managing Work Team Effectiveness," *Human Relations*, May 1996, pp. 643-676.

14. "Now Everyone Can Be a Boss: Creating Self-directed Work Teams Means Giving Shop-Floor Workers the Kind of Authority Once Reserved for Management," *Canadian Business*, May 1994, p. 48.

15. P. Booth, *Challenge and Change: Embracing the Team Concept*, Report 123-94, Conference Board of Canada, 1994.

16. See, for instance, T.D. Wall, N.J. Kemp, P.R. Jackson, and C.W. Clegg, "Outcomes of Autonomous Workgroups: A Long-Term Field Experiment," *Academy of Management Journal*, June 1986, pp. 280-304; and J.L. Cordery, W.S. Mueller, and L.M. Smith, "Attitudinal and Behavioral Effects of Autonomous Group Working: A Longitudinal Field Study," *Academy of Management Journal*, June 1991, pp. 464-476.

17. See J. Lipnack and J. Stamps, *The TeamNet Factor*, pp. 14-17; G. Taninecz, "Team Players," *Industry Week*, July 15, 1996, pp. 28-32; D.R. Denison, S.L. Hart, and J.A. Kahn, "From Chimneys to Cross-Functional Teams: Developing and Validating a Diagnostic Model," *Academy of Management Journal*, August 1996, pp. 1005-1023; and A.R. Jassawalla, "Building Collaborative Cross-Functional New Product Teams," *Academy of Management Executive*, August 1999, pp. 50-63.

18. "Cross-Functional Obstacles," *Training*, May 1994, pp. 125-26.

19. See, for example, M.E. Warkentin, L. Sayeed, and R. Hightower, "Virtual Teams Versus Face-to-Face Teams: An Exploratory Study of a Web-Based Conference System," *Decision Sciences*, Fall 1997, pp. 975-993; A.M. Townsend, S.M. DeMarie, and A.R. Hendrickson, "Virtual Teams: Technology and the Workplace of the Future," *Academy of Management Executive*, August 1998, pp. 17-29; and D. Duarte and N.T. Snyder, *Mastering Virtual Teams: Strategies, Tools, and Techniques* (San Francisco: Jossey-Bass, 1999).

20. K. Kiser, "Working on World Time," *Training*, March 1999, p. 30.

21. S.L. Jarvenpaa, K. Knoll, and D.E. Leidner, "Is Anybody Out There? Antecedents of Trust in Global Virtual Teams," *Journal of Management Information Systems*, Spring 1998, pp. 29-64.

22. A.B. Drexler and R. Forrester, "Teamwork—Not Necessarily the Answer," *HRMagazine*, January 1998, pp. 55-58.

23. R. Forrester and A.B. Drexler, "A Model for Team-Based Organization Performance," *Academy of Management Executive*, August 1999, p. 47. See also S.A. Mohrman, with S.G. Cohen and A.M. Mohrman, Jr., *Designing Team-Based Organizations* (San Francisco: Jossey-Bass, 1995); and J.H. Shonk, *Team-Based Organizations* (Homewood, IL: Business One Irwin, 1992).

24. See, for instance, D.L. Gladstein, "Groups in Context: A Model of Task Group Effectiveness," *Administrative Science Quarterly*, December 1984, pp. 499-517; J.R. Hackman, "The Design of Work Teams," in J.W. Lorsch (ed.), *Handbook of Organizational Behavior* (Englewood Cliffs, NJ: Prentice Hall, 1987), pp. 315-342; M.A. Campion, G.J. Medsker, and C.A. Higgs, "Relations Between Work Group Characteristics and Effectiveness: Implications for Designing Effective Work Groups," *Personnel Psychology*, 1993; and R.A. Guzzo and M.W. Dickson, "Teams in Organizations: Recent Research on Performance and Effectiveness," in J.T. Spence, J.M. Darley, and D.J. Foss, *Annual Review of Psychology*, vol. 47, pp. 307-338.

25. D.E. Hyatt and T.M. Ruddy, "An Examination of the Relationship Between Work Group Characteristics and Performance: Once More into the Breech," *Personnel Psychology*, Autumn 1997, p. 555.

26. This model is based on M.A. Campion, E.M. Papper, and G.J. Medsker, "Relations Between Work Team Characteristics and Effectiveness: A Replication and Extension," *Personnel Psychology*, Summer 1996, pp. 429-452; D.E. Hyatt and T.M. Ruddy, "An Examination of the Relationship Between Work Group Characteristics and Performance: Once More into the Breech," *Personnel Psychology*, Autumn 1997, pp. 553-585; and S.G. Cohen and D.E. Bailey, "What Makes Teams Work: Group Effectiveness Research from the Shop Floor to the Executive Suite," *Journal of Management*, vol. 23, no. 3, 1997, pp. 239-290.

27. R. Wageman, "Critical Success Factors for Creating Superb Self-Managing Teams," *Organizational Dynamics*, Summer 1997, p. 55.

28. M.A. Campion, E.M. Papper, and G.J. Medsker, "Relations Between Work Team Characteristics and Effectiveness: A Replication and Extension," *Personnel Psychology*, Summer 1996, p. 430.

29. M.A. Campion, E.M. Papper, and G.J. Medsker, "Relations Between Work Team Characteristics and Effectiveness: A Replication and Extension," *Personnel Psychology*, Summer 1996, p. 430.

30. V.F. Nieva, E.A. Fleishman, and A. Reick, *Team Dimensions: Their Identity, Their Measurement, and Their Relationships* (Research Note 85-12) (Washington, DC: U.S. Army, Research Institute for the Behavioral and Social Sciences, 1985).

31. M.R. Barrick, G.L. Stewart, M.J. Neubert, and M.K. Mount, "Relating Member Ability and Personality to Work-Team Processes and Team Effectiveness," *Journal of Applied Psychology*, June 1998, pp. 377-391.

32. M.R. Barrick, G.L. Stewart, M.J. Neubert, and M.K. Mount, "Relating Member Ability and Personality to Work-Team Processes and Team Effectiveness," *Journal of Applied Psychology*, June 1998, pp. 377-391.

33. M.R. Barrick, G.L. Stewart, M.J. Neubert, and M.K. Mount, "Relating Member Ability and Personality to Work-Team Processes and Team Effectiveness," *Journal of Applied Psychology*, June 1998, pp. 377-391.

34. For a more detailed breakdown on team skills, see M.J. Stevens and M.A. Campion, "The Knowledge, Skill, and Ability Requirements for Teamwork: Implications for Human Resource Management," *Journal of Management*, Summer 1994, pp. 503-530.

35. C. Margerison and D. McCann, *Team Management: Practical New Approaches* (London: Mercury Books, 1990).

36. E. Sundstrom, K.P. Meuse, and D. Futrell, "Work Teams: Applications and Effectiveness," *American Psychologist*, February 1990, pp. 120-133.

37. D.E. Hyatt and T.M. Ruddy, "An Examination of the Relationship Between Work Group Characteristics and Performance: Once More into the Breech," *Personnel Psychology*, Autumn 1997, p. 555.

38. T.B. Kinni, "Boundary-Busting Teamwork," *Industry Week*, March 21, 1994, pp. 72-78.

39. R.I. Beekun, "Assessing the Effectiveness of Sociotechnical Interventions: Antidote or Fad?", *Human Relations*, October 1989, pp. 877-897.

40. S.G. Cohen, G.E. Ledford, and G.M. Spreitzer, "A Predictive Model of Self-Managing Work Team Effectiveness," *Human Relations*, May 1996, pp. 643–676.

41. D. Eden, "Pygmalion Without Interpersonal Contrast Effects: Whole Groups Gain from Raising Manager Expectations," *Journal of Applied Psychology*, August 1990, pp. 394-398.

42. J.M. George and K. Bettenhausen, "Understanding Prosocial Behavior, Sales, Performance, and Turnover: A Group-Level Analysis in a Service Context," *Journal of Applied Psychology*, December 1990, pp. 698-709; and J.M. George, "State or Trait: Effects of Positive Mood on Prosocial Behaviors at Work, *Journal of Applied Social Psychology*, April 1991, pp. 299-307.

43. See S.T. Johnson, "Work Teams: What's Ahead in Work Design and Rewards Management," *Compensation & Benefits Review*, March-April 1993, pp. 35-41; and A.M. Saunier and E.J. Hawk, "Realizing the Potential of Teams Through Team-Based Rewards," *Compensation & Benefits Review*, July-August 1994, pp. 24-33.

44. P. Booth, *Challenge and Change: Embracing the Team Concept*, Report 123-94, Conference Board of Canada, 1994, pp. 14-15.

45. P. Booth, *Challenge and Change: Embracing the Team Concept*, Report 123-94, Conference Board of Canada, 1994, p. 14.

46. E.E. Lawler, *Pay and Organizational Development*, Reading, MA: Addison-Wesley, 1981; V. Vroom, *Work and Motivation*, New York: John Wiley, 1964; T.B. Wilson, "Group Incentives: Are You Ready?", *Journal of Compensation Benefits*, 6(3), 1990, pp. 25-29.

47. A.M. Mohrman, S.A. Mohrman, and E.E. Lawler, "The Performance Management of Teams," in William J. Bruns, Jr. (ed.), *Performance Measurement, Evaluation and Incentives* (Boston, MA: Harvard Business School Press, 1992), pp. 217-241; A.K. Gupta and V. Govingarajan, "Resource Sharing Among SBUs and Administrative

Implications," *Academy of Management Journal*, 29, 1986, pp. 695-714; E.E. Lawler and S.G. Cohen, "Designing Pay Systems for Teams," *ACA Journal*, 1, 1992, pp. 6-19; I.T. Kay and D. Lerner, "What's Good for the Parts, May Hurt the Whole," *HR Magazine*, 40(9), 1995, pp. 71-77.

48. J.S. DeMatteo, L.T. Eby, and E. Sundstrom, "Team-Based Rewards: Current Empirical Evidence and Directions for Future Research," *Research in Organizational Behavior*, 20, 1998, pp. 141-183.

49. J. Pfeffer and N. Langton, "The Effect of Wage Dispersion on Satisfaction, Productivity, and Working Collaboratively: Evidence from College and University Faculty," *Administrative Science Quarterly*, 38, 1993, pp. 382-407.

50. M. Bloom, "The Performance Effects of Pay Dispersion on Individuals and Organizations," *Academy of Management Journal*, 42, 1999, pp. 25-40.

51. K. Hess, *Creating the High-Performance Team* (New York: Wiley, 1987); J.R. Katzenbach and D.K. Smith, *The Wisdom of Teams* (Boston: Harvard Business School Press, 1993), pp. 43–64; and K.D. Scott and A. Townsend, "Teams: Why Some Succeed and Others Fail," *HRMagazine*, August 1994, pp. 62–67.

52. F. McGuire, "Empowering Employees," *Canadian Business Review*, Winter 1993, pp. 21-23.

53. E. Weldon and L.R. Weingart, "Group Goals and Group Performance," *British Journal of Social Psychology*, Spring 1993, pp. 307-334.

54. R.A. Guzzo, P.R. Yost, R.J. Campbell, and G.P. Shea, "Potency in Groups: Articulating a Construct," *British Journal of Social Psychology*, March 1993, pp. 87-106; S.J. Zaccaro, V. Blair, C. Peterson, and M. Zazanis, "Collective Efficacy," in J.E. Maddux (ed.), *Self-Efficacy, Adaptation and Adjustment: Theory, Research and Application* (New York: Plenum, 1995), pp. 308-330; and D.L. Feltz and C.D. Lirgg, "Perceived Team and Player Efficacy in Hockey," *Journal of Applied Psychology*, August 1998, pp. 557-564.

55. K. Jehn, "A Multimethod Examination of the Benefits and Detriments of Intragroup Conflict," *Administrative Science Quarterly*, June 1995, pp. 256-282.

56. K. Hess, *Creating the High-Performance Team* (New York: Wiley, 1987).

57. F. McGuire, "Empowering Employees," *Canadian Business Review*, Winter 1993, pp. 21-23.

58. T. Davis and M.J. Landa, "The Trust Deficit," *Worklife Report*, 4, 1999, pp. 6-7.

59. T. Davis and M.J. Landa, "The Trust Deficit," *Worklife Report*, 4, 1999, pp. 6-7.

60. Based on S.D. Boon and J.G. Holmes, "The Dynamics of Interpersonal Trust: Resolving Uncertainty in the Face of Risk," in R.A. Hinde and J. Groebel (eds.), *Cooperation and Prosocial Behavior* (Cambridge, UK: Cambridge University Press, 1991), p. 194; D.J. McAllister, "Affect- and Cognition-Based Trust as Foundations for Interpersonal Cooperation in Organizations," *Academy of Management Journal*, February 1995, p. 25; and D.M. Rousseau, S.B. Sitkin, R.S. Burt, and C. Camerer, "Not So Different After All: A Cross-Discipline View of Trust," *Academy of Management Review*, July 1998, pp. 393-404.

61. J.K. Rempel, J.G. Holmes, and M.P. Zanna, "Trust in Close Relationships," *Journal of Personality and Social Psychology*, July 1985, p. 96.

62. M. Granovetter, "Economic Action and Social Structure: The Problem of Embeddedness," *American Journal of Sociology*, November 1985, p. 491.

63. P.L. Schindler and C.C. Thomas, "The Structure of Interpersonal Trust in the Workplace," *Psychological Reports*, October 1993, pp. 563-573.

64. J.K. Butler Jr. and R.S. Cantrell, "A Behavioral Decision Theory Approach to Modeling Dyadic Trust in Superiors and Subordinates," *Psychological Reports*, August 1984, pp. 19-28.

65. D. McGregor, *The Professional Manager* (New York: McGraw-Hill, 1967), p. 164.

66. B. Nanus, *The Leader's Edge: The Seven Keys to Leadership in a Turbulent World* (Chicago: Contemporary Books, 1989), p. 102.

67. F.K. Sonnenberg, "Trust Me, Trust Me Not," *Industry Week*, August 16, 1993, pp. 22-28. For a more elaborate definition, see L.T. Hosmer, "Trust: The Connecting Link Between Organizational Theory and Philosophical Ethics," *Academy of Management Review*, April 1995, pp. 379-403.

68. See, for instance, M. Sashkin and K.J. Kiser, *Putting Total Quality Management to Work* (San Francisco: Berrett-Koehler, 1993); and J.R. Hackman and R. Wageman, "Total Quality Management: Empirical, Conceptual and Practical Issues," *Administrative Science Quarterly*, June 1995, pp. 309-342.

69. R.M. Stogdill, "Group Productivity, Drive, and Cohesiveness," *Organizational Behavior and Human Performance*, February 1972, pp. 36-43. See also M. Mayo, J.C. Pastor, and J.R. Meindl, "The Effects of Group Heterogeneity on the Self-Perceived Efficacy of Group Leaders," *Leadership Quarterly*, Summer 1996, pp. 265-284.

70. J.E. McGrath, *Groups: Interaction and Performance* (Englewood Cliffs, NJ: Prentice Hall, 1984).

71. This idea is proposed in S.E. Jackson, V.K. Stone, and E.B. Alvarez, "Socialization Amidst Diversity: The Impact of Demographics on Work Team Oldtimers and Newcomers," in L.L. Cummings and B.M. Staw (eds.), *Research in Organizational Behavior*, vol. 15 (Greenwich, CT: JAI Press, 1993), p. 68.

72. "People Programs Pay Dividends," *Plant*, May 2, 1994, pp. 1, 5.

## Chapter 7

1. This opening section is based on L. Kines and R. Ouston, "Police Board Sacks Chambers; Mayor Cites Lack of Confidence," *Vancouver Sun*, June 26, 1999, pp. A1-A2; I. Mulgrew, "Chief Grilled About Checks on a Police Board Member"; *Vancouver Sun*, July 1, 1999, pp. A1-A2; "What Chambers Told the Police Board," *Vancouver Sun*, July 1, 1999, p. B5; C. Sankar, "Councillor Suggests Chief Was Targeted," *Vancouver Sun*, July 2, 1999, p. A1.

2. See, for example, K.W. Thomas and W.H. Schmidt, "A Survey of Managerial Interests with Respect to Conflict," *Academy of Management Journal*, June 1976, p. 317.

3. Laura Ramsay, "Communication Key to Workplace Happiness," *Financial Post*, December 6/8, 1997, p. 58.

4. R. Nutt, "Tax Hurting High-Tech Recruiting, CEO Claims," *Vancouver Sun*, January 28, 2000, pp. F1, F12.

5. D.K. Berlo, *The Process of Communication* (New York: Holt, Rinehart & Winston, 1960), p. 54.

6. J.C. McCroskey, J.A. Daly, and G. Sorenson, "Personality Correlates of Communication Apprehension," *Human Communication Research*, Spring 1976, pp. 376-380.

7. See R.L. Daft and R.H. Lengel, "Information Richness: A New Approach to Managerial Behavior and Organization Design," in B.M. Staw and L.L. Cummings (eds.), *Research in Organizational Behavior*, vol. 6 (Greenwich, CT: JAI Press, 1984), pp. 191-233; R.E. Rice and D.E. Shook, "Relationships of Job Categories and Organizational Levels to Use of Communication Channels, Including Electronic Mail: A Meta-Analysis and Extension," *Journal of Management Studies*, March 1990, pp. 195-229; R.E. Rice, "Task Analyzability, Use of New Media, and Effectiveness," *Organization Science*, November 1992, pp. 475-500; S.G. Straus and J.E. McGrath, "Does the Medium Matter? The Interaction of Task Type and Technology on Group Performance and Member Reaction," *Journal of Applied Psychology*, February 1994, pp. 87-97; J. Webster and L.K. Trevino, "Rational and Social Theories as Complementary Explanations of Communication Media Choices: Two Policy-Capturing Studies," *Academy of Management Journal*, December 1995, pp. 1544-1572.

8. R.L. Daft, R.H. Lengel, and L.K. Trevino, "Message Equivocality, Media Selection, and Manager Performance: Implications for Information Systems," *MIS Quarterly*, September 1987, pp. 355-368.

9. D. Silverman, "Schism in Management Blamed for Compaq Woes," *Houston Chronicle*, May 30, 1999, pp. 1A, 14A.

10. S.I. Hayakawa, *Language in Thought and Action* (New York: Harcourt Brace Jovanovich, 1949), p. 292.

11. R.L. Simpson, "Vertical and Horizontal Communication in Formal Organizations," *Administrative Science Quarterly*, September 1959, pp. 188-196; and B. Harriman, "Up and Down the Communications Ladder," *Harvard Business Review*, September-October 1974, pp. 143-151.

12. P. Booth, *Challenge and Change: Embracing the Team Concept,* Report 123-94, Conference Board of Canada, 1994, p. 9.

13. D.M. Saunders and J.D. Leck, "Formal Upward Communication Procedures: Organizational and Employee Perspectives," *Canadian Journal of Administrative Sciences,* 10, pp. 255-268.

14. "Heard It Through the Grapevine," *Forbes*, February 10, 1997, p. 22.

15. See, for instance, J.W. Newstrom, R.E. Monczka, and W.E. Reif, "Perceptions of the Grapevine: Its Value and Influence," *Journal of Business Communication*, Spring 1974, pp. 12-20; and S.J. Modic, "Grapevine Rated Most Believable," *Industry Week*, May 15, 1989, p. 14.

16. K. Davis, cited in R. Rowan, "Where Did That Rumor Come From?", *Fortune*, August 13, 1979, p. 134.

17. L. Hirschhorn, "Managing Rumors," in L. Hirschhorn (ed.), *Cutting Back* (San Francisco: Jossey-Bass, 1983), pp. 49-52.

18. R.L. Rosnow and G.A. Fine, *Rumor and Gossip: The Social Psychology of Hearsay* (New York: Elsevier, 1976).

19. See, for instance, J.G. March and G. Sevon, "Gossip, Information and Decision Making," in J.G. March (ed.), *Decisions and Organizations* (Oxford: Blackwell, 1988), pp. 429-442; M. Noon and R. Delbridge, "News from Behind My Hand: Gossip in Organizations," *Organization Studies*, 14, no. 1 (1993), pp. 23-36; and N. DiFonzo, P. Bordia, and R.L. Rosnow, "Reining in Rumors," *Organizational Dynamics*, Summer 1994, pp. 47-62.

20. Jim Collins and Jerry Poras, *Built to Last: Successful Habits of Visionary Companies* (HarperCollins), 1994.

21. Material in this section is based, in part, on Jim Collins, "Forget Strategy, Build Mechanisms Instead," *INC.*, October 1997, pp. 45-48.

22. R.L. Birdwhistell, *Introduction to Kinesics* (Louisville, KY: University of Louisville Press, 1952).

23. J. Fast, *Body Language* (Philadelphia: M. Evan, 1970), p. 7.

24. See D. Tannen, *You Just Don't Understand: Women and Men in Conversation* (New York: Ballantine Books, 1991); and D. Tannen, *Talking from 9 to 5* (New York: William Morrow, 1995).

25. D. Goldsmith and P. Fulfs, "You Just Don't Have the Evidence: An Analysis of Claims and Evidence in Deborah Tannen's *You Just Don't Understand*," *Communications Yearbook*, 22, 1999.

26. N. Langton "Differences in Communication Styles: Asking for a Raise," in Dorothy Marcic, *Organizational Behavior: Experiences and Cases,* 4th ed. (St. Paul, MN: West Publishing Co.), 1995.

27. R.E. Axtell, *Gestures: The Do's and Taboos of Body Language Around the World* (New York: Wiley, 1991).

28. See M. Munter, "Cross-Cultural Communication for Managers," *Business Horizons*, May-June 1993, pp. 75-76.

29. N. Adler, *International Dimensions of Organizational Behavior*, 3rd ed. (Cincinnati, OH: Southwestern, 1997), pp. 87-88.

30. See, for instance, R. Hotch, "Communication Revolution," *Nation's Business*, May 1993, pp. 20-28; G. Brockhouse, "I Have Seen the Future," *Canadian Business*, August 1993, pp. 43-45; R. Hotch, "In Touch Through Technology," *Nation's Business*, January 1994, pp. 33-35; and P. LaBarre, "The Other Network," *Industry Week*, September 19, 1994, pp. 33-36.

31. A. LaPlante, "TeleConfrontationing," *Forbes ASAP*, September 13, 1993, p. 117.

32. "Virtual Pink Slips Start Coming Online," *The Vancouver Sun*, July 3, 1999, p. D15.

33. Based on B. Crosariol, "E-mail Nightmares," *Report on Business Magazine*, March 1996, pp. 41-42.

34. E. Church, "Employers Read E-mail as Fair Game," *The Globe and Mail*, April 14, 1998, p. B16.

35. E. Church, "Employers Read E-mail as Fair Game," *The Globe and Mail*, April 14, 1998, p. B16.

36. Based on P. Kuitenbrouwer, "Simmer...Then Raise to a Boil: A Family Stew over Succession at the McCain Foods Empire Spills into the Courts [1993 review]," *Financial Post Daily*, v. 10(205A) F 2 '98 Anniversary edition, p. 22; and Peter Newman, "Tales from a Mellower Harrison McCain: Four Years After Winning a Bitter Feud With His Brother, Harrison Acknowledges That 'Strained' Family Relations Still Exist," *Maclean's*, 111, no. 3, January 19, 1998, p. 50.

37. See, for instance, C.F. Fink, "Some Conceptual Difficulties in the Theory of Social Conflict," *Journal of Conflict Resolution*, December 1968, pp. 412-460. For an updated review of the conflict literature, see J.A. Wall, Jr. and R.R. Callister, "Conflict and Its Management," *Journal of Management*, 21, no. 3, 1995, pp. 515-558.

38. L.L. Putnam and M.S. Poole, "Conflict and Negotiation," in F.M. Jablin, L.L. Putnam, K.H. Roberts, and L.W. Porter (eds.), *Handbook of Organizational Communication: An Interdisciplinary Perspective* (Newbury Park, CA: Sage, 1987), pp. 549-599.

39. K.W. Thomas, "Conflict and Negotiation Processes in Organizations," in M.D. Dunnette and L.M. Hough (eds.), *Handbook of Industrial and Organizational Psychology*, 2nd ed., vol. 3 (Palo Alto, CA: Consulting Psychologists Press, 1992), pp. 651-717.

40. This section is based on S.P. Robbins, *Managing Organizational Conflict: A Nontraditional Approach* (Englewood Cliffs, NJ: Prentice Hall, 1974), pp. 31-55; and J.A. Wall, Jr., and R.R. Callister, "Conflict and Its Management," *Journal of Management*, 21, no. 3, 1995, pp. 517-523.

41. K.W. Thomas, "Conflict and Negotiation Processes in Organizations," in M.D. Dunnette and L.M. Hough (eds.), *Handbook of Industrial and Organizational Psychology*, 2nd ed., vol. 3 (Palo Alto, CA: Consulting Psychologists Press, 1992), pp. 651-717.

42. K.W. Thomas, "Conflict and Negotiation Processes in Organizations," in M.D. Dunnette and L.M. Hough (eds.), *Handbook of Industrial and Organizational Psychology*, 2nd ed., vol. 3 (Palo Alto, CA: Consulting Psychologists Press, 1992), pp. 651-717.

43. See R.J. Sternberg and L.J. Soriano, "Styles of Conflict Resolution," *Journal of Personality and Social Psychology*, July 1984, pp. 115-126; R.A. Baron, "Personality and Organizational Conflict: Effects of the Type A Behavior Pattern and Self-Monitoring," *Organizational Behavior and Human Decision Processes*, October 1989, pp. 281-296; and R.J. Volkema and T.J. Bergmann, "Conflict Styles as Indicators of Behavioral Patterns in Interpersonal Conflicts," *Journal of Social Psychology*, February 1995, pp. 5-15.

44. K.W. Thomas, "Conflict and Negotiation Processes in Organizations," in M.D. Dunnette and L.M. Hough (eds.), *Handbook of Industrial and Organizational Psychology*, 2nd ed., vol. 3 (Palo Alto, CA: Consulting Psychologists Press, 1992), pp. 651-717.

45. See A.C. Amason, "Distinguishing the Effects of Functional and Dysfunctional Conflict on Strategic Decision Making: Resolving a Paradox for Top Management Teams," *Academy of Management Journal*, February 1996, pp. 123-148.

46. See, for instance, R.A. Cosier and C.R. Schwenk, "Agreement and Thinking Alike: Ingredients for Poor Decisions," *Academy of Management Executive*, February 1990, pp. 69-74; K.A. Jehn, "Enhancing Effectiveness: An Investigation of Advantages and Disadvantages of Value-Based Intragroup Conflict," *International Journal of Conflict Management*, July 1994, pp. 223-238; and R.L. Priem, D.A. Harrison, and N.K. Muir, "Structured Conflict and Consensus Outcomes in Group Decision Making," *Journal of Management*, 21, no. 4, 1995, pp. 691-710.

47. J. Heinzl and P. Waldie, "Eaton's Drowning in Red Ink," *Globe and Mail*, February 28, 1997, p. B1; and John Heinz, Carolyn Leitch, John Saunders, Marina Strauss, and Paul Waldie, "Inside the Debacle at Eaton's," *Globe and Mail*, March 1, 1997, pp. B1, B4.

48. J. Hall and M.S. Williams, "A Comparison of Decision-Making Performances in Established and Ad-Hoc Groups," *Journal of Personality and Social Psychology*, February 1966, p. 217.

49. R.L. Hoffman, "Homogeneity of Member Personality and Its Effect on Group Problem-Solving," *Journal of Abnormal and Social Psychology*, January 1959, pp. 27-32; and R.L. Hoffman and N.R.F. Maier, "Quality and Acceptance of Problem Solutions by Members of Homogeneous and Heterogeneous Groups," *Journal of Abnormal and Social Psychology*, March 1961, pp. 401-407.

50. See T.H. Cox and S. Blake, "Managing Cultural Diversity: Implications for Organizational Competitiveness," *Academy of Management Executive*, August 1991, pp. 45-56; T.H. Cox, S.A. Lobel, and P.L. McLeod, "Effects of Ethnic Group Cultural Differences on Cooperative Behavior on a Group Task," *Academy of Management Journal*, December 1991, pp. 827-847; P.L. McLeod and S.A. Lobel, "The Effects of Ethnic Diversity on Idea Generation in Small Groups," paper presented at the Annual Academy of Management Conference, Las Vegas, August 1992; C. Kirchmeyer and A. Cohen, "Multicultural Groups: Their Performance and Reactions with Constructive Conflict," *Group & Organization Management*, June 1992, pp. 153-170; D.E. Thompson and L.E. Gooler, "Capitalizing on the Benefits of Diversity Through Workteams," in E.E. Kossek and S.A. Lobel (eds.), *Managing Diversity: Human Resource Strategies for Transforming the Workplace* (Cambridge, MA: Blackwell, 1996), pp. 392-437; and L.H. Pelled, K.M. Eisenhardt, and K.R. Xin, "Exploring the Black Box: An Analysis of Work Group Diversity, Conflict, and Performance," *Administrative Science Quarterly*, March 1999, pp. 1-28.

51. R.E. Hill, "Interpersonal Compatibility and Work Group Performance Among Systems Analysts: An Empirical Study," *Proceedings of the Seventeenth Annual Midwest Academy of Management Conference*, Kent, OH, April 1974, pp. 97-110.

52. D.C. Pelz and F. Andrews, *Scientists in Organizations* (New York: John Wiley, 1966).

53. This section is based on F. Sommerfield, "Paying the Troops to Buck the System," *Business Month*, May 1990, pp. 77-79; W. Kiechel III, "How to Escape the Echo Chamber," *Fortune*, June 18, 1990, pp. 129-130; B. Angelo, "Musical Chairs in Maryland," *Time*, August 26, 1991, p. 21; E. Van de Vliert and C.K.W. de Dreu,

"Optimizing Performance by Conflict Stimulation," *International Journal of Conflict Management,* July 1994, pp. 211-222; E. Van de Vliert, "Enhancing Performance by Conflict-Stimulating Intervention," in C. De Dreu and E. Van de Vliert (eds.), *Using Conflict in Organizations* (London: Sage Publications, 1997), pp. 208-222; and K.M. Eisenhardt, J.L. Kahwajy, and L.J. Bourgeois III, "How Management Teams Can Have a Good Fight," *Harvard Business Review,* July-August 1997, pp. 77-85.

54. See J.A. Wall, Jr., and R.R. Callister, "Conflict and Its Management," *Journal of Management,* 21, no. 3, 1995, pp. 523-526 for evidence supporting the argument that conflict is almost uniformly dysfunctional.

55. P. Kuitenbrouwer, "The Mail Must Go Through: Canada Post Is Trying Hard to Get Better by Improving Its Services and Changing Its Relationship with Employees," *Financial Post,* 91, no. 9, February 28/March 2, 1998, pp. 8-9.

56. K. Jehn, "A Multimethod Examination of the Benefits and Detriments of Intragroup Conflict," *Administrative Science Quarterly,* June 1995, pp. 256-282.

57. A.C. Amason, "Distinguishing the Effects of Functional and Dysfunctional Conflict on Strategic Decision Making: Resolving a Paradox for Top Management Teams," *Academy of Management Journal,* 39(1), pp. 123-148.

58. K.M. Eisenhardt, J.L. Kahwajy, and L.J. Bourgeois III, "How Management Teams Can Have a Good Fight," *Harvard Business Review*, July-August 1997, p. 78.

59. K.M. Eisenhardt, J.L. Kahwajy, and L.J. Bourgeois III, "How Management Teams Can Have a Good Fight," *Harvard Business Review*, July-August 1997, p. 78.

60. J.A. Wall, Jr., *Negotiation: Theory and Practice* (Glenview, IL: Scott, Foresman, 1985).

61. This model is based on R.J. Lewicki, "Bargaining and Negotiation," *Exchange: The Organizational Behavior Teaching Journal,* vol. 6, no. 2, 1981, pp. 39-40; and B.S. Moskal, "The Art of the Deal," *Industry Week,* January 18, 1993, p. 23.

62. R. Fisher and W. Ury, *Getting to Yes* (New York: Houghton Mifflin, 1981).

63. These suggestions are based on J.A. Wall, Jr., and M.W. Blum, "Negotiations," *Journal of Management,* June 1991, pp. 278-282; and J.S. Pouliot, "Eight Steps to Success in Negotiating," *Nation's Business,* April 1999, pp. 40-42.

64. For a negative answer to this question, see C. Watson and L.R. Hoffman, "Managers as Negotiators: A Test of Power Versus Gender as Predictors of Feelings, Behavior, and Outcomes," *Leadership Quarterly,* Spring 1996, pp. 63-85.

65. A.H. Eagley, S.J. Karau, and M. Makhijani, "Gender and the Effectiveness of Leaders: A Meta-Analysis," *Psychological Bulletin,* 117,1995, pp. 125-145.

66. A.F. Stuhlmacher and A.E. Walters, "Gender Differences in Negotiation Outcome: A Meta-Analysis," *Personnel Psychology,* 52, 1992, pp. 653-677.

67. D.M. Kolb and G.G. Coolidge, "Her Place at the Table," *Journal of State Government,* 64, no. 2, April-June 1991, 68-71.

68. "Women Must Be Ready to Negotiate for Equal Pay," *Financial Post,* October 5/7, 1996, p. 41.

69. "Women Must Be Ready to Negotiate for Equal Pay," *Financial Post,* October 5/7, 1996, p. 41.

70. "Women Must Be Ready to Negotiate for Equal Pay," *Financial Post*, October 5/7, 1996, p. 41.

71. "The Battle of the Sexes: Do Men and Women Really Have Different Negotiating Styles?", *CMA Management Accounting Magazine*, 71, no. 1, February 1997, p. 8.

72. C.C. Eckel and P.J. Grossman "Are Women Less Selfish Than Men?: Evidence from Dictator Experiments," *The Economic Journal*, May 1998, pp. 726-735.

73. I. Ayres, "Further Evidence of Discrimination in New Car Negotiations and Estimates of Its Cause," *Michigan Law Review*, 94, no. 1, October 1995, pp. 109-147.

74. B. Gerhart and S. Rynes, "Determinants and Consequences of Salary Negotiations by Male and Female MBA Graduates," *Journal of Applied Psychology*, 76, no. 2, April 1991, pp. 256-262.

75. See N.J. Adler, *International Dimensions of Organizational Behavior*, 3rd ed. (Cincinnati, OH: Southwestern, 1997), pp. 189-232; and J.M. Brett and T. Okumura, "Inter- and Intracultural Negotiation: U.S. and Japanese Negotiators," *Academy of Management Journal*, October 1998, pp. 495-510.

76. K.D. Schmidt, *Doing Business in France* (Menlo Park, CA: SRI International, 1987).

77. S. Lubman, "Round and Round," *The Wall Street Journal,* December 10, 1993, p. R3.

78. A.T. Mair, "Pixel Perfect," *Business in Vancouver*, March 17-23, 1998, pp. 13-14.

79. E.S. Glenn, D. Witmeyer, and K.A. Stevenson, "Cultural Styles of Persuasion," *Journal of Intercultural Relations,* Fall 1977, pp. 52-66.

80. J. Graham, "The Influence of Culture on Business Negotiations," *Journal of International Business Studies,* Spring 1985, pp. 81-96.

81. A.F. Westin aand A.G. Feliu, *Resolving Employment Disputes Without Litigation* (Washington: Bureau of National Affairs, 1988); and J.A. Wall, Jr., and M.W. Blum, "Negotiations," *Journal of Management,* June 1991, pp. 283-287.

82. C. Olsheski, "Resolving Disputes Has Just Become More Efficient," *Financial Post*, August 16,1999, p. D9.

83. T. Tillson, "Common Sense Resolution," *Canadian Business*, March 1997.

84. P. Fitzpatrick, "Disruption Looms as CN, CAW Talks Derail," *Financial Post Daily*, July 28, 1998, pg. 5.

85. See, for example, R.S. Schuler, "A Role Perception Transactional Process Model for Organizational Communication-Outcome Relationships," *Organizational Behavior and Human Performance*, April 1979, pp. 268-291.

86. J.P. Walsh, S.J. Ashford, and T.E. Hill, "Feedback Obstruction: The Influence of the Information Environment on Employee Turnover Intentions," *Human Relations*, January 1985, pp. 23-46.

87. S.A. Hellweg and S.L. Phillips, "Communication and Productivity in Organizations: A State-of-the-Art Review," in *Proceedings of the 40th Annual Academy of Management Conference*, Detroit, 1980, pp. 188-192.

# Chapter 8

1. Based on N. Reynolds, "Beowulf Smites Wizard to Take the Whitbread," *Electronic Telegraph*, 26 January 2000; N. Reynolds, "Harry Potter Beaten by Beowulf," *Electronic Telegraph*, 28 January 2000; N. Reynolds, "Literary Judge Who Put a Curse on Harry Potter," *Electronic Telegraph*, 27 January 2000; and "Harry Potter Versus Beowulf," *Globe and Mail* Web site, January 28, 2000.

2. Based on B.M. Bass, *Bass & Stogdill's Handbook of Leadership*, 3rd ed. (New York: Free Press, 1990).

3. J.R.P. French, Jr., and B. Raven, "The Bases of Social Power," in D. Cartwright (ed.), *Studies in Social Power* (Ann Arbor: University of Michigan, Institute for Social Research, 1959), pp. 150-167. For an update on French and Raven's work, see D.E. Frost and A.J. Stahelski, "The Systematic Measurement of French and Raven's Bases of Social Power in Workgroups," *Journal of Applied Social Psychology*, April 1988, pp. 375-389; T.R. Hinkin and C.A. Schriesheim, "Development and Application of New Scales to Measure the French and Raven (1959) Bases of Social Power," *Journal of Applied Psychology*, August 1989, pp. 561-567; and G.E. Littlepage, J.L. Van Hein, K.M. Cohen, and L.L. Janiec, "Evaluation and Comparison of Three Instruments Designed to Measure Organizational Power and Influence Tactics," *Journal of Applied Social Psychology*, January 16-31, 1993, pp. 107-125.

4. D. Kipnis, *The Powerholders* (Chicago: University of Chicago Press, 1976), pp. 77-78.

5. M. Folb, "Cause Celeb: From Deborah Cox to Maestro, Homegrown Talent Is Hocking Retail Fashion," *Marketing Magazine*, April 5, 1999, p. 13.

6. P.P. Carson, K.D. Carson, and C.W. Roe, "Social Power Bases: A Meta-Analytic Examination of Interrelationships and Outcomes," *Journal of Applied Social Psychology*, 23(14), 1993, pp. 1150-1169.

7. K. Kelley and E. Schine, "How Did Sears Blow This Gasket?", *Business Week*, June 29, 1992, p. 38.

8. G. Yukl and T. Taber, "The Effective Use of Managerial Power," *Personnel*, 37, 1983.

9. D. Hickson, C. Hinings, C. Lee, R. Schneck, and J. Pennings, "A Strategic Contingencies Theory of Intra-Organizational Power," *Administrative Science Quarterly*, vol. 16, 1971, pp. 216-229.

10. J.W. Dean Jr. and J.R. Evans, *Total Quality: Management, Organization, and Strategy* (Minneapolis-St. Paul, MN: West, 1994).

11. R.E. Emerson, "Power-Dependence Relations," *American Sociological Review*, 27, 1962, pp. 31-41.

12. H. Mintzberg, *Power in and Around Organizations* (Englewood Cliffs, NJ: Prentice Hall, 1983), p. 24.

13. R.M. Cyert and J.G. March, *A Behavioral Theory of the Firm* (Englewood Cliffs, NJ: Prentice Hall, 1963).

14. Adapted from J. Pfeffer, *Managing with Power* (Boston: Harvard Business School Press, 1992), pp. 63-64.

15. Adapted from R.M. Kanter, "Power Failure in Management Circuits," *Harvard Business Review*, July-August 1979, p. 67.

16. See, for example, D. Kipnis, S.M. Schmidt, C. Swaffin-Smith, and I. Wilkinson, "Patterns of Managerial Influence: Shotgun Managers, Tacticians, and Bystanders," *Organizational Dynamics*, Winter 1984, pp. 58-67; T. Case, L. Dosier, G. Murkison, and B. Keys, "How Managers Influence Superiors: A Study of Upward Influence Tactics," *Leadership and Organization Development Journal*, vol. 9, no. 4, 1988, pp. 25-31; D. Kipnis and S.M. Schmidt, "Upward-Influence Styles: Relationship With Performance Evaluations, Salary, and Stress," *Administrative Science Quarterly*, December 1988, pp. 528-542; G. Yukl and C.M. Falbe, "Influence Tactics and Objectives in Upward, Downward, and Lateral Influence Attempts," *Journal of Applied Psychology*, April 1990, pp. 132-140; B. Keys and T. Case, "How to Become an Influential Manager," *Academy of Management Executive*, November 1990, pp. 38-51; D.A. Ralston, D.J. Gustafson, L. Mainiero, and D. Umstot, "Strategies of Upward Influence: A Cross-National Comparison of Hong Kong and American Managers," *Asia Pacific Journal of Management*, October 1993, pp. 157-175; G. Yukl, H. Kim, and C.M. Falbe, "Antecedents of Influence Outcomes," *Journal of Applied Psychology*, June 1996, pp. 309-317; K.E. Lauterbach and B.J. Weiner, "Dynamics of Upward Influence: How Male and Female Managers Get Their Way," *Leadership Quarterly*, Spring 1996, pp. 87-107; K.R. Xin and A.S. Tsui, "Different Strokes for Different Folks? Influence Tactics by Asian-American and Caucasian-American Managers," *Leadership Quarterly*, Spring 1996, pp. 109-132; and S.J. Wayne, R.C. Liden, I.K. Graf, and G.R. Ferris, "The Role of Upward Influence Tactics in Human Resource Decisions," *Personnel Psychology*, Winter 1997, pp. 979-1006.

17. This section is adapted from D. Kipnis, S.M. Schmidt, C. Swaffin-Smith, and I. Wilkinson, "Patterns of Managerial Influence: Shotgun Managers, Tacticians, and Bystanders," *Organizational Dynamics*, Winter 1984, pp. 58-67.

18. S. Wetlaufer, "Organizing for Empowerment: An Interview with AES's Roger Sant and Dennis Bakke," *Harvard Business Review*, January-February 1999, pp. 110-123.

19. R.E. Quinn and G.M. Spreitzer, "The Road to Empowerment: Seven Questions Every Leader Should Consider," *Organizational Dynamics*, Autumn 1997, p. 38.

20. S. Wetlaufer, "Organizing for Empowerment: An Interview with AES's Roger Sant and Dennis Bakke," *Harvard Business Review*, January-February 1999, pp. 110-123.

21. C. Argyris, "Empowerment: The Emperor's New Clothes," *Harvard Business Review*, May-June 1998.

22. R.C. Ford and M.D. Fottler, "Empowerment: A Matter of Degree," *Academy of Management Executive*, 9, 1995, pp. 21-31.

23. Points are summarized from Robert C. Ford and Myron D. Fottler, "Empowerment: A Matter of Degree," *Academy of Management Executive*, 9, 1995, pp. 23-25.

24. T.D. Wall, N.J. Kemp, P.R. Jackson, and W.W. Clegg, "Outcomes of Autonomous Work Groups: A Long-Term Field Experiment," *Academy of Management Journal*, 29, 1986, pp. 280-304.

25. "Delta Promotes Empowerment," *The Globe and Mail*, May 31, 1999, Advertising Supplement, p. C5.

26. G.M. Spreitzer, "Psychological Empowerment in the Workplace: Dimensions, Measurement, and Validation,"

*Academy of Management Journal*, 38, 1995, pp. 1442-1465; G.M. Spreitzer, M.A. Kizilos, and S.W. Nason, "A Dimensional Analysis of the Relationship Between Psychological Empowerment and Effectiveness, Satisfaction, and Strain," *Journal of Management*, 23, 1997, pp. 679-704; and K.W. Thomas and W.G. Tymon, "Does Empowerment Always Work: Understanding the Role of Intrinsic Motivation and Personal Interpretation," *Journal of Management Systems*, 6, 1994, pp. 39-54.

27. D.E. Hyatt and T.M. Ruddy, "An Examination of the Relationship Between Work Group Characteristics and Performance: Once More into the Breech," *Personnel Psychology*, 50, 1997, pp. 553-585; B.L. Kirkman and B. Rosen, "Beyond Self-Management: Antecedents and Consequences of Team Empowerment," *Academy of Management Journal*, 42, 1999, pp. 58-74; P.E. Tesluck, D.J. Brass and J.E. Mathieu, "An Examination of Empowerment Processes at Individual and Group Levels," paper presented at the 11th annual conference of the Society of Industrial and Organizational Psychology, San Diego, 1996.

28. M. Kane, "Quality Control Can Save Firms Millions, New Data Suggests," *Vancouver Sun*, May 29, 1998, pp. H1, H6.

29. Based on W.B. Stevenson, J.L. Pearce, and L.W. Porter, "The Concept of 'Coalition' in Organization Theory and Research," *Academy of Management Review*, April 1985, pp. 261-263.

30. P.P. Poole, "Coalitions: The Web of Power," in *Research and Application, Proceedings of the 20th Annual Eastern Academy Conference*; D.J. Vredenburgh and R.S. Schuler (eds.), *Effective Management: Academy of Management*, Pittsburgh, May 1983, pp. 79-82.

31. J.K. Murnighan and D.J. Brass, "Intraorganizational Coalitions," in M.H. Bazerman, R.J. Lewicki, and B.H. Seppard (eds.), *Research on Negotiation in Organizations* (Greenwich, CT: JAI Press, 1991).

32. J. Pfeffer, *Power in Organizations* (Marshfield, MA: Pittman, 1981).

33. The following section is based on J.N. Cleveland and M.E. Kerst, "Sexual Harassment and Perceptions of Power: An Under-Articulated Relationship," *Journal of Vocational Behavior*, February 1993, pp. 49-67.

34. J. Goddu, "Sexual Harassment Complaints Rise Dramatically," *Canadian Press Newswire*, March 6, 1998.

35. "Car Dealership Settles Same Sex Harassment Lawsuit," *Associated Press*, June 28, 1999.

36. G. Keenan and J. McFarland, "Auto Industry a Bastion of Macho Behavior," *Canadian Press Newswire*, October 1, 1997.

37. "Harassment Barely Recognized in Japan," *Financial Post Daily*, May 15, 1996, p. 8.

38. "Energy Roughneck," *Canadian Business*, August 1996, pp. 20-25.

39. "Energy Roughneck," *Canadian Business*, August 1996, pp. 20-25.

40. S.A. Culbert and J.J. McDonough, *The Invisible War: Pursuing Self-Interest at Work* (New York: John Wiley, 1980), p. 6.

41. H. Mintzberg, *Power in and Around Organizations* (Englewood Cliffs, NJ: Prentice Hall, 1983), p. 26.

42. T. Cole, "Who Loves Ya?", *Report on Business Magazine*, April 1999, p. 54.

43. D. Farrell and J.C. Petersen, "Patterns of Political Behavior in Organizations," *Academy of Management Review*, July 1982, p. 405. For a thoughtful analysis of the academic controversies underlying any definition of organizational politics, see A. Drory and T. Romm, "The Definition of Organizational Politics: A Review," *Human Relations*, November 1990, pp. 1133-1154.

44. D. Farrell and J.C. Petersen, "Patterns of Political Behavior in Organizations," *Academy of Management Review*, July 1982, pp. 406-407; and A. Drory, "Politics in Organization and Its Perception Within the Organization," *Organization Studies*, 9, no. 2, 1988, pp. 165-179.

45. J. Pfeffer, *Power in Organizations* (Marshfield, MA: Pittman, 1981).

46. K.K. Eastman, "In the Eyes of the Beholder: An Attributional Approach to Ingratiation and Organizational Citizenship Behavior," *Academy of Management Journal*, October 1994, pp. 1379-1391; and M.C. Bolino, "Citizenship and Impression Management: Good Soldiers or Good Actors?", *Academy of Management Review*, January 1999, pp. 82-98.

47. See, for example, G. Biberman, "Personality and Characteristic Work Attitudes of Persons with High, Moderate, and Low Political Tendencies," *Psychological Reports*, October 1985, pp. 1303-1310; and G.R. Ferris, G.S. Russ, and P.M. Fandt, "Politics in Organizations," in R.A. Giacalone and P. Rosenfeld (eds.), *Impression Management in the Organization* (Hillsdale, NJ: Lawrence Erlbaum Associates, 1989), pp. 155-156.

48. D. Farrell and J.C. Petersen, "Patterns of Political Behavior in Organizations," *Academy of Management Review*, July 1982, p. 408.

49. S.C. Goh and A.R. Doucet, "Antecedent Situational Conditions of Organizational Politics: An Empirical Investigation," paper presented at the Annual Administrative Sciences Association of Canada Conference, Whistler, BC, May 1986; C. Hardy, "The Contribution of Political Science to Organizational Behavior," in J.W. Lorsch (ed.), *Handbook of Organizational Behavior* (Englewood Cliffs, NJ: Prentice Hall, 1987), p. 103; and G.R. Ferris and K.M. Kacmar, "Perceptions of Organizational Politics," *Journal of Management*, March 1992, pp. 93-116.

50. See, for example, D. Farrell and J.C. Petersen, "Patterns of Political Behavior in Organizations," *Academy of Management Review*, July 1982, p. 409; P.M. Fandt and G.R. Ferris, "The Management of Information and Impressions: When Employees Behave Opportunistically," *Organizational Behavior and Human Decision Processes*, February 1990, pp. 140-158; and G.R. Ferris, G.S. Russ, and P.M. Fandt, "Politics in Organizations," in R.A. Giacalone and P. Rosenfeld (eds.), *Impression Management in the Organization* (Hillsdale, NJ: Lawrence Erlbaum Associates, 1989), p. 147.

51. R.C. Ford and M.D. Fottler, "Empowerment: A Matter of Degree," *Academy of Management Executive*, 9, 1995, pp. 21-31.

52. M.R. Leary and R.M. Kowalski, "Impression Management: A Literature Review and Two-Component Model," *Psychological Bulletin*, January 1990, pp. 34-47.

53. W.L. Gardner and M.J. Martinko, "Impression Management in Organizations," *Journal of Management*, June 1988, pp. 321-338; D.C. Gilmore and G.R. Ferris, "The Effects of Applicant Impression Management Tactics on Interviewer Judgments," *Journal of Management*, December 1989, pp. 557-564; M.R. Leary and R.M. Kowalski, "Impression Management: A Literature Review and Two-Component Model," *Psychological Bulletin*, January 1990, pp. 34-47; S.J. Wayne and K.M. Kacmar, "The Effects of Impression Management on the Performance Appraisal Process," *Organizational Behavior and Human Decision Processes*, February 1991, pp. 70-88; E.W. Morrison and R.J. Bies, "Impression Management in the Feedback-Seeking Process: A Literature Review and Research Agenda," *Academy of Management Review*, July 1991, pp. 522-541; S.J. Wayne and R.C. Liden, "Effects of Impression Management on Performance Ratings: A Longitudinal Study," *Academy of Management Journal*, February 1995, pp. 232-260; and C.K. Stevens and A.L. Kristof, "Making the Right Impression: A Field Study of Applicant Impression Management During Job Interviews," *Journal of Applied Psychology*, October 1995, pp. 587-606.

54. M. Snyder and J. Copeland, "Self-Monitoring Processes in Organizational Settings," in R.A. Giacalone and P. Rosenfeld (eds.), *Impression Management in the Organization* (Hillsdale, NJ: Lawrence Erlbaum Associates, 1989), p. 11; E.D. Long and G.H. Dobbins, "Self-Monitoring, Impression Management, and Interview Ratings: A Field and Laboratory Study," in J.L. Wall and L.R. Jauch (eds.), *Proceedings of the 52nd Annual Academy of Management Conference*, Las Vegas, August 1992, pp. 274-278; and A. Montagliani and R.A. Giacalone, "Impression Management and Cross-Cultural Adaption," *Journal of Social Psychology*, October 1998, pp. 598-608.

55. M.R. Leary and R.M. Kowalski, "Impression Management: A Literature Review and Two-Component Model," *Psychological Bulletin*, January 1990, p. 40.

56. W.L. Gardner and M.J. Martinko, "Impression Management in Organizations," *Journal of Management*, June 1988, p. 333.

57. R.A. Baron, "Impression Management by Applicants During Employment Interviews: The 'Too Much of a Good Thing' Effect," in R.W. Eder and G.R. Ferris (eds.), *The Employment Interview: Theory, Research, and Practice* (Newbury Park, CA: Sage Publishers, 1989), pp. 204-215.

58. G.R. Ferris, G.S. Russ, and P.M. Fandt, "Politics in Organizations," in R.A. Giacalone and P. Rosenfeld (eds.), *Impression Management in the Organization* (Hillsdale, NJ: Lawrence Erlbaum Associates, 1989), pp. 155-156.

59. R.A. Baron, "Impression Management by Applicants During Employment Interviews: The 'Too Much of a Good Thing' Effect," in R.W. Eder and G.R. Ferris (eds.), *The Employment Interview: Theory, Research, and Practice* (Newbury Park, CA: Sage Publishers, 1989), pp. 204-215; D.C. Gilmore and G.R. Ferris, "The Effects of Applicant Impression Management Tactics on Interviewer Judgments," *Journal of Management*, December 1989, pp.

557-564; and C.K. Stevens and A.L. Kristof, "Making the Right Impression: A Field Study of Applicant Impression Management During Job Interviews," *Journal of Applied Psychology*, October 1995, pp. 587-606.

60. C.K. Stevens and A.L. Kristof, "Making the Right Impression: A Field Study of Applicant Impression Management During Job Interviews," *Journal of Applied Psychology*, October 1995, pp. 587-606.

61. S.J. Wayne and K.M. Kacmar, "The Effects of Impression Management on the Performance Appraisal Process," *Organizational Behavior and Human Decision Processes*, 48, 1991, pp. 70-78; S.J. Wayne and G.R. Ferris, "Influence Tactics, Affect, and Exchange Quality in Supervisor-Subordinate Interactions," *Journal of Applied Psychology*, 75, 1990, pp. 487-499; and G.R. Ferris, T.A. Judge, K.M. Rowland, and D.E. Fitzgibbons, "Subordinate Influence and the Performance Evaluation Process: Test of a Model," *Organizational Behavior and Human Decision Processes*, 58, 1994, pp. 101-135.

62. S.J. Wayne and R.C. Liden, "Effects of Impression Management on Performance Ratings: A Longitudinal Study," *Academy of Management Journal*, 38, 1995, pp. 232-260.

63. G.H. Dobbins and J.M. Russell, "The Biasing Effects of Subordinate Likeableness on Leaders' Responses to Poor Performers: A Laboratory and a Field Study," *Personnel Psychology*, 39, 1986, pp. 759-777; and T.R. Mitchell, and R. Wood, "Manager Behavior in a Social Context: The Impact of Impression Management on Attributions and Disciplinary Actions," *Organizational Behavior and Human Decision Processes*, December 1981, pp. 356-378.

64. D.V. Day, D.J. Schneider, and A.L. Unckless, "Self-Monitoring and Work-Related Outcomes: A Meta-Analysis," paper presented at the 11th Annual Conference of the Society of Industrial and Organizational Psychology, San Diego, CA, 1996; and M.A. Warech, J.W. Smither, R.R. Reilly, R.E. Millsap, and S.P. Reilly, "Self-Monitoring and 36-Degree Ratings," *Leadership Quarterly*, 9, 1998, pp. 449-473.

65. M.A. Warech, J.W. Smither, R.R. Reilly, R.E. Millsap, and S.P. Reilly, "Self-Monitoring and 36-Degree Ratings," *Leadership Quarterly*, 9, 1998, pp. 449-473.

66. D.V. Day, D.J. Schneider, and A.L. Unckless, "Self-Monitoring and Work-Related Outcomes: A Meta-Analysis," paper presented at the 11th Annual Conference of the Society of Industrial and Organizational Psychology, San Diego, CA, 1996.

67. A. Hochschild, *The Managed Heart: The Commercialization of Human Feeling* (Berkeley, CA: University of California Press, 1983); J. Van Maanen and G. Kunda, "Real Feelings: Emotional Expression and Organizational Culture," in L.L. Cummings and B.M. Staw (eds.), *Research in Organizational Behavior*, 11 (Greenwich, CT: JAI Press, 1989), pp. 43-103; and B.A. Turner, "Sociological Aspects of Organizational Symbolism," *Organization Studies*, 7, 1986, pp. 101-115.

68. A. Hochschild, *The Managed Heart: The Commercialization of Human Feeling* (Berkeley, CA: University of California Press, 1983); R.I. Sutton and A. Rafaeli, "Untangling the Relationship Between Displayed Emotions and Organizational Sales: The Case of Convenience Stores," *Academy of Management Journal*, 31, 1988, pp. 461-487; A. Rafaeli, "When Cashiers Meet Customers: An

Analysis of the Role of Supermarket Cashiers," *Academy of Management Journal*, 32, 1989, pp. 245-273; A. Rafaeli and R.I. Sutton, "The Expression of Emotion in Organizational Life," in L.L. Cummings and B.M. Staw (eds.), *Research in Organizational Behavior* 11 (Greenwich, CT: JAI Press, 1989), pp. 1-42; A. Rafaeli and R.I. Sutton, "Busy Stores and Demanding Customers: How Do They Affect the Display of Positive Emotion?", *Academy of Management Journal*, 33, 1990, pp. 623-637; A. Rafaeli and R.I. Sutton, "Emotional Contrast Strategies as Means of Social Influence: Lessons from Criminal Interrogators and Bill Collectors," *Academy of Management Journal*, 34, 1991, pp. 749-775; and R.I. Sutton, "Maintaining Norms About Expressed Emotions: The Case of Bill Collectors," *Administrative Science Quarterly*, 36, 1991, pp. 245-268.

69. H. Willmott, "Strength Is Ignorance; Slavery Is Freedom: Managing Culture in Modern Organizations," *Journal of Management Studies*, 30, 1993, pp. 515-552; and S. Fineman, "Emotion and Organizing," in S. Clegg (ed.), *Handbook of Organizational Studies* (London: Sage, 1996), pp. 543-564.

70. A. Hochschild, *The Managed Heart: The Commercialization of Human Feeling* (Berkeley, CA: University of California Press, 1983).

71. J. Van Maanen and G. Kunda, "Real Feelings: Emotional Expression and Organizational Culture," in L.L. Cummings and B.M. Staw (eds.), *Research in Organizational Behavior* 11 (Greenwich, CT: JAI Press, 1989), pp. 43-103.

72. V. Waldron and K. Krone, "The Experience and Expression of Emotion in the Workplace: A Study of a Corrections Organization," *Management Communication Quarterly*, 4, 1991, pp. 287-309.

73. C. Bains, "Safeway Clerks' Forced Smiles Seen as Flirtation," *Vancouver Sun*, September 3, 1998, pp. A1, A2.

74. This figure is based on G.F. Cavanagh, D.J. Moberg, and M. Valasquez, "The Ethics of Organizational Politics," *Academy of Management Journal*, June 1981, pp. 363-374.

75. R.M. Kanter, *Men and Women of the Corporation* (New York: Basic Books, 1977).

76. See, for instance, C.M. Falbe and G. Yukl, "Consequences for Managers of Using Single Influence Tactics and Combinations of Tactics," *Academy of Management Journal*, August 1992, pp. 638-652.

77. P.A. Wilson, "The Effects of Politics and Power on the Organizational Commitment of Federal Executives," *Journal of Management*, Spring 1995, pp. 101-118.

78. See, for example, M.A. Rahim, "Relationships of Leader Power to Compliance and Satisfaction with Supervision: Evidence From a National Sample of Managers," *Journal of Management*, December 1989, pp. 545-556.

79. J.G. Bachman, D.G. Bowers, and P.M. Marcus, "Bases of Supervisory Power: A Comparative Study in Five Organizational Settings," in A.S. Tannenbaum (ed.), *Control in Organizations* (New York: McGraw-Hill, 1968), p. 236.

80. J. Pfeffer, *Managing With Power* (Boston: Harvard Business School Press, 1992), p. 137.

81. See, for example, N. Gupta and G.D. Jenkins Jr., "The Politics of Pay," *Compensation & Benefits Review*, March/April 1996, pp. 23-30.

82. G.R. Ferris and K.M. Kacmar, "Perceptions of Organizational Politics," *Journal of Management*, March 1992, pp. 93-116.

83. A. Drory, "Perceived Political Climate and Job Attitudes," *Organization Studies*, vol. 14, no. 1, 1993, pp. 59-71.

## Chapter 9

1. Based on information in Gaye Emery, "Overcoming Success at IBM: When the Wheels Fall Off, Change Is Easier," *Business Quarterly*, Winter 1994, pp. 39-44; Paul Barker, "Dissecting the New IBM: The President and CEO of the Canadian Subsidiary Talks of the Company's Rise From 'Near Death,'" *Computing Canada*, May 26, 1997, p. 11; D. Akin, "Big Blue Chills Out: A Canadian Executive Leads the Campaign to Turn IBM Into Cool Blue," *Financial Post*, October 11, 1999, pp. C1, C6; and D. Steinhart, "IBM to Dish Out $1.6b in Cash Bonuses: Bonuses Amount to 25% of Company's 1998 Profit," *Financial Post*, February 1, 1999, pp. C1, C6.

2. P. Selznick, "Foundations of the Theory of Organizations," *American Sociological Review*, February 1948, pp. 25-35.

3. See L.G. Zucker, "Organizations as Institutions," in S.B. Bacharach (ed.), *Research in the Sociology of Organizations* (Greenwich, CT: JAI Press, 1983), pp. 1-47; A.J. Richardson, "The Production of Institutional Behaviour: A Constructive Comment on the Use of Institutionalization Theory in Organizational Analysis," *Canadian Journal of Administrative Sciences*, December 1986, pp. 304-316; L.G. Zucker, *Institutional Patterns and Organizations: Culture and Environment* (Cambridge, MA: Ballinger, 1988); and R.L. Jepperson, "Institutions, Institutional Effects, and Institutionalism," in W.W. Powell and P.J. DiMaggio (eds.), *The New Institutionalism in Organizational Analysis* (Chicago: University of Chicago Press, 1991), pp. 143-163.

4. "Organization Man: Henry Mintzberg Has Some Common Sense Observations About the Ways We Run Companies," *Financial Post*, November 22/24, 1997, pp. 14-16.

5. See, for example, H.S. Becker, "Culture: A Sociological View," *Yale Review*, Summer 1982, pp. 513-527; and E.H. Schein, *Organizational Culture and Leadership* (San Francisco: Jossey-Bass, 1985), p. 168.

6. This seven-item description is based on C.A. O'Reilly III, J. Chatman, and D.F. Caldwell, "People and Organizational Culture: A Profile Comparison Approach to Assessing Person-Organization Fit," *Academy of Management Journal*, September 1991, pp. 487-516; and J.A. Chatman and K.A. Jehn, "Assessing the Relationship Between Industry Characteristics and Organizational Culture: How Different Can You Be?" *Academy of Management Journal*, June 1994, pp. 522-553. For a description of other popular measures, see A. Xenikou and A. Furnham, "A Correlational and Factor Analytic Study of Four Questionnaire Measures of Organizational Culture," *Human Relations*, March 1996, pp. 349-371.

7. See, for example, G.G. Gordon and N. DiTomaso, "Predicting Corporate Performance From Organizational Culture," *Journal of Management Studies*, November 1992, pp. 793-798.

8. Y. Wiener, "Forms of Value Systems: A Focus on Organizational Effectiveness and Cultural Change and Maintenance," *Academy of Management Review,* October 1988, p. 536.

9. V. Hempsall, "Family Matters: Unique Culture and Strategic Acquisitions Key to St. Joseph Corp's Financial Success," *Canadian Printer,* June 1997, pp. 24-27.

10. R.T. Mowday, L.W. Porter, and R.M. Steers, *Employee-Organization Linkages: The Psychology of Commitment, Absenteeism, and Turnover* (New York: Academic Press, 1982).

11. The view that there will be consistency among perceptions of organizational culture has been called the "integration" perspective. For a review of this perspective and conflicting approaches, see D. Meyerson and J. Martin, "Cultural Change: An Integration of Three Different Views," *Journal of Management Studies,* November 1987, pp. 623-647; and P.J. Frost, L.F. Moore, M.R. Louis, C.C. Lundberg, and J. Martin (eds.), *Reframing Organizational Culture* (Newbury Park, CA: Sage Publications, 1991).

12. See J.M. Jermier, J.W. Slocum, Jr., L.W. Fry, and J. Gaines, "Organizational Subcultures in a Soft Bureaucracy: Resistance Behind the Myth and Facade of an Official Culture," *Organization Science,* May 1991, pp. 170-194; S.A. Sackmann, "Culture and Subcultures: An Analysis of Organizational Knowledge," *Administrative Science Quarterly,* March 1992, pp. 140-161; R.F. Zammuto, "Mapping Organizational Cultures and Subcultures: Looking Inside and Across Hospitals," paper presented at the 1995 National Academy of Management Conference, Vancouver, BC, August 1995; and G. Hofstede, "Identifying Organizational Subcultures: An Empirical Approach," *Journal of Management Studies,* January 1998, pp. 1-12.

13. T.A. Timmerman, "Do Organizations Have Personalities?", paper presented at the 1996 National Academy of Management Conference; Cincinnati, OH, August 1996.

14. S. Hamm, "No Letup—and No Apologies," *Business Week,* October 26, 1998, pp. 58-64.

15. A. Rose, "A Cut Above: Kitchener, Ontario Based MGI Has Carved Out a Market Selling Halal Beef to the Muslim World," *Report on Business Magazine,* May 1997, pp. 78-82.

16. See N.J. Adler, *International Dimensions of Organizational Behavior,* 3rd ed. (Cincinnati, OH: Southwestern, 1997), pp. 61-63.

17. S.C. Schneider, "National vs. Corporate Culture: Implications for Human Resource Management," *Human Resource Management,* Summer 1988, p. 239.

18. S.C. Schneider, "National vs. Corporate Culture: Implications for Human Resource Management," *Human Resource Management,* Summer 1988, p. 239.

19. James Harding, "Rising Star in China's Infant Corporate Culture: The Boss at State-Owned White Goods Maker Haier, Is Known for Smashing Fridges as a Lesson in Quality Control," *Financial Post Daily,* November 21, 1997, p. 69.

20. See C.A. O'Reilly and J.A. Chatman, "Culture as Social Control: Corporations, Cultures, and Commitment," in B.M. Staw and L.L. Cummings (eds.), *Research in Organizational Behavior,* 18 (Greenwich, CT: JAI Press, 1996), pp. 157-200.

21. T.E. Deal and A.A. Kennedy, "Culture: A New Look Through Old Lenses," *Journal of Applied Behavioral Science,* November 1983, p. 501.

22. J. Case, "Corporate Culture," *INC.,* November 1996, pp. 42-53.

23. T. Cole, "How to Stay Hired," *Report on Business Magazine,* March 1995, pp. 46-48.

24. R. McQueen, "Bad Boys Make Good," *Financial Post,* April 4, 1998, p. 6.

25. See, for instance, D. Miller, "What Happens After Success: The Perils of Excellence," *Journal of Management Studies,* May 1994, pp. 11-38.

26. This paragraph is based on information in "Nuclear Workers Thought They Were Best, Says ex-Hydro Boss," *Canadian Press Newswire,* August 24, 1997.

27. See C. Lindsay, "Paradoxes of Organizational Diversity: Living Within the Paradoxes," in L.R. Jauch and J.L. Wall (eds.), *Proceedings of the 50th Academy of Management Conference* (San Francisco, 1990), pp. 374-378; and T. Cox, Jr., *Cultural Diversity in Organizations: Theory, Research & Practice* (San Francisco: Berrett-Koehler, 1993), pp. 162-170.

28. "Texaco: Lessons from a Crisis-in-Progress," *Business Week,* December 2, 1996, p. 44; and M.A. Verespej, "Zero Tolerance," *Industry Week,* January 6, 1997, pp. 24-28.

29. A.F. Buono and J.L. Bowditch, *The Human Side of Mergers and Acquisitions: Managing Collisions Between People, Cultures, and Organizations* (San Francisco: Jossey-Bass, 1989); Y. Weber and D.M. Schweiger, "Top Management Culture Conflict in Mergers and Acquisitions: A Lesson from Anthropology," *The International Journal of Conflict Management,* January 1992, pp. 1-17; S. Cartwright and C.L. Cooper, "The Role of Culture Compatibility in Successful Organizational Marriages," *Academy of Management Executive,* May 1993, pp. 57-70; D. Carey and D. Ogden, "A Match Made in Heaven? Find Out Before You Merge," *Wall Street Journal,* November 30, 1998, p. A22; and R.J. Grossman, "Irreconcilable Differences," *HRMagazine,* April 1999, pp. 42-48.

30. J.R. Carleton, "Cultural Due Diligence," *Training,* November 1997, p. 70; and D. Carey and D. Ogden, "A Match Made in Heaven? Find Out Before You Merge," *Wall Street Journal,* November 30, 1998, p. A22.

31. "CIBC Exodus: Cultures Clash," *Financial Post,* June 8/10, 1996, pp. 12, 14.

32. K. Macklem and B. Critchley, "Speculation Growing over First Marathon Sale," *Financial Post,* May 20, 1999, p. C1.

33. E.H. Schein, "The Role of the Founder in Creating Organizational Culture," *Organizational Dynamics,* Summer 1983, pp. 13-28.

34. E.H. Schein, "Leadership and Organizational Culture," in F. Hesselbein, M. Goldsmith, and R. Beckhard (eds.), *The Leader of the Future* (San Francisco: Jossey-Bass, 1996), pp. 61-62.

35. See, for example, J.R. Harrison and G.R. Carroll, "Keeping the Faith: A Model of Cultural Transmission in Formal

Organizations," *Administrative Science Quarterly,* December 1991, pp. 552-582.

36. See B. Schneider, "The People Make the Place," *Personnel Psychology,* Autumn 1987, pp. 437-453; J.A. Chatman, "Matching People and Organizations: Selection and Socialization in Public Accounting Firms," *Administrative Science Quarterly,* September 1991, pp. 459-484; D.E. Bowen, G.E. Ledford, Jr., and B.R. Nathan, "Hiring for the Organization, Not the Job," *Academy of Management Executive,* November 1991, pp. 35-51; B. Schneider, H.W. Goldstein, and D.B. Smith, "The ASA Framework: An Update," *Personnel Psychology,* Winter 1995, pp. 747-773; and A.L. Kristof, "Person-Organization Fit: An Integrative Review of Its Conceptualizations, Measurement, and Implications," *Personnel Psychology,* Spring 1996, pp. 1-49.

37. R. Pascale, "The Paradox of 'Corporate Culture': Reconciling Ourselves to Socialization," *California Management Review,* Winter 1985, pp. 26-27.

38. "Who's Afraid of IBM?", *Business Week,* June 29, 1987, p. 72.

39. "Who's Afraid of IBM?", *Business Week,* June 29, 1987, p. 72.

40. D.C. Hambrick and P.A. Mason, "Upper Echelons: The Organization as a Reflection of Its Top Managers," *Academy of Management Review,* April 1984, pp. 193-206; B.P. Niehoff, C.A. Enz, and R.A. Grover, "The Impact of Top-Management Actions on Employee Attitudes and Perceptions," *Group and Organization Studies,* September 1990, pp. 337-352; and H.M. Trice and J.M. Beyer, "Cultural Leadership in Organizations," *Organization Science,* May 1991, pp. 149-169.

41. "The Cruickshank Redemption: Can the New Editor-in-Chief of the *Vancouver Sun* Save the Paper from Hopeless Mediocrity?", *B.C. Business Magazine,* 23, no. 12 (December 1995), pp. 28-35.

42. "Newspaper Sales Stabilizing," *Canadian Press Newswire,* January 16, 1998; and A. Wilson-Smith, "Chain Reaction: The Launch of a New National Daily Starts an Industry Upheaval," *Maclean's,* November 9, 1998, p. 44.

43. See, for instance, N.J. Allen and J.P. Meyer, "Organizational Socialization Tactics: A Longitudinal Analysis of Links to Newcomers' Commitment and Role Orientation," *Academy of Management Journal,* December 1990, pp. 847-858; J.P. Wanous, *Organizational Entry,* 2nd ed. (New York: Addison-Wesley, 1992); G.T. Chao, A.M. O'Leary-Kelly, S. Wolf, H.J. Klein, and P.D. Gardner, "Organizational Socialization: Its Content and Consequences," *Journal of Applied Psychology,* October 1994, pp. 730-743; and J.S. Black and S.J. Ashford, "Fitting In or Making Jobs Fit: Factors Affecting Mode of Adjustment for New Hires," *Human Relations,* April 1995, pp. 421-437; and B.E. Ashforth, A.M. Saks, and R.T. Lee, "Socialization and Newcomer Adjustment: The Role of Organizational Context," *Human Relations,* July 1998, pp. 897-926.

44. "McGarry Queen of the Xeroids Document Co CEO," *Financial Post Magazine,* June 1995 , pp. 14, 16+.

45. J. Impoco, "Basic Training, Sanyo Style," *U.S. News & World Report,* July 13, 1992, pp. 46-48.

46. B. Filipczak, "Trained by Starbucks," *Training,* June 1995, pp. 73-79; and S. Gruner, "Lasting Impressions," *INC.,* July 1998, p. 126.

47. J. Van Maanen and E.H. Schein, "Career Development," in J.R. Hackman and J.L. Suttle (eds.), *Improving Life at Work* (Santa Monica, CA: Goodyear, 1977), pp. 58-62.

48. D.C. Feldman, "The Multiple Socialization of Organization Members," *Academy of Management Review,* April 1981, p. 310.

49. J. Van Maanen and E.H. Schein, "Career Development," in J.R. Hackman and J.L. Suttle (eds.), *Improving Life at Work* (Santa Monica, CA: Goodyear, 1977), p. 59.

50. T. Cole, "How to Stay Hired," *Report on Business Magazine,* March 1995, pp. 46-48.

51. Information on Husky based on Bruce Livesey, "Provide and Conquer," *Report on Business Magazine,* March 1997, pp. 34-44.

52. J. Greenwood, "Job One: When Bobbie Gaunt Became Ford of Canada President Earlier This Year, the Appointment Put a Spotlight on the New Rules of the Auto Industry: It's Less About Manufacturing These Days Than About Marketing and Sales," *Financial Post Magazine,* June 1997, pp. 18-22.

53. D.M. Boje, "The Storytelling Organization: A Study of Story Performance in an Office-Supply Firm," *Administrative Science Quarterly,* March 1991, pp. 106-126; and C.H. Deutsch, "The Parables of Corporate Culture," *The New York Times,* October 13, 1991, p. F25.

54. A.M. Pettigrew, "On Studying Organizational Cultures," *Administrative Science Quarterly,* December 1979, p. 576.

55. A.M. Pettigrew, "On Studying Organizational Cultures," *Administrative Science Quarterly,* December 1979, p. 576. See also K. Kamoche, "Rhetoric, Ritualism, and Totemism in Human Resource Management," *Human Relations,* April 1995, pp. 367-385.

56. Cited in J.M. Beyer and H.M. Trice, "How an Organization's Rites Reveal Its Culture," *Organizational Dynamics,* Spring 1987, p. 15.

57. A. Rafaeli and M.G. Pratt, "Tailored Meanings: On the Meaning and Impact of Organizational Dress," *Academy of Management Review,* January 1993, pp. 32-55.

58. "Clear Visions: The Top 40 Under 40," *Financial Post Magazine,* April 1997, pp. 16-30.

59. M. Posner, "The 28 Billion Dollar Woman," *Chatelaine,* 70, no. 12 (December 1997), pp. 70-75.

60. J. Greenwood, "Job One: When Bobbie Gaunt Became Ford of Canada President Earlier This Year, the Appointment Put a Spotlight on the New Rules of the Auto Industry: It's Less About Manufacturing These Days Than About Marketing and Sales," *Financial Post Magazine,* June 1997, pp. 18-22.

61. V. Hempsall, "Family Matters: Unique Culture and Strategic Acquisitions Key to St. Joseph Corp's Financial Success," *Canadian Printer,* June 1997, pp. 24-27.

62. J. Harris, "Talk About a Revolution," *Canadian Business,* November 28, 1977.

63. V. Hempsall, "Family Matters: Unique Culture and Strategic Acquisitions Key to St. Joseph Corp's Financial Success," *Canadian Printer,* June 1997, pp. 24-27.

64. "DCACronyms," April 1997, Rev. D; published by The Boeing Co.

65. B. Schneider, "The People Make the Place," *Personnel Psychology*, Autumn 1987, pp. 437-453; D.E. Bowen, G.E. Ledford, Jr., and B.R. Nathan, "Hiring for the Organization, Not the Job," *Academy of Management Executive*, November 1991, pp. 35-51; B. Schneider, H.W. Goldstein, and D.B. Smith, "The ASA Framework: An Update," *Personnel Psychology*, Winter 1995, pp. 747-773; A.L. Kristof, "Person-Organization Fit: An Integrative Review of Its Conceptualizations, Measurement, and Implications," *Personnel Psychology*, Spring 1996, pp. 1-49; D.M. Cable and T.A. Judge, "Interviewers' Perceptions of Person-Organization Fit and Organizational Selection Decisions," *Journal of Applied Psychology*, August 1997, pp. 546-561; and J. Schaubroeck, D.C. Ganster, and J.R. Jones, "Organization and Occupation Influences in the Attraction-Selection-Attrition Process," *Journal of Applied Psychology*, December 1998, pp. 869-891.

66. This section is based on R. Goffee and G. Jones, *The Character of a Corporation: How Your Company's Culture Can Make or Break Your Business* (New York: HarperBusiness, 1998).

67. Jennifer Chatman's work, as reported in M. Siegel, "The Perils of Culture Conflict," *Fortune*, November 9, 1998, pp. 257-262.

68. The AT&T and Saturn examples are taken from B. Schneider; A.P. Brief and R.A. Guzzo, "Creating a Climate and Culture for Sustainable Organizational Change," *Organizational Dynamics*, 24 (4), 1996, pp. 6-19.

69. E. Schall, "Honk If You're Hungry," *National Post*, January 12, 1999, p. B3.

70. J.A. Chatman, "Matching People and Organizations: Selection and Socialization in Public Accounting Firms," pp. 459-484; and B.Z. Posner, "Person-Organization Values Congruence: No Support for Individual Differences as a Moderating Influence," *Human Relations*, April 1992, pp. 351-361.

71. J.E. Sheridan, "Organizational Culture and Employee Retention," *Academy of Management Journal*, December 1992, pp. 1036-1056.

## Chapter 10

1. Based on "Jobs Does the Job on Apple," *Financial Post Daily*, March 12, 1998, p. 18; "Apple Is Exciting Again, says Jobs," *Financial Post*, October 4/6, 1997, p. 14; "Amelio Resigns From Apple," *Financial Post Daily*, July 10, 1997, p. 5.

2. J. Carlton, *Apple: The Inside Story of Intrigue, Egomania, and Business Blunders* (New York: Random House, 1998).

3. J.P. Kotter, "What Leaders Really Do," *Harvard Business Review*, May-June 1990, pp. 103-111; and J.P. Kotter, *A Force for Change: How Leadership Differs From Management* (New York: Free Press, 1990).

4. R.J. House and R.N. Aditya, "The Social Scientific Study of Leadership: Quo Vadis?" *Journal of Management*, 23(3), 1997, p. 445.

5. R.N. Kanungo, "Leadership in Organizations: Looking Ahead to the 21st Century," *Canadian Psychology*, 39(1-2), 1998, p. 77. For more evidence of this consensus, see N. Adler, *International Dimensions of Organizational Behavior*, 3rd ed. (Cincinnati, OH: South Western College Publishing), 1997; R.J. House, "Leadership in the Twenty-First Century," in A. Howard (ed.), *The Changing Nature of Work* (San Francisco: Jossey-Bass), 1995, pp. 411-450; R.N. Kanungo and M. Mendonca, *Ethical Dimensions of Leadership* (Thousand Oaks, CA: Sage Publications, 1996); A. Zaleznik, "The Leadership Gap," *Academy of Management Executive*, 4(1), 1990, pp. 7-22.

6. K. Cameron and R.E. Quinn, *The Competing Values Framework*; R.E. Quinn, S.R. Faerman, M.P. Thompson, and M.R. McGrath, *Becoming a Master Manager: A Competency Framework* (New York: John Wiley and Sons, 1990); K. Cameron and R.E. Quinn, *Diagnosing and Changing Organizational Culture: Based on the Competing Values Framework*, 1st ed. (Reading, MA: Addison Wesley Longman Inc., 1999).

7. A. Bryman, "Leadership in Organizations," in S.R. Clegg, C. Hardy, and W.R. Nord (eds.), *Handbook of Organization Studies* (London: Sage Publications, 1996), pp. 276-292.

8. See, for instance, R.G. Lord, C.L. DeVader, and G.M. Alliger, "A Meta-Analysis of the Relation Between Personality Traits and Leadership Perceptions: An Application of Validity Generalization Procedures," *Journal of Applied Psychology*, 71, 1986, pp. 402-410; R.G. Lord and K.J. Maher, *Leadership and Information Processing: Linking Perceptions and Performance* (Cambridge, MA: Unwin Hyman, 1991); E.A. Locke and Associates, *The Essence of Leadership: The Four Keys to Leading Successfully* (New York: Lexington, 1991); and R.J. House, W.D. Spangler, and J. Woycke, "Personality and Charisma in the U.S. Presidency: A Psychological Theory of Leader Effectiveness," *Administrative Science Quarterly*, 36, 1991, pp. 364-396.

9. J.G. Geier, "A Trait Approach to the Study of Leadership in Small Groups," *Journal of Communication*, December 1967, pp. 316-323.

10. A. Bryman, "Leadership in Organizations," in S.R. Clegg, C. Hardy, and W.R. Nord (eds.), *Handbook of Organization Studies* (London: Sage Publications, 1996), p. 277.

11. S.A. Kirkpatrick and E.A. Locke, "Leadership: Do Traits Matter?" *Academy of Management Executive*, May 1991, pp. 48-60.

12. G.H. Dobbins. W.S. Long, E.J. Dedrick, and T.C. Clemons, "The Role of Self-Monitoring and Gender on Leader Emergence: A Laboratory and Field Study," *Journal of Management*, September 1990, pp. 609-618; and S.J. Zaccaro, R.J. Foti, and D.A. Kenny, "Self-Monitoring and Trait-Based Variance in Leadership: An Investigation of Leader Flexibility Across Multiple Group Situations," *Journal of Applied Psychology*, April 1991, pp. 308-315.

13. G. Yukl and D.D. Van Fleet, "Theory and Research on Leadership in Organizations," in M.D. Dunnette and L.M. Hough (eds.), *Handbook of Industrial & Organizational Psychology*, 2nd ed., vol. 3 (Palo Alto, CA: Consulting Psychologists Press, 1992), p. 150.

14. R.M. Stogdill and A.E. Coons (eds.), *Leader Behavior: Its Description and Measurement*, Research Monograph no. 88 (Columbus: Ohio State University, Bureau of Business

Research, 1951). This research is updated in S. Kerr, C.A. Schriesheim, C.J. Murphy, and R.M. Stogdill, "Toward a Contingency Theory of Leadership Based Upon the Consideration and Initiating Structure Literature," *Organizational Behavior and Human Performance,* August 1974, pp. 62-82; and C.A. Schriesheim, C.C. Cogliser, and L.L. Neider, "Is It 'Trustworthy'? A Multiple-Levels-of-Analysis Reexamination of an Ohio State Leadership Study, With Implications for Future Research," *Leadership Quarterly,* Summer 1995, pp. 111-145.

15. R. Kahn and D. Katz, "Leadership Practices in Relation to Productivity and Morale," D. Cartwright and A. Zander (eds.), *Group Dynamics: Research and Theory,* 2nd ed. (Elmsford, NY: Row, Paterson, 1960).

16. R.R. Blake and J.S. Mouton, *The Managerial Grid* (Houston: Gulf, 1964).

17. See, for example, R.R. Blake and J.S. Mouton, "A Comparative Analysis of Situationalism and 9,9 Management by Principle," *Organizational Dynamics,* Spring 1982, pp. 20-43.

18. See, for example, L.L. Larson, J.G. Hunt, and R.N. Osborn, "The Great Hi-Hi Leader Behavior Myth: A Lesson From Occam's Razor," *Academy of Management Journal,* December 1976, pp. 628-641; and P.C. Nystrom, "Managers and the Hi-Hi Leader Myth," *Academy of Management Journal,* June 1978, pp. 325-331.

19. See, for instance, P.M. Podsakoff, S.B. MacKenzie, M. Ahearne, and W.H. Bommer, "Searching for a Needle in a Haystack: Trying to Identify the Illusive Moderators of Leadership Behavior," *Journal of Management,* 1, no. 3, 1995, pp. 422-470.

20. F.E. Fiedler, *A Theory of Leadership Effectiveness* (New York: McGraw-Hill, 1967).

21. Cited in R.J. House and R.N. Aditya, "The Social Scientific Study of Leadership: Quo Vadis?" *Journal of Management,* vol. 23, no. 3, 1997, p. 422.

22. P. Hersey and K.H. Blanchard, "So You Want to Know Your Leadership Style?" *Training and Development Journal,* February 1974, pp. 1-15; and P. Hersey and K.H. Blanchard, *Management of Organizational Behavior: Utilizing Human Resources,* 6th ed. (Englewood Cliffs, NJ: Prentice Hall, 1993).

23. Cited in C.F. Fernandez and R.P. Vecchio, "Situational Leadership Theory Revisited: A Test of an Across-Jobs Perspective," *Leadership Quarterly,* vol. 8, no. 1, 1997, p. 67.

24. **For controversy surrounding the Fiedler LPC scale see** A. Bryman, "Leadership in Organizations," in S.R. Clegg, C. Hardy, and W.R. Nord (eds.), *Handbook of Organization Studies* (London: Sage Publications, 1996), pp. 279-280; A. Bryman, *Leadership and Organizations* (London: Routledge & Kegan Paul, 1986); and T. Peters and N. Austin, *A Passion for Excellence* (New York: Random House, 1985). **For supportive evidence on the Fiedler model, see** L.H. Peters, D.D. Hartke, and J.T. Pohlmann, "Fiedler's Contingency Theory of Leadership: An Application of the Meta-Analysis Procedures of Schmidt and Hunter," *Psychological Bulletin,* March 1985, pp. 274-285; C.A. Schriesheim, B.J. Tepper, and L.A. Tetrault, "Least Preferred Co-Worker Score, Situational Control, and Leadership Effectiveness: A Meta-Analysis of Contingency Model Performance Predictions," *Journal of*

*Applied Psychology,* August 1994, pp. 561-573; and R. Ayman, M.M. Chemers, and F. Fiedler, "The Contingency Model of Leadership Effectiveness: Its Levels of Analysis," *Leadership Quarterly,* Summer 1995, pp. 147-167; **for evidence that LPC scores are not stable, see** for instance, R.W. Rice, "Psychometric Properties of the Esteem for the Least Preferred Coworker (LPC) Scale," *Academy of Management Review,* January 1978, pp. 106-118; C.A. Schriesheim, B.D. Bannister, and W.H. Money, "Psychometric Properties of the LPC Scale: An Extension of Rice's Review," *Academy of Management Review,* April 1979, pp. 287-290; and J.K. Kennedy, J.M. Houston, M.A. Korgaard, and D.D. Gallo, "Construct Space of the Least Preferred Co-Worker (LPC) Scale," *Educational & Psychological Measurement,* Fall 1987, pp. 807-814; **for difficulty in applying Fiedler's model, see** E.H. Schein, *Organizational Psychology,* 3rd ed. (Englewood Cliffs, NJ: Prentice Hall, 1980), pp. 116-117; and B. Kabanoff, "A Critique of Leader Match and Its Implications for Leadership Research," *Personnel Psychology,* Winter 1981, pp. 749-764. **For evidence that Hersey and Blanchard's model has received little attention from researchers, see** R.K. Hambleton and R. Gumpert, "The Validity of Hersey and Blanchard's Theory of Leader Effectiveness," *Group & Organizational Studies,* June 1982, pp. 225-242; C.L. Graeff, "The Situational Leadership Theory: A Critical View," *Academy of Management Review,* April 1983, pp. 285-291; R.P. Vecchio, "Situational Leadership Theory: An Examination of a Prescriptive Theory," *Journal of Applied Psychology,* August 1987, pp. 444-451; J.R. Goodson, G.W. McGee, and J.F. Cashman, "Situational Leadership Theory: A Test of Leadership Prescriptions," *Group & Organization Studies,* December 1989, pp. 446-461; W. Blank, J.R. Weitzel, and S.G. Green, "A Test of the Situational Leadership Theory," *Personnel Psychology,* Autumn 1990, pp. 579-597; and W.R. Norris and R.P. Vecchio, "Situational Leadership Theory: A Replication," *Group & Organization Management,* September 1992, pp. 331-342; **for evidence of partial support for the theory,** see R.P. Vecchio, "Situational Leadership Theory: An Examination of a Prescriptive Theory," *Journal of Applied Psychology,* August 1987, pp. 444-451; and W.R. Norris and R.P. Vecchio, "Situational Leadership Theory: A Replication," *Group & Organization Management,* September 1992, pp. 331-342; and **for evidence of no support for Hersey and Blanchard, see** W. Blank, J.R. Weitzel, and S.G. Green, "A Test of the Situational Leadership Theory," *Personnel Psychology,* Autumn 1990, pp. 579-597.

25. M.G. Evans, "The Effects of Supervisory Behavior on the Path-Goal Relationship," *Organizational Behavior and Human Performance,* 5, 1970, pp. 277-298; M.G. Evans, "Leadership and Motivation: A Core Concept," *Academy of Management Journal,* 13, 1970, 91-102; R.J. House, "A Path-Goal Theory of Leader Effectiveness," *Administrative Science Quarterly,* September 1971, pp. 321-338; R.J. House and T.R. Mitchell, "Path-Goal Theory of Leadership," *Journal of Contemporary Business,* Autumn 1974, p. 86; M.G. Evans, "Leadership," in S. Kerr (ed.), *Organizational Behavior* (Columbus, OH: Grid Publishing, 1979); R.J. House, "Retrospective Comment," in L.E. Boone and D.D. Bowen (eds.), *The Great Writings in Management and Organizational Behavior,* 2nd ed. (New York: Random House, 1987), pp. 354-364; and M.G.

Evans, "Fuhrungstheorien, Weg-ziel-theorie" (trans. G. Reber), in A. Kieser, G. Reber, & R. Wunderer (eds.), *Handworterbuch Der Fuhrung*, 2nd ed., (Stuttgart, Germany: Schaffer Poeschal Verlag, 1995), pp. 1075-1091.

26. See R.T. Keller, "A Test of the Path-Goal Theory of Leadership With Need for Clarity as a Moderator in Research and Development Organizations," *Journal of Applied Psychology*, April 1989, pp. 208-212; J.C. Wofford and L.Z. Liska, "Path-Goal Theories of Leadership: A Meta-Analysis," *Journal of Management*, Winter 1993, pp. 857-876; M.G. Evans, "R.J. House's 'A Path-Goal Theory of Leader Effectiveness,'" *Leadership Quarterly*, Fall 1996, pp. 305-309; and C.A. Schriesheim and L.L. Neider, "Path-Goal Leadership Theory: The Long and Winding Road," *Leadership Quarterly*, Fall 1996, pp. 317-321.

27. L.R. Anderson, "Toward a Two-Track Model of Leadership Training: Suggestions From Self-Monitoring Theory," *Small Group Research*, May 1990, pp. 147-167; G.H. Dobbins, W.S. Long, E.J. Dedrick, and T.C. Clemons, "The Role of Self-Monitoring and Gender on Leader Emergence: A Laboratory and Field Study," *Journal of Management*, September 1990, pp. 609-618; and S.J. Zaccaro, R.J. Foti, and D.A. Kenny, "Self-Monitoring and Trait-Based Variance in Leadership: An Investigation of Leader Flexibility Across Multiple Group Situations," *Journal of Applied Psychology*, April 1991, pp. 308-315.

28. S. Kerr and J.M. Jermier, "Substitutes for Leadership: Their Meaning and Measurement," *Organizational Behavior and Human Performance*, December 1978, pp. 375-403; J.P. Howell and P.W. Dorfman, "Substitutes for Leadership: Test of a Construct," *Academy of Management Journal*, December 1981, pp. 714-728; J.P. Howell, P.W. Dorfman, and S. Kerr, "Leadership and Substitutes for Leadership," *Journal of Applied Behavioral Science*, 22, no. 1, 1986, pp. 29-46; J.P. Howell, D.E. Bowen, P.W. Dorfman, S. Kerr, and P.M. Podsakoff, "Substitutes for Leadership: Effective Alternatives to Ineffective Leadership," *Organizational Dynamics*, Summer 1990, pp. 21-38; P.M. Podsakoff, B.P. Niehoff, S.B. MacKenzie, and M.L. Williams, "Do Substitutes for Leadership Really Substitute for Leadership? An Empirical Examination of Kerr and Jermier's Situational Leadership Model," *Organizational Behavior and Human Decision Processes*, February 1993, pp. 1-44; P.M. Podsakoff and S.B. MacKenzie, "An Examination of Substitutes for Leadership Within a Levels-of-Analysis Framework," *Leadership Quarterly*, Fall 1995, pp. 289-328; P.M. Podsakoff, S.B. MacKenzie, and W.H. Bommer, "Transformational Leader Behaviors and Substitutes for Leadership as Determinants of Employee Satisfaction, Commitment, Trust, and Organizational Citizenship Behaviors," *Journal of Management*, 22, no. 2, 1996, pp. 259-298; P.M. Podsakoff, S.B. MacKenzie, and W.H. Bommer, "Meta-Analysis of the Relationships Between Kerr and Jermier's Substitutes for Leadership and Employee Attitudes, Role Perceptions, and Performance," *Journal of Applied Psychology*, August 1996, pp. 380-399; and J.M. Jermier and S. Kerr, "'Substitutes for Leadership: Their Meaning and Measurement'—Contextual Recollections and Current Observations," *Leadership Quarterly*, vol. 8, no. 2, 1997, pp. 95-101.

29. V. Smith, "Leading Us On," *Report on Business Magazine*, April 1999, pp. 91-96.

30. A. Bryman, "Leadership in Organizations," in S.R. Clegg, C. Hardy, and W.R. Nord (eds.), *Handbook of Organization Studies* (London: Sage Publications, 1996), pp. 276-292.

31. J.M. Howell and B.J. Avolio, "The Leverage of Leadership," in *Leadership: Achieving Exceptional Performance*, A Special Supplement Prepared by the Richard Ivey School of Business, *The Globe and Mail*, May 15, 1998, pp. C1, C2.

32. J.M. Howell and B.J. Avolio, "The Leverage of Leadership," in *Leadership: Achieving Exceptional Performance*, A Special Supplement Prepared by the Richard Ivey School of Business, *The Globe and Mail*, May 15, 1998, pp. C1, C2.

33. R.N. Kanungo, "Leadership in Organizations: Looking Ahead to the 21st Century," *Canadian Psychology*, 39(1-2), 1998, p. 78.

34. B.M. Bass, "Leadership: Good, Better, Best," *Organizational Dynamics*, Winter 1985, pp. 26-40; and J. Seltzer and B.M. Bass, "Transformational Leadership: Beyond Initiation and Consideration," *Journal of Management*, December 1990, pp. 693-703.

35. Robert House identified three: extremely high confidence, dominance, and strong convictions in his or her beliefs. House also notes that charismatic leaders demonstrate a high level of integrity and place the company goals above their own personal goals. He further notes that such leaders motivate employees by sharing a vision of an exciting, challenging future. They do this by describing what kind of organization they want the company to become, setting high performance standards, and expressing confidence that their employees can achieve that vision. To review House's vision, see R.J. House, "A 1976 Theory of Charismatic Leadership," in J.G. Hunt and L.L. Larson (eds.), *Leadership: The Cutting Edge* (Carbondale: Southern Illinois University Press, 1977), pp. 189-207; and "Building a Better Boss," *Maclean's*, September 30, 1996, p. 41. Warren Bennis, after studying 90 of the most effective and successful leaders in the United States, found that they had four common competencies: They had a compelling vision or sense of purpose; they could communicate that vision in clear terms that their followers could readily identify with; they demonstrated consistency and focus in the pursuit of their vision; and they knew their own strengths and capitalized on them. For this elaboration, see W. Bennis, "The Four Competencies of Leadership," *Training and Development Journal*, August 1984, pp. 15-19.

36. J.A. Conger and R.N. Kanungo, *Charismatic Leadership in Organizations* (Thousand Oaks, CA: Sage, 1998).

37. P.C. Nutt and R.W. Backoff, "Crafting Vision," *Journal of Management Inquiry*, December 1997, p. 309.

38. P.C. Nutt and R.W. Backoff, "Crafting Vision," *Journal of Management Inquiry*, December 1997, p. 312-314.

39. M. Naval, "Onvia.com Sets Eyes on Canada's Small Business Market," *Computer Dealer News*, December 10, 1999, p. 14.

40. Cited in L.B. Korn, "How the Next CEO Will Be Different," *Fortune*, May 22, 1989, p. 157.

41. J.C. Collins and J.I. Porras, *Built to Last: Successful Habits of Visionary Companies* (New York: HarperBusiness, 1994).

42. "Building a Better Boss," *Maclean's,* September 30, 1996, p. 41.

43. R.J. House, J. Woycke, and E.M. Fodor, "Charismatic and Noncharismatic Leaders: Differences in Behavior and Effectiveness," in J.A. Conger and R.N. Kanungo, *Charismatic Leadership in Organizations,* pp. 103-104; D.A. Waldman, B.M. Bass, and F.J. Yammarino, "Adding to Contingent-Reward Behavior: The Augmenting Effect of Charismatic Leadership," *Group & Organization Studies,* December 1990, pp. 381-394; and S.A. Kirkpatrick and E.A. Locke, "Direct and Indirect Effects of Three Core Charismatic Leadership Components on Performance and Attitudes," *Journal of Applied Psychology,* February 1996, pp. 36-51; and J.A. Conger, R.N. Kanungo, and S.T. Menon, "Charismatic Leadership and Follower Outcome Effects," paper presented at the 58th Annual Academy of Management Meetings, San Diego, CA, August 1998.

44. J.M. Howell and P.J. Frost, "A Laboratory Study of Charismatic Leadership," *Organizational Behavior & Human Decision Processes,* 43, no. 2, April 1989, pp. 243-269.

45. "Building a Better Boss," *Maclean's,* September 30, 1996, p. 41.

46. Cited in B.M. Bass and B.J. Avolio, "Developing Transformational Leadership: 1992 and Beyond," *Journal of European Industrial Training,* January 1990, p. 23.

47. J.J. Hater and B.M. Bass, "Supervisors' Evaluation and Subordinates' Perceptions of Transformational and Transactional Leadership," *Journal of Applied Psychology,* November 1988, pp. 695-702.

48. J.M. Howell and B.J. Avolio, "The Leverage of Leadership," in *Leadership: Achieving Exceptional Performance,* A Special Supplement Prepared by the Richard Ivey School of Business, *The Globe and Mail,* May 15, 1998, p. C2.

49. B.M. Bass and B.J. Avolio, "Developing Transformational Leadership: 1992 and Beyond," *Journal of European Industrial Training,* January 1990, p. 23; and J.M. Howell and B.J. Avolio, "The Leverage of Leadership," in *Leadership: Achieving Exceptional Performance,* A Special Supplement Prepared by the Richard Ivey School of Business, *The Globe and Mail,* May 15, 1998, pp. C1, C2.

50. J.M. Howell and B.J. Avolio, "The Leverage of Leadership," in *Leadership: Achieving Exceptional Performance,* A Special Supplement Prepared by the Richard Ivey School of Business, *The Globe and Mail,* May 15, 1998, p. C2.

51. R.J. House, "A 1976 Theory of Charismatic Leadership," in J.G. Hunt and L.L. Larson (eds.), *Leadership: The Cutting Edge* (Carbondale: Southern Illinois University Press, 1977), pp. 189-207; and R.J. House and R.N. Aditya, "The Social Scientific Study of Leadership: Quo Vadis?" *Journal of Management,* vol. 23, no. 3, 1997, p. 441.

52. "Corporate Cults," *Financial Post Magazine,* November, 1993, pp. 118-123.

53. J.A. Conger, *The Charismatic Leader: Behind the Mystique of Exceptional Leadership* (San Francisco: Jossey-Bass, 1989); R. Hogan, R. Raskin, and D. Fazzini, "The Dark Side of Charisma," in K.E. Clark and M.B. Clark (eds.), *Measures of Leadership* (West Orange, NJ: Leadership Library of America, 1990); D. Sankowsky, "The Charismatic Leader as Narcissist: Understanding the Abuse of Power," *Organizational Dynamics,* Spring 1995, pp. 57-71; and J. O'Connor, M.D. Mumford, T.C. Clifton, T.L. Gessner, and M.S. Connelly, "Charismatic Leaders and Destructiveness: An Historiometric Study," *Leadership Quarterly,* Winter 1995, pp. 529-555.

54. J.M. Kouzes and B.Z. Posner, *Credibility: How Leaders Gain and Lose It, Why People Demand It* (San Francisco: Jossey-Bass, 1993); C.C. Manz and H.P. Sims, "Super-Leadership: Beyond the Myth of Heroic Leadership," *Organizational Dynamics,* 19, 1991, pp. 18-35; and H.P. Sims and P. Lorenzi, *The New Leadership Paradigm* (Newbury Park: Sage, 1992).

55. C.C. Manz and H.P. Sims, "SuperLeadership: Beyond the Myth of Heroic Leadership," *Organizational Dynamics,* 19, 1991, pp. 18-35; H.P. Sims and P. Lorenzi, *The New Leadership Paradigm* (Newbury Park: Sage, 1992).

56. H.P. Sims and P. Lorenzi, *The New Leadership Paradigm* (Newbury Park: Sage, 1992), p. 295.

57. See, for instance, J.H. Zenger, E. Musselwhite, K. Hurson, and C. Perrin, *Leading Teams: Mastering the New Role* (Homewood, IL: Business One Irwin, 1994); and M. Frohman, "Nothing Kills Teams Like Ill-Prepared Leaders," *Industry Week,* October 2, 1995, pp. 72-76.

58. See, for instance, M. Frohman, "Nothing Kills Teams Like Ill-Prepared Leaders," *Industry Week,* October 2, 1995, p. 93.

59. See, for instance, M. Frohman, "Nothing Kills Teams Like Ill-Prepared Leaders," *Industry Week,* October 2, 1995, p. 100.

60. J.R. Katzenbach, and D.K. Smith, *The Wisdom of Teams: Creating the High-Performance Organization* (Boston, MA: Harvard Business School, 1993).

61. N. Steckler and N. Fondas, "Building Team Leader Effectiveness: A Diagnostic Tool," *Organizational Dynamics,* Winter 1995, p. 20.

62. R.S. Wellins, W.C. Byham, and G.R. Dixon, *Inside Teams* (San Francisco: Jossey-Bass, 1994), p. 318.

63. N. Steckler and N. Fondas, "Building Team Leader Effectiveness: A Diagnostic Tool," *Organizational Dynamics,* Winter 1995, p. 21.

64. See W.W. Burke, "Leadership as Empowering Others," in S. Srivastva and Associates, *Executive Power* (San Francisco: Jossey-Bass, 1986); J.A. Conger and R.N. Kanungo, "The Empowerment Process: Integrating Theory and Practice," *Academy of Management Review,* July 1988, pp. 471-482; J. Greenwald, "Is Mr. Nice Guy Back?" *Time,* January 27, 1992, pp. 42-44; J. Weber, "Letting Go Is Hard to Do," *Business Week,* November 1, 1993, pp. 218-219; and L. Holpp, "Applied Empowerment," *Training,* February 1994, pp. 39-44.

65. See, for instance, D.A. Waldman, "A Theoretical Consideration of Leadership and Total Quality Management," *Leadership Quarterly,* Spring 1993, pp. 65-79.

66. For problems with empowerment, see J.A. Belasco and R.C. Stayer, "Why Empowerment Doesn't Empower: The

Bankruptcy of Current Paradigms," *Business Horizons,* March-April 1994, pp. 29-40; L. Holpp, "If Empowerment Is So Good, Why Does It Hurt?", *Training,* March 1995, pp. 52-57; and M.M. Broadwell, "Why Command and Control Won't Go Away," *Training,* September 1995, pp. 63-68.

67. R.E. Kelley, "In Praise of Followers," *Harvard Business Review,* November-December 1988, pp. 142-148; E.P. Hollander, "Leadership, Followership, Self, and Others," *Leadership Quarterly,* Spring 1992, pp. 43-54; and I. Challeff, *The Courageous Follower: Standing Up to and for Our Leaders* (San Francisco: Berrett-Koehler, 1995).

68. R.E. Kelley, "In Praise of Followers," *Harvard Business Review,* November-December 1988, pp. 142-148.

69. A. Bandura, "Self-Reinforcement: Theoretical and Methodological Considerations," *Behaviorism,* 4, 1976, pp. 135-155; P.W. Corrigan, C.J. Wallace and M.L. Schade, "Learning Medication Self-Management Skills in Schizophrenia; Relationships with Cognitive Deficits and Psychiatric Symptom," *Behavior Therapy,* Winter, 1994, pp. 5-15; A.S. Bellack, "A Comparison of Self-Reinforcement and Self-Monitoring in a Weight Reduction Program," *Behavior Therapy,* 7, 1976, pp. 68-75; T.A. Eckman, W.C. Wirshing, and S.R. Marder, "Technique for Training Schizophrenic Patients in Illness Self-Management: A Controlled Trial," *The American Journal of Psychiatry,* 149, 1992, pp. 1549-1555; J.J. Felixbrod and K.D. O'Leary, "Effect of Reinforcement on Children's Academic Behavior as a Function of Self-Determined and Externally Imposed Contingencies," *Journal of Applied Behavior Analysis,* 6, 1973, pp. 141-150; A.J. Litrownik, L.R. Franzini, and D. Skenderian, "The Effects of Locus of Reinforcement Control on a Concept Identification Task," *Psychological Reports,* 39, 1976, pp. 159-165; P.D. McGorry, "Psychoeducation in First-Episode Psychosis: A Therapeutic Process," *Psychiatry,* November, 1995, pp. 313-328; G.S. Parcel, P.R. Swank, and M.J. Mariotto, "Self-Management of Cystic Fibrosis: A Structural Model for Educational and Behavioral Variables," *Social Science and Medicine,* 38, 1994, pp. 1307-1315; G.E. Speidel, "Motivating Effect of Contingent Self-Reward," *Journal of Experimental Psychology,* 102, 1974, pp. 528-530.

70. D.B. Jeffrey, "A Comparison of the Effects of External Control and Self-Control on the Modification and Maintenance of Weight," *Journal of Abnormal Psychology,* 83, 1974, pp. 404-410.

71. M. Castaneda, T.A. Kolenko, and R.J. Aldag, "Self-Management Perceptions and Practices: A Structural Equations Analysis," *Journal of Organizational Behavior,* 20, 1999, p. 102.

72. M. Castaneda, T.A. Kolenko, and R.J. Aldag, "Self-Management Perceptions and Practices: A Structural Equations Analysis," *Journal of Organizational Behavior,* 20, 1999, p. 102.

73. M. Castaneda, T.A. Kolenko, and R.J. Aldag, "Self-Management Perceptions and Practices: A Structural Equations Analysis," *Journal of Organizational Behavior,* 20, 1999, p. 102.

74. R.M. Kanter, *The Change Masters, Innovation and Entrepreneurship in the American Corporation* (New York: Simon & Schuster, 1983).

75. R.A. Heifetz, *Leadership Without Easy Answers* (Cambridge, MA: Harvard University Press, 1996), p. 205.

76. R.A. Heifetz, *Leadership Without Easy Answers* (Cambridge, MA: Harvard University Press, 1996), p. 205.

77. R.A. Heifetz, *Leadership Without Easy Answers* (Cambridge, MA: Harvard University Press, 1996), p. 188.

78. This section is based on D. Goleman, *Working With Emotional Intelligence* (New York: Bantam, 1998); and D. Goleman, "What Makes a Leader?" *Harvard Business Review,* November-December 1998, pp. 93-102.

79. "Women Find the Top Jobs in Canada Easier to Get at U.S.-owned Companies," *Vancouver Sun,* August 19, 1999, p. F5.

80. K. Hanson, "Glass Ceiling in Canada Cracked, But Still Here: Women Executives Disagree With Fiorina's Comment," *Financial Post,* July 21, 1999, pp. C1, C6.

81. To see a list of Canada's top 100 women-owned businesses, and information about these businesses and the women who run them, see "Top Women Owned Businesses," *Canadian Business,* October 8, 1999, pp. 112-130, or "100 Top Women Entrepreneurs," *Chatelaine,* November 1999, pp. 72-118.

82. J. Wells, "Stuck on the Ladder: Not Only Is the Glass Ceiling Still in Place, But Men and Women Have Very Different Views of the Problem," *Maclean's,* October 20, 1997, p. 60.

83. M.B. White, "Women of the World: Diversity Goes Global at IBM," *Diversity Factor,* Summer 1999, pp. 13-16.

84. Information in this paragraph based on Michelle Martinez, "Prepared for the Future: Training Women for Corporate Leadership," *HRM Magazine,* April 1997, pp. 80-87.

85. J. Wells, "Stuck on the Ladder: Not Only Is the Glass Ceiling Still in Place, But Men and Women Have Very Different Views of the Problem," *Maclean's,* October 20, 1997, p. 60.

86. J. Wells, "Stuck on the Ladder: Not Only is the Glass Ceiling Still in Place, But Men and Women Have Very Different Views of the Problem," *Maclean's,* October 20, 1997, p. 60.

87. K. Hanson, "Glass Ceiling in Canada Cracked, But Still Here: Women Executives Disagree With Fiorina's Comment," *Financial Post,* July 21, 1999, pp. C1, C6.

88. D. Maley, "Canada's Top Women CEOs," *Maclean's,* October 20, 1997.

89. D. Maley, "Canada's Top Women CEOs," *Maclean's,* October 20, 1997.

90. B.R. Ragins, B. Townsend, and M. Mattis, "Gender Gap in the Executive Suite: CEOs and Female Executives Report on Breaking the Glass Ceiling," *Academy of Management Executive,* February 1998, pp. 28-42.

91. M. Yamaguchi, "Japan's Slump Hurts Women's Prospects," *Vancouver Sun,* January 27, 1999, p. D3.

92. The material in this section is based on J. Grant, "Women as Managers: What They Can Offer to Organizations," *Organizational Dynamics,* Winter 1988, pp. 56-63; S. Helgesen, *The Female Advantage: Women's Ways of Leadership* (New York: Doubleday, 1990); A.H. Eagly and B.T. Johnson, "Gender and Leadership Style: A Meta-Analysis," *Psychological Bulletin,* September 1990, pp. 233-256; A.H. Eagly and S.J. Karau, "Gender and the

Emergence of Leaders: A Meta-Analysis," *Journal of Personality and Social Psychology,* May 1991, pp. 685-710; J.B. Rosener, "Ways Women Lead," *Harvard Business Review,* November-December 1990, pp. 119-125; "Debate: Ways Men and Women Lead," *Harvard Business Review,* January-February 1991, pp. 150-160; A.H. Eagly, M.G. Makhijani, and B.G. Klonsky, "Gender and the Evaluation of Leaders: A Meta-Analysis," *Psychological Bulletin,* January 1992, pp. 3-22; A.H. Eagly, S.J. Karau, and B.T. Johnson, "Gender and Leadership Style Among School Principals: A Meta-Analysis," *Educational Administration Quarterly,* February 1992, pp. 76-102; L.R. Offermann and C. Beil, "Achievement Styles of Women Leaders and Their Peers," *Psychology of Women Quarterly,* March 1992, pp. 37-56; T. Melamed and N. Bozionelos, "Gender Differences in the Personality Features of British Managers," *Psychological Reports,* December 1992, pp. 979-986; G.N. Powell, *Women & Men in Management,* 2nd ed. (Thousand Oaks, CA: Sage, 1993); R.L. Kent and S.E. Moss, "Effects of Size and Gender Role on Leader Emergence," *Academy of Management Journal,* October 1994, pp. 1335-1346; C. Lee, "The Feminization of Management," *Training,* November 1994, pp. 25-31; H. Collingwood, "Women as Managers: Not Just Different: Better," *Working Woman,* November 1995, p. 14; and J.B. Rosener, *America's Competitive Secret: Women Managers* (New York: Oxford University Press, 1995).

93. J. Howell and K. Hall-Merenda, "Leading From a Distance," in *Leadership: Achieving Exceptional Performance,* A Special Supplement Prepared by the Richard Ivey School of Business, *The Globe and Mail,* May 15, 1998, pp. C1, C2.

94. S. Mingail, "Computing Telework's Trade-offs," *Financial Post,* August 9, 1999, p. C8.

95. S. Mingail, "Computing Telework's Trade-offs," *Financial Post,* August 9, 1999, p. C8.

96. For a review of the cross-cultural applicability of the leadership literature, see R.S. Bhagat, B.L. Kedia, S.E. Crawford, and M.R. Kaplan, "Cross-Cultural Issues in Organizational Psychology: Emergent Trends and Directions for Research in the 1990s," in C.L. Cooper and I.T. Robertson (eds.), *International Review of Industrial and Organizational Psychology,* 5 (Chichester, England: John Wiley & Sons, 1990), pp. 79-89; and M.F. Peterson and J.G. Hunt, "International Perspectives on International Leadership," *Leadership Quarterly,* Fall 1997, pp. 203-231.

97. "Military-Style Management in China," *Asia Inc.,* March 1995, p. 70.

98. Cited in R.J. House and R.N. Aditya, "The Social Scientific Study of Leadership: Quo Vadis?" *Journal of Management,* vol. 23, no. 3, 1997, p. 463.

99. R.J. House, "Leadership in the Twenty-First Century," in A. Howard (ed.), *The Changing Nature of Work* (San Francisco: Jossey-Bass, 1995), p. 442.

100. R.J. House, "Leadership in the Twenty-First Century," in A. Howard (ed.), *The Changing Nature of Work* (San Francisco: Jossey-Bass, 1995), p. 442.

101. R.J. House and R.N. Aditya, "The Social Scientific Study of Leadership: Quo Vadis?" *Journal of Management,* vol. 23, no. 3, 1997, p. 463.

102. R.J. House, "Leadership in the Twenty-First Century," in A. Howard (ed.), *The Changing Nature of Work* (San Francisco: Jossey-Bass, 1995), p. 443.

103. Information in this paragraph based on K. Boehnke, A.C. Di Stefano, Joseph J. Di Stefano, and N. Bontis, "Leadership for Extraordinary Performance," *Business Quarterly,* Summer 1997, pp. 57-63.

104. This section is based on R.B. Morgan, "Self- and Co-Worker Perceptions of Ethics and Their Relationships to Leadership and Salary," *Academy of Management Journal,* February 1993, pp. 200-214; J.B. Ciulla, "Leadership Ethics: Mapping the Territory," *Business Ethics Quarterly,* January 1995, pp. 5-28; E.P. Hollander, "Ethical Challenges in the Leader-Follower Relationship," *Business Ethics Quarterly,* January 1995, pp. 55-65; J.C. Rost, "Leadership: A Discussion About Ethics," *Business Ethics Quarterly,* January 1995, pp. 129-142; and R.N. Kanungo and M. Mendonca, *Ethical Dimensions of Leadership* (Thousand Oaks, CA: Sage Publications, 1996).

105. J.M. Burns, *Leadership* (New York: Harper & Row, 1978).

106. J.M. Howell and B.J. Avolio, "The Ethics of Charismatic Leadership: Submission or Liberation?" *Academy of Management Executive,* May 1992, pp. 43-55.

## Chapter 11

1. Based on J. Cooper, "Partnerships for Change [Manufacturers and Retailers Can Make a Real Difference in the Community by Forging Close Ties with Food Banks and Other Relief Agencies]," *Canadian Grocer,* November 1997, pp. 12-13+; T. Ebden, "CIBC Bankrolls Youth Fund," *Canadian Press Newswire,* September 28, 1998; and S.P. Upham, "Packaging Values," *Financial Post,* July 17, 1999, p. D6.

2. See H.A. Simon, "Rationality in Psychology and Economics," *The Journal of Business,* October 1986, pp. 209-224; and A. Langley, "In Search of Rationality: The Purposes Behind the Use of Formal Analysis in Organizations," *Administrative Science Quarterly,* December 1989, pp. 598-631.

3. For a review of the rational model, see E.F. Harrison, *The Managerial Decision Making Process,* 5th ed. (Boston: Houghton Mifflin, 1999), pp. 75-102.

4. W. Pounds, "The Process of Problem Finding," *Industrial Management Review,* Fall 1969, pp. 1-19.

5. T. Barry, "Smart Cookies: Why CIBC Said Yes to the Girl Guides," *Marketing Magazine,* May 31, 1999, pp. 11, 14.

6. J.G. March, *A Primer on Decision Making* (New York: Free Press, 1994), pp. 2-7.

7. D.L. Rados, "Selection and Evaluation of Alternatives in Repetitive Decision Making," *Administrative Science Quarterly,* June 1972, pp. 196-206.

8. M. Bazerman, *Judgment in Managerial Decision Making,* 3rd ed. (New York: Wiley, 1994), p. 5.

9. See, for instance, L.R. Beach, *The Psychology of Decision Making* (Thousand Oaks: Sage, 1997).

10. See, for example, M.D. Cohen, J.G. March, and J.P. Olsen, "A Garbage Can Model of Organizational Choice," *Administrative Science Quarterly,* March 1972, pp. 1-25.

11. See J.G. Thompson, *Organizations in Action* (New York: McGraw-Hill, 1967), p. 123.

12. See H.A. Simon, *Administrative Behavior*, 3rd ed. (New York: Free Press, 1976); and J. Forester, "Bounded Rationality and the Politics of Muddling Through," *Public Administration Review*, January-February 1984, pp. 23-31.

13. W.H. Agor, "The Logic of Intuition: How Top Executives Make Important Decisions," *Organizational Dynamics*, Winter 1986, p. 5; W.H. Agor (ed.), *Intuition in Organizations* (Newbury Park, CA: Sage Publications, 1989); O. Behling and N.L. Eckel, "Making Sense Out of Intuition," *Academy of Management Executive*, February 1991, pp. 46-47; G. Klein, *Sources of Power: How People Make Decisions* (Cambridge: MIT Press, 1998); P.E. Ross, "Flash of Genius," *Forbes*, November 16, 1998, pp. 98-104.

14. O. Behling and N.L. Eckel, "Making Sense Out of Intuition," *Academy of Management Executive*, February 1991, pp. 46-54.

15. As described in H.A. Simon, "Making Management Decisions: The Role of Intuition and Emotion," *Academy of Management Executive*, February 1987, pp. 59-60.

16. W.H. Agor, "The Logic of Intuition: How Top Executives Make Important Decisions," *Organizational Dynamics*, Winter 1986, p. 9.

17. W.H. Agor, "The Logic of Intuition: How Top Executives Make Important Decisions," *Organizational Dynamics*, Winter 1986, p. 15.

18. A. Tversky and K. Kahneman, "Judgment Under Uncertainty: Heuristics and Biases," *Science*, September 1974, pp. 1124-1131; and J.S. Hammond, R.L. Keeney, and H. Raiffa, "The Hidden Traps in Decision Making," *Harvard Business Review*, September-October 1998, pp. 47-58.

19. K. McKean, "Decisions, Decisions," *Discover*, June, 1985, pp. 22-31.

20. A. Tversky and K. Kahneman, "Judgment Under Uncertainty: Heuristics and Biases," *Science*, September 1974, pp. 1124-1131.

21. See B.M. Staw, "The Escalation of Commitment to a Course of Action," *Academy of Management Review*, October 1981, pp. 577-587; and D.R. Bobocei and J.P. Meyer, "Escalating Commitment to a Failing Course of Action: Separating the Roles of Choice and Justification," *Journal of Applied Psychology*, June 1994, pp. 360-363.

22. A.J. Rowe, J.D. Boulgarides, and M.R. McGrath, *Managerial Decision Making*, Modules in Management Series (Chicago: SRA, 1984), pp. 18-22.

23. N.J. Adler, *International Dimensions of Organizational Behavior*, 3rd ed. (Cincinnati, OH: Southwestern, 1997), pp. 166-173.

24. See N.R.F. Maier, "Assets and Liabilities in Group Problem Solving: The Need for an Integrative Function," *Psychological Review*, April 1967, pp. 239-249; G.W. Hill, "Group Versus Individual Performance: Are N+1 Heads Better Than One?" *Psychological Bulletin*, May 1982, pp. 517-539; and A.E. Schwartz and J. Levin, "Better Group Decision Making," *Supervisory Management*, June 1990, p. 4.

25. See, for example, R.A. Cooke and J.A. Kernaghan, "Estimating the Difference Between Group Versus Individual Performance on Problem-Solving Tasks," *Group & Organization Studies*, September 1987, pp. 319-342; and L.K. Michaelsen, W.E. Watson, and R.H. Black, "A Realistic Test of Individual Versus Group Consensus Decision Making," *Journal of Applied Psychology*, October 1989, pp. 834-839.

26. See, for example, W.C. Swap and Associates, *Group Decision Making* (Newbury Park, CA: Sage, 1984).

27. I.L. Janis, *Groupthink* (Boston: Houghton Mifflin, 1982); W. Park, "A Review of Research on Groupthink," *Journal of Behavioral Decision Making*, July 1990, pp. 229-245; C.P. Neck and G. Moorhead, "Groupthink Remodeled: The Importance of Leadership, Time Pressure, and Methodical Decision Making Procedures," *Human Relations*, May 1995, pp. 537–558; and J.N. Choi and M.U. Kim, "The Organizational Application of Groupthink and Its Limits in Organizations," *Journal of Applied Psychology*, April 1999, pp. 297-306.

28. I.L. Janis, *Groupthink* (Boston: Houghton Mifflin, 1982).

29. M.E. Turner and A.R. Pratkanis, "Mitigating Groupthink by Stimulating Constructive Conflict," in C. De Dreu and E. Van de Vliert (eds.), *Using Conflict in Organizations* (London: Sage, 1997), pp. 53-71.

30. See N.R.F. Maier, *Principles of Human Relations* (New York: John Wiley & Sons, 1952); I.L. Janis, *Groupthink: Psychological Studies of Policy Decisions and Fiascoes*, 2nd ed. (Boston: Houghton Mifflin, 1982); and C.R. Leana, "A Partial Test of Janis' Groupthink Model: Effects of Group Cohesiveness and Leader Behavior on Defective Decision Making," *Journal of Management*, Spring 1985, pp. 5-17.

31. J.N. Choi and M.U. Kim, "The Organizational Application of Groupthink and Its Limitations in Organizations," *Journal of Applied Psychology*, 84, 1999, pp. 297-306.

32. J. Longley and D.G. Pruitt, "Groupthink: A Critique of Janis' Theory," in L. Wheeler, (ed.), *Review of Personality and Social Psychology* (Newbury Park, CA: Sage, 1980), pp. 507-513; and J.A. Sniezek, "Groups Under Uncertainty: An Examination of Confidence in Group Decision Making," *Organizational Behavior and Human Decision Processes*, 52, 1992, pp. 124-155.

33. C. McCauley, "The Nature of Social Influence in Groupthink: Compliance and Internalization," *Journal of Personality and Social Psychology*, 57, 1989, pp. 250-260; P.E. Tetlock, R.S. Peterson, C. McGuire, S. Chang, and P. Feld, "Assessing Political Group Dynamics: A Test of the Groupthink Model," *Journal of Personality and Social Psychology*, 63, 1992, pp. 781-796; S. Graham, "A Review of Attribution Theory in Achievement Contexts," *Educational Psychology Review*, 3, 1991, pp. 5-39; and G. Moorhead and J.R. Montanari, "An Empirical Investigation of the Groupthink Phenomenon," *Human Relations*, 39, 1986, pp. 399-410.

34. J.N. Choi and M.U. Kim, "The Organizational Application of Groupthink and Its Limitations in Organizations," *Journal of Applied Psychology*, 84, 1999, pp. 297-306.

35. S. Silcoff, "The Sky's Your Limit," *Canadian Business*, 70, no. 4, April 1997, pp. 58-66.

36. See D.J. Isenberg, "Group Polarization: A Critical Review and Meta-Analysis," *Journal of Personality and Social Psychology*, December 1986, pp. 1141-1151; J.L. Hale and F.J. Boster, "Comparing Effect Coded Models of Choice Shifts," *Communication Research Reports*, April 1988, pp. 180-186; and P.W. Paese, M. Bieser, and M.E. Tubbs, "Framing Effects and Choice Shifts in Group Decision Making," *Organizational Behavior and Human Decision Processes*, October 1993, pp. 149-165.

37. See, for example, N. Kogan and M.A. Wallach, "Risk Taking as a Function of the Situation, the Person, and the Group," in *New Directions in Psychology* 3 (New York: Holt, Rinehart and Winston, 1967); and M.A. Wallach, N. Kogan, and D.J. Bem, "Group Influence on Individual Risk Taking," *Journal of Abnormal and Social Psychology 65*, 1962, pp. 75-86.

38. R.D. Clark III, "Group-Induced Shift Toward Risk: A Critical Appraisal," *Psychological Bulletin*, October 1971, pp. 251-270.

39. A.F. Osborn, *Applied Imagination: Principles and Procedures of Creative Thinking* (New York: Scribner's, 1941). See also P.B. Paulus, M.T. Dzindolet, G. Poletes, and L.M. Camacho, "Perception of Performance in Group Brainstorming: The Illusion of Group Productivity," *Personality and Social Psychology Bulletin*, February 1993, pp. 78-89.

40. Based on information in Kevin Steel, "Wrapping the World in a Tortilla: The Successor to Bagel Barns and Sub Shops, Coming to a Strip Mall Near You," *Alberta Report*, January 12, 1998, p. 25.

41. I. Edwards, "Office Intrigue: By Design, Consultants Have Workers Conspire to Create Business Environments Tailored to Getting the Job Done," *Financial Post Daily*, December 16, 1997, p. 25.

42. Information in this paragraph from G. Crone, "Electrifying Brainstorms," *Financial Post*, July 3, 1999, p. D11.

43. T. Graham, "The Keys to the Middle Kingdom: Experts Will Tell You It Takes Years of Patient Effort to Crack the Chinese Market, But That's Not Always the Case," *Profit: The Magazine for Canadian Entrepreneurs*, December 1997/January 1998, p. 29.

44. See A.L. Delbecq, A.H. Van deVen, and D.H. Gustafson, *Group Techniques for Program Planning: A Guide to Nominal and Delphi Processes* (Glenview, IL: Scott, Foresman, 1975); and W.M. Fox, "Anonymity and Other Keys to Successful Problem-Solving Meetings," *National Productivity Review*, Spring 1989, pp. 145-156.

45. See, for instance, A.R. Dennis and J.S. Valacich, "Computer Brainstorms: More Heads Are Better Than One," *Journal of Applied Psychology*, August 1993, pp. 531-537; R.B. Gallupe and W.H. Cooper, "Brainstorming Electronically," *Sloan Management Review*, Fall 1993, pp. 27-36; and  A.B. Hollingshead and J.E. McGrath, "Computer-Assisted Groups: A Critical Review of the Empirical Research," in R.A. Guzzo and E. Salas (eds.), *Team Effectiveness and Decision Making in Organizations* (San Francisco: Jossey-Bass, 1995), pp. 46-78.

46. V.H. Vroom and P.W. Yetton, *Leadership and Decision Making* (Pittsburgh: University of Pittsburgh Press, 1973).

47. V.H. Vroom and A.G. Jago, *The New Leadership: Managing Participation in Organizations* (Englewood Cliffs, NJ: Prentice Hall, 1988). See also V.H. Vroom and A.G. Jago, "Situation Effects and Levels of Analysis in the Study of Leader Participation," *Leadership Quarterly,* Summer 1995, pp. 169-181.

48. See, for example, R.H.G. Field, "A Test of the Vroom-Yetton Normative Model of Leadership," *Journal of Applied Psychology,* October 1982, pp. 523-532; C.R. Leana, "Power Relinquishment Versus Power Sharing: Theoretical Clarification and Empirical Comparison of Delegation and Participation," *Journal of Applied Psychology,* May 1987, pp. 228-233; J.T. Ettling and A.G. Jago, "Participation Under Conditions of Conflict: More on the Validity of the Vroom-Yetton Model," *Journal of Management Studies,* January 1988, pp. 73-83; and R.H.G. Field and R.J. House, "A Test of the Vroom-Yetton Model Using Manager and Subordinate Reports," *Journal of Applied Psychology,* June 1990, pp. 362-366.

49. "Theatrics in the Boardroom: Acting Classes Are Not Widely Accepted as Management Tools," *Financial Post,* March 4/6, 1995, pp. 24-25.

50. K. Brooks and P. Thompson, "A Creative Approach to Strategic Planning," *CMA Management Accounting Magazine,* July/August 1997, pp. 20-22.

51. T.M. Amabile, "A Model of Creativity and Innovation in Organizations," in B.M. Staw and L.L. Cummings (eds.), *Research in Organizational Behavior*, 10 (Greenwich, CT: JAI Press, 1988), pp. 123-167; and T.M. Amabile, "Motivating Creativity in Organizations," *California Management Review*, Fall 1997, p. 40.

52. T.M. Amabile, *The Social Psychology of Creativity* 'New York: Springer-Verlag, 1983'; T.M. Amabile, "A Model of Creativity and Innovation in Organizations," in B.M. Staw and L.L. Cummings (eds.), *Research in Organizational Behavior*, 10 (Greenwich, CT: JAI Press, 1988), pp. 123-167; C.E. Shalley, "Effects of Productivity Goals, Creativity Goals, and Personal Discretion on Individual Creativity," *Journal of Applied Psychology*, 76, 1991, pp. 179-185; R.W. Woodman, J.E. Sawyer, and R.W. Griffin, "Toward a Theory of Organizational Creativity," *Academy of Management Review*, 18, 1993, pp. 293-321; G. Zaltman, R. Duncan and J. Holbek, *Innovation and Organizations* (London: Wiley, 1973).

53. G.R. Oldham and A. Cummings, "Employee Creativity: Personal and Contextual Factors at Work," *Academy of Management Journal*, 39, 1996, pp. 607-634.

54. Cited in C.G. Morris, *Psychology: An Introduction,* 9th ed. (Upper Saddle River, NJ: Prentice Hall, 1996), p. 344.

55. F.B. Barron and D.M. Harrington, "Creativity, Intelligence, and Personality," *Annual Review of Psychology*, 32, 1981, pp. 439-476; G.A. Davis, "Testing for Creative Potential," *Contemporary Educational Psychology*, 14, 1989, pp. 257-274; C. Martindale, "Personality, Situation, and Creativity," in J.A. Glover, R.R. Ronning, and C.R. Reynolds (eds.), *Handbook of Creativity* (New York: Plenum, 1989), pp. 211-232.

56. G.R. Oldham and A. Cummings, "Employee Creativity: Personal and Contextual Factors at Work," *Academy of Management Journal*, 39, 1996, pp. 607-634; see also F.B. Barron and D.M. Harrington, "Creativity, Intelligence, and Personality," *Annual Review of Psychology*, 32, 1981, pp. 439-476; H.G. Gough, "A Creative Personality Scale for the Adjective Check List," *Journal of Personality and Social*

*Psychology*, 37, 1979, pp. 1398-1405; C. Martindale, "Personality, Situation, and Creativity," in J.A. Glover, R.R. Ronning, and C.R. Reynolds, eds., *Handbook of Creativity* (New York: Plenum, 1989), pp. 211-232.

57. F. Barron and D.M. Harrington, "Creativity, Intelligence, and Personality," *Annual Review of Psychology*, 32, 1981, pp. 439-476; M. Basadur and C.T. Finkbeiner, "Measuring Preference for Ideation in Creating Problem Solving Training," *Journal of Applied Behavioral Science*, 21, 1985, pp. 37-49; M. Basadur, G.B. Graen, and S.G. Green, "Training in Creative Problem Solving: Effects on Ideation and Problem Finding and Solving in an Industrial Research Organization," *Organizational Behavior and Human Performance*, 30, 1982, pp. 41-70; H. Gardner, *Frames of Mind* (New York: Basic Books, 1993); M.A. Glynn, "Innovative Genius: A Framework for Relating Individual and Organizational Intelligences to Innovation," *Academy of Management Review*, 21, 1996, pp. 1081-1111; R. Helson, B. Roberts, and G. Agronick, "Enduringness and Change in Creative Personality and the Prediction of Occupational Creativity," *Journal of Personality and Social Psychology*, 69, 1995, pp. 1173-1183; B. Singh, "Role of Personality Versus Biographical Factors in Creativity," *Psychological Studies*, 31, 1986, pp. 90-92; and R.J. Sternberg, "A Three-Facet Model of Creativity," in R.J. Sternberg (ed.), *The Nature of Creativity: Contemporary Psychological Views*, (Cambridge, England: Cambridge University Press, 1988), pp. 125-147.

58. T.M. Amabile, "A Model of Creativity and Innovation in Organizations," in B.M. Staw and L.L. Cummings, eds., *Research in Organizational Behavior*, 10 (Greenwich, CT: JAI Press, 1988), pp. 123-167; T.M. Amabile, K.G. Hill, B.A. Hennessey, and E.M. Tighe, "The Work Preference Inventory; Assessing Intrinsic and Extrinsic Motivational Orientations," *Journal of Personality and Social Psychology*, 66, 1994, pp. 950-967; M.A. Glynn and J. Webster, "Refining the Nomological Net of the Adult Playfulness Scale: Personality, Motivational, and Attitudinal Correlates for Highly Intelligent Adults," *Psychological Reports*, 72, 1993, pp. 1023-1026; R. Kanfer, "Motivation Theory and Industrial/Organizational Psychology," in M.D. Dunnette, ed., *Handbook of Industrial and Organizational Psychology*, 1, 1990, pp. 75-170; R. Kanfer and P.L. Ackerman, "Motivation and Cognitive Abilities: An Integrative Aptitude-Treatment Interaction Approach to Skill Acquisition," *Journal of Applied Psychology Monograph*, 74, 1989, pp. 657-690.

59. T.M. Amabile, "How to Kill Creativity," *Harvard Business Review*, September-October 1998, pp. 76-87.

60. T.M. Amabile, "A Model of Creativity and Innovation in Organizations," in B.M. Staw and L.L. Cummings, eds., *Research in Organizational Behavior*, 10 (Greenwich, CT: JAI Press, 1988), pp. 123-167; T.M. Amabile and S.S. Gryskiewicz, *Creativity in the R&D Laboratory*, Technical Report no. 10 (Greensboro, NC: Center for Creative Leadership, 1987); and G.R. Oldham and A. Cummings, "Employee Creativity: Personal and Contextual Factors at Work," *Academy of Management Journal*, 39, 1996, pp. 607-634.

61. M.D. Mumford and S.B. Gustafson, "Creativity Syndrome: Integration, Application, and Innovation," *Psychological Bulletin*, 103, 1988, pp. 27-43.

62. E. De Bono, *Six Thinking Hats* (Boston: Little, Brown & Company, 1985); and E. De Bono, *The Mechanism of Mind* (New York: Simon and Schuster, 1969).

63. K. Brooks and P. Thompson, "A Creative Approach to Strategic Planning," *CMA Management Accounting Magazine*, July/August 1997, pp. 20-22.

64. Adapted from E. De Bono, *Six Thinking Hats* (Boston: Little, Brown & Company, 1985).

65. K. Brooks and P. Thompson, "A Creative Approach to Strategic Planning," *CMA Management Accounting Magazine*, July/August 1997, pp. 20-22.

66. Cited in T. Stevens, "Creativity Killers," *Industry Week*, January 23, 1995, p. 63.

67. T.M. Amabile, "How to Kill Creativity," *Harvard Business Review*, September-October 1998, pp. 76-87.

68. Cited in T. Stevens, "Creativity Killers," *Industry Week*, January 23, 1995, p. 63.

69. G.F. Cavanagh, D.J. Moberg, and M. Valasquez, "The Ethics of Organizational Politics," *Academy of Management Journal*, June 1981, pp. 363-374.

70. See, for example, T. Machan, ed., *Commerce and Morality* (Totowa, NJ: Rowman and Littlefield, 1988).

71. L.K. Trevino, "Ethical Decision Making in Organizations: A Person-Situation Interactionist Model," *Academy of Management Review*, July 1986, pp. 601-617; and L.K. Trevino and S.A. Youngblood, "Bad Apples in Bad Barrels: A Causal Analysis of Ethical Decision Making Behavior," *Journal of Applied Psychology*, August 1990, pp. 378-385.

72. See L. Kohlberg, *Essays in Moral Development: The Philosophy of Moral Development*, vol. 1 (New York: Harper & Row, 1981); L. Kohlberg, *Essays in Moral Development: The Psychology of Moral Development*, vol. 2 (New York: Harper & Row, 1984); and R.S. Snell, "Complementing Kohlberg: Mapping the Ethical Reasoning Used by Managers for Their Own Dilemma Cases," *Human Relations*, January 1996, pp. 23-50.

73. D. Todd, "Business Responds to Ethics Explosion," *Vancouver Sun*, April 27, 1998, pp. A1, A7.

74. L. Ramsay, "A Matter of Principle," *Financial Post*, February 26, 1999, p. C18.

75. G. Crone, "UPS Rolls Out Ethics Program," *Financial Post*, May 26, 1999, p. C4.

76. G. Crone, "UPS Rolls Out Ethics Program," *Financial Post*, May 26, 1999, p. C4.

77. D. Todd, "Ethics Audit: Credit Union Reveals All," *Vancouver Sun*, October 19, 1998, p. A5.

78. D. Todd, "Business Responds to Ethics Explosion," *Vancouver Sun*, April 27, 1998, pp. A1, A7.

79. D. Todd, "Business Responds to Ethics Explosion," *Vancouver Sun*, April 27, 1998, p. A7.

80. M. Friedman, *Capitalism and Freedom* (Chicago: University of Chicago Press, 1962).

81. R. Walker and S. Flanagan, "The Ethical Imperative: If You Don't Talk About a Wider Range of Values, You May Not Have a Bottom Line," *Financial Post 500*, 1997, pp. 28-36.

82. P. Foster, "Social Responsibility, Corporate Humbug," *Financial Post*, June 23, 1999, p. C7.

83. R. Walker and S. Flanagan, "The Ethical Imperative: If You Don't Talk About a Wider Range of Values, You May Not Have a Bottom Line," *Financial Post 500*, 1997, pp. 28-36.

84. W. Chow Hou, "To Bribe or Not to Bribe?" *Asia, Inc.*, October 1996, p. 104.

85. T. Donaldson, "Values in Tension: Ethics Away From Home," *Harvard Business Review*, September-October 1996, pp. 48-62.

86. P. Digh, "Shades of Gray in the Global Marketplace," *HRMagazine*, April 1997, pp. 91-98.

87. A. Swift, "Executives Warned to Stay Clean: Bata Leaves Corrupt Nigeria," *Canadian Press Newswire*, October 7, 1997.

88. A. Gillis, "How Can You Do Business in a Country Where Crooked Cops Will Kill You for a Song?" *Report on Business Magazine*, March 1998, pp. 59-68.

89. A. Gillis, "How Can You Do Business in a Country Where Crooked Cops Will Kill You for a Song?" *Report on Business Magazine*, March 1998, p. 60.

90. A. Gillis, "How Can You Do Business in a Country Where Crooked Cops Will Kill You for a Song?" *Report on Business Magazine*, March 1998, p. 60.

91. A. Gillis, "How Can You Do Business in a Country Where Crooked Cops Will Kill You for a Song?" *Report on Business Magazine*, March 1998, p. 64.

92. A. Gillis, "How Can You Do Business in a Country Where Crooked Cops Will Kill You for a Song?" *Report on Business Magazine*, March 1998, p. 66.

## Chapter 12

1. G. Mallet, "Spotlight on Success: The Canadian Woman Entrepreneur of the Year Awards," *Financial Post Magazine*, December 1997, pp. 82-91; and "Innovators Alliance: Ontario's Leading Growth Firms," *Profit: The Magazine for Canadian Entrepreneurs*, June 1999, pp. Insert 1-8.

2. See, for instance, R.L. Daft, *Organization Theory and Design*, 6th ed. (Cincinnati, OH: Thomsen, 1998).

3. See, for instance, L. Urwick, *The Elements of Administration* (New York: Harper & Row, 1944), pp. 52-53.

4. J.R. Brandt, "Middle Management: Where the Action Will Be," *Industry Week*, May 2, 1994, p. 31.

5. L. Surtees, "Cantel's New CEO Ringing in Change," *The Globe and Mail*, June 10, 1998, p. B1.

6. C. Sankar, "Decentralized Policing 'A Success'," *The Vancouver Sun*, January 5, 1999, p. B3.

7. D.B. Harrison, "Shaping the Organization of the Future," *Canadian Business Review*, Winter 1995, pp. 13-16.

8. A. Ross, "BMO's Big Bang," *Canadian Business*, January 1994, pp. 58-63.

9. G. Morgan, *Images of Organization* (Newbury Park, CA: Sage Publications, 1986), p. 21.

10. T. Burns and G.M. Stalker, *The Management of Innovation* (London: Tavistock, 1961); and J.A. Courtright, G.T. Fairhurst, and L.E. Rogers, "Interaction Patterns in Organic and Mechanistic Systems," *Academy of Management Journal*, December 1989, pp. 773-802.

11. H. Mintzberg, *Structure in Fives: Designing Effective Organizations* (Englewood Cliffs, NJ: Prentice Hall, 1983), p. 157.

12. J. Lee, "Sepp's Steps Up With Niche Foods and Acquisitions," *Vancouver Sun*, May 11, 1998, pp. C1, C3.

13. K. Knight, "Matrix Organization: A Review," *Journal of Management Studies*, May 1976, pp. 111-130; and L.R. Burns and D.R. Wholey, "Adoption and Abandonment of Matrix Management Programs: Effects of Organizational Characteristics and Interorganizational Networks," *Academy of Management Journal*, February 1993, pp. 106-138.

14. See, for instance, S.M. Davis and P.R. Lawrence, "Problems of Matrix Organization," *Harvard Business Review*, May-June 1978, pp. 131-142.

15. "Initiating and Managing Change in Your Organization Using a Form of Organizational Structuring Called the Soft Matrix," *CMA Management Accounting Magazine*, 69, no. 7, September 1995, pp. 28-31.

16. G.G. Dess, A.M.A. Rasheed, K.J. McLaughlin, and R. Priem, "The New Corporate Architecture," *Academy of Management Executive*, August 1995, pp. 7-18; C.Y. Baldwin and K.B. Clark, "Managing in an Age of Modularity," *Harvard Business Review*, September-October 1997, pp. 84-93.

17. P. Booth, "Embracing the Team Concept," *Canadian Business Review*, 21, no. 3, 1994, pp. 10-13.

18. M. Kaeter, "The Age of the Specialized Generalist," *Training*, December 1993, pp. 48-53.

19. R. Forrester and A.B. Drexler, "A Model for Team-Based Organization Performance," *Academy of Management Executive*, August 1999, pp. 36-49.

20. R. Forrester and A.B. Drexler, "A Model for Team-Based Organization Performance," *Academy of Management Executive*, August 1999, pp. 36-49.

21. See, for instance, E.A. Gargan, "'Virtual' Companies Leave the Manufacturing to Others," *New York Times*, July 17, 1994, p. F5; D.W. Cravens, S.H. Shipp, and K.S. Cravens, "Reforming the Traditional Organization: The Mandate for Developing Networks," *Business Horizons*, July-August 1994, pp. 19-27; R.T. King, Jr., "The Virtual Company," *Wall Street Journal*, November 14, 1994, p. 85; R.E. Miles and C.C. Snow, "The New Network Firm: A Spherical Structure Built on Human Investment Philosophy," *Organizational Dynamics*, Spring 1995, pp. 5-18; G.G. Dess, A.M.A. Rasheed, K.J. McLaughlin, and R.L. Priem, "The New Corporate Architecture," *Academy of Management Executive*, August 1995, pp. 7-20; D. Morse, "Where's the Company?", *Wall Street Journal*, May 21, 1998, p. R19; and G. Hamel and J. Sampler, "The e-Corporation," *Fortune*, December 7, 1998, pp. 80-92.

22. P. Jarvis, "Palmer Jarvis: Celebrating 25 Years," Promotion Supplement, *B.C. Business Magazine*, June 1994, Insert 1-30.

23. S. McKay, "Marriages of Convenience: Have You Noticed How Many Eligible Canadian Firms Have Been Wooed by Big Foreign Competitors Lately?" *Financial Post Magazine*, June 1997, pp. 26-36.

24. G.G. Dess, A.M.A. Rasheed, K.J. McLaughlin, and R. Priem, "The New Corporate Architecture," *Academy of Management Executive*, August 1995, pp. 7-18.

25. Why Do Canadian Companies Opt for Cooperative Ventures?", *Micro: the Micro-Economic Research Bulletin*, 4, no. 2, Summer 1997, pp. 3-5.

26. G.G. Dess, A.M.A. Rasheed, K.J. McLaughlin, and R. Priem, "The New Corporate Architecture," *Academy of Management Executive*, August 1995, p. 13. See also P. Lorange and J. Roos, "Why Some Strategic Alliances Succeed and Why Others Fail," *Journal of Business Strategy*, January/February 1991, pp. 25-30; and G. Slowinski, "The Human Touch in Strategic Alliances," *Mergers and Acquisitions*, July/August 1992, pp. 44-47.

27. "GE: Just Your Average Everyday $60 Billion Family Grocery Store," *Industry Week*, May 2, 1994, pp. 13-18.

28. H.C. Lucas Jr., *The T-Form Organization: Using Technology to Design Organizations for the 21st Century* (San Francisco: Jossey-Bass, 1996).

29. This section is based on L. Grant, "The Management Model That Jack Built," *Los Angeles Times Magazine*, May 9, 1993, pp. 20-22; P. LaBarre, "The Seamless Enterprise," *Industry Week*, June 19, 1995, pp. 22-34; D.D. Davis, "Form, Function and Strategy in Boundaryless Organizations," in A. Howard (ed.), *The Changing Nature of Work* (San Francisco: Jossey-Bass, 1995), pp. 112-138; R. Ashkenas, D. Ulrich, T. Jick, and S. Kerr, *The Boundaryless Organization: Breaking the Chains of Organizational Structure* (San Francisco: Jossey-Bass, 1995); and P. Roberts, "We Are One Company, No Matter Where We Are. Time and Space Are Irrelevant," *Fast Company*, April/May 1998, pp. 122-128.

30. See J. Lipnack and J. Stamps, *The TeamNet Factor* (Essex Junction, VT: Oliver Wight Publications, 1993); J.R. Wilke, "Computer Links Erode Hierarchical Nature of Workplace Culture," *The Wall Street Journal*, December 9, 1993, p. A1; and T.A. Stewart, "Managing in a Wired Company," *Fortune*, July 11, 1994, pp. 44-56.

31. This analysis is referred to as a contingency approach to organization design. See, for instance, J.M. Pennings, "Structural Contingency Theory: A Reappraisal," in B.M. Staw and L.L. Cummings (eds.), *Research in Organizational Behavior*, 14 (Greenwich, CT: JAI Press, 1992), pp. 267-309.

32. The strategy-structure thesis was originally proposed in A.D. Chandler, Jr., *Strategy and Structure: Chapters in the History of the Industrial Enterprise* (Cambridge, MA: MIT Press, 1962). For an updated analysis, see T.L. Amburgey and T. Dacin, "As the Left Foot Follows the Right? The Dynamics of Strategic and Structural Change," *Academy of Management Journal*, December 1994, pp. 1427-1452.

33. See R.E. Miles and C.C. Snow, *Organizational Strategy, Structure, and Process* (New York: McGraw-Hill, 1978); D. Miller, "The Structural and Environmental Correlates of Business Strategy," *Strategic Management Journal*, January-February 1987, pp. 55-76; and D.C. Galunic and K.M. Eisenhardt, "Renewing the Strategy-Structure-Performance Paradigm," in B.M. Staw and L.L. Cummings (eds.), *Research in Organizational Behavior*, 16 (Greenwich, CT: JAI Press, 1994), pp. 215-255.

34. See, for instance, P.M. Blau and R.A. Schoenherr, *The Structure of Organizations* (New York: Basic Books, 1971); D.S. Pugh, "The Aston Program of Research: Retrospect and Prospect," in A.H. Van de Ven and W.F. Joyce (eds.), *Perspectives on Organization Design and Behavior* (New York: John Wiley, 1981), pp. 135-166; R.Z. Gooding and J.A. Wagner III, "A Meta-Analytic Review of the Relationship Between Size and Performance: The Productivity and Efficiency of Organizations and Their Subunits," *Administrative Science Quarterly*, December 1985, pp. 462-481; and A.C. Bluedorn, "Pilgrim's Progress: Trends and Convergence in Research on Organizational Size and Environments," *Journal of Management*, Summer 1993, pp. 163-192.

35. See J. Woodward, *Industrial Organization: Theory and Practice* (London: Oxford University Press, 1965); C. Perrow, "A Framework for the Comparative Analysis of Organizations," *American Sociological Review*, April 1967, pp. 194-208; J.D. Thompson, *Organizations in Action* (New York: McGraw-Hill, 1967); J. Hage and M. Aiken, "Routine Technology, Social Structure, and Organizational Goals," *Administrative Science Quarterly*, September 1969, pp. 366-377; and C.C. Miller, W.H. Glick, Y. Wang, and G.P. Huber, "Understanding Technology-Structure Relationships: Theory Development and Meta-Analytic Theory Testing," *Academy of Management Journal*, June 1991, pp. 370-399.

36. See F.E. Emery and E. Trist, "The Causal Texture of Organizational Environments," *Human Relations*, February 1965, pp. 21-32; P. Lawrence and J.W. Lorsch, *Organization and Environment: Managing Differentiation and Integration* (Boston: Harvard Business School, Division of Research, 1967); M. Yasai-Ardekani, "Structural Adaptations to Environments," *Academy of Management Review*, January 1986, pp. 9-21; and A.C. Bluedorn, "Pilgrim's Progress: Trends and Convergence in Research on Organizational Size and Environments," *Journal of Management*, Summer 1993, pp. 163–192.

37. G.G. Dess and D.W. Beard, "Dimensions of Organizational Task Environments," *Administrative Science Quarterly*, March 1984, pp. 52-73; E.A. Gerloff, N.K. Muir, and W.D. Bodensteiner, "Three Components of Perceived Environmental Uncertainty: An Exploratory Analysis of the Effects of Aggregation," *Journal of Management*, December 1991, pp. 749-768; and O. Shenkar, N. Aranya, and T. Almor, "Construct Dimensions in the Contingency Model: An Analysis Comparing Metric and Non-Metric Multivariate Instruments," *Human Relations*, May 1995, pp. 559-580.

38. T. Fennell, "Paying the Price: How Asia's Financial Crisis Hurts Canadians," *Maclean's*, 110, no. 49, December 8, 1997, p.44.

## Chapter 13

1. Based on L. Young, "Rev Up: CAMI Shapes Cutting-Edge Supply Chain," *Materials Management & Distribution*, September 1998, pp. 20-21.

2. R.M. Steers and R.T. Mowday, "The Motivational Properties of Tasks," *Academy of Management Review*, October 1977, pp. 645-658; and D.G. Gardner and L.L. Cummings, "Activation Theory and Job Design: Review and Reconceptualization," in B.M. Staw and L.L. Cummings (eds.), *Research in Organizational Behavior*, vol. 10 (Greenwich, CT: JAI Press, 1988), p. 100.

3. J.R. Hackman and G.R. Oldham, "Motivation Through the Design of Work: Test of a Theory," *Organizational*

*Behavior and Human Performance*, August 1976, pp. 250-279.

4. J.R. Hackman, "Work Design," in J.R. Hackman and J.L. Suttle (eds.), *Improving Life at Work* (Santa Monica, CA: Goodyear, 1977), p. 129.

5. See "Job Characteristics Theory of Work Redesign," in J.B. Miner, *Theories of Organizational Behavior* (Hinsdale, IL: Dryden Press, 1980), pp. 231-266; B.T. Loher, R.A. Noe, N.L. Moeller, and M.P. Fitzgerald, "A Meta-Analysis of the Relation of Job Characteristics to Job Satisfaction," *Journal of Applied Psychology*, May 1985, pp. 280-289; W.H. Glick, G.D. Jenkins, Jr., and N. Gupta, "Method Versus Substance: How Strong Are Underlying Relationships Between Job Characteristics and Attitudinal Outcomes?", *Academy of Management Journal*, September 1986, pp. 441-464; Y. Fried and G.R. Ferris, "The Validity of the Job Characteristics Model: A Review and Meta-Analysis," *Personnel Psychology*, Summer 1987, pp. 287-322; S.J. Zaccaro and E.F. Stone, "Incremental Validity of an Empirically Based Measure of Job Characteristics," *Journal of Applied Psychology*, May 1988, pp. 245-252; R.W. Renn and R.J. Vandenberg, "The Critical Psychological States: An Underrepresented Component in Job Characteristics Model Research," *Journal of Management*, 21, no. 2, 1995, pp. 279-303; and J.R. Rentsch and R.P. Steel, "Testing the Durability of Job Characteristics as Predictors of Absenteeism over a Six-Year Period," *Personnel Psychology*, Spring 1998, pp. 165-190.

6. See R.B. Dunham, "Measurement and Dimensionality of Job Characteristics," *Journal of Applied Psychology*, August 1976, pp. 404-409; J.L. Pierce and R.B. Dunham, "Task Design: A Literature Review," *Academy of Management Review*, January 1976, pp. 83-97; D.M. Rousseau, "Technological Differences in Job Characteristics, Employee Satisfaction, and Motivation: A Synthesis of Job Design Research and Sociotechnical Systems Theory," *Organizational Behavior and Human Performance*, October 1977, pp. 18-42; and Y. Fried and G.R. Ferris, "The Dimensionality of Job Characteristics: Some Neglected Issues," *Journal of Applied Psychology*, August 1986, pp. 419-426.

7. Y. Fried and G.R. Ferris, "The Dimensionality of Job Characteristics: Some Neglected Issues," *Journal of Applied Psychology*, August 1986, pp. 419-426.

8. See, for instance, Y. Fried and G.R. Ferris, "The Dimensionality of Job Characteristics: Some Neglected Issues," *Journal of Applied Psychology*, August 1986, pp. 419-426; and M.G. Evans and D.A. Ondrack, "The Motivational Potential of Jobs: Is a Multiplicative Model Really Necessary?", in S.L. McShane (ed.), *Organizational Behavior*, ASAC Conference Proceedings, vol. 9, Part 5, Halifax, Nova Scotia, 1988, pp. 31-39.

9. R.B. Tiegs, L.E. Tetrick, and Y. Fried, "Growth Need Strength and Context Satisfactions as Moderators of the Relations of the Job Characteristics Model," *Journal of Management*, September 1992, pp. 575-593.

10. C.A. O'Reilly and D.F. Caldwell, "Informational Influence as a Determinant of Perceived Task Characteristics and Job Satisfaction," *Journal of Applied Psychology*, April 1979, pp. 157-165; R.V. Montagno, "The Effects of Comparison Others and Prior Experience on Responses to Task Design,"

*Academy of Management Journal*, June 1985, pp. 491-498; and P.C. Bottger and I.K.H. Chew, "The Job Characteristics Model and Growth Satisfaction: Main Effects of Assimilation of Work Experience and Context Satisfaction," *Human Relations*, June 1986, pp. 575-594.

11. J.R. Hackman, "Work Design," in J.R. Hackman and J.L. Suttle (eds.), *Improving Life at Work* (Santa Monica, CA: Goodyear, 1977), pp. 132-133.

12. D.A. Light, "Human Resources: Recruiting Generation 2001," *Harvard Business Review*, July-August 1998, pp. 13-16.

13. G.R. Salancik and J. Pfeffer, "A Social Information Processing Approach to Job Attitudes and Task Design," *Administrative Science Quarterly*, June 1978, pp. 224-253; J.G. Thomas and R.W. Griffin, "The Power of Social Information in the Workplace," *Organizational Dynamics*, Autumn 1989, pp. 63-75; and M.D. Zalesny and J.K. Ford, "Extending the Social Information Processing Perspective: New Links to Attitudes, Behaviors, and Perceptions," *Organizational Behavior and Human Decision Processes*, December 1990, pp. 205-246.

14. See, for instance, J. Thomas and R.W. Griffin, "The Social Information Processing Model of Task Design: A Review of the Literature," *Academy of Management Journal*, October 1983, pp. 672-682; M.D. Zalesny and J.K. Ford, "Extending the Social Information Processing Perspective: New Links to Attitudes, Behaviors, and Perceptions," *Organizational Behavior and Human Decision Processes*, December 1990, pp. 205-246; and G.W. Meyer, "Social Information Processing and Social Networks: A Test of Social Influence Mechanisms," *Human Relations*, September 1994, pp. 1013-1045.

15. "Born-Again Basket Case: Imperial Oil's Refinery in Dartmouth, NS, Used to Be One of the Least Efficient in North America. Now It's an Industry Leader, Using 46% Less Human Effort and Far More Flexible Work Rules," *Canadian Business*, 66, no. 5, May 1993, pp. 38-44.

16. See, for example, P. Kuitenbrouwer, "The Mail Must Go Through," *The Financial Post*, February 28, 1998, pp. 8-9.

17. J.E. Rigdon, "Using Lateral Moves to Spur Employees," *Wall Street Journal*, May 26, 1992, p. B1.

18. B.G. Posner, "Role Changes," *INC.*, February 1990, pp. 95-98.

19. C. Garfield, "Creating Successful Partnerships With Employees," *At Work*, May/June 1992, p. 8.

20. See, for instance, data on job enlargement described in M.A. Campion and C.L. McClelland, "Follow-Up and Extension of the Interdisciplinary Costs and Benefits of Enlarged Jobs," *Journal of Applied Psychology*, June 1993, pp. 339-351.

21. B. Livesey, "Glitch Doctor," *Report on Business Magazine*, November 1997, pp. 97-102.

22. W. Karl, "Bombardier Reaches Lofty Heights: The Challenge Now Is Maintaining Cruise Altitude," *Plant*, August 11, 1997, pp. 1, 12+.

23. J.R. Hackman and G.R. Oldham, *Work Redesign* (Reading, MA: Addison Wesley, 1980).

24. Cited in *U.S. News & World Report*, May 31, 1993, p. 63.

25. See, for example, J.R. Hackman and G.R. Oldham, *Work Redesign* (Reading, MA: Addison Wesley, 1980);

J.B. Miner, *Theories of Organizational Behavior* (Hinsdale, IL: Dryden Press, 1980), pp. 231-266; R.W. Griffin, "Effects of Work Redesign on Employee Perceptions, Attitudes, and Behaviors: A Long-Term Investigation," *Academy of Management Journal,* June 1991, pp. 425-435; and J.L. Cotton, *Employee Involvement* (Newbury Park, CA: Sage, 1993), pp. 141-172.

26. J.R. Hackman, "The Design of Work Teams," in J.W. Lorsch (ed.), *Handbook of Organizational Behavior* (Englewood Cliffs, NJ: Prentice Hall, 1987), pp. 324-327.

27. See, for instance, M. Sashkin and K.J. Kiser, *Putting Total Quality Management to Work* (San Francisco: Berrett-Koehler, 1993); and J.R. Hackman and R. Wageman, "Total Quality Management: Empirical, Conceptual, and Practical Issues," *Administrative Science Quarterly*, June 1995, pp. 309-342.

28. See, for example, P. Kuitenbrouwer, "The Mail Must Go Through," *The Financial Post*, February 28, 1998, pp. 8-9; T.H. Berry, *Managing the Total Quality Transition* (New York: McGraw Hill, 1991); D. Ciampa, *Total Quality* (Reading, MA: Addison-Wesley, 1992); W.H. Schmidt and J.P. Finnegan, *The Race Without a Finish Line* (San Francisco: Jossey-Bass, 1992); and T.B. Kinni, "Process Improvement," *Industry Week*, January 23, 1995, pp. 52-58.

29. M. Sashkin and K.J. Kiser, *Putting Total Quality Management to Work* (San Francisco: Berrett-Koehler, 1993), p. 44.

30. G. Keenan, "Lego: The Toy as Training Tool," *The Globe and Mail*, May 7, 1999, p. B25.

31. Gordon Arnaut, "The Taxpayer as Customer," in *The Total Quality Imperative*, an insert to *Report on Business*, January 1995.

32. S. Becker, "TQM Does Work: Ten Reasons Why Misguided Efforts Fail," *Management Review*, 82, 1993, pp. 30-34.

33. K. Doyle, "Who's Killing Total Quality?" *Incentive*, 16, 1992, pp. 12-19.

34. K. Doyle, "Who's Killing Total Quality?" *Incentive*, 16, 1992, pp. 12-19.

35. R.E. Numeroff, "How to Avoid Failure When Implementing a Quality Effort," *Tapping the Network Journal*, 3, 1992, pp. 1-14; R.E. Numeroff, "How to Prevent the Coming Failure of Quality," *Quality Progress*, 27, 1994, pp. 93-97.

36. T.Y. Choi and O.C. Behling, "Top Managers and TQM Success: One More Look After All These Years," *Academy of Management Executive*, 11, 1997, p. 37-47.

37. T.Y. Choi and O.C. Behling, "Top Managers and TQM Success: One More Look After All These Years," *Academy of Management Executive*, 11, 1997, p. 46.

38. B. Krone, "Total Quality Management: An American Odyssey," *The Bureaucrat*, Fall 1990, p. 37.

39. The following two examples are taken from *Profiles in Quality: Blueprints for Action From 50 Leading Companies* (Boston: Allyn & Bacon, 1991), pp. 71-72 and 76-77.

40. C. Bak, "Lessons From the Veterans of TQM," *Canadian Business Review*, Winter 1992, pp. 16-19.

41. M. Hammer and J. Champy, *Reengineering the Corporation: A Manifesto for Business Revolution* (New York: HarperBusiness, 1993). See also J. Champy, *Reengineering Management: The Mandate for New Leadership* (New York: HarperBusiness, 1995); and M. Hammer and S.A. Stanton, *The Reengineering Revolution* (New York: HarperBusiness, 1995).

42. M. Hammer and J. Champy, *Reengineering the Corporation: A Manifesto for Business Revolution* (New York: HarperBusiness, 1993). See also J. Champy, *Reengineering Management: The Mandate for New Leadership* (New York: HarperBusiness, 1995); and M. Hammer and S.A. Stanton, *The Reengineering Revolution* (New York: HarperBusiness, 1995).

43. R. Karlgaard, "ASAP Interview: Mike Hammer," *Forbes ASAP,* September 13, 1993, p. 70.

44. R. Karlgaard, "ASAP Interview: Mike Hammer," *Forbes ASAP,* September 13, 1993, p. 70.

45. "Born-Again Basket Case: Imperial Oil's Refinery in Dartmouth, NS, Used to Be One of the Least Efficient in North America. Now It's an Industry Leader, Using 46% Less Human Effort and Far More Flexible Work Rules," *Canadian Business*, 66, no. 5, May 1993, pp. 38-44.

46. "The Age of Reengineering," *Across the Board,* June 1993, pp. 26-33.

47. "The Age of Reengineering," *Across the Board,* June 1993, pp. 26-33.

48. N.D. Chander and Howard Armitage, "An Assessment of Business Process Reengineering Among Canadian Organizations," working paper, University of Waterloo.

49. N.D. Chander and Howard Armitage, "An Assessment of Business Process Reengineering Among Canadian Organizations," working paper, University of Waterloo.

50. N.D. Chander and Howard Armitage, "An Assessment of Business Process Reengineering Among Canadian Organizations," working paper, University of Waterloo.

51. "SaskTel Dials the Wrong Number; Employees Rebel at Being 'Re-engineered' by a Psychobabbling Yankee Consultant," *Western Report*, February 26, 1996, pp. 14-17; "The Ghost in the Machine (Re-engineering)," *Financial Post 500*, 1996, pp. 8, 16.

52. Cited in "The Bigger Picture: Reorganizing Work," *Industry Week*, August 2, 1993, p. 24.

53. "Reengineering Revisited: Survey of Top Financial Officers," *B.C. Business Magazine*, 23, no. 9, September 1995, p. 9.

54. A. Ehrbar, "'Reengineering' Gives Firms New Efficiency, Workers the Pink Slip," *Wall Street Journal,* March 16, 1993, p. A1.

55. Based on J. Wells, "Winning Colours," *Report on Business*, July 1992, pp. 26-35; "Canadian Jobs Lost in Plant Move (from Lindsay, Ontario to Pennsylvania)," *Plant*, February 10, 1997, p. 5; and "Top of the Class," *Canadian Packaging*, February, 1994, p. 26.

56. John Heinzl, "Crayon Maker Draws in an Older Kid," *The Globe and Mail*, March 5, 1998, p. B13.

57. "The Right Stuff: Pratt & Whitney Canada Inc. Uses Automated Technology and Modern Management Techniques to Build a Utopian Manufacturing Operation in Halifax," *Plant*, 55, no. 18, December 16, 1996, pp. 18-19.

58. S. Moffat, "Japan's New Personalized Production," *Fortune,* October 22, 1990, p. 44.

59. See E. Norton, "Small, Flexible Plants May Play Crucial Role in U.S. Manufacturing," *Wall Street Journal,* January 13, 1993, p. A1.

60. F. Pomeroy, "Workplace Change: A Union Perspective," *Canadian Business Review,* 22, no. 2, Summer 1995, pp. 17-19.

61. Information about Bestar was obtained from "Quality Comes out of Hiding," in *Labour-Management Innovation in Canada* (Ottawa: Minister of Supply and Services, 1994), pp. 26-29; "Bestar Embarks on $10m Expansion," *Financial Post Daily,* December 4, 1997, p. 19; and "Bestar Hammers Out Record Profit, Sales," *Montreal Gazette,* April 22, 1998, p. E3.

62. "Fewer Workers Had Jobs in June but They Made Slightly More Money," *Canadian Press Newswire,* August 29, 1996.

63. M. Kane, "Flexwork Finds More Favour," *Vancouver Sun,* May 15, 1998, pp. F1, F2.

64. M. Kane, "Flexwork Finds More Favour," *Vancouver Sun,* May 15, 1998, pp. F1, F2; Margot Gibb-Clark, "Royal Bank Scores with Flexible Work Programs," *The Globe and Mail,* May 15, 1998, p. B23.

65. E.J. Calvasina and W.R. Boxx, "Efficiency of Workers on the Four-Day Workweek," *Academy of Management Journal,* September 1975, pp. 604-610.

66. See, for example, J.C. Latack and L.W. Foster, "Implementation of Compressed Work Schedules: Participation and Job Redesign as Critical Factors for Employee Acceptance," *Personnel Psychology,* Spring 1985, pp. 75-92; and J.W. Seybolt and J.W. Waddoups, "The Impact of Alternative Work Schedules on Employee Attitudes: A Field Experiment," paper presented at the Western Academy of Management Meeting, Hollywood, CA, April 1987.

67. C. Goodale and A.K. Aagaard, "Factors Relating to Varying Reactions to the 4-Day Work Week," *Journal of Applied Psychology,* February 1975, pp. 33-38.

68. "Compressed Work Week Stressful for Women, says Stats Can," *Canadian Press Newswire,* January 7, 1997.

69. M. Kane, "Flexwork Finds More Favour," *Vancouver Sun,* May 15, 1998, pp. F1, F2.

70. L. Rubis, "Fourth of Full-Timers Enjoy Flexible Hours," *HRMagazine,* June 1998, pp. 26-28.

71. L. Rubis, "Fourth of Full-Timers Enjoy Flexible Hours," *HRMagazine,* June 1998, pp. 26-28.

72. See, for example, D.A. Ralston and M.F. Flanagan, "The Effect of Flextime on Absenteeism and Turnover for Male and Female Employees," *Journal of Vocational Behavior,* April 1985, pp. 206-217; D.A. Ralston, W.P. Anthony, and D.J. Gustafson, "Employees May Love Flextime, but What Does It Do to the Organization's Productivity?", *Journal of Applied Psychology,* May 1985, pp. 272-279; J.B. McGuire and J.R. Liro, "Flexible Work Schedules, Work Attitudes, and Perceptions of Productivity," *Public Personnel Management,* Spring 1986, pp. 65-73; P. Bernstein, "The Ultimate in Flextime: From Sweden, by Way of Volvo," *Personnel,* June 1988, pp. 70-74; and D.R. Dalton and D.J. Mesch, "The Impact of Flexible Scheduling on Employee Attendance and Turnover," *Administrative Science Quarterly,* June 1990, pp. 370-387.

73. D. Keevil, *The Flexible Workplace Study: Asking the Experts About Flexible Policies and Workplace Performance* (Halifax: Halifax YWCA in cooperation with Status of Women Canada, 1996).

74. L. Duxbury and G. Haines, "Predicting Alternative Work Arrangements From Salient Attitudes: A Study of Decision Makers in the Public Sector," *Journal of Business Research,* August 1991, pp. 83-97.

75. J.E. Fast and J.A. Frederick, "Working Arrangements and Time Stress," *Canadian Social Trends,* Winter 1996, pp. 14-19.

76. "Job Sharing, 1995," *The Daily Statistics Canada,* June 9, 1997.

77. K. Hanson, "Some Companies Go Beyond the Norm to Offer Services to Employees," *Financial Post,* October 8, 1999, p. C15.

78. M. Gibb-Clark, "Royal Bank Scores With Flexible Work Programs," *The Globe and Mail,* May 15, 1998, p. B23.

79. S. Shellenbarger, "Two People, One Job: It Can Really Work," *Wall Street Journal,* December 7, 1994, p. B1.

80. "Telecommuting in Europe," *Manpower Argus,* April 1997, p. 9.

81. S. Shellenbarger, "Two People, One Job: It Can Really Work," *Wall Street Journal,* December 7, 1994, p. B1.

82. See, for example, T.H. Davenport and K. Pearlson, "Two Cheers for the Virtual Office," *Sloan Management Review,* Summer 1998, pp. 61-65; E.J. Hill, B.C. Miller, S.P. Weiner, and J. Colihan, "Influences of the Virtual Office on Aspects of Work and Work/Life Balance," *Personnel Psychology,* Autumn 1998, pp. 667-683; and S. Fister, "A Lure for Labor," *Training,* February 1999, pp. 57-62.

83. "More Canadians Tailor Work to Suit Lifestyles," *Daily Commercial News,* December 23, 1996, p. A7.

84. S. Mingail, "Computing Telework's Trade-offs," *Financial Post,* August 9, 1999, p. C8.

85. Cited in R.W. Judy and C. D'Amico, *Workforce 2020* (Indianapolis: Hudson Institute, 1997), p. 58.

86. "Telecommuting in Europe," *Manpower Argus,* April 1997, p. 9.

87. Information in this paragraph based on H. Scoffield, "Nortel Leaves Employees at Home," *The Globe and Mail,* May 27, 1998, p. B24.

88. S. Mingail, "Computing Telework's Trade-offs," *Financial Post,* August 9, 1999, p. C8.

89. J. Cote-O'Hara, "Sending Them Home to Work: Telecommuting," *Business Quarterly,* Spring 1993, pp. 104-109.

90. N. Hulsman, "Farewell Corner Office," *BC Business,* June 1999, p. 48-55.

91. R. Hearn, "First Banker in Space," *Canadian Business,* August 1997, p. 15.

92. Cited in R.W. Judy and C. D'Amico, *Workforce 2020* (Indianapolis: Hudson Institute, 1997), p. 58.

93. L. Arnold, "Geographical, Organisational and Social Implications of Teleworking — Emphasis on the Social Perspectives," paper presented at the 29th Annual Meeting of the Canadian Sociological and Anthropological

Association, Calgary, Alberta, June 1994; K.S. Devine, L. Taylor, and K. Haryett, "The Impact of Teleworking on Canadian Employment," in A. Duffy, D. Glenday, and N. Pupo (eds.), *Good Jobs, Bad Jobs, No Jobs: The Uncertain Future of Employment in Canada* (in press); C.A. Hamilton, "Telecommuting," *Personnel Journal*, April 1987, pp. 91-101; and I.U. Zeytinoglu, "Employment Conditions in Telework: An Experiment in Ontario," Proceedings of the 30th Conference of the Canadian Industrial Relations Association, 1992, pp. 281-293.

94. L. Arnold, "Geographical, Organisational and Social Implications of Teleworking — Emphasis on the Social Perspectives," paper presented at the 29th Annual Meeting of the Canadian Sociological and Anthropological Association, Calgary, Alberta, June 1994.

95. I.U. Zeytinoglu, "Employment Conditions in Telework: An Experiment in Ontario," Proceedings of the 30th Conference of the Canadian Industrial Relations Association, 1992, pp. 281-293; and K.S. Devine, L. Taylor, and K. Haryett, "The Impact of Teleworking on Canadian Employment," in A. Duffy, D. Glenday, and N. Pupo (eds.), *Good Jobs, Bad Jobs, No Jobs: The Uncertain Future of Employment in Canada* (in press).

96. I.U. Zeytinoglu, "Employment Conditions in Telework: An Experiment in Ontario," Proceedings of the 30th Conference of the Canadian Industrial Relations Association, 1992, pp. 281-293.

97. K.S. Devine, L. Taylor, and K. Haryett, "The Impact of Teleworking on Canadian Employment," in A. Duffy, D. Glenday, and N. Pupo (eds.), *Good Jobs, Bad Jobs, No Jobs: The Uncertain Future of Employment in Canada* (in press); and C.A. Hamilton, "Telecommuting," *Personnel Journal*, April 1987, pp. 91-101.

98. K.S. Devine, L. Taylor, and K. Haryett, "The Impact of Teleworking on Canadian Employment," in A. Duffy, D. Glenday, and N. Pupo (eds.), *Good Jobs, Bad Jobs, No Jobs: The Uncertain Future of Employment in Canada* (in press).

99. K.S. Devine, L. Taylor, and K. Haryett, "The Impact of Teleworking on Canadian Employment," in A. Duffy, D. Glenday, and N. Pupo (eds.), *Good Jobs, Bad Jobs, No Jobs: The Uncertain Future of Employment in Canada* (in press).

100. C.A. Hamilton, "Telecommuting," *Personnel Journal*, April 1987, pp. 91-101.

101. L. Arnold, "Geographical, Organisational and Social Implications of Teleworking — Emphasis on the Social Perspectives," paper presented at the 29th Annual Meeting of the Canadian Sociological and Anthropological Association, Calgary, Alberta, June 1994.

102. N. Hulsman, "Farewell Corner Office," *BC Business*, June 1999, pp. 48-55.

103. Paul Weinberg, "The Space Race," *Report on Business Magazine*, November 1997, pp. 134-138.

104. "Accounting Firm Takes Away Personal Work Areas," *Vancouver Sun*, June 2, 1999, p. D14.

105. Information in this paragraph based on Paul Weinberg, "The Space Race," *Report on Business Magazine*, November 1997, pp. 134-138.

106. Paul Weinberg, "The Space Race," *Report on Business Magazine*, November 1997, pp. 134-138.

107. "Accounting Firm Takes Away Personal Work Areas," *Vancouver Sun*, June 2, 1999, p. D14.

## Chapter 14

1. G. Crone, "Canadian Tire Chief Takes Home $2.1m," *Financial Post*, April 7, 1999, p. C6; G. Livingston, "Managing Change Stressed for Retailers," *Vancouver Sun*, June 15, 1999, p. D2; S. Theobald, "Canadian Tire Store Makeovers Pay Off," *Canadian Press Newswire*, December 23, 1998; Z. Olijnyk, "Canadian Tire CEO Bachand Set to Retire," *Financial Post*, January 12, 2000, pp. C1,C10; Z. Olijnyk, "Bachand Leaves CTC Corp with $4.5m: Retirement Package," *Financial Post*, January 13, 2000, p. C6.

2. J. Lee, "Canadian Businesses Not Good at Adjusting, Survey Says," *Vancouver Sun*, December 14, 1998, pp. C1-2.

3. A. Levy, "Second-Order Planned Change: Definition and Conceptualization," *Organizational Dynamics,* Summer 1986, pp. 4-20.

4. K.L. Miller, "The Factory Guru Tinkering with Toyota," *Business Week,* May 17, 1993, pp. 95-97.

5. J.S. McClenahen, "Condit Takes a Hike," *Industry Week,* December 2, 1996, pp. 12-16.

6. Based on H.J. Leavitt, "Applied Organization Change in Industry," in W. Cooper, H. Leavitt, and M. Shelly (eds.), *New Perspectives on Organization Research* (New York: John Wiley, 1964); and P.J. Robertson, D.R. Roberts, and J.I. Porras, "Dynamics of Planned Organizational Change: Assessing Empirical Support for a Theoretical Model," *Academy of Management Journal,* June 1993, pp. 619-634.

7. P. Tellier, "Turning CN Around," *Canadian Business Review*, Spring 1995, pp. 31-32+.

8. P. Fitzpatrick, "CN's Tellier Took Home $1.3m," *Financial Post Daily*, March 26, 1998, p. 6.

9. D.B. Harrison, "Shaping the Organization of the Future," *Canadian Business Review*, vol. 22, 4, Winter 1995, pp. 13-16.

10. J. Powell, "Under Pressure: Take Two Former Natural Gas Monopolies. Make Them One. Tall Order," *Financial Post*, April 19/21, 1997, pp. 35, 36.

11. J. Powell, "Under Pressure: Take Two Former Natural Gas Monopolies. Make Them One. Tall Order," *Financial Post*, April 19/21, 1997, pp. 35, 36.

12. J. Powell, "Under Pressure: Take Two Former Natural Gas Monopolies. Make Them One. Tall Order," *Financial Post*, April 19/21, 1997, pp. 35, 36.

13. J. Powell, "Under Pressure: Take Two Former Natural Gas Monopolies. Make Them One. Tall Order," *Financial Post*, April 19/21, 1997, pp. 35, 36.

14. Information on Rusco based on "Reorganizing to Save the Company: Improving the Production Flow Became a Life and Death Situation for Rusco Canada Ltd.," *Plant*, February 10, 1997, p. 14.

15. Information on IMMI based on "Turnarounds of the Year," *Profit: The Magazine for Canadian Entrepreneurs*, December 1996/January 1997, pp. 64-71.

16. Information on Sutherland-Schultz Inc. based on George Koch, Micehla Pasquali, and Donna Green, "A Change for the Better," *Profit: The Magazine for Canadian Entrepreneurs*, December 1997/January 1998, pp. 58-61+.

17. Information on Suncor based on P. Spelliscy, "Changing the Corporate Culture from Downsizing to Growth," *Canadian Speeches*, June 1996, pp. 45-50.

18. M.A. Glynn, T.K. Lant, and F.J. Milliken, "Mapping Learning Processes in Organizations: A Multi-level Framework Linking Learning and Organizing," *Advances in Managerial Cognition and Organizational Information Processing*, 5, pp. 43-84, 1994.

19. B. Levitt and J.G. March, "Organizational Learning," *Annual Review of Sociology*, 14, 1988, pp. 319-340; J.G. March, "Footnotes to Organizational Change," *Administrative Science Quarterly*, 26, 1981, pp. 536-577; D. Levinthal and J.G. March, "A Model of Adaptive Organizational Search," reprinted in J.G. March, *Decisions and Organizations* (New York: Basil Blackwell, 1988), pp. 187-218; S. Herriot, D. Levinthal, and J.G. March, "Learning from Experience in Organizations," reprinted in J.G. March, *Decisions and Organizations* (New York: Basil Blackwell, 1988), pp. 219-227; T.K. Lant and S.J. Mezias, "Managing Discontinuous Change: A Simulation Study of Organizational Learning and Entrepreneurial Strategies," *Strategic Management Journal,* 1, 1990, pp. 147-179.

20. R.B. Duncan and A. Weiss, "Organizational Learning: Implications for Organizational Design," in B.M. Staw (ed.), *Research in Organizational Behavior*, 1 (Greenwich, CT: JAI Press, 1979), pp. 75-123; R.H. Miles and W. Randolph, "Influence of Organizational Learning Styles on Early Development," in J.H. Kimberly and R.H. Miles (eds.), *The Organizational Life Cycle* (San Francisco: Jossey-Bass, 1980); C. Argyris and D. Schon, *Organizational Learning* (Reading, MA: Addison-Wesley, 1978); M. Jelinek, *Institutionalizing Innovations: A Study of Organizational Learning Systems* (New York: Praeger, 1979); D. Epple, L. Argote, and R. Devadas, "Organizational Learning Curves: A Method for Investigating Intra-plant Transfer of Knowledge Acquired Through Learning by Doing," *Organization Science*, 2, 1991, pp. 58-70.

21. M.A. Glynn, Theresa K. Lant, and Frances J. Milliken, "Mapping Learning Processes in Organizations: A Multi-level Framework Linking Learning and Organizing," *Advances in Managerial Cognition and Organizational Information Processing*, 5, 1994 p. 46.

22. J.G. March, "Exploration and Exploitation in Organizational Learning," *Organization Science,* 2, 1991, p. 80.

23. C. Argyris and D. Schon, *Organizational Learning* (Reading, MA: Addison-Wesley, 1978).

24. "Corporate Culture Club: Companies Are Focusing on Employee Morale and Training to Boost the Bottom Line," *Maclean's*, December 12, 1994, pp. 42-43.

25. "Corporate Culture Club: Companies Are Focusing on Employee Morale and Training to Boost the Bottom Line," *Maclean's*, December 12, 1994, pp. 42-43.

26. H. Kluge, "Learning Leadership for a World of Change," *Canadian Speeches*, May 1993, pp. 48-52.

27. Based on P. Senge, *The Fifth Discipline: The Art and Practice of the Learning Organization* (New York: Doubleday, 1990), pp. 18-25. Not all of his roadblocks are listed.

28. K. Lewin, *Field Theory in Social Science* (New York: Harper & Row, 1951).

29. M. Young and J.E. Post, "Managing to Communicate, Communicating to Manage: How Leading Companies Communicate with Employees," *Organizational Dynamics*, Summer 1993, pp. 31-43.

30. L. Tabak, "Quality Controls," *Hemispheres*, September 1996, pp. 33-34.

31. L. Tabak, "Quality Controls," *Hemispheres*, September 1996, pp. 33-34.

32. L. Tabak, "Quality Controls," *Hemispheres*, September 1996, pp. 33-34.

33. L. Tabak, "Quality Controls," *Hemispheres*, September 1996, pp. 33-34.

34. A. Van den Broek, "All's Quiet on the Eastern Front: Times Have Changed for the Better at Historically Turbulent Irving Paper Inc.," *Plant*, 56, no. 17, November 24, 1997, pp. 10-11.

35. "Common Characteristics of Successful Companies," *Manitoba Business*, May 1996, pp. 25-29.

36. A.E. Reichers, J.P. Wanous, and J.T. Austin, "Understanding and Managing Cynicism About Organizational Change," *Academy of Management Executive*, 11, 1997, pp. 48-59.

37. R.H. Hall, *Organizations: Structures, Processes, and Outcomes*, 4th ed. (Englewood Cliffs, NJ: Prentice Hall, 1987), p. 29.

38. J. Lee, "Canadian Businesses Not Good at Adjusting, Survey Says," *Vancouver Sun*, December 14, 1998, pp. C1, C2.

39. D. Katz and R.L. Kahn, *The Social Psychology of Organizations,* 2nd ed. (New York: John Wiley & Sons, 1978), pp. 714-715.

40. J.P. Kotter and L.A. Schlesinger, "Choosing Strategies for Change," *Harvard Business Review,* March-April 1979, pp. 106-114.

41. See, for instance, W. Ocasio, "Political Dynamics and the Circulation of Power: CEO Succession in U.S. Industrial Corporations, 1960-1990," *Administrative Science Quarterly,* June 1994, pp. 285-312.

42. J.A. Ross, "Does Shuffling the Deck Work?", *Harvard Business Review*, November-December, 1997, p. 17.

43. See S. Shane, S. Venkataraman, and I. MacMillan, "Cultural Differences in Innovation Championing Strategies," *Journal of Management,* 21, no. 5, 1995, pp. 931-952.

44. P.S. Goodman and L.B. Kurke, "Studies of Change in Organizations: A Status Report," in P.S. Goodman (ed.), *Change in Organizations* (San Francisco: Jossey-Bass, 1982), pp. 1-2.

The page on which the keyterm is printed in boldface

# NAME AND ORGANIZATION INDEX

The page on which a weblink appears is printed in boldface.

# PHOTO CREDITS

Author photos: Laura F. Ospanik (Stephen P. Robbins) and Gary Schwartz (Nancy Langton)

## Chapter 1

Page 3, Jacque Boissinot/Canapress; page 5, Malone & Co. Photography, Inc. (top), Robert Wright Photography (bottom left), © 1999 Brian Coats/Brian Coats Photography (bottom right); page 14, Bombardier Canadian; page 16, Courtesy of Seagate Software; page 19, © John Dakers: EYE UBIQUITIOUS/CORBIS; page 21, Jay Dickman

## Chapter 2

Page 37, Derek Ruttan/Canapress; page 39, Vincent J. Musi; page 45, Courtesy of Fern Hill School; page 55, Moe Doiron/Canapress; page 57, Courtesy of Richard Branson/Virgin Airlines; page 64, Joyce Ravid; page 67, Paul Ekman, Ph.D., Professor of Psychology

## Chapter 3

Page 87, Courtesy of Procter & Gamble; page 92, Courtesy of Mainframe Entertainment Inc.; page 93, Montreal Gazette; page 95, Frank Gunn/Canapress; page 96, Reprinted with permission from the Globe & Mail; page 97, Tom Wagner/SABA Press Photos Inc.; page 98, Greg Girard/Contact Press Images Inc.; page 105, David Laundry/Canapress; page 106, Ed Quinn/SABA Press Photos Inc.; page 109, Yvonne Berg/Canapress; page 122, Gary Schwartz; page 126, Courtesy of Canadian Designer Linda Lundstrom

## Chapter 4

Page 137, AP Photos/Milt Savage, Canapress; page 139, Courtesy of Comingo; page 144, Jeff McIntosh/Canapress; page 149, Peter Redman/Financial Post; page 151, Adrian Wyld/Canapress; page 153, Mike Ridewood/Canapress; page 160, © Thierry Ledoux; page 167, Peter Blakely/SABA Press Photos Inc.; page 176, Courtesy of Nova Chemical Corporation

## Chapter 5

Page 199, Irene Vasque/Special to the Sun; page 207, Timothy Hursley; page 209, Nic Lehoux Photography; page 212, Chris Usher Photography; page 213, Courtesy of Thrifty Foods; page 214, Ken Miller Photography; page 216, Tanis Toohey; page 222, Dan Callis Photography

## Chapter 6

Page 241, Willow Mfg. Co. Ltd.; page 248, Courtesy of Xerox Canada Ltd.; page 250, Courtesy of Goldgrab Leadership Coaching; page 255, J. Mahler/Toronto Star; page 258, Courtesy of Hot Wheels®car model by Mattel Inc.; page 259, Motorola, Inc.; page 261, Tom Ebenson/Black Star; page 263, Prentice Hall Archives

## Chapter 7

Page 275, Ward Perrin/Vancouver Sun; page 276, Anne States/SABA Press Photos Inc.; page 277, Adrian Wyld/Canapress; page 279, Voldi Tanner; page 287, Todd Buchanan; page 288, Fred Mertz; page 291, Courtesy of John Bernard of Donna Cona; page 292, Andrew Brusso; page 298, Louis Psihoyos/Matrix International; page 314, Courtesy of the Bank of Nova Scotia

## Chapter 8

Page 325, AP Photo/Stefan Rousseau, PA; page 328, Joe Marquette/Canapress; page 331, Chuck Stoody/Canapress; page 332, Alan Levenson; page 336, Rhoda Baer Photography; page 337, Courtesy of Golden Valley Foods; page 340, Courtesy of Redwood Plastic Corp.; page 352, Teranet Land Information Services; page 354, Tobey Sanford/Courtesy of General Electric Company; page 372, Peter Southwick/Picture Quest

## Chapter 9

Page 379, Reprinted with permission from The Globe and Mail; page 386, Alan Levenson; page 392, Courtesy of Andree Beaulieu-Green; page 393, Burk Uzzle/Time Inc.; page 394, Reprinted courtesy of InSystems Technologies Inc.; page 399, Courtesy of Creo Products Inc. Copyright © 2000 Creo Products Inc.; page 400, Courtesy of Cyberplex Inc.; page 402, Mark Richards

## Chapter 10

Page 417, Stuart Ramson/Canapress; page 419, Dave Oleckio/Canapress; page 421, Shonna Valeska; page 425, Lexington Herald-Leader; page 434, Courtesy of Smed International Inc.; page 442, Courtesy of International Paper Industries; page 445, Frank Gunn/Canapress; page 449, Alan Levenson

## Chapter 11

Page 459, Courtesy of Kraft Canada Inc.; page 462, Courtesy of the Imperial Bank of Commerce; page 479, QLT Photo Therapeutics Inc.; page 472, Photo by Patrick Price; page 482, Ian Lindsay, Vancouver Sun; page 485, Courtesy of Perth Services Ltd.; page 487, Courtesy of United Parcel Service Canada Ltd.; Page 489, Courtesy of Nova Scotia Power

## Chapter 12

Page 507, Courtesy of Southmedic Inc.; page 511, Courtesy of Hydro Quebec/Robert Bourassa; page 515, Rob Nelson/Black Star; page 517, Courtesy of R.C.M.P. Surrey, BC; page 518, Olivier Vidal/Gamma-Liaison; page 528, Rex Rystedt Photography; page 531, Courtesy of Richmond Savings

## Chapter 13

Page 549, Cami Automotive Inc.; page 557, Courtesy of Honeywell Limited; page 550, Courtesy of Robert Meggy, President of Great Little Box Company; page 561, Reprinted with permission from The Globe and Mail; page 563, J. Chiasson/Gamma-Liaison Inc.; page 569, Bob Sacha Photography; page 576, Dick Hemingway

## Chapter 14

Page 585, Kevin Frayer/Canapress; page 588, Phill Snel/Canapress; page 590, Dick Hemingway; page 609, Randy Lagerway; page 611, Elder/Pono Press International; page 624, AP Photo/Stevan Morgain